The Handbook of Phonetic Sciences

B

Blackwell Handbooks in Linguistics

This outstanding multi-volume series covers all the major subdisciplines within linguistics today and, when complete, will offer a comprehensive survey of linguistics as a whole.

Published Works

FLETCHER AND MACWHINNEY
The Handbook of Child Language

GOLDSMITH
The Handbook of Phonological Theory

LAPPIN
The Handbook of Contemporary Semantic Theory

COULMAS
The Handbook of Sociolinguistics

HARDCASTLE AND LAVER
The Handbook of Phonetic Sciences

Forthcoming

SPENCER AND ZWICKY
The Handbook of Morphology

JOSEPH AND JANDA
The Handbook of Historical Linguistics

The Handbook of Phonetic Sciences

Edited by

*William J. Hardcastle and
John Laver*

BLACKWELL
Publishers

Copyright © Blackwell Publishers Ltd, 1997

First published 1997

2 4 6 8 10 9 7 5 3 1

Blackwell Publishers Ltd
108 Cowley Road
Oxford OX4 1JF
UK

Blackwell Publishers Inc.
238 Main Street
Cambridge, Massachusetts 02142
USA

British Library Cataloging in Publication Data

A CIP catalogue record for this book is available from the
British Library.

Library of Congress Cataloging-in-Publication Data

The Handbook of phonetic sciences / edited by William J. Hardcastle
and John Laver.
    p. cm. — (Blackwell handbooks in linguistics ; 5)
  Includes bibliographical references and index.
  ISBN 0–631–18848–7 (alk. paper)
    1. Phonetics—Handbooks, manuals, etc. I. Hardcastle, William
J., 1943– . II. Laver, John. III. Series.
P221.H28 1997
414—dc20   96–1454
                                                               CIP

Typeset in 10 on 12pt Palatino
by Graphicraft Typesetters Ltd, Hong Kong
Printed in Great Britain by T.J. Press, Padstow, Cornwall

This book is printed on acid-free paper

Contents

Contributors

William A. Ainsworth
University of Keele

Janet Mackenzie Beck
Queen Margaret College, Edinburgh

Rolf Carlson
Massachusetts Institute of Technology

Anne Cutler
Max-Planck-Institute for Psycholinguistics, Nijmegen

Bertrand Delgutte
Massachusetts Eye and Ear Infirmary, Boston

Donna Erickson
Ohio State University

Edda Farnetani
Centro di Studio per le Richerche di Fonetica del CNR, Padova

Osamu Fujimura
Ohio State University

Christer Gobl
University of Dublin

Björn Granström
Royal Institute of Technology, Stockholm

Hajime Hirose
Kitasato University

Raymond D. Kent
University of Wisconsin-Madison

Peter Ladefoged
University of California at Los Angeles

Johan Liljencrants
Royal Institute of Technology, Stockholm

Anders Löfqvist
Haskins Laboratories, New Haven

James M. McQueen
Max-Planck-Institute for Psycholinguistics, Nijmegen

Peter F. MacNeilage
University of Texas at Austin

Ian Maddieson
University of California at Los Angeles

Brian C.J. Moore
University of Cambridge

Ailbhe Ní Chasaide
University of Dublin

Francis Nolan
University of Cambridge

Sieb G. Nooteboom
Rijksuniversiteit te Utrecht

John Ohala
University of California at Berkeley

Joseph S. Perkell
Massachusetts Institute of Technology

Christine H. Shadle
University of Southampton

William M. Shearer
Northern Illinois University

Kenneth N. Stevens
Massachusetts Institute of Technology

Maureen Stone
University of Maryland

Kristin Tjaden
University of Wisconsin-Madison

Gary Weismer
University of Wisconsin-Madison

Introduction

This Handbook is designed as an advanced tutorial introduction for students with a basic grounding in phonetics who are interested in acquiring a foundation for independent graduate-level research in the phonetic sciences. Thirty leading researchers have contributed twenty-six invited chapters in five major sectors of the contemporary subject. An elementary knowledge of the field is assumed, and each chapter presents an overview of a key area of the expertise which makes up the wide range of the phonetic sciences today.

The phonetic sciences have always had a linguistic motivation, and a principal focus has always been the communicative function of spoken language. This remains a central and dominant aspect, but it will be evident from the list of contents that the phonetic sciences are obliged to draw on the techniques and data of many disciplines for which speech is only a partial interest.

This makes the phonetic sciences a necessarily interdisciplinary enterprise, and the modern phonetician needs to know something of anatomy, physiology, physics and engineering as well as being knowledgeable in general phonetic theory and phonology. The result is that, as well as being linguistically sophisticated, the chief methodology of the phonetic sciences is one of quantified experimentation. In the spectrum of knowledge, the phonetic sciences thus blend the perspectives of the social sciences with those of the life sciences, the natural sciences and the engineering sciences.

In its interdisciplinary nature, the current Handbook is broadly comparable in its scope to an early predecessor, the Manual of Phonetics edited first by Louise Kaiser in 1957 and later, in a second edition, by Bertil Malmberg in 1968 which also attempted a broad-ranging overview of the subject. But the phonetic sciences have grown very substantially over the last thirty years, both in the richness of data now incorporated from the non-linguistic areas mentioned above, and in the numbers of and range of researchers taking a professional interest in speech. The four-yearly International Congresses of Phonetic Sciences (ICPhS) are now routinely attended by some 1,000 international participants from every inhabited continent, compared for example, with the low number of hundreds, mainly from Europe, that attended ICPhS meetings in Helsinki and Munster in the early sixties. The structure of the book begins with an account of some of the major instrumental and experimental techniques commonly found in experimental phonetic laboratories. The next part explores normal and disordered aspects of the anatomy of speech and its physiological control. The largest part in the book concentrates on the phenomena of speech production and perception. The fourth part takes up the linguistic motivation of the subject, in an examination of some facets of linguistic phonetics. Finally, the concluding part returns to an experimental approach to speech, but this time in terms of an applied interest in speech engineering, discussing modern developments in speech technology. All the chapters contain extensive pointers to further reading. For readers with complementary interests in phonology, the companion volume to this Handbook of Phonetic Sciences, the Handbook of Phonology edited by Goldsmith (1994) is highly recommended.

Part I begins with a critical evaluation by Maureen Stone of the main non-acoustic instrumental techniques for measuring the physiology of the speech articulatory organs (e.g. the tongue, lips, jaw and velum). The techniques are grouped in terms of imaging techniques (e.g. X-rays, MRI, ultrasound), point-tracking techniques (e.g. Electromagnetic Midsagittal Articulometry, strain gauges, Optotrak, X-ray microbeam) and techniques for measuring complex behaviours (e.g. electropalatography, electromyography). Writing as a researcher with first-hand experience of most of these techniques, Stone outlines, for each technique, the main advantages and limitations for investigating the mechanisms of speech production.

Experimental approaches to speech production are explored further by Christine Shadle in her chapter on the aerodynamics of speech. She begins by introducing basic physical and mathematical concepts in aerodynamics and then applies these to the mechanisms of speech and other vocal tract activities. Aerodynamic behaviours are grouped in terms of respiration, turbulent air flow in fricatives, transient excitation in stops, and mechanical oscillation in voicing and whistling. Laboratory techniques for measuring flow velocity and pressure, including hot-wire anemometry, are evaluated along with techniques specially adapted to speech such as inverse filtering using the Rothenberg mask. The chapter concludes with a discussion and evaluation of some models of speech production incorporating aerodynamics.

Acoustic phonetics is the subject of the third chapter by Osamu Fujimura and Donna Erickson. They begin with a description of the sound spectrograph and exemplify by selected spectrograms the acoustic characteristics of the major classes of speech sounds (vowels, obstruents, nasals, laterals etc.). This is followed by a discussion of acoustic characteristics of suprasegmental phenomena such as intonation and phrasal organisation. New conceptual approaches to the organisation of syllables and coarticulatory phenomena are explored further in a concluding section.

The instrumental investigation of laryngeal structures is the subject of Hajime Hirose's chapter. In the first part of the chapter he describes specialized, newly developed techniques of investigation including laryngeal fiberscopy, high-speed digital imaging of vocal fold vibration, laryngeal electromyography, photoglottography and electroglottography. This is followed by a discussion of laryngeal structures including laryngeal muscles and the microstructure of the vocal folds and the mechanisms for the control of phonation.

Chapter 5 is a discussion of instrumental techniques for linguistic phonetic fieldwork by Peter Ladefoged. He outlines basic principles for gathering data for a description of the phonetic structures of a language and includes guidelines for preparing and recording data, selecting subjects and analysing the speech material. From personal experience, the author evaluates a number of key instrumental techniques suitable for fieldwork conditions including acoustic analysis based on a portable computer and techniques for obtaining aerodynamic, palatographic and electrolaryngographic records.

Part I concludes with an overview by William Shearer of the various types of statistical designs particularly suited to the fields of phonetics and speech pathology: single subject design, two group comparisons (involving either normal distributions or non-parametric groups) and correlations for two groups of data. Using examples drawn mainly from the clinical literature he discusses the relative advantages of the different types of factorial analysis. A numerical example of a factorial design using ANOVA is provided to illustrate issues such as the interpretation of interactions and post-hoc testing. The chapter concludes with a discussion of extraneous variables relevant to research in speech science.

Part II begins with a chapter by Gary Weismer on motor speech disorders. The chapter is motivated by the fact that the study of the disordered state can provide valuable and relevant data to inform models of speech production. He presents a comprehensive overview of recent research into the acoustic and physiological characteristics of the dysarthrias and apraxia of speech focusing on speech breathing, laryngeal and supraglottal behaviours. While recognising the important contribution that early work by Darley, Aronson and Brown at the Mayo Clinic made to the description of motor speech disorders, Weismer challenges the notion that 'speech pathology reflects neuropathology' and seeks instead a symptomatology based on measurable speech motor control deficits as a more productive starting point for a unified theory of the disorders. In his survey he clearly indicates the importance of instrumentally-based objective measures, which often provide subtle insights into speech motor control deficits that remain undetected by more traditional perceptually-based approaches.

Ray Kent and Kristin Tjaden in their chapter on brain functions underlying speech begin with an overview of the main structures of the central and peripheral nervous systems, placing particular emphasis on those critical areas most widely linked to speech and language processing (e.g. Broca's, Wernicke's and the Supplementary Motor Areas). The foundations of a neural model for speech production are then sketched using this neuroanatomical framework along with results from a variety of different sources: experiments on animal vocalisations, electrical stimulation of the cortex in humans, clinicoanatomical studies of individuals with neurogenic communication disorders, neuro-imaging studies of speech behaviour (using for example MRI, CT scans, etc.) and new developments in cognitive neuroscience. Using this approach the authors are able to suggest neural mechanisms for the control of speech production and to provide insights into several key issues in speech science such as functional localisation of spoken language in the brain; evolutionary perspectives on language capability; cerebral asymmetry for speech and the relationship between speech production and perception.

The theme of biological foundations underlying speech production is taken up also by Janet Mackenzie Beck in her chapter on organic variation of the vocal apparatus. She points to two main sources of variation in speech performance; phonetic variation resulting from differences in the way the individual uses their vocal apparatus and organic variation depending on individual differences in inherent characteristics of the vocal organs. The chapter focuses on organic variation bringing together information from a variety of sources, anatomical, physiological, anthropological. Three main types of differences in the structure of the vocal apparatus are discussed: the life-cycle changes within an individual; genetic or environmental factors which differentiate between individuals; and differences which result from trauma or disease.

Various different models and theories of speech production and perception are covered in Part III. Chapters on speech production begin with a discussion by Peter MacNeilage on the acquisition of speech. He focuses mainly on speech production but some current views on the acquisition of speech perception are noted briefly. He proposes an innovative theory in which the core event in the development of speech production is the acquisition of syllable-like 'Frames' consisting of rhythmic alternations between depression and elevation of the mandible. During the babbling stage, most of the variance in sound patterning is the result of these mandibular oscillations alone, with limited ability of other articulators (tongue, lips, soft palate) to actively change their positions, either within or between syllables. He argues that subsequent development of segmental production capabilities consists primarily of gradual modifications of these mouth opening and closing acts to expand the initially limited repertoire of vowels and consonants.

Articulatory processes are explored in detail by Joseph Perkell. He shows how multiple influences converge on structures such as the tongue, lips, mandible etc., each with different physical and physiological properties and large number of degrees of freedom, making control very complicated. Drawing on recent research using techniques of acoustic and physiological analysis, he addresses four main aspects of articulatory processes; their role in the 'speech chain'; their kinematic characteristics; how they are constrained by inherent physical and physiological properties of the mechanisms that produce them and perceive their acoustic consequences; and how they might be controlled.

In chapter 12 Edda Farnetani presents an overview of the current knowledge concerning coarticulation and connected speech processes. Current theoretical approaches to coarticulation are reviewed and the chapter covers new ground by developing the relationship between coarticulation (defined as continuous movements of different articulations for the production of successive phonetic segments overlapping in time and interacting with each other) and connected speech processes (traditionally viewed as rule-governed categorical processes such as assimilations, weak forms, elisions etc.). The relationship is considered particularly in the context of the claims from gestural phonology that connected speech processes are not substantially different from coarticulatory processes, i.e. they are continuous and do not imply qualitative changes in the categorical underlying units.

Theories and models of speech production are developed further by Anders Löfqvist particularly from the point of view of spatial and temporal control of speech movements. He points to the requirement of speech production to coordinate several subsystems, i.e. the respiratory system, the larynx, and the supralaryngeal articulators and draws on experimental results within an Action Theory framework to suggest how this coordination may be controlled. Other theoretical issues discussed include the coordinate spaces for speech motor control and the temporal cohesion of speech movements across changes in stress and speaking rate.

Another specialist area of theoretical importance is the larynx, particularly the nature of the voice source and how it varies in speech. In the chapter by Ailbhe Ní Chasaide and Christer Gobl, variations in the source due to laryngeal tension, configuration of the glottis, respiratory effort and even supraglottal activities are first outlined. This is followed by a detailed evaluation of methods used in the analysis and measurement of the voice source including inverse filtering (using either oral air-flow or the speech pressure waveform) and the use of voice source modelling. Innovative software such as a manual interactive method for inverse filtering is introduced. Voice source parameters that determine the overall shape of the glottal pulse are used to define different voice qualities (modal, breathy, whispery voice etc.). Finally the authors discuss the main linguistic and extralinguistic determinants of voice source variation.

The section on speech production concludes with an overview by Ken Stevens of various models and data that address articulatory, acoustic and auditory relationships. Estimates of acoustic consequences of changes in vocal tract shape are given for a variety of sound types such as vowels, sonorant consonants and obstruents. Data on acoustic/auditory relations are reviewed for the high-low and front-back dimensions for vowels and for vowel nasalisation, as well as for the voicing and place dimensions for consonants. Together with the chapter by Fujimura and Erickson it provides a comprehensive state-of-the-art survey of acoustic patterns for speech sounds.

The final three chapters in Part III deal with aspects in auditory processes and speech perception. Bertrand Delgutte begins with a detailed description of neural processing at the earliest stage of speech perception, the level of patterns of discharge from single auditory neurons and cochlear nucleus cells. He reports on studies which show that these neural discharges can reveal important information about phonetically relevant acoustic features such as formant pattern and voice pitch. Evidence is beginning to emerge as well for neural correlates of speech perception phenomena such as categorical perception. He concludes that many phonetic features are prominently and robustly encoded in neural responses, suggesting that the auditory system shows predispositions for the particular set of acoustic features used for phonetic contrasts.

The characteristics of the auditory system are further explored in the chapter by Brian Moore. He discusses the resolution of the auditory system in frequency and time as revealed by psychoacoustic experiments using paradigms such as masking, discrimination of pitch and temporal resolution. A consistent finding from these experiments is that the resolution of the auditory system in frequency and time usually substantially exceeds the resolution necessary for the identification and discrimination of speech sounds. As the author states 'this partly accounts for the fact that speech perception is robust and resistant to distortion of the speech and to background noise'.

James McQueen and Anne Cutler in their chapter on cognitive processes and speech perception focus on the process by which stored lexical knowledge is accessed during speech recognition. Drawing on extensive psycholinguistic research using a variety of methodologies they evaluate the role of acoustic-phonetic, prosodic and lexical information upon which listeners can draw prior to lexical access. Acoustic-phonetic information appears to be essential; only certain aspects of prosodic information are used (e.g. rhythmic for word boundary location) and there is no convincing evidence that lexical knowledge is used prelexically. They conclude that human word recognition appears to be primarily a bottom-up process.

The four chapters in Part IV cover different aspects of linguistic phonetics. Peter Ladefoged in his chapter on linguistic phonetic descriptions outlines the kind of phonetic framework that is necessary for the description of a language. In developing a set of linguistic phonetic features as the basis for such a framework, three principle functions of the framework are considered; the need to describe all linguistic contrasts, a description of the patterns that occur (e.g. grouping sounds into classes that share particular features) and defining a set of possible human sounds that can be used linguistically.

In chapter 20 Ian Maddieson develops the notion of phonetic universals. He describes two general approaches to the question of universals in phonetics; the 'mechanistic' and the 'ecological'. In the mechanistic approach, frequently observed patterns across languages are related to the fact that all human beings use a similar apparatus for speech production and perception and are subject to the same physical laws. A number of proposed mechanistic phonetic universals are discussed including those related to vowel height, consonant voicing and place. In the final part of the chapter, he discusses ecological models which emphasise contrastivity and connectedness as motivating factors in phonetic universals.

John Ohala's chapter explores the relation between phonetics and phonology.

In tracing the history of this relationship from the early part of this century he shows it has been affected by theoretical frameworks such as structuralist phonology, in which more attention was given to relations between sounds at the expense of the substance of sounds. It is proposed that in order to explain sound patterns in language, phonology needs to re-integrate scientific phonetics (as well as psychology and sociolinguistics). The author provides examples where principles of aerodynamics and acoustics are used to explain certain common sound patterns.

Part V is concerned with issues in speech technology. Most speech technology applications rely on digital signal processing (DSP) and Johan Liljencrants presents an overview of this area. He surveys frequently used DSP concepts and applications that are particularly relevant to the speech scientist. These include discrete and fast Fourier transforms, analog-to-digital conversion, filtering, the Z-transform, spectrum analysis, linear predictive coding (LPC) and pitch extraction.

An important application of speech technology is automatic speech recognition and Bill Ainsworth's overview outlines recent developments in this area. He discusses current issues in the development of robust speech recognition systems including the problem of time scale variation, and evaluates a number of techniques that have been adapted to deal with this, including dynamic time warping, Hidden Markov Models and neural networks. Techniques developed to deal with noise are also described together with the problems of training, feedback and error correction.

Chapter 25 by Francis Nolan discusses speaker recognition and forensic phonetics. He examines the ways in which the characteristics of an individual are encoded in the speech signal, and discusses how reliably identity can be inferred. Several sources of variation are explored and related to current issues in forensic phonetics. Practical applications of both speaker verification and speaker recognition are also discussed.

Part V concludes with a survey of speech synthesis systems by Rolf Carlson and Björn Granström. They review some of the more popular approaches to speech synthesis and show how it is no longer simply a research tool but has many everyday applications. They describe current trends in speech synthesis research and point to some present and future applications of text-to-speech technology.

We believe that the twenty-six chapters give a representative flavour of research across the phonetic sciences today. The distinguished group of international contributors offer students an invitation to the phonetic sciences, and the hard work of the authors will be amply repaid if readers feel that they have been stimulated to take a research interest in this vigorously growing interdisciplinary subject.

Bill Hardcastle and John Laver
Edinburgh, October 1995

NOTES

Goldsmith, J. (ed.) (1994) Handbook of Phonology, Blackwell, Oxford.

Kaiser, L. (ed.) (1957) Manual of Phonetics, North-Holland, Amsterdam.

Malmberg, B. (ed.) (1968) Manual of Phonetics, North-Holland, Amsterdam.

Part I Experimental Phonetics

1 Laboratory Techniques for Investigating Speech Articulation

MAUREEN STONE

Measuring the vocal tract is an exceedingly difficult task because the articulators differ widely in speed of movement, structural composition, dimensionality of movement, degree of complexity, shape, and location. There are large differences in shape and structural composition between soft tissue structures (tongue, lips, velum) and hard tissue structures (jaw, palate). Therefore, these structures differ significantly in movement dimensionality. For example, the fluid deformation of the tongue needs quite different measurement strategies from the rigid body movements of the jaw.

The second difficulty is the different speeds and locations of the articulators. An instrument with a frequency response adequate for the slow-moving jaw will not necessarily be adequate for the fast-moving tongue tip. As with articulator speed, differences in articulator location significantly affect the type of transduction system needed. Structures that are visible to superficial inspection, such as the lips, are much easier to record than structures deep within the oral cavity such as the velum.

The final and perhaps most important complication in measuring articulatory movement is the interaction among articulators. Some articulatory behaviors are more highly correlated than others, and distinguishing the contributions of each player can be quite difficult. The most dramatic example of this is the tongue-jaw system. It is clear that jaw height is a major factor in tongue tip height. However, this coupling of the two structures becomes progressively weaker as one moves posteriorly, until in the pharynx, tongue movement is only minimally coupled to jaw movement if at all. Thus, trying to measure the contribution of the jaw to tongue movement becomes a difficult task.

As a result, an instrument that competently measures one articulator is inadequate to measure another. A plastic pseudo-palate is an excellent means of determining where on the palate the tongue makes contact. A similar device that measured where on the tongue that contact occurs, even if made out of soft, flexible material, would be difficult to create because such a device would curtail the expansion, contraction, flexion and torsion occurring on the tongue surface.

It is also difficult to devise a transducer that can be inserted into the mouth, which will not in some way distort the speech event. Thus, the types of instruments used in the vocal tract need to be unobtrusive, such as by resting intimately against a surface (e.g., electropalatography (EPG)), by being small and positioned on non-contact surfaces (e.g., pellet tracking systems) or by not entering the vocal tract at all (e.g., imaging techniques).

Instruments that enter the oral cavity must meet certain criteria. They need to be unaffected by temperature change, moisture, or air pressure. Affixatives must be unaffected by moisture, must be able to stick to expandable, moist surfaces, and must be removable without tearing the surface tissue. Devising instruments that are non-invasive, unobtrusive, meet the above criteria, and still measure one or more components of the speech event is so difficult that most researchers prefer to study the speech wave and infer physiological events from it. However, since those inferences are based on some initial physiological data, it is critical that new physiological data be added and refined, lest models of the vocal tract and our understanding of speech production stagnate.

In recent times, physiological measurements have improved at an extraordinary pace. Imaging techniques have emerged on the scene and have revolutionized the way we view the vocal tract by providing recognizable images of structures deep within the pharynx. Point-tracking systems are transforming our ideas about coarticulation by revealing inter-articulator relationships that could only in the past be addressed theoretically. Finally, instruments with a relatively long history of use in speech science, such as electropalatography and electromyography, have been improved to provide better and more useful data.

This chapter considers three types of non-acoustic instruments for measuring speech physiology: imaging techniques, point-tracking techniques, and measures of complex behaviors.

1 Imaging techniques

The internal structures of the vocal tract are difficult to measure without impinging upon normal movement patterns. Imaging techniques overcome that difficulty because they register internal movement without directly contacting the structures. Four well-known imaging techniques have been applied to speech research: X-ray, computed tomography (CT), magnetic resonance imaging (MRI), and ultrasound. Imaging systems provide very different information from other physiological measures, i.e., an image of the entire structure, rather than a single point on the structure.

1.1 X-ray

X-ray is the most well known of the imaging systems and is important because until recently most of our knowledge about the behavior of the pharyngeal portion of the vocal tract came from X-ray data. To make a lateral X-ray image, an X-ray beam is projected from one side of the head through all the tissue, and is recorded on a plate on the other side. The resulting image shows the head from front to back and provides a lengthwise view of the tongue. A frontal or anterior/posterior (A/P) X-ray is made by projecting the X-ray beam from the front of the head through to the back of the head and recording the image on a plate behind the head. The resulting image provides a cross-sectional, or side-to-side, view of the tongue. Usually, soft tissue structures such as the tongue are difficult to measure with X-rays, because the beam records everything in its path including teeth, jaw, and vertebrae. These strongly imaged bony structures obscure the fainter soft tissue. A second problem with X-ray is that unless a contrast medium is used to mark the midline of the tongue, it is difficult to tell if the visible edge is the midline of the tongue or a lateral edge. This is particularly problematic during speech, because the tongue is often grooved. Finally, the potential hazards of overexposure preclude the collection of large quantities of data with ordinary X-rays. The X-ray Microbeam was devised to overcome this limitation by tracking points and vastly reducing the X-ray exposure.

Considerable research has been done using X-ray imaging. Most models of the vocal tract are based on X-ray data (cf. Fant, 1965, Harshman et al., 1977, Hashimoto and Sasaki, 1982, Maeda, 1990, Mermelstein, 1973, Wood, 1979). X-rays have also been used to study normal speech production (Kent and Netsell, 1971, Kent, 1972, Kent and Moll, 1972) and disorders (Subtelney et al., 1989, Tye-Murray, 1991).

1.1.1 Xeroradiography

1.1.1 Xeroradiography Xeroradiography is also a projection technique and uses a conventional X-ray tube to generate the X-rays. However, the image receptor is an aluminum plate coated with selenium, a photoconductive material. The image receptor for a standard X-ray is X-ray film.

The first stage in making a xeroradiograph is the formation of a "latent image" on the aluminum plate. The second stage is the development of that image into a xeroradiographic image. In stage one, the selenium coated aluminum plate is electrostatically charged prior to being exposed to the X-ray. The selenium coating acts as an insulator. When exposed to X-rays (or light) selenium's insulating ability decreases in proportion to the amount of X-ray exposure, discharging a proportional amount of static electricity. This effect is extremely well localized. The X-ray exposure at one point does not cause discharge nearby, so that the edges of an object are very well defined. The plate at this point contains an invisible electrostatic representation of an X-ray image, called a latent image. The plate is then taken to a light-tight chamber for stage two: development. To develop the xeroradiograph, an aerosol of electrically charged pigmented powder is sprayed on the latent image, transferred to paper, and fused (fixed) by heating. Positive and negative xeroradiographs can be made. However, the plate must be cleaned (heated and cooled) before reuse to prevent shadow contours from previous images (Zeman, 1976, Schertel et al., 1976).

The advantage of xeroradiography is the extreme clarity at the edges of a structure, even a soft tissue structure. The disadvantages are great, however. First it is a very slow procedure, requiring two stages and could only be used for steady state vocal tract measurements. Second the technique uses considerably more radiation than conventional X-rays (Schertel et al., 1976). Third, the machines are hard to maintain and are very sensitive to dust because of the static electricity. Fourth, these machines are quite old and hard to find. Thus, this technique does not seem well suited to speech research when compared to the other imaging techniques available.

1.2 Tomography

Tomography creates images in a fundamentally different way from projection X-ray. Tomographs, or pictures of slices of tissue, are constructed by projecting a thin, flat beam through the tissue in a single plane.

In order to interpret these data, four tomographic planes are used (see Figure 1.1). They are sagittal, coronal, oblique, and transverse. The midsagittal plane is a longitudinal slice, from top to bottom, down the median plane, or midline, of the body (dashed line). The parasagittal plane is parallel to the midline of the body but off-center. The coronal plane is a longitudinal slice perpendicular to the median plane of the body. The oblique plane is inclined between the horizontal and vertical planes. Finally, the transverse plane lies perpendicular to the long axis of the body, and is often called the transaxial plane, or the axial plane.

1.2.1 Computed Tomography (CT)   Computed tomography (CT) uses X-rays to image slices (sections) of the body as thin as 2 mm. Figure 1.2 depicts a CT scanner. The scanner rotates around the body, taking multiple images at different angles, of a single section of tissue. A computer then creates a composite, including any structures that were visible in some scans but obscured in others. Figure 1.3 shows a transverse section CT of the oropharynx at rest. Bone appears bright white in the image. The jaw can be seen at the top of the image, and a vertebra at the bottom. The hyoid bone is horseshoe shaped, in the middle of the image. The air in the vocal tract appears black, and the epiglottis can be seen within the vocal tract. The tongue and other soft tissue are gray. CT can image soft tissue more clearly than projection X-ray because it produces a composite X-ray. By digitally summing a series of scans, the composite section has sharper edges and more distinct tissue definition.

IMAGING TECHNIQUES

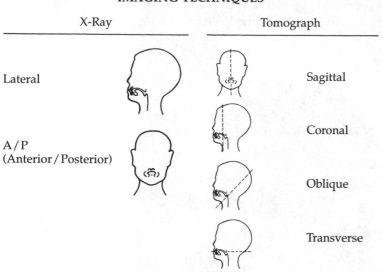

X-Ray	Tomograph

Lateral

A/P
(Anterior/Posterior)

Sagittal

Coronal

Oblique

Transverse

Figure 1.1 Scan types used in through-transmission and tomographic imaging. There are two X-ray angles contrasted with four tomographic scanning planes.

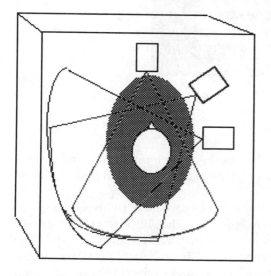

Figure 1.2 Schematic of patient lying in CT scanner with multiple scans being made and combined into an image.

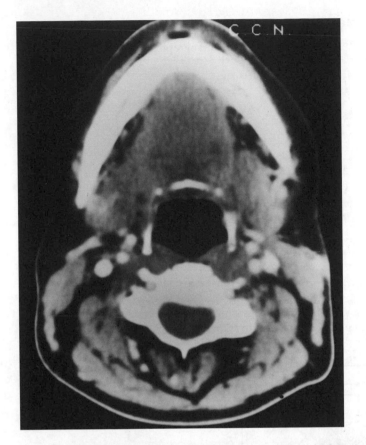

Figure 1.3   CT image of a transverse section of the oropharynx at rest.

Very few studies have used CT to image the vocal tract because of radiation exposure and because MRI provides much the same information. Those studies that do depict the vocal tract using CT include Kiritani et al., 1977, Muraki et al., 1983, Sundberg et al., 1987.

CT has three major limitations. The first is speed. Most current CT scans take 2.5 sec per frame, too slow for real-time speech. The newer CT's can take several scans per sec, so future technology may reduce this problem. The second limitation is the radiation exposure. CT is an X-ray. Therefore, only a limited amount of data can be collected on a single subject. Finally, the scan images are limited to the transverse and oblique planes because the scanning table can only be tilted roughly 45 degrees. On the positive side, CT can image the entire tract, sectioning multiple planes for analysis. In addition, the images are extremely clear and the edges are easy to measure. The sections are quite thin (2 mm), allowing composite three-dimensional vocal-tract shapes to be constructed by combining multiple sections.

1.2.2 Magnetic Resonance Imaging (MRI)   Another tomographic technique is magnetic resonance imaging (MRI), (sometimes called Nuclear Magnetic Resonance, NMR). MRI uses a magnetic field and radio waves rather than X-rays to image a section of tissue.

MRI is very good at differentiating different types of tissue, and therefore a number of studies have used it to view vocal tract anatomy (Christianson et al., 1987, Lufkin et al., 1983, McKenna et al., 1990). Several studies cross-validated or coupled MRI with other instruments, such as ultrasound (Takashima et al., 1989, Wein et al., 1990), X-ray (Lakshminarayanan et al., 1990, 1991) and glossometry (McCutcheon et al., 1990). The last study validated both instruments by using tongue-palate spacers to generate known tongue positions.

MRI also has been used to calculate vocal tract volumes (Baer et al., 1987, 1991, Lakshminarayanan et al., 1990, 1991, Moore, 1992, Tiede, pc). Lakshminarayanan used a newer technique that allowed scan times as low as 4 sec per image. This rapid rate was achieved through the use of a specially designed coil that highlighted the oral area, and a gradient-echo technique. The formant patterns generated by the resultant model were generally comparable to real acoustic data, but individual formants varied by as much as 500 Hz. The authors hypothesized that the error might be due to their width-to-area conversion algorithm or to their assumptions of cross-sectional tube area.

MRI is very useful for studying pathology that involves tissue changes, such as tumors, and highlights other speech related pathologies as well. Takashima et al. (1988) used MRI and ultrasound in the staging of tongue cancers. Cha and Patten (1989) described tongue postural abnormalities in patients with Amyotrophic Lateral Sclerosis (ALS). Wein et al. (1991) used sagittal images to demonstrate velopharyngeal insufficiency in 5 patients with varied pathologies.

An MRI scanner consists of electromagnets that surround the body and create a magnetic field. MRI scanning detects the presence of hydrogen atoms, which occur in abundance in water and, therefore, in tissue. In Figure 1.4, picture A represents a hydrogen proton spinning about an axis which is oriented randomly. B shows what happens when a magnetic field is introduced. The proton's axis aligns along the direction of the field's poles. Even when aligned, however, the proton wobbles, or precesses. In picture C, a short-lived radio pulse, vibrating at the same frequency as the wobble, is introduced. This momentarily knocks the proton out of alignment. D shows the proton realigning, within milliseconds, to the magnetic field. As it realigns, the proton emits a weak radio signal of its own. These radio signals are then assembled as an image indicating hydrogen density, or water content, thus clearly differentiating between different types of tissue.

Figure 1.5 shows a sagittal MRI image of [s]. The subject held the [s] for 45 seconds to make this image. The vocal tract appears black, as do the teeth, since neither contain water. The marrow in the palate, which is high in water content, and the fat surrounding the head, which is high in hydrogen, are bright white. Although the edges are not as crisp as CT, they are reasonably clear and easily measurable.

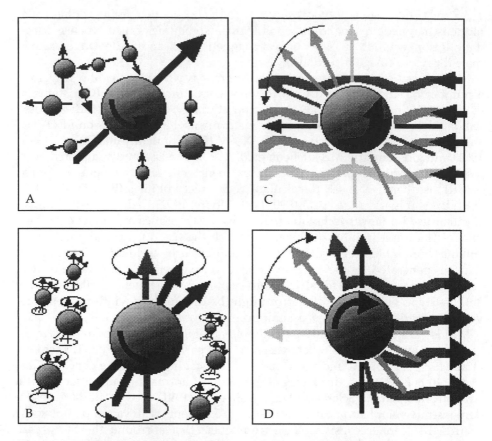

Figure 1.4   The effects of MRI scanning on hydrogen protons.

A new application of MRI, the Tagging Snapshot technique has been used by Kumada et al. (1992) and Niitsu et al. (1992) to examine tongue position at the beginning and end of a movement and to derive the direction of movement. In this technique, tagging stripes or a grid are superimposed on a slice of tissue. As the tissue changes shape and position, the stripes move and deform, reflecting the changes in the tissue (Figure 1.6). Thus, one can see compression and expansion within the body of the tongue.

As with CT, MRI has several drawbacks. The first is speed. The radio signal emitted by each proton is so weak that it must be summed over time. Image time for a good resolution picture takes from 3 seconds (Wein et al., 1991) to 6 minutes (Moore, 1992). Newer MRI scanners takes only 50 ms per scan, but resolution is still poor (64 × 64 pixels). However, this technology is improving, and MRI is progressing towards real-time. The second drawback is the width of the section. Whereas CT sections are 2 mm wide, MRI scans are usually at least 5 mm wide. A tomographic scan compresses a three-dimensional space

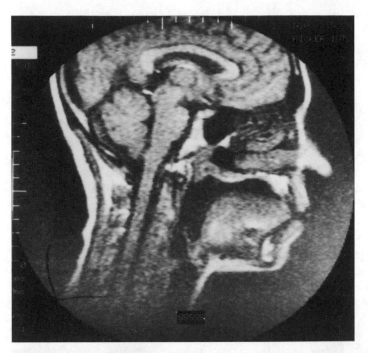

Figure 1.5   MRI image of a midsagittal section of the tongue during the production of [s].

(a)   (b)

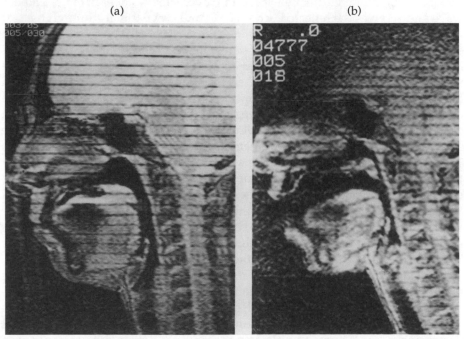

Figure 1.6   Tagging snapshot MRI. a) an MRI image of the vocal tract at rest.
b) the tongue is deformed into an /a/. The tags are no longer straight, but reflect
the compression and expansion occurring locally in the tongue.

into two dimensions, like displaying a cylinder as a circle. Therefore, in a slice that is 5 mm wide, items that are actually 5 mm apart in the cross-sectional plane of the image will appear to be in the same plane. Thus the hyoid bone and epiglottis might appear in the same slice even though one is several mm below the other. Narrower widths on MRI require longer exposure time. A third drawback is that many subjects, as many as 30 per cent, experience claustrophobia and cannot tolerate the procedure. Fourth, metal clamps, tooth crowns, and steel implants quench the signal creating a diffuse dark spot surrounding the metal.

A final drawback for both MRI and CT is that the subject must be lying supine or prone. This position changes the location of gravity with respect to the oral structures and normal agonist/antagonist muscle relationships. It is not clear what effect this would have on vocal tract shapes. One might speculate however, that the effects would be greatest when at rest, and minimal during speech, since acoustic constraints would probably ensure relatively stable vocal tract behaviors. Despite these non-trivial drawbacks, MRI and CT provide unique and valuable information by imaging both the soft and hard tissue of the vocal tract with no obscuration. In addition, MRI is the only imaging technique that can image any plane of the body, providing outstanding cross-sectional vocal tract information.

1.2.3 Ultrasound   Ultrasound produces an image by using the reflective properties of sound waves. A piezoelectric crystal stimulated by electric current emits an ultra high-frequency sound wave. The crystal both emits a sound wave and receives the reflected echo. The sound wave travels through the soft tissue and reflects back when it reaches an interface with tissue of a different density, like bone, or when it reaches air. The best reflections are perpendicular to the beam (Figure 1.7). In order to see a section of tissue rather than a single point, one needs a mechanical sector scanner or an array transducer. In a mechanical scanner transducer, multiple crystals rotate about a hub. The crystals are "on," or emit and receive waves, during a portion of the rotation cycle and "off" during the remainder of the rotation. This creates a wedge shaped image of up to 140 degrees (Figure 1.8a). In an array transducer, up to 128 crystals fire sequentially imaging a rectangular or wedge-shaped section of tissue the size of the transducer. In both cases, the returning echoes are processed by computer and displayed as a video image.

Figure 1.8b shows a sagittal (lengthwise) image of the tongue. To create such an image, the transducer is placed below the chin and the beam passes upward through a 1.9 mm thick section of the tongue. When the sound reaches the air at the surface of the tongue, it reflects back creating a bright white line. The black area immediately below is the tongue body. The border between the white reflection and the black tissue is the surface of the tongue. Interfaces within the tongue are also visible. Figure 1.8c depicts the tongue in coronal section. The smaller, cross-sectional tongue surface contains a small midsagittal depression. Genioglossus muscle and the muscles of the floor of the mouth

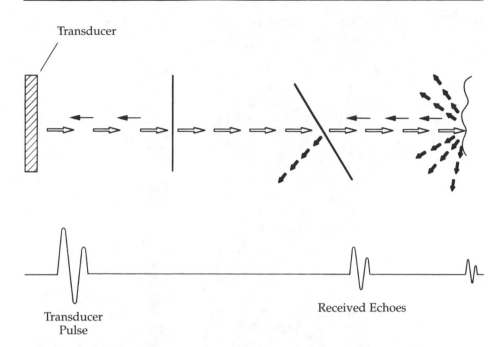

Figure 1.7 Schematic of ultrasound reflection patterns emanating from surfaces at different angles to the beam.

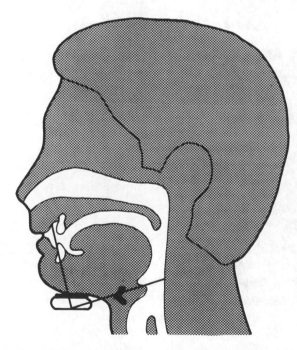

Figure 1.8a A schematic of the head indicating the approximate region captured by a midsagittal ultrasound scan.

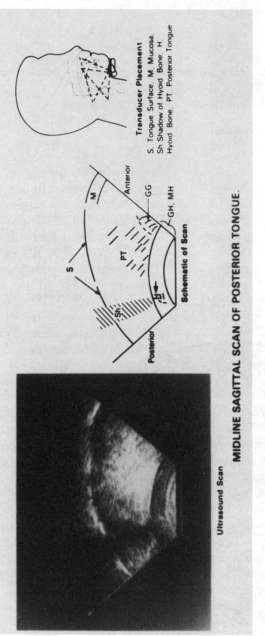

Figure 1.8b Midsagittal scan of the posterior tongue and shadow of the hyoid bone.

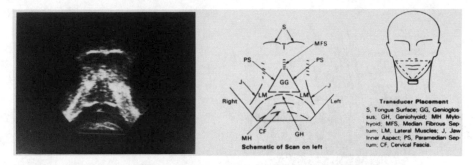

Figure 1.8c Coronal scan of the tongue.

appear as black areas. Measurement error on such images is less than .7 mm. The vocal folds may also be imaged by placing the ultrasound transducer at the front of the neck, at the thyroid notch (Adam's apple), and pointing it directly back in the transverse plane. A number of studies have used real-time ultrasound to study tongue movements during speech, (Stone et al., 1987, 1988, Stone, 1990, Watkin and Rubin, 1989, Wein et al., 1990), and swallowing (Sonies, 1991). Recently 3D tongue surface reconstructions have been made as well (Stone and Lundberg, 1996) as shown in Figure 1.9.

There are several disadvantages of ultrasound. The first is that about 1 cm of the tongue tip may not be imaged because the ultrasound beam is reflected by the interface between the floor of the mouth and the air above it, thus never reaching the tongue tip. The tip may be imaged, however, if there is a great deal of saliva in the mouth, or if the tongue is resting against the floor. The second disadvantage is the inability to see beyond a tissue/air or tissue/bone interface. Since the air at the tongue's surface reflects the sound wave, the structures on the far side of the vocal tract, beyond the air gap, like the palate and pharyngeal wall, cannot be imaged. Similarly, when ultrasound reaches a bone, the curved shape refracts the sound wave creating an acoustic shadow or dark area. Thus, the jaw and hyoid bones appear as shadows and their exact position cannot be reliably measured.

Ultrasound, however, is relatively fast. The scan rate is as fast as 60 scans/ sec and is recorded on 60 video fields per sec. It can image tongue movement for vowels and most consonants, although it is not fast enough to measure vocal fold vibration. A second advantage is that it involves no known bio-logical hazards, since the transduction process involves only sound waves. In addition, the real-time multiple-plane capabilities capture tongue movements, not just positions, allowing reconstruction of complex three-dimensional move-ments of the tongue surface. This is more complete, movement data on the tongue than can be obtained from any other instrument.

Imaging techniques provide more complete information about vocal tract behavior than are available from direct measures like point-tracking techniques or electropalatography, because imaging techniques measure the inaccessible

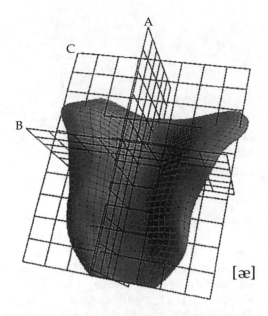

[æ]

Figure 1.9   A three-dimensional reconstruction of the tongue surface for the sound [æ] made from 60 coronal and oblique ultrasound images.

parts of the tract (e.g., the pharynx), and they measure planes rather than points. In the future, as scan rates increase, imaging systems will become more accessible and more widely used, providing expanded datasets and multiple perspectives.

2 Point-tracking measurements of the vocal tract

Point-tracking systems measure individual fleshpoints by affixing pellets to the articulators and tracking their movement during speech. Typically, multiple articulators can be measured at the same time, and tracking speed is fast, so that interarticulator timing measures are quite good. Three specific point tracking systems, the articulometer, the X-ray microbeam, and the Optotrak are significantly improving the quality of vocal tract measurements.

2.1 *Electromagnetic Midsagittal Articulometer (EMMA)*

The EMMA tracks fleshpoint movement by measuring the movement of small receiver coils through alternating magnetic fields. Several such instruments, using roughly similar principles have been developed in Germany (Schönle

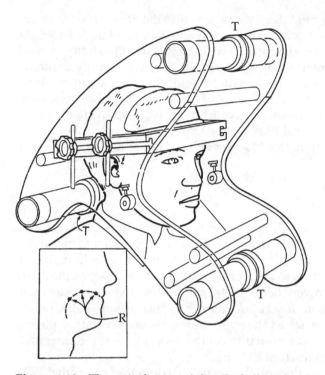

Figure 1.10   The articulometer (after Perkell et al., 1992, *Journal of the Acoustical Society of America*. (Reproduced with permission)

et al., 1987, 1989), Sweden (Branderud, 1985), and the United States (Perkell et al., 1988, 1992).

In the Perkell system, a clear plastic assembly, suspended from above, fits around the subject's head (Figure 1.10). Three transmitter coils (T) form an equilateral triangle. The transmitter coils each produce an alternating magnetic field. Each transmitter is driven at a different sinusoidal frequency to generate a different alternating magnetic field. The use of three transmitters, and therefore three overlapping fields, assures accuracy in locating the receiver coils (R). The best resolution in the field space is found in the center, i.e., in the oropharyngeal region, where measurement resolution is calculated at less than 1 mm. The receiver coils are small insulated coils attached with adhesive to articulatory structures at midline. As the alternating magnetic fields pass through the receiver coil, they induce an alternating signal in the receiver coils. The voltage of this signal is inversely related to the distance between the transmitter and the receiver coil. A computer algorithm calculates the actual location of the receiver coil as it moves in x–y space over time.

One disadvantage of this system is that only points are measured, so the behavior of the entire articulator is largely inferred. This is most problematic for the soft tissue structures like the lips, tongue and velum, whose movements are more fluid than rigid. A second disadvantage is that the data can only be collected at midline and are subject to error as the articulators rotate left-to-right.

The biggest advantages are the rapid tracking rate, and the ability to track multiple articulators simultaneously. Because of these two features, interaction among the articulators can be measured, and questions about interarticulator timing and programming can be asked. Although there has been some concern over possible health consequences from exposure to magnetic fields, the articulometer poses minimal biological hazards since it uses short exposure times and low field strengths. Nonetheless, its use is not recommended with pregnant women.

2.2 X-ray Microbeam

The X-ray Microbeam uses an extremely thin X-ray beam to track the motion of small gold pellets that are affixed to one or more articulators using dental adhesive. The beam is 0.4 mm thick and the pellets are 2–3 mm in diameter. Gold pellets are used because gold is an inert metal and because, as the X-ray dosage is very small, only a very dense metal can be detected. The system was designed to reduce radiation dosage to well below that of a dental X-ray, to avoid radiosensitive areas, such as the eyes, and to reduce secondary photon scatter. The X-ray beam focuses primarily on the pellets so that the surrounding tissue receives only minimal radiation.

The two-dimensional position of the beam is computer controlled. The X-ray beam originates at one side of the subject, passes through the subject's head, and is detected by a scintillation counter on the far side. Up to 1,000 pellet positions are sampled per sec. Thus, if 10 pellets are used, they can each be sampled 100 times per sec. Differential sampling rates are also possible. The pellets are sampled initially in rest position to determine baseline xy displacement. A computer algorithm causes the beam to scan the area in which the pellet is predicted to move. The prediction is based on the pellet's previous displacement, velocity, and acceleration. Each pellet is scanned in order. Positioning accuracy of the beam is 62 microns.

There are several advantages to the X-ray Microbeam. The rapid rate and accuracy of tracking make this an excellent system for examining timing-related coarticulatory effects, kinematic parameters such as velocity and acceleration, and the intercoordination of the articulators. In addition, the technique is unobtrusive and the low radiation dosage allows for reasonably large data sets to be collected on each subject.

A disadvantage of the X-ray Microbeam is that such a large, costly facility, and a large support staff, will always be either unique or rare. Therefore, it requires considerable travel for most investigators and their subjects to reach the facility. The second disadvantage is that although the radiation dosage is low, the use of X-ray and the known biological hazards must still be considered a limitation of the system. A final disadvantage is that with a 450 kV beam, the X-ray will not pass through silver and therefore subjects must have no fillings. A new or upgraded machine, however, could produce a 600 kV beam level that will pass through silver fillings but not gold pellets, allowing the pellets to be better imaged.

Two other limitations are common to both the articulometer and the X-ray Microbeam. First, only two-dimensional data are collected, and movements off-plane are lost or induce error. The second common problem is the difficulty of affixing pellets to the pharynx, velum and posterior tongue due to the gag reflex, thus limiting its use with some subjects.

2.3 *Strain gauges*

Strain gauges were developed for use in lip and jaw measurements in the early 1970s (Abbs and Gilbert, 1973, Barlow and Abbs, 1983, Muller et al., 1977). Strain gauge transducers are composed of two sequential, perpendicular, very thin cantilever beams (c. 0.13 mm) on which are mounted miniature strain gauges. From the end of the outer beam a rigid wire extends and is affixed to the articulator of interest at midline. The wire moves with the articulator. The perpendicular arrangement of the beams causes one to bend in response to anterior/posterior movement, and the other to bend in response to superior/inferior movement. The bending of the beams is converted into a proportional voltage by the strain gauges mounted on them. The changes in voltage produce an analog waveform that can be recorded on an FM recorder, printed out on an oscillograph, or digitized and entered into a computer. The waveform can be differentiated to yield velocity and acceleration data as well.

The method of attachment of the gauge to the jaw is of interest in both this instrument and the other jaw measurement instruments. Since the skin of the jaw moves with lower lip movement, an artifact in measures of jaw movement is created if the rigid wire is affixed to the skin below the chin, rather than to a mandibular tooth. Kuehn et al. (1980), used X-ray to calculate error in movement of a chin mounted transducer relative to movement of the lower incisor. They found some error in both labial and non-labial consonants with a chin mount. The tooth mount placement eliminated this problem. However, it may interfere with lip movement. Careful planning of speech materials and theoretical questions is needed to overcome these weaknesses.

More recent modifications and applications of strain gauge technology have been used to measure lip and jaw closing force in non-speech activities. Measurements of maximum voluntary closure force (Barlow and Rath, 1985), and controlled sustained closure force (Barlow and Burton, 1990) have provided normative data on lip and jaw forces. These data can be applied to dynamic models of lip and jaw movement and in comparisons of normal and disordered movements.

2.4 *Optotrak*

Another point tracking system, Optotrak, is a new and improved version of the older Watsmart. This device tracks the movement of points in three-dimensional (xyz) space. Thus, Optotrak can measure side-to-side movement as well as anterior-to-posterior and superior-to-inferior movement. The system consists of markers placed on surface structures, sensors that track their position, and a system unit that controls the timing of the marker emissions and the sensor processing. The markers are lightweight, flat, circular disks that come in two diameters, 4.75 mm and 16 mm. Embedded in the center of each marker is a small semiconductor chip that emits an infrared signal. Up to 256 markers can be used at one time. A strip of three sensors acts as a camera and tracks the movement of the markers. This is not a video system, in which marker position is filmed. Rather each sensor contains a lens and signal processing circuitry that records the infrared emissions of the marker. The sensors are pre-aligned so that they measure the position of each marker in three-dimensional space.

This instrument is particularly well suited to tracking lip and jaw motion in 3D and examining relationships between them and head position. Its advantage over the other two point-tracking systems is that it provides three-dimensional motion data. The third dimension allows measurement of rotation and provides a better understanding of speech kinematics and motor control. The system's disadvantage is that it is limited to external use, unlike the X-ray Microbeam and articulometer, because its sensors track LED's and must maintain "visual" contact with them. Therefore, it cannot be used inside the mouth and so does not reveal structures within the vocal tract.

Two more disadvantages are common to all point tracking systems. First, only fleshpoints are tracked, not the entire structure. For rigid structures such as the jaw, the entire structure can be reconstructed. However, the flexibility of soft tissue structures such as the tongue, lips and velum, is incompletely measured and represented. Second, the markers or their attached wires may interfere, at least minimally, with truly natural speech.

3 Measurement of complex behaviors

3.1 Electropalatography

Electropalatography (EPG) measures tongue–palate contact in real-time during speech. EPG is the only instrument that reveals the shape of tongue–palate contact patterns and their changes over time. Therefore, data from EPG provide a unique perspective on the interaction of the tongue and palate, as well as information on the cross-sectional vocal tract shape in the palatal area. A very thin (0.5 mm) acrylic pseudo-palate is molded to fit a palatal cast of the speaker. A series of very small electrodes (up to 96) are embedded in the palate and in some cases along the inner surface of the teeth (Figure 1.11). Thin wires (42 gauge) attached to each electrode, exit the palate by winding behind the back molars on each side and forward out through the corners of the lips.

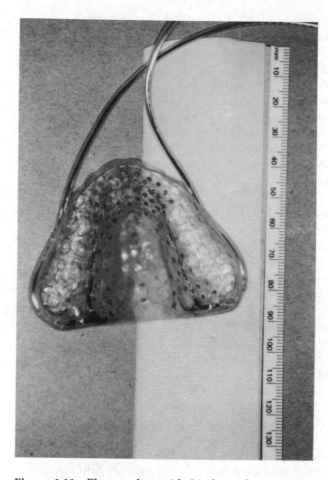

Figure 1.11 Electropalate with 96 electrodes embedded along the palatal surface and inner edges of the teeth.

A ground electrode, usually placed on the wrist, completes the circuit. The pseudopalate is electrically isolated from the computer, and the wires that connect to it are driven by an undetectable DC current. When the tongue contacts an electrode, the circuit is completed and the contact registered. The electrodes are sampled 100 or more times per second in most systems.

EPG has been in use for three decades (Fletcher et al., 1975, Hardcastle, 1972, 1974, Kiritani et al., 1977, Kuzzmin, 1962, Kydd and Belt, 1964, Palmer, 1973, Shibata, 1968). It has been used to study both normal and disordered subjects, and has been an instrument of choice when available because it is only minimally invasive yet provides unique information. Data analysis is also relatively straighforward using a PC (see Hardcastle et al., 1991 for a complete review). Normal studies using EPG include demographic studies of palatal growth (Hiki and Itoh, 1986), and normative data on children (Fletcher, 1989) and adults (Fletcher and Newman, 1991). EPG has also been used in conjunction with other instruments to add to its power. Such instruments include acoustical measures (Hoole et al., 1989), articulography (Hoole et al., 1993), ultrasound (Stone et al., 1991, 1992), aerodynamics (Hardcastle and Clark, 1981), fiberoptics, air pressure and transillumination (Manuel and Bateson, 1988).

There have been three major applications of EPG to linguistics. The first is the documentation of physiology for sounds involving lingual–palatal contact during speech production across languages. Alveolar sounds such as [t,d,l,n,s,z] flap, and trill, have been studied extensively in such languages as Japanese (Fujimura et al., 1972, Miyawaki et al., 1974, Mizutani et al., 1988), Italian (Farnetani, 1991, Farnetani and Faber, 1992, Farnetani et al., 1985), Catalan (Recasens, 1991), German (Kohler, 1976), and English (Hardcastle and Clark, 1981, Hardcastle and Barry, 1989, Manuel and Bateson, 1988, Palmer, 1973). Velar sounds are less studied since the traditional pseudo-palate usually ends before the soft palate (Hardcastle, 1985). However, some velo-palatography has been done (Suzuki and Michi, 1986).

The second area of interest has been fricatives. For intra-oral fricatives, the size and shape of the constrictions are difficult to ascertain, yet they are very important to the spectrum and energy of the noise produced. EPG provides the width, length, and curvature of the palatal portion of the constriction, as well as the upper surface of the vocal tract "tube" throughout the palatal region (Flege et al., 1988, Fletcher and Newman, 1991, Hardcastle and Clark, 1981, Hoole et al., 1989, 1993).

A third area of interest is coarticulation. The effects of neighboring vowels on tongue-palate contact during consonants reveals the nature of how we sequence sounds and strategies of motor control (Farnetani, 1990, Farnetani et al., 1985, Farnetani and Faber, 1992, Hardcastle and Roach, 1977, Marchal, 1983, 1988, Recasens, 1984a, 1984b, Gibbon et al., 1993).

Another contribution of EPG is to the study of disorders (cf. Gibbon, 1990). EPG has been used to study cleft palate (Fletcher, 1985, Michi et al., 1986, Hardcastle et al., 1989), open bite (Suzuki et al., 1981), deaf speech (Fletcher et al., 1979), apraxic speech (Hardcastle and Edwards, 1992) and as a biofeedback tool to allow deaf speakers (who have an essentially normal speech production system) to receive biofeedback as to the state of their vocal tract during speech (Dagenais and Critz-Crosby, 1992, Fletcher and Hasegawa, 1983, Fletcher et al., 1991). A review of literature on clinical aspects of EPG may be found in Nicolaidis et al. (1992) and Hardcastle et al. (1991).

Two other applications of EPG are in the study of speech compensation to changes in oral morphology (Hamlet and Stone, 1978) and the study of word recognition from EPG patterns (Fletcher, 1990).

EPG has two principal drawbacks. The first is that it provides information on only one component of the vocal tract event. This could, of course, be said of most of the instruments discussed here. The second, and more important drawback, is that EPG provides information only when the tongue touches the palate. Thus it is less useful when the jaw lowers the tongue away from the domain of the palate. This occurs during mid and low vowels, and as a result, the interpretation of EPG during continuous speech requires much inference (Stone et al., 1991).

3.2 *Electromyography (EMG)*

Electromyography (EMG) is the study of the electrical activity of a muscle. When a muscle contracts a chemical change occurs, resulting in electrical activity. The amount of electrical activity depends on the size and function of the muscle. A muscle is made up of a number of motor units. A motor unit is a bundle of muscle fibers, and is the smallest unit of activity for that muscle. As more motor units are activated, the muscle's contraction increases, and the EMG signal increases as well.

Instrumentation includes three types of electrodes: needle, surface, and hooked wire electrodes. Needle electrodes are used in small muscles because the large scale movements of large muscles may dislodge the needle and cause discomfort. Surface electrodes are affixed to the skin above the muscle and are the most comfortable of the three. If the muscle is bundled and superficial, as with Orbicularis Oris, this technique yields considerable success. Hooked wire electrodes are used in muscles that move substantially when they contract, because hooked wires maintain their position in the muscle quite well. A computer is used to average the output voltage of the electrodes.

Considerable research has focused on developing this technique and interpreting its data (Doble et al., 1985, Hirose, 1971, Kewley-Port, 1973, Palmer, 1989, Port, 1971). Applications to oral musculature research have involved studies of non-speech, speech, and speech disorders. Non-speech behaviors include correlating specific lip, tongue and jaw movements with EMG activity of corresponding muscles (Abbs et al., 1984, Miyawaki et al., 1975, Moore et al., 1988, Sauerland and Mitchell, 1975), and the study of reflexive vocal tract behaviors like swallowing (Palmer, 1989, Perlman et al., 1989).

EMG of normal and disordered speakers has been used to expose underlying motor control strategies for sequencing phonemes used in speech production (cf. Gay, 1977). The tongue has been studied extensively because it is composed entirely of muscles and deforms in complex ways when it moves (cf. Smith, 1971). Vowels have been of great interest because not only is the tongue the primary articulator for vowels, but also because the entire tongue, not just a part, is integral to their production (cf. Baer et al., 1988, MacNeilage and Sholes, 1964, Miyawaki et al., 1975, and Raphael and Bell-Berti, 1975). Other studies have examined velar muscles with respect to velopharyngeal function (Bell-Berti, 1976) and nasal sounds (Dixit et al., 1987), lip muscles (Abbs et al., 1984), and jaw muscles (Moore et al., 1988, Tuller et al., 1981). Hirose (1986) examined temporal patterns of muscle activity during speech in a dysarthric population.

There are several drawbacks with EMG. The first is that the signal is noisy, and therefore, difficult to interpret. Often, the signal is averaged over multiple repetitions of a speech token to provide a more recognizable peak (Hirose, 1971, Kewley-Port, 1973). Averaging masks token to token differences however (Cooper and Folkins, 1982). A second drawback is the insertion problem. In muscles that are not neatly bundled, such as the tongue, it is almost impossible to be sure that the signal comes from the muscle of interest. Even where muscles are bundled, different insertion locations will affect signal strength (Cooper and Folkins, 1981, Perlman et al., 1989). The third problem is that the procedure is physically uncomfortable. In a long session, the electrodes can cause tissue swelling and speech distortion.

Instrumental studies of physiology are challenging and, no single instrument provides total vocal tract information. However, the importance of these instruments lies in the critical role they play in cutting edge studies of speech motor control, speech disorders, phonetics, phonology and even speech processing. The data acquired by these instruments is in great demand for two reasons. First, the data keep increasing our knowledge of speech physiology, speech disorders and coarticulation strategies. They reveal how articulation and rhythm are organized and controlled, what aspects of speech are common among languages, and the nature of differences between speakers, languages and disorders. Second, the data are key in testing current theories and models. The facts or models of an age are often supported or disproved by the data from new instrumentation. Forty years ago, the sound spectrograph destroyed the notion that speech sounds were independent, concatenated segments. Today, measures of speech physiology are challenging our ideas of how vocal tract constrictions are achieved and what features of them are acoustically salient. Similarly, we wish to find out what components of the articulatory gesture are carried in the speech wave and decoded by the listener. A better understanding of how the vocal tract produces speech can also improve synthetic speech and provide strategies for machine recognition of speech. These and other issues, that are in the forefront of speech research, can be addressed and perhaps resolved using the instruments described in this chapter. The exciting leaps in knowledge provided by physiological data far outweigh the difficulties associated with the use of these instruments.

2 The Aerodynamics of Speech

CHRISTINE H. SHADLE

1 Introduction

Aerodynamics is the study of the motion of air. It is a subset of fluid mechanics, since air is only one possible fluid; it is a subset in another sense because mechanics includes statics as well as dynamics, but one must understand something about fluid statics in order to consider dynamics. Acoustics is the study of sound, and sound involves a particular type of wave travelling through a medium. Acoustics in air is therefore a part of aerodynamics; acoustics in water is a part of fluid dynamics, but not aerodynamics; acoustics in solids is not contained within fluid dynamics at all.

These distinctions may seem pedantic, but they are often blurred in speech research and result in some confusion. Aerodynamics in speech tends to be thought of as 'everything the air is doing that isn't sound.' In speech we ultimately care only about the sound that is radiated to the far field, well outside the vocal tract. Here, near the microphone or someone's ear, the air is essentially at rest except for the sound wave, and describing that wave is an acoustics-only problem. However, inside the vocal tract, the air is not at rest; we speak, for the most part, while exhaling, and the sound waves travel through that moving airstream. Further, most speech sounds are generated by that airstream: it sets the vocal folds vibrating which in turn chop up the steady airstream, and it can become turbulent and generate noise. The usual approach is to consider the larger picture – i.e. the non-acoustic aerodynamics – in order to define the acoustic sources that are operating, include these sources in a model that considers only acoustic waves, and thereafter ignore the moving stream of air. However, our understanding of the various types of sources is not very far advanced in some cases, and the limitations of these definitions need to be understood. Further, some sources continue to interact with the moving air, and thus are less suited to such a separation of 'acoustic' and 'aerodynamic' function.

We also need to consider the wider aspects of aerodynamics when we measure speech or any aspect of speech production. There can be obvious effects, like the need to avoid breath noise on a microphone, or more subtle effects, like the limitations of inverse filtering. One can devise certain methods of recording various parameters in speech that avoid pitfalls, but new measurement techniques are developed all the time. It is important to be aware of the issues involved.

Aerodynamics texts are rarely written with speech applications in mind, and tend also to be highly mathematical. In spite of the high level of mathematics required, there are topics that currently resist any analytical solution, and must be dealt with empirically. In this article mathematics is not avoided altogether, but the chief aim is to convey an appreciation for the physical mechanisms involved, provide a pointer to more detailed treatments of each subject, and describe some of the limitations in our current understanding of the aerodynamics of speech.

In Section 2 we describe some basic aerodynamic concepts and define the variables and non-dimensional parameters needed. In Section 3 we use these basic concepts to consider mechanisms of speech production, grouped in terms of the aerodynamic behavior(s) present. In Section 4 we consider measurement methods and their limitations, including methods in general use and those adapted for speech research. Finally, in Section 5 we discuss some models of speech production that incorporate aerodynamics.

2 Basic considerations

Air has a mass and a springiness or compressibility. It takes energy to move air or to compress it, and the air imparts energy to an object that stops it from moving or confines it to its container when it expands.

In a static situation – a set number of air molecules sealed in a container – the behavior of the air is described by its pressure, volume, and temperature, by the relation

$$PV = nRT \tag{1}$$

where P = pressure, V = volume, T = temperature, R = the universal gas constant, and n = mass of gas in moles. So, for this sealed-up gas, if the temperature increases, the pressure or the volume or both must also increase; if the temperature stays the same, any increase in pressure must be offset by a corresponding decrease in volume, and vice versa.

The temperature, T, affects the density, ρ, viscosity, v, and speed of sound, c, in a gas. Equation 1 can be used to derive the equations relating T to ρ, v, and c. Values of these parameters for humid air at body temperature have been computed and are listed in the Appendix.

We are treating the enclosed mass of gas as though the pressure everywhere within it were constant. This is not strictly true: the gas at the bottom of the container has the weight of the gas above pressing on it, so its pressure is slightly greater. Because the density of air is low, it takes a very tall container for this effect to be noticeable: an increase in altitude of 1 km decreases atmospheric pressure by only 10 per cent, for instance (Halliday and Resnick, 1966). But in a liquid, which is more dense, the effect is more noticeable, and this is exploited in the operation of the manometer, a basic instrument for measuring static pressure. In the manometer, a U-tube of constant inner diameter contains a liquid of known density ρ'. One end of the tube is attached to the gas with the pressure P to be measured; the other end is attached to a gas at a reference pressure P_0 (if that end is left open, the reference pressure is atmospheric pressure). The difference in the height of the liquid in each arm of the tube, h, is proportional to the difference in pressure:

$$P - P_0 = \rho'gh \tag{2}$$

where g is the gravitational acceleration. A denser liquid, with higher ρ', will show a smaller difference in height for the same pressure difference. Thus atmospheric pressure at sea level is 76.0 cm of mercury and 1,033 cm of water. The subglottal pressure during speech is commonly 5 to 30 cm H_2O above atmospheric pressure; for such a relatively small value, the pressure can be measured more accurately by using water.

A sound wave travelling through a fluid that is otherwise at rest consists of a longitudinal pressure-rarefaction wave. This means that particles of the fluid are alternately pressed together more tightly than normal and pulled apart further than normal. As the wave travels through the fluid, individual particles oscillate about their original positions, but do not have a net movement. The molecules in the compressed regions tend to move towards the rarefied regions, so that particles in the rarefied regions have higher velocity. This tendency towards reestablishing equilibrium moves the high- and low-pressure regions along at a speed regulated by the properties of the fluid: the speed of sound.

The ideal gas law given in (1) can be simplified when we are talking about the pressure and volume changes induced by a sound wave travelling through air. In this case the gas is undergoing an adiabatic process, which means that no heat flows into or out of the system. Then

$$PV^\gamma = \text{constant} \tag{3}$$

where V = volume and $\gamma = 1.4$ for air. Note that this is not the same as saying that the temperature remains constant; instead, it says that if the temperature changes, it must change back again quickly before any heat exchange can take place. When a sound wave travels through air, the pressure at a given location increases and then decreases. The temperature locally rises and falls, but the sound wave passes through so quickly that it behaves adiabatically.

Pressure and particle or volume velocity of the fluid as a function of time and location in space are the basic quantities used to describe a sound wave. They can also be used to describe a fluid in motion without a sound wave travelling through it. As the name indicates, particle velocity, v, is the velocity at a specific point in a fluid, and is expressed in units of distance per unit time; a particle at that location will have that velocity. The volume velocity, U, instead describes the rate of volume flow per unit time past a particular cross-sectional area. Any differences in particle velocity across that area will be averaged out by the description in terms of volume velocity.

There are many different types of fluid flow; recognizing which type occurs in a certain situation allows one to simplify the equations describing the fluid motion accordingly. One of the simplest types of flow to describe is steady, incompressible flow. Steady flow means that the flow does not change in time: if we measure pressure and particle velocity at a particular point, it will remain the same at that point. This means that the flow cannot be turbulent, since turbulence implies that pressure and velocity will vary randomly in space and time. But non-random changes over time are excluded as well: if the overall flowrate is very slowly increased and then decreased without producing turbulence, it is still not a steady flow.

Liquids are very nearly incompressible; gases, with their lower density, are compressible. Sound waves cannot exist unless a fluid is compressible. However, describing a fluid flow as incompressible does not mean we are restricting ourselves to liquids: it means that we are ignoring the compressible effects in our model. So, assuming steady, incompressible flow in a duct allows one to derive a form of Bernoulli's Equation relating the pressure and velocity at two places along the flow, assuming no work, heat transfer, or change of elevation occurs between those two places:

$$-gH_L = \frac{p_2 - p_1}{\rho} + \frac{v_2^2 - v_1^2}{2} \tag{4}$$

where g = the gravitational acceleration, H_L = head loss (or energy per unit weight lost to friction) from point 1 to point 2, p_1, p_2 = static pressure at points 1 and 2, v_1, v_2 = particle velocity at points 1 and 2, and ρ = density. We can use the relation of volume velocity to particle velocity $U = vA$ and the fact that the volume velocity will be the same at any point along the duct to rearrange the equation. The head loss is related to the internal energy of the fluid; because the fluid has friction, some energy is converted to heat. If we assume that the flow is frictionless, $H_L = 0$, and do some rearranging, we get:

$$U = \frac{A_2}{\sqrt{1 - (A_2/A_1)^2}} \sqrt{\frac{2(p_1 - p_2)}{\rho}} \tag{5}$$

where U = volume flow rate (m^3/s), A_1, A_2 = cross-sectional flow areas at points 1 and 2 (m^2), p_1, p_2 = static pressure at points 1 and 2 (Pa), and ρ =

density of the fluid (kg/m^3). Although this equation strictly applies only to frictionless, incompressible, steady flow, it is used in practice where these restrictions are violated to measure volume flowrates. The calibration procedures and empirical coefficients that can render such practice more accurate are discussed briefly in Section 4, and more extensively in Doebelin (1983).

All fluids are viscous; as a result, the head loss can become significant for flow along a length of pipe. It is proportional to the length of pipe and to the flow velocity squared, but the constant of proportionality is an empirically-determined friction factor that depends on the non-dimensional parameters of wall roughness and Reynolds number. The Reynolds number is defined as

$$Re = \frac{VD}{v} \tag{6}$$

where V = a characteristic velocity, D = a characteristic dimension, and v = the kinematic viscosity. For pipe flow, the V normally used is the average particle velocity in the center of the pipe (and, because of the averaging, is therefore typically capitalized in the literature, confusing it with volume) and D is the pipe diameter (Massey, 1984). Although we are not often called upon to compute the head loss in the vocal tract, the Reynolds number is used in models of speech production, and it is therefore important to understand what it means.

All fluid motion can be broadly classified into three regimes: laminar, unstable, and turbulent flow. For a particular geometry – take, for example, a constricted region in a duct – the flow progresses from one regime to the next as the Reynolds number is increased. For a particular size of that geometry, this could be observed simply by increasing the flow velocity. In laminar flow, at the lowest velocity range, individual particles follow paths that do not cross paths of other fluid particles. The particles nearest the walls of the duct will move the slowest, constrained by friction to stick to the non-moving walls. In the center of the duct the particles will move the fastest. In going through a constriction the flow will hug the walls of the duct, and the velocity gradient and therefore the velocity in the center of the duct will increase as the area decreases. Laminar flow is dominated by friction forces, and the empirical friction factor is highest for lowest Reynolds numbers.

As the flow velocity increases, inertial forces begin to dominate over friction forces. As the fluid enters the constriction, it overshoots a bit, and the moving flow separates from the walls. The vena contracta, thus formed, effectively reduces the area of the constriction. The region of transition from the fast-moving flow to the still flow near the walls is known as a boundary layer, and it can itself become unstable. In an unstable regime, any perturbations will tend to increase in amplitude.

If the Reynolds number is increased still further, the flow may pass through a sequence of unstable states, but eventually it becomes fully turbulent. Here inertial effects dominate. Paths of fluid particles cross each other unpredictably, so the flow as a whole has a random fluctuating component superimposed on the mean flow. This is very effective at mixing the flow.

For a particular geometry the characteristic velocity and dimension can be defined, and then a critical Reynolds number Re_{crit} can be found that marks the change from laminar to unstable flow regimes. This means that the flow regime can be predicted for any velocity in any size of that geometry. The value of Re_{crit} may differ though for a square instead of circular pipe, for instance, or a rectangular instead of·circular constriction. The behavior above Re_{crit} may also depend on geometry: for fully turbulent flow in smooth pipes the friction factor decreases with increasing Re, but for rough pipes it remains relatively constant (Massey, 1984).

Sound waves travelling through a fluid can be affected by the flow regime. First, turbulence can diffract and absorb sound waves, though it is questionable whether this is a significant effect for speech (see discussion in Davies et al., 1993). Second, the sound wave travelling through a moving medium will travel faster downstream than upstream relative to an observer at rest. We can gauge the strength of this effect by computing the average Mach number $M = V/c$, where V = the average particle velocity of the fluid. In a vowel, where average volume velocity $U = 200$ cm^3/s and the most constricted region has an area of approximately $A_c = 1$ cm^2, the Mach number in the constricted region will be $M = U/(A_c c) = 200/(1 \cdot 35,000) = 0.0057$. Since $M \ll 1$, this effect is not significant. However, for fricatives, a typical $U \approx 600$ cm^3/s and $A_c \approx 0.1$ cm^2, so $M = U/(A_c c) = 600/(0.1 \cdot 35,000) = 0.17$. Here the value of M relative to 1 indicates that the convection velocity is significant with respect to the speed of sound, and may have to be taken into account.

In addition to these effects that flow can have on sound travelling through it, flow can also generate sound, with different characteristics according to the type of flow that produced it.

An unstable flow regime can lead to a self-sustaining aerodynamic oscillation. One or more positive feedback paths must exist. The sound that can result is characteristically high-amplitude, narrow-bandwidth: a whistle. Its frequency and the parameters that control it are related to the underlying instability.

We spoke earlier of the boundary layer that can detach from the walls of an orifice. In fact, a boundary layer exists between any two regions with significantly different flow parameters: they may have different velocities (as with the fluid moving in the center of a duct and the still fluid clinging to the walls of the duct), different densities (as with the Gulf Stream, which is warmer and saltier than the surrounding water), or actually be two different as yet unmixed fluids (cream just poured into coffee). The boundary itself is unstable for certain ranges of the difference of the two parameter values. In this unstable range, any small perturbation of the boundary will tend to grow. At first this will appear as ripples on the boundary; the ripples grow larger and curl up into vortices, which continue to rotate while being convected downstream.

The length of time required to traverse the feedback path tends to determine the spacing between vortices, because the initial perturbations are reinforced at that interval. In general an integral number of vortices will be found between abrupt discontinuities such as the two ends of a sharp-edged orifice, or the distance between an orifice exit and an edge. These patterns, and the sound generated, will couple into the resonances of a surrounding cavity. Increasing the flow velocity will tend to increase the frequency of the sound produced, but not uniformly; it will remain steadily coupled into one resonance, then jump abruptly to the next higher one, with the jumps exhibiting hysteresis (Chanaud and Powell, 1965; Holger et al., 1977).

Turbulence also generates sound, but since the motion is more random than an unstable state reinforced by feedback, the sound that results is noise with a relatively flat spectrum. Such noise cannot be predicted precisely from moment to moment, but can only be characterized statistically, and modelled by a collection of idealized flow-generated noise sources: the flow monopole, dipole or quadrupole. These are analogous to idealized acoustic sources. The *acoustic* monopole can be thought of as produced by a pulsing sphere, which generates spherical sound waves. The acoustic dipole consists of two adjacent out-of-phase monopoles, which generate sound waves that interfere with each other; the result is a characteristic figure-eight directivity pattern. Solid objects such as a piston or a loudspeaker cone that act on the air can be modelled using these acoustic sources. In a *flow* source, the flow of air itself acts upon the surrounding air so that the far-field sound exhibits monopole, dipole or quadrupole properties. Theoretically, the noise generated by turbulence away from any solid boundaries can be modelled by flow quadrupoles; the noise generated by turbulence that results in a fluctuating force being applied to a solid object, by flow dipoles. As with acoustic sources, these can be thought of as collections of four and two flow monopoles, respectively, pulsing out of phase. In each case, the source strength depends upon the flow velocity. The total sound power of a flow quadrupole is proportional to V^8, that of a flow dipole, to V^6. However, the flow quadrupole is much less efficient than a flow dipole. It can be shown that the ratio of their total sound powers is proportional to the Mach number squared (Goldstein, 1976). Thus, for $M < 1$, if a flow generates both dipole and quadrupole sources, the dipole sources will have higher sound power even though the sound power of the quadrupole sources increases faster with an increased flow velocity.

If the far-field sound pressure of a jet is recorded for a variety of jet sizes and mean velocities, the results can best be compared by plotting a normalized spectrum. A spectrum typically shows a measure of amplitude, such as sound pressure level, versus frequency. Every variation of V and D would result in a different curve: a larger jet will produce higher-amplitude noise with the peak at a lower frequency than a smaller jet with same V. However, we can normalize the sound pressure level by dividing it by $V^8 D^2$, which reflects the theoretically predicted variation with V and D. We can also normalize the frequency axis by plotting instead the Strouhal number, St, where

$$St = \frac{fD}{V} \tag{7}$$

As a result of these normalizations, all jet spectra for any size and velocity (as long as $V < c$) fit the same curve, as shown in Fig 2.1 (solid line).

A similar collapse of data can be done for the noise produced by flow past a spoiler in a duct. The presence of the duct changes the dependence of source strength on V below the first cut-on frequency[1] (Nelson and Morfey, 1981). However, the principle of collapsing the data by using nondimensional parameters is the same. Here normalization by V^4 below cut-on and V^6 above cut-on frequency for the duct is used, and the resulting curve has a different shape from that of the free jet, as shown in Fig 2.1 (dashed line).

3   Aerodynamically distinct tract behaviors

In this section we consider the different mechanisms of speech production, grouping them from an aerodynamics point of view and proceeding from the simplest to the most complex. In each section we describe the physical events, and give parameter values typical for speech.

3.1   Breathing

Respiration is the simplest tract behavior aerodynamically because sound generation is not essential to the process and the time scales are relatively long.

The trachea extends about 11 cm below the larynx and then branches into the bronchial tubes. The bronchi continue to branch until the small, elastic-walled alveolar sacs are reached. The entire spongy mass is encased within the pleural sacs, which are suspended in the rib cage and surrounded on all sides by muscles. There are two sets of muscles that decrease lung volume when tensed: the internal intercostals, attached to the ribs, and the abdominal muscles. There are two sets that increase lung volume when tensed: the external intercostals, and the diaphragm, suspended across the bottom of the rib cage. We can thus actively breathe in and out by tensing and relaxing these sets of muscles in turn (as described by Hixon et al., 1973, and Hixon et al., 1976). But we can also use the elastic recoil force of the lung tissue itself as a passive mechanism for exhalation: if we cease to actively hold the rib cage expanded, we will passively exhale until the lung volume is small enough that the elastic recoil force no longer operates (see Fig 2.2). The lungs will not be empty at this point; the volume of air still in them is termed the functional residual capacity (FRC). To empty our lungs further we must actively tense muscles, and even doing so, we cannot empty them below a residual volume (RV).

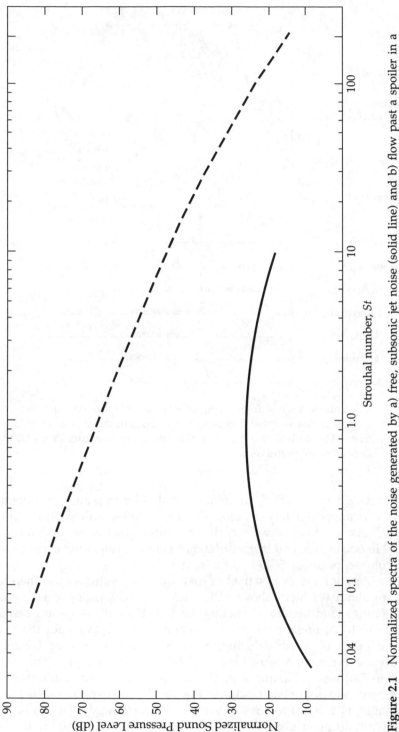

Figure 2.1 Normalized spectra of the noise generated by a) free, subsonic jet noise (solid line) and b) flow past a spoiler in a duct (dashed line), for various sizes of jets and spoilers. One-third octave sound pressure level is normalized by $V^8 D^2$ for a), by V^6 or V^4 for b). Levels of the two curves relative to each other are arbitrary. After Goldstein (1976) and Nelson and Morfey (1981).

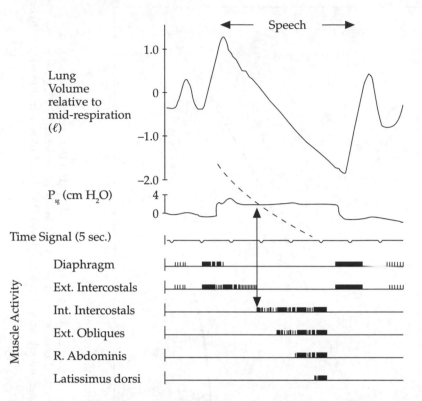

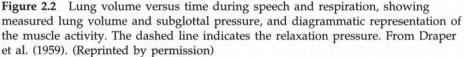

Figure 2.2   Lung volume versus time during speech and respiration, showing measured lung volume and subglottal pressure, and diagrammatic representation of the muscle activity. The dashed line indicates the relaxation pressure. From Draper et al. (1959). (Reprinted by permission)

The total lung capacity (TLC) in an adult male is approximately 7 liters of air. The RV is approximately 2 liters. The FRC varies with posture, but is typically 4 liters. The vital capacity is the maximum amount of air that can be exchanged in one breath, and is the difference between total lung capacity and residual volume, or about 5 liters (Ohala, 1990c).

Typical respiration involves actively expanding lung volume (and therefore inhaling) to about 0.5 liters above FRC, and passively letting elastic recoil deflate the lungs (and therefore exhaling) back to the FRC. A typical respiration rate is 15 to 20 breaths per minute (Thomas, 1973). We hold the vocal folds as far apart as possible during inspiration (maximum area is 52% of tracheal area according to Negus, 1949; tracheal area ranges from 3.0 to 4.9 cm^2 according to Catford, 1977a) and keep the tongue relaxed and velum down to provide a relatively unimpeded path for the air. During expiration the glottal area is smaller, but still of the order of 1 cm^2 (Sawashima, 1977); this is wide open compared to phonation, with an average glottal area of 0.05 to 0.1 cm^2.

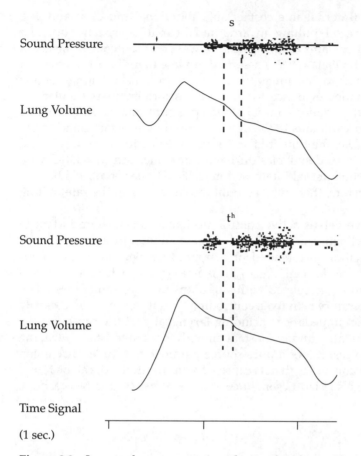

Figure 2.3 Lung volume versus time during the phrase 'Deem -oon real,' where the blank was filled in by [s] (top) and [tʰ] (bottom). From Ohala (1990). (Reprinted by permission of Kluwer Academic Publishers)

For short utterances of speech at normal level, normal expiration is sufficient. For louder and/or longer speech, we need to use muscles actively to inhale more deeply, to offset the greater relaxation pressure, and to expel air below the FRC. During speech our goal appears to be to hold the subglottal pressure P_{sg} approximately constant, at a level corresponding to the loudness level of speech. It ranges from 3 to 30 cm H_2O, as deduced by measuring esophageal pressure (Draper et al., 1959) or by using tracheal puncture to measure the pressure directly (Isshiki, 1964). The lung volume then decrements fairly steadily; during stops the rate of decrement decreases momentarily, and during fricatives it increases (see Fig 2.3).

The respiratory system can be modelled uncontroversially as a simple mechanical system, as described by Draper et al. (1959): a set of bellows, with one active force (external intercostals and diaphragm) pulling outwards on the handles, one active (internal intercostals and abdominal muscles) and one passive force (elastic recoil) pulling inwards, and a variable-resistance opening in the bellows. What remains controversial, however, is the control mechanism for such a model. Ohala (1990c) asserts that we either aim for a constant pressure to be applied to the lungs, or a long-term constant lung-volume decrement, and provides evidence to support the former. In particular, he argues that observed variations in subglottal pressure and in lung-volume decrement are due to variations in the downstream flow resistance and to the inertia of the system, i.e. the time it takes to reestablish equilibrium. It is also true, however, that stressed syllables during an utterance are correlated with bursts of activity in the internal intercostal muscles (Draper et al., 1959). Both passive and active factors, then, may account for variations in the rate of lung volume decrement.

The issue of passive versus active control mechanisms is also important in explanations of f_0 declination across the duration of an utterance. First, it is not clear whether declination is intended or a byproduct. Second, both respiratory and laryngeal muscles can affect f_0; it is not clear which produces declination. Variations in P_{sg} correlated with variations in f_0 are sometimes taken as evidence that respiratory activity is controlling f_0, but this is not necessarily the case since the tract impedance, including laryngeal posture, can affect P_{sg}. P_{sg} is a measurable quantity and is constant enough to seem to be a controlling parameter, but it is a result, not a pure source parameter. A fuller discussion of declination, which concludes that its cause remains unresolved, can be found in Ohala (1990c). (See also Maddieson, Phonetic Universals, and Nooteboom, Prosody of Speech.)

3.2 Frication

Fricatives are produced by making a tight constriction, with area of the order of 0.1 cm^2, somewhere in the vocal tract. The air emerging from the constriction forms a turbulent jet, and this jet produces noise. For unvoiced fricatives the vocal folds are held apart, giving a typical glottal area of 1 cm^2. This means that most of the subglottal pressure is dropped across the supraglottal constriction, rather than across the glottis (the obvious exception to this is [h], where the glottal constriction can be the only constriction. As a result, the vowel context can make [h] into an approximant, as in /ihi/.).

Although the area of the constriction is much smaller than any tract area used during a vowel, it is larger than the average glottal area during voicing and thus the volume flowrate is higher during unvoiced fricatives, ranging typically from 200 to 400 cm^3/s or more (for [h] it may be 1,000 – 1,200 cm^3/s). In a vowel-fricative transition usually the glottis opens before the supraglottal constriction is formed, resulting in a momentary maximum volume velocity (see Fig 2.4). Then, as A_c decreases, U decreases also and the pressure drop across the supraglottal constriction increases. (See also Stevens, Articulatory

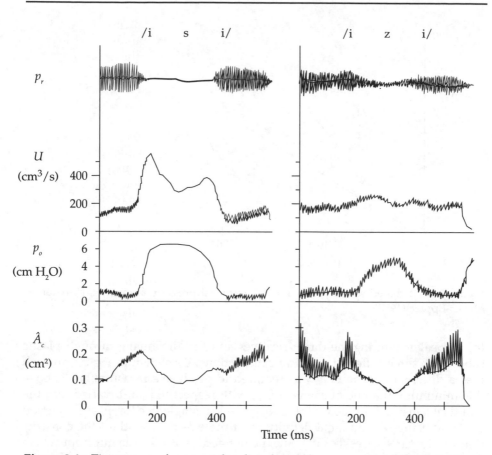

Figure 2.4 Time traces of measured radiated sound pressure p_r, volume velocity at the lips U, intraoral pressure p_o, estimated constriction area $\hat{A}_c$ for unvoiced and voiced fricatives. An adult male subject produced [pisi] (left) and [pizi] (right).

– ACOUSTIC – AUDITORY RELATIONSHIPS.) At some point frication begins; it would be useful to be able to predict precisely when. For voiced fricatives, with a lower mean U, the situation is even more complicated: turbulence noise is usually generated more weakly than in the unvoiced equivalent, but it is also effectively modulated by the voicing. This was first described by Fant (1960); the changes to the noise source spectrum as a result of the modulation have been described more recently (Shadle, 1995). Flanagan's model of fricatives (1972, pp. 248–59) incorporates modulation based on the Reynolds number, and is discussed further in Section 5. For both voiced and unvoiced fricatives, the first question must be: for what dimensions and flowrate does a turbulent jet form? This can be rephrased as, what is the critical Reynolds number for vocal tract geometries?

Meyer-Eppler (1953) conducted experiments to determine Re_{crit} for the fricatives [f, s, ʃ]. He measured radiated sound pressure (p_r) and oral pressure (p_0)

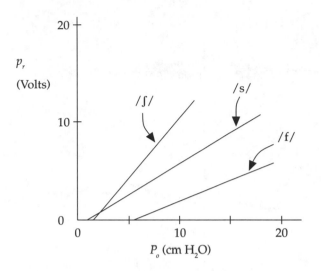

Figure 2.5   Radiated sound pressure p_r vs. intraoral pressure p_o for [f, s, ʃ]. After Meyer-Eppler (1953).

for a speaker uttering the three fricatives and for air flowing through plastic tubes with three different elliptical constrictions. As shown in Fig 2.5, in each case a different minimum p_0 was required to produce a measurable p_r; above this minimum, the rate of change of p_r with respect to p_0 also varied. For the elliptical constrictions, he was able to arrive at a single line for p_r as a function of Re by using two different definitions of the effective width of the constriction for the three cases. For this line, he defined Re_{crit} to be the intercept where $p_r = 0$, and found $Re_{crit} = 1{,}800$. He then generalized this to speech, on the assumption that the same value of Re_{crit} would work for all fricatives provided the effective width was properly defined in each case.

This idea has gained wide acceptance. Studies using various ducts and orifices have led to a range of Re_{crit} values, from 1,700 to 2,300 (Ishizaka and Flanagan, 1972; Catford, 1977a). There are two problems, however. Since it is so difficult to measure the cross-sectional shape of the constriction, there is no independent check of Re. We do not know what the effective width should be for a particular constriction shape. Second, using the Reynolds number to collapse data carries with it the assumption that the geometries and therefore the source mechanism are the same, and thus allows comparison for different sizes and flowrates. But constriction shape is definitely not the same for different fricatives. Are we then losing or gaining by collapsing them together?

There is evidence that there are different source types operating to produce different fricatives. The noise produced by the jet alone, generated by relatively inefficient flow quadrupoles, is quite weak for the jet sizes encountered in the vocal tract. Anything solid in the path of the jet, however, produces a much more efficient noise-generation mechanism. Stevens (1971) recognized this difference, and adapted the work of Heller and Widnall (1970) on flow spoilers to frication. By treating the tongue-constriction as a spoiler, he found an equation giving source strength in terms of the pressure drop across the constriction. Although he acknowledged that the location of the constriction in the tract could affect the power-law relationship of the radiated sound power to the pressure drop, this was seen to be due to changes in the proximity of tract resonances to the source spectrum peak rather than an effect on the source mechanism.

Based on more recent analysis of speech and work with mechanical models, it appears that a flow dipole mechanism is operating, but not necessarily at the tongue constriction (Shadle, 1990, 1991). There are at least two distinctly different fricative geometries that result in different sources. The obstacle case has an obstacle such as the teeth at approximately right angles to the jet axis. The source is localized at the upstream face of the obstacle. [s, ʃ] fall into this category. The wall case has an 'obstacle' such as the hard palate at a more oblique angle. The jet generates noise all along the wall, resulting in a much more distributed source. The fricatives [ç, x] and presumably all pharyngeal fricatives fall into this category. The weak front fricatives [f, θ] should also possibly be grouped in this category, since noise is clearly generated along the lips (Shadle, 1990). The 'wall' does not continue on very far, however, and so it may be that these sounds should be considered as a third category.

The geometry affects not only where noise is generated, but how much, or the spectral characteristics of the noise and the way it changes with flow velocity and area of the constriction. Rather than absorb these differences by means of effective width formulas, it would seem useful to express the acoustic properties of the noise in terms of the aerodynamic and articulatory parameters for each category. Some work has been done on this, e.g. source curves as a function of volume velocity have been measured for models of [ʃ, ç, x] (Shadle, 1990), and power laws have been determined for human speakers (Badin, 1989). Much remains to be done. For instance, it seems clear that ΔP across a constriction depends principally on the volume velocity through it and the constriction's shape and area. The amount of noise generated by it can be related to ΔP, but the particulars of the relationship will depend very much on what is present downstream of the constriction exit. The ways in which parameters of the obstacle affect that relationship need to be investigated further, as does the effect of the constriction shape on the jet shape and therefore the velocity and area of the jet at point of impingement on the walls or obstacle.

3.3 Transient excitation: stops

Stops are intrinsically transient. Complete closure is effected somewhere in the vocal tract, from glottis to the lips. As shown in Fig 2.6, for a supraglottal unvoiced stop the pressure upstream of the closure typically builds up rapidly

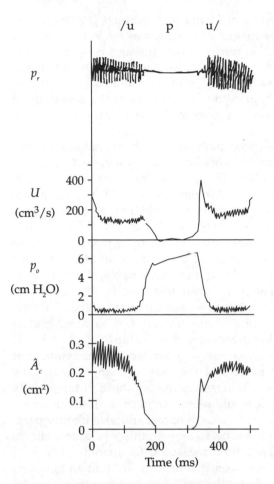

Figure 2.6   Time traces of measured radiated sound pressure p_r, volume velocity at the lips U, intraoral pressure p_o, and estimated constriction area $\hat{A}_c$ for the stop [p] in the context [upu]. An adult male was the subject.

for a short time, and then continues to increase more slowly, possibly reaching a plateau. The neck and cheeks expand slightly in response to this pressure, and the rate of decrease in lung volume eases slightly (Ohala, 1990c). When the stop is released, either at the place of closure or at the velum, the oral pressure drops suddenly, lung volume suddenly begins to decrease more rapidly, and air is pushed out of the vocal tract explosively. The expelled air may become turbulent, and the patch of turbulence travels downstream, gradually dissipating. Depending on the position of the vocal folds, this brief period of high airflow may result in aspiration noise being generated. (See also Stevens, ARTICULATORY – ACOUSTIC – AUDITORY RELATIONSHIPS.)

The closure must be held for a perceptible amount of time, from a minimum of 20–30 ms to 100 ms or more. The release burst and ensuing frication last for a short time, of the order of 5 ms, and the aspiration, if it occurs, may last 50 ms or more before voicing begins. Indeed, the voice onset time will be longest if aspiration is present, and this is not a coincidence. Glottal area during stops is largest for unaspirated voiceless stops; for other cases, the glottal area depends somewhat on position of the stop within the word (Sawashima, 1977). Differences in voice onset times thus appear to be largely related to the time it takes to adduct the vocal folds (Catford, 1977a). The wide-open glottis allows a high glottal volume velocity once the stop has been released, thus producing audible turbulence noise.

For a voiced stop, a pressure drop of at least 200 Pa must be maintained across the glottis for voicing to occur (Westbury, 1983). As a result the oral pressure does not increase as much as during an unvoiced stop. Fundamental frequency decreases as the pressure increases, and if closure is held long enough, vocal fold vibration may cease altogether. However, it appears that voicing during stops is extended by a combination of passive and active vocal tract expansion. The passive expansion occurs when cheek and neck tissue yields, puffing out slightly. We can control the degree of expansion somewhat by tensing or relaxing our cheek muscles; relaxed tissue yields more. The active expansion occurs by moving articulators: the larynx tends to move down, the soft palate up, and the tongue dorsum and blade down more during voiced than unvoiced stop closure. (See also Stevens, ARTICULATORY – ACOUSTIC – AUDITORY RELATIONSHIPS.) Both kinds of expansion serve to lower the pressure in the vocal tract, and therefore increase the transglottal pressure difference. Without such means, voicing can theoretically continue for approximately 60 ms after closure. With such means, voiced closure can extend theoretically to 200 ms or more – and in practice, voiced intervals of 100 ms or more are not uncommon (Westbury, 1983).

Sound production during and after the release has been modelled by Maeda (1987). He proposes a simple dynamic model that generates two different kinds of sources: an initial brief coherent source, followed by a longer frication source. The coherent source is caused by the assumption that when the closure is first opened, there is actually reverse flow into the sudden expansion, which causes a negative impulse of pressure. Although this flow monopole is predicted to last no more than 0.1 ms, it should be a very efficient sound source. The subsequent frication source is predicted to last from 1 to 5 or more milliseconds depending on the model parameter settings. Its strength would, of course, depend on the place of the constriction and the changing parameters.

Maeda demonstrated the coherent source with data from the utterance [mi]. The end of the [m] is released without a pressure buildup and therefore without the frication or aspiration sources, and shows a release bar on the spectrogram and extra negative-going radiated pressure. Flow visualization of [m] using the smoke technique and a high-speed camera shows a noticeable delay between opening the lips and the emergence of smoke, supporting Maeda's model (Pelorson, 1994).

3.4 Mechanical oscillation: trills and voicing

Since the walls of the tract and the articulators are for the most part not rigid, it is possible for the air stream to set up a mechanical oscillation. This has been thought to be due to the Bernoulli force operating in the narrowed region such as the true or false vocal folds, the uvula, tongue tip or lips: here the air flows with a higher particle velocity and therefore the pressure drops. An inwards force is applied to the surrounding structure, and if that structure is flexible enough and the force strong enough, it may be pulled closed (see, for example, Catford, 1977a). However, recent simulations of the aerodynamics in the larynx indicate that the Bernoulli force is a relatively small contributor compared to the power provided during the opening phase by the subglottal pressure (Liljencrants, 1991a). In any case, the closure of the 'valve' formed by the vocal folds, tongue tip, etc. interrupts the airflow and allows pressure to be built up behind the closure, so it blows open and the process can repeat. The frequency of repetition is determined by both aerodynamic and mechanical variables near, in and of the 'valve': the original upstream pressure, velocity through and area of the opening, and the mass, compliance and damping factors of the tissues making up the valve.

Studies of the flow patterns downstream of a periodically closing valve show that at each re-opening of the valve, a jet forms, which can curl up into vortices that are convected downstream (Shadle et al., 1991; Glendinning et al., 1990). Sound can be generated, but exactly where it is and how it should be modelled is a matter of some debate. It can be argued that the puffs of air emerging from the valve act like a pulsing point source, and can be modelled as a flow monopole, or, extending this to a one-dimensional model, a volume velocity source located at the exit from the valve. It can also be argued that a jet rolling up into vortices is a somewhat more complex entity. In mechanical models, the jet behavior changes somewhat according to downstream structures such as the false folds (Shadle et al., 1990; Pelorson et al., 1994). Such unstable behavior is more commonly associated with flow dipoles, and sound may be generated then at any downstream discontinuity (McGowan, 1988; Pelorson et al., 1994).

The situation is somewhat similar to that of reed instruments such as the clarinet, in which the reed vibrates enough to close off the flow of air periodically, and those vibrations couple into and excite the resonances of the clarinet tube. However, in the clarinet the natural frequency of the reed is well above the resonances of the tube, and so the pitch of the resulting sound is that of the lowest resonance (Benade, 1976). In the vocal tract, the natural frequency of the vocal folds is usually below that of the lowest formant, and so the pitch that results is that of the vocal fold vibration, in the range of 40 Hz (for creaky voice) to 1,000 Hz or more (for sopranos and children). For uvular and tongue-tip trills the mechanical oscillation is slower, in the range 20–35 Hz (Recasens, 1991; McGowan, 1992).

Vocal fold vibration has been extensively studied. There are many sets of muscles both in and around the vocal folds that can be adjusted to provide a very fine degree of control. The initial separation of the vocal folds, their length, and the tension of the three layers of the folds can all be separately controlled, in some cases by more than one mechanism. By these means the mode of vibration of the folds can be selected, and the frequency of vibration controlled within each mode.

The different modes of phonation are distinguished both by the pattern of movement of the vocal folds and by the resulting sound quality. The modes range from falsetto, in which the bulk of the folds are still and the margins vibrate, resulting in a relatively high-frequency sound with weak harmonics and a nearly sinusoidal glottal area function $A_g(t)$, to chest voice, in which a wave travels through the mucosa (the vocal fold cover) in the direction of the vocal tract's longitudinal axis, thus adding an extra component to the simple lateral motion of the folds. The closed phase for chest voice is a significant proportion of the total cycle, and upper harmonics of the fundamental carry a significant proportion of the total energy (Gauffin and Sundberg, 1989).

Within a mode, frequency of oscillation is primarily controlled by the length and tension of the folds and the subglottal pressure. (See Hirose, INVESTIGATING THE PHYSIOLOGY OF LARYNGEAL STRUCTURES.) The subglottal pressure is not an independent parameter in the way that the mechanical settings of the folds are: for instance, the minimum pressure required to achieve phonation appears to increase with f_0, and that relationship differs for singers and non-singers (Titze, 1992).

There are numerous models of the vocal folds. Of the self-oscillating models, the best known are the one-mass and two-mass models (Flanagan and Landgraf, 1968; Ishizaka and Flanagan, 1972). Variations on the mechanical structure of the folds have included increasing the number of masses (Titze, 1973, 1974), using a distributed rather than lumped model (Titze and Talkin, 1979), a collapsible tube model (Conrad, 1985), and a translating and rotating one-mass model (Liljencrants, 1991a). In all of these, sufficient degrees of freedom are included to allow different modes of vibration. The different parts of each fold are coupled, either directly (e.g. via a spring) or indirectly (e.g. controlled by the same aerodynamic parameter). The effect on the flow of the current shape of the folds is handled generally by computing the point of flow separation within the glottis, and allowing pressure, velocity and effective glottal area to vary accordingly.

It is difficult to test such models since it is impossible to compare 'output' for a human phonating with the same parameter 'settings'. It is accepted, however, that source-tract interactions occur in humans (Rothenberg, 1981; Guérin, 1983), and evidence of such interactions is sought for each model. For instance, one of the advantages of the two-mass over the one-mass model is that the two-mass model shows more realistic behavior when f_0 approaches and exceeds the frequency of the first formant.

There have been numerous studies of the detailed aerodynamics of the glottis using mechanical models. Most of these have been static rather than dynamic models owing to the experimental difficulties with the latter (see for example van den Berg et al., 1957; Ishizaka and Matsudaira, 1972; Scherer, 1981; Gauffin et al., 1983; Binh and Gauffin, 1983; Scherer and Guo, 1991). They present detailed measurements of the pressure-flow relationship in and near the glottis for converging and diverging glottis with a range of areas and, in some cases, the ventricles and false folds are modelled as well. The point of flow separation was also observed for each glottal shape and flow condition. These measurements were then used to compute empirical coefficients modelling, for instance, entry and exit loss. In cases where the models were deliberately made larger than lifesize to facilitate measurement the results were scaled using the Reynolds number. Results from all static models are used by making the quasi-static assumption that the dynamics can be modelled by considering a sequence of static configurations. In particular, this assumes that behavior in the opening and closing phases will be the same, depending only on the instantaneous glottal shape and area. Results obtained with dynamic models or measurements on phonating subjects, however, generally show this to be a poor assumption (e.g. Cranen and Boves, 1987; Shadle et al., 1991).

Phonation can be combined with turbulence noise generation at the glottis in breathy and in hoarse phonation. In both cases, the vocal folds oscillate but do not completely close. In breathy voicing a chink is left open near the arytenoid cartilages (Fritzell et al., 1986; Södersten and Lindestad, 1990; Södersten et al., 1991 and Stevens, ARTICULATORY – ACOUSTIC – AUDITORY RELATIONSHIPS, for the acoustics of breathy voice). Hoarseness is more variable; it may be caused by swollen folds resulting in slow oscillation, a node on one fold preventing a clean closure, or a paralyzed fold allowing a more significant gap (Hammarberg et al., 1984). In all of these cases there is a relatively inefficient conversion of the energy from the steady airstream into sound. Some work has been done to model hoarse phonation by, for instance, modifying the two-mass vocal fold model to generate a pathological model (Koizumi and Taniguchi, 1990).

For tongue-tip trills, the vibrating structure is not so finely controlled as the vocal folds, and partly as a consequence has a smaller range of frequency of vibration. Both unvoiced and voiced trills can be produced. In either case, the tongue blade and dorsum are held steadily in position and the tongue tip vibrates against the hard palate at a rate of between 20 and 35 Hz. Closure is seldom complete, judging from electropalatography data of Catalan speakers and Rothenberg mask data (showing a non-zero minimum flow) of English speakers (Recasens, 1991; McGowan, 1992).

McGowan simulated the tongue-tip trill by modelling the tongue tip as a hinged trap door in the spirit of the one-mass vocal fold model. Wall compliance was included for the tract upstream of the tongue tip, and proved to be an essential part of the model. The oscillation of the tongue tip is only self-sustaining if net energy is transfered from the airflow to the motion of the tip during each cycle; this is accomplished if the pressure is greater during the opening phase than during the closing phase. This asymmetry occurs in the model because of the compliance of the walls. When the tongue-constriction is closed and the oral pressure rises, the walls expand. When the tip is released, they deflate, but they do so relatively slowly, thus maintaining a higher pressure for a time as the constriction opens. The wall effect is apparently more important for a smaller glottal area, since that limits the extent of variation in glottal volume velocity.

McGowan did not attempt to model the details of the flow near the tongue tip, and suggested that this might be important for two reasons. First, the simulated traces were much smoother than the measured ones. Second, flow separation in the constriction could also result in energy exchange tending to sustain the oscillation. Finally, although he included an adducted-glottis condition to approximate the average glottal opening during voicing, he did not actually allow the glottal area to vary, whether under direct control or via a self-oscillating vocal fold model.

3.5 Aerodynamic oscillation: whistling

Whistling in speech occurs primarily in whistle languages (Busnel and Classe, 1976), but may also occur in whistly fricatives, both deliberately as in Shona (Clark et al., 1986) and accidentally in languages that do not use a whistle for linguistic purposes (Shadle and Scully, 1995). Whistle languages can be used over distances of up to a few kilometers, and consist basically of a loud whistle that follows the $F2$ pattern of the whistler's ordinary language, or duplicate f_0 patterns of lexical tone. Whistly fricatives have whistles and frication noise occurring together; the whistle peak occurs generally in the high-amplitude region of the frequency spectrum, in the fricatives [s, ʃ, z]. Both kinds of whistling are best understood by considering 'recreational' human whistling. Here there tends to be very little frication noise. The whistle may occur at $F2$ or $F3$, giving a frequency range of from 500 to 4,000 Hz (Shadle, 1983).

As described earlier, in order to produce a whistle sound there must be an unstable boundary layer and feedback that reinforces the instability. We would like to know when a whistle will occur and at what frequency, and therefore we need to know where the boundary layer forms and under what conditions it becomes unstable.

Because whistles are so geometry-dependent, the controlling parameters of a few classic geometries have been thoroughly investigated. Those that seem most applicable to the vocal tract are the orifice tone, the edge tone and the hole tone. The orifice tone, however, depends on sharp edges at the inlet causing the boundary layer to separate from the walls of the orifice. This is inconsistent with the shape of the lips, and the controlling parameter – length of the orifice – predicts too high a whistle frequency (Shadle, 1985).

The hole tone can be produced without sharp-edged inlets. It results from two orifices in a row. The first produces an unstable jet, which curls up into vortices in the region between the orifices. In the absence of surrounding walls, the distance between the orifices determines the feedback path length; with surrounding walls, the whistle couples into one of the resonances of that cavity (Chanaud and Powell, 1965). If the constriction formed by the tongue is the first orifice, and the rounded lips form the second orifice, the resonances of the cavity in between should control the whistle frequency; the lowest of these is in fact $F2$ (Shadle, 1985), consistent with whistle languages.

For whistly fricatives, the edge tone appears to be a more appropriate model. In this geometry, the unstable jet formed by an orifice strikes a solid object: a sharp edge of varying angle, or a cylinder. With laminar flow, the jet will divide smoothly around the object. When the jet becomes unstable, it tends to go to one side or the other of the object, alternating periodically and shedding vortices alternately. Here the orifice diameter and the distance to the edge are critical parameters (Powell, 1961, 1962; Holger et al., 1977). It appears that this mechanism could be at work with the whistly fricatives, with the tongue again forming the jet-producing constriction and the teeth serving as the edge. This is consistent with the role of the teeth in noise production, and simply indicates that some structure can exist in a turbulent flow (Shadle and Scully, 1995).

Because whistles are so sensitive to small changes in the geometry or flow rate, it is difficult to model them for the vocal tract where dimensions are difficult to determine and easily varied. They are also difficult to model for another reason: the whistle mechanism exhibits a complete interaction of 'source' and 'filter'.

4 Measurement methods

4.1 Basic methods

A steady-state or slowly varying pressure can be measured by use of the manometer, which was described earlier. The tap can be placed in a sealed tank of gas, or at a particular place of interest along a duct. In the latter situation, where there is a relatively steady flow along the duct, the tap must be designed so as to measure the desired static pressure without altering the flow by its presence. In general, having the tap flush with the wall, of a diameter much smaller than the duct diameter, and the edge of the tap abrupt rather than bevelled is sufficient. One must also pay attention to local variations in the pressure. For instance, there is a net loss in pressure across an orifice, and it is often of interest to measure this difference. However, in and near the orifice the pressure may rise over a short distance, then will drop substantially, and then over a longer distance will recover to the downstream value. To measure the pressure drop reliably, then, one must space the taps

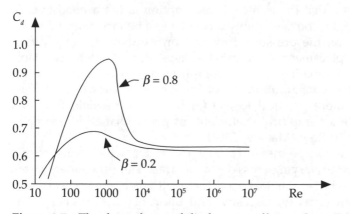

Figure 2.7 The dependence of discharge coefficient C_d on Reynolds number, Re, and on β, the ratio of orifice to pipe diameter (after Doebelin, 1983). (Reproduced with permission of McGraw-Hill, Inc.)

away from the orifice by an amount that depends on the orifice shape; for instance, for a thin orifice plate, the taps should be located at $2\frac{1}{2}$ diameters upstream and 8 diameters downstream of the orifice (Doebelin, 1983).

Pressure drop across a known orifice is often used to deduce flowrate. In some cases an existing orifice is measured and calibrated; in others, an orifice of known shape and area is inserted into a duct. In either case, the flowrate U is derived from the pressure drop measured at two taps for an incompressible fluid by:

$$U = \frac{C_d A_2}{\sqrt{1 - (A_2/A_1)^2}} \sqrt{\frac{2(p_1 - p_2)}{\rho}} \tag{8}$$

where U is flowrate in m^3/s, A_1 = pipe cross-section area (m^2), A_2 = orifice cross-section area (m^2), p_1, p_2 = the pressure measured at the two taps (Pa), ρ = the density of the fluid (kg/m^3), and C_d is a dimensionless discharge coefficient that depends on Reynolds number and the ratio of orifice to pipe diameter, as shown in Fig 2.7. Including C_d, an empirically-determined coefficient that varies with orifice shape and the locations of the pressure taps, allows actual areas to be used rather than flow areas as in (5), and includes frictional losses. Calibration to determine C_d for every new setup can be avoided by using standard dimensions for the orifice meter and relying on the extensive experimental data available (Doebelin, 1983).

Equation (8) can be modified for compressible fluids to give the weight flow rate rather than the volume flowrate. For a small pressure drop ($p_2/p_1 > 0.99$), this is sufficient. For isentropic (i.e. frictionless and adiabatic) flows with larger pressure drop, an equation for weight flow rate can be derived whose only empirical coefficient is C_d. For a sharp-edged orifice plate, however, enough turbulence is generated that the isentropic assumption is not a good one. In this case, an experimental compressibility factor Y must be incorporated in the equation; Y depends on the pressure drop and orifice diameter in a different way for different placement of the pressure taps. For a known and stable configuration the final equation, though complicated, can be quite accurate (Doebelin, 1983). If the configuration is not known or is known to change, however, it may be more practical to use (8) for incompressible flow and determine or estimate an empirical coefficient for every change in geometry or significant change in flow (Massey, 1984).

Volume velocity can also be measured by a rotameter, which consists of a float in a vertical tube of varying cross-sectional area. The flow enters at the bottom of the tube and blows the float up to the point where the vertical forces of differential pressure, gravity, viscosity, and buoyancy are balanced. The same equations for flow rate as a function of area apply, but since the float position rather than pressure drop is the output measured, and flow rate is linearly related to float position (for the typical tube tapering) but related to the square root of pressure drop, the rotameter has a greater accurate range than orifice flowmeters (approximately 10:1 rather than 3:1 maximum:minimum flow rate, respectively) (Doebelin, 1983).

Particle velocity can be measured by a number of methods. The pitot tube is a probe that is placed directly into the flow, pointing upstream. It measures two pressures: the stagnation pressure, by a tap at its upstream end, and the static pressure, via taps along its sides. The difference between these two pressures can be used to derive the particle velocity at the location of the upstream tap.

Although the pitot tube is quite accurate, it cannot measure very low flow velocities, nor will it register quickly fluctuating velocities, as in turbulence. Higher frequency variations in particle velocity can be measured by using a hot-wire anemometer, which consists of a very fine wire with current passing through it. When held in a moving fluid, the flow cools it and changes the resistance slightly. In the constant-temperature form of the instrument, the current is adjusted to keep the wire temperature constant, as measured by its resistance. The square of the current is then related to the flow velocity. Because the wire is so fine, it responds quickly, and fluctuating flow velocities (up to as much as 100 kHz, depending on the compensating circuit) can be measured. Also, the wire and its support can be made small enough to provide minimal disturbance to the flow. The difficulties with the technique are that the wires are very fragile; they will not register flow direction, but only its magnitude; and each hot-wire must be calibrated with known velocities in the fluid in which it is to be used (Doebelin, 1983).

High-frequency pressure fluctuations can be measured with a microphone, but in some situations this includes more than the sound wave and only the sound wave is wanted. The most familiar example is breath noise; the microphone can be moved further away or out of the breath stream, or a foam windscreen can be used that absorbs the mean flow before it deflects the microphone's diaphragm. Inside a duct with both sound waves and a non-zero mean flow, similar problems occur. Pressure transducers can be flush-mounted on the walls, or effectively extended into the flow by use of probes. A probe in a moving fluid can, however, in itself become a location for sound generation. A different way to measure fluctuating pressures is to use two hot-wires a known distance apart. Their two velocities can be used to compute a velocity gradient proportional to pressure. The cross-correlation of the two signals can be used to compute the time delay between the two sensors, and therefore the speed of propagation of a particular signal. By this means hydrodynamic and acoustic pressure disturbances can be separated out: the former travel at approximately the mean flow velocity, the latter at the speed of sound.

Fluctuating pressures can also be measured in terms of the force they exert on an object. Heller and Widnall (1970) used force transducers to deduce the source strength from the force applied by the flow to spoilers in a duct. Accelerometers can also be quite useful for measuring the effect of flow on solid bodies, provided they have a mass much less than that of the object they are attached to.

Flow visualization can be accomplished by many techniques. The flow can be seeded with visible particles such as smoke, and pictures taken of the patterns thus revealed. Alternatively, the difference in refractive index caused by differences in density can be made visible by three different optical techniques. The shadowgraph technique is the simplest, but registers only large density gradients such as in shock waves. The Schlieren technique is more sensitive, but cannot reliably be used for absolute measurements of density. Interferometry can be used for quantitative density measurements, but is quite complex to set up. All three methods depend on passing light through the flow (Massey, 1984).

If the time between successive photographs is known, the time of travel of vortices and rate of their growth can be computed. In general, flow visualization works best with flows that are essentially two-dimensional, for example, with rectangular rather than circular jets. Obviously, internal flows (i.e. flow in ducts) cannot be visualized unless at least one wall of the duct is clear and the flow is 'lit' by a means appropriate to the visualization method.

4.2 Speech-adapted methods

Ideally, in speech as in any other system, aerodynamic parameters should be measured without disturbing the flow producing them. Likewise, parameters not directly measured should be derived with due regard for the type of flow. However, the difficulties of accessing the vocal tract mean that many parameters cannot be measured directly, and a certain degree of pragmatism is therefore essential.

The aerodynamic parameters needed to model respiration tend to be more slowly-varying than those for the larynx and supraglottal system. The lung volume cannot be measured directly; it is inferred by measuring changes in body volume. Total body volume can be measured with a plethysmograph, in which the body is sealed in an airtight container. Changes in volume are deduced either by measuring changes in pressure within the container, or by measuring the flowrate through a single port into the container. Alternatively, the motion of the thorax and abdomen can be monitored by use of multiple position sensors, and the lung volume then deduced (Draper et al., 1959; Hixon et al., 1973, 1976; Ohala, 1990a).

Subglottal pressure can be measured directly by tracheal puncture (Isshiki, 1964) or by pressure transducers lowered through the glottis (Cranen and Boves, 1985, 1988). It can be inferred from esophageal pressure (Draper et al., 1959). All of these methods are invasive medical procedures requiring the presence of a physician, and thus cannot be done routinely. They can be invaluable to validate and evaluate other less invasive procedures, however. For instance, Cranen and Boves placed two pressure transducers above and two below the glottis. This allowed not only measure of the subglottal pressure, but use of the pressure gradient to deduce flow through the glottis, which could be compared to the glottal flow derived from simultaneous laryngograph, photoglottograph, and inverse filtering.

Supraglottal pressure can be measured directly much more easily than subglottal pressure by introducing a thin plastic tube at the side of the mouth and bending it behind the rear molars so that its open end is midsagittal and perpendicular to the longitudinal axis of the vocal tract. The pressure measured, P_0, should thus be the static pressure upstream of all labial, dental and alveolar constrictions. The tube is typically attached to a pressure transducer sensitive to 1–2 kHz, and referenced to atmospheric pressure (Scully, 1986). It can then be used as an estimate of the pressure drop across the constriction, ΔP_c, with the proviso that $P_0 \geq \Delta P_c$. During the stop [p], P_0 increases quickly as pressure in the tract behind the constriction equalizes with the lung pressure. The maximum value of P_0 measured during [p] can thus be used to estimate subglottal pressure, and the estimate can be extrapolated to the surrounding speech sounds. The exact value used depends on the respiratory model accepted, however: an assumption of constant pressure applied to lungs, or of constant lung-volume decrement, gives slightly different results (Scully, personal communication, 1994).

Volume velocity at the lips can be measured by a variety of masks containing flow or pressure transducers, some with nasal and oral airflow separately measured. The Rothenberg mask provides the least acoustic distortion: it measures the pressure drop across screens of known flow resistance (Rothenberg, 1973). Its frequency range is limited to 0–1.8 kHz partly by that of the transducers used, but also by acoustic resonances of the mask itself (Hertegård and Gauffin, 1992). Although it is relatively non-distorting acoustically within this range, the screening very likely massively disrupts any vortex pattern emerging from the mouth. Whether or not this is significant for the far-field sound is unknown at present.

The volume flow from the mouth measured by the Rothenberg mask is also commonly used to estimate the volume flow from the glottis, U_g, by inverse filtering; U_g is then related to activity of the vocal folds and the voicing source. Because it is not invasive and provides an essential source function, it has been used extensively. Possible limitations of the method are related to the source-filter model of speech production on which it is based, and are therefore considered in the next section.

Particle velocity has been measured within the vocal tract by using shrouded hot-wire anemometers during production of open vowels. Open vowels were necessary so that the hot-wire holder could be inserted and traversed across the tract (Teager, 1980; Teager and Teager, 1983). The shrouding was used to enable detection of flow reversal; whether it does that without undue distortion of the flow is a matter of some debate. The hot-wires can be expected to have a short life in such an environment, but the difficulties of calibration for low flow velocities and the inherent inability of a single hot-wire to detect flow reversal are more significant problems (see, for example, the extensive discussion printed as part of Teager and Teager, 1983, pp. 394–401).

The technique used by Heller and Widnall (1970) of mounting the flow spoilers on force transducers in order to measure the force generated by the flow directly is clearly not possible with an articulator like the tongue. However, accelerometers and other motion-sensing devices have been used in the vocal tract to measure motion of the velum, jaw, vocal folds and tongue. It is beyond the scope of this article to review such methods. However, when aerodynamic parameters must be inaccurately measured, or deduced from indirect measurement, or outright estimated, the presence of independently-obtained articulatory data can help put such estimates on a firmer footing. We describe such a process below.

In fricative consonants, the area of the constriction is a key parameter that is clearly related to the properties of the noise generated, although perhaps not so simply as has been proposed by Stevens (1971). It is difficult to derive this area from vocal tract imaging methods because it is so small. However, we can use an oral pressure tube and a Rothenberg mask simultaneously, and measure P_0 and U_m as a function of time during, say, a vowel-fricative-vowel transition. We can then estimate the area, A_c, by rearranging (8):

$$\hat{A}_c = KU_m \sqrt{\frac{\rho}{2P_0}} \tag{9}$$

where K is an empirical constant, nominally a shape factor, taken equal to 1 by, for example, Scully (1986). Since the constriction area has been assumed to be much less than the tract area ($A_c = A_2 \ll A_1$), K should correspond approximately to $1/C_d$.

An obvious limitation of this estimate is that P_0 does not measure the pressure drop across the constriction only: lip rounding will increase it while not affecting constriction area or, presumably, frication noise. A less obvious problem is that this form of the equation is based on steady, incompressible, frictionless flow, which we clearly do not have. Although (9) is used for flow measurement in cases that also violate these assumptions, that is done for particular geometries for which extensive empirical data exist. Not only are such data nonexistent for the vocal tract, but the geometry is continually changing. The little we do know indicates that if we use Reynolds numbers and area ratios appropriate for the transition to and from a fricative, Fig 2.7 predicts that the discharge coefficient C_d in (8) will traverse a range of values, from approximately 0.9 to 0.6, yet K is typically held constant.

It would be theoretically more valid to use an equation for compressible flow. For turbulence, however, recall that this equation involved a second empirically-derived coefficient dependent on geometry. It is circular reasoning to use a geometry-dependent parameter to estimate the area. That circularity and the inaccuracies involved in the measurement of ΔP in particular do not seem to justify the extra complexity. Scully (1986) resolves this dilemma by using the simple (9) to estimate area, but including an extra viscous term proportional to U rather than U^2 when computing the pressure drop, upon which many parameters such as flow resistance are based. In general, if the noise predicted by a simply-estimated area does not match measured noise very well, it is not clear if the fault lies with the model of the noise production mechanism, or with the estimation of the area upon which that model is based. Independently-deduced data on the area or the shape of the constriction can help clarify such issues.

A related problem occurs in estimating the flow resistance of constrictions, which is relevant for the glottis as well as for fricatives. A typical procedure is to use the average volume velocity through and pressure drop across a constriction to define an operating point on an essentially parabolic function. The incremental resistance is then defined as the slope of the tangent to the curve at the operating point (Heinz, 1956). Pressure fluctuations due to sound waves are assumed to be small excursions about that point which can be modelled linearly; for small sound pressure amplitudes, this assumption is borne out by the measurements of Ingard and Ising (1967). However, the flow resistance in practice is often deduced from constriction area and volume velocity alone (Badin and Fant, 1984), whereas constriction shape can influence the pressure drop and, therefore, the operating point (Shadle, 1985).

5 Models incorporating aerodynamics

The classical acoustic theory of speech production models the acoustic properties of the vocal tract as an analogous electrical network. In so doing, several assumptions are made: sources and filter are independent, the filter is composed of passive elements and constitutes a linear system, sound propagation is one-dimensional, and in the most restrictive models, there is no mean flow. In this type of model, all aerodynamic effects are essentially confined to the source functions. Because source and filter are independent, whistles or whistly fricatives cannot be generated, but this lack would not of itself be of undue significance for speech models for most languages. Unfortunately, problems of greater consequence do arise; it is instructive to consider the ways in which some existing models have approached greater physical realism by relaxing some of the assumptions.

All models of phonation must include mean flow as an input, and fluctuating volume velocity is generated as an output. However, tract models do not always include mean flow. How can fricatives then be generated? Scully (1990) includes mean flow in her synthesizer by having separate acoustics and aerodynamics blocks. The aerodynamics block computes static pressure and mean flow throughout the tract, including the lungs, and generates frication sources with strength related to the pressure drop across the constriction. These sources are then fed forward to the final source-filter model. The sources and filter cannot interact extensively, but some influence is possible via numerous interconnecting paths.

A somewhat different approach is taken by Flanagan and Ishizaka (1976), who derive the fluctuating glottal flow from the two-mass model and a mean flow from a dc atmospheric-pressure source. This arrangement allows respiration, as well as frication. Frication is then modelled by providing each transmission-line section with a noise pressure source parameterized by Reynolds number. A particular source would generate noise only if the area and volume velocity in that section resulted in $Re > Re_{crit}$. The amplitude of the noise source is modulated by a function proportional to Re^2, making the modulation observed in voiced fricatives possible (as demonstrated in earlier work based on a similar model, Flanagan, 1972). The noise source spectrum is flat, a reasonable simplification given the frequency range of the simulation (0–4 kHz). It now appears that the noise source should be located downstream of rather than at the section that produced it, but exactly where it should be cannot be determined from area and volume velocity alone. The location and spectrum of flow sources depend on velocity at point of impingement; the non-uniform velocity distribution across the tract and tract shape as well as cross-sectional area therefore become important, but are included so far only in numerical simulation models (Shadle, 1990).

Mean flow is also included in inverse filtering procedures using the Rothenberg mask, which are based on a similar model of independent source and a filter that is linear, time-invariant, and composed of passive elements only (Rothenberg, 1973). The major difficulty of estimating the vocal tract transfer function, and therefore the inverse filter, is discussed in Ní Chasaide and Gobl, VOICE SOURCE VARIATION.

However, serious problems remain. The source of sound due to phonation is assumed to be a one-dimensional volume-velocity source localized at the glottis. All studies visualizing the flow near the glottis of mechanical models, whether static or dynamic, show a jet, with reverse flow on either side; velocity is clearly highly non-uniform across the vocal tract. Is the plane source supposed to represent the average velocity across the tract, or the velocity of the jet alone? Further problems arise when considering the mean flow. Because the mask 'captures' steady (dc) as well as fluctuating flow, the dc component is presumed to equal the dc flow that passed through the glottis when the fluctuating component was generated, and to indicate incomplete closure. However, this mean flow will travel at the convection velocity through the vocal tract, whereas any sound generated near the glottis will travel at the speed of sound. A simple calculation shows that for a typical vowel, the sound will take about 0.5 ms to arrive at the lips, whereas the mean flow component will take about 170 ms (Davies et al., 1993). This disparity will vary with the tract area function and subglottal pressure, and so cannot be easily estimated and compensated for. While inverse filtering is undoubtedly useful, it appears that the waveform it generates has a more complex relationship to actual velocities existing near the glottis than was originally appreciated.

A recent model of sound propagation in the vocal tract (Davies et al., 1993) retains a separation of source and filter while relaxing many of the traditional assumptions. Sound propagation is not always one-dimensional, and it need not be isentropic near junctions; mean flow is allowed, and the speed of sound is adjusted accordingly, but flow sources are not generated by the model. Because the tract is not modelled as an electrical analog, but instead is divided up into different duct elements that affect sound propagation differently, more physical realism is possible while still remaining powerful conceptually.

Teager sought to relax the assumption of independent source and filter. His hot-wire data showed evidence of non-uniform velocity across the vocal tract during vowel production (Teager, 1980). He suggested that source-filter interaction was therefore essential to a speech production model, and described a jet-cavity interaction paradigm (Teager and Teager, 1983). Such an interaction is essential for modelling whistles. It is clear also that jets and separated flow exist in the vocal tract, even in non-whistling cases (Liljencrants, 1991b; Pelorson et al., 1994). It is not clear that such flow patterns always lead to radiated sound. Also, some speech sounds do not seem to require such complete aerodynamic interaction. In the end, though, the most serious objection to Teager's paradigm is that no quantitative model exists, reflecting the difficulties inherent in such an approach.

Full continuum simulations of the entire flow field represent another approach to including aerodynamics in a model of the vocal tract (e.g. Thomas, 1986; Iijima et al., 1990; Liljencrants, 1991b). These simulations must be regarded as another kind of model, for simplifications must be made here as well, restricting, for instance, the frequency range, spatial resolution, or wall motion. As a result such models are mostly restricted to the vicinity of the glottis. While non-uniform flow velocity can be minutely 'observed' by such means, there is no obvious way to separate acoustic and hydrodynamic motion, i.e. to predict the radiated sound from the internal fluid motion. Such models are not simple conceptually, but nevertheless provide a valuable addition to experiments with mechanical models and human subjects in increasing our understanding of the fluid dynamics of the vocal tract.

In summary, a variety of models exists that incorporates aerodynamics to a greater or lesser degree. Although it is difficult to model such effects as phonation (fluid-solid interaction) or frication (turbulence) because the underlying phenomena are incompletely understood and resist an analytical solution, the fact that aerodynamics underlies all aspects of speech production makes such efforts important.

ACKNOWLEDGEMENTS

I would like to thank Prof. Peter Davies and Dr. Celia Scully for helpful discussions, and Dr. Bob Damper, Prof. Bill Hardcastle and Prof. John Laver for their helpful comments on an earlier draft of this paper. Thanks also to Dr. Scully for the raw data incorporated in Figures 2.4 and 2.6, which was obtained as part of an EC SCIENCE award, CEC-SCI*0147C(EDB).

APPENDIX: CONSTANTS AND CONVERSION FACTORS

The following values hold for dry air at 37°C. Values for completely saturated air are given in parentheses where available. (From Batchelor, 1967, and Davies, 1991).

c	= speed of sound	=	35,300 cm/s	(35,900)
γ	= ratio of specific heats	=	1.400	(1.396)
R	= gas constant	=	2.87×10^6 erg/g	(2.977×10^6)
ρ	= density	=	1.139×10^{-3} g/cm³	(1.098×10^{-3})
μ	= absolute viscosity	=	1.89×10^{-4} g/cm-s	
v	= μ/ρ = kinematic viscosity	=	0.166 cm²/s	
P_0	= standard atmospheric pressure at sea level	=	760 mm Hg	(760)

NOTE

1 At frequencies below the first cut-on frequency only plane waves propagate, which excite the longitudinal modes. The first cut-on frequency, above which transverse as well as longitudinal modes can propagate, depends on the duct's cross-sectional shape and inversely on its largest cross-dimension. A circular duct 4 cm in diameter has a cut-on frequency of approximately 5 kHz (Kinsler et al., 1982). This is why using only cavity lengths and area ratios to compute formant frequencies works well up to 5 kHz, and less well above that.

Table 2.1 Pressure (force per unit area)

This conversion table for units of pressure should be interpreted as follows: 1 of the unit chosen from the leftmost column equals x of the unit chosen from the topmost row, where x is the value found at the intersection of the chosen row and column. For example, 1 bar = 10^5 Pa.

	dyn/cm^2	Pa	bar	atm	$cm\ H_2O$	$in\ H_2O$	$mm\ Hg$
dyn/cm²	1	0.1	10^{-6}	9.869×10^{-7}	1.0197×10^{-3}	4.015×10^{-4}	7.501×10^{-4}
Pa	10	1	10^{-5}	9.869×10^{-6}	1.0197×10^{-2}	4.015×10^{-3}	7.501×10^{-3}
bar	10^6	10^5	1	9.869×10^{-1}	1.0197×10^3	4.015×10^2	7.501×10^2
atm	1.013×10^6	1.013×10^5	1.013	1	1033.0	406.8	760.0
cm H₂O	980.71	98.071	9.8071×10^{-4}	9.865×10^{-4}	1	0.3937	0.7355
in H₂O	2491.0	249.1	2.491×10^{-3}	2.458×10^{-3}	2.54	1	1.868
mm Hg	1.333×10^3	133.3	1.333×10^{-3}	1.316×10^{-3}	1.3597	0.5353	1

1 μbar = 1 dyn/cm²; 1 Nt/m² = 1 Pa.
Values in this table are derived from Halliday and Resnick (1966).

3 Acoustic Phonetics

OSAMU FUJIMURA AND
DONNA ERICKSON

1 Spectrographic analysis

Spectrographic characteristics of consonants and vowels have been studied extensively in the history of speech research (Fant, 1970; Joos, 1948; Potter, Kopp, & Green, 1947). Among the most recent publications, a concise account of American English characteristics can be found in the textbook by Kent & Read (1992), in conjunction with relevant background issues of speech signal analysis. Ladefoged's textbook (Ladefoged, 1993) discusses both British and American forms of English. A more comprehensive treatise by Laver (1994), including articulatory and acoustic details of speech sound characteristics with references to a variety of languages, is recommended for further study. Another textbook by Ladefoged, *Elements of Acoustic Phonetics*, deals with selected issues of acoustics and signal processing for experimental phoneticians and has been revised substantially in the new edition.

In this chapter, only basic points of spectrographic interpretation will be discussed along with some remarks on theoretical issues. First, in this section, principles of spectrographic analysis of acoustic signals along with some basic concepts will be outlined. In Section 2, so-called segmental characteristics of individual consonants and vowels will be discussed. In Section 3, principles of speech organization will be discussed with a new perspective regarding syllables as the basic concatenative units. Finally in Section 4, what are generally called prosodic aspects of speech characteristics will be discussed.

1.1 Periodic signal

A periodic signal ideally repeats the same segment of time function exactly and for an infinite length of time. If the minimal repeated segment that can be identified in the time function representing a speech signal has the duration T, the fundamental frequency of this signal is its inverse $1/T = f_0$. This f_0 is the primary contribution to perceived voice pitch, even though the sensation of pitch is affected by other factors such as intensity and the shape of the spectral envelope. T is called the fundamental period of the periodic signal.

If (and only if) the waveform of the signal is sinusoidal, the sound contains only one frequency, say, f_0. In other words, the spectrum of a sinusoidal signal consists of only one frequency component (line spectrum), and its frequency is f_0. If the sound signal contains other frequency components, and if each of the other frequency components has a frequency that is an integer multiple of f_0 (such as $2f_0$, $3f_0$, or $4f_0$, etc., representing the second, third, and fourth harmonics), then the spectrum has a harmonic structure (comb spectrum), and each component is a harmonic component. The fundamental component is the first harmonic. Any of the harmonic components, including the first harmonic, may be sporadically missing, and still the fundamental frequency and period are the same. If the spectrum has a harmonic structure, the time function representing the composite sum of all frequency components is periodic and has the same fundamental period (T) and the same fundamental frequency (f_0) as the fundamental component has. The spectrum of the signal represents the Fourier transform of the original time function (apart from the effects of the weighting time function which we always use in practice): this implies a conversion of the independent variable from time to frequency.

1.2 Aperiodic signal

If the waveform is not periodic, the spectrum does not show harmonic structure. If the physical phenomenon of signal production is stationary, the spectrum of the generated signal may consist of discrete spectral lines representing a set of frequency components which are not mutually related in frequency by integer multiple relations. It may constitute a continuous spectrum, as would be the case for a single pulse as the time function. It may have some random structure, as in the case of white (Gaussian) noise, which changes randomly and exhibits a statistically constant (to the extent the signal is stationary) average envelope of amplitude. By a mathematical method of time-frequency conversion for non-periodic signals, any time function can be examined through a time window, usually with a gradually tapered weight placed around the center of the time window, to evaluate the (short-term) spectrum of the time function.

Mathematics tells us that there is always some uncertainty in the frequency specification of the spectral property of a signal, and the narrower the time window in selecting the time region, the wider the frequency window through which the spectral property can be evaluated. As a matter of order of magnitude, the product of the time window width (in seconds) and the frequency window width (in Hz) cannot be smaller than 1. Therefore, if we select to separate contiguous harmonic components in the frequency domain for a male voice with $f_0 = 100$ Hz, for example, by using a narrow bandpass filter with a

50 Hz bandwidth, then we should not expect to be able to determine the timing of an event like voice onset or offset by any better than ±10 msec accuracy, since the product of 20 msec and 50 Hz equals 1. If we use a wider bandwidth for the analysis filter, say 300 Hz, the typical wideband filter for spectrographs, the time resolution improves to a few milliseconds.

1.3 The spectrograph

Since speech signals are characterized by fairly fast temporal changes in the conditions of the sound production system, the concept of spectra that pertain to stationary sounds is not very useful in most speech research except in basic theoretical work, such as studies of physical mechanisms in vowel production, nasalization of vowels, etc. Visible speech (Potter, *et al.*, 1947) was invented in the late 1940s in conjunction with the development of magnetic sound recording techniques, to record and make permanently available the elusive characteristics of auditory signals for objective quantitative studies. The device, called a spectrograph, converts the single-variable time functions of speech signals, usually representing sound pressure as measured by a microphone, into a two-dimensional time-frequency display. Such a display is called a spectrogram, whether it is displayed on a computer screen or printed as a hard copy. The abscissa of the display represents time, and the ordinate represents frequency, and the amplitude of the signal that is contained in the vicinity of a specified time and frequency is represented by darkness at that spatial point on the display.

In consideration of the time-frequency uncertainty constraint discussed above, a wideband filter with a nominal bandwidth of 300 Hz is usually employed for speech analysis involving examination of consonantal properties, while a 45 Hz narrowband filter is used by tradition for studying voice f_0 contours (Potter, *et al.*, 1947). Fig 3.1 illustrates different intonation patterns associated with the same sentence, 'That's wonderful', depending on the conversational situation. Note that the voice pitch (f_0) pattern is drastically different among (a), (b), and (c) in the figure (see Section 4 for further discussion on prosodic control). Unless otherwise stated, all spectrograms in this chapter pertain to utterances by a young adult female who speaks a typical form of American English in Ohio.

Since harmonic structure may be assumed approximately for voiced signals, we may find an n-th harmonic with a frequency corresponding to n times f_0, where n is any integer (such as 5 or 10). The temporal change of a particular harmonic, if traceable, represents an amplified display of the fundamental frequency change (pitch contour) and often provides the most exact pitch evaluation. This is particularly true when the speech signal is changing rapidly either in articulation or voicing conditions (including irregularity of the vocal fold vibration), and automatic pitch extraction algorithms cannot be reliable. It should be noted that the concept of the fundamental frequency

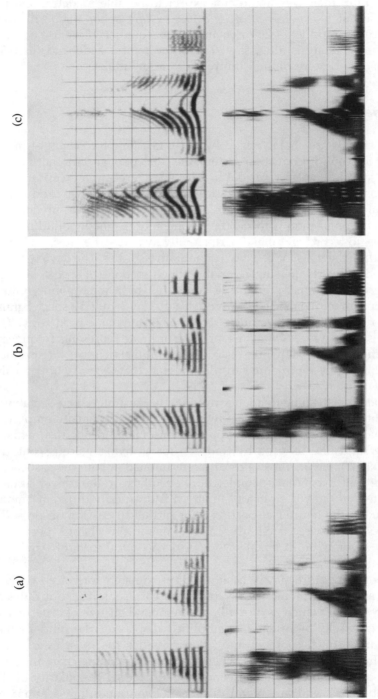

Figure 3.1 'That's wonderful' spoken with different intonation patterns: (a) a plain statement, (b) a question with surprise, (c) excitedly with prominence attached to both 'that' and 'wonderful'. Wideband (0–4 kHz) and narrowband (0–4 kHz) analyses. The calibration grid is given for every 500 Hz (vertical) and 0.1 second (horizontal, narrowband only).

(a)   (b)

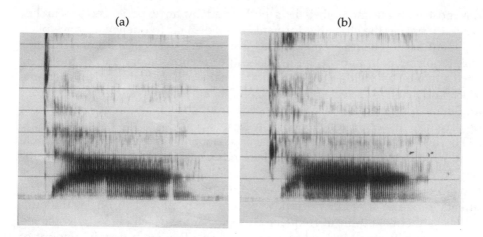

Figure 3.2 Wideband spectrograms (0–8 kHz) comparing English syllables (a) [dɑ] and (b) [gɑ], spoken in isolation.

(often called pitch in speech technology) as a one-dimensional time-varying quantity is based on the assumption that the signal is quasi-periodic and is sufficiently stationary. The speech signals or the vocal fold vibration in reality do not necessarily satisfy these assumptions, and therefore a single number f_0 is not always a valid measure even for a fairly stationary utterance of a sonorant sound. This may be particularly true when voicing is weak, for example toward the end of an utterance when the pulmonary pressure drops and the vocal folds become slack. Spectrograms can handle aperiodic signals and show deviations from stationary periodicity, including such phenomena as subharmonics and relatively rapid amplitude/frequency modulation (see Fujimura, 1988; Mazo, *et al.*, 1994; Estill, Fujimura, *et al.*, 1995), as well as partial periodicity limited in frequency range (see Fujimura, 1968).

In Fig 3.2, we compare the syllables (a) [dɑ] and (b) [gɑ], spoken in isolation. In the wideband spectrograms, each of the lowest four formants can be identified best in the transition from the stop to the vowel. The stationary frequency values toward the end of each utterance are approximately: for [dɑ], $F_1 = 1,100$ Hz, $F_2 = 1,700$ Hz, $F_3 = 2,700$ Hz, $F_4 = 3,700$ Hz; for [gɑ], $F_1 = 1,050$ Hz, $F_2 = 1,600$ Hz, $F_3 = 2,700$ Hz, $F_4 = 3,700$ Hz (as estimated visually from these figures).

We are often interested in fairly fast changes of the formant frequencies. The formant bar is a relatively wide, horizontal dark area (e.g. about 300 Hz-wide for an isolated formant if the filter bandwidth is 300 Hz). The harmonic structure in the so-called cross-section spectrum often does not reveal the true formant frequency defined as the resonance frequency of the vocal conduit, because the latter generally does not coincide with any of the harmonic frequencies due to the vocal fold vibration. Partly for this reason, the seemingly gross visual method of formant-bar evaluation using a wideband filter can be the most accurate method, if it is performed by an experienced researcher carefully tracing the changing formant bars. Formant frequency or voice pitch (f_0) identification using acoustic speech signals is a very complex and difficult task requiring both knowledge of speech production theory and of the utterance situation as well as the particular speaker. Some automatic algorithms work fairly well for selected speakers, but generally, the results obtained from automatic formant and voice fundamental frequency extraction methods must be carefully inspected for reliable conclusions.

The original analog spectrographs used a bandpass filter with selectable fixed bandwidths, combined with a heterodyne circuit, for continuously shifting, in effect, the center frequency of the filter passband. A horizontal line traversed the display area of the recording paper covering the required frequency range. A frequency window continuously moved up, from the minimum to the maximum in frequency, as the same speech signal was played back repeatedly from an analog magnetic disc, allowing a certain amount of frequency window overlap for adjacent scans. Modern spectrographs digitally store signals and use either digital hardware (or firmware) or a Fast Fourier Transform algorithm. A graphic display and a laser printer are typically used for the output. The amplitude spectrum is computed for each frequency range given a windowed segment of time function, drawing a brightness-modulated vertical line along the frequency (vertical) scale of the spectrogram. Flexible choices of time/frequency windows allow optimizing analysis parameters as well as the signal duration to be analyzed, and real-time analysis (with some delay depending on the size of the time window and the corresponding filter bandwidth) can be performed.

Spectrographic analysis software often offers waveform editing capabilities together with the time-function display, so that the user can listen to the cursor-selected segments of signals, splice different portions together (waveform editing), measure segmental durations and signal intensity, etc. Some software allows the user to evaluate automatically such speech signal parameters as formant frequencies and fundamental frequency, based on, or verified with, the subjective judgment using visual inspection of the spectrographic display, and log the measured or edited values of selected variables in computer files for data reduction using statistical analysis tools.

2 Segmental characteristics

2.1 Perceptual cues

The acoustic signal characteristics have been evaluated in terms of their perceptual effects in phoneme identification or discrimination tasks, using synthetic speech samples, of which specific acoustic characteristics are controlled quantitatively and independently for each parameter of synthesis specification.

This tradition of speech perception research started with the ground breaking work at Haskins Laboratories (Liberman, *et al.*, 1954; Delattre, *et al.*, 1955) soon after the invention of the spectrographic speech analysis technique (Potter, *et al.*, 1947). Cooper with his associates invented what they called Pattern Playback (Cooper, *et al.*, 1952), which aimed at playing the sound back from spectrographic patterns. This machine took manually painted optical control patterns for specifying the utterance message to be produced, as a cartoon-like schematization of spectrographic pattern as obtained by the spectrograph (visible speech).

This speech synthesizer, rudimentary by the current standards of speech synthesis using computer programs and relatively exact speech signal generation algorithms, did not allow voice source manipulation, and the fundamental frequency was fixed.[1] Nevertheless, it was effectively used for crucial discoveries of basic properties of speech signals in relation to phonetic perception. Following this strategy in speech research, many research groups have combined perceptual experimental techniques with speech synthesis. In some cases the relative importance of physical characteristics (multiple cues) have been identified using simultaneous control of parameters for high quality speech synthesis (Klatt, 1987). It should be noted here, however, that in speech perception, there are typically many interacting factors that determine the perceived phonetic qualities. For this reason, with unnatural synthetic speech, determining effective cues in relation to physical parametric specifications of the acoustic properties generally tends to be inconclusive or misleading, unless the cues are predominantly strong as was the case in the early pioneering work at Haskins Laboratories. To investigate further details, it is mandatory to first secure naturalness of the synthetic stimuli as the intended phonetic unit, and then control the parameter values in synthesis, deviating from the optimal specification, keeping other synthesis conditions the same.

Suppose there are two perceptual cues (such as voice onset time, see below, and f_0 inflection near the explosion of a stop-vowel syllable) that are known to influence a categorical opposition between two consonants in minimal contrast (with respect to one feature such as voiced *vs.* voiceless) and can be controlled continuously as signal parameters in speech synthesis. Then, the primary cue (voice onset time, in this case, see Lisker & Abramson, 1964) may be defined as the characteristic that overrides the perceptual effects of the other characteristic in a wide range of the latter's parameter values determining the consonantal identity. The secondary cue (e.g. f_0 inflection) determines the categorical identification consistently only when the primary cue (voice onset time) takes a value intermediate between the most preferable values for the two categories (see Fujimura, 1961b, 1971; Haggard, Ambler, & Callow, 1970).

Generally, however, perceptual cues interact with each other, and often coexistence of more than one cue is required for reliably identifying a minimal opposition with respect to a single feature. The perceptual cues for the /g/-identification in the context of back vowels in an utterance of a CV syllable is such an example. For example, the syllables /dɑ/ and /gɑ/ in isolation are not identifiable reliably by synchronized linear formant transitions (as in early experiments), while the same consonants in combination with front vowels are readily identifiable with such synthetic speech. But the phonemic identities as well as naturalness can be achieved effectively for back-vowel syllables by combining a burst and asynchronous piecewise linear formant transitions for the lowest three formants using a series formant synthesizer. Generally, also, the definition of a cue is dependent on the particular framework of phonetic description of the signals or the synthesis control scheme.

2.2 *Vowels*

The acoustic theory of vowel production (Fant, 1960) provides a standard model of vowel spectra in relation to the articulatory characteristics. The articulatory condition is described as the vocal tract configuration in terms of the cross-sectional area variation as a one-dimensional function of the distance from the glottis to the lip opening. The acoustic and perceptual validity of this approximation theory has been confirmed by various experimental studies, including direct acoustic measurements of the transfer functions of the resonant system (Fujimura & Lindqvist, 1971). Speech synthesis schemes called terminal analog synthesizers, based on this theory, have demonstrated a very high signal quality (Fant, Martony, Rengman, Risberg, & Holmes, 1961; see also Holmes, 1973, and Carlson and Granström, SPEECH SYNTHESIS). This standard acoustical theory also has provided the theoretical basis of many developments in computational speech technology.

The basic idea of the acoustical theory of speech production is that the acoustic system can be separated into two approximately independent parts: source and filter. The source for vowels and similar (sonorant) sounds is normally the modulated airflow produced by the pulmonary air pressure and the passively vibrating vocal folds (van den Berg, 1958). It is assumed that the filter is the acoustic system which serves basically as a plane-wave propagation medium in a tube (vocal conduit) with a variable cross-sectional area, which corresponds to variable characteristic impedance and resultant reflections at points along the length of the vocal tract. Also, the surrounding walls defining the tube insulate and reflect acoustic waves; the effects of cross-modes of acoustic waves traveling in the direction perpendicular to the tube axis are negligible due to the small cross-dimensions relative to the wave-lengths of interest. Both of these assumptions are only approximately met and result in limitations of accuracy in certain cases, and the second assumption about rigid walls was later removed by implementing an effective correction (with respect to the first formant frequency and bandwidth) to account for the yielding and dissipating walls of the vocal tract (Fant, 1972; also see Fujimura & Lindqvist, 1971).

The filter characteristics can be represented by a product of separate formant terms (summation in terms of dB). The set of lowest three or four formant frequencies (F-pattern) alone determines the phonetic vowel quality, in usual circumstances. Correction terms for the finite truncation of the formant series and the radiation characteristics (relating the volume velocity through the lips to the microphone signal) are usually treated approximately as a constant frequency function for a given utterance. The voice source spectrum is often assumed to have a constant envelope, allowing only variation of the fundamental frequency and overall amplitude (intensity) throughout the utterance. Thus, the vowel quality, at any point of the slowly changing vowel articulation (base function, see below) in speech, is described by the F-pattern as a quasi-stationary parameter (see Stevens & House, 1961 and Fant, 1970 for tutorial accounts). Such a vocalic function is seen in the wideband spectrogram (as seen, for example, in Fig 3.7) as the smoothly changing formant bars interrupted at syllable margins by consonantal perturbations (Öhman, 1966).

Voiced sounds such as vowels and other sonorants (see below) are spectrographically characterized by a vertical striation in wideband spectrograms as evidence of voice periodicity. In narrowband spectrograms, a horizontal striation separating individual harmonics of such periodic signals is usually observed.

2.3 Obstruents

Obstruents are typical (also called true) consonants. Phonologically, they are found commonly as representative elements in syllable margins. Phonetically, they are characterized by obvious acoustic obstacles along the vocal tract, in the form of either a complete blockage of the acoustic channel (stops) or constrictions causing generation of turbulent noise (fricatives), or a temporally sequential combination thereof (affricates). When the glottis is narrowed by vocal fold adduction, the vocal folds may maintain vibration under such vocal tract conditions, but the vibration tends to be weak and limited in duration, and it is relatively difficult to initiate vibration. Obstruents are more often voiceless than voiced in most languages (see, for examples of occurrence patterns, Maddieson, 1984a, and Ohala, THE RELATION BETWEEN PHONETICS AND PHONOLOGY). In addition, voiced obstruents tend to become phonetically (partially or totally) unvoiced when there is an adjacent unvoiced portion of the speech signal manifesting a boundary as a silent period, or a voiceless consonant as an unvoiced obstruent segment. The voiced fricative /z/ in English, for example, tends to appear as an unvoiced fricative (like a weak [s]) at the beginning or ending of a phonetic phrase, when there is either preceding or following voicing cessation (compare the utterance-initial /z/ and the word-final /z/ in Fig 3.3).

Stop consonants require some spectrographic 'gap' or obvious signal weakening, which varies in duration depending on the prosodic conditions. In

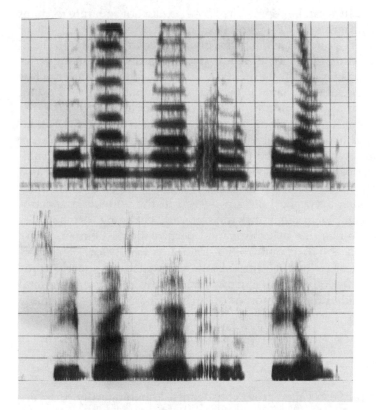

Figure 3.3 'Zebras live in the fields.' (lower panel: 8 kHz wideband with grid lines at every 1 kHz, upper panel: 2 kHz narrowband with grid lines at every 250 Hz and 0.1 sec.)

syllable final position, particularly, the phonological stop may not be produced by an articulatory (supralaryngeal) closure. A common alternative in syllable final position for the apical closure in English is a glottal stop, which shows a neutral formant transition. An articulatory closure in the oral part of the vocal tract produces a total silence when there is neither voicing (i.e. vocal fold vibration) nor nasal coupling (velum lowering), and a 'voice bar' when there is voicing but no nasal coupling, and a nasal murmur when there is nasal coupling and voicing.

Stop consonants are also called plosives. The articulatory explosion is characterized by a spectrographic 'burst' with an abrupt onset, or 'spike', generated by the articulatory release of the closure. In the case of dorsal stops, there is often observed more than one such spike in the spectrogram. Due to the movement of the crucial articulator, such as the lips for labial stops, the tongue tip for apical stops, and the tongue body for dorsal stops, there is always some formant transition from consonant (C) to vowel (V) when the consonantal gesture of closure and release is followed by a vowel gesture. (For further discussion of transitional movements see Stevens, ARTICULATORY – ACOUSTIC – AUDITORY RELATIONSHIPS.) A similar and reversed formant transition into the closure gesture is observed in a VC sequence, but the pattern is not necessarily symmetric with the CV transition, and their perceptual effects vary from language to language (see Ohde & Sharf, 1977; Fujimura, Macchi & Streeter, 1978).

The temporal change of the F-pattern characterizes the place of articulation, or the identity of the crucial articulator, as well as the concomitant (secondary) articulation such as lip rounding in apical/coronal or dorsal obstruents and tongue tip retroflexion in apical obstruents. The patterns of such formant transitions are inherent properties of the particular combination of the consonant(s) and the tautosyllabic vowel and are thus characteristic of the demisyllable. Note that the contextual influence (coarticulation) is not necessarily between adjacent phonemes, as observed in the lip gesture difference in the [s] of 'slay' (un-rounded [s]) vs. 'slow' (rounded [s]). A certain degree of approximation to the formant transition patterns often, in the case of a CVC syllable (where the pertinent C is a single consonantal phoneme), can be given in terms of what are called formant loci (Delattre, *et al.*, 1955). These frequency loci, or target values, were proposed to be inherent to the particular consonant regardless of the vowel, and the transition between C and V were viewed as straight-line frequency changes over a fixed amount of time for all formants (i.e. synchronous linear transition). In particular, F_2 and F_3 loci were described as the inherent property of the place of articulation for obstruents and nasals. Formant loci were not necessarily visible in the spectrogram nor to be produced in synthesis, but hidden ('cutback') as an abstract extension of the formant movement from the vowel to the consonant.

Fricatives are characterized by turbulent noise. The random signal, called frication, often shows some clear power concentration in a specific frequency range. The frequency range is largely characteristic of location along the vocal tract of the critical articulator for the consonant and the three-dimensional shape of the obstacle it faces directly (e.g. the shape of the alveolar ridge for [s]), but the physical conditions of the vocal tract downstream (e.g. the shape of the teeth for [s]) is also important (Shadle, 1990, 1991, also see Shadle, THE AERODYNAMICS OF SPEECH). These acoustic properties are shared by the frication noise (spike) at the explosion of stop consonants with the corresponding place of articulation (*cf.* Stevens & Blumstein, 1978; Kewley-Port, Pisoni, & Studdert-Kennedy, 1983). Strident fricatives show clear and strong as well as relatively context-independent spectrographic characteristics of frication. Non-strident fricatives produced at the front end of the vocal tract are weaker in intensity and show widely spread noise energy over a wide range, including the highest end, of the frequency range for speech signals. The turbulent noise for /h/, generated at or near the glottis, often accompanied by a frication near the constriction along the vocal tract for the adjacent vowel, is usually treated as a fricative, but physically it is an aspiration. The signal for this turbulent noise is often very weak, and tends to be voiced intervocalically. The vocal folds can maintain vibration under a partially abducted condition, while it is harder to initiate voicing with the same physical position of the vocal folds (Titze, 1994).

The turbulent noise often appears in higher frequency regions for strident fricatives, affricates, spirantization (see Section 3.2) and stops: [s] showing the noise power concentration around the fourth and higher formant regions of the speaker, and [ʃ] around the third and higher formant regions. When the fricative is voiced, all or part of the frication in these regions is amplitude-modulated due to the periodically interrupted airflow. Such a modulation may be observed in the wideband spectrogram as a vertical striation. Often in such a case, the narrowband spectrogram does not show any harmonic structure in the higher frequency regions, while the lowest frequency region clearly shows steady harmonic structure (see the final /z/ of 'zebras' in Fig 3.3). The vertical striation in the wideband spectrogram does not necessarily represent any periodicity of the signal, because periodically amplitude-modulated random noise is not periodic and has no harmonic structure in its spectrum. The fundamental component and some low harmonics as observed in the narrowband spectrogram are due to a superimposed voiced signal with a very low F_1, which explains the low amplitudes of higher harmonics for the periodic part of the signal (see Fant, 1956). In synthesis experiments, an amplitude modulation of turbulent noise seems to produce more natural voiced fricatives than simple superposition of voice source signal and spectrally shaped random noise.

A voiceless stop usually shows another succeeding segment of turbulent noise after the burst (short frication) at the articulatory release (with a continuous superpositional transition). This second component of random signal is produced at the glottis (and to some extent concomitantly at other constricted areas in the vocal tract) after the constriction at the place of articulation is sufficiently opened, and the glottis is sufficiently adducted for a following voicing gesture. This type of frication noise, called aspiration, is basically the same phenomenon as [h]. The time interval between the articulatory release of a stop consonant and voice onset, typically in a CV syllable context, is called voice onset time (VOT) (Lisker & Abramson, 1964). This interval includes the spike (the sound produced by the separation of the articulators), frication after the spike, and the aspiration following it. Some languages use aspiration distinctively in combination with voicing as well as without voicing (e.g. the Hindi four-way distinction, Dixit, 1978; Kagaya, 1975).

The VOT for a syllable-initial voiceless stop consonant varies somewhat systematically depending on the place of articulation and other segmental context (see e.g. Fischer-Jørgensen, 1963). Particularly salient in English is the difference among the initial stop, spirantized stop (i.e. /s/ + stop, see Section 3.2), and stop + /l/ or /r/, as in the paradigm 'kip', 'skip', and 'clip'. In a spirantized stop, i.e. /sp/, /st/, or /sk/ cluster in phonemic terms, the VOT is very small (the stop is un-aspirated), while a stop followed by a liquid /l/

or /r/ is associated with a very large (often 100msec or more) VOT. Fig 3.4 illustrates examples of a variety of onset cluster paradigms in spectrograms. The words, 'bit, pit, spit, split, splash, kip, skip, clip, till, still, trill', were produced in isolation (list form). The temporal patterns of these initial consonant clusters will be discussed in Section 3.2.

Affricates exhibit a combination of stop closure and frication generation at the same place of articulation. The combined duration is more like the corresponding single stop or fricative rather than the sum of them (see Fig 3.5 for spectrograms). Considering the distribution of stops, fricatives, and affricates in different places of articulation, the English [tʃ] may be interpreted as a palatal stop, minimally contrasting with /ʃ/ in terms of the stop/fricative distinction phonologically. This distinction is implemented phonetically with a prolonged frication for a stop consonant (in comparison with stops with other places of articulation) because of the vocal tract shape for the palatal stop formation (note that [k], also using the tongue body surface as the articulator, has a long frication as well as aspiration, but it does not contrast with a fricative in American English).

2.4 Sonorants

2.4.1 Glides Some sonorants, typically the semivowels [j] and [w], are vowels from the phonetic point of view, except that the spectral characteristics tend to change temporally more rapidly than syllable nuclei do. The temporal pattern of formant transition, particularly in a syllable final glide (diphthongization), varies greatly from language to language. Some languages use secondary (tongue body) articulation gestures, palatalization for example, with peripheral obstruent gestures roughly simultaneously superimposed. This results in contrasting obstruents (or sonorants) with and without such glides. This can occur either in syllable initial position (e.g. Japanese palatalization, see Miyawaki, 1972), or in syllable final position (e.g. Estonian palatalization, see Eek, 1973). In English, a typical syllable-initial palatalization occurs only in conjunction with the vowel /u/, as in 'cue' and 'student' (in some dialects), whereas in Japanese, it occurs with all back vowels /ɑ, o, u/. Such palatalization effects are properties of initial demisyllables as a whole from the phonetic point of view, affecting both the consonantal and vocalic gestures. Phonologically, it may be considered a feature of the onset or the nucleus depending on the language.

2.4.2 Intermittent obstruction From a phonological point of view, sonorants also function as elements of syllable margins. Phonetically, the vocal tract leaves a wide enough channel for the airflow through the main vocal tract, whether it is a midsagittal passage or lateral passage, or through the nasal passages, so that the vocal fold vibration is easily maintained. This results in the output signal with a relatively large acoustic power in comparison

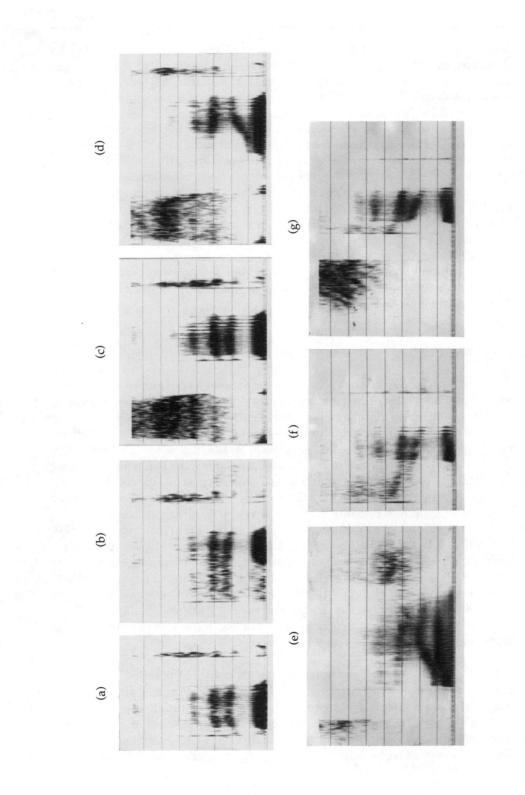

(a)   (b)   (c)   (d)

(e)   (f)   (g)

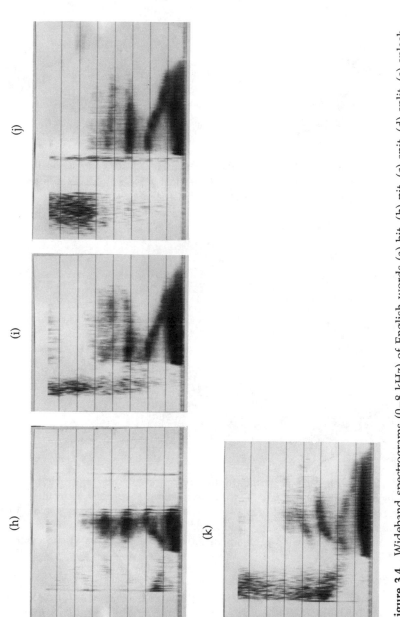

Figure 3.4 Wideband spectrograms (0–8 kHz) of English words (a) bit, (b) pit, (c) spit, (d) split, (e) splash, (f) kip, (g) skip, (h) clip, (i) till, (k) still, (l) trill, produced in isolation.

(a)   (b)

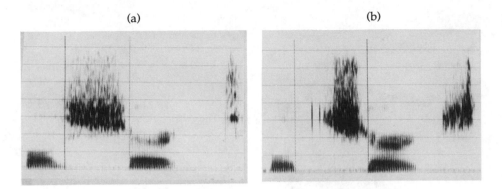

Figure 3.5 The word 'shirt' /ʃʌRt/ [ʃɝ:t] *vs.* 'church' /ʧʌRʧ/ [ʧɝ:ʧ] in 'I found a beautiful _____ today' (wideband 8 kHz). The vertical cursors delimit the intervals of voice cessation for the word-initial fricative and affricate.[2]

(a)   (b)

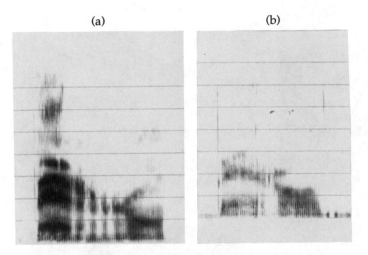

Figure 3.6 Spanish trilled /r/, orthographically represented by a double 'rr', *vs.* flap /ɾ/, orthographically a single 'r', forming a minimal contrast as in the pair of words 'perro' (dog) /pero/ and 'pero' (but) /peɾo/. The words were spoken in a carrier sentence 'Diga la palabra _____ otra vez' ('Say the word _____ one more time.') by a female speaker of Highland Mexican Spanish. Wideband spectrograms, 0–8 kHz.

with voiced obstruents. In some cases, the passage is opened intermittently, as in the trilled [r] (typically about 30 times a second) observed in many languages or dialects. In other cases, the interruption of the vocal tract channel occurs in a single ballistic motion of the articulator, sometimes (as in Spanish) minimally contrasting with the trill, as illustrated in Fig 3.6. The harmonic structure of the source signal is usually clearly visible, either as a vertical striation (when analyzed by a wideband filter) or horizontal striation (narrow-band filter), but since the trill repetition is not incomparably slower than the vocal fold vibration, the waveform in this case is quite complex.

Spectrographically, in English and many other languages, /r/ (rhotacized sounds) is characterized by an unmistakably low F_3. Interestingly, this low F_3 is observed for various phonetic variants of /r/, including syllable initial and final positions, and apical and uvular productions. These locations of special constriction both contribute to lowering of the third formant because they correspond to points along the vocal tract where the volume velocity nodes of the third resonance mode are located (see Chiba & Kajiyama, 1941; Fant, 1960). This gives a strong argument for the position that perceptual quality is the ultimate characteristic of a phonological unit, whether phoneme or feature. Note, however, that it does not imply that speech production processes aim at an acoustic or perceptual target by real-time adjustment via auditory feed-back. A given speaker uses a more or less fixed articulatory strategy for a given gesture in the given (typically intrasyllabic) context under normal circumstances of speech production, and it may be assumed that the articulatory pattern is reasonably stable at the control level for each syllable. How a phonological pattern emerges in history or is acquired in child language development, and how these development processes are related to phonetic behaviors, whether perception or production, is a different issue from how speech production is executed in normal speech circumstances. The auditory characteristics of the third formant lowering for /r/ is no doubt critical in determining how this phonologic element is associated with particular phonetic gestures in languages, but it does not imply that the motor execution in producing this phonetic element is adjusted in real time according to the auditory effects.

2.4.3 Nasals and nasalization   Nasal consonants and nasalized vowels are characterized by antiformants as well as formants. An antiformant (in other words antiresonance, or a pair of conjugate zeros of the transfer function, of the vocal tract filter) causes a selective absorption of acoustic energy at a frequency and its vicinity due to a resonance of a subsystem, such as the nasal cavity, that is coupled to the main acoustic tube (Hattori, *et al.*, 1958). The main tube, in the case of a nasalized vowel, is formed by the vocal tract from the glottis to the lip opening. In the case of the nasal consonants with an oral occlusion, the main tube extends from the glottis to the nostrils, and the oral cavity behind the articulatory closure constitutes the branching subsystem. The spectral effects of antiformants are opposite to those of formants (conjugate poles of the transfer function). An antiformant is created together with an extra formant at the same frequency when a branching subsystem is infinitesimally coupled to the main system, and the created formant and antiformant in each pair are separated from each other in frequency as the degree of acoustic coupling is increased. It should be noted that the subglottal system consisting of the trachea and the bronchi acts like the nasal branch for nasalized vowels, in the sense that the slight opening of the glottis introduces an additional pair or pairs of poles and zeros to the vocal tract filter transfer function. (See also Stevens, ARTICULATORY – ACOUSTIC – AUDITORY RELATIONSHIPS, on this point.)

In the case of nasalized vowels, as the velum is lowered continuously, the lowest of such nasal formant-antiformant pairs is created usually (though it varies depending on the configuration of the nasal sinuses) slightly above the bottom of the vowel F_1 range for the speaker. The lowest antiformant frequency goes up sometimes crossing the lowest (shifting oral) formant of the vowel, as the coupling of the branching tube increases by further lowering the velum. When this crossing takes place, there is seen an annihilation of the oral formant and the nasal antiformant. The extra lowest (nasal) formant usually stays in the lowest frequency range (Fujimura & Lindqvist, 1971). For a finite degree of coupling of the nasal subsystem to the oral main system, all resonances, i.e. both oral and nasal formants, depend on both the nasal and oral (as well as pharyngeal) tract configurations, and therefore all formants shift in frequency more or less as the degree of nasalization changes.[3] An antiformant of a nasalized vowel represents a mode of resonance of the oral cavity seen from the posterior open end at the coupling point, but its observed frequency may be affected by the mixture of the acoustic signals emitted through the nostrils and through the mouth orifice (see Fant, 1960).

In the case of the nasal murmur, the lowest antiformant corresponds to the lowest resonance (impedance minimum seen from the coupling point, i.e. at the uvula) of the oral cavity, and is low (in the first formant frequency range for low vowels) for [m] and higher (in the first formant frequency range) for [n], and very high (usually not identified) for [ŋ] (Fujimura, 1962). The spectrum of the nasal murmur for [ŋ] roughly represents the transfer characteristics of the acoustic system from the glottis to the nostrils, and is characterized by a somewhat denser population of formants (due to a longer effective tube) than the vowel F-pattern, and the resonances are typically characterized by a high degree of damping (wider formant bandwidths). Thus, the spectra of nasal murmurs in general are modifications of this spectrum for [ŋ] by the addition of formant-antiformant pairs due to the coupling of the terminated oral branch tube.

Antiformants may not be directly perceptible, if stationary sounds with and without them are compared in isolation. Since an antiformant is introduced together with an extra formant when a coupling to the branching tube is gradually increased, the effect is not simply that of a spectral zero but a combination of a zero and a pole arranged along the frequency scale. This means that, depending on which is higher in frequency, the spectrum envelope in the vicinity of this pole-zero or zero-pole pair is affected, resulting in a local disturbance of the spectral tilt and also some readjustment of relative amplitudes of the spectrum above the frequency range of this local disturbance. Also, as explained above, a temporary annihilation of the spectral peak and valley may occur. This is often the case at some point when either the oral configuration such as jaw opening temporally changes, causing formant movement, or the degree of nasalization changes due to velum movement in a nasalized vowel affected by a nasal consonant. The ear is sensitive to temporal spectral changes. Such temporal course of changes in the spectrum is complex, depending on the specific situation, but is often predictable for demisyllables containing a nasal element. Natural speech synthesis, therefore, presumably would have to be able to reproduce such spectral changes due to continuously changing nasalization.

A gross overall characterization of the effect of nasalization in a quasistatic sense is the low frequency boost and distortion of the spectral shape which deviates from natural formant patterns for vowels (Hattori, *et al.*, 1958). The wideband spectrograms sometimes show interesting blank regions, particularly in the first formant frequency range, for a short period, presumably revealing the changing pattern of formant-antiformant interaction (temporary annihilation). An example of this effect may be seen in Fig 3.11 (c) as a rising antiformant for the word 'Kent' (and less clearly in (d) 'rent') around 2 kHz to the right of the cursor in the nasalized vowel portion.

2.4.4 Laterals Laterals show a similar formant-antiformant pair in a higher frequency range (see Kent & Read, *ibid.* p. 137). The syllable initial /l/, like nasals, shows a short but steady sonorant articulation, followed by a rapid change to the tautosyllabic vowel gesture. The first formant for [l] is in the middle of the F_1 range. A very abrupt change from this F_1 to the vowel F_1, higher or lower, together with a positive F_3 transition,[4] gives a distinct perceptual quality of the initial /l/ in synthesis using a terminal analog. This abrupt F_1 change is due to the switching of the lateral acoustic channel(s) to the midsagittal channel at the release of the apical contact, which invariably characterizes English initial /l/ (see below). The inherent F_1 for [l] is distinctly higher than for nasal murmurs. Also, the lack of remaining nasal formant after the oral release along with the generally sharper oral formants in the immediately following vocalic portion distinguishes [l] from [n]. The F_3 locus for [l] in onset is high like other apical consonants. A comparison between 'Lynn' and 'nil', contrasting initial and final /l/ and /n/ is shown in Fig 3.18 (e, f) below. (For further acoustic details of vowel and consonant segments, see Stevens, ARTICULATORY – ACOUSTIC – AUDITORY RELATIONSHIPS.)

3 Speech Organization

3.1 *Speech as concatenated segments*

Traditionally, speech is depicted as a linear string of sound segments, which are categorized into two basic classes: vowels and consonants. Linguists have described speech organization principles from this point of view, studying functional characteristics of abstract sound units identified as phonemes (for a recent and comprehensive phonetic explanation along with extensive examples in many languages, see Laver, 1994). Phonemes are assumed to have inherent properties of articulatory gestures or acoustic signal characteristics, but observed properties may vary depending on the context. For phoneticians, in order to find inherent properties of phonemes, appropriate caution has to be exercised in collecting speech materials to control the utterance context reproducibly. In particular, in a laboratory exercise of acoustic phonetics, a phonetic contrast between different words, for example, must be a manifestation of a minimal phonological contrast with respect only to the sound unit that we are trying to characterize. For example, regarding the phoneme to be the sound unit under control, 'seed', /siJd/ and 'read' /riJd/ in English show a minimal contrast /s/ *vs.* /r/ in word-initial position. (For the use of the symbol /J/, see Section 3.1.1.)

3.1.1 Phonemes and phonemoids

By convention, phonemic transcriptions are surrounded by slashes. In this chapter, the symbols in this format are similar but not the same as phonemes, and we call them phonemoids. Phonemoids are transcriptive alphabetical symbols roughly reflecting some concepts of archiphonemes (Trubetzkoy, 1962) and of underspecification in some theories of nonlinear phonology. In particular, the capital letter /N/ represents a nasal consonant in syllable coda which shares the place of articulation with a concomitant obstruent in English (as in 'camp' /kaNp/, 'tent' /teNt/, 'honk' /hoNk/, and any syllable final (moraic) nasal in Japanese, as in /hoN/ [hoɴ] (book) and /haNpa/ [hampa] (odd piece). Also, capital letters like /J/ in the example words above represent syllable coda elements: for English and Japanese, /J/ is a palatalizing glide, /W/ is a rounding and velarizing glide, /H/ is a (monophthongal) vowel elongation element. In English, these vowels represented with glide phonemoids are the tense vowels, which are often in contrast with lax vowels represented by the same vowel symbols (but without the glide phonemoid). Thus, in American English, the vowel contrast in 'bet' and 'bait' is represented by /bet/ *vs.* /beJt/, 'dog', 'paw', and 'boat' by /dog/, /pɔH/, and /boWt/, and 'spat', 'spot', and 'spa' by /spat/, /spɑt/, and /spɑH/. Regarding the glide elements in this sense as phonetically vocalic but phonologically consonantal, any English words must be closed, i.e. must end with a consonantal phonemoid, unless it is reduced. The phonemoidal symbol /Q/ stands for a consonant elongation (gemination, roughly speaking) in Japanese and many other languages; it often occurs intersyllabically and can be implemented with some concomitant laryngeal gestures. /R/ is used for the rhoticized syllable-final sonorant, as in 'car' /KaR/, 'shirt' /ʃʌRt/, 'church' /tʃʌRtʃ/ etc. Likewise, /L/ is used for a lateral sonorant in syllable final position, as in 'call' /kɔL/, 'felt' /feLt/. These sonorant elements tend to integrate with the vowel gestures of the syllable nucleus.

3.1.2 Distinctive features

Jakobson, Fant, & Halle (1952), in their seminal publication, argued that it is a distinctive feature that constitutes the minimal

(a)   (b)

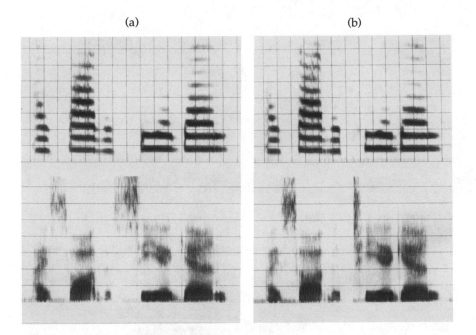

Figure 3.7 Wideband (lower, 1–8 kHz) and narrowband (upper, 1–2 kHz) spectrograms of (a) 'I saw the C again.' and (b) 'I saw the T again.'

functional unit of speech sound description. A minimal contrast, i.e. *ceteris paribus* comparison, according to them, is represented by a choice between permissible binary values (e.g. 1 *vs.* 0, or + *vs.* –, or acute *vs.* grave) of one of the distinctive features keeping other feature values the same. A phoneme is characterized as a 'simultaneous bundle' of distinctive features. Thus, 'bead' and 'deed', for example, contrast with each other with respect to the binary feature opposition of grave *vs.* acute that also characterizes the opposition between 'peak' and 'teak', 'mail' and 'nail', etc. The minimal contrast /s/ *vs.* /d/ in phonemic terms, according to their preliminary proposal, would be described as a combinatory contrast involving two features: (1) tense *vs.* lax which would group /s/ and /t/ together against /z/ and /d/, and (2) continuous *vs.* interrupted, which would group /s/ and /z/ together against /t/ and /d/.[5]

Such contrasting pairs in a word or word-like syllable paradigm would be recorded for laboratory studies to identify acoustic correlates of each feature opposition. For example, the key words 'C' /siʃ/ and 'T' /tiʃ/ may be put in the same carrier sentence to produce 'I saw the C again.' *vs.* 'I saw the T again.' spoken by the same speaker as consistently as possible with similar voice quality, speed of utterance, followed by a sufficiently large pause accompanied by inspiration, etc. Fig 3.7 shows wideband spectrograms of such a pair of utterances.

(a)

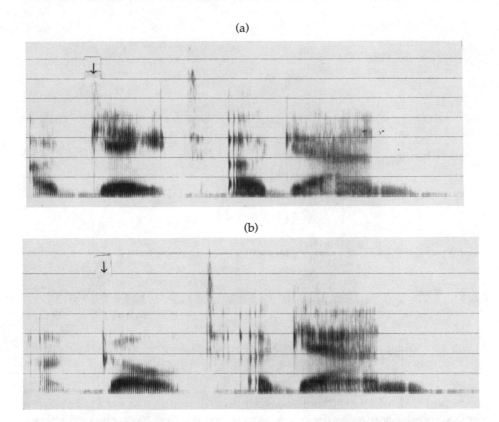

(b)

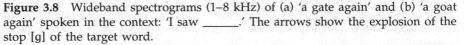

Figure 3.8 Wideband spectrograms (1–8 kHz) of (a) 'a gate again' and (b) 'a goat again' spoken in the context: 'I saw _____.' The arrows show the explosion of the stop [g] of the target word.

A number of sample pairs using a variety of controlled feature values would be examined to discover the inherent and invariant characteristics of the pertinent feature. But strictly speaking, the contrasting physical properties thus discovered are valid only for the context that was used for the comparison. For example, the target values of the second formant frequency (F_2) of initial dorsal *vs.* apical stops can be, and in fact are, different depending on whether the following vowel is a front vowel or a back vowel (Delattre, Liberman, & Cooper, 1955). Fig 3.8 compares the consonant /g/ in a word pair 'gate' /geJt/ *vs.* 'goat' /goWt/. The second and third formant bars appear to originate from different frequency values between the two cases ('gate' and 'goat'); the third formant goes down toward the vowel in the front-vowel context (a) from about 3,500 Hz, and goes up from about 2,200 Hz in the back-vowel context (b).

The same spectrographic properties for a given consonant may not be identified in materials spoken in different styles or by different speakers even of the same dialect; the invariant properties may be an abstract and holistic pattern rather than concrete target values (i.e. the point of origin or destination of formant bar movements), or even direction of formant movement. Traditionally, formant transition patterns are described for CV and VC movements, by following the movement from V to C whether it is leftward or rightward in the spectrogram. If the movement is upward toward the consonant, then the transition is positive, and if downward, it is negative [Delattre, *et al.*, 1955].

In the case of palatal/velar stops, like /k/ or /g/, a better characterization of this place of articulation is a 'bunching' of a pair of formants (typically but not necessarily F_2 (second formant) and F_3 (third formant), in their movement toward the consonant (either forward or backward from the vowel). For a syllable containing a front vowel, this bunching occurs at a relatively high frequency, and for a back vowel, at a lower frequency. The bunching of higher formants for [g] in the front vowel context Fig 3.8 (a) appears to involve also a lowered fourth formant.

3.1.3 Some additional considerations Phoneticians, in reality, must understand the characteristics of speech far beyond the special situation of minimal contrast. In fact, the abstract and relative nature of the distinctive features was emphasized in the original proposal of the distinctive feature theory (Jakobson, *et al., ibid.*). Based on experience of handling day-to-day speech phenomena, partly in response to the needs of speech technology, the recent tendency is to place more emphasis on effects of what is often called prosodic or supra-segmental conditions (Lehiste, 1970) or of situations under which real-life conversation takes place. Covering a wide variety of utterance situations for each segmental material implies a very extensive scope of experimental studies. To a large extent, acoustic phonetics these days depends on the recent availability of inexpensive and 'friendly' laboratory computers and software. Even so, it is becoming more and more difficult to follow the *ceteris paribus* strategy, since controlling the utterance conditions as well as speech materials conflicts with the desire to observe realistic speech.

In such studies, it is sometimes helpful to examine some of the articulatory movements, in addition to the acoustic or spectrographic signal, in order to understand changes due to prosodic conditions, given the same phonemic materials or word sequence. Generally, mandible position varies greatly depending just on the degree of prominence attached to the word: the more prominence, the lower the mandible. Due, at least in part, to the complex physical and physiological interaction among articulatory organs, other articulatory gestures such as tongue body position also change due to prominence in the particular utterance situation (such as contrastive emphasis or excitement) in a rather complex way. Some researchers assume that it is primarily the acoustic or auditory properties rather than articulatory states that are inherent to phonemic properties. However, quite often, formant frequencies also are considerably different for the same vowel in the same phonological context when prominence varies.

In order to understand properties of conversational speech, it is imperative that prosodic conditions are explicitly included in the descriptive framework. Given that complexity of the phenomena and the increasingly large number of factors that must be considered, insightful hypotheses couched in theoretically coherent and comprehensive descriptive frameworks have become increasingly important, along with powerful probabilistic inference tools such as neural networks (see for an advanced approach using neural networks, Jordan & Rumelhart, 1992; about the primary role of hypotheses, Josephson & Josephson, 1994).

Also, as we observe patterns of multidimensional articulatory gestures under different segmental and non-segmental conditions, we see that the concept of phonemic segments described as simultaneous bundles of features is not as effective as previously believed in interpreting observed physical phenomena. On the other hand, when prosodic conditions vary, much of the apparent 'disintegration' of the bundle of gestures manifesting individual features seems to be explained by temporal shifting of articulatory gestures of different articulators while maintaining constant elemental gestural patterns (see, e.g. accounts given by articulatory phonology, Browman & Goldstein, 1992). In this chapter, while the main theme is acoustic properties of speech sounds, some attention is also directed to speech production mechanisms in order to understand observed phenomena. At the same time, in order to accommodate part of the phonetic variability of feature manifestations, segmental concatenative units larger than phonemic segments are considered for interpreting acoustic signals. For a comprehensive theoretical model of utterance organization based on syllable concatenation instead of phonemes, see Fujimura (1992, 1994a, 1995a,b).

3.2 Demisyllabic analysis – syllable core and affixes

Traditionally, along with phonemic segments, a larger and separately utterable unit called a syllable has been recognized as useful for describing the chain of articulatory and acoustic events. In such an approach, a syllable would be represented as a linear string of phonemes, with a vowel at the center (syllable nucleus) surrounded by consonants (syllable margins). English has its typical syllable structure C_iVC_f, where C_i stands for a consonant or a consonant cluster in initial position and C_f stands for a consonant or a consonant cluster in final position. For example, 'Sam' /sam/ [sæm] is a monosyllabic word, where C_i = /s/, C_f = /m/, and V = /a/. The word 'splash' /splaʃ/ [splæʃ] is also monosyllabic, but the initial consonantal component (i.e. syllable onset) is a consonant cluster /spl/, from the phonemic point of view. As shown in Fig 3.9, the word 'sprinkler' can be pronounced as /spriŋ-kləR/ in two syllables, or as /spriŋ-kə-ləR/ in three syllables (perhaps more often referring to a person as opposed to a device).

This chapter adopts a new approach to describing syllable structure, based on what is called demisyllabic analysis (Fujimura, 1979). According to this

(a)   (b)

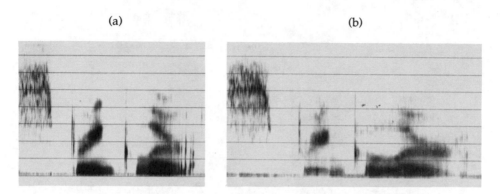

Figure 3.9 The word 'sprinkler' pronounced as (a) /spriŋ-kləR/ [spriŋklɚ] and (b) /spriŋ-kə-ləR/ [spriŋkələ], spoken in the context: 'There was a _____ on the lawn'.

analysis, a syllable in English can be decomposed into syllable core and optional syllable suffix(es).[6] Using a more recently coined term (Fujimura, 1994a)[7], the syllable suffix will be called 's-fix'. An s-fix often corresponds to a morphemic suffix, e.g. the 's' of 'kicks' /kik.s/ [kɪks], but this is not always the case, as seen in 'fix' /fik.s/ [fɪks], and 'lens' /len.z/ [lɛnz]. In the phonemoidal transcription, an s-fix is separated from the syllable core by a dot.

An English s-fix is always an apical (or coronal, phonetically)[8] obstruent involving a stop closure or a frication or both (as in the case of /st/ in 'text' /tek.st/ [tɛk.st], see below, and /t.s/ in 'acts' /ak.t.s/ [æk.t.s]). The voicing status of an s-fix must agree with that of the preceding core-final consonant (Fujimura, 1979).[9] Thus, in the words 'act' /ak.t/, 'lapse' /lap.s/, 'bend' /ben.d/, and 'labs' /lab.z/, the final consonants /t, s, d, z/, respectively, are all s-fixes, whereas the final /p, t, s/ in 'lamp', /laNp/, 'tent' /teNt/ and 'sense' /seNs/ are within the syllable core (coda) and not s-fixes. Note that the phonetic place of articulation for the nasal phonemoid /N/ varies depending on the final consonant, whereas in a form with an s-fix like /ben.d/, the /n/ could stand in a phonological opposition with /m/ or /ŋ/. Fig 3.10 illustrates examples of s-fixes, both voiceless (a-d) and voiced (e-g) depending on the coda voicing status.

An s-fix is phonetically (regardless of the morphological status) rather independent from the preceding (final) demisyllable, in the sense that splicing out the acoustic signal portion for the frication or stop gap (voice bar if voiced) together with the release burst results in a phonemically expected remainder of the syllable form (e.g. 'tack' /tak/ from 'tax' /tak.s/, 'men' /men/ from 'mend' /men.d/). Furthermore, if we splice the waveform segment of the s-fix taken out of one syllable and concatenate it to the waveform representing the core of a different syllable to form a new syllable, we obtain quite natural sounding syllables (e.g. 'tax' /tak.s/ from 'tacked' /tak.t/ and 'glimpse' /gliNp.s/).

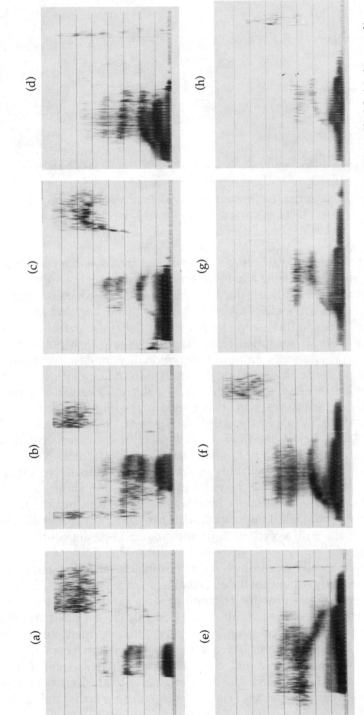

Figure 3.10 (a) 'fix' /fɪk.s/[fɪks], (b) 'text /tek.st/[tekst], (c) 'glimpse' /glɪNp.s/[glɪmps], (d) 'left' /lef.t/[left], (e) 'hammed' /ham.d/[hæmd], (f) 'lens' /len.z/[lenz], (g) 'lend' /len.d/[lenz], (h) 'lent' /leNt/[lɛⁿt].

The syllable core can be separated into the initial demisyllable and the final demisyllable in the spectrogram or the waveform, as a phonetic approximation. Roughly speaking, these demisyllables contain initial and mid-to-final parts, respectively, of the 'vowel segment'. The separation of the two demisyllables in a syllable core can be performed most consistently at the point in time where the initial CV transition changes into a more stationary vowel portion.[10] In Fig 3.11, the spectrographic pattern of monosyllabic words 'Ked, red, Kent, rent' /ked/, /red/, /keNt/, /reNt/ are divided by a cursor into the initial demisyllable (containing the beginning part of the vowel /e/, and the final demisyllable (containing the heavily nasalized vowel for the latter two) as well as the final stop consonant. Note that, in the latter two cases, the final transition from the nasalized vowel to the nasal murmur is not as abrupt as in the initial nasal to vowel switching. Depending on the utterance, there may not be any clear nasal murmur as a steady segment separable from the nasalized vowel (see Fig 3.15, below for such variants produced by the same speaker). Sometimes, it is difficult to determine whether there is a distinct nasal murmur or not in a word like 'Kent'. For this reason, in this chapter, the phonetic transcriptions for e.g. /teNt/ and /ten.d/, are symbolically given in the forms [tẽⁿt] and [tɛnd], respectively, indicating the continuous variance by the use of the small superscript (see also note 19).

An important point about the demisyllabic (and C/D, see Section 3.4) analysis is that the specification of temporal ordering of phonemic elements is not necessary within each demisyllabic component, i.e. initial or final demisyllable (onset or coda), after separating out syllable affixes (p-fixes or s-fixes). Traditionally in phonemic analyses, phonotactics deals with the linguistic constraints imposed on the temporal relations among constituents within a syllable in a given language. Generally, there is a strong tendency observed in most languages that a phonemic element that is assigned a higher value of a certain inherent phonetic property (which might be called sonority or vowel affinity) is placed closer to the vowel as the nucleus of the syllable than others assigned a lower value of sonority (vowel affinity). Thus, in the monosyllabic English word 'strains' /streJn.z/ [streɪnz], one may assume that there is a sonority hierarchy $|s|<|t|<|r|<|e|$ observed for the left of the syllable and $|z|<|n|<|J|<|e|$ for the right half (the phonemoidal unit surrounded by vertical lines indicating its sonority value). Such hierarchical values of phonemes may be expected to be consistent when we construct similarly ordered phonemic strings for many syllable forms in English.

If it were true that we could establish a strict hierarchy of phonemes in terms of sonority, then we could claim that temporal ordering of phonemes within a syllable in English were redundant, and all we needed to specify for each half of the syllable would be an unordered set of phonemes as the syllable constituents. This is not true, however, given such common counter-examples as 'tax' [tæks] *vs.* 'task' [tæsk], 'stock' [stɑk] *vs.* 'cost' [kɔst]. If /s/ should have a lower sonority value than a voiceless stop as indicated by the first members of these word pairs, then the second members should not occur

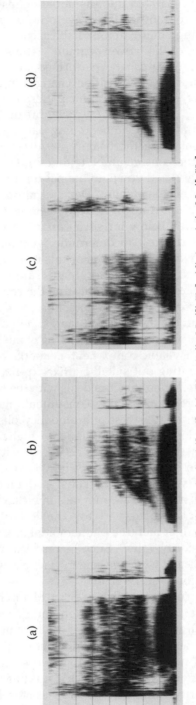

Figure 3.11 (a) 'Ked' /ked/[ked], (b) 'red' /red/[rɛd], (c) 'Kent' /keNt/[kɛ̃ʰt], (d) 'rent' /reNt/[rɛ̃ʰt].

in English.[11] The demisyllabic analysis (Fujimura, 1979) addresses this issue using a more abstract feature analysis than traditionally considered based on the assumption of phonemic segments as basically mutually independent concatenative units.[12] This chapter, including the phonemoidal transcription, adopts this analysis in part. First, in this analysis, each syllable is separated into two types of constituents: the syllable core and (optional) syllable affixes (s-fixes only at the end of syllables in English). Further, the /sp/, /st/, /sk/ clusters (in onset, coda, or s-fix) in English are treated as a set of integral consonants that are characterized by the manner feature {spirantized} (in parallel to {stop} and {fricative}) in the abstract (phonological) representation. This feature {spirantized}, which is one of the obstruent phonological features, phonetically evokes an apical/coronal frication gesture combined with the temporally subsequent oral closure gesture in both onset and coda (and also s-fix). Since the closure gesture may use different articulators in this situation, a concomitant place feature specifies the articulator for the oral closure, but the frication is produced always with the tongue tip/blade.

Such a description of phonetic implementation of phonetic gestures within each syllable based on inherent temporal properties of elemental articulatory gestures is comprehensively provided by the C/D model. Note that the unique but systematic phonemic minimal pair with respect to the temporal ordering of obstruents in syllable final position, such as 'task' [tæsk] *vs.* 'tax' [tæks], contrasts with the sonority-governed inversion in a pair like 'slip' [slɪp] *vs.* 'pulse' [pʌls]. This peculiarity can be readily explained by the separation of the final /s/ as an s-fix in the case of /tak.s/ as an apical (place-specified) fricative as opposed to the /sk/ as an integral obstruent element of the coda, specified as {spirantized, dorsal}, in /task/. Note also that phonetically, the initial /sp, st, sk/ exhibits peculiarly unaspirated stops, and therefore would require a special treatment in implementation if it were treated as a voiceless stop. Also, this feature specification scheme makes it possible to claim that within a core, place of articulation is never given more than once in each onset or coda (no place is specified in s-fixes in English). This is a critical condition for the claim that there is no temporal ordering specified for features in the phonological representation within a core. In contrast, p-fixes and s-fixes, when more than one member in one of these syllable components occurs, must be order-specified, but their phonological specifications are expected to be highly parsimonious (in English, s-fixes are specified by only one of the manner features as a unary obstruent feature specification, voicing and place being unspecified).

The lack of aspiration (i.e. short VOT) for the /sp/ cluster as opposed to the single consonant /p/, for example, reflects the tendency that the temporal stretch of each voice cessation tends to be assigned nearly the same value whether or not there is an additional frication gesture. The larger VOT after the explosion of the voiceless stop when a liquid, /l/ or /r/ is included in the onset (as in 'plea' as opposed to 'pea', for example) is also explained by this tendency. When an additional sonorant segment is added, the individual consonantal segment durations, as observed above, become smaller. This 'crushing' of multiple consonantal elements can be observed in articulatory studies as an overlapping of individual articulatory gestures, not necessarily affecting the time course (such as the maximum speed of movement) of each gesture (Fujimura, 1986; Browman & Goldstein, 1992; Kröger, 1993). Consequently, the same voice cessation period starting from the beginning of the stop closure covers more of the otherwise voiced period of the sonorant gesture that is added onto the CV gestural configuration.

It is generally observed that the demisyllables are relatively free from the influence of the rest of the syllable, even when the other (particularly final) demisyllable contains a sonorant element such as nasal, which tends to largely overlap with the vowel gestures. Furthermore, s-fixes are generally stable and easily separable as waveform segments from the tautosyllabic context. Spectrographic patterns of demisyllabic portions in carefully pronounced speech materials are also fairly stable. This implies that spectrograms can be read relatively successfully by memorizing all demisyllabic patterns.[13] Conceptually, in a paradigm as shown in Fig 3.11, it can be seen that the initial demisyllable of 'Ked' can be combined with the final demisyllable of 'rent' to produce 'Kent', and 'red' with 'Kent' to produce 'rent', with almost perfect intelligibility as well as naturalness. In practice, waveform splicing introduces undesirable acoustic discontinuities particularly in the middle of a voiced segment, partly due to the f_0 difference. In order to avoid this peripheral problem, a parametric analysis is used for separating source parameters from vocal-tract filter parameters.

In application work, such a system of concatenative synthesis with independent voice pitch control has been performed with the use of LPC analysis/synthesis techniques (Atal & Hanauer, 1971; also see Kent & Read, 1992; Ladefoged, forthcoming). An inventory of demisyllables (somewhat less than 1,000 items including s-fixes for English) is prepared. A pair of initial and final demisyllables can be more or less freely combined and smoothed at the junction in terms of LPC coefficients (log-area functions), in consideration of the physically inevitable (hard) coarticulation (Fujimura & Lovins, 1978; also see Section 3.3). Speech signals for any string of syllables can be formed, combined with a computed fundamental frequency contour for the desirable intonation pattern (Fujimura, Macchi, & Lovins, 1977; Macchi & Spiegel, 1990). Prosodic conditions can be controlled independently within a limited range of source characteristics. Demisyllabic units are also useful for automatic speech recognition based on time warping of stored template patterns (Rosenberg, Rabiner, Wilpon, & Kahn, 1983).

3.3 *Coarticulatory smoothing*

It is well recognized that phonemic segments cannot be assumed to have independent acoustic or articulatory properties because they vary depending on the context. One general process that is known to cause considerable variation of segmental properties is coarticulation (Lindblom, 1963). Coarticulation, in essence, refers to the temporal smoothing of a sequence of presumably inherent phonetic gestures in adjacent (or in some sense distant) entities (see Farnetani, COARTICULATION AND CONNECTED SPEECH PROCESSES, for a thorough discussion of this issue).

As a mathematical model, this process can be equated to some type of low-pass filtering of an underlying signal that is assumed to represent a segmental gesture sequence. Let us take an example of a syllable sequence

$$S = s_1 + s_2 + \ldots s_i + \ldots s_N,$$
$$\text{where } s_i = C_i^o V_i \, C_i^c \ (i = 1, \ldots N\text{-}1, N).[14]$$

Suppose there is a stationary target value fi^v of a formant frequency, say the second formant frequency F_2, for each vowel (syllable nucleus) V_i, and similarly fi^o for each onset consonant C_i^o, and fi^c for each coda consonant C_i^c, of s_i. For simplicity of the discussion, let us assume here that C_i^o and C_i^c are both single phonemic segments, according to the classical concept of phonemic segment concatenation and coarticulation.[15] Assume further that each syllable s_i is assigned a syllable duration D_i, and this duration is subdivided among the onset, vowel, and coda as $D_i = d_i^o + d_i^v + d_i^c$. Accordingly, we form a step function for this acoustic phonetic variable, representing, e.g. the second formant frequency (see Fig 3.12). This underlying time function (solid line, Fig 3.12 (a)) undergoes a smoothing process, which can be interpreted as a virtual low-pass filter. The resulting output signal (dashed lines) has no discontinuities (but see below).

This concept was used in Vaissière (1988) interpreting velum movement time functions observed by the x-ray microbeam system at the University of Tokyo. The best form of smoothing process may not be represented as a response function of a physically realizable filter. In other words, the current value of the output may be dependent on the future value of the input. This is justifiable even for a model of the physiological process of speech production, because the motor program is prepared at the cortical level for an organized string of syllables representing a phonetic phrase before the actual commands are physically executed (see Sternberg, *et al.*, 1988; Fujimura, 1990a).

There have been numerous observations in the literature which demonstrated marked deviations from the prediction of coarticulatory smoothing based on inherent target values of phonemes. It has been argued (see Fujimura & Lovins, 1978) that descriptions of such exceptions are characteristically contained within the same syllable, and furthermore within the demisyllable, or otherwise are conditioned by the prosodic conditions, such as stress pattern, around the adjacent syllable boundary (Kahn, 1980).

The process of coarticulation, if applied to the acoustic parameters, does not account for apparent discontinuities in the acoustic signals. Formant frequencies generally tend to change smoothly, but there are abrupt changes when the

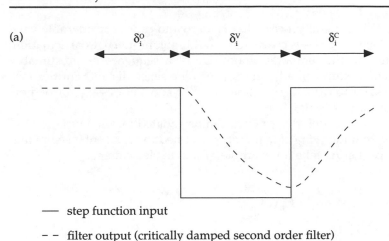

(a)

$\delta_i^o \qquad \delta_i^v \qquad \delta_i^c$

—— step function input

− − filter output (critically damped second order filter)

(b)

—— step function input

− − − smoothing filter output (Gaussian filter)

Figure 3.12 Mathematical models of the coarticulatory smoothing process. Two types of the smoothing filter are exemplified: (1) the critically damped second-order filter and (2) Gaussian filters. (a) compares the input step function (solid line) for concatenated phonemic segments (onset, vowel, and coda) for a syllable, according to the classical concept of segment concatenation and coarticulation, with the output function (dashed line). This filter is a physically realizable (critically damped second-order) filter. (b) compares a step function input with its output function through a Gaussian filter. This type of filter is not physically realizable (is realizable approximately with a delay). Using the Gaussian filter, (c) and (d) show different degrees of undershooting in the output signals when different parameter values or time constants are selected ($\sigma = 0.35$ for (c) and 1.0 for (d) in the standard formula for the Gaussian filter).

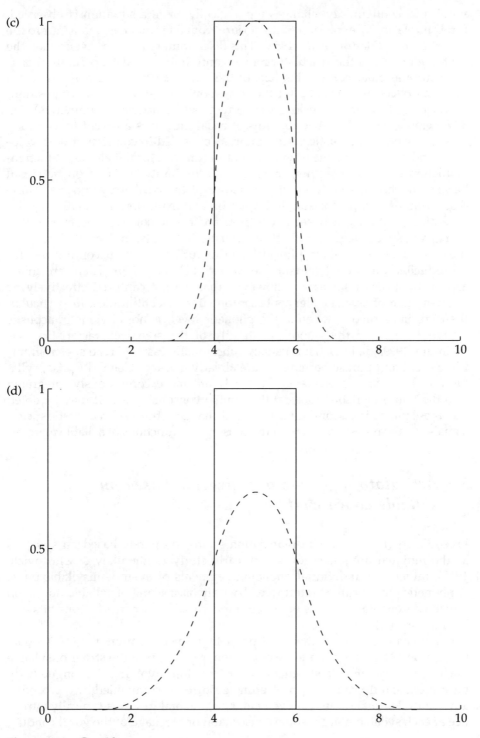

Figure 3.12 Cont'd

vocal tract configuration changes topologically. Such a situation is observed, for example, in the explosion of lip closure from an initial nasal murmur to the vowel gesture (Hattori, *et al.*, 1958). This discontinuity appears even when the center of gravity of the articulator moves continuously under gradually changing neuromuscular control, because of the nonlinearity of the mapping from articulatory control variables (or the corresponding center of gravity position) to vocal tract cross dimensions (or corresponding acoustic parameters). Fig 3.18 below exemplifies spectrograms of nasal murmurs adjacent to vowels.

Another type of acoustic discontinuity is observed in connection with voice onset and offset. While the laryngeal control function for the glottal adduction-abduction changes smoothly, there is a discontinuity in the acoustic signal because of the inherently nonlinear nature of the oscillatory process. These discontinuities, corresponding to implosion and explosion of articulatory closure along with voice onset and offset, are the major acoustic events that demarcate speech signals into clear acoustic segments, and most durational measurements in acoustic phonetic studies utilize such discontinuities for reproducible durational measurements (e.g. Lehiste, 1970). There are many aspects of speech information, however, that are not captured effectively by segmentation of acoustic signals based on such discontinuities. In particular, the phrasing structure (even at the phonetic level) is not obvious in acoustic signals because of the smooth continuity of the signal characteristics (see Fujimura, 1990a,b). In fact, it is usually substantially easier to read spectrograms if the word and phrase boundaries are already marked. Generally, also, syllable (or word) final consonants are weak and more continuously integrated into the vowel (syllable nucleus) than initial consonants are. It may be noted that these phonetic discontinuities or rapid changes observed in acoustic speech signals are always associated with the consonantal functions of syllable margins.

3.4 *Articulatory gesture organization based on syllable concatenation*

Prosodic control of speech organization seems to operate based on syllables as the minimal units (see for a very early study Kozhenikov & Chistovich, 1965), rather than individual phonemic segments or even demisyllabic units. A phonetic phrase can be interpreted basically as a string of syllable nuclei, on which consonantal gestures are superimposed as local perturbations at syllable margins (Öhman, 1966).

In a recently proposed theory of phonetic implementation, the C/D model (Fujimura, 1995a), the vocalic base function, representing the string of syllable nuclei, manifests the slowly changing articulation involving the tongue body movement and lip rounding-protruding gestures, accompanied by a prosodically controlled mandibular movement. Consonantal gestures typically introduce at each syllable margin some constriction or blockage of the vocal conduit, resulting in a gap (silence) or turbulent noise in the acoustic signal, or quick changes in the spectrogram. The manifestation of syllable margins are assisted by jaw approximation in cooperation with consonantal gestures of various articulators, while jaw opening control for syllable nuclei reflects primarily the prosodic status of the syllables. The first formant frequency, accordingly in acoustic signals, shows a general syntagmatic modulation reflecting the alternation of syllable nuclei and margins. In addition, most visibly in the spectrogram, a local voice cessation often occurs around the syllable boundary. In the examples of Fig 3.7 above ('I saw C/T again'), syllable margins are observed mostly as the breaks between voicing stretches indicated by striated dark regions in the low-to-mid frequency ranges of the spectrograms, and as a quick weakening of the darkness (due to the voiced stop [g] in this case). In general, however, there are many cases where syllable boundaries are not obviously located in the acoustic waveform or its spectrographic representation, such as when a syllable onset is not marked with a consonantal gesture (as in the beginning of the word 'again' in this figure). Depending on the prosodic and segmental context, the syllable nucleus may be voiceless, or no vowel segment may be observed spectrographically or articulatorily, rendering the vowel only an abstract phonological entity. In English, a syllabic sonorant, phonetically, may be identified for a prosodically reduced syllable. The last reduced syllables of words like 'button' and 'buckle' usually show no clearly identifiable vowel segment between the stop closure and the voiced sonorant, even in a context of sentence final rising intonation, as shown in Fig 3.13. In our phonemoidal transcription, the symbol /ə/ is used for the reduced (abstract) syllable nucleus,[16] and an ambisyllabic intervocalic single consonant is represented without any syllable boundary (-) indicated.

In the Tokyo dialect of Japanese, high vowels /i/ and /u/ often show no spectrographic segment as evidence of any vowel, when its surrounding consonants (or phrase boundary) are voiceless. The phonological distinction between the front and back vowels is identified by the spectral difference in the frication in such a contrast as 'Nasaimasu.' /na-saʃ-maˈsu/ [nasaimaˈsᵘ] ('He does.') *vs.* 'Nasaimasi.' /na-saʃ-maˈsi/ [nasaimaˈsⁱ] ('Please do.') in the sentence final position. If this sentence is pronounced with a rising intonation toward the end, however, the vowel manifests itself as a voiced vocalic segment with a high f_0, as shown in Fig 3.14 (b) in the question 'nasaimasu?' /na-saʃ-maˈsu?/ [na-sai-maˈ-su?] ('Does he?' or 'Will you?').[17] This contrasts with the English case of vowel deletion, as exemplified in Fig 3.13 (b,d), where the schwa does not appear as a distinct vowel segment phonetically even in a rising intonation situation.

3.5 Onset vs. coda

Characteristics of sonorants are typically very different between initial and final positions in the syllable, and depending on the prosodic conditions for

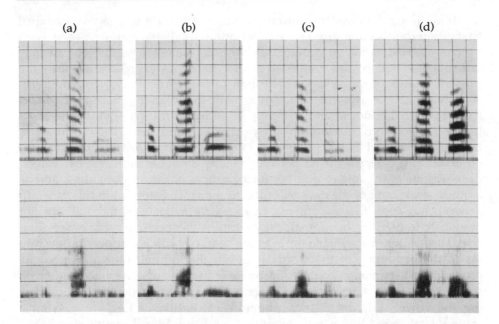

Figure 3.13   (a, b) 'button' /bʌtən/[bʌtn̩], (c, d) 'buckle' /bʌkəl/[bʌkl̩] spoken in the sentences 'I have the_____.' (a, c), and 'I have the_____?' (b, d).

the syllable. In initial position, sonorants typically exhibit clearer consonantal gestures, whereas in final position, they behave more like gliding vowels.[18] Typically, nasal consonants have a place distinction, between /m/ and /n/ as in English, but many languages have no place distinction in final position. In English, when a nasal is combined with a voiceless obstruent in coda, the place is specified for both nasal murmur and stop closure since they are always homorganic, and the articulatory closure is one integrated action. The nasal murmur is often very short or even nonexistent, as shown in Fig 3.15 for words uttered in isolation: 'camp' /kaNp/ [kæᵐp], 'pant' /paNt/ [pæⁿt], and 'tank' /taNk/ [tæⁿk] (also see comments in connection with Fig 3.11, in Section 3.2).[19]

For sonorants in coda, in general, articulatory gestures are more integrated with the tautosyllabic vowels. In the initial demisyllable, for example in 'lap', 'lip', etc., there is a spectrographic discontinuity separating the [l] segment from the vocalic segment, and the formant movement toward the vowel target in the vocalic portion is rather rapid. In the final demisyllable, in contrast, there is no clear discontinuity between the vowel and the lateral, and the vowel quality in the stationary portion is strongly affected by the l-characteristics with respect to formant frequencies, showing a much slower movement than in the initial demisyllable, reflecting, in particular, tongue body retraction (Sproat & Fujimura, 1993). In Fig 3.18, these points can be seen in (c) 'melt' *vs.* (a) 'men', and (e) 'nil' *vs.* (g) 'lint'. In some dialects (particularly in New

(a)   (b)

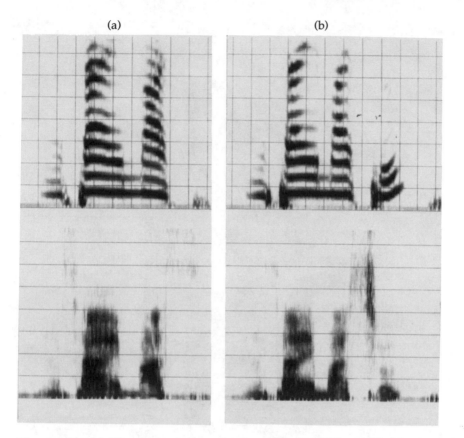

Figure 3.14 (a) 'Nasaimasu.' /na-saʃ-ma⌐su./[nasaima⌐sᵘ.] and (b) 'Nasaimasu?'
/na-saʃ-ma⌐su?/ [nasaima⌐su?], in Japanese, spoken by a 67-year old male speaker
(Tokyo dialect).

England), a schwa is inserted after a palatal glide preceding the lateral, forming an extra syllable in a word like 'oil'. In American English in many forms,
the front mid vowel as in 'bell' is often not a front vowel at all from a phonetic
point of view, while it is in a word like 'bed'.

In the case of the final 'r', as in 'shirt' and 'church', the phonetic transcription often treats the nucleus and coda integrated as a retroflexed vowel. In the
phonemoidal transcription of American English, the consontal elements corresponding to the phonemes/l/ and /r/ in coda are represented in capitals
/L/ and /R/.

From the phonemic point of view, the consonant /n/ in English words 'nil',
'Lynn', 'lint' is identical. Physically, the spectrographic properties of this nasal
element in these contexts are very different. It is known that the degree of
velum lowering is systematically less for initial position as opposed to final
position.[20] This tendency has been observed in many languages including

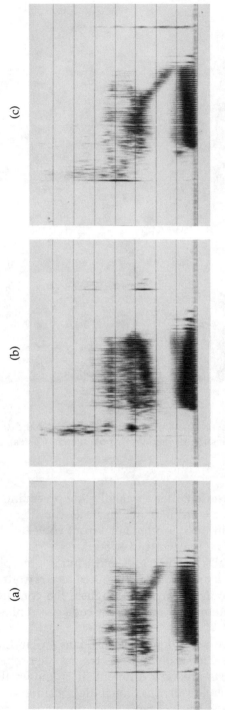

(a)   (b)   (c)

Figure 3.15 Wideband spectrograms (0–8 kHz) of (a) 'pant' /paNt/ [pæ̃ⁿt], (b) 'tank' /taNk/ [tæ̃ŋk], and (c) 'camp' /kaNp/ [kæ̃ᵐp].

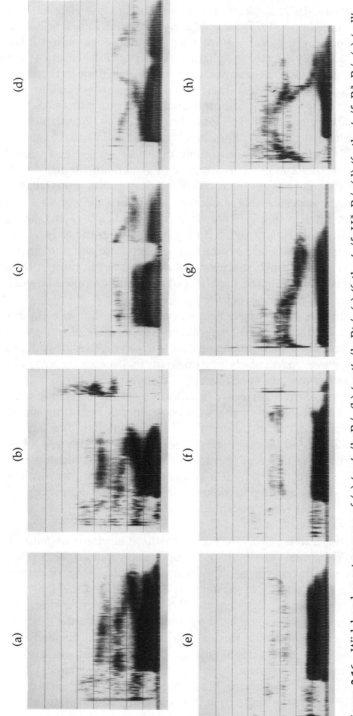

Figure 3.16 Wideband spectrograms of (a) 'car' /kɑR/, (b) 'cart' /kɑRt/, (c) 'father' /fɑHðəR/, (d) 'farther' /fɑRðəR/, (e) 'call' /kɔL/, (f) 'cold' /koWL.d/, (g) 'beer' /biR/, (h) 'peel' /pijL/.

English (Fujimura, 1977; Krakow, 1989) French (Benguerel & Cowan, 1975), and Japanese (Fujimura, 1977). Acoustically, in American English, the nasal murmur (defined by the oral closure with simultaneous velum lowering) is typically considerably shorter in syllable initial position than in syllable final position when there is no concomitant voiceless obstruent in the latter. When there is a tautosyllabic voiceless (therefore core-internal) obstruent, as in 'lint' or 'dance' or examples in Fig 3.15, the final nasal murmur tends to be short or even virtually nonexistent. The total duration for such syllables (e.g. 'lent' /leNt/) are similar to those without involving the coda nasal (e.g. 'let' /let/), and it is much shorter than a form containing an s-fix (e.g. 'lend' /len.d/). The dominant perceptual cue in many dialects of American English for the nasal element in such a case is the heavy nasalization of the tautosyllabic vowel. Malécot (1956) interpreted this situation as a phonemic contrast of oral *vs.* nasal vowel in English. Fig 3.17 shows a paradigm 'ten' /ten/ [tɛ̃^{n}n], 'tend' /ten.d/ [tɛ̃^{n}nd], 'tent' /teNt/ [tɛ̃^{n}t]. It may be seen that the form /ten.d/ with the s-fix /d/ is very similar to /ten/ if we separate out the final plosion, whereas /teNt/ has a much shorter nasal murmur (even though there is one distinctly in this utterance) and the effect of nasalization of the vowel is rather differently seen in (c) than in (a,b).

Fig 3.18 compares nasal consonants in onset and coda. In coda, the vowel to consonant transition may be fairly abrupt, as in most of our examples except when the nasal element is concomitant with a voiceless obstruent gesture. Sometimes, however, particularly in conversational speech, the vowel-to-nasal pattern may not show any spectrographic discontinuity.

An obvious qualitative difference (allophonic variation) among onset, coda, and ambisyllabic situations of the same consonants including stops (Kahn, 1980), has been observed in different dialects of English (see e.g. Bladon & Al-Bamerni, 1976; Maddieson, 1985). A well known variant is observed in American English as a 'flapping' (more exactly tapping, see Ladefoged, Cochran, & Disner, 1977) of /t/ and /d/ as a single consonant in intervocalic position (ambisyllabic /t/, according to Kahn, 1980) when the following syllable is reduced, as in 'butter' and 'pudding'.

In word-final position, as in 'pat', the apical closure is very weak in comparison with the initial /t/ as in 'tap', and there is often (depending on the dialect) no apical contact at all, the oral stop being replaced, or supplemented, by a characteristic laryngeal gesture such as a glottal stop or a constriction formed by the false vocal folds (Fujimura & Sawashima, 1971).

Another interesting case is English /l/, as mentioned earlier. Like other consonants, this phoneme is realized by a weaker consonantal gesture in coda than in onset. Sometimes, the final /l/ is said to be vocalicized (e.g. Wells, 1982; Hardcastle & Barry, 1985), losing the apical gesture altogether. In contrast, the initial/l/ seems always characterized by an apical contact, the sides (or one side) of the tongue blade providing an open acoustic channel (Ladefoged, 1993). At the same time, however, the English lateral consonant is characterized by dorsal retraction and blade narrowing, and the dorsal gesture

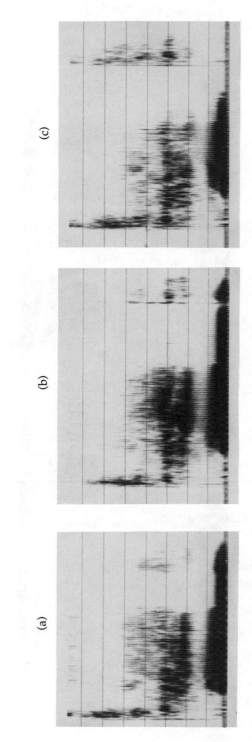

Figure 3.17 (a) 'ten' /ten/[tɛⁿn], (b) 'tend' /ten.d/[tɛⁿnd], (c) 'tent' /teNt/[tɛⁿt], uttered in list form.

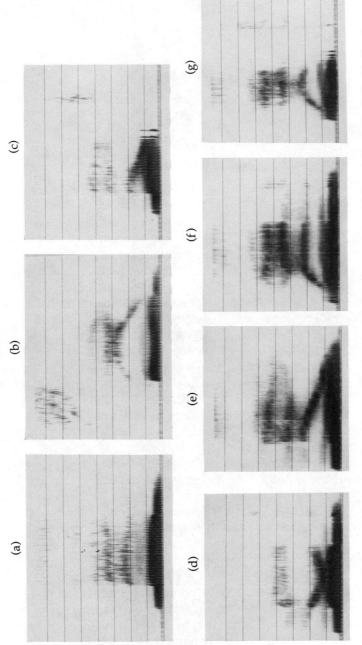

Figure 3.18 Some examples of nasal consonants comparing onset and coda: (a) 'men' /men/ [mɛ̃ⁿn], (b) 'Sam' /sam/ [sæ̃m], (c) 'melt' /meLt/ [meLt], (d) 'none' /nʌn/ [nʌ̃n], (e) 'nil' /niL/ [nɪl], (f) 'Lynn' /lin/ [lɪ̃n], (g) 'lint' /liNt/ [lɪⁿt].

(a)   (b)

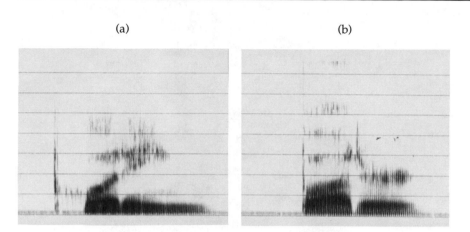

Figure 3.19 Wideband spectrograms (0–8 kHz) of (a) 'pudding' /pudiŋ/[pʊɾĩŋ], and (b) 'butter' /bʌtəR/[bʌɾɚ], showing American English taps (so called flaps).

is characteristic of this consonant even in a back vowel context in final position as an additional tongue retraction gesture (Sproat & Fujimura, 1993). This 'vocalic' aspect of the l-gesture in coda shows its peak activity at a time closer to the center of the syllable and has a stronger influence on the tautosyllabic vowel than when it occurs in coda. Depending on the dialect, there may be a partial loss of phonemic distinction of vowels in this context (see Veatch, 1992), as in the well-known cases of nasals in coda. Recasens & Farnetani (1990) discuss allophonic variation of /l/ in Catalan, Italian, and English.

It can be said generally that syllable-final consonants have stronger influence on the articulation of the nucleus than the initial consonants do. This results in a great variety of vocalic properties of final demisyllables. In phoneme-based schemes of speech synthesis by rule (Holmes, Mattingly, & Shearme, 1964; Liberman, Ingemann, Lisker, Delattre, & Cooper, 1959; Klatt, 1987b; Hertz, Kadin, & Karplus, 1985), this means that the choice of target values for formant frequencies for the vowel must be specified by context-sensitive allophonic rules. Sometimes, the context to be looked up in this anticipatory process must extend over several phonemic segments ahead, but it rarely involves consideration of heterosyllabic segmental contexts. A typical example of such a long-distance tautosyllabic contextual dependence is the American English 'pint' /paJNt/ [pãĩ̃-t] *vs.* 'pined' /paJn.d/ [pãĩnd], where the former has, in some dialects (often noted in parts of Canada), a less low vowel gesture than the latter, while the only phonemic difference is the /t/-/d/ opposition at the end of the string. Even without such a distinction in vowel quality, when the waveform is truncated by digital waveform editing before the oral stop, the latter sounds perfectly natural as 'pine', whereas the former sounds still like 'pint'.[21] Our examples here pertain to a speaker of Midwest American dialect, and do not show the vowel quality difference.

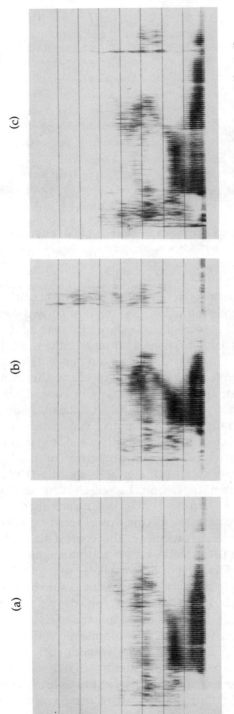

(a)   (b)   (c)

Figure 3.20 Wideband spectrograms of (a) 'pine' /paɪn/ [paɪ̃n], (b) 'pint' /paɪNt/ [paɪ̃nt], and (c) 'pined' /paɪn.d/ [paɪ̃nd].

3.6 Phenomena around the syllable boundary

There are phonetic phenomena that are unique in situations across the syllable boundary. In American English, as mentioned above, the so-called t-flapping occurs under conditions specified across a syllable boundary. In British English (RP), a phonemoidal /R/ in final position in the lexical representation manifests itself as an initial /r/ when the following word has no initial consonant (as in 'her own'), similar to the liaison in French (Selkirk, 1972).

In addition, there is a wide range of assimilation processes that take place across a syllable or word boundary. In Swedish, a syllable final /r/ is integrated with any (phonemically adjacent) apical dental consonant(s) making the latter a retroflex alveolar, and this effect spreads over the word boundary (as in 'under ett års tid' (under one year's time, i.e. for one year) [ʊnder ɛtːɔʂ ʈiːd], where both /s/ and /t/ are rhotacized under the influence of the preceding /r/ in the word 'år' [ɔr] (year). In Japanese, a geminate consonant (with some laryngeal gesture) is used usually word-medially in contrast to a single initial consonant, as in /si-ta/ [sʲita] (did) *vs.* /siQ-ta/ [sʲitːa] (got acquainted).[22] Similarly, in Japanese (Hattori, 1961) a nasal glide without place specification occurs in syllable final position as in /ha-da/ [hada] (skin) *vs.* /haN-da/ [handa] (solder) or /haQ-pa/ [hapːa] (leaf) *vs.* /haN-pa/ [hampa] (odd piece), assimilating in place to the following initial consonant resulting in a homorganic nasal consonant or a nasalized semivowel or vowel, according to the manner of articulation of the following onset. Such phenomena generally can be described as a temporal spreading of a phonetic gesture in a particular way depending on the language.[23]

The behavior of gesture spreading is often continuously variable depending on the prosodic context such as the strength of the word/phrase boundary involved, speed and style of utterance, and is at least in a large part a matter to be described within phonetics (see Fujimura & Lovins, 1978; Browman & Goldstein, 1985; Hardcastle & Barry, 1985; Keating, 1988; Boyce, 1990; Manuel, 1990; Browman & Goldstein, 1992; Kohler, 1992; Fujimura, 1995b; Veatch, 1993; Cohn, 1993; Kröger, 1993). Since such phonetic behaviors critically depend on the particular language, descriptions in acoustic phonetics must be given specifically for the given language. Phonetics, contrary to the statement in early generative phonology (see Chomsky & Halle, 1968), contains language-specific parameters.

4 Prosodic characteristics

4.1 Stress, accent, and intonation

Different languages use different prosodic means for distinguishing words. English traditionally has been called a stress language, but the acoustic correlate of the lexical distinction is manifested primarily in the voice fundamental frequency (f_0) change (Fry, 1955; Fry, 1958; Bolinger, 1958). In the contemporary phonological literature, the adjusted word stress patterns (stress subordination) in English, implemented in f_0 contours, have been described as intonation patterns. Different systems of lexical accent and their implications in phrasal phonology and phonetics have been discussed (see, *inter alia* Chomsky & Halle, 1968; Liberman, 1975; Maeda, 1976; Liberman & Prince, 1977; Pierrehumbert, 1980; Ladd, 1986; Beckman & Pierrehumbert, 1986 for English; Nishinuma & Rossi, 1981; Vaissière, 1971, 1983 for French; Öhman, 1967; Gårding, 1979, 1983; Bruce, 1979 for Swedish; 't Hart & Collier, 1979 for Dutch; Shi, 1988 for Chinese; Hattori, 1961; McCawley, 1968; Haraguchi, 1977; Fujisaki & Hirose, 1982; Poser, 1984; Fujisaki, Hirose, & Sugito, 1986; Pierrehumbert & Beckman, 1988; Fujimura, 1991; Kubozono, 1993 for Japanese).

An intonation computation would combine timing specifications with tone value specifications to produce continuous f_0 contours (see Pierrehumbert, 1981; Anderson, Pierrehumbert, & Liberman, 1984). Speech synthesis by rule (or text-to-speech) systems perform such computations, but in the current technology, the resultant speech is obviously artificial while the word identifiability (intelligibility) may be very high. These computational schemes usually assign inherent segmental durations for phonemes/allophones or demisyllables, subject to modifications due to the prosodic environment. Intonation theories may assume an inherent duration specified for each tone in the tone tier, and when these tones are linked to syllables with externally given timing and duration values of a syllable string, the temporal gaps would be filled by a simple interpolation scheme.

The theory of articulatory phonology proposes to compute the temporal patterns based on crucial articulatory gestures, mutually related in timing according to a biological oscillatory principle called task dynamics (Saltzman, 1995; Browman & Goldstein, 1992). This theory, however, has not specified algorithms of prosodically organizing the phrasal temporal patterns. A general computational model of syllable timing is included in the C/D (converter-distributor) model of phonetic implementation based on syllable and boundary strengths (Fujimura, 1992; Fujimura, 1995a,b).

There is a significant interaction between the articulatory control for implementing phonological feature specifications and the f_0 control. Voiceless consonants tend to cause locally raised f_0 in its temporal vicinity (see t'Hart, Collier, & Cohen, 1990), and tongue position for vocalic gestures may be linked to some extent with local f_0 changes (see Lehiste & Peterson, 1961; Honda, 1983). Such an interaction may largely reflect the physical and physiological constraints of the natural speech production system; nevertheless, acoustic and auditory signals contain such f_0 modulations as part of the phonetic information, and in certain situations, the perceptual identity of the consonantal feature (such as voiced/voiceless) may be determined by the local f_0 contour (Fujimura, 1971; Haggard, *et al.*, 1970). Furthermore, such a concomitant effect can be phonologized to establish a target value of the phonological feature (Honda & Fujimura, 1991).

Combining task forces from different traditions, recent efforts have formulated a practical transcription system called ToBI (Silverman, Beckman, Pitrelli, Pierrehumbert, Ostendorf, Wightman, *et al.*, 1992) for English f_0 patterns. Intonation phenomena as manifestations of prosodic control in speech utterances, however, are by no means limited to patterning of the f_0 contour. In particular, expressive utterances often use vocal means that escape the accounts of available descriptive framework. A semantic focus placed on a particular word or phrase often results in what is called prominence of a syllable, which shows an f_0 increase, or sometimes f_0 suppression. The latter case, in particular, seems accompanied by characteristic and temporally changing voice source spectrum envelope with a selective emphasis in the mid frequency range by an increase of more than 10dB (Silverman, Pierrehumbert & Talkin, personal communication; also see Fujimura, *et al.*, 1994).

Phonological functions of dynamic control of voice quality (often called voice register, including temporal perturbation as well as spectral envelope changes), have been reported in the literature (see e.g. Henderson, 1965; Thongkum, 1988; for related instrumental techniques, see Ladefoged, Maddieson, & Jackson, 1988). Temporal perturbation of voice periodicity, sometimes involving sub-harmonic generation as typically observed in vocal fry situations in daily speech, also can characterize emotional expressions (see, e.g. Williams & Stevens, 1972; Erickson & Fujimura, 1992; Spring, Erickson, & Call, 1992; Mazo, 1992). For an overall discussion of voice quality control, see Laver (1980); for a physiological and acoustic study of voice qualities in singing and speech, see Estill, *et al.*, (1995). (For voice source characteristics of voice quality, see Ní Chasaide and Gobl, VOICE SOURCE VARIATION.)

4.2 *Phrasal organization of gestural events, temporal modulation*

It is well recognized by phonologists (see e.g. Selkirk, 1984) that the (postlexical) phonological tree structure is independent from, though related to, syntactic (surface) structure. Most phonetic evidence is provided by studies of intonation patterns as mentioned above. There is, however, evidence also in articulatory data comparing identical word sequences uttered in different prosodic situations (Fujimura, 1990a). In the C/D model, the prosodic representation in the form of a metrical tree (Liberman & Prince, 1977), augmented by numerical utterance specifications, is converted into a linear string of syllable/boundary pulses. The magnitudes (and time values derived therefrom) of syllable/boundary pulses represent the prosodic control pattern.

The beginning of a phonetic phrase tends to be marked by stronger gestures, while the ending is marked by time-scale elongation (Keating, 1995). Also, prominence attachment (as in the case of informational focus or contrastive emphasis) tends to introduce a phrase boundary (Fujimura, 1990a,b).

Temporal modulation such as phrase final elongation, a gradual declination of articulatory excursions as well as voice intensity over a phrasal unit, and various f_0 changes near the end of a phrase provide important perceptual and spectrographic cues for parsing and comprehending speech utterances. In addition, segmental alterations of various kinds, some of which are often described as allophonic changes, seem to assist the parsing process by identifying the edges of words (Church, 1987). It should be emphasized that perceptually clear phrase boundaries are not necessarily marked phonetically as silent periods. Phonetic phrase boundaries are not consistently used according to the phonological phrase structures. The strength of each phonetic phrase boundary is continuously, rather than categorically controlled.

Prosodic cues seem primarily important for very early phases of language acquisition, and also for second language learning. Spectrographic representation methods were historically motivated primarily for assisting verbal communication by the deaf, but the goal was primarily identifying the visual pattern for each word. The display of spectrographic patterns was designed to optimize the clarity of syllabic identities, suppressing effects like gradual intensity change that are not useful for lexical identification. Acoustic phonetic studies now have a different emphasis: understanding prosodic organization.

ACKNOWLEDGMENTS

This work was in part supported by funds provided by ATR Human Information Processing Research Laboratories and ATR Interpreting Telecommunications Research Laboratories. The authors also wish to acknowledge substantive assistance of Jennifer Flaherty and Catita Williams in preparing the spectrograms for this article. Finally, editorial suggestions offered by Professors William Hardcastle and John Laver are gratefully acknowledged.

NOTES

1   These shortcomings of the Playback were overcome by a later invention of a vocoder-type speech synthesizer also using an optical control pattern, based on mechanical resonances of an array of piezoelectric birefringence crystals (Fujimura, 1958).

2   The use of /R/ is explained in Section 3.1.1 in connection with our use of phonemoidal transcription.

3   There are also significant effects on formant frequencies of the constriction formed by the lowered velum approaching the back surface of the tongue, see Maeda (1992).

4   Positive in the direction from V to C; See Section 3.1.2.

5   These feature names were used in the original proposal by Jakobson, *et al*. Current literature does not use the same feature system, and there

is no exact agreement among specialists. In this chapter, features are used only for explanation of the basic concept and are not exactly defined. Also, it should be noted that the term 'prosodic' in this chapter, along with most contemporary phonological and phonetic literature, is used with a very different meaning from the same term used in the original distinctive feature theory.

6   Although English has only s-fixes, p-fixes (syllable prefixes) occur to the left of the syllable core in other languages.

7   This term was proposed by Cari Spring (personal communication) in order to avoid confusion with the morphological suffix.

8   Phonetically, 'apical' in the strict sense refers to the articulation by the tongue tip, and 'coronal' by the blade region of the tongue, the pertinent region of the roof of the mouth being alveolar or postalveolar in either case, and postalveolar or palatal when the blade is the crucial articulator. In the phonological literature (see, e.g. Chomsky & Halle, 1968), 'coronal' is commonly used to refer to the place including both articulations, unless a further distinction is used in the language under discussion. In this article, as an abstract cover term, 'apical' refers to the involvement of the tip/blade region of the tongue in articulation. English has a distinction between interdental (also called dental according to IPA) and alveolar, the latter being either apical or coronal phonetically. In this article for a functional representation, the English phonemoids /θ, ð/ and /s, z, t, d, n/ are all referred to as apical (deviating from the standard usage in phonetics (see, e.g.

Ladefoged, 1993), /ʃ, ʒ, ʧ, ʤ/ as palatal, and /k, g/ as velar, in terms of place of articulation; /θ, ð/ are treated as a separate class called 'interdental' in terms of manner, as opposed to fricative, stop, nasal, etc. The phonetic (and phonemoidal) affricates /ʧ, ʤ/ are treated phonologically as palatal stops in the C/D model version of the demisyllabic analysis (Fujimura, 1995b), the affrication being considered a matter of phonetic implementation, in opposition to the palatal fricatives /ʃ, ʒ/. Obstruents are stop, fricative, or interdental. The phonetic affricates /t.s, d.z/, which occur only syllable-finally except for obviously non-English words, are treated with the s-fixes /s/ and /z/. For an argument supporting the different treatments of [ʧ] and [ts] in English, see Wang & Peterson (1958).

9   There is one morphological class of exceptions to this voicing agreement principle of s-fixes involving the final voiceless 'th' in a voiced coda environment, as in 'width', 'warmth', etc. Also, the word 'dreamt' [drɛmt] is singly exceptional. Note, however, that all these examples satisfy the sonority contour principle, or more specifically the general condition (Fujimura, 1995b) that a syllable must contain no more than one continuous voicing stretch. It should also be mentioned that, phonetically, word-edge voicing tends to drop for obstruents in general (as in the phonetically unvoiced /z/ of 'Gibbs'), thus making these exceptions perceptually less outstanding.

10   It is not always the case that such a point can be found in the spectrogram. In the text-to-speech

synthesis work using demisyllables as the concatenative units, a fixed time interval such as 30msec is measured off from the voice onset or any spectral discontinuity delimiting the acoustic vowel segment (Macchi, 1980).

11   Note that these 'exceptions' are not caused by morphological affixation, since these examples are all monomorphemic. Phonemic theories, therefore, do not adopt the idea that temporal ordering of phonemic segments in a syllable is redundant, and they must treat phonemes to be, in principle, specified in their ordering of occurence in each syllable. In fact, in many phonological theories, syllables are considered to be epiphenomenal, given the strong interaction between the integrity of each syllable and the segment order within a syllable. Phonotactics is significant, as the sonority hierarchy holds statistically among most lexicons of languages. Vowels tend to be found in all syllables in their middle parts, and obstruents tend to be more marginal than sonorant consonants if consonant clusters are allowed.

12   A recently proposed general principle of linguistic description, called Optimality Theory (see Prince & Smolensky, forthcoming, and McCarthy & Prince, forthcoming) may offer a very different solution to this problem. This theory claims that rules, which are expressed as constraints (not in ordered derivational rules), are generally violable but there is a strict hierachy established for rules in terms of relative preference for violation when there is a conflict between two rules.

13   This, of course, does not imply that it is *necessary* to memorize all demisyllabic patterns independently

in order to be able to read spectrograms.

14   The symbol + in this formula represents a sequential concatenation of syllables. The superscripts o and c refer to onset and coda, respectively, excluding syllable affixes (p-fixes or s-fixes). If there are affixes, the general form of syllable structure is (denoting a p-fix or its cluster by C_i^p and an s-fix or its cluster by C_i^s), $\sigma_i = C_i^p C_i^o V_i C_i^c C_i^s$ (i = 1, ... N-1, N).

15   More exactly, we may assume that we are considering one of the many articulatory or other phonetic dimensions that is pertinent to the discussion, to represent a temporal sequence of gestures of each syllable within that dimension (see for a more specific model of this type Fujimura, 1994b; 1995a). In such multidimensional models, corresponding to the nonlinear theories (considering multiple tiers for representing vocalic base functions separately from consonantal perturbation functions), the subdivision of syllable duration assumed immediately below does not apply, but the basic equation of syllable string does apply as long as the model adopts a prosodic organization scheme based on syllable concatenation.

16   There are English words that have phonetically front vowels in reduced syllables, as in the second syllable of 'pudding' (see Fig 3.19 (a)), which we transcribe with /ɪ/.

17   The symbols ∏and ? in both phonemoidal and phonetic transcriptions here denote the accent (pitch drop) and the final pitch rise, respectively. Similarly, the dot at the end of the major phrase indicates a pitch fall. The syllable boundary symbol is omitted when these occur. The elided

syllables [sᵘ] and [sⁱ] are phonetically completely voiceless and show no phonetic vowel segment, but the spectral quality of the frication is perceptually and spectrographically clearly different, the latter showing palatalization.

18 There are reasons to say that initial consonants are generally pronounced more clearly with larger force of articulation than the phonemically corresponding final consonants (see e.g. Ohala & Kawasaki, 1984, and Keating, 1995).

19 When a phonetic segment is short of a relatively obscure spectrographically or auditorily, the symbol for the segment is given as a superscript, as it is here, to indicate that the nasal element is neither a full nasal segment or just nasalization of the vowel.

20 Often, it is difficult to differentiate word-initial/final and syllable-initial/final status, but Fujimura (1977) shows for Japanese materials that word-medial syllable-initial nasals contrast with syllable final nasals, and argues that this higher velum position is consistent with the general characterization of initial consonants to be more forcibly articulated.

21 Some special caution must be exercised in such waveform editing experiments. Generally, the truncation point must coincide with a zero-crossing point of the waveform to avoid an introduction of a spurious spike, unless special techniques are used for tapering the amplitude continuously.

22 In the phonemoidal transcription in this chapter, the minus sign represents the syllable boundary, and a blank space a word boundary.

23 Cohn (1993) argues that phonological *vs.* phonetic processes of spreading with respect to nasalization can be distinguished by temporal patterns of a phonetic measure (nasal airflow).

4 Investigating the Physiology of Laryngeal Structures

HAJIME HIROSE

1 Introduction – basic laryngeal functions

In humans, there are four basic laryngeal functions: airway protection which is particularly important during deglutition, effort closure for fixation of the trunk while moving the upper extremities, airway opening for respiration, and phonation.

The most basic function of the larynx is to protect the airway. This function can be best understood by an appreciation of its origin determined by primitive needs (Negus, 1949). The most primitive larynx is found in the bichir lungfish (polypterus) living in rivers which periodically become dry. The primary lung developed as downgrowths of the pharyngeal pouch in response to their need for oxygen under conditions where the source of supply in water is limited. Development of the lung needed to be protected from the invasion of water and food during periods of submersion and, therefore, the primary larynx evolved as a protective mechanism. In the lungfish, the larynx developed as a simple, circular group of muscle fibers within the upper end of the trachea, constituting an encircling sphincter band. When this simple sphincter closed, the lung could be effectively isolated and its closure during deglutition prevented invasion by food or water.

During the course of evolution, the encircling sphincter became a more complicated structure, and in higher animals like the human, laryngeal sphincteric closure is accomplished by a valvular adduction mechanism at both false vocal fold and true vocal fold levels.

The sphincteric closure essentially serves as a protective mechanism for the airway but it also serves those physiologic functions which are dependent on air being trapped at the larynx when accompanied by increases in or maintenance of intra-thoracic and intra-abdominal pressure. Such functions include coughing, defecation, micturition, and fixation of the trunk for the stable movement of the upper extremities.

Another important modification during evolution was the development of the laryngeal opening or abductor mechanism and the cartilagenous framework of the larynx. Thus, the larynx was able to open the airway when necessary. Basically, the glottis widens during inspiration and narrows during expiration. This movement may be almost imperceptible during quiet respiration, but it becomes more prominent as the depth of respiration increases.

Finally, phonation developed as a principal function of the larynx in which the vocal folds are used as a flutter valve. This type of flutter valve is only seen in vertebrates possessing the respiratory requirements of an effective bellows. This is possible only in vertebrates which have a diaphragm; that is the mammals. Among all mammals, only humans have acquired the potential for the production of meaningful sounds, i.e., speech, by using the laryngeal valve as a source of vibration.

2 Methods of investigating laryngeal function in speech

Studies of laryngeal function rely heavily on the methods of investigation. In recent years, various kinds of observation techniques for the assessment and analysis of laryngeal behavior during speech production have been developed. The following is a brief description of the systems currently in use to assess laryngeal dynamics.

2.1 Fiberoptic observation and measurement of vocal fold movement

Many techniques have been used for the observation of the larynx. The most simple and popular method for otolaryngologists is the indirect mirror technique, but using this conventional laryngeal mirror, the larynx can be observed only while the subject's mouth is kept open. Even then photographs cannot easily be taken. The rigid tele-endoscope became available later, and laryngeal photography could be readily undertaken. Figure 4.1 shows a view of the larynx taken during phonation and deep inspiration using a tele-endoscope.

However, there was still a difficulty in the assessment of laryngeal dynamics during speech. In order to find out what happens during speech or singing in natural circumstances, the flexible fiberscope was devised during the late 1960s (Sawashima and Hirose, 1968).

The flexible fiberscope basically consists of a hard tip that houses an objective lens and two bundles of glass fibers: the light guide and the image guide.

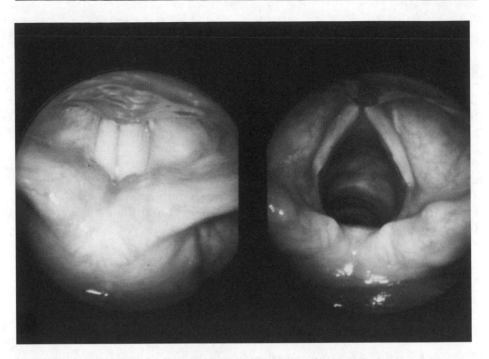

Figure 4.1   The laryngeal views obtained using a rigid tele-endoscope.

The light guide conducts the light for illumination of the field of view from the light source to the object-end of the scope. The image guide is a bundle of aligned or coherent glass fibers which transmits the image from the objective lens to the eye-piece of the scope.

Specific requirements in the design of the fiberscope were: (1) that it have an outside diameter small enough to pass through the nostril; (2) that it can obtain an image with a resolution good enough for the analysis of glottal gestures; and (3) that it should be provided with a light source of sufficient brightness (Sawashima, 1977). In recent years, these requirements have generally been satisfied.

Prior to the insertion of the fiberscope, surface anesthesia is applied to the nasal mucosa and to the epipharyngeal wall. After insertion, the tip of the scope is placed down near the tip of the epiglottis to obtain a good laryngeal view. Figure 4.2 illustrates the positioning of the fiberscope in an adult male.

2.2 High-speed digital imaging of vocal fold vibration

Until recently, precise observations of the pattern of vocal fold vibration have generally been made using an ultra-high-speed movie system. Ultra-high-speed

Figure 4.2 Positioning of the fiberscope for laryngeal observation.

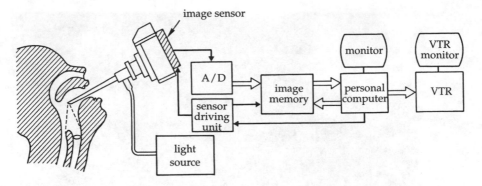

Figure 4.3 Block diagram of the digital imaging system for the analysis of vocal fold vibration.

photography can provide good resolution images of the vibrating vocal folds. However, this system is usually massive and costly, and it is always very time-consuming to carry out frame-by-frame analysis of the film obtained.

In the late 1980s, a new method of digitally imaging vocal fold vibration was developed using a solid-state image sensor attached to a conventional camera system (Hirose, 1988). In this system, a lateral viewing laryngeal tele-endoscope is attached to a single-lens reflex camera. A MOS-type solid-state image sensor consisting of 100 × 100 picture elements is attached to the lid of the camera at the position of the film plate. Under computer control, an image scan is made during the opening of the shutter, and image signals are stored in an image memory through a high-speed A/D converter. After data storage, the images can be reproduced and displayed on a monitor CRT screen. By reducing the number of horizontal scan lines, image data with a maximum rate of 2,000 to 4,000 frames can be obtained.

Figure 4.3 shows a block-diagram of the present system, which consists of a laryngeal tele-endoscope, a single-lens reflex camera, a special purpose image memory, a personal computer and an ordinary video recorder. The image memory has a 1-megabyte memory and a high-speed, 8 bit A/D converter. The image memory samples and stores image data until the memory becomes full. Then the image data are transferred to the personal computer via a parallel I/O unit. The time required for the transfer is 15 sec. After the transfer, a slow motion display of the image data can be accomplished under the control of the personal computer. The images are displayed on a TV monitor and can be recorded on an ordinary video recorder. As a light source, a pair of 250 W halogen lamps are used.

Data recording is made in the same manner as in still photography of the larynx. The larynx is visualized through a view finder and the camera shutter is released to start data acquisition. During the shutter opening of approximately 150 msec, 200 to 400 data frames are stored in the computer memory.

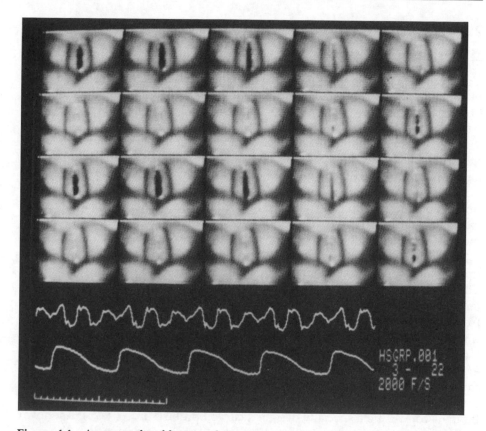

Figure 4.4 An example of laryngeal images recorded using the digital imaging system. Male subject: sustained phonation of /e/ at a fundamental frequency (f_0) of approximately 200 Hz. Frame rate: 2,000 frames/second.

Other physiological data, such as electroglottographic (EGG) signals, can also be recorded simultaneously, along with the speech signal.

Figure 4.4 shows the vocal fold vibration of a normal male subject taken at a rate of 2,000 frames per second. Twenty consecutive frames are displayed from the top-left corner to the bottom-right. The opening and closing phases of the vocal fold vibration are easily identifiable. In this example, the subject phonated with a fundamental frequency of 200 Hz, so approximately 2 cycles are displayed in the figure. The two curves shown below the pictures are the acoustic signal at the top and EGG signal at the bottom.

A pilot system using a fiberscope has also been developed more recently (Hirose et al., 1988). In this system, a CCD-type image sensor is used. The light source for the fiberscope system is a 300 W xenon lamp. The sampling rate of the picture elements is 20 MHz. A film rate of 2,000 per second can be achieved with 200×14 picture elements. This type of system makes it possible to observe vocal fold vibration during speech samples containing consonantal gestures.

2.3 Laryngeal electromyography

Electromyography (EMG) is a technique for providing graphic information about the time course of the electrical activity of the muscle fibers that accompanies muscle contraction and subsequent effects, including the development of tension. (See Stone, LABORATORY TECHNIQUES FOR INVESTIGATING SPEECH ARTICULATION.)

Since EMG was established as a scientific discipline, it has been widely used in various fields for studying muscular function and coordination. In particular, EMG has proved to be useful for research into kinesiological aspects of human behavior, where the analysis of the parameters of the individual motor unit action potential may not play an important role. Rather, EMG kinesiology is much more concerned with the biomechanical analysis of various movements or gestures (Harris, 1981).

The EMG system consists of some sort of probe or electrodes for picking up the action potentials, amplifying equipment, recording equipment, and ultimately a graphic display, which may have signal processing facilities. For laryngeal EMG in the study of speech dynamics, so-called hooked-wire electrodes are used, in which a pair of thin electrically shielded wires are threaded through a needle and inserted in the target muscles (Hirose, 1985). Intrinsic laryngeal muscles, such as the cricothyroid, thyroarytenoid, and lateral cricoarytenoid muscles are reached percutaneously as are two extrinsic laryngeal muscles, the sternohyoid, and sternothyroid muscles. The posterior cricoarytenoid and interarytenoid muscles are reached perorally with indirect laryngoscopy using a specially designed curved probe (Hirose, 1976). As shown in Figure 4.5, the wire-bearing tip of the needle is kept drawn into the shaft of the probe until it is brought closely to the point of insertion, at which time it is pushed out by pulling the trigger of the probe.

It should be emphasized that progress in the strategy of the computer processing of EMG data has led to better analysis of the temporal pattern of the activity of pertinent laryngeal muscles with reference to speech signals (Kewly-Port, 1973).

2.4 Photoglottography (transillumination of the glottis)

Photoglottography (PGG) is a technique for recording glottal area variation by measuring the amount of light passing through the glottis.

In 1960, Sonesson first reported the use of a photo-electric device applied to the normal human subject for assessing the glottal area variation. In his method, a DC light source was placed against the anterior neck, while a light-conducting rod was inserted into the hypopharynx through the mouth under topical

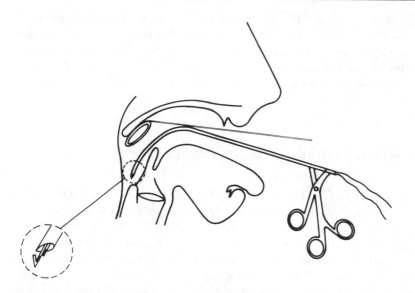

Figure 4.5 Peroral insertion of wire electrodes using a curved probe under indirect laryngoscopy.

anesthesia. A photomultiplier tube was attached to the other end of the rod so that the illuminating light passing through the glottal aperture was transmitted through the light-conducting rod to the photomultiplier tube. The output of the tube was displayed on a cathode ray oscilloscope and the record was called a photo-electric glottogram or photoglottogram. Using this technique, he measured the open period, the opening phase, and the closing phase of the glottal vibratory cycle for sustained phonation. He claimed that the results obtained from his method were in good agreement with the results obtained from high-speed motion picture analysis.

Since Sonesson's technique imposed considerable limitations on articulatory movements, further modification was made by other investigators. For example, Frøkjær-Jensen (1967) introduced a small photo-sensor attached to the tip of the thin flexible plastic tube through the nasal cavity to the hypopharynx, thus making transillumination possible during speech articulation.

Sawashima (1968) reversed the positions of light source and photo-sensor relative to the glottis. He used a fiberscopic illumination as a light source while observing the laryngeal gesture, and picked up the photo-electric signals through a photo-sensor attached to the anterior neck.

These modifications have extended the application of the photoglottographic technique to studies on glottal adjustments as well as on the patterns of vocal fold vibration during speech production. It has been assumed that the data obtained by this technique provides a good approximation of the glottal area function, although it is impossible to calibrate the instrument to measure the absolute area of the glottis. Also, it should be taken into consideration that several sources of artefacts may exist during data assessment. A shift in the positioning of the instruments relative to the larynx may be a major source of artefacts. Interruption of the light by the epiglottis during speech utterance should also be carefully monitored during recording to minimize incorrect interpretation of the obtained results.

2.5 Electroglottography (laryngography)

Electroglottography (EGG) is a technique for registering glottal vibratory movements by measuring changes in electrical resistance across the neck. In this technique, a pair of plate electrodes are placed on the skin on both sides of the neck above the thyroid cartilage. A weak high frequency electrical current is applied to the electrodes, and a small fraction of the electrical current passes through the larynx. The transverse electrical resistance of the larynx varies depending on the opening and closing of the glottis, and a modification in the amplitude of the transglottic current occurs in correspondence with the vibratory cycles of the vocal folds. The amplitude modification of the current is detected from which electrical glottograms are obtained.

In a typical model described by Fourcin (1981), each electrode has a guard ring and an inner conductor. One of the electrodes has a 4 MHz transmitting voltage applied between the center conductor and guard ring. The other serves as a current pick-up. According to Fourcin, typically about 30 mW is dissipated at the subject's neck with only microwatts being involved at the level of the vocal folds. Contact between the vocal folds increases current flow as contact area increases, but movement of the vocal folds without contact, giving an increase in glottal area, will not necessarily change the current flow. For this reason, Fourcin claimed that the term "glottograph" is inappropriate, and he proposed that it should be called a "laryngograph".

In making comparisons between electrical and photo-electric glottograms, Frøkjær-Jensen (1968) concluded that the opening of the glottis seemed to be better represented in photo-electric glottograms, whereas the closure of the glottis, particularly its vertical contact area, was probably better reflected in EGG.

One of the advantages of EGG is that the procedure is carried out with a minimum discomfort for the subject. As stated above, EGG record reflects the glottal condition during closure better than during the open period, and the presence or absence of glottal vibration, as well as the accurate fundamental frequency can be readily determined. However, since it is difficult to estimate to what extent the glottal condition contributes to the electrical resistance or impedance variations between the electrodes, a quantitative interpretation of EGG seems to be less direct than PGG.

3 Laryngeal structures and the control of phonation

3.1 Laryngeal framework and laryngeal muscles

The framework of the larynx consists of four different cartilages: the epiglottis, thyroid, cricoid, and arytenoid cartilages. The thyroid and cricoid cartilages are connected by the cricothyroid joint, while the arytenoid and cricoid cartilages are connected by the cricoarytenoid joint. The movement of the thyroarytenoid joint changes the length of the vocal folds. Movements of the arytenoid cartilage on the surface of the cricoarytenoid joint contribute to the abduction-adduction of the vocal folds. The main movement of the cricoarytenoid joint is a rotation (abduction-adduction) of the arytenoid cartilage around the longitudinal axis of the joint. Other possible movements of the arytenoid are a small degree of sliding motion along the longitudinal axis of the joint and a rocking motion around a fixed point at the attachment of the posterior cricoarytenoid ligament (Leden and Moore, 1961). (For further details of the anatomy of laryngeal structures, see Kahane and Folkins, 1984; Hirano, 1991; and Bless and Abbs, 1983.)

Movements of the cricothyroid and cricoarytenoid joints are controlled by the intrinsic laryngeal muscles. Elongation and stretching of the vocal folds is achieved by contraction of the cricothyroid muscle (CT). Movements of the arytenoid cartilage and the resultant abduction-adduction of the vocal folds are controlled by the abductor and adductor muscles. The posterior crico-arytenoid muscle (PCA) is the only abductor muscle, while another three – the interarytenoid (INT or IA), lateral cricoarytenoid (LCA), and the thyroarytenoid (TA) muscle – are the adductor muscles. Contraction of the cricothyroid muscle may also result in a small degree of glottal abduction. The vocalis muscle (VOC), which is the medial part of the thyroarytenoid muscle, contributes to the control of the effective mass and stiffness of the vocal folds rather than to abduction-adduction movements.

The entire larynx is supported by the extrinsic laryngeal muscles and the ligaments, of which suprahyoid and infrahyoid muscles form the important members. These muscles contribute to the elevation and lowering of the larynx, which may relate to the pitch control of voice, as well as to articulatory adjustments such as jaw opening (Erickson et al., 1977).

3.2 Layered structure of the vocal fold

The layered structure of the vocal fold edge described by Hirano (1974) is shown in Figure 4.6. As can be seen in the figure, the vocal fold consists of the mucosa epithelium, the lamina propria mucosa, and the vocalis muscle. In the lamina propria, the superficial layer is the loose connective tissue, and the intermediate and deep layers correspond to the so-called vocal ligament. Based

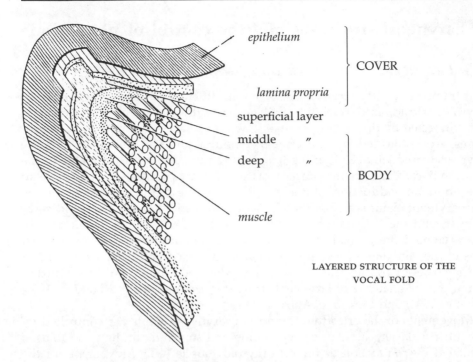

Figure 4.6   Schematical presentation of the layered structure of the human vocal fold.

on the concept of this layered structure, Hirano proposed a structural model of the vocal fold. In his model, the vocal fold basically consists of the three layers – cover, transition, and body. The cover consists of the epithelium and the superficial layer of the lamina propria; the transition includes the intermediate and the deep layers; and the body includes the vocalis muscle. For simplification, the transition can be considered as part of the body so that the entire structure can be regarded as cover and body.

This cover-body model proposed by Hirano is quite useful for explaining variation in the mode of vocal fold vibration with different laryngeal adjustments and with various pathological conditions. Contraction of CT elongates the vocal fold, and its effective mass decreases. Due to the elongation of the vocal fold, the stiffness of both cover and body increases. This is the situation of the vocal fold for phonation in the light or head register. Contraction of VOC, in contrast, shortens the vocal fold, its effective mass being increased. At the same time, stiffness of the body increases, while that of the cover decreases. Contraction of VOC in combination with different degrees of contraction of CT usually takes place for phonation in the modal or chest register. Thus the difference in the mode of vocal fold vibration between the head and the chest registers can be accounted for by the different conditions of the cover and body of the vocal fold (Hirano, 1974).

3.3 *Vocal fold vibration during phonation*

According to the almost universally accepted myoelastic-aerodynamic theory of vocal fold vibration during phonation, one cycle of the vibration of the vocal fold is produced as follows (See also Stevens, ARTICULATORY/ACOUSTIC/AUDITORY RELATIONSHIPS.):

(a) The bilateral vocal folds are appropriately approximated towards the midline by the activation of the adductor laryngeal muscles accompanied by suppression of the abductor muscle.

(b) Air is then forced through the vocal tract from the lungs and the vocal folds are sucked together by the combined effect of Bernoulli's aerodynamic law and the elasticity of the tissues (See Shadle, THE AERODYNAMICS OF SPEECH).

(c) When the vocal folds have been sucked together, the flow of air from the lungs continues but the flow through the glottis ceases and the subglottal air pressure rises.

(d) When the subglottal air pressure becomes greater than the medial compression of the vocal folds, the folds are blown apart and a puff of air escapes into the supraglottal space. Consequently, the subglottal pressure falls and the vocal folds return to their adducted position at the beginning of the vibratory cycle as a result of their tissue elasticity.

(e) A second cycle starts as a repetition of the first cycle.

Several preconditions are required for normal phonation. The transglottal pressure (the difference between the subglottal and supraglottal pressure) and the airflow must be high enough, the glottal width small enough and the glottal resistance sufficiently low.

4 Laryngeal adjustments for different phonetic conditions

The basic features of laryngeal adjustments for different phonetic conditions can be classified as follows:

(1) abduction vs. adduction of the vocal folds;
(2) constriction of the supraglottal structures;
(3) adjustment of the length, stiffness and thickness of the vocal fold;
(4) elevation and lowering of the entire larynx.

4.1 Abduction vs. adduction of the vocal folds

This type of adjustment is used for the distinction between respiration and phonation, as well as for the voiced versus voiceless distinction during speech production. For deep inspiration, the vocal folds are fully abducted by an increase in the activity of PCA and a suppression of the adductor muscles. For quiet respiration, the extent of the glottal opening is approximately half that for deep inspiration and the vocal fold position observed in laryngoscopy in quiet respiration is described as the intermediate position. In this condition, the activities of both the abductor and the adductor muscles are minimal.

The general picture of the glottal condition in the abduction vs. adduction dimension during speech is that the glottis is closed or nearly closed for voiced sounds including vowels, whereas it is open for voiceless sounds, the degree of the glottal opening and its timing relative to the articulatory gestures varying with different phonetic environments.

The principal mechanism underlying abduction vs. adduction of the vocal folds during speech production is reciprocal activation of the abductor and adductor muscle groups. The reciprocal activity pattern between the two groups of laryngeal muscles has been revealed by recent EMG studies combined with fiberoptic observation. In particular, reciprocity between PCA and INT is found to be important for realization of the voiced-voiceless distinction. The reciprocity between PCA and the adductor muscles has been observed for different languages, including American English (Hirose and Gay, 1972), Japanese (Hirose and Ushijima, 1978), Danish (Hirose et al., 1979) and French (Benguerel et al., 1978).

Figure 4.7 shows an example of averaged EMG curves of the INT and PCA, for a pair of test words /əp'ʌp/ and /əb'ʌp/ produced by an American English speaker. It can be seen that PCA activity is suppressed for the voiced portion of the test words, whereas it increases for the production of the inter-vocalic voiceless stop /p/ as well as for word-final /p/. On the other hand, INT shows a reciprocal pattern when compared with that of PCA in that its activity increases for the voiced portion and decreases for the voiceless portion of the test words.

Figure 4.8 shows a typical example of the relationship between the glottal size and the pattern of the averaged laryngeal EMG activity of PCA and INT for the production of the Japanese test word /ise:/. The glottal width (GW), measured by means of fiberoptic analysis, increases for the voiceless consonant /s/, for which PCA activity increases and INT activity is reciprocally suppressed.

Some languages, such as Hindi and Chinese, show a phonemic distinction between aspirated and unaspirated stops. Previous EMG and fiberoptic studies revealed that the degree and timing of glottal abduction-adduction gestures are well controlled by coordinated laryngeal muscle activities (Sawashima and Hirose, 1983). In particular, the degree and timing of PCA activation seem

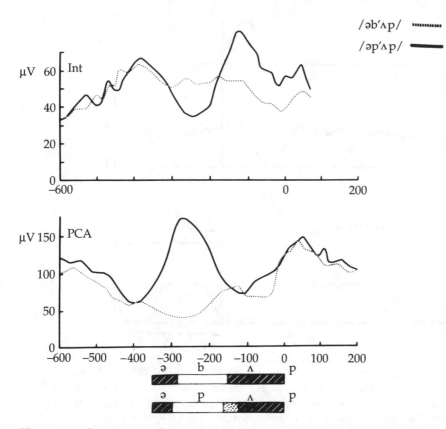

Figure 4.7 Superimposed averaged EMG curves of INT and PCA for the utterances /əp'ʌp/ (solid line) and /əb'ʌp/ (dotted line). The line-up point for averaging (zero on the abscissa) indicates the voice offset of the stressed vowel.

quite important for the distinction between different phonemic types associated with glottal opening i.e., arytenoid separation at the vocal processes observed by a fiberscope.

Figure 4.9 shows the relationship between the pattern of PCA activity and the time course of the glottal width measured at the vocal process, for the three labial stop types showing arytenoid separation: voiceless aspirated, voiceless unaspirated and voiced aspirated. The curves are lined up at the articulatory release taken as time 0 on the abscissa, and durations of oral closure and aspiration are also illustrated (Hirose, 1977). The figure shows good agreement not only in degree but also in timing between PCA activity and the opening gesture of the glottis. Thus, we must fully realize that, in addition to the control of the degree of glottal abduction vs. adduction, the control of laryngeal timing is also essential in phonetic realization of different types of consonants. As explicitly discussed by Abramson (1977), various languages of the world make extensive use of the timing of the valvular action of the

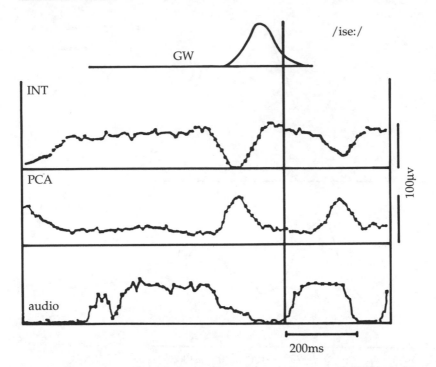

Figure 4.8 Time curves of the glottal width (GW), the smoothed and integrated EMG curves of the INT and PCA, and the speech envelope (audio) for the test world /ise:/ produced by a Japanese subject. The curves are aligned on the same time axis. The vertical line indicates the voice onset for the vowel /e/.

larynx relative to supraglottic articulation in order to distinguish classes of consonants, although certain nonlaryngeal features such as pharyngeal expansion may also be linked with laryngeal timing.

It should be noted, however, that adjustment of glottal width is only one parameter that determines whether or not the vocal folds will vibrate during the consonantal interval. In addition, there must be an adequate glottal airflow through the glottis for generating vocal fold vibration, the amount of which will depend on both subglottal pressure and on the configuration of the supraglottal articulators. Further, the physical properties of the vocal folds, particularly the stiffness, is an important factor that relates to initiation-cessation as well as the mode of vocal fold vibration.

In order to clarify the relationship between transglottal pressure difference and the glottal configuration during the production of voiceless consonants, a physiological experiment was performed in which the sub- and supraglottal pressure was measured by means of pressure transducer systems and the glottal size was estimated using the photoglottography technique (Löfqvist and Yoshioka, 1980). The data were obtained at the offset of the vibration at oral closure of voiceless consonants /s/ and /t/, at the onset of the vibration

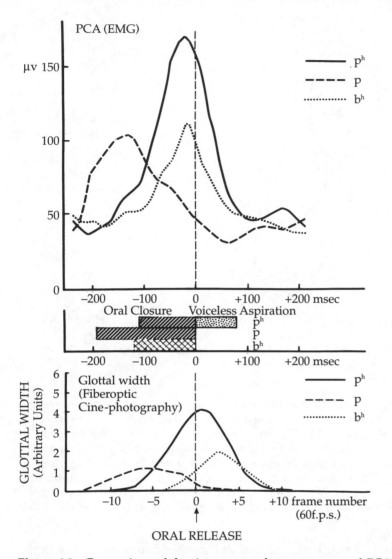

Figure 4.9 Comparison of the time courses between averaged PCA activity and glottal opening gesture. All curves are lined up at the oral release.

after the oral release, and during the maximum glottal opening for each consonant. The transglottal pressure (ΔP) was calculated by subtracting the subglottal pressure value from the supraglottal value.

Figure 4.10 shows the relationship between the ratio of the transglottal pressure to the subglottal pressure (ΔP/Ps) and the relative size of the glottal width (GW) for word-initial /s/ and word-initial /t/. In this figure, the 90 per cent range of the distribution is represented by circles for each of the following sets of data: the voice offsets for /s/ and /t/, and voice onsets after /s/ and /t/.

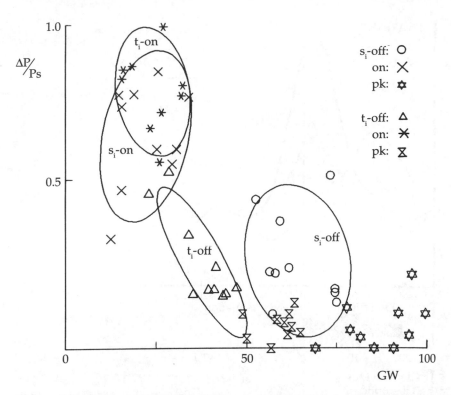

Figure 4.10 Pattern of data distribution for word-initial /s/ and /t/ representing the relationship between transglottal pressure (ΔP) vs. subglottal pressure (Ps) ratio and relative glottal width (GW) (The largest glottal opening during the consonantal period of [s] was taken as 100%, and relative glottal width was calculated as a percentage of that value for each token). In the figure, the 90% range of distribution is circled for each of the following data sets: voice offset for /s/ and /t/ (s_i-off and t_i-off) and voice onset after /s/ and /t/ (s_i-on and t_i-on), respectively. The symbol for "pk" indicates the coordinate for values at the time of maximum glottal opening for each token.

It can be seen here that both /s/ and /t/ demonstrate a difference in the physiological conditions for the cessation and initiation of voicing related to obstruent production. Namely, in both cases, voicing following the consonantal closure period occurred with a relatively small glottis and a higher ΔP/Ps ratio compared to those values with which voicing ceased around the implosion of the consonant.

It can also be seen that there is a subtle difference in the patterns of the distribution of data between the fricative /s/ and stop /t/ in terms of the laryngeal conditions for voice offset. In the case of /s/, the vocal fold vibration ceases with a relatively wider glottis than for /t/, whereas the ΔP/Ps ratio is comparable. On the other hand, there is no apparent difference between /s/ and /t/ distribution for the initiation of vocal fold vibration.

Thus, it appears that there is a hysteresis in the glottal mechanism defined by the initiation and cessation of oscillation. That is, vocal fold vibration tends to be maintained at the implosion of obstruents with relatively favorable physiological conditions for oscillation, while vibration does not start after the voiceless period until more favorable conditions are obtained by a narrowing of the glottis. These more favorable conditions are associated with an elevation of the transglottal pressure difference, although the reason why the vocal folds continue to vibrate with a wider glottis for /s/ than for /t/ is still unclear (Hirose and Niimi, 1987).

4.2 Constriction of the supraglottal structures

A typical example of supraglottal laryngeal constriction with the open glottis is observed in whispered phonation. In whisper, there is arytenoid separation at the vocal process with an adduction of the false vocal folds taking place with a decrease in the size of the anterior-posterior dimension of the laryngeal cavity. For this type of laryngeal adjustment, PCA continues to be active and the thyropharyngeal activation is also observed most likely for realization of supraglottal constriction (Tsunoda et al., 1994). This particular gesture for whispering is considered to contribute to the prevention of the vocal fold vibration by the transglottal airflow, as well as to facilitate the generation of turbulent noise in the laryngeal cavity.

Supraglottal laryngeal constriction with closed glottis is typically observed for glottal stop production. A similar gesture is often seen for the syllable-final stops in American English (Fujimura and Sawashima, 1971). The gesture prevents the air from the lungs from passing through the glottis. In laryngeal EMG, it has been observed that LCA appears to show a high degree of activity for this particular gesture together with activation of TA.

A lesser degree of supraglottal constriction with the closed glottis can be regarded as characterizing the laryngeal gesture known as "laryngealization". This type of adjustment may be observed for the production of Korean forced or tense stops and the so-called stød in Danish, where strong activation of VOC has been reported (Sawashima and Hirose, 1983).

4.3 Adjustment of the length, stiffness and thickness of the vocal folds with respect to pitch control

The best example of this type of laryngeal adjustment is control of the pitch of the voice, f_0, during phonation. f_0 control at the larynx is considered to be achieved mainly by adjusting the effective mass and the stiffness of the vocal folds. The main contributor to pitch regulation is CT, while TA also appears to participate to some extent. The activity of CT increases to raise pitch and decreases to lower pitch. As mentioned earlier, contraction of CT elongates the vocal folds, resulting in a decrease in the effective vibrating mass and an increase in the stiffness of both the cover and body of the vocal folds. Contraction of TA results in a thickening of the vocal folds, their effective mass being increased. The stiffness of the body increases while that of the cover decreases.

It has been observed that in the chest or modal register, a rise in pitch is characteristically achieved by contraction of both CT and TA. The most remarkable difference in muscle control between the chest and head registers is observed in the activity of TA. In the head register, as compared to the chest register, there is a marked decrease in TA activity, accompanied by an increase in CT activity. The difference in the muscle control between the two registers results in a difference in the physical conditions of the cover and body of the vocal folds, which is reflected in the mode of vocal fold vibration (Hirano et al., 1970).

In the realization of pitch accent in Japanese, different types of tones in tone languages such as Chinese, and word stress in English and other languages, CT is found to be uniquely related to f_0 changes. In particular, the increase in longitudinal tension and stretch of the vocal folds is obtained by CT activation. Figure 4.11 compared the curves of averaged CT activity and f_0 contours for five test words having different stress positions. It is obvious for all words, that CT activation occurs slightly ahead of the pitch peak associated with the stressed syllable.

Although the mechanism of pitch elevation seems quite clear, the mechanism of pitch lowering is not so straightforward. The contribution of the extrinsic laryngeal muscles such as sternohyoid is assumed to be significant, but their activity often appears to be a response to, rather than the cause of, a change in conditions. The activity does not occur prior to the physical effects of pitch change.

4.4 Elevation and lowering of the entire larynx

This type of laryngeal adjustment is typically observed in the action of swallowing, as well as during speech for vocal pitch control and voiced vs. voiceless distinction. However, the contribution of these movements for phonetic distinctions still needs to be investigated, except for specific laryngeal adjustment such as ejective and implosive sound production in which the entire larynx is elevated or lowered respectively and for generating or maintaining vocal fold vibration while the vocal tract is closed.

5   Current main issues and the direction of future research

The science of speech production is an inherently interdisciplinary endeavor. Thus, in recent years, multidisciplinary approaches, including physiological,

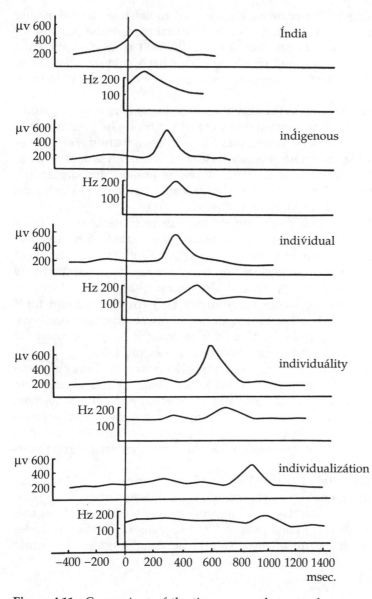

Figure 4.11 Comparison of the time courses between the averaged EMG curves of CT and f_0 contours for test words having different stress positions.

engineering, and linguistic aspects have attempted to disclose the fine nature of laryngeal behavior in voice and speech production. For the purpose of facilitating the exchange of information among different research domains, a series of conferences on vocal fold physiology have been held since 1981, and the proceedings of the latest conference were published in 1994 (Fujimura, 1994).

In the domain of physiological research, simultaneous recordings of multiple parameters are widely performed. For example, ultra-high-speed observation of the vocal fold vibratory pattern was made in combination with precise acoustic measures together with the assessment of other physiological parameters such as EGG (Childers et al., 1983). From an engineering standpoint, numerical simulation and modeling of the voice source based on physiological data were often reported (Bickley, 1991; Cranen, 1991).

Another important issue is to investigate the nature of pathological voice production. Evaluation of abnormal voice quality associated with laryngeal diseases has attracted the interest of laryngologists, and the measurement of many different acoustic parameters has been proposed to quantitatively represent the degree of voice abnormality (Imaizumi, 1985).

Further, simultaneous recordings of vibratory patterns of the vocal folds and voice signals have led to a direct comparison between the temporal variation in vocal fold vibration and perturbation of voice, thus giving a physiological basis of abnormal voice production (Kiritani et al., 1993).

As for future research, it seems that basic studies on laryngeal structure and function are still needed. In particular, we still lack details of neural control in the human larynx, including; 1) efferent nerve cell distribution in the brainstem, and exact neural pathways to the laryngeal muscles from the central nervous system, 2) the control of the larynx by the autonomic nervous system, and 3) the cerebellar control of laryngeal timing, etc. In future research, these points need to be investigated.

In addition, further study is needed of the physical properties of the laryngeal framework, for example the network of blood vessels within the larynx, the surface microstructure and the physical properties of the laryngeal mucosa, and the vocal fold vibratory patterns in different laryngeal conditions under different emotional states. All of these should be suitable topics for future basic research.

5 Instrumental Techniques for Linguistic Phonetic Fieldwork

PETER LADEFOGED

1 Introduction

There are remarkably few extensive phonetic descriptions of languages. A few well known languages, such as English, French and Japanese have recently become well documented from the phonetic point of view, because of the needs of speech synthesis systems. But in places where there is no commercial need for detailed phonetic knowledge, often only the most prominent phonetic features of the language have been described. There have been no comprehensive phonetic investigations of many major languages, such as Navajo (and, indeed, virtually all American Indian languages), Swahili, Malayalam, and hundreds of others. The lack of phonetic work is especially unfortunate in the case of less prominent languages that are no longer being spoken as a first language, and will not be available to be recorded in the near future. Hale, Krauss, Watahomigie, Yamamoto, Craig, Jeanne, and England (1992) estimate that over half the 6,000 languages currently spoken in the world will not be spoken by the end of the next century. This chapter will consider what kind of phonetic fieldwork must be undertaken in order to record a substantial part of the phonetic structures of such languages.

Most phonetic fieldwork differs from typical linguistic fieldwork not only by being more limited in scope, but also by being more limited in time. Linguists going out to examine a single language are usually prepared to spend several months on the process. But with adequate preparation phoneticians can record the phonetic structures with only a comparatively short time in the field. There are four basic tasks in making a description of the phonetic structures of a language. First one must decide what to describe; second, suitable speakers must be found; third (the major concern of this paper), the necessary phonetic data must be recorded and analyzed. Lastly the results must be written up as a coherent whole, a topic that will not be discussed in this paper, but which should always be held in mind. For ease of exposition we will consider each of the first three tasks separately. In practice, all these components overlap (especially the writing, which should be carried out throughout the fieldwork; it should never be left till the investigation is completed). We will focus principally on aspects of phonetic fieldwork that have not been described in readily available literature, and have little to say about well known techniques such as spectrographic analysis and other laboratory techniques that are familiar to all phoneticians.

2 Linguistic phonetic structures

The first requirement for a phonetic description of a language is a good account of the phonology. Of course, it is also true that in order to describe the phonology one needs to know the phonetics. The two things go hand in hand, providing us with a chicken and egg problem as to which must come first. Obviously they actually evolve together. But it is usually phonological knowledge that precedes detailed phonetic observation. Some people still have a lingering feeling, based on older works such as Pike's (1947) *Phonemics*, that a linguist should go into the field, make detailed phonetic transcriptions of some speakers, and then sort out the sounds into phonemes. But it seldom works out like that. Only rarely does one notice a phonetic difference between two sounds in a corpus, and then examine the corpus to see if they are in contrast.

Most of a linguistic phonetician's work involves describing the sounds of languages that have been the subject of previous linguistic work. On the few occasions when I have myself described a language that has not been the subject of previous linguistic analysis (e.g. Igbirra, as described in Ladefoged, 1964), it has clearly not been a case of my observing phonetic differences, and then seeing if they are phonemically contrastive. Instead, in my attempts to learn the language, it has been the native speaker who has pointed out that certain utterances mean different things, usually by commenting on my mispronunciations when I have managed to say one word while attempting to say another. After the phonological contrasts have been observed, then the phonetic differences involved can be described.

When trying to record the phonetic structures of a language, the ideal situation is if the fieldwork can be undertaken together with a linguist who has already analyzed the language. It is often possible to cooperate with local working linguists and their consultants to get phonetic data that they might otherwise disregard. But even if there are no local working linguists, phoneticians can usually prepare themselves reasonably well by reading everything that is available; fieldwork should never be undertaken without previous knowledge of all the literature. There will no doubt still be phonological points to be cleared up when the particular speakers being recorded do not behave as anticipated. But the phonological description of a language must have been fully worked out before an adequate phonetic description can be made. Linguistic phonetics follows phonology rather than preceding it.

This is a different attitude to fieldwork from that taken by some linguists. Kelly and Local (1989), for example, advise fieldworkers to avoid reading anything about a language they are going to investigate. I find this attitude presumptuous. Other people usually know more than I do. Previous linguists may have missed some phonetic points that I might be fortunate enough to note. They may also have described some sounds incorrectly, but that does not hinder me from making my own observations. My own practice is to try to find out as much as I can about a language, reading all the available literature on it and its neighbors.

A complete phonetic description of a language would be one that was sufficient for a computer to turn the output of a phonological description of an utterance into natural-sounding speech. Making a description of this kind is an enormous undertaking, which has only recently been attempted for languages such as English. The kind of detailed phonetic description required for synthesizing natural-sounding speech is well beyond the scope of the fieldwork we envisage. We will assume that when describing the phonetic structures of a language it is sufficient (at least to begin with) to consider each of the phonologically contrasting items in comparable contexts. This would involve recording the complete set of vowel and consonant contrasts of each language as well as the principal dynamic phonetic patterns.

It would be nice if it were possible to record all the desired items in naturally occurring speech, but this is impossible. There is no way in which one can sit around waiting for half a dozen speakers to use each of a set of words such as "heed," "hid," "head," "had," etc. in spontaneous speech. Accordingly it is necessary to prepare word lists. The form of the word list developed will vary from language to language, depending on particular features of the language. The general structure of the basic word list should be to place all the vowels and all the consonants in matched environments so that contextual influences are equalized. It is often appropriate to use words illustrating consonants initially before a low central vowel such as [a], and at least two sets of words illustrating vowels, one following a dental or alveolar stop, and one following a labial stop. Supplementary word lists are also needed to look at additional contextual variation in vowels, the relative durations of segments, and features such as the spreading of nasality from [+nasal] segments. Lexical suprasegmental features must be recorded. Tone and stress contrasts are usually fairly easy to illustrate in citation forms, but one has to ensure that the variation that occurs in different prosodic domains is also captured. Therefore phrases or sentences illustrating features such as tonal sandhi and stress shifts must be included.

It cannot be emphasized too strongly that the preparation of good word lists is the key to linguistic phonetic fieldwork. However much one prepares one inevitably finds that on returning from the field and doing the analysis of the data some things have been omitted or not adequately covered. I am often only too aware that I should have recorded additional material further illustrating contrasts or allophonic distributions that I had not considered important when out in the field. But adequate preparation can avoid many pitfalls. One cannot spend too much time checking word lists and making sure that all the contrasts and all the interesting allophonic distributions are included. I find it useful to make consonant, vowel and suprasegmental charts, and words illustrating each item (much as the "Illustrations" of languages in the *Journal of the International Phonetic Association*) even before going out into the field. When the time comes to work with speakers of the language, it often turns out that they do not know some of the words, or pronounce them differently. But it pays to have thought the whole process through before beginning work with native speakers.

Citation forms and carefully controlled sets of phrases and sentences provide the best overall view of the phonetic structures in a language, but they do not provide sufficient information on the rhythm of the language, and on larger units such as contrasting intonation patterns. In an effort to record at least some material that would illustrate these properties, a short narrative or other material containing longer stretches of speech should be included. This might be a local folk tale, a short autobiographical narrative, or perhaps something more standardized. We have found that a suitable way of recording a short text is to ask speakers to repeat a story that has been told to them. If the story is illustrated by a series of pictures, then the pictures can be used as prompts in the subsequent re-telling.

3 Linguistic consultants

Probably the questions asked most often by people considering doing phonetic fieldwork are "How many speakers do I need, and how do I find them?" There are no set answers to these questions. It is clear that it is no longer appropriate to present data based on instrumental records of only a single speaker, as some misguided phoneticians have done in the past (Ladefoged, 1968). But beyond that it depends on the language and the local circumstances. One wants a group of people who all speak in the same way, so that it is a single dialect of a language that is being described, but who do not all belong to the same family, so that there is sufficient diversity for any familial idiosyncrasies to be noticeable. For quantitative phonetic work an absolute minimum of three people of each sex is essential; and it is definitely preferable to have at least half a dozen women and men. Of course, in the case of languages with few native speakers, or when the field worker has limited time in the field, it may not be possible to get sufficient numbers; but it is difficult to provide meaningful measurements without a sample of at least six people of each sex.

The best speakers for phonetic research are usually not the old people who know the language well. These people may be the most helpful for finding appropriate illustrative words; but even when eliciting phonological contrasts, they can be troublesome because they have their own agenda. They are often eager to tell stories or sing songs, and they nearly always want to make sure that all the details of the meaning are understood, and that notice is taken of all the homophones of each word. These points may be useful and fascinating for other linguists, but usually all the phonetician wants is to be sure that the gloss has been noted faithfully enough to allow another linguist to be able to repeat the data gathering by eliciting the same form. Once the material to be recorded has been established, it is preferable to use younger speakers, with stronger voices (and all their teeth). School children in their teens often make excellent consultants; they enjoy playing teacher and correcting the fieldworker's mistakes.

4 Instrumental techniques

The major concern of this paper is the instrumental phonetic techniques that are needed for a good description of the phonetic structures. The use of phonetic instrumentation in the field is comparatively recent. There is a story about Daniel Jones, the great British phonetician who dominated the field in the first half of this century. When he was about to go off on a field trip someone asked him what instruments he was going to take with him. He pointed to his ears and said: "Only these." It is surely true that by far the most valuable assets a phonetician can have are a trained set of ears. It is also true (and Daniel Jones would certainly have agreed) that the ears should be coupled to highly trained vocal organs that are capable of producing a wide range of sounds. There is no substitute for the ability to hear small distinctions in sounds. There is also no substitute for the ability to pronounce alternative possibilities, so that one can ask a speaker which of two pronunciations sounds better. One of the most efficient procedures for getting results in the field is to test different hypotheses by trying out various vocal gestures of one's own.

Nevertheless, however well trained they might be, phoneticians who now go out with only their ears and their own vocal apparatus are doing themselves a dis-service. There are three ways in which instrumental aids can be valuable supplements to the field phonetician. Firstly they can sometimes suggest new descriptive possibilities; we have, for example, learned a number of facts about the unusual voiceless nasals that occur in the Tibeto-Burman language Angami by observing records of the airflow from the mouth and the nose (Bhaskararao and Ladefoged, 1991). Secondly instruments allow permanent records to be made so that one can demonstrate the facts to those who do not have access to speakers of the language being described. Thus readers might believe descriptions of the curious consonant clusters that occur in Khoisan languages without any instrumental evidence; but it is nice to have records so that they can see for themselves (Ladefoged and Traill, 1994). Thirdly, instruments enable one to make quantitative descriptions. However good one's ears, one cannot, for example, measure and report the duration in milliseconds of the aspiration of stops in different contexts; and without measurements one cannot prove that there is a statistically significant difference between one group of stops and another, or between the sounds of one language and another.

4.1 Acoustic data

For almost half a century the most important instrument available to the phonetician has been the tape recorder. Before World War II phoneticians had to rely on their notes and their skill in making phonetic transcriptions. But since that time few phoneticians would start a fieldwork investigation of a language without having some means of making recordings. We will begin this section with a discussion of techniques for making recordings.

Recordings can be like audible notebook jottings, or like more formal finished papers that demonstrate the sounds of a language. In either case a recording should *always* begin with a statement of the date, the place, the names of the speakers, and the material. These things will no doubt be written on a label; but labels can come off and tapes can easily get put into the wrong box, and become virtually useless unless they have been properly identified. When recording on a portable tape recorder it is also advisable to record a known signal such as a tuning fork at the beginning and the end of a recording session. This provides a useful check on the speed of the recording.

If it is possible, all the preliminary labeling procedures should be carried out before setting up to record the language consultant. The whole process of making a fieldwork recording should be done with as little fuss and as inconspicuously as possible. (Of course, recordings should not be made surreptitiously. The speakers must be asked if they mind being recorded.) One can often make good recordings unobtrusively by walking in with a tape recorder in one pocket or slung over the shoulder, and a microphone in another pocket, already connected and ready to be produced at the appropriate moment.

Tape recordings should be of the highest quality possible. Interviews sometimes have to take place amidst noises such as background talking and household sounds that the fieldworker can ignore. But on a recording for linguistic phonetic purposes anything other than the voice of the language consultant can be a distraction. We have found that when trying to make a high quality recording it is often a good idea to go off outside. But this may prove less convenient on windy days. It is possible to protect the microphone itself from the effect of the wind by using a wind-shield, a protective covering of foam rubber or a similar substance. But it is more difficult to deal with the noise of the wind in the trees, although much can be achieved by finding a large enough open space. Both in everyday parlance and in the technical acoustic terminology, the best recordings are often those made in a free field, rather than in a noisy, reverberant room.

The intensity (loudness) of the speech being recorded should be as high as possible without overloading the tape recorder. This requires proper use of the microphone. The intensity varies with the square of the distance between the source of the sound and the microphone. A baby crying ten feet away may be one quarter of the loudness of a speaker who is five feet from the microphone; but the same baby will be only one hundredth of the loudness of a speaker who is one foot from the microphone. If recordings must be made in circumstances where there is a lot of background noise, make sure that the speaker is a close but constant distance away. We have found so-called lip-microphones fastened to a headset to be excellent for recording one speaker at a time. They are usually designed so that they cancel sounds coming from the other side, which makes them suitable for recording even in a slightly noisy room. When recording a group of people, arrange them in a small circle. If you have somebody else to operate the tape recorder and watch the signal level, then you can move around and control the recording by holding the microphone just in front of the speaker who should be speaking. If you are alone, place the microphone on something soft at least a few feet from the tape recorder.

Check the signal level frequently while making the recordings, as speakers often vary their loudness. The signal should always be at the highest permissible level, so as to make sure that it is as far above the background noise as possible. Finally, after making a recording, play it back and verify that you have proper written notes to explain what is on it. As soon as you can, play all your recordings right through, checking them against a complete text. (We try to do this every night, so that we never accumulate data that is not useful.)

What sort of machine should be used for making field recordings? DAT (digital) recorders are superior to analog (cassette) recorders; virtually any DAT recorder will be more than adequate for linguistic phonetic purposes. Cassette recorders can vary widely in quality, and it is important that the one chosen should meet certain specifications. Firstly it should have a good frequency response – that is to say it should be able to reproduce the complete range of frequencies recorded with the same relative intensities as when they were originally produced. People in their prime can hear sounds with frequencies around 20,000 Hz, but this ability declines with age. No language relies on distinctions that can be heard only by young adults, and a frequency range up to 12,000 Hz should be sufficient for linguistic purposes. Any DAT recorder will be able to record this range, but only so-called professional cassette recorders will. Secondly the tape recorder should have a good S/N (signal to noise) ratio. The difference between the maximum signal that can be recorded without overloading and the noise that is present in the absence of any signal should be at least 45 db. DAT recorders have about twice this range, but even professional quality cassette recorders often only just exceed it. Thirdly speed variations, whether of the short term kind known as flutter, or the day to day kind due to variations in the batteries and motors, should be less than 0.1 per cent. This is usually no longer a problem for any recorder, as long as the batteries are not run down. In addition, the tape recorder, like any other piece of apparatus taken into the field, should be tough and reliable. It should be possible to drop it on the floor and kick it around for a few minutes without too much damage. We have heard stories of professional tape recorders that have been fished out of rivers, dried out, and found to be still working. The stories are probably apocryphal, but they provide a good standard to aim for.

Before going into the field, the tape recorder should be thoroughly checked out. If it has rechargeable batteries, make sure that they are not only fully charged, but also are capable of maintaining their charge for as long as is required. In any case, spare batteries are a necessity that should not be forgotten. We have found rechargeable batteries useful when we have a vehicle available, as they can be recharged with the aid of a unit that plugs into the dashboard. On analog recorders (as opposed to DAT machines) the heads should be cleaned and demagnetized (simple procedures that may increase the frequency response by as much as 5,000 Hz), and the frequency response checked. Record frequencies from 50 Hz to 15,000 Hz at about half octave intervals, checking with a meter that they are all being produced by the signal generator at the same level. Then observe on a meter the relative intensities of these signals when they are played back, so as to make sure that the tape recorder really has a full frequency range. A plot of the frequency response of a Sony Professional cassette recorder used on a field trip is shown in Figure 5.1. In addition, check the S/N ratio, and, if the necessary equipment is available, the speed constancy.

As portable computers become more available, the days of dependence on tape recorders may be passing. Direct recording onto portable computers may be used, with the tape recorder being regarded simply as a backup. As with the tape recorders discussed above, the computer battery can be kept charged with the aid of a unit plugged into a vehicle's dashboard. Even when considered just as devices for reproducing sounds, computers are much more versatile than tape recorders. Fieldworkers want to be able to record word lists or short paragraphs and then to play back selected pieces over and over again, so that they can hear subtle nuances of sounds that are new to them. They also want to be able to hear one sound, and then, immediately afterwards, hear another that may contrast with it. Both tasks can be done somewhat cumbersomely and tediously using tape recorders. But they are trivial, normal operations on any computer equipped with a means for digitizing and editing recorded sounds. Figure 5.2 is an illustration of a computer screen while using the commercially available program SoundEdit™ with a MacRecorder. Clicking on the icon representing a speaker in either of the windows on the screen will play the utterance in that window. This makes it easy, or at least easier, to hear the difference between the two words shown in this illustration, exemplifying the contrast between so-called stiff and slack syllables in Bruu, a Mon Khmer language spoken in Thailand. Comparison of the two words is also aided by being able to see from the waveforms that the stop at the beginning

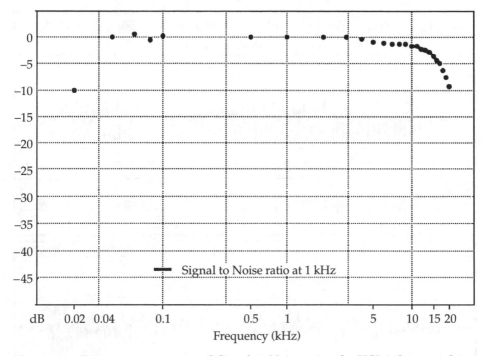

Figure 5.1 Frequency response and Signal to Noise ratio of a UCLA Sony used in recent fieldwork.

of the word in the lower window is slightly more aspirated than the stop in the upper window.

It is worth considering at this point some of the specifications of a computer system suitable for use in linguistic fieldwork. Sound waves have to be stored on a computer as a series of numbers (samples) representing the amplitude of the wave at regular intervals. There are two factors affecting the fidelity with which a given wave is stored. The first is the rate at which the amplitude of the wave is sampled. The sample rate must be at least twice the frequency of the highest frequency component in the wave. The second is the accuracy of the representation of the amplitude of each sample. If each amplitude can be represented as any one out of 1,024 possible numbers, then the stored wave can be more like the original sound wave than if each amplitude has to be represented as one out of only 256 possible values.

Bearing this in mind, we can now determine the sample rate and sample size required for a computer system that is to be used for phonetic fieldwork. As we noted earlier in discussing tape recordings, a frequency range from 60 Hz to 12,000 Hz is sufficient for most linguistic investigations. In fact, although some speech sounds (particularly voiceless stops and fricatives) may differ significantly in the amplitude of the frequency components in the 10,000 to 20,000 Hz range, the major differences (even in voiceless stops and fricatives)

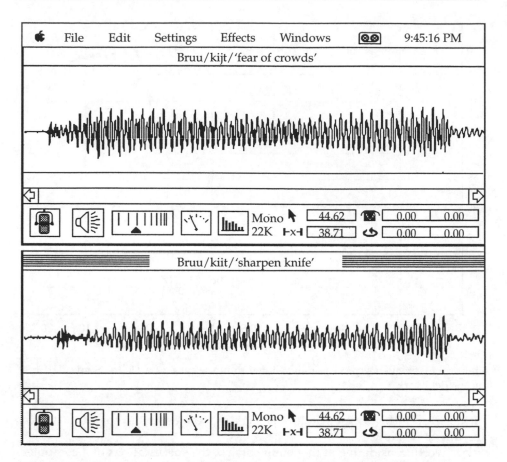

Figure 5.2 Computer screen showing two words in Bruu, a Mon Khmer language. Either word can be played by clicking on the speaker icon in its window.

are below 8,000 Hz; and for the analysis of vowels and similar sounds it is preferable to record as digital signals *only* frequencies below 4,000 Hz, so that (as will be discussed below) the recorded frequency range can be analyzed using the smallest possible steps. The implications of these requirements are that it is advisable to be able to record speech onto a computer in two different ways, one with a comparatively high fidelity from a speech point of view, capturing frequencies up to 12,000 Hz (although speech high fidelity could perhaps be regarded as up to only 8,000 Hz), and the other ensuring that only frequencies up to 4,000 Hz were recorded. In order to allow some tolerance in the system, the sample rate should be 2.5 times the highest frequency present. Accordingly, the computer system should be capable of sampling speech at 20–24,000 Hz for high quality listening and analysis, and at 10,000 Hz for the analysis of vowels and similar sounds.

The minimum sample size is more difficult to determine. DAT recorders and compact discs used in high fidelity audio systems specify amplitudes in terms of 32,000 possible levels (16 bits), which allows for the maximum signal level recorded to be 96 dB above the system noise. There is no doubt that a Signal/Noise ratio of this magnitude is highly desirable, but it is fully useful only in studio recordings. In most fieldwork situations, it is difficult to record in an environment in which the background noise is as much as 48 dB below the level of a speaker who is as close as possible to the microphone. There is always a baby crying in the next room, or the wind in the trees, or some other noise that cannot be avoided. Accordingly, when recording onto a computer from a well-made analog recording, 256 possible levels (8 bits) providing a 48 dB Signal/Noise ratio may be sufficient, provided that a great deal of care is taken to ensure that the full range is used (i.e. that the original signal is always re-recorded at the maximum level possible without overloading). In linguistic fieldwork, in which citation forms or specific sentences are produced in controlled circumstances, it is often possible to ensure that a maximum signal is recorded. In these situations, 8 bit systems providing a 48 dB Signal/Noise ratio (such as the MacRecorder used by the SoundEdit program illustrated above) are satisfactory for preliminary work. As we noted above, 48 dB is about the Signal/Noise ratio of a good laboratory tape recorder. Few portable cassette recorders (even so-called professional models) have a better Signal/Noise ratio. But it is often not possible to get the speaker to maintain a constant level, or multiple speakers may be being recorded, some having strong voices and others not. In these situations, it is essential to have a system with as great a Signal/Noise ratio as possible, making a 16 bit system highly preferable. In any case, the added margin of safety provided by 16 bit systems is always desirable.

In addition to being useful as a sophisticated playback device, a computer can provide several types of analysis that a fieldworker might find convenient. The most useful display of the general acoustic characteristics of a sound is a spectrogram. Figure 5.3 shows the kind of spectrogram that can be produced on a portable computer without a color (gray scale) screen. The figure is an unretouched copy of the printout from a battery operated printer used in the field. As portable computer screens and printers improve so that they produce better gray scale or color output, this kind of display will become even more useful.

The display in Figure 5.3 was created by another commercially available program, Signalyze. Spectrograms generated by this program on a color screen on a laboratory computer are much more impressive. But even the quality of the display in Figure 5.3 can be very useful to the fieldworker. The words shown illustrate the four contrastive sibilants that occur in Toda, a Dravidian language spoken in the Nilgiri Hills in India. Each of these words ends in a different sibilant. The overall spectral characteristics of these sibilants are evident. The laminal dental sibilant at the end of the first word has the highest frequency, and the retroflex sibilant at the end of the last word has the lowest.

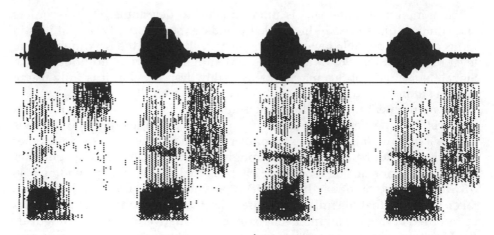

Figure 5.3   A spectrogram of [koṣ, poṣ, poʃ, poṣ] "money, milk, language, clan name" in Toda, made under field conditions.

The apical alveolar and (laminal) palatoalveolar sibilants at the ends of the second and third word have very similar spectral characteristics. (The lowering of the spectral energy peak at the end of the second word is a non-distinctive feature, being simply due to the closure of the lip for the consonant at the beginning of the next word.) These two sibilants are distinguished primarily by their on-glides. The increasing second formant at the end of the third word is due to the raising of the blade and front of the tongue for this laminal sound. In the last word, the lowering of the third formant is probably due to the sublingual cavity that is formed by raising the tip of the tongue for this retroflex sibilant. A great deal of information can be obtained even from these low quality spectrograms, actually produced under field conditions and computer cut and pasted into this paper. Of course, still more information can be obtained from high quality spectrograms produced by this or another program on a laboratory computer at a later date.

Another kind of analysis that is very useful to the fieldworker is one that indicates the pitch. The Signalyze program discussed above will generate good displays of the fundamental frequency (and it will produce narrow band spectrograms, which are sometimes even more useful for pitch analysis when a creaky voice quality or other unusual spectral characteristics are involved). But a number of other programs will also provide similar information. Figure 5.4 shows the fundamental frequency in a pair of words with contrasting tones in Sukuma, a Bantu language, as analyzed by a public domain modification of SoundWave, written at the University of Uppsala, Sweden.

The final kind of computer analysis of speech sounds that will be illustrated here is one for determining the formant frequencies, the principal aspects of vowel quality. A common way of obtaining formant frequencies is by inspection and peak picking using superimposed LPC and FFT displays of the kind

Figure 5.4 The tonal contrast between /ku'laamba/ "to lick", and /kulaamba/ "to be dear", in Sukuma, a Bantu language spoken in Tanzania.

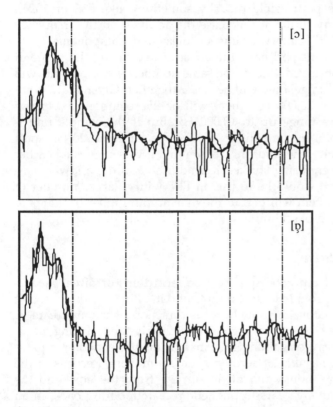

Figure 5.5 Superimposed FFT and LPC spectra of two Assamese vowels, made using a portable computer in the field.

shown in Figure 5.5. The original display was also produced by the Uppsala version of SoundWave mentioned above (slightly further modified at UCLA). The figure shows analyses of two Assamese (Indo-Aryan) vowels that are very similar in quality; one is between the IPA reference vowels [ɔ] and [o], and the other is a vowel with a tongue position like that in [ɑ], but a lip position more like that in [u]. In each of these two vowels, there are two formants close together; but the more rounded vowel in the lower part of the figure has a very sharp decrease in spectral energy immediately above the second formant. The third formant is not clear in either of these vowels.

When making an FFT it is important to remember the system limitations. In effect, an FFT provides the amplitudes of the spectral components that are present on the assumption that these components are all multiples of a wave with a frequency depending on the number of points in the FFT. The greater the number of points in the FFT, the longer the wave length, thus the lower the frequency of this wave, and the smaller the interval between calculated components. But any program calculating an FFT will have a certain maximum number of points permissible (usually something like 512 or 1024). Accordingly, the only way to further increase the accuracy in the frequency domain (i.e. to decrease the interval between measured components) is to *decrease* the sample rate. This will have the effect of decreasing the range of frequencies that can be observed. But, as the same number of components will be calculated within that range, they will be closer together. Given a 512 point FFT and a sample rate of 20,000 Hz, there will be 256 components spaced about 40 Hz apart in the range up to 10,000 Hz. But if the sample rate is reduced to 10,000 Hz, the 256 components will be spaced about 20 Hz apart in the range up to 5,000 Hz. It was for this reason that it was suggested earlier that if vowel formants were being studied it is advisable to use a lower sampling rate. The alternative would be to use an FFT with a larger number of points, but no analysis system will permit the maximum number of points to be increased beyond some fixed limit.

4.2 Aerodynamic data

Acoustic analyses made from good quality tape recordings or direct recording onto a computer can provide large amounts of data. But they often do not indicate important articulatory facts such as the direction of the airstream or the timing of movements of the vocal organs, particularly those during voiceless closures. The best way of gaining information on these phonetic parameters is by recording a number of aerodynamic parameters. Records of the pressure of the air in the mouth and of the airflow from the nose and the lips have been used for many years in phonetic research, dating back, in an unquantified way, to the kymograph tracings of Rousselot (1924–5), Scripture (1923), and other early experimental phoneticians. For many years we have been able to make good, calibrated, records of these variables (Ladefoged, 1967). Now this ability is available to the field phonetician.

The principal aerodynamic parameters with which we will be concerned are: (1) the pressure of the air in the mouth behind any bilabial closure; (2) the pressure of the air in the pharynx, behind any alveolar, velar or uvular closure; (3) the subglottal pressure; (4) the flow of air in and out of the nose; (5) the flow of air in and out of the mouth.

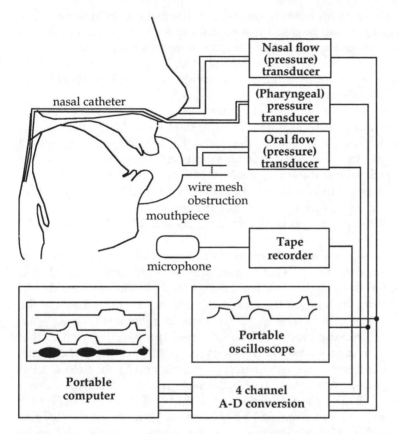

Figure 5.6 Apparatus for obtaining aerodynamic records in the field.

Examples of the use of some of these parameters for elucidating articulatory descriptions of West African languages have been given by Ladefoged (1968). In these examples the data were recorded live by subjects in the laboratory using a four channel inkwriter. Nowadays it is possible to record such data in the field using a portable computer. One type of system for use in the field is shown in Figure 5.6. It will record the audio signal and up to three physiological signals. Typically these include either the pressure of the air in the pharynx obtained by passing a tube through the nose, or the pressure of the air in the mouth using a more convenient tube between the lips, and the oral and nasal air flow. In investigations of prosodic features it is sometimes appropriate to record an approximation to the subglottal pressure by means of a tube with a small balloon on the end of it in the esophagus.

We will begin our discussion of a system for recording aerodynamic parameters in the field by noting some general requirements of such a system. It should obviously be light weight, compact, and battery operated. As with the tape recorder, it should be rugged enough to withstand the pounding it is likely to get while being transported into places where there are no roads. The air pressure devices should be capable of measuring ± 25 cm H₂O. The air flow devices should be constructed so that they measure ingressive and egressive air flow rates up to 2 litres/second. They should have a flat frequency response, so that they do not give different readings for sounds with identical flow rates said on different pitches.

There are also a number of practical points to take into consideration when making pressure and flow recordings. The tubes used should be short and as thick as the speaker can conveniently tolerate, so that they have a high enough frequency response to show some voicing vibrations. Long thin tubes act as acoustic filters and cut out the small pressure variations associated with voicing. Generally, tubes should be sealed at the end, with small holes at the sides near the tip to let the pressure in. Tubes that are open at the end often become full of mucus. We have found infant feeding tubes, size 12 French, to be suitable.

When recording the pressure of the air in the mouth one end of the tube should be connected to the pressure transducer, and the other end should be held (by the speaker) so that it is just behind the lips. The speaker should be discouraged from sucking on the end of the oral tube, as this leads to the tube becoming full of saliva, which will lower its frequency response.

The pharyngeal pressure tube should be inserted through the nose so that its open end rests on the back wall of the pharynx about 1 cm below the uvula. The speaker should first be given a practical demonstration by the field-worker of how easy it is to pass a tube through the nose into the pharynx. Take a clean, sterile, tube. (Tubes should be cleaned with disinfectant and boiled for 30 minutes if they have to be reused.) Hold it about 12 cm from the tip, and moisten it with saliva. If it has a slight natural curve, make sure that this curve is pointing downwards. Then, still holding the tube about 12 cm from the end, push it straight (i.e. horizontally, not upward) back into the nose until some obstruction is reached. It is advisable to be fairly rapid about this part of the proceedings. Many people find the most difficult part of the process to be the irritation that may occur while they are tentatively pushing just inside the nostril. Once an obstruction has been reached, take a mouthful of water, and while pushing the tube gently further in, swallow a small quantity. Keep pushing gently, swallowing, and breathing in through the nose until the tube has passed over the top of the velum into the pharynx. A large ingressive breath will cause the velum to lower more, and may help the tube go round and into the mouth. If there is any difficulty in getting the tube to pass round the velum, twist it slightly, first one way then another, all while swallowing or taking a deep breath through the nose, and gently pushing. Remember to hold your hand high above the level of the nose, so that the tube is never pushed upward, but always goes straight back (and, hopefully, down). Nearly everybody finds it easier to pass the tube through one nostril rather than the other, so if at first you don't succeed, try again with the other one.

For an average male adult about 15 cm of the tube should be inserted into the nose in order to locate the open end properly. It is a good idea to make a mark by putting a thread around the tube at slightly more than this distance before beginning the experiment. As soon as the tube is located properly in the pharynx the speaker should relax quietly for a moment in order to avoid a gag reflex. Check the location of the tube by using a flashlight (a small, focused pen light) while looking into the speaker's mouth. It may be necessary to use some object such as a spoon or a spatula to depress the speaker's tongue in order to see the end of the tube. If it is correctly located about 1 cm below the uvula, fasten the tube to the cheek just outside the nose with a small sticking plaster. When recording pharyngeal pressure through a nasal catheter, it is necessary to keep the tube free from mucus. Before attaching the end to the pressure transducer, connect it to a rubber bulb and blow some air through it. Repeat this procedure at frequent intervals throughout the recording.

A similar procedure can be used for passing a tube into the esophagus so as to estimate the subglottal pressure. In short phrases the esophageal pressure is a very good indication of the pressure below the vocal cords; but in longer sentences there will be a shift of the baseline upwards due to the changes in the relaxation pressure of the air in the lungs. In any case it is usually possible to get a fairly precise measure of the relation between the pressure recorded in the esophagus and that in the trachea by recording the pressure in the mouth with a tube between the lips during the pronunciation of voiceless bilabial stops. During a voiceless stop the pressure in the mouth will be the same as that in the trachea, so the esophageal pressure record can be calibrated from the oral pressure record. For recording subglottal pressure it is necessary to pass 30–35 cm of tube through the nose. Put markers on the tube at these distances before beginning, so that the position of the end can be estimated. A tube that is to be passed into the esophagus should be sealed by having a small balloon about 1 cm on the end of it. The cut off end of a condom can be used for this purpose, tying it on to the end of the tube with thread. When the tube is in the esophagus the balloon end should be inflated slightly.

In the system we have been describing, the pressure in the esophagus, or the pharynx, or behind the lips, has been recorded through tubes connected to pressure sensors mounted on the apparatus outside the mouth. An alternative technique is to use miniature pressure transducers which can be placed at the ends of the tubes passed through the nose into the esophagus or the pharynx or between the lips into the oral cavity. Miniature transducers are more convenient in many ways, particularly for recording esophageal or pharyngeal pressures; but they require more complex electronics, are more expensive, and have to be treated with more care than fieldwork conditions often allow. In general, for recording gross changes of air pressure of the kind that are associated with articulatory movements, externally mounted transducers are sufficient.

Pressure recordings may be calibrated using a water manometer, or more simply (and only slightly less accurately) by connecting one arm of a tube in

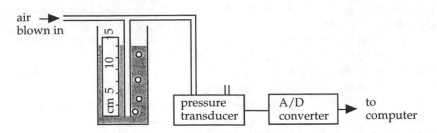

Figure 5.7   Calibrating a pressure transducer.

the form of a T piece to the pressure transducer, and the center of the T to a tube attached to a ruler in a container of water as shown in Figure 5.7. Blow into the other arm of the T until bubbles come out of the tube. At this time the pressure exerted on the transducer will be equivalent to the depth of the open end of the tube in the water. Repeat this procedure with varying depths, so that signals are produced over the entire range of interest (probably up to 15 cm H_2O). When these signals are reproduced a scale can be created showing the relation between the variations in the signal and the set of known pressures.

Variations in airflow are slightly more difficult to record than variations in air pressure. The most suitable way of measuring the rate of air flow in speech is by measuring the slight increase in pressure that occurs when the air flows through a fine wire mesh. Rothenberg (1973, 1977) has described a mask with built in stainless steel gauze that provides the appropriate kind of resistance. This system measures egressive or ingressive flows by converting them to small positive or negative pressures which can be transduced. It can be calibrated by connecting it to a commercially available flow meter, a device containing a ball in a tube; the greater the airflow, the higher the ball rises in the tube. With a little practice one can learn to blow steadily at a number of different rates, so that one can observe the flow meter readings that correspond to different signals, as shown in Figure 5.8. More accurate measure can be made in the laboratory by using a vacuum cleaner controlled by a variable voltage, reversing the drive to the fan, so that the device blows instead of sucking.

In fieldwork situations it may be necessary to have a face mask that can be used by speakers with very different features from those of the standard speaker of American English for whom the commercially available form of the Rothenberg mask was designed. Suitable masks can be made by taking a small rubber mixing bowl (available from a dental supply house) and cutting an opening in the bottom so as to connect it to a tube containing a stainless steel mesh. The frequency response of the system is not as good as that of the Rothenberg mask; but it is often more satisfactory for recording the overall airflow from the mouth.

For recording airflow from the nose a divided Rothenberg mask can be used. Alternatively, because it is often especially difficult to provide an

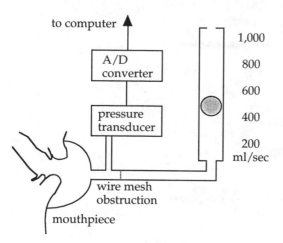

Figure 5.8   Calibration of oral airflow.

airtight division for speakers with different features, nasal airflow can be recorded separately. The flow of air from the nose is usually very small indeed, and it is simplest to gather it by two tubes ending in bulbs (nasal olives) lightly inserted into the nostril. A good fit into the nostril can be achieved using malleable earplugs with tubes going through them. These tubes are then joined and led out from the face mask into a tube containing a wire gauze. In practice it is difficult to collect air from both nostrils if one nostril is also being used for a catheter in the esophagus or the pharynx. If a calibrated record of the nasal airflow is required, this nostril must be sealed off completely, and the nasal flow recorded through the other one. Alternatively, if it is sufficient to record just the relative amount of nasal airflow at different moments (as, for instance, when recording different degrees of nasalization), then the build up of the air pressure in one nostril can be recorded directly, the other nostril through which the air may be flowing providing the (uncalibratable) resistance. In any case, whether one nostril or both are used, the small pressure build up is measured and used as an indication of the flow.

Figure 5.9 illustrates nasal and oral airflow recorded in this way, so as to show the aerodynamic features of Angami voiceless nasals (Bhaskararao and Ladefoged, 1991). In most South East Asian languages with voiceless nasals (e.g. Burmese), the last part of phonologically voiceless nasals is actually voiced, the vocal cords vibrate before the oral closure is released, while there is still nasal airflow. But as can be seen in Figure 5.9, in Angami these nasals are aspirated, with the oral closure being released while there is voiceless nasal airflow. These sounds are discussed in Blankenship, Ladefoged, Bhaskararao, and Chase (1993).

We can see that the value of a portable computer in phonetic fieldwork extends beyond its use in recording and analyzing sounds. It can also be an

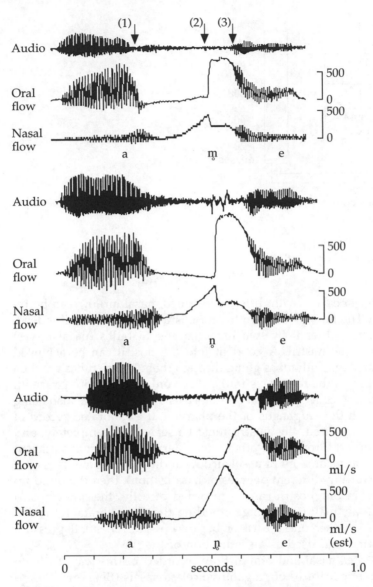

Figure 5.9 The voiceless aspirated nasals in Angami.

important part of a system for recording aerodynamic data. The parameters we have been discussing can be digitized along with the audio signal from a microphone. The sample rate required for digitizing the physiological parameters depends on the kind of information that is being sought. Records of the oral airflow can be filtered so as to remove the formant resonances and reveal the shape of the waveform produced at the glottis (Rothenberg, 1977; Javkin, Antoñanzas-Barroso, and Maddieson, 1987). If this is the intent, then an appropriate face mask such as that described by Rothenberg (1977) will have to be used, and the oral airflow should be digitized at 5,000 Hz. But if the intent is to use the physiological parameters to show the gross movements of the vocal organs, then a sample rate of 500 Hz is sufficient.

The system in Figure 5.6 also shows two of the channels being monitored on a battery operated portable oscilloscope. This is a luxury that it is very pleasant to have when recording aerodynamic data in the field. This device makes it possible to check the calibration voltages and signals as they are being recorded, and to do simple maintenance tasks when required. (We used one to find a fault in the ignition system of our vehicle when a short circuit occurred while out in the Kalahari Desert.) Equally importantly a portable storage oscilloscope combined with a camera for photographing the screen, provides a back up system for recording in the event of a computer failure. The value of back up systems cannot be overemphasized. As all fieldworkers know, things often go wrong. We routinely go on fieldwork trips with a second small (cheaper) tape recorder, two cameras, spare pressure transducers, and spare parts for anything that might break.

4.3 Laryngeal actions

Many aspects of glottal activity can be deduced from aerodynamic records, or observed in acoustic analyses. We have seen above how airflow records can be used to illustrate characteristics of aspiration in Angami; and Ladefoged, Maddieson, and Jackson (1988) have exemplified ways of quantifying phonation types such as breathy voice and creaky voice using acoustic analyses.

More direct observations of laryngeal activity can be made using an electroglottograph, which (substantially) provides a signal proportional to the degree of contact between the vocal cords. The signal actually reflects the electrical impedance between two electrodes placed on the surface of the neck, one on either side of the larynx. Consequently, it is affected by movements of the larynx beneath the skin, as well as by the opening and closing of the vocal cords, and by the degree of force with which they are thrust together.

The electroglottograph signal can be recorded on a computer in the same way as the aerodynamic signals described above. Figure 5.10 shows the aerodynamic and laryngeal activity that occurred during the pronunciation of the Montana Salish phrase /ʧ'ʧen'/ "Where to". The top line shows, on an expanded time scale, the laryngeal activity that occurred in the final laryngealized nasal /n'/. In this case this sound is realized with final creaky voice and a glottal stop. (Other speakers often produce this sound with a few periods of creaky voice after the glottal stop as well.)

The larynx record also reflects the laryngeal movements associated with the ejective [ʧ']. It cannot be taken as a direct indication of larynx raising and lowering, both because the gross movements of the larynx do not affect glottal impedance in a way that is directly proportional to larynx movement, and

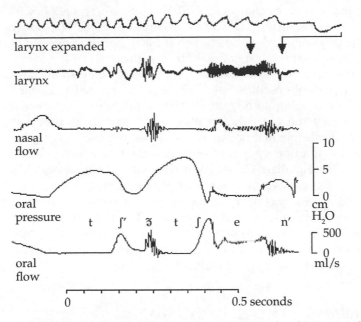

Figure 5.10   Laryngeal and aerodynamic records of Montana Salish.

because this record has been band-pass filtered (30–5,000 Hz). If it had not been filtered, the small changes due to the opening and closing of the glottis (which were the major focus of the investigation) would have appeared insignificant in comparison with the large changes associated with the movements of the larynx. Nevertheless, the record clearly shows that there is greater laryngeal activity during the closure of the ejective than there is for other sounds. Both the larynx record and the nasal flow record show that there is an epenthetic (non-contrastive) nasalized vowel after the ejective.

The aerodynamic records show that in this case the ejective [ʧ'] did not have a higher oral pressure than the pulmonic affricate [ʧ] that follows it. The comparatively slow decreases in the pressure and the corresponding increases in the oral flow are typical of affricates.

4.4 Recording the place of articulation

Fieldworkers want to know not only the manner but also the place of articulation. Photographs of the lips can be very informative particularly if a mirror is used so that a full face and side views are recorded simultaneously. Figure 5.11 shows the contrast between the bilabial and labiodental fricatives /ɸ, f/ in Kwangali (Bantu) recorded in this way. As discussed more fully in Ladefoged (1990), a salient aspect of the difference is that, for the labiodental, the lower lip is drawn back behind the upper teeth. This may be observed most clearly

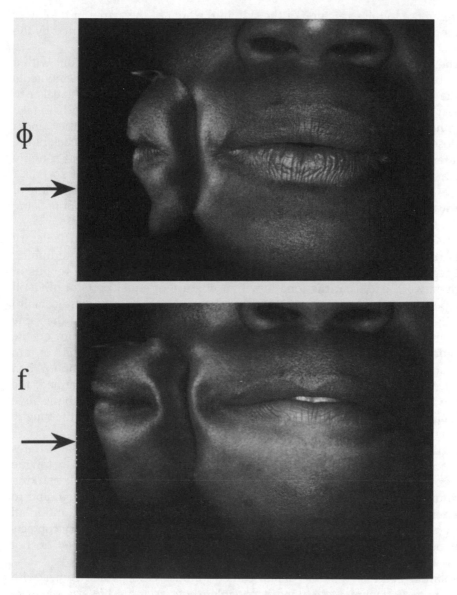

Figure 5.11   Photographs of the lips during the pronunciation of bilabial and labiodental fricatives /ɸ, f/ in Kwangali.

by reference to the stretching of the skin in the area of the arrow in the lower photograph, which does not occur at the corresponding point indicated by the arrow in the case of the bilabial.

The best way of recording lip positions is with a video camera. But with a little practice it is quite possible to take photographs at appropriate moments in the words being investigated using an ordinary camera. Ask the speaker to repeat the sound in a phrase, over and over again, while you get ready to take the photograph. Have a tape recorder running, and make sure that the camera is close to the microphone, so that there is a clear recording of the click of the shutter when you eventually take the photograph. You can find out roughly when the photograph was taken by playing the recording at half speed. A more precise determination of the time can be made from examination of the waveform or spectrogram of the utterance. If a computer system is being used, this can easily be done in the field.

Palatography is a well known traditional method of obtaining articulatory data (Abercrombie, 1957; Ladefoged, 1957). The best method of determining the region of the upper surface of the vocal tract contacted by the tongue in a given word is to coat the tongue with a mixture of equal parts of olive oil and powdered charcoal (Dart, 1991). Then ask the speaker to say a word containing the sound to be investigated and no other consonants made in the same articulatory region. When this has been done, the marking medium on the tongue will have been trasferred to the upper articulator. Insert a mirror into the mouth, and use it to view and photograph the place of articulation. When all the required pictures of the roof of the mouth have been obtained, the procedure can be reversed. Paint the upper surface of the mouth with the olive oil and charcoal mixture, and observe (and photograph) the part of the tongue that is making the contact.

Figure 5.12 (from Spajić, Ladefoged, Maddieson, and Sands, 1993) illustrates a pair of contrasting words recorded during fieldwork on Dahalo. The tongue has contacted the roof of the mouth and has transferred the black marking medium to the post-alveolar area in the case of the word on the left, and to the denti-alveolar area for the word on the right. Note that in these and in all such photographs, the contact areas reflect the sum of the articulatory contacts that occurred in the pronunciation of the words investigated; they do not show the position at any one particular moment.

Polaroid makes a suitable dental camera, model CU5, which comes with mirrors and attachments making it possible to get accurate life size pictures, as in Figure 5.12. Alternatively, a video camera can be used. There are a number of advantages to using a video camera. Firstly it is cheaper to buy and to use than the special purpose Polaroid camera. Secondly it can be held further away from the subject's face (about 120 cm, using an 8x zoom lens) and still fill the frame; this makes it less intimidating for the speaker. Thirdly, the image can be fed directly into a computer for further processing.

Figure 5.13 shows a picture of the upper surface of a speaker's mouth, exactly as it was captured on the computer screen, except for the scales that

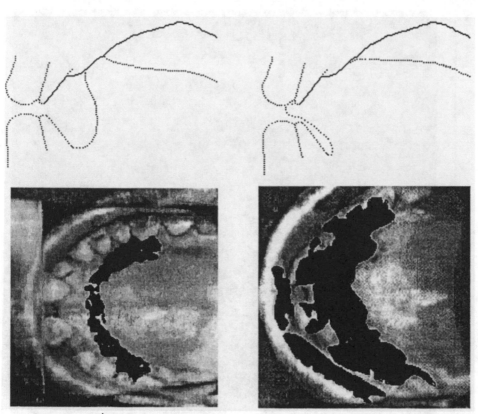

[tʰokke]   [t̪aːmi]

Figure 5.12 Palatograms and sagittal sections showing the contact between a laminal dental (right) and apical alveolar stop in Dahalo (left). The area of contact has been made darker to aid in making the contrast visible, but it is otherwise identical to the unretouched photograph.

have been added around the outside of the photograph. Two rulers were held against the speaker's teeth, one in the sagittal and one in the coronal plane. As the mirror was not exactly at a 45° angle to the plane of the teeth, it may be seen that the posterior anterior dimension is slightly foreshortened. In the horizontal dimension, 10 mm on the ruler in the photograph is equivalent to 20 mm on the scale; but in the vertical dimension, 11 mm on the ruler is equivalent to 20 mm on the scale. This can be corrected quite easily by using a graphics program that permits separate horizontal and vertical scaling of the image. In the particular case shown in Figure 5.13, reducing the horizontal dimension by 50 per cent and the vertical dimension by 55 per cent will produce a life-size image, as shown in the lefthand half of Figure 5.14.

Palatograms should be accompanied by diagrams showing the shape of that

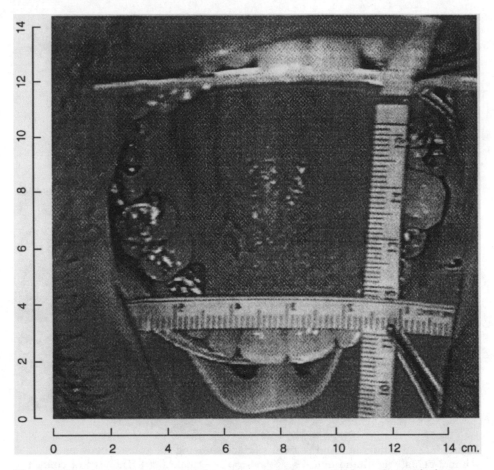

Figure 5.13   A computer image of a mirror placed so as to show the roof of a speaker's mouth, and rulers that have been placed in the plane of the teeth. The scales around the outside of the photograph were added in the computer graphics program.

particular speaker's mouth in the form of a traditional sagittal section. Diagrams of this kind can be based on dental impressions of the oral cavity made in the field. It is best to use an alginate impression material, as other substances which set harder cannot be manipulated suitably. There is no reason for the impression to be made using a tray of the kind that dentists use. All that is needed is an impression of the inner surfaces of the roof of the mouth; as the outer surfaces of the teeth play no role in the production of speech, we can simply neglect them. The easiest way to make an impression is to mix a sufficient quantity of the material and place it on the back of the palatography mirror. Get the speaker to lean slightly forward, and then insert the mirror with the material on it into the mouth. Press the mirror firmly against the

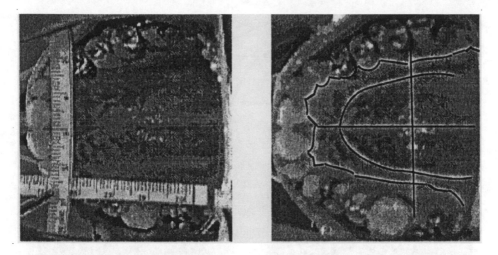

Figure 5.14 Photographs of the roof of a speaker's mouth, (a) as in Figure 5.13, but reduced and transformed into an undistorted life-size view, and (b) with contours drawn as explained in the text.

upper teeth, allowing some of the material to flow out of the mouth around the upper lip. A good impression for phonetic purposes should be made with sufficient material to indicate (at least roughly) the shape of the upper lip and the curvature of the soft palate. The palate will, of course, be in a lowered position, as the speaker will have been breathing through the nose while the impression material is setting. The impression material around the lips sets slightly more slowly than that inside the mouth, where it is slightly warmer. When the material around the lips is firm, it is quite safe to remove the mirror from the mouth, first rocking it back and forth, raising and lowering it slightly, so as to break the seal.

If an alginate impression is to be kept for any length of time it must be immersed in water so as to prevent it from drying and shrinking. Otherwise, take it off the mirror and trim the base flat so that it is parallel to the plane of the teeth. If the mirror really was pressed firmly against the upper teeth while the impression was being made, this should involve no more than the removal of excess material from around the sides. The impression may then be cut in half in the mid-sagittal plane, so as to form an outline for drawing the mid-line of the upper surface of the vocal tract. The exact positions of movable structures such as the lips and the soft palate have to be estimated, but if care has been taken to have sufficient impression material around the lips and as far back in the mouth as possible, the sagittal diagram will be reasonably accurate. Palatograms should always be accompanied by diagrams of this kind, as in Figure 5.12. It has long been established that sagittal sections provide the most useful representations of speech sounds.

It is possible to provide even more information from dental impressions of

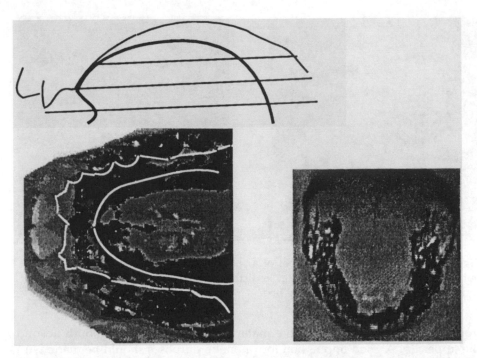

Figure 5.15   Palatogram (bottom left) and linguagram (bottom right) produced during an utterance of the Serbian word [dʒaːk] "student". The upper part of the figure shows a reconstructed sagittal section (see text).

the roof of the mouth. The right hand portion of Figure 5.14 shows records in which the impression material has been used to construct contour lines at fixed distances from the plane of the teeth. Lines showing points 6 mm and 12 mm above the plane of the teeth have been superimposed on the undistorted life-size photograph. In order to draw contour lines of this sort, put the two halves of the impression material together again, and place them between two spacers with a known height. Using these spacers as guides, cut the impression material horizontally, with the blade of the knife parallel to the surface corresponding to the plane of the teeth. Draw a line around the cut edges of the impression material, which will represent a contour at the height of the spacers up from the plane of the teeth. Repeat the process with the remainder of the impression material so as to get additional contour lines. In order to place the contour lines accurately on the photograph it will be necessary to draw two guide lines on both them and the photograph, one corresponding to the midline between the frontal incisors, and the other to a line between two teeth that can be seen on both the impression material and the photograph. These lines are also shown in the righthand photograph in Figure 5.14.

All this information can be put together as shown in Figure 5.15, which is part of an investigation of palatalization in Serbian (Spajić, forthcoming).

In interpreting such records it must be remembered that although the upper surface of the palate may have been accurately mapped, no such accuracy is possible when considering the photographs of the tongue. The photograph of the tongue in this figure shows it when it has been slightly stuck out of the mouth, and is therefore not in the same shape as it was when producing any of the sounds. However, consideration of the contact areas on both the tongue and the palate allows us to reconstruct where the tongue must have moved at some point during the word. It may be seen that the tip and forward part of the blade of the tongue are the articulators. Close to the mid-sagittal plane the contact on the roof of the mouth was on the posterior part of the alveolar ridge, at a level corresponding to the area between the two contour lines. There has also been some contact on the roof of the mouth slightly further back, particularly on the midline itself. The speaker had a number of prominent rugae (small ridges) in this area, which have not been indicated on the diagram of the midsagittal section. The sides of the tongue contacted the roof of the mouth at a level above that of the 12 mm contour. Accordingly, this must be a palatalized sound, with the midline of the tongue being in the vicinity of the area shown by the heavy black line.

We may conclude this section by noting a few practical points in connection with palatography. Firstly, care should be taken in selecting appropriate words. We are often interested in comparing the places of articulation of different sounds. Accordingly words must be chosen that contain these articulations, and do not contain any other similar articulations that might overlap with them. Thus when investigating the difference between [s] and [ʃ] in English one should use words such as "sop-shop" rather than "sot-shot." Similarly one should use either a range of vowels ("seep-sheep, sip-ship, same-shame, Sam-sham, sop-shop, etc.") or, if this is not possible, just open vowels which will not obscure the consonant contacts. As with all instrumental phonetic investigations, time spent selecting suitable words is a good investment.

When doing palatography, one should allow the speaker to practice the task extensively. It is important to get the speakers to relax after the upper surface of the mouth has been painted, so that when they say the word being investigated they do so naturally. It also requires practice to stick the tongue out of the mouth the same way every time. It is obviously important to date and label the photographs as soon as they are taken. When using a video camera, photography can be begun just before the speaker says the word, thus ensuring an audio record of the particular token photographed. In addition, it is preferable to make records of several different speakers saying a few utterances rather than one or two speakers repeating a large number of different utterances. Ideally one would like to get a dozen speakers of the same dialect each repeating a dozen times all the contrasts to be investigated. But making palatographic records is fairly time consuming, and in a world in which resources are limited one may have to be satisfied with half a dozen speakers saying each word once. We hope, however, that gone are the days when phoneticians such as Ladefoged (1964) made general statements about a language based on the palatographic records of a single speaker. We need to find out the properties of the language that a group of speakers have in common, rather than the details of an individual's pronunciation.

5 Concluding comment

The best kinds of instrumental investigations are those that are quantifiable, and to which one can apply statistical techniques such as analysis of variance. Differences *between* individuals have been shown to be much greater than differences *within* an individual's repetitions (Johnson, Ladefoged, and Lindau, 1993b), which is why, if a choice is necessary, it is preferable to record six different individuals saying a single utterance rather than one individual repeating an utterance six times. What we are interested in as linguistic phoneticians are the differences between languages, which means that we must have records of groups of speakers who can be considered to represent the different language. When we are trying to show that there are differences between particular sounds in different languages, we need to show that these differences are statistically large in comparison with differences among the speakers in each group, and also that they are large in comparison with differences among repetitions by a single speaker. When we have done this, we can say that the sounds in the languages represented by the groups really are phonetically different. And that's what linguistic phonetics is all about.

ACKNOWLEDGMENTS

This paper includes some material from a short presentation at the XIIth International Congress of Phonetic Sciences (Ladefoged, 1991), as well as some material from an earlier paper by Ladefoged and Traill (1984). My thanks are due to Tony Traill for his wonderful collaboration in the earlier paper. Many members of the UCLA Phonetics Lab have also contributed helpful comments. My colleague Ian Maddieson has offered much useful advice, and Sinisa Spajić has been particularly helpful in developing palatographic techniques. Support for this work was provided by NSF.

6 Experimental Design and Statistics in Speech Science

WILLIAM M. SHEARER

1 Overview and trends in speech science research

Experimental designs and statistical applications in speech science are characterized by methodology that has a high level of control, both in selection of subjects (i.e., sampling and matching procedures) and in regulation of the experimental environment. This more precise methodology tends to refine the measurements and reduces the potential effects of extraneous variables. It also allows for the achievement of valid results through the use of relatively small numbers of subjects and comparatively uncomplicated statistical treatments.

In the past there has been an acknowledged dichotomy between the basic research in the laboratory of the speech scientist and the applied research conducted in the field by for example a speech clinician. In this chapter most of the examples will be taken from the clinical literature. This difference has been assumed not only in principle, but also in methodology. The designs applied by the speech scientist have tended to be more in the nature of basic research and were more narrowly experimental in nature; those of the clinician tended to be quasi-experimental, limited by the constraints of clinical field conditions, and encompassing larger groups in order to compensate for the wide variance among clinical samples. More recently, however, some trend has appeared toward bringing clinical problems routinely into the laboratory for more precise analysis.

This trend has perhaps come about as a result of simpler and more easily managed computer enhanced laboratory instrumentation, as well as the need to quantify clinical disorders for more objective diagnostic analysis and accountability of intervention techniques. With improved techniques, clinical characteristics can be analyzed more quickly and efficiently in the laboratory, involving a much briefer and less tedious participation from clinical subjects.

This is not to suggest, however, that all clinical problems can or should be brought into the laboratory; field studies, such as those conducted among groups of school children, must still use somewhat less sensitive measures, larger numbers of subjects, and statistical treatments suitable for larger variances in the data. For example, in a study to test story comprehension abilities in young and adolescent school children: "The main participants in the study were 240 students, with 60 enrolled in each of the following grade levels: four, six, eight, and ten." (Nippold, Martin, and Erskine, 1988, p. 20).

In keeping with the apparent trend toward using both clinical and normal (control group) subjects in speech science research an increasingly more popular design for these applications is the factorial design, in which two groups (the clinical and normal groups) are measured under several test conditions. Inclusion of the control group adds another dimension to the analysis, reducing the chances for a type 1 error, and yielding an extra analysis for possible interaction effects between the groups and treatments. The resulting statistic has greater efficiency and power than the basic single factor designs, or the simple comparisons from traditional t tests.

2 Types of statistical design

All designs, broadly speaking, can be divided into those that intend to find differences (comparisons) and those that are to show correlations (relationships). The common types of design used in experimental phonetics cover a wide range of applications, from those involving little or no variance and using only one subject, to those that encompass a wide span of individual differences by averaging groups of pooled data. As a rule, the greater the individual differences in scores, the more subjects will be required in order to get a good estimate of the true average group score. Statistical treatments vary from the descriptive presentation of one variable, to multivariate analyses covering many factors interacting upon each other.

2.1 Completely descriptive studies

The simplest and most direct presentation of results employs only a graphic display of the data, with no computational statistics at all. Kuehn, Templeton, and Maynard (1990), for example, reported that neural spindle cells were present in certain speech muscles, but not in others. There were no numerical data in the analysis. Results consisted of a sample microphoto of muscle tissue to indicate the analysis procedure and a list of muscles that did and did not contain spindles. The results stated simply that spindles were found in the tensor palatine and palatoglossus, but were not found in the levator palatine, palatopharyngeus, uvula, salpingopharyngeus, or the superior constrictor.

2.2 Single subject designs

The single subject design is as yet not a widely used procedural method, but appears to be growing in general acceptance. It is a good choice to be considered when distinctive individual differences within a small group of subjects negate the use of a mean score to represent the results. Although an average score can of course be computed for any set of data, it sometimes does not represent a central tendency for the group and is therefore statistically meaningless. In this situation the single subject design can be applied advantageously, using the data from each individual subject in graphic form to show the outcome.

The term *single subject* is somewhat of a misnomer, in that most examples of this design actually incorporate from one to five or six subjects. When conducted properly it has exceptionally good validity because it demands the use of absolute baselines in raw data measures with little or no variances.

2.3 Traditional single subject designs

In its simplest form this methodology is described as an A B design, in which the A condition refers to the baseline measurement for the subject and the B condition refers to the measures during the experimental trials. Single subject designs are especially good for measuring shifts in speech behavior under different conditions, but are also used very effectively to display the results of training experience.

Figure 6.1 displays the result from a typical single subject study, in which a speaker is first tested in the neutral, or baseline condition, followed by the treatment condition, where the effect of the independent variable (delayed auditory feedback) is shown similar to that described by Harrington (1988). In this case, the data are in the form of nonfluencies, which are shown to change in the treatment condition (i.e., delayed auditory feedback). The basic

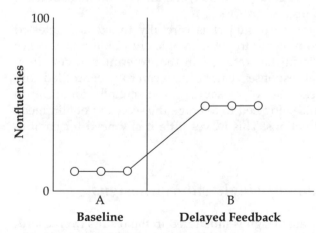

Figure 6.1 Proportions of nonfluencies in one normal speaker are shown for talking during the baseline (normal) condition and under delayed auditory feedback.

elements of the study are displayed as an A B design, which indicates that a baseline is first measured, followed by part B measures for the treatment condition. The results are stated in a definitive statement, usually without computational statistics, in which the reader is referred directly to the graph to support the conclusions. In this example the nonfluency level of the normal speaker is clearly shown to increase under the delayed feedback condition.

The earlier examples of single subject designs were comparatively rigid, and limited only to a specific set of circumstances in the classic psychophysical mode. More recently, however, single subject designs have shown more creative applications in contrast to the earlier straight-line results. Nevertheless, the flexibility and potential scope of these applications are still considered to be greatly underutilized (Connell and Thompson, 1986). Some examples are designed to display trends or even changes in variability as the main result. A variety of practical illustrations and a comprehensive discussion of this type of design is presented by Hegde (1987) and by McReynolds and Thompson (1986).

The potential weakness of the single subject design is in the assumption that the few subjects studied are representative of the population as a whole. Although this assumption is not unreasonable for many types of measure, the designs tend to emphasize the individual differences rather than the generality of their results. In some cases these applications are based on the concept that the normal physical mechanism would behave in a certain way more or less automatically, regardless of which subjects are used. In other cases, it is based on the observation that it is not possible to describe a representative group average for some phenomena, because there is too much individual difference from one subject to the next. This latter condition is expressed by Soloman et al. (1989), in a study to show laryngeal differences during two types of whispering who ". . . concluded that the notion of average behavior is meaningless in this context. Rather, the analysis demonstrated a predominance of combinations . . ." (p. 167).

In the single subject design each subject is carefully tested and retested (usually there are 3 pretests) in order to get a completely stable base level of response, then the subject is further retested in the experimental condition to determine a uniform set of responses. Under these carefully controlled conditions, the scores within each set of measures are essentially identical; in most cases there is no variance, no need to average the scores to obtain mean values, and no standard deviations. This leaves little if any need for computational statistics.

2.4 Practical variations of single subject designs

A very practical variation of the design is illustrated in the results from Gierut (1990), displaying the baseline and performance levels for each of two treatment methods, based on each of six subjects. In this example there are fully stable readings both for the baseline and the test conditions.

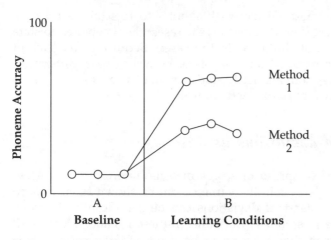

Figure 6.2   The effects of 2 methods of learning new phonemes is shown for one child. The subject was first tested in method 1, then later tested with method 2.

2.5 *Two group comparisons*

2.5.1 Normal distributions   When groups of subjects are compared, the usual assumption is that each group can be represented by an average score. The individual differences are averaged to represent the group, in which variances (primarily the standard deviations) are taken into account in making the comparisons. In the laboratory setting, the subjects can usually be carefully selected for participation, and there is usually a close cluster of scores around the mean. With this close conformity, normal distribution statistics can be applied with relatively few subjects, i.e., as few as 5 per group. Although the familiar t test is still widely used for this type of comparison, it is no longer the primary statistic of choice, because most types of research in today's speech science laboratories involve more than two treatment conditions and usually two or more groups in the study. Consequently, the t test has come to be more often used in secondary types of comparisons in conjunction with an analysis of variance.

2.5.2 Nonparametric groups   When only two groups are to be compared it is not uncommon to find sets of data that do not fit a normal pattern, i.e., the scores do not cluster around the mean. This calls for nonparametric treatments, such as the Mann-Whitney U or the Wilcoxon Matched Pairs H test. Unlike normal distributions, nonparametric data are not easily expanded into multifactor designs, and must be treated in simpler form, such as two-group comparisons or one-way analyses.

Non-parametric statistics are appropriately used in many laboratory studies in which measures are recorded in the form of ranked data or where a rank order transformation is the most rational presentation, especially with smaller numbers of subjects. It is most efficient with about 7 to 10 scores per group. When a nonparametric test is used, however, the researcher is obliged to state why this was the statistic of choice, as in the case: "Because of the lack of homogeneity of variance required for analysis of between-group differences with parametric statistics, nonparametric statistics were used for these analyses." (Humes and Christopherson, 1991, p. 689).

2.6 Using standard deviations as data

Sometimes the variations or spread of scores may assume the role of a dependent variable, where changes in the variance can be shown as an important result. Differences in standard deviations can be significantly different, even though the means are essentially the same. In these instances, the standard deviations, rather than the means, may be used as data to be treated statistically. In a study to compare the variations in vocal measures in normal and hearing impaired children, and to compare boys and girls, Ryalls and Larouche (1992) reported that "Hearing impaired subjects had significantly different standard deviations from normally hearing subjects." In addition, girls were found to have significantly larger standard deviations than boys in fundamental frequency (Ryalls and Larouche, 1992, p. 163). Although this type of analysis has been largely ignored by researchers, and is rarely mentioned in statistical texts, it provides an excellent medium for comparison when variation itself is the main point of the study.

2.7 Correlations for two groups of data

Correlations are an entirely different type of design from the comparative studies, although the same data can sometimes be used for either type of result. The advantage of correlation studies is that one measure can be predicted from the other. This type of predictive feature is used on a regular basis when dealing with topics such as the ages of children or elderly persons, since age is a logical predictor of changes in speech behavior. The validity of the correlation design depends upon the number of pairs of scores and also upon the assumptions of the researcher. That is, the researcher is responsible for making a logical association between different types of measures; small correlations, for example, can sometimes be found between such illogical sets of data as fundamental frequency and house numbers.

Correlations based upon laboratory data are frequently accompanied by scattergrams to illustrate trends based upon a discrete number of data points. The most common correlation, the Pearson r, assumes that the distribution of the population is normal and fairly large – i.e., preferably more than 30 pairs of scores. A good alternative, using rank order data, especially with 10 to 20 pairs of scores, is the Spearman rho.

The correlation is commonly used to indicate reliability between test-retest scores, to the point where the term *correlation* has come to be synonymous with reliability. Although this concept works well in most cases, the closer definition of reliability is the ability to achieve identical scores when the same test is used again on the same subjects. When all scores are nearly identical, however, the correlation is not always the best indicator of reliability. When all scores are very close together, the retest scores are likely to vary by only a point or two above or below the original values. In this situation the scores are very consistent (i.e., reliable) although the actual correlation value may be quite low. In these circumstances the standard error might be preferable.

Misleading assumptions can sometimes be implied in correlations by basing the result upon the level of significance rather than the value of the correlation itself. Thus a correlation of .30 may have a .001 level of significance, even though only 9 per cent of the scores in this case would actually be related. The percentage of predictability – the 9 per cent in this case – is obtained by squaring the r value. Thus an r of .30 squared becomes a .0900, or 9 per cent. This result is called the R^2. In order for the R^2 to have adequate predictability, the r value should preferably be .70 or higher, with the degree of predictability shown by its corresponding R^2 value. Thus an r of .70 will have an R^2 of .49, indicating that 49 per cent (about half) of the scores can be predicted from each other. From this example, it is clear that correlations lower than .70 will have relatively poor predictive value, even though their level of confidence might appear very strong.

2.8 *Multiple comparisons of one factor*

As more independent groups of data are added to the study the design evolves from the simple t test models into a one way analysis of variance, with the separate groups of data layed out across one main independent variable. Comparing fundamental frequency from four types of speakers would be an example of a single factor design for independent measures. The repeated measures design, on the other hand, compares the means of several tests made on the same group of subjects, such as measures of fundamental frequency from one group under three or more speaking conditions. Single factor designs with repeated measures tend to be less common, especially in clinical studies, because of the customary addition of a control group, thus forming a two factor design. This is found to be more frequently used in today's laboratory studies than the single factor repeated measures. The addition of a control group strengthens the repeated measures design considerably, reducing the chances of a type 1 error.

Although repeated measures designs are very efficient in using the same subjects for all tests, the advantage of the ANOVA for independent measures is that it eliminates possible development of test experience effect with the same subjects across successive trials. When each subject is tested only in one condition, subjects are usually matched or assigned randomly to the test conditions in order to reduce the chances of sampling error.

In speech science the single factor analysis of variance (ANOVA) with independent measures is relatively common, because a number of subjects are often assigned randomly to one of several different test conditions. In the more traditional basic research experiments, the subject groups are selected to be relatively homogeneous, such as undergraduate students, having similar age, gender, background, and normal speech and hearing. The statistic tells us whether one of the test conditions has a mean score higher than at least one of the others. This statistic is classed as having *independent measures* because none of the subjects takes more than one test. When each subject takes all of the tests, the statistic is called a *repeated measures* design.

The primary advantage of the simple repeated measures design is in its efficiency, wherein a relatively small number of subjects can be used for all tests. Validity and reliability are good in this design, since each subject in effect acts as its own control throughout the various test conditions. The primary type of extraneous variable – the serial effect – can be effectively controlled by either counterbalancing or randomizing the sequence of test procedures. However, in cases where the fatigue factor is severe, the subjects' performance on the last test in the sequence may be so poor as to invalidate that part of the data. To some extent the simple one way repeated measures design appears to have given way to the two way design, which incorporates both a control group and clinical group, instead of simply a clinical population alone.

In more recent speech science studies repeated measures designs are usually stacked on top of each other in order to test more than one type of subject, i.e., one clinical group and a control group to be tested under several conditions. This more complex design is called a *factorial design*. It is also described as a two factor design with repeated measures on one factor, or a treatments-by-groups design.

2.9 *Multifactor comparisons: factorial designs*

Well designed laboratory studies that are clinically based, often include a control group for comparison, where both types of subjects are tested under several of the same conditions. When two or more groups of subjects are incorporated into this type of study the factorial design has emerged as the method of choice. With increased interest in testing clinical populations under laboratory conditions, the use of this design is increasingly evident in the speech science literature. In this design the different groups are independent measures, and the treatments (i.e., tests) are the repeated measures. The design is described as a two factor design, with repeated measures on one factor (Winer, Brown, and Michels, 1991). In other terms, the "groups" factor is sometimes referred to as the "between subjects" factor, and the treatments are called the "within subjects variable".

This can be shown by the arrangement in Figure 6.3.

Measurements (Treatments)

Groups	1	2	3
A Clinical Group			
B Control Group			

Figure 6.3 Data arrangement for a factorial design for 2 groups of subjects measured under 3 treatment conditions is shown. This is described as a 2 factor design with independent measures on one factor (groups) and repeated measures on the second factor (treatments).

The factorial design has many advantages.

1   This design is uniquely suited for comparing different types of subjects under several test conditions. Quite often it is used for comparing clinical subjects with a control group through an array of tests, and as more studies are devoted to the analysis of aging on speech behavior and speech perception, the design is often used in comparing several age groups as well. Adding the control group in the design helps to increase the validity of the results, by comparison to a normative set of data.

2   The factorial design yields three F test results, with only one statistical computation. This increases the power of the test and reduces the chance for error that might otherwise be caused by making several separate computations (such as multiple t tests) on the same data. The F tests yield results for differences between groups, differences between treatments, and a groups-by-treatments interaction analysis.

3   The third advantage is that the basic design is easily expanded to accommodate either more types of subjects or more types of test conditions. It is typically used either as a two factor arrangement, showing one group factor and one treatment factor, or as a three factor design, showing one group factor and two types of treatment factors. This same general model, expanded into a three factor design, with repeated measures on the two treatment factors, is seen in Figure 6.4.

When multifactor designs are used it is strongly recommended that all factors be clearly explained to show how the variables are arranged and how the results were derived. Fortunately, many researchers already observe this practice: "... a three factor (group X time interval X category) analysis of variance ANOVA with repeated measures on time intervals and categories

Treatment Conditions

Groups	Condition A 1	2
	Condition B 1 2	1 2
A Clinical Group		
B Control Group		

Figure 6.4   A 3 factor design with repeated measures on 2 factors is shown. The first factor consists of two groups of subjects. The second factor includes 2 test conditions (such as loud and soft speech), and the third factor is shown with 3 parts (such as 3 different vowel productions).

was applied to the verbal fluency scores" (Adams, Reich, and Flowers, 1989, p. 873).

One purpose of the interaction analysis has traditionally been to determine whether some inconsistency existed, thus negating the significance of the primary (main effects) findings. In this context the interaction has been viewed mainly as a check on validity by detecting unexpected performance in one of the test groups. More recently, however, the interactions often represent the principal results of the whole experiment. In essence it says that although group A performs higher than group B, this difference is not found uniformly in all test conditions. The analysis of these unexpected contrasts among group scores may point out more subtle differences that have not been brought out in the analysis of main effects.

In using the factorial design it is helpful for the researcher to form a visual image of the mechanics of the statistic, rather than simply entering the numbers into the computer. Although the analyses of the main effects fall out clearly in the results, the interactions require special thought and consideration. Interactions have received a more thorough treatment in recent texts than in previous works. Keppel (1982) has an especially good discussion of interactions, and Winer, Brown, and Michel's 1991 presentation of interactions is considerably expanded from the previous edition in 1971.

The outcome of the main aspects of the design are often quite predictable:

1   When the study includes both a clinical and a control group, the main effects difference between groups is sometimes taken for granted. The clinical group, as expected, typically does not score the same as the normals. This is shown in a significant F test result for overall differences between groups. In many cases this is simply an indicator of face validity of the test data, rather than an important new finding.

2   The second F result indicates the difference between the next set of main effects – the different test conditions or treatments. This result, however, may still not be the primary measure of interest.

3   The next result is in the F score for interactions. This result indicates whether the different groups scored in a parallel manner across the array of tests. In other words, one group usually scores higher than the other by a fairly uniform margin through all tests. If the group scores are not parallel, the F result is found to be significant, and the post hoc analysis of where the irregularity occurs becomes a matter of special interest in the study.

2.9.1 A numerical example of the factorial design   Our simplified data are to represent those from a study by Karnell, Linville, and Edwards (1988), in which the timing sequence of velar movement, peak intraoral air pressure, and jaw closure are analyzed from repeated bilabial plosive syllables. One group of data was from a normal adult, and the other was from a speaker who had a repaired cleft palate. Both speakers were considered to have speech within the normal range. A simplified version of their study can be shown as a 2 (speakers) × 3 (events) factorial, with independent measures for the two speakers, and repeated measures on the three physiological speech events. The dependent variable was the times in milliseconds prior to production of the sound. The purpose of the study was to find whether the two types of speakers would have different timing of the articulation mechanisms, and also whether there would be any speaker-by-event interaction. The following data were reported:

Table 6.1   Mean times in milliseconds for each event prior to speech production for a plosive syllable are shown, adapted from part of a study by Karnell et al. (1988).

Groups	peak velar elevation	peak air pressure	peak jaw elevation	Totals
1. Normal	20	20	110	150
2. Rep. Palate	27	12	85	124
Totals	47	32	195	

All three of the F test results were significant: The normal speaker had significantly longer articulation times, there was a significant difference among the three event times, and there was a significant groups-by-events interaction.

In this example some difference between the two types of speakers could be anticipated, because of the cleft palate consideration for the group 2 data. The difference in timed events was also anticipated because articulation events were already observed not to occur at precisely the same times. The remarkable aspect of the result, however, was found in the groups-by-events interaction, that revealed that the impaired palate performance was similar to the normal palate in some respects, but not in others. This was found in the significant F score for the groups-by-events interaction.

2.9.2 Analysis of the factorial design

Step 1 The statistical computation is an analysis of variance (ANOVA) for a two factor design with repeated measures on one factor (Winer, Brown, and Michels, 1991) (This has also been called a treatments-by-groups design). The complete analysis of variance should first be made to determine whether either of the main effects and/or the interaction is significant. If neither the main effects nor the interaction are significant, then the analysis need go no further. The results of the ANOVA are shown in Table 6.2.

Table 6.2 Results of an analysis of variance for a 2 factor design with repeated measures on 1 factor, adapted from Karnell et al. (1988).

Factor	df	F	p
Groups	1	15.03	.002
Events	2	531.2	.001
Groups-by-Event	4	17.1	.001

Step 2

2.9.3 Interpretation of the F test results

　a　We see that, as expected, there is a significant difference between groups. Group 1 had longer time intervals overall than did group 2, as shown by the totals on the right side of Table 3, i.e., 150 compared to 124.

　b　There is also a significant difference between speech events. Treatment 3 time interval (jaw opening) is considerably longer than the other treatment times.

　c　Finally, there is a significant Groups-by-Events interaction. This indicates that one of the means could not be predicted simply by the fact that group 1 data had longer overall time than group 2. The means for group 2 means do not appear to be parallel to those of group 1 across all three treatments. This gives us a clue to a possible significant interaction; group 2 time intervals are lower than those of group 1, except for the velum measure.

2.9.4 Interpretation of the interactions

　a　The Graphic Presentation: A graph of the means for each group such as Figure 6.5 can be used as an initial step in the interpretation, in order to find visually which set of scores does not appear to be in parallel, giving the researcher a clear determination of exactly what is causing the significant interaction. The data points that are not in parallel, are causing the significant interaction result.

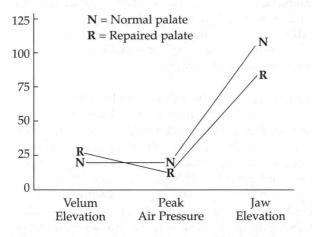

Figure 6.5 Timing in milliseconds for 3 speech events prior to syllable production is shown for 2 types of speakers, adapted from data by Karnell et al. (1988).

It can be seen in the graph that the velum time for group 2 appears to be out of parallel with the rest of the times. In the other measures, the group 2 times are below the group 1 times.

When the group scores are found to form parallel values the results indicate a relatively uniform group difference across all treatments, with no interaction. We have determined from the graph, therefore, that the velum time could be the source of the significant interaction result. In some cases, the graph itself may be presented to show this result descriptively, in lieu of further computation.

b Statistical Analysis of the Interaction: Post hoc testing can also determine which of the means fall outside of the parallel pattern by comparing the difference scores across the rows of means. When the rows of means are in parallel the difference scores will all be about the same and no interaction effect would be found. Determination of which difference scores vary significantly from the rest will reveal which pairs of means are responsible for the significant interaction result in the initial analysis of variance. This additional computation can be made as a one way analysis of variance along the row of difference scores.

Step 3

2.9.5 Post hoc testing At this stage the analysis of the potential results requires particularly careful judgement on the part of the researcher because the results must have a reasonable interpretation in terms of the hypothesis of the study. Keppel (1982) notes that there is no standard way to proceed at this point, except, as he puts it "to peel off the layers" of the design to understand what is happening in the interaction. Generally, it is recommended that the analysis should stay within the bounds of analyzing either separate rows or separate columns until the differences are found that can not be explained entirely by the main effects of the design. Although it is statistically possible to compare any mean anywhere in the study with any other mean, these are not always interpretable.

In this example, Karnell et al. chose to point out the contrast between the velum and intraoral air pressure times as the main result. They approached this conclusion by computing separate single factor ANOVAs on the data from group 1 (normal) and group 2 (cleft palate). They concluded that although the velar and air pressure time intervals were the same for group 1, they were significantly different for group 2. This yields a clearly presented difference between the group 1 and group 2 data. Alternative post hoc techniques, such as tests for multiple comparisons would of course also have been reasonable for the situation. Here the point is illustrated, however, that it is the researcher's judgement as to what is the most meaningful aspect of the results that determines the way in which the interaction should be described. In this case Karnell et al. wished to show that, although the speech samples were both judged to sound normal, a significant difference in the cleft palate timing pattern existed.

2.10 Post hoc statistical tests

The Newman Keuls test is still the most popular post hoc test, despite the fact that the Tukey test is the most strongly recommended by some statisticians, and that the Newman Keuls has been criticized as not maintaining its stated probability levels in some situations. In further consideration of the most appropriate post hoc analysis, Keppel (1982) notes that the Newman Keuls is likely to have more power when there are very few means to compare, whereas the Tukey is best for paired data, and finally the Scheffe is best if there are a larger number of comparisons to be made.

When the t is used for post hoc analysis, however, there is always the question of increasing the probability for error by re-analyzing the same data, thus creating the stronger chance for finding a difference when there is not really one there (a type 1 error). For this reason a modification of the t is used in these circumstances, by use of the Bonneferrone t test technique, or the t test for the least significant differences (Winer, Brown, and Michels, 1991). If you have a completely randomized blocks design, all subjects are considered to be equal, and randomly assigned to the experiment. In this case all cell means are theoretically equal, and a t test can logically be made between any two means anywhere in the total matrix of the analysis of variance.

All post hoc tests for comparisons are much the same in terms of their basic purpose and, to some extent, their fundamental structure. Post hoc tests are designed around the principle of non-additivity of the probability for making a type 1 error, i.e., finding a significant difference that does not really exist. The Bonneferrone adjustment for the probability level in post hoc t testing illustrates the concept very well. As a general rule, the number of t tests that can be made post hoc should not exceed the degrees of freedom in the treatments row of the design. Thus, if the ANOVA involves sampling fundamental frequency at four different times of the day, there are three degrees of freedom, which would allow three t tests between these means, using the $p < .05$ probability for error. If more t tests are needed, the p level must be shifted to a smaller value. Special tables are available for setting the new probability levels, but simply reducing the probable error from .05 to .02 will stay safely within the Bonneferrone criteria.

2.11 Influences of newer instrumentation on data collection

More precise and simplified instrumentation, such as the Visipitch, are now combined with computer technology, so as to provide nearly automatic data in what were previously very tedious measurement areas. These have included average fundamental frequency, vowel formants, consonant burst, jitter, shimmer, perturbation rate, and signal-to-noise ratio of vocal productions (Nittrouer et al., 1990). Similarly, the introduction of computerized palatography (Hamlet, 1988) and digital readout of interlabial pressures (Hinton and Luschei, 1992) has allowed for more plentiful data analysis in these once cumbersome areas, and has contributed toward better interjudge reliability and speed of measurement. These more accurate measures tend to narrow the standard deviations by reducing random variance, and give our traditional statistics somewhat more power, because differences are less likely to be obscured by large variances among the scores. As data are collected more routinely from direct readings on speech samples digitized by the computer, analyses that had previously been tremendously difficult are now conducted as a relatively simple task.

2.12 Influences of computer technology on data analysis

Recent developments in computer technology have led to considerably increased hard disk storage capacity and RAM (working storage). One might have predicted that with larger, more powerful computers, the statistics themselves would have evolved in more elaborate and exotic directions, and that not only the statistics themselves but the interpretations as well might require the workings of the computer's processors. For the most part, however, the opposite has been true; although some studies may present custom-made statistical treatments, most results are shown in terms of familiar designs and formulas that follow standard texts and can readily be interpreted by the reader.

Descriptive statistics in the form of computer structured charts and graphs are increasingly common in our scientific literature, and have greatly reduced many abstract concepts into easily designed graphics. Further trends appear to be toward more orthographic displays, such as 3-D bar charts, and exploded pie charts, which had previously required the skills of professional draftsmen.

In addition to graphic implementations, the impact of the computer has been to add more statistical options for the researcher during the process of data analysis and interpretation. The researcher now has the easy capability of trying several preliminary trial runs of different statistics, using the same data, simply by selecting a different item on the menu screen or pushing a different key. Once the data are stored they can easily be arranged and analyzed in several different ways. The probability levels, too, are usually calculated automatically by the computer, so that the results can always be selected to show the strongest level of confidence. This is a departure from traditional research theory, in which the appropriate statistic and level of confidence was preplanned in the design. The present range of selection, however, also places a stronger responsibility on the researcher for making meaningful interpretations from the conclusions that might emerge when all possible calculations are tried. Particularly, if non-orthogonal comparisons are made, some apparent results may make no logical sense, and strong discretion must be exercised where multivariate analyses are involved (Keppel, 1991).

3 Extraneous variables

In spite of the well controlled nature of speech science experimental methods, certain types of unpredicted and unwanted variables still tend to appear. When extraneous variables enter the study, they bias the data and detract from the validity of the results. In extreme cases, the extraneous variable may, in a sense, replace one of the independent variables, where, for example, instead of measuring the relative difficulty of different tests the study may inadvertently be measuring the relative fatigue of the subjects. Although these variables can be reduced or eliminated in most instances, sometimes their effect does not appear until the results are analyzed.

3.1 Extraneous variables related to subjects' abilities

Several types of extraneous variables tend to be related to certain types of subjects, such as young children, patients with neurological problems or brain injury, and elderly populations. These subjects are more inclined to demonstrate rather wide and inconsistent variations in performance due to pronounced differences in abilities, endurance, and fatigue. These conditions can easily contribute to data bias due to floor/ceiling effects and serial effects.

3.1.1 Ceiling and floor effects

3.1.1 Ceiling and floor effects   When research involves the analysis of performance, the endurance levels and test capabilities of some subjects cannot always be accurately estimated before the study. Tests that are appropriate for some subjects tend to be too easy for others. Conversely, tests for the more capable groups may yield only random attempts at answers from the younger ages. In these cases there is always the potential danger of both ceiling effects and floor effects to interfere with the collection of valid data.

Ceiling effects indicate that the test is too easy, making it impossible to show improvement on the retest. When the task, for example, is made easy enough for children with short attention spans, it may be so easy for the older age groups as to be really no test for them at all. When a test is too easy it does not represent the subject's true achievement score; there is no way to show improvement in the test because the subjects are already at the highest possible score (i.e., the ceiling). When this effect appears during the analysis of data there is little to do except to note it in the results. In a study on verbal comprehension for three age groups of children, Gibbs noted "the very high performance for the older children on the . . . test may reflect ceiling effects." (Gibbs, 1991, p. 617).

Floor effects are relatively common because tests that work well for the average subject may be unexpectedly difficult for other subjects during the study. When the test is too difficult, some subjects perform at the bottom of the test measurement, and there is no way to show that their score got worse when additional difficulty was introduced to the test condition. Sometimes, however, the test is simply too difficult for some of the subjects to achieve results. In a test of synthetic syllable perception it was concluded: "Because attempts at breaking the pattern were unsuccessful, it was clear that the task required too much concentration for the child and that their scores on the task would be meaningless." (Lehman and Sharf, 1989, p. 808).

A similar situation was noted in a study of coarticulation, where it was concluded "this interaction, therefore, likely reflects floor effects for subjects' incorrect responses." (Katz, Krepke, and Tallal, 1991, p. 1229).

When some question arises as to the possibility of floor or ceiling effects in the test procedure it is critically essential to conduct a pilot study prior to the main project, in order to set the test materials at the proper level for all groups of subjects, or to exclude those subjects who cannot meet the test criteria.

Serial effects are characteristic of repeated measure designs, as compared to independent group designs. When a subject takes a series of tests consecutively, the scores tend either to get better as the subject becomes more experienced, or to get worse as the subject becomes increasingly tired or bored. When testing motivated mature subjects, their scores usually get better as they gain more test experience or as learning increases with each successive test. Children, on the other hand, tend to tire or become bored easily, and their scores usually get worse with further testing. In most cases this situation can be handled by counterbalancing the order of treatments, in which the serial effect is spread equally among treatments. By this technique the first test is given as test 1 for some subjects, test 2 to others, and test 3 is given first to the rest of the subjects, etc. Nevertheless, the fatigue factor is sometimes too great to be counterbalanced, and exceptionally poor performance by some subjects on some of the last trials distort the result. "Other potential explanations include fatigue produced by the repetitive time-gated test materials." (Craig, 1992, p. 237).

When there is some likelihood of this condition, in which counterbalancing may not solve the extraneous problem, the time periods between tests must be extended to the point where there can reasonably be no carry-over of behavior from one test to the next.

3.2 Extraneous variables related to subjects' experiences

Another type of extraneous variable involves different attitudes or strategies among the subjects in the experimental testing situation. These are described under the headings of the *test experience effect*, the *Hawthorne effect*, and the *intervening variable effect*. These refer to the unexpected performance of some subjects due to their perception of the test situation, causing them to perform quite differently than their normally expected level pattern.

The test experience effect refers to the tendency of subjects who have taken many tests to become sophisticated in the test situation, and to respond in a manner based on their previous testing experiences. Experienced research subjects may anticipate the procedures or perform according to criteria learned in other studies. This applies both to humans and laboratory animals, that also tend to respond with behavior learned in previous experiments. For this reason it is advantageous to find subjects with no previous experience or background in similar experiments, and to instruct them on how to view the test situation. These are sometimes described as "naive" subject groups. In other circumstances, where subjects have a variety of experimental backgrounds a training session is included in the procedure, to make sure that all subjects start at the same level, regardless of previous experience.

Intervening variables refer to test strategies and attitudes of the subjects that may affect the manner in which they respond. Some subjects may, for example, simply select the longest answer or the first choice as being the best one. Others may avoid test items that take too long, or try to give standard responses to all trial conditions. Standardized responses are particularly common where subjects are reluctant to reveal their personal preferences or weaknesses. To reduce this factor the wording of instructions and questionnaire items should not imply any judgemental values, and the subjects should be assured of the confidentiality or anonymity of their responses. Instructions are frequently prewritten and read aloud so that all subjects receive identical information to start the test with the same mental set. In other instances, subjects are selected and paid in order to insure a more consistent level of dedication, objectivity, and perseverance for completing the experimental trials.

The Hawthorne effect is named after an electrical plant near Chicago, Illinois, and states that when the experimenter takes an interest in subjects' performances, they tend to do better, regardless of the trial conditions. Workers at the Hawthorne plant were being evaluated to determine the relationship between better lighting and better productivity. The experimenters could not understand why productivity improved as the lighting conditions got increasingly worse. The workers, however, were simply becoming motivated toward more production as they received more special attention by the research team.

Similarly, some types of subjects may push themselves to perform unusually well under difficult test conditions in order to impress the experimenter. To dispel the Hawthorne effect, the instructions to the subjects should specify that "there are no high or low scores to the test" and that the subjects should perform in their usual natural manner in all test conditions. The Hawthorne effect is particularly prevalent among subjects with certain types of speech pathologies, such as stutterers who become completely fluent during the experiment or dysphonic speakers who display markedly clear phonation for the voice samples.

To avoid this effect, the speaker's habitual speech can be observed for comparison during a brief conversation or comments prior to the test session. A more realistic sample can sometimes be brought out directly by explaining that higher performance is not the aim of the study.

4 Statistical software

Recent jumps in storage capacity in the order of megabytes and computational speeds up to 50 megahertz for the desk top computers have led researchers to rely more consistently upon their own software rather than linking into mainframe computers. This trend appears evident in spite of earlier predictions toward greater linking into the larger mainframe units. Although mainframe computers have also been periodically upgraded, their accessibility has in many cases declined because of capacity levels of use during peak hours. These emerging conditions have encouraged software producers to adapt some of their earlier mainframe statistical packages for use in desk top machines. These include SPSS, BMDP, and SYSTAT. In addition to the major brands, an increasing number of new computer packages are currently appearing on the market, and lower costs are making them increasingly affordable to laboratory facilities with limited budgets. The smaller packages, however, may not include multi-factor statistics, especially in the larger repeated measures designs.

Unfortunately, two primary obstacles still hamper the full use of this otherwise convenient technology. The primary obstacle is the necessity of a tutorial period for learning the characteristics of the software. In spite of the informal tone of the newer instruction manuals the new user tends to be unsuccessful and frustrated with initial efforts at using an unfamiliar package. Many researchers are reluctant to devote much time away from the research projects and deadlines in order to learn a new software methodology. In addition, many packages require a complicated process for inserting into the hard drive. Consequently, researchers may postpone the implementation of their own statistical software because of time considerations. Fortunately, a trend toward more user friendly menu driven software, following the example set earlier by word processors, is beginning to appear in statistical packages.

Another area of user frustration is in the lack of standardization among statistical instructions and concepts presented in the manuals. Some references refer to group means, which are called test replications in other texts. Eventually, perhaps a more uniform terminology will develop through user demands in the marketplace. An encouraging trend toward standardization, however, is in the tendency for many manual writers to use Winer, Brown, and Michel's (1991) examples and descriptive terms in their texts.

4.1 Comprehensive statistical packages for the microcomputer

The term *comprehensive* package refers to statistical software that contains the three major aspects for analysis: a full array of computational statistics, a data base storage system, and a graphics capability for illustrating the results. Many statistical packages are designed to accept data files from ASCII format, from database programs such as Lotus 1,2,3, or even from the ASCII files of word processors, such as Wordstar or Word Perfect.

The microcomputer versions of the full comprehensive packages require about 10 megabytes of RAM storage, with SAS requiring somewhat more than SPSS. BMDP is essentially comparable to SPSS, but tends to use less intuitive commands, and is therefore a bit more difficult to learn. The SYSTAT microcomputer package has versions both for the IBM compatible systems and the MacIntosh models.

One of the most widely used programs is SPSS. The Windows version tends to be more user-friendly than the DOS version, which appears in the spreadsheet mode. The OS/2 version, however, is gaining popularity because of its ability to accommodate larger data samples. The PC+ version has the advantage of a somewhat smaller storage requirement, and has fewer extra features, making it slightly easier for the new user to handle.

Data Desk runs on the MacIntosh. It offers a wide array of menu choices, and has the advantage of the MacIntosh intuitive command system that is helpful for new users. Number Cruncher has a very good selection of statistics, but comes with four manuals and tends to be difficult to master without guidance. The instruction format has a step-by-step itemized procedure, although the steps do not work intuitively without considerable rereading of the text and some tutorial experience.

The SPSS package is equally imposing for the part-time user, but many research facilities have technical advice available to give help through the more complicated areas, and regional SPSS workshops are also available. Nevertheless, the investment of the researcher's time in mastering the technical details of the software is often critical.

Part II Biological Perspectives

7 Motor Speech Disorders

GARY WEISMER

There are many neurological diseases that produce symptoms of disordered speech production. These symptoms are not typically associated with language problems (such as in the aphasias), but reflect deficits in the "control" of any or all levels of the speech mechanism. These are the problems we refer to as "motor speech disorders".

1 Preamble

It is not unreasonable to say that the systematic study of motor speech disorders was born with the publication in 1969 of two papers by Darley, Aronson, and Brown of the Mayo Clinic. Sporadic studies of various neuromotor speech disorders had been published prior to the Mayo work (e.g., Canter, 1963, 1965a,b; Zentay, 1937; Scripture, 1916; Lehiste, 1965), but a coherent rationale for the study of dysarthria (other than the obvious clinical one) had not been set forth. Darley et al. (1969a,b) provided this rationale in the form of a hypothesis concerning the **localizing** value of perceptual impressions of dysarthric speech. According to this hypothesis, different types of neurological pathology would be associated with unique kinds of speech production phenomena which in turn would be revealed in perceptual impressions of speech. The perceptual impressions were quantified by psychophysical scaling of multiple dimensions of speech production performance, the dimensions being chosen by Darley, Aronson, and Brown on the basis of their formidable clinical experience with dysarthric patients. These dimensions, some of which are listed in Table 7.1, clearly covered a wide range of speech production phenomena and were capable of providing a comprehensive, quantitative profile of the speech production deficit in neurogenic speech disorders. Darley et al.'s hypothesis was confirmed not on the basis of the individual dimensions, but rather on the unique **clustering** of the multiple perceptual dimensions. These clusters, which are listed in Table 7.2 along with their respective

Table 7.1 Selected perceptual dimensions used in the Mayo Clinic studies of dysarthria (from Darley, Aronson, & Brown, 1975)

Articulation dimensions	Pitch dimensions
Imprecise consonants	Monopitch
Vowels distorted	Pitch level
Irregular articulatory breakdown	Voice tremor
Phonemes prolonged	

Prosodic dimensions	Loudness dimensions
Rate (abnormally slow or rapid)	Monoloudness
Reduced stress	Excess loudness variation
Excess and equal stress	Loudness decay
Phrases short	

Voice quality dimensions	Speech breathing dimensions
Harsh voice	Audible inspiration
Strained-strangled voice	Grunt at end of expiration
Breathy voice	Forced inspiration/expiration
Hypernasality	
Voice stoppages	

dysarthria types, were appealing not only because they drastically reduced the dimensionality of the perceptual analysis, but also because they appeared to be explainable in terms of the underlying, unique pathophysiologies of the various neurological diseases under study.

FLACCID dysarthria was characterized by the clusters **phonatory incompetence**, **resonatory incompetence**, and **phonatory-prosodic insufficiency**. According to Darley et al. (1975), flaccid dysarthria resulted from lower motoneuron disease, meaning that the lesion was located *in* the cranial nerve motoneurons (i.e., the motor nucleus of C. V, the facial motor nucleus [associated with C. VII), the nucleus ambiguus [associated with C. IX, X, and XI], and the hypoglossal nucleus [associated with C. XII]), the ventral horn nuclei of the spinal cord serving the muscles of the head, neck, and respiratory system, the nerves leading from the motoneurons to the periphery (as, for example, in Bell's palsy, a lesion of C. VII), the junction of the motor end plate and the muscle fiber (as in Myasthenia Gravis), or some combination of the above. All of these possible sites-of-lesion share the effect of producing muscle weakness and/or paralysis, which was taken by Darley et al. (1975) as an explanation for the **phonatory** and **resonatory incompetence** features of flaccid dysarthria: weak or paralyzed muscles should not be able to generate the force required for adequate closure of the glottis during vocal fold vibration or of the velopharyngeal port during non-nasal sounds. **Phonatory-prosodic insufficiency** was attributed to hypotonia of the laryngeal muscles, hypotonia being a general feature of muscles in lower motoneuron disease.[1]

SPASTIC dysarthria was characterized by the clusters **prosodic excess**, **prosodic insufficiency**, **articulatory-resonatory incompetence**, and **phonatory stenosis**. Spastic dysarthria was associated with upper motoneurone lesions, that is, (typically) bilateral damage *above* the level of the cranial nerve or spinal motoneurones, in the region of the corticobulbar and/or corticospinal tracts. According to Darley et al. (1975), upper motoneuron damage differs from lower motoneurone damage because the former disrupts movement patterns, whereas the latter affects only the function of the affected muscles. A prominent neurological sign in spasticity is *hypertonicity*, which Darley et al. took to explain the **phonatory stenosis** cluster. In other words, excessive tone in the laryngeal muscles was assumed to be responsible for the perceptual impression of effortful phonation, as indexed by several scaled dimensions such as *harsh voice, strained-strangled quality*, and so forth. **Prosodic insufficiency** was formed from the intercorrelations of perceptual dimensions such as *monoloudness, monopitch*, and *reduced stress*; reduced range of movement, likely in laryngeal structures and possibly in supralaryngeal structures as well, was suggested as the physiological basis of this cluster. **Prosodic excess** was formed from the dimensions *excess and equal stress* and *slow rate*, and was said to be caused by the slow individual and repetitive movements seen in spasticity. **Articulatory-resonatory incompetence**, a cluster also invoked for flaccid dysarthria (see above), reflected the dimensions *hypernasality, vowels distorted*, and *imprecise consonants*, and was thought to be the result of "reduced force of movement of palate, tongue, and lips" (Darley et al., 1969b, p. 467). This underlying mechanism was believed to be related to the 'reduced range of movement' explanation for the **prosodic insufficiency** cluster.

ATAXIC dysarthria was associated with three clusters, **articulatory inaccuracy**, **prosodic excess**, and **phonatory-prosodic insufficiency**. Ataxic dysarthria may result from damage to the cerebellum as well as to pathways leading to and from the cerebellum. The classic description of the symptomatology of cerebellar dysfunction was provided by Holmes (1917), who noted problems in controlling the range and force of movements, inability to produce accurate movement goals (movement errors), decomposition of complex movements into simple components, slowness of movement, hypotonia, and difficulty in proper phasing of agonist and antagonist muscles (as in repetitive motion tasks, such as rapid and continuous pronation-supination of the wrist). Darley et al. (1969b, 1975) invoked this set of behaviors to explain the speech clusters identified above. For example, **articulatory inaccuracy**, which was formed from the dimensions *irregular articulatory breakdown, vowels distorted*, and *imprecise consonants*, was explained in terms of the movement accuracy problems experienced by persons with cerebellar damage. **Prosodic excess**, consisting of such dimensions as *excess and equal stress* and *phonemes prolonged*, was thought to be due to the slow movement characteristic of cerebellar disease, and **phonatory-prosodic insufficiency** was explained in terms of hypotonia (see above, flaccid dysarthria).

HYPOKINETIC dysarthria, resulting from Parkinson's disease or the various forms of Parkinsonism (i.e., associated with carbon monoxide poisoning, syphilis, arteriosclerosis, Shy-Drager syndrome, and so forth: see Duvoisin, 1986), was characterized by the single cluster **prosodic insufficiency**. In Parkinson's disease a lesion in the substantia nigra, a cluster of mesencephalic cells that produce the neurotransmitter dopamine, results in a reduction of dopaminergic influence in the cells of the basal ganglia (i.e., the caudate, putamen, and pallidal nuclei) (For a description see Kent and Tjaden, BRAIN FUNCTIONS UNDERLYING SPEECH.). This specific disruption of the normal balance of neurotransmitters causes movements to be initiated with great difficulty and executed with extremely small range; these 'micromovements' may appear to be quite rapid at times, as exemplified by the quick shuffling gait often seen in Parkinson's patients. According to Darley et al., **prosodic insufficiency** in hypokinetic dysarthria can be explained in terms of these rapid, small range movements. Some of the dimensions contributing to the **prosodic insufficiency** cluster in hypokinetic dysarthria included *variable rate, reduced stress, short rushes of speech,* and *imprecise consonants*. Although this cluster appears in other dysarthria types as well (in *spastic dysarthria*, and in *ataxic* and *flaccid dysarthria* in slightly different form, as reviewed above), the component dimensions may vary across dysarthria type.

HYPERKINETIC dysarthria is the term used by Darley et al. to describe the motor speech disorder associated with extrapyramidal lesions that cause involuntary movements. There are several different disorders in this category, including (but not limited to) dystonia, chorea, and athetosis. Darley et al. chose to separate these disorders into so-called 'quick' versus 'slow' hyperkinesias, using chorea and dystonia as prototypes of the 'quick' and 'slow' types, respectively. More specifically, quick hyperkinesias will involve very rapid involuntary movements which do not result in fixed, abnormal body postures, whereas slow hyperkinesias are characterized by slowly developing contractions that often distort the posture of the head, neck, trunk, or limbs for some length of time. Athetosis, which is one of the forms of cerebral palsy, is often conceptualized as a combination of quick and slow hyperkinesia. The hyperkinetic dysarthria of chorea had a complex and comprehensive pattern of speech breakdown, and was described by six clusters. These included **phonatory stenosis** (where 'stenosis' implies a squeezed, strained voice quality), **prosodic insufficiency, resonatory incompetence, articulatory-resonatory incompetence, prosodic excess,** and **articulatory inaccuracy**. The perceptual dimensions underlying these clusters are similar to those identified above for the other dysarthria types. The first four of these clusters also seemed to form an intercorrelated 'supercluster,' which was thought to result from co-occurring hypertonus and reductions in range and force of movement. The pervasive prosodic disturbance in this dysarthria was regarded by Darley et al. (1975, p. 207) as partly, if not largely, a compensatory reaction to the choreic pathophysiology: "As they proceed, patients are seemingly on guard against anticipated speech breakdowns, making compensations from time to time as they feel the imminence of glottal closure, respiratory arrest, or articulatory hindrance."

The hyperkinetic dysarthria of dystonia was described by four clusters, including **articulatory inaccuracy**, **prosodic excess**, **prosodic insufficiency**, and **phonatory stenosis**. As in previous dysarthria types, **articulatory inaccuracy** was interpreted to be the result of errors in movement goals, and **phonatory stenosis** was attributed to hypertonus. Darley et al. puzzled over the co-existance of **prosodic excess** and **insufficiency** in the same dysarthria type, but suggested that slowness of movement and limited range of movement – the stated underlying basis of these clusters – can co-exist in the same disorder (see Kent, 1990, p. 383, for relevant commentary).

Darley et al. also studied several disorders in which the neurological deficit was apparently more diffuse than in the five dysarthrias described above. For example, amyotrophic lateral sclerosis (ALS) is a disease in which both lower and upper motoneurone lesions are common. In keeping with their system, Darley et al. identified the dysarthria in ALS as *spastic-flaccid*. Similarly, multiple sclerosis (MS) often involves cerebellar and upper motoneuron lesions (among others), and therefore caused a dysarthria labeled as *spastic-ataxic*. These labelling decisions for dysarthrias in diseases involving more than one motor system were entirely consistent with Darley et al.'s (1975, p. 229) belief that ". . . speech pathology reflects neuropathology."[2]

Finally, Darley et al. were careful to separate *apraxia of speech* from the dysarthrias. Apraxia of speech was clearly a motor speech disorder, but not one resulting from paralysis, weakness, incoordination, and/or involuntary movement. Rather, apraxia of speech was conceptualized as a motor programming disorder, precisely because the orofacial control of patients diagnosed with this disorder did not seem to show the kinds of deficits observed in patients with dysarthria. Moreover, patients with apraxia of speech showed certain behaviors, such as difficulty initiating utterances, groping for articulatory positions, and sensitivity to variables such as phonetic complexity and utterance length, that seemed to suggest a programming disorder. Patients with apraxia of speech often had lesions in Broca's area, or perhaps in fibers of the internal capsule or thalamus, and frequently showed signs of aphasia coexisting with the speech apraxia. A common scenario would have a patient suffering a cardiovascular accident (CVA) with damage to Broca's area, resulting in aphrasia plus apraxia of speech closely following the insult. Over time the aphasia would likely become less severe, and the apraxia of speech may emerge as a more persistent residual of the CVA. Darley et al. did not construct a perceptually-derived set of clusters for apraxia of speech, perhaps because they believed the disorder should be described and diagnosed by different criteria than those applied to the dysarthrias. There is evidence, however,

Table 7.2   Clusters of perceptual dimensions reported by Darley et al. (1969b) for the five dysarthria types. See text for additional details

Flaccid:	phonatory incompetence; resonatory incompetence; phonatory-prosodic insufficiency
Spastic:	prosodic excess; prosodic insufficiency; articulatory-resonatory incompetence; phonatory stenosis
Ataxic:	articulatory inaccuracy; prosodic excess; phonatory-prosodic insufficiency
Hypokinetic:	prosodic insufficiency
Hyperkinetic:	phonatory stenosis; prosodic insufficiency; resonatory incompetence; articulatory-resonatory incompetence; prosodic excess; articulatory inaccuracy

that patients diagnosed with a 'pure' form of apraxia of speech (i.e., with no coexisting aphasia) have orofacial control deficits in nonspeech tasks similar to those observed among dysarthric patients (McNeil, Weismer, Adams, and Mulligan, 1990). This finding raises questions concerning the basis of the classification difference between apraxia of speech and dysarthria. A complete review of the history and characteristics of apraxia of speech has been presented by Rosenbek, Kent, and LaPointe (1984).

The Mayo framework provided a sharp focus for research in the area of motor speech disorders. The work suggested a whole range of physiological studies to validate the explanation of the clusters listed in Table 7.2, and a deeper exploration of the acoustic and perceptual bases of the perceptual dimensions. The work also provided a rational guide for the clinician attempting to modify the speech production deficit in dysarthria: identify the most prominent perceptual cluster in the profile of a speech production deficit, and focus therapeutic efforts there to make maximal gains in habilitation or rehabilitation.

Whereas the heuristic value of the Mayo studies is obvious, there is reason to believe that the explicit and implicit framework of the system is also constraining. For example, the notion that "speech pathology reflects neuropathology" is almost certainly responsible for the continued use of diagnostic tests in the speech clinic that emphasize classic signs of neuropathology in the orofacial system (see Gerratt et al., 1992), rather than systematic evaluation of the *speech production* deficit. Contrary to the position adopted by Darley et al., the classic symptoms of certain neurological diseases do not necessarily appear to account for aberrant speech production characteristics (Neilson and O'Dwyer, 1983; O'Dwyer and Neilson, 1988). Moreover, a careful analysis of the literature on the relationship of orofacial, nonverbal performance to normal and disordered speech production skills fails to reveal a compelling case for conducting the non-speech evaluations, if one is interested in understanding the speech production deficit (Weismer and Forrest, 1992). Finally, although there have been many studies that have used the Mayo perceptual system or a variant thereof to study motor speech disorders, the status of perceptual analysis as a 'localizing' tool can be questioned on a number of grounds.[3]

The remainder of this chapter will be devoted to 1) some discussion of how motor speech disorders should be defined, and 2) a survey of what has been learned about motor speech disorders since the publication of the Mayo studies. The chapter will conclude with a brief consideration of contemporary issues in motor speech disorders. Other recent reviews of motor speech disorders can be found in Putnam (1988) and Kent (1990).

2 What is a motor speech disorder?

The speech pathology literature contains several formal definitions of motor speech disorders (see, for example, Darley et al., 1975; Netsell, 1984; and Hunker and Abbs, 1984), all of which share the theme that there must be some form of damage and/or dysfunction to nervous system structures serving the speech mechanism. As straightforward as this may seem, there are several points of controversy concerning a proper definition of a motor speech disorder. We will address two of these points, one being the use of diagnosis labels that imply the presence of neurological dysfunction when none can be demonstrated with certainty, and the other being the status of *speech production* symptoms in the diagnosis of a motor speech disorder.

2.1 Diagnosis labels

In cases such as Parkinson's disease or ALS, the lesion locations and behavioral effects are fairly well understood. When a patient who is diagnosed with one of these diseases (or others where the lesions and effects are fairly clear) has or subsequently develops a speech production problem that cannot be attributed to other concurrent diseases (such as cancer), it is fairly straightforward to label the deficit as a motor speech problem. There are certain diseases, however, whose symptoms are consistent with neurogenic dysfunction but whose underlying neuropathology is unknown or controversial. The specific point of controversy in at least one of these disorders, *spasmodic dysphonia*, is whether or not the symptoms can be explained within a psychogenic framework. Spasmodic dysphonia, which typically has a slow onset in adulthood, is a laryngeal disorder characterized by intermittent voice stoppages (somewhat like stuttering blocks) superimposed on a fluctuating abnormal voice quality; the disorder is typically only obvious during speech, and not during other forms of phonation (such as laughing or singing) (Cannito, 1991). The older literature typically regarded spasmodic dysphonia as a psychogenic disorder, largely because the disease onset was often coupled with an emotionally traumatic event in the patient's life and the symptoms were highly variable and situation dependent (see Aronson and Lagerlund, 1991, for a commentary on this dispute). In the last decade there has been a substantial amount of experimental work designed to demonstrate the presence of neuromuscular abnormalities in persons with symptoms of spasmodic dysphonia (see Finitzo and Freeman, 1989; Cannito, Kondraske, and Johns, 1991; and Ludlow and Connor, 1987). The fairly clear presence of such abnormalities has led researchers to seek the underlying lesion location, with mixed success. Some patients clearly show some deviation from normality on brain imaging and/ or region blood flow mapping studies (Finitzo and Freeman, 1989), but the explanations for the correspondence of the particular brain regions identified as abnormal and the symptoms of spasmodic dysphonia are decidedly ad hoc (see discussion in Cannito et al., 1991, pp. 217–221). There seems to be some agreement that the unknown lesion locations are above the level of the brainstem motor nuclei, and that the neuropathophysiology is consistent with a dystonia. The problem, therefore, is this: If a definition of motor speech disorders requires that a lesion of the central or peripheral nervous system be present, should spasmodic dysphonia be defined as a motor speech disorder? This definitional problem is more than an academic exercise, as it may have influence on such diverse matters as subject inclusion criteria in research studies, models and theories of disordered speech production, and justification of insurance payments for speech therapy.

Another example of this definitional problem is found in the literature on childhood articulatory disorders. The term 'developmental apraxia of speech' (DAS: alternately, 'developmental verbal dyspraxia,' among others) has been used for at least 40 years to describe those children with severe, difficult-to-remediate articulation deficits involving multiple sound errors, possible articulatory groping, possible oral nonverbal apraxia, and inferred motor programming problems (see reviews in Love, 1992, pp. 95–111; Marquardt and Sussman, 1991; and Hall, Jordan, and Robin, 1993, pp. 2–8). These children seem to separate from those with delayed phonologies, due to the severity and relative intractability of the problem. Most writers regard DAS as a motor speech disorder, but as Love (1992, p. 96) has pointed out, the evidence for this classification is not compelling: "... there is yet no convincing evidence of localized and lateralized brain lesions similar to those found in the adult, nor is there unequivocal evidence of minor and inconsistent neurologic signs ... in all children studied to date." Whereas there are other possible types of brain dysfunction that would not show up in imaging studies but would qualify as neurological dysfunction (see Marquardt and Sussman, 1991), the identification of DAS as a neurogenically-based disorder is, at best, inferential.[4] As in the case of spasmodic dysphonia, the categorization of DAS as a motor speech disorder has important clinical and scientific implications. Perhaps more importantly, the use of a disorder label (apraxia) that implies some brain damage or dysfunction in the absence of reasonable evidence could have a profound and unnecessary educational and social impact on a child.

2.2 Status of speech production symptoms in definition of motor speech disorders

Some writers (Netsell, 1984; Dworkin, 1991; Hunker and Abbs, 1984) have chosen not to require a phrase indicating the *perception* of speech abnormality in their definitions of dysarthria. If a person has damage to central and/or peripheral nervous system structures involved in speech movement control but does not sound abnormal, does the person have dysarthria? We believe the answer in many cases is "yes," for the following reasons.

Speakers with known neurological disease can be shown to have abnormal speech production characteristics, even in the absence of relevant perceptual evidence. One example of this can be found among a small group of patients who had recently been diagnosed with ALS (based on a variety of limb and bulbar symptoms) but who were not perceived to have abnormal speech (originally reported in Weismer, Mulligan, and DePaul, 1986).[5] Acoustic analysis showed that several articulatory characteristics were unlike those derived from age-matched, normal speakers. For example, Figure 7.1 shows five repetitions of the first (F1) and second (F2) formant trajectories of the diphthong /aɪ/, extracted from the sentence "Buy Bobby a poppy" spoken by one normal speaker and one speaker with recently diagnosed ALS (age = 31 years). In both the upper and lower plots the set of curves originating around 500 Hz are the F1's, and the set of curves originating around 1,250 Hz are the F2's. Note the overall longer duration and shallower slopes of the trajectories produced by the ALS speaker. The shallow trajectory slopes, a feature seen in many dysarthric speakers (see Weismer and Martin, 1992; and Weismer, Martin, Kent, and Kent, 1992), are noteworthy because of their consistency across repetitions in a speaker perceived to have normal speech production. Figure 7.2 displays mean slope (labeled as 'transition rate') data for all five normal and five ALS speakers for four transitions, including the falling and rising F2 transitions seen in the /uɪ/ sequence derived from "The potato stew is in the pot" and the F1 and F2 transitions show in Figure 7.1. Above each transition labeled and schematized on the *x*-axis, the left and right columns of points plot normal and ALS mean data, respectively; the numbers on the *x*-axis indicate the number of the formant trajectory (e.g., uɪ2 shows the F2 trajectory, aɪ1 shows the F1 trajectory). The distribution of means is clearly overlapping for the /uɪ/ transitions, but completely or nearly completely non-overlapping for the /aɪ/ transitions. The nearly separate distributions of means across groups for /aɪ/ are not likely due to subject sampling error, especially because we have evidence of essentially normal transition slopes among these ALS speakers for a different vocalic sequence (/uɪ/). These measures for /aɪ/ suggest some early deterioration of speech production capabilities among these recently-diagnosed patients, and seem to validate the application of the 'dysarthric' categorization to these speech samples. It is not unusual, even in dysarthric speakers who show clear evidence of a speech disorder, for only

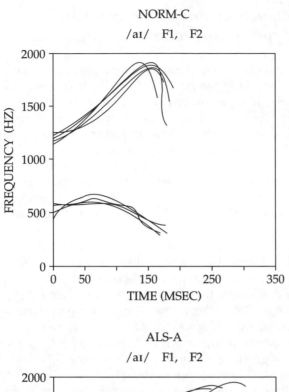

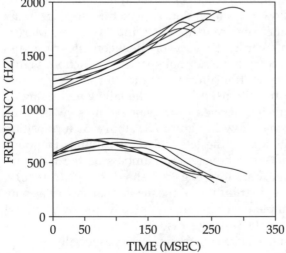

Figure 7.1 F1 and F2 trajectories for the diphthong /aɪ/ in the utterance "b**uy** Bobby a poppy," spoken at a conversational rate by a neurologically-normal speaker (top) and a 31-year-old speaker with ALS. Five repetitions are shown for each speaker.

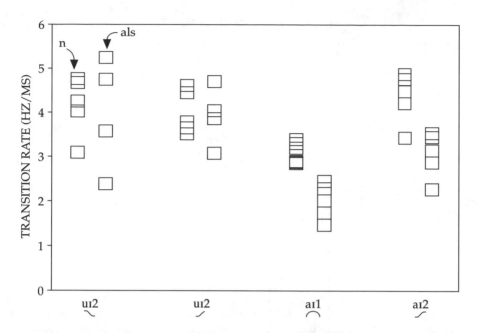

Figure 7.2 Mean Transition rate (slope of formant transition) for four different trajectories, shown for neurologically-normal subjects ('n': left column above each trajectory) and subjects with ALS who presented with no perceptual evidence of dysarthria ('als': right column above each trajectory). Data are shown for the falling and rising parts of the /uɪ/ transition from "... st<u>ew</u> <u>is</u> ...," and the falling F1 and rising F2 transitions in /aɪ/ (see Figure 7.1). Each point plots the mean value for a single subject.

certain segments to be affected by the neurogenic disease process. These segment-specific effects have been investigated only minimally, but may hold the key to vulnerabilities of the speech mechanism to neuropathology.

Another example of this phenomenon is shown in Figure 7.3, which plots the percentage of voiceless stop closure intervals for which vocal fold vibration continued for more than 20 msec following the offset of the preceding vowel. Weismer (1984) had shown previously that young adult speakers reliably terminate vocal fold vibration within 20 ms of the offset of a vowel preceding a voiceless stop closure. Conversely, neurologically-normal geriatric speakers (between 65 and 81 years of age) and speakers with Parkinson's disease did not, producing many voiceless stops with voicing continuing some 50–70 msec into the closure interval. In Figure 7.3 data for the five individual speakers with ALS, none of whom was above the age of 32, show the *frequent* failure to terminate vocal fold vibration within 20ms following the offset of vowels preceding a voiceless stop (percentages are based on a minimum of 30 analyzed stops per speaker, derived from sentence repetition material); group data are plotted for the neurologically-normal speakers, as no single speaker

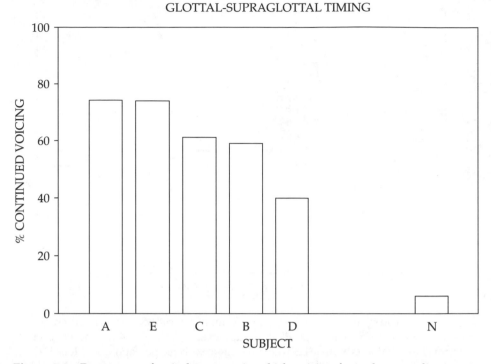

Figure 7.3 Percentage of voiceless stops in which voicing from the preceding vowel continued for more than 20 msec into the closure interval. Percentages are shown for five individual subjects with ALS and no perceptible dysarthria (subjects A, E, C, B, D), ranked from most to least frequent occurrence of continued voicing. Normal data, indicated above 'N', are pooled across subjects because of the infrequent occurrence of continued voicing.

produced more than 10 per cent of his voiceless stops with 'continued voicing.' Again we have clear evidence of speech production abnormalities even in the absence of perceptual abnormalities.

  These data argue strongly for the diagnosis of dysarthria in these individuals with ALS. A well-known and somewhat exaggerated clinical example of this phenomenon is often noted in patients with Parkinson's disease, who can be perfectly intelligible in highly structured situations (such as experiments, or clinical sessions) but very unintelligible in conversational settings (see Weismer, 1984). The patients do not lose their dysarthria in structured situations, but rather are able to control their disordered speech mechanisms to eliminate perceptual evidence of speech production difficulties. Parkinson patients who sounded 'normal' in the Weismer (1984) study consistently showed speech production anomalies on acoustic analysis. This raises an important distinction, which brings us back to the definitional issue noted above: The dysarthria label is only appropriate, in our opinion, when the patient who sounds 'normal' can be shown to have deficits of *speech production*, as revealed by acoustic or physiological analysis. Subtle deterioration of orofacial muscle control in *nonspeech* tasks (e.g., instability in holding a submaximal force in the tongue, or perhaps some reduction of maximum strength in the lips or jaw), even in the presence of known neurological disease, is not enough to warrant the label 'dysarthria.' In our opinion, the label 'dysarthria' is only appropriate when there is an effect on speech *production* performance, not simply on structures of the speech mechanism.

3 Current knowledge about motor speech disorders: a brief review

Since the publication of the Mayo studies, there have been many research efforts to learn more about the physiological and acoustical characteristics of the various dysarthrias and apraxia of speech. The literature is fairly large, so only broad summaries will be offered here.[6]

3.1 Speech breathing

Speech breathing problems among dysarthric and apraxic patients are known to be fairly common, but the relevant research literature is fairly sparse. There is an older literature (e.g., Ewanowski, 1964; Mueller, 1971; Hardy, 1964, 1966) showing decrements in certain partitions of lung volume among Parkinson and cerebral palsied individuals. More recent studies have employed the respiratory kinematics technique of Hixon and his colleagues (Hixon, Goldman, and Mead, 1973; Hixon, Mead, and Goldman, 1976) to investigate more detailed aspects of possible speech motor breathing problems. Issues of importance in these studies include the way in which the chest wall is used to produce the driving pressure for vocal fold vibration, use of lung volume range during speech, and the inferred effect of the former and latter on such phenomena as phrasing and speaking rate.

Speech breathing in patients with Parkinson's disease has been studied by Murdoch, Chenery, Bowler, and Ingram (1989) and Solomon and Hixon (1993). Interestingly, although many of the 33 patients participating in these studies had a relatively advanced form of the disease and perceptible speech problems, the data do not suggest much in the way of speech breathing difficulties in Parkinson's disease. Patients in both studies had aberrant behavior for vegetative breathing and some nonspeech respiratory measures (such as vital capacity, or forced expiratory volume over one second [FEV1]), but these were not predictive of speech breathing patterns. The lung volume range used for speech by Parkinson's patients was similar to the range used by normal speakers; moreover, the use of the chest wall in achieving lung volume change for

speech was not grossly different for the patients and normal speakers. Selected motion–motion patterns for Parkinson patients and neurologically normal speakers are shown in Figure 7.4, taken from Murdoch et al. (1989, p. 622).
In these graphs the two straight, diagonal lines with slope = −1.0 represent
chest wall configurations at *roughly* 40 per cent (all points along the lower line)
and 60 per cent (upper line) of the vital capacity (VC), respectively. The multiple,
thinner lines on each plot show the expiratory excursions of the chest wall
for multiple utterances (where chest wall = rib cage, and the diaphragm–
abdomen, or all structures outside the lung capable of producing volumetric
change of the lungs: see Hixon et al. (1973) and Weismer (1985, 1988) for
additional details on interpretation of these diagrams). A line oriented on a
perfect vertical would reflect only rib cage contribution to the volume change,
whereas a line on a perfect horizontal would reflect only diaphragm–abdominal
contribution to the volume change; orientations between these two cases reflect proportionate contributions of the two parts to lung volume change. Any
movement of an utterance line beginning on the top diagonal line and ending
on the bottom diagonal line, regardless of orientation, signals a roughly 20 per
cent change of lung volume. Most normal subjects initiate utterances around
60 per cent VC and terminate them in the vicinity of 40 per cent VC, as shown
in the right half of Figure 7.4 and previously by Hixon et al. (1973). The data
from Parkinson patients in Figure 7.4 show a number of examples of utterances initiated at lung volumes somewhat higher and lower than the typical
normal utterance, but for the most part the lung volume ranges used for
speech are not clearly different from normal. Note also the angle of line
orientations for Parkinson utterances, which are not dramatically different for
the two speaker groups. There is probably more intersubject variation among
the Parkinson patients (note S13's predominant use of the abdomen, and S15's
nearly exclusive use of the rib cage) compared to the normal speakers in this
figure, but there is a good deal of inter-subject variability among some of the
other normal speakers studied by Murdoch et al. (1989, see for example Figure
7a, p. 622). Solomon and Hixon (1993) reported that the chest wall configuration used for speech was less distorted from its presumed relaxed configuration in Parkinson, as compared to normal subjects. This was attributed primarily
to a stiffer rib cage in Parkinson patients, perhaps a reflection of the typical
rigidity (a type of hypertonia) seen in Parkinson's disease. There were other
minor abnormalities in the chest wall tracings examined by both Murdoch
et al. (1989) and Solomon and Hixon (1993), but as the latter authors pointed
out, these did not seem to be related to abnormalities in the acoustic end
product of speech.

In a similar study of patients with motoneuron disease, Putnam and Hixon
(1984) found that patients tended to initiate utterances at slightly lower lung
volumes than normal speakers, and sometimes produced irregular contributions of the chest wall parts to the lung volume change. A variety of explanations were considered for these findings, but again the dominant impression
was one of largely intact speech breathing even though reasonable inferences

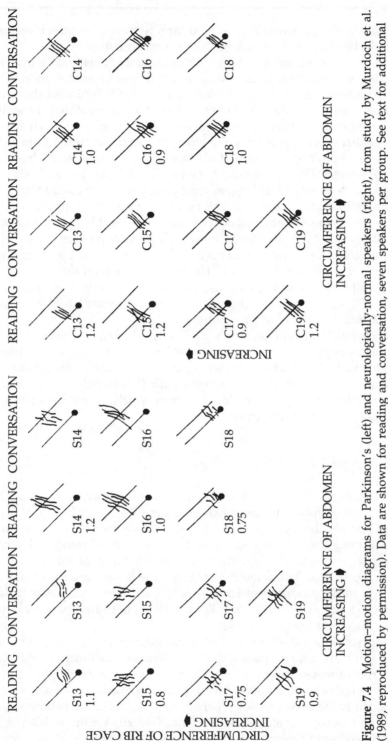

Figure 7.4 Motion–motion diagrams for Parkinson's (left) and neurologically-normal speakers (right), from study by Murdoch et al. (1989, reproduced by permission). Data are shown for reading and conversation, seven speakers per group. See text for additional details.

of respiratory muscle weakness, derived largely from non-speech respiratory data, could be made for the patients with motor neuron disease.

Aspects of phrasing and speaking rate can also be considered partly within the domain of speech breathing. Speaking rate disorders are common in motor speech disorders (e.g., Yorkston, Beukelman, and Bell, 1988), but the extent to which these rate anomalies are influenced by speech breathing difficulties is unknown. Moreover, because many speakers with motor speech disorders have laryngeal valving problems, the effect of speech breathing difficulties on phrasing and speaking rate cannot always be separated cleanly from laryngeal involvement. This is illustrated well in a study by Till and Alp (1991), who showed how laryngeal hypovalving (excessive transglottal airflow during phonation) could affect respiratory behavior in a group of dysarthric speakers. These speakers (including persons with vocal fold paralysis, stroke, head injury, and ALS) produced shorter breath groups and fewer syllables per breath group as compared to normal speakers, as did the speakers with Parkinson's disease in Solomon and Hixon (1993). A high incidence of laryngeal hypovalving among the Parkinsonian speakers studied by Solomon and Hixon (1993) is also likely, as suggested by the perceptual labels 'breathy' and 'hoarse' applied to many of their subjects.

Speech breathing in conjunction with laryngeal behavior needs to be studied in greater depth among additional speakers with motor speech disorders. Although available studies seem to indicate only subtle speech breathing deviations from normal among speakers with Parkinson's disease and ALS, clinical experience suggests that this is an area worthy of further investigation in a variety of dysarthric speakers.

3.2 Laryngeal behavior

Examination of the 38 perceptual dimensions employed by Darley et al. (1969a) reveals a large number (10) intended to reflect disordered laryngeal function in motor speech disorders. Many of these dimensions relate to voice quality (such as *breathy voice*, *strained-strangled voice*, and *harsh voice*) and problems with pitch control (*pitch breaks*, and *voice tremor*). Much of the contemporary focus on the loss of 'naturalness' (referred to as *bizarreness* by Darley et al., 1969a) in neurogenically-disordered speech (see Yorkston, Beukelman, and Bell, 1988, pp. 353–370) is also an acknowledgement of the common laryngeal disorders in motor speech disorders.

Electromyographic and movement data for neurogenically-disordered laryngeal behavior are rather sparse, and are often in the form of case studies. Because recordings of laryngeal muscle activity and movement of the vocal folds are technically demanding, investigators have developed alternate techniques to study the pathophysiology of neurogenic laryngeal disorders. Gerratt, Hanson, and Berke (1986; see also Hanson, Gerratt, Karin, and Berke, 1988) have employed simultaneous photoglottography (PGG) and electroglottography

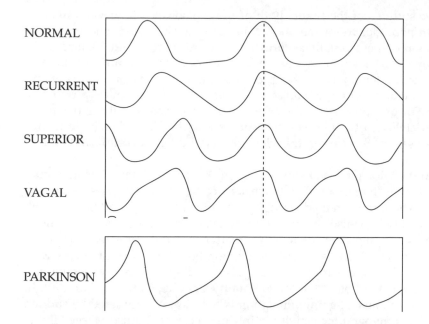

Figure 7.5 Photoglottography traces for normal speaker, and speaker with damage to recurrent laryngeal nerve, superior laryngeal nerve, vagal nerve, and speaker with Parkinson's disease. The top four traces are taken from Hanson et al. (1988, reproduced by permission) and the bottom trace from Gerratt et al. (1986, reproduced by permission). Each trace can be interpreted in terms of the time-varying glottal area, and hence vocal fold motion, throughout individual glottal cycles.

(EGG) to study vocal cord motion in patients with damage to the nerves supplying the laryngeal muscles (lower motoneuron disease) and in patients with Parkinson's disease. Vocal cord motion in lower motoneuron diseases might show slowness or unusual rapidity for the opening or closing phase of a glottal cycle, depending on the precise location of the nerve damage. The contrast between vocal cord vibration characteristics in one form of lower motoneuron disease (recurrent nerve paralysis) and Parkinson's disease is instructive of the difficulty in mapping underlying movement control problems onto speech symptoms. Lower motoneuron disease produces flaccidity whereas Parkinson's disease is characterized by rigidity, a form of hypertonia. As seen in Figure 7.5, the vocal folds are blown apart rapidly in recurrent nerve paralysis, probably because the flaccid tissue offers little resistance to displacement by the subglottal pressure; the folds then return toward the midline somewhat slowly because of decreased tissue elasticity. Conversely, the apparently rigid folds of the patient with Parkinson's disease (inferred from a thickened and bowed appearance) resist displacement by the developing subglottal pressure, but snap back rapidly toward the midline because of the relative stiffness of the tissue. Both of these disorders, however, are associated with poor closure of the vocal folds during phonation, and both may thus be classified perceptually as 'breathy' (see also Hirose and Joshita, 1991). Till and Alp (1991), recognizing the multiplicity of laryngeal movement disorders that may underly a single symptom (e.g., hypovalving of the airstream), have argued that grouping of subjects by *symptom* may be a more productive heuristic than grouping by *disease*. Recent observations of substantial inter-patient variability in the phonatory disorder associated with a single neurological disease – ALS – support this view (Strand, Buder, Yorkston, and Ramig, 1993).

The symptomatology-based categorization of laryngeal disorders as 'hypovalvular' versus 'hypervalvular' (such as occurs in many cases of spastic dysarthria, where the 'strained-strangled' voice is heard) will often be useful, but voice quality may also fluctuate between states from moment to moment. Voice quality ranging from extremely breathy to vocal stoppage (produced by adductor spasms) can be heard in a single breath group in persons with Huntington's chorea, athetoid cerebral palsy, and spasmodic dysphonia (see the interesting reanalysis of the Mayo data by Cannito, 1991, pp. 290–294). In spasmodic dysphonia, ongoing phonation is sometimes modulated by sudden bursts of electromyographic activity in intrinsic laryngeal muscles (see Finitzo and Freeman, 1989), which possibly reflect the underlying mechanism for voice stoppages. Acoustic evidence (Ramig, 1986) has revealed both adductory and abductory voice stoppages in sustained phonation of patients with Huntington's disease, as well. Again, these data suggest the wisdom of focussing more on symptomatology of motor speech disorders as a unifying concept, rather than the Mayo model of disease entity. It is possible, for example, that a symptom-based perspective on research in motor speech disorders would reveal a small set of commonly-occurring speech motor control deficits. The identification of such a set could be the starting point for a more unified theory of motor speech disorders.

L.O. Ramig and her colleagues have argued that, at least in the dysarthria associated with Parkinson's disease, treatment directed at increasing phonatory intensity may produce beneficial effects throughout the speech mechanism. The treatment method, referred to as the Lee Silverman Voice Treatment (LSVT) program (see Ramig, 1995), requires the patient to engage in high-effort exercises to increase phonatory intensity, throughout a relatively brief but intensive sequence of therapy sessions. Several published reports (e.g., Ramig, Bonitati, Lemke, and Horii, 1994; Ramig, Countryman, Thompson, and Horii, 1995) make the claim that the LSVT produced gains among patients with hypokinetic dysarthria, as revealed by a variety of measures of speech production. Importantly, some of the measures (such as average speaking fundamental frequency f_0, variability of f_0, and perceptual scalings of speech intelligibility) were not treated directly, supporting the idea of a highly focussed treatment (i.e., focussed on phonatory intensity) having "spreading effects" to other aspects of speech production. The idea of "spreading effects" in treatment is very much consistent with an older theory of treatment advanced by Rosenbek and LaPointe (1985), wherein the targets of treatment are underlying physiological abnormalities rather than the symptoms – usually defined perceptually – those abnormalities produce. Rosenbek and LaPointe (1985) also believed that a treatment focussed on underlying physiological problems would be likely to affect a number of surface symptoms, some of which might not be related in an obvious way to the physiological deficit.

Whether or not Ramig and her colleagues have demonstrated meaningful treatment effects with the LSVT is open to question. All of the statistical effects reported in the experiments cited above (Ramig et al., 1994, 1995) were based on group data; in this research program there are no single-case designs showing true control over the treatment variables. Moreover, some of the statistically-significant group effects are small enough to raise the question of their "clinical" significance (see, especially, f_0 effects reported in Ramig et al., 1994). Nevertheless, the LSVT or other treatment strategies that target a presumed, focussed physiological basis of a variety of speech production deficits should be investigated further.

Finally, laryngeal behavior for segmental distinctions (Weismer, 1980; Löfqvist, 1980) is often disrupted in motor speech disorders. The evidence for this includes short obstruent voiceless intervals in the speech of Parkinson's patients (Weismer, 1984), an inability among patients with ALS to stop vocal fold vibration at the interface of a voiceless obstruent and vowel (Weismer, Mulligan, and DePaul, 1986, and see above), and the prominent contribution of obstruent voicing feature errors to speech intelligibility deficits in several forms of dysarthria (Kent, Kent, Weismer, Sufit, Rosenbek, Martin, and Brooks, 1990; Kent, Kim, Weismer, Kent, Rosenbek, Sufit, Brooks, and Workinger, 1994). In our experience, phonetic 'microfeatures,' such as the coordinated onsets of the laryngeal devoicing gesture and the vocal tract closure for stops (Löfqvist and Yoshioka, 1981), are *typically* abnormal in most motor speech disorders. These microfeature phenomena do not appear to contribute greatly to speech intelligibility deficits, but do reflect one aspect of the speech motor control disturbance in dysarthria and apraxia of speech. Moreover, the microfeature abnormalities seen early in certain progressive diseases such as ALS and Parkinson's disease may be precursors of more serious deterioration of speech production, and therefore speech intelligibility.

3.3 Supraglottal behavior

Vocal tract activity in motor speech disorders is poorly understood, largely because of a paucity of relevant data. Investigations of *non*speech performance in vocal tract structures have been fairly common, but Weismer and Forrest (1992) have criticized this line of work, citing 1) the frequent failure to show meaningful links between nonspeech orofacial motor control and speech motor control, and 2) the lack of a theoretical framework to motivate the study of nonspeech orofacial control for insight to *speech* motor control. Indeed, the contemporary emphasis on task-specific motor control processes as opposed to effector-oriented control (e.g., Kugler and Turvey, 1987; and Löfqvist, THEORIES AND MODELS OF SPEECH PRODUCTION) would seem to require the study of *speech* movements, or the acoustic output of the vocal tract, to understand disordered speech motor control.

A selected summary of relevant studies of articulatory behavior in motor speech disorders, adapted and expanded from Weismer and Martin (1992), is listed in Table 7.3 (see also Hirose, 1986). This summary includes studies of electromyographic, kinematic, palatographic, aerodynamic, and acoustic characteristics of motor speech disorders. A common finding across studies and methods is that speakers with motor speech disorders often produce individual movements or changes in overall vocal tract shape with reduced displacements and velocities. This often results in the dysarthric speaker having a compressed phonetic working space for speech production. A static index of this space is easily furnished by the classic plot of first versus second formant frequencies, as exemplified in the work of Lehiste (1965), Ziegler and von Cramon (1983b), and Weismer et al. (1986). In terms of dynamic behavior, the velocity reduction seems to be captured well by lower-than-normal slopes of second formant (F2) transitions (Kent et al., 1989; Weismer, 1991; Weismer, Martin, Kent, and Kent, 1992), which are also correlated highly with speech intelligibility deficits (Kent et al., 1989). The average F2 slope derived from a variety of vocalic nuclei (see Weismer, Kent, Hodge, and Martin, 1988; Weismer and Martin, 1992) may therefore serve as a global index of dysarthria severity, simultaneously reflecting the degree of articulatory motor involvement and the loss of speech intelligibility.

The reductions of articulatory displacement and velocity, typically demonstrated for vocalic gestures, may be expected to compromise the integrity of consonantal articulations. This explanation has been used in the case of spirantization of stop consonants, where reduced vocalic gestures are assumed to result in incomplete stop consonant obstructions to the vocal tract airstream (Weismer, 1984; Ackermann and Ziegler, 1991). Although spirantization was originally thought of as a 'signature' characteristic of Parkinsonian dysarthria (Logemann, Fisher, Boshes, and Blonsky, 1978), it appears to be frequent in other motor speech disorders as well (e.g., Weismer et al., 1986).[7]

Articulatory behavior in motor speech disorders may in some cases not only be reduced, but also *uncoordinated*. As pointed out by Kent and Adams (1989), the identification of coordination problems in motor speech disorders (or any speech disorder) is complicated by the lack of agreement concerning a definition of coordination. Coordination may involve the regular, not necessarily synchronous, timing of two or more articulators in the service of some acoustic goal (Kent and Adams, 1989). Table 7.3 contains several examples of studies (Kent and Netsell, 1978; Ziegler and von Cramon, 1983a; Ziegler and von Cramon, 1986) in which persons with motor speech disorders did not satisfy this definition, and thus could be said to produce uncoordinated articulatory

Table 7.3 Survey of speech production deficits in motor speech disorders. Terms such as 'restricted', 'slow', and so forth, use normal as the reference. PD = Parkinson's disease, AD = Ataxic dysarthria, ALS = Amyotrophic lateral sclerosis, TBI = Traumatic brain injury, CP = Cerebral palsy, SpD = Spastic dysarthria, AOS = Apraxia of Speech.

Study	Artic Deficits
1 Kent & Netsell (1975)	*Restricted A–P tongue movement in one AD
2 Kent & Netsell (1978)	*Large jaw movements, restricted A–P movements of tongue in athetoid CP *Dyssynchrony of VP and lingual movements
3 Kent, Netsell, & Bauer (1975)	*restricted ranges of tongue, lip, & jaw movement in different dysarthrias (TBI, AD, CP) *slow articulatory movements *non-uniform velocity patterns
4 Kent, Netsell, & Abbs (1979)	*Equal and excess stress in AD *Loss of duration contrasts
5 Farmer (1980)	*VOT abnormalities in CP between long and short vowels
6 Hirose et al. (1981, 1982)	*Slightly slower velocities of lip, tongue dorsum, and velar movement in PD *reduced range of movement
7 Hunker et al. (1982)	*Reduced lip displacement in PD
8 Kent & Rosenbek (1982)	*Prolonged acoustic vowel steady states and transitions in AD *Spirantization in PD
9 Neilson & O'Dwyer (1983)	*Aberrant EMG signals from orofacial muscles of CP adults, but repetition to repetition variability of EMG no greater than normal
10 Ziegler & von Cramon (1983a)	*Articulatory difficulty when successive gestures conflict in TBI
11 Ziegler & von Cramon (1983b)	*collapsed acoustic vowel space in TBI *lack of acoustic transitions

Table 7.3 Cont'd

Study	Deficits
12 Weismer (1984)	*Spirantization in PD *Short voiceless intervals *Faster-than-normal speaking rates
13 Hardcastle et al. (1985)	*Spatial distortion in lingua-palatal contact patterns in dysarthria
14 Weismer et al. (1986)	*Reduced transition slopes in ALS *Spirantization in ALS *Collapsed acoustic vowel space
15 Ziegler & von Cramon (1986)	*collapsed vowel space in SpD *acoustic evidence of slow movement *difficulty with complex gestures
16 Caruso & Burton (1987)	*Longer stop closures & vowels in ALS
17 Kent et al. (1989)	*Reduced F2 slopes in ALS
18 Forrest et al. (1989)	*minimal jaw movement in PD *reduced articulatory velocities *reductions in transition extent *most abnormal movements and acoustics in complex gestures
19 Caliguiri (1989)	*reduced displacement and velocity of lower lip elevation for /va/ repetitions in PD
20 Moore & Scudder (1989)	*decoupling of EMG activity in bilaterally paired jaw muscles in PD *Tonic digastric activity in PD
21 Ackerman & Ziegler (1991)	*Reduced ability to create articulatory occlusion for consonants in PD, more so for unstressed environments
22 Weismer (1991)	*Reduced transition extents and slopes in PD

Table 7.3 Cont'd

Study	Deficits
23 Weismer et al. (1992)	*Shallow F2 slopes in ALS *Exaggerations of certain transition characteristics in ALS
24 Liss & Weismer (1992)	*Highly variable coupling across repetitions between consonantal and vocalic gestures in AOS
25 Gracco et al. (1992)	*Glottal-supraglottal discoordination for stop consonants in PD, inferred from pressure-flow measures *Slow labial opening and closing gestures in PD, inferred from pressure-flow measures
26 Ackermann, Hertrich, & Scharf (1995)	*Decreased velocity/displacement of lower lip movements in patients with ataxic dysarthria, as compared to normal *Inability of patients to scale lower lip gestures, especially those of brief duration

behavior. There are at least an equal number of studies, however, where the articulatory problem seemed to be largely one of reduction, and not coordination. It is possible that coordination problems are not a chronic aspect of motor speech disorders, but are only revealed when articulatory requirements are relatively complex (Ziegler and von Cramon, 1986; Forrest, Weismer, and Turner, 1989).

Articulatory coordination in motor speech disorders has not been studied much, largely because the technical requirements of monitoring multiple articulators prevent the collection of large amounts of data (e.g., the cineradiographic studies of Kent and his colleagues: see Katz et al., 1990, for a promising technique that poses no known health hazard). Coordination difficulties can also be inferred, however, by careful analysis of the acoustic output of the vocal tract. Liss and Weismer (1992) have studied the formant trajectories of utterance repetitions produced by adults with apraxia of speech, and suggested that trial-to-trial variability can be explained by variable coupling between adjacent vowel and consonant gestures. An example is given in Figure 7.6, which shows five F2 trajectories from a neurologically-normal speaker, and a speaker with apraxia of speech. The trajectories are derived from the word "build" (vocalic nucleus = /ɪl/) in the sentence "Build a big building" with

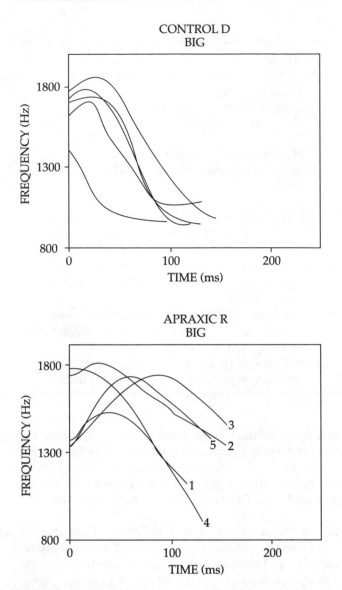

Figure 7.6   Five F2 trajectories produced by a neurologically-normal subject (top) and a subject with apraxia of speech (bottom). The vocalic nucleus from which the trajectories were derived was the /ɪ/ in the word "build" (from the utterance, "build a big building," spoken with emphatic stress on the word "big"). Reproduced by permission from Liss and Weismer (1992).

stress on the word "big." Note the typical shape of the normal speaker's trajectories, which start well above 1,500 Hz and have a steep falling transition following a brief flat or rising segment. All of the apraxic speaker's trajectories also have this descending transition, the onset of which is variably delayed relative to the onset of the whole trajectory. Liss and Weismer (1992) argued that the delay of the major transition is evidence of a 'pulling apart' of the vocalic and consonantal gestures. This pulling apart of the gestures, or *segmentalization*, is evidenced by the extremely low starting frequencies of the three trajectories with the most delayed descending transitions (F2 trajectories #2, 3, and 4 in Figure 7.6). Weismer et al. (1992) have presented examples of this kind of segmentalization for dysarthric speakers with ALS. Recent quantitative analysis (Weismer and Kent, 1993) has shown how the starting frequency of a trajectory can serve as an index of the degree of segmentalization, which in turn predicts the amount of delay to the major transition of a vocalic nucleus. This is an example of how acoustic analysis can be used to reveal interesting aspects of coordination difficulties in motor speech disorders.

Finally, there has been a limited amount of work on the electromyographic characteristics of supraglottal musculature in persons with motor speech disorders. Moore and Scudder (1989) have summarized the difficulties with this work, especially observations of agonist–antagonist cocontraction taken as evidence of underlying pathophysiology (e.g., Leanderson, Meyerson, and Persson, 1972) when in fact co-contraction is a typical feature of normal motor control. Moore and Scudder (1989) reported a loss of synchrony between the left and right side jaw muscles in Parkinsonian dysarthrics, as well as a general pattern indicative of uncoordinated muscular actions. On the other hand, there is evidence that speakers with congenital athetosis (a form of cerebral palsy) produce sentence-to-sentence repetitions with orofacial muscular activity that is aberrant, *but no more inconsistent than the muscular activity of normal speakers* (Neilson and O'Dwyer, 1983). Clearly, additional work combining electromyographic, kinematic, and acoustic methods is required to understand speech motor coordination in the service of acoustic goals. The specification of acoustic goals is necessary, as pointed out by Kent and Adams (1989), to clarify the meaning of 'discoordination' in dysarthric and apraxic speech production.

4 Contemporary issues in motor speech disorders

We have already alluded to several contemporary issues in motor speech disorders, but it is helpful to conclude this chapter in a forward-looking manner by summarizing research frontiers in the area.

The concept of speech intelligibility must be explored in an aggressive fashion, to understand in a detailed manner how motor speech disorders affect the transmission of information. Kent et al. (1989) have designed an intelligibility test with special sensitivities to the speech production deficits in dysarthria.

Moreover, listener responses can be analyzed to obtain a 'phonetic error profile' showing the particular phonetic characteristics that make an important contribution to the overall speech intelligibility deficit. This type of analysis has already demonstrated that very different phonetic error profiles may underlie similar global intelligibility deficits, that certain gender effects may be prominent in some profiles, and that the relationship between disease type and the phonetic error profile may be quite complex (see R. Kent et al., 1990; J. Kent et al., 1992; R. Kent et al., forthcoming). Statistical modeling of speech intelligibility deficits, including acoustic and phonetic predictor variables, should be developed to understand the detailed basis of this index of communication problems. Moreover, the relationship between speech intelligibility in highly controlled conditions, such as in the single-word test of Kent et al. (1989), and somewhat more realistic conditions (prepared sentences, or spontaneous speech) is basically unknown. This is an especially important issue in motor speech disorders, where speech production can vary greatly depending on the material to be spoken. An especially interesting issue concerns the influence of speaking rate on speech intelligibility in motor speech disorders. Because speaking rate is so often affected in motor speech disorders and is manipulated in therapy settings to achieve improved speech intelligibility, knowledge of the link between rate and intelligibility would seem to be critical to a management plan. Surprisingly, there are few data addressing this relationship. Yorkston, Hammen, Beukelman, and Traynor (1990) have reported increases in speech intelligibility at slowed rates for patients with ataxic and hypokinetic dysarthria. On the other hand, Turner, Tjaden, and Weismer (1995) found an inconsistent relationship between rate and speech intelligibility in dysarthric patients with amyotrophic lateral sclerosis (see also Turner and Weismer, 1993). Clearly more knowledge of the transformations between speaking rate, vocal tract acoustic output, and perceptual measures of speech intelligibility is needed to put clinical strategies on firmer, scientific grounds. A complete analysis of the problems associated with modeling of speech intelligibility deficits in motor speech disorders can be found in Weismer and Martin (1992).

Earlier in the chapter, we mentioned the difficulty of specifying coordination problems in motor speech disorders, and of understanding the relationship between electromyographic, kinematic, and acoustic phenomena in dysarthria and apraxia of speech. One approach to resolving these phenomena is to embed observations of neurogenically-disordered speech production within the interpretative framework of existing theories of normal speech production. Surprisingly, there has been very little communication between those investigators attempting to develop general speech production theories, and those interested in neurogenically-disordered speech production. One of the challenging frontiers of research in motor speech disorders will be the attempt to reconcile observations of impaired speech production with these general theories. Weismer, Tjaden, and Kent (1995a,b) have suggested that current theories of speech production do a poor job of accounting for deficits in motor speech disorders, but have general axioms that can be modified and broadened to benefit the understanding of both normal and disordered speech.

It should also be pointed out that the study of motor speech disorders may inform models of normal speech motor control, in much the same way as studies of normal speech production might inform the understanding of motor speech disorders. In many cases of motor speech disorders, there is extensive variability in kinematic and acoustic measures across repetitions of a given utterance. As discussed by Weismer, Tjaden, and Kent (1995a,b), this variability has often been considered as the noisy product of a poorly controlled system. An alternative view, however, is that it is lawful and can be described as such if the right measures are isolated. In several papers (Weismer et al., 1995a,b) we have shown that certain aspects of variability in formant trajectories can be modeled statistically using just a few variables. The discovery of additional variables may provide insight to those models of normal speech production (e.g., Saltzman and Munhall, 1989) that seek to account for articulatory variability in terms of sequences of gestures that can slide back and forth in time (see also Löfqvist, THEORIES AND MODELS OF SPEECH PRODUCTION). Thus the study of speech production characteristics in motor speech disorders should not be viewed as subsidiary to studies of normal speech production, but as equal to the task of developing a comprehensive model of speech production processes both in the normal and disordered state.

NOTES

The writing of this chapter was supported in part by Public Health Service Grant No. DC00319, through the National Institutes of Deafness and other Communication Disorders

1   Tone, as assessed clinically, is the subjective impression of resistance of a limb to passive displacement. The limbs of neurologically-intact individuals offer some mild resistance to passive displacement; *hypotonia* is the impression of minimal or no resistance to displacement, whereas *hypertonia* is the impression of excessive resistance to displacement (as in upper motoneuron disease, or Parkinson's disease). The assessment of tone in the speech mechanism is substantially more complicated as compared to the limbs, partly as a result of the inaccessibility of the structures (e.g., the tongue, or laryngeal muscles), and partly because the generally accepted mechanism of normal and disordered tone involves an intramuscular structure (the muscle spindle) whose presence in certain orofacial muscles is questionable. See Barlow and Abbs (1984) and Neilson, Andrews, Guitar, and Quinn (1979) for additional information on muscles spindles and tone in the speech mechanism, and Brooks (1986, pp. 151–159) for an excellent review of the mechanisms and measurement of tone.

2   It is important to be clear on what Darley et al. meant by this statement.

Out of context, the statement could be regarded as trivial, because if a neurological disease produces a disturbance in speech production, then of course speech pathology will reflect neuropathology. Darley et al. meant something much more specific, namely that the observed speech pathology is a direct reflection of the classic and partially unique neuropathologies associated with the various neurological diseases. The impact of this viewpoint on the field of speech pathology cannot be underestimated, especially in the domain of clinical evaluation of motor speech disorders.

3   It is beyond the scope of this chapter to explore the current status of the Mayo system in great depth, but it should be noted that Darley et al. (1969a,b) were very much oriented to the diagnostic role of the speech-language pathologist, and almost certainly provided important diagnostic input to the attending physician, who did not have access to the kinds of brain imaging techniques available today. Thus, both the neurologist and the speech-language pathologist of thirty years ago depended very much on perceptual examinations to make their diagnoses; the speech-language pathologist listened to speech and observed orofacial nonspeech motor control, whereas the neurologist evaluated limb strength, range of motion, alternating motion rates, and so forth, when conducting his or her examination. These kinds of evaluations still take place today, but brain imaging techniques would seem to lessen the need for the speech-language pathologist's **diagnostic** contribution to the neurology workup. In any case, there is also the question of whether the Mayo system is effective when other

clinicians use it. Zyski and Weisinger (1987) attempted to replicate the 'localizing' finding of Darley et al. by blinding trained speech-language clinicians to patients' neurological diagnosis, and asking them to identify dysarthria type based on perceptual analysis of speech samples; identification accuracy in this experiment was very poor. Nevertheless, Duffy (1995, pp. 3–4; 8–9), in his recent textbook which can be considered as an update of the Mayo perspective put forth by Darley et al. (1975), still argues for the localizing value of (perceptual) speech symptoms in dysarthria.

4   Marquardt and Sussman (1991, p. 342) have summed up the definitional problem with DAS quite nicely: ". . . neurological insult and maturational dysfunction are the only proposed etiologies [for DAS], but studies have not found clear evidence of neurological deficits. Evidence for a neurological basis then rests on behavioral symptomatology and the argument for brain dysfunction becomes tautological: developmental apraxia is ascribed to neurological origins on the basis of apractic symptoms, which in turn are assigned to the brain dysfunction."

5   The perceptual study, not reported in the original presentation (Weismer et al., 1986), involved scaling of the 'normalcy' of utterances produced by the five ALS speakers who took part in the study, as well as other selected speakers with normal neurological histories or those with known neuropathologies and obvious dysarthrias. Judges were asked to scale the normalcy of sentence production using a seven-point, equal-appearing interval scale, where 1 = most abnormal and 7 = normal. 'Normalcy' was defined for

the judges as meeting the criteria of intelligibility, articulatory accuracy, and naturalness expected from speakers without neurological disease. The judges were three graduate students who had experience treating persons with motor speech disorders. The scale values of the utterances produced by the ALS patients described here were essentially the same as those for utterances produced by the neurologically-normal speakers.

6 There have also been further studies of the perceptual characteristics of motor speech disorders (Carrow, Rivera, Mauldin, and Shamblin, 1974; Joanette and Dudley, 1980; Yorkston, Hammen, Beukelman, and Traynor, 1990; Workinger and Kent, 1991; Platt et al., 1980a,b) which will not be reviewed further in this chapter.

7 Our experience is that spirantization can be observed in nearly every type of dysarthria originally described by Darley et al. (1975), as well as in apraxia of speech. This would follow from the claim that reductions in F2 slopes of vocalic nuclei are a common feature of motor speech disorders.

8 Brain Functions Underlying Speech

RAY D. KENT AND KRISTIN TJADEN

Brain imaging abbreviations used in text:
> CT — computerized tomography; also known as CAT (computerized axial tomography).
> fMRI — functional magnetic resonance imaging (see MRI).
> MRI — magnetic resonance imaging; also known as nuclear magnetic resonance (NMR), particularly among physicists.
> PET — Positron emission tomography.
> rCBF — regional cerebral blood flow.
> SPECT — Single photon emission tomography.
> CT and MRI are used to image structure; fMRI, PET, and SPECT are used to image function or metabolism, one index of which is rCBF.

1 General neuroanatomy for speech

The brain functions that underlie speech reflect a complex neuroanatomy and neurophysiology. It is not possible to consider here the relevant neuroanatomy in any detail, but a general overview may be helpful for readers who are not familiar with neuroanatomy or those who would benefit from a brief review of terminology (especially because of terminological differences in writings on neuroanatomy). Human neuroanatomy is exceedingly complex, and the overview will be necessarily simplified and selective. More detailed information is available from additional sources cited in the text. Similarly, neurophysiology will be only selectively considered, but references to the literature should help the interested reader to seek additional information. General reviews of related material are available in Barlow and Farley (1989), Buckingham (1984), Caplan (1987), Kean (1988), Larson (1988), Musiek and Lamb (1992), Smith (1992), and Square and Martin (1994).

Figure 8.1 provides a general orientation to the human nervous system. Figure 8.1a illustrates the intact neuraxis, or central nervous system (CNS).

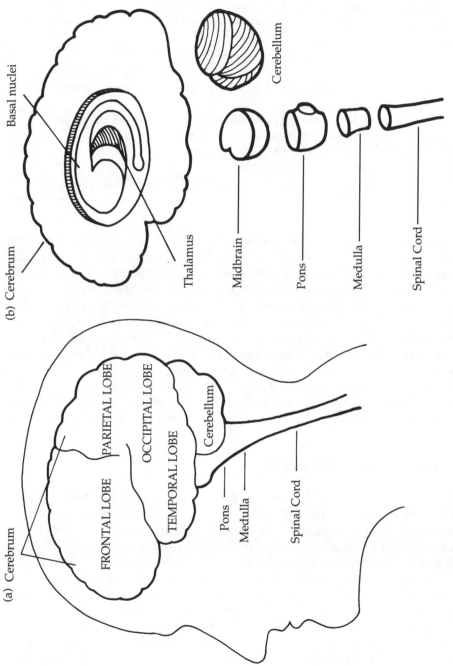

(a) Cerebrum

FRONTAL LOBE

PARIETAL LOBE

OCCIPITAL LOBE

TEMPORAL LOBE

Cerebellum

Pons

Medulla

Spinal Cord

(b) Cerebrum

Basal nuclei

Thalamus

Midbrain

Pons

Medulla

Spinal Cord

Cerebellum

Figure 8.1 (a) Lateral view of the intact CNS; (b) lateral view of the exploded CNS, showing major subdivisions.

Table 8.1 The six layers of the cerebral cortex. This is the commonly used description, but other systems have been published

Layer	Neuronal type and comments
I	This outermost layer is called the plexiform or molecular layer and consists primarily of diffusely distributed small fibers and few cell bodies.
II	Second layer from the outside, consisting of small pyramids.
III	Medium and large pyramids; relatively few fibers.
IV	Granular layer, composed of star cells.
V	Deep layer of large pyramids.
VI	Deepest layer, composed of medium pyramids and spindle cells.

The CNS consists of the brain and spinal cord, and is contained within the protective coverings of bone (cranium or vertebral column) and meninges (the tissues of the dura, arachnoid, and pia mater). Aside from their protective role, the tissues that surround the brain impose a limit on the expansion of the cranial contents. Because the cranium is closed through suturing of the cranial bones, hemorrhage or tumors carry great risk of death to brain cells through compression. The peripheral nervous system (PNS) consists of the 31 paired spinal nerves (which emerge from the spinal cord) and the 12 paired cranial nerves (which emerge from the base of the brain).

Figure 8.1b shows an exploded view of the major structures, including the cerebral hemispheres, thalamus, brainstem (midbrain, pons, and medulla), cerebellum and spinal cord. Each of these is considered briefly below.

1.1 Central nervous system

1.1.1 Cerebral cortex
The cortex is the thin (2–3 mm) bark that covers the cerebral hemispheres. This bark has a gray or dark color owing to the high concentration of neuronal cell bodies. The neurons are arranged in six cytoarchitectural layers as described in Table 8.1 (Bindman and Lippold, 1981). The underlying tissue of the hemispheres has a predominantly whitish color imparted by the myelin coating of the axonic processes. Although the cerebral hemispheres have a homogeneous appearance on superficial examination, microscopic studies reveal regional differences in neuronal type, laminar structure, and connections to adjacent and remote brain tissues. Some of these differences were recorded by Brodmann (1914) in a classic cortical map of numbered cytoarchitectural regions (Figure 8.2). Because these regional differences appeared to reflect differences in the functions of different parts of the brain, the Brodmann areas have been used to describe various localized

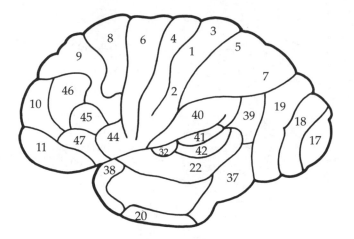

Figure 8.2 Selected Brodmann areas of the cerebral cortex.

functions. That is, discrete zones of the cortex have been identified through both microanatomic studies of cellular structure and functional or clinical studies that reveal regional differences in the brain's control of behavior.

The parcellations of the cortex that are most widely known for language functions are Broca's area (identified with Brodmann Area 44) and Wernicke's area (typically identified with Brodmann Areas 22, 37 and 42). Broca's area was named after Paul Broca who proposed that this cortical region was responsible for speech production. Wernicke's area was named after Carl Wernicke who described a cortical region that apparently was central to language comprehension. Wernicke also proposed an early and influential model in which Broca's and Wernicke's areas were part of a neural system for language. For a historical summary of this model, see Caplan (1987). Whitaker (1995) provides historical notes on brain-language studies that predate Broca and Wernicke, noting that Alexander Hood in 1824 "did a better job [than Broca] of analyzing expressive language functions and correlating them to frontal lobe anatomy" (p. 165). Whether or not Broca and Wernicke fully deserve the recognition, to this day many writers of both popular articles and specialized texts acknowledge Broca's and Wernicke's areas as the primary centers of language. A following section will review the degree to which recent evidence supports this position. Although the neural regulation of speech, not language, is the primary focus of this chapter, it is necessary to understand speech as a modality of language expression.

The cerebral cortex is a highly convoluted surface, and the major gyri (outfoldings) and sulci (infoldings) are frequently used as landmarks for anatomic descriptions (Figure 8.3). The two cerebral hemispheres are separated by the deep Longitudinal Fissure, which gives the brain a decided right-left pairing. Each hemisphere in turn has numerous fissures, but the two most commonly identified in gross neuroanatomy are the Central Fissure (or the Fissure

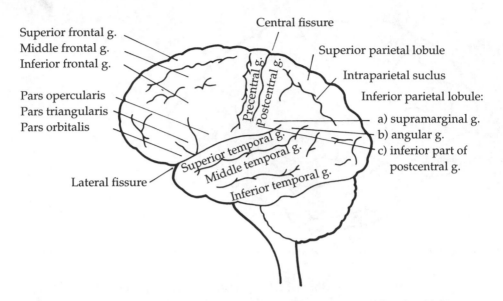

Figure 8.3 Major gyri (g.) and sulci of the cerebral cortex. Identified structures are those most relevant to speech and language functions.

of Rolando) and the Lateral Fissure (or the Fissure of Sylvius). Lesser sulci are not as readily identified because of large individual differences in their configuration (Ono et al., 1990). Each hemisphere is comprised of four visible lobes: frontal, parietal, occipital, and temporal (Figure 8.1a). An internal lobe, the limbic lobe, can be seen upon removal of the overlying cerebral tissue.

1.1.2 Intrinsic circuitry of the cerebral cortex   Cortical neurons communicate with one another both locally (e.g., interlaminar connections) and remotely (e.g., corticocortical pathways or fasciculi). One of the most influential models of cortical connectivity was proposed by Hubel and Wiesel (1962, 1977) from their studies of visual cortex in the cat and monkey. Essentially, their model was that excitatory input from the thalamus was received primarily in Layer IV. The Layer IV neurons send information to neighboring neurons in a pattern of converging, vertical connections. The result is a sequence that proceeds from excitation of simple cells in one layer to complex physiological patterns in other regions of the cortex. This model has been supported in a number of light and electron microscopy studies (Hendry, 1987). The implications of this model are that (1) the excitation is spread vertically to all cells in a column, and (2) the cells in this vertical organization are also subject to direct afferent inputs and intrinsic inhibitory inputs.

1.1.3 Major corticocortical pathways   Corticocortical pathways (fasciculi) are the means of communication for remote areas of the cortex. This rich

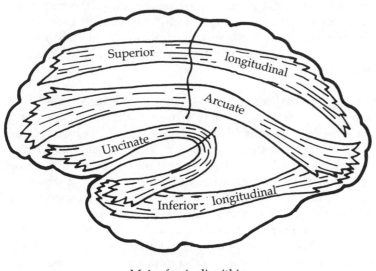

Major fasciculi within
cerebral hemisphere

Figure 8.4 Selected association tracts of the cerebral cortex.

network of hemispheric communication consists of two primary fiber types. Association fibers connect cortical areas of an individual hemisphere and commissural fibers join the two cerebral hemispheres. Association fibers are typically classified as short and long fibers. Short fibers function as communication linkages for adjacent gyri while long fibers connect distant areas of a single hemisphere. Figure 8.4 illustrates the major association fibers.

The largest of the association bundles, the superior longitudinal fasciculus, connects the cortex of the frontal, parietal, occipital, and temporal lobes while the inferior longitudinal fasciculus connects the temporal and occipital lobes. The association fiber bundle most frequently mentioned in respect to speech and language functions is the arcuate fasciculus which transfers neural information between Broca's and Wernicke's areas. Lesions of this structure may cause a dissociation of Broca's and Wernicke's areas resulting in a type of aphasia often classified as conduction aphasia. Additional association fibers include the cingulum, which lies on the medial aspect of each hemisphere. This structure connects the frontal, parietal, and temporal lobes within each hemisphere and is functionally part of the limbic system.

Commissural fiber bundles include the large corpus callosum as well as the anterior, middle, and posterior commissures. The corpus callosum connects analogous areas of the two cerebral hemispheres and provides a communication link between the two hemispheres. The corpus callosum consists of four parts, a trunk (main portion), splenium (posterior end), genu (anterior end), and the rostrum (which extends from the genu to the anterior commissure).

Severing this structure may result in functional separation of the two hemispheric lobes. Studies investigating such "split brain" conditions have revealed a significant amount of information regarding hemispheric specialization of function. The evidence for cerebral asymmetry of function will be reviewed in Section 2 (Neural Control of Speech Production).

1.1.4 Basal nuclei   The basal nuclei (also known as the basal ganglia, although the term *ganglia* is reserved by many writers for cell body masses in the PNS) are a set of nuclear masses (that is, aggregates of neuronal nuclei) situated near the top of the brain stem (Figure 8.5). They are difficult to visualize because the nuclei have a complicated three-dimensional configuration. Another difficulty is that different authors include different sets of structures as comprising the basal nuclei. The definition used here is quite conservative; the basal nuclei include the caudate ("tail"), putamen ("stone"), globus pallidus ("pale globe"), subthalamic nucleus ("under the thalamus"), and substantia nigra ("black substance"). The caudate, putamen, and globus pallidus are shown in Figure 8.5; the subthalamic nucleus and substantia nigra are smaller structures not clearly seen in this section of the brain. Even with this conservative definition, terminological confusions may be encountered because the literature often uses terms that designate various combinations of these three structures. For example, lenticular ("lenslike") nucleus is the name given to the putamen and globus pallidus, which lie closely together in a shape that suggests a lens. The term striatum refers to the caudate and putamen, which have a striated appearance under microscopy. Input to the basal nuclei is primarily through the striatum, and output to other structures is largely through the globus pallidus (sometimes called the pallidum) and the substantia nigra. Pallidal outflow is primarily to the thalamus, which, in turn, projects to the cortex. Thus, the cortex and basal nuclei form a circuit consisting fundamentally of the following pathway: cortex → striatum → pallidum → cortex.

The basal nuclei are most commonly recognized for their role in motor control. Ito (1989) describes the function as one of stabilization of motor systems. Large and complicated systems, such as the human motor control system, require stabilization in order to operate effectively. By virtue of their connections within the motor control circuits of the brain, the basal nuclei are well-situated to exercise stabilization. Furthermore, some of the major disorders associated with damage to the basal nuclei, such as hypokinesia in Parkinson's disease and hyperkinesia in chorea, may be viewed as deficiencies in stabilization.

Other views of the motor function of the basal nuclei include: regulating the execution of movement (Delong et al., 1984), directing actions (Passingham, 1987), and converting sensory information into a form that can be used to guide movement, as well as gating sensory inputs to other motor areas (Lidsky et al., 1985). Passingham (1987) reviews reasons why cortical-subcortical circuits involving the basal nuclei are suitable for directing action, and why corticocortical circuits are not.

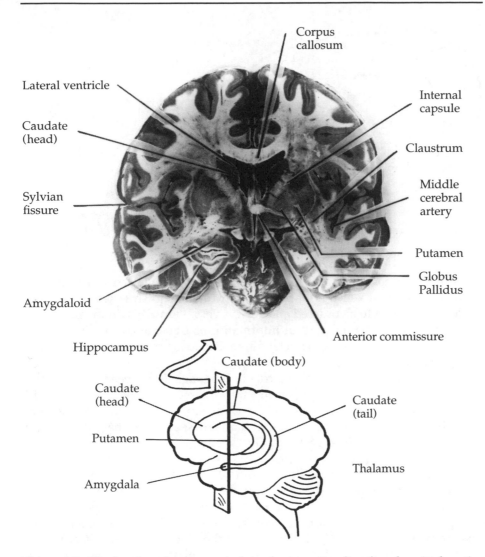

Corpus
callosum

Lateral ventricle

Internal
capsule

Caudate
(head)

Claustrum

Middle
cerebral
artery

Sylvian
fissure

Putamen

Globus
Pallidus

Amygdaloid

Hippocampus

Anterior commissure

Caudate (body)

Caudate
(head)

Caudate
(tail)

Putamen

Amygdala

Thalamus

Figure 8.5 The basal nuclei, shown in lateral perspective (inset) and sagittal section of the brain.

Very different conceptions have been published concerning the ways in which cortical information is processed as it is conveyed through the basal nuclei (Parent and Hazrati, 1995). The parallel-processing hypothesis states that the information derived from distinct cortical areas is maintained in a segregated form by virtue of multiple, parallel channels that run through the basal nuclei. The information-funneling hypothesis proposes that the information from distinct cortical areas converges in the basal nuclei, so that information projected from the basal nuclei back to the cortex combines the original

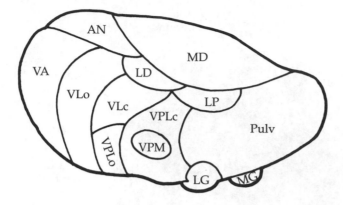

Figure 8.6   Major thalamic nuclei. See Table 8.2.

functional submodalities. Parent and Hazrati (1995) reviewed evidence for a third conception in which multiple modular units are distributed in the basal nuclei conforming to an ordered and repetitive pattern. This arrangement was thought to insure that (a) cortical information is transmitted in a highly specific manner, and (b) the basal nuclei can modulate neuronal activity in several brain systems.

The basal nuclei also may play a role in language. It has been reported that damage to these structures, especially the putamen, can be associated with language disturbance (Crosson, 1992; Damasio et al., 1982). In addition, dysarthrias can result from basal nuclei damage (see Darley et al., 1975; Duffy, 1995; and Weismer, MOTOR SPEECH DISORDERS).

1.1.5 Diencephalon (especially thalamus)   The diencephalon is commonly divided into four parts, the dorsal thalamus, the ventral thalamus, the epithalamus, and the hypothalamus. For our purposes, the general term "thalamus" is appropriate for characterizing the first three of these structures. Thalamus means "meeting place" or "chamber." This structure is appropriately named given that all sensory (excluding olfaction) and select motoric information destined for the cerebral cortex is integrated in this structure. Thus, the thalamus is a key link between subcortical and cortical structures in sensory and motor systems.

The thalamus is a paired structure located at the most rostral or superior end of the brainstem, enclosed by the cerebral hemispheres. Structurally, this nuclear body can be divided into anterior, medial, and lateral masses. Figure 8.6 illustrates the individual nuclei of these masses and their relative position in the thalamus.

Each thalamic nucleus serves as a sensory or motor integration center. Tables 8.2 and 8.3 summarize the major connections of these nuclei. It is apparent from these tables that the thalamus has complex subcortical and cortical

Table 8.2 Summary of thalamic nuclear groups and their corresponding individual nuclei

Nuclear Group	Named Nuclei
Anterior	no named nuclei
Medial	Mediodorsal (MD)
Lateral	Lateral Dorsal (LD)
	Lateral Posterior (LP)
	Pulvinar
Ventral	Ventral Lateral (VL)
	Ventral Anterior (VA)
	Ventralposterolateral (VPL)
	Ventralposteromedial (VPM)
	Medial Geniculate Body (MGB)
	Lateral Geniculate Body (LGB)
Intralaminar	Sheet-like Nuclei
	Centromedian (CM)

connections including connections with the basal nuclei and cerebellum. Nuclei specifically thought to be involved in speech and language production include the lateral posterior and pulvinar nuclei of the lateral mass. Although the relationship between these structures and speech and language function is unclear, it has been suggested that these nuclei serve as a relay between Broca's and Wernicke's areas. Other "motor" nuclei include the ventral anterior (VA) and ventral lateral (VL) nuclei of the ventral mass. These nuclei receive input from the cerebellum and the basal nuclei and project to premotor and motor cortex. In addition, the centromedian nucleus (CM), a part of the internal medullary lamina, has connections with the basal nuclei and motor cortex. These motor nuclei are thought to play an important role in the planning of voluntary movements. Botez and Barbeau (1971) and Crosson (1992) review evidence for the participation of the thalamus in speech and language functions.

In contrast to the specific sensory and motor integration function of the thalamus, the hypothalamus is involved in endocrine, autonomic, and behavioral functions such as release of hormones, control of food and water intake, sexual behavior, diurnal rhythms, and mediation of emotional responses. The hypothalamus is commonly divided into three regions including the supraoptic, tuberal, and mammillary regions. Although not directly involved in speech and language functions, the mammillary bodies are thought to play a role in

Table 8.3   Summary of thalamic connections

Nuclei	Input	Cortical Connections
Anterior Nuclear Group	Limbic System	Cingulate Gyrus
Mediodorsal Nucleus	Olfactory cortex Spinothalamic (pain) afferents	Frontal Association Cortex
Lateral Dorsal	Limbic System	Cingulate Gyrus
Lateral Posterior and Pulvinar	Superior Colliculus	Parietal, Temporal and Occipital Association Cortex
Ventral Lateral Ventral Anterior	Cerebellum Globus Pallidus Substantia Nigra	Motor and Pre-motor Cortex
Ventralpostero-lateral Nucleus Ventralpostero-medial Nucleus	Medial Lemniscus Spinothalamic Tracts Trigeminal fibers Taste fibers	Primary Sensory Cortex (and Motor Cortex)
Medial Geniculate Body	Inferior Colliculus	Auditory Cortex
Lateral Geniculate Body	Retinal ganglion cells	Primary Visual Cortex
Sheet-like Nuclei	Spinal Cord	(diffuse)
Centromedian	Globus Pallidus	Motor Cortex

the formation of memories. The hypothalamus may also act to mediate bodily functions via emotional factors.

1.1.6 Cerebellum   Cerebellum means "little brain" which appropriately describes this structure situated at the base of the occipital lobe. The cerebellum is one of the phylogenetically oldest structures of the brain. It is comprised of a superficial cerebellar cortex, which is the primary afferent center of the cerebellar white matter, and three sets of paired deep cerebellar nuclei, which comprise the major efferent portion of the cerebellum. Figure 8.7 illustrates the major fissures and subdivisions of the cerebellum.

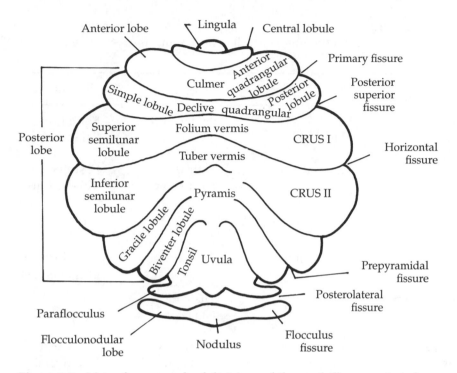

Figure 8.7 Major fissures and subdivisions of the cerebellum, as viewed schematically from the posterior aspect.

In contrast to the distinct cytoarchitectural areas of the cerebral cortex, the cerebellar cortex is uniform in its entirety. In fact, cortical gray matter from one area cannot be differentiated from that of another area and is even similar across species. The cerebellar cortex is characterized by the presence of many narrow, leaf-like folia with several fissures which serve to identify functional areas. Important landmarks include the primary fissure separating the anterior and posterior lobes, as well as the posterolateral fissure which divides the posterior and flocculonodular lobes. The cerebellum is also divided on the sagittal plane into a medial region known as the vermis and the large paired lateral hemispheres.

Afferent information is conveyed to the cerebellar cortex via the middle and inferior cerebellar peduncles (or "feet") from the spinal cord, vestibular system and motor cortical areas. This information is then transferred to the deep cerebellar nuclei via Purkinje cells, which are the sole source of output for the cerebellum. Efferent information leaves the deep cerebellar nuclei via the superior cerebellar peduncle destined for the spinal cord, thalamus (VA and VL) and cerebral cortex. Table 8.4 summarizes the major input and output relationships of the cerebellum.

Table 8.4   Summary of primary input and output relations of the cerebellum including intervening cerebellar nuclei and the associated function

Input	Cerebellar Nuclei	Projection	Function
Vestibular Nerve	Vestibular Nucleus	Spinal Cord	Equilibrium Balance
Spinal Cord Tracts	Fastigial Nucleus	Reticular Formation	Posture Muscle tone
	Vestibular Nucleus		
Spinal Cord Tracts	Interpositus Nucleus	Red Nucleus	Coordination of movement
Sensory Cortex		VA and VL Thalamic Nuclei	
Premotor Cortex	Dentate Nucleus	VA and VL Thalamic Nuclei	Coordination of movement
Motor Association Cortex		Red Nucleus	

The role of the cerebellum in speech motor control seems to be to coordinate the various muscle groups to produce a smooth flow of movement. Lesions of the cerebellum may result in decomposition of movement into component parts as well as errors in rate and range of movement. Because of the cerebellum's complex interconnections with the cortex and spinal cord, it has been hypothesized that the lateral cerebellum, which receives input from the premotor and association cortical areas acts to preprogram a movement, whereas the intermediate cerebellum (vermis) acts to update the evolving movement via its input from the sensorimotor cortical and spinal inputs. Recent discussions of selected topics on cerebellar function are: (1) effects of cerebellar pathology (Diener and Dichgans, 1992); (2) cerebellar regulation of movement (Thach et al., 1992); (3) cerebellar control of timing patterns (Jueptner et al., 1995; Keele and Ivry, 1990); (4) cerebellar function in computational, cognitive and language skills (Daum and Ackermann, 1995; Leiner et al., 1991; Silveri et al., 1994); and (5) conceptualizing the cerebellum as being specifically responsive to certain sequences of events in its input, and, in turn, producing sequences of signals in its output (Braitenberg, Heck, and Sultan, forthcoming).

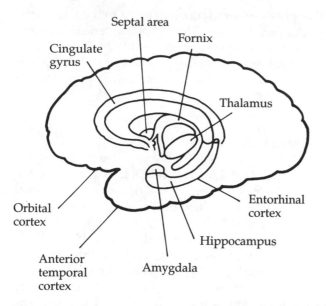

Septal area
Fornix
Cingulate gyrus
Thalamus
Orbital cortex
Entorhinal cortex
Hippocampus
Anterior temporal cortex
Amygdala

Figure 8.8 Structures comprising the limbic system.

1.1.7 Limbic system The limbic system is one of the most recently described major structures of the human brain. The term limbic means "border." The limbic lobe is a ring of cortex on the medial aspect of the cerebral hemispheres. The cortical areas of this lobe, including the cingulate gyrus, parahippocampal gyrus, and septal cortex, are interconnected via the cingulum (Figure 8.8). Structures included as part of the limbic system are the limbic lobe, the hippocampus ("sea horse"), amygdala ("almond"), the septal area, the mammillary ("breastlike") bodies (sometimes including the entire hypothalamus), and the anterior nuclei of the thalamus. The precise role of this structure in speech and language functions is unknown. However, the limbic system is thought to be important in emotional and visceral responses and thus may provide a motivational aspect to communication. A later section will emphasize the role of some limbic structures in intention.

1.1.8 Midbrain, pons and medulla The major brainstem structures include the midbrain, pons and medulla. These structures serve essential life functions including thermoregulation, respiration, swallowing, and digestion. It has been proposed that speech motor control follows directly from these basic centers of swallowing and respiration. Evidence for the role of central pattern generators (CPG's) in speech production will be discussed later. The pons and medulla also house the cranial nerve nuclei from which the cranial nerves originate and proceed or terminate. An important structure found within the brainstem is the reticular formation, which has both descending and ascending components. The descending reticular formation consists of a number of diffusely located nuclei that provide extrapyramidal input to the autonomic nervous system and to the voluntary muscles. The ascending reticular formation (also known as the reticular activating system) is a similarly diffuse group of nuclei that receive inputs from several sensory systems. The ascending reticular formation projects largely to the thalamus, which, in turn, projects to the cortex. This system regulates alertness and sleep.

1.2 Peripheral nervous system

1.2.1 Cranial nerves

The twelve cranial nerves and their associated brainstem nuclei are summarized in Table 8.5. Seven of the twelve paired cranial nerves are especially pertinent to speech production. These are cranial nerves V, VII, VIII, IX, X, XI, and XII. Nolte (1981) provides an excellent detailed description of the functional components of each cranial nerve. Leblanc (1995) is especially valuable for its presentation of cranial nerve anatomy through magnetic resonance imaging, computed tomography, and dissection photographs.

For present purposes, the cranial nerves may be thought to serve either sensory, motor, or combined sensory/motor functions. Motor or efferent portions of cranial nerves originate in numerous brainstem nuclei and then proceed to exit the brainstem to innervate musculature of the head, neck, and shoulders as well as abdominal and thoracic viscera. In contrast, the afferent portions of the various cranial nerves carry sensory information from receptors located in the periphery to additional brainstem nuclei. Sensory information is then relayed via the thalamus (except for Cranial Nerve I) to sensorimotor cortex. The following section briefly describes the major motor and sensory functions of those cranial nerves important for speech production.

The Trigeminal Nerve (V) innervates the muscles of mastication and relays general sensory information from the face; primary brainstem nuclei include the Trigeminal Motor Nucleus as well as the Main Sensory.

The efferent portion of the Facial Nerve (VII) innervates the muscles of facial expression via the Facial Motor Nucleus and provides taste information from the anterior 2/3 of the tongue via the Solitary Nucleus.

The Statoacoustic Nerve (VIII) is classically considered to be sensory in nature and contains vestibular and cochlear portions which play an important role in balance and hearing, respectively. However, more recent research has disclosed efferent pathways. Brainstem nuclei of this nerve include the Vestibular Nucleus and Cochlear Nucleus.

The Glossopharyngeal Nerve (IX) innervates various pharyngeal muscles via Nucleus Ambiguus which are important for swallowing. Taste information is conveyed from the posterior 1/3 of the tongue to the Solitary Nucleus. This cranial nerve also plays a role in salivation via the Inferior Salivatory Nucleus.

The efferent portion of the Vagus nerve (X) innervates intrinsic laryngeal and pharyngeal muscles via Nucleus Ambiguus to produce phonation. The Vagus also innervates thoracic and abdominal viscera via the Dorsal Motor Nucleus

Table 8.5 Summary of the cranial nerves, including: Roman Numeral designation; name; origin or termination in the CNS; major function (SS = special sensory, GS = general sensory, VS = visceral sensory, VM = visceral motor, BM = branchial motor, SM = somatic motor); sensory or motor ending in the PNS; and general location within CNS

Number	Name	Origin or termination in CNS	Major function	CNS Location
I	Olfactory	Olfactory epithelium	SS: olfactory epithelium	Telencephalon
II	Optic	Ganglion cells of retina	SS: ganglion cells of retina	Diencephalon
III	Oculomotor	Oculomotor nucleus	SM, VM: eye muscles	Midbrain
IV	Trochlear	Trochlear nucleus	SM: eye muscles	Midbrain
V	Trigeminal	Spinal and main sensory nuclei	GS: skin and head, dura mater	Mid pons
		Mesencephalic nucleus	GS: muscle spindles, mechanoreceptors	
		Trigeminal motor nucleus	BM: jaw muscles, tensor tympani	
VI	Abducens	Abducens nucleus	SM: eye muscles	Inferior pons
VII	Facial	Spinal trigeminal nucleus	GS: outer ear	Pons-medulla junction
		Solitary nucleus	SS: taste buds in anterior tongue	
		Solitary nucleus	SS: portion of nasopharynx	
		Superior salivatory nucleus	VM: salivary glands, lacrimal gland	
		Facial motor nucleus	BM: muscles of facial expression, stapedius	

Table 8.5 Cont'd

Number	Name	Origin or termination in CNS	Major function		CNS Location
VIII	Statoacoustic	Cochlear and vestibular nuclei	SS:	Organ of Corti, vestibular receptors	Pons-medulla junction
IX	Glossopharyngeal	Spinal trigeminal nucleus	GS:	outer ear	Medulla
		Solitary nucleus	SS:	taste of posterior tongue	
		Solitary and spinal trigeminal nuclei	VS:	carotid body and sinus, oropharyngeal mucosa	
		Inferior salivatory nucleus	VM:	parotid gland	
		Nucleus ambiguus	BM:	pharynx (stylopharyngeus)	
X	Vagus	Spinal trigeminal nucleus	GS:	outer ear	Medulla
		Solitary nucleus	SS:	taste in epiglottis	
		Solitary and spinal trigeminal nuclei	VS:	thoracic and abdominal viscera, membranes of larynx and pharynx	
		Dorsal motor nucleus	VM:	thoracic and abdominal viscera	
		Nucleus ambiguus	BM:	larynx and pharynx	
XI	Spinal accessory	Accessory nucleus, spinal cord	BM:	sternocleidomastoid, trapezius	Cervical cord
XII	Hypoglossal	Hypoglossal nucleus	SM:	muscles of tongue	Medulla

and relays sensory information from these structures to the Solitary Nucleus. Taste information from the epiglottis is also relayed to the Solitary Nucleus.

The spinal portion of the Spinal Accessory nerve (XI) innervates the trapezius and sternocleidomastoid muscles of the neck and shoulder via the Accessory Nucleus which function to turn the head and move the shoulders. The cranial portion of this nerve innervates muscles of the velum via Nucleus Ambiguus.

The Hypoglossal Nerve (XII) innervates all intrinsic muscles of tongue as well as select extrinsic muscles via the Hypoglossal Nucleus.

1.2.2 Spinal nerves The peripheral nervous system also includes the 31 paired spinal nerves which exit the spinal cord to innervate distal and axial musculature. In contrast to the cranial nerves, all spinal nerves contain a sensory and motor root or portion. Sensory information is relayed from the periphery to the dorsal horn of the spinal cord where the information eventually ascends in the spinal cord via various fiber tract systems to terminate in thalamic nuclei before reaching the cortex. Similarly, the motor roots of the spinal nerves originate in the ventral horn of the spinal cord and continue to exit the spinal cord to innervate muscles of the trunk and appendages. The spinal cord is selectively enlarged in both the cervical and lumbar regions due to the large number of nerve fibers supplying the appendages. In contrast, the mid-levels of the spinal cord are thinner due to the fewer nerve fibers needed to subserve axial musculature.

Lesions of the PNS result in a clustering of symptoms typically known as Lower Motor Neuron Syndrome (LMNS) which is characterized by a complete or partial paralysis of select muscle groups as well as muscle atrophy and muscle fasciculations, loss of spinal reflexes of those muscles subserved by affected spinal nerves, and sensory deficits. Lesions including the cranial nerves or their brainstem nuclei may result in "flaccid dysarthria." See Weismer, MOTOR SPEECH DISORDERS in this volume for a description of this motor speech disorder.

2 Neural control of speech production

The literature on speech production is replete with reference to processes such as linguistic input, motor programming, coordination and execution. These and other functions are summarized in Table 8.6, which lists major functions underlying speech, presumed neural structures for each function, and major disorders associated with each function. Information in this table will be mentioned in various sections to follow. The table is given primarily as a heuristic device, and not as a definitive summary of neural regulatory processes. Stage descriptions of neural processing are quite popular in the literature, but it can be difficult to establish the functional independence of the postulated stages in a multistage description. Some or all of the listed functions are mentioned in several recent discussions of speech neural control, including Fujimura (1990),

Table 8.6   General scheme of functions, neural substrates and associated neurogenic disorders of spoken language

Function	Primary Neural Structures	Disorder
Intention	Fronto-limbic formations of the forebrain	Mutism
Linguistic-symbolic processing	Cortico-cortical connections	Aphasia, apraxia of speech
Motor speech programming or planning	Wernicke's area, Broca's area, premotor cortex, supplementary motor area, inferior parietal lobule, inferior dorsolateral cortex, cerebellum, basal nuclei	Apraxia of speech
Coordination	Basal nuclei, cerebellum, motor cortex	Dysarthria
Execution	Pyramidal and extrapyramidal motor pathways	Dysarthria

Kent et al. (1996), Square and Martin (1994), Van der Merwe (forthcoming). The listing of neural structures for each major process reflects general directions in the literature, but the associations between structures and processess should be considered hypothetical. A given structure sometimes is associated with more than one regulatory process. For example, the cerebellum may participate in both motor programming and motor coordination. The following sections discuss various aspects of the neural regulation of speech, beginning with a look at nonverbal vocal communication.

2.1 Neural control of nonverbal vocal communication in animals and humans

The use of sound as a signalling system is common to many species, including insects, birds, reptiles, amphibians, and a variety of mammals. However, the repertoire of sounds is quite small in most nonhuman species, and learning usually plays a small or doubtful role in the acquisition of the species-typical sounds. Human languages have large sound repertoires and, in general opinion, are acquired by learning (but see Piatelli-Palmarini, 1989, for an opposing view). Learning does appear to be important in many avian species (Williams, 1989). Because animals are often used as models in physiological studies of vocalization, similarities and differences between humans and animals must be kept in mind when data from animals are generalized to humans. Jurgens (1992), Kaas (1987), and Ploog (1992) offer concise summaries of some important issues in cross-species and evolutionary comparisons.

2.1.1 *Evidence for an evolutionary corticalization of vocal motor control*

Among the major evolutionary accomplishments of humans, two of the most frequently cited are right handedness and specialization of the left hemisphere. These two features have been theoretically linked, and they have special relevance for the study of the neural control of speech. The following review highlights some of the primary discoveries and controversies pertaining to evolutionary processes in vocalization.

It has been hypothesized that there is an evolutionary progression of vocal control along the neuraxis. Lower species are thought to have neural control vested exclusively in subcortical structures. Within the primates, neural control ascends to the level of the cingulate gyrus. But only humans have genuine voluntary control over vocalization in the cerebral cortex. This hypothesis could help to explain why chimpanzees, who can learn sign language, have not demonstrated a facility for vocal communication that approaches human speech. If chimpanzees lack the cortical mechanisms for vocal control, then it should be difficult for them to yoke cortical processes of symbol manipulation with vocal ouput. It is also possible that nonhuman primates lack the vocal tract apparatus needed for language (Lieberman, 1984).

Brain asymmetry in vocal control is a much-explored aspect of animal vocalization. Songbirds, especially, have been noted for their asymmetric control of the syrynx (the sound-producing organ, roughly analogous to the human larynx). One of the puzzling pieces in the evolutionary puzzle of speech and language was the apparent lack of hand preference in nonhuman primates. Until recently, it was commonly accepted that nonhuman primates do not exhibit humanlike handedness preferences. MacNeilage and colleagues (MacNeilage, 1987; MacNeilage et al., 1987, 1993) have questioned the earlier research on this problem. They acknowledged that nonhuman primates use the two hands about equally often, an observation often cited as evidence that these animals lack a manual preference. However, closer examination reveals that hand selection in nonhuman primates is task dependent. Reaching is done largely with the left, but object manipulation is accomplished more often with the right. MacNeilage et al. (1993) theorized that handedness is rooted in postural actions. Prosimians used the left hand primarily for reaching and the right hand largely for postural support. These hand specializations were reflected by corresponding specializations in the contralateral hemisphere, so that the right hemisphere processed visual-spatial information while the left hemisphere processed information concerned with posture and position. Left hemisphere dominance, then, results from postural requirements but has been carried over to other kinds of activities including language. (Hellige, 1993, reviews general issues pertaining to hemispheric interaction in information processing.)

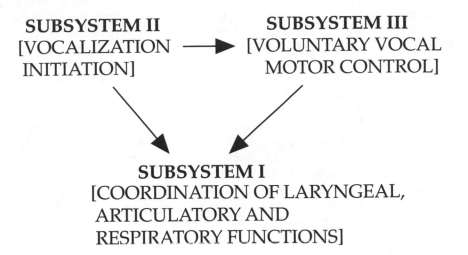

Figure 8.9   Jurgens' (1992) three-subsystem model of the neural control of vocal utterances.

2.1.2 *Studies of nonverbal vocal behavior in humans and animals*

Animal studies have been a major source of information on the neural control of vocalization. Of particular importance have been invasive studies that cannot be performed on humans. One limitation to the animal studies is that because animals do not speak, caution should be exercised in generalizing the results of animal studies to statements about the neural control of human speech. Animals do not speak, but they parallel humans in important ways: (1) many mammals, birds and reptiles vocalize; (2) some animals appear to have a highly lateralized neural control of vocalization; (3) some animals, especially songbirds, learn conspecific calls through exposure and imitation; (4) vocalizations generally involve a coordinated control of respiratory, phonatory and oral-nasal structures, possibly with a rhythmic substrate. In addition, some animals have neural connections that are similar to those in humans. Of particular importance is the demonstration that chimpanzees, but not cats or monkeys, resemble humans in having a direct projection from the precentral gyrus to the nucleus ambiguus (Kuypers, 1958a, 1958b, 1960; Jurgens, 1976; Larson, 1988).

From a consideration of both animal and human studies, Jurgens (1992) described a three-subsystem model for the neural control of vocal utterances that holds much relevance for understanding the neural control of human speech. Jurgens' model is diagrammed in Figure 8.9. Each subsystem is described below.

Subsystem I, primarily responsible for the coordination of respiratory, laryngeal and upper-airway actions, includes the reticular formation and the phonation-related motor and sensory nuclei of the brain stem and spinal cord.

In addition to its role in coordinating muscle activity, this subsystem may possess the subroutines needed for genetically preprogrammed vocal patterns.

Subsystem II, initiates vocal utterances and selects among fixed vocal patterns. This subsystem is hierarchically organized as follows:

Lowest level: periaqueductal gray and neighboring tegmentum.

Middle level: subcortical limbic structures including the hypothalamus, midline thalamus, amygdala, bed nucleus of stria terminalis, preoptic region and septum. As noted earlier, these structures participate in the regulation of emotion. They serve to relate external stimuli to internal stimuli geared to motivation.

Highest level: anterior cingulate cortex, which serves to exercise voluntary control over emotional states.

Subsystem III is composed of the motor cortex and its primary input and output structures, cerebellum, ventrolateral thalamus, primary somatosensory cortex, putamen, nucleus ruber and pyramidal tract. This subsystem regulates voluntary fine control over vocal patterns.

Jurgens' model may hold value as a means of correlating observations on animal and human vocalizations. There does appear to be general merit in recognizing functions such as initiation, voluntary fine motor control, and coordination. These functions are included in Table 8.6.

2.2 *Cerebral asymmetry related to speech*

A strict definition of functional lateralization is that the function in question is isolated to either the left or right hemisphere. Some caution should be observed in evaluating data purported to demonstrate lateralization. Particularly in studies of speech and language, the results do not necessarily show complete isolation to one side of the brain, but rather privileged or predominant processing by that side. Numerous studies have shown cerebral asymmetry in language, but this is not to say that language is exclusively represented in one hemisphere. For right-handers, the left hemisphere is thought to be dominant for language, but the right hemisphere does possess at least a limited language ability.

Evidence for this comes from an investigation by Ryding et al. (1987) who monitored cerebral activity of both hemispheres via regional cerebral blood flow (rCBF) of patients with past transient ischemic attacks. Three activation conditions were tested, including a rest condition, humming a nursery rhyme, and reciting the days of the week (automatic speech). During the automatic speech task, subjects showed greater rCBF increases in the right hemisphere relative to the left but humming evoked no assymetries. To explain the results for automatic speech, the authors suggested that speech may pose a greater difficulty for the right hemisphere. In contrast, Formby et al. (1989) and Lechevalier et al. (1989) reported no differences in cerebral hemispheric activation during speech tasks. Bottoni et al. (1994) reported bilateral activation during a comprehension task involving metaphors but not during either a lexical decision task or during comprehension of "literal" sentences. Soderfelt et al. (1994), using PET, observed bilateral activation of the posterior temporal regions for both signed (when the "listener" watches the speaker) and spoken language. Also using PET, Demonet et al. (1994) demonstrated that a word task resulted in activation of the left hemisphere as well as the right angular gyrus. A phoneme task activated only the left hemisphere in right-handed subjects. Karbe et al. (1995) used PET and MRI to examine regional metabolic activation during single-word repetition in 15 speakers. They reported bilateral activation of the entire planum temporale, but an asymmetric increase in the left Brodmann's area 22.

Any statements about lateralization should be accompanied by information about subject sex, language and culture. Females may have a greater degree of bilateral representation than males. Shaywitz et al. (1995) concluded from echo-planar fMRI studies that females had more diffuse (bilateral) patterns of activation than males during a rhyming task. The possibility of hormonal regulation of hemispheric cognitive activity is described in a study of cross-gender hormone therapy (Cohen and Forget, 1995). A general review of sex and cultural differences in cortical asymmetry is outside the scope of this paper, but these factors should be considered in any general formulation of brain representation of language. For discussions of cultural or language differences in hemispheric asymmetry, see Tsunoda (1975, 1989), Hu et al. (1990), and Wray (1992). Gender or sex differences are reviewed in Geschwind and Galaburda (1987) and Wray (1992). Suffice it to say that sweeping generalizations about hemispheric asymmetries for language may fail if cultural-linguistic and gender/sex differences are neglected.

Why is asymmetry desirable? As Kertesz (1989) points out, a structure with pure symmetry is likely to result in a duplicative representation. On the other hand, asymmetrical representation permits greater adaptability based on complementary functions. In speech, for example, complementary functions may be segmental vs prosodic (short-term vs long-term) operations. Each hemisphere is able to operate on the kind of information for which its temporospatial analyses are most suitable. This lateral complementarity could reduce error (by separating types of information in initial processing) while affording adaptable integration of information sources. Peters (1992) notes that asymmetry could also hold advantages for motor control, especially for rapid and precise movements such as those for speech. If speech motor control were bilaterally represented, then the performance of synchronized movements in the bilateral speech musculature would require a highly reliable interhemispheric coordination. Unilateral control could ensure temporally and spatially precise actions of the speech muscles. Peters (1992), commenting particularly on the asymmetry of the right and left laryngeal nerves, hypothesized that the longer length of the left recurrent laryngeal nerve should be reflected by a central asymmetry – otherwise neural signals issued along the left and right branches of this nerve would not be synchronized.

2.3 *Functional localization of speech within the brain*

The work of Penfield and Roberts (1959) suggesting cortical localization of function for speech and language production has had significant influence on the neurologic disciplines. Such a view suggests that specific cortical areas are associated with distinct aspects of behavioral function. Conversely, behavioral deficits in the periphery point to specific lesion sites in the brain. This hypothesis has been supported by numerous clinical and research reports. Recent advances in structural and functional neuroimaging techniques allow for refinement of earlier research findings. For an extensive introduction to brain imaging methods, see Orrison et al. (1995). Lauter (1995) provides an extensive review of the literature pertaining to neuroimaging techniques used to study speech production. Lefkowitz and Netsell (1993) offer a MRI atlas for the neural structures of speech. Users of the World Wide Web can access BrainMap (an electronic environment for metanalysis and modeling of human brain function). BrainMap is supported by the Research Imaging Center, The University of Texas Health Science Center, San Antonio, Texas (http://ric.uthscsa.edu/services).

Neuroimaging procedures have been used in various ways to study speech production, including investigations of neurologically compromised subjects and neurologically intact individuals. Investigations of more general motor behaviors (e.g., finger tapping) have also been generalized to speech production. However, despite the numerous technological advancements, the reader is cautioned that these techniques have not been perfected in their application. Methodological complications and variations make it extremely difficult to evaluate the significance of findings as well as to generalize results across investigations. Lauter (1995) evaluates neuroimaging techniques applied to speech production, and Tikofksy (1984) considers these techniques relative to aphasia diagnosis.

In addition to the primary motor cortex, several cortical areas have typically been associated with speech and language production including Broca's area, Wernicke's area, and the supplementary motor area (SMA) or premotor Area. (Note: some writers consider SMA and the premotor area to be the same, but others make a distinction between them). The following section will highlight the evidence demonstrating roles these cortical areas play in speech and language production. It should be noted that the literature has emphasized regional activation more than regional inhibition, so that the contemporary understanding of brain function is somewhat biased toward activation accounts. It is likely that future studies will offer a more complete description of brain function, including information on relative patterns of activation and inhibition.

2.3.1 Broca's area   Broca's area (Brodmann's area 44) has long been implicated in speech production. Specifically, it is thought that this cortical area is important for the production of fluent, well-articulated speech (see, however,

Mohr et al., 1978; Smith and Fetz, 1987). Evidence for this position comes from studies employing structural imaging techniques such as CT scans and MRI which have identified lesions involving but not limited to Broca's Area in the brains of individuals with specific speech deficits. This disorder, termed "Broca's aphasia," is characterized by nonfluent, effortful speech comprised of short, agrammatic phrases. Recently, Alexander et al. (1990) proposed a refined classification system for Broca's aphasia employing three distinct categorizations based on site and extent of lesion as well as speech symptomatology.

Results from studies employing functional neuroimaging tools have been contradictory in their conclusions regarding Broca's area. Early investigations reported no significant increases in regional cerebral blood flow (rCBF) in Broca's area during automatic naming tasks (Ingvar and Schwartz, 1974; Larsen et al., 1978). Yet other investigators have reported increased rCBF in Broca's Area while subjects read both silently and aloud (Lassen et al., 1978; Leblanc et al., 1992; Wise et al., 1991). In addition, a recent magnetoencephalographic study, which detects weak magnetic fields generated by active brain tissue, demonstrated activity in or close to Broca's area in association with overt vocalization in a picture naming task (Salmelin et al., 1994). It is possible that these contradictory results are due to methodological differences between the investigations as well as the fact that there are large individual differences across subjects and data are typically reported as group averages. However, such studies suggest that Broca's area may not have as primary a role in speech production as was once thought (Smith and Fetz, 1987). Paulesu et al. (1993) concluded that Broca's area is crucial to the operation of a sub-vocal rehearsal system used in tasks such as short-term memory for letters. They observed activation in Broca's area even though overt speech was not involved in the tasks they studied.

An adjacent area of cortex, left inferior frontal cortex, has been shown to be activated during tasks of word generation (Peterson et al., 1988; McCarthy et al., 1993). McCarthy et al. (1993), using echoplanar magnetic resonance imaging, observed significant activation associated with word generation in a cortical region described as "gray matter along a sulcus anterior to the lateral sulcus that included the anterior insula, Brodmann's area 47, and extending to area 10" (p. 4952). Activation in this region was interpreted to reflect word association or semantic processing (or both) but also speech (response) production. Activation was not observed during covert word generation or listening to words, nor was it seen during nonspeech movements of the mouth, tongue or jaw. In a PET study, Petrides et al. (1995) observed increased rCBF in frontal cortical area 45 during a verbal recall task. The authors suggested that in addition to its role in speech, this area is important for recall of verbal information from long-term memory. Similarly, Demb et al. (1995) used fMRI to study regional activation during a semantic encoding task and reported activation of prefrontal cortex (including Brodmann's areas 45–47). They interpreted their observations as evidence that this cortical area is part of a semantic executive system that plays a role in on-line retrieval of semantic information. (Also see D'Esposito et al., 1995, for fMRI data indicating that prefrontal cortex is involved in human working memory.)

Note: Additional comments on Broca's area in relation to the supplementary motor area are offered in the following section.

Additional evidence that Broca's Area is involved in organizing the motor output of speech comes from studies of a disorder variously termed a form of dysarthria, a type of apraxia, or aphemia (Schiff et al., 1983). This disorder is characterized by a lasting dysarthria in the absence of a persisting aphasia. The lesion area includes a small region in the posterior section of the inferior frontal lobe, the pars opercularis and inferior motor strip or the deep white matter of the anterior limb of the internal capsule.

Another disorder of primary interest in identifying the cortical regions involved in speech production is oral apraxia, or impaired ability to perform voluntary movements of the tongue, lips, larynx and other oral musculature (for a detailed discussion of performance deficits, see Poeck and Kerschensteiner, 1975). Tognola and Vignolo (1980) concluded from CT studies that oral apraxia results primarily from lesions to the following areas of the left hemisphere: frontal and central (Rolandic) opercula, neighboring portions of the first temporal convolution, and the anterior region of the insula. These structures, illustrated in Figure 8.10, may be considered as critical to the neural control of oral movements.

2.3.2 Wernicke's area

While Broca's area is purported to be a center for speech production, Wernicke's area (associated with Brodmann areas 22, 37 and 42) is thought to be a central mechanism for language comprehension. The traditional neuropsycholinguistic approach suggests that Wernicke's Area is the storage center of sound or phonological representations of words (Caplan, 1987). That is, the auditory representations as stored in Wernicke's Area are accessed subsequent to auditory presentation of language stimuli. Lesions involving this cortical area presumably result in deficits in language comprehension as well as expressive deficits characterized by fluent, incomprehensible speech. This disorder has been termed Wernicke's aphasia. The bulk of evidence in which structural imaging techniques were used to examine lesions relative to behavioral and cognitive tests suggests that a language center is located in the general cortical area of Wernicke's area. However this area is thought to differ in both size and relative location across individuals (Caplan, 1987; Howard et al., 1992).

Functional neuroimaging techniques also have been used to investigate the role of Wernicke's Area in speech and language. Petersen et al. (1988) found increased rCBF in the left temporoparietal cortex during passive hearing of spoken words while fixating a cross-hair versus fixating alone. Similarly, Howard et al. (1992) found increased rCBF in Wernicke's area (left superior and middle temporal gyrus) for subjects listening to spoken words versus a control condition in which subjects heard the same words recorded backwards (essentially nonsense words). In their search for localization of separate written

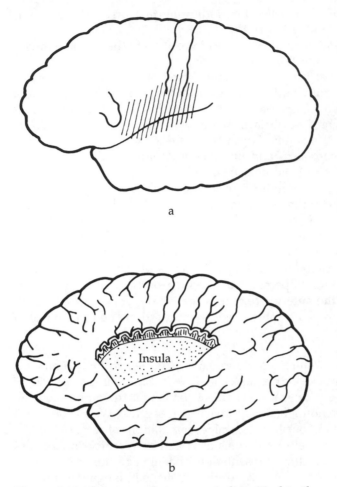

Figure 8.10 Structures that appear to be critical to the neural control of oral movements: (a), frontal and central opercula and neighboring regions of the first temporal convolution, and (b) insula.

word and spoken word lexicons, Howard et al. (1992) hypothesized that during a simple reading task and during single word repetition, subjects might access a word's semantic representation (resulting in increased blood flow in Wernicke's Area) although this may not be necessary for either reading or word repetition. The results indicated no single cortical area which showed significant increases in rCBF for both word reading and repetition. The authors suggest that representations of word meanings are not well localized but depend on activation of semantic features and connections between them, distributed over a large region of cortex.

2.3.3 Supplementary motor area   A possible role of the supplementary motor area (SMA) or premotor area (Brodmann Area 6) is indicated by PET studies of humans performing a variety of motor tasks (Deiber et al., 1991). Greater activity in the SMA was observed for tasks that required the internal generation of movement, as opposed to tasks in which movement was based on external cues. If speech is considered to consist of internally generated movements, then participation of SMA in speech control is expected. Additional investigations revealed increased rCBF in the SMA during repetitive, sequential motor tasks such as finger movements relative to sustained isometric contractions, suggesting the SMA is important for the execution of complex, sequential movements (Orgogozo et al., 1979; Roland et al., 1980). Tanji and Shima (1994) identified a group of cells in the caudal SMA of monkey that became active in relation to the performance of a sequence of multiple movements in a certain order. It was concluded that these cells are responsible for a signal pertaining to the order of forthcoming multiple movements. Data that suggest a refined view of localization have been reported in a PET investigation by Stephan et al. (1995). They observed rCBF for tasks involving both imagined and executed movements. Functionally distinct areas of SMA were identified, with the more rostral part of the posterior SMA showing increased activation during imagined movements. A caudoventral portion of the SMA was then activated during executed movements. Similarly, areas 44 (Broca's area) and 45 were more active during imagined than executed movements. A ventral premotor area (area 6) was active during both imagined and executed movements, and an area presumed to be SII was activated only during movement activation. It is noteworthy that Broca's area was similar to SMA in becoming active in a task of imagined nonspeech movements.

Jonas (1981) investigated the possible role of the SMA in speech production by reporting results of isotope brain scans of two patients with expressive speech deficits characterized by short phrases of reduced intensity, dysfluencies, and periods of muteness. Brain scans for both patients revealed regions of abnormal hyperactivity in the left SMA. Based upon these results the author concluded that the SMA might be important for initiation of speech, suppression of automatic speech, pacing, and fluency of phonation and articulation. A review of studies by Caplan (1987) suggests the SMA is involved in control of activation and initiation of speech. Studies of nondisordered speakers reveal increased rCBF in the SMA during verbal and nonverbal naming tasks (Posner et al., 1988; Wise et al., 1991). It is also noteworthy that vocalization may be elicited in humans most effectively by electrical stimulation of the SMA (Penfield and Welch, 1951).

2.3.4 Cortical networks in speech production   It is interesting that stimulation of the presumed motor centers of speech has been reported to both evoke simple vocalizations (Penfield and Roberts, 1959) as well as to disrupt ongoing vocalization (Ojemann, 1983). Electrical stimulation does not elicit words or even consonant-vowel syllables. On the other hand, stimulation of the limbic system and other diencephalic structures can elicit nearly the entire sound repertoire of monkeys (Larson, 1988). Perhaps the control of speech is accomplished through extensive neural circuits, so that stimulation of any one region is insufficient to elicit the structured vocalizations of speech. This interpretation is compatible with the observation that speech production tasks such as overt naming are associated with widespread cortical activation (Salmelin et al., 1994). Friston et al. (1991) proposed a network model of intrinsic versus extrinsic word generation based on cerebral activity as measured by PET. The proposed model consists of three neuronal systems including a pool that stores word representations in a distributed mode, an afferent system which conveys sensory input to this pool, and a modulating system which alters the sensitivity or responsivity of neurons in the pool. Based upon PET scans, the authors suggest the location of a distributed word store to be in the left superior temporal region (Wernicke's area) and the modulation site as the left dorsolateral prefrontal cortex (DLPFC). By examining the correlation between these two regions in terms of cerebral activity, the authors concluded that the DLPFC is responsible for modulating the responsivity of a neural system in the superior temporal gyrus and may also have a role in attentional and intentional states that underly the intrinsic generation of words.

Paulesu et al. (1993) describe the functional neuroanatomy of the "articulatory loop" involved in verbal short memory tasks such as memory for letters and rhyming judgments for letters. In the design of their experiment, short-term memory for letters was considered to involve both subvocal rehearsal and a phonological store. In contrast, rhyming judgment for letters was thought to involve only subvocal rehearsal. Therefore, a comparison of activation patterns for the two tasks was a means of determining the primary location of the phonological store. Paulesu et al. observed that phonological processing was associated with bilateral activation in Brodmann area 44, superior temporal gyri (Brodmann areas 22 and 42), supramarginal gyri (Brodmann area 40), and the insulae. These structures were thought to comprise the functional anatomy of the articulatory loop. It was also noted that Brodmann area 40 was activated in the short-term memory task but not the rhyming task. Therefore, this area was taken to be the primary location of the phonological store. Interestingly, activation was seen in the SMA, cerebellum and sensorimotor cortex (Brodmann areas 4, 3, 2, 1), even though overt speech was not produced in the experimental tasks. The authors concluded that, "The activation of SMA, cerebellum and possibly of sensory-motor areas suggests that these structures were automatically engaged as part of a more general neuronal network devoted to language planning and execution" (p. 344).

Large-scale cortical networks have been a popular theme of recent neural theories of cognition. Bressler (1995) comments that this concept yields an effective framework for the integration of data from neuroanatomical, neuropsychological and neurophysiological studies of distributed functioning of the cerebral cortex. According to this concept, elementary functions can be considered to be localized in discrete cortical regions, and complex functions would involve parallel processing of information in widespread cortical networks.

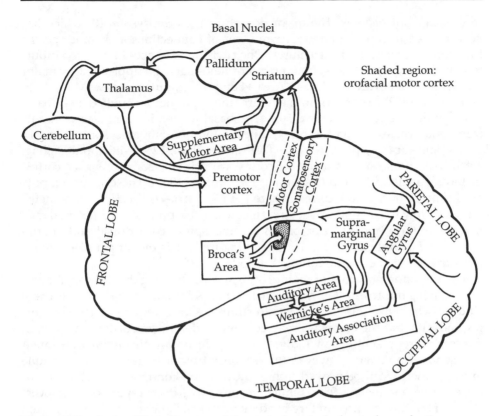

Figure 8.11 A simplified diagram of the neural control of speech production.

Activity in the large-scale cortical networks could be dynamically organized by control processes operating at cortical and subcortical levels. Large-scale networks for speech production presumably would involve both cortical and subcortical structures, including those neural structures listed in Table 8.6.

Similar ideas have been developed in the theory of neuronal group selection (Edelman, 1993; Friston et al., 1994). This theory proposes that variant populations of neurons are organized by the interaction of genetic and experiential factors. An important concept in this theory is "re-entrant signalling," an exchange of signals along parallel and reciprocal connections among neuronal groups. The theory of neuronal group selection has been used to account for perception, motor responses, language and consciousness.

2.4 A summary diagram of major neural pathways in speech production

The simplified diagram in Figure 8.11 is in some respects an elaboration of Jurgens' model shown in Figure 8.9. It resembles Jurgens' model in having three major subsystems. The major departure is in Subsystem III, which has been revised to represent a greater number of connections and some specific functions of certain brain structures. One revision is to show increased inputs to motor cortex, specifically, from premotor fields such as supplementary motor area, premotor cortex, Brodmann Area 44 and the cingulate cortex (Muakkassa and Strick, 1979). As shown in the figure, these premotor inputs deliver basal nuclei influence to the motor cortex. The basal nuclei, in turn, receive inputs from motor cortex, premotor cortex, supplementary motor area, somatosensory cortex, and superior parietal lobule (Alexander et al., 1986; Miller and Delong, 1988). Additional inputs to motor cortex are primary somatosensory cortex, including areas 1, 2 and 5 (Asanuma, 1989; Jones, 1987). These diverse inputs are funneled into motor cortex, where neurons project directly to motoneur-ones and to various brain structures, including the premotor cortex, thalamic nuclei, striatum, red nucleus, brainstem and spinal cord dorsal and ventral horns. The neural circuitry portrayed in Figure 8.11 is one of parallel connections involving the motor cortex as a node.

A better understanding of motor cortex itself is being gained through studies involving intracortical microstimulation of nonhuman primate cortex. These studies, which use minute currents to stimulate local regions of laminar cortex, indicate that the cortex is organized into "efferent microzones" with each microzone representing an individual muscle or an elemental movement (Wiesendanger, 1986). However, the response from a single muscle or simple muscle synergy can be evoked from multiple, non-contiguous areas of motor cortex (Wiesendanger, 1986). Similar results have been reported for a fMRI study of the control of voluntary hand movements. Sanes et al. (1995) reported overlapping cortical representations for different finger and wrist movements. They also reported multiple activation sites in the precentral gyrus for all movements (finger and wrist). These results are inconsistent with the classical view that motor function for different parts of the body is systematically mapped on the motor cortex in a one-to-one fashion (the "motor homunculus").

Huang et al. (1988) reported evidence of multiple efferent microzones in the orofacial motor cortex of nonhuman primates. Moreover, they observed two interesting results: (1) face representation in motor cortex partly enclosed and overlapped the cortical regions for jaw and tongue movement, and (2) although microstimulation typically evoked contralateral facial movements, some ipsilateral responses were observed. They concluded that the proximal representations of face, jaw and tongue, together with both contralateral and ipsilateral responses, could be a basis for the unilateral and bilateral integration of oral movement. The effects of lesions to motor cortex corroborate this newer concept of organization. The initial consequence of such a lesion is a temporary contralateral paresis, which gives way to a persisting disturbance in the execution of fractionated movements performed by the distal musculature (Freund, 1987).

As a crude analogy, the motor cortex is a redundant keyboard in which the keys represent specific muscles or muscle synergies. A given muscle or synergy can be represented by more than one key. Damage to the keyboard disrupts the corresponding muscle responses, but these responses sometimes can be elicited in the context of other movements, given the principle of multiple representation.

Classically, the motor cortex was regarded as the exclusive origin of the pyramidal tract, which in turn was regarded as the highest level of motor control. The newer understanding differs considerably (Davidoff, 1990): (a) the motor cortex is the origin for only about 60% of the pyramidal tract neurons, with the remainder having origins in Brodmann's Area 6 and the parietal lobe (b) the pyramidal tract contains many fibers that originate in the cortex and affect *sensory* transmission at subcortical and spinal level, and (c) as described above, movement does not begin in the motor cortex; rather, the motor cortex is a funnel for movement information from other cortical and subcortical sites.

2.5 Pattern generators for speech

In recent years, it has been proposed that the center for sequential speech production resides in central pattern generators (CPG) present in the brainstem. This proposal stems from research supporting the presence of such mechanisms or "pacemakers" which provide the necessary rhythm for cyclic life functions such as respiration, locomotion, and mastication (Chandler and Goldberg, 1984; Grillner and Wallen, 1985). It has been hypothesized that speech, viewed as a higher level complex function, evolved from lower level functions, such as mastication, whose centers reside in the brainstem. Evidence contrary to such a view comes from investigations showing that patterns of muscle activation during speech production differ from those muscle patterns utilized for chewing or nonspeech tasks (Gentil and Gay, 1986; Moore et al., 1988; Smith and Denny, 1990).

However, Gracco (1992) suggests that lower level rhythmic functions such as chewing and locomotion do not necessarily share similar motor patterns with speech production per se, but rather, share similar mechanisms for implementation as well as similar organizational principles. Gracco (1992) proposes that a central rhythm generator acts to provide a framework for the sequencing of speech patterns. These speech patterns, in turn, are comprised of phonemes with inherently distinct durational differences resulting in the continuous modulation of rhythm. Although this theory is an elegant way of accounting for organizational principles of speech production, neurophysiological evidence has yet to corroborate such a mechanism for speech production.

Experimental evaluation of the CPG hypothesis should take into account the possibility that the central rhythm generator may interact with other neural circuitry to produce appropriate patterns of activity. Feldman and Smith (1989) proposed that modulation of breathing pattern in mammals is accomplished by three interactive neural circuits. The first circuit, a pacemaker-driven oscillator, relies on endogenously rhythmic bursting neurons. A second circuit for pattern generation transforms the rhythmic drive from the first circuit to produce a spatiotemporal pattern of motoneuronal activity. Finally, coordinating circuitry integrates respiratory patterns with other functions, such as locomotion. Respiratory support for vocalization could be explained by this model. Rhythmic bursting neurons would provide the fundamental rhythm, but the actual spatiotemporal pattern of motoneuronal activity would be shaped by the pattern-generating circuitry and the coordinating circuitry. Experimental confirmation of this model would not require evidence of invariant rhythms. It is also possible that rhythmicity in speech reflects biomechanical properties, such that movements are performed at rates that allow a muscle energy minimum (Sorokin et al., 1980).

2.6 Production-perception linkages in speech

This important aspect of the neural representation for speech is unfortunately one of the most poorly understood. Production and perception are the two essential facets of speech, but little is known about how these facets relate to one another. Are both undergirded by a common representation in the brain, and if so, what is this common representation? Or do they have separate representations that are coordinated by neural mechanisms? The uncertainty mirrors the nearly separate development of theories of speech perception and speech production (Kent, forthcoming). There are some exceptions, such as the much disputed motor theory (Liberman et al., 1967; Liberman and Mattingly, 1985) and the theoretical combination of event perception (Fowler, 1986) and action theory (Kelso et al., 1986). But even in these theories, very little is said about underlying brain functions that unite the perceptual and productive aspects of speech. Not surprisingly, accounts of the neurobiology of speech perception are quite silent about speech production (Miller and Jusczyk, 1989).

Some neural mechanisms suitable for linkage of production and perception have been described. One is a proximity of neurons for motor and sensory functions in structures such as the cerebrum and the cerebellum. A second is the function of "multimodal" neurons, or cells that respond to more than one stimulus modality. Still another is a neural organization featuring parallel, recurrent pathways. These are discussed in more detail in the following.

One possibility for sensory-motor interaction is the proximity of motor and sensory neurons in the CNS representation of various parts of the body. The adjacency of the motor cortex and somatosensory cortex is one example. Although the Central Fissure is often taken as a dividing line, motor and sensory neurons may in fact be found in the same general area. For example, proximity of sensory and motor neurons has been reported for the cerebellum. Huang et al. (1991) found that the auditory area of Crus II of the cerebellar hemisphere in both rat and cat is surrounded by orofacial somatosensory receptive fields. These investigators also noted that cerebellar granule cells in the posterior vermis and the hemispheres respond phasically to auditory stimuli. One interpretation is that the cerebellum is involved in event timing. This suggestion agrees with clinical impressions of ataxic dysarthria, which is commonly described as having altered patterns of syllable timing or stress (Darley et al., 1969; Kent et al., 1979; Kluin et al., 1988). Moreover, the notion of cerebellar participation in event timing is congruent with the conclusion reached by Keele and Ivry (1990) that a major role of the cerebellum is to provide temporal computations that can be used for a variety of perceptual and motor functions.

The second possibility is that some neurons may respond to more than one type of stimulation, allowing for bisensory or multisensory convergence of peripheral stimulation. For example, Bruce et al. (1981) reported the following percentages for sensory responses of neurons in superior temporal sulcus in macaques: 41 per cent were exclusively visual, 21 per cent both visual and auditory, 17 per cent visual and somesthetic, and 17 per cent visual, auditory and somesthetic. For other examples, see the review by Meredith and Stein (1986). As Stein and Meredith (1990) point out, separate sensory channels enable the organism to dissociate stimuli by modality, but multisensory convergence in the CNS allows cross-modality integration. This capability could be particularly important in speech, which has a plurimodal sensory foundation (Kent et al., 1990). Nottebohm (1991) noted that in songbirds, the pathways that control song production respond to auditory stimulation ("an observation that blurs the demarcation between what is an auditory and what is a motor circuit" p. 206).

The third possibility of sensory-motor integration relies on complex neural circuitry that permits comparison among various neural representations. Studies of the avian song system illuminate the interaction between sound production and perception and provide examples of the neural circuitry that might accomplish the desired integration. Many song birds learn conspecific songs through exposure and practice, apparently comparing their own vocal efforts with those of the adult birds. Williams (1989) described the neural circuitry underlying birdsong development as having multiple loops, multiple modalities, multiple representations of song, and multiple neural mechanisms. Of particular interest was the observation that the neural system has two primary branches. The first, a descending branch, extends to the motoneurons for respiration and vocalization. The nuclei of this branch continue to grow during song development and appear to be indispensable for song production in the adult bird. This branch also is characterized by long and variable latencies among its nuclei. The second branch forms a recursive loop between two nuclei of the descending branch. The recursive branch has one nucleus that attains its maximum size in early song learning and then declines. This branch is characterized by short latencies with little variability. Auditory activity can be recorded in both branches of this system – including the motoneurones controlling the vocal organ. Williams suggests that the short-latency recurrent branch allows for comparisons of different song representations. If these results can be extended to speech development in humans, the implications include the following. First, different parts of the neural circuitry may reach their maximum sizes or functional maturation at different ages (which could be related to the concept of a "sensitive period" for speech development; Lenneberg, 1967; Locke, 1993). Second, the neural circuitry that supports sound learning may contain different representations of speech sounds, such as auditory, motor, tactile, and kinesthetic representations. Third, recurrent branches may allow for the comparison of these different representations of speech, although the reliance on comparative mechanisms is expected to decline with maturation. The evidence on speech production is that adults are either highly flexible in using different sensory information to control speech, or that they rely minimally on such information in the short-term (Kent et al., 1990).

These are not the only possibilities for sensory-motor interaction, nor are they mutually exclusive. The complicated functions underlying speech production and perception may be accomplished by more than one neural mechanism.

There are few data on humans that speak directly to any of these alternatives. However, Ojemann (1983), reviving the cortical stimulation techniques of Penfield and Roberts, stimulated cortical language areas in patients undergoing neurosurgery for epilepsy. One of his most controversial discoveries pertained to a cortical region that he concluded was involved in both speech perception and speech production. Ojemann found that sites at which stimulation disrupted the ability to mimic sequences of orofacial movements also were sites at which stimulation disrupted the phoneme identification. The converse was true as well: sites at which stimulation interfered with phoneme identification were sites at which stimulation disturbed orofacial sequencing. Ojemann concluded that "this relationship seems to identify a cortical area that has common properties of speech perception and generation of motor output, one with the common functions described by the motor theory of speech perception" (p. 195).

3 Conclusion

Neuroscience and speech science are at the threshold of what should be a highly productive era. This chapter has described some of the foundations for a neural model of speech. Many of the details are unknown, and there may well be major revisions even in the fundamental bases. However, at the least, the field has developed to the point that information can be effectively combined from different methods, including animal studies, electrical stimulation of cortex in humans, clinicoanatomic studies of individuals with neurogenic speech disorders, neuroimaging studies of normal subjects, and developments in cognitive neuroscience. A particular difficulty in the study of speech is that it is a form of skilled motor behavior closely tied to language. An understanding of speech therefore requires a knowledge of both motor control and language, both of which are served by complicated neural systems. Distinguishing speech and language processes is not always an easy matter. The interaction between speech regulation and language operations may be reflected in some shared neural processes. New conceptions of brain function underlying language are therefore an important backdrop for a consideration of speech motor control. Examples of recent papers on brain functions underlying cognitive and language processes are Bressler (1995), Damasio (1989), Edelman (1993), and Kean (1992).

Finally, it should be acknowledged that the information reviewed in this chapter is only a fraction of a large and rapidly growing literature. The neurosciences have experienced explosive growth. The rapid increases in knowledge carry great potential for a deeper understanding of how the brain controls speech.

ACKNOWLEDGMENTS

This work was supported in part by NIH research grant DC00319 from the National Institute on Deafness and Other Communication Disorders.

9 Organic Variation of the Vocal Apparatus

JANET MACKENZIE BECK

1 Introduction

1.1 The relevance of organic variation for phonetic science

The theoretical study of phonetics has been based on many assumptions. One of the chief amongst these is the notion that all speakers use speech production systems which can be treated as if they were essentially equivalent in terms of their anatomical geometry. This assumption is helpful when the aim is to identify the common strands of phonetic performance which allow a similar phonetic analysis to be made for a range of speakers producing the "same" linguistic content. The focus on commonality does, however, mask much of the intricacy and subtlety of individual phonetic performance. As phonetic science has become more sophisticated in its investigative techniques, allowing us to investigate speech output in finer detail, so individual differences in speech performance have become more apparent, and the motivation to examine the underlying causes of such differences has grown.

It may be useful to draw an explicit distinction between two major sources of variation in speech performance, which we may call phonetic and organic factors, following Laver (1980:9). Phonetic variation results from differences in the way in which an individual uses his or her vocal apparatus, whilst organically based variation depends on individual differences in shape and proportion of the vocal organs. The word "organic" will be used here to describe any factors which are to do with anatomical structure or morphology, and with the constraints which that structure imposes on the potential for physiological action. A study of organic features in this sense may be seen as analogous to the study of architecture, being concerned principally with the mechanical properties of the materials, or tissues, which form the vocal apparatus, and the way in which they are arranged. Organic variation, therefore, may encompass any anatomical features for which individual differences in size, shape or mechanical properties may be observed.

The most casual inspection of the general population will show how assumption-laden any notion of vocal tract equivalence must be. Even amongst the genetically related members of a family, there will almost always be differences in the size and shape of the dental arches, the palatal contour, the relationship of the upper and lower jaws and the size of the larynx. All these factors have implications for an individual's speech production, and to ignore them is to ignore a rich store of information which may help to explain at least some of the observed individual differences in speech production. It seems unfortunate, therefore, that in the study of phonetics "Inter-speaker differences of anatomy within the normal distribution have been largely ignored" (Laver 1991:211).

Organic variations with implications for phonetics vary from relatively minor differences between individuals, such as differences in dentition, which may cause subtle differences in anterior tongue placement and fricative airflow in front oral fricatives, to the more substantial differences in overall size and shape of the vocal organs associated with normal growth from childhood to maturity, to gross anomalies of the vocal tract such as are found in cleft palate or oral cancer. These latter distortions may impose serious limitations on potential phonetic performance. In addition to such relatively longer-term organic characteristics, we are all, at one time or another, subject to more transient changes within the vocal apparatus. Examples of these are the mild oedema of the vocal folds which might occur during a common cold or as a result of hormonal fluctuations during the menstrual cycle, a broken tooth, or a mouth ulcer, any of which might cause subtle day-to-day changes in speech output.

The aim of this chapter is to begin to explore organic variation as it affects the vocal apparatus, by bringing together some of the phonetically relevant information concerning human growth and variation. For general information on aspects of the anatomy of the vocal apparatus the reader is referred to standard references such as Hardcastle (1976), Dickson and Maue-Dickson (1982) and Kahane (1988). The chapter provides a broad overview of some of the types and sources of organic variation which affect speech output, in a form which should be easily accessible by the phonetician with a basic knowledge of the vocal apparatus. It cannot attempt to be exhaustive, but seeks to alert students of phonetics to some of the potential organic bases for inter- and intra-speaker variation in phonetic performance. In the interests of conciseness, only a selection of illustrative references is presented. A fuller review of some of the relevant literature may be found in Beck (1988).

It will be clear that the focus so far has been upon the structure rather than the functional control of the vocal apparatus. There are, of course, also many individual differences in physiological activity and neurological control of speech, but it would not be realistic to include all these aspects within the scope of this chapter. (Further discussion can be found in Perkell, ARTICULATORY PROCESSES and in Kent and Tjaden, BRAIN FUNCTIONS UNDERLYING SPEECH.)

1.2 Sources of individual variation

In summary, individual differences in vocal apparatus structure derive from three types of sources: life cycle changes within an individual, genetic or environmental factors which differentiate between individuals and differences which result from trauma or disease.

1.2.1 Intra-individual variation: life cycle changes
It is self-evident that the vocal apparatus, in common with every other part of the body, undergoes a complex process of change throughout the life span. Age-related changes in the vocal apparatus can be seen as falling into three main phases. In the first phase, which corresponds to the period between birth and puberty, there are major changes in the vocal apparatus which accompany general patterns of growth and development. There are no very salient differences between the sexes in terms of morphology or size of the vocal apparatus during this first phase. The second phase, from puberty to maturity, is characterised by a major growth spurt associated with the onset of puberty and by the fact that male and female patterns of growth and development are typically different. It is during this phase that the major differentiation between the male and female vocal apparatus emerges. Overall growth of the vocal apparatus during these two phases reflects fairly accurately the general body growth curves for males and females (see Figure 9.1). During the final phase, from maturity to senescence, growth processes are active in maintenance and repair only, and the only significant changes which occur are the result of the decreasing efficiency of these maintenance and repair processes, leading to degenerative change.

1.2.2 Inter-individual variation: genetic and environmental conditioning
While some differences between individuals may be due to sampling at different points in the life cycle, this is obviously not the whole story. Given any group of people of the same age and gender, there will still be marked differences in vocal tract morphology. This is partly because there is considerable variation in the precise nature and timing of the changes which occur during development and ageing. The varying developmental patterns which result in organic differences are influenced by both endogenous and environmental factors, but the ways in which they interact in order to co-ordinate growth and development are still only imperfectly understood.

1.2.3 Variation arising from trauma or disease
In addition to the organic variation arising as a result of what we think of as normal development or degeneration of the vocal apparatus, there may also be changes within the vocal apparatus which result from traumatic injury or disease. Although these may be defined as "abnormal", they are nevertheless common enough that a high proportion of the population will suffer from some trauma- or disease-related change in their vocal organs at some time in their lives, even if such

a. Standard height growth curves for British children

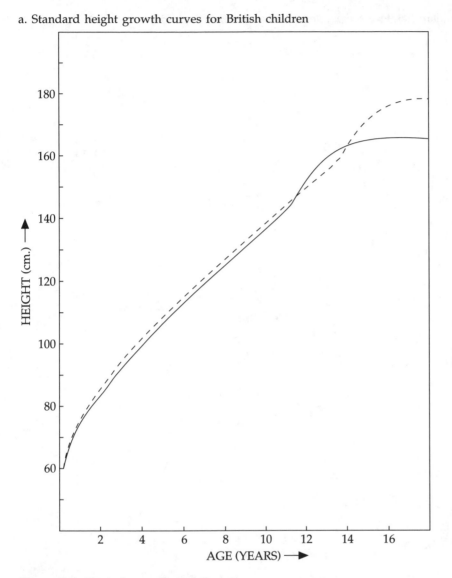

Figure 9.1   Typical overall growth patterns
(both adapted from Tanner 1978: 169, 170, 177, 178)
Female growth patterns are indicated by the solid lines, and male growth patterns
by the broken lines.

b. Standard height growth velocity curves for British children

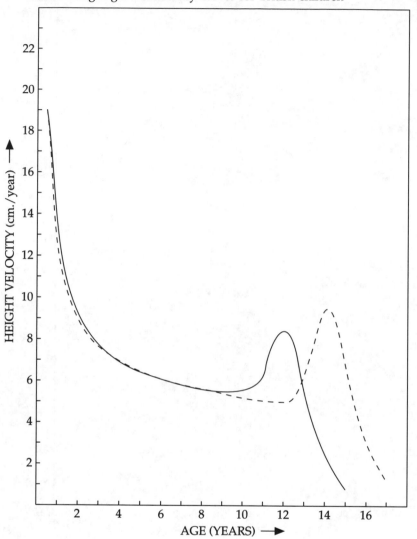

changes are transient in nature. It therefore seems appropriate to consider such changes as being relevant to general phonetic science, and not solely within the domain of speech and language pathology.

These three sources of organic variation will be considered in more detail in turn, starting with a discussion of the processes of growth, development, maturation and ageing which affect all of us as we progress through life.

2 Life cycle changes in the vocal apparatus

This section will focus on each major area of the vocal apparatus in turn, progressing from lungs and thorax to the larynx, and thence upwards through the resonating cavities. The principle organic changes occurring within each phase of the life cycle will then be summarised.

Discussion of age-related changes within each part of the vocal apparatus will include a description of skeletal aspects, followed by a description of soft tissue changes. Although the extraordinary plasticity of bone growth means that in the longer term it is a mistake to think of the skeleton as rigid or immutable, it is fair to say that at any given point in the life cycle the skeleton does behave as a rigid framework supporting the overlying soft tissues. Soft tissues are subject to constant observable distortion during normal movement of the body, and are prone to significant and short-term alterations in size and consistency in response to infection, hormones or physiological state, whereas bones are not. When an individual is studied over a short time period the overall shape and size of that person's vocal apparatus will thus be determined principally by his or her skeletal structure. Each section will therefore begin by considering the growth patterns of the underlying skeletal structures.

2.1 The respiratory system: the lungs and thorax

2.1.1 Skeletal framework: thoracic skeleton   At birth, the whole of the thoracic skeleton and the shoulder girdle is relatively high, as the small size of the pelvis causes the abdominal contents to be compressed upwards towards the diaphragm (Sinclair 1978:119). Rapid pelvic development during the first two or three years of life allows the abdominal contents, and hence the thorax, to drop. The thoracic skeleton grows to accommodate the lungs, and follows a similar curve (Altman and Dittner 1962:334). The circumference of the thorax seems to be slightly larger in males than in females in childhood, and this difference increases dramatically at puberty. In adulthood the sternum is shorter in females, and in a slightly higher position relative to the vertebral column. Females also have rather more mobility of the upper ribs, allowing greater expansion of the upper part of the thorax (Davies and Davies 1962:285). This is assumed to be an evolutionary adaptation for pregnancy, when the lower thorax and diaphragm are constricted by the uterus.

The angle of the ribs has important implications for the efficiency of respiration. In the adult, the ribs are angled downwards, and chest diameter is increased by pulling the ribs to a more horizontal position. During the first two years of life the ribs lie more horizontally (Sinclair 1978:121, Kahane 1988), so that raising the ribs has little effect on chest volume. The infant is thus much more dependent on diaphragmatic breathing. Thoracic wall movement increases progressively up to the age of seven, by which time the angle of the ribs is similar to that in adults (Kahane 1988). In old age the state of the ribs again impedes efficient respiration, as the rib cartilages become calcified and thus lose their ability to twist and allow proper elevation of the ribs during inspiration.

2.1.2 Soft tissues: lungs, bronchioles, bronchi and trachea

At birth, the lungs are very small, both in mass and volume. During the first few weeks of life they expand greatly, and by the end of the first year the lungs have trebled in weight and increased six-fold in volume (Sinclair 1978:89). After the first rapid period of growth the lungs follow the general growth curve (Boyd 1952). The internal structure of the lungs shows considerable change following birth. Most of the alveoli of the lung are formed after birth, and the number of alveoli increases until some time between 8 years and puberty (Kahane 1988, Emery 1979). The density of elastic fibres in the terminal airways increases concomitantly, allowing the lungs to recoil more easily during expiration.

About 50 per cent of the solid matter of the lungs is made up of collagen (Bouhuys 1977), which probably functions to prevent over-extension of the lungs. Changes in the quality of the collagen network occur in old age, as the collagen molecules form cross links and become less flexible. The lung structure becomes less mobile, progressively impairing respiratory function. This, in association with increasing rigidity of the thoracic skeleton, results in a reduction of vital capacity from a range of approximately 3.5 to 5.9 litres in young adult males to a range of 2.4 to 4.7 litres after the age of 60 years (Sinclair 1978:223)

2.2 The phonatory system: the larynx

2.2.1 General features

Laryngeal growth during childhood has been relatively little studied. The position of the larynx in the new born is very high relative to other structures of the vocal tract, and the epiglottis makes contact with the soft palate. This contact is lost through progressive lowering of the epiglottis and larynx during the first year of life. At the age of six months the epiglottis and palate are well separated, although they make contact during swallowing, and by 12 to 18 months the contact even during swallowing is inconsistent.

2.2.2 Skeletal framework: laryngeal cartilages

Dickson and Maue-Dickson (1982:176) report that growth of the laryngeal cartilages is more or less linearly related to growth in height in both sexes, and that a rapid increase in size of the male cartilages at puberty results in significant adult sex differences. Maue (1970) and Maue and Dickson (1971) both cited in Dickson and Maue-Dickson (1982:142, 148) give some measurements for male and female laryngeal carti-lages which are summarised in Figure 9.2. It is clear that significant growth during childhood is followed by marked sexual differentiation of the carti-laginous laryngeal skeleton at puberty (Kahane 1988), following the general growth curve.

During ageing, laryngeal cartilages are subject to calcification, with conse-quent changes in elasticity of the cartilages. The age of onset of calcification varies considerably. It may begin in men in their thirties, but the thyroid cartilage may still be unaffected in some 70-year olds. In women, ossification generally begins later and is less extensive (Pantoja 1968, Greene and Mattheson 1989, Kahane 1987).

2.2.3 Soft tissues: the vocal folds

The whole larynx is extremely small at birth, but reported vocal fold length measurements are rather discrepant, varying between 2.5 and 9 mm (Negus 1949, Terracol et al. 1956, Hirano et al. 1983). Growth seems to be most rapid in the first five years, and again during the pubertal growth spurt, especially in males.

There seems to be less disagreement about average adult vocal fold length, which is usually reported to be between 23–25 mm in males, and about 17 mm in females (Greene and Mattheson 1989, Romanes 1978). Hirano et al. (1983) report slightly smaller adult measurements, suggesting a total vocal fold length of 17–21 mm in males, and 11–15 mm in females. This is based on data for Japanese subjects, but it may be that there are geographical differences in laryngeal dimensions which reflect genetic variation between populations.

The relative proportions of the ligamental and cartilaginous parts of the vocal folds are usually reported to be broadly similar in both sexes, with the ligamental part constituting about two thirds of the total vocal fold length in adults. Hirano et al. (1983) have, however, shown that the ratio of cartilaginous to ligamental portions of the vocal fold changes throughout childhood, and that there is a slight gender difference in the adult ratio. In new-borns, the cartilaginous portion of the vocal fold constitutes only slightly less than half the total length of the vocal fold, but disproportionate growth of the ligamental portion results in a relative as well as an absolute increase in size of the ligamental vocal fold. This is slightly more marked in boys, so that in adult males the ligamental portion of the vocal fold constitutes a little more than two thirds of the vocal fold length.

The structure of the vocal fold at birth is very immature. The fibres of the vocalis muscle are poorly developed, and von Leden (1961) suggests that neuro-muscular maturation of the larynx is not complete before three years. The tissue layers which make up the vocal ligament are also poorly differentiated, and adult tissue layer relationships are not seen until after puberty.

In new-born infants there seems to be no clearly differentiated vocal liga-ment, and the entire lamina propria seems to be rather uniform and pliable.

a. Average dimensions of adult laryngeal cartilages (based on data from Dickson and Maue-Dickson 1982, pp. 142–148)

CARTILAGE	DIMENSION	FEMALE	MALE
Thyroid	height (A)	38mm	44mm
	anterior-posterior (B)	29mm	37mm
	weight	4gm	8gm
Cricoid	height (C)	19mm	25mm
	weight	2.89gm	5.8gm
Arytenoids	height (D)	13mm	18mm
	anterior-posterior (E)	10mm	14mm
	weight	0.20gm	0.39gm

b. Gender differences in contour of the thyroid cartilage
i. Superior view (adapted from Dickson and Maue-Dickson 1982, p. 142)
ii. Lateral view (adapted from Kahane 1988, p. 13).

i.   ii.

Figure 9.2   Summary of adult gender differences in laryngeal cartilages

The only areas of increased fibre density are at the ends of the ligamental portion of the vocal folds, and probably represent precursors of the maculae flavae. By four years of age an immature vocal ligament is present, but the differentiation between the elastic intermediate layer and the collagenous deep layer of the lamina propria does not begin until between 6 and 12 years. By 15 years of age a clear differentiation is typically observed. Full maturation may not occur before 20 years of age; before this the vocal ligament is thinner than in the adult, with a looser fibre arrangement. The epithelium shows no significant changes during development (Hirano et al. 1981, Hirano et al. 1982).

After reaching maturity there may be continuing changes in tissue thickness and consistency (see Figure 9.3). Oedema of the outer connective tissue cover of the vocal folds, together with a decrease in elastic fibres and an increase and distortion of collagen fibre content in the deeper layers, combine to alter the mechanical properties of the vocal folds (Hirano et al. 1982, Kahane 1983, Honjo and Isshiki 1980). Some of these changes may be more marked in men, but findings are inconsistent.

Yellowish or greyish discoloration of the vocal folds seems to occur quite often in older age groups (Honjo and Isshiki 1980, Mueller et al. 1985), and may indicate a degree of fatty degeneration or keratinization of the epithelium. These localised changes in the mechanical properties of the vocal folds may cause dysperiodic vibration, which would be perceived as harshness. Any significant change in overall mass or stiffness of the vocal folds may also affect fundamental frequency (see Figure 9.16).

Atrophy of the laryngeal musculature, especially of the vocalis muscle which forms the bulk of the body of the vocal fold, is also a commonly reported feature of the ageing larynx, which may be more marked in males (Honjo and Isshiki 1980, Mueller et al. 1985). The decrease in muscle mass and strength may prevent complete adduction of the folds, with consequent air wastage resulting in a whispery phonation and lower intensity. Decreased vocal fold mass may also be associated with an increase in fundamental frequency.

The mechanical structure of the conus elasticus supporting the vocal folds seems also to be subject to degenerative change in old age, especially at the point of union with the vocalis muscle, with males once again being more susceptible (Kahane 1987).

2.3 Resonating cavities: pharynx, oral cavity and nasal cavity

2.3.1 Skeletal determinants of the resonating cavities The most important of these is probably the skull, together with the cartilages and bones of the facial skeleton. The skull is usually described as consisting of two parts; the cranium, which encloses and protects the brain, and the facial skeleton. Structurally, these parts form a cohesive whole, but functionally they are rather

A. Females, 20–29 years

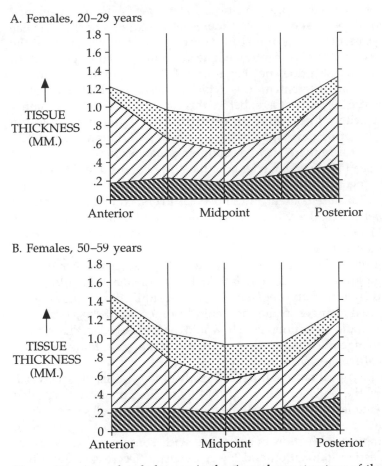

Figure 9.3   Age related changes in the tissue layer structure of the vocal folds. (based on data from Hirano et al. 1982:274)

different, and this difference is reflected in their disproportionate growth patterns. At birth, the cranium is 8 to 9 times the size of the face, and its relative size increases still further during the first 6 to 12 months of life as it grows more rapidly than the rest of the skull. Thereafter, facial growth is greater, and continues longer, so that in an adult the cranium is only 2 to 3 times the size of the face (Watson and Lowrey 1967, see Figure 9.4). Growth of the base of the skull, which provides points of articulation with the vertebral column and allows passage of the respiratory and digestive tracts and the spinal cord, is allied with the facial skeleton in terms of its growth behaviour.

2.3.2 The cranium   Growth of the cranium, as might be expected, reflects quite accurately the growth of the brain, being most rapid during the first one or two years of life, and virtually complete by 10–12 years (Watson and Lowrey 1967, Sinclair 1978, Tanner 1978). The cranium is significantly smaller in females,

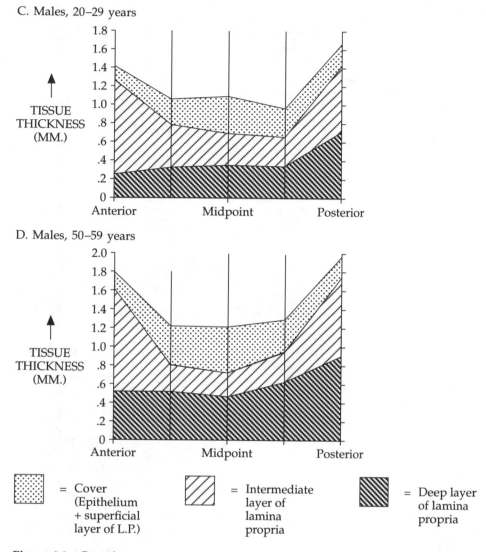

C. Males, 20–29 years

D. Males, 50–59 years

TISSUE THICKNESS (MM.)

Anterior   Midpoint   Posterior

▨ = Cover
(Epithelium
+ superficial
layer of L.P.)

▨ = Intermediate
layer of
lamina
propria

▨ = Deep layer
of lamina
propria

Figure 9.3   Cont'd

and the frontal bone may be more prominent (Wei 1970, Ingerslev and Solow 1975).

2.3.3 The facial skeleton   The facial skeleton imposes much more direct limits on the morphology of the resonating cavities of the vocal tract, and is therefore of more immediate relevance to phonetics. The main constituent parts and landmarks of the facial skeleton are shown in Figure 9.5.

There is a large and often controversial literature concerning development of the facial skeleton. Disagreement about normal patterns of growth arise

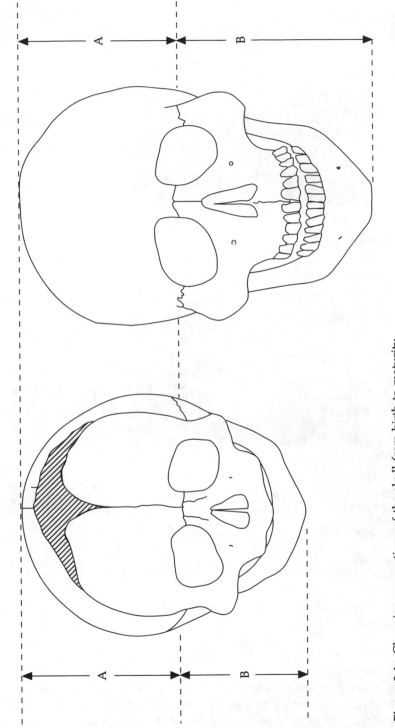

Figure 9.4 Changing proportions of the skull from birth to maturity
Newborn and adult skulls are drawn so that the cranial height is the same, showing the proportionately larger face in the adult.
(adapted from Sinclair 1978:94)

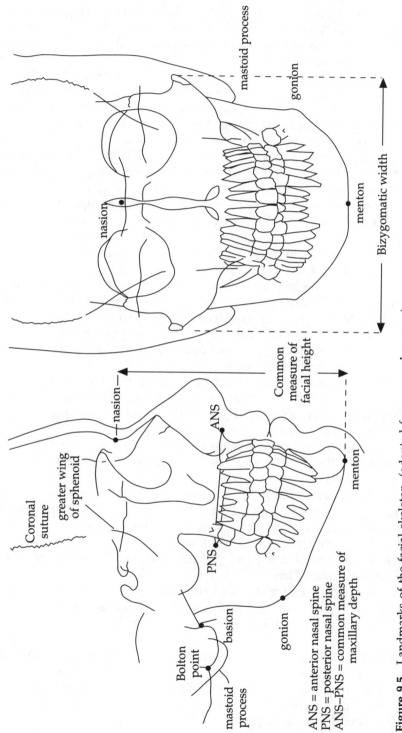

Figure 9.5 Landmarks of the facial skeleton. (adapted from several sources)

partly from the high degree of real variability in facial morphology and growth, and partly from the variety of cephalometric techniques used. A further problem is that descriptions may be biased towards an ideal view of growth, since many studies use only children of "good dental health" (e.g. Walker and Kowalski 1972:111) or normal occlusal relationships (Shah et al. 1980).

Variability in facial structure obviously has a large genetic component, as evidenced by the observation that different ethnic groups show very different facial characteristics, but facial growth patterns also display a high degree of plasticity, responding quite readily to environmental factors. A certain amount of flexibility in the growth patterns of the various parts of the facial skeleton is presumably an adaptive response to the need for very complex co-ordination of growth of the many bones and cartilages which make up the facial skeleton. The growth of each part must be carefully timed so as to maintain functional harmony of the overall facial structure, and it may be that the best way of achieving this harmony is for each growth area to be especially sensitive to its skeletal and soft tissue environment. The problem of co-ordinating growth is not, of course, unique to the face, but the complexity of the skeleton in this area makes it particularly crucial. The observation that facial characteristics are highly prone to disturbance by a wide variety of genetic and environmental abnormalities (Martin 1961), ranging from Down's Syndrome to foetal alcohol syndrome, is indicative of the level of sensitivity to growth disturbance displayed by the facial skeleton. Some examples of disturbed growth in this area will be described later in this chapter.

The facial skeleton and the cranial base follow the general body-growth curve much more closely than does the cranium. In early childhood, growth is closely related to development of the muscles of mastication, the tongue and the dentition. There is a pronounced adolescent growth spurt in most measurements (Hunter 1966, Dermaut and O'Reilly 1978, Shah et al. 1980), but the precise timing of the growth spurt may depend on the measurements used, the sex of the subjects and their genetic background. In females, facial growth is usually almost completed in the late teens, but facial growth in males may continue into the mid-twenties (Hunter 1966). The growth of the mandible seems to show the closest correlation with overall body growth curves (Hunter 1966). Generally, growth in facial width is completed earlier than growth in the anteroposterior dimension, and vertical growth of the face may continue into the third decade of life.

The various component sections of the facial skeleton will be considered separately, although vocal tract configuration depends as much on the relationship between these sections as on the shape or absolute size of each.

<u>Palate and maxilla</u>   Growth in size of the maxilla (upper jaw) and palate is quite complex. Watson and Lowrey (1967) differentiate three anatomical regions of the nasomaxillary complex, which all show different growth patterns. During the first year of life there is generalised growth of maxilla and palate, but after this period, growth becomes more localised.

i. Length of the anterior portion of the palate and maxilla becomes fixed in early infancy, and palatal width becomes fixed at 4 to 5 years of age. Thereafter, alveolar width is increased by apposition of bone at the external surface of the alveolar bone.

ii. Bizygomatic width (see Figure 9.5) has a very different pattern of growth, increasing at a smoothly and steadily diminishing rate until adulthood. Growth in this dimension is particularly pronounced in males.

iii. Maxillary width keeps pace with palatal and bizygomatic widths. Height and length of the maxilla increase concurrently, as growth proceeds in a forward and downward direction.

Figure 9.6a summarises palatal dimensions for American Caucasians (Shapiro et al. 1963, Redman et al. 1966). Unfortunately these findings were not related to measurements of any other part of the craniofacial skeleton, nor to overall body growth. It can be seen that there is significant sexual differentiation, and this accords with data for Danish subjects (Ingerslev and Solow 1975). Figure 9.6b shows the changing proportions of the palatal vault which result from these growth patterns. There seems to be considerable variability in the timing and extent of the maxillary growth spurt, at least for females (O'Reilly 1979).

The maxilla shows some degenerative changes in old age, especially in the area of tooth insertion. As teeth are lost, the requirement for bone thickness in the tooth socket area is reduced, and bone tends to be lost.

The mandible   Growth of the mandible (lower jaw) seems to be highly sensitive to a variety of factors. It seems to respond more to growth hormone than most other bones (Bevis et al. 1977), and may also be more responsive to testosterone. It is also very sensitive to the muscular forces imposed upon it (Watson and Lowrey 1967). Mandibular growth seems to be subordinate to maxillary growth, following growth of the maxilla in such a way as to produce adequate occlusion.

The mechanism of mandibular growth is complex and very variable (Bjork 1966, Enlow and Harris 1964, Sinclair 1978:77). Increase in length follows the general bodily growth curve quite closely, with a greater and longer lasting growth spurt in males than in females, so that sexual dimorphism in mandibular length becomes quite marked by adulthood (Hunter 1966, Walker and Kowalski 1972, Ingerslev and Solow 1975). Figure 9.7, adapted from Enlow and Harris (1964) and Sinclair (1978:77), shows the main areas of mandibular growth and remodelling. Growth results primarily in a length increase, although width also increases to allow proper articulation with the skull. During the prepubertal phase, there is considerable appositional growth at the head of the mandible. Bone growth behind the ramus, accompanied by bone resorption at the front of the ramus, gradually increases the space available for the dentition. The angle between the ramus and the body of the mandible is gradually reduced from about 140° in infancy to 120° in adulthood. The greatest contribution to overall facial growth at the time of puberty is made by the mandible. During this period, most growth continues in the ramus, but there

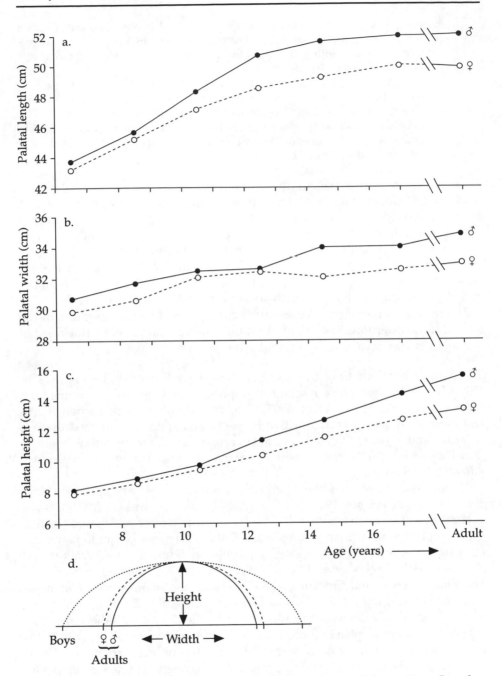

Figure 9.6   Developmental changes in palatal dimensions and proportions (based on data from Redman et al. 1966)

a, b and c. Graphic representations of palatal dimensions vs. age

d. Relationship between palatal height and width for 6–7 year-old boys, women and men, normalised for height.

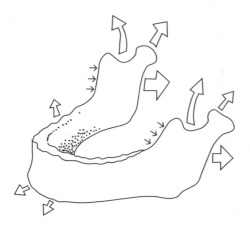
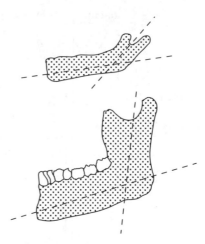

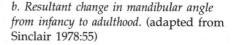
⇉ = Resorption   ⇨ = Direction of growth

a. Schematic diagram of the main axes of
mandibular growth and remodelling.
(adapted from Enlow and Harris 1964:50
and Sinclair 1978:58)

b. Resultant change in mandibular angle
from infancy to adulthood. (adapted from
Sinclair 1978:55)

Figure 9.7   Patterns of mandibular growth.

are also marked increases in the length of the body and the vertical distance
between the chin and the incisors.

As the mandible grows, the bone remodelling allows teeth to move forwards to create space for the eruption of the molar teeth, and the incisor teeth
gradually incline forwards (Sinclair 1978:78).

As with the maxilla, loss of teeth is associated with bone resorption in the
alveolar margin, so that the angle of the mandible becomes more obtuse, as in
infancy, and may reach about 140 degrees (Sinclair 1978:218).

Dentition   The first primary teeth usually appear at about 6 months of age.
The age of eruption is variable, but usually all have emerged by the age of
2½ years. The eruption of the permanent teeth is also very variable, but usually
begins between 5½ and 6 years, and is complete, with the exception of the third
molars, at around 12 years. The third molars, or wisdom teeth, do not normally erupt until between 18 and 21 years. Typical ages of tooth eruption are
shown in Figure 9.8. The age of eruption of the permanent dentition is slightly
earlier in girls, in line with the general trend towards earlier maturity in girls.

Tooth loss through disease is a common feature of old age. The gums begin
to recede from the crowns of the teeth in early adulthood, and since the enamel
covering the crown of the tooth cannot regenerate, the enamel covering becomes gradually more worn from contact with hard food stuffs and decay
resulting from plaque and infection.

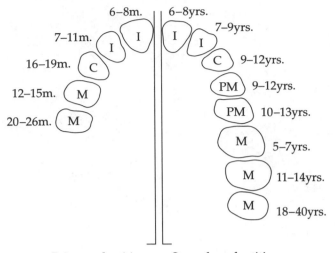

Primary dentition   Secondary dentition

I = incisors, C = canines, PM = premolars, M = molars

Figure 9.8   Typical ages of tooth eruption.

<u>Nasal cavity</u>   There is little data available on growth and development of the nasal cavity, but the poor development of the nasal bone at birth, and the marked enlargement of the nasal bone at puberty, together with other changes in proportions of the facial skeleton, point to major changes in the internal structure of the nose between birth and maturity. The oral-nasal port will be influenced by the lumen of the pharynx, the size and carriage of the tongue, and the mass of lymphoid tissue which is present at any given stage in development. All these factors may have major consequences for the balance of oral and nasal resonance, since the relative sizes of the posterior entrances to the oral and nasal cavities are thought to be important determinants of nasal resonance (Laver 1980), but it is unfortunately hard to evaluate their precise effects.

2.3.4 Jaw relationships   It was mentioned earlier that growth of the mandible tends to accommodate itself to maxillary growth so that the upper and lower teeth meet (or occlude) in the correct relationship. This accommodation process is not infallible, however, and minor problems of occlusion are very common. Whilst some of these may be transient results of uncoordinated growth between the maxilla and mandible during childhood which are corrected by later stages of mandibular growth, a significant proportion persist into adulthood.

In "normal" occlusion of the teeth, the back surfaces of the maxillary incisor teeth are in contact with the front surfaces of the mandibular incisor teeth. Each lower tooth contacts the corresponding upper tooth, but is relatively slightly further forward so that it also overlaps the adjacent upper tooth. The

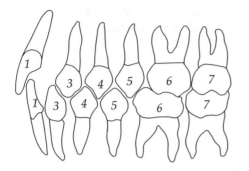

a. Lateral view
(adapted from Foster 1990)

b. Cross section between the molar teeth

Figure 9.9   Schematic representation of normal occlusion
For occlusion to be classified as normal the relationship of upper and lower teeth must be as shown above, and there should be no missing or misplaced teeth.

only exceptions to this are the lower central incisors, which occlude only with the upper central incisors. The vertical overlap (overbite) of mandibular and maxillary incisors is as shown in Figure 9.9, with an overlap of between one third and two thirds (Foster 1990). The horizontal gap (overjet) between the point of the upper incisors and the nearest point of the lower incisors is about 3 mm. Although this is an accepted description of "normal" occlusion, it might be better described as "ideal", as such a high proportion of the population deviates from this ideal, having some degree of malocclusion (Foster 1990). This will be discussed further in the section concerned with inter-individual variations.

2.3.5 Nasopharynx   The bony nasopharynx appears to expand its volume primarily through vertical growth, and there are some indications that this vertical growth is influenced by any soft tissue obstruction of the airway that may occur (Tourne 1991).

2.3.6 Soft tissues: soft palate, lymphoid tissue, tongue   The soft tissue structures which are most significant in terms of their effect on resonating cavity volume are the walls of the pharynx, the soft palate and related muscular arches, the lymphoid masses which form the adenoids and tonsils, the tongue, and the lips.

Pharyngeal walls   Soft tissue development of the pharyngeal walls seems to have been little studied, but the muscular walls of the pharynx can be assumed to expand quite rapidly as an adaptation to the skeletal and postural changes which occur during infancy. As the head is gradually held in a more upright position with greater extension of the neck, and the larynx adopts a lower position in the neck, pharyngeal volume increases dramatically. At puberty there is another period of pharyngeal enlargement, which is more marked in males, as the larynx descends further. In old age, the general tendency for muscles to atrophy and for mucosal linings to degenerate throughout the body are likely also to affect the pharynx.

Soft palate   Growth of the soft palate is most rapid during the first two years of life, continuing more slowly to the age of 18 years. Length increases from about 20 mm at 3 months to 35 mm at 18 years of age, with a relatively smaller increase in thickness (Kahane 1988:26–27). Growth progresses in such a way that the velum remains about one third longer than the anterior–posterior dimension of the nasopharynx.

Tonsils and adenoids   Growth of the tonsils and adenoids, in common with most lymphoid tissue, shows an unusual growth pattern, reaching a maximum before puberty, and thereafter declining in mass (Sinclair 1978). Tonsils and adenoids reach a maximum size at about 6 years, and then normally regress, becoming insignificant in adults. The discrepancy between this pattern of growth and that of the skeletal framework of the oral and pharyngeal cavities serves to exaggerate the effects of the skeletal growth spurt on the size of the resonating cavities.

The tongue   The tongue, because of its flexible and mobile mass, is notoriously difficult to measure, which may explain the paucity of comment on tongue growth and development. As mentioned earlier, the tongue is entirely contained within the oral cavity at birth, lowering to a relatively stable position within the neck by about the fourth year of life (Laitman and Crelin 1975:214). Later in childhood, descent of the hyoid bone as the neck elongates allows the tongue to descend more, and further enlarges the oral cavity (Bosma 1963:101). At birth the tongue effectively fills the oral cavity at rest, but the facial skeleton enlarges relatively more than the tongue (Bosma 1963:101), so that the oral cavity gradually enlarges. Hopkin's (1967) study of tongue dimensions suggested that the adult tongue is only twice the size of the newborn infant's, but any two dimensional representation of tongue size must be treated with some caution. The tongue grows differentially at its tip, acquiring what Bosma describes as a "limb like mobility". Eruption of teeth, enlargement of the oral cavity and maturation of chewing and swallowing patterns are all associated with a more retracted tongue posture.

Lips   There is little specific reference in the literature to growth of the labial aperture and labial musculature, but Kahane (1988) suggests that the facial muscles are better developed at birth than most other striated muscles, and links this to their importance in early feeding.

2.4 Summary of vocal apparatus changes occurring during the three phases of life

It may be helpful at this point to summarise the overall effect which all these changes have on vocal apparatus size and shape during childhood, adolescence and senescence, as a lead into a discussion of the consequences of growth and change for speech production.

2.4.1 Birth to puberty It is between birth and puberty that the most obvious changes in size and configuration of the vocal tract occur. At birth, the respiratory system and the larynx are poorly developed, so that phonatory control is rather limited. The human vocal tract is similar to that of other mammals, in that the tongue is held forward within the oral cavity, the larynx lies fairly high in the neck, and the epiglottis can slide up to contact the soft palate. The pharyngeal space is thus very small, and does not constitute a modifiable resonating cavity of any significance during vocalisation. The articulators in the oral region, i.e. the lips, jaw and tongue, are mobile, but immature muscular control limits their voluntary use in modifying vocalisations. The lack of teeth during the first months of life also influences articulatory potential and may have an effect on tongue posture.

The most dramatic changes occur during the first five years. After this time, the configuration of the vocal tract changes more slowly, apart from the temporary changes in dentition as permanent teeth replace the primary dentition, which may have significant, though transient, effects on front oral articulation. By the end of the first decade of life the respiratory system and the larynx are becoming more mature, and the vocal tract approximates to its adult form. Muscular development and increased neuromuscular control allow progressively finer phonetic control of the vocal apparatus during speech.

2.4.2 Puberty to maturity The most striking characteristic of vocal apparatus development during the adolescent years is the rapid increase in size of some areas, which is more marked in males, leading to the emergence of sexual differentiation. The most significant sex-related differences which are evident by early adulthood are to do with overall size of the vocal apparatus, the relative size of the larynx, and the relative proportions of the resonating cavities. Both sexes show some growth in vocal tract size during this period, and full maturation of the larynx and respiratory system will influence the range of phonation available to each individual. A rapid reduction in the mass of lymphoid tissue forming the tonsils will affect the configuration of the oropharyngeal and nasopharyngeal areas. Growth of the vocal apparatus at puberty in girls can be seen mostly as a scaling up of the pre-pubertal vocal apparatus, but in males there are significant changes in the relative proportions of the vocal apparatus. The male larynx increases rapidly and disproportionately, and the pharyngeal cavity increases its size relative to the oral cavity.

2.4.3 Maturity to senescence General ageing of the body is associated with some quite specific changes in the vocal apparatus. Respiratory function is impaired by connective tissue changes in the lungs and thoracic skeleton, and by degeneration of muscle and neuromuscular control. There are marked changes in the larynx, due to calcification of cartilages, muscular atrophy, and degenerative changes in the mucosal covering of the vocal folds. Muscular atrophy and mucosal changes will also affect the form and function of the supralaryngeal vocal tract, and the progressive loss of bone from the maxilla and mandible, together with loss of teeth, may alter the contours of the resonating cavities.

As illustration of the general morphological changes, Figure 9.10 shows a tracing of a lateral xeroradiograph of an adult male vocal tract, together with comparative tracings of lateral radiographs of the vocal tract at various stages during development.

2.5 Consequences of growth and change for speech production

Following this summary of organic changes during the life cycle, we can now draw some links between these and changes in phonetic output. There has been relatively little research in this area, partly due to the fact that it is very hard to extricate the relative contributions of organic and sociolinguistic factors when comparing different age and sex groups. The well-documented influences on verbal output of culture and style (e.g. Scherer and Giles 1979) complicate the research design.

This section offers a brief overview of reported age- and sex-linked differences in speech output which may be at least partially related to organic features, but the possibility of cultural determination cannot be excluded. It is well established that gender can be accurately judged from auditory recordings both in adults (Schwartz and Rine 1968, Coleman 1971), where there are obvious organic bases, and in young children (Meditch 1975), where potential organic determinants are less obvious. Age, too, is reasonably well judged on the basis of auditory recordings (Ptacek and Sander 1966). It seems likely that at least some of the features which allow sex and age identification do reflect organic differences, but the task of differentiating those strands of speech quality which are specifically influenced by organic changes in the vocal apparatus from those which are learned remains largely to be done.

Most existing reports of age- and gender-related aspects of speech production focus on suprasegmental aspects of speech, and these will be summarised briefly.

2.5.1 Phonation characteristics

<u>Subjective impressions</u> Subjective comments of phonatory quality are difficult to interpret, but do indicate some common life cycle trends. Very poorly

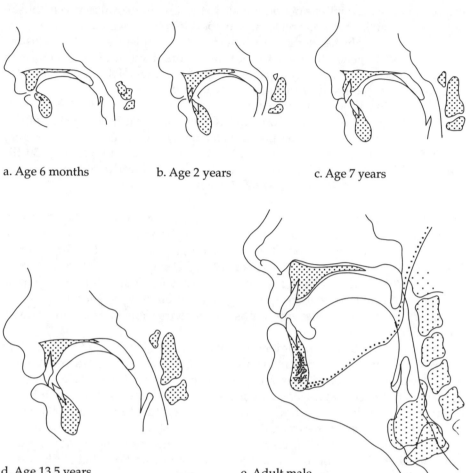

a. Age 6 months   b. Age 2 years   c. Age 7 years

d. Age 13.5 years   e. Adult male

Figure 9.10 Changing proportions of the vocal tract with age
a, b, c and d are cephalometric tracings, and show no velic closure. (adapted from Kahane 1988, p. 24). e is a xeroradiographic tracing, showing velic closure during production of [ə].

controlled, variable vocal behaviour at birth becomes rapidly more consistent during the early years of life (Wäsz-Hockert et al. 1968, Stark et al. 1975). Phonation changes at puberty are more obvious in boys, who are having to adjust to much greater changes in laryngeal structure, and who are often described as having a "husky" or "hoarse" voice quality (Greene and Mattheson 1989, Aronson 1980), with pitch breaks and fluctuations. Adolescent girls may also display some "huskiness", which may be due to hormonal changes at puberty (Greene and Mattheson 1989). Huskiness is also described as a consequence of the hormonal changes which may occur during menstruation and pregnancy in adult women (Greene and Mattheson 1989:197). Such impressionistic descriptions of voice quality are difficult to evaluate, but "huskiness" may usually be interpreted as whisperiness, i.e. fricative turbulence of the airflow through the glottis, resulting from incomplete vocal fold closure. "Hoarseness" is generally used to indicate a combination of this inefficient, whispery phonation with dysperiodicity of fundamental frequency and/or irregularity of the intensity of the laryngeal waveform.

The voice in old age has been given such labels as "weak", "tremulous", "hollow", "thin", "hoarse" and "breathy" (Greene and Mattheson 1989, Helfrich 1979), but the extent of deterioration in voice quality with age seems to be very dependent on the individual's general state of health and fitness, and on the way in which the voice has been used throughout life (Ramig and Ringel, 1983, Greene and Mattheson 1989:69–70).

Fundamental frequency   There is a clear theoretical relationship between laryngeal size and mean fundamental frequency, and a considerable amount of empirical evidence to support the expected general trends (Fairbanks et al. 1949, Mysak 1959, Hollien and Jackson 1967, Montague et al. 1974, Benjamin 1981; see also Helfrich 1979 for an extensive review). Figure 9.11 is a graphic summary of reported average speaking f_0 at different ages, showing the different sex curves. These general trends do, of course, encompass considerable individual variation.

There seems to be general agreement that old age is associated with a slight drop in f_0 in females, which may be due to several factors. Mass increase of the vocal folds due to oedema, as reported by Honjo and Isshiki (1980), would certainly be expected to lower f_0. A generalised loss of muscle tone, ossification of laryngeal cartilages and hormonal changes in old age may all have some effect. The relationship between f_0 and age is less clear in males. The overall trend of studies reviewed in Helfrich (1979:82) was for a slight increase in f_0 after the sixth decade of life, although not all studies reflect this (Wilcox and Horii 1980). This may be an artefact of cross-sectional data collection, or it may be linked to increased stiffness of the vocal folds or vocal fold atrophy (Honjo and Isshiki 1980).

Once speech is established, f_0 range seems to remain relatively constant during childhood, and then to increase between adolescence and adulthood (Helfrich 1979:84). It might be expected that reduced phonatory efficiency and flexibility in old age would be associated with decreased f_0 range, but research findings are inconsistent (Mysak 1959, Hollien et al. 1971, Benjamin 1981). It may be that different measurement procedures can partially explain this disagreement, but the sociolinguistic background and emotional state of speakers may also be important (Helfrich 1979:84).

Intensity   There seem to be few reports on speech intensity changes during childhood, although it might be expected that increased respiratory efficiency would be associated with increasing maximum intensity. Similarly, intensity may be expected to fall as respiratory capacity decreases in old age (Ptacek

a. Females

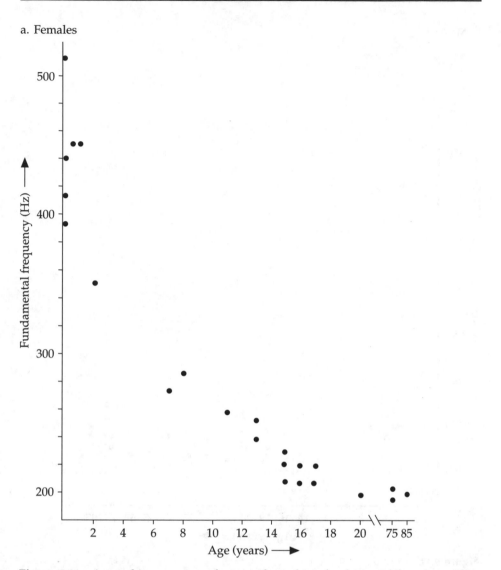

Figure 9.11 A graphic summary of reported speaking fundamental frequency (f_0) as a function of age.

et al. 1966). A complicating factor affecting habitual intensity in old age may be hearing loss, which could sometimes cause speakers to use inappropriately loud voices (Ryan and Burk 1974, Helfrich 1979:86). Studies in this area should therefore be careful to draw a distinction between maximum possible intensity and habitual intensity.

Waveform perturbations   Pitch has been reported to be very unstable in infancy (Stark et al. 1975) and at puberty (Helfrich 1979:85), with rapidly varying

b. Males

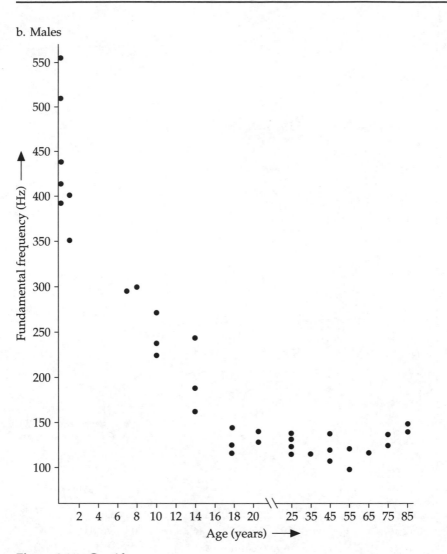

Figure 9.11   Cont'd

f_0. Several studies have found indications of increased pitch perturbation (jitter) in aged voices (Benjamin 1981, Linville and Fisher 1985) although the increase may be rather small and jitter may be related more to general state of health than to chronological age (Ramig and Ringel 1983, Ringel and Chodzko-Zajko 1987). Intensity perturbation (shimmer) may also increase in old age (Ramig and Ringel 1983, Beck 1988).

Helfrich (1979:85) attributes the pitch perturbations at all ages to lack of cortical control, but variations in the tissue layer structure of the vocal fold are also likely to be important, since these can affect the efficient functioning of the vocal fold as a vibrating body. This may be especially important in the elderly age groups, where the histology of the vocal fold may be markedly degenerate.

2.5.2 Resonance characteristics The dramatic changes in vocal tract size and configuration which occur in early childhood have direct consequences for the potential range of phonetic production, but it is extremely difficult to extricate the contributions of neuromuscular maturation, language development and organic change to overall phonetic output of young children.

There are some indications that, at least for women, age-related changes in the resonating cavities of the vocal tract may have detectable acoustic effects (Linville and Fisher 1985). The authors suggest that these effects may be explained by continuing growth of the craniofacial skeleton in adulthood, and by a lowering of the larynx in old age.

3 Interpersonal variation

The physical characteristics of any individual depend upon the precise patterns of growth during development. It is not feasible to attempt a full discussion of the mechanisms by which the timing, amount and pattern of growth displayed by an individual are controlled, and the aim here is simply to outline some of the factors which are known to have some influence on growth, as illustration of the complexity of the growth process and the many points at which it may be disturbed.

Factors which have been shown to influence growth fall into two classes: those which are endogenous to the individual, which generally means they are under genetic control, and those which can be loosely classified as environmental. Useful summaries of the genetic and environmental factors which may influence growth can be found in Sinclair (1978) Tanner (1978), and Rona (1981). The relative contributions of endogenous and environmental factors is much disputed, and as with any nature/nurture debate, the results of studies in this area will depend on which factors are held constant. If individuals with similar or identical genetic make-up are compared, then it may be shown that environmental factors are responsible for dramatic differences in overall growth. If, on the other hand, environmental factors are held constant, then the enormous contribution of genetic factors may be clearly demonstrated. Normally it is impossible to fully extricate the effects of endogenous and environmental influences, and both obviously play major roles in determining the final shape and size of an individual. Genetic factors will determine the maximum growth potential of each person, whilst environmental factors will determine the extent to which that potential is fulfilled.

3.1 Sources of interpersonal variation

3.1.1 Endogenous factors

Whilst studies of genetically identical twins make it clear that the genetic make up of a person plays a major role in determining his or her overall size, shape and rate of growth and maturation, investigation of which genes are responsible is hampered by the fact that the growth process involves so many stages at which genetic control of cells may affect growth. Very many genes play a part in the process, by controlling such factors as the rates of cell division, the rates of intercellular matrix synthesis, the rates of hormone production, or the sensitivity of cells to hormonal effects.

One growth phenomenon which has a clear genetic basis is the differentiation between males and females, including the timing of onset and the duration of the pubertal growth spurt and the earlier skeletal maturation (Sinclair 1978:142).

Hormonal factors, which play a major part in growth control, are ultimately under genetic control unless there is medical intervention of some sort, and a useful summary of hormonal control of growth can be found in Tanner (1978: Chapter 7).

3.1.2 Environmental factors

Environmental factors which may be implicated in inhibiting growth potential include poor nutrition, low socioeconomic status, emotional disturbance, large family size, being a younger sibling and disease (Garn and Clark 1975, Tanner 1978). There is also clear evidence that a general trend towards increased size and earlier maturity has been operational in many countries over at least the last century (Tanner 1978:150–151, Rona 1981). This trend seems to have slowed or stopped in Britain and some other countries, but is still continuing elsewhere. Various factors have been proposed as explanations for this phenomenon, including climatic change, a reduction in disease, improved nutrition, and genetic factors.

3.1.3 Integration and co-ordination of growth

The growth process is something of an organisational miracle, and the resilience of development to adverse factors is extraordinary. Waddington (1957) used the term "canalisation" to describe the strong tendency for development to return to its original course if anything causes a temporary diversion in the normal stream of development. It is as if the architectural plans of the adult body are laid down in the genes, but the exact timing and sequence of the building stages needed to produce the adult form are fairly flexible. If development is disrupted for a while, later developmental stages can usually be modified to make up for lost time, through a "catch-up" growth phenomenon. If the rate of catch-up growth is inadequate to allow full compensation for growth delay by the normal time of cessation of growth, then maturity may be delayed to allow a longer period of growth. One interesting feature of catch-up growth is that it is more efficient in females than in males, but the reasons for this are not clear (Sinclair 1978:158).

The mechanisms by which canalisation and associated phenomena such as catch-up growth are controlled are very poorly understood, although it has been suggested that the pattern of growth and development is to some extent under neural control (Tanner 1978:159). The widely varying growth patterns of different parts of the body and different tissue types must be co-ordinated most exactly if a properly proportioned body is to develop. Some physical characteristics can be clearly linked to specific gene effects, but a certain amount of plasticity is necessary if these physical traits are to harmonise properly. Different parts of the face, as mentioned earlier, must exert some kind of mutual growth control if they are to fit together adequately. In general, the ability of parts of the body which are under different genetic control to grow in such a way as to form an integrated whole is remarkable, although major genetic imbalances may prevent normal development and integration. Down's Syndrome is an obvious example of such a major, global imbalance in growth and development, and this is discussed further below.

3.2 *Illustrations of organic variations with phonetic relevance*

Two types of organic deviation from the mean will be used to illustrate the way in which non-standard anatomy may have implications for phonetic output. The first example concerns individuals who have dental malocclusions; these may be partially genetically conditioned, but environmental or behavioural factors may also play a role. The second concerns people with Down's Syndrome, whose genetic make-up causes a disturbance of craniofacial growth.

3.2.1 Malocclusion A malocclusion is defined as the abnormal relationship of one or more teeth to adjacent teeth in the same jaw, or to their normal antagonist in the opposing jaw (Hopkin 1978). The term is commonly used more loosely to describe any dento-facial anomaly, embracing any variations in morphology and relationships of the jaws and related craniofacial structures which can affect occlusion of the teeth.

Malocclusions are worthy of comment in the context of this chapter because there is a strong probability that variations in dentition will affect articulatory patterns, even if they do not cause obvious speech abnormalities, and also because they are very common. Precise incidence figures are hard to give, since studies vary so much in their standards of normality, but it is likely that at least 50 per cent of individuals display at least a mild degree of malocclusion (Hopkin 1978, Foster 1990). Many of these will involve only the misplacement of a few teeth, and do not result from significant growth imbalances between the mandible and maxilla, but they may still have subtle effects on both the auditory/acoustic characteristics of some segmental articulations and on the precise nature of the muscular adjustments which are necessary to achieve any given lingual articulation. The effects of orthodontic treatment upon speech production should also be considered. In the short term, speakers may have to adapt articulatory patterns to the presence of intrusive orthodontic appliances. In the longer term, the desired occlusal rehabilitation may itself demand some modification of long established patterns of speech production.

The most commonly used classification of malocclusions was developed by Angle in 1899, and is based on the antero-posterior relationship of the maxillary and mandibular dental arches. The three main classes are summarised below.

> Class I: this class shows normal arch relationships, but malpositioning of one or more teeth.
> Class II: in this class the mandibular arch is posterior to the maxillary arch. This class is further subdivided according to whether all the maxillary incisors protrude abnormally (= division 1) or only the lateral incisors (= division 2).
> Class III: in this class the mandibular arch is anterior to the maxillary arch.

These types of malocclusion are shown schematically in Figure 9.12. Angle class I malocclusions, where the jaw relationship is essentially normal but there is a variable degree of crowding, spacing or malpositioning of teeth, account for about 60 per cent of all malocclusions; Angle class II division 1 account for 25 per cent; the remaining malocclusions are fairly evenly spread between Angle class II division 2 and Angle class III (Hopkin 1978). In terms of the implications for speech, Angle classes II and III are likely to be more important, because of disturbances in tongue-to-palate relationships.

The development of abnormal jaw relationships is interesting, because although familial trends and ethnic differences show the importance of genetic factors, there is also a large body of evidence suggesting that the development of occlusal patterns is very sensitive to diet, behavioural habits and to the influence of disturbances in structure and function of other parts of the vocal apparatus (Foster 1990). Habits such as thumb or finger sucking, for example, may distort both the dentition and the palatal contour. Chronic obstruction of the pharyngeal airway may also affect the occlusal pattern and incisors angle, with improvements in occlusal pattern being evident following removal of tonsils or adenoids. This may be partly due to the fact that mouth breathing reduces the usual restraining forces imposed by the labial musculature, and partly due the adoption of unusual head and tongue postures in an attempt to maintain an open pharynx (Behlfelt 1990, Linder-Aronson et al. 1993). Malocclusion therefore offers a very clear illustration of the supremacy of the primary function of respiration over speech during development of the apparatus shared by the respiratory and speech mechanisms. The need to maintain an airway may result in a speech mechanism (and possibly a masticatory system) which is not maximally efficient.

a. Angle class I

b. Angle class II

c. Angle class III

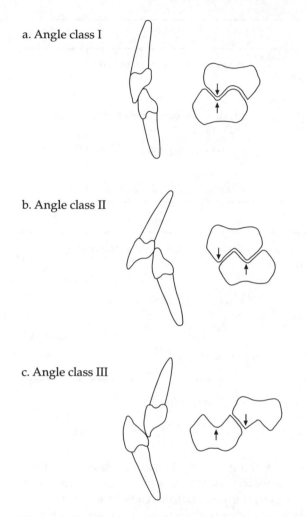

Figure 9.12 A schematic representation of Angle classes of malocclusion. (adapted from Hopkin 1978)

There have been some studies which have attempted to correlate speech output with specific patterns of malocclusion (Peterson-Falzone 1988, Bloomer 1971), but results are somewhat variable. Speakers seem to have an extraordinary capacity to compensate for malocclusal problems and still to produce acceptable speech, but some trends associated with abnormal tongue-to-palate relationships can be identified, and are summarised in Figure 9.13.

3.2.2 Down's Syndrome Down's Syndrome is characterised by the presence of an additional chromosome, and one of its effects seems to be a disruption of the narrow canalisation of growth and development mentioned earlier.

ANGLE CLASS II	
Retracted tip/blade articulation (becoming less retracted following corrective surgery)	Wakumoto et al. (in press)
"Interdental lisp" and "lateral lisp" more common	Blyth 1959, cited in Peterson-Falzone 1988:450
/s/ is realised with more incisal opening. Tongue tip may be protruded	Subtelny et al. 1964
Bilabial closure may be impaired	Bloomer 1971, Witzel et al. 1980

ANGLE CLASS III	
Advanced tongue tip/blade articulation (becoming less advanced following corrective surgery)	Wakumoto et al. (forthcoming)
Labiodentals may be realised as dentolabial. Alveolar consonants may be realised as linguolabial.	Witzel et al. 1980
/s/ may be produced with lower jaw position and retracted tongue posture	Guay et al. 1978

Figure 9.13 Reported phonetic consequences of malocclusion.

This results in increased variability in many physical characteristics. There are, none the less, some features of craniofacial anatomy which may be described as characteristic of the Down's Syndrome population. These are tabulated in Figure 9.14, together with predictions about the phonetic consequences which might be expected to result from these organic features. It should be noted that the prediction of a tendency towards an apparently "palatalised" quality is based on reports that the chromosomal imbalance in Down's Syndrome tends to result in palatal constriction of the vocal tract due to under-development of the mid-face, with relatively normal development of the tongue and lower jaw. This contrasts with descriptions sometimes offered, which suggest that front oral constriction may be the result of an over-large tongue.

Figure 9.15 shows the results of a study of the vocal characteristics of a group of adult women with Down's Syndrome, compared with an age-matched control group, and it can be seen that many of these predictions are borne out by the findings. A full description of this study may be found in Beck (1988), but the results suggest that organic features in these speakers make a very substantial contribution to their overall speech quality.

ORGANIC FACTOR	PREDICTED PHONETIC CONSEQUENCES
Thick, everted lips	Protruded labial setting
Maxillary underdevelopment	Protruded jaw setting. Tongue advanced relative to palate and upper teeth
Short, narrow palate + normal or large tongue	Advanced tip/blade articulations Fronted and raised tongue body setting
Pharynx reduced in anterior-posterior dimension	Pharyngeal constriction
Mucosal disorders affecting the vocal folds	Irregular vocal fold vibration and poor adduction →harshness, whisperiness
Generalised muscular hypotonia	Lax tension settings, increased nasality, open jaw, lowered larynx, minimised range of articulation

Figure 9.14   Characteristic organic features of the vocal apparatus in Down's Syndrome and predicted phonetic consequences.

4 Variation resulting from trauma or disease

The vocal organs, in common with the rest of the body, have to withstand a constant barrage of attack. The vocal apparatus is particularly vulnerable to the effects of environmental agents, sharing as it does the routes of ingress for both the respiratory and digestive systems. It is subject to invasion by infectious agents of various sorts, and has to withstand abrasion and chemical and thermal irritation caused by food passing through the mouth and pharynx as well as the effects of airborne irritants inhaled into the respiratory system. As an adaptation to this, the mucosal lining of the vocal tract is highly efficient at repair and regeneration.

Although the body's ability to repair and maintain its structure is extraordinary, tissues do vary in their ability to regenerate themselves. Disease processes and traumatic injuries themselves, and the defensive mechanisms marshalled by the body to combat disease or injury, may all involve some degree of organic change. Such change is complex and varied, and the range of alterations which may occur can be illustrated by reference to a few examples.

4.1 *Illustrative examples of the phonetic consequences of disease or trauma*

Any organic change which results from disease or injury to the vocal apparatus may have implications for speech production if it alters the morphology of

VOCAL SETTING	MEAN SCALAR DEGREE (Max. = 6)	AS PREDICTION? (See Figure 9.14)
Lip spreading	0.7	× *Lip rounding expected*
Protruded jaw	1.6**	√
Advanced tip/blade	1.45	√
Fronted tongue body	2.6**	√
Raised tongue body	1.5	√
Pharyngeal constriction	1.4**	√
Harshness	2.7**	√
Whisperiness	3.7**	√
Lax vocal tract	.95**	√
Tense larynx	1.6	× *Lax larynx expected*
Minimised range: lips	2.2**	√
Minimised range: jaw	1.9**	√
Minimised range: tongue	3.0**	√
Nasal	3.7**	√
Open jaw	.75**	√
Lowered larynx	.75	√

Figure 9.15 Observed Vocal Profile characteristics for 20 adult women with Down's Syndrome.
** indicates vocal characteristics which are significantly different from an age-matched control group.

the vocal organs and the resonating cavities, or if it alters the consistency and mechanical properties of the tissues which form the vocal apparatus. Tooth loss is a familiar example; the incisors are particularly vulnerable to traumatic injury, and their loss may cause minor difficulties with front oral articulations. These difficulties are usually transient, as most people adapt quickly to changes in dentition, but subtle differences in fricative quality may continue. Common examples associated with infection include inflammation of the tonsils, blockage of the nasal cavity and laryngitis. More extreme, although fortunately less common, examples of disease-related changes include tumours of the tongue, pharynx or larynx. In these cases, the surgical treatment itself may lead to much more severe phonetic disturbance.

4.1.1 Laryngeal disorders Phonetic output of the larynx is especially sensitive to trauma or disease because normal, regular arrangement of vocal fold tissues with varying degrees of stiffness and elasticity is essential for efficient, regular vibration. Any disruption of the tissue layers may interfere either with the mode of laryngeal vibration, or with the ability of the folds to adduct fully so as to limit air leakage during phonation (Hirano 1981). Structural alterations of the vocal folds can be classified in terms of the mechanical alterations involved and hence the predicted mode of phonation which would be expected (Mackenzie, Laver and Hiller 1991), and these predictions can be tested. Figure 9.16 is a summary of the structural changes associated with some vocal fold pathologies, and two examples from this list can be used to illustrate a possible relationship between mechanical state and vibratory pattern, as measured from the acoustic laryngeal waveform. Figure 9.17 shows acoustic profiles for two women with contrasting vocal fold disorders.

Case 1 is a woman with Reinke's oedema. This is a chronic condition, often associated with a history of smoking, characterised by fluid accumulation in the tissue at the glottal edge of both vocal folds, but without stiffening. The predicted acoustic consequence of such a symmetrical mass increase would be a reduced f_0, without any necessary increase in jitter or shimmer, and it can be seen that the acoustic results fit the predictions, with mean f_0 being the only acoustic parameter which falls outside 2 standard deviations of the normal control values.

Case 2 is a woman with a benign unilateral sessile polyp on her vocal fold, causing an asymmetrical increase in mass with no significant stiffening. The presence of an asymmetrical mass increase would be expected to result in increased jitter and/or shimmer as well as a reduction in f_0. Again, it can be seen that the acoustic results accord well with predictions.

Such relationships between phonetic output and structural state can be utilised in the assessment of voice disorder, and further discussions of the relationship between structural changes within the vocal folds and phonatory output can be found in Hirano (1981) and Mackenzie, Laver and Hiller (1991). Although the examples given above illustrate pathological changes, which might not be typical of the general population, most people are familiar with the effects of temporary infective inflammations of the vocal folds on their voices.

5 Conclusion

This chapter has indicated some of the sources of variability within the human vocal apparatus and has given some illustrative examples of instances where known organic features may be linked to specific patterns of phonetic production. During our life-span, each one of us will undergo a series of gradual

Pathology	Mass change	Stiffness change	Protrusion into glottis	Asymmetry	Disrupted tissue layer geometry →
	Mass increase →f_0 decrease	*Increased stiffness →f_0 increase*	*Incomplete adduction → whisperiness*	*Asymmetry of mass, stiffness or contour → irregular V.F. vibration*	*irregular V.F. vibration*
Epithelial:					
hyperplasia	+			+	
keratosis	(+)	+	(+)	+	
carcinoma-in-situ	+	+	(+)	+	
squamous carcinoma	+	+	+	I	+
verrucous carcinoma	+	+	+	+	+
adult papilloma	+	+	+	+	+
Lamina propria:					
Reinke's oedema	+		NL		
vocal nodules	+		+	(+)	
vocal polyps: sessile	+	+	+	(+)	(+)
acute laryngitis	+		NL		
chronic hyperplastic laryngitis	+	+	NL		
fibroma		+	+	+	+
vocal polyps: pedunculated	+	+	+	(+)	+

Figure 9.16   A summary of characteristic mechanical changes in a variety of voice pathologies, indicating predicted patterns of phonation.

a. Reinke's oedema

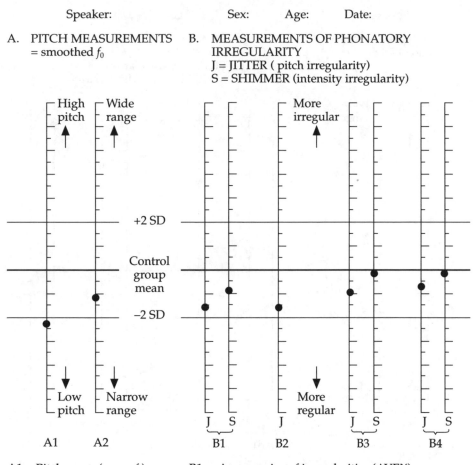

ACOUSTIC PROFILE

Speaker: Sex: Age: Date:

A. PITCH MEASUREMENTS   B. MEASUREMENTS OF PHONATORY
   = smoothed f_0 IRREGULARITY
                              J = JITTER (pitch irregularity)
                              S = SHIMMER (intensity irregularity)

A1 = Pitch mean (mean f_0)   B1 = Average size of irregularities (AVEX)
A2 = Pitch variability (SD f_0)   B2 = Standard deviation of irregularities (DEVEX)
                                      B3 = Percentage of substantial irregularities (RATEX)
                                      B4 = Percentage of substantial reversals in
                                           pitch/intensity contour (DPF)

"ACOUSTIC ANALYSIS OF VOICE FEATURES" Research Project.
(MRC Grant No. G8207136) Centre for Speech Technology Research,
Department of Linguistics, University of Edinburgh.

Figure 9.17 Acoustic profiles of two women with vocal fold pathology.
(a) Rienke's oedema and (b) sessile vocal polyp.

b. Sessile vocal polyp

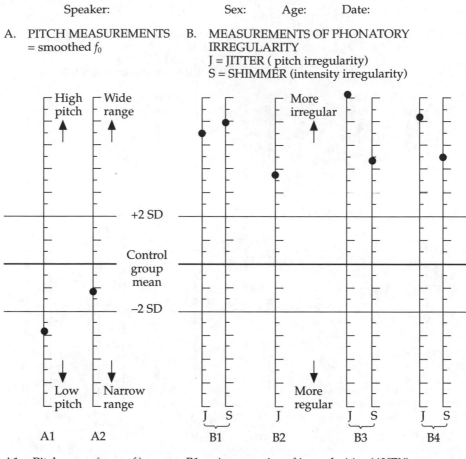

ACOUSTIC PROFILE

Speaker: Sex: Age: Date:

A. PITCH MEASUREMENTS   B. MEASUREMENTS OF PHONATORY
    = smoothed f_0 IRREGULARITY
                                 J = JITTER (pitch irregularity)
                                 S = SHIMMER (intensity irregularity)

A1 = Pitch mean (mean f_0)
A2 = Pitch variability (SD f_0)

B1 = Average size of irregularities (AVEX)
B2 = Standard deviation of irregularities (DEVEX)
B3 = Percentage of substantial irregularities (RATEX)
B4 = Percentage of substantial reversals in
     pitch/intensity contour (DPF)

"ACOUSTIC ANALYSIS OF VOICE FEATURES" Research Project.
(MRC Grant No. G8207136) Centre for Speech Technology Research,
Department of Linguistics, University of Edinburgh.

Figure 9.17   Cont'd

changes in vocal anatomy and physiology which are the inevitable result of development and degeneration. Many processes are involved in the creation of such changes, and they will interact in subtly different ways so that each one of us is endowed with a unique vocal apparatus. In addition, the consequences of illness or trauma of various kinds may include alterations in the organic state of the vocal apparatus. These alterations may be transient, lasting for a few hours or days, as in inflammation following sudden vocal misuse at a football match, for example, or they may be longer-term. In other words, day-to-day variations in vocal anatomy, in response to environmental factors and state of health, may be superimposed upon the types of inter-speaker differences which arise from normal variability in the cycle of development and dissolution.

Since the output of the vocal instrument at any given time depends upon its form and upon its potential for phonetic adjustment, anyone concerned with speech should be aware of the kinds of inter- and intra-personal variation in the vocal apparatus which may occur. The complex interplay between details of individual vocal tract architecture and speech production, both within the normal population and within the area of speech pathology, is largely unexplored. The ability of widely differing speech production systems to produce utterances which, although different in terms of phonetic detail, are yet similar enough to allow cognitive recognition of linguistic "sameness" is remarkable, and prompts many questions to do with both the nature and the communicative importance of these subtle differences.

In simplistic terms, organically derived speech differences may fall into two categories. In the first, people with organically different vocal tracts might produce some utterances which appear perceptually to be genuinely identical, although the underlying muscular adjustments of the articulators are different. Acoustically this is feasible, since equivalent auditory outputs could theoretically be produced by different vocal tracts as long as the articulators are appropriately adjusted. To illustrate this, let us imagine two speakers who are organically identical except that speaker A has a high, arched palate, and speaker B has a rather shallow palate and hence a small oral cavity volume. Both might be able to produce the initial CV sequence of the word "yam", [jam] with a very similar acoustic output, but the mandibular and lingual movements in each case would be rather different. Speaker A would have to make a relatively large upwards movement of the tongue to create sufficient approximation between the front of the tongue of the palate for the approximant [j], but would be able to produce a fairly open vowel without significant jaw opening being necessary to produce the required oral cavity volume. Speaker B, on the other hand, would need less upward movement of the tongue to constrict the oral cavity for [j], but might need to lower the jaw quite markedly to facilitate sufficient tongue lowering for the vowel to be acoustically equivalent to that of speaker A.

The second type of difference occurs where two organically different speakers produce utterances which, whilst they may be perceived as phonetically similar enough to have linguistic equivalence, show minor differences in auditory quality. This is much more typical. Going back to the previous "yam" example, it is actually rather unlikely that speakers with very different palatal volumes will be able to produce speech which is really perceptually identical. The fact that speaker B has to lower his jaw to produce enough oral cavity volume for the vowel [a] is likely to have consequences for the degree of labial opening, and this may affect both the vowel and the nature of transitions to the final nasal consonant. This might well cause minor but detectable differences in the auditory quality.

Such hypothetical examples raise many interesting questions, which, if answered, could inform discussion of many problems in the field of phonetics. For example, how do morphological anatomical relationships within the vocal apparatus influence the dynamics and trajectories of articulatory movements? Can we improve our understanding of the relationships between articulatory factors and acoustic output if we take individual organic characteristics into consideration? To what extent is an individual's potential range of phonetic output constrained by his or her organic status? What are the implications of the trading relationships between organic and phonetic factors in speech acquisition and speech pathology? What is the basis for the concept of phonetic quality in general phonetic theory?

We can begin to answer this last, pivotal, question for general phonetic theory by noting, following Laver (1994:426–7), that "The auditory quality of every speaker's voice arises from the balance in that speaker between on the one hand organic effects of the dimensions and geometry of the vocal apparatus, and on the other the phonetic adjustments of that apparatus which the speaker habitually makes." When a given phonetic quality is produced by two speakers with different vocal tract dimensions, the balance between organic and phonetic contributions to voice quality will be different, but we can say that they share a *configurational equivalence.* Analogously, one could posit a *phonatory equivalence* between two speakers with whispery voice, where in one it was produced as a result of a learned, phonetic adjustment, and in the other by virtue of semi-paralysis of one vocal fold, preventing full closure of the glottis (Laver, ibid.).

Organically-based speech differences are also interesting in the broader field of communication. We know little about the extent to which they impair intelligibility and acceptability of speech. It is likely that for the majority of organic deviations intelligibility is less of a problem than acceptability. Listeners are very willing to make judgements about a wide variety of personal and social attributes on the basis of speech quality, including social, geographical and educational background, physical stature, personality and emotional state, as well as age and gender (Laver 1991, Scherer et al. 1991, Thomson 1995); such judgements may have profound implications for an individual's own self image, as well as for his or her interactions with others. Misattributions where, for example, a voice quality associated with an organic condition is interpreted as a paralinguistic signal, and vice versa, are probably fairly common.

It is interesting to speculate to what extent lives may be affected by speech and voice qualities which are derived chiefly from organic states, and over which an individual has very little control. An obvious example would be that of a speaker whose voice, for some organic reason, was harsh. Given that harshness is a phonation type which is often interpreted as a signal of anger or aggression, it is entirely possible that such speakers might be unjustly judged as having aggressive personalities, with significant consequences for daily interactions with listeners making such judgements. Similar but more subtle misattributions could well be common throughout the population of speakers and listeners. We cannot, at the moment, begin to assess the potential misattributions and consequent distortions of self image which might result from habitual speech patterns associated with such minor organic deviations as an unusually small or large larynx, idiosyncrasies of palatal contours and their relationship with tongue volume, or dental malocclusion.

Some of the applications of speech science demand an especially good understanding of minor organic differences between speakers. The development of systems for automatic speaker verification, for example, might benefit from a better appreciation of the phonetic limitations imposed by any speaker's organic idiosyncrasies, as well as from an understanding of the phonetic implications of the commoner sorts of short-term organic fluctuation to which we are all prone.

The increasing sophistication of measurement techniques within speech science, coupled with a heightened awareness of the importance of organic variation in shaping phonetic output, should lead to opportunities for more rigorous research in this area.

Part III   Models of Speech Production and Perception

10 Acquisition of Speech

PETER F. MACNEILAGE

1 Introduction

In 3 or 4 years of untutored development an infant goes from a state of total helplessness to the possession of what is probably the most elegant behavior system in living forms, namely speech. The apparently effortless nature of this miracle has induced Chomsky and many others to place its causes almost totally within the organism, even though it is known that life experience is crucial to its normal manifestation. This effectively finesses the problem of understanding how the organism and its world conspire to produce the outcome. This review attempts to marshall the current information relevant to dealing with that problem. The concern of phonetics is primarily with how the speech production and perception systems work. The main focus of this chapter will be the acquisition of speech production. There are other recent reviews of acquisition of speech perception available (Kuhl, 1987; Juscyck, 1992) but not of production (though note Vihman, 1996). Within production, this review will focus on the segmental level. For a review of the acquisition of prosody see Vihman (1995).

1.1 The metatheoretical context: nature versus nurture

The nature versus nurture question is the fundamental question of the developmental sciences. Any work that attempts to go beyond sheer description of the (what happens when?) variety must either explicitly or tacitly concern itself with this question. Unfortunately, it has always been difficult even to formulate this question in an agreed-upon manner. Nevertheless, tackling the problem head-on seems to be the only path towards a coherent survey of the field of developmental phonetics. Although a detailed consideration of this question is beyond the scope of this chapter, something may be gained by examining some metaphors and analogies that have been used to characterize different ways of posing this basic question.

From the moment of conception onward, the developing organism is subject to a multitude of complex interacting developmental influences, first prenatal and then postnatal. The fact that there tend to be certain invariant stable outcomes of the developmental process in particular organisms encourages one to believe that these outcomes are pre-ordained, the connotation being that they are relatively uninfluenced by details of their developmental history. The field of developmental phonetics has been strongly influenced by the field of linguistics which tends to hold the view that the units and structures of language have an a priori status. Chomsky has been the most prominent advocate of this view in modern linguistics, advocating an innate universal grammar, including a phonological component (e.g. Chomsky, 1972).

However, if one takes the most specific reading of such a claim namely that linguistic phenomena are *genetically determined* then this claim cannot be justified. This has been pointed out by Stent (1981) in the context of the development of the nervous system, the structure in which a universal grammar would be instantiated. He states that ". . . the viewpoint that the structure and function of the nervous system of an animal is specified by its genes provides too narrow a context for actually understanding developmental processes and thus sets a goal for the genetic approach that is unlikely to be reached." (p. 186). He adds that ". . . too narrow means that the role of the genes, which thanks to the achievements of molecular biology, we now know to be the specification of the primary structure of protein molecules, is at too many removes from the processes that actually build nerve cells and specify neural circuits which underlie behavior to provide an appropriate conceptual framework for posing the developmental questions that need to be answered." (pp. 186–87). (For additional discussion of neurogenesis see Edelman, 1992.)

Stent points out that "Those who speak of a genetic specification of the nervous system, and hence of behavior, rarely spell out what it actually is that they have in mind. On information-theoretic grounds, the genes obviously cannot embody a neuron-by-neuron circuit diagram, and even if they did, the existence of an agency that reads the diagram in carrying out the assembly of a neuronal Heathkit would still transcend our comprehension." (p. 187). A weaker claim regarding genetic specification is that the genes contain a "program", a controlling entity, the structure of which "can be brought into 1-to-1 correspondence with a sequence of developmental phonemena". (p. 187) For example, Bickerton (1983) speaks of a language "bioprogram" underlying the evolution of grammar. However, according to Stent, few developmental phenomena fit this metaphor. Instead "Development belongs to that large class of regular phenomena that share the property that a particular set of antecedents generally leads, via a more or less invariant sequence of intermediate steps, to a particular set of consequents" (p. 187). In short development is "a historical phenomenon under which one thing simply leads to another." (p. 189). Appropriate analogies for this process according to Stent are the establishment of ecological communities upon colonization of islands, or growth of secondary forests. "Both of these examples are regular phenomena in the sense that a more or less predictable ecological structure arises via a stereo-typic pattern of intermediate steps in which the relative abundances of various types of flora and fauna follow a well-defined sequence." (p. 189). However he emphasizes that "The regularity of these phenomena is obviously not the consequences of an ecological program encoded in the genome of the parti-cipating taxa." (p. 189).

A similar metatheoretical analysis of developmental biology to that of Stent has been provided for a more general audience by Dawkins (1986). He notes the use of a "blueprint" metaphor, similar to the "program" metaphor, by those who believe in the a priori nature of form in embryology. According to this view, espoused by the preformationist school of embryology, there is a one-to-one relation between genetic structures and eventual outcomes. Dawkins considers a "recipe" metaphor, which characterizes the view of the other school of embryologists, the epigeneticists, to be more realistic. A recipe for making a cake "... is a set of instructions which, if obeyed in the right order, will result in a cake." (p. 295). From this standpoint, it makes no sense to look for a straightforward relation between parts of the finished product and particular ingredients – to ask, for example, where is the egg yolk? However, to Dawkins the analogy is too simple: "To simulate 'baking' of a baby, we should imagine not a single process in a single oven, but a tangle of conveyor belts, passing different parts of the dish through 10 million different miniaturized ovens, in series and in parallel, each oven bringing out a different combination of flavors from the 10,000 basic ingredients." (p. 297).

From these considerations it can be concluded that saying a phenomenon is genetically determined, while not necessarily totally inappropriate, typically adds little to the understanding of the development of the phenomenon. An apparently weaker though otherwise similar claim about a relatively stable developmental phenomenon is that it is "innate". "Innateness is generally thought of as inherent, internal, autonomous, fixed, in some sense preformed." (Oyama, 1993). However, as Oyama has pointed out, this term has a num-ber of different meanings, and even if defined by a particular investigator is often not used accordingly (Oyama, 1985; 1990. See the companion papers to Oyama, 1990 for a discussion of the use of the innateness concept in lan-guage development.)

It is crucial to emphasize that the evolutionary *history* of organisms includes their external environments. As Tooby and Cosmides (1988) point out: "The environment of an animal – in the sense of which features of the world it depends on or uses as inputs – is just as much the creation of evolutionary processes as the genes are. Thus the evolutionary process can be said to store information necessary for development in both the environment and the genes." (pp. 5–6. See also Tooby and Cosmides, 1995.) And in modern humans at least, there are several thousand different language environments each equally crucial to the acquisition of speech in infants subject to them.

Oyama (1993) has introduced the concept of "Developmental Systems" in an attempt to give environmental factors a more realistic role in developmental

theory: "These systems consist of the genes and all other relevant developmental influences, inside and outside the organism; the cell, with its complex
structures and constituents, the organism's own changing physiology, morphology and behavior, many aspects of the animate and inanimate environment . . ."
"These factors are interdependent and mutually constraining." (p. 11). "This
changes the concept of biology itself . . . by moving from insulation and isolation to explicit inclusion of environmental factors, as integral to the complex
system that is responsible for ontogenetic formation. There is also a shift from
internalism and autonomy to systematic interaction and mutual interdepend-
ence; from necessity and stasis to developmental contingency and change. At
the same time, learning must be rethought. No longer is it a matter of shaping
from the outside, constrained only by species nature; rather it is generated by
this same changing set of mutually constraining and selecting factors. Species-
typical learning is species-typical because the life cycle is such that particular
configurations of organisms, processes and contexts recur at times when the
organisms are in particular developmental states, having had particular developmental pasts. One wishes to know how these cycles are repeatedly accomplished." (pp. 11–12).

It should be noted that Oyama's stance is not an attempt to argue for a *more
important* role of environmental factors relative to organismic factors. In her
view; "nature and nurture are not complementary. That is, they are not separate sources of developmental form and control that must somehow be brought
together in ontogeny, added together like the complementary angles that make
up 90 degrees, or even interacting as separate entities . . . This vision of the
patchwork phenotype only leads to fruitless attempts to quantify the 'contributions' of genes and environment to the finished product. This 'product' is
not a static result, however, but a dynamic one that is perpetually changing."
(p. 13).

Oyama's conception of development, which seems basically consistent with
those of Stent and Dawkins, is the one which will be used in this chapter. The
present view, as mentioned earlier, is that the phenomena of speech development cannot be adequately discussed unless some explicit stance on the
nature–nurture question is adopted. In the author's opinion, this is the best
stance available.

1.2 Historical perspectives

1.2.1 Production Study of the acquisition of speech production came of
age with the English translation in 1968 of Roman Jakobson's monumental
1941 monograph "Kindersprache, Aphasie und Allgemeine Lautgesetze" (Child
Language, Aphasia and Phonological Universals). In the structuralist tradition
of linguistics, Jakobson believed that the sound level of language consisted of
a system of oppositions or contrasts mediated by a limited inventory of innate

distinctive features. On the basis of rather fragmentary evidence, Jakobson proposed that the sound forms of words developed in an invariant universal sequence motivated by a principle of maximization of perceptual distance. It was proposed that the first word was [ba], characterized by a maximally front labial closure for the consonant and a maximally back and open vowel. Following this, a lingual consonant contrasting with the labial consonant would be produced and a high vowel contrasting with a low vowel would be produced, and so on. Production of the first words was considered to be separated by a silent period from an earlier functionally unrelated babbling period during which the infant produced all the sounds of all the world's languages without favor.

Although the explicit and unequivocal form of Jakobson's theory no doubt had a positive formative influence on the field, and made for a concise treatment of the issues in secondary sources, almost every aspect of it has since been shown to be wrong, as we will see. The babbling repertoire has been found to be a good deal more limited than proposed. The sound form of the first words is highly similar to immediately preceding and concurrent babbling forms. A prespeech silent period is not typical. The distinctive feature is not a functional unit, and perceptual contrast is not an important motivating factor in early sound choice.

At the same time that the translation of Jakobson's work was becoming available, Chomsky was developing the implications of his grammatical theories for language learning. In his main work on phonology (Chomsky and Halle, 1968) it was asserted that "... a system of hypotheses concerning the essential properties of human language ... must be assumed to be available to the child learning a language as an a priori, innate endowment." (p. 4). The argument for an innate universal grammar is based mainly on what has come to be called "the poverty of the stimulus" – the apparent inadequacy of the child's postnatal experience in preparing him/her to use language. But, as Bever (1984) has pointed out, this could also be called in philosophical terms "the argument from ignorance": as an experiential basis for language learning is not obvious, then language must be primarily unlearned. This type of stance, as Oyama has pointed out, begs the question of how language development actually occurs.

There were two initial attempts to apply the generative linguistic approach of Chomsky, including use of distinctive features and various notation devices and rule forms, to speech acquisition. The first was David Stampe's "Natural Phonology" (Stampe, 1969; Donegan and Stampe, 1979). He postulated a set of automatic phonological rules which he called "natural processes". These natural processes were considered to be innate consequences of limitations of the human speech production and perception capabilities. All children were considered to begin the task of speech in possession of these natural processes, and speaking a particular language required suppressing, limiting or ordering a subset of these processes. For example if an infant produced [tu] with an initial stop consonant instead of the word "Sue" with an initial fricative, he/

she was considered to be using the natural process of "Stopping". Suppression of this process was then considered necessary to attain the correct production – [su]. This approach appeared to be an improvement on Jakobson's approach in that it was responsive to the presence of various typical infant sound patterns. And from the phonetic point of view it is an improvement on Jakobson's total omission of any role of production constraints in early speech attempts. But what has not always been recognized is that it was primarily descriptive in character and did not offer an explanation of why some particular patterns were most frequently observed.

The second attempt to apply the generative linguistic approach to speech acquisition was that of Smith (1973). On the basis of his son Amahl's phonological development he postulated an adult-like underlying representation and a set of realization rules accounting for the discrepancy between his son's output forms and adult forms. The rules were considered to be psychologically real and to form a universal template representing the child's linguistic competence. According to Vihman (1996, p. 24) Smith identifies four functions served by realization rules; "vowel and consonant harmony, consonant cluster reduction, systemic simplification (or merger of contrasting adult phonemes) and grammatical 'simplification' (e.g. his son's use of a fixed 'dummy' prefix for unstressed initial syllables of adult words)." Smith rejects the possibility that articulatory difficulties may play a major role in determining the patterns of mispronunciation, citing evidence that sounds that cannot be produced in one context may nevertheless be produced in another. However Braine (1976) in a review of Smith's book concludes that articulatory explanations cannot be so easily dismissed. And it is interesting to note that utterances consistent with the output forms of Smith's realization rules (e.g. absence of consonant clusters, vowel and consonant harmony, frequent use of neutral vowels) are highly characteristic of prespeech babbling, when they are unlikely to, as yet, reflect realization rules operating on adult forms. In addition a number of authors have made arguments critical of Smith's claim that his son did in fact have an entirely adult-like underlying representation.

One development of generative phonology in recent years has been Nonlinear Phonology which has made available a somewhat richer conceptual apparatus than Chomsky and Halle provided (Goldsmith, 1990). The term nonlinear refers to the fact that this approach could now go beyond the characterization of relationships between adjacent segments, and could now be applied to phenomena such as metrical patterns, tone sandhi and consonant and vowel harmony, the latter of course being common in early speech. (See Bernhardt, 1992 for a tutorial in nonlinear phonology for readers interested in speech acquisition.) Macken (1992; 1995) is a prominent exponent of this approach.

The prosodic phonology approach of Natalie Waterson (1971; 1987) motivated by Firth's (1948) analysis, to some extent anticipated the development of nonlinear phonology in placing emphasis on phenomena that transcended the segmental level. She stressed the importance of viewing the infant's output as holistic, the value of considering the infant's system on its own terms, and the likelihood that the infant's perceptual representations are schematic and incomplete and heavily dependent on the relative salience of various aspects of the input. All these themes struck a responsive chord in later work.

From the phonetic standpoint, all of these linguistic approaches to speech acquisition, with the exception of that of Waterson, raise a single basic issue. They all posit an autonomous level of innate phonological organization independent of the phonetic level. They all posit an a priori predominance of phonological form over phonetic substance. This formalist influence comes from the field of adult phonology.

In the 1970s there was a reaction against this formalistic adult-centered perspective in the direction of a more eclectic "Cognitive" orientation, reflected initially in the work of Menn (e.g. 1978; 1983) and of Ferguson and his colleagues on the Stanford Child Phonology Project (e.g. Ferguson, 1986; Ferguson and Farwell, 1975; Macken and Ferguson, 1983). This development resulted partly from the failure of Jakobson's universal order hypothesis and was influenced by increasing evidence that there could be considerable individual differences in acquisition patterns. From this perspective, the infant was regarded as a problem solver, bringing his/her particular package of propensities to the task and adopting various "strategies" in the development of adult-level production. Universal innate phonological knowledge was de-emphasized and phonetic factors were accorded more importance.

In the past decade or so, beginning with the work of Locke (1983) there has been an increasing emphasis on fitting the acquisition of speech production into a more biological perspective (e.g. Kent and Bauer, 1985; Kent, 1992; Lindblom, 1992; Studdert-Kennedy, 1987, 1991). In this approach, the uniqueness of language is not assumed a priori, mental concepts are de-emphasized, and perceptuomotor constraints are emphasized. There is some consensus on an aim of deriving phonological form from phonetic substance and developing explanations based on knowledge independent of the facts to be explained (Lindblom, 1992).

2 Stage 1 Prebabbling (0–7 months)

A convenient beginning for an outline of speech development is provided by Thelen's (1991, p. 340) identification of three components which are involved:

> First, there are the natural categories of sounds that emerge when the oral, facial, respiratory, and ingestive apparatus at particular stages of anatomical and functional maturation are combined and activated. Second, perceptual biases make infants sensitive to certain features of the sound and visual environment and to the proprioception of their own vocal behavior. And third, infants select from the universe of possible natural categories of sounds by matching their own motor output to the sights and sounds of the natural language environment.

Thus, at the most basic level we have productive propensities, perceptual propensities, and their interaction, in the development of an environmentally sensitive vocal repertoire.

The phenomena of vocal development are of course embedded in a social matrix of interaction, from prenatal stages onward, between the infant and significant others, in which the infant's own acts and the response of others to these acts play an important role. The world is not there just as a display screen for passive absorption, but as something to be acted upon, noting the consequences for both self and others. The social matrix, always a strong motivator for the infant, is the source of meaning, in a broad sense earlier, but subsequently of specifically lexical and grammatically encoded meaning. Phonetic knowledge thus emerges in a broader context of overall knowledge, within which it comes to serve its social interfacing purpose. (See Locke, 1993 for an attempt to sketch out this overall scene.)

2.1 Speech perception

Work on the acquisition of speech perception effectively dates from Eimas et al's landmark 1971 paper in which they showed that one month old infants could discriminate between stimuli with voice onset times that put them on each side of the phoneme boundary between [p] as in "bat" and [ph] as in "pat". This finding was interpreted as evidence for an innate speech-related capacity for perceptual categorization of phonemes. Subsequent work showed that very young infants could distinguish sounds that straddled virtually every perceptual boundary used to contrast a phoneme with a near neighbor in languages (See Kuhl, 1987 for a summary). Subsequent research showing that infants could discriminate in a similar manner between nonspeech stimuli and that other animals such as chinchillas (Kuhl and Miller, 1975) can make similar distinctions has suggested that such capacities, rather than being only part of an innate endowment for speech, may be basic to mammalian audition.

Later work in this area shifted from questions of discrimination to the more germane question of when an infant shows evidence of forming a phonetic category. In a summary of this work, Kuhl (1987) concludes: "By 6 months of age, infants appear to be natural categorizers." (p. 351). She reviews studies showing that infants can learn the equivalence of particular vowels across talkers of different sex and age, the equivalence of particular consonants across vocalic contexts, the equivalence of particular features occurring in different segments, and the equivalence of instances of a particular prosodic feature. Work by Kuhl and Meltzoff (1982) also showed that by the age of four months infants looked selectively at the video of a speaker producing the vowel they were hearing rather than the video associated with another vowel, showing some *visual* representation of phonetic categories.

Most recently, work by Kuhl and her colleagues (e.g. Kuhl, 1993) has shown that by 6 months of age infants have formed language-specific vowel categories. After identifying language specific prototypic vowel qualities or "hot spots" determined by adult preferences, it has been shown that infants regard similar stimuli as more similar after pretesting with a prototype vowel than with a non-prototype vowel. Kuhl (1993) describes this acquired similarity effect surrounding prototype sounds as a "perceptual magnet effect".

In the past few years, there has been increasing interest in the infant's ability to perceptually represent more holistic properties of spoken input such as intonation, stress and syllabification (see Jusczyk, 1992 for a review). Part of this shift has come with the realization that it is probably at these levels that the first sound-meaning relationships are forged. But it has also been motivated by the thought that in development the infant may need to first cut into input at a more global level, so to speak, before forming more local representations. The classic segmentation question (Lindblom, 1982) as it applies to parcelling out *words* in particular from the continuous stream of speech has become an important question (Jusczyk, 1992).

One of the more interesting findings has been that neonates show a selective sensitivity to their own mother's voices (deCasper and Fifer, 1980) and to their own language (Mehler et al, 1988) revealing a role of prenatal experience (Lecanuet and Granier-Deferre, 1993). Studies in the first 6 months have shown that infants' responsiveness to changes in stimulus sets from training session to test session seem to be on the basis of syllable-sized units rather than intrasyllabic structure (Jusczyk, 1992). On the basis of cross-language studies on 6 month old infants, Jusczyk (1992) also concludes that "infants recognize utterances in the native language on the basis of prosodic cues before they become sensitive to its segmental characteristics". (p. 30).

In a series of studies, Fernald and her colleagues (e.g. Fernald, 1992) have found a good deal of cross-cultural uniformity in the prosodic properties of speech to infants leading to the conclusion that this form of speech "has evolved as a species-specific parenting behavior." (p. 418). These researchers have found that caretakers "speak consistently more slowly and with higher pitch when interacting with infants, in smooth, exaggerated intonation contours quite unlike the choppy and rapid-fire speech patterns used when addressing adults." To praise an infant, mothers typically use wide-range pitch contours with a rise-fall pattern. To elicit an infant's attention they also use wide range contours, but often ending with rising pitch (for example in utterances such as "Look at X"). When soothing an infant, mothers tend to use long, smooth, falling pitch contours, in marked contrast to the short, sharp intonation patterns used in warning or disapproval.

2.2 Production

Infants begin life with a well developed capacity to cry, though there is some difference of opinion as to whether this function should be placed on the same track as speech development. There is a good deal of consensus that there are three subperiods of speech-related vocal development (Oller, 1980; Stark, 1980, 1983; Koopmans-van Beinum and Van der Stelt, 1986; Roug et al, 1989). These stages have been summarized by Vihman (1995). In the first stage, from 0–2 months, "The most common nonreflexive, nondistress sounds are the 'quasi-resonant nuclei' described by Oller, vocalizations with normal phonation but limited resonance, produced with a closed or nearly closed mouth. These elements give the auditory impression of a syllabic nasal or nasalized vowel. In stage 2, from 2–4 months the first comfort sounds, apparently vocalizations typically produced in response to smiling and talking on the part of an interlocutor, may have a consonant-like overlay, usually produced in the velar area where resting tongue and palate are in close contact. These vocalizations are at first produced singly but may then appear in series, separated by glottal stops . . .". In a third "vocal play" period, from 4–7 months, "the child appears to gain increasing control of both laryngeal and oral articulatory mechanisms." Both periodic and aperiodic sound sources of the vocal tract are explored (Roug et al, 1989): Prosodic features such as pitch level and pitch change (resulting in "squeals" and "growls") and loudness (resulting in "yells" and possibly whisper) are manipulated, as are consonantal features, yielding friction noises, nasal murmurs, and bilabial and (ingressive) uvular trills ("raspberries" and "snorts"). "Fully resonant nuclei" (adult-like vowels) begin to be produced in this period, as does "marginal babbling", in which consonant-like and vowel-like features occur but lack the mature regular-syllable timing characteristics of canonical babbling (Oller, 1980; 1986).

2.3 *Perception–production relationships*

In Kuhl and Meltzoff's 1982 study of cross-modal perception, described earlier, infants aged 4–5 months were observed to sometimes imitate the [i] and [a] stimuli with appropriate formant patterns. In addition Papousek and Papousek (1989) have shown that 2–5 month old infants show approaches to imitation of the absolute value of adult fundamental frequencies, and other characteristics. These findings should be viewed in the context of the findings of Meltzoff and others (e.g. Meltzoff and Moore, 1993) that neonates can imitate adult facial expressions and hand gestures. Although *vocal* imitation has not been shown to occur this early, these results, taken as whole, indicate a fundamental role of mimetic input–output processes in development of the behavioral repertoire of humans, even at very early developmental stages.

3 Stage 2   Babbling (7–12 months)

3.1 *Output patterns*

The primary aim of the remainder of the chapter is to use a particular phonetic conception of the acquisition of babbling and subsequent speech production as a framework for consideration of phonetic aspects of these phenomena. Use of this framework has led to a relatively comprehensive characterization of the articulatory level of babbling, and it can also serve as a frame of reference for consideration of the subsequent course of acquisition of speech production. The conception is that of "Frames, then Content" (MacNeilage and Davis, 1990a). According to this conception, a "Frame" for speech, in the form of a rhythmic open-close alternation of the mandible, may have evolved from cyclical ingestive events, such as chewing, via an intermediate stage of visuofacial communicative cyclicities (e.g. lipsmacks) widespread in other primates. This frame is considered to provide a universal motor base for speech acquisition, and to dominate vocal output at the babbling stage. Subsequent acquisition of speech production is considered to involve increasing ability to modulate frames by providing internal "Content" primarily by means of independent tongue actions. A cornerstone of this framework is evidence that when infants mature into adults they possess a mode of production in which syllabic frames and segmental content elements are independently controlled. In serial ordering errors of adult speech, consonants and vowels always obey "frame" constraints against occupying each other's positions in syllable structure. Levelt (1992) has concluded that: "Probably the most fundamental insight from modern speech error research is that a word's skeleton or frame and its segmental content are independently generated." (p. 10). The fact that speech error research is the main psycholinguistic approach to the study of adult speech production makes the significance of this finding clear. This frame/content mode of organization can thus be seen as the target of the speech acquisition process. The frames, then content perspective provides a developmental complement to this accepted conception of adult speech organization.

A typical infant, at the age of 7 to 8 months begins to babble. Babbling is produced by a rhythmic alternation between opening and closing of the mouth accompanied by phonation. This behavior typically continues from 4 to 5 months until the advent of words, and then accompanies early words for a number of months. Because of the linguistic orientation of this field in its early stages, and the later cognitive emphasis on the infant as a *lexical* problem-solver, the question of the actual nature of babbling has received a good deal less attention than early word production. However the increasing awareness that the structure of early words is highly similar to the structure of babbling, prompted primarily by the work of Cruttenden (1970), Oller et al (1976), Locke (1983) and Vihman et al (1985, 1986) has stimulated a good deal of recent work on the topic. Nevertheless the present thesis is that the potential explanatory power of the phenomena of babbling for the understanding of word acquisition has scarcely been tapped. In the author's opinion we have been deprived of this power by the historical accident of the early dominance of formal linguistics in this field. Thus rather than babbling being simply a matter of "ephemeral sound productions" or "external phonetics" (Jakobson, 1968, p. 27) babbling may be our best single route to the understanding of acquisition of speech. It shows us the simpler forms from which later forms must derive, thus providing a stronger basis for developmental inferences than any currently available to the student of perceptual development. In the author's view, it may even provide an important missing link in our attempt to understand the *evolution* of speech (MacNeilage and Davis, 1993; MacNeilage, 1994, 1995).

The intuition of the casual listener that the "bababab" they hear in the adjacent aisle in the supermarket is highly rhythmic, is an important one because it indicates there is a superordinate rhythmic controller in the earliest babbling – a controller that we retain throughout our life. Beyond that, there is an extremely strong tendency to begin a babbling episode with a consonant and terminate it with a vowel. (For the moment, the words "consonant", "vowel" and "syllable" will be used in a purely descriptive mode, with no commitment regarding their reality as independent action units.) For example in a recent study of six infants there were ten times as many initial consonants in babbling episodes as final consonants (Davis and MacNeilage, 1995). Initial vowels are favored somewhat more than final consonants (by a 3:1 ratio in the above study). Consonant clusters are virtually unknown. Utterances consisting of a single syllable, usually a consonant-vowel (CV) syllable tend to be most common. Frequency of multisyllabic utterances decreases with their length though an utterance with 10 or more syllables is not rare.

There is a good deal of agreement on the broad subclasses of consonants and vowels that the listener to babbling is most likely to transcribe. Though most work has been done on English, work done in other language environments seems to produce broadly similar results. (See Locke, 1983 for consonantal data and MacNeilage and Davis, 1990b for vowel data.) From the standpoint of babbling (and the rhythmic organization of speech in general) what are often called semivowels, (or glides, most commonly [w] and [j]), are better regarded as semi-consonants as they tend to alternate with vowels as consonants do. In the following analysis they will be grouped with consonants. Typical results on consonants can be seen in the tabulation of three studies of babbling in English-speaking environments given by Locke (1983, p. 4). The most favored consonants involving the upper articulators are labial and coronal stop consonants. Although some individual infants show strong preferences for velar stops, a typical infant develops this capacity slowly, beginning some time after the onset of babbling. Stops tend to be voiceless unaspirated in initial position, and voiced intervocalically.

After stops, labial and coronal nasals are the next most frequent consonantal category, though typically a good deal less frequent than stops. Glides may occur in the closing phases of the mouth open-close cycle with frequencies roughly similar to those of nasals.

There have been fewer studies of vowel frequencies in babbling than consonant frequencies, due apparently to qualms about the reliability of vowel transcriptions. Nevertheless, even in the presence of detailed disagreements, such studies can obviously show the relative frequencies of use of different broad regions of the vowel space. The most frequent occurrences are in the lower left quadrant of the vowel space – mid and low front and central regions. In addition high front vowels have higher frequencies than high back vowels (MacNeilage and Davis, 1990b).

All the above generalizations may at present be too heavily weighted towards English. As we will see, there is evidence of various cross-linguistic effects during the *later* part of the babbling period, but there is relatively little solid cross-linguistic evidence available for babbling prior to 10 months of age.

The fact that the rhythmic quality of babbling tends to be maintained throughout the typical utterance tells us that the mandible *is* an independent variable at this early stage. It provides a frame for the entire course of most babbled utterances. However it is important to ask whether movements of other articulators in babbling are more or less confined to single segments as they are in adults, or, as one might expect from an immature motor system, less confined in the time domain. Some consensus is developing from studies with Davis (Davis and MacNeilage, 1994, 1995) using large (>1,000 syllables) samples from each infant (7 infants) that there are three basic patterns of co-occurrence between consonant types and following vowel types, suggesting that these two major classes are *not* under independent control. Two of the patterns involve the tongue. Consonants transcribed as [t], [d] and [n] and the palatal glide [j] tended to occur with front vowels, and velars [k], [g], [ng] tended to occur with back vowels. Both of these tendencies were attributed to the tendency of the infant tongue to not move large distances in short periods of time. The third tendency was for labials [p], [b], and [m] to co-occur with central vowels. Because there seems to be no direct mechanical linkage that would link the lips with a central position of the tongue it was suggested that this co-occurrence was produced by "Pure Frames"; that is, instances of mandibular oscillation alone, with no necessary separate lip movement, and no movement of the tongue from its central resting position within the mandible (MacNeilage and Davis, 1990a). Extending this metaphor, instances of co-occurrence of tongue-front consonants with front vowels were called "Fronted Frames" and instances of co-occurrence of velars with back vowels were called "Backed Frames". In both cases it was argued that the tongue could be prepositioned before an utterance even began, and not actively moved during the syllable. A summary of these patterns of consonant-vowel co-occurrence is given in Figure 10.1.

Some agreement regarding the existence of these patterns but also some dissent comes from other studies using smaller samples of utterances from individual infants. (Vihman, 1992; Boysson-Bardies, 1993; Oller and Steffans, 1993). None of these studies involved infants under ten months of age. Some methodological differences from study to study make them difficult to compare with each other and with the studies of Davis and MacNeilage.

The main study of this issue with Davis was the 1995 study. Six infants in an English language environment were studied over a period of 4 to 6 months, from the onset of babbling onwards. Over 25,000 syllables were analyzed. All

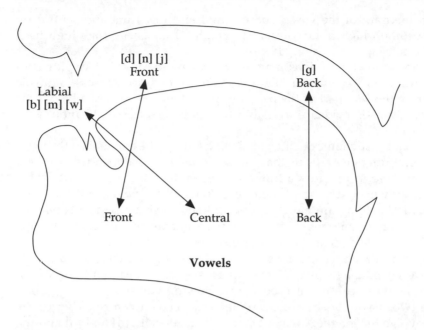

Figure 10.1 Schematic view of the 3 types of consonant-vowel co-occurrence constraints.

Table 10.1 Mean ratios of observed to expected frequences of various CV types in 6 subjects

| | | | Consonants | |
		Alveolar	Labial	Velar
	Front	1.28	.55	1.01
Vowels	Central	.83	1.39	.92
	Back	.72	1.23	1.34

18 findings (six subjects, three hypotheses) were in the expected direction, embedded in highly significant trends in most cases. Table 10.1 summarizes the results of the study. Ratios in the individual cells represent the relation between the observed co-occurrence frequencies and those expected on the basis of the frequencies of the individual consonant and vowel types represented by each cell, in the overall corpus. (For example, if labial consonants constituted 30 per cent of consonants in the corpus and central vowels constituted 40 per cent, the expected proportion of co-occurrences of labial consonants

with central vowels in the corpus is .3 × .4 = .12.) The results for the three predictions (for fronted, pure and backed frames) are shown in the diagonal of the table. These results suggest that major exceptions to these trends may be relatively rare in infants who are intensively studied.

A further result of this study (Davis and MacNeilage, 1995) was that if the data of this study are split into roughly equal early babbling and later babbling subsets, the patterns of CV co-occurrence constraints are virtually identical in the two subsets. This suggests that the phenomena are characteristic of babbling in general, not just early babbling. The results of an earlier Davis and MacNeilage study (1990) of a 14 to 20 month old infant, with 750 words at the end of the study period, suggest that these patterns may continue to be present in early words.

The analysis of the organization of babbling presented so far concerns the nature of *intra*syllabic patterns. The second main question is that of the nature of *inter*syllabic patterns. Following the earlier suggestions of Oller (1980) and Stark (1980) it was thought that there were two stages in the organization of multisyllabic babbling; a stage of reduplicated babbling from about 7 to 10 months, in which the infant repeats the same syllable, and a following stage of variegated babbling, from 10 to 12 months and typically beyond, in which an infant varies the consonants and/or the vowels within a multisyllabic utterance. This seemed a plausible sequence – apparently proceeding from easier organizational patterns to harder ones. A case study of Elbers' (1982) showed this pattern in a single infant. But some more recent studies (Smith, Brown-Sweeney and Stoel-Gammon, 1989; Mitchell and Kent, 1992) have shown that there is typically a good deal of variegation from the early stages of babbling onwards. These studies primarily involved consonant variegation. Davis and MacNeilage (1995) also studied vowel variegation and found that if one considers pairs of consecutive syllables the modal amount of intersyllabic variegation in the group of 6 subjects was about 50 per cent and differed little from the first to the second half of the 4 to 6 month period studied.

The question can be raised as to whether intersyllabic patterns are like intrasyllabic patterns in that they reflect a strong influence of mandibular variation relative to variation in other articulators. If so, then it can be hypothesized (MacNeilage and Davis, 1990b) that more variation should take place in what can be called the *vertical* dimension of articulation than in the *horizontal* dimension. For example successive vowels might be more likely to vary in height than in the front–back dimension because variation in mandibular depression may be the main source of intersyllabic vowel variegation. Similarly, consonants might vary more in manner of articulation, at least insofar as it is related to amount of vocal tract constriction, than in place of articulation. This might be so because variation in mandibular elevation between syllables might occur more readily than variation in the front back position of the tongue, or alternation between tongue and lip constrictions. Some studies seem to favor this possibility. Hodge (1989) found spectrographic evidence that the tongue height dimension was used more than the front–back dimension in vowels, and Mitchell and Kent (1992) observed a favoring of the manner dimension in consonantal variegation. However Smith, Brown-Sweeney and Stoel-Gammon (1989) observed more consonantal place variegation than manner variegation. In a case study of a single infant Davis and MacNeilage (1994) found more height variegation than front–back variegation in vowels, but a trend towards more consonantal manner variegation than place variegation did not reach statistical significance.

These hypotheses were also evaluated in the six case studies described earlier (Davis and MacNeilage, 1995). The question was whether the observed frequencies of vertical variegation from one syllable to the next (for all instances in which successive syllables varied) were higher than those expected from the overall frequencies of the two participating vowels or consonants in the entire corpus. In this analysis, only consonantal data involving stops, nasals and glides (the most frequently occurring categories) were analyzed, and manner variation was considered to only involve alternation between stops and nasals, on the one hand, and glides on the other. In all 12 cases (six subjects, two hypotheses) vertical variegation significantly exceeded horizontal variation ($p < .001$ in all cases).

Another important aspect of the organization of variegated babbling is that vowels are typically more free to vary than consonants. This was shown in a study of five 13 month old subjects by Kent and Bauer (1985). In addition, all six subjects in the study of Davis and MacNeilage (1995) showed an excess of vowel variegation over consonant variegation in two-syllable sequences in which variegation occurred. The median ratio of vowel variegation to consonant variegation was 2:1 in the Kent and Bauer study and 1.5:1 in the Davis and MacNeilage study.

Most of these various facts about the rhythmic organization of babbling, the consonantal and vocalic composition of babbled utterances, and the serial organization of consonant-vowel alternations can be summarized by the term "Frame Dominance" (Davis and MacNeilage, 1995). This concept will be used as a basis for the subsequent consideration of the nature of early words, for, as was already noted, the composition of early words closely reflects the composition of preceding and concurrent babbling.

3.2 *The role of input*

For a long time it was believed, from the innatist perspective (e.g. Lenneberg, 1967) that infants began to babble at the same time regardless of their auditory experience. Instead it has been shown more recently that, "The differences between deaf and hearing infants in onset of well formed syllables are so great that they could provide the basis for a screening evaluation for severe and profound hearing losses." (Oller and Steffens, 1993). (See the papers of Kent et al, 1987; Oller and Eilers, 1988; Oller et al, 1985; Stoel-Gammon, 1988; and Stoel-Gammon and Otomo, 1986 for details). Deaf infants typically do not begin to produce instances of canonical babbling until several months after normal infants, and the babbling repertoires are reduced relative to those of normals. The visual modality may also be important for the development of a normal babbling repertoire. Mills (1984) found that blind infants differed from normal infants in not having significantly more labial than alveolar consonants in their first words. In contrast, one prominent feature of the babbling repertoires of deaf infants is the extremely high proportions of labial consonants (Locke, 1983). It seems that in the absence of input from one of the two modalities, there may be, naturally enough, relatively more use of the other. Locke and Pearson (1990) found that an infant who was tracheostomized from the age of five months to 20 months, subsequently "produced primitive vocal forms and a restricted range of articulatory movements." (Locke, 1990, p. 629). According to parental report, speech developed only gradually in succeeding months, and, as in deaf infants, labial sounds were relatively frequent. Thus it seems that both auditory and visual experience of the ambient language and motor-auditory experience of one's own speech production apparatus are important in development of speech production.

Another earlier belief about babbling, supported in Locke's influential monograph (1983) was that the sounds produced in normal babbling were independent of the ambient language environment. However a number of studies, primarily by Boysson-Bardies and colleagues have now shown conclusively that there are language-specific effects on babbling, some occurring as early as 8 months of age. In one study of Boysson-Bardies and colleagues (Boysson-Bardies, Sagart and Durand, 1984) French listeners showed the ability to distinguish recorded samples of French eight month old babies from samples of Arabic and Cantonese Chinese. In a second study (Boysson-Bardies, Sagart, Halle and Durand, 1986) long term power spectra derived from recordings of groups of French, English and Arabic adults and eight month old infants were obtained, and it was shown that the overall spectral shapes of the infant groups tended to match those of the appropriate adult groups. A third study based on large numbers of F1–F2 patterns of vowels of groups of eight month old Arabic, Cantonese, (English) English and French infants, and groups of adults, revealed language-specific spectral "centers of gravity" shared by infants and adults of each language community (Boysson-Bardies, Halle, Sagart and Durand, 1989). In more recent work (Boysson-Bardies and Vihman, 1991) significant differences in the relative frequencies of various consonantal attributes, reflecting relative frequencies of these attributes in the ambient language have been found in comparisons of groups of English, French, Swedish and Japanese infants ranging from 10 to 17 months of age. For example, even at 10 months of age, labial production was higher in English and French groups than in Swedish and Japanese groups.

Effects involving syllable structure and position of segments in syllables were also observed. In the environment of Yoruba, a language in which nouns begin with vowels, an infant initiated 50 per cent of his utterances with vowels, a percentage much higher than observed in the Western languages and in Japanese (Boysson-Bardies, 1993). In the environment of Japanese, a language in which all syllable-final consonants are alveolar nasals, infants showed a much higher frequency of such syllable-final forms than in the other languages (Boysson-Bardies and Vihman, 1991).

How are these various effects of experience and the lack of it to be interpreted? The findings make it clear that, in statistical terms, effects of language-related experience are shown in segmental aspects of vocal output and syllable structure of infants before they produce their first words. In addition, the results from deaf, blind and tracheostomized infants are inconsistent with any simple claim that prespeech capacities are purely innate. But what *is* the role of experience? The studies of Boysson-Bardies and colleagues have shown that infants are sensitive to the relative frequencies of sounds and sound patterns of the ambient language during the babbling period. However such a frequency-based sensitivity to input is obviously not sufficient to account for the overall language-specific babbling patterns. It is true that sounds similar to those favored in babbling are virtually always to be found in some quantity in the ambient language. However there are also other sounds typically well represented in the adult language that are *not* favored in babbling. Almost all languages have at least one fricative, most often /s/, and at least one liquid (Maddieson, 1984a) but fricatives and liquids are rare in babbling. In addition high front and high back vowels are almost always present in languages, and often attributed a crucial role as "point vowels" (Lieberman, 1984) occupying two of the three corners of the vowel space, but they are not favored in babbling. And the fact that early babbling sound preferences seem to be similar despite differences in the patterns of relative frequencies of sounds in the ambient language shows that more than input frequencies of sounds is involved. These patterns presumably reflect the relative availability of various movement possibilities in the infant. Presumably the value of fricatives, liquids and high vowels as perceptual indicants of contrast associated with the sending of different messages accounts for their relatively high frequencies in languages, though not in babbling.

In summary, early babbling patterns are the combined result of rather general aspects of normal input, including self-input, and a set of normally developing output propensities, and both are essential to the development of normal vocal output. As Oyama would point out, it will not do to simply use the term "innate", at least in the sense of independent of experience, in talking about babbling. But as she would also presumably point out, neither can experience or any simple scenario of interaction between innate and experiential factors be invoked to describe the outcome.

Can anything further be said about the movement propensities. According to the frame/content theory of evolution of speech production (MacNeilage, 1995) the propensity for mandibular oscillation to accompany phonation in humans evolved from basic functional properties of the mandible present in ancestral forms. In this context, the evidence for frame dominance in babbling is regarded as an instance of ontogeny recapitulating phylogeny. In addition, in this phylogenetic context it is not surprising that apart from the mandible the main role in the production of babbling patterns is played by the anterior region of the tongue, as this region perhaps plays a more versatile role in ingestive history than any other part of the tongue.

3.3 Pre-speech organization of input–output relations

Learning to speak the ambient language basically involves developing a set of input–output relationships, direct and indirect. The direct relationship is evident in our ability to imitate. The ability of a typical adult to "shadow" utterances – that is, to repeat what is heard at remarkably short latencies – (Porter and Castellanos, 1980) testifies to the continuing importance of a direct input–output linkage throughout life. Indirect input–output relationships are evidenced when we spontaneously utter a word, the auditory representation of which we originally learned from the input. A distinction between these two types of capability is emphasized here not only because of its relevance to speech acquisition, but because it seems absolutely fundamental to any functional approach to speech. One crucial difference between speech and the vocal communication systems of other primates is that learning is necessary for an infant to acquire the vocal component of the ambient language. In contrast, as Jurgens (1992) points out, "At present there is not a single well documented case in the literature to demonstrate that vocal learning takes place in mammals below humans." (p. 36) Recently, Donald (1991) has argued persuasively that the first step in the cognitive evolution of hominids beyond the level of the other great apes was the development of a mimetic capacity in homo erectus, including a specific capacity for vocal mimesis. The importance of this link, even in *adult* humans who might be assumed to have no further use for it, is shown, as mentioned before, by our shadowing ability, and by aphasic disorders in which repetition is spared in the absence of a spontaneous speech capacity, and vice versa (McCarthy and Warrington, 1984). This link is presumably responsible for the ability of infants to reflect the ambient language in their output before they begin to control it from the lexicon in their first words.

Consider the nature of the input–output capabilities before the first word is said. The situation at the beginning of babbling can be illustrated schematically in Figure 10.2a. Auditory input comes from both the infant (IA) and adults (AA). The auditory trace of each instance of self-input is presumably closely linked to the motor output pattern that precedes and accompanies it during each utterance. There is also proprioceptive feedback from speech movements (P). In addition to the fact that auditory self-input has a motor-proprioceptive context, self-input and adult input are differentiated from each other in auditory terms by the fact that the infant vocal tract generates a spectrum centering on higher frequencies than does the adult vocal tract. Consequently the recognition of similarities between adult forms and infant forms necessary for an

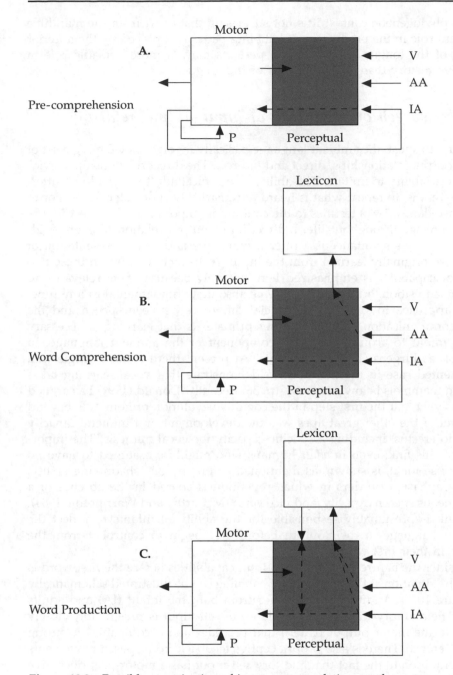

Figure 10.2 Possible organization of input–output relations at three stages of infant vocal development. a. Pre-Comprehension. b. Word Comprehension. c. Word Production. (P; proprioceptive: IA; infant auditory: AA; Adult auditory: V; Visual.)

infant to begin to reflect the ambient language in his/her output must involve the establishment of equivalences across these two different spectral families. Visual input from others is also indicated (V). We have seen the importance of the various components of this schema in the problems of deaf, blind and tracheostomized infants, discussed earlier.

There is no lexicon at the beginning of babbling because the infant probably has virtually no ability to understand words by linking particular incoming packages of segmental information to particular concepts. Auditory representations are sufficient to have enabled babbled output, in the normal infant, and occasionally an infant of this age may imitate at least a simplified adult utterance. Nevertheless the main auditory-motor linkages at this stage probably involve relations between auditory representations of the infant's own input and output. However the presence of shading in the box labelled "Perceptual" (and in the corresponding boxes below it) is meant to denote the likelihood that associations between similar adult and infant inputs are being formed. As noted earlier, some imitative capacity is present as early as 4 months. And the evidence of ambient language effects on babbling by 10 months of age shows that adult input can have a specific effect on output. Furthermore, Werker and her colleagues (e.g. Werker and Tees, 1984) have shown that at about 8–10 months infants begin to lose the discriminative capacities shown at earlier stages when the stimuli to be distinguished do not play a role in signalling message differences in the ambient language. For example infants in English-speaking environments show a decline in ability to discriminate among sounds associated with retroflex stop consonants in Hindi and uvular stops in Salish, while infants in these particular language environments do not. Such language-specific perceptual representations are presumably relevant to output. Nevertheless, as we have seen, language-specific effects on *output* in the first year are relatively subtle. Their demonstration requires some data-crunching. And sounds unusual in languages are apparently virtually non-existent in babbling.

According to Vihman (1995) "The first signs of language comprehension are typically reported within the first year." However, experimental studies attempting to show that infants comprehend specific words within the first year have not been particularly successful (e.g. Oviatt, 1980; Thomas et al, 1981). Assuming nevertheless that word perception precedes word production, an input route to the lexicon must then be added to the schematic picture before an output route, as shown in Figure 10.2b before one year of age. Comprehension, in its simplest terms, means associating recurring *adult* sound patterns with the recurring real world contexts that accompany them ("bye bye" with someone leaving, "doggie" with the form of a dog). The diagonal dashed lines from the AA input to the arrow to the lexicon denote the likelihood that the main linkages between audition and lexical concepts are formed from *adult* input. This schematic view of input–output organization prior to the first words will hopefully help us understand what happens when spoken words develop.

4 The first fifty words (12–18 months)

The typical infant produces his/her first words at around 1 year of age and for the next few months typically goes through what has come to be called the 50 word stage. This development is rather gradual and its time course is often irregular. Infants sometimes seem to have words and then lose them.

When an infant begins to *produce* words, a link from the lexicon to motor propensities is required (See Figure 10.2c.) and it is presumed that this link is made via the perceptual representation rather than directly between lexicon and motor representation. More generally, connections become established between some self-generated vocal output pattern and some world situation (departure, or appearance of the dog) so that when appropriately motivated the infant will produce the vocalization in the presence of the situation. The new link from the lexicon to the auditory representation system probably at first involves primarily representations of adult forms because it was those forms that were primarily involved in the initial auditory-lexical linkages made when the child was listening to adults. But what is now necessary is linkages between adult and infant perceptual representations (Figure 10.2c: double arrow within the perceptual box) because motor control routines for production are at this stage primarily linked to infant perceptual representations.

There is a general consensus that around this time the infant has a more complete auditory-phonetic representation of words than he/she is able to produce. But unfortunately little is known of the nature of speech-related auditory representations at this time. Little is known about units of representation or about the relative status of adult and infant-related representations and – if separate – how separate they might be. It seems important here to further emphasize the distinction being made between two aspects of prior development: 1) making a sound and hearing *it*; and 2) listening to adult words and comprehending *them*. Saying words seems to necessitate bringing these two previously somewhat separable subsystems together. From this perspective, learning to speak words involves three things: 1) Developing better perceptual representations of words whether self-produced or other-produced; 2) Increasing the ability to make the sounds; and 3) developing rules relating the more diverse and advanced representations of adult forms (which includes management of the relations between adult and infant auditory representations) to the less diverse and advanced motor representations of infant forms. The first two of these will tend to develop relatively slowly. The third may change quite rapidly as the infant shifts from one mapping of perceptual to motor forms to another, under the pressure of developing more general mapping rules as the size of the lexicon increases, and the perceptual and motor capabilities increase.

A fact relevant to the schematic view just presented is that infants are often able to repeat words better than they can spontaneously produce them. According to the above view, such repetition can be achieved by some kind of relatively direct transcoding from auditory analysis to motor propensities. One might expect that this mode of activation might be "richer" than activation from the lexicon because contact with the lexicon is presumably based on some simplified conception of the information involved. On the other hand it should be borne in mind that repeating what an *adult* says involves, according to the present conception, transcoding from adult to infant perceptual representations.

In attempts to understand lexical input-output relationships in early word production, use is often made of a "Two Lexicon" model (See Menn and Matthei, 1992). This term is a misnomer. The model does not apply to the lexicon itself (the store of words with their meanings) but involves a distinction between an adult based level of input representation, such as results from AA input in Figure 10.2, and an infant-based output representation in which the relative role of perceptual and motor representations is not specified. The present conception attempts to be more specific by distinguishing between adult-based and infant-based *perceptual* representations and assuming that they must somehow be linked in order for motor patterns for words to be produced.

In conceptions of adult speech, it is accepted that for both comprehension and production, a short term memory store is required (See Levelt, 1989, for production; and Baddeley, 1986, for comprehension). The most well known conception of this stage of processing is the "Phonological Loop" of Baddeley:

> This system appears to comprise two components, a memory store, capable of holding phonological information for a period of one or two seconds, coupled with an articulatory control process. (Baddeley, 1995, p. 761)

In this context, perceptual and motor components of Figure 10.2 can be seen as including a developing phonological loop capacity. The required coupling between memorial (related to perception) and articulatory (motor) components is designated in Figure 10.2 by the arrow going from the motor to the perceptual box, as well as the one going in the opposite direction. Instances of even slightly delayed imitation in infants are presumably evidence of the existence of the phonological loop. The phonological loop is regarded by Donald (1991) as one manifestation of the emerging hominid mimetic capacity. Baddeley asserts that "evidence is consistent with the hypothesis that the phonological loop has evolved, probably from more basic auditory perception and verbal production mechanisms, as a device for language acquisition." (1995, p. 762). The activation of Broca's area in recent brain imaging studies of a number of tasks involving verbal short term memory without overt speech, as well as in speech tasks (Demonet, Wise and Frackowiack, 1993) is consistent with this claim of a dual role of an articulatory component in input analysis and output. This dual role will eventually have to be factored into conceptions of speech acquisition.

4.1 The relation between babbling and speech

As Macken points out, "literally dozens of studies have shown . . . (that) . . . the same sounds and sound patterns characterize both babbling and words." (1992, pp. 252–3). Some of these studies have been reviewed by Locke (1983, Ch. 2). In the most influential study, Vihman et al (1985) concluded, from an analysis of 9 infants in English-speaking environments, that; ". . . in terms of the distribution of consonants, vocalization length and phonotactic structure, we find striking parallellism between babbling and words within each child . . ." (p. 15). This fact is represented schematically in Figure 10.2c. Production of first words is shown as involving the establishment of contact between the lexicon and a set of pre-existing input–output capabilities.

There is some evidence that infants even show an exaggeration of their babbling preferences in their first words. The favored number of syllables in babbling is one, the favored consonant is a stop consonant and the favored mode of consonant repetition is reduplication. There is evidence (Vihman et al, 1985; Boysson-Bardies et al, 1992) that these preferences actually increase in the first words and in concurrent babbling. It is tempting to surmise that with the onset of the demand to interface the lexicon with the motor system, the infant enters a conservative motor phase in which he/she focuses mainly on the simplest of the available motor capacities.

However there is also a tendency, shown in four languages by Boysson-Bardies et al (1992) to have more labial stops than alveolar stops in the first words even when alveolars are more frequent in babbling. According to the frames, then content perspective (MacNeilage and Davis, 1990a) this also is a case of regression to a more simple form, as labial stops only involve mandibular oscillation while alveolar stops also involve tongue action. The higher frequencies of alveolars in English *babbling* may be due to the fact that there are many more alveolars than labials in the ambient language. This is an important interpretation because it goes beyond the circular reasoning inherent in defining simplicity in terms of frequency. It predicts that first words will show an increment in labials in *all* languages while the ratio of labials to alveolars to labials in prespeech babbling will be linked to ambient language frequencies.

4.2 A whole word stage of production control?

The period of the first 50 words has also often been called the whole-word stage (Ferguson and Farwell, 1975). The whole-word was suggested as a unit of contrast by Ferguson (e.g. Ferguson, 1986) in opposition to the claim of Jakobson that the distinctive feature was the unit of contrast in the first words. The whole-word was also suggested as a unit of *production* by Ferguson (1986). Evidence cited was that the same consonant could be stable in one word and variable in a similar word, the same adult consonant could be represented by different subfamilies of consonants in different words, and that sets of features may typically be produced for a particular word but in different phonotactic arrangements in different individual tokens. Effects of neighboring vowels on consonants may be responsible for many of the word-specific consonantal variation noted in the first two types of example, and the third example is in fact evidence of independent control of motor subcomponents of a word rather than holistic control. Because the first words are so similar in form to babbling, it seems unlikely that their motor organization needs to be characterized in very different terms.

4.3 *Individual differences*

The generalizations presented so far regarding the structure of babbling and first words are considered to be relatively comprehensive. Nevertheless, infants can differ considerably in their favored patterns. While most infants' patterns are relatively susceptible to transcription in terms of standard segmental categories, some children proceded "by global approximation to long phrases rather than by attempts at single words or short phrases. Their early attempts at speech are characterized by variable and often "loose" articulation which is extremely hard to transcribe; Ann Peters dubbed these children "mush mouthed kids" (Menn, 1983, p. 6). Vihman (1995) distinguishes between two types of approach to the production of early words, though not claiming that this dichotomy is exhaustive. In perhaps the most typical approach, termed "Controlled Expansion" development of approximations to adult segmental forms is relatively versatile and the overall repertoire can more easily be expressed in terms of phonological rules. Another approach, termed "Crystallization" seems to initially focus on one or a small number of relatively fixed overall patterns ("Vocal Motor Schemes") such as a pattern involving palatalized release of consonants, or consonant reduplication, or final [i] production.

4.4 *Perceptual influences on early word patterns*

While it is clear that motor constraints are the main source of variance in early word patterns, perceptual factors may also play a role. Echols has provided evidence for the hypothesis that the perceptual salience of stressed and final syllables is a factor in production by showing that these syllables are least often omitted and most accurately produced (Echols and Newport, 1992; Echols, 1993). In an interesting finding regarding the segmental level, she has shown that where stop consonants are inappropriately reduplicated across syllables differing in stress, the consonant chosen tends to be more closely related to the one in the stressed syllable of the target form.

5 Beyond the first fifty words

Some time around 18 months of age, the typical infant begins to add to his/her lexical repertoire at an extremely fast pace, acquiring several new words per day. One gets the impression, though it has not been specifically documented, that the infant also increases in phonological "mobility" at this stage, increasing the rate at which he/she moves towards correct adult speech. In any event there is at least a lexical acquisition landmark here, and around this time an infant may also begin to put words together, thus showing the first signs of grammatical organization of output. The purpose of this section is to discuss, from a phonetic perspective, what kinds of steps in speech production the infant is taking at this time and later.

From the description given so far we can deduce that, in terms of inventory, the typical English-speaking infant needs to develop the capacity to reliably produce a number of fricatives, the affricates [tʃ] and [dʒ], the liquids [l] and [r], and a number of phonetic variants of stop consonant voicing. These sounds need to be produced in a number of environments including consonant cluster environments. In addition to the development of new sounds, this involves "a gradual weakening of restrictions on the co-occurrence of phones and the realization of more combinations of syllable structure with phonetic content." (Menn, 1983, p. 30) Judging from the prominence of contextual constraints on sound forms in babbling and early speech, it seems like the main form of development might be rather gradual changes in the ability to produce sounds independent of context.

The main body of phonological work on speech acquisition has involved the statement of rules summarizing the relations between the simplifications present in infant words and the adult models the infant is trying to match. It is commonly assumed that the amount of simplification is initially very great because an infant's perceptual representations are well ahead of their motor capabilities. There is only space here to consider a small sample of these rules – those that raise the main theoretical issues. On the right hand side of Figure 10.3 a number of typical rules are given at the top of the page with specific examples below. It will be observed that the segment is the unit in terms of which most rules are stated. Menn (1983) has emphasized that "a rule is no more than a description of a hypothesized regularity of behavior." Nevertheless phonological rules are often treated in the literature as if they have explanatory status. A not uncommon statement is that a rule "accounts for" the regularity that it summarizes. Such circular "explanations" are often accompanied by the claim that the phonological component of an infant's words is autonomous and not related to word phonetics. For example, adopting a stance reminiscent of Hockett (1955) who likened speaking to crushing a set of Easter eggs and mixing the consequent debris, Moscowitz (1991) complains of the infant's "phonetic muddying of the phonological waters" (p. 148) impeding the search for underlying innate phonological laws. This is a sore point for many phoneticians because they are involved in the task of deriving form

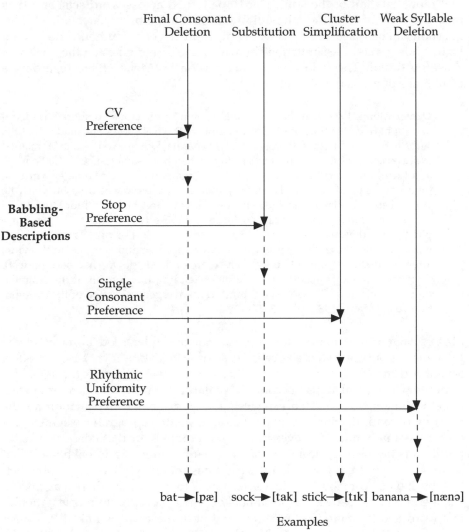

Figure 10.3 Two alternative descriptions of simplified versions of adult words produced by infants.

from substance or, in other words, attempting to explain phonological organization in terms of phonetic constraints. The left hand side of Figure 10.3 gives a number of alternative babbling-based names for the phenomena they are linked to. This shows rather clearly that these output regularities are all typical of babbling, and is meant to suggest that nothing is lost in characterizing *output forms* if one replaces the terms at the top of the diagram with these babbling-based terms.

The phonological names nevertheless have the merit of emphasizing that

infant output involves rule-governed modifications of the presumed perceptual representation of the adult words, patterned across word sets, and they
raise the issue of how these modifications should be best characterized. This
question can be discussed by considering another very common child phonological rule termed "Assimilation" by which one sound takes on the quality of
a nearby sound. The following is a discussion by Menn (1983) regarding a
child's use of a nasal assimilation rule:

> Daniel (Menn, 1971) had the two words "down" and "stone" rendered as [deʊn]
> and [don] from the time of his first attempts at them. Then, . . . he made all of the
> stops in the word nasal if the final stop was nasal. "Down" and "stone" remained
> lexical exceptions to this rule; that is, after he had been saying [naens] for "dance"
> and [nein] for "train" for two weeks he still maintained the two older words in
> their nonassimilated form. Eventually there was a period of time in which he
> varied between [naeʊn] and [daeʊn] for "down" and between [non] and [don]
> for "stone". Finally the assimilated forms for these two words took over com-
> pletely and they were no longer lexical exceptions to the rule. From the adult
> point of view, these two words were poorer approximations to the adult model
> after the rule had applied to them than before (indeed "down" had been perfect).
> Therefore the generalization involved in extending the domain of the assimila-
> tion rule to include "down" and "stone" is an overgeneralization of the assimila-
> tion rule. (Menn, 1983, pp. 26–27)

Menn (1983) argues that assimilation cannot be understood in terms of the
phonetics of output (what she calls "ease of articulation") because the effect
acts at a distance (across vowels) rather than on two adjacent forms (as for
example when labial stops "become" alveolar in front of vowel environments
(Stoel-Gammon, 1983)). Menn suggests a memory-based explanation for the
favoring of reduplication, arguing that it is easier to reprogram a segment just
used than a new one. However it has been pointed out that consonant reduplication is the most typical form of consonant sequencing in babbling. What
seems to be required, given that the child has indicated that they "know better" by having previously said [daeʊn] and [don] is that there has been a
change in linkage between a presumably correct perceptual representation of
this word and its motor instantiation, and now the word is linked to *another*
available method of uttering it. The change is phonetically based in that the
alveolarity of the first consonant is still apparently recognized in the new
linkage (all examples given involve alveolar consonants), and nasal reduplication is an output routine available from earliest babbling (you could call it an
instance of a "Reduplication Preference" rule of babbling). In addition it is
unlikely that the assimilation *was* phonetically discontinuous. Mattyear et al
(1994) have recently shown in an acoustical study that vowels between nasal
consonants are heavily nasalized in babbling even though this fact is not readily available to listeners. Obviously we need a theory which allows us to
understand why and how and when such reorganizational changes take place
in the young word learner. But is there anything to be gained by regarding

such events as evidence for an *autonomous* phonological component independent of phonetic constraints?

Many rule-governed changes in a child's word forms are considered to happen rather suddenly, although documentation of the overall temporal aspect of rule development is not at all easy. However, more commonly, rules are seen to develop more slowly, starting out in one or a few words and then spreading to others, as in the above example. Thus at a given time one might have, metaphorically speaking, some precocious forms and some fossil forms. Menn has argued that fossil forms are also a problem for an "ease of articulation" perspective, because she believes there is no phonetic reason why a rule shouldn't change lexical items across the board if it changes any. However most work on child phonology has paid scant attention to vowels, and existence of strong CV co-occurrence constraints has only recently become obvious. It is of interest to note that in the nasal assimilation example given above the examples of words that first became subject to the rule contained front vowels in an alveolar interconsonantal environment, but the "holdout" forms had *back* vowels – vowels strongly disfavored in this environment according to Davis and MacNeilage (1995). It seems possible that much more understanding of the patterns of rule growth and replacement could be gained from a systematic consideration of the vocalic environments of the consonants concerned.

Consider another example illustrating problems at the interface between child phonology and child phonetics. A second source of overgeneralization described by Menn (1983) results from a change in the structural description of a rule:

> Here is an example from Amahl (Smith, 1973, pp. 152–153): "At stage 1, /s/ and /l/ were normally neutralized as [d] together with all the other coronal consonants . . ." . . . Then, "/l/ began to appear in A's speech before any coronal consonant" – for example, 'lady' was rendered either [de:di] or [le:di]. So /l/ was optionally excepted from the general treatment of coronals in certain environments. "Then at stage 5 /s/ (and shortly afterwards /ʃ/) became /l/ before any coronal consonant . . . : 'sausage' [lɔdɪd]; 'shade' [le:t] . . ."

Here the new rule for realizing /l/ as [l] in some environments had added /s/ and /ʃ/ to its domain. So it had generalized by a change in structural description: the input to the rule had originally been /l/, but later included /l, s, ʃ/. What makes this an overgeneralization? Smith says: "Now originally two words such as 'side' and 'light' were both [dait], but after the appearance of /l/ before any coronal consonant they became distinct as [dait] and [lait] respectively. However once /s/ was liquidized, the two words fell together again – perfectly regularly, as [lait]." (p. 27) Once again, one can conclude that at some point between concept and movement, the mapping rules have changed, but in contrast with the above instance of nasal assimilation, the change has occurred at a point closer to the input representation than the output representation. But again, phonetic factors are involved in the causality.

The sounds [s] and [ʃ] are similar in place of articulation to [l] and [d], otherwise they would not be incorporated with these sounds into a functional unit. Again, what is to be gained by regarding such events as evidence of an autonomous phonological component?

There seems to be an important difference between these two rule change scenarios, from the phonetic standpoint. In the case of nasal assimilation there is a shift to an alternative available output form. In the case of Amahl, there is presumably an extension of the perceptual category that dominates [l] production. This distinction between output choice of a form that has been available since the beginning of babbling and a new development in perceptual categorization would seem to be quite basic.

Some types of modifications between input and output involve what Menn (1983) has described as "fairly violent rearrangements of sounds of adult words to match 'templates' of preferred sound patterns." (p. 19). In an example involving vowels, Vihman (1976) reported that her daughter, learning Estonian, went through a stage in which she produced words containing two different vowel sounds only if the first vowel was lower and more back than the second:

> /ema/ (mother) → [ami] or [ani]
> /isa/ (mother) → [asi]
> /liha/ (meat) → [ati]

In another example, involving consonants, Menn (1983, p. 80) described a Spanish child, Si, who "could produce disharmonic sequences in a word only if one target consonant was a labial and another was a dental. Adult words which met this criterion were produced so that the labial preceded the dental; much deletion and occasional metathesis (reversal of order) occurred." Examples:

> manzana → [mana]; pelota → [patda]
> zapato → [patda]; elefante → [batte]
> Fernando → [wanno]; sopa → [pwata]

A question that has not been raised from the phonological standpoint is the question of why these *particular* patterns should be favored and not others. Is it just a coincidence that the favored patterns reported by Vihman and Macken were both also observed in the speech of the only infant beyond the 50 word stage who has been studied by the present author (Davis and MacNeilage, 1990) – an infant in an *English* language environment? In a manner reminiscent of Vihman's daughter, the vowel [a] in syllable 1 and the vowel [i] in syllable 2 were by far the most popular vowels in their respective positions in the words of this infant. It was also noted that preferences for vowels generally favored in babbling (vowels in the lower left quadrant of the vowel space) were more highly favored in syllable 1 of disyllable words than in either syllable 2 of these words or in monosyllables. It was as if the infant was more free to produce relatively new vowels at the ends of words than within them.

Davis and MacNeilage also found, in a corpus of 1011 examples in this same infant, about three times as many instances of labial–alveolar consonant sequences as alveolar–labial sequences in words (unpublished observations). If one considers this result together with the tendency to favor labials in first words, described earlier, one might again suggest that the infant was more free to produce relatively less favored sounds in the terminal phase of an utterance than in its initiation. In summary, although speculative, one might suggest a phonetic principle of "terminal modification", or, in more colloquial terms, a "start easy, end hard" principle as a possible alternative approach to the patterns observed by Vihman, Macken and Davis and MacNeilage. Thus in this instance, as in the ones defined earlier, it seems possible to provide a phonetic account of at least some aspects of these instances of phonological rules. It is likely that as we come to understand more about output organization and the perceptual organization that underlies it – collectively, the phonetics of early speech – we will have less and less need for postulation of independent phonological causal factors. Will there nevertheless be a residue, and if so, what will it be due *to*, or, to avoid the pun, how will *it* be explained?

6 Conclusion: present and future

In many ways, the picture painted here of this area of knowledge is a disappointing one. The three subdisciplines, those concerned with speech production phonetics, speech perception phonetics and phonology tend to go their separate ways with little cross-fertilization. And each sub-area can be criticized for aspects of its own approach. Those concerned with speech production have done little to collect large comprehensive databases (e.g. consonants *and* vowels) which make statistical regularities in the acquisition process available, and have made limited use of acoustical analysis beyond the purely descriptive level. Those concerned with perception have paid virtually no attention to the infant beyond the first year, and their approach has been dominated by the search for adult perceptual capacities, rather than being infant-centered. Phonologists have made no serious attempts to throw off the shackles of circularity (description as explanation) that seem to come with the assumption of a priori order. The most miraculous aspect of speech acquisition resides in the development of the input–output relations involved in forming a true *system* of lexico-phonetic linkages. Perhaps it is time for a *concerted* multidisciplinary effort to understand this aspect of speech acquisition. And perhaps the unifying theoretical perspective should be the one that has been most successful in the understanding of other miracles of nature – the Neodarwinian theory of evolution by natural selection.

More specifically I would suggest that in the field of acquisition of speech production in particular we need to replace "Plato's problem" regarding development with "Bernstein's problem". Macken (1995, p. 671) states Plato's problem, a central theme in Chomsky's approach to language acquisition, as follows:

> How is it that human beings, whose contacts with the world are brief and personal and limited are nevertheless able to know as much as they do. How does a child come to master a complex, abstract system like language, when the evidence to the child is so sparse?

Bernstein's problem (Bernstein, 1967) is stated by Thelen (1995) as follows:

> How can an organism with thousands of muscles, billions of nerves, tens of billions of cells, and nearly infinite possible combinations of body segments and positions ever figure out how to get them all working toward a single smooth and efficient movement without invoking some clever "homunculus" who has the directions already stored? (p. 80)

One might argue that the problem of speech is different than the problem of other bodily movements. But is it? We don't need innate units of bodily movement control. In fact, to suggest them would be a bit ridiculous. Is speech so different?

ACKNOWLEDGMENTS

Preparation of this paper was supported in part by a grant from N.I.C.H.D (#HD-27733). I wish to thank Barbara Davis, Randy Diehl and Richard Meier for comments on the manuscript. I am grateful to Marilyn Vihman for providing me with a pre-publication form of her monograph.

11 Articulatory Processes

JOSEPH S. PERKELL

1 Introduction

This chapter is concerned with articulatory processes – the articulatory forces and movements that implement the conversion of linguistic messages into sound. The study of articulatory processes is at the heart of some of the most fundamental research issues in speech and language: the nature of discrete, phonological representations of utterances and their psychological reality; the function of the speech motor control system that converts an underlying phonological representation into sequential and sometimes overlapping articulatory commands; and the constraining influences of properties of the production and perception mechanisms on phonological processes, motor control strategies and speech kinematics.

The chapter addresses several aspects of articulatory processes: their role within the entire sequence of message generation and transmission by a speaker and reception and understanding by a listener (called the "speech chain" – Denes and Pinson, 1973); their kinematic characteristics and how those characteristics might help to convey a linguistic message; how the processes may be shaped by the properties of the mechanisms that produce them and perceive their acoustic consequences; and how they are controlled. In order to present a coherent account of articulatory processes, they are viewed from the perspective of a theoretical framework which hypothesizes that speech movements are programmed to generate an *intelligible signal* by achieving sequences of *goals* that are defined as *combinations of articulatory and acoustic parameters* (Perkell et al., 1995; Section 4, below).[1]

2 Articulatory processes: planning and execution

Utterances can be thought of as being generated in two stages: planning and execution (which may overlap in time). Articulatory processes take place in the motor execution stage; however, since the output of the planning stage can be considered to be the input to the execution stage, it is helpful to take a brief look at the pre-motor planning stage.

Imagine that a friend has called you to announce an upcoming vacation trip. In response to this announcement, you select and order lexical items to form the sequence "Do you really want to go gambling, when you could go camping?". You plan to transmit information about the syntactically-governed prosodic structure by choosing among a number of alternative prosodic shapes – for example, by: assigning prominence to the first syllables of "really", "gambling" and "camping"; increasing the duration and raising the fundamental frequency (f_0) of "ing" in "gambling" to signal the occurrence of additional following prosodic constituents; and assigning rising intonation to "camping" to express incredulity. In addition, you make situation-dependent settings of postural parameters (Perkell et al., 1992b). The term "postures" refers to baseline settings of parameters such as overall rate, sound level and f_0, upon which modifications are superimposed to signal a variety of linguistic and paralinguistic cues. These baseline settings are adjusted by the speaker in response to the changing needs of the listener, which are determined by transmission conditions as diverse as environmental noise, the listener's familiarity with the language, speaker and subject matter and whether or not the listener can see the speaker's face.[2] You also plan a certain amount of articulatory "reduction" (Kohler, 1991; discussion below), and modification of parameters that convey additional information, such as emotional state (Williams and Stevens, 1972).

In this example, it's a costly, long distance call over a somewhat noisy line and your friend's announcement has upset you a bit. To get your message (and feeling of incredulity) across in an effective manner, you plan to speak loudly and with an elevated, exaggerated intonation (f_0) pattern. You reduce the planned utterance (somewhat, but not too much because of the noisy phone line) by eliminating and modifying certain sounds, in order to help get the message across efficiently, without wasting a lot of time and expending very much effort. Like modification of rate and loudness, reduction has selective effects on different parts of the sound sequence (Kohler, 1991). The result of these adjustments is a representation of the planned utterance that can be characterized phonetically as [djə ˈrɪli wɑnə go ˈgæmblɪŋ wɛn jə kəd go ˈkæmpɪŋ]. You can reduce certain parts of the utterance because you and your friend are both native speakers of the same language, and your friend has a lot of implicit knowledge that will help him understand the utterance in its modified form. (The "knowledge-based" speech recognition capability of listeners allows for a lot of variation in production – Lindblom, 1994.) You plan to fully articulate "gambling" and "camping" because they are "focus words". Thus, planning results in sequences of phonetic goals that are modified to meet situation-dependent communicative needs (Nooteboom and Eefting, 1992; Lindblom, 1990; Charles-Luce, forthcoming).

More generally, as part of the planning process, a number of temporal parameters are determined as well, including sound segment durations and the intervals between stressed syllables. The durations of individual sound segments depend on a number of factors including phonologically-based quantity differences (Lehiste, 1970; Engstrand and Krull, 1994), intrinsic durations, overall speaking rate, number of syllables in the foot, and position in the phrase (Lindblom and Rapp, 1973; Klatt, 1976; Crystal and House, 1988a; van Santen, 1992). Some of the intrinsic temporal structure of (movements for) individual sounds is probably due to characteristics of the production mechanism, such as the biomechanical response properties of the articulators. On the other hand it is very likely that many of the temporal aspects of speech production are planned explicitly to fulfill communicative requirements, such as pre-pausal lengthening of the final sound segments in a phrase (Cooper and Paccia-Cooper, 1980; Wightman et al., 1992).

Observations of speech errors, e.g., saying *"emeny"* instead of "enemy", provide a persuasive form of evidence that planning is a distinct operation. Such errors can include sound substitutions, exchanges, shifts, additions and omissions (Fromkin, 1971; Shattuck-Hufnagel, 1979; 1983; 1992; Dell, 1986; Levelt, 1989). Their occurrence indicates that phonetic segments are manipulated in speech planning, and the systematicity of the errors provides one form of evidence about the feature-based nature of underlying representations of utterances (Shattuck-Hufnagel and Klatt, 1979).

The planning unit (amount of speech output that is planned at once) may correspond to the "breath group", which is the phrase that is spoken between the beginning and end of the expiratory limb of a speech respiration cycle (Lieberman, 1968; Weismer, 1988). The duration of a breath group can vary from a fraction of a second to a significant fraction of a minute.

In a different vein, it has been observed that most speech errors occur within an intonational phrase (defined in Boomer and Laver, 1968, as a stretch of speech with a coherent intonation contour and one and only one nuclear tone). It is possible that different types or levels of planning take place over different levels of constituents.

For the rest of this chapter, it is assumed that the result of the pre-speech stage is a motor plan that specifies a sequence of discrete phonetic goals for the speech production apparatus and includes timing information. The sequence of goals incorporates modifications of "canonical" acoustic and articulatory characteristics of the sounds, due to the above-mentioned influences of prosody and posture. From this point of view, articulatory processes comprise the execution stage of speech production; they are motor actions that convert the planned sequence of discrete goals into changing forces and smooth articulatory movements that result in a fluctuating sound output. Some of these discrete goals may be characterized best in terms of static articulatory and acoustic targets; others may be characterized more appropriately in terms of movement of articulatory and acoustic parameters.[3]

3 Examples of articulatory processes

In more functional terms, articulatory processes consist of manipulations of respiratory, laryngeal and vocal-tract structures to create sound sources and filter those sources. The respiratory system consists of the rib cage and lungs, respiratory muscles including the intercostals, diaphragm and those of the abdominal wall, and the inertial load of the contents of the abdominal cavity and other structures. It provides the energy for sound production in the form of a relatively constant level of subglottal air pressure, with superimposed fluctuations to help signal prominence by changing the sound level. The larynx, containing the smallest structures and possibly the most rapidly-contracting muscles, comprises one important mechanism for generating sound. Voicing is the most prominent laryngeal sound source. Vibration of the vocal folds is turned on and off, segment by segment, via adjustments in vocal-fold adduction and tension and stiffness of the folds, along with changes in transglottal air pressure that occur with the formation and release of supraglottal constrictions. Characteristics such as the fundamental frequency of vocal-fold vibration (f_0) and aspects of voice quality, such as the amount of breathiness, are regulated on both a suprasegmental basis (over intervals spanning multiple phonetic segments) and a segmental basis by prosodic and postural influences. The supraglottal vocal tract contains structures of intermediate size. Movements of the tongue body, tongue blade, lips, mandible and velum are coordinated to generate sound sources at narrow constrictions and to shape the acoustic filter formed by the vocal-tract airway, to produce strings of phonetic segments that can occur sequentially at a rate as high as about 15 per second.

Table 11.1 is a schematic, simplified representation of many of the articulatory processes (actions that have to be controlled) for a single short utterance, the word "camber". The left-most column lists components of the production mechanism, and each one of the remaining columns corresponds to a phonetic segment. Most of the cells contain a brief description of the important contribution of the production mechanism component to generating the sound and differentiating that sound from others. The cells containing an asterisk show cases for which some actions are not strongly constrained by communicative needs; during these intervals, the articulations can (sometimes must and often do) anticipate future requirements. This behavior, called "anticipatory coarticulation", is described in detail in Farnetani, COARTICULATION AND CONNECTED SPEECH PROCESSES (see also, Perkell and Matthies, 1992; Boyce, Krakow and Bell-Berti, 1991 for an alternative view; and Guenther, 1995a, 1995b). The top six rows describe actions of the vocal-tract articulators; the next two describe actions of the larynx, and the bottom row describes actions of the respiratory system.[4] Most of these actions consist of muscle contractions that lead to appropriately-timed movements with acoustic and in some cases aerodynamic consequences, to achieve goals that are characterized in articulatory and acoustic terms. Since the articulators are relatively slowly moving, a rapid succession of phonetic segments can only be produced with movements of individual articulators that overlap in time. Consequently, the movements of the different articulators are asynchronous (see Farnetani, COARTICULATION AND CONNECTED SPEECH PROCESSES on coarticulation). Because of this asynchrony and because segmental and suprasegmental processes involve some of the same articulators, the discrete nature of this table does not actually reflect what is observed in the articulation and the sound output.

4 Characteristics of articulatory processes

One of the main propositions of this chapter is that articulatory processes are shaped by a balance of influences from production and perception. It is believed that different production subsystems and individual articulators tend to change their states or move at somewhat different rates. Presumably these different characteristic rates are determined, at least in part, by the structures' different biomechanical properties, which have evolved mainly to optimize their more basic, life-supporting functions. For instance, it might take longer to set the relatively massive respiratory system into motion than to adduct the vocal folds. Depending on the choice of control strategy, such as one that minimizes expended effort (Nelson, 1983 – see below), and the biomechanical response properties, each articulatory structure should have a "preferred" rate of movement. Such preferred rates may contribute to some properties of utterances. For example, the preferred rate for cyclical movements of the mandible may help to determine average syllable rate. On the other hand, the fact that the various biomechanical structures and subsystems are well coordinated in normal speech production means that the speech motor control system deals effectively with any possible biomechanical differences in order to generate a perceptually-usable, intelligible acoustic signal.

Unfortunately, there are serious obstacles to quantifying the balance among constraints that arise in production and perception. Observations of acoustic and articulatory kinematic data have revealed a lot of variability, within and across languages and speakers, which makes it difficult to find convincing evidence for individual constraints. Another problem is that very little is actually known about articulatory dynamics – the quantitative relations among the forces generated by the articulatory muscles, the inertial and resistive properties of the articulators against which the forces are working, and the resulting movements. Given this situation, it is difficult to determine the relative influences of biomechanics and motor control mechanisms on speech kinematics[5] and control strategies, and how control strategies may also be constrained by perceptual and intelligibility requirements.

Some of these points are examined below in light of a theoretical framework (Perkell et al., forthcoming), which is based on ideas proposed by a number of researchers. According to the framework, the sound patterns of languages

Table 11.1 Some of the segmental events for the word "camber" (with stress on the first syllable). The cells containing an asterisk show cases for which some actions are not strongly constrained by communicative needs.

	k	æ	m	b	r
tongue body	rise to contact roof of mouth to achieve closure and silence	release contact to generate a noise burst; move down to vowel position	begin movement toward /r/ position	*	maintain /r/ position
tongue blade	*	maintain contact with floor of mouth to stay out of the way	begin retroflexion or bunching in anticipation of /r/	*	maintain retroflexed or bunched configuration
lips	begin spreading for the vowel /æ/	maintain position for vowel, then begin toward closure	achieve and maintain closure	maintain closure	release rapidly and round somewhat
mandible	move upward to support tongue movement	move downward to support tongue movement	move upward to support lower lip movement	*	move downward slightly to aid lip release

soft palate	maintain closure to contain pressure buildup	begin downward movement to open velopharyngeal port for /m/	begin closing movement toward onset of /b/	reach closure at right instant to begin /b/, (move upward during /b/ to help expand v.t. walls – voicing)	*
vocal-tract walls	stiffen to contain air pressure buildup	*	*	relax, perhaps expand actively to allow continuation of voicing for /b/	*
vocal-fold position	abduct maximally, with peak occurring at /k/ release	adduct to position for voicing	maintain position	maintain position	maintain position
tension on vocal folds	begin to raise tension to signal stress on following vowel	achieve maximum tension for the f_0 peak that signals stress	lower tension to lower f_0	maintain tension	maintain tension
respiratory system	increase subglottal air pressure to obtain a burst release for the /k/	maintain subglottal air pressure for increased sound level to signal stress	return to the previous value of subglottal pressure	maintain pressure	maintain pressure

and thus the goals of speech movements are determined partly by quantal, non-linear relations between articulation and sound (Stevens, 1972; 1989) and between one aspect of articulation and another (Fujimura and Kakita, 1979; Perkell, 1996). The goals are also influenced by other principles, such as a compromise between sufficient perceptual contrast and economy of articulatory effort (Lindblom and Engstrand, 1989), which leads to the prediction that the goal definitions correspond to regions (as opposed to points) in acoustic and articulatory space. Thus the goals are characterized by some parameter variation, which is possible in part because listeners can understand variable speech. In speech planning, goal specifications are modified by prosodic influences and by situation-dependent adjustments in postural settings for average speaking rate and sound level and by adjustments in the degree of clarity (reduction). During production, the sequence of modified goal specifications is converted to smooth, appropriately-timed articulatory movements by the speech motor control system; this control and the resulting kinematics are constrained in part by the dynamical properties of the articulators, and by the need to produce an intelligible signal.

With such ideas in mind, the following sub-sections discuss articulatory processes involving the respiratory, laryngeal and vocal-tract subsystems. These discussions are not meant to be comprehensive; for reviews from other perspectives, see MacNeilage (1972), Perkell (1980), Folkins and Kuehn (1982), Weismer (1988), Smith (1992) and Stevens (in preparation).

4.1 Respiratory and laryngeal actions

The role of respiration during speech is the generation of a relatively constant level of subglottal air pressure between 5 and 10 cm H_2O for comfortable sound levels, with superimposed modifications to change the overall sound level, and fluctuations to help signal prosodic parameters such as the sound-level cue to emphatic stress. These objectives are achieved by controlling the volume of the lungs, through the combined actions of inspiratory and expiratory muscles of the rib cage, the inspiratory action of the diaphragm, and the expiratory action of the abdominal muscles, which serve to push the abdominal contents against the diaphragm and thereby decrease lung volume. These muscular actions work against three types of passive forces. (1) The elastic properties of the lung tissue tend to make the lungs collapse, exerting a volume-decreasing force on the rib cage. (2) The lung volume is normally con-strained from decreasing by the semi-rigid structure of the rib cage. (3) Depending on the speaker's body posture, the effect of gravity on the abdominal contents tends either to flatten the diaphragm and increase lung volume (speaker upright) or make the diaphragm assume a more dome-like shape and decrease lung volume (speaker supine). At high lung volumes the net effect of the passive forces is to decrease lung volume. This effect diminishes in magnitude with decreasing lung volume until an equilibrium point is reached, below which passive forces tend to increase lung volume (Hixon, Mead and Goldman, 1976; Hixon and collaborators, 1987; Weismer, 1988).

Thus, achieving the subglottal pressure levels and fluctuations used during the speech respiration cycle involves a precisely-controlled, constantly changing balance between the actions of inspiratory and expiratory muscles as they work against changing values of passive forces. Speech breathing strategies, reflected in the range of lung volumes used and the relative contributions of the rib cage and abdomen, vary according to a number of factors, including body posture, age, sex, body type, type of speech, state of health and individual speaker (Hixon and collaborators, 1987). The amount of air inspired corresponds approximately to the anticipated duration of the breath group (Winkworth et al., 1994), and speech-like patterns of respiration have been observed when subjects were mentally rehearsing utterances without actually speaking (Conrad and Schönle, 1979). Such observations support the idea that there is an intimate link between the speech planning process and the programming of the respiratory cycle.

Laryngeal mechanisms are treated in detail in Hirose, INVESTIGATING THE PHYSIOLOGY OF LARYNGEAL STRUCTURE. Within appropriate ranges of transglottal air pressure, and tension, stiffness and adduction of the vocal-folds, they will vibrate (Stevens, 1977), causing the quasi-periodic interruption of airflow that is the voicing sound source for vowels and some consonants. With other ranges of the same parameters, the air flow through the glottis will become turbulent, and an aspiration noise will be generated. More extreme parameter settings will, on the one hand, cause the tight glottal closure and the complete cessation of flow of a glottal stop, or on the other hand, the unrestricted, essentially silent flow of quiet respiration. Modulation of f_0 is one of the main mechanisms used for signaling the prosodic structure of utterances. Along with changes in subglottal air pressure, laryngeal adjustments are also used to help convey prosodic information via changes in sound level.

Segmental articulations of the larynx consist mainly of the adducting and abducting movements and stiffness adjustments of the vocal folds that turn the voice source on and off, and the modifications of vocal fold tension that cause the f_0 fluctuations used to differentiate vowel sounds from one another in tone languages. For the frequently-occurring devoicing gesture of an intervocalic voiceless aspirated stop consonant (/p/, /t/, /k/) in English, the vocal folds begin to abduct around the beginning of supraglottal vocal-tract closure. The increasing separation of the folds along with their increasing stiffness act in combination with a drop in the level of trans-glottal air pressure to cause a rapid cessation of vocal-fold vibration. At about the time of the release of the consonant, the vocal folds reach their peak opening and begin to adduct. As the folds begin to come together, a glottal aspiration noise source is generated. Aspiration noise continues as the folds continue to adduct over a period of tens of milliseconds to a degree of separation at which voicing begins. Thus the beginning of vocal-fold abduction seems to be synchronized approximately with oral stop closure and the beginning of adduction seems to be synchronized approximately with stop release.

Modifications of the glottal airflow waveform contribute to perceived differences in pitch, loudness and voice quality. However, even within a given speech condition, glottal airflow waveforms can vary widely across speakers with normal voices. Figure 11.1 (from Holmberg et al., 1988) shows glottal volume velocity vs. time waveforms for six female and six male speakers from the vowel /æ/ in a syllable from the string /pæpæpæpæpæ/ spoken in comfortable, soft and loud voice. The shape and amplitude of the waveform varies considerably among females and among males, and most of the waveforms have substantial DC offsets. For example, in loud voice for male C, the magnitude of the AC portion of the waveform is nearly 0.5 l/s, and in his soft voice, the DC component approaches the same magnitude. The DC flow component is due to incomplete vocal-fold adduction and the presence of a posterior "chink" between the arytenoid cartilages (Rothenberg, 1973; Karlsson, 1985; Holmberg et al., 1988; Koike and Hirano, 1973; Södersten and Lindestad, 1990), which causes increased subglottal coupling and an increase in the bandwidth and a decrease in the amplitude of F1. Incomplete adduction also tends to make the flow waveform have a more sinusoidal shape and a steeper spectral slope, which correlate with an increase in the perceived breathiness of the voice (Klatt and Klatt, 1990).

4.2 Vocal-tract actions: articulator contributions to vowel and consonant production

Vocal-tract articulations perform two functions: supra-glottal sound source creation and acoustic filtering. Sound sources can be created with actions of the tongue body, tongue blade and lips in several ways that are described below. These and laryngeal sound sources are filtered by modifying the shape of the vocal-tract to produce distinctive resonance patterns for different vowels and consonants. (See Stevens, ARTICULATORY/ACOUSTIC/AUDITORY RELATIONSHIPS).

4.2.1 Aspects of vowel articulations   The tongue is the most prominent vocal-tract articulator, in terms of its anatomical complexity, influence on the area function and role in forming vowel and some consonant sounds. It consists of the tongue body (including the tongue root) and the tongue blade, which are capable of being controlled somewhat independently. Even parts of individual muscles, such as the genioglossus, can be made to contract separately (Miyawaki, 1974). This fact, in combination with the anatomical arrangement of the extrinsic and intrinsic musculature of the tongue and its particular situation within the right-angle shape of the vocal tract may account for the wide range of possible speech sounds that is unique to humans (Lieberman et al., 1972; Maeda and Honda, 1993). Actions of the extrinsic tongue muscles are largely responsible for positioning the tongue body within

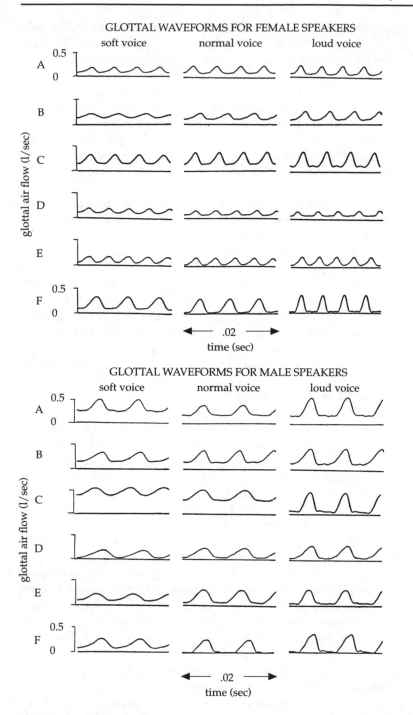

Figure 11.1 Glottal volume velocity vs. time waveforms for six female and six male speakers from the vowel /æ/ in a syllable from the string /pæpæpæpæpæpæ/ spoken in comfortable (labeled "normal"), soft and loud voice (Holmberg et al., 1988).

the vocal tract to differentiate vowels from one another. Figure 11.2 shows lateral x-ray tracings of the vowels /u/, /i/, /U/, /e/, /I/, /A/, and /æ/, as produced in the context /h@'tV/ by a speaker of American English (Perkell, 1969).

As in classical descriptions (Ladefoged, 1971), the vowels /i/ and /ɪ/ in Figure 11.2 are produced with a high, fronted tongue body; /u/ and /ʊ/ are produced with a high, backed tongue body; /ɑ/ with a low tongue body and /ɛ/ with a relatively "neutral" tongue-body position. Although /æ/ is usually described as "low", in this example, the tongue-body is in a position close to that for /ɛ/. The positions for /i/, /u/ and /ɑ/ are near the extremes of the articulatory space.

Figure 11.3 indicates how some of the tongue shapes in Figure 11.2 may be produced, according to the behavior of a physiologically-oriented tongue model (Perkell, 1974; 1996). The figure shows shapes resulting from "contraction" of the modeled posterior genioglossus, hyoglossus and styloglossus muscles. In each panel the dashed tongue contour represents the "rest" configuration, and the solid tongue contour shows the shape of the tongue produced by contraction of one of the muscles, which is modeled by the group of simulated muscle elements indicated by heavy solid lines. Contraction of the posterior portion of the genioglossus (a) pulls the base of the tongue forward toward the genioid tubercle of the mandible, producing a somewhat /i/-like tongue shape with a vocal-tract constriction in the anterior palatal region. Contraction of the hyoglossus (b) pulls the oral part of the tongue dorsum downward and backward and causes the pharyngeal part of the dorsum to bulge backward toward the pharyngeal wall, constricting the pharyngeal region and producing a tongue configuration very much like the vowel /ɑ/. Because of the way the fibres of the styloglossus run forward into the ventral aspect of the tongue blade, contraction of the styloglossus (c) produces an upward bulging of the tongue dorsum and a posterior movement of the tongue body, which results in a constriction in the velopalatal region. This configuration looks very much like the tongue shape for the vowel /u/. The location of the maximum vocal-tract constriction for /u/ is more anterior than the location of the styloglossus entry into the sides of the tongue, and the constriction happens to affect the area function in a way that is optimal for producing the formant pattern for /u/ (in combination with lip rounding). This modeling result and analyses of x-ray tracings (Wood, 1979) lead to the hypothesis that the anatomical arrangement of the vocal-tract musculature, in combination with area-function-to-acoustic relations, predisposes languages to select constriction locations for the point vowels that fortuitously result in formant patterns with distinctive acoustic properties (Jakobson et al., 1969; Wood, 1979; Perkell, 1996).

In order to test phonetic hypotheses about muscle actions, it should be possible to use electromyographic (EMG) recordings. Unfortunately, while EMG data can be helpful for studying some of the basic physiology underlying speech production (Smith, 1992), they are often less useful in phonetically-related investigations. It is very difficult to sample adequately all of the muscles

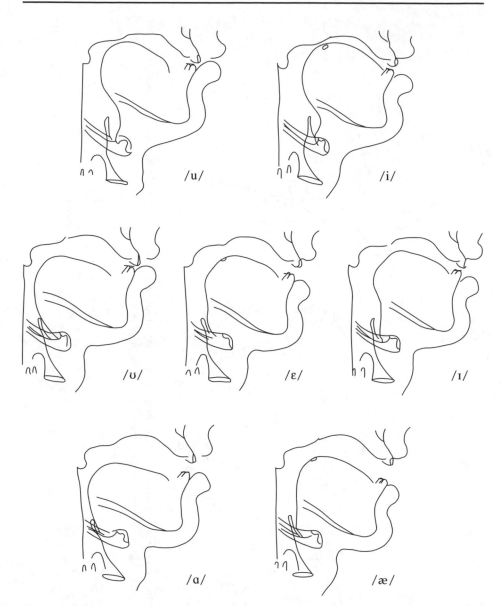

Figure 11.2 Lateral x-ray tracings of the vowels /u/, /i/, /ʊ/, /ɛ/, /ɪ/, /ɑ/, and /æ/, as produced in the context /hə'tV/ by a speaker of American English.

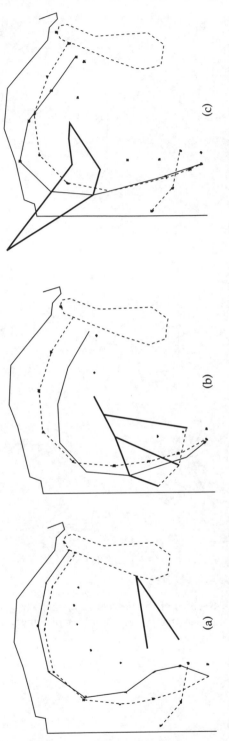
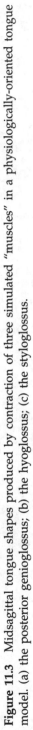

(a)

(b)

(c)

Figure 11.3 Midsagittal tongue shapes produced by contraction of three simulated "muscles" in a physiologically-oriented tongue model. (a) the posterior genioglossus; (b) the hyoglossus; (c) the styloglossus.

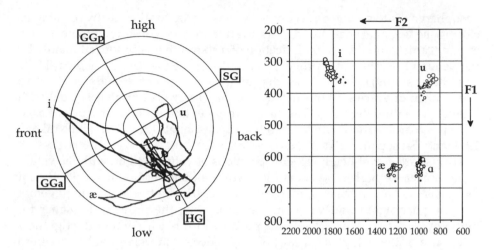

Figure 11.4 Left half – the activity levels of four muscles in production of the vowels /i/, /u/, /ɑ/ and /æ/ (after Kusakawa et al., 1993). The muscle activity levels are arranged in antagonistic pairs: posterior genioglossus (GGp) – hyoglossus (HG) and styloglossus (SG) – anterior genioglossus (GGa). Right half – the F1–F2 vowel quadrilateral. (From Maeda and Honda, 1993)

that contribute to any given movement, and relations between EMG activity and phonetically-important characteristics of the area function usually appear to be very indirect. This has been particularly true for the tongue, with its complicated, interdigitating muscular anatomy. One notable exception to these observations is a comprehensive EMG study of the extrinsic tongue muscles (from a single speaker of American English – Baer et al., 1988) that has been shown to have particularly interesting phonetic implications (Maeda and Honda, 1994; Honda, 1996). The left half of Figure 11.4 is a plot of the activity levels of four muscles in production of the vowels /i/, /u/, /ɑ/ and /æ/ (after Kusakawa et al., 1993). The muscle activity levels are arranged in pairs; within each pair, posterior genioglossus (GGp) – hyoglossus (HG) and styloglossus (SG) – anterior genioglossus (GGa), the muscle actions are antagonistic to one another. The relative muscle activity levels for the four vowels form a quadrilateral that is very much like the F1–F2 quadrilateral shown in the right half of Figure 11.4. Maeda and Honda (1994) have used the EMG data along with an articulatory model to predict the approximate F1–F2 pattern for the full set of 11 vowels produced by the subject. Thus in spite of the apparent complexity of the tongue anatomy and articulatory-to-acoustic relations, the authors are able to speculate that "the mappings from the muscle activities (production) to the acoustic patterns (perception) are simple and robust." (Maeda and Honda, 1994, p. 51.) If such findings can be replicated with additional speakers, they should have a significant impact on theories that are concerned with the relation between speech production and perception, at least for vowels.

The primary role of movements of the velum and the lateral walls of the nasopharynx is to couple or decouple the nasal and vocal tracts by opening or closing the velopharyngeal port. Nasalization may be considered to be a "secondary" articulation, i.e., a modification of a sound that is produced mainly by the action of a different, "primary" articulation of the tongue or lips (Halle and Stevens, 1991). As long as the language does not include contrastive nasalization of vowels, phonemically non-nasal vowels can be nasalized with little effect on intelligibility. The most prominent cause of such vowel nasalization is coarticulation with adjacent nasal consonants (Bell-Berti and Krakow, 1991 and Farnetani, COARTICULATION AND CONNECTED SPEECH PROCESSES). There also are vowel-height-specific positions of velum height, with the velum being higher for high vowels than low vowels (Bell-Berti et al., 1979). Recent work has shown that the amount of pressure exerted between the raised velum and the pharyngeal wall varies in the same way: the pressure is higher for high vowels (Moon et al., 1994). The purpose of this variation in the tightness of closure of the velopharyngeal port (as reflected in velar height variation) may be to constrain vowel nasalization. Because of the differences in the acoustic impedance of the oral cavity between high and low vowels, the same cross-sectional area of the velopharyngeal port will cause more nasalization of high vowels than low vowels (Stevens, forthcoming; Chen, 1996).

The lip configuration for vowels ranges from rounded (see the vowels /u/ and /ʊ/ in Figure 11.2) to spread. The purpose of lip rounding is to lengthen the vocal tract and constrict the terminal part of the area function, causing a decrease in formant frequencies. As with the velum, movements of the lips are mechanically quite independent of the tongue, providing a separate degree of freedom in the area function. The existence of multiple degrees of freedom of the area function has implications for speech motor control, since the same resonance pattern (acoustic transfer function) can be produced with more than one area function configuration (Atal et al., 1978; discussion below in Section 5).

4.2.2 Variation in vowel production   Consistent with the idea that phonetic goals correspond to regions in articulatory and acoustic space, Figure 11.5 shows an example of the extent of variability of tongue body articulations in production of the vowels /i/, /u/ and /ɑ/ by a speaker of American English (Perkell and Cohen, 1989). Each data point shows the midsagittal location of a transducer attached to the posterior tongue dorsum during one of many repetitions of the labeled vowel. The ellipses enclosing the distributions for each vowel are oriented in a direction that is approximately parallel to the vocal tract midline at the place of maximum constriction for the vowel, in the pharynx for the /ɑ/, velo-palatal region for the /u/ and anterior palatal region for the /i/. The finding of more variation in the direction parallel than perpendicular to the vocal-tract midline is consistent with the articulatory-to-acoustic relations for these vowels: their formants are relatively insensitive to some variation in constriction location (Stevens, 1972; 1989) and highly sensitive to variation in degree of constriction (Fant, 1960; Perkell and Nelson, 1985). It has also been observed that dorsal-ventral variation can be greater

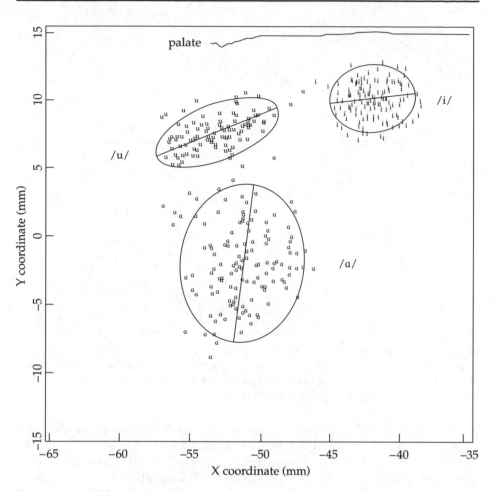

Figure 11.5 Midsagittal location of a transducer attached to the posterior tongue dorsum for a number of repetitions of the vowels /i/, /u/ and /ɑ/ by a speaker of American English.

where the vocal-tract cross-sectional area is large, since it causes less of a percentage change in the area and consequently has less influence on the acoustics (Perkell and Nelson, 1985; Gay et al., 1992). Thus, at least for some sounds, the nature of observed variation is influenced by basic properties of the production mechanism and articulatory-to-acoustic relations.

Vowel articulations can also vary across speakers (Johnson et al., 1993b). Since vowel formants are determined by the area function, the amount of tongue body displacement required to differentiate vowels from one another can depend on individual morphological factors such as vocal-tract size and shape of the palatal vault. Figure 11.6 shows coronal sections of maxillary casts through the first molar teeth from six speakers with differently-shaped

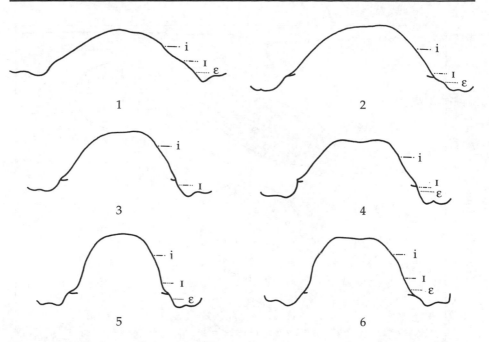

Figure 11.6 Tracings of coronal sections of maxillary casts through the first molar teeth from six speakers. Small tick marks along the right side of each contour show the location of the edge of tongue-to-palate contact for the vowels /i/, /ɪ/ and /ɛ/. Subject 3 had no tongue-to-palate contact for /ɛ/.

palatal vaults. Small tick marks along the right side of each contour show the location of the edge of tongue-to-palate contact for the vowels /i/, /ɪ/ and /ɛ/, as determined by direct palatography (Perkell, 1979). The speaker with shallowest palatal vault (1) uses the smallest adjustments of tongue height to create the area function differences required for the vowels, and the speaker with one of the steepest vaults (3) uses the largest adjustments. A kinematic study of the production of the vowel /u/ has suggested that such morphological differences may also underlie a speaker's choice of motor control strategies (Perkell et al., 1995).

4.2.3 *Aspects of consonant articulations*   Figure 11.7 shows midsagittal x-ray tracings of vocal-tract configurations for the consonants /p/, /t/, /k/, /s/, /d/, /z/ and /n/. Stop consonants such as /k/, /t/, /d/, /n/ and /p/ are produced by completely occluding the vocal tract at a single place of articulation with the tongue body, tongue blade or lips. If the velo-pharyngeal port is open, the result is a nasal stop consonant. If the port is closed, the stop is a plosive, with a low-amplitude or silent portion during which vocal-tract air pressure is built up and then released with a rapid opening movement that causes a noise burst. Fricatives in English such as /s/, /ʃ/, /f/ and their voiced counterparts are produced by creating a narrow constriction, usually by placing the grooved tongue body, tongue blade or lower lip against some

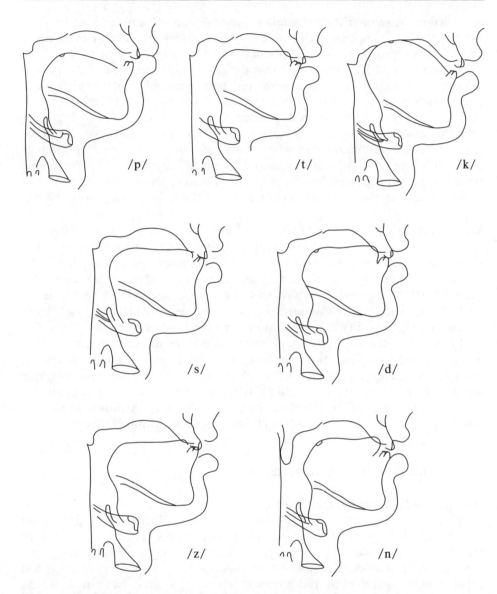

Figure 11.7 Lateral x-ray tracings of vocal-tract configurations for the consonants /p/, /t/, /k/, /s/, /d/, /z/ and /n/.

portion of the dorsal wall of the vocal tract. With an appropriate level of air pressure behind the constriction and configuration of the constriction, air flow through the constriction becomes turbulent, producing frication noise (Stevens, 1971). In the case of /s/, the airstream is directed at the barrier formed by the lower incisors, which increases the amplitude of the fricative noise (Shadle, 1985); this role of the lower incisors appears to be responsible for a relatively invariant mandible position for /s/. The formation of a precisely-configured constriction for some fricatives implies that their control is more complex than for the simple, complete occlusion of a stop. There are several even more complicated types of consonant articulations. For example, affricates such as /ʧ/ are produced by completely occluding the vocal tract and then quickly releasing the front part of the closure and more gradually releasing the back part, which results in a brief frication noise (Stevens, 1993a). Trills are produced by bringing articulators in proximity to one another with a degree of internal stiffness that causes an interaction with the air stream to produce several cycles of a vibratory movement and modulation of the amplitude of the emitted sound. Clicks are produced by occluding the vocal tract in two places, expanding the enclosed cavity to create a partial vacuum and then rapidly releasing the anterior constriction first (Ladefoged and Traill, 1994).

4.2.4 The supporting role of the mandible   The only part of the mandible that participates directly in determining the vocal-tract area function is the lower teeth. However, the mandible has the important role of supporting the tongue and lower lip, and as mentioned above, its position is important for the production of sounds in which a jet of air impinges on the lower incisors, such as /s/ and /t/. Consequently, mandible movements have significant effects on lingual and labial articulations for both vowels and consonants. The participation of the supported tongue and lips in coarticulation implies that at any moment in time, the mandible (like the thyro-arytenoid muscle in the example given below in Section 5) is under the influence of multiple temporally- and spatially-overlapping articulatory goals. Since such goals can conflict with one another, the control strategies have to include a means for resolving such conflicts (Perkell, 1980; Saltzman and Munhall, 1989).

4.3 Articulatory kinematics

It is generally believed that differences in the kinematic characteristics of articulatory movements (such as displacements, velocities and durations) help to signal a variety of prosodic and segmental cues. A broad overview of the literature indicates that articulatory kinematics may be governed by systematic relations among factors such as peak velocity, displacement, precision of movement termination and forces of contact required by various kinds of speech sounds and different degrees of stress and clarity. However, it is currently difficult to construct a comprehensive, systematic account of these inter-relations.

Studies of articulatory kinematics have examined a number of parameters, measured for points on the articulators in the midsagittal plane with a variety of techniques (Kent and Moll, 1969; Houde, 1968; Müller and Abbs, 1979; Abbs, Nadler and Fujimura, 1988; Perkell et al., 1992a), or for movements of the vocal-tract walls in one of several dimensions with cineradiography (Perkell, 1969) or ultrasound (Ostry and Munhall, 1985; Stone, 1991). Basic measures include movement distance, movement duration, locations of movement end-points, peak velocity and acceleration. The ratio of peak velocity to distance approximates the relative amount of underlying muscle contraction (sometimes referred to as muscle or articulator "stiffness"). Simple indices of velocity profile shape, such as peak velocity/average velocity can reflect differences in movement optimization criteria (Nelson, 1983; Munhall et al., 1985). Skewness of the velocity profile indicates the proportion of the movement spent in acceleration vs. deceleration (Adams, 1990). The number of velocity peaks in a movement and the third derivative of displacement versus time, called "jerk", are inverse indices of smoothness.

The syntactic structure of utterances and lexical stress impose prosodic constraints on segmental-level timing and on the magnitudes of muscle tensions and articulatory movements. For example, stressed syllables may be accompanied by a combination of increased duration and extremity of articulation for the vowel nucleus, and increased sound level and f_0 inflection. Among a number of examples at the segmental level, a /w/ is characterized mainly by movement of the lip rounding gesture, while an /u/ is characterized more by the steady state of lip rounding. A certain velocity of lip separation may be necessary to produce a clear burst noise in the release of a /p/. Therefore, depending on factors such as stress and the type of speech sound, it may be important to keep the value of a particular kinematic parameter within a certain range in order to maintain distinctiveness of a particular acoustic cue.

In comparison to normal (citation) speech, clear speech has been shown to be characterized, among other things by: greater intelligibility, greater intensity (by 3–5 db in vowel nuclei), longer sound segments, an expanded vowel space, tighter acoustic clustering within vowel categories, greater distinctiveness of VOT between voiced and voiceless stop consonants and released word final stops (Picheny et al., 1986; Moon and Lindblom, 1994; Moon, 1991).

The velocity and extent of articulatory movements have been shown to be related to a number of factors including: characteristics of different classes of consonants (Munhall, Ostry and Parush, 1985; Gracco, 1994), stress (MacNeilage et al., 1970; Harris, 1971; Munhall et al., 1985; Vatikiotis-Bateson and Kelso, 1990; Beckman and Edwards, 1994), interactions among articulators (Sussman et al., 1973), and speaking rate (Lindblom, 1963; Amerman et al., 1970; Kent et al., 1974; Gay, 1974; Gay et al., 1974; Kuehn and Moll, 1976; Ostry and Munhall, 1985; Harris et al., 1986; Adams, 1990). Vowel durations change more with rate than consonant durations (Gay et al., 1974), probably because vowels can be reduced more than consonants without disrupting intelligibility (Guenther, 1995a). Speech movements have also been shown to be similar to other movements in demonstrating orderly relationships among movement duration, distance and velocity (Ostry et al., 1987; Linville, 1982; Nelson et al., 1984; Vatikiotis-Bateson and Fletcher, 1992; Flanagan et al., 1990). Some limited spectral analyses of displacement vs. time signals indicate that muscle-generated movements of vocal-tract structures have very low bandwidths, ranging up to between 7 and 11 Hz (Nelson, 1977). (Aerodynamically-generated movements, such as the initial very rapid separation of the lips in the release of a /p/ – Fujimura, 1961a – can have much higher bandwidths.)

In Kuehn and Moll's (1976) study of speaking rate, it was found that to increase rate, some speakers increased articulatory velocities and produced little articulatory undershoot, while others did not increase velocities and did not completely reach articulatory targets. There was a positive relationship between articulatory velocity or displacement and tongue or jaw size. On the other hand, differences in oral structure size were considered, but rejected as an explanation for the inter-subject differences in strategies for increasing rate. In a kinematic study of tempo and prosody, Edwards et al. (1991) found that two of four subjects decreased the velocity of a phrase-final mandible closing gesture in producing a slow speech condition, while the other two delayed the onset of the closing gesture without decreasing velocity. The latter two subjects had generally longer syllable durations than the former two. As an explanation, Edwards et al. (1991) hypothesized a lower limit on velocity that may be physiologically- or perceptually-based (to preserve phonetic identity).

Adams et al.'s (1993) study of rate and clarity showed that normal and faster-than-normal speech was produced with symmetrical unimodal velocity profiles, most consistently for consonant release movements of the tongue tip, while slower-than-normal speech had asymmetrical multi-peaked (i.e., less smooth) velocity profiles. The rate-induced kinematic differences also included changes in the ratio of peak velocity to maximum displacement. Such changes were interpreted as indicating a rate-related modification of the control strategy. In the clear speech condition, maximum displacements and peak velocities were greater than in the normal condition. However, these differences were not accompanied by evidence of a separate control strategy that the authors thought might correspond to a different mode for producing clear speech.

Additional examples indicate further how articulatory movements may vary in different speech modes. Harris et al. (1986) observed movement trajectories of the tongue blade and Bell-Berti and Krakow (1991) observed trajectories of velum height vs. time in which, at normal rate, there were steady states corresponding to a given segment. Those steady states were absent at an increased rate, presumably making the trajectory smoother. In a palatographic study, Farnetani (1991) found that consonants produced in continuous speech had reduced areas of palatal contact relative to those in isolated words. This finding indicates that tongue-palate contact forces were diminished in continuous speech.

Despite the observed regularities, there are differences between studies and among subjects in the kinematic effects of speaking rate (Kuehn and Moll, 1976; Kelso et al., 1985; Munhall et al., 1985; Linville, 1982; Edwards et al., 1991), stress (Macchi, 1985 vs. preceding references; Vatikiotis-Bateson and Kelso, 1990), and phonetic factors (Adams et al., 1993). Some of the differences between studies may be due to different: (a) elicitation procedures, measurement techniques and analyses, (b) numbers of subjects, and (c) comprehensiveness with respect to articulatory structures and test materials. Differences among subjects within the same study may have to do with idiosyncratic interpretation of instructions and morphological differences (Kuehn and Moll, 1976; Perkell et al., 1995), abilities to perform tasks (Kelso et al., 1985) and individual "performance limits" (Nelson et al., 1984; Edwards et al., 1991; see further discussion below). As mentioned earlier, findings of such differences may also be related to the fact that speakers are able to communicate effectively with highly variable patterns of articulation and sound output.

4.4 Articulatory dynamics

A clearer understanding of the phonetic significance of differences in kinematic parameter values should be gained from learning more about underlying dynamics. As Stevens (forthcoming) points out,

> An understanding of . . . timing constraints in speech production (as well as the response of listeners to time-varying signals of the kind that occur in speech) is of basic importance in the study of language, since this knowledge may eventually provide some basis for explaining the constraints that exist in the sequential patterns of features that are allowed in various languages, and in some of the modifications that occur in utterances that are produced in a rapid or casual manner.

However, Stevens (forthcoming) also observes that

> . . . aspects of speech production relating to the constraints on the rates of movement of the various articulatory structures have not been well quantified. Consequently only rough estimates can be made of the rates at which different kinds of articulatory movements can be made or the rates at which articulatory states can be changed.

Table 11.2 shows ranges of estimated minimum movement durations for different vocal-tract structures. The durational estimates (from Stevens, forthcoming) are based on acoustic measurements and some work by other investigators (Rothenberg, 1968; Hixon and collaborators, 1987 for the respiratory system; Fujimura, 1961 for lip movements).

The durational values for changes of state of the different structures in Table 11.2 are generally within a factor of two of one another, indicating superficially that simple differences in size and mass do not account entirely for how the structures are employed in speech production. Obviously, it is possible to coordinate the state changes of the structures well enough, in spite of their possibly different dynamical properties. The fact that the respiratory system can be driven to change subglottal pressure in about the same time that it takes for state changes of other, smaller structures indicates that speakers make efficient use of respiratory biomechanics to achieve phonetic goals (Weismer, 1988). Greater insight about how speech motor control strategies deal with dynamical constraints will require a much deeper understanding of the dynamical properties of the different subsystems, one that goes well beyond comparing relative sizes and masses and considers the underlying forces.

Most of the speech articulators are capable of generating higher forces (expending greater amounts of effort) than are common in speech. This is

Table 11.2   Estimated minimal durations of articulatory movements (from Stevens, forthcoming).

Articulatory structure	Type of cyclical change (from one steady state to another and back)	Estimated duration of a complete rapid cycle (ms)	Duration of a uni-directional change (ms)
Respiratory system	Between two values of subglottal pressure	300	100
Vocal folds	Tension alternation to change between two values of f_0	200–300	100
Vocal folds	Abduction-adduction alternation for devoicing-voicing	80–150 (closing time shorter than opening time)	50 (closing)
Tongue body	Between two vowel targets	200–300	100
Velum	Raising and lowering to close and open the velo-pharyngeal port	200–300	
Lips	Rounding		50–100
Mandible	Raising-lowering	150	
Lips or tongue blade or tongue body plus mandible	Opening-closing for a stop consonant	150–200	

obvious for chewing forces generated by the mandibular closing muscles, and it has also been found for the lips (Müller et al., 1977; Barlow and Rath, 1985), and the tongue (McGlone et al., 1967). Higher levator veli palatini (velum elevating) EMG levels have been observed for a blowing task than for the production of oral plosive consonants (Kuehn and Moon, 1994). Velocities for single maximally-rapid mandibular movements have been observed that are several times higher than those of speech-like movements (Nelson et al., 1984).

Midsagittal-plane trajectories of points on the tongue dorsum (Houde, 1968; Perkell, 1969) indicate that consonant closures of the tongue body are almost always produced with relatively smooth, curved movements and sliding contact, as opposed to movements straight toward and then abruptly away from the place of closure. This appears to be the case even when context might "prefer" two straight-line trajectories joined by a complete, sharp reversal (such as in /aga/), which the articulators should be able to generate. Since the amount of effort expended to produce a smooth, curved trajectory should be less than that required for a sharp reversal (Nelson, 1983), it is very likely that the preference for sliding contacts is at least partly attributable to the use of an effort-minimizing strategy. Such economy of effort may interact with clarity to influence strategies for phenomena such as reduction (Lindblom, 1990).

Assuming a uni-dimensional, frictionless dynamic model, peak velocity can be considered to be a measure of expended effort (Nelson, 1983; Munhall et al., 1985). There are effort measures based on more complex models (Flash and Hogan, 1985; Kawato, 1991); however, the parameters of speech movements are more complex than those of any such model. So until more advanced production models are developed (see below), effort measures based on the simplest model may provide some useful initial insights into hypotheses about expended effort.

Figure 11.8 shows a distance, time, peak-velocity three-dimensional performance space, with a concave surface that is the minimum "effort" bound for a model with an acceleration limit of 1g and negligible friction (Nelson, 1983). The top ends of the vertical lines emerging from the minimum cost surface represent values of peak velocity (effort), distance and time (movement duration) for up and down strokes of a subject's mandible during normal speech production. The speech data are distributed above the central part of the surface, which "represents the region of good trade-off between movement time, distance and effort". Such data indicate that "there is a consistent economy of movement in the way the jaw moves during speech, even though this is obviously not the primary objective of these movements" – which is achieving phonetic goals (Nelson, 1983, p. 142).

In measures of increasingly-rapid "accelerando" sequences of speech-like and non-speech mandible movements from three speakers, Nelson et al. (1984) found large inter-subject differences in maximum movement distance, duration, peak velocity and acceleration. Figure 11.9 (from Nelson et al., 1984) shows movement distance versus time data for individual strokes from accelerando sequences produced by one of the subjects. Part (a) is from a speech-like "sa-sa" trial, and part (b) is from a "wag" movement trial without speech. The U, D symbols denote data from up and down strokes respectively. These plots represent two-dimensional top-down views of a three-dimensional space as shown in Figure 11.8. The solid curve represents a theoretical minimum-time limit for frictionless movements using a constant acceleration-deceleration magnitude of 1.5g. The set of straight lines radiating from the curve show minimum peak velocity effort levels.

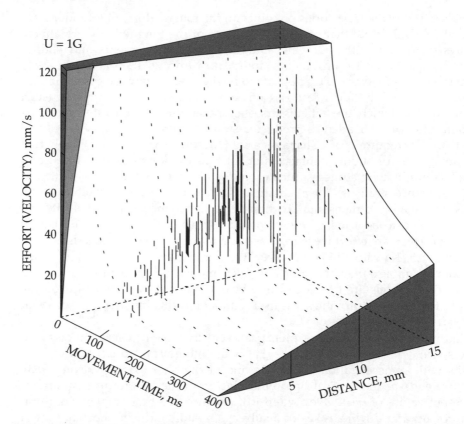

Figure 11.8 A distance, time, peak-velocity three-dimensional performance space, with a concave surface that is the minimum "effort" bound for a model with an acceleration limit of 1g and negligible friction. The top ends of the vertical lines show values of peak velocity, distance and time (movement duration) for up and down strokes of a subject's mandible during normal speech production (Nelson, 1983).

> The similarity of the "sa-sa" and "wag" data near the end of the sequences (i.e., near the minimum-time bound) may be largely due to the impact of the steep effort gradient in this region. For points at the beginning of the sequences, the effort gradient is low, and the physical constraint on large variations in these data is correspondingly low. The variation of the "sa-sa" data in this portion of the space is much less than the "wag" data, possibly because of phonetic constraints present only in the speechlike task. As the movement time gets below about 100 ms [faster than usually used in speech], however, the fact that the effort gradient is getting large makes it more likely that the control strategies for both tasks are being constrained to trade off distance for time in a similar way. (Nelson et al., 1984, p. 950)

The large differences among the subjects in this study, in combination with the result shown in Figure 11.9, lead to the speculation that different speakers

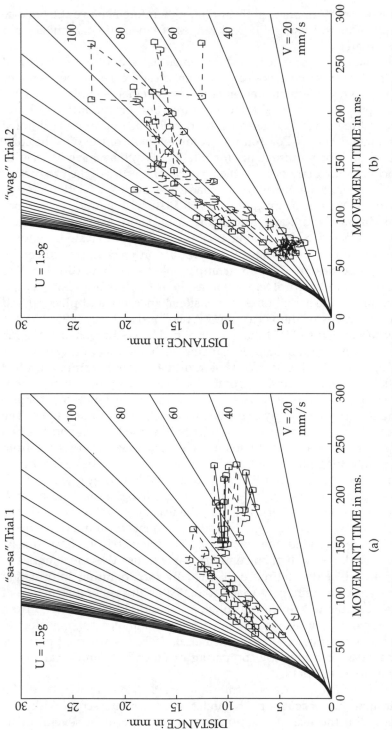

Figure 11.9 Movement distance versus time data for individual strokes from accelerando sequences. (a) A speech-like "sa-sa" trial, (b) A "wag" movement trial without speech. The U, D symbols denote data from up and down strokes respectively (Nelson et al., 1984). These plots represent two-dimensional top-down views of a three-dimensional space as shown in Figure 11.8. The solid curve shows a theoretical minimum-time limit of 7.5g. The set of straight lines radiating from the curve show minimum peak-velocity "effort" levels.

may have different performance limits and may therefore achieve the balance between clarity and effort using different ranges of kinematic parameters and even different strategies.

While such results are consistent with the idea that economy of effort and performance limits exert some degree of constraint on strategies of speech motor control, the underlying model in Nelson (1983) is extremely simple in relation to the physical properties of vocal tract structures, and far too little work has been done along these lines. Furthermore, there could be important additional constraints in other domains. For example, complexity of control (i.e., the computational load) and/or requirements for intelligibility may have at least as much influence on control strategies as the physical properties of the production mechanism. Before much headway can be made with such speculations, it will be necessary to obtain further insight into articulatory dynamics by extending analyses to include additional articulators, using more realistic dynamical models. Such analyses are challenging because of the complicated anatomy and nonlinear dynamical properties of the production mechanism; currently, many of these properties are difficult or impossible to measure directly. One promising approach to this problem involves the use of a simulation that attempts to account for the actual three-dimensional anatomy and physical and physiological properties of the vocal tract (Wilhelms-Tricarico, 1995; 1996).

The four panels in Figure 11.10 show a simplified three-dimensional tongue model that represents the first step in realizing such a simulation (Wilhelms-Tricarico, 1995; 1996). The illustrated version of the model is composed of 42 large-strain finite elements that incorporate contractile fiber directions, a nonlinear muscle model, inertial properties and a volume constancy constraint – for simulating the actual anatomy and dynamical behavior of the tongue. The tongue tip is at the right; the base of the tongue is at the bottom and the two upward projections are the styloglossus muscles. The dashes projecting from the model indicate magnitude and direction of node velocities. The figure shows four frames from the first 90 ms of a tongue-lowering gesture, computed with activation of the genioglossus anterior, hyoglossus (and a small amount of genioglossus posterior). Thus far, the feasibility of the methods has been demonstrated by realizing some typical movements in simulation experiments, which have included the use of inputs derived from EMG measurements (Baer et al., 1988). It is currently possible to use these techniques to implement a model of the entire vocal tract. By incorporating information from magnetic resonance imaging (Baer et al., 1991), the general structure of the model can be adapted to the morphology of individual speakers, from whom kinematic data can also be obtained with techniques such as electromagnetic midsagittal articulometry (Perkell et al., 1992a). Thus the properties of such a model can be refined by comparing its kinematics and a calculated acoustic output to actual data.

Recent work has begun to demonstrate how such modeling will be useful for gaining insight into articulatory dynamics and their interaction with control strategies. With the use of a simulation of the mandible, several of its muscles and a hypothesized control structure, it has been shown that patterns

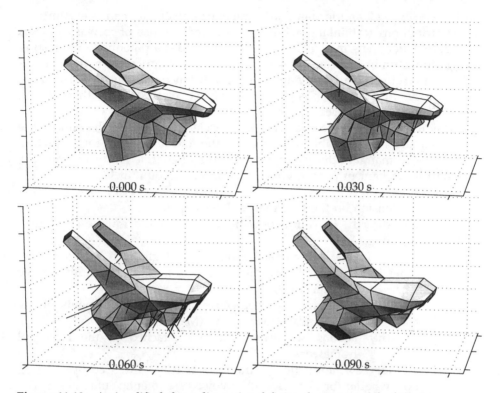

Figure 11.10 A simplified three-dimensional finite element model of the tongue that incorporates: contractile fiber directions, a non-linear muscle model, inertial properties and a volume constancy constraint (Wilhelms-Tricarico, 1995; 1996).

of actual VCV mandible movements, which can appear to be due to the control of anticipatory coarticulation, may instead be attributable solely to the dynamical properties of the system (Perrier et al., 1996; Laboissière et al., forthcoming; Ostry et al., forthcoming).

While it may be reasonable to hypothesize that, "Under most circumstances, the principal timing limitation is that imposed by the neuromuscular processes, that is, the time constants of the response to the muscle contractions", the requirement for inter-articulator coordination and the perceptual needs of listeners are additional candidates as factors that constrain timing (Stevens, forthcoming). A deeper understanding of these constraints will require much more work, including comprehensive studies of articulatory kinematics, dynamics and control.

5 Control of articulatory processes

The chapters by Löfqvist and Kent provide general discussions of many of the issues that are relevant to speech motor control. The control modeling of

Jordan (1990; 1992) and Jordan and Rumelhart (1992) has made very important contributions to thinking about learning and the use of forward models in speech. Guenther's model (1995a; 1995b) provides a potentially interesting integration of findings on speech sound acquisition, coarticulation, motor equivalence, rate effects, variability and velocity/distance relationships. The more limited focus in this section is on certain aspects of the control that interact with articulatory processes.

Consider the thyro-arytenoid (vocalis) muscle, which forms the bulk of the vocal fold and is responsible for stiffening the fold and partly for adducting it. In order to maintain the appropriate degree of contraction of this muscle, the control mechanism probably has to take into account at least:

(1)   the tension on the fold that is determined:
    (a)   directly, by contraction of the cricothyroid muscle in controlling f_0 and
    (b)   indirectly, by forces acting on the cartilaginous framework from:
        (i)   segmental movements of the tongue and mandible above (Honda, 1983)
        (ii)   respiratory (prosodically-influenced) movements of the lungs and trachea below (Maeda, 1976)
        (iii) actions of various muscles attached to the laryngeal framework
(2)   the degree of adduction of the folds that is influenced by:
    (a)   whether or not a sound is voiced (segmental influence)
    (b)   the desired sound level (prosodic and postural influences)
(3)   the tension in and commands to other intrinsic laryngeal muscles that also affect the state of the folds

This example illustrates that the number of degrees of freedom that have to be controlled in speech is large, and the control problem appears to be immensely complicated.[6] As Löfqvist points out in THEORIES AND MODELS OF SPEECH PRODUCTION, very little is known about the control of even the most basic articulations; however, there are some findings and hypotheses about control that are relevant to a discussion of articulatory processes. These concern mechanisms for the coordination of multiple articulators to achieve segmental articulatory and acoustic goals.

One part of the solution to such complexity is that the control of movement appears to be hierarchical (Ghez, 1991; Gracco, 1987). The parameters that are being controlled ("controlled variables") may be represented differently at different levels of the control hierarchy. For an arm movement, as an example, the controlled variables may be the position of the hand in some external coordinate system, the joint angles and the activities of the muscles. It is thought that feedback of various types of information (about spatial location, joint angle, muscle tension, velocity of movement, etc.) is used at all levels, primarily in sub-programs or controllers that reduce the number of degrees of freedom to be controlled by higher levels. In the case of speech it is necessary to control multiple constrictions for some acoustic transfer functions, multiple articulators for each vocal-tract constriction, and multiple muscles for each articulatory movement.

5.1 What are the variables that are controlled by the speech motor system?

Ultimately, the objective of speech articulations is to produce an acoustic signal with properties that will enable the listener to understand what is said. On the other hand, for the speaker's motor control system, the goals may be specified in terms of more than one type of parameter, and they may vary in kind from one sound segment to the next. Possible examples include steady state and time varying patterns of formant frequencies and articulatory configurations for vowels and glides, and patterns of articulator contact, noise bursts, silent intervals, aspiration sounds and rapid formant transitions for consonants. The acoustic characteristics of these sounds are determined by (a) levels of muscle tension, (b) resulting forces and movements, (c) ensuing aerodynamic events, (d) properties of the sound source and filter. So, while the desired results are particular acoustic patterns that will lead to comprehension by the listener, hypothetically, the motor control variables for the speaker could be parameters related to any of (a)–(d).

How does the speaker (and her/his motor control system) assure that perceptually-important acoustic goals are achieved? It is very unlikely that the motor control system uses auditory feedback moment-to-moment to control individual segmental movements. The neural processing times would probably be too long, and a major portion of the movements for many vowels occurs during preceding consonant strings, when relatively little or no sound is being generated.

The difficulty that prelingually-deafened individuals have in learning how to speak fluently attests to the importance of auditory information for speech acquisition (Levitt, Stromberg, Smith and Gold, 1980; Osberger and McGarr, 1982; Smith, 1975). On the other hand, although some aspects of the speech of postlingually-deafened speakers are affected, such speakers often sound intelligible for decades following hearing loss (Cowie and Douglas-Cowie, 1983; Lane and Webster, 1991). These observations support the hypothesis that, in adults, auditory feedback is used to maintain ("validate" or "calibrate") a robust internal model of relation between speech motor commands and the sound output. The model is used by programming mechanisms that achieve acoustic targets without the closed-loop, moment-to-moment use of auditory feedback (Jordan, 1990; 1992; Jordan and Rumelhart, 1992; Lindblom et al., 1979; Perkell et al., 1992b). The speaker establishes and refines this model during speech acquisition and maturation, which begins in the infant and can continue into puberty (Kent, 1976a; Kent and Forner, 1980).

While phonetic goals may have acoustic components, the goals may also be characterized in terms of the types of orosensory feedback that are generated in the speaker – sensations that reflect muscle tensions, articulator contact forces and movements and intraoral air pressures and flows (review by Kent, Martin and Sufit, 1990), particularly as they provide information about aerodynamically-critical aspects of sound source generation and acoustically-critical parts of the area function. Orosensory goals would vary from one sound segment and one articulator to the next. For the consonant /p/ the orosensory goals may be lip contact and an increase of intra-oral air pressure; for vowels they may be patterns of muscle tension and contact between the tongue surface and vocal-tract walls, especially as they correspond to the production of relatively narrow constrictions.

As cited by Löfqvist, THEORIES AND MODELS OF SPEECH PRODUCTION, in bite-block experiments, there appear to be rapid adjustments of vowel productions in response to immobilization of the mandible at unusual degrees of opening with a bite block (Lindblom et al., 1979). On the other hand, when Hamlet and Stone (1976) altered oral morphology by placing a 4 mm thick palate in speakers' mouths for two weeks, adjustments of vowel articulations continued for that long. The apparent differences between compensation times in these two results could be due to relatively uninteresting methodological differences; however, one methodological difference may be significant. The artificial palate created a completely new configuration of the oral cavity and blocked a major source of tactile feedback (from receptors in the palatal mucosa). This may have been much more of a disturbance than the bite block, which still allows subjects to use tactile feedback from a normally-shaped hard palate. The artificial palate result is compatible with other bite block studies in which compensation was more difficult under reduced or absent oral sensation and speakers may have needed to rely more on auditory feedback (Hoole, 1987). If, as suggested above, auditory feedback is not used moment-to-moment, compensations that need it could take more practice to succeed (McFarland and Baum, 1995; Baum et al., 1996). The fact that one of Hamlet and Stone's subjects could compensate much more rapidly to re-insertion of the palate a month later (Hamlet et al., 1976) is compatible with the idea that an alternative set of motor command-to-acoustic mappings was acquired (as part of the internal model referred to above) during the original two-week adaptation period and was retained for later recall, as in the learning of other complex motor-sensory skills.

5.2 Synergistic mechanisms for simplifying the control of articulatory processes

The results of speech perturbation experiments (Abbs and Gracco, 1984; review by Löfqvist, THEORIES AND MODELS OF SPEECH PRODUCTION) provide evidence of mechanisms that use orosensory and internal feedback in the control of synergistic actions of multiple articulators for achieving functionally-specific segmental goals. For example, if the lower lip is unexpectedly impeded in its upward movement toward a bilabial closure for a /p/, the upper lip may move further downward than planned with an increased velocity to complete the closure (Abbs et al., 1984). The use of such synergisms should significantly reduce the number of degrees of freedom that have to be controlled to achieve phonetic goals.

Evidence of articulatory synergisms also comes from motor equivalence experiments, which involve observation of many repetitions of the same behavior without the use of external perturbations. The term "motor equivalence" refers to the finding that the same goal is reached in more than one way (Hughes and Abbs, 1976). Theoretically, across multiple repetitions, there can be trading relations (complementary covariation) in the relative contributions of: (1) multiple muscles to the same movement, (2) multiple movements to the same acoustically-critical vocal-tract cross-sectional area and (3) two area-function constrictions to the same acoustic transfer function.

Figure 11.11a (from Abbs and Gracco, 1984) shows an example of a possible trading relation between two lower lip elevator muscles in multiple tokens of a lower-lip raising movement, i.e., motor equivalence at the muscle-to-movement level. As reflected in the EMG signal levels, when one muscle contracts more, the other one contracts less, and vice-versa. Figure 11.11b (from Abbs et al., 1984) shows trading relations in contributions of upper and lower lip movements for three repetitions of closure for a /p/, i.e., motor equivalence at the movement-to-area function level. In the three panels in Figure 11.11b the upper and lower lips move different, complementary amounts to achieve the invariant goal of lip closure. (For a critical review of literature on studies of these two kinds of motor equivalence, including methodological issues, see Folkins and Brown, 1987.)

Figure 11.12 (from Maeda, 1991) shows plots of tongue position (front-back) vs. jaw position (low-high) for the production of the vowels /a/ and /i/ by two speakers of French. The values on the axes are in standard deviations of the distribution of all of the data from that speaker. For each subject, the points lie near a separate line for each of the two vowels, indicating varying and complementary contributions of relatively independent (horizontal) tongue and (vertical) jaw displacements to the vowel productions.

There is also some preliminary evidence to support the idea that there can be trading relations in contributions of two relatively independent parts of the vocal-tract area function to the same acoustic transfer function. Such findings may be interpreted to support the idea that phonetic goals have an acoustic component. The left half of Figure 11.13 illustrates this idea for production of the vowel /u/ in American English. The /u/ is produced by constricting the area function in the velo-palatal region with tongue-body raising, and constricting the area function in the labial region with lip rounding. As schematized by the double-headed arrows, a very similar acoustic transfer function can be produced with a bit more tongue raising and a bit less lip rounding and vice versa. So, for example, if some source of variation were to cause the tongue body to be too low, an acceptable /u/ could be produced with increased lip

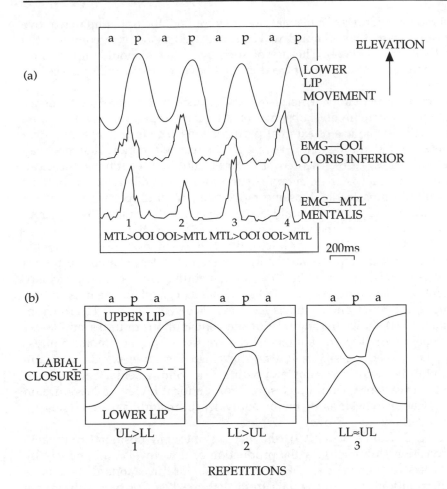

Figure 11.11 (a) An example of a possible trading relation between two lower lip elevator muscles in multiple tokens of a lower-lip raising movement. When one muscle contracts more, the other one contracts less, and vice-versa (Abbs and Gracco, 1984). (b) Trading relations of upper and lower lip movements. In the three repetitions the upper and lower lips move different, complementary amounts to achieve lip closure for a /p/ (Abbs et al., 1984).

rounding. This kind of motor equivalence is a variation-constraining strategy that takes advantage of the fact that a particular acoustic goal can be achieved with more than one combination of articulatory settings (Atal et al., 1978). The right half of the figure shows scatter plots of mid-vowel locations of transduced points on the tongue body, upper lip, lower lip and lower incisor for multiple repetitions of /u/ by one speaker. In data like these from five of six speakers, Perkell et al. (1993; 1995) have shown negative correlations between lip rounding and tongue-body raising. Such results support the idea that there can be motor

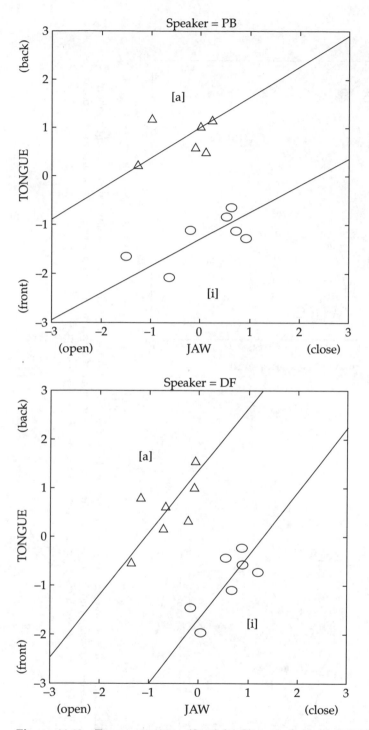

Figure 11.12 Tongue position (front–back) vs. jaw position (low–high) for production of the vowels /a/ and /i/ by two speakers of French. The values on the axes are in standard deviations of the distribution of all of the data from each speaker (Maeda, 1991).

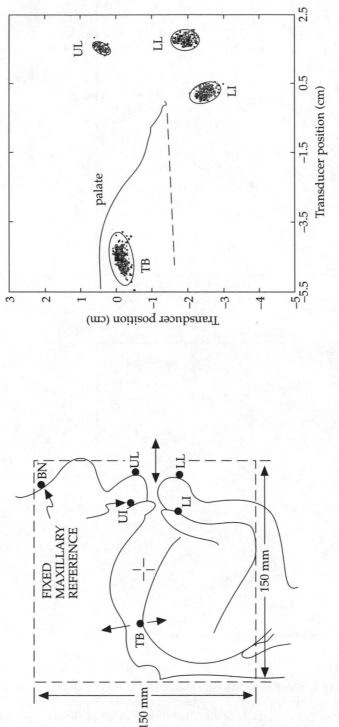

Figure 11.13 Left half – A midsagittal x-ray tracing of the vowel /u/; the double-headed arrows illustrate a trading relation between tongue-body raising and lip rounding. Right half – Scatter plots of mid-vowel locations of points on the tongue body, upper lip, lower lip and lower incisor for multiple repetitions of /u/ by one speaker.

equivalence in the transformation between the vocal-tract area function and the acoustic transfer function; thus, speech motor programming may include acoustic goals.

Abbs et al. (1984) and others have hypothesized that control mechanisms are acquired to accomplish the kind of synergistic coordination that is observed in perturbation and motor equivalence experiments. Such controllers, consisting of functionally-specific combinations of efferent and afferent neural components, are organized via learning so that they automatically compute time-varying commands to individual muscles to achieve specific phonetic goals on the basis of relatively simple inputs. In principle, when such a mechanism is combined with the use of an internal model of the relation between articulatory commands and acoustic results (see above), this concept should be extendible to include synergisms for achieving acoustic goals as well as orosensory goals. Thus synergistic mechanisms may be available to reduce the number of controlled degrees of freedom at several levels in the control hierarchy.

6 Summary and conclusions

Articulatory processes are actions of the respiratory, laryngeal and vocal-tract systems that convert linguistic messages to an intelligible signal. The linguistic message is encoded in acoustic characteristics of individual sound segments and in superimposed prosodic patterns of sound level, fundamental frequency and duration. Important additional influences are listener needs, which are determined by factors such as the level of environmental noise and the listener's familiarity with the language, speaker and subject matter. The speaker's response to listener needs is to modify clarity (adjust the amount of reduction) and the "postural" parameters of overall rate and sound level. All of these influences, segmental, prosodic, postural and level of clarity converge on the same sets of structures, each with its very different physical and physiological properties and large number of degrees of freedom. Thus the task of controlling articulatory processes appears to be immensely complicated. Pre-planning seems to play a large role in this control; it is hypothesized that the results of such planning are appropriately-timed sequences of acoustic-phonetic goals that are defined in articulatory and acoustic terms, and are modified by influences such as prosody, clarity and posture. As with other forms of movement, it is likely that the motor control of articulatory processes is hierarchical. Lower levels include learned, individual controllers for synergisms that achieve specific acoustic-phonetic goals and thus reduce the number of degrees of freedom that have to be controlled by higher levels.

Kinematic adjustments are used to help convey some linguistically-contrastive information; however, the large amount of variability inherent in speech and the lack of truly comprehensive kinematic data currently make it difficult to provide a systematic account of articulatory kinematics. Some preliminary ideas about articulatory dynamics indicate that the biomechanical response properties of articulators and effort minimization strategies have roles in shaping the control of articulatory processes; on the other hand, it is very likely that perceptually-related factors are at least as important in this regard.

Many of these observations are consistent with a theoretical framework in which the goals of speech movements are defined in terms of articulatory and acoustic parameters, and the control strategies that achieve those goals are influenced by dynamical constraints and intelligibility requirements. However, these ideas depend as much on speculation as they do on established knowledge. Additional, comprehensive data on articulatory kinematics, more realistic modeling of articulatory dynamics and control, and a deeper understanding of the role of perception and mechanisms of speech understanding should shift this balance toward more of a reliance on facts.

NOTES

I am very grateful for helpful comments from: Suzanne Boyce, Peter Guiod, Frank Guenther, Eva Holmberg, Mike Jordan, Jim Kobler, Harlan Lane, Anders Löfqvist, Melanie Matthies, Clay Mitchell, Stefanie Shattuck-Hufnagel, Ken Stevens, Mario Svirsky, Alice Turk and Yi Xu. Preparation of this chapter was supported by N.I.H. Grant DC01925.

1 It is recognized that there are alternative frameworks (Browman and Goldstein, 1986; 1989 and Saltzman and Munhall, 1989; discussion by Löfqvist in this volume) and that too little is known currently about speech production to decide that any one theory is more valid than others.

2 Articulatory processes also produce visual cues for speechreading, which is beyond the scope of this chapter.

3 According to the somewhat different perspective taken by Articulatory Phonology (Browman and Goldstein, 1989) and task-dynamic modeling (Saltzman and Munhall, 1989) phonetic goals and articulatory processes are one and the same.

4 In order to be able to describe articulatory processes in a convenient way in this chapter, the terms "actions" and "articulations" are used interchangeably to refer to activities of the vocal-tract, laryngeal and respiratory systems. More often in the literature, such actions of vocal-tract and laryngeal structures are called "articulations".

5 Note that in contrast to "dynamics", the term "kinematics" refers to readily observable properties of movements such as displacements, distances, velocities and accelerations, without consideration of the underlying forces.

6 The convergence of multiple influences on individual articulators and subsystems also has to be taken into account in experimental design and analysis, particularly when studying the effect of some external perturbation or environmental change. For example, the speaker's response might well be a change in a postural setting that can be misinterpreted as a modification of a parameter value of a phonetic goal (Perkell et al., 1992b).

12 Coarticulation and Connected Speech Processes

EDDA FARNETANI

1 Context dependent variability in speech

1.1 Coarticulation

During speech the movements of different articulators for the production of successive phonetic segments overlap in time and interact with one another. As a consequence, the vocal tract configuration at any point in time is influenced by more than one segment. This is what the term "coarticulation" describes. The acoustic effects of coarticulation can be observed with spectrographic analysis: any acoustic interval, auditorily defined as a phonetic segment, will show the influence of neighboring phones in various forms and degrees. Coarticulation may or may not be audible in terms of modifications of the phonetic quality of a segment. This explains why descriptive and theoretical accounts of coarticulation in various languages became possible only after physiological and acoustical methods of speech analysis became available and widespread, that is, during the last thirty years. Recent reviews of theories and experimental data on coarticulation have been provided by Kent (1983), Harris (1983), Fowler (1980, 1985), and Farnetani (1990).

Table 12.1 shows how coarticulation can be described in terms of: 1) the main articulators involved; 2) some of the muscles considered to be primarily responsible for the articulatory–coarticulatory movements; 3) the movements that usually overlap in contiguous segments; 4) the major acoustic consequences of such overlap. As for lingual coarticulation, the tongue tip/blade and the tongue body can act quasi-independently as two distinct articulators, so that their activity in the production of adjacent segments can overlap in time.

Jaw movements are not included in the table since the jaw contributes both to lip and to tongue positioning, i.e. is part of two articulatory subsystems. Jaw movements are analyzed especially when the goal of the experiment is to establish the role of the jaw in shaping the vocal tract and thus distinguish between active and passive tongue (or lip) movements, or to investigate how

Table 12.1   Coarticulation

| | Level of description | | |
Articulator	Myomotoric	Articulatory	Acoustic
LIPS	Orbicularis Oris/ Risorius	Lip rounding/ spreading	Changes in F1, F2 and F3
TONGUE	Genioglossus and other extrinsic and intrinsic lingual muscles	Tongue front/back, high/low displacement	Changes in F2, F1 and F3
VELUM	(Relaxation of) Levator Palatini	Velum lowering	Nasal Formants and changes in Oral Formants
LARYNX	Posterior Cricoarytenoid/ Interarytenoid, Lateral Cricoarytenoid	Vocal fold abduction/ adduction	Aperiodic/Periodic signal Acoustic duration

the jaw contributes to or compensates for coarticulatory variations (see Perkell, ARTICULATORY PROCESSES).

The present account will center on coarticulation at the supraglottal level. For laryngeal activity see Hirose, INVESTIGATING THE PHYSIOLOGY OF LARYNGEAL STRUCTURES and Ní Chasaide and Gobl, VOICE SOURCE VARIATION. For detailed accounts of the relationship between vocal tract activity and the acoustic signal, see Fant (1968) and Fujimura and Erickson, ACOUSTIC PHONETICS and Stevens, ARTICULATORY/ACOUSTIC/AUDITORY RELATIONSHIPS.

Typical examples of coarticulation in terms of muscle activity and of articulatory movements are illustrated in Figures 12.1, 2 and 3.

Figure 12.1 illustrates coarticulation at the myomotoric level. It shows electromyographic (EMG) activity of the muscles during the production of /əpɪb//əpɪp/ (From Hirose and Gay, 1972). It can be seen that the activity of *orbicularis oris* for the production of the first /p/ is overlapped by the activity of the *genioglossus* for the production of the following front vowel. Moreover the activity of the laryngeal muscles responsible for abducting and adducting the vocal folds also overlap: the onset of lateral cricoarytenoid (LCA, adducting) occurs when the posterior cricoarytenoid activity (PCA, abducting) is at its peak, that is at the middle of the /p/ closure.

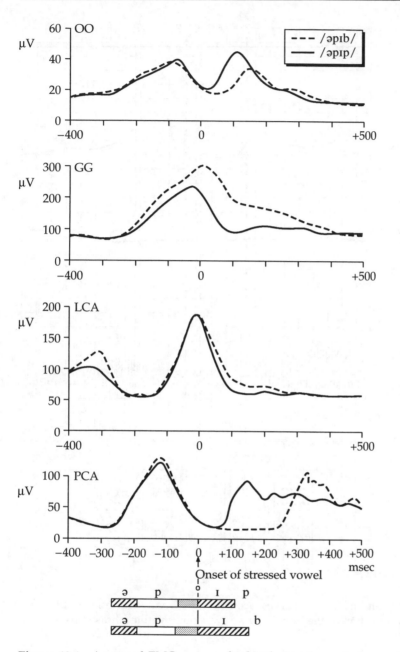

Figure 12.1 Averaged EMG curves of orbicularis oris, genioglossus, lateral and posterior cricoarytenoid muscles in utterances /əpɪp/ /əpɪb/ produced in isolation by an American subject. The line up point is the acoustic onset of /ɪ/ (from Hirose and Gay, 1972).

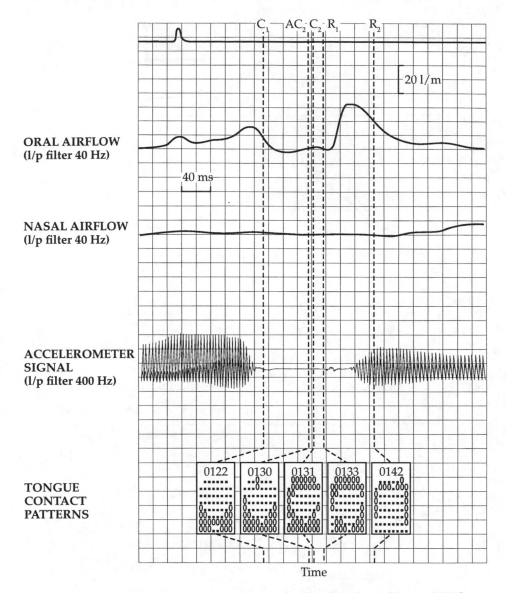

Figure 12.2   Oral and nasal flow curves, acoustic signal, and synchronized EPG activity in the production of the English word 'weakling' within phrase (from Hardcastle, 1985).

Figure 12.3   (Opposite) Acoustic signal, oral and nasal flow curves and synchronized EPG curves during /ana/ /ini/ produced in isolation by an Italian subject (from Farnetani, 1986).

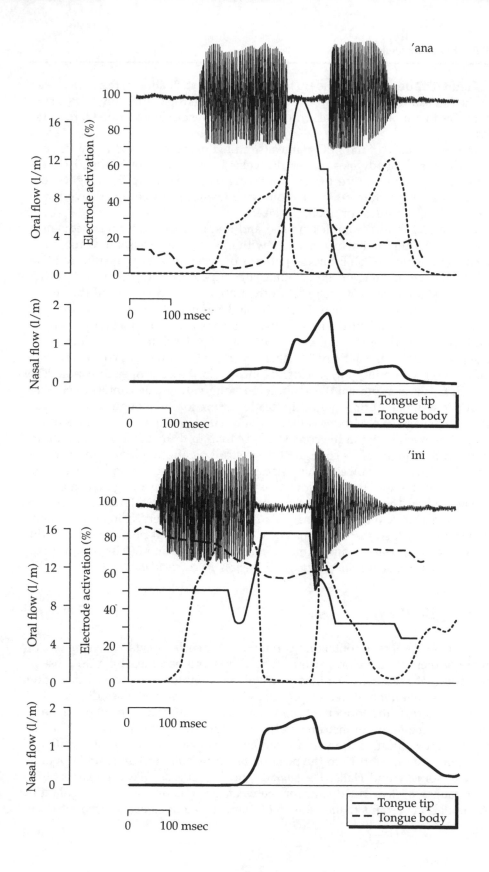

Figure 12.2 describes tongue-tip tongue-body coarticulation in the /kl/ cluster of the English word "weakling", analyzed with electropalatography (EPG) synchronized with oral and nasal airflow and the acoustic signal (from Hardcastle, 1985).

In the sequence of the EPG frames (sampled every 7.5 msec) it can be seen that the tongue body closure for the velar consonant is overlapped by the tongue tip/blade gesture for the following /l/, detectable by a light front contact as early as frame 130. The following frames show complete overlap of /k/ and /l/ closures for about 20 msec.

Figure 12.3 shows examples of velar and lingual coarticulation in sequences /'ana/ and /'ini/ in Italian, analyzed with EPG and oral/nasal flow measurements (Farnetani, 1986). From the patterns of nasal flow it can be inferred that in /'ana/ the opening of the velopharyngeal port for the production of /n/ occurs just after the acoustic onset of the initial /a/ and lasts until the end of the final /a/; in /'ini/ there is only a slight anticipation of velopharyngeal opening during the initial /i/, but after the consonant the port remains open until the end of the utterance. Thus in /'ana/ velar C-to-V coarticulation is extensive both in the anticipatory (before /n/) and in the carryover direction (after /n/), while in /'ini/ it extends mostly in the carryover direction. The two EPG curves represent the evolution of tongue-to-palate contact over time. It can be seen that during tongue tip/blade closure for /n/, tongue body contact (the percentage of electrodes contacted in the mid and the back regions of the palate) is much larger in the context of /i/ than in the context of /a/, indicating that the tongue body configuration is strongly affected by the movements associated with the vowels. These patterns describe V-to-C lingual coarticulation, that is, the effects of the vowel on the articulation of a lingual consonant.

The central theoretical issues in the studies of coarticulation concern its *origin, function,* and *control.* Coarticulation has been observed in all languages so far analyzed, so that it can be considered a universal phenomenon; at the same time it appears to differ among languages. Thus another important issue is how to account for *interlanguage differences in coarticulation.*

1.2 Assimilation

Assimilation refers to contextual variability of speech sounds, by which one or more of their phonetic properties are modified and become similar to those of the adjacent segments. We may ask whether assimilation and coarticulation refer to qualitatively different processes, or to similar processes described in different terms (the former reflecting an auditory approach to phonetic analysis, and the latter an instrumental articulatory/acoustic approach). The answers to this question are various and controversial. In order to illustrate the problem, we can start from the position taken by standard generative phonology (Chomsky and Halle, *The Sound Pattern of English*, 1968, hereafter SPE). SPE makes a clear-cut distinction between assimilation and coarticulation. Assimilation pertains to the domain of linguistic competence, is accounted for by phonological rules, and refers to modifications of features (the minimal categorical-classificatory constituents of a phoneme). Hence assimilatory processes (although widespread among languages) are part of the grammar and are language-specific. Coarticulation by contrast results from the physical properties of the speech mechanism and is governed by universal rules; hence it pertains to the domain of performance and cannot be part of the grammar. Chomsky and Halle describe coarticulation as "the transition between a vowel and an adjacent consonant, the adjustments in vocal tract shape made in anticipation of a subsequent motion etc." (SPE, p. 295) Accordingly, both the *distribution* (universality vs language specificity) and the *quality* of the contextual change (mere articulatory adaptation vs intentional phonetic modification) should allow one to distinguish the two processes.

Quite often context-dependent changes involving the same articulatory structures have different acoustic and perceptual manifestations in different languages so that it is possible to distinguish what can be considered universal phonetic behavior from language particular rules. A classical example is the difference between vowel harmony, an assimilatory process present in a limited number of languages (such as Hungarian) and the process of vowel-to-vowel coarticulation, attested in many languages and probably present in all (Fowler, 1983). In other cases cross-language differences are not easily interpretable, and inferences about the nature of the underlying processes can be made only by manipulating some of the speech parameters, for example segmental durations. In a study of vowel nasalization in Spanish and American English, Solé and Ohala (1991) were able to distinguish phonological (language specific) from phonetic nasalization by manipulating speech rate. They found a quite different distribution of the temporal patterns of nasalization in the two languages as a function of rate: in American English the extent of nasalization on the vowel preceding the nasal was proportional to the varying vowel duration, while in Spanish it remained constant. They concluded that the spread of nasalization as vowel duration increases in American English, must be intentional (phonological), while the short and constant extent of nasalization in Spanish must be an automatic consequence of the speech mechanism, since it reflects the minimum time necessary for the lowering gesture of the velum. But the interpretation of contextual changes in terms of a strict dichotomy between universal and language-specific variations fails to account for the many cross-language data showing that coarticulation differs in degree across languages: a typical example is Clumeck's study on velar coarticulation, which was found to differ in temporal extent across all the six languages analyzed (Clumeck, 1976). In this case, what criterion can be used to decide in which language the patterns are unintentional and automatic, and in which they are to be ascribed to the grammar?

Likewise, within a language, context-dependent variations may exhibit different articulatory patterns which can be interpreted either as the result of different underlying processes, or just as quantitative variations resulting from the same underlying mechanism. For example, Figure 12.4 shows the variations of the articulation of the phoneme /n/ as a function of the following

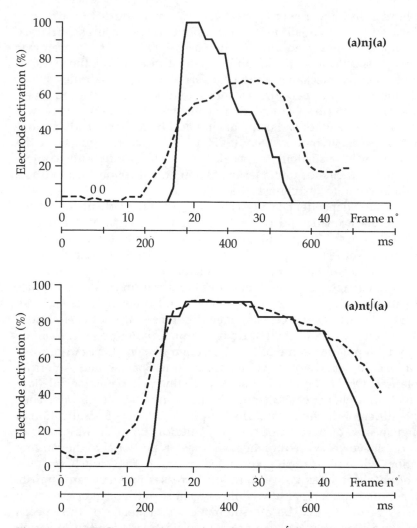

Figure 12.4 EPG curves during /anja/ and (antʃa/ produced by an Italian subject. Continuous lines: tongue-tip/blade contact; dashed lines: tongue body contact, (from Farnetani, 1986).

context, a palatal semivowel (in /anja/) and a postalveolar affricate consonant (in /antʃa/). The utterances are pseudowords produced in isolation by an Italian speaker, and analyzed with EPG.

In each graph in Figure 12.4 the two curves represent the evolution of the tongue-to-palate contact over time. We can see that in /anja/, as the tongue tip/blade (continuous line) achieves maximum front contact for /n/ closure, the tongue body (dashed line) moves smoothly from /a/ to /j/ suggesting overlapping activity of two distinct articulators, and two distinct goals. In /antʃa/, instead, the typical /n/ configuration has disappeared; the front contact has decreased by some percentage points, and the back contact has appreciably increased; the cluster seems to be produced with one tongue movement. These differences may indicate that two distinct processes are at work in the two utterances: anti-cipatory coarticulation of /j/ on /n/ in the former, and place assimilation of /n/ to /ʧ/ in the latter. Another possible interpretation is that both patterns are instances of coarticulation: they differ because the gestures overlapping /n/ are different and impose different constraints on its articulation; the greater amount of /n/ palatalization in /anʧa/ than in /anja/ would simply be the outcome of such different constraints.

Current theories of coarticulation offer controversial views on whether there are qualitative or quantitative or even no differences between assimilatory and coarticulatory processes. It will be seen that at the core of the different positions are different answers to the fundamental issues addressed above, i.e. the domain, the function and the control of coarticulation.

1.3 Connected speech processes

In speech the phonetic form of a word is not invariable, but can vary as a function of a number of linguistic, communicative and pragmatic factors (e.g. information structure, style, communicative situation): these variations are generally referred to as *alternations*, and the phonetic processes accounting for them have been termed *connected speech processes* (Jones, 1969; Gimson, 1970). According to Gimson (p. 287), these processes describe the phonetic variations that characterize continuous speech when compared to a word spoken in isolation. The author makes a detailed list of connected speech processes in English, among them: place assimilations (within and across word boundaries), assimilations of manner and voicing, reduction of vowels to schwa in unaccented words, deletions of consonants and vowels. According to the author, the factors that contribute to modify the phonetic properties of a word are "the pressure of its sound environment or of the accentual or rhythmic group of which it forms part", and the speed of the utterance (p. 287).

Kohler (1990) proposes an explanatory account of connected speech processes in German. His analysis focuses on the difference between careful and casual pronunciation of the same items and interprets all connected speech processes as a global phenomenon of reduction and articulatory simplification. These processes include /r/ vocalization (/r/ is vocalized to [ɐ] when it is not followed by vowel), weak-form, elision and assimilation. From an analysis of the sound categories most likely to undergo such changes, he infers that connected speech processes result in large part from articulatory constraints (minimization of energy), which induce a reorganization of the articulatory gestures. He also proposes a formalization of the processes in terms of sets of phonetic rules which generate any reduced segmental pronunciation.

The two accounts, although substantially different in their perspectives, have in common the assumption that connected speech processes imply modifications of the basic units of speech (elimination and replacements of articulatory gestures, changes in articulation places, etc.). Thus the difference between connected speech processes and the phonological assimilations described in 1.2 is that the latter occur independently of how a word is pronounced (SPE, p. 110), while the former occur in some cases (rapid, casual speech), but are absent in others.

Certain theories of coarticulation also consider connected speech processes and propose their own accounts. Experimental research in this field started only recently, but some interesting data are beginning to emerge, as will be seen below in section 2.4.4.

2 Theoretical accounts of coarticulation

2.1 Pioneering studies

That speech is a continuum, rather than an orderly sequence of distinct sounds as listeners perceive it, was pointed out by Sweet, as long ago as the last century (Sweet, 1877, cited by Wood, 1993). Sweet saw speech sounds as points "in a stream of incessant change" and this promoted the view that coarticulatory effects result from the transitional movements conjoining different articulatory targets and is reflected acoustically in the transitions to and from acoustic targets. Menzerath and de Lacerda (1933) showed that segments can be articulated together, not merely conjoined to each other (the term "coarticulation" is attributed to these authors). The pioneer acoustic analysis of American English vowels conducted by Joos (Joos, 1948) revealed that vowels vary as a function of neighboring consonants not only during the transitional periods but also during their steady state. Referring to temporal evolution of the second formant, Joos observed that "the effect of each consonant extends past the middle of the vowel so that at the middle the two effects overlap" (p. 105). In his theoretical account of the phenomenon he contests the "glide" hypothesis, which attributes coarticulation to mechanical factors, i.e. the inertia of vocal organs and muscles. According to that view, since no shift from one articulatory position to another can take place instantaneously, a transition intervenes between successive phones. Joos proposes instead the "overlapping innervation wave theory" (p. 109): each command for each segment is an invariant "wave" that "waxes and wanes smoothly"; "waves for successive phones overlap in time".

As will be seen below, these two early hypotheses on the sequential ordering of speech segments have been highly influential in the development of coarticulation theories.

2.2 Coarticulation as speech economy

2.2.1 Speech variability   The theoretical premise at the basis of Lindblom's theory of speech variability is that the primary scope of phonetics is not to describe how linguistic forms are realized in speech, but to explain and derive the linguistic forms from "substance-based principles pertaining to the use of spoken language and its biological, sociological and communicative aspects" (Liljencrants and Lindblom, 1972, p. 859).[1] Accordingly, in his theory of "Adaptive Variability" and "Hyper-Hypo-Speech" (Lindblom, 1983, 1988, 1990), phonetic variation is not viewed as a mere consequence of the inertia of the speech mechanism, but rather as a continuous adaptation of speech production to the demands of the communicative situation. Variation arises because the production strategy at the basis of any instance of speech varies, being the result of the interaction between system-oriented and output-oriented motor control. Some situations will require an output with a high degree of perceptual contrast, others will require much less perceptual contrast and will allow more variability. Thus, the acoustic characteristics of the same item will exhibit a wide range of variation reflected along the continuum of over- to under-articulation, or hyper- to hypo-speech.

2.2.2 Low-cost and high-cost production behavior

2.2.2 Low-cost and high-cost production behavior What is the function of coarticulation within this framework? Coarticulation, manifested as a reduced displacement and a shift of movements towards the context, is a low-cost motor behavior, an economical way of speaking. Its pervasiveness indicates that the speech motor system, like other kinds of motor behavior, is governed by the principle of economy.

In his study of vowel reduction, Lindblom (1963) introduced the notion of *acoustic target*, an ideal context-free spectral configuration (represented for vowels by the asymptotic values towards which formant frequencies aim). Lindblom's study showed that targets are quite often not realized: his data on CVC syllables indicated that the values of formant frequencies at mid-vowel point change monotonically with changes in vowel duration. At long durations, formants tend to reach the target values; as duration decreases, the formant movements are reduced (target undershoot) and tend to shift towards the values of the adjacent consonants, as shown in Figure 12.5.

The continuous nature of the process indicated that vowel reduction is an articulatory process, largely dependent on duration, rather than a phonological process. The direction of the change towards the context, as well as the different degree of undershoot as a function of the extent of the CV transitions (the amount of vowel reduction is minimal when the consonant-to-vowel distance is small), indicated that reduction is a coarticulatory process rather than a centralization process towards a schwa-like configuration.[2]

Lindblom's account of the relation between duration, target undershoot and coarticulation was that reduction is the automatic response of the motor system to an increase in rate of motor commands. When successive commands on one articulator are issued at very short temporal intervals, the articulator has insufficient time to complete the response before the next signal arrives, and has to respond to different commands simultaneously. This induces both vowel shortening and reduced formant displacement. Subsequent research showed that the system response to high rate commands does not automatically result in reduced movements (Kuehn and Moll, 1976; Gay, 1978), and that reduction

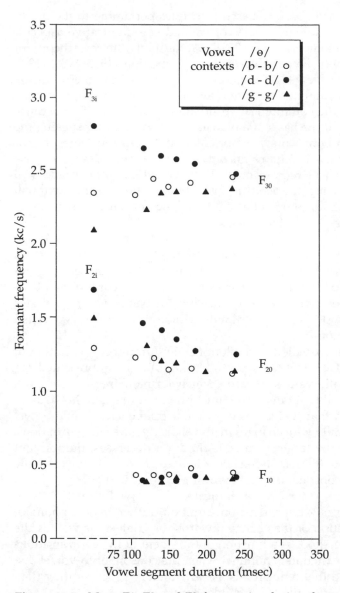

Figure 12.5 Mean F1, F2 and F3 frequencies during the steady state of the Swedish vowel /ɵ/ plotted against vowel duration. The vowel is in the contexts of /b/, /d/ and /g/. As the vowel shortens, the F2 and F3 frequencies shift towards the formant values of the /bV/, /dV/ and /gV/ initial boundaries, F2i and F3i (from Lindblom, 1963).

can occur also at slow rates (Nord, 1986). This indicated that speakers can adapt to different speaking situations and choose different production strategies to avoid reduction/coarticulation or to allow it to occur (these were the premises of Lindblom's hyper-/hypo-speech theory, as mentioned in 2.2.1).

In the recent, revised model of vowel undershoot (Moon and Lindblom, 1994), vowel duration is still the main factor, but variables associated with speech style, such as the rate of formant frequency change, can substantially modify the amount of formant undershoot. The model is based on an acoustic study of American English stressed vowels produced in clear speech style and in citation forms (i.e. overarticulated vs normal speech). The results on vowel durations and F2 frequencies indicate that in clear speech the vowels tend to be longer and less reduced than in citation forms, and in the cases where the durations overlap in the two styles, clear speech exhibits a smaller amount of undershoot. A second finding is that clear speech is in most cases characterized by larger formant velocity values than citation forms. This means that for a given duration, the degree of context-dependent undershoot depends on speech style and tends to decrease with an increase in velocity of the articulatory movements. In the model (where the speech motor mechanism is seen as a second-order mechanical system) it is proposed that undershoot is controlled by three variables reflecting the articulation strategies available to speakers under different circumstances: duration, as expected, input articulatory force and time constant of the system. An increase in input force and/or an increase in speed of the system response (i.e. a decrease in stiffness) contribute to increase the movement amplitude/velocity, and hence to decrease the amount of context-dependent undershoot. Thus, clear speech reflects an undershoot-compensatory reorganization of articulatory gestures.

Another experiment (Lindblom, Pauli and Sundberg, 1975) shows that a low-cost production strategy, characterized by coarticulatory variations, is the norm in natural speech. The authors analyzed apical consonants in VCV utterances. Using a numerical model of apical stop production, the authors showed that the best match between the output of the model and the spectrographic data of natural VCV utterances produced in isolation, is a tongue configuration always compatible with the apical closure but characterized by a minimal displacement from the preceding vowels. In other words, among a number of tongue body shapes that facilitate the tongue tip closure, the tongue body always tends to take those requiring the least movement and an adaptation to the configuration of the adjacent vowels.

Lindblom's hypothesis that the more speech style shifts towards the hypo-speech pole the larger will be the amount of coarticulation is confirmed by a number of studies on connected speech: Krull (1987, 1989), for Swedish; Duez (1991) for French; Farnetani (1991) for Italian.

2.2.3 *Phonological adaptations*   Lindblom (1983) makes a clear distinction between coarticulation/target-undershoot and assimilation. The former, as seen above, is a continuous motor process, increasing in magnitude in connected

spontaneous speech, the latter is a categorical change, a language-specific grammatical rule. Assimilation is a consequence of coarticulation, an adaptation of language to speech constraints (see Ohala, THE RELATION BETWEEN PHONETICS AND PHONOLOGY).

2.3 Coarticulation as "creature" of the Language Grammar

The evolution of featural phonology after SPE, is marked by a gradual appropriation of coarticulation into the domain of linguistic competence.

2.3.1 The theory of feature-spreading
Daniloff and Hammarberg (1973), and Hammarberg (1976) were the promotors of the "feature spreading" account of coarticulation. According to Hammarberg (1976), the view that coarticulation is a purely physiological process due to mechano-inertial constraints of the speech apparatus entails a sharp dichotomy between intent and execution, and implies that the articulators are unable to carry out the commands as specified. The only way to overcome this dichotomy is to assume that coarticulation itself is part of the phonological component. The arguments in support of this assumption are that: 1) phonology is prior to phonetics; 2) phonological segments are abstract cognitive entities, and cannot be altered by the speech mechanism (in order to be altered they would have to be physical): all that the physical mechanism can do is to execute higher level commands. Therefore the variations attributed to coarticulation must be the input to the speech mechanism, rather than its output. How? Segments have both inherent properties (the phonological features) and derived properties. These latter result from the coarticulation process, which alters the properties of a segment. Phonological rules stipulate which features get modified, and the phonetic representation, output of the phonological rules and input to the speech mechanism, specifies the relevant details of articulation and coarticulation. This departure from Chomsky and Halle's view of coarticulation was probably necessary, in face of the emerging experimental data on coarticulation: data on anticipatory lip protrusion, (Daniloff and Moll, 1968) and on velar coarticulation, (Moll and Daniloff, 1971) showed that coarticulatory movements could be initiated at least two segments before the influencing one. This indicated that coarticulation is not the product of inertia. Another reason (Hammarberg, 1976) was that coarticulation could not be accounted for by universal rules as assumed in SPE, owing to cross-language differences such as those pointed out by Ladefoged (1967) between English and French in the coarticulation of velar stops with front and back vowels.

Why does coarticulation occur? The function of coarticulation is to smooth out the differences between adjacent sounds: if phonemes were executed in their canonical forms, the speech mechanism would introduce transitional sounds between executions of contiguous segments. Coarticulatory modifications accomodate the segments so that when they are realized, the transitions between them are minimized. Thus coarticulatory rules serve to reduce what the vocal tract introduces when we speak. Notice that, according to SPE (see 1.2), and to the "glide" hypothesis of coarticulation (see 2.1), the transitions between segments are the effects of coarticulation, while here they are what the coarticulation rules have to minimize. In Daniloff and Hammarberg's view anticipatory coarticulation is always a deliberate phonological process, while carryover coarticulation can be in part the effect of the inertia of the speech organs and in part a feed-back assisted strategy that accomodates speech segments to each other. The authors acknowledge that no clear phonological explanation in terms of feature spreading can be found for a number of contextual variations such as the lengthening of vowels before a voiced consonant, or the lack of aspiration in obstruent stops after /s/.

2.3.2 Henke's articulatory model According to Daniloff and Hammarberg (1973) the articulatory model of Henke (1966) best accounts for experimental data on the extent of coarticulation. Henke's model contrasts with another well known account of coarticulation, the articulatory syllable model proposed by Kozhevnikov and Chistovich (1965). This model was based on data on anticipatory labial coarticulation in Russian. Segments seemed to coarticulate within, but not across, C_nV sequences. The C_nV-type syllable was thus viewed as the articulatory domain of coarticulation, and its boundaries as the boundaries of coarticulation. Unlike the C_nV model, Henke's model does not impose top-down boundaries to anticipatory coarticulation. Input segments are specified for articulatory targets in terms of binary phonological features (+ or −), with features unspecified in the phonology being given a value of 0 (Moll and Daniloff, 1971). Coarticulatory rules assign a feature of a segment to all the preceding segments unspecified for that feature, by means of a look-ahead scanning mechanism. The spread of features is blocked only by a specified feature. So, the nasality feature inherent in a nasal consonant [+nasal] will be anticipated to all the preceding segments unspecified for nasality. Likewise, after the nasal, if a segment specified as [−nasal] follows, the feature [−nasal] will be applied immediately to the first unspecified segment after the nasal. Obviously a look-ahead mechanism intrinsically impedes carryover coarticulation, for which, as seen above, Daniloff and Hammarberg devised other explanations.

2.3.3 Feature specification and coarticulation: towards the concept of coarticulation resistance A number of experimental results, such as those mentioned in 2.3.1, are compatible with the hypothesis of feature spreading and the look-ahead mechanism, but many others contradict the spatial and/ or the temporal predictions of the model. First, the model cannot explain the quite extensive carryover effects observed in a number of studies on V-to-V coarticulation (for example Recasens, 1989; Magen, 1989). The other disputed aspects of the theory are: 1) the adequacy of the concept of specified vs unspecified features for blocking or allowing coarticulation to occur; 2) the hypothesis that a look-ahead mechanism accounts for the temporal extent of anticipatory coarticulation (this point will be developed below in section 2.4.3).

As for the first issue, it appears that segments specified for a contradictory feature in asymmetric V_1CV_2 type sequences can nonetheless be modified by coarticulation. Data on lip rounding in French (Benguerel and Cowan, 1974) and English (Sussman and Westbury, 1981) indicate that, in an /iC_nu/ sequence type, rounding movements for /u/ can start during /i/, specified as [–round]. Also data on lingual coarticulation indicate that tongue displacement towards a vowel can begin during a preceding cross-consonantal vowel even if this is specified for conflicting features with respect to the following vowel, for example /a/ vs /i/ (Öhman, 1966, for Swedish and English; Butcher and Weiher, 1976, for German; Farnetani, Vagges and Magno Caldognetto, 1985, for Italian; Magen, 1989, for American English). Most interestingly, these transconsonantal V-to-V effects appear to vary in degree across languages, indicating that the *same* vowel categories in different languages are subject to different constraints that favor or disfavor coarticulatory variations (see Manuel and Krakow, 1984, comparing Swahili, Shona and English; Manuel, 1987, comparing three Bantu languages; Choi and Keating, 1991, comparing English, Polish, Russian and Bulgarian).

As for phonologically unspecified segments, some experimental data are compatible with the idea that they completely acquire a contextual feature.

Figure 12.6 illustrates how the Japanese vowel /e/, unspecified for nasality, acquires the nasality feature in a symmetric context as predicted by the feature spreading model. The figure shows the amount of velum height during the vowel /e/ in Japanese, surrounded by oral consonants (a), by nasal consonants (c), and in a mixed environment (b). It can be seen that during /e/ the velum is as high as for oral consonants in (a), and as low as for nasal consonants in (c): in both cases the velum height curve runs nearly flat across the vowel. In the asymmetric example (b) the curve traces a trajectory from a high to a low position during the /e/ preceded by /s/ and the reverse trajectory during the /e/ followed by /d/. The symmetric sequences show that /e/ is completely oral in an oral context and completely nasalized in a nasal context, indicating that this vowel has no velar target of its own and acquires that of the context. The trajectories in the asymmetric sequences do not contradict the hypothesis that this vowel has no target for velar position, but contradict the assumption that contextual features are spread in a categorical way. Accordingly, /e/ would have to be completely nasalized from its onset when followed by a nasal, and completely oral when followed by an oral consonant, and this does not seem to occur (see panel b).

Many other data indicate that phonologically unspecified segments may nonetheless exhibit some resistance to coarticulation, indicating that they are specified for articulatory targets. English data on velar movements (Bell-Berti, 1980; Bell-Berti and Krakow, 1991) show that the oral vowels are not articulatorily neutral to velar height, and have their own specific velar positions

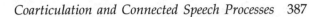

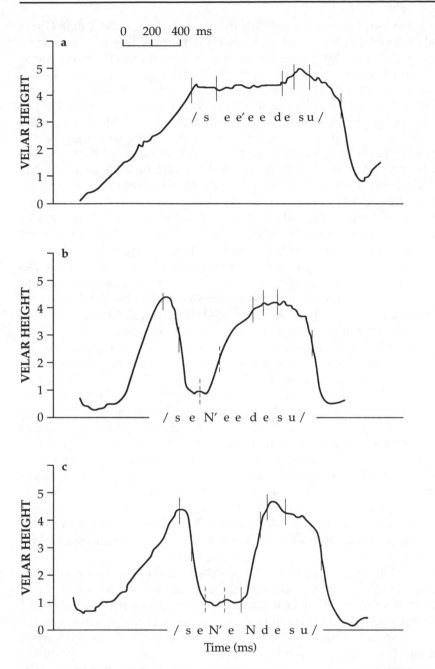

Figure 12.6 Velar movements observed with fiberscope during Japanese utterances containing the vowel /e/ in oral and nasal contexts (from Ushijima and Sawashima, 1972).

even in a non-nasal environment. As for lip position, Engstrand's data (1981) show that in Swedish /u-u/ sequences with intervocalic lingual consonants, protrusion of the upper lip relaxes during the consonants and the curve forms a "trough" between the vowels, suggesting that such consonants are not completely neutral to lip position. For lingual coarticulation, troughs in lingual muscles' activity during /ipi/ sequences were first observed in the 1974 study by Bell-Berti and Harris. Analogously, at the articulatory level, Engstrand (1983) observed that the vertical movement of the tongue in /ipi/ sequences shows troughs during the consonant, indicating that bilabial voiceless stops may be specified for lingual position, possibly to meet the aerodynamic requirements for the bilabial release burst to occur, and for avoiding turbulence noise during the transition to V2.

Subsequent research on lingual consonants in Catalan, Swedish and Italian (Recasens, 1983, 1984a, 1987; Engstrand, 1989; Farnetani, 1990, 1991) showed that consonants unspecified for tongue body features coarticulate to different degrees with the surrounding vowels. During the production of coronals, the amount of tongue body coarticulation tends to decrease from alveolars to postalveolars and from liquids to stops to fricatives (Farnetani, 1991, data on Italian); a similar trend is observed in Swedish (Engstrand, 1989).

Figure 12.7 is an example of how different consonants coarticulate to different degrees with the surrounding vowels /i/ and /a/ in Italian, as measured by EPG. The trajectories represent the amount of tongue body contact over time during intervocalic coronals /t/, /d/, /z/, /ʃ/, /l/ and bilabial /p/ in symmetric VCV sequences. The /i-i/ trajectories exhibit troughs of moderate degree for most consonants; /z/ shows the largest deviation from the /i/ to /i/ trajectory (see points V1 and V2), indicating that the production of this consonant requires a lowering of the tongue body from the /i/-like position. In the context of /a/ (see points V1 and V2 in this context), /p/ appears to fully coarticulate with this vowel, as it shows no contact; also /l/ strongly coarticulates with /a/. For /t/, /d/, /z/ the tongue body needs to increase the contact to about 20 per cent. During /ʃ/ it can be seen that the tongue body contact reaches the same value (between 50 per cent and 60 per cent) in the two vocalic contexts, indicating that this consonant is maximally resistant to coarticulation.

The overall data on tongue body V-to-C coarticulation indicate that no alveolar consonant fully coarticulates with the adjacent vowels, which suggests the presence of a functional and/or physical coupling between tip/blade and body. The differences in coarticulation across consonants can be accounted for by consonant specific production constraints imposed on the tongue body. Fricatives must constrain tongue dorsum position to ensure the appropriate front constriction and the intraoral pressure required for noise production; the production of stops and laterals imposes lesser constraints, and allows for a wider range of coarticulatory variations. As will be seen in 2.3.4, Keating (1988), on the basis of coarticulatory data, will propose that English /s/ be specified as [+high] for tongue body position.

The notion of coarticulation resistance was introduced by Bladon and

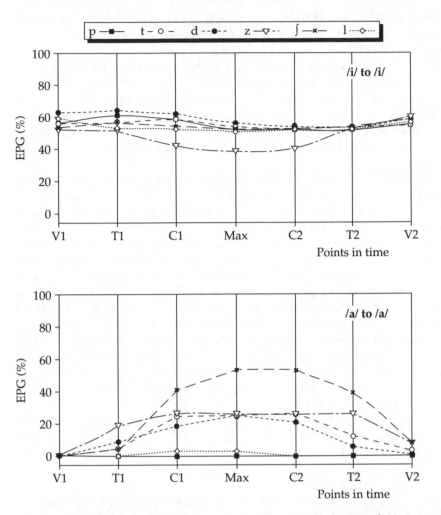

Figure 12.7 Tongue body EPG contact at various points in time during symmetric (C)VCV isolated words in Italian. V1, V2 correspond to vowel mid-points; T1, T2 to offset of V1 and onset of V2 respectively; C1, C2 correspond to onset and release of consonant closures/constrictions respectively; Max refers to the point of maximum contact during the consonant (from Farnetani, 1991).

Al-Bamerni (1976) in an acoustic study of V-to-C coarticulation in /l/ allophones (clear vs dark vs syllabic /l/). The data indicated that coarticulatory variations decrease continuously from clear to syllabic /l/. These graded differences could not be accounted for by binary feature analysis, which would block coarticulation in dark /l/, specified as [+back]. The authors propose a numerical index of coarticulation resistance to be attached to the feature specification of each allophone. A subsequent study on tongue tip/blade displacement in alveolars (Bladon and Nolan, 1977) confirmed the idea that feature specification alone cannot account for the observed coarticulatory behavior.

All these studies show that the assignment of contextual binary features to unspecified segments through phonological rules fails to account for the presence vs absence of coarticulation, for its graded nature, and for the linguistically relevant aspects of coarticulation associated with this graded nature i.e. the different degree of coarticulation exhibited by the *same* segments across languages. Explanation of these facts requires factors outside the world of phonological features: *articulatory constraints* and *aerodynamic-acoustic constraints*. Manuel (1987, 1990) proposes that interlanguage differences in coarticulation may be controlled by perceptual *output constraints* (see 2.3.4).

2.3.4 *The window model of coarticulation*   Keating (1985, 1988a, 1988b, 1990) proposes a new articulatory model which can account for the continuous changes in space and time observed in speech, and for intersegment and interlanguage differences in coarticulation.

On one hand Keating agrees that phonological rules cannot account for the graded nature of coarticulation. At the same time she contests the assumption that such graded variations are to be ascribed to phonetic universals as automatic consequences of the speech production mechanism (Keating, 1985). One example is the duration of vowels as a function of the voiceless vs voiced consonantal context. Vowels tend to be shorter before voiceless than before voiced stops, but these patterns are not the same across languages. Keating shows that in English the differences in vowel durations are relevant and systematic, while in other languages such as Polish and Czech they are unsystematic or even absent. Therefore each language must specify these phonetic facts in its grammar.

Keating's proposal is that all graded spatial and temporal contextual variations, both those assumed to be phonological, and those assumed to be universal and physically determined, be accounted for by the *phonetic* rules of the grammar.

The windows   Keating's model marks a substantial departure from the feature-spreading model, first because it assumes that phonological underspecification (i.e. unspecified features) may persist into the phonetic representation, and second because underspecification in this model is not a categorical, but a continuous notion. Input to the window model is the phonological representation in terms of binary features. Unspecified segments may be left unspecified, or can acquire specifications through a number of language specific phonological rules. For instance, English /s/ is assumed to acquire the feature [+high] through fill-in rules, owing to aerodynamic constraints requiring a high tongue body position for its production; there are context-sensitive rules, such as those that specify Russian /x/ as [−back] before high vowels; in some languages there may be assimilation rules like those proposed in the feature-spreading model (see below for expansion).

Implementation rules interpret the output of the phonological component in space and time and provide a continuous phonetic representation. For a given articulatory or acoustic dimension a feature value is associated with a range

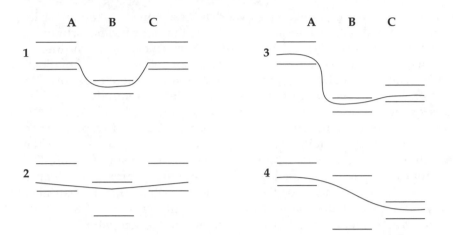

Figure 12.8 Windows and paths modeling articulator movements in three-segment sequences (selected from Keating, 1988a). The effects of narrow vs. wide windows on the interpolation contours can be observed in both the symmetric (1, 2) and the asymmetric (3, 4) sequences.

of values called a *window*. Windows have their own duration, and a width representing the entire range of contextual variability of a segment. Window widths depend first of all on phonological information: specified features are associated with narrow windows and allow for *little* contextual variation, unspecified features are associated with wide windows and allow for *large* contextual variation. Quantitative information on the maximum amount of contextual variability observed in speech will determine the exact window width for a given dimension, so that all the intermediate degrees between maximally wide and maximally narrow windows are possible.

Adjacent windows are connected by "paths" (or contours), which are interpolation functions between windows, and are constrained by the requirements of smoothness and minimal articulatory effort. Paths should represent the articulatory or acoustic variations over time in a specific context. Figure 12.8 shows some selected sequences of windows and contours.

Wide windows contribute nothing to the contour and allow direct interpolation between the preceding and the following segment. For instance, in VCV sequences, if C is unspecified for tongue body position, its associated window will not be seen as a target, and will allow V-to-V interpolation (and coarticulatory effects) to occur (see sequence 4 in Figure 12.8). If instead C is specified, its associated narrow window will allow local V-to-C effects but will block V-to-V effects: in this case the contour will be constrained to take place quickly between the two narrow windows (see sequences 1 and 3 in Figure 12.8). It can be seen that the middle window of sequence 2 is not as wide as to allow direct interpolation between the first and the third segment: according to Keating, such patterns indicate that the segment is not completely unspecified. An example of "not quite unspecified" segments are English vowels with respect to phonetic nasality. Keating shows that these vowels (phonologically unspecified for nasality) are associated with wide but not maximal windows, and in some contexts they reveal their inherent specification. According to Keating, this occurs because underspecification is categorical at the phonological level, but continuous in the surface representation, and therefore allows for a variety of window widths: in any case wide windows specify very little about a segment. On this crucial point, Boyce, Krakow and Bell-Berti (1991) argue that, if supposedly unspecified segments are associated in production with characteristic articulatory positions, it becomes hard to reconcile the demonstration of any kind of target with the notion of underspecification. The authors propose instead that phonologically unspecified features can influence speech production in another way: they may be associated with cross-speaker variability (as shown in their lip-protrusion data during unspecified consonants), and cross-dialectal variability (see below, for a compatible account proposed by Keating for cross-language phonetic differences).

Cross-language differences　According to Keating, interlanguage differences in coarticulation may originate from phonology or from phonetics. Phonological differences occur when, for a given feature, phonological assimilatory rules operate in one language and not in another. Phonetic differences are due to a different phonetic interpretation of a feature left unspecified. Speech analysis will help determine which differences are phonological and which are phonetic.

In a study of nasalization in English using airflow measurement, Cohn (1993) compared the nasal flow contour in nasalized vowels in English with the contour of nasal vowels in French and of nasalized vowels in Sundanese. In French vowels nasality is phonological, in Sundanese it is described as the output of a phonological spreading rule. Cohn found that in the nasalized vowels of Sundanese the flow patterns have plateau-like shapes very similar to the French patterns. In nasalized English vowels, instead, the shapes of the contours describe smooth, rapid trajectories from the [−nasal] to the [+nasal] adjacent segments. The categorical vs the gradient quality of nasalization in Sundanese vs English indicates that nasalization is indeed phonological in Sundanese (i.e. the output of phonological assimilatory rules), while in English it results from phonetic interpolation rules.[3]

Languages may also differ in coarticulation because the phonetic rules can interpret phonological underspecification in different ways in different languages, allowing the windows to be more or less wide. In this case interlanguage differences are only quantitative. "Window width is to some extent an idiosyncratic aspect that languages specify about the phonetics of their sounds and features" (Keating, 1988a, p. 22).

Manuel (1987) disagrees with Keating's proposition that all phonetic changes have to be accounted for by grammatical rules simply because they are not universal. Referring to interlanguage differences in V-to-V coarticulation, Manuel proposes that language-particular behavior, apparently arbitrary, can itself be deduced from the interaction between universal characteristics of the motor system and language specific phonological facts, such as the inventory and distribution of vowel phonemes. Her hypothesis is that V-to-V coarticulation is regulated in each language by the requirement that the perceptual contrast among vowels is preserved, i.e. by *output constraints*, which can be strict in some languages and rather loose in others. Languages with smaller vowel inventories, where there is less possibility of confusion, should allow more coarticulatory variations than languages with a larger number of vowels, where coarticulation may lead to articulatory/acoustic overlap of adjacent vowel spaces. This hypothesis was tested by comparing languages with different vowel inventories (Manuel and Krakow, 1984; Manuel, 1987). The results of both studies support the output constraints hypothesis. Thus, if the output constraints of a given language are related to its inventory size and to the distribution of vowels in the articulatory/acoustic space, then no particular language specific phonetic rules are needed, since different degrees of coarticulation across languages can be to some extent predictable.

Connected speech   Keating does not deal with the problem of phonetic variations due to factors other than the segmental phonetic context, for instance with the phonetic differences characterizing different speaking styles. In the present version of the model, windows have no internal temporal structure allowing them to stretch or compress in time, and their width is intended to represent all possible contextual variations. So at present, samples of strongly coarticulated informal speech and samples of clear speech cannot be differentiated. A recent neural network model proposed by Guenther (1994b) allows targets (viewed as regions in the orosensory coordinates) to increase or reduce in size, as a function of rate and accuracy in production, and thus overcomes the present limitations of the window model. On the other hand, if the windows associated with specified features were allowed to stretch in width in continuous informal speech, then the relation between feature specification at the phonological level and window width at the phonetic level would become much weaker.

2.4 *Coarticulation as coproduction*

The coproduction theory has been elaborated through collaborative work of psychologists and linguists, starting from Fowler (1977, 1980, 1985), Fowler, Rubin, Remez and Turvey (1980), and Bell-Berti and Harris (1981). In conjunction with the new theory, Kelso, Saltzman and Tuller (1986), Saltzman and Munhall (1989), Saltzman (1991) have developed a computational model, the *task-dynamic model*, whose aim is to account for the kinematics of articulators in speech. Input to the model are the *phonetic gestures*, the dynamically defined units of *gestural phonology*, proposed as an alternative to segments and features by Browman and Goldstein (1986, 1989, 1990a, 1990b, 1992).

The present account centers on four topics: the nature of phonological units, coarticulation resistance, anticipatory coarticulation and connected speech processes.

2.4.1 *The dynamic nature of phonological units*   The central point of Fowler's criticism of feature-based theories (Fowler, 1977, 1980) is the dichotomy between the abstract, discrete and timeless units posited at the level of language knowledge, and the physical, continuous and context-dependent movements at the level of performance. In other words, she contests the assumption that what speakers know about the phonological categories of their language is substantially different from the units they use when they speak. According to Fowler, all current accounts of speech production need a translation process between the abstract and the physical domain: the speech plan supplies the spatial targets to be reached, and a central clock specifies when the articulators have to move to the targets: "The articulator movements are excluded from the domain of the plan except as it is implied by the different successive articulatory positions" (Fowler, 1977, p. 99). An alternative proposal that overcomes the dichotomy between linguistic and production units and gets rid of a time program separated from the plan is to *modify the phonological units* of the plan. The plan must specify *the act* to be executed, not only describe "an abstract summary of its significance" (Fowler et al., 1980, p. 381). These units, the gestures, must be serially ordered planned actions, specified dynamically, and context-free. It is their specification in terms of dynamic parameters (such as force, stiffness) that automatically determines the kinematics of the speech movements. Gestures have their own intrinsic temporal structure, which allows them to overlap in time when executed; the degree of gestural overlap is controlled at the plan level. So gestures are not altered by adjacent gestures, they just overlap (i.e. are coproduced) with adjacent gestures.

Figure 12.9 illustrates coproduction of gestures. The activation of a gesture increases and decreases smoothly in time, and so does its influence on the vocal tract shape. In the figure, the vertical lines delimit a temporal interval (possibly corresponding to an acoustic segment) during which gesture 2 is prominent, i.e. has maximal influence on the vocal tract shape, while the overlapping gestures 1 and 3 have weaker influences. Before and after this interval (i.e. during the implementation and relaxation period of gesture 2, respectively) its influence is less, while that of the other two gestures supervenes.

The view of gestures as intervals of activation gradually waxing and waning in time, echoes the early insight of Joos (1948) who proposed the "innervation wave theory" to account for coarticulation (cf. 2.1).

2.4.2 *Coarticulation resistance*   Gestures are implemented in speech by coordinative structures, i.e. by transient functional dependencies among the articulators that contribute to a gesture. These constraints are established to ensure invariance of the phonetic goal; for instance, upper lip, lower lip, and jaw are functionally linked in the production of bilabial closures, so that one

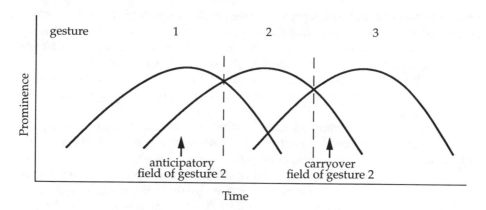

Figure 12.9 Representation of a sequence of three overlapping gestures (from Fowler and Saltzman, 1993). Notice the similarity of this representation of gestural activation and gestural overlap to actual data on EMG activity and overlap illustrated in Figure 12.1.

will automatically compensate for a decreased contribution of another due to perturbation or coarticulatory variations (see Löfqvist, Theories and Models of Speech Production and Perkell, Articulatory Processes).

How are coarticulatory variations accounted for within the gestural framework? According to Fowler and Saltzman (1993) variations induced by coproduction depend on the degree to which the gestures share articulators, i.e. on the degree of spatial overlap. When subsequent gestures share only one articulator, such as the jaw in /VbV/ sequences, the effects of gestural interference will be irrelevant, and temporal overlap between vocalic and consonantal gestures will take place with minimal spatial perturbations. The highest degree of spatial overlap occurs when two overlapping gestures share the articulators directly involved in the production of gestural goals, and impose competing demands on them. In Bell-Berti and Harris (1981) it is proposed that gestural conflict be resolved by delaying the onset of the competing gesture so that the ongoing goal can be achieved, i.e. the conflict is resolved at the plan level. Browman and Goldstein (1989), Saltzman and Munhall (1989) propose that the phasing of gestures may be context free and that the output of a gestural conflict may be simply a blend of the influence of the overlapping gestures. According to Fowler and Saltzman (1993), the outcome of gestural blending depends on the degree of "blending strength" associated with the overlapping gestures: "stronger" gestures tend to suppress the influence of "weaker" gestures, while the blending of gestures of similar strength will result in an averaging of the two influences. Fowler and Saltzman's account of coarticulation resistance implies that gestures with a high degree of blending strength resist interference from other gestures, and at the same time themselves induce strong coarticulatory effects, in agreement with experimental findings (Bladon and Nolan, 1977; Recasens, 1984b; Farnetani and Recasens,

1993). On this account, the highest degree of blending strength appears to be associated with consonants requiring extreme constrictions, and/or placing strong constraints on articulator movements, while a moderate degree of blending strength appears to be associated with vowels (see a compatible proposal by Lindblom, 1983, that coarticulatory adaptability, maximal in vowels and minimal in lingual fricatives, varies as a function of the phonotactically based sonority categories).

The coproduction account of coordination and coarticulation also implies that speakers do not need a continuous feedforward control of the acoustic output and consequent articulatory adjustments. Likewise, cross-language differences do not result from on-line control of the output. Languages may differ in degree of coarticulation in relation to their inventories, but these differences are consequences of the different gestural set-up, i.e. the parameters that specify the dynamics of gestures and their overlap, which are learned by speakers of different languages during speech development.

2.4.3 *Anticipatory extent of coarticulation*   According to the coproduction theory, gestures have their own intrinsic duration. Hence the temporal extent of anticipatory coarticulation must be constant for a given gesture. Compatibly, Bell-Berti and Harris (1979, 1981, 1982), on the basis of experimental data on lip rounding and velar lowering, proposed the "frame" model of anticipatory coarticulation (also referred to as the time-locked model): the onset of an articulator movement is independent of the preceding phone string length and begins at a fixed time before the acoustic onset of the segment with which it is associated. Other studies, however, are consistent with the look-ahead model (see 2.3.2) and indicate that the onset of lip rounding or velar lowering is not fixed, but extends in the anticipatory direction as a function of the number of neutral segments preceding the influencing segment (see, for lip rounding coarticulation, Daniloff and Moll, 1968; Benguerel and Cowan, 1974; Lubker 1981; Sussman and Westbury, 1981; and for velar coarticulation, Moll and Daniloff, 1971). Yet, other results on velar coarticulation in Japanese (Ushijima and Sawashima, 1972; Ushijima and Hirose, 1974) and in French (Benguerel, Hirose, Sawashima and Ushijima, 1977a) indicate that velar lowering for a nasal consonant does not start earlier in sequences of two than in sequences of three oral vowels preceding the nasal. An important finding of Benguerel et al. (1977a), apparently disregarded in the literature, was the distinction between the velar lowering associated with the oral segments preceding the nasal, and a subsequent more rapid velar lowering for the nasal which causes the opening of the velar port. Al-Bamerni and Bladon (1982) made similar observations on velar coarticulation in CV_nN sequences in English: the speakers seemed to use two production strategies, a single velar opening gesture (one-stage pattern), and a two-stage gesture whose onset was aligned with the first non-nasal vowel and whose higher velocity stage was coordinated with the nasal consonant. Perkell and Chiang (1986) and Perkell (1990) were the first to observe two-stage patterns in lip rounding movements, which converged

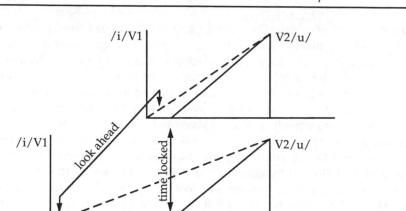

Figure 12.10 Schematic representation of the three models of anticipatory lip rounding coarticulation proposed by Perkell (see text for description).

with Al-Bamerni and Bladon's observations: in /iC$_n$u/ utterances there was a gradual onset of lip protrusion linked to the offset of /i/, followed by an increase in velocity during the consonants with an additional protrusion closely linked with /u/, and quite invariant. The authors interpreted the composite movements of the two-stage patterns as a mixed coarticulation strategy, and proposed a third model of anticipatory coarticulation, the *hybrid model*. Accordingly, the early onset of the protrusion movement would reflect a look-ahead strategy, while the rapid increase in protrusion at a fixed interval before the rounded vowel would reflect a time-locked strategy. Figure 12.10 compares the three models of anticipatory coarticulation. Perkell's data on three English subjects (Perkell, 1990) indicated that two of the three subjects used the two-stage pattern, compatible with the hybrid model.

Boyce, Krakow, Bell-Berti and Gelfer (1990) argue that many of the conflicting results on the extent of anticipatory coarticulation stem from the assumption that phonologically unspecified segments are also articulatorily neutral (see 2.3.3 on this problem); a number of studies have attributed the onset of lip rounding or velar lowering to anticipatory coarticulation without testing first whether or not the phonologically neutral segments had specific target positions for lips or velum. The authors also argue against the hypothesis put forth by Al-Bamerni and Bladon that the occurrence of one-stage and two-stage patterns of anticipatory coarticulation might occur randomly. The data by Bell-Berti and Krakow (1991) on velar lowering show, through comparisons between vowels in nasal vs oral context, that the early onset of velar lowering in the two-stage patterns is associated with the characteristic velar positions of the oral vowels, while the second stage, temporally quite stable, is associated with the production of the nasal consonant; therefore the two-stage patterns do not reflect a mixture of two coarticulation strategies, but simply a vocalic gesture followed by consonantal gestures. Moreover the study shows that the patterns of velar movements do not change randomly, but depend on speech rate and the number of vowels in the string, the two-movement patterns prevailing in longer utterances and the one-movement patterns in shorter utterances. These variations, according to the authors, simply reflect different degrees of blending between the vocalic and the consonantal gestures, which sum together into a single movement when they are temporally adjacent.

In a subsequent study on four American speakers, Perkell and Matthies (1992) tested whether the onset of the initial phase of lip protrusion in /iC$_n$u/ utterances is related to consonant specific lip targets, as proposed by Boyce et al. (1990), and whether the second phase, from the maximum acceleration event, is indeed stable, as predicted by the hybrid and coproduction models, or is itself affected by the number of consonants. In agreement with Boyce et al. (1990), the movement patterns in the control /iC$_n$i/ utterances showed consonant-related protrusion gestures (especially for /s/), and in /iC$_n$u/ utterances it was found that lip movements begin earlier when the first consonant in the string is /s/, thus confirming the hypothesis of consonant contribution to the onset of lip movements. The analysis of the second-phase movement, i.e. of the /u/ related component of lip protrusion, revealed that the interval between the acceleration peak and the onset of /u/ was not fixed, but tended to vary as a function of consonant duration for three of the subjects (although the correlations were very low, with R^2 ranging from 0.057 to 0.35). According to the authors, the timing and the kinematics of this gesture reflect the simultaneous expression of competing constraints, that of using the same kinematics (as in the time-locked model), and that of starting the protrusion gesture for /u/ when it is permitted by the relaxation of the retraction gesture for /i/ (as in the look-ahead model). The variability between and within subjects would reflect the degree to which such constraints are expressed. Also recent data on three French subjects (Abry and Lallouache, 1995) indicate that the lip protrusion movement (from the point of maximum acceleration to that of maximum protrusion) varies in duration as a function of the consonant interval. However, its duration does not decrease from /iC$_1$y/ to /iy/ utterances, as would be predicted by the look-ahead model; in other words the lip protrusion movement can expand in time, but cannot be compressed (see Farnetani, in press, for a more detailed account of the "movement expansion" model proposed by these authors).

The possibility that the slow onset of the protrusion movement occurring around the offset of /i/ may reflect a passive movement due to the relaxation of the retraction gesture of /i/, rather than an active look-ahead mechanism has not yet been explored. Sussman and Westbury (1981), did observe that in /iC$_n$u/ sequences the onset of lip protrusion occurred before the onset of *orbicularis oris* activity, and suggested that the movement might be the passive result of the cessation of *risorius* activity, and simply reflect a return of lips to a neutral position. We believe that this problem should be investigated further.

All cross-language studies indicate that anticipatory coarticulation varies across languages: Clumeck (1976) observed that the timing and amplitude of velar lowering varies across the six languages analyzed; Lubker and Gay (1982) showed that anticipatory lip protrusion in Swedish is much more extensive than in English; a study by Boyce (1990), on lip rounding in English and Turkish, indicated that while the English patterns were consistent with the coproduction model, the plateau-like protrusion curves of Turkish marked lip rounding coarticulation as a phonological process (in agreement with Cohn's interpretation of nasality in Sundanese – see 2.3.4).

2.4.4 *Connected speech processes*

<u>Articulatory model</u> According to Browman and Goldstein (1990b, 1992) gestural phonology can give an explanatory and unifying account of apparently unrelated speech processes (coarticulation, allophonic variations, alternations) that in featural phonology require a number of separate and unrelated phonological rules. Here the phonological structure of an utterance is modeled as a set of overlapping gestures specified on different tiers (the vocal tract variables, see Figure 12.11). Quantitative (gradient) variations in overlap, or quantitative variations in gestural parameters can account for a large number of allophonic variations as a function of stress and position, as well as for the alternations observed in connected speech. Connected speech processes such as assimilations, deletions, reductions (or weakenings) can be accounted for by an *increase in gestural overlap* and a *decrease in gestural amplitude*. In casual rapid speech, subsequent consonantal gestures can so far overlap as to hide each other when they occur on different tiers, or to completely blend their characteristics when they occur on the same tier. Hiding gives rise to perceived deletions and/or assimilations, while blending gives rise to perceived assimilations. For example, the deletion of /t/ in a rapid execution of the utterance "perfect memory" is only apparent; Xray trajectories reveal the presence of the /t/ gesture, overlapped by the following /m/ gesture. Figure 12.11 shows a schematic gestural representation of part of the utterance "perfect memory" spoken in isolation (a), and within a fluent phrase (b).

In the figure the extent of each box represents the duration (or activation interval) of a gesture. It can be seen that within each word the gestures always overlap, but in version (b) the labial closure for the initial /m/ of word 2

'per<u>fect mem</u>ory'

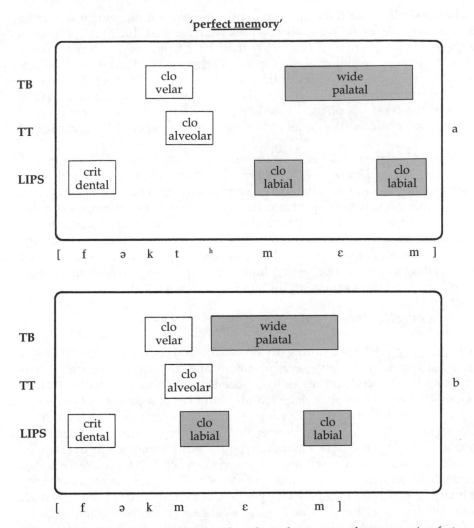

Figure 12.11   Representation of the phonological structure of utterance 'perfect memory' produced in isolation (a) and in continuous speech (b). Vocal tract variables are from top: tongue body, tongue tip and lips (from Browman and Goldstein, 1989).

overlaps and hides the alveolar gesture for final /t/ of word 1. According to the authors, hidden gestures may be extremely reduced in magnitude or completely deleted. "Even deletion, however, can be seen as an extreme reduction, and thus as an endpoint in a continuum of gestural reduction, leaving the underlying representation unchanged" (Browman and Goldstein, 1990b, p. 366).

An example of within-tiers blending is the palatalization of /s/ followed by a palatal in the utterance "this shop": the articulatory analysis should show a smooth transition between the first and the second consonant, not the substitution of the first with the second. Finally, in CVCV utterances with unstressed schwa as first vowel, the gestures on the consonantal tier can overlap the schwa gesture so far as to completely hide it, giving the impression of deletion of the unstressed syllable.

Data   As for experimental data, an increase in coarticulation and reduction in rapid, fluent speech has been shown in a number of acoustic and articulatory studies (see 2.2.2) and this is consistent with both gestural theory and Lindblom's hyper-/hypo-speech account.

The proposition that position dependent allophonic variations are continuous rather than categorical changes, is supported by experimental data on contrast neutralization (in generative phonology contrast neutralization is accounted for by rules that delete the feature(s) responsible for the contrast). Beckman and Shoji (1984), in an acoustic-perceptual experiment on vowel contrast neutralization in devoiced syllables in Japanese, show that contrast is not completely neutralized: listeners in fact are able to recover the underlying vowels /i/ and /u/, possibly from coarticulatory information present in the preceding consonant. Port and O'Dell (1985), in an acoustic-perceptual study on neutralization of voicing contrast in word-final obstruents in German, showed that voicing is not completely neutralized and that listeners are able to distinguish the voiced from the voiceless consonants with better-than-chance accuracy.

Also the majority of English data on alveolar-velar place assimilation in connected speech is consistent with the proposition that the nature of changes is gradient. EPG studies on $VC_1\#C_2V$ sequences, where C_1 is an alveolar stop, (Kerswill and Wright, 1989; Wright and Kerswill, 1989; Nolan, 1992) show an intermediate stage between absence of assimilation and complete assimilation, which the authors refer to as residual alveolar gesture. It is also shown that the occurrences of partial and complete assimilations increase from careful/slow speech to normal/fast speech. Most interestingly, a perceptual study reveals that the rate of correct identification of C_1 decreases (as expected) from unassimilated to assimilated alveolars, but never falls to 0, suggesting that also in the cases of apparently complete assimilation (i.e. absence of alveolar tongue-to-palate contact), listeners can make use of some residual cues to the place distinction. The data are in agreement with the hypothesis that in English the assimilation of alveolars to velars is a continuous process. This is confirmed in a recent investigation on clusters of alveolar nasals + velar stops (Hardcastle, 1994). Some other data, however, (Barry, 1991; Nolan and Holst, 1993) challenge some of the assumptions of gestural phonology. The cross-language study by Barry (1991) on English and Russian alveolar-velar clusters confirms that assimilation in English is a graded process. In Russian, instead, assimilation never occurs when C_1 is an oral stop; when C_1 is a nasal, assimilation may be continuous or categorical, depending on syllabic structure. The data of Nolan and Holst (1993) on /s#ʃ/ sequences, do show intermediate articulations between two-gesture and one-gesture patterns, as predicted by gestural phonology. Accordingly, the one-gesture or static patterns should reflect complete spatio-temporal overlap, i.e. show a blending of the /s/ and /ʃ/ influences and a duration comparable to that of a single consonant. Contrary to this hypothesis, the preliminary results indicate that the static patterns have the spatial characteristic of a typical /ʃ/, and are 16 per cent longer than an initial /ʃ/. Recent EPG and durational data on Italian clusters of /n/ + oral consonants of different places and manners of articulation, seem to indicate that both categorical and continuous processes may coexist in a language, the occurrence of the one or the other depending on cluster type and individual speech style. Moreover, the finding that in Italian the alveolar-velar assimilation in /nk/ clusters is always categorical, indicates, in agreement with Barry (1991), that the assimilatory process for the same cluster type may differ qualitatively across languages (Farnetani and Busà, 1994).

3 Summary

This excursus on the problem of contextual variability shows, on one hand, the incredible complexity of the speech production mechanism, which renders the task of understanding its underlying control principles so difficult. It shows, on the other hand, the enormous theoretical and experimental ongoing progress, as reflected in continuously evolving and improving models, and in increasingly rigorous and sophisticated research methodologies.

We started with the questions of the origin, function and control of coarticulation, and the consequent question of the relation between coarticulation and other context dependent processes. At the moment there is no single answer to these questions. For generative phonology, assimilations, connected speech processes and coarticulation are different steps linking the domain of competence with that of performance, with no bottom-up influences from the physical to the cognitive structure of the language. For both the theory of "adaptive variability" and the theory of gestural phonology the origin of coarticulation lies in speech (in its plasticity and adaptability for the former, in its intrinsic organization in time for the latter). Both theories assume that the nature of speech production itself is at the root of linguistic morpho-phonological rules, which are viewed as adaptations of language to speech processes, sometimes eventuating in historical sound changes. However, there is a discrepancy between the two theories on the primacy of production vs perception in the control of speech variability. Gestural phonology considers acoustics/perception as the effect of speech production, whilst the theory of "adaptive variability" sees acoustics/perception as the final cause of production, hence perception itself contributes to "shape" production.

Two general control principles for speech variability have been repeatedly advocated: economy (by Lindblom and by Keating) and output constraints (advocated by Lindblom for the preservation of perceptual contrast across styles within a language and extended by Manuel to account for interlanguage differences in coarticulation). Manuel's proposal is supported by a variety of V-to-V coarticulation data and by other cross-language experiments (for example, the lip protrusion data of Lubker and Gay, 1982). But other data do not seem to be consistent with this account: anticipatory nasalization has a limited extent not only in French, which has nasal vowels in its inventory (Benguerel et al., 1977a), but also in Italian (Farnetani, 1986), and Japanese (Ushijima and Hirose, 1974), which have a restricted number of oral vowels and no contrastively nasal vowels. Probably other principles are at work besides that of perceptual distinctiveness – among them, that of preserving the exact phonetic quality expected and accepted in a given language or dialect.

If we confront the various articulatory models with experimental data, it seems that the overall results on coarticulation resistance are more consistent with the gestural model than with others, although certain patterns of coarticulation resistance (Sussman and Westbury, 1981; Engstrand, 1983) could be better explained if aerodynamic/acoustic constraints, in addition to articulatory constraints, were taken into account. The challenging hypothesis of gestural phonology that connected speech processes are not substantially different from coarticulation processes (i.e. are continuous and do not imply qualitative changes in the categorical underlying units) is supported by a large number of experimental results. However, recent data, based on both spatial and temporal parameters, indicate that assimilation can also be a rule-governed categorical process.

As for anticipatory coarticulation, no model in its present version can account for the diverse results within and across languages: the review shows that languages differ both quantitatively and qualitatively in the way they implement this process. English and Swedish seem to differ quantitatively in lip rounding anticipation (Lubker and Gay, 1982); while the plateau-patterns observed in some languages (Boyce, 1990; Cohn, 1993) suggest that the process is phonological in some languages and phonetic in others.

Most intriguing in the data on anticipatory coarticulation are the discrepancies among the results for the same language (on nasalization in American English: cf. Moll and Daniloff, 1971 vs. Bell-Berti and Harris, 1980, vs. Solé and Ohala, 1991). Such discrepancies might be due to different experimental techniques, or the different speech material may itself have conditioned the speaking style or rate and hence the coarticulatory patterns. The discrepancies might also reveal actual regional variants, suggesting ongoing phonetic changes, yet to be fully explored.

NOTES

I thank Michael Studdert-Kennedy for his extensive comments on the form and substance of this work, and Björn Lindblom, Daniel Recasens and Bill

Hardcastle for their valuable suggestions.

This research was supported in part by ESPRIT/ACCOR, WG 7098.

1   This position is shared by many other speech scientists (see Ohala, The Relation Between Phonetics and Phonology).

2   See Fourakis (1991) for a recent review of the literature on vowel reduction.

3   Notice the different definitions of the term *phonetic* given by Keating and by Cohn on the one hand, and by Solé and Ohala (1991) on the other: according to the former phonetics pertains to competence, it is knowledge of the phonetic aspect of a language; for the latter phonetics pertains to the speech mechanism, therefore what is phonetic is unintentional and automatic. Thus the actual data on nasalization in English (Cohn's and Solé and Ohala's) may be not so diverse as the two different accounts would suggest.

13 Theories and Models of Speech Production

ANDERS LÖFQVIST

> *"The purpose of models is not to fit the data*
> *but to sharpen the questions"*
> Samuel Karlin
> (11th R.A. Fisher Memorial Lecture,
> Royal Society, 20 April 1983)

1 The speech signal and its description

For the purpose of this chapter, it is convenient to view speech as audible gestures. A speaker creates variations in air pressure and air flow in the vocal tract by making valving actions with different parts of the vocal tract: the glottis, the velum, the tongue, the lips, and the jaw. The changes in pressure and flow give rise to the acoustic signal that we hear when perceiving speech. Most of the variations in the acoustic signal are made intentionally by the speaker to convey linguistic information. Other properties convey what is called paralinguistic information, such as attitudes and emotions, social and geographical dialect characteristics. In addition, there are properties reflecting biological features of the speaker such as sex and age. The resulting acoustic signal is thus shaped by contributions from many different sources that are all overlaid on each other. The fact that listeners can usually identify these different sources suggests that they are recoverable from the acoustic signal.

In describing speech and language, it is common to use one of two modes that can be referred to as the linguistic and the dynamic mode (see Pattee, 1977, for a further elaboration of this distinction). In the linguistic mode, the units of language are described without a temporal domain. For example, most phonological descriptions use a set of symbols that can be arranged in different ways to produce different messages. Although the primitives used for this type of analysis vary depending on the theoretical framework being adopted, the units are commonly described as being discrete and serially ordered. The dynamic mode is used for describing articulatory and acoustic properties of speech. Here, the focus is on the time-varying properties of articulatory movements and/or the spectral characteristics of the speech signal.

This necessarily implies a temporal domain. The linguistic units of speech can no longer be described as discrete, since a salient feature of speech production is that the units show considerable articulatory influence and overlap. This is commonly referred to as coarticulation, coproduction, blending or aggregation (cf. Farnetani, COARTICULATION AND CONNECTED SPEECH PROCESSES; Perkell, ARTICULATORY PROCESSES). Thus, the movements associated with different production units blend seamlessly with each other and in the articulatory record there are no boundaries between units. Consequently, the movements necessary for the production of a given unit differ according to its context, and likewise its acoustic properties vary according to context. A further result of this overlap is that at any one point in time, the vocal tract is an aggregate of different production units (cf. Fowler and Smith, 1986; Saltzman and Munhall, 1989; Löfqvist, 1990). The obvious acoustic consequence is that a single temporal slice of the signal contains influences from several production units (see Fant, 1962, for an early discussion).

Throughout the history of the study of speech, much effort has been devoted to arguments about these two modes of description (cf. Ohala, THE RELATION BETWEEN PHONETICS AND PHONOLOGY). One famous depiction of their different natures is provided by Hockett (1955), who makes an analogy between speech production and a row of raw Easter eggs on a conveyor belt, being smashed between the two rollers of a wringer. The implication is that the units of speech are distinct and serially ordered (perhaps also invariant and displaying their essential properties) before they are all smeared together in the process of articulation: "The flow of eggs before the wringer represents the impulses from the phoneme source; the *mess* that emerges from the wringer represents the output from the speech transmitter." (Hockett, 1955, p. 210; italics added.) We should note that Hockett does not imply that it is impossible to recover the original eggs that went into the mess. He duly comments that an inspector examining the passing mess could "decide, on the basis of the broken and unbroken yolks, the variously spread-out albumen, and the variously colored bits of shell, the nature of the flow of eggs which previously arrived at the wringer" (ibid.) and further notes that the inspector represents the hearer.

While Hockett's Easter egg analogy would seem to represent an extreme case, it is not unique. Rather, it represents a class of theories which have been called translation theories, because they view speech production as translating a mental representation into something completely different during the process of articulation (cf. Fowler, Rubin, Remez, and Turvey, 1980; Fowler, 1993). Hockett's view is also understandable from its epistemological context. The discovery of coarticulation was made around the beginning of this century, and Menzerath and de Lacerda (1933) published the first systematic treatise on the subject. Not only did they show large contextual variability for productions of the same sound, but they also showed, as had others before them, that it was impossible to draw boundaries between sounds in the articulatory record (cf. Hardcastle, 1981; Farnetani, COARTICULATION AND CONNECTED SPEECH

Processes, for historical reviews). These findings caused some consternation among speech scientists, since it had often been assumed that the same sound would be articulated in the same way irrespective of its context – an assumption that seems to reappear at certain intervals over time. Hence, the search was on to find the invariant, or essential, properties of the phoneme in production (or acoustics). In a review of theories of speech production, Peter MacNeilage neatly sums up the shift in emphasis that has come to dominate work on speech motor control:

> . . . it becomes clear that the more basic problem in speech production theory is not the one considered central to most theorists; namely, why articulators do not always reach the same position for a given phoneme. It is, How do articulators always come as close to reaching the same position as they do? One of the main conclusions of this paper is that the essence of the speech production process is not an inefficient response to invariant central signals, but an elegantly controlled variability of response to the demand for a relatively constant end. (MacNeilage, 1970, p. 184)

Before continuing, we should also note another shift of emphasis in the study of speech motor control. Much work in speech physiology was carried out within a paradigm in which two general issues dominated: chain versus comb models for the serial ordering of articulatory movements, and the role of peripheral feedback in speech production (Lashley, 1951; Kozhevnikov and Chistovich, 1965; Keele, 1968; see Kent, 1976b, for a review of these issues). Briefly, in a chain model, the central motor commands to the articulators to produce a segment were supposed to be triggered by feedback from the periphery upon the completion of the articulatory movements for the previous one. In a comb model, the commands to the articulators for successive segments were assumed to be sent according to a plan or temporal scheme. In practice, one limitation in this approach was a tendency to subsume the question of feedback under the question of serial order, and phrase the alternatives as either a chain model incorporating feedback or a comb model without feedback. Of the two remaining alternatives, one was perhaps automatically ruled out, i.e. a chain model without feedback, but the possibility of a comb model incorporating feedback was not generally explored, in spite of the wealth of physiological studies of sensorimotor mechanisms (e.g. Granit, 1970; Matthews, 1972). In such a model, the role of feedback would not necessarily be limited to the sequencing of movements but rather would be important in the shaping of movements as well. A further limitation was an insistence that signals from peripheral receptors go to higher centers with the resulting problem of apparently inadequate loop time. Another possibility could be that information from the periphery goes to lower levels of the nervous system such as the spinal cord or the brain stem; we will later explore the idea that these levels may play a crucial role in integrating signals from the periphery with signals from higher centers.

While coarticulation has been taken as a fundamental characteristic of speech and the basis for the rapidity with which information can be conveyed (Liberman, Cooper, Shankweiler, and Studdert-Kennedy, 1967), it is also likely to be a fundamental characteristic of most motor activities. Presumably, the reason why it has received so much attention in speech science is that speech can, at one level, be described as a succession of discrete segments, making it possible to study how the "canonical" forms of these segments are altered in the process of articulation. Very similar patterns of contextual variability can be found in typing. In typing, the goal is to produce a sequence of keystrokes, and it may thus be easier to define the targets in typing than in speech production. The movements of the fingers towards the keys show large contextual variability in both space and time (Salthouse, 1986). For example, successive keystrokes are made faster by fingers on alternate hands than by fingers on the same hand. The likely reason is that when alternate hands are used, there is no conflict between the fingers used for the strokes, since the two hands can operate independently. The time needed for a keystroke depends on the context in which a character occurs. The range of these contextual influences in typing appears to be limited to two or three characters. In contrast, coarticulatory influences in speech have been claimed to span up to six segments, but the size of the temporal window for coarticulatory influences remains under debate (cf. Farnetani, COARTICULATION AND CONNECTED SPEECH PROCESSES). The differences between strokes made by the same or alternating hands in typing are similar to coarticulation in speech, where the different parts of the vocal tract can operate relatively independently of each other.

2 Concepts and issues in movement control

During speech, parts of the vocal tract are briefly coupled in a functional manner to produce the acoustic characteristics of speech sounds. For example, the production of the bilabial voiceless stop /p/ requires the following set of actions. The lips are closed by joint activity of the jaw and the lips. The velum is elevated to seal off the entrance into the nasal cavity. The glottis is widened and the longitudinal tension of the vocal folds is often increased to prevent glottal vibrations. These articulatory and laryngeal actions all contribute to a period of silence in the acoustic signal and an increase in oral air pressure associated with the stop consonant. Speech production thus involves control and coordination of different parts of the vocal tract. How this is achieved is not well understood. Speech motor control should properly be seen as an instance of the control of coordinated movements in general. As a preliminary to this discussion, we shall briefly review a line of experiments on speech production that will provide a suitable empirical and experimental background. After this review, the remaining parts of this section discuss a number of issues in the control of movement and their implications for speech motor control.

2.1 What happens when speech movements are perturbed?

Daily activities such as walking and picking up and moving objects often require rapid actions to cope with unexpected events such as stumbling or hitting an object with the hand. One valuable experimental paradigm for understanding movement coordination and control is to introduce unexpected perturbations to motor acts in a systematic manner. In a standard experiment, a subject is attached to a small motor that can be activated during some trials to generate a brief load. The rationale for this research is that the nature and time course of the response to the load may reveal the motor organization and reflex structure of the motor act. This paradigm has been applied to different types of motor behavior in humans such as posture control (e.g. Nashner and McCollum, 1985), hand and finger movements (e.g. Traub, Rothwell, and Marsden, 1980; Rothwell, Traub, and Marsden, 1982; Cole, Gracco, and Abbs, 1984), and respiratory control (Newsom Davis and Sears, 1970). A number of studies have also used this method to study speech motor control (Folkins and Abbs, 1975; Folkins and Zimmermann, 1982; Abbs and Gracco, 1984; Kelso, Tuller, Vatikiotis-Bateson, and Fowler, 1984; Gracco and Abbs, 1985, 1988, 1989; Shaiman, 1989; Shaiman and Abbs, 1987; Kollia, 1994; Munhall, Löfqvist, and Kelso, 1994).

From these speech perturbation studies, some general conclusions can be drawn. First, compensations are rapid. Electromyographic responses can occur 20–30 ms after load onset. The latency is not fixed, however, but depends on when the load was applied with respect to onset of activity in the muscles responsible for the movement in question (Abbs, Gracco, and Cole, 1984). The short latencies suggest that the responses are not due to reaction time processes. Second, compensations are mostly task-specific. That is, they are neither stereotypic nor evident throughout the system, but rather tailored to the needs of the ongoing motor act. For example, when the jaw is loaded during the transition from a vowel to a bilabial stop, compensatory responses are made in the upper and lower lips to achieve the labial closure. On the other hand, when the jaw is loaded during the transition from a vowel to a dental fricative or a dental stop, a response is seen in the tongue (Kelso, Tuller, Vatikiotis-Bateson, and Fowler, 1984; Shaiman, 1989). We should add a word of caution here, however, since task specificity is not always consistent across speakers. In particular, one of the subjects in the study by Shaiman (1989) showed increased lower lip movement in addition to jaw and tongue compensatory movements when the jaw was perturbed during the utterance /ædæ/, which does not require lip activity. Similarly, the study by Kelso, Tuller, Vatikiotis-Bateson, and Fowler (1984) found increased upper lip EMG activity in perturbed productions of /bæz/. Third, compensations are flexible and distributed among articulators involved in a specific task. Thus, when the jaw is loaded in the production of a bilabial stop, responses can occur in the jaw itself and/or in the upper and lower lips (Shaiman, 1989). Fourth, compensations are functional and effective in the sense that the intended goal is normally achieved. For example, Munhall, Löfqvist, and Kelso (1994) perturbed the lower lip at the transition from the first vowel to the medial bilabial voiceless stop in the utterance /i pip/. The system was able to overcome the load, making the intended closure of the vocal tract and increasing the air pressure in the oral cavity: recordings of oral pressure revealed no differences in pressure between load and control productions.

While the results of these studies clearly indicate that the articulatory system is capable of rapid and functional responses to external loads, such loads may, nevertheless, affect the timing between different articulatory systems (Löfqvist and Gracco, 1991; Saltzman, Löfqvist, Kinsella-Shaw, Rubin, and Kay, 1992). For example, Munhall, Löfqvist, and Kelso (1994) also examined laryngeal responses to lower lip perturbations during the production of a voiceless bilabial stop. In addition to lip and jaw actions to achieve the labial closure, a laryngeal response was evident by a delay of the onset of glottal abduction, measured relative to the onset of the preceding vowel. This delay was presumably made to maintain lip-larynx coordination at the onset of labial closure, and resulted in an increased acoustic duration of the preceding vowel. However, the period of bilabial closure for the stop was shortened by the perturbation while the laryngeal abduction–adduction movement increased in duration. The normal phasing between the oral and laryngeal movements was consequently disrupted at the release of the oral closure. As a result, Voice Onset Time increased in the perturbed trials since it depends in part on the timing between the oral and laryngeal events in stop production (e.g. Löfqvist and Yoshioka, 1984; Löfqvist, 1992).

2.2 Planning and execution of movements

While it is convenient to discuss movement control in terms of a plan and its execution, there is reason to believe that a clear separation between plan and execution is often not possible. One problem here concerns the representations used in speech planning. Current phonological representations would seem to require a great deal of detail to be filled in during the conversion into a phonetic representation, in particular temporal information (cf. Zsiga, 1993, for a recent discussion). Another issue is how much motoric detail a plan can contain, an issue that will be taken up in more detail in section 2.3. Theories of speech planning have often used cases of speech errors, slips of the tongue or spoonerisms, as evidence (see also Perkell, Articulatory Processes). An example of such an error is when someone says "queer old dean" instead of the intended "dear old queen". Based on analysis of such speech errors, several models of the speech planning process have been proposed (e.g. Garrett, 1980; Levelt, 1989; Dell, Juliano, and Govindjee, 1993). These findings obviously suggest that utterances are planned, since it would otherwise be difficult to explain how an upcoming word could be exchanged with one that is preceding it. Both words would have to be activated at the same time for such an exchange to occur. Still, the nature of this plan is not clear. Using Hockett's Easter egg analogy, the plan in these models of speech production would seem to correspond to the organization of the eggs before they are smashed between the rollers. That is, the smashing process does not appear to be part of the plan.

2.3 Distributed control

The nervous system is made up of a complex network of interacting neurons and centers at different levels of the system. In motor control, one important function must involve integrating signals from higher centers with signals from the periphery which indicate the current state. This involves selecting the appropriate muscles, activating them to a suitable degree, and establishing a proper sequence of activation. The integrative function for limb control is located in the spinal cord (cf. Humphrey and Freund, 1991; McCrea, 1992). Only at this level is all the relevant information present. The activity of the neural pool in the spinal cord is constantly changing as a function of central and peripheral inputs. Hence, a given central command will have different results depending on the current state of the pool. From the perspective of movement planning and execution, the executive and integrative function is thus played by lower levels of the nervous system. Indeed, it is not entirely clear that a general division between central and peripheral processes is possible. A metaphor would be that an intended movement is realized successively in more motoric detail as it is passed down through the system until it reaches the final common path from the motor neurons to the muscles. Speech production would seem to share the same form of control, where the brain stem plays the integrative role (see Kent and Tjaden, BRAIN FUNCTIONS UNDERLYING SPEECH). The rapid and functional compensations following perturbations to articulators are in agreement with such a distributed system.

2.4 Coordinate spaces

One persistent problem in movement control concerns the coordinate space in which movements are planned and represented (see Hollerbach, 1990, for a general discussion, and Munhall, Ostry, and Flanagan, 1991, for discussion of speech movements). In unrestrained reaching movements, the hand usually traverses a relatively straight path in an extrinsic cartesian coordinate system. If the same movement is described in an intrinsic coordinate system represented by the joint angles of the shoulder and elbow, a plot of elbow angle versus shoulder angle typically shows a curved path. One can similarly compare articulator path shapes observed during speech production in extrinsic versus intrinsic coordinates. For example, jaw movements can be represented in extrinsic or intrinsic coordinate space, where the latter involves at least rotation and translation of the jaw, possibly also yaw. For tongue movements, the situation is even more complex. Due to its mechanical linkage to the jaw, movements of the tongue are partly due to jaw rotation and translation, and partly to the activities of intrinsic and extrinsic tongue muscles. Moreover, the tongue has a hydrostatic skeleton, like an elephant's trunk, and not like the joints of the legs, the arms, and the jaw (cf. Smith and Kier, 1989).

Straight-path trajectories in extrinsic space have often been cited as evidence that movements are planned in extrinsic space. For speech, this argument can possibly be bolstered by the fact that the result of the speech production process is a time-varying acoustic signal. It has been argued that speech movements are controlled with respect to such acoustic effects. The acoustic effects depend on the transfer function of the vocal tract. Planning and control of speech movements in an acoustic coordinate system thus seems plausible. We should perhaps add, however, that tongue movements usually do not follow straight lines in extrinsic coordinate space but rather show curved paths, cf. Figure 13.1 (Houde, 1968; Perkell, 1969; Kent and Moll, 1972; Schönle, 1988; Munhall, Ostry, and Flanagan, 1991; Löfqvist, Gracco, and Nye, 1993; Löfqvist and Gracco, 1994; Perkell, ARTICULATORY PROCESSES).

However, one traditional cause for concern is that control in extrinsic space requires the motor control system to solve the so-called inverse problem. A solution to the inverse problem entails going backwards from the desired movement trajectory to the muscle forces required to produce the movements. In arm movement control, the inverse problem involves mapping backwards from the desired movement goal in extrinsic space to the required muscular forces. For speech, the same mappings would be involved, perhaps with the added step of going from acoustic coordinates to vocal tract coordinates. The inverse problem is mathematically ill-posed in the sense that it is unclear whether a solution exists, is unique, and depends continuously on initial conditions (Tikhonov and Arsenin, 1977). One component of the inverse problem for arm movements is that the arm has excess degrees of freedom – seven (e.g. Alexander, 1992). Excess degrees of freedom in this context imply that the number of controlled spatial variables for the arm is less than the number of controlled joint angular variables. In such a case, the mapping from spatial variables to joint variables is indeterminate, since the same final position of the hand can be achieved by very many possible combinations of joint movements and, consequently, of very many different combinations of muscle activity patterns (there are 22 distinct muscles in the arm). In speech, the problem is the one-to-many mapping from acoustic signal to vocal tract area function as well as the excess degrees of freedom of the articulatory system. Models of speech production arguing for acoustically-based targets would assume implicitly that speech movements are planned in acoustic space. Interestingly, when the acoustic properties of the vocal tract are changed experimentally, e.g. by having subjects wear a dental prosthesis, speakers do not compensate

Average receiver trajectories for /aka/

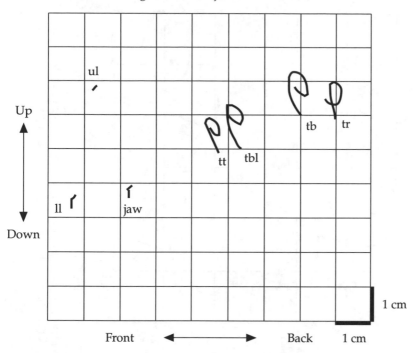

Figure 13.1a Trajectories of receivers placed on the upper and lower lips, the jaw, and on four positions on the tongue during production of the sequence /aka/. All four tongue receivers move counterclockwise. See Löfqvist, Gracco, and Nye (1993), and Löfqvist and Gracco (1994) for experimental details.

immediately for the induced changes (Hamlet and Stone, 1976, 1978). Rather, such a manipulation requires some time for adjustment, possibly indicating that an inverse mapping has to be solved anew. These results might superficially seem to contradict the finding of immediate compensations when jaw movements are constrained by a bite-block held between a subject's teeth (Lindblom, Lubker, and Gay, 1979; Lubker, 1979; Fowler and Turvey, 1980). Note that the bite-block does not necessarily change the transfer function of the vocal tract in the same way as a dental prosthesis.

Recent work using parallel processing (Jordan, 1990; Jordan and Rumelhart, 1992) suggests that the traditional computational concerns about the inverse problem may be exaggerated (see section 2.7). We should also remember that speech and most other skilled movements are highly learned motor activities. Depending on what definition we use for mastering speech, it takes human infants two or three years to acquire it. Thus, in many instances of movement control, the motor system may not have to perform an exhaustive inverse computation, since learning can reduce the number of possible actions. Furthermore, much of the discussion about the inverse problem has received

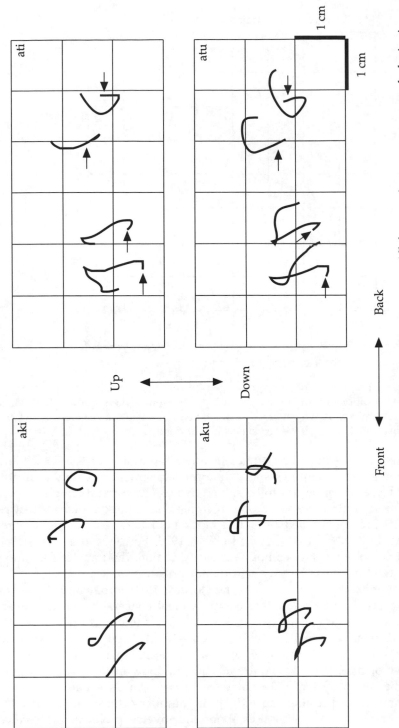

Figure 13.1b Trajectories of four tongue receivers during different VCV sequences. All four receivers move counterclockwise in the sequences with a velar consonant. The arrows identify the onset of the trajectories in the sequences with a dental stop.

input from the field of robotics, but natural systems may "take a loan" on physics and evolution to solve this problem. Brains and nervous systems are not general purpose devices, but rather special purpose devices that have evolved to solve ecologically significant problems in a world governed by relatively stable and predictable physical forces.

In an attempt to alleviate the inverse problem, some investigators have argued that motor control is formulated in terms of muscular coordinates. One such model is the equilibrium-point model (Asatryan and Feldman, 1965; Feldman, 1966; see Bizzi, Hogan, Mussa-Ivaldi, and Giszter, 1992, and commentaries for a review). According to the equilibrium-point model, the target of the movement is specified by the length and stiffness of agonist–antagonist muscle pairs working across a joint. This specification is made via central commands. We noted in section 2.4 that the tongue is a muscular hydrostat lacking joints. Equilibrium-point control of the tongue would nevertheless seem possible. By specifying relationships between the three major extrinsic tongue muscles the tongue can be moved up and down, forward and backward. Control of tongue shape can similarly be made by changing the relation between on the one hand the transverse and vertical muscles, and on the other hand the longitudinal muscles. There is some experimental evidence for such a control model. For example, Bizzi and colleagues (Polit and Bizzi, 1979) studied arm movements in monkeys who had been deprived of sensory information from the arm. The animals could still reach a visually presented target using the arm without kinesthetic or visual feedback about arm position. They could even do so when the arm was momentarily perturbed in the opposite direction, slowing the movement. Initially, it was thought that the target was set once and for all before the initiation of movement. In a later study (Bizzi, Accornero, Chapple, and Hogan, 1984), the perturbation was applied in the opposite direction during the reaching task. That is, the perturbation moved the arm towards the target position and thus assisted the movement. Contrary to expectations, this did not result in the arm reaching the target faster. Instead, after the perturbation had been released, the arm moved away from the target and returned to the position on its trajectory before the perturbation was applied. Hence, the target is apparently not specified at the onset of movement but rather continuously updated.

Using an equilibrium-point approach, the muscles controlling movement in a joint can be modeled as a mass-spring system. This has certain attractive features (cf. Cooke, 1980). One of them is that movement will proceed in the face of transient perturbations (cf. section 2.1). Another one is equifinality, i.e. the intended goal will be reached from different initial conditions (see also Perkell, ARTICULATORY PROCESSES).

2.5 *Coordinative structures*

The speech perturbation studies suggest another property of movement control. In coordinated action, the level of control is not the individual muscles but rather task-dependent groupings of muscles. For example, perturbations to the jaw during the formation of a labial closure are compensated for by any combination of lip and jaw activity. It thus appears that individual articulators can be flexibly marshaled during speech to perform the intended closure in the vocal tract (cf. Gracco and Abbs, 1986).

Such task-dependent groupings of muscles have been called coordinative structures or synergies. This particular view of movement control owes much of its initial formulation to the Russian physiologist N. Bernstein (Bernstein, 1967). Further discussion and elaboration of these concepts are found in Greene (1972), Gelfand, Gurfinkel, Fomin, and Tsetlin (1971), Turvey (1977, 1990), Kelso, Holt, Kugler, and Turvey (1980), Kugler, Kelso, and Turvey (1980), and Lee (1984). A synergy is defined as "those classes of movements which have similar kinematic characteristics, coinciding active muscle groups and conducting types of afferentation" (Gelfand, Gurfinkel, Tsetlin, and Shik, 1971, p. 331). According to Lee (1984), synergies can be defined by coherent patterns of muscle activity and/or movement, and in terms of spatial, temporal and scaling properties. Spatially, the same set of muscles should be activated. In the temporal domain, synchronicity, stable order or stable phase relationships should hold between events. Relations among events should demonstrate a scaling relationship. Such a definition requires appropriate measurements for a synergy to be recognized. For speech, the arguments for synergies have mostly been based on temporal and spatial relationships between muscle and/or movement patterns. As will be discussed in section 3, there are some intriguing experimental problems in defining synergies using timing and scaling properties. The most convincing evidence for coordinative structures would appear to come from the perturbation studies reviewed in section 2.1. In particular, a theory of coordinative structures predicts task-specific responses.

Coordinative structures should be seen as linkages between muscles that are set up for the execution of specific tasks. For example, Kelso, Tuller, and Harris (1983) had subjects make flexion-extension movements of the index finger in synchrony with stressed and unstressed syllables. They noted a coupling between speech and finger movements. When producing a stressed syllable, the subjects also increased the amplitude of the finger movements. Similarly, when the finger was mechanically perturbed, a change in the acoustic speech signal was also observed. The authors argue that these findings can be accounted for by a coordinative structure comprising the vocal tract and the hand, set up for the execution of a specific task. Thus, when one member of the synergy was perturbed, other members also showed a change. We should note that the functionality of this particular coupled change is not entirely clear. Perhaps we should entertain another interpretation of these results.

Movements such as walking and swimming are rhythmic, and such movements can be effectively modeled by coupled oscillators producing many different patterns of organization (cf. Cohen, Rossignol, and Grillner, 1988; see also Stewart and Golubitsky, 1992, chapter 8, for a discussion of locomotion in terms of coupled oscillators). According to the oscillator model, a perturbation to a coupled system would manifest itself throughout the system. This class of models is very powerful for simulating coordinated rhythmic movements such as those found in locomotion, swimming, and chewing. The question arises, however, whether such rhythmic patterns are a property of normal speech movements.

One attractive feature of coordinative structures is that they can provide a principled solution to the problem of controlling many degrees of freedom. We noted above that the arm has several degrees of freedom which, on the one hand, provides flexibility in the control of arm movements, but on the other hand introduces the problem of indeterminacy in managing all the degrees. A coordinative structure can be described as a set of constraints between muscles that are set up to make the set of muscles behave as a unit. Thus, control is simplified in the sense that the individual muscles need not be controlled independently of each other but rather as a functional unit. It is obvious, however, that while control may be simplified at one level, complexities arise on other levels. If coordinative structures are task-specific and set up for brief periods of time to execute a given movement, there must be a way for the system to keep track of these different coordinative structures, to put them together and break them apart at the appropriate time. For example, in the production of a sequence of a bilabial stop and a vowel, the jaw and the lips are engaged in making and releasing the labial closure for the consonant, whereas for the vowel, the lips may not be directly involved while the jaw and the tongue shape the vocal tract. Thus, the degree of coupling between the lips, the jaw, and the tongue is changing.

2.6 *A gestural approach to speech production*

Records of speech movements generally show a succession of opening and closing movements at different locations in the vocal tract. One approach to understanding speech motor control is to posit underlying gestures as the building blocks of speech. A gesture can be defined briefly as a class of functionally equivalent movement patterns (cf. Saltzman and Munhall, 1989). Again, a word of caution is in order, since introducing underlying representations always carries a certain risk – such representations have a tendency to show an unprincipled rate of multiplication. Parsimony and a judicious use of Occam's razor is often desirable in science, although we are also well advised to keep in mind that the famous razor has been described as an instrument used by scientists to cut their own throats. Still, using gestures as underlying representations has certain advantages. It can possibly bypass the translation problem by providing the underlying linguistic units with more motoric detail. In this view, a segment should be viewed as a set of gestures (see Löfqvist, 1990, for a defense of the segment).

Munhall and Löfqvist (1992) examined how the two successive laryngeal movements in the utterance "Kiss Ted", for the /s/ and the /t/, were affected by variations in speaking rate. At a slow rate, two independent movements were found. At fast rates, a single movement was observed. Interestingly, at intermediate rates, a blend of the two gestures was seen. These blends could be reasonably well modeled by adding together two underlying gestures at different degrees of overlap. By varying speaking rate, it was thus possible to view the gestures both in isolation and as aggregates. Hence, the assumed underlying gestures could be readily observed. Similar effects of speaking rate on velar movements have been presented by Boyce, Krakow, Bell-Berti, and Gelfer (1990).

Using underlying gestures to account for movement control is not a new idea. Aiming movements have often been shown to be composed of a number of submovements (e.g. Woodworth, 1899). Here, a large initial movement is followed by smaller corrective movements. It has been suggested by Milner and Ijaz (1990) that irregularities in the tangential velocity of aiming movements can be accounted for by linearly superimposing submovements to create a single composite movement. Similarly, when a subject is suddenly required to switch to a new target after a reaching movement has started, the initial movement is not aborted. Rather, a second movement is blended with the first one (Flash, 1990), and the resulting tangential velocity of the movement can be modeled by adding two underlying movements. For speech, Öhman (1966, 1967) showed evidence of gestural blending in VCV sequences when the vowels and medial consonant shared the same articulator: In the sequences /aga/ and /igi/, the tongue shape during the closure for the /g/ is a blend of the gestures for the vowels and the consonant (cf. Saltzman and Munhall, 1989, for simulation of such patterns using gestural blending). Thus, blending of gestures may be a general strategy that the motor system applies in implementing successive elements of movements.

2.7 Some new tools: connectionist models

The nervous system consists of a very large number of individual processing units, neurons, with very many interconnections. Compared to the central processor of a modern computer, each of these processing units is slow. In contrast to most computers, though, the neurons of nervous systems perform their processing in parallel, making up for the slowness of the individual units. Models borrowing the parallel processing (neural network) approach have become more common in the last decade and offer potentially useful and interesting tools for modeling speech processes. (While there is a large and rapidly increasing literature on neural networks, the standard references are still Rumelhart and McClelland (1986) and McClelland and Rumelhart (1986).) Although such models have some similarities to natural nervous systems, they are not brain models – they are modeling tools. A typical neural network consists of one layer of input units, one layer of output units, and one layer of intermediate, or hidden, units. The units are interconnected with each other and the connections can increase and decrease the activation level of the receiving unit. The activation level of a given unit thus depends on the weighted sum of its inputs. In a pattern recognition task, a task where neural nets have proved especially useful, the object is to make the network respond to a pattern applied to the input units with a certain pattern at the output units. For example, one task could be to have the network produce speech in response to an alphabetic input. During a training period, the network "learns" to associate input and output patterns by adjusting the weights of the connections between the units. After training, the network shows some similarities with natural systems such as generalization of responses to patterns not in the training set and graceful degradation of performance when units are eliminated. (For further description of neural nets, see Ainsworth, SOME APPROACHES TO AUTOMATIC SPEECH RECOGNITION.)

Jordan and Rumelhart (1992) describe the application of neural nets to the inverse problem in movement control (cf. section 2.4). This approach involves two steps. First a forward model of the system under study is learned. A forward model produces the consequence of a given action based on the current state, e.g. what happens with the hand when there is motion at the joints of the arm. The counterpart of a forward model is an inverse model. An inverse model produces an action as a function of the current state and a desired consequence. In the second step, the inverse model and the forward model are composed and an identity mapping is learned across the composed network. When learning the identity mapping, the network also finds an inverse model.

One important factor in learning in both natural and artificial systems is constraints. Jordan (1990) discusses some general constraints on movements that are most likely identical across systems. Such constraints can be taken as minimization of cost functions, defined in terms of, for example, energy, time, and smoothness. Principles of least-effort are intuitively attractive in motor control (cf. Nelson, 1983), and have often been invoked in reference to speech motor control (e.g. Lindblom, 1983). A persistent problem in speech has been to obtain the actual costs. Models may offer some insights in this area.

As a tool in studying processes of speech production, neural nets have been used to model articulatory movements from EMG signals (Hirayama, Vatikiotis-Bateson, Kawato, and Honda, 1992; Vatikiotis-Bateson, Hirayama, Honda, and Kawato, 1992). In this approach, a network is first trained to learn correlations between articulator position, velocity, EMG and articulator acceleration. This produces a forward model. The forward model is then incorporated into a recurrent network that is driven by EMG signals and predicts articulator position and velocity over time as output. Bailly, Laboissière, and Schwartz (1991) describe a similar system for speech synthesis, where a forward model of the articulatory system is incorporated into a control system that drives an articulatory synthesizer.

Guenther (1994) presents a connectionist model of speech production that integrates and provides a unified account for a number of experimental findings regarding the effects of changes in speaking rate and phonetic context on speech movement kinematics. In this model, the movement targets of different articulators for the production of a given sound are expressed using convex hulls; a convex hull is a region in orosensory space. The size of the hulls serves as an index of the precision needed to produce a given sound. The place of constriction or closure for a consonant is associated with smaller hulls than those for vowels. A change in speaking rate can be modeled by making the hull for a sound larger or smaller; a shrinking hull is associated with a decrease in speaking rate. The change of the size of the hull is larger for vowels than for consonants. Consequently, in the model an increase in speaking rate is associated with an increased movement velocity for vowels but with no change, or even a decrease in velocity, for consonants, as has been found in several experimental studies.

Connectionism is a rapidly expanding field that cuts across many different approaches to modeling (cf. Farmer, 1990). At present, most connectionist models of speech production are limited to statistical patterns of input-output relationships. They are not "complete" models in the sense that they incorporate the biomechanics of the articulators but rather lump everything into a single network.

3 Serial control of speech movements

During normal speech production, movements of the articulators have to be made in the proper sequence to produce an acoustic signal that transmits the intended message. Figure 13.2 shows aerodynamic and articulatory records of three productions of the utterance "It's a papaya", spoken at a conversational rate. The top trace shows the air pressure in the oral cavity; there are three local increases in pressure associated with the voiceless consonants of the utterance. The middle trace shows the vertical movements of the lower lip; the lip moves upwards for the labial closure of the two stop consonants. The bottom trace shows the opening in the glottis; the glottis opens three times for the production of the voiceless consonants; the glottal movements for the stop and the fricative in /ts/ blend together. The signals for the three productions have been temporally aligned at the first peak glottal opening, associated with the cluster /ts/. The duration of the three productions differ. This can be seen by comparing the temporal location of the highest lower lip position for the second /p/ in "papaya" across productions. The order of occurrence of this point for the three productions is (in terms of line thickness) the thin line, the thick line, and the medium line. The difference in utterance duration is visible in all the three signals for that utterance, i.e. the movements of the lower lip and the glottis as well as the increase in oral air pressure all shift together. This is, in a sense, self-evident, since if it didn't occur, the intelligibility of speech would break down. The temporal coordination between articulatory move-

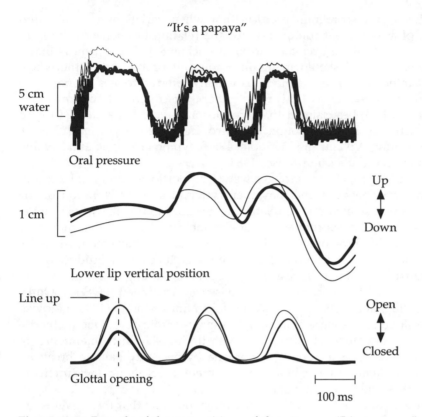

Figure 13.2 Records of three repetitions of the utterance "It's a papaya". The curves represent, from top to bottom, oral air pressure, lower lip vertical position, and glottal opening.

ments has to be maintained within certain limits for speech to be intelligible, across changes in speaking rate. How this temporal cohesion is achieved is not well understood, however. It has been suggested that variations in speaking rate result in a scaling between the different articulatory movements that are involved in the production process. This suggestion is based on the following theoretical view. If someone is writing a word on a paper with a pencil or on a blackboard with a piece of chalk, different parts of the body are used. When the word is written on paper, writing involves movements of the hand and around the wrist; when it is written on the blackboard, the arm moves around the shoulder joint. Since the written pattern on the blackboard can be seen as a scaled version of the one on paper, it has generally been argued that there is a single underlying representation of the movement pattern that is instantiated by different parts of the body using a scaling relation. The alternative view, that each pattern is stored as a separate entity, is at least intuitively implausible and inefficient. Thus, the claim is that the pattern is stored as a "generalized motor program" that can be reparameterized (see Schmidt, 1975).

A generalized motor program predicts that when variations in speed and amplitude of a movement complex occur, the relationship between the individual movements should remain virtually unchanged. The reason is that a submovement interval should maintain a constant proportion of the whole movement interval. Hence, the model is usually referred to as a proportional duration model (see Heuer, 1991, for a general discussion of such models). Initially, several studies claimed that proportional timing was indeed found for motor activities like locomotion, (Shapiro, Zernicke, Gregor, and Diestel, 1981) handwriting (Viviani and Terzuolo, 1980), typing (Terzuolo and Viviani, 1979), and speech (Tuller and Kelso, 1984).

Gentner (1987) proposed a stronger test of proportional duration by examining if the ratio between one movement interval and the duration of the whole movement sequence is unrelated to the duration of the whole movement sequence. The proportional duration model predicts that this should be the case, since the duration of all the components of a movement sequence should maintain a constant proportion of the overall duration. Studies applying this statistical analysis suggest that proportional timing does not occur in speech or any other motor activity that has been examined (cf. Sock, Ollila, Delattre, Zilliox, and Zohair, 1988; Wann and Nimmo-Smith, 1990; Löfqvist, 1991). The slope of the regression usually deviates from zero. One methodological uncertainty facing students of speech timing should be mentioned in this context. Studies of temporal phenomena by necessity have to break up the flow of articulatory movements into discrete intervals for measurement. To delimit these intervals, movement onset and offset, and peak velocity of movement are commonly used. It is, of course, possible that these events are not the ones that the nervous system uses for controlling movements. Kelso, Saltzman, and Tuller (1986) suggested that the proper metric for constant relative timing is phase as measured on a phase plane, rather than ratio of articulatory intervals, and presented some evidence in support of this notion. In a phase plane representation, position is plotted against velocity. In a vowel-labial consonant-vowel sequence, a phase plane plot of the jaw or the lower lip shows an elliptical orbit. Using this kind of representation, movement onsets for different articulators can be defined in terms of phase relationships. Further studies have, however, failed to replicate their findings (Lubker, 1986; Nittrouer, Munhall, Kelso, Tuller, and Harris, 1988; Nittrouer, 1991). These results have implications for theories of speech motor control based on coordinative structures. When discussing coordinative structures in section 2.5, we noted that a definition based on temporal relations requires fixed intervals or scaling among components. One interpretation of scaling is proportional timing which, as we have seen, does not appear to occur, or, at least the scaling is not linear. An important task for speech motor control is to define the metric that governs temporal relations among speech movements.

While constant proportionality thus does not appear to be a proper description of speech movement timing, movements still show temporal cohesion as exemplified by the material presented in Figure 13.2. Another way of analyzing

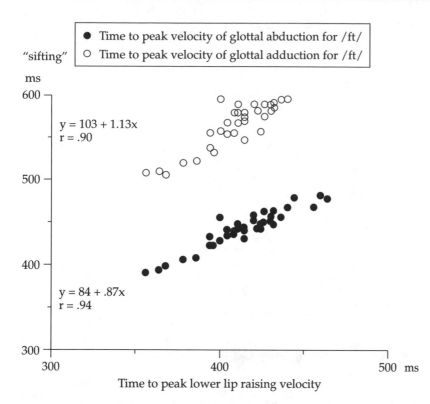

Figure 13.3a Plot of temporal intervals during productions of the word "sifting". The intervals are defined in Figure 13.3b.

the temporal properties between speech movements is illustrated in Figure 13.3. Figure 13.3a shows a plot of articulatory intervals during several normal productions of the utterance "It's a sifting again". Figure 13.3b shows how these intervals have been defined. The interval plotted along the x-axis in Figure 13.3a is measured from the peak glottal opening for the voiceless consonant cluster in "It's" (identified by the vertical dashed line in Figure 13.3b) to the peak velocity of the lower lip raising movement for the labiodental fricative /f/ in "sifting". On the y-axis are plotted two intervals that are both measured from the same instance of peak glottal opening. One of these intervals ends at the peak velocity of the glottal abduction movement for the fricative+stop sequence in "sifting", while the other one ends at the peak adduction velocity of the same laryngeal action. The movements of the lower lip and the glottis are both made to create a period of voiceless frication noise in the acoustic signal. The intervals plotted in Figure 13.3 are thus temporally related to each other in the production of the specific utterance, and one would expect that they should covary. As variations in the overall duration of the utterance occur between productions, the intervals measured for the lower lip

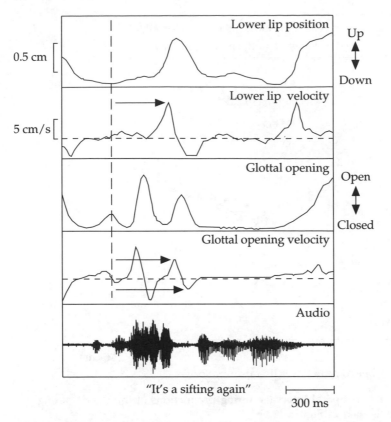

Figure 13.3b   A single production of the utterance "It's a sifting again". The signals represent lower lip vertical movement, glottal opening, and audio. The vertical dashed line occurs at peak glottal opening for the voiceless consonant cluster in "It's" and serves as an anchor point for measuring articulatory intervals. The three intervals identified by the horizontal arrows represent (from top to bottom) time to peak velocity of lower lip raising for the /f/ in "sifting", time to peak velocity of glottal abduction for /ft/, and time to peak velocity of glottal adduction for /ft/.

and the larynx should change together; remember that they have been measured from the same temporal reference point, peak glottal opening for the voiceless consonants /ts/. As is evident from Figure 13.3a, this is indeed the case. Their covariation can be indexed by the high correlation between them. At the same time, it is also apparent from Figure 13.3a that they do not scale linearly, since the intercepts of the regressions are not at, or close to, zero. This type of analysis has been used to index temporal cohesion in speech production between the lips and the jaw (see Gracco, 1988, 1994; Gracco and Abbs, 1988) and also between oral and laryngeal movements (e.g. Löfqvist and Yoshioka, 1984; Gracco and Löfqvist, 1994). One possible statistical problem should be mentioned in this context. In using correlations, one has to be aware of the possibility of correlating intervals that form a part-whole relationship. Such a relationship would in itself result in a correlation coefficient of about .7 (cf. Benoit, 1986; Munhall, 1985).

Speech movements thus show temporal cohesion even though they do not appear to follow a proportional duration model. What are the rules governing this cohesion? Admittedly, not very much is known about this problem, although a reasonable assumption is that intervals that are important for the integrity of the speech signal will show relatively less variability than others. A recent experiment by Saltzman, Löfqvist, Kinsella-Shaw, Kay, and Rubin (1992, 1995) tried to shed some light on this issue using the perturbation paradigm discussed above (see also Gracco and Abbs, 1989). As a subject was producing the pseudo-word "pæsæpæpple", a mechanical load was applied to the lower lip, pulling the lip downwards; the load was applied at different points in time during the production of the utterance. They found that the temporal intervals between the successive bilabial closing movements for the stop consonants were systematically affected by the perturbation. Most of the timing changes occurred during the lip opening phases of these intervals; these phases are associated with the production of the vowels. The closing phases were relatively resistant to temporal distortion, suggesting that their durations were, in some sense, more actively controlled.

In discussions about timing control of speech movements, a confusing issue has been whether timing is intrinsic or extrinsic. According to an extrinsic timing model, time is metered out by a central clock or time keeper that is, in a sense, outside the movement itself. Proponents of intrinsic timing argue that time may not be represented outside the movement but is rather "inside" it (cf. Fowler, 1980; Kelso and Tuller, 1987). It seems safe to conclude that the solution depends on the level of description being adopted. According to the equilibrium-point model of movement control, the end point of the movement is specified in terms of the relationship between the stiffness or activation thresholds of agonist and antagonist muscles. The duration of the movement trajectory thus depends on the dynamical system defined among muscles, and there may be no timing device keeping track of the progression of the movement. In this sense, time is not represented outside the movement by a time-keeper but is rather intrinsic to it. However, for movements to be properly executed and sequenced, the equilibrium points have to be reset continuously. These changes have to be made at the appropriate points in time and the system must have some time-keeping mechanism to make them. At this level, the time keeping should thus more properly be considered extrinsic.

What are the properties of the clock or time keeper? Again, applying mechanical perturbations to movements may provide some clues. For rhythmic movements, phase resetting analysis can be used (see Winfree, 1980, and Glass and Mackey, 1988, for general discussion). In this type of experiment, one measures the temporal shift that is introduced by a perturbation relative to the timing pattern of the pre-perturbation rhythm. If a phase shift is found, the implication is that a central clock does not drive the periphery in a unidirectional manner. Rather, the central–peripheral coupling is bi-directional, since feedback from the periphery affects the clock. Studies of rhythmic finger movements (Kay, Saltzman, and Kelso, 1991) suggest that mechanical perturbations do introduce shifts in the phasing of such movements. Results reported by Saltzman (1992) and by Saltzman, Löfqvist, Kay, Rubin, and Kinsella-Shaw (1992, forthcoming) indicate that this is also the case for speech, at least when the speech task consists of the repetition of a single consonant-vowel syllable.

4 Summary

The theoretical and empirical approaches to speech production that we have discussed in this chapter converge in their focus on understanding how the different parts of the vocal tract are flexibly marshaled and coordinated to produce the acoustic signal that the speaker uses to convey a message. A variety of experimental paradigms are currently being applied to the problem of coordination and control in motor systems with excess degrees of freedom. Progress in speech motor control is likely to benefit from input from other areas of movement control and in using a combined strategy of empirical studies and mathematical modeling.

NOTE

I am grateful to Vincent L. Gracco, Laura L. Koenig and Elliot Saltzman for discussions and comments on earlier versions of this manuscript. This work was supported by Grant DC-00865 from the National Institute on Deafness and Other Communication Disorders.

14 Voice Source Variation

AILBHE NÍ CHASAIDE AND
CHRISTER GOBL

1 Introduction

This chapter deals with acoustic aspects of voiced phonation. More specifically, it focuses on the voice source which is typically defined as the airflow (or
volume velocity) through the glottis, and it varies over time in a periodic way
which reflects the rapid opening and shutting cycles of the vibrating vocal
folds. (The source for voiceless sounds is not dealt with here.) The glottal
airflow signal constitutes the input signal to the vocal tract which acts as an
acoustic filter. The configuration of the supraglottal vocal organs determines
the specific resonance characteristics of this filter. For a given source signal, a
large number of segments may be differentiated from each other on the basis
of the particular patterning of resonances and antiresonances that different
supraglottal filters impart.

Figure 14.1 shows a schematic illustration of the speech production process
for two vowels [u] and [i]. The source spectrum is identical in both cases: it
contains all harmonic components and has a constant slope of −12 dB per
octave. This means that the amplitude of the harmonics decreases monotonically with increasing frequency, so that for every doubling of frequency, the
amplitude has dropped by 12 dB. We should note that this is the ideal case.
The true source spectrum does not have a constant slope, and may present
dips depending on the precise shape of the glottal pulse.

The filtering effect of the vocal tract (referred to as the transfer function) is
rather different for the two vowels, due to the different positions adopted by
the tongue and the lips. Source harmonics which fall at or near the peaks of
the transfer function will be amplified by the filter. Harmonics which do not
come near to the peaks will not be amplified and may be attenuated. Consequently, the output of the filter, i.e., the oral airflow, has a spectrum exhibiting
peaks and dips rather than the relatively evenly falling source spectrum, and
these determine the different segmental qualities of the sounds we hear (in
this instance the difference between [u] and [i]). Finally, the radiated sound

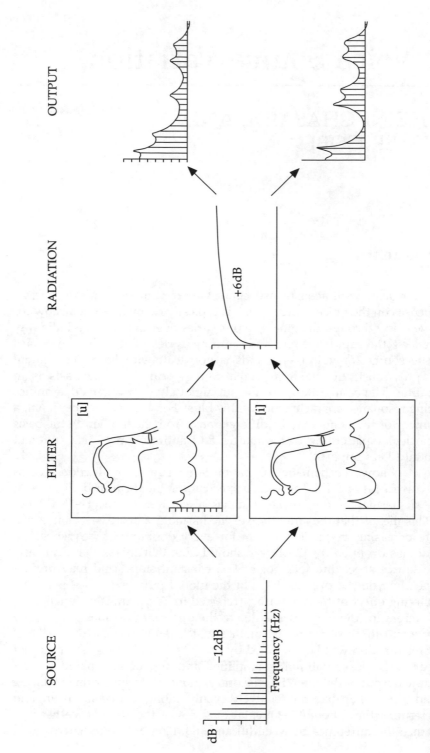

Figure 14.1 A schematic illustration of the speech production process for the vowels [u] and [i].

pressure at the lips has a spectrum that is tilted by approximately +6 dB per octave in comparison to the spectral slope of the oral airflow.

The illustration in Figure 14.1 is of an idealised source which is assumed to be constant for the two vowels. In real speech, the source varies dynamically in a way that reflects the configuration of the glottis, the degree and type of any laryngeal tension that may be present, the respiratory effort being used, and even the aerodynamic consequences of any supraglottal stricture. Gobl (1988) illustrates how the source may vary in the course of a single utterance spoken with a neutral, modal mode of phonation. The variation is even greater if the speaker chooses to switch between different modes of phonation (e.g., breathy voice, creaky voice, etc.) as is often done for paralinguistic signalling of emotion and attitude. Different speakers may also vary considerably in terms of the habitual type of phonation they use.

Over the years, much work has been carried out on the acoustics of the filter, (see Fujimura and Erickson, ACOUSTIC PHONETICS) which corresponds to much of the segmental differentiation of place and manner of articulation. Concerning the voice source, a good deal is known about f_0 variation, and how it varies as a function of intonation, tone and stress. Relatively little is known about other aspects of the voice source and how it varies in speech. (There are of course also many studies on the intensity variation of the speech signal. Although the amplitude of the speech output to some extent reflects the amplitude of the source, one should bear in mind that the total amplitude of the speech output is a function of both source and filter.)

In the next section, ways of analysing and measuring the voice source are discussed. This is followed in Section 3 by brief illustrations of how the source varies for a number of different voice qualities. In Section 4 we give an overview of the factors that determine voice source variation in speech and language.

2 Analysing the voice source

2.1 *Obtaining glottal flow: inverse filtering*

Most experimental studies of the voice source have been based on inverse filtering. This technique is effectively a reversal of the speech production process. The speech signal is passed through a filter whose transfer function is the inverse of the supraglottal transfer function. In principle this yields the voice source in its prefiltered form, as the filtering effect of the vocal tract is cancelled. Figure 14.2 illustrates this process in the frequency domain (in terms of the signal's frequency components) and in the time domain (in terms of the glottal airflow, or its derivative). Cancellation of lip radiation is not shown here for reasons that are explained below.

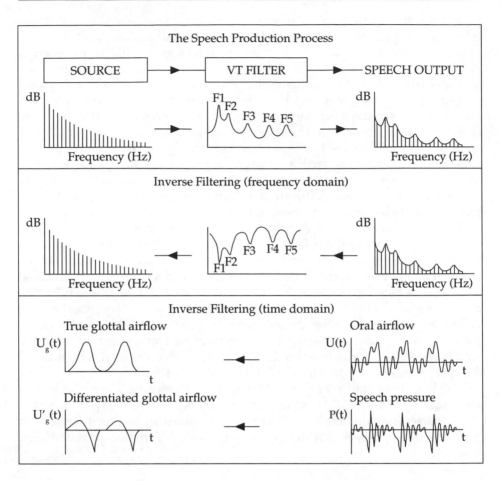

Figure 14.2   Schematic representation of inverse filtering in the frequency and time domains.

The inverse filter should contain a specification of the frequencies and band-widths of the antiresonators (complex-conjugate zeros) required to cancel the formants (complex-conjugate poles) of the vocal tract transfer function at any given instant in time. It is important to get the number of poles right for the bandwidth determined by the sampling frequency. The average spacing between the poles is determined by the length of the vocal tract: for a typical male with a vocal tract of 17.5 cm we can expect one formant on average per 1000 Hz. The specification of the precise frequency and bandwidth is very critical for the lower formants, especially F1. Any error here will result in some distortion of the glottal pulse. Minor errors in the higher formants have little effect on the main pulse shape or its corresponding frequency spectrum (Gobl, 1988).

An all-pole function adequately describes the transfer function for many sounds such as vowels. For certain sounds such as nasals and laterals the vocal tract transfer function contains zeros as well as poles and in principle these zeros should be cancelled by the inclusion of corresponding poles in the inverse filter. As it is often difficult to estimate the zeros of the transfer function, most researchers tend, in practice, to use an all-pole model for all sounds. Although this simplifies the inverse filter specification, it does mean that sounds whose spectrum contains zeros are less accurately filtered.

To obtain the true glottal flow from the speech pressure wave, the filtering effect of the radiation at the lips needs to be cancelled as well. The radiation characteristics can be relatively accurately approximated by a first order differentiation (see, however, Fant, 1960: 44–45, for a more detailed description). The spectral consequence of the differentiation is a relative boosting of higher frequencies by 6 dB per octave. This effect can easily be cancelled by a simple integration of the signal (a real pole at zero frequency), as this is the inverse of differentiation. If the effect of the lip radiation is not cancelled, the output of the inverse filter will correspond to the differentiated glottal flow, also referred to as the glottal flow derivative. Many researchers opt to work with this signal rather than the true glottal flow. The emphasis of higher frequencies by 6 dB per octave permits a more precise modelling of the spectral slope of the source signal. It is also convenient for resynthesis purposes to lump the lip radiation with the source: one does not need first to remove it and then reintroduce it.

Inverse filtering based on the speech pressure waveform can yield detailed temporal and spectral information. However, the recording equipment and room are critical, and shortcomings in either condition can lead to disappointing results (see, for example, discussion and comments in Ladefoged, Maddieson, Jackson and Huffman, 1987). Ideally, an anechoic chamber should be used. The recording equipment must preserve the phase characteristics of the signal even at very low frequencies, which effectively means that a digital or FM recorder is needed unless the recording is done straight to computer. Analog tape recorders introduce phase distortion, and suggestions have been made by numerous authors on how this might be compensated for (Hedelin, 1986; Holmes, 1975; Hunt, 1978; Ljungqvist and Fujisaki, 1985).

Inverse filtering can also be carried out on recordings of oral airflow. In this case, a special airflow mask with a built-in differential pressure transducer must be used. Many studies have employed the circumferentially vented pneumotachograph mask designed by Martin Rothenberg (Rothenberg, 1973). When oral airflow is inverse filtered, the output is the true glottal flow. If the differentiated glottal flow is required, a real zero at zero frequency (a first order differentiator) is added to the inverse filter. The main advantage of using oral airflow recordings is that absolute values of the airflow rate can be measured, which is not possible from recordings of the speech pressure wave. This is particularly useful for measuring the "DC-leakage" during phonation where the glottal cycle lacks complete closure during the so-called closed phase. The main disadvantage with this approach arises out of the limited frequency response of the mask. In the best case, e.g., the Rothenberg mask, the frequency response is limited to slightly over 1 kHz (see Hertegård and Gauffin, 1992; Badin, Hertegård and Karlsson, 1990). As a consequence, it does not provide for detailed spectral analysis of the source.

For a successful source analysis, it is of course essential that the estimate of the vocal tract transfer function be accurate. Many of the systems proposed for estimating the inverse filter involve fully automatic procedures, typically based on LPC analysis in one form or another. Unfortunately, they often do not yield satisfactory results for detailed source analysis, particularly where the vocal tract filter is undergoing rapid change or where the source involves a non-modal mode of phonation. At present, the most accurate source signal is obtained by using a method where the user interactively fine-tunes the formant frequencies and bandwidths of the inverse filter. Figure 14.3 is a slightly modified screen display illustrating the time and frequency domain information which guides the user in cancelling the formant peaks (in the frequency domain) and corresponding formant oscillations (in the time domain). The upper window shows the speech waveform, with a cursor marking the pulse under analysis. The second and third windows show (a) the speech waveform and (b) the inverse filter output (the differentiated glottal flow) for this pulse. The lowest window shows the corresponding spectra for (A) the speech waveform and (B) the differentiated glottal flow. The points marked as crosses in the lowest window indicate the formants, determining the complex zeros of the inverse filter. Using the mouse, each of these points can be moved in a horizontal or vertical direction to manipulate the frequency and bandwidth respectively. With each manipulation, the screen is instantaneously updated to show the new inverse filtered waveform (b) and its spectrum (B). For further details on this particular implementation, see Ní Chasaide, Gobl and Monahan (1992).

At present no automatic procedure can achieve the level of accuracy that the trained researcher can. Using the combined time and frequency information, many aspects of the source can be measured more accurately than would otherwise be possible. Yet there are also disadvantages with this method. In fine tuning the filter, it is sometimes necessary to compromise between the time and frequency information, and here it is vital that a consistent approach be adopted. This of course demands considerable skill and experience, and entails a risk that different experimenters will adopt different strategies leading to inconsistent results. Even with a trained researcher, there is some risk of circularity with this procedure. As the experimenter has certain expectations of what the glottal flow should look like, it could lead to an avoidance of unlikely-looking but valid pulse shapes. But probably the greatest problem of all is that the manual interactive method is not suited to the analysis of large amounts of data. As the analysis typically proceeds on a pulse-by-pulse basis, it is extremely time-consuming. This, and the high degree of vigilance needed, has resulted in these types of studies being limited to small amounts of carefully analysed data.

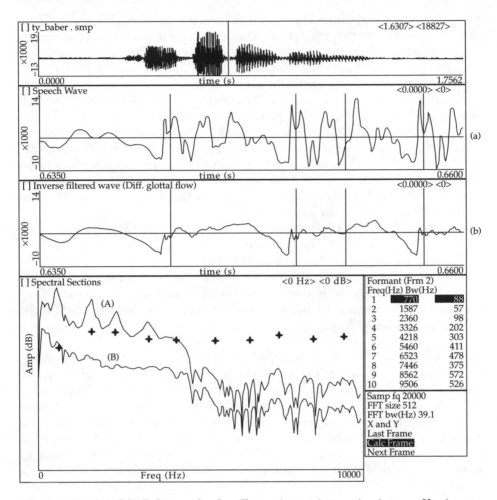

Figure 14.3 (Modified) Screen display illustrating an interactive inverse filtering method.

2.2 *Voice source models*

As stated above, the output signal of the inverse filter is an estimate of the glottal airflow or its derivative. Visual inspection may yield a first gross impression of some characteristics, whether the voicing is efficient, breathy, etc., but for fine comparisons precise measurements are required. These can be made directly from the source signal, as was done by Holmberg, Hillman and Perkell (1988) and by Huffman (1987). An alternative method involves matching a source model to the output of the inverse filter, and deriving the measurements from the modelled waveform.

For this approach to be successful, it is important that the model be a good representation of the true source and that it be flexible enough to capture the important variations that may occur. Traditionally, the voice source in speech synthesis (see Carlson and Granström, SPEECH SYNTHESIS) was implemented as a low-pass filtered impulse train (Klatt, 1980a; Liljencrants, 1969). The only control parameters of this simple type of voice source are f_0 and the amplitude of the impulse. Its main drawback is that the spectral slope cannot be controlled. It is always perfectly regular, falling off monotonically at −12 dB per octave. Another drawback is that the phase characteristics of the filtered impulse are very different from that of the typical glottal pulse. The impulse response of the low-pass filter is time-reversed in comparison to the typical glottal waveform. This means that the main discontinuity of the waveform (corresponding to the main excitation) occurs at the rising branch rather than at the falling branch of the glottal pulse.

These drawbacks resulted in an inflexible and often unsatisfactory voice quality in speech synthesisers, and have prompted the development of more elaborate voice source models. The new voice source models all have a larger number of control parameters and more accurate representations of the glottal waveform. They are therefore more capable of capturing the frequency characteristics (e.g., the spectral slope) as well as the phase characteristics of the natural glottal waveform.

2.2.1 The LF model

A model which has gained popularity in recent years, and which is used below for a number of illustrations is the LF model of differentiated glottal flow (Fant, Liljencrants and Lin, 1985). In addition to f_0, this model has four parameters and a requirement of area balance (see below) which determine the waveshape. As can be seen in Figure 14.4, the model is made up of two segments. The first is an exponentially growing sinusoid used for modelling the differentiated flow from the time point of glottal opening t_o, to the time point of main excitation t_e. Three parameters determine the shape of this segment. These parameters are: (1) E_0 which is a scale factor, (2) $\alpha = -B\pi$ where B is the "negative bandwidth" of the exponentially growing sinusoid (i.e., the larger the α the faster the increase in amplitude) and (3) $\omega_g = 2\pi F_g$ where $F_g = 1/2t_p$ and t_p is the time of the opening branch (the time from glottal opening to maximum airflow).

The second segment is an exponential function which is used to model the differentiated flow from the time point of the main excitation, t_e, to the time point of glottal closure, t_c. This part of the glottal cycle is termed the return phase and determines the residual airflow (or dynamic leakage) after the main excitation when the vocal folds close. In the LF model, the control parameter of the return phase is TA. TA is the time constant of the exponential curve, which is determined by the projection on the time axis of the tangent at time t_e (see Figure 14.4).

The description of the LF model assumes that $t_c = t_o$, i.e., the time point of glottal closure is the same as the time point of glottal opening for the forthcoming pulse period. This implies that the model lacks a closed phase. In

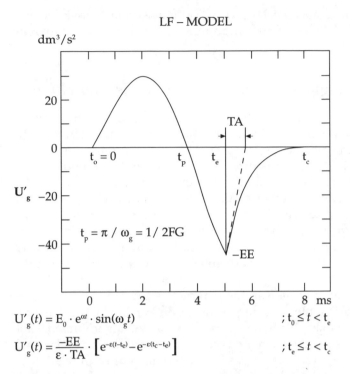

$$U'_g(t) = E_0 \cdot e^{\alpha t} \cdot \sin(\omega_g t) \qquad\qquad ; t_0 \le t < t_e$$

$$U'_g(t) = \frac{-EE}{\varepsilon \cdot TA} \cdot \left[e^{-\varepsilon(t-t_e)} - e^{-\varepsilon(t_c - t_e)} \right] \qquad\qquad ; t_e \le t < t_c$$

Figure 14.4 The LF model of differentiated glottal flow.

practise, for normal (small) values of TA, the exponential curve will fit closely to the zero line, providing, to all extents and purposes, a closed phase. This saves one parameter without any significant loss in flexibility. Furthermore, in order to unambiguously determine the pulse shape, the four LF parameters E_0, α, ω_g and TA are complemented by a requirement of area balance. In other words, the positive area of the LF pulse (from t_0 to t_p), should always equal the negative area (from t_p to t_c). In terms of the true glottal flow, this means that the baseline of consecutive pulses is kept constant.

2.2.2 Other voice source models A number of other parametric voice source models have been proposed in the literature (see Ananthapadmanabha, 1984; Fant, 1979a, 1979b, 1982; Fant et al., 1985; Hedelin, 1984; Klatt and Klatt, 1990; Ljungqvist and Fujisaki, 1985; Rosenberg, 1971; Rothenberg, Carlson, Granström and Lindqvist-Gauffin, 1974). These models can be divided into two groups on the basis of whether they model the true glottal flow pulse or the differentiated one. They also differ in the number of parameters and in the functions they use to generate the glottal waveshape. Another important difference among them concerns whether or not they include a segment to model the return phase of the glottal pulse.

Fairly detailed comparisons of many of these voice source models can be found in Ananthapadmanabha (1984) and in Ljungqvist and Fujisaki (1985). Figure 14.5 summarises some of the important features of seven different models.

2.3 Measuring the glottal signal: source model matching

As mentioned earlier, a method of extracting source measurements involves matching a voice source model to the inverse filter output, and deriving the measurements from the modelled waveform. This procedure has certain advantages over measuring parameters directly from time and amplitude points of the inverse filter output. First of all, the model matching allows us to take both time and frequency domain information into account, as the spectrum of the model can be calculated. This is particularly useful for capturing important features such as the return phase (see Section 2.4) which have important spectral consequences, but which are extremely difficult to measure accurately directly from the waveform. A further advantage is that the modelled source signal can be quickly implemented in synthesis, and in principle this should facilitate perceptual testing of the various parameters measured.

As with inverse filtering, the matching of the model can be done automatically (e.g., Chan and Brookes, 1989), but present automatic algorithms do not always yield reliable results. Again, more accurate measurements are obtained if a manual interactive approach is adopted as can be illustrated in relation to Figure 14.6, the screen display which guides the user in the matching process.

The mid panel of this figure shows the inverse filtered waveform (differentiated glottal flow) for the pulse specified in the top panel. Superimposed on this pulse, one can also see a matched LF pulse (thick line), whose contour is determined by four time points (vertical lines) and one amplitude point (horizontal line), which are manually set by the experimenter. The four time points are: (1) the time of glottal opening, t_o; (2) the time of peak glottal flow, t_p; (3) the time of the excitation, t_e; (4) the time point on the basis of which the return phase is estimated, t_r (equals $t_e + TA$). The amplitude point (5) is the amplitude of the excitation, EE. The spectrum corresponding to the inverse filtered pulse is shown in the bottom panel and superimposed on it is the spectrum of the LF model pulse (thick line). The model pulse is optimised by making fine adjustments to the time and amplitude points in order to find the best overall agreement in both the time and frequency domains.

2.4 Some important voice source parameters

The LF parameters outlined in Section 2.2 determine the overall shape of the glottal pulse. For our analysis, we need to measure very specific aspects of this waveform, i.e., those aspects that are thought to be acoustically and perceptually important, and which can be more readily related to the underlying physiological events. Once the matching procedure has been satisfactorily completed,

	Model	Single flow derivative discontinuity	Provision for multiple flow derivative discontinuities	Provision for continuous flow derivative	Waveform realization
Amplitude, width and skewing of the glottal flow	(a)	yes	(yes)*	no	sinusoidal
	(b)	yes	no	no	sinusoidal
Independent control of flow derivative discontinuity	(c)	yes	no	yes	sinusoidal
Modeling of activity in the glottal closed phase	(d)	yes	no	yes	
	(e)	yes	no	yes	sin+polyn.
	(f)	yes	no	yes	exp.×sin.
	(g)	yes	yes	yes	polynomial

* Rosenberg proposed several models, some of which allow multiple discontinuities.

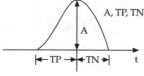

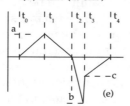

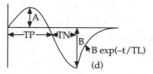

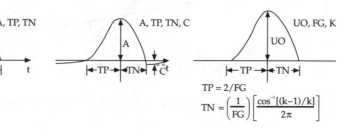

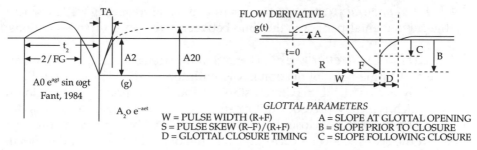

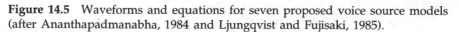

Figure 14.5 Waveforms and equations for seven proposed voice source models (after Ananthapadmanabha, 1984 and Ljungqvist and Fujisaki, 1985).

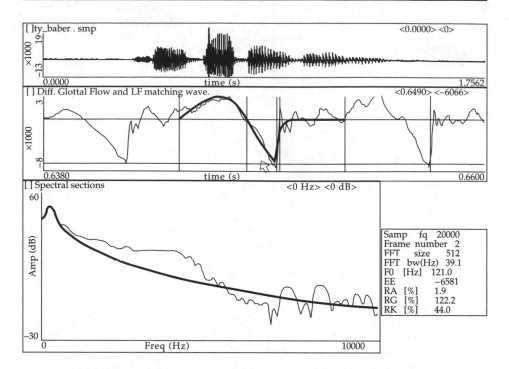

Figure 14.6   Screen display of the voice source matching method.

these source parameters can be calculated. We outline some of the most important parameters here, illustrating in Figure 14.7 how changes in the glottal waveform affect the acoustic spectrum. One must remember however that it is difficult to give a very precise specification of the spectral consequences of the individual source parameters, as they frequently interact in complex ways. The reader should also remember that the precise definition of these parameters depend on the model used. Here we define the parameters in terms of the LF model, which was used for a number of illustrations later in this chapter.

2.4.1   *Fundamental frequency*, f_0

The fundamental frequency $= 1/T_0$, where T_0, the fundamental period, is the time between two consecutive excitations.

2.4.2   *Excitation strength*, EE

The excitation strength is the negative amplitude at the time-point of maximum discontinuity of the differentiated flow. It normally occurs at the maximum slope of the falling branch of the glottal pulse, which typically precedes full closure. At the production level it is determined by the speed of closure of the vocal folds and by the airflow through them. At the acoustic level it corresponds to the overall intensity of the signal. This parameter is the one that is most similar to the amplitude parameter of the traditional simple impulse source.

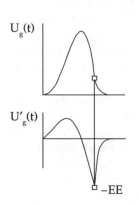

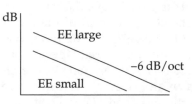

EE

RA

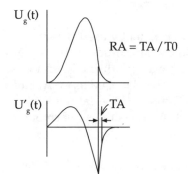

RK and RG

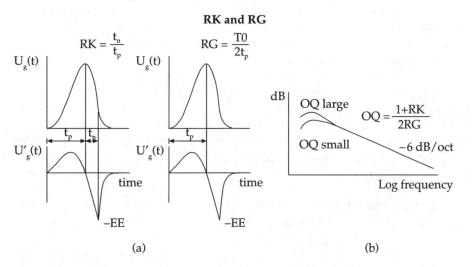

(a) (b)

Figure 14.7 The voice source parameters EE, RA, RK and RG, in terms of the true and differentiated glottal flow, showing how changes in these parameters affect the acoustic spectrum (for explanations, see text).

2.4.3 Dynamic leakage, RA   The dynamic leakage is the residual flow during the return phase, which occurs from the time of the excitation to the time of complete closure (or maximum closure if there is a DC leakage). In terms of the true glottal flow, the return phase shows up as a "rounding of the corner" of the closing branch of the pulse. In terms of the LF model, RA is equal to TA/T_0 where TA is the time constant of the exponential function modelling the return phase (see Figure 14.4). At the production level, RA relates to the sharpness of the glottal closure, that is, to whether the vocal folds make contact in an instantaneous way or in a more gradual fashion along their entire length and depth. Differences in dynamic leakage are important acoustically because they affect the spectral slope of the signal. The frequency characteristics of the exponential function of the return phase are approximately those of a first order low-pass filter. The cutoff frequency, FA, is inversely proportional to TA: $FA = 1/2\pi TA = f_0/2\pi RA$, i.e., the cutoff frequency of the filter is inversely correlated with the amount of dynamic leakage.

2.4.4 Open quotient, OQ   The open quotient is a frequently used parameter. In terms of the source spectrum, it mainly controls the amplitude of the lower components. A related parameter which tends to covary with the open quotient is UP, the peak volume velocity of the glottal pulse (labelled as A, A, and U0 respectively in the first three glottal models of Figure 14.5). A large value in either of these corresponds to an increased level of the very lowest harmonics of the source spectrum.

2.4.5 Glottal frequency, FG   The glottal frequency is defined as $1/2t_p$ (Fant, 1979a), i.e., it is a frequency determined by the time period of the opening branch of the glottal pulse. A more practical expression of this parameter is RG, essentially the same as FG, but normalised to f_0, so that $RG = FG/f_0$. RG tends to vary inversely with OQ and UP. Consequently, a high RG is found with attenuated levels of the lowest end of the spectrum. The higher the RG value, the more it will approach the frequency of the second harmonic, H2, and the more it will contribute to boosting its level. A high RG and a relatively strong H2 tend to be characteristic of tense or pressed phonation. Low RG values are found where UP is high, where it contributes to boosting H1. Thus RG contributes (with OQ and UP) to the relative amplitude of H1 and H2 in the speech output, a measure frequently used in the linguistic literature (see more on this below).

2.4.6 Glottal symmetry/skew, RK   Quite a lot of attention has also been given to the skewing of the pulse. In comparison to the underlying glottal area function, the glottal flow pulse is typically skewed to the right, i.e., the opening phase tends to be longer than the closing phase. This would appear to be due to the inertive loading of the vocal tract. The acoustic consequences of pulse skewing are somewhat complex. It affects mainly the lower part of the source spectrum so that a more symmetrical pulse shape has the effect of boosting the lower harmonics. However, the degree of skewing also determines the depth of the notches (weakened or missing harmonics) in the source spectrum: the more symmetrical the pulse, the deeper the spectral dips. The locations of the notches are determined by the open quotient together with the pulse shape (cf. Flanagan, 1972: 236–242). It may be the case that the perceptual importance of the skewing has been relatively overestimated. Skewing is typically highly correlated with the excitation strength, and its perceptual contribution is easily confused with that of the excitation strength. The risk of such confusion is particularly high if a voice source model is used which lacks direct control of the excitation strength. In other words, we would suggest that the excitation strength is fundamentally a more important parameter than the skewing of the pulse.

2.4.7 Aspiration noise, AH

2.4.7 Aspiration noise, AH   A parameter which is often not explicitly included in voice source models is the aspiration noise. The importance of mixed excitation (periodic excitation mixed with aspiration noise) has been mentioned on several occasions (Dolansky and Tjernlund, 1968; Fujimura, 1968; Gobl, 1989; Gobl and Ní Chasaide, 1988; Hunt, 1987; Klatt, 1986a; Ladefoged and Antoñanzas-Barroso, 1985; Pandit, 1957; Rothenberg, 1974), but the noise component is difficult to estimate quantitatively. Most of the voice source models discussed above generate a perfectly harmonic spectrum, and thus do not directly include control of aspiration noise in the voiced excitation. Even if a voice source model does not explicitly incorporate a parameter for aspiration noise, a noise generator can always be used together with any source model to provide the noise component of the voiced excitation. Issues like the actual spectral content of the aspiration noise, strategies for controlling the level of aspiration noise, and the question of how to modulate the noise within a glottal period have been discussed by, for example, Klatt and Klatt (1990); Makhoul, Vishwanathan, Schwartz and Huggins (1978); Rothenberg et al. (1974).

The pulse-to-pulse stability of source parameters is also an important factor in determining voice quality. Traditionally, measures such as jitter and shimmer have been used to quantify pulse-to-pulse stability. Jitter is the random variation in f_0 and shimmer equals fluctuations of the pulse-to-pulse amplitude. Shimmer is often measured from the speech waveform amplitude, which can lead to errors as it is to some extent influenced by source-filter interaction effects. Ideally, shimmer should be measured directly from the amplitude of the glottal waveform, for example, EE. High levels of jitter and shimmer have often been found to correlate with hoarse voice. Note, however, that other source parameters are also likely to exhibit instability in certain circumstances, a fact which is probably also of perceptual importance. For examples, see the illustration of a pathological voice in Figure 14.13 and of a normal creaky voice in Figure 14.9.

Gobl (1988) has shown that many of the above mentioned source parameters tend to covary. EE is highly correlated with the negative amplitude of the speech waveform and other source parameters are often correlated with

EE. For example, the return phase typically varies inversely with EE, so that if the excitation is weaker, RA is higher. There is generally also covariation between RA and RK, so that a long return phase (and a low EE) corresponds to a more symmetrical pulse shape. Several of these tendencies have been corroborated by subsequent work (Pierrehumbert, 1989; Fant, 1994) but are not invariably present as indicated in Gobl and Ní Chasaide (1992). As our state of knowledge increases, it may become possible to predict many of the source parameters from a few of the more basic ones (hopefully the more easily measured ones) and this is an approach currently being pursued by Fant (1994). Although it is too soon to know how far the correlations he posits can be generalised, these approximations should nevertheless in the short term yield major improvements in applications such as speech synthesis.

2.5 *Spectral measurements relevant to the voice source*

In the preceding section, we have concentrated on time domain measurements of the glottal source, linking these to their expected spectral consequences. Frequency domain measurements can also be carried out on the output of the inverse filter. As is probably clear from the description of source parameters above, one may need to distinguish the very lowest frequencies from higher regions in any attempt to characterise and compare source spectra. The picture can be further complicated by the appearance of spectral notches, or even additional subglottal pole/zero pairs. Specific glottal pulse shapes (very symmetrical) can give rise to notches, and might be found, for example, in breathy voice. Furthermore, the more the glottis is abducted, the greater the coupling to the subglottal system and the greater the likelihood of subglottal resonances showing up in the source spectrum.

The spectral tilt is probably the most fundamental parameter one would want to measure in the source spectrum. Obtaining it is not always a simple matter as has been demonstrated by Jackson, Ladefoged, Huffman and Antoñanzas-Barroso, (1985; 1986), who explored the possibility of fitting a single regression line to source spectra. One possible method for comparing source spectra, which takes account of changing levels in different frequency regions is illustrated in Figure 14.12, and explained in Section 3.

Spectral measurements based on the speech output signal can also be very useful. For identical speech items, differing only in voice quality, average spectra (as in Figure 14.11) or even long term average spectra can help to demonstrate source differences. A measure frequently used is the comparison of the level of the first harmonic (H1) with the level of some higher frequency component. A comparison of H1 and F1 levels has been used in a number of studies (see, for example, Ní Chasaide and Gobl, 1993; Kirk, Ladefoged and Ladefoged, 1984 and Figure 14.10). Another popular measure has involved the comparison of the level of the first two harmonics (see, for example, Bickley, 1982; Fischer-Jørgensen, 1967; Maddieson and Ladefoged, 1985). A very dominant H1 has been widely found to be highly correlated with a breathy mode of phonation whereas a relatively strong H2 can be correlated with tense or creaky voice.

Measurements based on the speech output waveform are particularly attractive to linguists working in the field, in that they do not require the level of technical facilities which the execution of inverse filtering and model matching require. However, it is important to bear in mind that although these types of measurements reflect differences in the source spectrum, they are also sensitive to other factors and can therefore not be used to infer the actual slope of the source spectrum. It is important for the experimenter to be aware of the other factors that can affect the level of different frequencies of the output spectrum, as the speech materials must be carefully chosen to take account of them. First of all, the frequencies of the formants affect their levels, and so a comparison of H1 and F1 levels would clearly not be appropriate across different vowel qualities. Formant levels are also partially determined by the degree of damping present. A high degree of damping is found where there is little or no closed phase in the glottal pulse, as for example, in breathy voice. Supraglottal factors may also affect the degree to which formants are damped. In any case, formant damping affects the levels of the output spectrum in a way that does not directly reflect the slope of the source spectrum.

All of these spectral measures are also sensitive to f_0 differences, or more precisely, to any shift in the ratio of f_0 to F1 frequencies. For example, the comparison of H1 and H2 levels may be a valid measure when F1 is high and f_0 low. However, when F1 is low or f_0 is high (or in the worst case where both of these factors pertain), the levels of H1 or H2 may be boosted depending on their proximity to the F1 peak. In such cases the relative levels of H1 and H2 are influenced by filter as well as by source factors, and so are no longer reliable indicators of the mode of phonation.

3 Some commonly occurring voice qualities

As a backdrop to Section 4 we present here a brief sketch of a few commonly occurring voice qualities. The aim is not only to show how these voice qualities may differ acoustically, but also to illustrate different kinds of measurements that are useful. The voice qualities we deal with are modal voice, breathy voice, whispery voice, creaky voice, tense voice and lax voice as described in Laver (1980). (Note that although we are concerned here only with the laryngeal aspects of voice quality, the last two mentioned may involve greater or lesser degrees of tension in the entire speech apparatus, and not purely of the phonatory system.)

The physiological descriptions here are in terms of three hypothesised parameters of muscular tension; adductive tension, medial compression and longitudinal tension (see illustration in Figure 14.8 from Laver, 1980). These

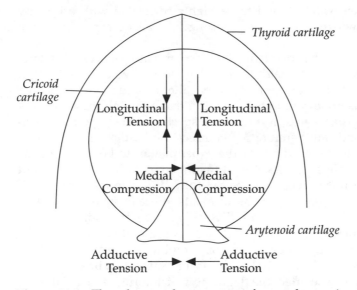

Figure 14.8   Three laryngeal parameters of muscular tension as described in Laver (1980).

determine the configuration and tension settings of the vocal folds, and inter-act with aerodynamic factors related to subglottal pressure and glottal airflow to yield a variety of voice qualities. For a fuller description the reader is re-ferred to that text. (See also the descriptions of voice quality in Catford (1964) and Ladefoged (1971).) *Adductive tension* is defined as the force by which the arytenoids are drawn together, so that the cartilaginous glottis is adducted. It is controlled by the interarytenoid muscles. *Medial compression* is defined as the force by which the ligamental glottis is closed, through the approximation of the vocal processes of the arytenoids. It is primarily controlled by the lateral cricoarytenoid muscle, but the external thyroarytenoid muscle can also be involved. *Longitudinal tension* is the tension of the vocal folds, and is mediated primarily by contraction of the vocalis and of the cricothyroid muscles, whose main function is to control pitch (see also Hirose, Investigating the Physio-logy of Laryngeal Structures).

Some of the acoustic characteristics of these voice qualities are illustrated in Figures 14.9–12, and were derived using the analysis techniques outlined in Section 2. The speech materials were produced by a male phonetician, well acquainted with the Laver system for characterizing voice qualities (see above). Figure 14.9 shows source parameter values; Figures 14.10 and 14.11 show spectral measures of the speech output signal for the vocalic interval of the relatively unstressed word *strikes*. For four of the qualities, a schematic rep-resentation of the source spectra is shown in Figure 14.12, measured at the mid point of the stressed /a/ in the nonsense word *babber*. The aim here was to facilitate comparison of spectral slopes by showing the extent to which the

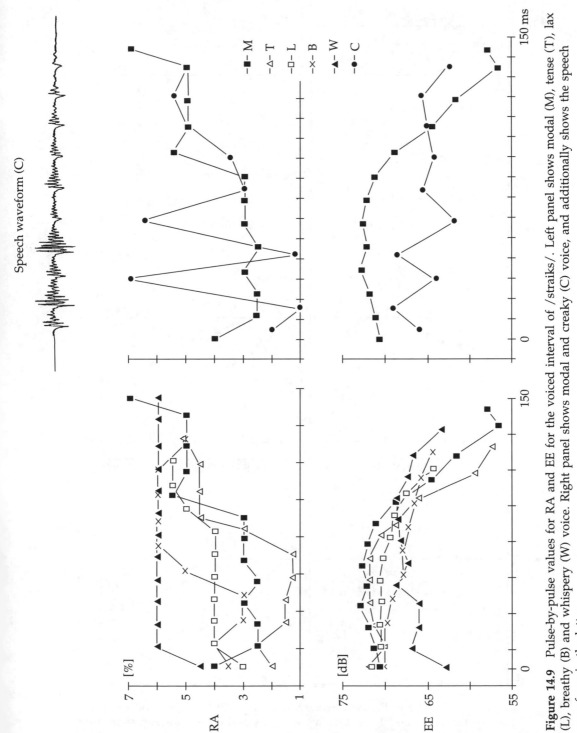

Figure 14.9 Pulse-by-pulse values for RA and EE for the voiced interval of /straiks/. Left panel shows modal (M), tense (T), lax (L), breathy (B) and whispery (W) voice. Right panel shows modal and creaky (C) voice, and additionally shows the speech waveform in the latter.

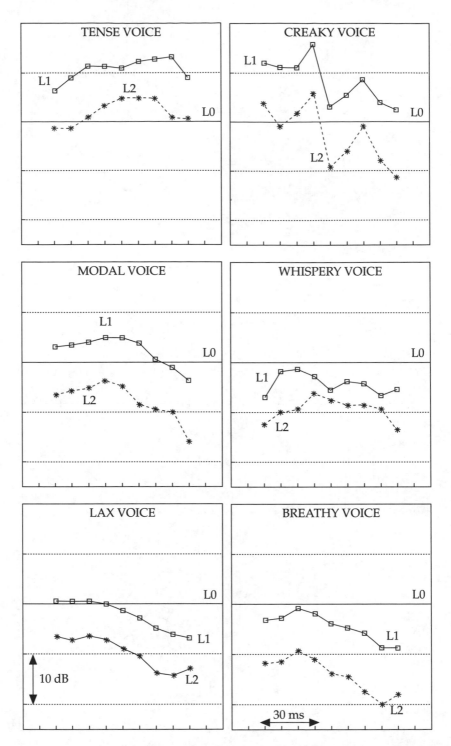

Figure 14.10 F1 and F2 levels relative to the level of H1 (L_1–L_0 and L_2–L_0) are shown for tense, modal, lax, breathy, whispery and creaky voice qualities for a 90 ms interval in /straiks/.

slope for each quality deviates from the "ideal" source (i.e., –6 dB per octave for the differentiated glottal flow). To achieve this, the spectra were "flattened" by adding 6 dB per octave relative to the amplitude of the first harmonic (L_0). The source spectrum was then divided into four frequency bands: 0–1, 1–2, 2–3, 3–4 kHz. (For the vowel in question there is one formant in each band. Harmonics above 4 kHz were not measured.) The average of the normalised (linear) amplitudes of all harmonics within a frequency band was then calculated and plotted relative to L_0. This average represents the deviation from the "ideal" source slope, indicated by the horizontal line at 0 dB in Figure 14.12. For further details, see Gobl (1989) and Gobl and Ní Chasaide (1992).

Modal voice is the neutral mode of phonation to which other voice qualities are compared, and "which phonetic theory assumes takes place in ordinary voicing, when no specific feature is explicitly changed or added" (Laver, 1980: 95). For this quality, adductive tension, medial compression and longitudinal tension are thought to be moderate. Both the ligamental and the cartilaginous part of the glottis vibrate as a single unit. The vocal fold vibration is further described by Laver as regularly periodic and efficient, with full glottal closure and thus, without audible glottal frication noise. Some recent studies have, however, shown that incomplete glottal closure may be very common even in what is perceived as modal voice (see, for instance, Södersten, 1994) and particularly in female speech.

The slope of the source spectrum for modal voice in Figure 14.12 is somewhat greater than the "ideal" case. Nevertheless, it is in relative terms a fairly efficient mode of phonation. It is important to remember that within utterances spoken with modal (or indeed any) voice quality, there may be considerable dynamic variation of the source (see, for example, Gobl, 1988). In certain environments there may be considerable convergence of modal and breathy/whispery voice, as can be seen in the few periods preceding the voiceless consonant /k/ in Figure 14.9. This is a contextual effect which appears to affect all the voice qualities looked at, and is discussed in detail in Ní Chasaide and Gobl (1993).

Breathy voice is thought to involve minimal adductive tension, weak medial compression and low longitudinal tension. The vocal folds vibrate very inefficiently and they never come fully together. Thus, there is a considerable constant glottal leakage with some audible frication noise. The high dynamic leakage of this voice quality is evidenced by high RA values. Consequently, FA is much lower than for modal voice, particularly in the stressed vowel of *babber*, where we find a value of 500 Hz for breathy voice compared to 1,500 Hz for modal. The glottal pulse is also more symmetrical (high RK) for breathy voice, and has a high open quotient (OQ). Together, these suggest a high rate of airflow through the vocal folds, as would be expected for this voice quality, and this is indeed what our calculated UP (peak glottal flow) values show. This would yield a relative boosting of the lowest harmonic, a spectral feature which has been widely reported for this voice quality. The consequent sharp slope in the lower end of the source spectrum can be seen clearly in Figure

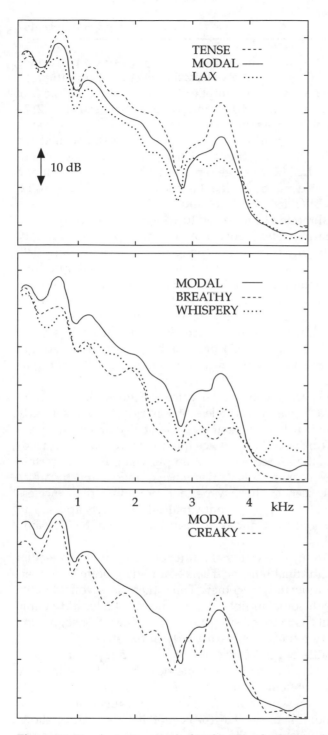

Figure 14.11 Average spectra for the voiced portion of /straiks/ shown for tense, modal, lax, breathy, whispery and creaky voice qualities.

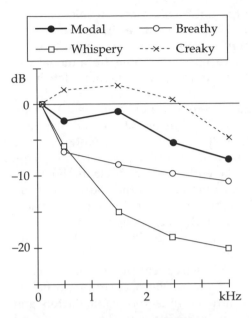

Figure 14.12 Schematic source spectra for four voice qualities in *babber* showing within four frequency bands the average deviation from a constant −12 dB/octave slope.

14.12. In the speech output signal, we see in Figure 14.10 the clear dominance of H1 for breathy voice as compared to the dominance of F1 in modal voice. This particular spectral measure captures not only the relative boosting of L_0, but also the high degree of damping of F1, which would be expected for the breathy voice quality, where the vocal folds are abducted. These effects can also be observed in the average spectra of Figure 14.11.

Whispery voice is characterised by low adductive tension, moderate to high medial compression and moderate longitudinal tension. As a consequence, there is a triangular opening of the cartilaginous glottis, whose size varies with the degree of medial compression. In weak whisper the medial compression is moderate and the opening may include a part of the ligamental glottis as well as the cartilaginous. Whisper with increasingly higher intensity has increasingly higher medial compression and smaller glottal opening, until only the cartilaginous glottis is open. Laryngeal vibration is assumed to be confined to that portion of the ligamental glottis which is adducted, and the whispery component to the triangular opening between the arytenoids. It is very inefficient and there is a considerable degree of audible frication noise.

As pointed out by Laver (1980: 133–134), whispery and breathy voice form an auditory continuum with no clear borderline between them. In auditory terms they would be distinguished in terms of the relative dominance of the periodic and noise components: in breathy voice, the periodic component is dominant, whereas in whispery voice the noise component would be relatively greater (see further comments on these two qualities in Section 4).

The source measurements for whispery voice are fairly similar to those of breathy voice, being in many cases more extreme deviations from modal values. Whispery voice differs mainly from breathy voice in having a lower RK and OQ, showing a more skewed glottal flow pulse, with a relatively shorter closing branch. The calculated UP values were also noticeably less than for breathy voice. As UP is highly correlated with H1 level (L_0), we find that there is less boosting of the fundamental than for breathy voice. Note that this difference does not show up in the source spectra of Figure 14.12, as these have been normalised to L_0. In terms of the entire source spectrum, however, the fundamental component remains very dominant, as the source spectrum has an even greater slope than does breathy voice. Probably for this reason, the measurements of L_1 and L_2 relative to L_0 in the output signal (Figure 14.10) do not look very different to those of breathy voice. Of course, bandwidth differences also affect the levels of the spectral output.

Creaky voice is thought to involve high adductive tension and medial compression, but little longitudinal tension. Pitch has been observed to be extremely low, and would appear to be controlled by aerodynamic factors and not by varying the longitudinal tension, as in the other qualities. The f_0 and amplitude of consecutive glottal pulses is further known to be very irregular. Because of the high adductive tension, only the ligamental part of the vocal folds is vibrating. The folds are relatively thick and compressed, and the ventricular folds may also be somewhat adducted, so that their inferior surfaces come in contact with the superior surfaces of the true folds. This would thus create an even thicker vibrating structure. The mean airflow rate has been observed to be very low.

Although every voice quality varies dynamically in the course of an utterance, creaky voice is particularly variable. Creakiness, in the sense of irregularity of successive glottal pulses appears intermittently. It did not show up in the stressed word *babber*, but did in the relatively unstressed word *strikes* (see right hand panel in Figure 14.9 where the speech waveform for creaky voice is also shown). Here, there is an alternation of two very different types of glottal pulse. One has a reasonably high EE (which however is still lower than for model or lax voice), a very low RA, and consequently a high FA, suggesting a fairly instantaneous glottal closure and strong higher frequencies. The other type of pulse shows rather opposite tendencies: EE is very low and RA is very high, and these should have rather different effects on the acoustic spectrum. Both types of pulse are characterised by a low OQ, a low RK and a relatively high RG (values are more extreme for the first type of pulse). In the stressed word *babber*, source values were not unlike those of the strong pulse described above, but differed mainly in that EE was considerably higher. The short open phase found generally for this voice quality correlates well with the known low airflow rate observed for creaky voice, and would have the consequence of reducing the levels of the lower harmonics relative to the rest of the spectrum.

This effect can be seen clearly in the schematic source spectrum in Figure 14.12 and in the average spectra of the speech output signal in Figure 14.11. Similarly in Figure 14.10, we find a very dominant F1 relative to the H1 level. Note that the pulse-to-pulse variation is to some extent smoothed out by the 30 ms Hamming window used in the FFT calculations for this figure. The relatively long closed phase of the glottal pulse should also contribute to narrow formant bandwidths, and this can probably also be inferred from the sharp peaks in the average spectra of Figure 14.11. The relatively high RG observed for this voice quality would also tend to boost the region of H2 relative to H1, a feature which has been noted in the literature as a characteristic of creaky voice.

Tense voice involves a higher degree of tension in the entire vocal tract as compared to the neutral setting. At the laryngeal level, the two parameters which show a particular increase in tension are adductive tension and medial compression. This would correspond to the term pressed phonation used by many authors. The increased muscular tension associated with tense voice is likely to affect the respiratory system (resulting in a raised subglottal pressure) as well as the supralaryngeal tract. Acoustically, this voice quality (measured only for *strikes*) exhibited a very low RA showing a very sharp full closure of the vocal folds. The related frequency measure FA was higher than for all the other qualities looked at in this context, and so one would expect strong higher frequencies. The glottal pulse was also more skewed for tense voice (lowest RK values), had a small open quotient (OQ) and a high RG. The picture of a highly skewed pulse with instantaneous closure and a long closed phase accords well with the physiological description of high adductive tension and medial compression. These source values suggest that the lower harmonics should be attenuated relative to higher frequencies. This effect shows up clearly in Figure 14.11, and we observe in Figure 14.10 that F1 dominates the spectrum. As with creaky voice, the high RG will affect the ratio of H1 to H2 by relatively boosting the latter. For this speaker, there is considerable similarity between tense and creaky voice parameters, if one ignores the pulse-to-pulse variability sometimes found for the latter.

Lax voice involves a lesser degree of tension in the entire vocal tract and typically tends to have opposite characteristics to tense voice. At the laryngeal level there is a reduced degree of adductive tension and medial compression. Phonation may therefore be similar to breathy voice, sounding softer and lower pitched than modal voice: however, the amount of change in these tension parameters is often less than for breathy voice. Source measurements show parameter values similar to those of breathy voice. Excepting the extremely low RG values, differences found between lax and breathy voice suggest that, of the two, lax voice is the closer to modal voice.

For all voice qualities, the reader should bear in mind that they are not fixed entities. Non-modal qualities may occur to a greater or lesser degree, i.e., may be further from or closer to modal voice. Voice qualities can also be of a compound type, as for example in whispery creaky voice (for more on this, see Laver, 1980).

As was mentioned for modal voice, there may be considerable dynamic variation even within utterances considered to have been spoken with a single voice quality. The same point holds across voice qualities: a non-modal quality may be nearer or closer to the modal depending on context. For example, our data suggest that differences were greater in the stressed than in the relatively unstressed syllable. Another example is the creakiness in creaky voice, which is intermittent and appears to be associated with particular environments. As far as we can tell at this point, it seems unlikely that a good implementation of a voice quality change in synthesis will be achieved by a single set of transformations, but will require context-sensitive rules.

4 Determinants of voice source variation

Individuals differ in the voice quality that they may habitually use. Even within the speech of the individual there are considerable dynamic changes in the voice. Some aspects of source variation are within the speaker's control, and may be linked to the linguistic content of utterances or to the speaker's paralinguistic signalling intent. Some source differences serve a sociolinguistic function insofar as social, regional or linguistic groups may tend towards frequent use of particular voice qualities. But beyond linguistic, paralinguistic and sociolinguistic influences, individuals' voices are shaped by many factors, some of which are not within their control, such as the physical properties of their vocal apparatus. This section presents an overview of some of these functions of voice quality variation.

4.1 Linguistically determined variation of the source

Variations in the voice source may be associated with segmental or suprasegmental elements of the linguistic code. The voice qualities most frequently mentioned as partaking in linguistic contrasts are modal voice, creaky voice (also called laryngealised) and breathy voice (also called murmured, or in the case of consonants, voiced aspirated). For the latter quality Laver (1980) suggests, that in terms of his classifications, whispery rather than breathy voice may be involved. However, as there is considerable variability in the realisations of breathy voiced segments, it is likely that they lie at different points on the breathy to whispery voice continuum (see below and also Section 3), and they will simply be referred to here as breathy voiced. Other more extreme voice qualities also occur, such as the very harsh "growl" described by Rose (1989) for the Zhenhai variety of Wu Chinese. This last would appear to involve the ventricular folds as well as epiglottalisation, and would sound like a pathological voice quality to an English speaker's ear. The terms tense and lax have also been used to describe contrasts based on voice quality, but as is clear from Maddieson and Ladefoged (1985), the terms can be misleading, and likely to be used in a phonological rather than in a phonetically accurate sense. Thus, the authors speculate, tense might signify modal voice in one language (e.g., Wa, a Mon-Khmer language of Southwest China, where it contrasts with a lax quality which may be phonetically breathy voiced) but creaky voice with raised larynx in another language (such as Yi, also spoken in Southwest China, where the contrasting lax quality would appear to be modal voice).

4.1.1 *Source variation associated with segmental contrasts*   The contrastive use of voice quality for vowels or consonants is fairly common in South East Asian, South African, and Native American Languages, and these have been the focus of a number of studies carried out at UCLA. Although both vowels and consonants may employ voice quality contrasts in a given language, Ladefoged (1982) points out that it is very rare to find contrasts at more than one place in a syllable. The term register is often used to describe voice quality contrasts, but is a phonological cover term, and subsumes any other phonetic features (such as vowel quality, vowel duration and small or exaggerated f_0 differences) which are often associated with such contrasts in particular languages. As a practical consequence of the facilities available (especially in field work) most investigations of linguistically contrastive source effects have tended to concentrate on spectral measurements based on the speech waveform, such as those outlined in Section 2.5. However, for the reasons mentioned there, using these kinds of measurements to characterise an essential voice quality difference can be problematic where there are concomitant differences in formant frequencies or in f_0.

For vowels, contrasts are typically of a two way kind, e.g., the breathy voiced vs. modal voiced vowels in Gujerati (for instrumental descriptions, see Fischer-Jørgensen, 1967; Bickley, 1982). A more unusual case is the six way opposition described for !Xóõ, a Khoisan language spoken by Bushmen in Southern Africa (Ladefoged, 1982; Traill, 1985). This language distinguishes modal and breathy voiced vowels. Each of these qualities can occur with additional creakiness, to give creaky voice and breathy creaky voice. (We should note here that the latter would be termed whispery creaky voice in Laver's system, where the combination of breathiness and creakiness is regarded as an impossible combination within his definitions.) Finally, both modal and breathy voiced vowels can occur with an additional strident quality. Strident here would appear to be fairly similar to the "growl" of Wu mentioned above (see discussion in Rose, 1989).

In the case of consonants, voice quality contrasts have been reported for stops, nasals, liquids and approximants. A modal vs. breathy voice contrast of nasals is reported for Tsonga and for other Bantu languages of Moçambique and South Africa (Traill and Jackson, 1987). Breathy voiced stops are characteristic of many Indo-Aryan languages including Nepali, Gujerati and Hindi, where they may contrast with (modal) voiced, voiceless unaspirated and voiceless aspirated stops. For a description of the contrasts of Hindi, see Dixit (1987).

Note that where consonants are described as having contrasting voice qualities, the acoustic manifestation oftens appears to be primarily located at the onset or offset of the vowel. The acoustic effect in these cases is attributed to laryngeal differences associated with the consonant, but affecting the initial or final portion of the vowel. Dixit (1987) is at pains to point out that although glottal abduction in the voiced aspirated stop occurs about half way through the closure, the stop interval should not itself be regarded as different from that of the normally voiced stop. In a similar vein, Traill and Jackson (1987) show for the breathy voiced nasals of Tsonga, that the acoustic effects are mostly associated with the vowel onset, and that vocal fold abduction for the breathy voiced nasal begins during the nasal consonant. The phonological domain of particular voice quality contrasts is not always clearcut, and there may be reasons for preferring to treat a particular contrast as concerning the vowel, the consonant, or the syllable. In the Jalapa de Diaz dialect of Mazatec, Mexico, contrasts involving modal voice, breathy voice and creaky voice qualities are found. Two possible analyses are suggested by Kirk, Ladefoged and Ladefoged (1984). One is to view the language as having a three way contrast at the level of the syllable. Alternatively, it can be viewed as having an opposition of modal and breathy voiced vowels, and of modal and creaky voiced consonants. For a discussion of the domain of the voice quality contrast in the Wu dialect of Chinese, see Jianfen and Maddieson (1989).

As was pointed out in Section 3, voice qualities differ from each other in a scalar rather than in a discrete way. For any given voice quality, e.g., breathy voice, it will occur to differing degrees across languages or even for different speakers of one language/dialect. Maddieson and Ladefoged (1985) point out that the ratio of breathiness to voicing for breathy voiced segments is greater in Hindi than in Yi and greater in Yi than in Tsonga. Concerning cross-speaker variation, Ladefoged hypothesises that although speakers of a single dialect may vary in the degree of breathiness they employ for a breathy voiced segment, all speakers produce the contrast by using different degrees along a continuum. Thus, for a speaker with an intrinsically breathy voice, a modal vs. breathy voiced contrast would be achieved by increasing the breathiness where relevant. It is therefore not surprising that attempts to find (from data illustrating linguistic contrasts) measures that allow classification of voice quality in absolute terms have not met with success.

Discussion so far has only been of cases where voice quality is considered to have a contrastive function, i.e., is taken to be the main phonetic feature on which a phonological contrast rests. Differences can also occur which would not be considered (phonologically) distinctive. One such case is described for Swedish in Ní Chasaide and Gobl (1993), where the voiced/voiceless nature of an intervocalic stop can greatly influence the quality of the offset of a preceding stressed vowel. This type of effect was not found for comparable French and German data. And although the source quality difference observed in Swedish is likely to contribute perceptually to the stop contrast, it would not constitute the primary cue.

Classes of consonants differing in manner of articulation would appear to have intrinsically different voice source characteristics. For a description of differences amongst voiced stops, fricatives, nasals and laterals, see Ní Chasaide, Gobl and Monahan (1993). This type of variation most likely reflects the supraglottal configuration and resulting aerodynamic conditions pertaining to the different classes of segments, and as such, one would expect it to be universal. Although it may be relatively uninteresting to the linguist concerned with the contrastive material on which phonological systems are based, we do need to know more about it, both as baseline material for descriptive analyses and for improved speech synthesis.

4.1.2 Source variation associated with suprasegmental contrasts

Suprasegmental phenomena such as intonation, tone and stress have been extensively studied, though primarily in terms of f_0 (and to a lesser degree amplitude) variation. These relatively well understood aspects were explicitly excluded from the present coverage (see Nooteboom, PROSODY OF SPEECH: MELODY AND RHYTHM). However, it is worth noting that many other aspects of the glottal pulse will vary as a function of f_0 and voice level. But voice source variation plays a role in the suprasegmental systems of languages quite beyond that which is strictly dependent on f_0 and voice level.

Among tonal languages it is not unusual to find that a particular voice quality is associated with specific tones. One of the seven tones in Hmong, a Sino-Tibetan language, is described as having a breathy voice quality (Huffman, 1987). The yin and yang tones of the Wu dialect of Chinese described by Jianfen and Maddieson (1989) are also characterised by specific voice qualities. The yang tones differ from the yin in that they employ breathy phonation and begin with a lower f_0 onset. See also Rose (1989) on the rather different realisations of yin/yang tones in the Zhenhai variety of Wu.

As f_0 differences tend to be associated with different voice qualities in any case, it is hardly surprising to find register correlates of tonal contrasts and vice versa. Despite such correlations, many authors are at pains to point out that f_0 and voice quality are separately controllable, and that variation in one does not allow prediction of variation in the other. The link between voice quality and f_0 may have historical implications, and the likelihood of tonal contrasts having evolved from earlier voice quality contrasts has been discussed by Maddieson and Hess (1987), Jianfen and Maddieson (1989), and by Rose (1989). Not surprisingly, there are cases where contrasts in specific languages are open to competing analysis as involving primarily register or tone. See for example the lively debate concerning the so-called register contrast of Mon (Lee, 1983; Diffloth, 1985; Thongkum, 1987). Maddieson and Hess (1987) suggest that the six tones of Lisu should be interpreted as a four way tonal contrast, with a register contrast in two of the tones. Rose (1989) argues for an interpretation of the yin/yang difference in tones of the Zhenhai dialect of Wu as a register contrast, which interacts with a three way tonal contrast.

Variation in source parameters other than f_0 may also be relevant to the description of intonation. Pierrehumbert (1989) carried out a pilot study on the interaction of intonational and voice source variables. Her findings show that the glottal pulse for high tones (in pitch accents) has a greater open quotient (OQ) but a higher degree of skew (lower RK) than for low tones. These results do not hold, however, across utterances produced at different voice levels: a higher voice level results in a higher f_0 but a reduced OQ. She points out that a better understanding of the interaction of pitch and voice source variables will ultimately be required for the adequate phonetic realisation of intonation in synthetic speech. Fant and Kruckenberg (1989) have demonstrated how creaky voice is used as a phrase boundary marker for speakers of Swedish. This can alternate with the insertion of pauses in read texts. In a similar vein, Laver (1980) suggests that creaky voice in conjunction with a low falling intonation is used by speakers of Received Pronunciation of English to regulate turn taking, by signalling that the speaker's contribution is completed.

There may also be correlates of stress in particular languages. Gobl (1988) has described the source characteristics of a word in focal, prefocal and postfocal position of an utterance. The dynamic range of the source excitation (EE) was considerably greater when the word was in focal position than in the other environments, being stronger for the vowel and weaker for the surrounding voiced consonants. This is effectively an enhancement of the vowel-consonant distinction in the stressed syllable.

4.2 Paralinguistic aspects of voice source variation

Whatever the habitually favoured voice quality of a speaker, temporary shifts are a means of signalling the speaker's mood, emotion and attitude to the listener or to the content of the message. As paralinguistic communication is a voluntary, convention-bound system of affective signalling, it can be readily used to mislead the listener. For example, speakers can adopt a tone of voice that signals interest in a topic which they find truly boring, or can feign indifference to cover a very real but controllable anger or other emotion.

A number of impressionistic observations can be found in the literature, concerning the paralinguistic significance of different voice qualities. Laver (1980) suggests that for speakers of English, breathy voice is associated with intimacy, whispery voice with confidentiality, and harsh voice with anger. Although the communicative function of certain voice qualities may tend to be universal, in many cases it is culturally determined. Thus for example, whereas sustained creaky voice is used by certain speakers of English to signal bored resignation, the same voice quality is used in Tzeltal (a Mayan language) to express commiseration or complaint (see Laver, 1980: 126).

Studies on the acoustic correlates of emotional states are summarised by Kappas, Hess, and Scherer (1991) for the following emotions: boredom-indifference, displeasure-disgust, irritation-cold anger, rage-hot anger, sadness-dejection, worry-anxiety, fear-terror, and joy-elation. These studies have tended to concentrate on the acoustic parameters of f_0 (changes in the mean value, range, contour type, variability) and intensity (changes in the mean value). Increased mean values and increased variability of f_0 and intensity were found for many of these emotions, and it is clear that many more fine-grained types of measurements will be needed if we are to differentiate, as listeners do, the various emotions that may be acoustically signalled. As pointed out in this and other studies, research in this area faces major methodological difficulties, particularly in eliciting appropriate speech samples. For example, many studies have employed actors' portrayals of emotions and the considerable inter-subject variability found in these studies suggests that they may vary not only in their style of acting, but also in their ability to simulate emotions. Furthermore, actors' portrayals may differ from spontaneous, naturally occurring emotions. When dealing with extremes of emotions it is likely that voice quality changes are involuntary, having their origin in the physiological changes brought about by the emotional state itself. As such, they are extralinguistic and presumably universal, and do not belong to the conventional learnt system of affective signalling.

Listeners' reactions to manipulated synthetic speech may prove an additional fruitful research method in this difficult field, particularly as certain speech synthesisers now permit control of many important source parameters and not simply of f_0 and intensity. In this type of experimentation it is important to take account of the linguistic content of test utterances. The linguistic and paralinguistic functions interact in complex ways, and an inappropriate choice of linguistic elements might yield a bias in the attribution of affective colouring to voice parameters. The interaction of linguistic and paralinguistic aspects of communication has been looked at by Scherer, Ladd and Silverman (1984), and by Ladd, Silverman, Tolkmitt, Bergmann and Scherer (1985).

4.3 Sociolinguistic function of voice source differences

Voice quality may also have a sociolinguistic function, serving to differentiate among linguistic, regional and social groups. Supralaryngeal as well as phonatory features may be used to this end. As anyone who has taught a foreign language will attest, cross-language differences in voice quality are an important aspect of a convincing accent, but difficult to teach as they are virtually never described in the linguistic or applied linguistic literature. This can lead to cultural misperceptions, as the native speaker is likely to interpret the foreigner's voice quality in terms of his/her own paralinguistic system for affect or attitude signalling.

Within a particular language or dialect group, voice quality features may signal social subgroups. In Edinburgh English a greater incidence of creaky voice is associated with a higher social status, whereas whispery and harsh qualities are linked to a lower social status (Esling, 1978). In Norwich, working and middle class accents are differentiated on the basis of habitual phonatory and supralaryngeal settings (Trudgill, 1974). Other social groupings may also tend towards different voice qualities. Rose (1989) suggests that the extremely harsh "growl" mode of phonation found in the Zhenhai dialect of Wu differs in terms of the sex and age of the speaker, being least harsh for women, and most harsh for old men. In investigating differences which are correlated with sex and age, it is of course important to distinguish between truly sociolinguistic markers and differences which are due to laryngeal anatomy.

4.4 Extralinguistic determinants of the voice source

There are other factors which determine the quality of the voice, many of them beyond the control of the speaker. Differences in the size, shape and muscular tone of the laryngeal structures play a major role. The voices of men, women and children reflect mostly anatomical differences, although intrinsic, anatomy-based features may be enhanced or reduced depending on the socio-cultural context. For example, women working and competing in a male environment may choose to adopt a mode of phonation more similar to that of the male. As is shown by the typically poor quality of synthesised women's and children's voices, our understanding here lags behind that of the male voice. For some descriptions of the female voice see Karlsson (1992a), Holmberg et al. (1988) and for child vs. adult male differences, see Gobl (1988).

Voice quality is also affected by the individual's physical and mental health. There has been considerable study of certain acoustic correlates (mostly f_0 and intensity) of psychiatric illnesses such as depression and schizophrenia. For a summary of studies on the vocal indicators of depression, see Scherer (1987). Pathologies of the laryngeal structures also affect vocal quality and many studies of the voice have been medically motivated. Figure 14.13 illustrates a number of source parameters (f_0, EE, RA, RK) for a female speaker with vocal fold nodules, as compared to a normal speaker matched for age, sex and accent. The pathology appeared to be particularly associated with the initiation of voicing, where the vibratory cycle was grossly perturbed in a number of ways. f_0 was very high, the pulse excitation was weak (low EE). There tended to be a considerable degree of dynamic leakage (high RA) and the pulse shape was generally more symmetrical (high RK). Probably as important as the actual values was the unstable nature of the glottal pulse during this initial interval, evident from the considerable pulse-to-pulse fluctuations for all parameters. At a certain point (somewhere between the 10th and 20th glottal cycle) the phonatory pattern switched abruptly. Pitch dropped by about an octave to normal values and the other source parameters indicated a more normal and stable glottal pulse. For further details of this study, see Kane and Ní Chasaide (1992).

Over and above the linguistic and non-linguistic factors mentioned so far, voice quality also carries uniquely personal information and serves an important function in allowing us to identify speakers and tell them apart (see Nolan, SPEAKER RECOGNITION AND FORENSIC PHONETICS).

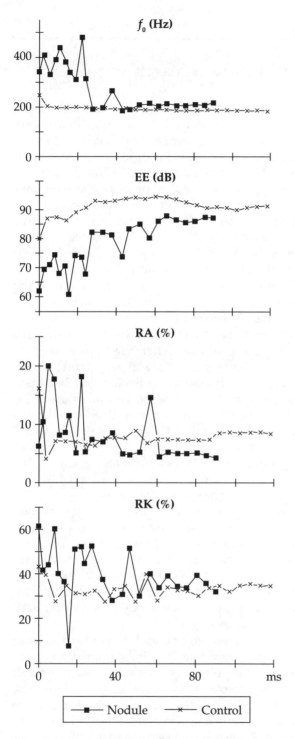

Figure 14.13 Values of f_0, EE, RA and RK compared for a speaker with vocal fold nodules and a normal speaker, from the initiation of voicing (following stop release) in the nonsense word *baa*.

5 Possible directions of future research

The human voice has evolved as a vehicle for conveying many different types of information, and human listeners have developed the ability to detect very small, very subtle voice quality changes, and interpret their function. In spite of improvements in recent years in the techniques for describing and modelling source variation, our abilities lag far behind what the human ear can effortlessly do. At this stage of play, we can but appreciate the scale and complexity of the research that will be needed to gain a full understanding of how the voice is used in speech and language. Most of the studies to date have been very limited, either in the quantity of data analysed, or in the kinds of source measures made. Advances in the field have been particularly hampered by the lack of availability of suitable analysis tools. The manual interactive techniques outlined in Section 2, permit a fine grained analysis of the source, but because of their labour-intensive nature, are not suitable for the large scale studies that would be ideally needed for progress in this field.

The research agenda must therefore be directed not only at descriptive studies, but also at devising new techniques or enhancing current ones to automate the acquisition of accurate source data. Work aimed at automating the analysis of the source without sacrificing accuracy is currently being explored by Gobl, Monahan, Fitzpatrick and Ní Chasaide (1994). Another approach currently being pursued by Fant (1994) is to exploit the likely correlations among source parameters (explained in Section 2.4). This will of course not involve the same degree of accuracy but would provide useful first estimates and could be used for larger quantities of data. As our state of knowledge concerning correlations between source parameters advances, we may be able to infer more of the fine detail from the more gross measures.

As in other areas of speech research, acoustic analysis must be supplemented by physiological experiments, to elucidate underlying production processes. The technique for high-speed digital imaging of vocal fold vibration, described by Hirose, INVESTIGATING THE PHYSIOLOGY OF LARYNGEAL STRUCTURES, offers exciting prospects in this area. Research in this field should also soon show the benefits of rigorous perceptual testing, now that speech synthesisers are increasingly incorporating more sophisticated source models, permitting separate control of many important parameters.

An improved understanding of the voice source and of how it varies in speech would open the door to many applications. The most immediate application of providing a more natural and potentially variable voice in speech synthesis would greatly enhance the acceptability of synthesis-based devices. In the past, an inappropriate voice quality has often led to a rejection of these devices, even by those who would most benefit from them, e.g., the vocally handicapped (see also Carlson and Granström, SPEECH SYNTHESIS). One can envisage at some future date the possibility of customised voices in handicap-aids, designed to match the original voice quality of the user. When reasonably accurate automatic analysis procedures become available, one can envisage many other applications in areas such as speaker recognition and verification. And with an increased understanding of the range and types of variation found in normal and pathological voices, such techniques might also facilitate an acoustic screening procedure for voice disorders.

NOTE

The authors would like to acknowledge that some of their work discussed in this chapter was carried out within the framework of the ESPRIT/Basic Research Actions ACCOR I, ACCOR II, SPEECH MAPS and VOX. We are also grateful to Peter Monahan and Liam Fitzpatrick for their assistance with some of the figures presented here.

15 Articulatory–Acoustic–Auditory Relationships

KENNETH N. STEVENS

1 Introduction

The process of communication by means of speech involves the generation of sound by a speaker and interpretation of that sound by a listener. In preparation for production of sound, the speaker plans the utterance in a linguistic form, one component of which is a concatenation of words that are organized into phrases and larger units. The words are represented in the mental lexicon as structured sequences of segments each of which is characterized by discrete classes of features. The linguistic representation then initiates commands to the muscles that are responsible for respiration and for manipulating the various laryngeal and supraglottal structures. The sound that reaches the ear of the listener is processed by the peripheral auditory system and the output of this processing forms the basis for lexical access and ultimately interpretation of the utterance.

One of the central problems of research in speech science is to model the relation between the continuously varying speech signal produced by a speaker and the discrete linguistic representation in terms of words, segments, and features. Of particular interest are two kinds of discreteness: discreteness in time (e.g., the acoustic representation of the word *sick* has three segmental units), and discreteness in terms of phonological categories (e.g., *sick* contrasts with *seek* in the vowel segment and with *sit* in the final consonant segment).

The exercise of examining the relations between articulation and sound and between speech-like sounds and auditory responses can potentially shed light on these questions. The sound produced by the vocal tract can be described in terms of a number of parameters such as relative frequencies of formants, descriptors of the waveform of glottal excitation, amplitude and spectrum of turbulence noise, fundamental frequency changes, etc. These parameters change as the positions and states of the various articulators are manipulated. As has been discussed elsewhere (Stevens, 1972; 1989), the changes in the acoustic parameters as the articulatory parameters vary through ranges of values are often not monotonic. The relation between an acoustic parameter and an articulatory parameter often shows a region in which the acoustic parameter is relatively stable, and an adjacent region where there is an abruptness or discontinuity in the relation. The same type of relation is also often observed between certain acoustic parameters and some aspects of the auditory response to the different acoustic patterns. That is, as an acoustic parameter is manipulated, there are abrupt changes in the auditory response for certain graded values of the parameter.

These acoustic–articulatory and auditory–acoustic relations provide some basis for the two types of discreteness noted above. As the positions of the articulators change with time, there will be points in time where acoustic discontinuities or dislocations occur, and other points where there are local extrema (maxima or minima) in some acoustic parameters such as formant frequencies. These points in time can be regarded as markers for segmental units. The quantal acoustic properties in the vicinity of these discontinuities or extrema help to define the features of these segmental units.

This view of the role of acoustic–articulatory–auditory relations in helping to define the correlates of segmental units provides motivation for the discussion in this chapter.

2 Articulatory–acoustic relations

The production of speech sounds can be described as a process involving (1) the generation of sound sources, and (2) the filtering of these sound sources by the airway above the glottis (Fant, 1960). The sound sources are usually created by forming a narrowing of the airway at or above the glottis, and causing a rapid flow of air through the constriction. The generation of sound can occur through three different mechanisms: modulation of airflow through vocal-fold vibration, turbulent airflow near a constriction, and generation of a transient due to rapid release of pressure in the vocal tract (see also Shadle, THE AERODYNAMICS OF SPEECH). Filtering of the sound sources can be described in terms of transfer functions relating the spectrum of the vocal-tract output to the spectrum of the sources. This transfer function is usually dominated by peaks at the natural frequencies of the vocal tract, particularly the natural frequencies of the portion of the vocal tract that is downstream from the sources, or frequencies determined by upstream portions of the tract that are closely coupled to the sources.

In the following sections we describe the characteristics of the various sources and of the vocal-tract filtering that shapes the sources to produce the sound pressure at a distance from the speaker.

2.1 Sound sources in the vocal tract

2.1.1 Sources at the glottis   When the vocal folds are positioned sufficiently close together and a subglottal pressure is applied, vibration of the
vocal folds is initiated. The changing shape of the folds during a cycle of
vibration is illustrated by the succession of coronal sections in Figure 15.1
(Baer, 1975). The cycle begins with the folds approximated at their superior
edges. The sub-glottal pressure produces abducting forces on the lower surfaces of the folds (shown by the arrows in panel 1 of the figure), and causes
these surfaces to displace laterally. This lateral movement of the inferior surfaces eventually causes the upper edges to move apart, resulting in airflow
through the glottis. When this airflow occurs, the pressure in the glottis decreases, and consequently there is a reduction in the lateral forces on the lower
surfaces. The restoring force due to the vocal-fold stiffness then causes these
surfaces to reverse direction and to displace inwards (panels 4 and 5 of Figure
15.1). The lower surfaces eventually come together and the airflow is cut off,
and these surfaces are once again subjected to the abducting force from the
subglottal pressure. The upper edges come together somewhat later in the
cycle. The cycle of vibration then begins again. Maintenance of vibration requires a certain minimum subglottal pressure that is about 3 cm H_2O (Titze,
1992).

The airflow through the glottis during a cycle of vibration has a waveform
like that shown in Figure 15.1. The volume velocity waveform is skewed somewhat to the right because the mass of the air in the glottis and in the subglottal
and supraglottal airways causes the volume velocity to lag behind the area
change (Rothenberg, 1981). This lag causes the airflow to increase more slowly
during the opening phase and to decrease more rapidly during the closing
phase, as the figure shows.

The frequency of glottal vibration is determined primarily by the stiffness
and mass of the folds, although the subglottal pressure can also have a small
influence on the frequency. The principal mechanism for changing the frequency is to stretch the vocal folds by increasing their length. This stretching
is accomplished through contraction of the cricothyroid muscle. The frequency
can also be influenced by contraction of the vocalis muscle which is embedded
within the vocal folds, but the relation between vocalis muscle contraction and
frequency is less direct (Hirano et al., 1969 and Hirose, INVESTIGATING THE
PHYSIOLOGY OF LARYNGEAL STRUCTURES).

The periodic pulses of volume velocity, schematized in Figure 15.2a, form
a source of excitation of the vocal tract during glottal vibration. The spectrum
of these pulses has the form shown in Figure 15.2b. At high frequencies, above
about 500 Hz, the amplitudes of the harmonics decrease as $1/f^2$ (f = frequency) if there is an abrupt discontinuity of the slope of the waveform at the
instant of closure. At frequencies below 500 Hz, the amplitudes of the harmonics decrease less rapidly with increasing frequency.

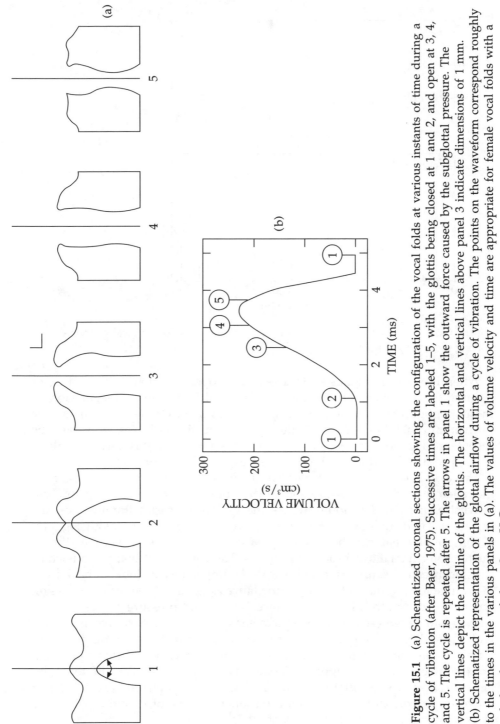

Figure 15.1 (a) Schematized coronal sections showing the configuration of the vocal folds at various instants of time during a cycle of vibration (after Baer, 1975). Successive times are labeled 1–5, with the glottis being closed at 1 and 2, and open at 3, 4, and 5. The cycle is repeated after 5. The arrows in panel 1 show the outward force caused by the subglottal pressure. The vertical lines depict the midline of the glottis. The horizontal and vertical lines above panel 3 indicate dimensions of 1 mm. (b) Schematized representation of the glottal airflow during a cycle of vibration. The points on the waveform correspond roughly to the times in the various panels in (a). The values of volume velocity and time are appropriate for female vocal folds with a subglottal pressure of about 8 cm H_2O.

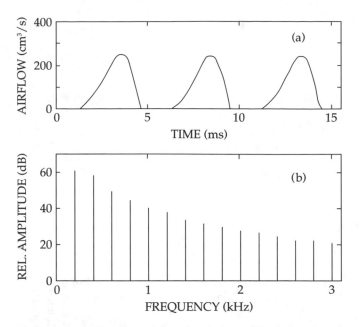

Figure 15.2   Waveform (a) and spectrum (b) of glottal airflow typical of modal voicing for a female voice.

When the glottis is adjusted to a relatively open position by spreading or rotating the arytenoid cartilages apart, the vocal folds will no longer vibrate. In this configuration, the aero-dynamic forces cannot provide sufficient energy to maintain vibration. The flow through the open glottis will, however, be turbulent, and noise is generated as a consequence of this turbulent flow. Noise produced in this manner is called aspiration noise.

This noise source can have two components: (1) a component that can be modelled as a sound-pressure source distributed over a region up to 3 cm downstream from the glottis, where the glottal airstream impinges on the ventricular folds (false vocal folds) and on the surface of the epiglottis; and (2) a component that can be modeled as a volume-velocity source due to fluctuations in the flow through the glottis. The component that is modeled as a sound-pressure source is in series with the impedance Z_b looking back from the source toward the glottis. This impedance Z_b is that of a short transmission line terminated in the glottal impedance. This sound-pressure source in series with Z_b can be represented as an equivalent volume-velocity source in parallel with Z_b, and can be combined with the second volume-velocity component to form an equivalent noise source. The estimated spectrum of this equivalent noise source is shown in Figure 15.3 (Stevens, forthcoming). For different glottal areas A_g and subglottal pressures P_s, this noise spectrum is scaled up or down in proportion to $P_s^{1.5} A_g^{0.5}$, for a reasonable range of P_s and A_g observed in normal speech production (Stevens, 1971).

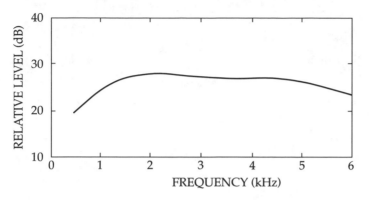

Figure 15.3 Spectrum of aspiration noise source. This spectrum is estimated from measurements with models (Shadle, 1985; Pastel, 1987). The source is modeled as an equivalent volume-velocity source to permit comparison with the periodic glottal source.

During modal vocal-fold vibration, with a periodic waveform and spectrum shown in Figures 15.1 and 15.2, it is expected that some turbulence noise will be generated in the flow. If we assume an average glottal area of 0.04 cm² during modal vibration, then the estimated spectrum of this equivalent volume-velocity noise source is as shown by the lower solid line in Figure 15.4. The spectrum of the periodic source for modal vibration is shown for comparison (upper solid line), and is well above the spectrum of the noise source for frequencies up to 5 kHz.

When the vocal folds are partially abducted at the vocal processes (the forward tips of the arytenoid cartilages), vibration can still be maintained, but the waveform is modified, as schematized in Figure 15.5a. The modified waveform differs from the waveform for modal vibration in several ways. The average flow is larger, and, since the vocal folds do not come together during the cycle, the airflow does not have a sharp change in slope when it reaches a minimum flow. The net effect of this abducted configuration on the spectrum of the flow is shown in Figure 15.5b. The periodic component of the spectrum is reduced at high frequencies, and the amplitude of the noise component is increased, as shown by the dashed lines in Figure 15.4. The net result is that the noise spectrum can become comparable to the periodic component at middle and high frequencies. This mode of glottal vibration is called breathy voicing. When the glottis is spread still more, vocal-fold vibration will cease, as noted above, and only the noise component will remain, as in Figure 15.3.

Adduction of the vocal folds by contraction of the lateralis muscle can produce a sufficiently large compression force that the subglottal pressure cannot push the folds apart, and no sound is generated at the glottis. For a somewhat smaller adducting force, a condition of pressed voicing can occur. The glottal volume-velocity waveform for this configuration has narrower pulses than for

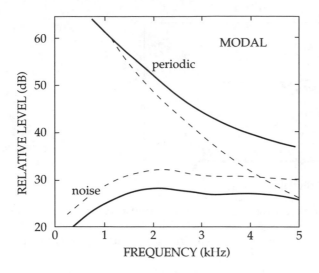

Figure 15.4 Calculated spectra and relative amplitudes of periodic volume-velocity source and turbulence-noise source for two different glottal configurations: a modal configuration in which the glottis is closed over one-half of the cycle (solid lines), and a configuration in which the minimum glottal opening is 0.1 cm^2 (dashed lines). The spectrum for the periodic component gives the amplitude of the individual harmonics. The noise spectrum is the spectrum amplitude in 50-Hz bands. The calculations are based on theoretical models of glottal vibration and of turbulence noise generation (Shadle, 1985; Stevens, 1993).

modal vibration, and a more abrupt termination of each pulse. The spectrum has a somewhat greater amplitude at high frequencies and a lower amplitude for the first one or two harmonics than the spectrum in Figure 15.2 for modal vibration. The component due to turbulence noise is negligible.

When a narrow constriction is formed in the airway above the glottis, during the production of a consonant, pressure can build up behind the constriction, assuming that the glottis is not completely adducted. For an obstruent consonant produced in this manner, there is a reduced pressure drop across the glottis. Vocal-fold vibration can be maintained only if this pressure drop does not decrease below a certain critical value. Continued vibration can be facilitated for an interval of a few tens of milliseconds if the volume of the vocal tract behind the constriction is actively expanded by lowering the larynx and/ or advancing the tongue root, thereby preventing the supraglottal pressure from decreasing too rapidly (Rothenberg, 1968; Westbury, 1979).

2.1.2 *Frication noise*

When a sufficiently narrow constriction is formed in a region of the vocal tract above the glottis, there is a possibility of turbulence noise generation in the vicinity of the constriction when there is airflow through the constriction. The amplitude, spectrum, and location of this sound-pressure

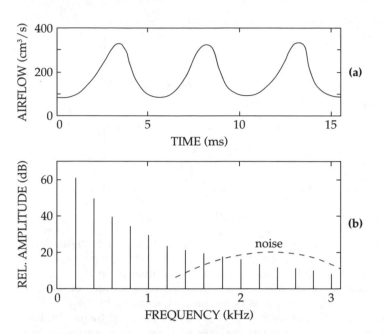

Figure 15.5 Waveform (a) and spectrum (b) of glottal airflow typical of breathy voicing for a female voice. The spectrum shows noise components at high frequency, as indicated by the dashed line.

source depend upon the pressure drop across the constriction, the cross-sectional area of the constriction, and the locations of any obstacles in the airstream downstream from the constriction. The volume velocity U through the constriction is related approximately to the cross-sectional area A and the pressure drop ΔP by the equation

$$\Delta P = \frac{\rho U^2}{2A^2},$$ (1)

where ρ = density (van den Berg et al., 1957). This equation is valid within about 20 percent for most constriction shapes, as long as the area A is not too small (i.e., not less than about 0.01 cm^2). (See also Shadle, THE AERODYNAMICS OF SPEECH.)

The amplitude of the turbulence noise source for a given airflow through the constriction is greatest if the air stream impinges directly on an obstacle. This condition is approximated during the production of a fricative consonant like /s/ or /ʃ/. The amplitude and spectrum of the sound-pressure source for this situation has been estimated from measurements with mechanical models (Shadle, 1985; Pastel, 1987; Stevens, 1993b). This spectrum is shown in Figure 15.6, for a mechanical model in which air flows through a tube containing a narrow constriction. For the upper spectrum, the volume velocity through the

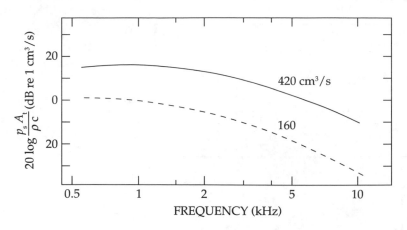

Figure 15.6 Spectrum of sound-pressure source p_s for a mechanical configuration in which air flows through a narrow constriction in a tube and impinges on an obstacle 3 cm downstream from the constriction, for two values of airflow. The diameter of the (circular) constriction is 0.32 cm; the cross-sectional area of the tube is 5.0 cm². The sound-pressure source p_s is normalized by dividing by the characteristic impedance $\rho c/5$. Spectrum of p_s is in 300-Hz bands of frequency. For 0 dB on the ordinate, $\frac{5A_t}{\rho c} = 1$ cm³/s. When the area A_t of the tube downstream from the constriction is different from 5 cm², the curves should be scaled up by 20 log $\frac{A_t}{5}$ dB. Curves are based on experimental data of Shadle (1985). (From Stevens, forthcoming.)

constriction is 420 cm³/s and the cross-sectional area of the constriction is 0.08 cm². For a different volume velocity U and cross-sectional area A, this spectrum should be scaled up or down in proportion to $U^3 A^{-2.5}$, as illustrated for a lower volume velocity in Figure 15.6. Also, when there is not an obstacle directly in the airstream, the amplitude of the noise can be reduced by up to 10–15 dB. As the figure shows, the spectrum of the noise source has a broad peak in the mid-frequency range, and decreases at high frequencies. As will be shown later, this source is filtered by the airway, particularly the part of the airway downstream from the constriction.

2.1.3 Transient sources   When a complete closure is made by an articulator in the oral cavity and there is an increased or decreased pressure behind the constriction, rapid release of the constriction causes an acoustic transient to be generated at the instant of release. This transient is a consequence of the abrupt airflow as the compressed air behind the constriction is released. It occurs at the release of stop consonants (Maeda, 1987; Massey, 1994), and is particularly salient at the release of certain clicks (Ladefoged and Traill, 1994) and affricate consonants. The transient can be modeled as an abruptly changing volume-velocity source at the constriction, with a brief duration of less than 1 ms. (For further details see Shadle, THE AERODYNAMICS OF SPEECH.)

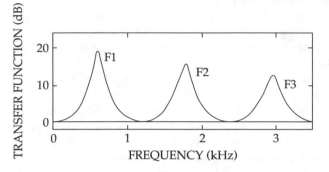

Figure 15.7   Transfer function for a vocal tract with uniform cross-sectional area and length 15 cm (omitting the effect of the radiation impedance).

2.2 *Vowels and sonorant consonants*

There is a large class of speech sounds that are produced with a sound source at or near the glottis and with no buildup of pressure due to airflow through a narrow constriction in the airway above the glottis. For these sounds the properties of the sound source at the glottis are relatively uninfluenced by the configuration of the vocal tract above the glottis. Differentiation between sounds produced in this manner is achieved either by manipulating the properties of the glottal source in the manner described in Section 2.1, or by manipulating the filtering of the source through adjustment of the shape of the airways above the glottis. Two types of filtering can be distinguished: (1) with a vocal tract shape that is relatively unconstricted in the oral or pharyngeal region, and (2) with a relatively narrow constriction or closure in the oral region. The first class consists of the vowels, and the second class encompasses the sonorant consonants, including liquids, glides, and nasal consonants. For the consonant [h], the vocal tract above the glottis may also be relatively unconstricted, but the glottis is spread. There is a much larger airflow than for vowels, with consequent turbulence noise generation near the glottis. For all of these sounds, the filtering can be described by a transfer function, which is the ratio of the amplitude of the acoustic volume velocity at the mouth (or at the nose, or both) to the volume velocity of the source, as a function of frequency.

2.2.1 Non-nasal vowels   When the velopharyngeal port is closed, the transfer function for vowels can usually be approximated by an all-pole function (Fant, 1960). The poles of the transfer function are the natural frequencies of the vocal tract, or the formants. A typical transfer function, for a vowel with a uniform vocal-tract cross-sectional area, as it might be produced by an adult female, is shown in Figure 15.7. The formants are manifested as peaks in the transfer function.

The frequencies of the formants, particularly the first two formants F1 and F2, are dependent on the shape of the airway between the glottis and the lips, and this shape in turn is determined by the position of the tongue body and the lips. For purposes of determining its acoustic behavior, the shape of the airway is specified by the cross-sectional area as a function of the distance from the glottis, called the area function. The average spacing of the lowest three or four formants is dependent on the overall length ℓ of the vocal tract, and is given approximately by $\frac{c}{2\ell}$, where c is the velocity of sound. The third and higher formant frequencies tend to be less sensitive to tongue-body position than the first two formant frequencies. When the tongue body and lips are positioned such that the cross-sectional area of the vocal tract is uniform, the frequencies of the formants are approximately equal to $\frac{c}{4\ell}, \frac{3c}{4\ell}, \frac{5c}{4\ell}, \ldots \ldots$

The relation between tongue-body and lip position on the one hand and the formant frequencies on the other is a complex one, but there are some general principles governing this relation. One approach to examining this articulatory-acoustic relation is through a perturbation analysis (Chiba and Kajiyama, 1941; Schroeder, 1967; Fant, 1980). For a given area function, each natural frequency or formant can be characterized by a distribution of the amplitude of sound pressure and volume velocity over the length of the vocal tract. When the area function is modified by making a small perturbation of cross-sectional area over a local region of the vocal tract, a given natural frequency is displaced upward or downward by an amount that depends on the location of the perturbation in relation to the maxima in these distributions. In particular, when a small decrease in cross-sectional area is made in a region where the distribution of volume velocity is a maximum for a formant (or the distribution of sound pressure is a minimum), then the frequency of that formant will be displaced downward. Likewise if the decrease is in a region where there is a minimum in the volume-velocity distribution, then the shift in the frequency of the formant is upward. When the cross-sectional area is increased rather than decreased in these local regions, the frequency of the formant shifts in the opposite direction.

Application of these principles to a vocal tract with a uniform cross-sectional area is illustrated in Figure 15.8. The area function is shown at the top left, and below it are the distributions of volume-velocity and sound-pressure amplitude for the first three formants. The volume velocity is constrained to be a maximum at the open end and a minimum at the closed (glottis) end. To the right are curves showing the relative amounts of shift of the first three formants (ΔF1, ΔF2 and ΔF3) when a small local decrease in cross-sectional area is made at different points along the length of the uniform tube. A local increase in the cross-sectional area will, of course, lead to values of ΔF1, ΔF2 and ΔF3 that are opposite in sign to the changes resulting from a local decrease in area. One can observe a symmetry in these functions: a given perturbation in the posterior half of the vocal tract yields formant shifts that are equal and opposite to those obtained with a similar perturbation at a symmetrically located point in the anterior half of the tract. Alternatively, it is

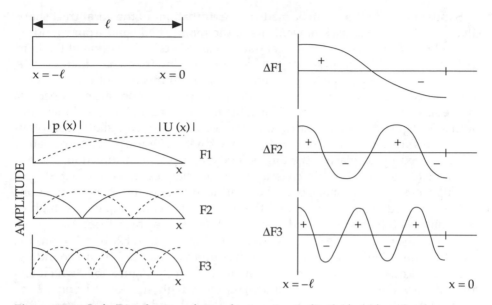

Figure 15.8 Left: Distribution of sound-pressure amplitude $|p(x)|$ and volume velocity amplitude $|U(x)|$ in a uniform tube (shown at the top) for the first three natural frequencies F1, F2, and F3. Tube is closed at left-hand end and open at right-hand end.

Right: Curves showing the relative magnitude and direction of the shift ΔFn in formant frequency Fn for a uniform tube when the cross-sectional area is decreased at some point along the length of the tube. The abscissa represents the point at which the area perturbation is made. The – sign represents a decrease in formant frequency and the + sign an increase.

noted that perturbations of opposite sign at symmetrically located points enhance the formant shifts produced by one such perturbation.

These perturbation functions can be used to infer how the formants shift as a result of different movements of the tongue body and lips (Mrayati et al., 1988). For example, narrowing of the area function over the posterior half of the length of the vocal tract and widening over the symmetrical anterior half gives rise to an increase in the first-formant frequency. In terms of tongue-body position, this change in shape (relative to a uniform vocal tract) is achieved by displacing the tongue body downward. This movement is assisted by lowering the jaw. On the other hand, narrowing of the area function in the anterior half of the vocal tract and widening it in the posterior half causes the first-formant frequency to decrease. This change in the area function is accomplished by raising the tongue body in the oral cavity. For both of these movements – tongue-body lowering and tongue-body raising – there are limits to the amount of movement consistent with maintaining an airway that is not too constricted.

Similar interpretations can be made for perturbations of the vocal-tract shape that arise from front–back movements of the tongue body and from rounding of the lips. For example, if the vocal tract is narrowed in the region of the hard palate, Figure 15.8 shows that the second-formant frequency increases. A fronting movement of the tongue body gives rise to this type of change in the area function. Likewise, narrowing in the pharyngeal region causes a decrease in the second-formant frequency. When the narrowing is at the lips, the second-formant frequency also decreases, and this decrease is enhanced by a concomitant narrowing in the posterior part of the oral cavity. These types of perturbation are achieved by displacing the tongue body in a posterior direction.

Estimates of the acoustic consequences of changes in vocal-tract shapes through perturbation analysis leads, then, to the following general relations between tongue-body position and the first two formant frequencies: high or low tongue-body positions lead, respectively, to low or high F1; front or back tongue-body positions lead, respectively, to high or low F2. In addition, the low F2 with a high back tongue-body position is enhanced by lip rounding. These relations are summarized in schematic form in Figure 15.9, which is a plot of F2 versus F1. The four combinations of high and low F1 and F2 are marked by points at the corners of a quadrilateral, and the area functions that give rise to these combinations are superimposed on the plot. These area functions are shown as concatenations of uniform tubes with different lengths and cross-sectional areas.

These four vowels represent extremes in the vowel space in that it is not possible to form vowel configurations for which the formant frequencies lie outside of the quadrilateral defined by the four points in Figure 15.9. For the front vowels, the tongue-body position is adjusted so that second-formant frequency has a maximum value that is as close to F3 as possible, consistent with maintaining a vowel-like configuration. On the other hand, for the back vowels, the tongue-body position and lip rounding are adjusted to produce a minimum value of F2. When the tongue body is positioned so that F2 has a maximum or minimum, it is expected that F2 would be relatively insensitive to small perturbations in tongue-body position (Stevens, 1972; 1989).

Other vowels that may be distinctive in a given language have formant frequencies that lie either on the sides of the quadrilateral in Figure 15.9 or inside the quadrilateral. The F1 and F2 values for some of the vowels in English are plotted in Figure 15.10 (Peterson and Barney, 1952). Also shown in a separate panel of the figure is a plot of F2 versus F3 for the same vowels. This part of the figure shows that the range of F3 values across the vowels is considerably narrower than the F2 range. Rounded vowels ([u ʊ ɔ]) have a somewhat lower F3 than unrounded vowels, and F3 is higher for the palatalized vowel [i] than for the other front vowels. The frequencies in Figure 15.10 are average values for adult female speakers. They would be 10–20 percent lower for adult male speakers on the average, because the overall vocal tract length is usually greater for males than for females.

The modeling of a vowel as a quasiperiodic volume-velocity source filtered

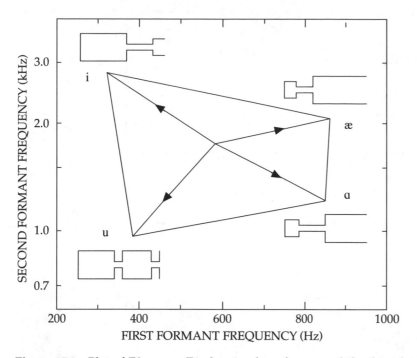

Figure 15.9 Plot of F2 versus F1 showing how formants shift when the shape of an acoustic tube is perturbed in different ways. The mid-point represents equally spaced formants for a uniform tube of length 15.4 cm. The lines with arrows indicate how the formant frequencies change when the tube is modified as shown by the diagrams. The corners of the diagram are labeled with vowel symbols corresponding roughly to the tube shapes. Dimensions are selected to approximate the vocal-tract size of an adult female speaker.

by an all-pole transfer function is an approximation that accounts for the principal attributes of vowel spectra under most conditions. There are, however, several situations in which this simple model requires some modification. These include: (1) the existence of an opening through the velopharyngeal port to the nasal cavity; (2) a shaping of the tongue blade and tongue body so that there is more than one acoustic path around or under the tongue; and (3) a glottal opening that is large enough to provide acoustic coupling to tracheal resonances. The first and second of these influences will be considered in later sections of this chapter. The effect of acoustic coupling to the trachea is to introduce pole-zero pairs into the transfer function. These pole-zero pairs appear as additional peaks and valleys in the spectrum of a vowel. The additional peaks occur in the vicinity of resonances of the subglottal system. For adult speakers, the first three of these resonances are in the frequency ranges 600–800 Hz, 1,400–1,800 Hz, and 2,000–2,500 Hz (Ishizaka et al., 1976; Cranen and Boves, 1987; Klatt and Klatt, 1990).

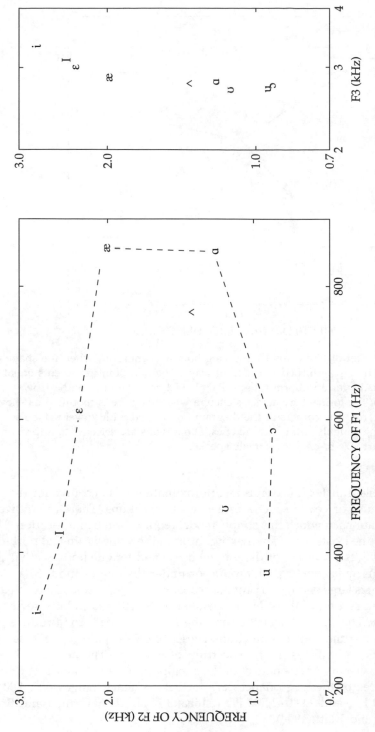

Figure 15.10 Average values of F1, F2, and F3 for American English vowels for adult female speakers. The left panel plots F2 versus F1, and the right panel F2 versus F3. Data from Peterson and Barney (1952).

Figure 15.11 gives examples of spectra of vowels (produced by female speakers) in which these spectral perturbations due to tracheal coupling are apparent. The arrows indicate the approximate locations of the subglottal resonances. In some spectra a sharp minimum is apparent adjacent to an extra peak, but this evidence for a zero is not always clear.

The tracheal resonance that is evident most consistently in the examples in Figure 15.11 and in other examples is the one in the range 1,400–1,800 Hz. When the second vocal-tract resonance F2 becomes close to this tracheal resonance or passes through it, the tracheal resonance can cause a perturbation in the amplitude and frequency of the F2 prominence, particularly for speakers who have particularly strong evidence for a tracheal resonance. This tracheal resonance provides a natural boundary in the F2 value between back and front vowels.

2.2.2 Sounds produced with an aspiration noise source

When there is an aspiration noise source in the vicinity of the glottis, it has been noted that this source can be represented as an equivalent volume-velocity source, with a spectrum as shown in Figure 15.3. The transfer function for this source is essentially the same as that for the periodic glottal source, except that there are modifications in the formant bandwidths and frequencies due to the partially open glottis. The bandwidths, particularly for the lowest two or three formants, may be considerably wider than those for modal glottal vibration.

The spectrogram of the utterance [əhet], shown in Figure 15.12, illustrates the differences in the spectrum for a given vocal-tract configuration for the two types of sources. The spectra below the spectrogram show the differences in the source spectrum as well as differences in the bandwidths of the lower formants. The first formant is highly damped when there is aspiration because of the large acoustic losses at and below the glottis in this low-frequency range. At high frequencies, in the range of F4 and F5, the spectrum amplitude of the aspiration noise (left panel) is comparable to the spectrum amplitude in the adjacent interval where the source is from glottal vibration (middle panel). Immediately after onset of glottal vibration, there is breathy voicing, with a reduced amplitude of the second harmonic relative to the first harmonic, and a widened bandwidth of F1 compared with that in the middle of the vowel (right panel).

2.2.3 Transitions into and out of consonants

Production of a consonant is usually achieved by forming a narrow constriction in the oral portion of the vocal tract. This constriction is made with one of three different articulators: the lips, the tongue blade, or the tongue body. The narrowing can result in complete closure of the airway or just a partial closure. The changes in vocal-tract shape that occur as this constriction is formed or is released give rise to changes in the formant frequencies, called formant transitions. The pattern of movements of the different formants depend upon which articulator forms the constriction, how the articulator is shaped, and where the articulator is placed.

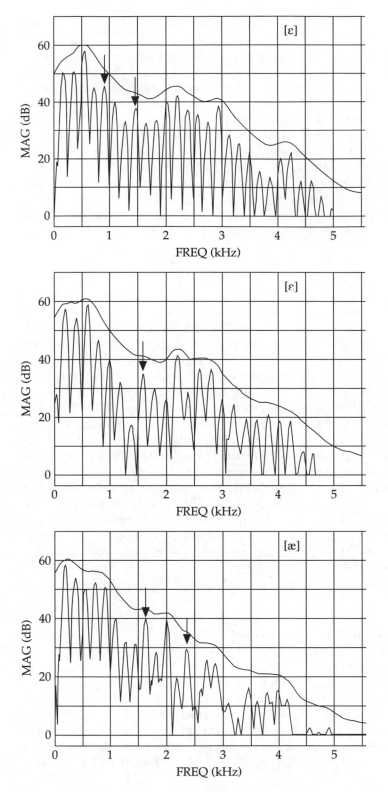

Figure 15.11 Examples of spectra of vowels produced by female speakers, in which one or more prominences due to subglottal resonances are evident. The arrows identify these prominences. The lines above the spectra are obtained by smoothing the spectra.

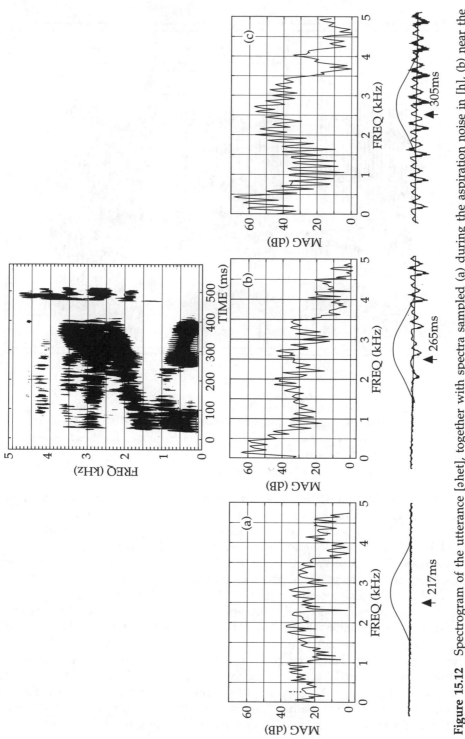

Figure 15.12 Spectrogram of the utterance [əhetl], together with spectra sampled (a) during the aspiration noise in [h], (b) near the onset of glottal vibration, and (c) in the vowel. The waveforms are shown below the spectra.

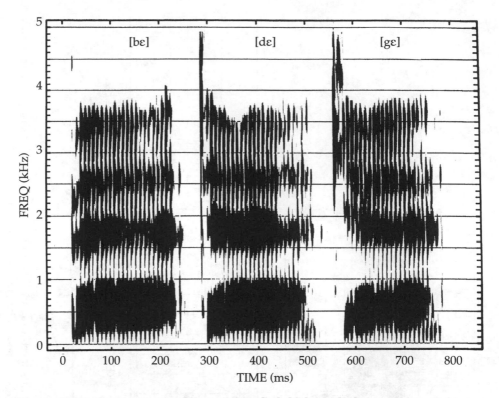

Figure 15.13   Spectrograms of the syllables [bɛ], [dɛ] and [gɛ], from left to right. These spectrograms illustrate the different transitions of F2 and F3 following the release of the different consonants. The first-formant frequency F1 rises following the release for all the consonants.

Spectrograms illustrating the different patterns of change of formant frequencies for different voiced stop consonants are given in Figure 15.13.

The formation of a consonantal constriction in the oral cavity with the lips, the tongue blade or the tongue body always causes the first-formant frequency to decrease. This observation can be derived from the perturbation concepts described above, since any narrowing is in the anterior portion of the vocal tract where there is a maximum in the velocity distribution for F1. The movements of the second and third formants depend where in the oral cavity the constriction is formed, as illustrated in Figure 15.13. The shifts in F2 and F3 for different places of articulation are shown schematically in Figure 15.14 when the unconstricted vocalic configuration has a uniform area function. A labial constriction is formed by narrowing the vocal tract at the anterior end, and this narrowing is often accompanied by a raising of the mandible, causing a modest tapering of the area function over the anterior part of the vocal tract, as the figure shows. The F2 and F3 values for this configuration are lower than

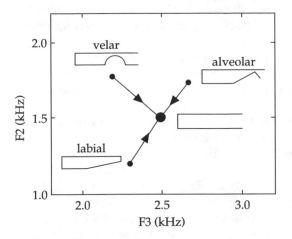

Figure 15.14   Illustrating the direction of movements of F2 and F3 when a consonant produced with a constriction at different places in the oral cavity is followed by a vowel with a uniform vocal-tract shape. The formant frequencies for the vowel are 1,500 and 2,500 Hz. The area functions for the various vocal-tract configurations for the consonants and the vowel are schematized.

the values for the idealized vowel. An alveolar constriction, which is formed by raising the tongue blade and raising the mandible, results in an increase in F2 and F3, since the constriction is formed in a region where there is a maximum in the sound-pressure distribution for both F2 and F3. Both F2 and F3 are resonances of the cavity behind the constriction for an alveolar consonant. The schematized shape for this consonant is given in the upper right portion of Figure 15.14. A velar constriction is made by raising the tongue body, and for the uniform tube the narrowing occurs in a region where F2 is displaced upward (near a maximum in sound pressure) and F3 is displaced downward (near a minimum in sound pressure), as shown in the figure. The arrows in Figure 15.14 depict the direction of movement of F2 and F3 when the consonant configuration is released into the neutral vowel (although the shape of this trajectory is not necessarily the linear shape schematized in the figure).

The act of creating the consonantal constriction with a particular articulator allows some freedom in the shaping of regions of the vocal tract that are not directly involved in producing the constriction (Öhman, 1966). These portions of the vocal tract can be manipulated in anticipation of segments adjacent to the consonant, such as the following vowel. For example, if a labial stop consonant is produced in a syllable with a following front vowel, the tongue body can be displaced forward during the time the lips are closed, so that the vocal-tract shape is different from the schematized shape for a labial consonant in Figure 15.14. The values of F2 and F3 for the labial configuration are shifted relative to the values in Figure 15.14 for a following neutral vowel. Likewise, if the labial consonant precedes a back vowel, the tongue body can be shifted back during the consonant closure, in anticipation of the following vowel. (For further discussion on coarticulatory effects, see Farnetani, COARTICULATION AND CONNECTED SPEECH PROCESSES.)

Shown in Figure 15.15 are the estimated starting F2 and F3 frequencies for labial, alveolar, and velar stop consonants as they occur immediately preceding eight different vowels in American English. In each part of the figure, the vowel labels identify F2 and F3 values for the steady-state vowels, as shown in Figure 15.10. In each panel the estimated F2 and F3 values at the release of one of the consonant types are joined to the vowel into which the consonant is released, with the arrow indicating the direction of movement from consonant to vowel.

The values of F2 and F3 for consonants in Figure 15.15 are estimated from several sources of data, and have been adjusted to show consistent monotonic behavior across front and back vowels (Stevens et al., 1966; Kewley-Port, 1982; Sussman et al., 1991). The frequencies are intended to represent the natural frequencies of the vocal tract when it is in the consonantal position preceding the different vowels, and they may be slightly different from the measured average values of F2 and F3 during the first one or two glottal pulses following the consonantal release. For each consonant, the F2 and F3 values are enclosed by separate contours for the three groups of vowel contexts: front vowels ([i ɪ ɛ æ]), back unrounded vowels ([ɑ ʌ]), and back rounded vowels ([u ʊ]).

For labial consonants, the range of starting frequencies for F2 before different vowels is about 800 Hz. When a labial consonant precedes a back vowel, the starting frequencies of F2 and F3 are similar to the formant frequencies for the vowels; that is, the transitions of the formants are small. When a labial consonant is produced before a front vowel, the F2 starting frequency is significantly below that for the vowel, and F3 is also lower for the most fronted vowels [i] and [ɪ]. In general, the starting frequency for F2 is in the range normally occupied by back vowels, so that when there is a following front vowel, F2 must cross over the region separating back from front vowels. In the case of the vowel [i], the movement of the point in the F2–F3 plane following the release follows a curved trajectory, reflecting the fact that the front cavity resonance at release is F2, but this resonance shifts to F3 as the lip opening increases. The back-cavity resonance remains fixed during this maneuver; it is F3 at the time of release and then shifts to being affiliated with F2.

The range of starting frequencies is more constrained for alveolar consonants (Figure 15.15b). Apart from the high front vowel [i] and the high back rounded vowel [u], the consonantal F2 and F3 values are relatively tightly clustered. When an alveolar consonant precedes a back vowel, F2 falls, and passes through the region that separates front from back vowels. The starting frequencies for velar consonants (Figure 15.15c) cluster into three groups depending on whether the vowel is a front vowel, a back unrounded vowel, or a back rounded vowel. For velar consonants before back vowels, F2 falls and F3 rises, whereas when the following vowel is a front vowel both F2 and F3 tend to fall.

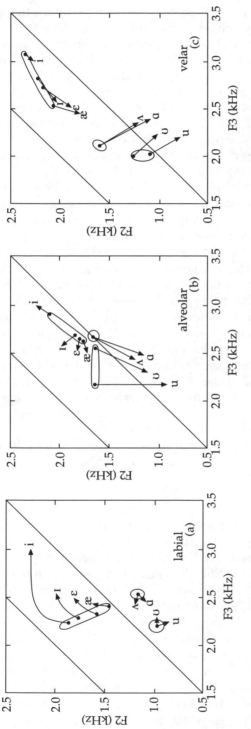

Figure 15.15 Showing the approximate trajectories of F2 and F3 movements in the F2–F3 plane when consonants with different places of articulation are followed by different vowels. The vowel targets are identified by the vowel symbols. For each consonant (labial, alveolar, or velar) the movement of F2 and F3 when the consonant is released into the vowel is indicated by a line with an arrow. The starting points of the F2 and F3 movements for three classes of following vowels are identified by closed contours: front vowels, unrounded back vowels, and rounded back vowels. The vowel formant frequencies are from Peterson and Barney (1952). The data on formant movements for consonants are taken from various sources, including unpublished measurements. Some smoothing has been applied to the data. These charts apply to adult male speakers. For adult females, the frequencies should be scaled up by 10–20 percent.

When a stop consonant closure is formed following a vowel, the transitions of the formants are usually similar to (but not always identical to) those for a consonant–vowel sequence. However, these transitions at the consonant closure can also be influenced by the vowel that follows the consonant.

The formant transitions for fricative consonants produced with the same labial, alveolar, and velar constrictions are similar to those shown in Figure 15.15, although the transitions tend to be less extreme, i.e., the formant starting frequencies are closer to F2 and F3 for the vowel than they are for stop consonants. When the place of articulation for a consonant produced with the tongue blade is different from alveolar, the F2 and F3 starting frequencies will be shifted somewhat from the values given in Figure 15.15b.

The patterns of formant movements for different consonant–vowel combinations in Figure 15.15 are based on data from English, but are expected to be characteristic of languages for which there is no contrast in tongue-body position for consonants, such as palatalization, velarization or pharyngealization. When such a contrast does exist, it is expected that the F2 and F3 starting frequencies for a given consonant will be much more constrained (Öhman, 1966).

When the vocal-tract constriction for a consonant is formed in the pharyngeal region, the perturbation principles discussed in Section 2.2.1 predict a pattern of formant movements quite different from that for consonants with a constriction in the oral region of the vocal tract. The most salient difference is that the first-formant frequency does not decrease when a pharyngeal constriction is formed, since such a constriction is made in the posterior half of the vocal-tract area function (Klatt and Stevens, 1969). A constriction in the lower pharyngeal region is expected to cause a greater increase in F1 than a constriction in the uvular region. Typical values of F2 and F3 for these consonants adjacent to the three vowels [i ɑ u] are given in Figure 15.16 (Alwan, 1986). Pharyngeal consonants ([ħ] in the figure) show a rising F3 into the following vowel whereas uvulars ([χ]) do not, and both pharyngeals and uvulars have a rising F2 when the vowel is [i].

2.2.4 Nasal vowels and consonants

When the soft palate is lowered to create a velopharyngeal opening, the acoustic coupling to the nasal cavity causes modifications in the vocal-tract transfer function and hence in the spectrum of a vowel. Since there are substantial individual differences in the morphology of the nasal cavity, the effects of this nasal coupling on the vowel spectrum can be quite variable, particularly in the middle and high-frequency range. At lower frequencies, however, there are several acoustic consequences of nasalization that are more consistent across different speakers, although not all of these attributes may be evident in all cases. One such effect is an increased bandwidth of the first formant that occurs because of greater acoustic losses in the nasal cavity, which has a large surface area covered with mucosa. Another acoustic consequence of nasalization is the introduction of additional peaks in the spectrum, due to pole-zero pairs in the transfer function (Dang et al., 1994). One such peak usually occurs in the frequency range 800–1,100

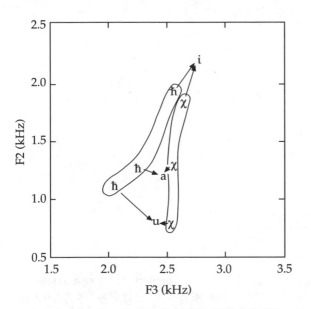

Figure 15.16   This chart is organized like those in Figure 15.15, except that the consonants are the pharyngeal fricative [ħ] and the uvular fricative [χ], and only three vowels are shown. Data are from Alwan (1986), and are averages for several male and female speakers of Arabic.

Hz (Stevens, forthcoming), depending on the area of the velopharyngeal opening. Another peak has been observed at lower frequencies in nasal vowels in French, usually below the first formant (Delattre, 1954), and this could be caused by a resonance of the maxillary sinuses (Maeda, 1982a) or by enhanced low-frequency energy in the glottal spectrum.

These three acoustic manifestations of nasalization for a vowel are schematized in the spectra in Figure 15.17. The solid line is a hypothetical spectrum envelope in the lower frequency range for a non-nasal vowel. The dashed line shows how the spectrum envelope would be modified by each of these effects: widened F1 bandwidth (leading to a reduced prominence of the F1 peak), additional pole-zero pair due to the nasal cavity proper, and an enhancement at low frequencies. The overall effect of these individual spectral modifications is to flatten the spectrum in the vicinity of the first formant (Maeda, 1982b). This spectrum flattening is the result of widening the F1 bandwidth and "filling in" the spectrum above and below F1 so that the prominence of F1 as an isolated peak is lessened.

The spectrograms and spectra in Figure 15.18 illustrate the contrasting acoustic properties of nasal and non-nasal vowels in French. In each of the two words *combat* and *engage*, the first vowel is a nasal vowel and the second is non-nasal. The spectra of the two nasal vowels (top spectra) show an enhanced first harmonic and a greatly increased first-formant bandwidth, compared with

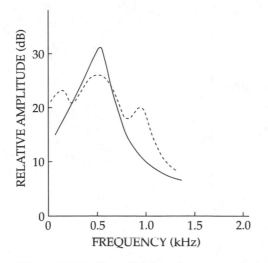

Figure 15.17   The solid line shows a typical spectrum envelope for a non-nasal, non-high vowel in the F1 region. The dashed line illustrates how this spectrum is modified when the same vowel is nasalized. The overall effect of nasalization is a flattening of the spectrum in the F1 region.

the non-nasal vowels (bottom spectra). Evidence for an additional resonance in the vicinity of 1,000 Hz is obscured, since F2 for the vowel is also in this frequency range.

A nasal consonant is produced by making a complete closure with one of the articulators, while maintaining an open velopharyngeal port. Sound is radiated from the nose. During the closure interval, the transfer function from glottal volume velocity to nose volume velocity contains poles that are the natural frequencies of the combined vocal and nasal tracts, together with zeros at frequencies for which the impedance looking into the oral tract from the region of the velopharyngeal opening is zero. Typically, the lowest resonance is around 250–300 Hz (for an adult speaker) and the next one is in the vicinity of 800–1,000 Hz. This latter resonance is called the nasal resonance, since it is due primarily to the nasal cavity. The next highest pole is at a frequency that is approximately equal to the second formant that would occur for a non-nasal consonant configuration, since the effect of nasal coupling on the second and higher formants is relatively small. This frequency depends upon the place of articulation of the consonant and on the following vowel, as shown in Figure 15.15. The spectral prominence due to this formant may be obscured, however, by the presence of a zero that is nearby in frequency. The frequency of this zero is roughly equal to $\frac{c}{4\ell_f}$, where ℓ_f is the length of the front cavity from the velopharyngeal opening to the point of oral closure. This frequency is expected to be in the range 1,000–1,200 Hz for a labial consonant and 1,500–1,800 Hz for an alveolar consonant.

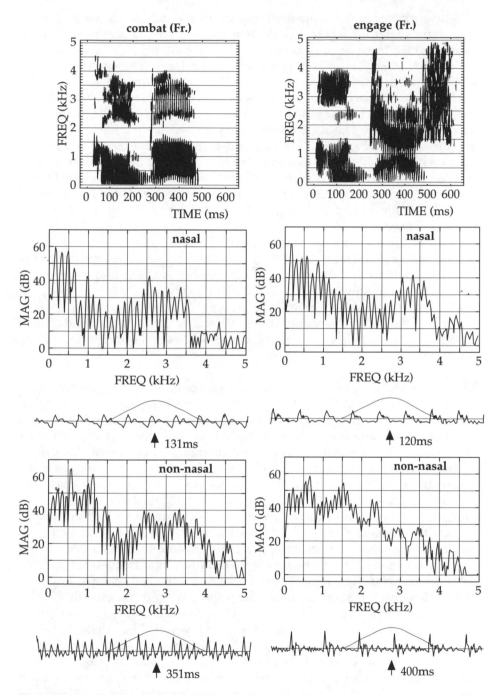

Figure 15.18 Spectrograms and spectra illustrating the acoustic attributes of nasal and non-nasal vowels in French. The left column shows a spectrogram of the word *combat*, and the two spectra below are sampled in the nasal vowel and in the non-nasal vowel, respectively. Similar displays in the right column are for the word *engage*.

These attributes in the frequency range up to about 2,000 Hz are evident in the spectra shown in Figure 15.19. Three pairs of spectra are given, corresponding to the three nasal consonants [m] (in *a mill*), [n] (in *a knock*), and [ŋ] (in *sing out*). Also shown is a spectrogram of *a knock*. The spectrum in the upper panel in each case is sampled in the nasal murmur just before the release into the vowel, and the lower spectrum is sampled in the vowel just after the consonant release. The low-frequency first resonance is evident in all the nasal murmurs. The nasal resonance is labeled as *FN*. The true second formants F2 and F3 are also labeled, and these frequencies are roughly in accord with the values on the chart in Figure 15.15. The movement of F2 and F3 following the release of [n] can be seen in the spectrogram. Evidence for the zero in the spectrum of the nasal murmur can be seen at about 1,100 Hz for [m], 1,500 Hz for [n] and around 2,100 Hz for [ŋ], although the last of these is not well-defined.

A salient acoustic attribute at the release of a nasal consonant is the abrupt increase in spectrum amplitude in the middle and high-frequency range as the output shifts abruptly from the nose to the mouth, and the frequency of the zero shifts rapidly downward. As Figure 15.19 shows, the jump in spectrum amplitude in the frequency range of F2 is about 20 dB, when upper and lower spectra are compared. This abrupt amplitude change is due to the rapid change in the first-formant frequency at the release as well as to the abrupt downward shift in the zero.

2.2.5 Liquids and glides

Like the vowels, the liquids and glides are produced with a source at the glottis, but with a constriction in the airway that is relatively narrow. The constriction is not so narrow however, that it creates a significant pressure drop when the vocal folds are vibrating with a modal configuration. The constriction is narrow enough, however, that the airflow creates a resistance that increases the acoustic losses and hence increases the bandwidth of certain formants. As a consequence, when the vocal tract is in the most constricted configuration for such a consonant the spectrum has some peaks that are less salient than others. The formant with the increased bandwidth is usually F2 or F3. The constriction also has the potential effect of loading the glottal source, resulting in a reduced amplitude of the source and a greater downward tilt of the source spectrum at high frequencies (Bickley and Stevens, 1986). This influence on the source, combined with the low first-formant frequency that occurs when the vocal tract is constricted in the oral region, causes liquids and glides to have a low-frequency spectrum amplitude that is reduced relative to that of an adjacent vowel. Thus there are three general properties of liquids and glides that distinguish them from vowels: a reduced low-frequency spectrum amplitude, an additional decrease in amplitude at high frequencies, and a reduced prominence of the second or third formant peak. All of these attributes are not necessarily present in all instances of these sounds. In addition to these properties, the spectra for liquids ([l] and [r]) have some irregularities at high frequencies (in the F3 range) that

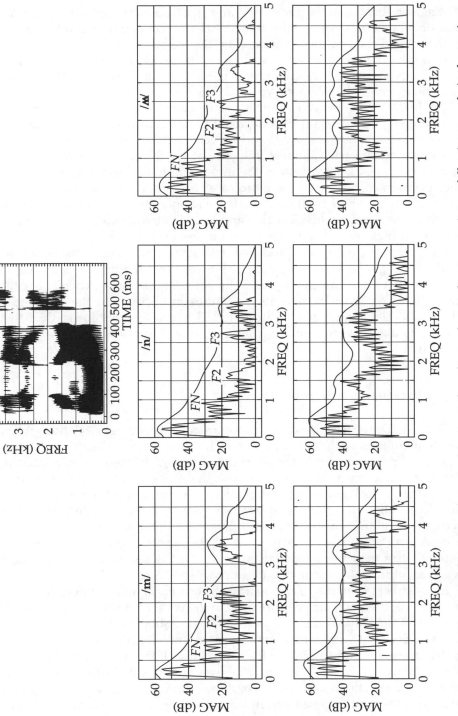

Figure 15.19   Illustrating how the spectrum changes at the release of a nasal consonant into a following vowel. At the top is a spectrogram of the utterance a *knock*. In the column below the spectrogram are two spectra: one sampled in the nasal murmur for [n] and the other sampled immediately following the release. The formant frequencies F2 and F3 are labeled, as is the nasal formant *FN*. Similar pairs of spectra are given in the left column for the utterance a *mill* and in the right column for the utterance *sing out*. The solid line above each spectrum is a smoothed version of the spectrum. The increase in spectrum amplitude in the F2 region is about 20 dB as the consonant-vowel boundary is crossed.

distinguish them from the glides ([w] and [j]). These irregularities arise from additional pole-zero pairs in the transfer function because of multiple acoustic paths around the constriction formed by the tongue blade.

Examples of spectra sampled at the most constricted point during each of the liquids and glides in American English are compared with the spectra sometime later in the following vowel, in the top and bottom panels in Figure 15.20. In each case, the consonant is produced in a symmetrical intervocalic position with the vowel selected to have F1 and F2 values similar to those for the consonant. In this way, a comparison can be made between the vowel and consonant spectra with minimal influence of the formant frequencies on the spectrum shapes. Comparison of the upper and lower panels indicates how the spectrum changes from the more constricted region for the consonant to the more open vowel configuration. For example, there is rapid increase in spectrum amplitude in the F2 region and at higher frequencies for both [l] and [r], with a high-frequency F3 for [l] and a lower F3 for [r].

The glides [w] and [j] are produced with vocal-tract configurations similar to those for the high vowels [u] and [i], except that the tongue-body height (and, in the case of [w], the degree of lip rounding) is more extreme. For the back glide [w], the narrowed airway causes an increase in the bandwidth of F2. The high-frequency amplitude for [j] is considerably lower than that for the following vowel, presumably due to an increased tilt in the glottal spectrum.

2.3 Obstruent consonants

In Section 2.2, we have described some articulatory–acoustic relations when the configuration of the vocal tract is such that the airflow does not cause a significant pressure drop in the supraglottal airway. For those configurations, the acoustic source is always at or near the glottis, and the pressure drop across the glottis is equal to the subglottal pressure. When the constriction in the airway above the glottis is sufficiently narrow, a pressure drop can occur across the constriction. The increased pressure behind the constriction causes a decreased pressure drop across the glottis, and the transglottal pressure becomes less than the subglottal pressure. This is the condition that exists when an obstruent consonant is produced.

An obstruent consonant has two acoustic attributes that distinguish it from sounds produced with no pressure drop in the vocal tract above the glottis: (1) because of the reduced transglottal pressure, the strength of vocal-fold vibration is reduced or vocal-fold vibration ceases, and (2) turbulence noise is generated due to the rapid airflow at the constriction. If the size of the constriction is maintained at a small non-zero value over an interval of time of a few tens of milliseconds, the noise source continues throughout this interval, and a fricative consonant is generated. If a complete closure is formed to produce a stop consonant, then turbulence noise is produced at the constriction for a

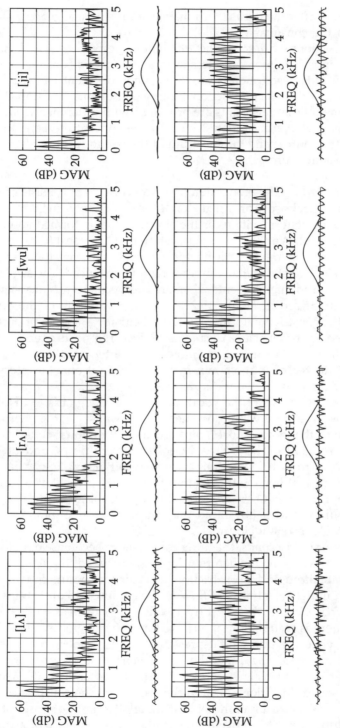

Figure 15.20 The top panels show spectra sampled during the constricted interval for liquids and glides in various vowel environments, as shown. The spectra in the bottom panels are sampled during the initial or middle parts of the following vowels. The waveforms are shown below the spectra, together with the time windows for the spectra. The time intervals from top spectrum to bottom spectrum are as follows: for [lʌ], 36 ms; for [rʌ], 93 ms; for [wu], 97 ms; for [ji], 101 ms. Speaker is adult female.

brief interval of time after the release. A transient source may also occur at the time of release of the consonant.

In the next two sections we describe the articulatory, aerodynamic and acoustic events for the most common voiceless stop and fricative consonants. We then consider how this description is modified when different laryngeal adjustments are made during the production of these consonants. The transitions of the formants when these consonants are produced with different articulators have been discussed above in Section 2.2.5, and we concentrate here on the time variation of the sources and the spectrum of the sound resulting from the frication and transient sources.

2.3.1 Stop consonants

2.3.1 Stop consonants The production of a stop consonant consists of two events: a closure and a release of an articulator. If the consonant is in intervocalic position, there are formant transitions as the closure is being formed and after the release has occurred. We assume in this section that the vocal folds remain in a state appropriate for modal voicing for a vowel, and that there are no active adjustments of this state when the consonant is produced. The sequence of mechanical and aerodynamic events when an intervocalic stop consonant is produced are summarized in Figure 15.21. The time variation of the cross-sectional area of the constriction formed by the articulator is shown in part (a) of the figure: the cross-sectional area decreases rapidly, the closure remains for 80-odd ms, and then the area increases. Immediately after closure occurs, the intraoral pressure increases (also shown in Figure 15.21a) and the pressure across the glottis decreases. As the intraoral pressure increases, the force from this pressure causes the walls of the vocal tract and of the glottis to displace outwards. The flow due to outward movement of the walls, U_w, together with the flow U_g through the glottis and U_c through the supraglottal constriction, is plotted in Figure 15.21b. These curves depict average flows, and do not show fluctuations due to glottal vibration. The actual glottal flow is schematized in part (c) of the figure. When the transglottal pressure drops below a threshold value of about 3 cm H_2O, vocal-fold vibration ceases. The decrease in transglottal pressure is sufficiently rapid that only one or two glottal pulses occur following the consonant closure.

After a few tens of milliseconds, the intraoral pressure becomes equal to the subglottal pressure. At the time when the closure is released, there is a rapid outward flow of air through the constriction. This airflow occurs in two successive phases: an initial brief transient flow as the compressed air is released, and a longer peak in flow as the vocal-tract walls displace back to their rest position and as there is resumption of airflow through the glottis. Vocal-fold vibration begins when the transglottal pressure increases above a threshold value of about 3 cm H_2O. These aerodynamic events following the release result in a sequence of acoustic sources: (1) a transient source, (2) a brief turbulence noise source (frication noise) in the vicinity of the constriction, (3) a possible brief interval of aspiration noise at the glottis, and (4) onset of the quasiperiodic volume-velocity source at the glottis. This sequence of acoustic sources is shown schematically in Figure 15.22.

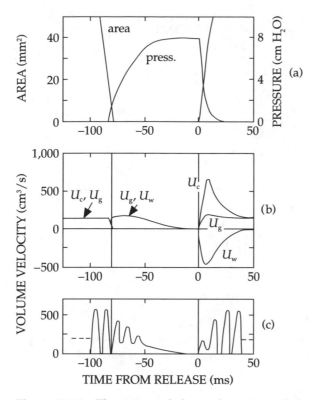

Figure 15.21 The top panel shows the estimated change in cross-sectional area of the consonantal constriction when a voiceless unaspirated alveolar or labial stop consonant is produced in intervocalic position. The calculated intraoral pressure, based on an aerodynamic and mechanical model of the vocal tract, is also displayed. The middle panel gives the calculated airflows during the production of the consonant: the flows U_c through the constriction, U_g through the glottis, and U_w due to outward movement of the vocal-tract walls. The bottom panel shows estimates of the instantaneous flow, and depicts each glottal pulse in the vicinity of the consonant interval. The vertical lines in the bottom two panels show the times of closure and opening. The subglottal pressure is 8 cm H_2O.

The detailed aerodynamic and acoustic events depend on the rate of closure or release of the articulator forming the stop consonants. The rates of change of cross-sectional area shown in Figure 15.21 are typical of labial and alveolar stop consonants. The rates for velar consonants are slower, and the slower release leads to a longer burst and a longer time interval from the release to the onset of glottal vibration.

These various sources are filtered by the vocal tract, and the output shows spectral peaks, with the degree of prominence of each peak depending on the spectrum and location of the source. The transient and frication noise sources excite primarily the resonances of the part of the airway that is downstream

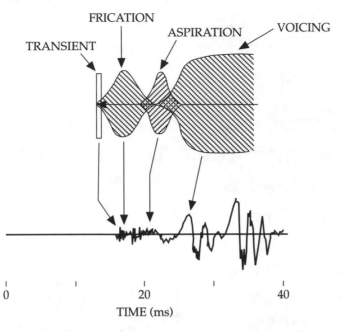

Figure 15.22   Schematic representation of sequence of events at the release of a voiceless unaspirated stop consonant. A typical waveform (with time scale) is shown at the bottom.

from the constriction, whereas the aspiration or periodic source at the glottis excites all of the vocal-tract resonances.

The waveform and spectrogram for the utterances ['bɑpə], shown in Figure 15.23, illustrate some of the acoustic attributes of an unaspirated labial stop consonant [p] as it occurs before a reduced vowel. In this example, there is a time interval of about 12 ms from the consonant release (shown by an arrow on the waveform) to the onset of the first glottal pulse. The falling second-formant transition as the consonantal closure is formed, and the rising F2 transition after the labial release are evident in the spectrogram.

The spectrum sampled over a brief time interval following the release of the burst of the unaspirated consonant [p] in ['bɑpə] is shown in Figure 15.24a. Overlaid on this spectrum is the spectrum of the vowel averaged over a 4-ms interval in the second period of the following vowel. The spectrum of the burst has no major spectral prominences, reflecting the fact that there is no acoustic cavity anterior to the constriction to filter the noise and transient sources at the constriction. Minor spectral peaks are evident in the conson-ant spectrum as a consequence of weak excitation of the vocal tract behind the consonant constriction. Because there is no enhancement of the source by a front-cavity resonance, the burst spectrum for [p] is relatively weak, and is lower in amplitude than the spectrum peaks in the following vowel.

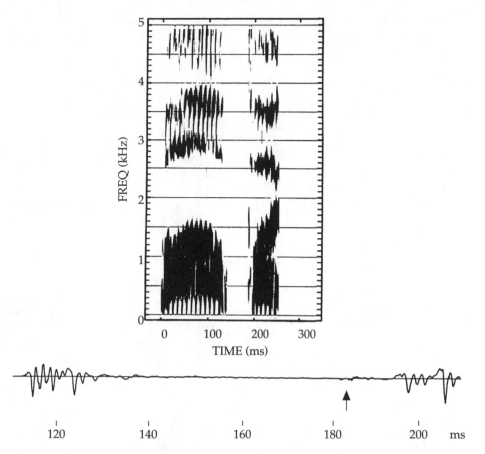

Figure 15.23 At the top is a spectrogram of the utterance ['bapə], illustrating the acoustic attributes of a voiceless unaspirated [p]. The waveform of the portion of the utterance from near the end of the first vowel to the first few glottal periods of the second vowel is shown below, with the consonant release marked by an arrow.

Similar pairs of spectra of the consonant burst and the following vowel (second glottal period) are shown for unaspirated [t] and [k] in Figures 15.24b and 15.24c. In the case of the alveolar consonant [t], there is a major spectral peak in the frequency range 3,500–4,000 Hz, due to a resonance of the short cavity anterior to the constriction formed by the tongue tip. The amplitude of this spectrum peak is 10–15 dB greater than the amplitude of the spectrum peak that is in the same frequency range for the vowel. In the case of [k] (Figure 15.24c), the major spectrum peak is at 1,500 Hz, reflecting a resonance of a front cavity with a length of about 6 cm. The amplitude of the peak is about equal to the amplitude of the F2 spectrum peak in the following vowel. A second resonance of this cavity is evident at about 4,500 Hz. The location of the tongue-body constriction for [k] is dependent on the following vowel, and

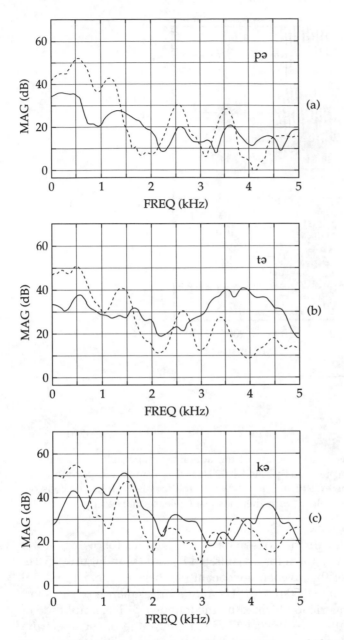

Figure 15.24   Each panel shows the spectrum sampled in the burst at the release of a voiceless unaspirated stop consonant (solid line), together with the spectrum near the second glottal period in the vowel (dashed line). The spectra are obtained by averaging a series of four spectra (6.4-ms time window) sampled at 1-ms intervals. From top to bottom, the consonants are labial, alveolar, and velar, and the following vowel is [ə]. Adult male speaker.

hence the vowel influences the frequency location of the major mid-frequency peak in the spectrum of the burst. When [k] is followed by a front vowel, the frequency of the spectral prominence for the burst is usually in the vicinity of F3 for the vowel, rather than F2, as shown in the figure.

Theoretical studies of models, together with data of the type given in Figure 15.24, show that the spectrum of the burst at the release of a stop consonant has distinctive characteristics depending on which articulator produces the consonantal closure and where that articulator is positioned. The spectrum of the burst has no major prominences for a labial stop, has a peak in the F4 or F5 range for an alveolar stop, and has a prominence in the F2 or F3 region for a velar stop.

2.3.2 Fricative consonants   When a fricative consonant is produced, the cross-sectional area of the constriction becomes narrow enough that continuous turbulence noise is generated in the vicinity of the constriction. The time variation of the cross-sectional area when a fricative consonant is in intervocalic position has the form shown in Figure 15.25a. When the fricative consonant is voiceless, it is necessary to spread the glottis in order to provide sufficient airflow to generate the frication noise. A typical time course of the glottal opening for the inter-vocalic fricative is also given in Figure 15.25a. The time variation of the supraglottal and glottal constriction areas are shown by two sets of lines. The solid lines are the areas that would exist if there were no increase in intraoral pressure. The increased intraoral pressure creates forces on the surface of the supraglottal articulator and on the surface of the glottis, causing an increase in the two areas. The calculated modified area traces are shown by the dashed lines. The pressures and flows resulting from this pattern of change of the areas can be calculated approximately using equation (1), with the result shown in Figures 15.25b and 15.25c.

As Figure 15.25b shows, the transglottal pressure decreases as the constriction is formed and increases at the release, and consequently there is cessation of glottal vibration during this time interval. Frication noise is generated throughout the time when there is an increased intraoral pressure.

An example of the fricative [s] in an intervocalic context is shown in the spectrogram in Figure 15.26. The transitions of the first and second formants into and out of the consonant are evident, as is the frication noise and the cessation of glottal vibration. The spectrum of the frication noise is displayed below the spectrogram, together with the spectrum of the vowel shortly after the onset of glottal vibration. The frication noise has a spectrum similar to that of the [t] burst in Figure 15.24b, with a broad high-frequency peak. This peak is in the F5 range here, and is about 20 dB higher in amplitude than the corresponding peak in the adjacent vowel.

Typical spectra for several fricatives in English are shown in Figure 15.27. These spectra have contrasting shapes as the place of articulation changes from labiodental to dental to alveolar to palato-alveolar. The labiodental and dental fricatives have no major spectral prominence, at least up to 8 kHz, since there

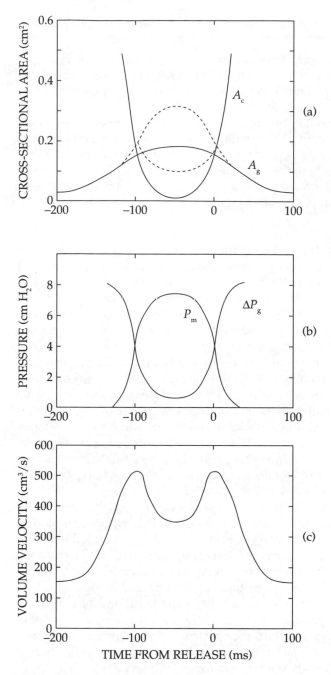

Figure 15.25 (a) Schematized time variation of cross-sectional area of vocal-tract constriction A_c and glottal constriction A_g for production of a voiceless fricative consonant in intervocalic position. The solid lines indicate what the constriction areas would be if there were no increase in intraoral pressure, and the dashed lines show how the areas are modified by forces on the structures due to the increased intraoral pressure. (b) Calculated intraoral pressure P_m and transglottal pressure ΔP_g. (c) Calculated airflow.

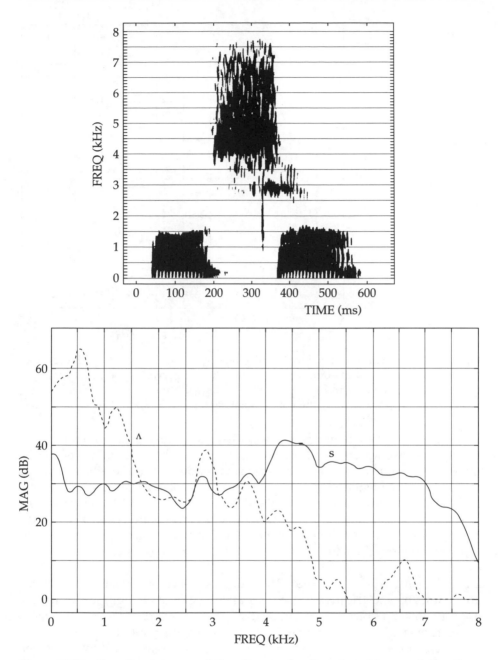

Figure 15.26 Top: Spectrogram of the utterance [ʌsʌ] produced by an adult male speaker. Bottom: The solid line is the measured spectrum for [s]. The dashed line is the spectrum sampled in the vowel near the second glottal period. Spectra are measured as in Figure 15.24, except that the averaging time for the spectrum of [s] is 100 ms.

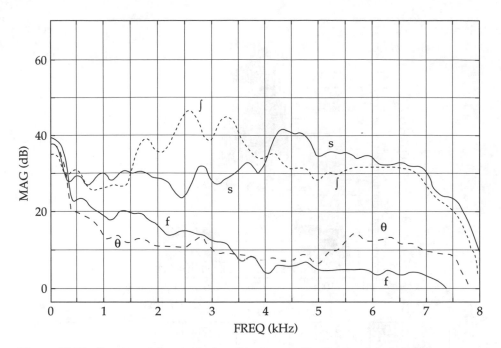

Figure 15.27 Spectra of four voiceless fricatives in English, as labeled. The spectra are obtained with a 6.4 ms time window over a time interval of 100 ms. The fricatives were produced in isolated VCV syllables, with the vowel [ʌ]. The spectra are given with approximately the correct relative amplitudes. Adult male speaker.

is basically no front-cavity resonance. There are only small differences between these two spectra, and the spectrum amplitude at high frequencies (in the F4 and F5 range) is below the spectrum amplitude of the adjacent vowel in the same frequency range. For the palato-alveolar fricative [ʃ], there are spectral peaks corresponding to F3 and F4, at 2,600 and 3,300 Hz, and there is some noise excitation of F2. The F3 and F4 peaks are resonances of the narrow passage formed by the tongue blade and of the cavity in front of the constriction formed by the anterior surface of the tongue blade.

2.3.3 *Voicing for obstruents* The articulatory-acoustic relations discussed above for stop and fricative consonants assume glottal configurations that are appropriate for a voiceless unaspirated stop consonant or for a voiceless fricative consonant. When these glottal configurations are combined with the constricting gestures of one of the articulators in the oral cavity, vocal-fold vibration is inhibited during most of the time interval in which the constriction is formed. Various adjustments of the glottal state and/or of the pharyngeal volume can be used to facilitate glottal vibration during the constricted interval or to introduce aspiration noise at the glottis either before the constriction is formed or after it is released.

For example, vocal-fold vibration will continue throughout the closure interval for a stop consonant if the transglottal pressure is maintained at a sufficiently high value, assuming that the glottis is not strongly abducted or adducted. This condition is achieved by actively expanding the vocal-tract volume in the pharyngeal region, either by advancing the tongue root or by lowering the larynx, or both. For a fricative consonant, glottal vibration is maintained if the glottis is only partially spread, and can also be facilitated if the pharyngeal volume is actively expanded. An example of a voiced unaspirated stop consonant in intervocalic position is given in Figure 15.28a. The spectrogram shows the continuing glottal vibration throughout the closure interval. The spectra sampled in the closure interval and in the adjacent vowel show the drop in amplitude of the first-formant prominence and the significant reduction in amplitude at high frequencies due to the attenuation of sound through the vocal-tract walls and neck in the high-frequency range. The spectrum of the burst, in the bottom panel of Figure 15.28a, again shows the relatively weak amplitude and flat spectrum characteristic of a labial (as in Figure 15.24a).

A voiceless aspirated stop consonant is normally produced in prevocalic position by spreading the glottis during the closure interval, so that the glottal opening is at maximum at the time of release of the consonant. In the 60-odd ms following the release, the glottis returns to a modal configuration, and aspiration noise is generated at the glottis during the initial few tens of ms. In some languages, voiceless aspirated stop consonants contrast with voiced aspirated stops, in which glottal vibration continues through much of the closure interval, and then the glottis is spread to cause aspiration noise to be generated following the release.

Spectrograms and spectra of voiceless and voiced aspirated stop consonants are shown in Figures 15.28b and 15.28c, together with spectra sampled at selected points in the utterances. The spectrum of the aspiration noise in [p] (middle spectrum) is similar to that for [h], discussed earlier in Section 2.2.2, in that it has prominent formant peaks (in contrast to the spectrum at onset). For the voiced aspirated consonant, there is greater low-frequency energy in the aspiration. In both consonants, the bottom spectra show that there is a time interval when breathy voicing occurs, in which the amplitudes of the second and higher harmonics are reduced in relation to the amplitude of the first harmonic. This attribute of breathy voicing was noted in Section 2.1.1 and in Figure 15.5.

3 Acoustic–auditory relations

3.1 *Vowels*

In Section 2.2.1 we observed that the pattern of formant frequencies for vowels depends on the position of the tongue body and the configuration of the lips.

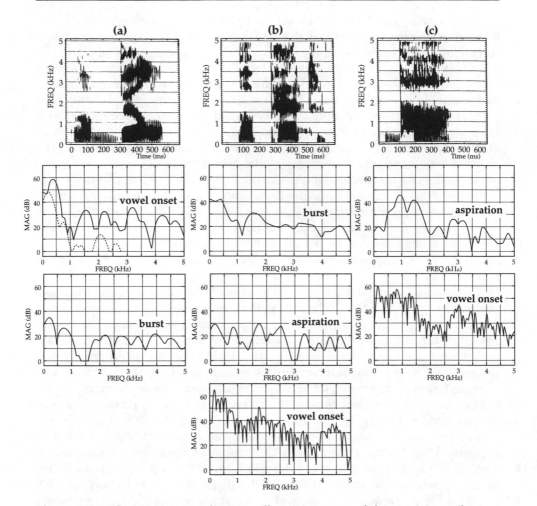

Figure 15.28 Spectrograms and spectra illustrating some of the acoustic attributes of (a) a voiced unaspirated stop consonant (in the utterance *a bill*), (b) a voiceless aspirated stop consonant (in *a pet*), and (c) a voiced aspirated stop consonant (in *dha*). Spectrograms are given at the top. In (a) the top panel shows the spectrum (6.4 ms window) sampled in the middle of the consonant (dashed line) and in the second glottal pulse after release. The bottom panel is the spectrum of the burst. In (b) the spectra are the burst (top), the aspiration (middle), and immediately after voicing onset (bottom, with a 26-ms window). In (c) the top spectrum is in the aspiration and the bottom spectrum is immediately after voicing onset (26-ms window).

To produce a pattern with a high first-formant frequency, the tongue body must be low, and to produce a low F1 the tongue body is in a raised position in the oral cavity. Likewise, the second-formant frequency is high and close to F3 when the tongue body is in a fronted position, and is low and distant from F3 when the tongue body is backed. For non-low vowels, this attribute of a low F2 is enhanced if the lips are rounded.

This classification of vowels as high or low or as front or back also appears to be grounded in basic auditory responses to stimuli that contain spectral prominences similar to those for vowels. Chistovich and her colleagues (Chistovich and Lublinskaya, 1979; Chistovich et al., 1979) carried out a series of experiments in which listeners adjusted the frequency of a single-formant stimulus so that there was a match in quality to a two-formant stimulus (with frequencies F_a and F_b). Various parameters of the two-formant stimulus were manipulated, including the frequency spacing F_b–F_a between the formants and the relative amplitudes of the two spectral prominences. When the spacing between the two formants was greater than about 3.5 Bark, listeners adjusted the frequency of the one-formant matching stimulus to be equal to F_a or F_b, or else they showed great variability in setting the frequency of the matching stimulus, depending on the relative amplitudes. A different pattern of response was obtained when F_b–F_a was less than about 3.5 Bark. The matching formant was adjusted to F_b when the amplitude of that spectral prominence was substantially greater than that of F_a, and vice versa. However, when the amplitudes of the two prominences were similar (within a range of about 30 dB), the matching frequency was intermediate between F_a and F_b. In this case, then, the listeners tended to match to the "center of gravity" of the two-formant stimulus rather than to one formant or the other. Based on these experiments, one can conclude that when two spectral prominences are separated by less than about 3.5 Bark, there is some kind of auditory integration of the two prominences, whereas each prominence maintains a separate auditory representation when the separation is greater than 3.5 Bark.

These results of auditory matching experiments help to provide an auditory basis for the classification of vowels. For example, Syrdal and Gopal (1986) used the data from Peterson and Barney (1952) to show that the F3-F2 values for vowels from a wide range of American English speakers are less than 3 Bark for front vowels and more than 3 Bark for back vowels. Their analysis of the Peterson and Barney data also showed that vowels separated into high and non-high categories according to whether F1-f_0 was less than or greater than 3 Bark, where f_0 = fundamental frequency. Evidence for the relevance of F1-f_0 (in Bark) as a normalized measure of vowel height has been reported by Traunmüller (1981).

Further evidence that vowel quality for front vowels is determined by the "center of gravity" of the complex of higher formants (F2-F3-F4) comes from experiments reported by Carlson et al. (1970). They showed that a vowel that is judged to have a quality similar to a multi-formant front vowel can be synthesized with a two-formant vowel in which F1 for both vowels is the same. To obtain a match in vowel quality, subjects placed the second formant (F2′) of the two-formant synthetic vowel at a frequency that was usually between F2 and F3, and was sometimes between F3 and F4, depending on the values of F2 and F3 in relation to F4. However, when the spacing between F2 and F3 was greater than 3.0 Bark (as it is for back vowels), F2′ was set equal to F2 for the multi-formant vowel.

3.2 Nasalization

As has been shown in Section 2.2.4, one of the ways that a vowel spectrum can be modified to produce a class of sounds that contrasts with non-nasal vowels is through nasalization. The various acoustic consequences of acoustic coupling to the nasal cavity through the velopharyngeal port have been summarized in Section 2.2.4. Several experiments have examined the perceptual consequences of introducing these acoustic attributes into synthetic utterances. For example, it has been shown that listeners judge a vowel to be nasal when (1) the spectrum amplitude at low frequencies is enhanced (Delattre, 1954); (2) the bandwidth of the first formant is increased (Hawkins and Stevens, 1983; Chen, 1995); and (3) a pole-zero pair is introduced to create an additional prominence in the vowel spectrum above the first formant (Hawkins and Stevens, 1985; Chen, 1995).

Maeda (1982b) has pointed out that all of these acoustic consequences of forming a velopharyngeal opening for a vowel contribute to a single global acoustic property: flattening the spectrum in the frequency range extending up to about 1,500 Hz. (See also Stevens, 1985a.) The nature of this spectral flattening for nasal vowels has been illustrated in Figure 15.17. Maeda proposed a metric for quantifying the degree of "flatness" of the spectrum in this frequency range, but noted that some refinement of this metric is necessary.

3.3 Distinction between aspirated and unaspirated stop consonants

As has been discussed in Section 2.3.3, the distinction between voiced and voiceless stop consonants in pre-stressed position is marked in part by a difference in the time from the consonant release to onset of glottal vibration (voice-onset time, or VOT), this time being greater for the voiceless cognate. When the VOT is manipulated in a synthetic consonant-vowel syllable to be greater than about 25 ms, the consonant is heard as voiceless, and when it is less than 25 ms it is heard as voiced. Experiments with nonspeech stimuli consisting of two sounds with different onset times have examined the ability of listeners to judge the temporal order of the two sounds (Hirsh, 1959; Pisoni, 1977, and Moore, ASPECTS OF AUDITORY PROCESSING RELATED TO SPEECH

PERCEPTION). These experiments have shown that a difference in onset times of at least 20 ms is needed for listeners to reliably judge the temporal order and to perceive the two onsets as successive rather than simultaneous events. One can conclude from these results with nonspeech stimuli that this 20-ms limitation is a basic property of the perceptual system, and this property appears to be exploited in establishing a system of phonetic contrasts between voiceless stop consonants with a longer VOT and unaspirated stop consonants with a short VOT. (See also Delgutte, AUDITORY NEURAL PROCESSING OF SPEECH.)

3.4 *Place for consonants*

When a consonant is produced with a narrow constriction in some region of the oral cavity, the transitions of the formants when the consonant is released into the following vowel are different for different places of articulation for the consonant, as has been discussed in Section 2.2.3. If the consonant is an obstruent, the spectrum of the frication noise that is produced also varies with the place of articulation, as illustrated in Figures 15.24 and 15.27. A number of experiments have examined listener responses to synthetic consonant-vowel syllables in which these formant transitions and noise spectra were manipulated. The stimuli that elicit coronal responses (i.e., responses of t or d to stop consonants and s to fricative consonants) tend to be those for which the spectrum amplitude at high frequencies (range of F4 or higher) near the vowel onset is greater than or equal to that just after the vowel onset (Blumstein and Stevens, 1980; Ohde and Stevens, 1983; Stevens, 1985b). Labial responses are obtained when the spectrum amplitude at high frequencies in the consonant noise is weaker than that in the following vowel. Responses of k or $\int$ (sometimes classified as *compact* consonants) are obtained when the spectrum of the noise has a narrow prominence in the F2 or F3 range, with an amplitude that is comparable to that of the corresponding formant peak in the following vowel. These acoustic attributes for labial, alveolar, and velar stop consonants have been illustrated in Figure 15.24.

A general conclusion from these and other results is that the identification of place of articulation for an obstruent consonant in a CV syllable is determined by the spectrum of the noise portion and by the nature of the spectrum change at the transition into the vowel (Stevens, 1985b). A *compact* consonant has a spectrum with a midfrequency prominence that is narrower than an auditory critical band, whereas *diffuse* consonants like p or t do not. (See also Moore, ASPECTS OF AUDITORY PROCESSING RELATED TO SPEECH PERCEPTION and Delgutte, AUDITORY NEURAL PROCESSING OF SPEECH.) The labial and coronal consonants can usually be distinguished on the basis of whether or not there is a broad high-frequency prominence with an amplitude that is comparable to or greater than the high-frequency spectrum amplitude in the following vowel.

4 Summary

In this chapter we have given a number of examples that show how certain acoustic characteristics of the radiated sound change as the articulatory parameters describing the vocal-tract shapes are manipulated through a range of values. In some of these examples, an abrupt change or discontinuity in the acoustic attributes occurs when a consonant is produced by forming or releasing a narrow constriction in the vocal tract. This abrupt change may be due to a reduction in the amplitude of the glottal source, or to the rapid introduction of a frication noise source, or to a switching of the output from the mouth to the nose. In other examples involving obstruent consonants, adjustments in the positioning and shaping of the constriction can cause quantal changes in the vocal-tract resonance that receives major excitation from the frication noise source. Examples are the spectra of the stop bursts and fricative noise in Figures 15.24 and 15.27. In the case of vowels, there appear to be tongue-body and lip positions for which the second formant achieves a relatively stable maximum or minimum value that is only weakly sensitive to the positioning of the tongue body.

Examination of the perception of sounds with speechlike properties shows that as certain dimensions of the stimuli are manipulated through a range of values, listener responses change in a discontinuous manner. These dimensions include the spacing between two formants or between F1 and f_0, spectral "flattening" in the first-formant region, the timing of a stop consonant release and onset of glottal vibration, and the prominence of spectral peaks in frication noise in relation to those of an adjacent vowel.

It appears that the non-monotonicity of these articulatory–acoustic and auditory–acoustic relations forms one basis for the design of a set of phonetic categories that are used in languages. Discontinuities or abruptnesses in these relations are utilized to form consonantal landmarks in the signal, and acoustic parameters in the vicinity of the landmarks provide cues for some of the features of the consonant. In the case of vowels, both articulatory–acoustic and auditory–acoustic relations play a role in defining front–back and height distinctions and the nasal–non-nasal distinction.

16 Auditory Neural Processing of Speech

BERTRAND DELGUTTE

1 Introduction

In speech communication, the listener identifies the phonetic structure of the utterance produced by the speaker on the basis of the waveform of the acoustic signal. This complex decoding act involves both general auditory mechanisms as well as specialized language processing mechanisms. This chapter outlines what is known about the earliest stages of speech perception based on recordings from single auditory neurons in response to speech and speech-like stimuli. Such single-unit data make it possible to trace neural representations of the speech signal through subsequent stages of auditory processing. This survey updates and extends previous reviews of the neural processing of speech (Sachs, 1984; Sachs et al., 1988; Delgutte, 1982; Smoorenburg, 1987; Greenberg, 1988). It incorporates recent results on speech processing by central auditory neurons, and emphasizes the neural representation of dynamic features of speech.

Pioneered in the early 1970s (Kiang and Moxon, 1974; Kiang, 1975; Hashimoto et al., 1975), studies of speech coding in the auditory nerve have considerably matured, and a great deal of information is now available on responses to most phonetic categories, including vowels (Sachs and Young, 1979; Young and Sachs, 1979; Delgutte and Kiang, 1984a), stops (Miller and Sachs, 1983; Sinex and Geisler, 1983; Carney and Geisler, 1986), nasals (Deng and Geisler, 1987), and fricatives (Delgutte and Kiang, 1984b). These physiological studies have motivated the development of peripheral auditory models for speech processing, many examples of which can be found in recent volumes (Carlson and Granström, 1982; Schouten, 1987, 1992; Ainsworth, 1992; Cooke et al., 1993). The last decade has witnessed the first detailed studies of the encoding of speech at the next stage of auditory processing, the cochlear nucleus (Palmer et al., 1986; Kim et al., 1986; Blackburn and Sachs, 1990; Winter and Palmer, 1990). Some information is also available on the responses of midbrain and cortical auditory neurons (Watanabe and Sakai, 1973, 1978; Palmer et al., 1990;

Steinschneider et al., 1994, 1995; Eggermont, 1995). This survey necessarily reflects these limitations in our knowledge: it emphasizes speech coding in the auditory nerve and cochlear nucleus, even though the most important processing in speech perception may well occur at more central stages.

Because speech has many properties in common with other acoustic stimuli, the neural processing of speech can be studied using both speech stimuli and nonspeech analogs. For example, voiced speech shares periodic excitation with music and animal vocalizations. Speech, music and sounds produced by animals in motion all show pronounced amplitude modulations at very low frequencies (2–16 Hz). In many cases, very simplified stimuli can be understood as speech. For example, sine-wave speech (a sum of frequency-modulated sine waves that match the first 2–3 formants of an utterance) is intelligible under certain circumstances (Remez et al., 1981). Sine-wave speech has been valuable for understanding the encoding of vowels in the auditory nerve (e.g. Reale and Geisler, 1980; Sachs and Young, 1980). The frequency-modulated (FM) sounds used by bats for echolocation resemble the formant transitions of speech (Suga, 1992). FM sounds have long been used in studies of central auditory neurons (Suga, 1964; Whitfield and Evans, 1965). Among these nonspeech analogs, species-specific vocalizations are particularly germane because there may exist general neural mechanisms for the perception of conspecific communication sounds, including human speech (Ehret, 1992).

While these analogies are useful, speech differs in many important respects from nonspeech analogs. For example, while sine-wave speech may be intelligible, it is not spontaneously identified as speech, in part because it lacks the periodic amplitude modulation of voiced sounds. While bat FM sounds may resemble formant transitions on spectrographic displays, FM rates for bat echolocation sounds often exceed 10 MHz/sec, which is three orders of magnitude greater than rates for typical formant transitions. Moreover, formant transitions are not true FM sounds in that the actual component frequencies do not vary, only the peak of the spectral envelope does. Thus, nonspeech analogs should be closely scrutinized for their similarities and differences with speech when using these analogs as models for investigating the neural processing of speech.

While no single acoustic property is unique to speech, speech is characterized by particular combinations of acoustic properties occurring in specific frequency ranges that set it apart from other acoustic stimuli (Stevens, 1980). First, speech shows an alternation between relatively intense segments corresponding to vowels and weaker segments corresponding to consonants. This more or less regular amplitude modulation occurring at a 3–4 Hz rate is essential for speech understanding (Houtgast and Steeneken, 1973). Second, the spectral envelope of speech shows pronounced maxima (corresponding to formants) interleaved with minima at intervals of 1,000–1,200 Hz. Third, speech shows both nearly periodic segments corresponding to sonorants such as vowels, and irregular (noise-like) segments corresponding to obstruents such as fricative consonants and bursts of stop consonants. Thus, speech is characterized by a triple alternation in amplitude envelope, spectral envelope, and fine spectral structure. In order to get a realistic picture of the neural encoding of speech, it is necessary to use stimuli possessing all of these characteristics.

A methodological issue in studying the neural substrates of speech perception is the degree to which the mechanisms involved are specific to humans. Perceptual studies generally use human subjects, while single-unit studies must use animal models (usually cats or small rodents, more rarely monkeys). There is a long-standing debate between proponents of specialized speech perception mechanisms and those who favor general auditory mechanisms (Liberman et al., 1967; Stevens and Blumstein, 1978; Kuhl and Miller, 1978; Delgutte, 1982; Bregman, 1990; Liberman and Mattingly, 1989; Miller and Jusczyk, 1990; Kluender, 1990). The evidence is broadly consistent with the view that speech perception *at the phonetic level* requires no more than an adaptation of general auditory mechanisms to a particular class of stimuli rather than specialized neural mechanisms. Cats (Dewson, 1964), chinchillas (Kuhl and Miller, 1978; Kuhl, 1981), monkeys (Sinnott et al., 1976; Kuhl and Padden, 1982), and certain birds (Kluender et al., 1987; Dooling et al., 1989) can discriminate speech sounds in ways that can be strikingly similar to humans. When processing at the more peripheral stages of the auditory nervous system is considered more specifically, the general layout of the cochlea and brainstem auditory pathways is largely similar in most species of mammals including humans (Moore, 1987). Many physiological properties of auditory neurons are similar in unrelated species such as rodents, bats, and cats, suggesting that they may represent very general neural mechanisms common to most mammals including humans. Thus, it is likely that a great deal can be learned about the neural processing of human speech by studying responses of single units in non-human mammals. At the very least, physiological studies using animal models are relevant to the issue of whether speech perception at the phonetic level requires specialized neural mechanisms.

Speech is made up of a wide variety of phonetic elements (speech sounds and features) that differ in both temporal and spectral characteristics. Such diversity is essential for speech to function effectively as a communication signal. Distinctions among major phonetic categories such as vowels, stops, nasals and fricatives are based primarily on dynamic features such as temporal envelope characteristics (onsets and offsets, silent intervals, durations) and changes in the gross distribution of spectral energy. Distinctions among vowels and place-of-articulation distinctions among consonants depend on more detailed spectral features such as the formant pattern, and how this pattern changes with time (formant transitions). Voicing and pitch information depend on waveform periodicity or, equivalently, harmonicity of the spectral pattern. This chapter follows this tripartite classification of the acoustic characteristics of speech: Section 2 discusses the neural encoding of dynamic features, Section 3 the spectral pattern, and Section 4 pitch and voicing. Section 5 describes specific attempts to identify neural mechanisms underlying categorical perception, context dependence and trading relations. In each section, the responses of auditory-nerve fibers are described first, followed by those of central auditory neurons.

2 Coding of rapid changes in amplitude and spectrum

Much information in speech is available in rapid changes in amplitude and spectral characteristics that are apparent in spectrographic displays (Fant, 1973). The temporal relationships among these discrete events, as well as their spectral distribution provide phonetic information. For example, stop consonants are characterized by two events occurring in rapid succession: a rapid increase in amplitude primarily in the high frequency region corresponding to consonantal release (burst onset), and an increase in amplitude in the low frequency region corresponding to the onset of voicing. The time interval between these two events is the voice onset time (VOT), which is an important cue for voicing distinctions among stop consonants (Lisker and Abramson, 1964). Not only the spectro-temporal distribution of these events, but also their amplitude envelope is phonetically important. For example, affricate consonants (as in "chop") have abrupt increases in amplitude of the frication noise, while fricative consonants (as in "shop") have a more gradual onset. More generally, rapid changes in amplitude and spectrum point to time intervals that are rich in information about the identity of the neighboring phonetic segments, including vowels and consonants (Delattre et al., 1955; Blumstein and Stevens, 1980; Stevens, 1980). These events are particularly important in continuous speech, where they may help segment utterances into perceptually-manageable chunks.

2.1 *Representation in the auditory nerve. Adaptation*

Rapid changes in amplitude and spectrum are prominently represented in the discharge patterns of auditory-nerve fibers (ANFs). Figure 16.1A shows the activity of the auditory nerve in response to a speech utterance whose spectrogram is shown in Figure 16.1B. In this *neurogram* display, each trace shows the average response of a small number of ANFs displayed as a *post-stimulus time histogram* (PSTH). PSTHs represent the rate of discharge averaged over short intervals, or "bins" as a function of time following stimulus onset. The bin width in Figure 16.1A is 1 msec. Fibers are arranged according to their *characteristic frequency (CF)*, the frequency to which they are most sensitive. For pure-tone stimuli, each fiber responds to a limited range of frequencies at a given sound level (Kiang et al., 1965). This frequency selectivity is due to the mechanical tuning of the basilar membrane and hair cells in the cochlea. There is a precise mapping between the CF of an ANF and its

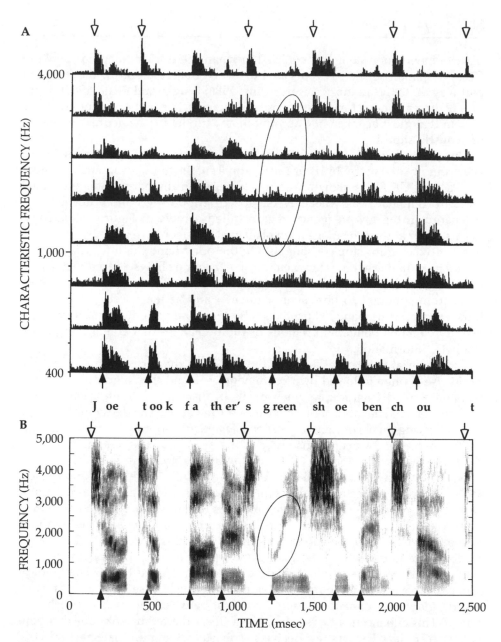

Figure 16.1 Neurogram and spectrogram for a speech utterance produced by a female speaker. A. Neurogram display of the activity of the cat auditory nerve in response to the utterance. Each trace represents the average post-stimulus-time histogram for 2–7 auditory-nerve fibers whose CFs are located in a $\frac{1}{2}$ octave band centered at the vertical ordinate. All histograms were computed with a bin width of 1 msec, and have been normalized to the same maximum in order to emphasize temporal patterns. The stimulus level was such that the most intense vowels were at 50 dB SPL. B. Broadband spectrogram of the utterance. Filled arrows point to rapid increases in amplitude in the low frequencies (and their neural correlates on top), while open arrows point to rapid increases in amplitude in the high frequencies. The ovals show the second-formant movement in "green" and its neural correlate.

place of innervation along the cochlea (Liberman, 1982b). This mapping between CF and spatial position is replicated at every major station in the auditory pathway up to the auditory cortex (Irvine, 1986; Brugge and Reale, 1985). Thus, the CF dimension is a fundamental organizing principle of the auditory nervous system that must be taken into account in any model for the neural processing of acoustic stimuli.

The rapid spectral and amplitude changes pointed to by arrows in the spectrogram of Figure 16.1B are also apparent in the neurogram of Figure 16.1A. Low-CF fibers show an abrupt increase in discharge rate, associated with a prominent peak whenever the spectrogram shows an abrupt increase in energy in the low-frequency region (filled arrows in Figure 16.1). These events occur at the transitions from obstruent to sonorant segments, and at the onset of voicing for stop consonants. On the other hand, high-CF fibers show a rise/peak in discharge rate when the spectrogram shows a rapid increase in energy in the high-frequency region (open arrows). This occurs at the transitions from sonorant to obstruent segments, and at the onset of the release burst for stop consonants. Thus, the spatio-temporal pattern of auditory-nerve activity contains pointers to regions of rapid changes that contain important phonetic information.

These neural pointers differ from those seen in the spectrogram in that the rapid rise is often followed by a prominent peak and then a gradual decay in instantaneous discharge rate. Such peaks in discharge rate are seen for any stimuli that have an abrupt onset such as a tone burst. The decay in discharge rate following an abrupt onset is called *adaptation*, and may be caused in part by the depletion of neurotransmitter at the synapses between hair cells and ANFs in the cochlea (Smith, 1979). Following an adapting stimulus, the responses to subsequent stimuli are depressed (Smith, 1979; Harris and Dallos, 1979). Adaptation occurs on different time scales, ranging from a few milliseconds to several seconds and even minutes (Smith, 1979; Kiang et al., 1965).

Adaptation plays several roles in the encoding of speech in the auditory nerve (Delgutte, 1980; Delgutte and Kiang, 1984c; Delgutte, 1986). First, peaks in discharge rate resulting from adaptation point to spectro-temporal regions that are rich in phonetic information, as shown in Figure 16.1. Second, adaptation increases the temporal precision with which onsets are represented. Third, adaptation enhances spectral contrast between successive speech segments. This enhancement arises because a fiber adapted by stimulus components close to its CF is less responsive to subsequent stimuli that share spectral components with the adapting sound. On the other hand, stimuli with novel spectral components stimulate "fresh", unadapted fibers, thereby producing an enhanced response. A fourth role of adaptation is to encode phonetic contrasts based on characteristics of the amplitude envelope. For example, for a majority of auditory-nerve fibers, the abrupt onset of affricate consonants results in a more prominent adaptation peak than the more gradual onset of fricative consonants having the same spectral characteristics (Delgutte, 1980; Delgutte and Kiang, 1984c).

The roles of adaptation in speech coding can be placed into the broader context of a functional model for the auditory processing of speech proposed by Chistovich et al. (1982). Chistovich et al. hypothesized that two separate systems operate in parallel: a tonic system that continuously delivers a running spectral representation of the stimulus, and a phasic system that detects acoustic transients (onsets and offsets) in individual frequency bands. The phasic system has two functions: by itself, it provides important temporal cues to the identity of phonetic segments, and it also provides pointers for sampling the output of the tonic system at times that are particularly important.

Delgutte (1986) showed how adaptation in auditory-nerve fibers leads to a simple and robust implementation of the phasic system proposed by Chistovich et al. (1982). Using a model of the peripheral auditory system incorporating adaptation, he showed that peaks in discharge rate such as those visible in Figure 16.1 can be reliably detected in the response patterns of model ANFs by means of a template matching technique. For a corpus of French stop-vowel syllables produced by both male and female speakers, peaks in discharge rate were consistently detected at the burst onset for high-CF (> 1 kHz) model fibers, while peaks at voicing onset were detected for low-CF fibers. Thus, the model was able to reliably measure VOT by computing the time interval between these high-CF and low-CF events. This line of research was further developed by Wu et al. (1992) and Schwartz et al. (1982), who introduced many refinements in the model and showed that the phasic system encodes other phonetic events besides VOT.

In summary, adaptation produces prominent features in the response of the auditory nerve to the rapid changes in amplitude and spectrum in speech. Adaptation should not be seen as an epiphenomenon reflecting the inability of neurons to sustain high discharge rates for long periods of time, but as the first stage in a phasic neural system specialized for the processing of acoustic transients.

2.2 Representation in central auditory nuclei

Little is known about the encoding of dynamic features of speech in the central nervous system. The available data on the response of the central auditory neurons to speech stimuli (Watanabe and Sakai, 1973, 1978; Steinschneider et al., 1994, 1995; Eggermont, 1995), as well as more extensive data on their responses to dynamic nonspeech stimuli (reviewed by Langner, 1992) suggest that the prominent representation of acoustic transients initiated at the level of the auditory nerve is further enhanced in the central nervous system, consistent with the ideas of Chistovich et al. (1982).

Many central auditory neurons respond primarily at the onset of tone-burst stimuli, giving little or no sustained response (for reviews, see Rhode and Greenberg, 1992; Irvine, 1986; Brugge and Reale, 1985). Such "onset" neurons are found at virtually every major stage of processing in the auditory pathway, beginning with the cochlear nucleus (CN). At first sight, onset neurons might appear to provide appropriate processing for the phasic system postulated by Chistovich et al. (1982). However, onset cells in the CN tend to discharge to every pitch period of vowel stimuli (Kim et al., 1986; Palmer and Winter, 1992). Thus, these cells signal many more events in addition to the major changes in amplitude and spectrum that are apparent in Figure 16.1. The response of CN onset cells can be understood if we consider their sensitivity to amplitude-modulated (AM) tones. In response to these stimuli, neural discharges tend to occur at a particular phase within the modulation cycle, a phenomenon known as *phase locking*. For CN onset cells, phase locking is most precise for modulation frequencies in the 100–400 Hz range (Frisina et al., 1990). These best modulation frequencies closely coincide with the range of fundamental frequencies of human voice. These observations suggest that the precise phase-locking of CN onset cells to the pitch period may result from the pronounced AM that voiced speech shows at the fundamental frequency.

Many cells at more central locations than the CN in the auditory pathway also show preferred sensitivity to a particular range of AM frequencies, but their best modulation frequencies are generally lower than for CN cells. For example, a majority of cells in the inferior colliculus (IC), the principal auditory nucleus in the midbrain, have best modulation frequencies in the 10–300 Hz range (see review by Langner, 1992). Most cortical neurons have best modulation frequencies in the 3–100 Hz range. Cells with best modulation frequencies in the 10–50 Hz range would not be expected to phase lock to the pitch period of speech stimuli. On the other hand, these cells are likely to respond vigorously to the major changes in amplitude and spectrum associated with phonetic events. The multiple-unit recordings of Steinschneider et al. (1994) from the primary auditory cortex of the awake macaque are consistent with this hypothesis. Steinschneider et al. found a population of units that showed a "double onset" pattern in response to [da] and [ta] syllables: These units respond with a transient burst of activity at the consonantal release, and a second burst at the onset of voicing. A similar response pattern has been observed by Watanabe and Sakai (1973) for one IC neuron in response to a [ta] syllable. Thus, cells may exist that directly encode the VOT of stop consonants in their response patterns, consistent with the phasic cells postulated by Chistovich et al. (1982). Such cells are found in the primary auditory cortex, and possibly in the auditory midbrain as well.

In summary, physiological studies of central auditory neurons generally support the Chistovich et al. (1982) notion of a phasic system that encodes rapid changes in amplitude and spectrum. Systematic studies are needed to determine the neural mechanisms leading to these phasic responses, as well as the exact nature of the phonetic events encoded by these cells at different stages in the central auditory pathway. The possibility of higher-order neural circuits that would respond to combinations of onsets occurring at different times in different frequency bands also needs to be investigated. In the next section, we turn to the other component of the Chistovich et al. (1982) model, the tonic system that delivers a running spectral representation.

3 Coding of spectral patterns

Techniques for the physical analysis of speech such as spectrograms or linear prediction provide spectral representations for successive time frames of the waveform. Experience with speech synthesis and recognition suggests that such short-time spectral representations contain sufficient information for speech understanding (e.g. Flanagan, 1972). For certain classes of speech sounds such as vowels or fricative consonants, the spectrum can be approximately constant over many time frames. Such steady-state stimuli provide an appropriate starting point for studies of the neural representation of the spectral patterns of speech. The most important features for vowel perception are the frequencies of the spectral maxima associated with the first two or three formants (Peterson and Barney, 1952; Carlson et al., 1975).

3.1 Rate-place representation in the auditory nerve

The simplest neural codes for the representation of speech spectra are *rate-place* schemes, which display the amount of neural activity (average discharge rate) as a function of CF. Rate-place schemes, which constitute modern formulations of Helmholz's (1863) place theory of hearing, are based on the frequency selectivity of the cochlea and the tonotopic organization of the auditory nervous system. Because virtually every major station in the auditory pathway from the auditory nerve to the cortex is tonotopically-organized (Irvine, 1986; Brugge and Reale, 1985), rate-place schemes provide very general neural representations of the short-time spectrum.

The ability of rate-place schemes to represent the spectra of steady-state vowels was investigated in a classic paper by Sachs and Young (1979). Sachs and Young recorded the activity of a large number of ANFs in the same cat in response to a vowel stimulus, and analyzed how the average discharge rate varies as a function of fiber CF. Their results, reproduced in Figure 16.2 for the vowel [ɛ], show that, for low stimulus levels, discharge rate is maximum for fibers whose CFs are close to the frequency of one of the first three formants. Thus, for these low levels, rate-place schemes provide a good representation of the formant pattern. As stimulus level increases, the representation of the formants degrades. For higher levels still well within the conversational range, the rate-place pattern takes on a lowpass shape with little or no information about the positions of the formants. Similar degradations in the representation of the formant frequencies occur when moderate-level background noise is introduced, even if such noise does not impair intelligibility (Sachs et al., 1983; Delgutte and Kiang, 1984d).

The results of Sachs and Young (1979) illustrate a very general "dynamic range" problem in auditory neuroscience (Evans, 1981): The dynamic range of

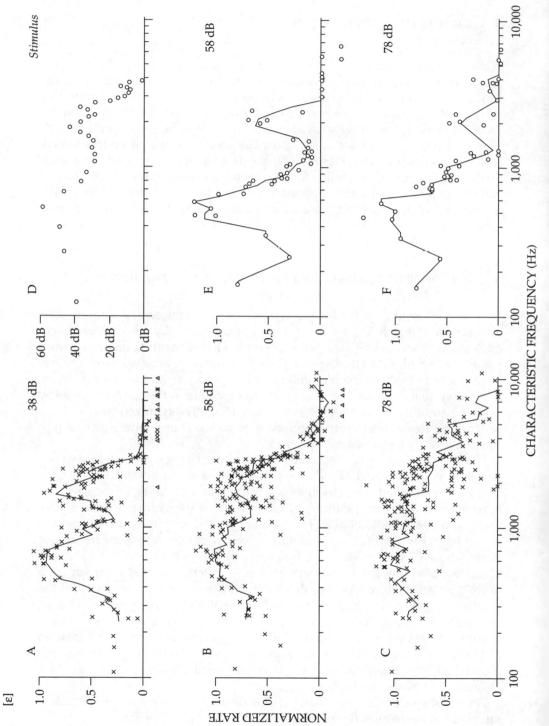

single ANFs is much smaller than the wide (> 100 dB) range over which listeners can understand speech and discriminate sound intensities. Specifically, the discharge rates of ANFs only increase over a 20–40 dB range of stimulus levels between threshold and a level where discharge rate reaches a maximum (Kiang et al., 1965; Sachs and Abbas, 1974). In response to vowels, the discharge rates of fibers with CFs close to a formant reach their maximum at moderate sound levels. With further increases in level the rates of fibers with CFs between formants also reach their maximum, so that the dips between formants in the rate-place profiles are eliminated. While the Sachs and Young results pose a serious challenge to rate-place schemes, several factors need to be considered before reaching any conclusion as to the viability of these schemes for speech encoding.

The first factor is that the data of Figure 16.2A–C represent only the responses of the subset of auditory-nerve fibers that discharge vigorously in the absence of intentionally-applied acoustic stimuli. These high spontaneous rate (SR) fibers form a majority of ANFs, and always have the lowest thresholds for pure tones at the CF (Liberman, 1978). There is a minority of fibers that have low SRs, and thresholds that can be as much as 40–60 dB higher than those of high-SR fibers with the same CF (Liberman, 1978). Low-SR and high-SR fibers differ not only in threshold but also in many other characteristics such as dynamic range (Schalk and Sachs, 1980; Winter et al., 1990), morphology and position of their synaptic terminals on inner hair cells (Liberman, 1982a), and patterns of projections to the cochlear nucleus (Liberman, 1991). These variations in SR and threshold among ANFs constitute an organizing principle possibly as important as tonotopic organization, which must be taken into account in descriptions of responses to speech stimuli.

Because low-SR fibers have higher thresholds and wider dynamic ranges than high-SR fibers, their discharge rates continue to grow at stimulus levels for which the responses of high-SR fibers have reached their maximum. Figure 16.2E–F, from Sachs and Young (1979) shows rate-place patterns for low-SR fibers in response to the vowel [ε] presented at conversational speech levels. Despite the smaller number of these high-threshold fibers, the rate-place patterns show local maxima at the first two formant frequencies up to the highest level that was investigated (75 dB SPL). Thus, high-threshold fibers

---

Figure 16.2 (Opposite) (Modified from Sachs and Young, 1979). A–C. Normalized average discharge rate against CF for a large sample of auditory-nerve fibers from the same cat in response to a synthetic [ε] vowel. Each symbol shows the average rate for one fiber having a spontaneous discharge rate (SR) greater than 1/sec. The line is a moving-window average of the data points. Average discharge rates are normalized so that 0 corresponds to SR, and 1 to the maximum rate for a pure tone at the CF. Each panel shows data for one stimulus level. D. Power spectrum of the [ε] stimulus, which had a fundamental frequency of 128 Hz and a duration of 400 msec. The formant frequencies are 512, 1792, and 2432 Hz. E and F: Same as B and C respectively for fibers with SRs smaller than 1/sec.

provide a rate-place representation of the formant pattern for moderate and high stimulus levels, while low-threshold fibers provide this information for low stimulus levels. Delgutte (1982) proposed a rate-place scheme that gave a good representation of the formants over a broad range of levels by adaptively weighting information from low- and high-threshold fibers depending on stimulus level. Delgutte (1987) further showed that a very similar scheme arises when modeling psychophysical performance in intensity discrimination based on statistical descriptions of auditory-nerve activity. Thus, the same rate-place model that accounts for basic psychophysical tasks such as masking and intensity discrimination can also be applied to speech encoding over a wide dynamic range (Delgutte, 1995). Similar ideas have been expressed by Winslow et al. (1987), who further proposed a neural circuit based on patterns of synaptic connections in the cochlear nucleus that could implement level-dependent adaptive weighting.

Feedback is another factor that needs to be considered in assessing the viability of rate-place schemes for speech encoding. The activity of ANFs is modulated by feedback pathways from the brainstem. The best understood of these feedback systems is the medial olivocochlear (MOC) pathway, which consists of neurons whose cell bodies are located in the superior olivary complex, and whose axons terminate on outer hair cells in the cochlea (Warr, 1992; Guinan, 1996). Stimulation of MOC neurons shifts the dynamic range of ANFs by as much as 15–30 dB towards higher intensities for stimulus frequencies near the CF (Wiederhold and Kiang, 1970; Guinan and Gifford, 1988). Thus, fibers that would discharge at their maximum rate in the absence of efferent stimulation become capable of encoding stimulus level when MOC neurons are stimulated. These effects are particularly striking for transient signals in continuous background noise, where stimulation of the MOC pathway can exert a strong anti-masking effect (Winslow and Sachs, 1987; Kawase et al., 1993). These physiological experiments describe MOC effects in an open-loop condition. In natural conditions, MOC effects would be induced through reflex action, possibly modulated by central control (Warren and Liberman, 1989). This mode of activation might lead to further signal processing capabilities. For example, MOC neurons innervating cochlear regions in which the signal-to-noise ratio is particularly low might be selectively activated. Although the role of MOC feedback in speech encoding has not been directly investigated, results with tonal stimuli strongly suggest that this role is likely to be important, particularly in the presence of background noise.

To summarize, while rate-place profiles for low-threshold (high-SR) fibers provide a poor representation of the formant frequencies of vowels at conversational speech levels, rate-place coding cannot be discounted as a general scheme for spectral representation because high-threshold fibers and feedback systems are likely to provide the necessary information for high intensities and low signal-to-noise ratios. A major advantage of rate-place schemes is that they are equally effective for obstruent sounds such as fricative consonants as for vowels (Delgutte, 1980; Delgutte and Kiang, 1984b).

3.2 Temporal representation in the auditory nerve

An alternative to rate-place schemes for the encoding of speech spectra are temporal schemes, which can be seen as modern formulations of Wever and Bray's (1930) volley principle. Because ANF discharges are phase-locked to low-frequency (< 5 kHz) pure tones (Rose et al., 1967; Johnson, 1980), intervals between these discharges tend to occur at integer multiples of the stimulus period. Such interspike interval information can in principle be used to derive very precise estimates of the tone frequency (Siebert, 1970; Goldstein and Srulovicz, 1977). Phase locking is not limited to pure tones, but also occurs for complex periodic tones, including steady-state vowels (Young and Sachs, 1979; Reale and Geisler, 1980; Delgutte and Kiang, 1984a). In this case, the temporal patterns of discharge of single fibers contain information about the frequency content of the stimulus.

When discussing temporal schemes for auditory processing, it is important to be specific about time resolution. Any viable scheme must be able to track short-time variations in the spectrum of speech. For example, rate-place schemes typically average the instantaneous rate of discharge over 5–40 msec moving frames similar to those used for speech analysis and synthesis (Flanagan, 1972). These time frames are consistent with psychophysical estimates of temporal resolution (e.g. Moore et al., 1988). In contrast, detection of phase locking of ANF discharges requires an analysis with a much finer time resolution. For example, in order to clearly demonstrate phase locking to a 5-kHz stimulus, temporal resolution finer than 50 µsec is required. In the following, the term *temporal scheme* will be restricted to models of auditory processing that make use of such fine time information. Thus, both rate-place and temporal schemes make use of information distributed in time, albeit on different scales.

Figure 16.3 shows the spatio-temporal patterns of discharge of the auditory nerve for the steady-state vowel [æ] presented at 60 dB SPL. This neurogram shows PSTHs arranged by CF as in Figure 16.1A, but differs in that it has a much finer time resolution, thereby revealing the phase locking of neural discharges to the stimulus waveform. The duration of the time axis is 20 msec, corresponding to two periods of the stimulus. Figure 16.3 demonstrates two important points. First, the fine time patterns of discharge depend systematically on CF. Thus, the frequency selectivity of the cochlea, which is the basis for rate-place coding, also plays an important role in shaping temporal patterns of response. The second point is that a majority of fibers convey formant information in their discharge patterns. Specifically, for fibers with CFs between 500 Hz and 1,300 Hz, peaks in the response patterns are separated by intervals of approximately 1.2 msec, which is the reciprocal of the first formant frequency F1 = 750 Hz. For CFs between 1,300 Hz and 1,800 Hz, response patterns show peaks at intervals of 0.7 msec, which is the reciprocal of F2 = 1,450 Hz. For higher CFs, more complex response patterns are observed, with some periodicities related to F1, others to F2, and yet others to the fundamental

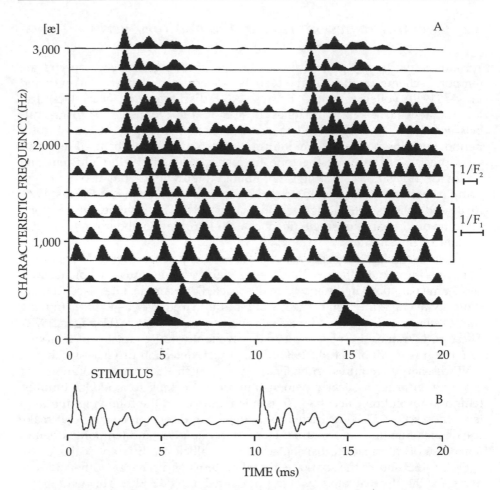

Figure 16.3 A. Neurogram display of the auditory-nerve activity in response to a synthetic [æ] vowel presented at 60 dB SPL. Each trace shows a smoothed period histogram for one auditory-nerve fiber whose CF was approximately equal to the vertical ordinate. The histogram bin width is 50 μsec, and its base period is 20 msec, corresponding to two pitch periods of the vowel stimulus. Brackets indicate CF regions in which ANFs phase-lock primarily to the first or second formant frequency. B. Waveform of two pitch periods of the [ae] stimulus, which had a 100-Hz fundamental. The power spectrum is shown in Figure 16.5A.

frequency f_0. Thus, the temporal response patterns of the majority of ANFs provide information about the formant frequencies and the fundamental frequency.

The results shown in Figure 16.3 are typical for vowels at moderate to high stimulus levels (Young and Sachs, 1979; Delgutte and Kiang, 1984a): The general rule is that fibers tend to phase lock to the formant frequency that is closest to their CF. There are however considerable variations in the extent and positions of the CF regions in which ANFs phase lock to a particular formant frequency depending on the formant pattern of each vowel (Delgutte and Kiang, 1984a). For example, for *low* vowels (e.g. [a] or [æ]), which have a high F1, low-CF fibers (< 500 Hz) phase lock to the low-frequency harmonic of f_0 closest to the CF rather than to the first formant. No such low-CF region is found for *high* vowels such as [i] and [u]. For *diffuse* vowels such as [i], for which F1 and F2 are widely separated, fibers with CFs between F1 and F2 primarily phase lock to the CF or to f_0. This intermediate CF region is lacking in *compact* vowels such as [a]. Thus, there exist correlates of phonetic features in the spatio-temporal patterns of discharge of ANFs.

While Figure 16.3 demonstrates that fine temporal patterns of discharge contain a great deal of information about the stimulus spectrum, generation of this display requires an independent time reference that precisely indicates the onset of each pitch period. Such a time reference would not be directly available to the central nervous system during speech perception. Figure 16.4A shows an alternative display based on interspike intervals, which does not require such a time reference. Each trace shows the *all-order* interspike interval distribution (also known as *autocorrelation histogram*) for one ANF. As in Figure 16.3, the fibers are arranged by CF. This display is an instance of the interval-place representation proposed by Licklider (1951) in his duplex theory of hearing. Licklider pointed out that the all-order distribution of neural interspike intervals is formally identical to an autocorrelation function if the neural discharges are modeled as a train of impulses. The autocorrelation function can be implemented using coincidence detectors and delay lines, elements which are known to exist in the central nervous system. If the autocorrelation function is evaluated for different lags using separate neural circuits differing in the length of their delay lines, a scheme for transforming a temporal code into a place code is obtained. Licklider proposed that an array of such neural circuits computes the autocorrelation function of the spike train in every CF region, forming a two-dimensional ("duplex") representation of neural activity as in Figure 16.4A along both CF (or cochlear place), and autocorrelation lag (or interspike interval). Much of the information about formant frequencies available in the neurogram of Figure 16.3 is also apparent in the interval-place representation of Figure 16.4A. Specifically, for fibers with CFs between 500 and 1,300 Hz, the first 3 peaks in the interspike interval distribution are approximately at 1/F1 and its multiples, while for CFs between 1,300 Hz and 1,800 Hz, the first 6 peaks are approximately at 1/F2 and its multiples. Thus, short interspike intervals (< 5 msec) may provide sufficient information for vowel identification (Palmer, 1990; Cariani and Delgutte, 1993). Longer intervals provide information about the fundamental frequency, a point to which we return in Section 4.1.

3.3 *Temporal processing schemes*

Because temporal patterns of discharge of ANFs provide rich, highly-redundant information about the spectra of sonorants, many different

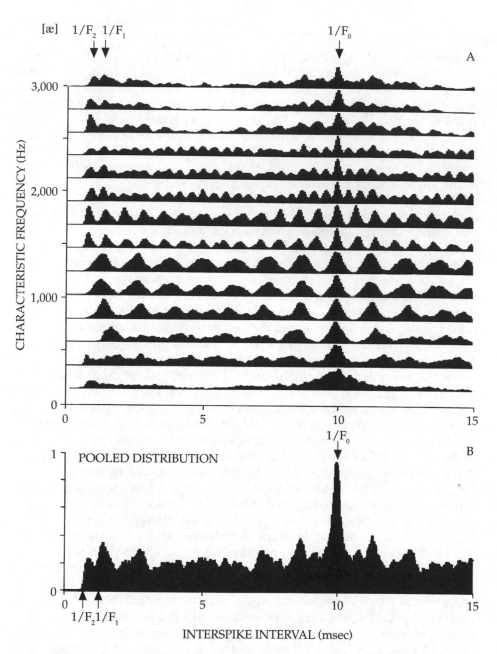

Figure 16.4 A. Interval-place representation of the response of the auditory nerve to the same [æ] stimulus as in Figure 16.3. Each trace shows an all-order interspike interval (also called autocorrelation histogram) for one auditory-nerve fiber. Fibers are arranged vertically by CF as in Figure 16.3. The histogram bin width is 50 μsec. Arrows indicate interspike intervals corresponding to the reciprocal of the first and second frequencies. B. Pooled interspike interval distribution obtained by summing all-order interspike interval histograms for 57 auditory-nerve fibers whose CFs ranged from 200 to 15,000 Hz.

processing schemes have been proposed for extracting this temporal information. The goal of these schemes is to derive a compact representation that contains essential information for intelligibility for a wide range of stimulus conditions. The scheme that has received the most attention in the literature is the *Average Localized Synchronized Rate (ALSR)* proposed by Young and Sachs (1979). The ALSR is closely related to the central spectrum model of Srulovicz and Goldstein (1983). In these models, the temporal pattern of discharge of each ANF is processed by a central (neural) filter whose center frequency matches the fiber CF. The central filter selects the frequency components of the response that are close to the CF and possibly its harmonics. The time-average output of each central filter is then displayed as a function of CF to form the ALSR or central spectrum. Because the ALSR for a particular CF is based on fine temporal information from ANFs innervating a specific cochlear place, it combines temporal and place information and constitutes a *temporal-place* model of auditory processing (Young and Sachs, 1979). Figure 16.5B shows the ALSR for the vowel [æ] derived from the neurogram of Figure 16.3. The ALSR shows pronounced peaks near the frequencies of the first 2–3 formants. In general, the ALSR provides a good representation of the formant frequencies over a wide range of stimulus levels for many different classes of speech sounds, including steady-state vowels (Young and Sachs, 1979; Delgutte, 1984), whispered vowels (Voigt et al., 1982), vowels in background noise (Sachs et al., 1983; Delgutte and Kiang, 1984d), and formant transitions of stop consonants (Miller and Sachs, 1983; Delgutte and Kiang, 1984c). However, the ALSR poorly encodes the spectra of sounds such as fricative consonants that have intense frequency components above 3 kHz because there is little or no phase-locking at these high frequencies (Delgutte and Kiang, 1984b).

The ALSR is important because it demonstrates that a simple temporal scheme can provide a spectrum-like representation that contains essential information for speech intelligibility, at least in the low-frequency region. On the other hand, the ALSR makes use of only a small fraction of the temporal information available in the auditory nerve, and the particular form of information reduction performed by the ALSR may not be the most physiologically plausible. In particular, there is no physiological evidence for the existence of central filters matched to the CFs of auditory-nerve fibers.

One alternative to temporal-place schemes is the pooled (also known as "ensemble", "summary", or "aggregate") interspike interval distribution, which is obtained by summing interspike interval histograms across the tonotopically-arranged ensemble of ANFs (Ghitza, 1988; Palmer, 1990; Meddis and Hewitt, 1991, 1992; Delgutte and Cariani, 1992). Because this scheme eliminates explicit place information by integrating across all cochlear places, it is an example of a *purely temporal* scheme for spectral representation. Figure 16.4B shows the pooled interspike interval distribution for the vowel [æ] derived from the interval-place representation of Figure 16.4A. The Fourier transform of the pooled distribution (Figure 16.5C) shows peaks at the frequencies of the first 2–3 formants, indicating that essential information for vowel identification

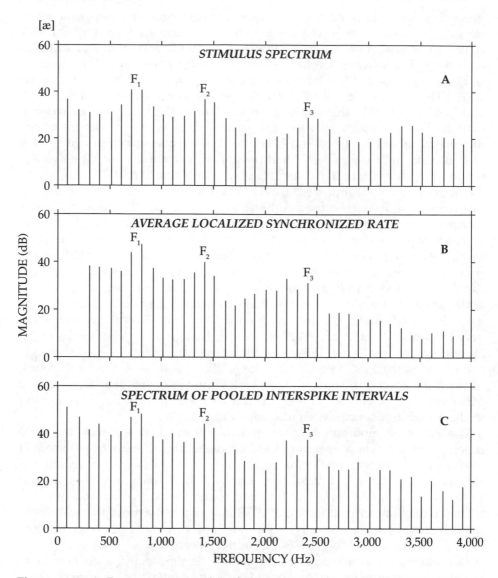

Figure 16.5   A. Power spectrum of the [æ] vowel stimulus of Figures 16.3 and 16.4. The frequencies of the first three formants are 750, 1,450, and 2,450 Hz. B. Average localized synchronized rate (ALSR) computed from period histograms such as those of Figure 16.3 for 57 ANFs. The ALSR at frequency F was evaluated by averaging the F-components of the period histograms for all ANFs whose CFs lie in a 0.4–octave band centered at F (Young and Sachs, 1979). C. Power spectrum of the pooled interspike interval distribution shown in the bottom of Figure 16.4.

is available in this representation. In general, purely temporal schemes such as the pooled interval distribution do well for low-frequency sounds such as vowels and voiced formant transitions (Sinex and Geisler, 1983; Delgutte, 1984; Carney and Geisler, 1986; Geisler and Gamble, 1989; Palmer, 1990), but have difficulty for high-frequency sounds such as fricative consonants (Delgutte and Kiang, 1984b). It should also be noted that the vast majority of cells at the most peripheral stages of the auditory nervous system show sharp frequency tuning, so that there is no evidence for wide-scale spatial integration in the brainstem.

A third alternative to temporal-place and purely temporal schemes is a class of *spatio-temporal coincidence* schemes that rely on differences in spike arrival times for ANFs innervating different places along the cochlea (Loeb et al., 1983; Shamma, 1985, 1988; Deng et al., 1988; Carney, 1994). These schemes differ in the detail of their assumptions about how sensitivity to coincidence is achieved. Although these schemes have not been as thoroughly tested against physiological data as the other two classes of schemes, it appears that some of them provide sufficient information for encoding at least sonorant spectra (Deng et al., 1988; Shamma, 1985). From the point of view of central processing, these schemes assume the existence of cells sensitive to the coincidence of spikes across their spatially-distributed inputs, a notion for which physiological evidence is mounting (Carney, 1990; Rothman et al., 1993; Joris et al., 1994; Palmer et al., 1994). Unlike schemes based on interspike intervals, spatiotemporal coincidence schemes do not require long neural delays, and make use of precise temporal relationships imposed by cochlear mechanics among the discharges of ANFs tuned to different CFs. This class of schemes appears to be a promising avenue for research into central auditory mechanisms for processing acoustic stimuli.

In conclusion, a wide variety of processing schemes have been proposed for the temporal representation of the short-time spectra of speech sounds. For the most part, these schemes are effective for low-frequency stimuli such as vowels and voiced formant transitions, but many of them have difficulty with high-frequency sounds such as fricatives and the bursts of stop consonants. The available physiological data from ANFs do not allow us to rule out any of these schemes, so that the most valid scheme can only be identified by examining how speech sounds are processed by the central nervous system.

3.4 Rate-place and temporal representations in the cochlear nucleus

The functional organization of the central auditory system is considerably more complex than that of the auditory nerve. Whereas the auditory nerve can be considered as a two-dimensional array of fibers organized along CF and sensitivity (threshold), auditory nuclei in the brainstem contain many different types of cells interconnected by a complex pattern of projections (reviewed by

Irvine, 1986). This organization is best understood for the cochlear nucleus, which contains at least six major types of cells, with some of these major cell types being further divided into sub-types. These cell types are defined by a wide set of properties, including morphology, cytochemistry, intrinsic cell-membrane characteristics, regional distribution within the CN, patterns of synaptic inputs, central projections, and responses to acoustic stimuli (for reviews, see Young, 1984; Cant, 1992; Rhode and Greenberg, 1992). Because most of these cell types cover the entire range of CFs, the CN effectively provides multiple, parallel spectro-temporal representations of the acoustic stimulus. Elucidating the functions of these parallel representations is a major task for auditory neuroscience.

Investigations of how different cell types in the cochlear nucleus respond to speech sounds (Palmer et al., 1986; Kim et al., 1986; Blackburn and Sachs, 1990; Winter and Palmer, 1990; Palmer and Winter, 1992) have focused on how the spectra of steady-state vowels are encoded. The unit type that has been the most thoroughly studied is the *primary-like* unit, whose response pattern resembles that of ANFs. Primary-like responses are recorded from bushy cells (Rhode et al., 1983; Rouiller and Ryugo, 1984), which receive giant synaptic terminals ("end bulbs") from auditory-nerve fibers. These giant endings provide multiple synapses that ensure very secure synaptic transmission, so that the response patterns of primary-like neurons closely resemble those of their ANF inputs. In particular, primary-like units show precise phase locking to pure tones similar to that of ANFs (Bourk, 1976; Rhode and Smith, 1986), with some cells even showing enhanced phase locking for low frequencies (Joris et al., 1994). Consistent with this precise phase locking, primary-like units provide a good representation of vowel formants in their fine temporal patterns of discharge (Palmer et al., 1986; Winter and Palmer, 1990; Blackburn and Sachs, 1990). On the other hand, rate-place codes for primary-like units suffer from the same dynamic range limitations as they do for low-threshold ANFs (Blackburn and Sachs, 1990). Bushy cells project to nuclei in the superior olive that play a role in the processing of binaural information (Cant, 1992). The precise phase locking of bushy cells is well adapted to this binaural processing function because interaural differences in phase are known to be an important cue for sound localization (Durlach and Colburn, 1978). Of course, the function of bushy cells in binaural circuits does not preclude their playing an additional role in speech processing.

Another CN unit type whose responses to vowels have been studied in some detail is the *chopper* unit, thus called because its response pattern shows pronounced peaks spaced at regular intervals. Chopper responses are recorded from stellate cells, which receive small synaptic terminals from many auditory-nerve fibers (Rhode et al., 1983; Rouiller and Ryugo, 1984). As such, stellate cells are more likely than bushy cells to integrate information across ANFs. Chopper units poorly phase lock to pure tones above 1 kHz (Bourk, 1976; Rhode and Smith, 1986). Consistent with this poor phase locking, the fine temporal discharge patterns of chopper units provide information about the first formant frequency, but not about higher formants whose frequencies exceed 1 kHz (Blackburn and Sachs, 1990). In contrast, chopper units provide a better rate-place representation of vowels for conversational speech levels than do low-threshold ANFs (Blackburn and Sachs, 1990). In particular, the rate-place representation for a sub-class of choppers, the "transient" choppers, is nearly invariant over a 40 dB range of stimulus levels. Thus, chopper units (particularly transient choppers) encode the spectrum of vowels in rate-place profiles over a wide range of sound levels despite the limited dynamic range of their ANF inputs. One hypothesis for explaining the enhanced dynamic range of choppers is that they might receive an orderly convergence of inputs from ANFs having the same CF, but differing in thresholds (Winslow et al., 1987). Another (not mutually exclusive) conception is that chopper neurons receive inputs from ANFs with different CFs exerting mutually inhibitory influences (Rhode and Greenberg, 1994).

In summary, different cell types in the cochlear nucleus show distinct response patterns to vowel stimuli. Primary-like units provide a precise encoding of formant frequencies in their fine temporal patterns of discharge. Chopper units give a rate-place representation of vowel spectra over a wide range of stimulus levels. Thus, chopper and primary-like units provide complementary information about the short-time spectra of speech stimuli. The methods used for characterizing the responses of chopper and primary-like units to speech stimuli are also applicable to other types of cells in the cochlear nucleus and to cells in more central auditory nuclei. Such detailed characterizations are needed for elucidating the functions of the different cell types and neural circuits in speech processing.

4 Coding of pitch and voicing

The previous section focused on how the spectral envelope associated with the resonant properties of the vocal tract is encoded in the auditory nerve and cochlear nucleus. The fine spectral structure associated with voicing is also important in speech communication. Over short times, voiced sounds have nearly periodic waveforms. This periodicity, and the corresponding harmonicity of the spectral pattern produce a prominent pitch sensation. Variations in pitch throughout an utterance convey information about stress, grammatical structure, and speaker's attitude. Pitch may also be important for communication in the presence of competing sounds because differences in pitch help segregate voices from each other (Darwin, 1992). Pitch sensations produced by complex periodic waveforms are not unique to human speech, but are also important in music and animal vocalizations. Thus, neural mechanisms for the perception of the pitch of voice are likely to be a special instance of a general mechanism found in both humans and non-human animals for the perception of the pitch of complex acoustic stimuli. Such pitch percepts are heard even when the stimulus has no energy at the fundamental frequency (for review, see De Boer, 1976). Such missing-fundamental stimuli are of practical as well as theoretical interest because the fundamental component of speech is often lacking (as in telephone communication) or masked by low-frequency background noise in every day situations.

4.1 Temporal representation of pitch

As for the spectral envelope, the pitch of complex tones might be encoded in either the temporal or the spatial patterns of discharge of auditory neurons. The coding of voice pitch in interspike intervals of ANFs is perhaps the most directly demonstrated. For every fiber in Figure 16.4A, the largest peak in the interspike interval distribution occurs at 10 msec, the pitch period of the [æ] vowel, which has a fundamental of 100 Hz. This maximum at 10 msec is even more salient in the pooled interval distribution of Figure 16.4B because it is present in all fibers, while formant-related periodicities occur only in particular CF regions. Thus, for this vowel, pitch corresponds to the most frequent interspike interval in the auditory nerve. Cariani and Delgutte (1996) have shown that this result holds not only for periodic stimuli such as steady-state vowels, but also for a wide variety of inharmonic stimuli devised by psychoacousticians to test theories of pitch perception (see also Evans, 1983). These physiological results lend support to models of pitch perception based on interspike intervals (Licklider, 1951; Srulovicz and Goldstein, 1983; Moore, 1990; van Noorden, 1983; Meddis and Hewitt, 1991).

If pitch were coded in interspike intervals of ANFs, a key question is how such interval information might be processed by the central nervous system. The vast majority of cells in the cochlear nucleus show interspike intervals related to fundamental frequency of complex periodic sounds, including vowels (Kim et al., 1986; Greenberg and Rhode, 1987; Palmer and Winter, 1992; Rhode, 1995; Cariani, 1995). Particularly interesting are the responses of onset cells, which respond primarily to the onset of tones at their CF. Most onset cells phase lock to low-frequency (< 1 kHz) tones, much as if each stimulus cycle constituted a separate onset. In response to steady-state vowels, certain onset cells show very precise phase-locking to the fundamental, basically discharging once for each stimulus cycle (Kim et al., 1986; Palmer and Winter, 1992). Thus, the temporal discharge patterns of these cells are considerably simplified compared to the responses of ANFs, which typically show multiple peaks per cycle (Figure 16.3). Such simplification might aid later stages of processing in extracting pitch information. Thus, onset cells might be a component of a neural circuit involved in pitch processing, although they do not by themselves extract pitch. The hypothesis that onset cells play a role in pitch extraction needs to be tested by examining the response of these cells to inharmonic stimuli used in psychophysical experiments on pitch perception.

4.2 Rate-place representation of pitch

Alternatives to purely temporal models of pitch perception are place or "pattern recognition" models that determine pitch by identifying harmonic relationships among stimulus components (e.g. Goldstein, 1973; Terhardt, 1974). These models require an input spectral representation in which low-frequency partials are resolved, but they do not specify how such a representation might be obtained physiologically. The simplest possibility is that this representation is provided by a rate-place code. Another possibility (not discussed here) is that a temporal-place scheme such as the ALSR might produce the required representation (Srulovicz and Goldstein, 1983; Delgutte, 1984; Miller and Sachs, 1984).

At first sight, the possibility that pitch might be derived from rate-place information appears unlikely because the patterns of average discharge rate against CF measured by Sachs and Young (1979) for vowel stimuli fail to show peaks at harmonics of the fundamental frequency, even for low stimulus levels where dynamic range limitations are not an issue (Figure 16.2A). However, this negative result is likely to depend strongly on both the fundamental frequency and the species. The fundamental frequency used by Sachs and Young was 128 Hz, which is typical for a male voice. Hirahara et al. (1996) have found some evidence for rate-place cues to pitch for higher f_0s (> 200 Hz), appropriate for the voices of women and children. Evidence for rate-place cues to harmonic spectral patterns is also available for nonspeech stimuli with relatively high f_0s (Evans and Wilson, 1973; Smoorenburg and Linschoten, 1977). Another factor that needs to be considered is species differences in the frequency selectivity of the ear. Psychophysical data suggest that the human ear is more selective than the cat ear. (Pickles, 1979, 1980). Delgutte (1995) showed that, when a rate-place model for the cat ear is modified to incorporate the human cochlear frequency map (Greenwood, 1990), the modified model does show peaks in discharge rate at the frequencies of the first 5 harmonics of f_0s in the range of male voices. Thus, the lack of rate-place cues to f_0 in the Sachs and Young (1979) data for the cat might not hold for the human auditory nerve. Interestingly, the f_0s of cat vocalizations are near 600 Hz (Watanabe and Katsuki, 1974), in a range where rate-place cues are clearly available in the auditory nerve of this species. Thus, rate-place coding might provide a general representation for the pitch of complex tones with fundamental frequencies within the range of vocalization of each species. This hypothesis is in harmony with the view that the perception of virtual pitch and the perception of conspecific vocalizations are intimately linked (Terhardt, 1974).

In summary, information about the pitch of voice is clearly available in temporal representations, and may also be available in rate-place representations, particularly for the higher f_0s. In general, temporal schemes are more plausible for the encoding of pitch than for the encoding of the formant pattern because the degradation of phase locking with increasing frequency is less likely to be a limitation in the range of fundamental frequencies of the human voice.

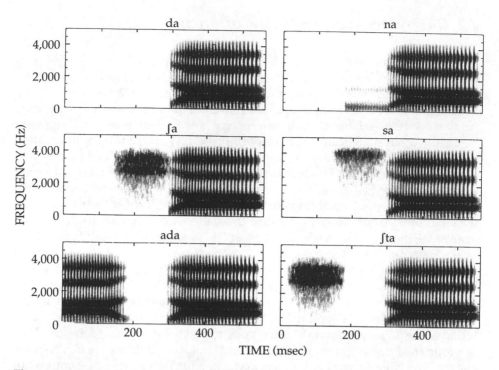

Figure 16.6   Broadband spectrograms of 6 synthetic speech stimuli designed for studying the context dependence of the neural response to speech. The spectrograms are aligned so that the common [da] segment occurs at the same time.

5 Neural correlates of speech perceptual phenomena

5.1 Context dependence in speech perception

A major issue in speech perception arises in the search for invariant acoustic correlates of phonetic categories (Liberman et al., 1967; Stevens and Blumstein, 1978; Repp, 1982). For the most part, it has not been possible to identify acoustic properties that reliably characterize a given speech sound (or phonetic feature, or syllable, or word) for all contexts. Conversely, in many cases, a given acoustic segment can be heard as different phonetic categories depending on context (Liberman et al., 1967). This context dependence is not unique to speech, but exists for the perception of objects through any sensory modality (Gibson, 1966; Marr, 1982). Nervous systems may have evolved very general mechanisms to handle such context-dependence in the stimulus.

Neural mechanisms such as adaptation, facilitation, and long-lasting inhibition may underlie certain context-dependencies in speech perception. Figure 16.6 shows spectrograms for a set of stimuli designed to investigate the

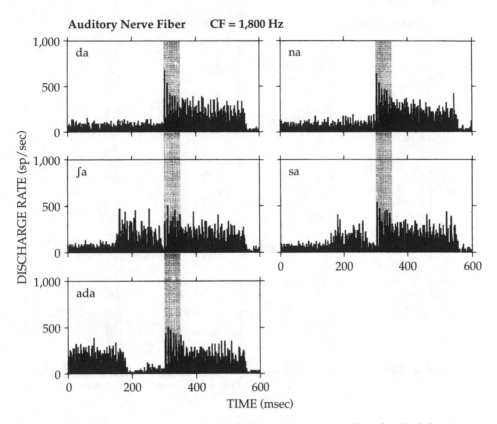

Figure 16.7 Response patterns of a high–SR auditory-nerve fiber for 5 of the 6 stimuli of Figure 16.6 presented at 60 dB SPL. The shaded area indicates the interval of formant transitions. The PST histograms have a bin width of 1 msec.

context-dependent encoding of speech (Delgutte and Kiang, 1984c). These six stimuli share a common part which, by itself, sounds like [da]. They differ in that this common part is preceded by different contexts, yielding stimuli sounding like [na], [ʃa], [sa], [ada] and [ʃta] as well as the basic [da]. Figure 16.7 shows the response patterns of an auditory-nerve fiber for five of these stimuli. For [da], the response pattern shows a clear peak resulting from adaptation at the beginning of the formant transitions. The amplitude of this peak is reduced for the stimuli in which the context elicits a pronounced response (particularly [ʃa] and [ada]). Thus, the contrast between these stimuli is more salient in the neural response, where differences are present during both the context and the transitions, than in the acoustic waveform, where differences occur only during the context. In general, the greater and longer-lasting the response to the context, the smaller the response to the formant transitions (Delgutte, 1980; Delgutte and Kiang, 1984c), consistent with the properties of auditory-nerve adaptation (Smith, 1979).

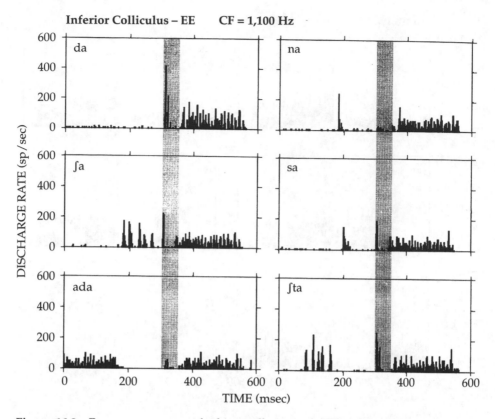

Figure 16.8   Response patterns of a binaurally-excited (EE) inferior-colliculus unit for the stimuli of Figure 16.6 presented diotically at 60 dB SPL. The PST histograms have a bin width of 1 msec.

Central auditory neurons exhibit more complex forms of context-dependencies than auditory-nerve adaptation. An example is shown in Figure 16.8 for an inferior-colliculus neuron in response to the stimuli of Figure 16.6. The response pattern for [da] shows a pronounced peak at the onset of the formant transition, followed by a pause and then relatively sustained activity during the steady-state [a]. The peak at the onset of the transitions is both decreased in amplitude and altered in shape for all the other stimuli. These findings differ from those of Figure 16.7 in that, whereas for the ANF the peak amplitude is always inversely related to the amount of activity in response to the preceding context, this simple relationship does not hold for the IC neuron. In particular, the peak in discharge rate is almost entirely eliminated for [na] despite the weak response during [n]. This strong effect of a context which, by itself produces virtually no spike discharges suggests that a form of long-lasting inhibition may be involved. This interpretation is consistent with evidence for long-lasting inhibition in IC neurons in response to pairs of click stimuli presented in succession (Carney and Yin, 1989). Overall, the temporal interactions for this neuron are considerably more complex than those resulting from simple adaptation.

Evidence for complex temporal interactions is not limited to the IC, but is also available for both more peripheral stages of processing such as the CN, and more central sites such as the auditory cortex. Rupert et al. (1977) and Caspary et al. (1977) studied the responses of single units in the dorsal cochlear nucleus to brief excerpts from sustained vowels presented in rapid succession. They found that the response to a particular vowel could be suppressed when preceded by another vowel that, by itself, produced no response. Even though these artificial stimuli show abrupt spectral changes that never occur in natural speech, these results point to the existence of inhibitory interactions clearly distinct from adaptation, and lasting for durations comparable to those of speech sounds. This conclusion is supported by studies of "forward masking" in CN neurons using pairs of tone stimuli presented in succession (Boettcher et al., 1990; Palombi et al., 1994; Shore, 1995). These studies show that for certain unit types, particularly chopper, onset, and build-up neurons, forward masking does not obey the functional relationships established by Smith (1979) for adaptation in ANFs, suggesting the existence of additional inhibitory or facilitatory mechanisms. Evidence for inhibitory temporal interactions is also available for neurons in the cat primary auditory cortex (Calford and Semple, 1995).

The significance of these context-sensitive interactions in neural responses is that they might underlie certain trading relations in speech perception (Delgutte, 1982). Trading relations arise when multiple acoustic cues contribute to a phonetic distinction, such that a change in one cue can be compensated for by an opposite change in another cue without changing the phonetic identity of the stimulus (Repp, 1982). For example, two cues for the [aʃa]-[atʃa] distinction are the rise time of the frication noise and the duration of the silent interval preceding the noise (Dorman et al., 1979). Using a model of peripheral auditory processing incorporating adaptation, Delgutte (1982) showed that both decreasing the rise time and increasing the duration of the silent interval result in a more prominent adaptation peak at the onset of the frication noise in the response patterns of model ANFs. Thus, in this case, the model neural response showed greater invariance over different realizations of the phonetic category than did the acoustic stimulus.

Adaptation in ANFs is admittedly too simple a neural mechanism to explain more than a handful of trading relations in speech perception. However, neurons in the CN and IC possess more complex forms of temporal interactions that might account for more general trading relations and context dependencies. Some of these neurons may be sensitive to combinations of stimulus components that are widely separated in both time and frequency, thereby providing the neural machinery necessary for the perception of highly context-dependent stimuli such as speech.

5.2 *Categorical perception*

Human listeners are often better at resolving small differences between speech stimuli that lie near the perceptual boundary between two phonetic categories than they are at resolving stimuli that are far from the boundary (Liberman et al., 1967; Abramson and Lisker, 1970). One of the best-studied examples of such natural perceptual boundaries is for stop consonants differing along a VOT continuum (e.g. [da] vs. [ta]). In many languages, stimuli with VOTs shorter than 20–40 msec are heard as voiced (e.g. [da]), while stimuli with longer VOTs are heard as unvoiced (e.g. [ta]) (Abramson and Lisker, 1970). Pairs of stimuli having VOTs near the 20–40 msec boundary are more easily discriminable than stimuli having either shorter or longer VOTs (Abramson and Lisker, 1970). This enhanced psychophysical acuity for VOTs near the perceptual boundary is not unique to humans, but is also found for chinchillas (Kuhl and Miller, 1978; Kuhl, 1981), monkeys (Kuhl and Padden, 1982), and birds (Dooling et al., 1989; Kluender, 1991), suggesting that it may reflect a very general property of the vertebrate auditory system. Such natural perceptual boundaries may be the basis for certain forms of categorical perception, and may have guided the evolution of the repertoire of sounds used for speech communication (Kuhl, 1981).

A neural correlate of the perceptual boundary along the VOT continuum was identified by Sinex and his colleagues in the discharge patterns of chinchilla ANFs (Sinex and McDonald, 1988, 1989; Sinex et al., 1991). Figure 16.9 shows representative results. Each panel shows the population response patterns of a sample of low-CF fibers for a pair of stimuli differing in VOT along a [da]-[ta] continuum. The two stimuli in the middle panel span the category boundary between [da] and [ta], while both stimuli in the top panel are normally identified as [da], and both stimuli in the bottom panel as [ta]. The population response to stimuli with VOTs of 30–40 msec shows a rapid rise/peak in discharge rate that is stable across all low-CF fibers. This rise is either less rapid or less stable in response to stimuli that have either lower or higher VOTs. As a result of these differences, the population response patterns are more clearly distinct for the pair of stimuli whose elements belong to two different phonetic categories than for pairs whose elements belong to the same category. Thus, there exists a correlate of the enhanced psychophysical acuity near the 30–40 msec VOT boundary in the response pattern of the *population* of ANFs.

A neural correlate of categorical perception along the VOT continuum was also identified by Steinschneider et al. (1994, 1995) in the primary auditory cortex of the macaque. We have seen in Section 2.2 a class of "double onset" units in the auditory cortex respond to stop-vowels syllables with two bursts of activity: a first burst at consonantal release, and a second one at voicing onset (Steinschneider et al., 1994). In response to stimuli differing in VOT along a [da]-[ta] continuum, a subset of this class of multi-units only shows

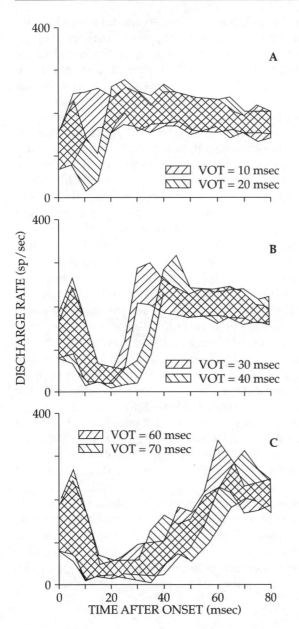

Figure 16.9 (From Sinex et al., 1991). Comparison of the population ANF responses elicited by pairs of synthetic syllables differing in VOT by 10 msec. Each cross-hatched area encloses the mean ±1 standard deviation of the PST histograms of 11 low-CF (<1 kHz) ANFs from one chinchilla. A. Population response patterns for two stimuli clearly identified at [da]. B. Population response patterns for two stimuli located near the phonetic boundary between [da] and [ta]. C. Population response patterns for two stimuli identified at [ta].

the second burst of activity if the VOT exceeds 30–40 msec (Steinschneider et al., 1995). In effect, the second burst of activity is suppressed, perhaps through a form of long-lasting inhibition, when it occurs less than 30–40 msec after the first burst. Regardless of the mechanism involved, responses to stimuli identified as [da] show a single burst of activity, while responses to [ta] stimuli show two bursts.

The auditory-nerve correlate of categorical perception found by Sinex et al. (1991) and cortical correlate of Steinschneider et al. (1995) differ fundamentally in that the former is a property of the population of ANFs, while the latter is found for single recording sites. Nevertheless, the cortical correlate can be interpreted as a transformation of the auditory-nerve correlate. Such a transformation might be accomplished by coincidence-detector neurons that would discharge only when they receive nearly simultaneous inputs from ANFs spanning a wide range of CFs. The cortical correlate of Steinschneider et al. (1995) may be appealing because its behavior is consistent with that of a feature detector. However, only a fraction of cortical units show the categorical effect, so that, in principle, stimuli within a phonetic category could be easily discriminated using VOT information from the majority of units that do not show a categorical effect. This difficulty does not arise for the auditory-nerve correlate of Sinex et al. (1991) because it inherently depends on the entire population of fibers. Overall, the results of Sinex et al. (1991) and Steinschneider et al. (1995) offer promise that relatively simple neural mechanisms might underlie certain forms of categorical perception, and provide further support for the view that properties of the auditory system may have influenced the selection of the repertoire of phonetic features (Kuhl, 1981).

Since this chapter was written, a new study of the encoding of VOT in the primary auditory cortex has been published (Eggermont, 1995). As Steinschneider et al. (1994, 1995) found for the unanesthetized macaque, Eggermont found that single units in the auditory cortex of the anesthetized cat respond with "double onset" patterns to long-VOT stimuli, and with a single onset for short VOTs. However, for the neural population as a whole, there was no tendency for the cross-over between the two response patterns to occur at VOTs near the 30-msec phonetic boundary, in contrast to the Steinschneider et al. reports. This negative result illustrates the need for caution when seeking correlates of perceptual phenomena in single "feature detector" neurons, as opposed to populations of neurons.

6 Conclusion

Taken together, studies of the neural processing of speech show that a rich array of cues to phonetic distinctions is available in the discharge patterns of ANFs and CN cells. However, much less is known about which of these cues are actually utilized by more central stages in the auditory nervous system, and if they are used, how this information is processed. For example, while fine time patterns of discharge of ANFs contain highly-redundant information about the formant pattern of vowels, there is little agreement as to which schemes might be used for processing this information in the central nervous system.

Despite this limitation in our knowledge, two major conclusions emerge from this survey of neural processing of speech. First, many features of the neural responses to speech stimuli can be understood in terms of responses to simpler stimuli that share some acoustic characteristics with speech. For example, ANF responses to pure tones and two-tone stimuli help to understand responses to vowels. Responses of brainstem auditory neurons to AM stimuli help to elucidate responses to acoustic transients in speech. Thus, there is no evidence that speech is treated as a "special" stimulus in the auditory nerve, the brainstem or the midbrain. This observation suggests that a productive approach to understanding the neural processing of speech is to combine speech stimuli with nonspeech analogs in order to identify general neural mechanisms.

The second major conclusion is that the acoustic characteristics of speech that are phonetically the most important are prominently and robustly encoded in neural responses. For example, a majority of ANFs phase lock to one or more of the formant frequencies of vowels, providing a very robust representation of the formant pattern. Phonetically-important changes in amplitude and spectrum are encoded by prominent peaks in discharge rate in the response patterns of ANFs, and may produce even more prominent responses for phasic cells in the central nervous system. For stimuli differing along a VOT continuum, pairs of stimuli that are psychophysically the most discriminable produce the most distinct neural responses. These observations support the view that the auditory system shows predispositions for the particular set of acoustic features used for phonetic contrasts.

For the most part, physiological studies of the auditory processing of speech have not helped to address fundamental issues in speech perception such as variability in acoustic correlates of phonetic categories or the nature of internal representations. It might be hoped that, since the auditory system can easily distinguish phonetic elements, invariant correlates of phonetic categories might be more easily identified from neural responses than from the acoustic signal. In certain respects, this task may in fact be more difficult for neural responses. For example, stimulus level generally has a strong effect on neural responses to acoustic stimuli, while speech perception remains remarkably stable over a very wide range of levels. On the other hand, it is clear that the responses of auditory neurons at the level of the brainstem and above are much more than smeared reflections of the spectrogram, and that there exists a wide variety of neural mechanisms adapted for processing highly context-dependent stimuli such as speech. These mechanisms include adaptation, long-lasting inhibition, coincidence detection, and lateral inhibition. Some neural correlates of classic speech perceptual phenomena such as categorical perception and trading relations are beginning to emerge. Further studies of the neural processing of speech, particularly those dealing with the central auditory system, are likely to contribute much more to our understanding of fundamental issues in speech perception.

Practical benefits of physiological studies may come even earlier than their theoretical contributions to our understanding of speech perception. Because single-unit techniques provide detailed, signal-oriented descriptions of neural responses, they may be more likely to inspire novel signal processing algorithms than traditional psychophysical models. Neurophysiological studies together with computational and psychophysical approaches may help in developing hearing aids and auditory implants that would provide better speech reception in adverse environments. They may also aid in the design of artificial systems for the coding, transmission and recognition of speech that perform more like the auditory system.

NOTE

I thank P.A. Cariani and T. Hirahara for assistance in collecting physiological data, and B.E. Norris for expert figure preparation. M.C. Brown, P.A. Cariani, B.M. Hammond, J.R. Iversen, S. Kalluri, R.Y. Litovsky and M.F. McKinney made valuable comments on the manuscript. Preparation of this chapter was supported by NIH Grants DC00119 and DC02258.

17 Aspects of Auditory Processing Related to Speech Perception

BRIAN C.J. MOORE

1 Introduction

This chapter reviews selected aspects of auditory processing, chosen because they play a role in the perception of speech. Although there are certainly specialized brain mechanisms for speech perception, the initial analysis of speech and non-speech sounds is probably similar, with many processes being shared between the two. For example, the frequency selectivity of the ear, as measured in simple masking experiments, plays a role in determining the internal representation of speech sounds, and in particular the extent to which formant frequencies are represented. It turns out that the resolution of the auditory system in frequency and time, as measured in psychoacoustic experiments, usually markedly exceeds the resolution necessary for the identification or discrimination of speech sounds. This partly accounts for the fact that speech perception is robust, and resistant to distortion of the speech and to background noise.

2 Frequency selectivity

Frequency selectivity refers to our ability to resolve the sinusoidal components in a complex sound, and it plays a role in many aspects of auditory perception. However, it is often demonstrated and measured by studying masking. Masking may be defined as:

(1) The process by which the threshold of audibility for one sound is raised by the presence of another (masking) sound.

(2) The amount by which the threshold of audibility of a sound is raised by the presence of another (masking) sound. The unit customarily used is the decibel.

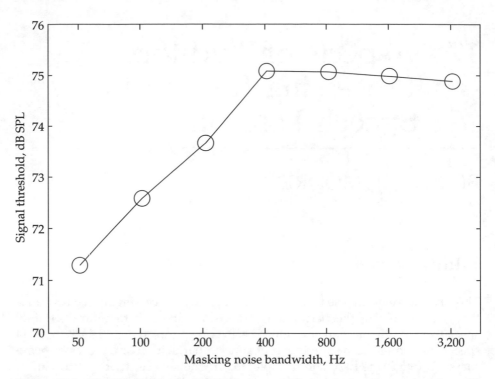

Figure 17.1   The threshold of a 2,000-Hz sinusoidal signal plotted as a function of the bandwith of a noise masker centered at 2,000-Hz. Data from Moore et al. (1993b).

It has been known for many years that a signal will most easily be masked by a sound having frequency components close to, or the same as, those of the signal. This led to the idea that masking reflects the limits of frequency selectivity: if the selectivity of the ear is insufficient to separate the signal and the masker, then masking will occur.

2.1 The critical band concept

Fletcher (1940) measured the threshold of a sinusoidal signal as a function of the bandwidth of a bandpass noise masker. The noise was always centered at the signal frequency, and the noise power density was held constant. Thus, the total noise power increased as the bandwidth increased. This experiment has been repeated several times since then. An example of the results, taken from Moore et al. (1993b), is given in Figure 17.1. The threshold of the signal increases at first as the noise bandwidth increases, but then flattens off, so that further increases in noise bandwidth do not change the signal threshold significantly.

To account for these results, Fletcher (1940) suggested that the peripheral auditory system behaves as if it contained a bank of bandpass filters, with over-lapping passbands. These filters are now called the "auditory filters". Fletcher suggested that the basilar membrane provided the basis for the auditory filters. Each different point on the basilar membrane corresponds to a filter with a different center frequency, and the center frequency changes progressively with position along the basilar membrane (see Delgutte, AUDITORY NEURAL PROCESSING OF SPEECH). Recent data are consistent with this point of view (Moore, 1986).

When trying to detect a signal in a noise background, the listener is assumed to make use of a filter with a center frequency close to that of the signal. This filter will pass the signal but remove a great deal of the noise. Only the com-ponents in the noise which pass through the filter will have any effect in masking the signal. It is usually assumed that the threshold for the signal is determined by the amount of noise passing through the auditory filter; specifi-cally, threshold is assumed to correspond to a certain signal-to-noise ratio at the output of the filter. This set of assumptions has come to be known as the "power spectrum model" of masking (Patterson and Moore, 1986), since the stimuli are represented by their long-term power spectra, i.e. the relative phases of the components and the short-term fluctuations in the masker are ignored. The assumptions of this model do not always hold (Moore, 1993), but it works well in many situations.

In the band-widening experiment described above, increases in noise band-width result in more noise passing through the auditory filter centered at the signal frequency, provided the noise bandwidth is less than the filter band-width. However, once the noise bandwidth exceeds the filter bandwidth, fur-ther increases in noise bandwidth have little effect on the noise passing through the filter. Fletcher called the bandwidth at which the signal threshold ceased to increase the "critical bandwidth".

In analysing the results of his experiment, Fletcher made a simplifying as-sumption. He assumed that the shape of the auditory filter could be approx-imated as a simple rectangle, with a flat top and vertical edges. For such a filter all components within the passband of the filter are passed equally, and all components outside the passband are removed. The width of this passband is equal to the critical bandwidth described above. The term "critical band" is often used to refer to this hypothetical rectangular filter. However, the audit-ory filter is not rectangular; rather, it has a rounded top and sloping skirts. The next section outlines how the shape of the auditory filter at a given center frequency can be estimated.

2.2 *Estimating the shape of the auditory filter*

Most methods for estimating the shape of the auditory filter at a given cen-ter frequency are based on the assumptions of the power spectrum model of masking. The threshold of a signal whose frequency is fixed is measured in the presence of a masker whose spectral content is varied. It is assumed, as a first approximation, that the signal is detected using the single auditory filter which is centered on the frequency of the signal, and that threshold corresponds to a constant signal-to-masker ratio at the output of that filter. The methods described below are both based on these assumptions.

2.2.1 Psychophysical tuning curves (PTCs)

These involve a procedure which is analogous in many ways to the determination of a neural tuning curve (see Delgutte, AUDITORY NEURAL PROCESSING OF SPEECH). To determine a PTC, the signal is fixed in level, usually at a very low level, say, 10 dB SL. The masker can be either a sinusoid or a narrow band of noise. For each of several masker frequencies, the level of the masker needed just to mask the signal is determined. Because the signal is at a low level it is assumed that it will produce activity primarily in one auditory filter. It is assumed further that at threshold the masker produces a constant output from that filter, in order to mask the fixed signal. Thus the PTC indicates the masker level required to produce a fixed output from the auditory filter as a function of frequency. Normally a filter characteristic is determined by measuring the output from the filter for an input varying in frequency and fixed in level. However, if the filter is linear the two methods give the same result. Thus, assuming linearity, the shape of the auditory filter can be obtained simply by inverting the PTC. Examples of some PTCs are given in Figure 17.2.

There are several problems in interpreting the PTC as a direct measure of the auditory filter shape. One problem is that the auditory filter is not strictly linear; rather, its shape changes with stimulus level. It is not yet clear what aspect of stimulus level determines the filter shape, but it seems likely that the shape of the PTC is affected by the fact that the masker level changes markedly with frequency. The steep high-frequency slope of the PTC may overestimate the effective frequency selectivity available at a given stimulus level (Verschuure, 1981; Moore and O'Loughlin, 1986; Moore, 1993).

A second problem is that the listener may not attend to just one auditory filter. When the masker frequency is above the signal frequency the listener may attend to a filter centered just below the signal frequency, which gives a higher signal-to-masker ratio. Similarly, when the masker frequency is below the signal frequency the listener may attend to a filter centered above the signal frequency. This is known as "off-frequency listening", and there is now good evidence that humans do indeed listen "off-frequency" when it is advantageous to do so. The result of off-frequency listening is that the PTC has a sharper tip than would be obtained if only one auditory filter were involved (Johnson-Davies and Patterson, 1979; O'Loughlin and Moore, 1981).

2.2.2 The notched-noise method

Patterson (1976) has described a method of determining auditory filter shape which limits off-frequency listening. The

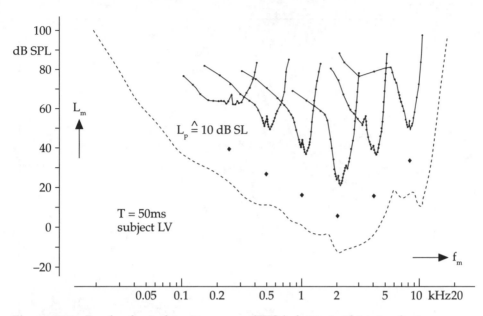

Figure 17.2 Psychophysical tuning curves (PTCs) determined in simultaneous masking, using sinusoidal signals at 10 dB SL. For each curve, the solid diamond below it indicates the frequency and level of the signal. The masker was a sinusoid which had a fixed starting phase relationship to the brief, 50 ms, signal. The masker level, L_m, required for threshold is plotted as a function of masker frequency, f_m, on a logarithmic scale. The dashed line shows the absolute threshold for the signal. From Vogten (1974), by permission of the author.

signal is fixed in frequency, and the masker is a noise with a bandstop or notch centered at the signal frequency. The width of the notch is varied, and the threshold of the signal is determined as a function of notch width. Since the notch is symmetrically placed around the signal frequency, the method cannot reveal asymmetries in the auditory filter, and the analysis assumes that the filter is symmetric on a linear frequency scale. This assumption appears not unreasonable, at least for the top part of the filter and at moderate sound levels since PTCs are quite symmetric around the tips. For a signal symmetrically placed in a bandstop noise, the optimum signal-to-masker ratio at the output of the auditory filter is achieved with a filter centered at the signal frequency.

As the width of the spectral notch is increased, less and less noise passes through the auditory filter. Thus the threshold of the signal drops. Assuming that threshold corresponds to a constant signal-to-masker ratio at the output of the filter, the change in signal threshold with notch width can be used to estimate the shape of the filter; full details are given in Glasberg and Moore (1990).

A typical auditory filter derived using this method is shown in Figure 17.3. It has a rounded top and quite steep skirts. Unlike the simple rectangular

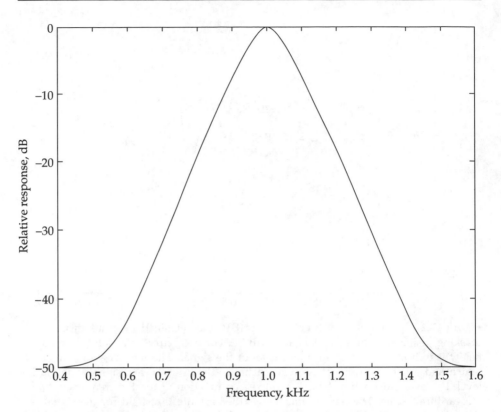

Figure 17.3   A typical auditory filter shape determined using the notched-noise method. The filter is centered at 1 kHz. The relative response of the filter (in dB) is plotted as a function of frequency.

filter, a filter with this shape cannot be completely specified with a single number, the critical bandwidth. However, some sort of summary statistic is useful, and one common measure is the bandwidth of the filter at which the response has fallen by a factor of two in power, i.e. by 3 dB. The 3-dB bandwidths of the auditory filters derived using Patterson's method are typically between 10 per cent and 15 per cent of the center frequency. An alternative measure is the equivalent rectangular bandwidth (ERB), which is equal to the bandwidth of an ideal rectangular filter with the same peak transmission as the auditory filter, and which passes the same power for a white noise input. The ERBs of the auditory filters derived using the notched-noise method are typically between 11 per cent and 17 per cent of the center frequency. These values are quite close to the estimates of the critical bandwidth obtained in other ways. However, the values at low frequencies tend to be smaller than the traditional critical bandwidth estimates. Figure 17.4 compares the ERB of the auditory filter, obtained from several experiments using the notched-noise method, with the traditional critical bandwidth function. An equation

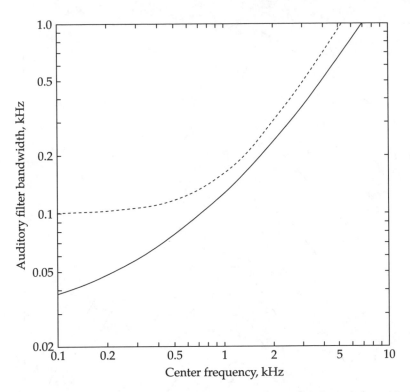

Figure 17.4   The dotted curve shows the traditional value of the critical bandwidth as a function of frequency. The solid curve shows the value of the ERB of the auditory filter as a function of frequency.

describing the value of the ERB as a function of frequency is (Glasberg and Moore, 1990):

$$ERB = 24.7(4.37F + 1), \tag{1}$$

where the ERB is in Hz, and F is frequency in kHz.

The notched-noise method has been extended to include conditions where the spectral notch in the noise is placed asymmetrically about the signal frequency. This allows the measurement of any asymmetry in the auditory filter, but the analysis of the results is more difficult, and has to take off-frequency listening into account (Patterson and Nimmo-Smith, 1980; Patterson and Moore, 1986; Moore and Glasberg, 1987). The results show that the auditory filter is reasonably symmetric at moderate sound levels, but becomes increasingly asymmetric at high levels, the low-frequency side becoming shallower than the high-frequency side. The relative response of the auditory filter centered at 1 kHz is shown in Figure 17.5 for a range of input sound levels from 20 to 90 dB SPL.

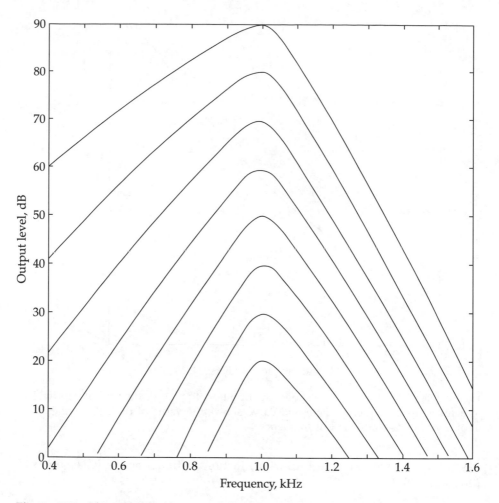

Figure 17.5 The relative response of the auditory filter centered at 1 kHz, plotted for input sound levels ranging from 20 to 90 dB SPL.

2.3 *Excitation patterns*

The auditory filter represents frequency selectivity at a particular center frequency, equivalent to a particular place on the basilar membrane. However, to gain some insight into the representation of sounds in the peripheral auditory system, it is often useful to describe the pattern of activity across different auditory filters (equivalent to the pattern across place on the basilar membrane). This distribution is called the excitation pattern (Zwicker, 1970).

Moore and Glasberg (1983) have described a way of deriving the shapes of excitation patterns using the concept of the auditory filter. They suggested that the excitation pattern of a given sound can be thought of as the output of the auditory filters as a function of their center frequency. This idea is illustrated in Figure 17.6. The upper portion of the figure shows auditory filter shapes for five center frequencies. Each filter is symmetrical on the linear frequency scale used, but the bandwidths of the filters increase with increasing center frequency, as illustrated in Figure 17.4. The vertical line represents a 1-kHz sinusoidal signal whose excitation pattern is to be derived. The lower panel shows the output from each filter in response to the 1-kHz signal, plotted as a function of the center frequency of each filter; this is the desired excitation pattern.

To see how this pattern is derived, consider the output from the filter with the lowest center frequency. This has a relative output in response to the 1-kHz signal of about -40 dB, as indicated by point "a" in the upper panel. In the lower panel, this gives rise to the point "a" on the excitation pattern; the point has an ordinate value of -40 dB and is positioned on the abscissa at a frequency corresponding to the center frequency of the lowest filter illustrated. The relative outputs of the other filters are indicated, in order of increasing center frequency, by points "b" to "e", and each leads to a corresponding point on the excitation pattern. The complete excitation pattern was derived by calculating the filter outputs for filters spaced at 10-Hz intervals. In deriving the excitation pattern, excitation levels were expressed relative to the level at the tip of the pattern, which was arbitrarily labelled as 0 dB. To calculate the excitation pattern for a 1-kHz sinusoid with a level of, say, 60 dB, the level at the tip would be labelled as 60 dB, and all other excitation levels would correspondingly be increased by 60 dB.

Note that, although the auditory filters were assumed to be symmetric on a linear frequency scale, the derived excitation pattern is asymmetric. This happens because the bandwidth of the auditory filter increases with increasing center frequency. This method of deriving excitation patterns is easily extended to the case where the auditory filters are asymmetric (Moore and Glasberg, 1987). Note, however, that whereas it is the lower side of the auditory filter which gets less steep with increasing level (see Figure 17.5), it is the upper branch of the excitation pattern that becomes less steep with increasing level, as illustrated in Figure 17.7. This happens because the upper side of the excitation pattern is determined by the lower side of the auditory filter and vice versa.

The representation of sounds in the peripheral auditory system is most appropriately indicated by plotting excitation patterns on a scale related to the ERB of the auditory filter, i.e. where the abscissa is number of ERBs. A function relating number of ERBs, E, to frequency is (Glasberg and Moore, 1990):

$$E = 21.4\log_{10}(4.37F + 1), \tag{2}$$

where F is frequency in kHz. Such a scale is similar conceptually to the Bark scale proposed by Zwicker and Feldtkeller (1967), but it differs numerically,

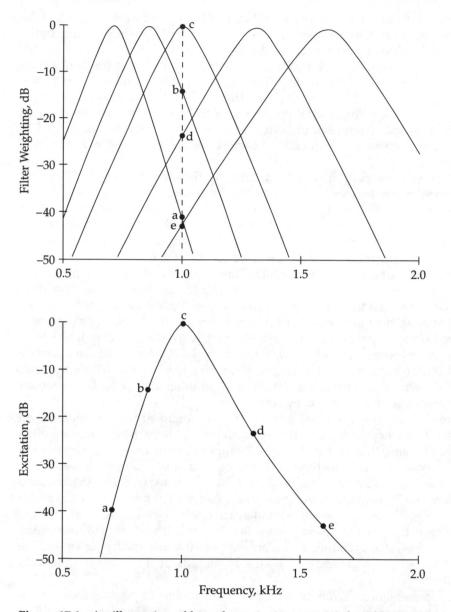

Figure 17.6   An illustration of how the excitation pattern of a 1-kHz sinusoid can be derived by calculating the outputs of the auditory filters as a function of their center frequency. The top half shows five auditory filters, centered at different frequencies, and the bottom half shows the calculated excitation pattern. From Moore and Glasberg (1983).

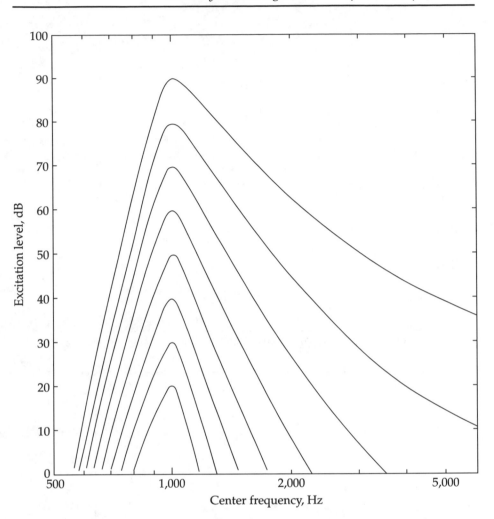

Figure 17.7 Psychoacoustical excitation patterns for a 1-kHz sinusoid at levels ranging from 20 to 90 dB SPL in 10 dB steps.

since the value of the ERB is smaller than the traditional critical bandwidth at low frequencies (see Figure 17.4).

The lower part of Figure 17.8 shows the excitation pattern for a synthetic vowel, /ɪ/, plotted on an ERB scale, for two different overall levels, 50 and 80 dB. The spectrum of the vowel is shown in the upper part of the figure, on a linear frequency scale. Several aspects of the excitation patterns are noteworthy. Firstly, the lowest few peaks in the excitation patterns do not correspond to formant frequencies, but rather to individual lower harmonics; these harmonics are resolved in the peripheral auditory system, and can be heard out as separate tones under certain conditions (Plomp, 1964a; Moore and Ohgushi, 1993). Hence

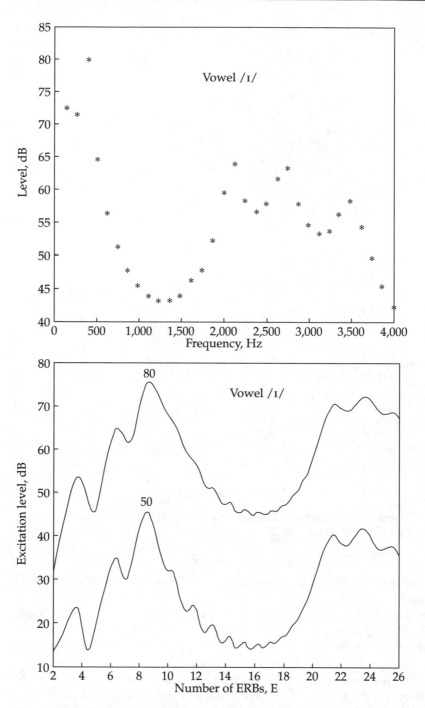

Figure 17.8   The spectrum of a synthetic vowel /ɪ/ (top) plotted on a linear frequency scale, and the excitation patterns for that vowel (bottom) for two overall levels, 50 and 80 dB. The excitation patterns are plotted on an ERB scale.

the center frequency of the first formant is not directly represented in the excitation pattern; it must be inferred from the relative levels of the peaks corresponding to the individual lower harmonics.

A second noteworthy aspect of the excitation patterns is that the second, third and fourth formants, which are clearly separately visible in the original spectrum, are not well resolved. Rather, they form a single prominence in the excitation pattern, with only minor ripples corresponding to the individual formants. The perception of this vowel probably depends more on the overall prominence than on the frequencies of the individual formants. Finally, it should be noted that changes in auditory filter shape with level have only a minor effect on the excitation patterns over the range of levels from 50 to 80 dB, the range of normal conversational speech.

2.4 Across-channel processes in masking

It has been assumed so far that, when detecting a signal in a background noise, the subject attends to the single filter that gives the highest signal to masker ratio. While this assumption appears reasonable in many situations, it clearly fails in others. Furthermore, it is obvious that speech perception usually requires comparison of the outputs of different auditory filters. This section reviews recent data on across-channel processes in auditory masking, and speculates on their relevance for speech perception.

2.4.1 Co-modulation masking release   Hall et al. (1984) were among the first to demonstrate that across-filter comparisons could enhance the detection of a sinusoidal signal in a fluctuating noise masker. The crucial feature for achieving this enhancement was that the fluctuations should be correlated across different frequency bands. One of their experiments was similar to the experiment of Fletcher (1940), described earlier. The threshold for a 1-kHz, 400-ms sinusoidal signal was measured as a function of the bandwidth of a noise masker, keeping the spectrum level constant. The masker was centered at 1 kHz. They used two types of masker. One was a random noise; this has irregular fluctuations in amplitude, and the fluctuations are independent in different frequency regions. The other was a random noise which was modulated in amplitude at an irregular, low rate; a noise lowpass filtered at 50 Hz was used as a modulator. The modulation resulted in fluctuations in the amplitude of the noise which were the same in different frequency regions. This across-frequency correlation was called "co-modulation" by Hall et al. (1984). Figure 17.9 shows the results of this experiment.

For the random noise (denoted by R), the signal threshold increases as the masker bandwidth increases up to about 100–200 Hz, and then remains constant, as expected (see Figure 17.1). The auditory filter at this center frequency has a bandwidth of about 130 Hz. Hence, for noise bandwidths up to 130 Hz, increasing the bandwidth results in more noise passing through the filter.

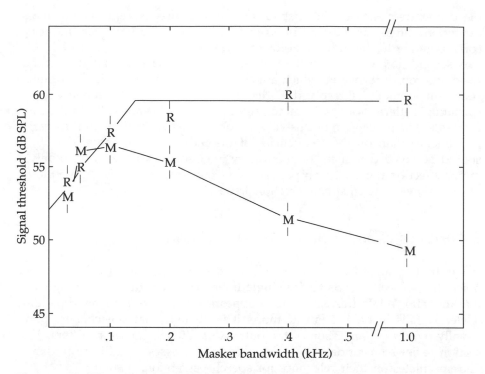

Figure 17.9 The points labelled "R" are thresholds for a 1-kHz signal centered in a band of random noise, plotted as a function of the bandwidth of the noise. The points labelled "M" are the thresholds obtained when the noise was amplitude modulated at an irregular, low rate. From Hall et al. (1984), by permission of the authors and the Journal of the Acoustical Society of America.

However, increasing the bandwidth beyond 130 Hz does not increase the noise passing through the filter, so threshold does not increase. The pattern for the modulated noise (denoted by M) is quite different. For noise bandwidths greater than 100 Hz, the signal threshold decreases as the bandwidth increases. This indicates that subjects can compare the outputs of different auditory filters to enhance signal detection. The fact that the decrease in threshold with increasing bandwidth only occurs with the modulated noise indicates that fluctuations in the masker are critical and that the fluctuations need to be correlated across frequency bands. Hence, this phenomenon has been called "co-modulation masking release" (CMR).

It seems likely that across-filter comparisons of temporal envelopes are a general feature of auditory pattern analysis, which may play an important role in extracting signals from noisy backgrounds, or separating competing sources of sound. As pointed out by Hall et al. (1984): "Many real-life auditory stimuli have intensity peaks and valleys as a function of time in which intensity trajectories are highly correlated across frequency. This is true of speech, of interfering noise such as 'cafeteria' noise, and of many other kinds of environmental stimuli". The experiments reviewed above suggest that we can exploit these coherent envelope fluctuations very effectively, and that substantial reductions in signal threshold can result.

The importance of CMR for speech perception remains controversial. Some studies have suggested that it plays only a very minor role in the detection and identification of speech sounds in modulated background noise (Grose and Hall, 1992; Festen, 1993). However, for synthetic speech in which the cues are impoverished compared to normal speech (sinewave speech; see Remez et al., 1981), comodulation of the speech (amplitude modulation by a sinusoid) can markedly improve the intelligibility of the speech, both in quiet (Carrell and Opie, 1992) and in background noise (Carrell, 1993).

2.4.2 Profile analysis Green and his colleagues (Green, 1988) have carried out a series of experiments demonstrating that, even for stimuli without distinct envelope fluctuations, subjects are able to compare the outputs of different auditory filters to enhance the detection of a signal. They investigated the ability to detect an increment in the level of one component in a complex sound relative to the level of the other components; we will call the other components the "background". Usually the complex sound has been composed of a series of equal-amplitude sinusoidal components, uniformly spaced on a logarithmic frequency scale. To prevent subjects from performing the task by monitoring the magnitude of the output of the single auditory filter centered at the frequency of the incremented component, the overall level of the whole stimulus was varied randomly from one stimulus to the next, over a relatively large range (typically about 40 dB). This makes the magnitude of the output of any single filter an unreliable cue to the presence of the signal.

Subjects were able to detect changes in the relative level of the signal of only 1–2 dB. Such small thresholds could not be obtained by monitoring the magnitude of the output of a single auditory filter. Green and his colleagues have argued that subjects performed the task by detecting a change in the shape or profile of the spectrum of the sound; hence the name "profile analysis". In other words, subjects can compare the outputs of different auditory filters, and can detect when the output of one changes relative to that of others, even when the overall level is varied.

Speech researchers will not find the phenomenon of profile analysis surprising. It has been known for many years that one of the main factors determining the timbre or quality of a sound is its spectral shape. Our everyday experience tells us that we can recognise and distinguish familiar sounds, such as the different vowels, regardless of the levels of those sounds. When we do this, we are distinguishing different spectral shapes in the face of variations in overall level. This is functionally the same as profile analysis. The experiments on profile analysis can be regarded as a way of quantifying the limits of our ability to distinguish changes in spectral shape. In this context, it is noteworthy that the differences in spectral shape between different vowels are generally far larger than the smallest detectable changes as measured in profile analysis experiments.

2.4.3 Modulation discrimination interference
In some situations, the detection or discrimination of a signal is *impaired* by the presence of frequency components remote from the signal frequency. Usually, this happens when the task is either to detect modulation of the signal, or to detect a change in depth of modulation of the signal. Yost and Sheft (1989) showed that the threshold for detecting sinusoidal amplitude modulation (AM) of a sinusoidal carrier was increased in the presence of another carrier, amplitude modulated at the same rate, even when the second carrier was remote in frequency from the first. They called this modulation detection interference (MDI). They showed that MDI did not occur if the second carrier was unmodulated.

Moore et al. (1992) determined how thresholds for detecting an increase in modulation depth (sinusoidal AM or FM) of a 1,000-Hz carrier frequency (the target) were affected by modulation of carriers (interference) with frequencies of 230 Hz and 3,300 Hz. They found that modulation increment thresholds were increased (worsened) when the remote carriers were modulated. This MDI effect was greatest when the target and interference were modulated at similar rates, but the effect was broadly tuned for modulation rate. When the target and interfering sounds were both modulated at 10 Hz, there was no significant effect of the relative phase of modulation of the target and interfering sounds.

The explanation for MDI remains unclear. Yost and Sheft (1989) suggested that MDI might be a consequence of perceptual grouping; the common AM of the target and interfering sounds might make them fuse perceptually, making it difficult to "hear out" the modulation of the target sound. However, certain aspects of the results on MDI are difficult to reconcile with an explanation in terms of perceptual grouping. One would expect that widely spaced frequency components would only be grouped perceptually if their modulation pattern was very similar. Grouping would not be expected, for example, if the components were modulated out of phase or at different rates, but, in fact, it is possible to obtain large amounts of MDI under these conditions.

An alternative explanation for MDI is that it reflects the operation of "channels" specialised for detecting and analysing modulation (Kay and Mathews, 1972; Schreiner and Urbas, 1986). Yost et al. (1989) suggested that MDI might arise in the following way. The stimulus is first processed by an array of auditory filters. The envelope at the output of each filter is extracted. When modulation is present, channels are excited that are tuned for modulation rate. All filters responding with the same modulation rate excite the same channel, regardless of the filter center frequency. Thus, modulation at one center frequency can adversely affect the detection and discrimination of modulation at other center frequencies.

The purpose of the hypothetical modulation channels remains unclear. Since the physiological evidence for such channels comes from studies of animals, we can assume that they did not evolve for the purpose of speech perception. Nevertheless, it is possible, even likely, that speech analysis makes use of the modulation channels. There is evidence that amplitude modulation patterns in speech are important for speech recognition (Steeneken and Houtgast, 1980). Thus, anything that adversely affects the detection and discrimination of the modulation patterns would be expected to impair intelligibility. One way of describing MDI is: modulation in one frequency region may make it more difficult to detect and discriminate modulation in another frequency region. Thus, it may be the case that MDI makes speech recognition more difficult in situations where there is a background sound that is modulated, such as one or more people talking. However, this is no direct evidence to support this supposition.

3 The perception of pitch

Pitch is usually defined as that attribute of auditory sensation in terms of which sounds may be ordered on a musical scale. In other words, variations in pitch give rise to a sense of melody. For speech sounds, the variations in voice pitch over time convey intonation information, indicating whether an utterance is a question or a statement, and helping to identify stressed words (see Nooteboom, PROSODY OF SPEECH). Voice pitch can also convey information about the sex, age, and emotional state of the speaker (Rosen and Fourcin, 1986).

Pitch is related to the repetition rate of the waveform of a sound; for a pure tone this corresponds to the frequency and for a periodic complex tone to the fundamental frequency. There are, however, exceptions to this simple rule. Since voiced speech sounds are complex tones, this section will concentrate on the perception of pitch for complex tones.

3.1 The phenomenon of the missing fundamental

Although the pitch of a complex tone usually corresponds to the frequency of the fundamental component (f_0), that component does not have to be present for the pitch to be heard. Consider, as an example, a sound consisting of short impulses (clicks) occurring 200 times per second. This sound has a low pitch, which is very close to the pitch of a 200-Hz pure tone, and a sharp timbre. It contains harmonics with frequencies 200, 400, 600, 800 . . . etc. Hz. However, if the sound is filtered so as to remove the 200-Hz component, the pitch does not alter; the only result is a slight change in the timbre of the note. Indeed, all except a small group of mid-frequency harmonics can be eliminated, and the low pitch still remains, although the timbre becomes markedly different.

Schouten (1970) called this low pitch associated with a group of high harmonics the "residue". He pointed out that the residue is distinguishable, subjectively, from a fundamental component which is physically presented or from a fundamental which may be generated (at high sound pressure levels) by nonlinear distortion in the ear. Thus it seems that the perception of a residue pitch does not require activity at the point on the basilar membrane which would respond maximally to a pure tone of similar pitch. Several other names have been used to describe residue pitch, including "periodicity pitch", "virtual pitch" and "low pitch". This chapter will use the term residue pitch. Even when the fundamental component of a complex tone is present, the pitch of the tone is usually determined by harmonics other than the fundamental. Thus the perception of a residue pitch should not be regarded as unusual. Rather, residue pitches are normally heard when listening to complex tones, including speech. For example, when listening over the telephone, the fundamental component for male speakers is usually inaudible, but the pitch of the voice can still be easily heard.

3.2 The principle of dominance

Ritsma (1967) carried out an experiment to determine which components in a complex sound are most important in determining its pitch. He presented complex tones in which the frequencies of a small group of harmonics were multiples of a fundamental which was slightly higher or lower than the fundamental of the remainder. The subject's pitch judgements were used to determine whether the pitch of the complex as a whole was affected by the shift in the group of harmonics. Ritsma found that: "For fundamental frequencies in the range 100 Hz to 400 Hz, and for sensation levels up to at least 50 dB above threshold of the entire signal, the frequency band consisting of the third, fourth and fifth harmonics tends to dominate the pitch sensation as long as its amplitude exceeds a minimum absolute level of about 10 dB above threshold."

This finding has been broadly confirmed in other ways (Plomp, 1967), although the data of Moore et al. (1984, 1985) show that there are large individual differences in which harmonics are dominant, and for some subjects the first two harmonics play an important role. Other data also show that the dominant region is not fixed in terms of harmonic number, but depends somewhat on absolute frequency (Plomp, 1967; Patterson and Wightman, 1976). For high fundamental frequencies (above about 1,000 Hz), the fundamental is usually the dominant component, while for very low fundamental frequencies, around 50 Hz, harmonics above the fifth may be dominant (Moore and Glasberg, 1988; Moore and Peters, 1992). For speech sounds, the dominant harmonics usually lie around the frequency of the first formant.

3.3 Discrimination of the pitch of complex tones

When the repetition rate of a complex tone changes, all of the components change in frequency by the same ratio, and a change in residue pitch is heard.

The ability to detect such changes in pitch is better than the ability to detect changes in a sinusoid at the fundamental frequency (Flanagan and Saslow, 1958) and can be better than the ability to detect changes in the frequency of any of the sinusoidal components in the complex tone (Moore et al., 1984). This indicates that information from the different harmonics is combined or integrated in the determination of residue pitch. This can lead to very fine discrimination; changes in repetition rate of about 0.2 per cent can often be detected for fundamental frequencies in the range 100–400 Hz.

The discrimination of pitch is usually best when low harmonics are present (Hoekstra and Ritsma, 1977; Moore and Glasberg, 1988). Somewhat less good discrimination (typically 1–4 per cent) is possible when only high harmonics are present (Houtsma and Smurzynski, 1990). Pitch discrimination can be impaired (typically by about a factor of two) when the two sounds to be discriminated also differ in timbre (Moore and Glasberg, 1990); this would be the situation with speech sounds, where changes in pitch are usually accompanied by changes in timbre.

In speech, intonation is typically conveyed by differences in the pattern of f_0 change over time. When the stimuli are dynamically varying, the ability to detect pitch changes is markedly poorer than when the stimuli are steady. Klatt (1973) measured thresholds for detecting differences in pitch for an unchanging vowel (i.e. one with static formant frequencies) with a flat f_0 contour, and also for a series of linear glides in f_0 around an f_0 of 120 Hz. For the flat contour, the threshold was about 0.3 Hz. When both contours were falling at the same rate (30 Hz over the 250-ms duration of the stimulus), the threshold increased markedly to 2 Hz. When the steady vowel was replaced by the sound /ya/, whose formants change over time, thresholds increased further by 25–65 per cent.

Data obtained in a more natural speech context were presented by Pierre-humbert (1979). She started with a natural nonsense utterance "ma-MA-ma-ma-MA-ma", where the prosodic pattern was based on the sentence "The baker made bagels". The stressed syllables (MA) were associated with peaks in the f_0 contour. She then modified the f_0 of the second peak, over a range varying from below to above the f_0 of the first peak. Subjects listened to the modified utterances, and were required to indicate whether the first or second peak was higher in pitch. The results reflected what she called "normalization for expected declination"; when the two stressed syllables sounded equal in pitch, the second was actually lower. For first peak values of 121 and 151 Hz, the second peak had to be shifted over a range of about 20 Hz to change judgements from 75 per cent "second peak lower" to 75 per cent "second peak higher". This indicates markedly poorer discriminability than found for steady stimuli. In a similar vein, 't Hart (1981) presented evidence suggesting that about a 19 per cent difference was necessary for successive pitch movements in the same direction to be reliably heard as different in extent.

It may be concluded that the pitch changes that are linguistically relevant are much larger than the limits of pitch discrimination measured psychophysically using steady stimuli. This is another reflection of the fact that speech is conveyed using robust cues that do not severely tax the discrimination abilities of the auditory system.

4 Temporal analysis

Time is a very important dimension in hearing, since almost all sounds change over time. For speech, much of the information appears to be carried in the changes themselves, rather than in the parts of the sounds which are relatively stable. In characterizing temporal analysis, it is essential to take account of the filtering that takes place in the peripheral auditory system. Temporal analysis can be considered as resulting from two main processes: analysis of the time pattern occurring within each frequency channel; and comparison of the time patterns across channels. Each of these processes will be considered in turn.

A major difficulty in measuring the temporal resolution of the auditory system is that changes in the time pattern of a sound are generally associated with changes in its magnitude spectrum – the distribution of energy over frequency. Thus, the detection of a change in time pattern can sometimes depend not on temporal resolution per se, but on the detection of the spectral change. Sometimes, the detection of spectral changes can lead to what appears to be extraordinarily fine temporal resolution. For example, a single click can be distinguished from a pair of clicks when the gap between the two clicks in a pair is only a few tens of microseconds, an ability that depends upon spectral changes at very high frequencies (Leshowitz, 1971). Although spectrally based detection of temporal changes can occur for speech sounds, this chapter will concentrate on experimental situations which avoid the confounding effects of spectral cues.

There have been two general approaches to avoiding the use of cues based on spectral changes. One is to use signals whose magnitude spectrum is not changed when the time pattern is altered. For example, the magnitude spectrum of white noise remains flat if a gap is introduced into the noise. The second approach uses stimuli whose spectra are altered by the change in time pattern, but extra background sounds are added to mask the spectral changes. Both of these approaches will be considered.

4.1 Within-channel temporal analysis using broadband sounds

The experiments described below all use broadband sounds whose long-term magnitude spectrum is unaltered by the temporal manipulation being performed. For example, interruption or amplitude modulation of a white noise does not change its long-term magnitude spectrum, and time-reversal of any sound also does not change its long-term magnitude spectrum.

4.1.1 The detection of gaps in broadband noise The threshold for detecting a gap in a broadband noise provides a simple and convenient measure of temporal resolution. Although white noise excites many different frequency channels in the auditory system, it is generally assumed that this task depends primarily on within-channel processes, rather than on comparisons across channels (although the fact that the gap occurs synchronously in all channels may well be important, and information may be combined across channels at some level higher than the cochlea). The gap threshold is typically 2–3 ms (Plomp, 1964b; Penner, 1977). The threshold increases at very low sound levels, when the level of the noise approaches the absolute threshold, but is relatively invariant with level for moderate to high levels. The smallest detectable gap is thus markedly larger than temporal gaps that are relevant for speech perception (for example, "sa" and "sta" may be distinguished by a temporal gap lasting several tens of milliseconds).

4.1.2 The discrimination of time-reversed signals As mentioned above, the long-term magnitude spectrum of a sound is not changed when that sound is time reversed (played backwards in time). Thus, if a time-reversed sound can be discriminated from the original, this must reflect a sensitivity to the difference in time pattern of the two sounds. This was exploited by Ronken (1970), who used as stimuli pairs of clicks differing in amplitude. One click, labelled A, had an amplitude greater than that of the other click, labelled B. Typically the amplitude of A was twice that of B. Subjects were required to distinguish click pairs differing in the order of A and B: either AB or BA. The ability to do this was measured as a function of the time interval or gap between A and B. Like white noise, click pairs have a broad spectrum that would excite many auditory channels, but again it is generally assumed that this task depends primarily on within-channel processes. Ronken found that subjects could distinguish the click pairs for gaps down to 2–3 ms. Thus the limit to temporal resolution found in this task is similar to that found for the detection of a gap in broadband noise. It should be noted that, in this task, subjects do not hear the individual clicks within a click pair. Rather, each click pair is heard as a single sound with its own characteristic quality. For example, the two click pairs AB and BA might sound like "tick" and "tock".

4.1.3 Temporal modulation transfer functions The experiments described above each give a single value to describe temporal resolution. A more general approach is to measure the threshold for detecting changes in the amplitude of a sound as a function of the rapidity of the changes. In the simplest case, white noise is sinusoidally amplitude modulated, and the threshold for detecting the modulation is determined as a function of modulation rate. The function

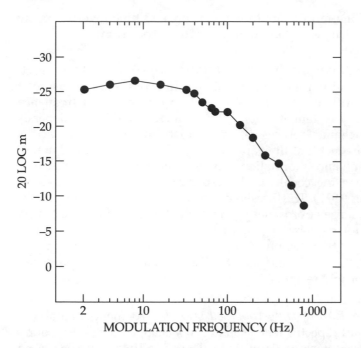

Figure 17.10   A temporal modulation transfer function (TMTF). A broadband white noise was sinusoidally amplitude modulated, and the threshold amount of modulation required for detection is plotted as a function of modulation rate. The amount of modulation is specified as 20log(*m*), where m is the modulation depth. The higher the sensitivity to modulation, the more negative is this quantity. Data from Bacon and Viemeister (1985).

relating threshold to modulation rate is known as a temporal modulation transfer function (TMTF) (Viemeister, 1979). An example of the results is shown in Figure 17.10 (data from Bacon and Viemeister, 1985). The thresholds are expressed as 20log*m*, where *m* is the modulation index (*m* = 0 corresponds to no modulation and *m* = 1 corresponds to 100 per cent modulation). For low modulation rates, performance is limited by the amplitude resolution of the ear, rather than by temporal resolution. Thus, the threshold is independent of modulation rate for rates up to about 16 Hz. As the rate increases beyond 16 Hz, temporal resolution starts to have an effect; performance worsens, and for rates above about 1,000 Hz the modulation is hard to detect at all. Thus, sensitivity to modulation becomes progressively less as the rate of modulation increases. The shapes of TMTFs do not vary much with overall sound level, but the ability to detect the modulation does worsen at low sound levels. Over the range of modulation rates important for speech perception, below about 50 Hz (Steeneken and Houtgast, 1980), the sensitivity to modulation is rather good.

4.2 Within-channel temporal analysis using narrowband sounds

The experiments described above all used broadband stimuli. It has often been assumed that the results depend primarily on within-channel processes, but there is no guarantee that this is the case. In addition, these experiments provide no information regarding the question of whether the temporal resolution of the ear varies with center frequency. This issue can be examined by using narrowband stimuli that excite only one, or a small number, of auditory channels.

4.2.1 Discrimination of time-reversed sinusoids
Green (1973) used time-reversed stimuli where each stimulus consisted of a brief pulse of a sinusoid in which the level of the first half of the pulse was 10 dB different from that of the second half. Subjects were required to distinguish two signals, differing in whether the half with the high level was first or second. Green measured performance as a function of the total duration of the stimuli. The threshold was similar for center frequencies of 2 and 4 kHz, and was between 1 and 2 ms. However, the threshold was slightly higher for a center frequency of 1 kHz, being between 2 and 4 ms.

It is interesting that performance in this task was actually a non-monotonic function of duration. Performance was good for durations in the range 2–6 ms, worsened for durations around 16 ms, and then improved again as the duration was increased beyond 16 ms. For the very short durations, subjects listened for a difference in quality between the two sounds – rather like the "tick" and "tock" described earlier for Ronken's stimuli. At durations around 16 ms, the tonal quality of the bursts became more prominent, and the quality differences were harder to hear. At much longer durations the soft and loud segments could be separately heard, in a distinct order. It appears, therefore, that performance in this task was determined by two separate mechanisms, one based on timbre differences associated with the difference in time pattern, and the other based on the perception of a distinct succession of auditory events.

4.2.2 Detection of temporal gaps in narrowband noise
When a temporal gap is introduced into a narrowband sound, the spectrum of the sound is altered. Energy "splatter" occurs outside the nominal frequency range of the sound. To prevent the splatter being detected, the sounds are presented in a background sound, usually a noise, designed to mask the splatter.

Several researchers have measured thresholds for detecting gaps in narrowband noises (Fitzgibbons, 1983; Shailer and Moore, 1983; Buus and Florentine, 1985). Generally, gap thresholds were found to improve with increasing center frequency. However, in these experiments, the bandwidth of the stimuli used increased with increasing center frequency. Noise bands have inherent fluctuations in amplitude, and the rapidity of these fluctuations increases with increasing bandwidth. Gap thresholds for noise bands may be partly limited by the inherent fluctuations in the noise (Shailer and Moore, 1983, 1985; Green, 1985). Randomly occurring dips in the noise may be "confused" with the gap to be detected. The confusion is maximal for dips comparable in duration to the gap. In practice, this means that noise with a narrow bandwidth, and hence slow fluctuations, creates the greatest confusion and gives the largest gap thresholds. The data are consistent with this view: gap thresholds for narrowband noises increase with decreasing noise bandwidth (Shailer and Moore, 1983, 1985). Furthermore, gap thresholds measured with noise of constant bandwidth show little effect of center frequency (Shailer and Moore, 1985; de Filippo and Snell, 1986; Eddins et al., 1992).

Gap thresholds for narrowband noises tend to decrease with increasing sound level for levels up to about 30 dB above absolute threshold, but remain roughly constant after that.

4.2.3 Detection of temporal gaps in sinusoids

Shailer and Moore (1987) studied the ability of subjects to detect a temporal gap in a sinusoid. To mask "splatter" associated with the introduction of the gap, the sinusoid was presented in a continuous noise with a spectral notch at the frequency of the sinusoid. The results were strongly affected by the phase at which the sinusoid was turned off and on to produce the gap. Only the simplest case will be considered here, called "preserved phase" by Shailer and Moore. In this case the sinusoid was turned off at a positive-going zero crossing (i.e. as the waveform was about to change from negative to positive values) and it started (at the end of the gap) at the phase it would have had if it had continued without interruption. Thus, for the preserved-phase condition it was as if the gap had been "cut out" from a continuous sinusoid. For this condition, the detectability of the gap increased monotonically with increasing gap duration.

Shailer and Moore (1987) found that the gap threshold was roughly constant at about 5 ms for center frequencies of 400, 1,000 and 2,000 Hz. Recently, gap thresholds for sinusoids have been measured for center frequencies of 100, 200, 400, 800, 1,000 and 2,000 Hz using a condition similar to the preserved-phase condition of Shailer and Moore (Moore et al., 1993a). The gap thresholds were almost constant at 6–8 ms over the frequency range 400–2,000 Hz, but increased somewhat at 200 Hz, and increased markedly, to about 18 ms, at 100 Hz. Individual variability also increased markedly at 100 Hz.

Overall, the results of experiments using narrowband stimuli indicate that temporal resolution does not vary markedly with center frequency, except perhaps for a worsening at very low frequencies (200 Hz and below).

4.3 Temporal analysis based on across-channel processes

Studies of the ability to compare timing across different frequency channels can give very different results depending on whether the different frequency components in the sound are perceived as part of a single sound or as part of more than one sound. Also, it should be realised that subjects may be able to *distinguish* different time patterns, for example a change in the relative onset time of two different frequencies, without the subjective impression of a change in time pattern; some sort of change in the quality of the sound may be all that is heard. The studies described next indicate the limits of the ability to compare timing across channels, using highly trained subjects.

4.3.1 The discrimination of Huffman sequences Patterson and Green (1970) and Green (1973) have studied the discrimination of a class of signals which have the same long-term magnitude spectrum, but which differ in their short-term spectra. These sounds are called Huffman sequences. Essentially, they are brief broadband sounds, like clicks, except that the energy in a certain frequency region is delayed relative to that in other regions. The amount of the delay, the center frequency of the delayed frequency region, and the width of the delayed frequency region can all be varied. If subjects can distinguish a pair of Huffman sequences differing, for example, in the amount of delay in a given frequency region, this implies that they are sensitive to the difference in time pattern. Green (1973) measured the ability of subjects to detect differences in the amount of delay in three frequency regions: 650 Hz, 1,900 Hz and 4,200 Hz. He found similar results for all three center frequencies: subjects could detect differences in delay time of about 2 ms regardless of the center frequency of the delayed region.

It should be noted that subjects did not report hearing one part of the sound after the rest of the sound. Rather, the differences in time pattern were perceived as subtle changes in sound quality. Further, some subjects required extensive training to achieve the fine acuity of 2 ms, and even after this training the task required considerable concentration.

4.3.2 Detection of onset and offset asynchrony in multicomponent complexes Zera and Green (1993) measured thresholds for detecting asynchrony in the onset or offset of complex signals composed of many sinusoidal components. The components were either uniformly spaced on a logarithmic frequency scale, or formed a harmonic series. In one stimulus, the "standard", all components started and stopped synchronously. In the "signal" stimulus, one component was presented with an onset or offset asynchrony. The task of the subjects was to discriminate the standard stimulus from the signal stimulus. They found that onset asynchrony was easier to detect than offset asynchrony. For harmonic signals, onset asynchronies of less than 1 ms could generally be detected, whether the asynchronous component was leading or lagging the other components (although in the latter case, thresholds increased markedly for delays in the higher harmonics, presumably because for the higher harmonics several harmonics fall within the passband of a single auditory filter and produce a masking effect on the asynchronous component). Thresholds for detecting offset asynchronies were larger, being about 3–10 ms when the asynchronous component ended after the other components, and 10–30 ms when the asynchronous component ended before the other components. Thresholds for detecting asynchronies in logarithmically spaced complexes were generally two to fifty times larger than for harmonic complexes.

The difference between harmonically and logarithmically spaced complexes may be explicable in terms of perceptual grouping. The harmonic signal was perceived as a single sound source, i.e. all of the components appeared to belong together. The logarithmically spaced complex was perceived as a series of separate tones, like many notes being played at once on an organ. It seems that it is difficult to compare the timing of sound elements that are perceived as coming from different sources. The high sensitivity to onset asynchronies for harmonic complexes is consistent with the finding that the perceived timbres of musical instruments are partly dependent on the exact onset times and rates of rise of individual harmonics within each musical note (Risset and Wessel, 1982).

Overall, the two sets of experiments reviewed above indicate that remarkably small asynchronies between frequency channels can be detected, both for short duration sounds (Huffman sequences), and for asynchronies in the onsets of longer duration sounds (complex tones). The smallest detectable asynchronies are generally much smaller than required for distinctions in speech. For example, voiced and unvoiced initial plosives can be distinguished on the basis of the time delay between the onset of the sound (the release burst) and the onset of voicing; the delay is typically close to zero for voiced plosives and is several tens of milliseconds for unvoiced plosives.

4.3.3 Judgement of temporal order   The ability to judge the temporal order of a sequence of sounds depends strongly on whether the task requires actual *identification* of the order of individual elements or whether it can be performed by *discrimination* of different orders or by attaching well-learned labels to different orders. In the latter case, resolution can be rather fine. With extended training and feedback, subjects can learn to distinguish between and identify orders within sequences of nonrelated sounds lasting only 10 ms or less (Warren, 1974). For sequences of tones, the component durations necessary for labelling different orders may be as low as 2–7 ms (Divenyi and Hirsh, 1974). This is the type of acuity that would be expected for speech sounds, since these consist of well-learned sequences to which consistent labels have been attached.

When the task is to identify the order of sounds in a sequence, performance is generally markedly worse. For example, Hirsh (1959) found that, for pairs of unrelated items, trained subjects required durations of about 20 ms per item for correct order identification. When the number of items in the sequence is increased, the durations required for order identification tend to increase also.

4.3.4 Change detection and contrast effects   The auditory system seems particularly well suited to the analysis of changes in the sensory input. When a complex stimulus is changed in a certain way, for example by increasing the level of a single frequency component, the changed aspect stands out perceptually from the rest. A powerful demonstration of this effect may be obtained by listening to a stimulus with a particular spectral structure and then switching rapidly to a stimulus with a flat spectrum, such as white noise. A white noise heard in isolation may be described as "colorless"; it has no pitch and has a neutral sort of timbre. However, when a white noise follows immediately after a stimulus with spectral structure, the noise sounds "colored". The coloration corresponds to the inverse of the spectrum of the preceding sound. A harmonic complex tone with a flat spectrum may be given a speech-like quality if it is preceded by a harmonic complex having a spectrum which is the inverse of that of a speech sound, such as a vowel (Summerfield et al., 1987).

5 Overview

This chapter has reviewed several aspects of auditory perception that are relevant to the perception of speech. These aspects have included frequency selectivity, the perception of pitch, and temporal analysis. A recurring theme has been the finding that the basic discrimination abilities of the auditory system, measured using simple non-speech stimuli, are very good when considered relative to the acoustic differences that distinguish speech sounds. This partially accounts for the robust nature of speech perception.

NOTE

I thank Joseph Alcántara, Tom Baer, Michael Shailer and Michael Stone for helpful comments on an earlier version of this chapter.

18 Cognitive Processes in Speech Perception

JAMES M. McQUEEN AND ANNE CUTLER

1 Introduction

The recognition of spoken language involves the extraction of acoustic-phonetic information from the speech signal, and the mapping of this information onto cognitive representations. To develop accurate psycholinguistic models of this process, we need to know what information is extracted from the signal, and when and how it is integrated with stored knowledge.

An essential assumption in all models of spoken language understanding is the mental lexicon. The lexicon is certainly not a list of orthographic word forms. Instead, it is usually characterised as a dictionary in which a variety of information is contained in each entry: phonological and orthographic form information; morphological structure; syntactic, semantic and pragmatic information. A lexical entry may in fact not represent an individual word: groups of word forms (such as those corresponding to the different inflections of a verb) may share a lexical entry, and multi-word phrases such as idioms may have their own entries. Where we refer below to the accessing of words in the mental lexicon, we do so as a shorthand; we mean the accessing of lexical entries.

Whatever the exact structure and organisation of lexical entries, however, lexical access has to be central to any cognitive model of speech recognition. There is an infinite number of possible sentences that a listener might hear, but a finite number of words. Syntactic, semantic and pragmatic processes can therefore only operate for interpretation of utterances via the intermediary process of word recognition. An account of the cognitive processes involved in speech perception should thus be set in the context of lexical access and word recognition. In this chapter, we therefore ask what sources of information are involved in the pre-lexical processing of the speech signal, that is, in the processing which takes place prior to and for lexical access.

There are three types of information that might be involved in lexical access: acoustic-phonetic (information specifying segmental structure); lexical (information about the words of the input language); and prosodic (information specifying supra-segmental structure). Of these three, only acoustic-phonetic information has a mandatory role to play in pre-lexical processing. Since it is acoustic-phonetic information which primarily distinguishes words one from another, this has to be what provides the principal means of access to the lexicon. However, there has been considerable disagreement about how acoustic-phonetic information is used in the access process, as discussed in section 2. There are no *a priori* reasons, however, to assume that either lexical or prosodic information must be involved in the generation of a lexical access code. Both sources of information may only play a role after words have been accessed in the lexicon. In sections 3 and 4, we ask if these two sources of information do influence the lexical access process, and if so, how?

2 Acoustic-phonetic information

2.1 Units of perception

There are two ways in which acoustic-phonetic information might be used in the process of lexical access. One possibility is that phonetic segments are extracted explicitly, in some pre-lexical level of representation, with a classification of the speech signal into "units of perception" (Healy and Cutting, 1976; McNeill and Lindig, 1973). Units which have been postulated include acoustic-phonetic features (Eimas and Corbit, 1973; Marslen-Wilson, 1987; Marslen-Wilson and Warren, 1994; Stevens, 1988), phonemes (Foss and Blank, 1980; McClelland and Elman, 1986), context-sensitive allophones (Wickelgren, 1969), syllables (Cole and Scott, 1974; Mehler, 1981), and articulatory gestures (Liberman and Mattingley, 1985). Alternatively, acoustic-phonetic information could be used implicitly, in a direct mapping of the signal onto the lexicon with no explicit classification into pre-lexical units. Klatt (1980b, 1989) has suggested a template-matching process, where spectral information, as analysed by the peripheral auditory system, is mapped directly onto a lexicon of spectral templates of diphone sequences.

In some experiments, alternative perceptual units have been compared. Foss and Swinney (1973) and Segui, Frauenfelder and Mehler (1981) demonstrated that syllable monitoring was faster than phoneme monitoring. Listeners were quicker to detect a pre-specified target in a list of words and nonwords when that target was a syllable than when it was a phoneme. These findings suggested that the syllable functions as a basic perceptual unit. Norris and Cutler (1988), however, claimed that these results were artifactual. The subjects could detect syllables using only a partial analysis of the signal. In their experiment, Norris and Cutler (1988) included foil items, which contained phonetic near-matches of syllabic and phonemic targets. When subjects were thus required to analyse each stimulus fully, phoneme monitoring was faster than syllable monitoring. This finding, however, does not confirm that the phoneme is the unit of perception, only that phonemic information tends to become available, for a phonetic decision, more rapidly than syllabic information.

Other studies have provided evidence in favour of several different units. Selective adaptation effects have been taken as evidence of acoustic feature detectors (Eimas and Corbit, 1973, but these effects now appear to be due to general auditory adaptation: Kuhl and Miller, 1978; Sawusch and Jusczyk, 1981). Results from duplex perception experiments have been taken as evidence for the extraction of articulatory gestures during speech perception (Liberman and Mattingley, 1985). Data showing that listeners integrate co-articulatory information for segments over time can be taken as support for a phonemic unit of perception (Fowler, 1984). Subjects are faster to detect syllable targets when the targets match the syllabification of the target-bearing word than when they mismatch (Mehler, Dommergues, Frauenfelder and Segui, 1981), as would be predicted if the syllable were the unit of perception. Dupoux and Mehler (1990) found that phoneme monitoring to word-initial targets was faster in high- than in low-frequency monosyllables, but that there was no frequency effect in disyllables. These results suggest that pre-lexical processing involves extraction of syllabic information (the structural complexity of disyllables could delay lexical access, relative to that for monosyllables, and hence reduce the contribution of the lexicon, as characterized by the word frequency effect). But these results can also be explained by a pre-lexical process of rate normalization that does not involve syllabic information *per se*. Finally, features have been claimed to be the basic perceptual units on the grounds that lexical entries contain underspecified phonological representations rather than phoneme strings (Lahiri and Marslen-Wilson, 1991). If segments are not represented lexically there is no need to extract them pre-lexically; instead phonological features extracted from the signal could be mapped directly onto the lexicon.

No definitive answer to the unit of perception question is available. Instead, the results suggest that there is in fact no one basic unit. Many different "units" can be used by listeners, depending on the demands of the listening situation (Pisoni and Luce, 1987). It is therefore perhaps impossible to establish whether any particular units are always constructed during normal comprehension. But even if there is no basic unit, this does not mean that lexical access must be a direct mapping of the unanalysed speech stream onto the lexicon. The assumption that acoustic-phonetic information is transformed into more abstract pre-lexical representations (whatever their exact form) is supported by the need for speech normalization.

2.2 Normalization

The acoustic cues to segments are far from invariant. They vary greatly depending on a large number of factors, including: coarticulation (the realization of segments depends upon both preceding and following phonological context;

Fowler, 1984; see also Farnetani, Coarticulation and Connected Speech Processes); speech rate (e.g. temporal cues such as Voice Onset Time [VOT] change depending on speed of articulation, requiring rate-dependent processing; Miller, 1981; Gordon, 1988); and variation between speakers due to differences in sex, age and dialect. Some authors have argued that this variation is dealt with by the extraction of acoustic cues which are invariant (Stevens and Blumstein, 1981); others that the variation is lawful, and can be exploited by the listener (Elman and McClelland, 1986). In either case, however, it is clear that the perceptual system must be able to deal with this variability. The same physical signal must be interpretable as different segments, and different signals must be interpretable as the same segment (Repp and Liberman, 1987). It seems clear that normalization should take place pre-lexically, prior to lexical access.

In a study of speech rate effects, for example, Miller, Green and Schermer (1984) demonstrated that subjects labelled more ambiguous consonants, midway between /b/ and /p/ and embedded in the continuum *bath-path*, in a contextually congruent manner (i.e. more *bath* responses in a bathing context), but only when subjects were explicitly told to attend to the sentence context. These effects were absent in a speeded response condition, which focused the subjects' attention on the target words. Speaking rate was also varied, resulting in shifts in the category boundary between /b/ and /p/, but the task demand manipulation did not influence this rate-dependent boundary placement. Miller and Dexter (1988) also used the phonetic categorization task to examine effects of lexical status and speaking rate. They found that under speeded response conditions, there was no tendency to label ambiguous initial consonants in a lexically-consistent manner (e.g. as /b/ in a *beef-peef* continuum and as /p/ in a *beece-peace* continuum). Listeners could not ignore the rate manipulation, however: even under speeded response instructions they based their decision on the early portion of the syllable, treating it as if it was physically short (the /b/ – /p/ boundary shifted to a smaller VOT for fast responses). These studies neatly demonstrate that rate normalization is a mandatory feature of pre-lexical processing. The analysis of acoustic information specifying speech rate appears to be essential for accurate lexical access (Miller, 1987).

Other research on normalization has explored effects of between-speaker variability. Mullennix, Pisoni and Martin (1989) showed that listeners could identify words more easily in lists spoken by a single speaker than when the same word-lists were spoken by 15 different speakers, and that this effect was more marked when the speech signal was physically degraded. Normalization across speakers thus appears to operate at a low level, like rate normalization. Mullennix and Pisoni (1990) have further shown that speaker normalization, again like rate normalization, is mandatory. Subjects could not ignore voice variability when categorizing unambiguous initial phonemes in lists of words spoken by one or several speakers, nor could they ignore the variability in the initial consonants when categorizing the words as being spoken by either a male or female speaker. Asymmetries in this interference suggested that extraction of phonetic and speaker information are independent but closely related processes: phonetic decisions appear to be at least partially contingent upon the process of speaker normalization.

In a related series of experiments (Goldinger, Pisoni and Logan, 1991; Martin, Mullennix, Pisoni and Summers, 1989; Palmeri, Goldinger and Pisoni, 1993), speaker variability has been shown to affect recall. This suggests that information about speakers' voices is retained in long-term memory. These authors argued that their results contradict the view that normalization entails a mapping of the input onto abstract linguistic representations with the consequent loss of information about the speaker's voice. Rather, this information appears to be preserved. But these data are not inconsistent with a process of linguistic abstraction: they suggest only that speaker information is not discarded during recognition. These results are nevertheless consistent with the suggestion that the mapping of the signal onto the lexicon should be viewed as a collection of interacting parallel processes, extracting different pieces of information, rather than as a unified process extracting a transcription composed of abstract units at a single level of representation.

2.3 *Summary*

Acoustic-phonetic information clearly plays a fundamental role in lexical access. Evidence from speech normalization suggests that there is an intermediate level of prelexical processing, mediating between the raw acoustic input and the mental lexicon. It has not been possible, however, to determine which linguistic unit, if any, is constructed at this level of processing. There is support for several different processing units. But the search for a single "unit of perception" is perhaps futile. Evidence that seems to support a particular unit is very often obtained when the subject is required to make responses based at that level of representation. Nevertheless, it is clear that pre-lexical processing entails the transformation of acoustic-phonetic information into more abstract representations. The form of these representations remains to be determined. One important constraint on pre-lexical representations is that they must have a "shared vocabulary of representation" (Connine and Clifton, 1987) with the lexicon (or at least there has to be a very direct mapping between these representations). The form of lexical representations may thus constrain the form of pre-lexical representations.

3 Lexical information

Is lexical information involved in pre-lexical processing? Discussion of this question is best done in the context of two competing theories. Interactive models hold that lexical information is brought to bear pre-lexically. We will focus on one particular model of this class, TRACE (McClelland and Elman, 1986; McClelland, 1991). This interactive activation model has three levels of processing units, corresponding to features, phonemes and words. Units within a level compete with each other via lateral inhibitory connections. Units at lower levels activate the units at higher levels with which they are consistent via facilitatory connections. Thus, during recognition, activation of a feature node leads to activation of consistent phoneme nodes, which in turn activate word nodes. Importantly, higher level nodes also facilitate lower level units. Activated word units boost the activation of their constituent phonemes: this top-down facilitation instantiates the claim that lexical information influences pre-lexical processing.

We will contrast the TRACE model with an autonomous model which holds that lexical information is not involved in pre-lexical processes. In the Race model (Cutler and Norris, 1979; Cutler, Mehler, Norris and Segui, 1987), phonetic decisions can be based either on pre-lexical processing (the pre-lexical route) or on phonological information, stored in the lexicon (the lexical route). The two routes race with each other when a phonetic decision is being made. Whichever route produces an output first wins the race. But processing is strictly bottom-up only, so the lexicon cannot influence pre-lexical processing. Below, we will describe how the TRACE and Race models, as instances of interactive and autonomous theories, account for lexical involvement in various tasks.

3.1 Lexical effects

3.1.1 Monitoring   Phoneme monitoring is sensitive to phonetic factors. Foss and Gernsbacher (1983) have shown an effect of vowel length: the longer the vowel, the longer the reaction time (RT) on the preceding target consonant. Another factor is the phonological similarity of the target phonemes to preceding phonemes (Newman and Dell, 1978; Dell and Newman, 1980). Detection of target phonemes in sentences is slower when the word preceding the target-bearing word begins with a phoneme closely related to the target. Several studies, however, have failed to find lexical effects. Foss, Harwood and Blank (1980) found that monitoring was no faster to words than to nonwords, and that the frequency of occurrence of the target-bearing word did not influence RT. Segui, Frauenfelder and Mehler (1981) also failed to find an RT advantage for word responses over nonword responses, and Segui and Frauenfelder (1986) did not find a frequency effect when subjects were required to monitor only for word-initial phonemes ("standard" phoneme monitoring).

These results support the claim that phoneme monitoring is based on pre-lexical processing which is open to the influence of phonetic information but not lexical information. But there are some studies which have demonstrated lexical effects. Segui and Frauenfelder (1986), for instance, did obtain a word-frequency effect when subjects were required to monitor not just for word-initial targets, but for targets which could appear anywhere in the words ("generalized" phoneme monitoring). Rubin, Turvey and van Gelder (1976) also found a word-nonword effect: subjects were faster to detect e.g. /b/ in *bat* than in *bal*.

Lexical effects appear to be present only in some experiments. Stemberger, Elman and Haden (1985) took this variability as support for interactive models like TRACE. Lexical influences are taken to result from top-down facilitation from word nodes increasing the level of activation of target phoneme nodes, thus speeding responses to targets in words relative to nonwords. Where there are no lexical effects, it is assumed that responses are being made from the phoneme-node level, without top-down facilitation from the lexical level.

Cutler et al. (1987) describe how these lexical effects support the Race model. When the lexical route is available, there are two competing routes for word responses. Thus phonetic decisions will tend to be faster to words than to nonwords because there will be a proportion of trials in which the lexical route wins the race. Cutler et al. examined word-nonword effects in a series of experiments, using only monosyllabic target-bearing items. Lexical effects were found to come and go. Responses to targets in words were faster than those to targets in nonwords only when task monotony was reduced. It was argued that task monotony determines attentional focus in the Race model: given a monotonous list, subjects attended to the signal, and based their responses on the output of the pre-lexical route; given a less monotonous list, subjects attended to lexical route output, producing lexical effects.

Both models can therefore account for the lexical effect, and its variability, in phoneme monitoring. In another task, rhyme monitoring, where subjects detect words and nonwords which rhyme with a prespecified cue, responses are faster to words than to nonwords, and responses are faster to high- than to low-frequency rhyming words (McQueen, 1993). Again both models can explain these lexical effects.

3.1.2 Phonemic restoration

If the medial /s/ of *legislatures* is replaced with a cough, listeners report hearing a cough and the complete *legislatures*, with the absent phoneme perceptually restored (Warren, 1970). Low-level factors influence the effect: if the replacing noise is acoustically similar to the removed phoneme, the illusion is more likely to occur (Samuel, 1981a, 1981b; Warren and Obusek, 1971); and there is more restoration for fricatives and stops (which are more noise-like) than for liquids, vowels and nasals (Samuel, 1981a, 1981b).

Samuel (1981a) found that several lexical factors influenced the extent of the illusion: there was more restoration for longer than for shorter words; there was a more reliable illusion in words than in phonologically legal nonwords; and presenting an intact version of the target word before the target word also increased restoration. Samuel (1987) found further that there was more restoration for items with several possible restorations (e.g. *egion*: *legion* or *region*) than for items with a unique restoration (e.g. *esion*: *lesion*). He also found that there was more phonemic restoration in words which become unique early, moving left-to-right through the word (e.g. *boysenb*rry*) than in words which became unique late (e.g. *indel*ble*). Samuel explained these results in terms of a partially interactive model, in which top-down expectations are confirmed by the bottom-up signal, lexical information being used to facilitate perceptual decisions made at lower levels.

An autonomous account of the data is however also possible. If the illusion is due to attention being focused on lexical information, then the lexical effects can be explained without recourse to top-down connections. In Race model terms, restoration occurs because subjects are using the lexical route. Just as with the monitoring tasks, the evidence for lexical involvement in phoneme restoration does not allow us to distinguish between the two models.

3.1.3 *Phonetic categorization* In the phonetic categorization task, with a continuum of sounds from /d/ to /t/ in the contexts *deep-teep* and *deach-teach*, for example, a lexical effect would be shown by an increased proportion of /d/ responses in the ambiguous region of the continuum when the voiced endpoint formed a word (*deep*), and an increased proportion of /t/ responses when the unvoiced endpoint formed a word (*teach*). This effect was originally demonstrated by Ganong (1980). In the TRACE model, this effect is again accounted for by top-down connections. In the Race model, the effect again reflects the operation of the race between pre-lexical and lexical routes.

Fox (1984) replicated this effect, and showed that there were no lexical effects for fast categorization responses. Connine and Clifton (1987) found both a lexical shift and an RT advantage for word responses relative to nonword responses in the boundary region. They further showed that the lexical effect was not due to postperceptual bias: it was not equivalent to an effect obtained using monetary reward to bias subjects' responses. Lexical effects have also been reported by Burton, Baum and Blumstein (1989), who found that the categorization of a word-initial continuum depended on the acoustic-phonetic quality of the continuum, and by Miller and Dexter (1988), who showed that lexical involvement in categorization was not mandatory, in contrast to rate-normalization processes (see above).

McQueen (1991a) and Pitt and Samuel (1993) have found lexical effects for phonemes in word-final position (e.g. for an /ʃ/–/s/ continuum in contexts such as *fish-fiss* and *kish-kiss*). McQueen (1991a) also replicated Burton et al.'s (1989) finding that lexical effects in the categorization task only appear when the materials are of poor acoustic quality. Pitt and Samuel (1993), however, have shown that poor stimulus quality is not a necessary condition for a lexical effect: lexical shifts were obtained with high-quality materials in both word-initial and word-final categorization. The basic lexical effect in this task is consistent with both types of model.

3.2 Test cases

Both models can account for lexical effects in several tasks. Are there any test cases which might allow us to distinguish between the two models? Can we establish whether or not lexical information is used in pre-lexical processing? Several attempts have been made to contrast divergent predictions of the TRACE and Race models.

3.2.1 Phoneme monitoring

Frauenfelder, Segui and Dijkstra (1990) have presented evidence from the phoneme monitoring task which challenges the interactive position. TRACE predicts that activation of a lexical candidate will both boost the activation of its constituent phonemes by top-down facilitation and inhibit the activation of nonconstituent phonemes because of phoneme-to-phoneme inhibition. As this study showed, there are strong facilitatory effects on the detection of targets (such as /p/ in *olympiade*), which occur after the word becomes unique, relative to matched nonwords (e.g. *arimpiako*). In TRACE terms, this could be due to top-down facilitation of /p/ from the word node. If this were the case, detection of /t/ in *vocabutaire* should be inhibited relative to detection of /t/ in a matched nonword such as *socabutaire*, because of top-down facilitation of /l/ from the activated *vocabulaire* node followed by inhibition of other phoneme nodes by the /l/ node. No such inhibition was found, contrary to the TRACE account. This result is not problematic for the Race model, however. It predicts that performance on nonwords is insulated from lexical information because all nonword decisions have to be made via the pre-lexical route.

3.2.2 Word-final categorization

McQueen (1991a) showed that the lexical effect in categorization of word-final ambiguous fricatives, in contexts such as *fish-fiss* and *kish-kiss*, was larger for faster responses. This finding has recently been replicated by Pitt and Samuel (1993). This reaction time effect is predicted by the Race model, where for word-final fricatives the lexical route can be assumed to be faster, on average, than the pre-lexical route. But the TRACE model assumes that lexical effects should build up gradually over time (McClelland and Elman, 1986), and thus predicts exactly the opposite pattern of results, that the lexical effect should be larger for slower responses.

3.2.3 Compensation for coarticulation

One result appears to support interactive models. Mann and Repp (1981) showed that stops midway between /t/ and /k/ were more often categorized as /k/ after /s/, but as /t/ after /ʃ/. The perceptual system appears to compensate for fricative-stop coarticulation. Elman and McClelland (1988) replicated this effect for ambiguous word-initial stops following fricative-final words such as *christmas* and *foolish*, and, most importantly, they showed that the effect occurred when the word-final fricatives were replaced with an ambiguous fricative. When the

/s/ in *christmas* was replaced with an ambiguous sound /?/, midway between /s/ and /ʃ/, there were again more /k/ responses to the ambiguous stops. With *fooli?*, there were more /t/ responses.

Elman and McClelland claimed that this effect was strong evidence in favour of interactive models like TRACE. Lexical information appears to be influencing a compensation process that can be assumed to be operating pre-lexically. This seems to be direct evidence against the autonomous assumption that information flow is bottom-up. But autonomous models can account for Elman and McClelland's results. Norris (1993) and Chater, Shillcock, Cairns and Levy (submitted) have shown that connectionist recurrent net models, which are sensitive to temporal context but which have strictly bottom-up information flow, can simulate the compensation for coarticulation effect. During training, these networks learn to use contextual information, and thus become sensitive to sequential dependencies. They recognise /s/ in *christma?*, for example, because in training (on a large corpus of conversational English) /s/ was more likely after schwa than /ʃ/. These models successfully simulate both Elman and McClelland's results, and those of McQueen (1991b). The effect is not, after all, a test case that might allow us to distinguish between interactive and autonomous models. Note that this demonstration also shows that effects which appear to be due to specific lexical entries may in fact be due to knowledge about regularities of the spoken language as a whole. Further research is required to establish which "lexical effects" are indeed due to the involvement of stored information about specific lexical entries.

3.3 Attentional effects

The previous section has shown that the little evidence there is which distinguishes between interactive and autonomous models supports the Race account. Lexical information does not appear to be involved in pre-lexical processing. Further evidence in support of this conclusion has come from an analysis of attentional effects. In addition to the task monotony effect in phoneme monitoring, that lexical effects tend to be absent when listeners hear only monosyllabic items (Cutler et al., 1987, see above), other attentional effects have been found with this task. In a comparison of standard and generalized phoneme monitoring, Frauenfelder and Segui (1989) found that responses were faster to target-bearing words that were preceded by associatively-related words than to those preceded by unrelated words, but only in generalized monitoring. In standard monitoring, subjects can attend to the initial sounds alone, but in generalized monitoring, where there was no prior cueing of the possible target position, subjects have to rely more heavily on lexical information.

Pitt and Samuel (1990a) explicitly examined attentional effects in phoneme monitoring. They manipulated the proportion of occurrences of targets in a particular position in disyllabic words in a generalized phoneme monitoring task: that is, they varied the probable location of the target phoneme. Subjects were faster and more accurate in detecting, for example, initial-position targets when they appeared in lists in which 75 per cent of the targets were in this position than when they appeared in an unbiased baseline condition; target detection in other (non-predicted) locations was worse than in the baseline condition. These authors argued that the manipulation of expected target location induced a strategy of attending to that location.

Nusbaum, Walley, Carrell and Ressler (1982) and Samuel and Ressler (1986) have examined the role of attention in the phoneme restoration effect. The lexical status of stimuli could cause subjects to attend to word-level representations rather than to individual phonemes. But if subjects could be trained on potential targets and cued as to the identity and location of the critical phoneme then the illusion could perhaps be removed. Samuel and Ressler (1986) found that training and cueing did indeed inhibit the restoration illusion.

Eimas, Marcovitz Hornstein and Payton (1990) asked subjects to identify unambiguous item-initial stops in words and nonwords, which were presented at the end of a neutral phrase. There were no lexical effects. However, when subjects also performed a secondary task which required lexical knowledge (such as lexical decision) on the target items subsequent to the identification decision, reliable lexical effects emerged. The concurrent task, which focused attention on the lexicon, appeared to produce lexically-mediated performance in the phonetic task. Eimas and Nygaard (1992) showed further that lexical effects in phoneme monitoring did not emerge in sentential contexts, even with a secondary lexical task. They occurred only in random word strings, and then only when a secondary task was being performed. Eimas and Nygaard argued that when subjects were given meaningful contexts, the secondary decisions were based on higher-level representations, and the phonetic decisions were based on pre-lexical processing. It is only in neutral contexts, where listeners must use lexical information to perform the secondary task, that attention is directed to the lexical level for phoneme monitoring.

These attentional effects show that, in contrast to rate or speaker information, lexical information plays no mandatory role in pre-lexical processing. Attentional manipulations can encourage or discourage listeners from using lexical information during phonetic decision-making. But listeners cannot avoid using rate and speaker information, even when they are asked to ignore this information. As Cutler et al. (1987), Eimas et al. (1990) and Eimas and Nygaard (1992) have argued, these results are more in keeping with the Race model than with TRACE. An attentional mechanism fits more parsimoniously into the Race model framework, requiring only that attention, in response to task demands, can be focused on the output of one or other route. Shifting attention to one or other level of representation naturally entails shifting attention to one or other route. In the TRACE framework, however, attentional modulation of lexical involvement has to be modelled in terms of a gain control, increasing or decreasing the amount of top-down facilitation. Adjusting the gain in this way does not naturally follow from a shift of attention from one level of representation to the other.

3.4 Summary

As claimed by the Race model, lexical information is not used to constrain the process of lexical access. Although many results can be handled by both models, a few findings are problematic for the TRACE account. Furthermore, attentional modification of lexical involvement, though not contradicting either model, is more consistent with the Race account. It might be argued that no Race model explanation of compensation for coarticulation has been offered. Lexical involvement in compensation for coarticulation was accounted for by autonomous recurrent networks. But the Race model has recently been considered to be part of a fuller account of spoken-word recognition which includes the recurrent network responsible for compensation effects: the Shortlist model (Norris, 1994).

Shortlist is a two-stage model of spoken-word recognition (for a fuller description, see Norris, 1994). In the first stage, lexical hypotheses, consistent with the segmental information in the input, are activated. This stage can be modelled using the type of recurrent net which can explain the compensation for coarticulation results. This stage encapsulates pre-lexical processing in the model: it is capable of rate normalization (Norris, 1990), and, in accordance with the empirical evidence, the lexical access code is based on acoustic-phonetic information specifying segmental structure. Since phonetic decisions can be based on the output of this stage, it instantiates the pre-lexical route of the Race model. In the second stage, the activated lexical hypotheses (constituting a "shortlist" of candidate words) compete with each other via a process of lateral inhibition, until one word (or a series of words in the case of continuous speech recognition) dominates the activation pattern, and can then be recognised. This stage instantiates the lexical route of the Race model. The Shortlist model thus provides an account both of the compensation for coarticulation results and the lexical effects that can be explained by the Race model. Information flows only bottom-up in Shortlist, and thus the model embodies the claim that lexical information does not influence pre-lexical processing.

Note that we are not claiming that lexical information is not involved in lexical access, just that it is not involved in the processing which takes place prior to lexical access. The lexical information specifying the structure of the vocabulary and the form-based relationships between words has an important role to play in word recognition. There is growing evidence that multiple lexical hypotheses are activated during the recognition process (Marslen-Wilson, 1987, 1990; Shillcock, 1990; Swinney, 1981; Zwitserlood, 1989). Recent evidence suggests that once words consistent with the input speech have been activated, they then compete (Goldinger, Luce and Pisoni, 1989; Goldinger, Luce,

Pisoni and Marcario, 1992; McQueen, Norris and Cutler, 1994; Norris, McQueen and Cutler, 1995; Slowiaczek and Hamburger, 1992; Vroomen and de Gelder, 1995). Accessed words compete with each other until one word dominates the others: this one word can then be recognised. This competition process is instantiated, in different ways, in several models of spoken-word recognition: the Neighborhood Activation Model (Luce, 1986), TRACE, and, as described above, Shortlist. Lexical information, such as the extent to which one word overlaps with other words, and the nature and number of words embedded within other words, is thus crucially important in the process of word recognition, but only after lexical access has taken place.

4 Prosodic information

The third type of information whose role in lexical access we will investigate is prosodic information. By prosody we mean variations in fundamental frequency, timing structure and intensity across an utterance, and we confine ourselves here to prosodic variation which is not solely the direct consequence of a segmental decision.

By this restriction we in fact exclude a very large amount of prosodic variation. Speech is realised as sound, and sounds must perforce be uttered with a certain fundamental frequency (f_0), a certain amplitude, and a certain duration. Phonetic segments may vary in intrinsic f_0, and listeners certainly exploit this information (see Silverman, 1987, for a review). Likewise segments may be longer or shorter in one context than in another simply due to properties of that immediate context: effects of adjacent segments, for example, or of the position of occurrence within a word; again, we exclude this source of prosodic variation.

Furthermore, in many languages inter-segmental contrasts are realised solely in duration (vowels have three levels of duration in Estonian, for example). Analogous to this, we argue, is the case of lexical tone in languages such as Mandarin, Vietnamese or Yoruba, in which two morphemes consisting of the same sequence of segments are distinguished by f_0 variation. In many languages, tone realisation can be in part contextually dependent (which is of course also true of coarticulated segments); but it remains the case that, for example, a CV syllable with a rise-fall tone can be a *different lexical item* from the same CV with a level tone. And although tone is best conceptualised as a property of syllables, it is actually realised to all intents and purposes on syllabic nuclei, i.e. vowels; thus it is conceivable that a recogniser could process a given vowel with a rise-fall tone and the same vowel with a level tone simply as different segments, irrespective of context. There is as yet little experimental evidence available on spoken-word recognition in tone languages, but what evidence there is supports a parallelism between segmental processing and the processing of tonal information.

For instance, lexical information can affect tone categorisation in just the same way as it affects segment categorisation. In the segment categorisation study of Ganong (1980), listeners' category boundaries between /t/ and /d/ shifted to produce more /d/ responses preceding /iːp/ but more /t/ responses preceding /iːtʃ/; similarly, in a tone categorisation study by Fox and Unkefer (1985), listeners' category boundaries between two tones of Mandarin Chinese shifted as a function of which endpoint tone produced a real word given the syllable the tone was produced on. (This was of course only true when the listeners were Mandarin speakers; English listeners showed no such shift.) Lexical priming studies in Cantonese also suggest that the role of a syllable's tone in word recognition is analogous to the role of the vowel (Cutler and Chen, 1995). Nevertheless, there is evidence (Cutler and Chen, in press) that tonal information is not processed in conjunction with vocalic information; listeners can detect the difference between two CV syllables with the same onset and the same tone but a different vowel more rapidly than they can detect the difference between two CV syllables with the same onset and the same vowel but a different tone.

The above types of prosodic information we will exclude from further consideration; the principal question at issue here concerns prosodic information which is not segmentally constrained, and the use of which is, therefore, in principle optional. We will consider two aspects of prosodic structure: lexical stress and sentence rhythm. These neither exhaust the canon of prosodic variation, nor, more importantly, can they lay claim to universal validity: for example, many languages do not have lexical stress. They are chosen chiefly because they have both been the subject of considerable research effort.

4.1 Lexical stress

The term *lexical stress* itself suggests that stress pattern can have a lexically distinctive function. Indeed, pairs of unrelated words differing only in stress pattern do exist, although in the world's lexical stress languages such pairs are extremely rare. In English, for instance, although stress oppositions between verb and noun forms of the same stem (*decrease, conduct*) are common, there are very few such pairs which are lexically clearly distinct (such as *forbear, or insight/incite*).

Due to the greater acoustic reliability of stressed syllables, stress can affect recognition: stressed syllables are more readily identified than unstressed syllables when cut out of their original context (Lieberman, 1963), and distortions of the speech signal are more likely to be detected in stressed than in unstressed syllables (Cole and Jakimik, 1980; Browman, 1978; Bond and Garnes, 1980). Detection of word-initial target phonemes can also be faster on stressed than unstressed syllables, although only when acoustic differences are relatively large, as for instance in spontaneous speech; such differences do not arise with laboratory-read materials (Mehta and Cutler, 1988).

Studies of English vocabulary structure show that stress pattern information could be of use in word recognition. A partial phonetic transcription which includes stress pattern information applies to a smaller candidate set of words than one which does not (Aull, 1984; Waibel, 1988). An automatic recognition algorithm operating at this level of phonetic specification performs significantly better with stress pattern information than without (Port, Reilly and Maki, 1988). But stress information does not facilitate human word recognition: neither visual nor auditory lexical decision is facilitated by prior specification of stress pattern, nor does whether or not a bisyllabic word conforms to the canonical English word class pattern (initial stress for nouns, final stress for verbs) affect how rapidly its grammatical category is judged (Cutler and Clifton, 1984).

Mis-stressing, to be sure, inhibits word recognition. English listeners presented with English spoken by Indian speakers, including stress patterns unorthodox by British English standards, tend to interpret the input in conformity with the stress pattern, often in conflict with the segmental information (Bansal, 1966). Puns are unsuccessful if they require a stress shift (Lagerquist, 1980). Deliberately mis-stressed words are responded to more slowly in recognition tasks than correctly stressed words (Bond and Small, 1983; Cutler and Clifton, 1984). The mis-stressing used in such studies, however, was not simply a prosodic manipulation. Pairs of English words with stress-pattern opposition usually also differ vocalically. Thus *OBject* and *obJECT*, *CONtent* and *conTENT* have quite different vowels in their first syllables – the stressed syllables have a full vowel, while the unstressed syllables have schwa. Just as the vowel difference in *cot* and *cut* is lexically significant, so may observed effects of stress simply reflect the lexical significance of different vowels resulting from stress differences. To English listeners, the vowel quality distinction is indeed more crucial than the purely prosodic distinction; cross-splicing vowels with different stress patterns produces unacceptable results only if vowel quality is changed (Fear, Cutler and Butterfield, 1995). In Fear et al.'s study, listeners heard tokens of, say, *autumn*, which has primary stress on the initial vowel, and *audition*, which has an unstressed but unreduced vowel, with the initial vowels exchanged; they rated these tokens as insignificantly different from the original, unspliced, tokens.

To investigate *prosodic* effects on word recognition in a lexical-stress language, it is necessary to control for vowel quality. Although most unstressed syllables in English have a neutral (schwa) vowel, a reasonably large class of polysyllabic words with exclusively full vowels does exist. *Nutmeg* and *typhoon* are two such words. In their mispronunciation experiment, Cutler and Clifton (1984) explicitly compared bisyllabic words in which the unstressed syllable contained schwa (*wisdom*, *deceit*) with words like *nutmeg* and *typhoon*. Word recognition was clearly inhibited by mis-stressing for the former group. The words with full vowels, however, were only harder to recognize when mis-stressed if their citation form pronunciation had initial stress. That is, *nutMEG* was much harder to recognize than *NUTmeg*; but *TYphoon* was not significantly more difficult than *tyPHOON*. (In English, the demands of sentence rhythm can cause stress to shift in words like *typhoon*; they are in practice encountered sufficiently often in initially-stressed form for this form perhaps to have achieved the lexical status of an optional pronunciation.) Similarly Taft (1984), using a monitoring task, found that SW (strong, weak) words produced slower responses when mis-stressed (*cacTUS*), but mis-stressing of WS words (*SUSpense*) actually led to response times which were somewhat faster than those with the correctly stressed words. Slowiaczek (1990) also demonstrated increased recognition difficulty for pronunciations like *nutMEG*.

The process of word recognition includes several subsidiary operations, however, and there are at least two ways in which prosody could be relevant in recognition. These correspond to the commonly drawn distinction between lexical access and lexical retrieval. On the one hand, lexical prosody, i.e. stress marking, could be an essential part of the access code by which lexical entries are located; on the other, it could be part of the phonological code listed for a word in the lexicon and consulted only in retrieval, i.e. once access has been achieved. The mis-stressing results do not distinguish between these two possibilities. If prosodic information is present in the lexical access code, *nutMEG* could be hard to recognize because the initial access attempt will encounter no match, and successful access will only be achieved after the code has been recomputed. If prosody does not play a role in access, however, *nutMEG* could be hard to recognize because the complete phonological form in the accessed lexical entry fails to match the input.

If prosody participates in lexical access, in much the same way that segmental identity does, then minimal stress pairs, i.e. words with identical segments but different prosody, should generate distinct lexical access codes, and be, in practice, not confusable. In fact, the rarity of minimal stress pairs itself suggests that lexical stress may hardly ever exercise such constraint. Experimental evidence supports this, by suggesting that the lexical access code does not draw on the information available from English word prosody. Using the cross-modal priming paradigm (Swinney, 1979), in which listeners hear a sentence and at some point during the sentence perform a visual lexical decision, Cutler (1986) showed that strings like *forbear* are functionally homophonous: both *FORbear* and *forBEAR* facilitate recognition of words related to *each* of them (e.g. *ancestor*, *tolerate*). In other words, listeners did not distinguish between these two word forms in initially achieving access to the lexicon.

Where English listeners *can* use stress information, they do use it; so when Connine, Clifton and Cutler (1987) asked listeners to categorize an ambiguous initial consonant in either *DIgress-TIgress* (in which *tigress* is a real word) or *diGRESS-tiGRESS* (in which *digress* is a real word), they reported /t/ more often for the initial-stress items, /d/ more often for the final-stress items. In other words, they were using the stress information (both that in the signal and that in their stored representations of these words) to resolve ambiguity in a difficult perceptual situation. As we pointed out in section 3.3, however, evidence that a given source of information is used in a phonetic categorization task does not constitute evidence that it is used pre-lexically; this holds as true for prosodic correlates of stress (although they could in principle be processed in a bottom-up way) as for information about lexical identity (which implies top-down flow of information). The listeners in Connine et al.'s study had the opportunity to consult the phonological code listed in two lexical entries, and to use the prosodic information contained therein to motivate their phonetic categorisation decision.

In fact, it may well make good sense for the listener not to make early use of lexical stress for lexical access. In order to know the stress pattern of a word, the listener's word recognition system must know how many syllables the word has; in effect, therefore, it could not begin the process of lexical access until the end or nearly the end of the word if it were to need stress pattern information before access could be attempted. Perhaps, therefore, lexical prosody does not participate in the *pre-lexical* access code simply because the information it provides cannot outweigh the disadvantage of delayed initiation of access.

4.2 Sentence rhythm

The characteristic rhythm of English – in which language most of the relevant experimental evidence is again to be found – is based on stress. Rhythmic patterns are accompanied by segmental variations: by far the majority of unstressed syllables in English contain weak (reduced) vowels. And again, rhythmic effects in the recognition of spoken English largely reduce to effects which can be interpreted in terms of segmental processing. Consider, for instance, the effects observed in speech segmentation. In continuous speech, word boundaries are rarely reliably marked, and listeners in practice adopt explicit procedures which assist with the location of points at which lexical access attempts should most usefully be commenced; in English, and in rhythmically similar languages such as Dutch, the procedure is based on the assumption that strong syllables are most likely to be word-initial. The evidence for this comes partly from studies of word boundary misperceptions, in which listeners most commonly err by assuming strong syllables to be word-initial and weak syllables to be non-initial (Cutler and Butterfield, 1992; Vroomen, van Zon and de Gelder, in press), and word-spotting studies, in which real words embedded in nonsense bisyllables are harder to detect if detecting them requires processing segments from two consecutive strong syllables, i.e. across the canonical point of speech segmentation (Cutler and Norris, 1988; McQueen et al., 1994; Norris et al., 1995; see also Vroomen and de Gelder, 1995; Vroomen et al., in press).

In all of these studies the effective parameter was vowel quality rather than prosodic stress *per se*. In Cutler and Norris' (1988) original word-spotting study, for example, prosodic stress was not varied. Thus detection of the word *mint* was compared in *mintayf* and *mintef*; both bisyllables had the same stress pattern (initial stress). The difference was solely in the vowel which occurred in the second syllable, and it was this vowel which affected listeners' responses: *mint* was much harder to detect when the second vowel was strong, as in *mintayf*.

Although we interpret these rhythmic effects as reflecting exploitation of vowel quality, i.e. segmental information, it is also relevant that the strong/ weak vowel difference in English is the manifestation of language rhythm. In other languages with different rhythmic patterns, segmentation procedures also exploit rhythmic structure (see, e.g. Cutler, Mehler, Norris and Segui, 1992; Cutler and Otake, 1994; Otake, Hatano, Cutler and Mehler, 1993). In fact, rhythm allows a single, universally valid description of the different segmentation procedures used across languages. Important for the present discussion is that these effects thus indicate a way in which the lexical access process is indeed affected by prosodic structure (although in English the segmental reflections of rhythmic structure make a purely segmentally-based segmentation procedure feasible). The heuristic procedures which listeners use to facilitate word boundary location both in English and in other languages amount to a direction of attention to certain portions of the input rather than to other portions.

It is not only for speech segmentation purposes that such effects may be observed. A series of studies using the phoneme monitoring task provide evidence that listeners also use the overall prosodic contour of a sentence to direct attention to words bearing sentence accent. Response time to detect the initial phoneme of an acoustically constant word token is faster when the word occurs in a prosodic context consistent with sentence accent falling at that point than when it occurs in a context consistent with lack of accent (Cutler, 1976; Cutler and Darwin, 1981). Listeners can derive sufficient information to perform this attentional focus even when f_0 variation has been removed (Cutler and Darwin, 1981), although when dimensions of prosodic information conflict – such that, for example, the rhythm predicts accent where the f_0 contour predicts lack of accent – listeners refrain from deriving predictive information from prosody at all (Cutler, 1987). Similarly, the initial phonemes of nonsense words are detected more rapidly in contexts in which sentence rhythm predicts that the syllables containing the target will be accented (Shields, McHugh and Martin, 1974). Pitt and Samuel (1990b) presented acoustically constant versions of disyllabic minimal stress pairs at the ends of auditory lists in which all the disyllabic items had the same stress pattern; detection of a phoneme in these words was again faster when the syllable containing the target phoneme was predicted to be stressed, suggesting that listeners used the predictive information to attend selectively to stressed syllables.

The utility of prosodic information in human speech processing seems, therefore, to depend on the type of prosodic information involved. Information about word identity directly encoded in the stress pattern of a word is, as we saw above, not used in the computation of the initial lexical access code. Information about the general prosodic pattern-class of words, on the other hand, is used, and it is used in such a way as effectively to guide initiation of the access process. In a language such as English, this latter decision process can in practice be effected via vowel identity, i.e. via the segmental information alone, and thus does not depend on prosodic information. But this decision process is nevertheless highly similar to the process which exploits predictive sentence-level prosody. Rhythmic information directs attention to strong syllables (i.e. effectively to syllables containing full vowels) for the purpose of lexical segmentation; strong syllables are the most likely locations of word onsets in English. Predictive prosodic information directs attention to accented words or syllables, and effectively speeds processing and results in faster responses to the presence of target phonemes. In the final section we will consider the implications of this pattern of findings for the architecture of the human speech recognition system.

5 Conclusions

Each type of information we have discussed plays a different role in the processing which takes place for lexical access. Acoustic-phonetic information has a central and mandatory role in pre-lexical processing. The recognition system must deal with the variability of acoustic-phonetic information in the speech signal; and normalization processes such as those dealing with speech rate and speaker variability appear to operate always, outside of attentional control. These features suggest that pre-lexical processing entails the abstraction of segmental information from the speech signal. Although it is unclear precisely which representational units are abstracted pre-lexically, it seems clear that they constitute the basis of the lexical access code.

Lexical information, on the other hand, appears to play no role in pre-lexical processing, contrary to the claims of interactive models such as TRACE (McClelland and Elman, 1986), but consistent with autonomous models like Shortlist (Norris, 1994). Top-down connections from lexical to pre-lexical levels of processing are not required. Lexical effects which do occur in tasks requiring phonetic decisions can be explained either by a race between pre-lexical and lexical procedures (as in the Race model, Cutler et al., 1987) or by a pre-lexical mechanism which is sensitive to the sequential dependencies in speech (as in the recurrent net explanation of apparent lexical involvement in compensation for coarticulation). Both these mechanisms are instantiated in the Shortlist model. Furthermore, lexical effects in phonetic tasks are influenced by attentional manipulations. The modulation of lexical involvement by attention is more parsimoniously explained by autonomous than by interactive models.

Prosodic information, finally, plays an intermediate role. Information specifying the rhythmic structure of the language is used to constrain the process of lexical segmentation, and information about sentence-level accent can be used predictively, to benefit the processing of a word in an accented position. Prosodic information about lexical stress, however, does not appear to be used pre-lexically.

The direction of attention to some parts of the signal rather than others, which is how prosody is exploited pre-lexically, may seem analogous to potential lexical constraints on the pre-lexical access code. But the two are fundamentally different. The prosodic information which is used is present in the speech signal (information specifying vowel quality, sentence accent pattern, and so on), while lexical information has to be constructed from the signal via contact with a higher-level representation. In other words, prosodic information can be used bottom-up, while lexical information can only be used top-down. This means that prosodic information, like acoustic-phonetic information, can be used immediately, to benefit on-line processing. Top-down processing, on the other hand, is likely to be time-delayed, since lexical representations have to be accessed before they can influence processing. (Note that the prosodic information which cannot be computed on-line without delaying access, that is, lexical stress information, is precisely the type of prosodic information which appears not to be used *pre*-lexically.)

Furthermore, as Massaro (1989) has pointed out, lexical information, if used top-down, can act to distort the acoustic-phonetic information available in the signal. In the TRACE model, Massaro argues, top-down activation can eventually obliterate bottom-up evidence. The recognition system would surely be better designed if bottom-up information were not lost, and remained available to be used in perceptual decisions. Prosodic information available bottom-up, however, cannot distort the other information available in the signal.

In conclusion, it appears that human word recognition is an autonomous process. Information that is available in the speech signal is used to generate the lexical access code. This is largely acoustic-phonetic information specifying segmental structure, but includes information specifying the rhythmic structure of the input language and sentence-level prosodic information. Lexical information, however, does not appear to influence pre-lexical processing.

Part IV   Linguistic Phonetics

19   Linguistic Phonetic Descriptions

PETER LADEFOGED

This chapter will be concerned with the kind of phonetic framework that is necessary for the description of a language. Essentially this means determining the set of phonetic parameters that are to be used in phonological descriptions. Accordingly, before we can begin discussing the parameters themselves, we must consider what belongs in the phonology of a language. We must decide which differences in utterances are part of the language, and which are extra-linguistic. This is sometimes not as simple as it might seem, as speech conveys many kinds of information simultaneously. Whenever we talk we convey not only linguistic information about the topic under discussion, but also sociolinguistic information about the group to which we belong. As Shaw (1916) puts it in the preface to *Pygmalion*: "It is impossible for an Englishman to open his mouth without making some other Englishman despise him." There is no general agreement as to whether this kind of indexical information should be considered within the phonology. It may be part of a specific language, but it is not clear whether all the ways in which one accent (or, indeed, one language) is distinguished from another necessarily involve the same aspects of speech sounds as those that are used for distinguishing one word or sentence from another within a language. Some differences between accents are conveyed by phonetic differences of the same kind as those that change the meanings of words. There are obvious cases such as the fact that I pronounce the word "glass" as [glɑs] whereas speakers from elsewhere might say [glæs]. But some of the sociolinguistic functions of speech cannot be described entirely in terms of the same phonetic properties as those that are required for specifying phonological oppositions. Differences in accents can be maintained by subtle shifts in vowel quality that are noticeable over a long stretch of speech, but which would not be sufficient for distinguishing the meanings of words or phrases. There is no theoretical reason why speech systems should be expected to use the same devices for phonological and sociolinguistic purposes. In this chapter we will be concerned with only those differences between sounds that are known to have a phonological function.

In addition to small sociolinguistic phonetic phenomena, several other aspects of speech will not here be considered part of the phonology. Sometimes utterances are best regarded as vocal signals rather than vehicles for conveying linguistic information. This is true, for example, of a sergeant yelling orders on a parade ground. Superficially there may be lexical items arranged in some syntactic pattern; but the actual words are not important; barks or grunts would do as well. Another of the functions of speech is to convey the attitude of the speaker. This is not codified in the same way as linguistic information. Emphasis, for example, is often a gradient matter; the louder the shout the more emphatic the utterance. Similarly, sarcastic, simpering, or loving intonations are not part of language and should not be described within the phonology. They are simply attitudinal affects. Nor should we consider emotional effects that may be reflected in speech. Many of them seem to be universal, general human traits, but to the extent that they are not the same in all languages, they are aspects of particular cultures rather than particular languages. Finally, there are the aspects of speech that convey personal identity; these are obviously not part of language. We will take it that phonology is concerned only with linguistic information, and that this can be defined as all the encoded aspects of speech except those that convey information about the speaker's identity, attitude, emotions, or sociolinguistic background, in so far as these are not conveyed by syntactic or lexical devices.

Another way of regarding this problem is to say that we need a phonetic framework that can describe all linguistic contrasts. These include lexical contrasts, which have to be characterized at the surface phonetic level. English "ram, ran, rang", for example, must be considered to end in distinct segments, regardless of whether [ŋ] is phonologically specifiable as /ng/ at some higher level. Morphological and syntactic contrasts must also be specified within the phonetic framework. Often this involves no more than using the same phonetic devices as are used for describing lexical contrasts. But intonation and other suprasegmental phenomena must be specifiable in linguistic phonetic terms when they are used for syntactic purposes, as, for example, when distinguishing sentences such as: "When danger threatens your children, call the police" and "When danger threatens, your children call the police." Similarly there are syntactic differences underlying what is sometimes called contrastive stress, as exemplified by italics in sentences such as: "The glass is on the *table*" and "The *glass* is on the table." In syntactic terms this is a change in the focus of the sentence. In many other languages differences of focus are conveyed by affixes; and in all languages they should be considered part of the linguistic information. However, although intonation patterns such as these are part of the language, many others that are described in studies of intonation (e.g. by Pierrehumbert 1979, 1980) are not what we would consider to be linguistically contrastive, and are therefore not part of the phonology.

The linguistic phonetic framework must also provide for another aspect of phonology, the description of the patterns of sounds that occur. In order to account for both the patterns of sounds within languages, and those that occur across languages, it is necessary to group sounds into classes that share particular features. Phonological features thus serve two different purposes: they group sounds together in the rules that describe and elucidate phonological patterns, and they distinguish linguistic contrasts such as items in the lexicon. There is no intrinsic reason why the features required for the one purpose should be the same as those required for the other. In fact it may be that certain languages (e.g. !Xóõ, according to Traill 1985) have little or no phonology – i.e. few alternations explicable in terms of rules – although they obviously have lexical items that have to be given distinct representations. Similarly, there are phonological alternations in languages that depend on some feature that is not actually used to distinguish words in that language. Thus in many languages the release of a final stop may be phonologically relevant in that it marks syntactic units, but it does not distinguish lexical items.

Phonological features are also required for a third task, namely, defining the set of possible human sounds that can be used linguistically. An important task for phonological theory is to explain why languages have certain contrasting sounds and not others. One of the major pieces of work of this kind published recently is that of Maddieson (1984a). A proper theory of phonology must account for both the inventories that Maddieson observes, and the rules that other phonologists find in the world's languages. Many contemporary phonologists (e.g. Clements 1985, Halle 1988) are more interested in the types of rules that can occur than in the formal statements that constrain the set of possible linguistic sounds. But both are important tasks for phonology.

The remainder of this chapter will be concerned with determining a set of linguistic phonetic features for use within a complete phonological theory. We will do this while bearing in mind that features have three distinct functions: they provide a means for distinguishing the distinct utterances of a language; they group sounds into classes that can be used in descriptions of phonological patterns; and they form a set that determines the range of possible linguistic sounds.

In order to construct a valid set of features of this kind we must consider how languages get to be the way they are. Languages are the products of speakers and listeners; and the acts of speaking and listening leave their mark on languages in different ways (Martinet 1955, Lindblom 1984). From a speaker's point of view, one of the goals of using a language is to communicate without undue articulatory effort. From a listener's point of view, a language should contain sufficiently distinct sequences of sounds so that the message is readily interpretable. The notions of economy of articulatory effort and auditory distinctiveness are both important in the formation of phonological patterns. Because sounds that were produced in similar ways usually have a similar acoustic structure, features that group sounds in articulatory terms will usually also group them in acoustic terms. But this is not always true. Nasalized vowels share an articulatory activity (lowering of the soft palate), but there is no prominence in the acoustic spectrum that they all share. Furthermore, the reverse is not always true; some segments can sound very similar although they were produced in quite different ways. Different forms of

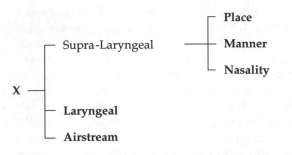

Figure 19.1   The first part of a hierarchy of linguistic phonetic features.

rhotic sounds are examples. There are thus two different kind of features: those that have an auditory basis, and those that group sounds in articulatory terms. We will consider the more well known articulatory features first.

1 The hierarchy of articulatory features

Linguistic phonetic features form a hierarchical structure, a notion that has been firmly entrenched in phonological theories, at least since the seminal paper by Clements (1985). This notion has been used to account for constraints on phonological processes such as the spreading of a feature from one segment to another. But if our phonological theory is to be able to determine human phonetic capabilities, it must also show what kinds of full phonological specifications are possible, and what are not. The concept of a hierarchical structure is equally important in the way it defines what constitutes a possible segment.

We will consider the feature hierarchy in small sections. The first section is as shown in Figure 19.1. This figure formalizes some very traditional phonetic concepts. But it also formalizes, in a new way, some of the constraints on interactions among the terms listed. A formal aspect of importance in this theory is the distinction between those branches of the tree that are labeled in bold face and those that are not. Bold face indicates features that must be specified if the node above them is specified. The hierarchy is dominated by an X, a root node or single segment slot in many phonological descriptions. Immediately below this are three terms, supra-laryngeal, laryngeal and airstream. Two of these, laryngeal and airstream, are in bold face, indicating that every segment must have some laryngeal state, and some airstream. The supralaryngeal possibility is not in bold face because, as Keating (1988a) has pointed out, the output of the phonological component of a grammar may contain sounds that are completely unspecified for certain features. Segments such as a glottal stop or [h] may have no supra-laryngeal specifications. When these sounds are actually produced, phonetic interpretation rules will ensure that a complete account of the sound could be given, perhaps by interpolating values from those of the neighboring sounds.

The supralaryngeal node dominates three possibilities, Place, Manner, and

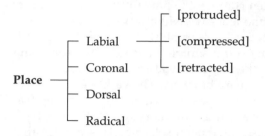

Figure 19.2 Another section of the feature hierarchy.

Nasality, all of which are in bold face, as each of them must be specified if the Supralaryngeal node is specified. The five bold face terms in Figure 19.1 therefore reflect the standard practice of articulatory phonetic description as seen in many textbooks. Abercrombie (1967), for example, notes that consonants can be described in terms of the place of articulation, the manner of articulation, the oro-nasal process, the state of the glottis, and the airstream mechanism. The same organization is apparent in Pike (1943), and has been taken over by Ladefoged (1971, 1993).

The five terms in bold face in Figure 19.1 may be called hyper-features. As we will see, the first two hyper-features correspond to the traditional terms place and manner, interpreted in a slightly different way, with the emphasis on the active articulator, and the allocation of places to sounds irrespective of whether they are consonants or vowels. The third hyper-feature, Nasality, is regarded by traditional IPA phoneticians as part of the manner of articulation (e.g. in the IPA consonant chart); but here, in accordance with the usual generative phonology tradition, Nasality is regarded as a separate process, so that, as with the other hyper-features, it is applicable to consonants and vowels alike. When this is done it is possible to describe, for example, the nasalization of vowels before nasal consonants as involving the spreading of the feature value [+nasal]. The Laryngeal hyper-feature has long been recognized as a separate entity by all phoneticians, although the structures that it dominates may not be the same as that suggested later in this chapter. The final hyper-feature, Airstream, is often not considered as an independent node by generative phonologists, who usually regard the Laryngeal hyper-feature as specifying all the glottalic aspects of sounds, and the Place and Manner hyper-features as specifying a velaric airstream when necessary. As will become apparent later, there are advantages in setting up an additional hyper-feature in accordance with the IPA tradition.

1.1 Place of articulation

The features that are immediately dominated by the Place node are shown in Figure 19.2, along with the values that are dominated by one of them, the Labial node. This diagram allows us to make clear another formal distinction within the theory. Many writers often confuse the name of a feature with its value, but in this view of linguistic phonetics we will always distinguish carefully between them. Thus in the preceding paragraph we spoke of "the spreading of the feature value [+nasal]" where others might have said "the spreading of the feature nasal". In this chapter, the names of features will be capitalized', and the values of features will be in square brackets. The values always form a set of mutually exclusive properties. The possible values of one of the features, Labial, are shown in Figure 19.2. If the Supralaryngeal node has been selected, then the Place node will also have been selected. This implies that one of the features below it must be chosen, and that that feature will have a particular value. But the Place features (a shorthand way of saying the features dominated by the Place node) are not in bold, as only one of them need be selected so that the Place node can be given some value.

The Place node dominates four possibilities which define the active articulators. The IPA tradition, and that adopted in many textbooks, such as Ladefoged (1993), has been to regard place of articulation as a continuum from the glottis to the lips, with major points indicated, but with little or no structure defined among the points along the continuum. This is not the appropriate way of organizing linguistic phonetic features. The arguments advanced by Halle (1983), Sagey (1986), Gorecka (1989) and many others are correct in emphasizing the importance of the active articulator. In this way one can make more satisfactory statements concerning what double articulations are possible, and what articulators are free to make secondary articulations. Perhaps equally importantly, the notion of adjacent articulations can be given more meaning, if the description first indicates the active articulator. Thus a velar and a uvular stop are really adjacent articulations, differing only by a comparatively small movement of the body of the tongue, specifiable in terms of the same feature Dorsal; but a sublaminal retroflex and a velar stop are far apart, one being a type of coronal articulation, and the other involving dorsal activity, making them very distinct sounds and not really "adjacent" although they might be in adjacent columns on a consonant chart.

As is shown in Figure 19.2, Labial articulations are of three different types. The first, which involves the vertical movement of one lip towards the other, we will regard as the modal or neutral form of labial compression; this is the movement involved in a normal bilabial stop. The second is rounding, the drawing of the corners of the lips together, which is the movement involved in the labial–velar approximant [w], a sound which also involves a high back tongue gesture. A third possibility might be that the lips can be protruded without necessarily drawing the corners forward. But from a phonological point of view, rounding and protrusion do not seem to be distinct gestures; they may be combined in ways that are specific to individuals, or perhaps (as suggested by Linker 1982) in ways that are characteristic of languages. But they do not distinguish linguistic information. A truly different lip gesture is that involved in labiodental sounds, in which the lower lip is retracted so that it approaches the upper teeth. These three values correspond to what, in a different context, Keating (1984) calls major phonetic categories. They can be regarded as the three named values within the Labial continuum: [protruded], [compressed], and [retracted].

A constraint that should be made evident by the feature system is the fact that bilabials can be accompanied by lip protrusion, whereas labiodentals cannot. Labiodentals can be *followed* by a high back rounded (i.e. labial–velar) approximant, and in this sense can be rounded; but while the lower lip is being retracted for a labiodental it cannot be simultaneously protruded. It is interesting in this respect to note the details of the lip movements that occur in some of the languages that contrast bilabial and labiodental fricatives. In Ewe (as shown by the photographs in Ladefoged, 1968), the bilabials [ɸ,β] are made with simple lip compression, whereas the labiodentals [f,v] are clearly distinguished by actively raising the upper lip, a gesture that makes them sound even further from any impression of lip rounding that might be associated with the bilabials. In Venda the reverse procedure occurs. The labiodentals [f,v] do not have a distinctive raising of the upper lip; but the bilabials [ɸ,β] do sometimes have a slight lip protrusion that emphasizes their non-retracted character, and makes them sound slightly rounded.

The notion of a continuum within the feature Labial is captured in Figure 19.2 by regarding Labial as a three valued feature, the three named possibilities being [protruded], [compressed], and [retracted]. These values are also sufficient to account for the differences in lip shape that distinguish the Swedish high front rounded vowels [y] and [ʉ]. Both these vowels have a value for Labial, [y] being [protruded], and [ʉ] being [compressed].

The phonological representation of labial gestures in terms of the three values [protruded], [compressed], and [retracted] involves a simplification of the phonetic facts. These three values are not really on a single dimension. The opposite of protruded lips is not a retracted lower lip; it is spread lips, in which *both* lips are retracted by drawing back the corners. Consequently it is a distortion to regard the formation of labiodentals as involving the opposite of protrusion; in forming labiodentals the lower lip is slightly retracted while the upper lip is not. Nonetheless the use of these three terms as oppositions within a single feature is completely appropriate. The question we must ask is whether it allows us to capture a phonological truth, or whether it simply obscures the phonetic facts. The answer is evident when we recall the purpose of these representations. We are trying to set up a system for representing just the phonological facts of languages. The simplification of the physiological phonetic facts allows us to see patterns of sounds that are otherwise not evident, and it is therefore fully justified. By regarding the spreading of the lips in a non-rounded vowel as equivalent to the retracting of the lower lip in the formation of the labiodental we can see a phonological universal: labiodentals cannot be contrastively protruded. If we had used two binary features, one to specify the difference between labials and labiodentals, and the other to specify that between sounds with lip protrusion and sounds with lip spreading, we would not have been able to make this point, except by an *ad hoc* statement.

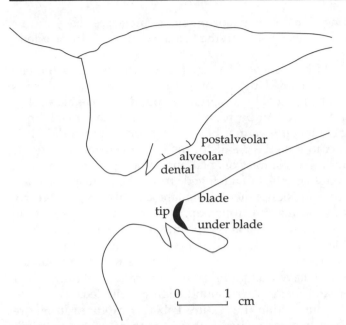

Figure 19.3 The parts of the vocal tract involved in the definition of Coronal articulations.

Putting this another way, we are making the claim that the differences between sounds made with spread lips and labiodentals are a matter of phonetic detail which does not play any role in phonological descriptions.

When we come to consider Coronal articulations, it becomes obvious that many points are still not clear, particularly with regard to the interactions between the tip, blade, and front of the tongue. As these terms themselves do not necessarily mean the same thing for all phoneticians, we had better begin by considering how they will be used. There is no way in which one can be precise about these matters both because the tongue is a continuous body with no relevant anatomical landmarks and because people vary considerably in the shapes of their mouths. The terms will be used as indicated in Figure 19.3.

The tip of the tongue at rest is considered to be just the part that has a primarily vertical aspect (i.e. largely parallel to the surfaces of the teeth) plus a small area about 2 mm wide on the upper surface. Sounds made with the tip of the tongue are said to be apical. The underside of the tip of the tongue is used in some articulations; sounds made in this way are said to be sublaminal. Behind the tip is the blade, which is the defining part of the tongue for sounds that are said to be laminal. It is difficult to say how far back the blade extends before what is called the front of the tongue begins. Probably the most useful definition of the blade of the tongue from a linguistic phonetic point of view is in terms of its relation to the roof of the mouth. It is the part of the tongue below the center of the alveolar ridge when the tongue is at rest. This, of

Table 19.1 The likelihood of different combinations of values of the features Apicality and Anterior

Apicality	Anterior		
	[dental]	[alveolar]	[postalveolar]
[laminal]	(1) ***	(2) *	(3) **
[apical]	(4) *	(5) ***	(6) **
[sublaminal]	(7)	(8) ?	(9) *

See text for discussion of the entries in each cell.

course, requires us to define the alveolar ridge – an equally difficult task. The center of the ridge is the point of maximum slope behind the upper teeth in the curvature of the mid-line sagittal section of the vocal tract. In practice this is often difficult to determine but it is probably the most useful point that can be approximated in a wide selection of individuals. Laminal sounds are made with the part of the tongue that has its center, when the tongue is at rest, immediately below the center of the alveolar ridge. The laminal area extends forward to about 2 mm behind the tip of the tongue, and backward to a point about 2 mm behind the point on the tongue below the center of the alveolar ridge.

Given these definitions of the tongue blade and of the alveolar ridge it is clear that palatal sounds are not Coronal. True palatal sounds are not articulated with the blade of the tongue raised; a more posterior part of the tongue, traditionally known as the front (of the body) of the tongue is used. It is also the front of the tongue, not the blade, that is operative in the high front vowel [i]. There are a few rare vowels, such as the Swedish [i], in which the blade of the tongue plays a subsidiary role, but in by far the majority of cases it is clear that high front vowels cannot be said to be Coronal.

The determination of the center of the alveolar ridge also enables us to define three parts of the upper surface of the vocal tract that are relevant to the discussion of Coronal articulations. Sounds made on the teeth are obviously dental; those that are made behind the teeth but in front of the center of the alveolar ridge are alveolar; and those that are made immediately behind the center of the alveolar ridge are postalveolar.

These distinctions allow us to define the two features dominated by the Coronal node: Apicality, which specifies the action of the lower, active, articulator; and Anterior, which specifies the part of the upper, passive, articulator that is involved. Each of these features has three named values as shown in Table 19.1. This table also shows estimates of the likelihood of different combinations of the two features. As Maddieson (1984a) notes, the published data on this matter are not very reliable. Many writers do not distinguish between apical and laminal gestures, or between dental and alveolar sounds. In descriptions of many languages, for example, English and French, this is quite appropriate, as there is a great deal of individual variation; Dart (1991) has shown that although many speakers of English have basically alveolar articulations for [d], about one third of her sample of 20 speakers did not; and although many speakers of French have something like a laminal dental articulation for [d], again about one third do not.

Table 19.1 shows estimates of the likelihood of the various possible combinations for the different values of Apicality and Anterior, enabling us to assess whether these are truly independent features. Among languages that distinguish alveolar and dental sounds, and thus require a phonological specification of these features, most languages have laminal dentals and apical alveolars. To signify this, cells 1 and 5 in Table 19.1 are marked with three asterisks. The alternative possibility in which the dentals are apical and the alveolars are laminal, occurs in only a few languages, so cells 2 and 4 in the table have only a single asterisk. Although the members of these two pairs of articulatory combinations might appear to be equally distinct from an articulatory point of view, the acoustic distinction between apical dental and laminal alveolar is far less than that between laminal dental and apical alveolar.

Sublaminal dental sounds (cell 7) have not been observed in any known language, and have therefore not been marked at all in Table 19.1. They are highly improbable phonological elements, although they are not impossible sounds to produce. Similarly, it is doubtful if it is ever necessary to classify sounds as being sublaminal and alveolar, and this combination (cell 8) is therefore marked with a question mark. Given all this, we might well ask whether Apicality is really a feature with three possible phonological values. A possible answer comes from considering the third column. All three possibilities for post-alveolar sounds have been observed, although not as phonologically contrastive items. Cells 3 and 6, laminal post alveolar and apical postalveolar, may be said to specify the difference between [ɕ] and [ʂ] in languages such as Polish. This is also the principal phonetic difference between the phonologically contrastive laminal postalveolar stops and nasals (in IPA terms, palatoalveolars) and apical postalveolar stops and nasals (IPA retroflex sounds) in Australasian languages such as Nunggubuyu and Wangurri. There are no attested phonological contrasts between apical postalveolars (cell 6) and sublaminal postalveolars (cell 9) the former occurring in Hindi and other Indo-Aryan languages, and the latter in Telugu and other Dravidian languages spoken in Southern India (Ladefoged and Bhaskararao 1983). They are clearly distinct sounds, and it is not at all improbable that these differences should be phonologically distinct within a single language.

Table 19.2 shows the contrasts that occur in various languages; examples of contrasts in these languages are given in Ladefoged and Maddieson (1996). Of the nine possibilities shown, only a few languages such as Nunggubuyu

Table 19.2 Languages illustrating the use made of different combinations of the possible values of the features Apicality and Anterior

Apicality	Anterior		
	[dental]	[alveolar]	[postalveolar]
[laminal]	Malayalam Nunggubuyu	Temne	Malayalam Nunggubuyu
[apical]	Temne	Malayalam Nunggubuyu	Hindi Nunggubuyu
[sublaminal]			Malayalam

contrast more than three. But it would take somewhat procrustean efforts to classify all the contrasts with two binary features, or even in terms of one binary feature and one three-valued feature. If we are to retain the ability to compare the phonological description of one language with that of another, we need two features, each with three possible values.

Any three-valued feature can, of course, always be replaced by two binary features. But, when this is done, it is no longer evident from the formal structure itself that a segment cannot be specified as being, for example, both [dental] and [postalveolar]. In addition, the use of three-valued features in Table 19.2 shows how Malayalam uses the three way possibilities along the diagonal between Apicality and Anterior to maximize contrasts among similar sounds, a fact that would not be evident if four binary features were used to classify these sounds, as suggested by Mohanan and Mohanan (1984). Furthermore, the three way division of the feature Anterior offers an appropriate way of showing the low level allophonic variations that occur in English words such as "eighth, eight, tray" which in many pronunciations have dental, alveolar, and postalveolar allophones of /t/. However, neither Anterior nor Apicality presents a strong basis for arguing the case for multi-valued features. Generally speaking, phonological processes involving these two features can be adequately expressed using binary values.

We noted earlier that the feature Apicality refers to properties of the active articulator, the tip or blade of the tongue; whereas Anterior refers to the passive articulator, the site on the roof of the mouth of the articulation. As both features are dominated by the major node Coronal, it is a constraint of the theory that one of the three sites of the passive articulator can be specified only when one of the three possibilities for the active articulator is also specifiable. Gorecka (1989) has a more far reaching proposal, which is tantamount to reviving in a fuller form the traditional notions of active and passive

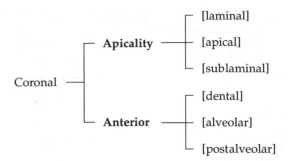

Figure 19.4   The expansion of the feature Coronal.

articulators. She proposes a feature hierarchy in which there are two sister nodes, Site (= passive articulator) and Articulator (= active articulator), instead of the hyper-feature Place. This seems a retrograde step, in that the theory would then permit a great number of combinations of Site and Articulator that never occur, making it possible, for example, to specify labial alveolar or apical palatal sounds, which most people can learn to make.

Gorecka does not address the problem of why possible combinations such as labial alveolar or apical palatal sounds do not exist. She does suggest that truly impossible articulations, such as laminal pharyngeals, are ruled out by physiological constraints that are not part of a linguistic theory. But even given that our linguistic theories exist alongside other theories, such as a theory of possible physiological gestures, it is not clear why these particular physiological constraints should be permitted to be outside linguistics. We have already relied on a physiological basis for other parts of the theory. When we say that there are four and only four types of articulatory gestures (labial, coronal, dorsal and radical) we are encapsulating within our linguistic theory a part of the theory of possible physiological gestures. A feature theory should, in itself, provide an account of what is, and what is not, linguistically possible. It is part of linguistics, not physiology, that no language has sublaminal uvular stops, just as it is part of linguistics that labial articulations can be combined with dorsal articulations. Accordingly we should have a feature theory with a constrained notion of possible types of Coronal and other articulations.

The above discussion can be summarized by reference to a further fragment of the feature hierarchy, shown in Figure 19.4. This allows us to give another example of the constraints imposed by the hierarchical structure in the kind of linguistic phonetic specification being outlined here. If a sound is specified as being Coronal it must have potential values for both the feature Apicality and the feature Anterior. For this reason, both these features are in bold in Figure 19.4. The values may be plus or minus if binary oppositions are being maintained, or [laminal], or [apical] or [sublaminal], and [dental], or [alveolar] or [postalveolar] in a three valued system. The values may be specified by default whenever Coronal is specified. But it is not possible to have a sound that

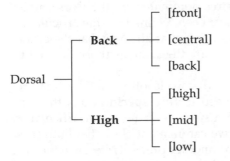

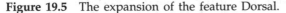

Figure 19.5   The expansion of the feature Dorsal.

is Coronal and does not have potential values for both Apicality and Anterior. It is only when a sound is, say, Labial and not Coronal, that neither Apicality nor Anterior is specifiable. Thus at an abstract level in the phonology, the higher place nodes may act as cover features, designating sets of values of the terminal features. But Coronal is not itself a terminal feature. If it were then it would have to be defined in terms of some properties; and this cannot be done independently of the characteristics of Anterior and Apicality or (Distributed in the SPE system).

Any of the features dominated by the hyper-feature Place may not need to be further distinguished in many phonological statements. It is often sufficient to characterize a sound as being simply Labial, Coronal, Dorsal or Radical. In such usages these terms are acting as cover features, or unary features. But although the phonologies of most languages do not need to make subtler distinctions, the phonological feature set has to provide finer distinctions, such as that between bilabial and labiodental sounds, because a few languages (e.g. Ewe and Venda) make use of them. Generally speaking we can use a set of default feature specification rules to fill in the lower level feature values, making it clear that, for example, Labial sounds are by default [bilabial] if they also have the value [stop], and by default [labiodental] if they also have the value [fricative]. A complete set of default feature specification rules will not be given here, as the hierarchy of features which is being proposed has not yet been sufficiently tested. Interesting work on these lines for a different feature set has been done by Dogil (1988).

The next feature, Dorsal, dominates the two features necessary for specifying sounds involving the body of the tongue. As is shown in Figure 19.5, these two features, Back and High, are in bold, as they both must have some value if a sound is Dorsal. The Dorsal node differs from the Labial and Coronal nodes we have been discussing by virtue of its role in classifying both consonants and vowels. For some vowels, one aspect, the degree of lip rounding, is specified by a feature dominated by the Labial node; and for a few rare vowels (e.g. American English and Chinese r-colored vowels) the role of the tip or blade may require specification of one or more Coronal features. But nearly all vowels can be described in terms of features dominated by the Dorsal node. The terms High (Low) and Back (Front) have been retained for the articulatory features as shown in Figure 19.5, although it is not at all clear that the classes of vowels defined by tongue body positions are the same as those defined by the traditional use of these terms.

The interactions between consonants and vowels often involve features dominated by the Dorsal node and we need feature specifications that link vowels and consonants appropriately. By using the same set of articulatory features for both vowels and consonants we can make it clear that both these classes of sounds have a great effect on one another precisely because they are produced within the same mouth. We need a phonetic theory that allows us to explain why velar consonants are more likely to have an advanced articulation before high front vowels than before back vowels. The same theory should make it evident that high vowels are more likely to be lowered by uvular consonants (as occurs in Serer, Squamish, Quechua, Montana Salish, and many other languages) than for the reverse to occur so that mid vowels are raised by uvulars (which never happens). The feature set proposed here allows explanatory statements of this kind. The features High and Front are multi-valued features, each describing an ordered set of possibilities. In this way high back vowels may be associated with velar consonants, mid back vowels with uvular consonants, and low back vowels with pharyngeal consonants. For front and central vowels the associations with consonants are less clear. High front vowels are akin to palatals. But mid front and central vowels have less consonant-like properties, and low front vowels cannot be said to be associated with any particular types of consonants. From a phonological point of view, they may be left unspecified with respect to these features, allowing the auditory features Height and Brightness, which we will consider later, to account for interactions among vowels.

True palatal consonants requiring the feature specification [front] are rare. Many of the sounds that are called palatals are more properly categorized as laminal postalveolars. For example, the symbol [ɲ] is not really appropriate for the nasal segment in the French word "agneau", nor is the symbol [ʎ] for the lateral segment in the Italian word "figlio". But true palatals, that is, sounds in which the body of the tongue is raised towards the hard palate well behind the postalveolar region occur, in, for example, Ngwo (see palatographic data in Ladefoged 1968, reprinted in Ladefoged and Maddieson 1996). Mohanan and Mohanan (1984) report that in one dialect of Malayalam there is a contrast between palatoalveolar (i.e. laminar postalveolar) nasals and true palatal nasals. Hardman (1966) gives clear evidence of contrasts between true palatal, velar, and uvular stops in Jaqaru.

If we take it as axiomatic that more complex segments are less likely to occur than simple segments, then we can account for the comparative rarity of palatals by following a suggestion made by Keating and Lahiri (1993), and considering them to be complex segments. They are complex in that they have both Coronal and Dorsal attributes, having both the blade and the front of the tongue raised. This solution is in accord with palatographic data such as that

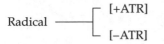

Figure 19.6   The possible values of the feature Radical.

of Doke (1931) for Shona [ɲ]. But it does not agree with the palatographic data for Ngwo, nor with the x-ray data for Hungarian palatals in Bolla (1980); both these sources show no Coronal articulation (the tongue blade is not actively raised) for the palatal stops. The feature system in Figure 19.5 allows for the two possibilities; palatals can be classified as either [high, front] Dorsal sounds or as complex segments that are both Coronal and Dorsal, as suggested by Keating and Lahiri (1993).

The final place node, Radical, classifies articulatory gestures made with the root of the tongue, as shown in Figure 19.6. This feature is relevant in the descriptions of comparatively few languages. Furthermore, it seems that the phonologies of even these languages require only two values, which may be referred to as [advanced tongue root] as opposed to [epiglottal], or [+ ATR] as opposed to [− ATR]. As was first shown by Ladefoged (1964), the vowel harmony sets in languages such as Igbo can be described in terms of the advancement of the tongue root. This feature is also relevant in the specification of so-called pharyngeal consonants in Arabic and other Semitic languages, although in these cases it is the value [epiglottal] that is more appropriately specified. The strident vowels of some Khoisan languages (Snyman 1975, Traill 1985, Ladefoged and Traill 1980) can also be classified as [epiglottal].

There are a number of sounds that have two active articulators, so that they form complex segments characterized by segments dominated by two place nodes. One of the justifications for the division of the traditional places of articulation into four groups, each dominated by a single node, is that this framework allows us to specify all and only the combinations that can occur. As has been noted by Sagey (1986), complex segments formed by combinations of the place nodes within a single segment are not uncommon. Labial plus Dorsal articulations as in [k͡p, ɡ͡b] are the best known; Coronal plus Dorsal articulations occur in clicks; and Radical plus Dorsal articulations occur in some Caucasian fricatives (Catford 1977b). We have also noted that palatal sounds can sometimes be considered as complex segments with Coronal and Dorsal attributes. Furthermore, what are traditionally known as secondary articulations (labialization, palatalization, velarization, pharyngealization) can be regarded as combinations of two different places involving different strictures.

1.2 *Manners of articulation*

More work is needed in the characterization of the hyper-feature Manner. The hierarchical structure of the features dominated by this node is extremely hard

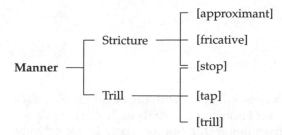

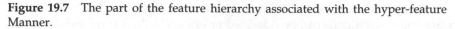

Figure 19.7   The part of the feature hierarchy associated with the hyper-feature Manner.

to formalize. Many contemporary phonologists maintain that there are two important articulatory manner features, one specifying the opposition Sonorant – Obstruent, and the other the opposition Continuant–Noncontinuant (stop). Neither of these pairs of oppositions is defined in the traditional way by Chomsky and Halle (1968). Before their work the term Sonorant meant just voiced non-obstruent sounds. For Chomsky and Halle sonorants also include [h, ʔ] and voiceless nasals and laterals, providing a natural class that is not as useful as the classical grouping. The other differences from classical usage are in the term stop, which used to mean a complete stoppage of the airstream, and therefore excluded nasals, and the term continuant, which used to mean a sound that could be continued, and therefore included nasals. In contemporary phonological usage nasals are regarded as stops. This is a comparatively minor terminological change, which leads to useful phonological groupings.

   A serious problem with feature theories of the SPE type is that there is no way of defining the natural class of fricatives such as [ʃ,θ,s,f] in terms of a single property that they have in common. It is, of course, not sufficient to include a feature Sibilant (Strident) because not all fricatives are sibilants. It is more appropriate to set up an articulatory feature, Stricture, with [fricative] as one of its named values as shown in Figure 19.7. There are many advantages to having a feature Stricture with the three possibilities [stop, fricative, approximant]. These items form a set of mutually exclusive possibilities; and, as we have been noting, it is an important aspect of any phonology that it should be able to make clear what can and what cannot co-occur. Furthermore, as noted earlier (Ladefoged 1971:55): "These values form a linearly ordered set, by means of which we [can] give an explanatory account of lenition phenomena, in which stops weaken to fricatives, and a further weakening gives rise to approximants." This phenomenon is exemplified in the pronunciation of the Danish words "lade foged" (barn steward). The original voiced stops in these words have weakened, first to fricatives [ð] and [ɣ], and then to approximants (frictionless continuants) eventually becoming (at least in the case of the velar consonant) omitted altogether in modern Danish. Progressive changes from stop through fricative to approximant are not easy to explain in terms of binary features. In the system being proposed here the Danish changes (and similar variations in other languages such as Spanish) are simply assimilations in which the intervocalic stops become more and more like the surrounding approximants.

Ladefoged (1971:55) rejected the notion of a single feature with the values [stop, fricative, approximant] because it did not permit fricative to be regarded as a separate feature that could be added to stops for the characterization of affricates. Now, however, formalisms have been developed (Goldsmith 1979, Halle and Vergnaud 1980) that allow us to note sequential attributes of a segment within a single slot in the CV structure. Steriade (1993) has formalized these notions more precisely by requiring all stops (and only stops) to be given a feature specification for both closure and release. In this way affricates can be assigned the correct feature values in the correct order.

We now need to formalize the relationship between the different degrees of Stricture and the kinds of trills that are found. Trills can occur with friction (as they do in Czech) or without as in most occurrences of these sounds, in which case the value of the Stricture feature may be said to be [approximant]. The one value of Stricture that is entirely incompatible with any form of trill is the [stop] value. A way of capturing this situation is to set up a feature Trill with three values [stop], [tap], [trill], the first of these values overlapping with one of the values of the feature Stricture. This grouping also has the merit that it shows that stops can more easily become taps (as in American English) than they can become trills; and that taps and trills can alternate (as they do in some forms of Scottish English) more readily than trills and stops. There seems to be a good case for saying that taps are, in some sense, in between trills and stops.

We should also consider whether the distinction between a tap and a flap is worth pursuing. Earlier Ladefoged (1971) noted that "A flap is . . . distinguished from a tap by having one articulator strike another in passing while on its way back to its rest position, as opposed to striking immediately after leaving its rest position [in a tap]." It now seems that this may be only an incidental difference between taps and flaps, because flaps (if defined as in the quoted sentence) always have a more retracted articulation than taps. It may therefore be appropriate to consider a flap as a tap with a different place specification. There is no phonological reason for distinguishing between the two. However, this is not a completely satisfactory solution, as the dynamics of the two gestures are so very different. A tap involves a small movement of the tip of the tongue, whereas a flap necessitates a backward movement of the body of the tongue, as well as a large upward and backward movement of the tip. A tap has the same transition into and out of it; a flap does not.

1.3 Laterality

All theories of phonetic description recognize the necessity to provide for the distinction between central and lateral sounds. Many phonologists and most

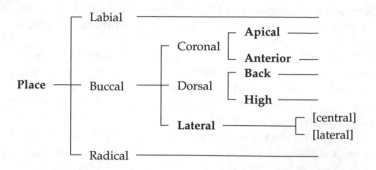

Figure 19.8   The location of the feature Lateral within the feature hierarchy.

traditional phoneticians would consider the feature Lateral to be under Manner in the hierarchy. But before we do this, we should consider the constraints on its applicability. Different values of the feature Lateral can occur with each of the values of Stricture, and with at least the [tap] value of the feature Trill. Distinctions between central and laterally released stops are common (e.g. in Mayan languages). Such differences could be regarded as sequential attributes of a single segment, as is appropriate for affricates. But it is less clear that this solution can be adopted in the case of clicks, which are also stops that utilize the central-lateral opposition. Most languages with clicks (Xhosa, !Xóõ) contrast a central alveolar click [!] with a lateral alveolar click [ǁ]. An independent specification of the feature Lateral is also required in the case of fricatives. Zulu, for example, has both a central alveolar fricative [z] and a lateral alveolar fricative [ɮ]. The third possible value of the feature Stricture, [approximant] supports a [central] vs. [lateral] contrast in many languages, including most forms of English, as in [ɹ] and [l]. Contrasts between taps with [central] vs. [lateral] specifications (i.e. [r] and [ɺ]) occur in Bantu languages such as Chaga.

There are more constraints on the places of articulation that can occur with the value [lateral]. It is not true that, as Chomsky and Halle (1968) suggested, only Coronal sounds can be specified for laterality. Dorsal sounds can be lateral, in that velar laterals occur in Mid-Waghi and other languages spoken in Papua New Guinea (Ladefoged, Cochran and Disner 1977). These sounds definitely have articulatory contact only in the velar region, and a narrowing of the tongue from side to side, so that air escapes laterally. But neither Labial nor Radical sounds can be contrastively [lateral]. The most appropriate way to express these constraints on the feature Lateral is to regard it as being dominated by the hyper-feature Place, as shown in Figure 19.8.

An additional node, Buccal (belonging to the mouth), has been added to include both Coronal and Dorsal segments. These features dominate the features Apical, Anterior, Back and High, as described above. But they also have a sister node, Lateral, in bold face, indicating that whenever a sound has any form of Buccal specification, it must also have a value for the feature Lateral.

1.4 Nasality

The hyper-feature Nasality is fairly straightforward. It dominates a single terminal feature, Nasal, which applies to both consonants and vowels. From a phonological point of view, this is clearly a binary feature, in that sounds are either [+ nasal] or [− nasal]. At one time (Ladefoged 1971) it was considered that Chinantec (Merrifield 1963), has surface contrasts between oral, lightly nasalized and heavily nasalized sounds, but later research has shown that some of these sounds are sequences, the contrasts being of the form [a - ã - ãn], with the final consonant being very short. Again we must also note that there are co-occurrence constraints on this feature; among consonants only stops can be contrastively [+nasal] or [−nasal].

1.5 Laryngeal features

Before we look at the terms dominated by the Laryngeal node, we must consider the phonological relations that we want these features to capture. Virtually all phonologists regard the opposition voiced–voiceless as an important aspect of natural classes of sounds. (A notable exception is Halle, who for many years (Halle and Stevens 1971, Halle 1988) has advocated feature systems that replace the functions of the feature Voiced with various combinations of the four features Stiff, Slack, Spread and Constricted.) Another widely recognized set of phonological possibilities is that for variations in Voice Onset Time (VOT). Although there may be low level phonetic differences, from a phonological point of view there are only three possibilities: aspirated, voiceless unaspirated, and voiced (Keating 1984). We also need to be able to categorize differences in phonation types. Again, from a phonological point of view we need recognize only three types: breathy voice, modal voice and creaky voice (Ladefoged, Maddieson and Jackson 1988). Closely tied in with the phonation types are the movements of the glottis that produce the glottalic airstream mechanism. Finally we must not overlook the obvious fact that specifications of tone and intonation can be regarded as part of the hyperfeature Laryngeal, although no attempt will be made here to give a system for the representation of these aspects of language.

These considerations lead to a specification of the feature Laryngeal as shown in Figure 19.9. The three phonation types are part of the five possible values of Glottal stricture that are used by languages. Sounds can have the vocal cords tightly together, as in a glottal stop, or they can be far apart as in voiceless sounds, or they can have one of the three phonation types: breathy voice, modal voice and creaky voice. Although some phoneticians (Laver 1980, Catford 1977a) have shown how terms similar to these may be combinable from the phonetic point of view, the named terms form a set of phonologically mutually exclusive possibilities. There is never any need to classify a segment as

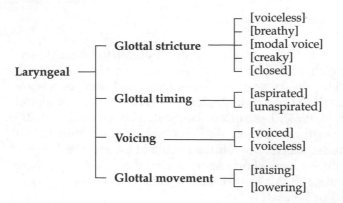

Figure 19.9 The part of the feature hierarchy dominated by the feature Laryngeal.

being phonologically both [breathy] and [creaky]. We should also note that [breathy] sounds are in some sense between [voiceless] and [modal voice] sounds. In this way we can regard the breathy voiced quality of the /h/ in English "ahead" as being due to an assimilatory process. Similarly [creaky] sounds are in between the [modal voice] and the [closed] value of Glottal Stricture. Allophonic variations between glottal stops and creaky voice occur in Mazatec (Kirk, Ladefoged and Ladefoged 1994), Hausa (Lindau 1984) and many other languages. These factors point to there being an ordered set of five possibilities: [voiceless], [breathy], [modal voice], [creaky] and [closed]. These are all clearly mutually exclusive possibilities; if a sound has breathy voice, as in murmured sounds, it cannot be phonologically creaky, and so on. It might be that the five named types of glottal stricture can be regarded as the product of two ternary oppositions, as suggested by Stevens (1988). It is certainly appropriate to consider these glottal states as resulting from two physiological attributes of the vocal cords, their stiffness and their aperture. However from a linguistic phonetic point of view, the named values of the feature Glottal Stricture operate as a linearly ordered set of five mutually exclusive possibilities.

Variations in Voice Onset Time (VOT) are here regarded as a property of Glottal Timing. It is possible to consider aspiration as an extreme form of voicelessness, making a sixth term in the Glottal Stricture set. But data provided by Dixit (1989) indicates that the degree of aspiration is not simply related to the degree of glottal stricture, as was once thought (Kim 1970, Ladefoged 1971). Furthermore, despite the fact that many languages (e.g. Thai and Eastern Armenian) have sets of stops with the three possibilities, voiced, voiceless unaspirated, aspirated, Glottal Timing is best regarded as a binary feature, with only the possible values [+ aspiration] and [– aspiration]. We already have other features that will distinguish between voiced and voiceless sounds, and there are no convincing examples that show that a three term series is necessary for phonological reasons. There would need to be a rule whereby, for example, voiced stops become voiceless unaspirated stops in the same circumstances as voiceless unaspirated stops become aspirated (i.e. [b → p] and [p → pʰ] in the same circumstances). Failing the occurrence of such a rule, it is better to consider Glottal Timing to be a binary feature. This allows us to formulate simple explanatory statements showing how both voiced and voiceless aspirated stops (i.e. [bʰ, pʰ] etc.) act together to form a natural class.

Figure 19.9 also illustrates another important point that we will consider in detail later, namely the fact that not all features have articulatory (physiological) values. We need a separate feature, Voice, which specifies whether the vocal cords are vibrating, as in breathy, modal, and creaky sounds, or voiceless, as in both spread and closed types of glottal stricture. The feature Glottal Stricture does not provide a direct way of explaining why most sounds are either voiced or voiceless. There has to be a separate feature accounting for these two very natural classes of sounds. Glottal stops are [voiceless], despite the fact that the glottal gesture involved is absolutely the opposite of that in most other voiceless sounds. We will consider Voice as a feature that is best defined in terms of its auditory properties.

The closed glottis can be moved upward and downward, so as to produce a glottalic airstream mechanism. There are two possibilities, which are obviously mutually exclusive: ejective and implosive. Voiceless ejectives occur in many languages, for example Amharic, Navajo and Xhosa; voiced ejectives are unknown. Voiced implosives are many times more common than voiceless implosives, occurring in, for example, Sindhi and Kalabari. Both voiced and voiceless implosives occur at the same place of articulation in Owerri Igbo (Ladefoged, Williamson, Elugbe and Uwalaka 1976). The likelihood of the different combinatory possibilities is not adequately accounted for in the feature hierarchy given here.

It might be appropriate to consider other interactions among laryngeal gestures, such as the alternations between voiced plosives and implosives that occur in widely different languages such as Thai and Zulu. We could also note the well known connection between voiceless sounds and high pitch. But there are also converse facts to be acknowledged. Fully voiced stops (as well as voiceless unaspirated and aspirated stops) contrast with both voiced and voiceless implosives in Owerri Igbo (Ladefoged, Williamson, Elugbe and Uwulaka 1976), making it impossible to equate full voicing with implosion. In most tone languages both high and low tones occur in syllables with both voiced and voiceless consonants, so we do not want a complete identification of high tone with voicelessness. Nevertheless it is important to bear in mind that there are a number of commonly observed interactions among features whereby a particular value of one feature enhances a distinction that is primarily signaled by another featural opposition, as suggested by Stevens and Keyser (1989). Possible enhancing interactions should be formalized within a complete phonetic theory, although it is not yet clear how this should be done.

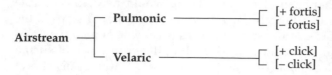

Figure 19.10   The part of the feature hierarchy dominated by the Airstream feature.

1.6 Airstream mechanisms

The final hyper-feature shown in Figure 19.1 is Airstream. The feature set outlined here departs slightly from traditional phonetic descriptions, in that this hyper-feature is regarded as dominating only two possibilities, pulmonic and velaric, as shown in Figure 19.10. Glottalic airstreams are here considered to be properties of the hyper-feature Laryngeal.

It might seem as if there were no need to specify the presence of the pulmonic airstream mechanism, as it is present in all sounds. It is, however, necessary to note that some sounds have an increase in lung power associated with them. For example, Dart (1987) has shown quite conclusively that Korean so-called fortis stops have a significant increase in pulmonic pressure, as well as differences in phonation type.

The possible classificatory values for the Pulmonic feature have been called [+ fortis] and [− fortis]. More apt descriptive names might have been [+ heightened subglottal pressure] and [− heightened subglottal pressure], a pair of terms suggested by Chomsky and Halle (1968). These terms have been avoided here, because they have also been used to describe other phenomena, such as the opposition between aspirated and unaspirated sounds, a usage for which there is no physiological foundation (see Ladefoged 1971:96). Another possibility rejected here is to use the terms [+ stress] and [− stress], although the most common manifestation of stress is an increase in subglottal pressure much of the kind used in Korean fortis stops. From a phonological point of view stress is usually a property of a larger unit than a segment, and therefore not like the features we have been considering. There are very few occasions on which it is appropriate to describe a consonantal element of the CV structure as having a value of the feature Pulmonic; segments such as the Korean fortis stops seem to be very rare.

The feature Velaric, with its two possible values [+ click] and [− click] provides the natural classes required in the description of Khoisan and Nguni languages. It would be possible to classify these sounds simply as examples of multiple articulations, as suggested by Sagey (1986); but there seems to be no phonological advantage in doing this, other than an apparent economy of description. The velaric airstream mechanism occurs in conjunction with the pulmonic airstream mechanism, in that clicks are accompanied by velar or uvular stops of some kind. Clicks may also require a simultaneous specification of the glottalic airstream mechanism, as in Zhulhõasi [k!ˣʼ] in which there is an affricated velar ejective accompanying an alveolar click (Ladefoged and Traill 1993). The features dominated by the Airstream node are in bold, as one of them must always be specified; but, as in the case of the Place features, some sounds require the specification of more than one of them.

2 Auditory features

So far we have been considering only features that specify articulatory distinctions. But phonological features may be based on physiological or acoustic facts. There are several important natural classes that are the result of sounds having an acoustic structure such that they have certain auditory properties in common. It is somewhat ironic that this great insight of the Prague school, much touted by Jakobson, Fant and Halle (1951), should now be overlooked by the phonologists who are their successors. The present situation arises partly because of the view of phonology propounded by Chomsky and Halle (1968), in which features are considered to be mental entities. From this point of view it is just a matter of exposition as to whether features are defined in articulatory or acoustic terms. But this is simply not true. Segments may occasionally act together because of some abstract mental property, due to the outcome of historic process. But it is much more common for them to be grouped into natural classes because of specific properties relating to the way they are heard, or to the way they are produced. Of course all features have both articulatory and acoustic properties in the somewhat irrelevant sense that as soon as a feature has been defined in terms of one set of properties, it is possible to infer the other set of properties. Features are linguistic units that (among other things) characterize the lexical items of a language. These lexical items have to be capable of being both spoken and heard; and the features that characterize them must have both kinds of properties. But it does not follow from this that we should consider the linguistic function of a feature as being *required* in both domains or that we can define it equally well in either way. A similar view has been expressed by Lieberman (1970).

Table 19.3 lists some auditory features. The first is the feature Voice, which has two possible values, [+ voice] and [− voice], determined by the presence or absence of an acoustic structure with well defined harmonics. It might seem as if vocal cord vibration could be considered to be an articulatory action, thus making Voice definable in articulatory terms. In some senses this is so, but the vibrations are not themselves articulatory gestures; they are only the consequence of certain muscular actions. Furthermore, as we have noted, completely opposite articulatory gestures can produce the same value, [− voice], which occurs in both [h] and [ʔ]. There is no doubt that we need to consider such sounds as belonging to the same natural class; but it is not because they have some articulation in common.

One of the most well known auditory features is Grave, which groups some labial and velar sounds in accordance with their spectral characteristics. Sounds

Table 19.3   A set of features that have non-specific articulatory properties, but determine auditorily based natural classes.

Feature	Traditional terms	Possible values	Brief description
Voice	Voiced	[+voice]	periodic low frequency energy
	Voiceless	[–voice]	absence of such energy
Grave		[+grave]	aperiodic low frequency energy
		[–grave]	absence of such energy
Sibilant	Sibilant	[+sibilant]	aperiodic high frequency energy
		[–sibilant]	absence of such energy
Height	High vowel	[high]	low F1
	Mid-high	[mid high]	mid low F1
	Mid-low	[mid low]	mid high F1
	Low vowel	[low]	high F1
Brightness		[+brightness]	high (F2'-F1)
		[–brightness]	low (F2'-F1)
Sonorant		[+sonorant]	periodic energy with well-defined formants
		[–sonorant]	absence of such energy

such as [p,k,f,x] are produced in very different ways, but they sound similar because they have a comparatively large amount of aperiodic acoustic energy in the lower part of the spectrum. This similarity is reflected in historical changes such as English [x] to [f] in words such as "rough, tough," or the parallel phenomena in Danish whereby "lugt" becomes "luft" (Basböl 1974). These changes are completely inexplicable in articulatory terms. Phonological alternations involving the feature Grave have been described by Hyman (1975) who shows that different vowel allophones occur before Grave consonants in Fe?fe?. Other cases of phonological alternations include spirantization in Hebrew undergone by the Grave consonants /p, b, k/. There seems to be no doubt that Grave consonants form a natural class.

Chomsky and Halle discarded the feature Grave because they found it did not provide a satisfactory basis for characterizing differences in place of articulation. This is undoubtedly true; from an articulatory point of view the feature Grave does not distinguish the appropriate natural classes. But this does not mean that it fails to characterize a natural class of sounds from an auditory point of view. Throwing out Grave just because it does not have a useful articulatory correlate is as bad as it would be to throw out Nasal just because it does not have a unified set of acoustic correlates that form a basis for a natural class.

Note that the feature Grave as defined in Table 19.3 is not exactly the same as the feature proposed by Jakobson, Fant and Halle (1951). Their definition was "the predominance of one side of the significant part of the spectrum over the other." It was intended to include both consonants and vowels. The feature Grave as defined here is in practice restricted to obstruents (and, perhaps, voiceless approximants) because it stipulates that the auditory characteristic of a Grave sound is that there is salient *aperiodic* energy in the lower part of the spectrum. In speech, this type of energy occurs only in stop bursts and fricatives (and, perhaps, a voiceless labial-velar approximant). There is no auditory property of this sort that links particular vowels with particular consonants. Note also that this definition of Grave implies that [– grave] sounds are not necessarily Acute in the old Jakobsonian sense. All sounds that do not have a significant amount of aperiodic energy in the lower part of the spectrum are [– grave], irrespective of whether they have a significant amount of aperiodic energy in the upper part of the spectrum or whether they do not have any aperiodic energy at all.

Another auditory feature that is of importance in grouping consonants may be called Sibilant, following the traditional phonetic usage. It is not exactly equivalent to the Jakobsonian feature Strident in that the feature Strident has also been used to distinguish [f,v] from [ɸ,β], thus resulting in the rather unnatural class of strident sounds [f,v,s,z,ʃ,ʒ]. So as to make the difference in definition plain, it is preferable to retain the traditional term Sibilant, which has been used for a few centuries (e.g. by Holder 1669, and many phoneticians after him) to identify the class of sounds [s,z,ʃ,(ʒ)].

It is interesting to consider whether it might be possible to give an articulatory definition of this feature, in that Sibilant sounds are always pronounced with the jaw raised so that there is a very narrow gap between the upper and lower front teeth. The high frequency aperiodic acoustic energy that gives rise to the auditory characteristics of this feature is due to the jet of air striking this narrow gap (Catford 1977a, Shadle 1985, 1991). However, the fact that sibilant sounds have an articulatory attribute in common is an unlikely cause for their acting together in historical changes and morphological alternations. There is no evidence showing that jaw position is a salient characteristic of sounds causing them to be grouped together, whereas the auditory grouping of these sounds is evident in the perceptual confusion data of Miller and Nicely (1955) and its re-analysis by Shepard (1972).

It is appropriate at this point to consider further what is at issue in claiming that a certain feature (e.g. Sibilant) should be defined in auditory rather than articulatory terms. It is not a matter of whether there is or is not a feature of this kind. There is little doubt that sibilants form a natural class of sounds that act together in phonological rules. Nor is it a matter of formal evaluation of rules. Given that there is a feature Sibilant the system for evaluating its use within a phonology will be the same irrespective of its phonetic attributes. What is at stake is whether the auditory definition provides a better explanation for the grouping than a definition in terms of the articulatory attributes. Until there is some evidence for the shared articulatory properties being the reason for this grouping, it seems preferable to continue to maintain that the well attested salient auditory characteristics are the basis for the natural class.

The most outstanding features of the auditory type are properties of vowels. There is good evidence (e.g. Johnson, Ladefoged and Lindau 1993) that in producing vowels the targets at which speakers aim are defined by auditory properties, not by vocal tract configurations. From an auditory point of view, vowels such as [i e a o u] differ in terms of two auditory properties, which may be called Height and Brightness. Height is a well known term for describing an aspect of vowel quality, but it should be emphasized that here it is being regarded as simply an auditory property. As such, it cannot be defined in anything other than impressionistic terms reflecting a listener's judgments. It is like pitch, for which the only definition offered by the Acoustical Society of America is that it is that property of a sound that enables it to be ordered on a scale going from low to high. In the case of vowel Height the definition is that it is the property that enables a vowel to be ordered on an auditory scale of vowel height going from low to high. But just as pitch can be related to fundamental frequency, so can vowel Height be related to measurable acoustic parameters. It is generally agreed that the acoustic features that listeners attend to are formant frequencies and amplitudes. The major acoustic correlate of the auditory property vowel Height is the frequency of the first formant (F1).

We are not used to thinking of vowels simply as sounds to be judged in terms of auditory qualities. Our difficulties are further compounded by the fact that the auditory features we have considered so far, such as Grave and Strident, operate in a binary way. They are either present or absent, and we do not have to think in terms of scales, as we do for vowels. We all realize that the notes on a piano are arranged on a scale going from low to high. But most people find difficulty in thinking of any properties other than musical scales on which sounds can be ordered; loudness is the only other auditory property that is generally recognized. Nevertheless it is a fact that some pairs of sounds – [i] and [e] for example – are more alike than others – for example [i] and [a]. Accordingly there must be some property or properties of vowel sounds that enable listeners to make these judgments. These properties may, of course, be in the articulatory domain. It may be that listeners are simply referring their auditory impressions to their tacit knowledge of the articulations required to produce vowels, as suggested by the motor theory of speech perception (Liberman and Mattingley 1985). But there is no reason to believe that the auditory judgments that people make are in fact equivalent to their articulatory gestures.

The second auditory property of vowels has been termed Brightness ("Helligkeit") following Trubetzkoy (1969), and more recently Fischer-Jørgensen

(1985b). The acoustic correlates of Brightness are not fully established (it is another topic on which more research remains to be done), but we will take it to be (F2'-F1), the difference in frequency between the first formant and F2', a form of the second formant frequency modified so as to account for the influence of higher formants. Suitable formulae for calculating F2' are discussed by Bladon and Fant (1978). In a description of feature geometry as applied to vowels Odden (1991) has investigated the phonological possibilities of an auditory/acoustic feature which he calls Back-Round, which is very much akin to what we are here calling Brightness.

From an articulatory point of view, there is no reason why front unrounded and back rounded vowels should be more common than the reverse combinations. From an auditory point of view, the choice of these particular vowels is part of the tendency among languages to ensure sufficient perceptual contrasts. Phonologists who regard all features as having only articulatory definitions have no explanation for the remarkable facts of vowel distribution. But it should be emphasized that the notion that vowels should be specified in terms of auditory features does not mean that articulatory features do not also have a role in the description of vowels. The action of the body of the tongue in the production of a vowel is specifiable in terms of physiological features that are also applicable to consonants (and thus show the relations between vowels and consonants). There should be no doubt that in order to form the correct phonological classes, vowels have to be characterized in *both* physiological and auditory terms.

The next auditory feature listed in Table 19.3 is Sonorant, a feature which is defined in a slightly different way from the definition given by Chomsky and Halle (1968). In many languages sounds such as [m,n,l,r] act together as a class. For instance, in English these sounds are syllabic after a stop or a fricative, as at the ends of the words "table, tassel, sudden, prism, hidden", but not (for most of us) after other sonorants as in "film, kiln". The feature Sonorant is hard to define meaningfully in articulatory terms. The notion of "spontaneous voicing" (Chomsky and Halle 1968) does not get at the essence of what it is that causes vowels, nasals, laterals and some approximants to be grouped together. Better articulatory statements can be made in terms of the function of the articulatory system as a whole: sonorant sounds are those in which the vocal cords are vibrating and there is no significant build up of oral pressure. But if we are to claim that the feature Sonorant has this kind of articulatory basis, then we must claim that vocal cord vibrations and lack of pressure are both sensed by a speaker, and then combined so that together they are considered to form a salient psychological percept. This is a rather far-fetched notion for which there is no evidence. The fact that a feature can be defined in a certain way does not necessarily mean that this definition is any help in explaining why the feature groups sounds together into a natural class. Sonorant sounds are clearly related by having a periodic, well-defined, formant structure. They behave the same way within a language not because they are made alike, but because they sound alike.

Similar observations can be made about the feature Rhotacized, which is associated with a lowering of the frequencies of the third and fourth formants. As has been shown by Lindau (1985) many forms of *r* share this auditory characteristic, although they may have been produced by very different articulatory means. There is, however, a complicating factor in that Lindau also shows that some forms of *r* do not have this acoustic structure; they are linked to some (but not all) of the other r sounds by having a similar articulation.

Finally within this section we must note some differences between the auditory and the articulatory features that we have been discussing. As we noted earlier, linguistic phonetic features have three major functions: they specify the distinct utterances within a language; they permit the grouping of sounds into natural classes so that phonological patterns can be described in terms of rules; and they form part of a phonetic theory defining the set of possible segments in human language. The articulatory features serve all three of these functions, but the auditory features are more limited, serving only the second, expressing patterns in phonological rules. They are not necessary for characterizing linguistic items such as the words in the lexicon, nor for constraining the set of possible linguistic sounds.

3 The limits of linguistic phonetic theory

The theory of linguistic phonetics we have been developing in this chapter is obviously incomplete. We should now consider whether it can ever be complete. It seems likely that there will always be a small residue of sounds that cannot be accommodated within a formal framework. It is always possible to give some sort of description of any speech sound, however complex or exotic; any competent phonetician who can reproduce the sound can give an accurate account of the necessary vocal gestures. The problem lies in describing all sounds within a coherent theory of linguistic phonetics. This theory must use a specific set of terms to distinguish all possible linguistic contrasts. It must do this using phonologically appropriate features. It must also include a way of specifying all and only the set of possible speech sounds. These are tough constraints on a theory.

There are a number of examples of sounds that occur in only one or two languages which, if they were all included, would considerably complicate the feature hierarchy. Catford (1977b) has described bidental fricatives, in which the turbulence is caused by the flow of air between the clenched teeth. As far as is known, these sounds are used to form only a few linguistic contrasts in the Shapsug dialect of Adyghe (West Circassian). Traill (1991) has shown that there is an active pulmonic ingressive airstream mechanism, drawing air inwards, as an accompaniment of one of the clicks in !Xóõ. Even in the one dialect which uses this sound, it occurs in only a very few words. Another unusual sound occurs in Pirahã, a Mura language spoken by approximately

100 people in Brazil. According to Everett (1982) this language has "a voiced, lateralized apical-alveolar/sublaminal-labial double flap with egressive lung air. In the formation of this sound the tongue tip [first] touches the alveolar ridge and [then] comes out of the mouth, almost touching the upper chin as the underblade of the tongue touches the lower lip."

These sounds are more unusual than some others that are also not readily accommodated within the feature hierarchy we have been discussing. Maddieson (1989) has described a small group of Oceanic (Austronesian) languages that have linguo-labial stops, nasals and fricatives in which the tongue is protruded so as to make contact with the upper lip. This entails the possibility of a [+ laminal] specification along with one of the values of the feature Labial, which is not possible within the feature hierarchy we have been discussing, despite the fact that these are relatively common sounds in the languages in question. In this last case it seems quite clear that some modification of the hierarchy is required; but what should we do about the other unusual sounds mentioned above?

It is hard to find a scientific justification for not providing specific features for all these sounds so that they could be described within the general phonetic framework. We can only say that all theories describing the real world have fuzzy edges. But how frequent does a sound have to be before it is included? It is one thing to disregard what might (to our ethnocentric ears) seem like a freak sound occurring rarely and in only one language. But if it occurs in a few words in three languages is that sufficient to qualify for feature status? Or would ten languages be required? Any addition complicates the theory. It is just a matter of the price. We always have to decide whether the extra coverage is worth the cost.

We have made considerable progress in our goal of defining the set of possible linguistic sounds. A hierarchy with dominance relations as defined above expresses some of the essential constraints required by a theory of linguistic phonetics. The permissible feature combinations are severely limited by the rules concerning paths through the hierarchical structure. They show that only Labial sounds can be [protruded], only Coronal sounds can be [laminal], only Dorsal sounds can be specified for High or Back, only Coronal or Dorsal sounds can have a value for Lateral, and so on. These are all obvious constraints but they are not formally recognized without a definitional hierarchy of the kind described above. There are also constraints built in as a result of using multi-valued features. About half of the terminal features that have been described are multi-valued. If we had used binary features, additional combinations of terms, such as *[+high, +low], would have to have been ruled out as definitionally impossible. The introduction of unmotivated binary features would also have eliminated the advantages of linearly ordered sets (such as [high], [mid], [low]), which enables us to write more explanatory rules.

There are, however, many additional limitations on the set of possible phonological segments that have not yet been formalized. Some of these are absolute constraints. For example, if a segment is [+voice] it must also have one of the values [creaky], [modal] or [breathy] for the feature Glottal Stricture. Some other combinations of feature values are best regarded as phonological impossibilities. For example ejective nasals (to use a shorthand label for [stop], [+nasal], [ejective] segments) can be made, but they certainly do not appear. Some constraints are fairly complex. For example, if the Glottalic airstream is [ejective] then the Glottal Stricture must be [stop], and the articulatory Stricture must be [stop] or [fricative] as ejective approximants do not occur. There are also combinations of values of features which distinguish the sounds of one language from those of another, but which are not used contrastively within a single language. For example no language contrasts a voiceless alveolar lateral fricative [ɬ] and a voiceless alveolar lateral approximant [l̥]; but Maddieson and Emmorey (1984) have shown that some languages consistently use one of these possibilities and others the other. Distinctions such as these should be given some special status in a theory providing an account of all possible phonologically contrastive segments.

What is needed in order to complete this part of linguistic phonetic theory is a set of rules showing, perhaps by co-indexing, those feature combinations that are impossible and those that are highly unlikely. Underlying this there should be a theory of phonetic naturalness, a formal statement of the old idea of ease of articulation combined with some measures of auditory distinctiveness. We are a long way from being able to say what is and what is not phonologically possible; but the features discussed here are a step towards organizing our knowledge. Languages have lived a long time. They have developed intricate phonological structures, and grown complex. We cannot expect that a simple theory of linguistic phonetics will be sufficient.

NOTE

My thanks are due to my colleagues at the UCLA Phonetics Laboratory, who have helped develop these ideas, although they may not agree with them. The general scheme outlined in this paper is similar to that in a forthcoming book *The Sounds of the World's Languages* (Ladefoged and Maddieson, 1996); I am particularly indebted to Ian Maddieson for his suggestions concerning the placement of features specifying the glottalic airstream mechanism.

20 Phonetic Universals

IAN MADDIESON

1 Introduction

There are two general approaches to the question of universals in phonetics. One approach is based on drawing a distinction between the learned and the automatic or 'mechanical' aspects of speech behaviour. The second on considering the way that the phonetic aspects of language must be structured in order to satisfy the functional demands of communication. For convenience, these two approaches may be distinguished as the 'mechanistic' and the 'ecological', but they are not as disjunct as the labels attached to them may suggest. Nonetheless, because research efforts tend to be directed more toward one or the other there are two rather separate literatures on them. This chapter will be structured as a discussion of these two approaches in turn.

2 Learned versus inherent patterns

From the mechanistic viewpoint the particular way a given human language sounds is due to the interaction of two classes of processes. One class of processes is responsible for language-specific details, according to phonetic regularities governing the relationship between the phonological structure of the language and linguistically-relevant physical phonetic parameters. The other class shapes the sound patterns in ways that are necessarily universal, that is, they are the result of inherent properties of the mechanisms by which speech is produced and processed, and of the general physical laws under which the universe operates. The phonological structures and the language-specific rules must be learned as part of the process of acquiring a command of the individual language concerned. By contrast, it would be meaningless to talk of a speaker learning the processes that shape universals since these are simply part of the context within which speech exists.

As an example of the kind of distinction being drawn, consider a pair of English words such as 'pill' and 'kill'. The consonants at the beginnings of these words are usually pronounced with a substantial amount of aspiration, slightly longer with /k/ than with /p/. The fact that aspiration occurs here is a language-specific property of English; this can be expressed by saying that English speakers must learn a rule specifying that voiceless plosives are aspirated when they are initial in a stressed syllable. Other languages have a different distribution of aspiration, or lack it altogether. In contrast to this language-specific pattern, the fact that the duration of the aspiration is on average longer with the velar plosive than the bilabial is usually attributed to factors that are inherent in the use of this place contrast. This is because parallel variations in the duration of the voice onset interval can be found in languages that have no aspiration, such as Spanish and Hungarian, or have contrasting aspirated and unaspirated voiceless plosives, such as Cantonese and Hindi (Lisker and Abramson 1964).

As in this example, much of the work on 'mechanistic' universals has been based on the simple observation of patterns of repeated similarity across languages. When a pattern is seen to be widely repeated, the assumption is often made that it must in some way be a consequence of the fact that human beings all make use of the same basic equipment for speaking and listening and are subject to the same physical laws. Subsequently, a search may be conducted for an explanation of the pattern in these terms. One result of this mode of working, as well as the lack of precision of many of the existing models of speech processes, is that there are a good many putative universals for which no accepted explanation is available. As our understanding of speech production and perception mechanisms grows, it is increasingly likely that genuinely universal patterns can be predicted from more precise models of the processes involved. However, at the present time competing explanations have been proposed for many putative universals. For as long as this remains true, some uncertainty must be associated with the claim that a given pattern is in fact appropriately considered universal.

We can illustrate this point with the commonly observed place-related differences in voice onset time mentioned above in connection with English 'kill' and 'pill'. One type of explanation focuses on the velocity of movement of the articulators concerned. The releasing movement of a velar closure is slower than that for a bilabial closure, in part because the rotational movement of the jaw accelerates the movement of the lower lip in comparison with the back of the tongue (Kuehn and Moll 1976). The distance from the pivot point of the rotation is greater for the lip than for the tongue back. Hence for a given amount of angular motion of the jaw the lower lip will move further in the same time than a point on the tongue does, as shown schematically in Figure 20.1. (This is probably not the only factor involved since differences between the two articulators in their mass and compliance may also contribute to a faster labial than velar release, as will be discussed.) A different articulator speed affects voice onset time in the following way: Because the oral aperture through which air is escaping increases at a slower rate after a velar stop release, a longer time elapses before the crucial transglottal pressure difference required to initiate voicing is attained. This proposed explanation appeals to

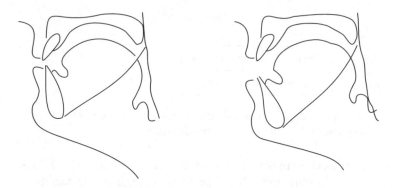

Figure 20.1 Schematic representation of the effect of jaw rotation. A 10° shift in jaw angle moves the lips apart more than the tongue back and velum.

the mechanical constraints on the jaw, general laws of fluid dynamics, and the physiology of the vocal folds – clearly universal properties.

An alternative account would explain the voice onset difference between 'pill' and 'kill' as resulting from different closure durations for stops at different places of articulation (itself a putative universal, which will be discussed further below), coupled with a stable duration for the vocal fold abduction gesture. This stable duration would be a learned feature of English voiceless stops in this particular position. Weismer (1980) measured the mean duration of the entire voiceless interval (from offset of voicing at the formation of the stop closure to onset of voicing after the release and the aspiration interval) for English words with initial /p/ and /k/, spoken in a carrier phrase, and found it to be the same in these two cases. This, as well as other evidence cited by Weismer, suggests that there is an abduction–adduction cycle of the vocal cords for voiceless stops which is longer in duration than the closure and has a constant time course, anchored to the onset of closure. If this is correct, then rate of articulator movement may have nothing to do with the different aspiration durations. A shorter hold of the closure for a velar stop than for a bilabial stop will automatically increase the time interval of the following aspiration by the amount of the difference, as is schematically shown in Figure 20.2. Such a precise trade-off between component durations is suggested by data on English from two classic studies. Umeda (1977) measured the mean closure duration of /k/ as 20 ms shorter than the closure of /p/ (69 vs 89 ms); Lisker and Abramson (1964) measured the aspiration duration for /k/ as 22 ms longer than that for /p/ (80 vs 58 ms).

When these competing accounts are considered together, it appears that there may not be a single universal accounting for a relationship between place of articulation and onset of voicing. The first explanation predicts a difference between bilabials and velars only if the vocal folds are together at, or very soon after, the release of the oral occlusion, and not if the vocal folds are still in an open position at the release. Note that if the vocal folds are not

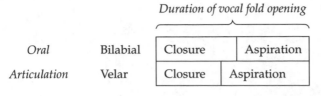

Figure 20.2 Schematic representation of place differences in aspirated stops from constant vocal cord abduction plus different closure duration.

brought together until some 50 ms or more after the velar closure for /k/ has been released, it is unlikely that supraglottal pressure is high enough to delay the initiation of voicing. Intraoral pressure drops very rapidly once the closure is broken, and the tongue dorsum can be expected to have lowered by some 4 to 5 mm by 50 ms after release. Weismer's proposal for fixed vocal fold opening duration fits the situation better. The case is different for /b/ and /g/ because the vocal folds are adducted in these consonants; the explanation offered by Weismer does not apply. The fact that Lisker and Abramson (1964) found a similar difference of about 20 ms in the voice onset time between both the English consonant pairs /b/ ~ /g/ and /p/ ~ /k/ may therefore be coincidental. These two differences may be the result of different processes which in English operate in disjunct environments, but produce superficially similar outcomes.

We therefore stress that observing a pattern of cross-language similarities is only a very preliminary step. Understanding the basis on which the pattern is founded is the primary goal. What seems to be a unified pattern may have several causes, and conversely a single effect may have different outcomes depending on variations in other factors. Finding an apparent counterexample to a proposed universal may not invalidate its status as a universal unless all relevant factors are constant. And a pattern that is 'mechanical' in one context may be generalized to others and thus become part of what a speaker must learn about a language.

In the next section, a brief catalogue of some of the most widely suggested 'mechanistic' universals will be provided. In each case a very short discussion of proposed factors on which the universal pattern might depend will be provided together with references to some of the most important work on the topic.

3 A brief catalogue of proposed mechanistic phonetic universals

3.1 Universals relating to vowel height

Several universals relating to vowel height have been proposed. Other things being equal, higher vowels have higher f_0 than lower vowels. This correlation,

Table 20.1 Vowel Height and f_0 in Iaai (values rounded to nearest integer).

	Women (3 speakers)			Men (2 speakers)		
	n	f_0	*s.d.*	*n*	f_0	*s.d.*
High [i, y, u]	43	240	22	37	152	15
Mid [e, ɤ, o]	41	233	15	40	144	12
Low [æ, a, ɔ]	37	224	19	37	136	13

sometimes referred to as the intrinsic pitch of vowels, has been documented in a large number of languages (Whalen and Levitt 1995). We add here data from Iaai, using an equal number of vowels in the high, mid and low classes. f_0 was measured at the mid-point of vowels in words spoken in isolation. These results are given in Table 20.1.

One class of explanations suggests that the intrinsic pitch effect arises because of a mechanical linkage between the supralaryngeal and laryngeal tissues, resulting in increased tension on the vocal folds as the tongue is raised (Ohala 1978). However, there are puzzling discrepancies between results obtained when different regions of the vowel space are examined, and some evidence that the level of activity of the cricothyroid muscle – the muscle most involved in the active control of f_0 differences – is itself positively correlated with vowel height (Honda and Fujimura 1991). This suggests that the intrinsic pitch effect may involve some active targeting of different f_0 values for different vowels. One possibility is that in a high vowel the (low) F1 is close enough to the f_0 value to produce a perceptual integration of the two, usually believed to occur when two spectral components are closer together than 3.5 Bark (see Stevens, Articulatory-Acoustic-Auditory Relationships in this volume). Since high vowels appear higher in pitch, speakers might then mimic this effect in their production. Another suggestion is that the intrinsic pitch effect is a consequence of the perceptual reliance on a speaker's characteristic f_0 as a calibration tool for interpreting the speaker-dependent variation in F1 and other formants (Hoemeke and Diehl 1994). On this view, if a high vowel is produced with a higher f_0, it triggers an interpretation that the vowel is higher than would otherwise be the case, reinforcing the percept of its height. (The calibration works as follows: A high mean f_0 indicates that a speaker has a small vocal tract and all formants will be on the high side of average; they must therefore be equated with lower values from larger speakers. The imputed lower F1 correlates with a perceptually higher vowel.)

Other things being equal, higher vowels are shorter than lower vowels. This observation, like most others concerning segment durations, is traditionally based on measures of the intervals between acoustic landmarks. The effect, sometimes known as intrinsic vowel duration, is usually explained as due to the fact that a greater distance must be moved by the tongue and jaw to go from a consonantal constriction to a lower vowel and back again than is required for a higher vowel (Catford 1977a). There are few studies that address this point, although Lindblom (1967) showed that short and long Swedish /ɑ/ vowels take longer than the /i/ vowels of the corresponding length category and that differences in the magnitude of mandibular movement are implicated in this difference. However, the magnitude of the vowel durational difference was actually less than might have been expected from the differences in movement. In his experiment, the vowels were surrounded by bilabial consonants, and some reorganization of the coordination between lip and jaw movements seems to be involved in limiting the durational differences.

Other things being equal, higher vowels also have a greater tendency to devoicing than lower vowels. Jaeger (1978) catalogued a number of cases from language descriptions where either only high vowels were devoiced in a particular environment, or higher vowels showed a greater tendency to occur voiceless than lower ones. This pattern is attributable to aerodynamic conditions: since the higher the vowel is the more constricted the oral passage is, a higher vowel creates greater impedance to oral airflow and therefore tends to raise supraglottal pressure. Thus over a certain range of laryngeal settings the pressure differential across the glottis in a high vowel will fall below the critical level required to initiate or sustain voicing, whereas a lower vowel would permit the voicing to occur.

3.2 *Universals related to consonant voicing*

A number of other proposed universals relate to the voicing state of consonants. Most often these are discussed in connection with obstruents, as these are the consonants that most often provide an opportunity to contrast voiced and voiceless cognates. Other things being equal, the vowel before a voiced consonant is longer than that before its voiceless counterpart. For example, in English, the vowel in 'bid' is longer than that in 'bit'. It is often remarked that the difference is greater in English than in other languages, but some difference is reported in a wide variety of languages, and not just in closed syllables (as the Italian data below illustrates). The general effect is often explained as a consequence of the need to make a more forceful gesture of closure for a voiceless consonant, since the unimpeded flow of air through an open glottis provides greater resistance to the formation of an oral seal (Chen 1970). The resulting more forceful gesture results in a faster movement of the articulators and a more rapid achievement of the consonantal target position. There are several problems with this explanation. First of all, studies of articulatory movements show that the *onset* of the closing movement occurs earlier when the consonant is voiceless, so that more than a faster rate of closure is involved. We will return to this point later. Secondly, sonorant consonants in the coda are also affected; thus in a pair of words such as 'build' and 'built' both components of the [ɪl] sequence differ in length, and this effect extends to nasals in pairs such as 'send' and 'sent'. Raphael et al (1975) found that the length difference in the nasals was actually twice as great as that in the vowels in this pair. The articulatory closure is made as the nasal is initiated, and since the nasal itself is voiced in both environments there is unlikely to be any great difference in the resistance to closure between these two cases.

Other phoneticians have suggested that this type of durational difference is due to a perceptual mechanism. One proposal is that the continuity of voicing from a vowel into a voiced obstruent might make it harder to determine the end of the vowel, creating an 'auditory illusion' of greater length. Consequently, speakers internalize a longer vowel target in such words (Javkin 1976). Another interpretation is that the vowel length difference is due to exploitation of a perceptual contrast effect to signal the voicing distinction. This idea relates the vowel length difference to another observational universal, namely that the acoustic duration of voiced consonants, especially obstruents, is shorter than that of corresponding voiceless ones. A longer preceding vowel makes the duration of a (short) voiced consonant appear even shorter in much the same way as, in the visual domain, changing the brightness of a background colour can change the perception of the brightness of an item in the foreground (Kluender, Diehl and Wright 1988; but see Fowler 1992). In this way the salience of the voicing distinction might be enhanced.

It is possible that the difference in consonant durations may account for the vowel duration pattern without appealing to enhancement of a perceptual contrast. Suppose that in a CVCV structure a normal production strategy is to control the duration of some longer unit, for example by fixing the phasing between the acoustic onsets of the vowels. With this requirement, a longer intervening consonant must 'borrow' duration from the preceding vowel. An explanation of this general kind seems to account quite well for the shorter vowels that occur before geminate consonants in Italian in comparison with their singleton counterparts (Smith 1995). An unpublished study by Dunn (1993) suggests that taking the consonant duration as primary also provides a good account of the differences attributable to voicing in Italian. Some of her results comparing intervocalic /p/ and /b/ production and the preceding vowel in the nonsense words 'tapa' and 'taba' are shown in Table 20.2. Dunn used an LED tracking system to follow the lip movements in these sequences and also made the conventional measurements of acoustic durations. Reading down the rows of Table 20.2, we see that mean acoustic vowel duration (from the burst for /t/ to the labial closure) is on the order of 15 ms shorter before /p/ than before /b/. This matches very closely with the difference in the latency of the onset of the articulatory movement of the lips toward closure, i.e. the time between the /t/ burst and the beginning of the labial closing gesture. In other words, the lips start to close about 15 ms sooner to form a /p/. Once closed, they stay together longer. In fact, the /p/ – /b/ closure duration difference is longer than the difference in the preceding vowel.

Table 20.2   Acoustic and articulatory measures of intervocalic /p/, /b/ for two Italian speakers (after Dunn 1993). All values are means of 20 repetitions.

	Speaker A			Speaker B		
	tap a	*tab a*	*p/b diff*	*tap a*	*tab a*	*p/b diff*
Acoustic vowel duration (ms)	157	173	−16	191	208	−17
Latency of movement onset for consonant (ms)	100	115	−15	131	145	−14
Acoustic consonant duration (ms)	99	76	+23	118	86	+32
Peak velocity of consonant closure (mm/sec)	275	210	+65	335	305	+30
Duration of onset movement (ms)	67	65	+2	78	79	−1
Held duration of articulatory peak (ms)	60	53	+7	73	51	+22
V-onset to V-onset interval (ms)	256	249	+7	309	294	+15

Although the closing velocity is indeed faster in forming a /p/, the duration of the closing movement is the same for /p/ and /b/, suggesting that the movement rate is not affecting the preceding segment durations, but is rather part of a strategy to maintain the longer closure for the voiceless consonant by making a more forceful closure. The peak articulatory position is held longer for /p/ than for /b/, especially by speaker B. Finally, the interval from the articulatory onset of the first /a/ vowel to the onset of the second is shown. This is longer with /p/ than with /b/, suggesting that /p/ also 'borrows' some duration from the second vowel, particularly again for speaker B. Adding together the earlier onset of the closing movement for an intervocalic /p/ and the later onset of the movement toward the second vowel after /p/ we obtain a close match with the added acoustic duration of /p/ compared with /b/.

It is thus possible to view the voicing-dependent differences in vowel duration as due to the interaction of larger-scale timing principles which function to create similar durations for similarly-structured words and a voicing-dependent effect on the inherent duration of the closure of stops. Timing principles of this type, though not universal, are common. The burden of explanation is therefore shifted to the consonant duration difference; a reasonable proposal is that this has an aerodynamic basis. Vocal fold vibration cannot be sustained when there is high resistance to airflow above the glottis, as in the case of a stop. A variety of manoevres to expand the size of the oral cavity, such as lowering the larynx, can reduce the supraglottal resistance. (See Shadle, THE AERODYNAMICS OF SPEECH and Stevens, ARTICULATORY–ACOUSTIC–AUDITORY RELATIONSHIPS.) Similarly, a shortened duration of closure and a less extensive contact area both help to increase the likelihood that vocal fold vibration will continue through the closure until the moment of release (The shortened duration just limits the length of time that voicing needs to be sustained, whereas a less extensive contact leaves more surface area to absorb rising intraoral pressure). These patterns are not mechanical *consequences* of producing voicing, but are good ways of using vocal tract mechanics given a goal of realizing voicing in a stop consonant.

Another familiar observational universal is the tendency for the fundamental frequency (f_0) to be higher after a voiceless consonant than after a voiced one (other factors affecting f_0 being equal). This observation has been much discussed, and like other universals, interpreted in various ways. For many, it is viewed solely as the consequence of 'the lowering effect of voiced consonants' (Mohr 1971). But there are probably (at least) two separate effects, one a lowering process and another which is responsible for raising pitch after voiceless consonants. The lowering is sometimes argued to be due not to the fact of voicing alone but to a process that lowers the f_0 when obstruency and voicing are combined (Hombert 1978). For example, as noted above, keeping the vocal folds vibrating when there is a closure in the oral cavity is problematical. It can be assisted by lowering the larynx, and this lowering might incidentally mimic some aspect of the active pitch control regimen. After all, there is known to be an association between the height of the larynx, usually measured by the height of the thyroid notch, and active control of pitch (Ewan and Krones 1974, Riordan 1980). Ohala (1980) reasoned that if this was the explanation, then no lowering should be found following ordinary voiced nasal consonants as these allow a relatively high volume of air to continue to flow through the glottis, since the nasal passage is open. As predicted, she found that in the Hindi speaker she studied, voiced stops did have a lowered f_0, producing a rising f_0 onset to the following vowel, but after nasals the f_0 trajectory was flat. However, Maddieson (1984b) found that in Burmese, voiced nasals and laterals had a rising onset like that of voiced stops. Bickley and Stevens (1986a, b) showed that vocal fold vibration drops in frequency, presumably due to aerodynamic conditions, when the oral escape channel is constricted but not closed by an experimenter-controlled manipulation. If the escape is sufficiently narrowed in the nasals and laterals of certain languages this may account for lowering sometimes being observed with consonants of these types.

The link between voicing and lowered f_0 has received much more attention

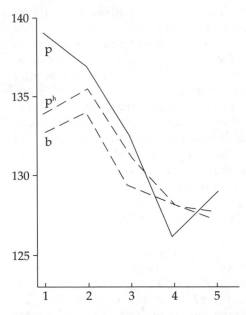

Figure 20.3 Mean f_0 contours in Hz after consonants differing in voicing, averaged across the five tonal categories of Thai (measurements taken at 5 equally spaced intervals through the duration of the vowel).

than its counterpart – the association between voicelessness and raised f_0. In fact, in most studies which have measured both, the amount that f_0 is raised after a voiceless obstruent is considerably greater than the amount of lowering seen after a voiced obstruent (comparing values at the vowel onset to a target f_0 later in the following vowel). Data from a male speaker of Thai, based on Gandour and Maddieson (1976), are shown in Figure 20.3. As this is a tonal language, with a high functional load for tones, there is good reason for taking the target pitch on the following vowel to be relatively controlled. Yet mean onset of f_0 after /p/ is about 7 Hz higher than after /b/, and the decline is sharper after /p/ than is the rise after /b/. Informal suggestions have been made that raised f_0 occurs because of high transglottal air flow when a stop or other obstruent constriction is released while the vocal folds still remain apart. Since an increased flow – such as that resulting from an unexpected push on the chest while speaking – does increase f_0 (Ladefoged 1967b, Sonesson 1982), the raised f_0 may be the result of the beginning of the vowel being produced while the vocal folds are not yet fully adducted. A slightly wider aperture between the folds would allow greater flow but the folds would still be close enough to vibrate. In this case it might be anticipated that voiceless aspirated stops would show greater f_0 elevation than voiceless unaspirated ones. As the Thai data in Figure 20.3 show, this is far from a universal finding, so other factors must also be involved.

An alternative theory is based on the observation that the cricothyroid muscles can be actively involved in the production of voiceless consonants. Contraction of these muscles increases the distance between the attachments of the vocal folds, thereby stretching the folds longitudinally and increasing the frequency of their vibration when other conditions are appropriate for voicing to occur (Sonesson 1982). Cricothyroid activity is thus the principal way of increasing f_0 for intonational peaks, high tones and other upward pitch excursions (See Hirose, INVESTIGATING THE PHYSIOLOGY OF LARYNGEAL STRUCTURES). In a study of three subjects (two speakers of American English and one of Dutch), Löfqvist, Baer, McGarr and Seider Story (1989) showed that the level of electrical activity in the cricothyroid muscles is also higher during voiceless stops, affricates and fricatives than during their voiced counterparts. Moreover, since the peak of this activity occurs relatively early in the acoustic duration of the voiceless consonants, Löfqvist et al argue that it is directly associated with their voicelessness, and that the tensing of the vocal folds assists in inhibiting vocal fold vibrations. The raising of f_0 is incidental; because the relaxation time of these muscles is relatively long the folds are still somewhat tensed at the vowel onset following voiceless consonants. A persuasive detail is that the speaker and consonant class with the smallest cricothyroid activity difference (the affricates of one of the English speakers) also shows the smallest f_0 difference between voiced and voiceless cases. However, as with f_0 lowering, there seem to be language or speaker-based differences. Löfqvist et al's results are consistent with an electromyographic study by Dixit and MacNeilage (1980) of one Hindi speaker, but Collier, Lisker, Hirose and Ushijima (1979) report no relevant difference between the voiced and voiceless stops and fricatives of a speaker of Dutch.

There thus seem to be a number of mechanisms which can result in higher f_0 after a voiceless consonant than after a voiced one. f_0 lowering with voicing may be a consequence of a lowered larynx position, or due to the aerodynamic effects of a supraglottal constriction. Aerodynamic effects may raise f_0 after voiceless consonants with an open glottis, and devoicing strategies that involve tensing the vocal folds will also be likely to raise f_0 after voiceless consonants. The particular effects that come into play will produce somewhat differing patterns both with respect to the amount of f_0 difference and the classes of sounds involved, but in no case will f_0 be higher after a voiced consonant than after a voiceless one. The variability noted in the correlation of consonant voicing and lowered f_0 is one factor that lead Kingston and Diehl (1994) to suggest that there is much more of a language-specific, learned, nature to this correlation, rather than a universal basis for it. (They interpret several other proposed phonetic universals in the same way).

3.3 Universals related to consonant place

Several observational universals relate place of articulation and the duration of consonants or their environments. Most of the measurements related to this

Table 20.3   Stop consonant closure durations (in ms) and place of articulation.

English (6 speakers) *(Stathopoulos and Weismer 1983)*				English (TIMIT: 630 speakers) *(Byrd 1993)*			
p-	96	b-	92	p	69	b	64
t-	82	d-	76	t	53	d	52
k-	72	g-	68	k	60	g	54

issue have been on stops; the longer closure of bilabial than of velar stops was mentioned in section 2 above. It has been informally suggested that this pattern is connected to the air pressure in the cavity behind the closure. The smaller this cavity is, the more rapidly the pressure will rise following closure and the sooner intraoral pressure will reach equality with pulmonic pressure (primarily because smaller cavities have smaller surface area). If the consonant gesture is timed in some way that directly relates to the time of the pressure peak, then broadly speaking, the further back in the oral cavity a stop closure is formed, the shorter its acoustic closure duration will be. An experiment by Ohala and Riordan (1979, see also Ohala 1983), showed that intraoral pressure becomes high enough to suppress voicing on average about 25 ms earlier for alveolar /d/ than for /b/, and about 15 ms earlier for /g/ than for /d/.

Comparing English bilabial, alveolar and velar stops in word-medial position of disyllabic nonsense words with second syllable stress, Stathopoulos and Weismer (1983) did find a monotonic relationship between the backness of the place and the shortness of the closure, as shown in Table 20.3. A similar pattern has been found, at least in certain environments, in other languages, for example in Ṣtandard Chinese word-initial unaspirated stops (Ren 1985), Swedish word-final short stops (Elert 1964: 143) and Florentine Italian intervocalic voiced stops following stress (Vagges, Ferrero, Magno-Caldognetto and Lavagnoli 1978). However, in many studies coronal stops have shorter closure durations than velars while labials remain longest. Byrd (1993) found this overall pattern in TIMIT, the large American English read-sentence database including 630 speakers, as also shown in Table 20.3 (note that the flap allophones of /t, d/ are excluded from this count).

This alternative pattern might be attributed to differences in the compressibility of the articulators. Bilabials are formed by closure between two soft surfaces which undergo a good deal of compression as they contact, velars involve contact between two somewhat compressible articulators – the tongue back and the soft palate, whereas dentals and alveolars involve a hard surface on one side of the contact. When the upper articulator is a yielding surface, there is likely to be a less rapid rebound from the ballistic movement that creates the contact, just as a ball bounces back more rapidly from a hard surface than a soft one. Air pressure and tissue compressibility effects may interact to create the pattern noted by Fischer-Jørgensen (1964) for Danish, in which bilabials are longest in their closure duration but alveolars and velars are of comparable duration. Since many factors affect durations, and there are also language-specific positional variations in stops to consider, it is often the case that inconsistent rankings are found even within a single language. And languages with multiple places for coronal stops, such as those of Australia, provide particular challenges for interpretation, as in the Rembarrnga data provided by McKay (1980) in which palato–alveolar stops are the longest, and postalveolars the shortest.

A more uniform observation is that the delay in voice onset following the release of a stop is dependent on how far back the place of articulation of the stop is; the further back, the longer the VOT. The English data in Byrd (1993) agree with this, with overall mean VOT for bilabials of 32 ms, for alveolars of 39 ms and for velars of 46 ms. Similar rankings are found in a wide range of languages, although results are not uniform. In general, voiceless bilabial plosives do have the shortest VOT, and velar VOT's are consistently longer than bilabials. However, uvulars are not consistently longer than velars, and the VOT of stops in the coronal region is highly variable, depending both on the part of the tongue used to form the constriction and its profile behind the constriction, as well as on what seem to be controlled differences in the way that the release itself is made (Ladefoged and Maddieson 1995). As noted in section 2, place-dependent VOT durations may have different causes under different circumstances. In the case of unaspirated stops, a short VOT for bilabials may be due to the rapid separation of the lips at release, both of them being mobile and moving away from one another, and accelerated by the effect of jaw opening. A long VOT for velars may result from the relatively great length of the contact in the sagittal plane. The long closure separates more slowly, often even reclosing momentarily to produce the 'double bursts' characteristic of velars. These different speeds of separation mean that the high intraoral pressure is dissipated more rapidly at the release of a bilabial stop than at the release of a velar. Hence, the transglottal pressure difference required for voicing to be (re-)initiated is reached earlier. However, as also noted above, explanations based on rate of separation do not apply well to aspirated stops, since the articulators are fully separated long before the aspiration ends.

3.4 Universals related to prosodic units

A number of universal tendencies can be observed in relation to the prosodic structure of languages. A very widespread pattern is that some phonetic components are longer in a position before a boundary, such as at the end of a sentence or an intonational phrase than they are in other positions. Beckman and Edwards (1990) are able to separate out phrase-final and word-final lengthening processes in English. Lengthening in these types of positions functions as a means of demarcating the ends of constituents, and presumably has a perceptual rather than a physiological basis. A longer syllable at the end of a constituent not only directly helps to mark the end of the constituent but also provides a better host for other markers of constituent structure such as tonal or voice quality changes, for example, the high-tone question-marker of Hausa (Lindau 1986). Pre-boundary lengthening may apply to a segment or syllable not in absolute final position, as in many Bantu languages which lengthen the penultimate syllable at the ends of sentences and, within sentences, at the ends of some major clauses. In this case, the lengthening may be positioned earlier in order to avoid the strongest impact of amplitude and pitch declination in the absolute final position.

Declination refers to an underlying downward trend of some trait over the length of an utterance or part of an utterance (see Nooteboom, PROSODY OF SPEECH). Declination of f_0 and overall acoustic amplitude appear to be universal, and there are some indications that declination of articulatory amplitude may also be typical (Vayra and Fowler 1992, Krakow 1993). Local perturbations – for example, for stressed syllables – may be superimposed on this overall decline, but successive local perturbations themselves often conform to a pattern of declination. In almost every language in which pitch patterns have been studied over utterances longer than word-length, the f_0 pattern follows an overall downward trend, at least within certain spans and at least for some unmarked utterance types. It seems likely that this declination is, broadly speaking, associated with the baseline decline in the subglottal pressure that occurs as lung volume decreases over the course of an utterance. Important experiments reported in Gelfer, Harris, Collier and Baer (1985) and Gelfer, Harris and Baer (1987) showed that the Dutch-speaking subjects they studied controlled the rate of subglottal pressure decrement, as it remained constant with different rates of lung volume decrement arising from use of low air flow segments (/m/) versus high air flow segments (/f/). f_0 declination was correlated with the declination of subglottal pressure, not with lung volume declination, nor with activity of the cricothyroid muscle. They therefore conclude that subglottal declination 'is a controlled variable in sentence production, and that f_0 declination is a consequence.' The same authors conclude that the overall decline of acoustic amplitude is also a consequence of the declination of subglottal pressure. This effect, combined with anticipation of the open glottal position of normal respiration, produces a common tendency for elements in utterance-final position to become devoiced.

Phonetic universals have also been sought for smaller prosodic units such as the syllable, but few of the marks of syllable affiliation have been found to have cross-linguistic generality. One possible exception is shortening in closed syllables. In many languages a vowel in a closed syllable is shorter than a matched vowel in an open syllable (Maddieson 1985). Thus, the /ei/ in '*grey towel*' will tend to be longer than that in '*great owl*'. This effect may be observed most readily in languages where medial single and geminate consonants of the same type contrast (assuming that the geminate closes the preceding syllable). In this environment the influence of syllabification is isolated from

Table 20.4 Duration of stressed /a/ before single and geminate consonants in Italian. (Mean of three speakers, after Farnetani and Kori (1986))

	Vowel duration	
Consonant type	*before single C*	*before geminate C*
-l-	211	133
-n-	212	138
-s-	222	129

other durational modifications. Some results for Italian, where this effect is very strong, are given in Table 20.4. Since there are languages in which geminate consonants do not have a shorter preceding vowel than single consonants, such as Japanese (Homma 1981, Smith 1995) and perhaps Sinhala (Letterman 1994), it is clear that this is not an automatic effect of the syllabification. As suggested above, what may be at work here is a strategy for keeping words with equal syllable count similar in overall duration. (A possible advantage of doing this would be to keep the information density in the signal more uniform.)

3.5 *Some general comments*

The various observational universals described briefly in the preceding sections illustrate a variety of situations. In some cases, such as f_0 raising after voiceless consonants and place-dependant VOT differences of stops, a number of 'mechanical' factors work together to produce phonetic patterns that are broadly uniform in direction. In others, such as place-dependant patterns of stop closure duration, competing factors lead to expectation of conflicting trends. For some cases, such as final lengthening, a perceptual basis for a pattern seems more explanatory than an aerodynamic or physiological one. All these observations illustrate the point that 'universals' are not fixed attributes of languages. Rather, they are reflections of the overall context within which language is produced and heard. This is a fluctuating and dynamic set of conditions of which mechanical and perceptual constraints are only a part. Although these conditions set some boundaries and shape more likely and less likely outcomes, they do not result in linguistic homogeneity.

4 Ecological models

A somewhat different perspective on the issue of phonetic universals is based on what is here called an ecological view of the matter. Rather than considering primarily factors such as the physiological and aerodynamic conditions that rule during the production of a given sound or utterance, or the perceptual processing of a given sound or utterance, the ecological perspective considers a larger view of the functionality of language. Spoken language must, among other requirements, be constructed to conform to two overarching principles which might be labeled Contrastivity and Connectedness. A language must show variation in sound – rather than being an undifferentiated noise – if it is to convey any other message than simply 'I'm speaking'. It must also be possible to identify recurrent parts of the signal and recognize them as representing the same word (or morpheme or other meaningful constituent). That is, both speakers and listeners need to be able to identify the same message as being the same, and different messages as being different. These requirements create the property that is usually labeled phonological contrast; utterances must contain parts that are differentiated from each other and recognizable when they recur. The need for contrastivity is responsible for such things as the alternation of louder and quieter sounds that is the basis of syllabification and for the selection of elements with good characteristic 'signatures' in both their motor and auditory patterns so that they may be recognized and memorized.

Equally, a language needs to be produced as a continuous stream, its parts connected to each other just as essentially as they must be differentiated from each other. Moreover, since the position in which a given word or other element will occur is variable, the form of any item must be adapted for variable environments. These considerations place some limits on the degree to which articulatory displacements are made, especially in adjacent parts of an utterance. Moving an articulator to an extreme displacement (e.g. sticking the tongue out as far as possible between the teeth) makes it harder to connect to the next position – unless it is the same, and variability of context ensures that it will more frequently not be the same. Connectedness therefore favours moderate articulatory displacements over extreme ones. However, some variation in articulatory instantiation of a given word facilitates its concatenation with other items in contexts that themselves vary. Nonetheless, beyond a certain level, variation begins to conflict with the need to be able to identify repetitions of the same item. Variation will therefore tend to remain within limited bounds.

Note that, although these comments could be made about a segmental level of analysis, and will be discussed below in the light of such an analysis, it is not necessary to presuppose that any such level exists. The observations above hold whether one regards segments as 'emergents' that arise from a self-organizing system (Lindblom 1992), whether one believes that the human system is pre-adapted in some way to a segmental analysis of speech (Ohala 1992b), or whether one believes that there is no level of segmental organization (Local 1992). Connectedness requires flexibility in production, and favours less extreme articulations under any interpretation of the units involved.

Contrastivity and connectedness as described here are related to the idea

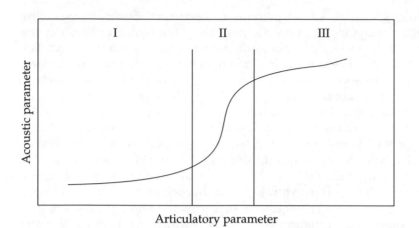

Figure 20.4   Schematic relationship between an articulatory and an acoustic parameter as discussed by Stevens (1972, 1989).

that, in their phonetic structure, languages must maintain a balance between auditory distinctiveness and ease of articulation. Lindblom (1986, 1990) has argued that the interaction of these two principles generates many of the patterns described as markedness relations between different segments or segment inventories. We argue that there is a requirement for articulatory as well as auditory distinctiveness, and suggest a different perspective on the question of ease of articulation, in which the value of 'unity in diversity' is stressed. The Quantal Theory of Stevens (1972, 1989) provides one window on the issue of contrastivity. This proposes that nonlinearities in the relationships between articulatory parameters and the resulting acoustic/auditory responses are a key to this issue. In Figure 20.4, based on Stevens (1989: 4), the horizontal axis represents changes in some articulatory parameter on a linear scale, for example, steps in increasing the distance between the lips. The vertical scale represents changes in some acoustic or auditory parameter, for example, the overall amplitude of the signal, in response to this change. Region II is an area where there are large changes in the acoustics for small shifts in articulation, as at the release of a labial closure. Within regions I and III there is relatively little difference in the acoustics for articulatory shifts of equivalent size, but the difference between Region I and Region III is large. In the example we have used this might correspond to the acoustic difference between stop and vowel. Over a small but crucial range of lip movement the acoustic output demonstrates a relatively sharp change in amplitude. Many other pairs of parameters are similarly related. Stevens suggests the general principle that segment sequences are selected so that they cross regions such as Region II in this figure, producing rapid changes that serve as landmarks in the acoustic stream.

In whatever way concepts such as connectedness and contrastivity are formulated, they are attempts to capture some of the ambient factors that govern the overall design of the sound patterns of languages. Such factors in the 'ecology' of language shape phoneme frequency, the structure of phoneme inventories, and the pattern of contrast distribution, among other matters. For example it has often been noted that phoneme inventories are constructed in such a way as to appear built on a foundation of use of basic parameters, which are found in almost all languages including those with very small numbers of segmental distinctions. As increasing numbers of distinctions are made, additional ways of making them are added. For example, we may observe that vowel systems start from height variations; a few languages have only two or three distinctive vowels, and contrast these on the height dimension alone. No language is known which does not have some distinctions of height. Other languages with as few as three vowels and all those known with five or more also show front/back distinctions among their vowels, with typically a redundant association between rounding and backness which enhances the acoustic distinction (contrastivity) between front and back. Only languages with relatively large numbers of distinct vowel qualities disrupt this association between rounding and backness and permit these parameters to be independently varied, yielding front rounded and back unrounded vowels in contrast with the more frequently encountered front unrounded and back rounded types. Nasalization, pharyngeal volume, and voice quality differences are other more elaborated distinctions among vowels (Ladefoged and Maddieson 1995, see also Ladefoged, LINGUISTIC PHONETIC DESCRIPTIONS.)

There is generally a good correlation between the relative frequency of a segment type in terms of its appearance in the inventories of languages around the world and its frequency within the lexicon of particular languages. The UPSID archive (Maddieson 1984a), currently containing data on 453 languages, provides a basis for determining which are the most frequent sound types in the world's languages. It may be inferred that these sound types meet the ecological criteria better than others (though their frequency is not by itself evidence of this fact). Among consonants, 80 per cent or more of languages have p, *t, k, m, *n, *s, j (where * indicates a class of coronal consonants that includes dental and alveolar places). Over 50 per cent have b, *d, g, ŋ, h, *l, w, and some form of *r. In a count of lexical items in a sample of 25 languages of widely varied genetic and geographical groupings the most common individual syllable-onset consonants were /k/ (10 languages), /*t/ (5 languages), /l/, /s/ (2 languages each) and /m/, /n/, /d/, /h/, /r/ and /tɕ/ (1 language each). All except /tɕ/ are among the most common consonants crosslinguistically, but an interesting fact that emerges from this study is the greater favouring of /k/ relative to other common consonants. In a similar way, although /i/, /a/ and /u/ are all found in over 80 per cent of the UPSID language sample, lexical counts show that, in many languages, /a/ is far more frequent than any other vowel (Maddieson 1992). We might therefore say that the optimal syllable is /ka/.

The listing of most common consonants also illustrates a basic structural principle; inventories tend to be built by the intersection of repeated characteristics.

Table 20.5 A grid of some of the most common consonants.

	bilabial	*dental/alveolar*	*velar*
voiceless plosive	p	t	k
voiced plosive	b	d	g
nasal	m	n	ŋ

For example, nine of the most common consonants can be laid out on a grid with three rows, as in Table 20.5. By replicating essentially identical articulatory gestures, the task of learning motor 'images' of sounds is reduced in complexity, and we may also infer that the places of articulation represented are those that are most easily connected to other sounds in the stream of speech. Note that there is one 'modal' place represented for each of the three main independent oral articulators, the lips, tongue tip and tongue body (granted the conflation of dental and alveolar). More extreme coronal or dorsal articulations, such as interdental, linguo-labial, or uvular are rare by comparison. This again illustrates that the construction of inventories starts from basic elements and extends to include less basic elements as inventory size increases (Lindblom and Maddieson 1988).

A related principle that has been widely discussed is that of 'dispersion'. In early formulations (Liljencrants and Lindblom 1972, Lindblom 1986), the idea was that contrastive elements within a given phonetic domain should be expected to be *maximally* separated from each other. For example, a three vowel system would be expected to consist of the vowels /i, a, u/, where /i, u/ have the lowest possible first formant values but differ by having opposite extreme values of the second formant, and /a/ has the highest possible first formant. If a language had a larger number of distinct vowels, /i, a, u/ would remain in the same position and the others would be added between the extreme values, giving, say, a system containing /i, e, ɛ, a, ɔ, o, u/. Analysis of tone systems with different numbers of level tones suggests instead that contrastive elements are not maximally separated, and that increasing numbers of contrasts may be accommodated by moving the end-points of the scale further apart rather than by fitting more steps in between fixed end-points. Data in Table 20.6 from two Hausa–Nupe bilinguals (hence, controlled for speaker differences in pitch range) shows that the two lower tones of Nupe are essentially on the same levels as the two tones of Hausa, but the third tone of Nupe – the high tone – is substantially higher.

That something similar is found with vowels is indicated by Figure 20.5, comparing the values of the first two formants of /i, a, u/ in a dialect of Bavarian German with many other vowels and in Tausug, an Austronesian language of the Philippines, which has only these three vowels. Although the vowels being compared have been written the same in the two languages, the

Table 20.6 Mean f_0 (in Hz) of tones in matched environments in Hausa and Nupe as spoken by two bilingual speakers (after Maddieson 1991)

Hausa			Nupe		
			high	135	}14
high	123	} 20	mid	121	
low	103		low	98	}23

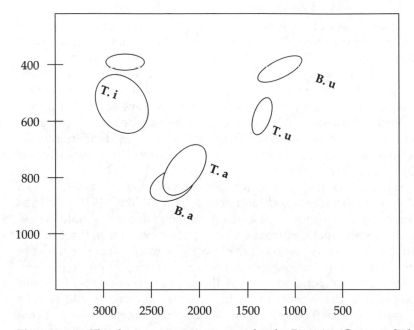

Figure 20.5 The three most extreme vowels of a Bavarian German dialect with 13 distinct long vowels (B.) and the three vowels of Tausug (T.) plotted in F1/F2 space (based on Disner 1983). The ellipses enclose approximately 95 percent of the variance in the data, which is from 8 male speakers of Bavarian and 4 of Tausug.

high vowels are markedly lower in Tausug than in the German dialect. Although few such comparisons have been made, it seems likely that when there are few vowels the phonetic realizations of the most distinct vowels are in general closer together in a space defined by the first two formants than is the case in a language with more vowels. These two examples show that contrastivity is satisfied by less than a maximal separation; however the difference between the end-points of any scale looked at cannot be extended indefinitely far apart. Comfortable limits are soon reached (with three or four tone levels and five or six vowels), and contrast will then tend to be extended by use of other parameters (duration, dynamic patterns, differences in source spectrum, etc).

This section has outlined some of the major ecological considerations that the sound systems of languages must meet and briefly discussed a few of the consequences of these requirements in terms of observed patterns across languages. Research on 'ecological' universals is perhaps less developed than research on 'mechanistic' universals. This may be because the theories that describe the ecological setting are broader in scope than those that address 'mechanistic' universals, and therefore developing tests of their predictive power is more challenging.

21 The Prosody of Speech: Melody and Rhythm

SIEB NOOTEBOOM

1 Introduction

The word *'prosody'* comes from ancient Greek, where it was used for a "song sung with instrumental music". In later times the word was used for the "science of versification" and the "laws of metre", governing the modulation of the human voice in reading poetry aloud. In modern phonetics the word 'prosody' and its adjectival form 'prosodic' are most often used to refer to those properties of speech that cannot be derived from the segmental sequence of phonemes underlying human utterances. Examples of such properties are the controlled modulation of the voice pitch, the stretching and shrinking of segment and syllable durations, and the intentional fluctuations of overall loudness. On the perceptual level these properties lead amongst other things to perceived patterns of relative syllable prominences, coded in perceived melodical and rhythmical aspects of speech. In modern generative phonology (Selkirk, 1984; Nespor and Vogel, 1986), the word 'prosody' has been given a somewhat different meaning, as it refers to nonsegmental aspects of abstract linguistic structure, such as a particular type of constituent structure and the presence or absence of accents, that are, at least potentially, systematically reflected in the phonetic rendition of utterances. Of course, the phonetic and phonological meanings of the word prosody might be considered two sides of the same coin: although phonologists give primacy to an abstract description of the phenomena concerned, they look for empirical evidence in the realm of speech. Phoneticians rather start from observations on real speech, but the abstract notions they come up with to account for the observed phenomena are phonological by nature. In this chapter we will take our starting position in the phonetic domain.

From a phonetic point of view we observe that human speech cannot be fully characterised as the manifestation of sequences of phonemes, syllables or words. In normal speech we hear for example that pitch moves up and down in some non-random way, providing speech with recognizable melodical properties. We also hear that segments or syllables are shortened or lengthened, apparently in accordance with some underlying pattern. We hear that some syllables or words are made to sound more prominent than others, that the stream of words is subdivided by the speaker into phrases made up of words that seem to belong together, and that, one level higher up, these phrases can be made to sound as if they relate to each other, or, alternatively, as if they have nothing to do with each other.

Properties of speech that cannot be derived from the underlying sequence of phonemes are often called suprasegmental properties of speech, including whether speakers speak softly or loudly, whether they speak in a normal, a hoarse or a breathy voice, whether they articulate carefully or slurringly, or even whether they would speak with an unusual posture of the vocal tract and the larynx so as to disguise their voice. Typically prosodic features of speech are not reflected in normal orthography, nor in conventional segmental phonetic transcriptions. In this chapter the treatment of prosody on the phonetic level will be limited to speaker-controlled aspects of voice pitch, organized in perceived speech melody or intonation, and speaker-controlled aspects of speech timing, organized in the perceived rhythmical structure of speech. Such melodical and rhythmical aspects of speech seem to have a variety of communicative functions, most of these closely tied to the fact that they mediate between the abstract and time-free mental structures underlying speech utterances and the production and perception of speech developing in real time.

Section 2 will discuss the melodical structure of speech, section 3 the rhythmical structure of speech, and in section 4 some communicative functions of speech prosody will be discussed.

2 The melody of speech

2.1 Introduction

This section deals with speech intonation, in its strict interpretation as "the ensemble of pitch variations in the course of an utterance" ('t Hart, Collier and Cohen, 1990:10), concentrating on those pitch variations that are related to perceived speech melodies, and thereby paying less attention to pitch variations that are related to the segmental structure of speech. As the knowledgeable reader will notice, the subject is approached following the ideas of 't Hart et al. (1990), giving primacy to the perceptual structure of intonation. The reader is referred to their book for a much fuller account and argumentation, based on more than 25 years of intonational research. One should also notice that the insights presented here are claimed to have validity only for so-called intonation languages such as the Germanic languages, Romance languages, and Japanese. Tone languages such as Chinese, in which lexical forms are distinguished by differences in level and/or movement of pitch on a particular vowel phoneme, are not dealt with in this chapter.

Obviously, the approach by 't Hart et al. is not the only one in the world. Other attempts to come to grips with the structure of intonation in terms of the actual course of pitch in speech utterances and its perceptual and linguistic correlates, can be found in Fujisaki and Sudo (1971) for Japanese, Maeda (1976), O'Shaughnessy (1976; 1979), Pierrehumbert (1980) for American English, Brown, Currie and Kenworthy (1980) for British English, Bruce (1977) for Swedish, and Thorsen (1980; 1985) for Danish. What these approaches all have in common is that they strive for some kind of stylized approximation of the apparently capricious pitch fluctuations found in natural speech, hence making reality more tractable by data reduction. In the approach by 't Hart et al. it is demonstrated that one can find a reliable basis for such stylization in the way pitch contours are perceived by native listeners, and that intonation can be described in terms of sequences of standard discrete pitch movements, supposedly corresponding to voluntary actions on the part of the speaker.

2.2 *Speech pitch, production and perception*

In strict terms, pitch is the perceptual correlate of f_0, the fundamental frequency or repetition frequency of a sound. One should be aware, however, that rather often the notion "pitch" is used to refer to f_0 or the repetition frequency itself. In speech f_0 is determined by the rate of vibration of the vocal cords located in the larynx. The physiological and acoustic mechanisms by which f_0 is controlled are rather intricate and will not be dealt with here. An excellent account of these mechanisms is given in Borden and Harris (1983). Rate of vibration of the vocal cords, and thereby f_0, is measured in Hertz (Hz; 1 Hz is 1 cycle per second). The range of f_0 for each individual speaker mainly depends on the length and mass of the vocal cords. For males in conversational speech this range is typically between approximately 80 and 200 Hz, for females between approximately 180 and 400 Hz, and for young children this range can be even considerably higher. Within this range each speaker has to a large extent active control over f_0: a speaker can choose to speak on a high or a low pitch, and can produce pitch rises and falls. However, many details of the actual course of pitch in speech are not actively controlled by the speaker, but are rather involuntary side-effects of other speech processes, often related to the production of particular speech sounds. For example, other things being equal, high vowels like /i/ and /u/ have a higher intrinsic pitch than low vowels like /a/ (Peterson and Barney, 1952; Ladd and Silverman, 1984; Steele, 1986). In vowels following voiceless consonants the voice pitch starts higher than in vowels following voiced consonants (Ohde, 1984; Silverman, 1986). These involuntary aspects of speech pitch superimpose small perturbations on the course of pitch, and often, in the visual analysis of measured pitch fluctuations in speech utterances, make it difficult to identify those pitch variations that are responsible for the perceived speech melody. This is illustrated in Figure 21.1, presenting the measured course of pitch in a rather lengthy

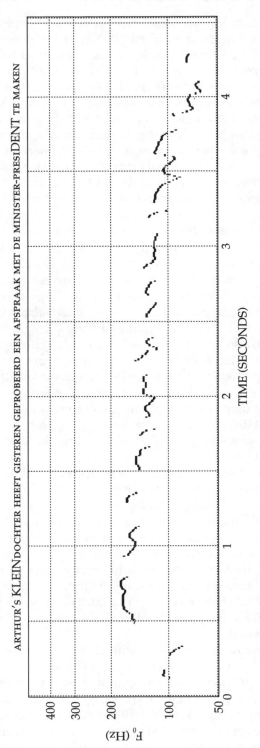

ARTHUR'S KLEINDOCHTER HEEFT GISTEREN GEPROBEERD EEN AFSPRAAK MET DE MINISTER-PRESIDENT TE MAKEN

Figure 21.1 Measured course of pitch in a Dutch sentence, with only two voluntary pitch movements, an accentuating rise on the syllable "KLEIN" and an accentuating fall on the syllable "DENT". All other pitch movements are involuntary side-effects of other speech processes. Note also that the continuity of pitch is interrupted during all voiceless consonants.

Dutch utterance. In fact, this sentence was spoken with only two accent-representing pitch movements, one on "KLEIN" in "KLEINdochter" and one on "DENT" in "presiDENT". All the other pitch movements do not seem to contribute to the perceived speech melody. These other pitch movements are thought to be involuntary side-effects of other processes of articulation.

In Figure 21.1 it can also be seen that the course of pitch is discontinuous. It is interrupted during the production of voiceless consonants like /k/, /p/, /t/. One should note that, while listening to fluent speech, one does not hear these interruptions of f_0 during stop consonant silent intervals as pauses or perceptual interruptions of the course of pitch. Although such interruptions of f_0 contribute to the perceived character of the consonants concerned, as listeners, we have the illusion that the speech and its intonation or melody are uninterrupted. In fact, interruptions of the sound of speech during for example silent intervals of voiceless consonants are only perceived as interrupting the stream of speech and the speech melody when they are longer than, roughly, 200 ms. This is in accordance with the observation that silent gaps longer than this effectively prohibit perceptual integration of preceding and following speech sounds. Sensory information about the preceding speech sound has faded away during the silent gap and therefore is not available for perceptual integration when the following speech sound arrives (Huggins, 1975; Nooteboom, 1979). It should also be noted that, when the pitch after a silent interval is considerably higher or lower than before, the listener perceives a rise or fall in pitch, as if human perception unconsciously bridges the silent gap by filling in the missing part of the pitch contour. It is only when the virtual pitch change becomes unnaturally steep, that this illusion breaks down and is supplanted by perceptual disintegration of the stream of speech, potentially leading to the perception of a second speaker interrupting the first (Nooteboom, Brokx and de Rooij, 1978).

In quasi-periodic complex sounds like voiced speech, pitch is perceived on the basis of the frequency interval between harmonics present in the signal. We might think of some central processing mechanism, finding the common divisor of a number of candidate-harmonics detected in the signal (Goldstein, 1973). The third to the sixth harmonics are most effective, thereby constituting a dominance region for periodicity pitch (Ritsma, 1967). The lowest harmonic or fundamental (i.e. f_0 itself) does not need to be physically present for pitch to be perceived (Schouten, 1940; note that, if the fundamental were necessary, normal male speech would have no perceivable pitch over the telephone, where frequencies below 300 Hz are generally filtered out) (see also Moore, ASPECTS OF AUDITORY PROCESSING).

Human pitch perception is, for signals with clearly defined periodicity, remarkably accurate, the differential threshold (just noticeable difference) being in the order of 0.3 to 0.5 per cent (Flanagan and Saslow, 1958). In natural speech, accuracy of pitch perception varies considerably as a function of the clarity of periodicity in the signal. This clarity of periodicity covers the whole range from the absence of any periodicity in silent gaps or voiceless fricatives, via ill-defined periodicity in voiced fricatives and in hoarse or overly breathy voices, and during rapid pitch changes, to well defined periodicity in vowels with sufficient loudness, produced with well-vibrating vocal cords and without rapid pitch changes. For this reason, which has to do more with the highly variable nature of human speech than with perceptual acuity, it is not feasible to give a general figure of how accurately pitch in speech can be determined, either by humans or by machines. However, it is safe to assume that during most vowel sounds in normal speech with a normal loudness level, pitch can be determined with an accuracy of a few percent.

For the study of intonation, pitch distances are more relevant than absolute pitch: we can recognize the same melody in different pitch ranges, for example those of a male and a female speaker. For this reason it is often useful to measure pitch in semitones rather than in Hertz, the semitone scale being just one possible log scale derived from the Hertz scale. The distance D in semitones between two frequencies f_1 and f_2 is calculated as:

$$D = 12 * \log_2(f_1/f_2) = 12/\log_{10}2 * \log_{10}\frac{f_1}{f_2}$$

One semitone roughly corresponds to a frequency difference of 6 per cent. The reader should be aware, however, that the semitone scale, although adequate for predicting pitch distances, is not adequate for predicting equal perceptual prominences made by pitch movements in different (for example male and female) registers. A psychoacoustic scale derived from the frequency selectivity of the auditory system, associated with distances along the basilar membrane, appears to be more appropriate for this purpose. This psychoacoustic scale can be approximated by the so-called Equivalent Rectangular Bandwidth (ERB) scale, calculated as:

$E = 16.7 \log_{10}(1 + f/165.4),$
$f = 165.4 (10^{0.06E} - 1),$

in which E is the ERB-rate (number of ERBs used to express the difference between two frequencies) and f is frequency in Hz (Hermes and van Gestel, 1991, see also Moore, ASPECTS OF AUDITORY PROCESSING).

Precisely because in speech perception pitch distance is more relevant than absolute pitch, the differential threshold of pitch distance is more relevant than the differential threshold of pitch itself. It has been estimated that only pitch differences of more than three semitones can be discriminated reliably ('t Hart, 1981; 't Hart, Collier and Cohen, 1990:29). This would suggest that pitch differences smaller than three semitones cannot play a role in speech communication, but Rietveld and Gussenhoven (1985) showed that pitch differences of 1.5 semitones create reliable differences in the perception of prominence.

2.3 Perceptual equality: close-copy stylizations

It has been assumed above that there are many apparently capricious details in the pitch fluctuations in speech utterances that are not actively controlled

by the speaker, but are rather involuntary side-effects of other speech production processes. It was also assumed that such involuntary pitch movements do
not contribute to the perceived speech melody. A priori this is a bold assumption, comparable to the assumption that involuntary, segmentally conditioned,
variations in speech sound durations are irrelevant to the perceived rhythmical structure of speech. As we will see later, the latter assumption does not
hold. But the earlier assumption with respect to pitch fluctuations does hold.
This can be shown by using the technique of analysis-by-synthesis, replacing
the original pitch course of an utterance by an artificial one, using for example
an LPC-analysis-resynthesis system (Atal and Hanauer, 1971) or the more
recent Pitch Synchronous Overlap and Add method (PSOLA: Hamon, 1988;
Charpentier and Moulines, 1989, see also Carlson and Granström, SPEECH
SYNTHESIS).

A first step in this demonstration is the so-called 'close-copy stylization' of
pitch in speech utterances, as applied by de Pijper (1983) to British English.
Figure 21.2 gives the natural, measured f_0 curve of an English utterance together with its close-copy stylization. A *close-copy stylization* is defined as a
synthetic approximation of the natural course of pitch, meeting two criteria: it
should be perceptually indistinguishable from the original, and it should contain the smallest possible number of straight-line segments with which this
perceptual equality can be achieved. Note that the graphical representation of
the close-copy stylization continues through the voiceless portions in the utterance. In the actual resynthesis voicing, and therewith pitch, will be suppressed
in these voiceless portions. de Pijper (1983) has convincingly demonstrated in
a formal experiment using 64 native speakers of British-English as his subjects,
that the capricious pitch curves of natural utterances can be simplified to
sequences of straight-line segments in the time – log f_0 domain, without there
being any noticeable difference between original and close-copy pitch curves.
This is an important finding, because it justifies the description of intonation
in terms of rather simple approximations. One should notice that there is no
reason why this finding should be limited to approximations with straight-line
segments. If, for example, one were to conduct a similar study using some
well-defined curvilinear approximations such as cosine-functions (e.g. Fujisaki
and Sudo, 1971), one would obtain a similar outcome: there seems to be no fundamental reason to use straight-line segments in describing intonation. However, as we will see below, there is a practical reason. Straight-line segments
easily lend themselves to a description of intonation in terms of neatly segmented discrete units ('t Hart et al., 1990:71).

2.4 *Perceptual equivalence: towards standard pitch movements*

Close-copy stylization is based on perceptual equality. It is only a first step in
the description of intonation. If we have someone imitate the intonation or

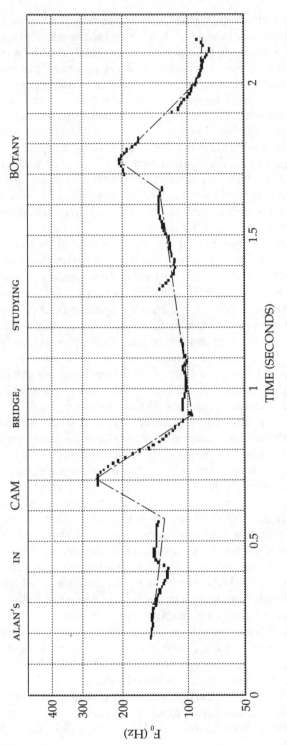

Figure 21.2 Measured course of pitch (dotted line) in a British-English utterance together with a so-called "close-copy" stylization (interrupted line), containing the smallest possible number of straight-line segments with which perceptual equality between original and close-copy can be achieved.

speech melody of an utterance, either with the same words or with different words, or even with no words at all by humming, we obtain a pitch curve that will definitely not be perceptually equal to the original. It will be easy to hear many differences. But yet we, or a panel of native listeners, can hear whether the imitation is successful in conveying the same melodic impression. Apparently, intonation is organized in terms of melodic patterns that are recognizable to native speakers of the language. This calls for a unifying notion different from perceptual equality. For this other notion 't Hart et al. use the term *perceptual equivalence*. Two different courses of f_0 are perceptually equivalent when they are similar to such an extent that one is judged a successful (melodic) imitation of the other ('t Hart et al., 1990:47). Perceptual equivalence implies that the same speech melody can be recognized in two realizations despite easily noticeable differences, in the same way that the same word can be recognized from different realizations.

The powerful notion of perceptual equivalence now allows us, for any intonation language, to set up, by various sorts of generalizations, an inventory of standard pitch movements. Combinations of these generate pitch contours that are perceptually equivalent to naturally-occurring pitch curves. Figure 21.3 gives a measured pitch curve for a British English utterance, together with its close-copy stylization and a standardized stylization. Notice that, in order to arrive at this standardized stylization, a grid is set up with three equidistant lines in the time − log f_0 domain. These three equidistant lines are slightly tilted, thus simulating the phenomenon of *declination*, making the pitch slowly drift down during all stretches where there are no abrupt changes in pitch that affect the perceived melodic properties of the utterance.

Declination has been attested as a rather general phenomenon in many languages. In its uninterrupted form it is generally constrained to rather brief sentences. In longer sentences, particularly in spontaneous speech, it is regularly interrupted by a "declination reset", giving a new high start to the pitch of the next chunk of speech. It is assumed by 't Hart et al. (1990) that the production of declination is not under voluntary control, whereas declination resets are voluntarily controlled by speakers. Other researchers are inclined to believe that at least part of the declination is due to a voluntary down step (Cf. Liberman and Pierrehumbert, 1984; Ladd, 1988). Speakers prefer to let these resets coincide with important boundaries in the constituent structure of the utterance ('t Hart et al., 1990:Chapter 5). It is often not easy to estimate declination from pitch curves measured from naturally spoken utterances, because of the capriciousness of the pitch fluctuations, the variability of the size of pitch movements, and the occurrences of declination resets. 't Hart et al. suggest that the declination should be estimated by first making a close-copy stylization and then by trying to replace the stretches of relatively low pitch by pieces of a single straight-line, a tentative baseline. The tilt of this baseline would then give an estimate of the declination and would, in resynthesis, give the same perceptual result as the original declination.

The three equidistant lines in Figure 21.3, to be called basic pitch levels

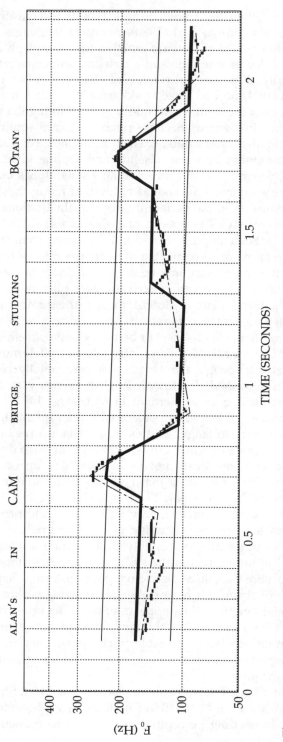

Figure 21.3 Measured course of pitch (dotted line), close-copy stylization (interrupted line), a grid of three declination lines (solid lines), and standardized stylization (bold line) in a British-English utterance.

(topline, midline, baseline) from now on, are typical for the description of British English (See also Brown et al., 1980). For other languages this may be different. For the description of Dutch intonation for example, it appears that two such basic pitch levels, a topline and a baseline, suffice as reference lines for defining virtually all perceptually relevant rises and falls ('t Hart et al., 1990:76). Adriaens (1991) needed three equidistant basic pitch levels with one extra pitch line between the topline and midline, for defining the major standard pitch movements in German. Because pitch levels are equidistant in the time – log f_0 domain, distances can be fixed in semitones. For British English a distance of 12 semitones between baseline and topline gives satisfactory results. For Dutch, 6 semitones and for German 7.5 semitones between baseline and topline are adequate. One should notice that fixing these differences is a very severe reduction in the variability of pitch fluctuations. It is imaginable that for different styles of speech one should use different distances between pitch levels. Such changes would not, however, change the perceptual equivalence in terms of recognizable melodic patterns of the language.

Standard pitch movements can now be defined as more or less rapid transitions from one pitch level to another. Each standard pitch movement is fully characterized by its *direction* (up or down), its *size* (the number of semitones covered by the pitch movement), its *rate of change* (in semitones per second), and its *timing* (in ms after syllable onset or before syllable offset). Number and characterizations of standardized perceptually relevant pitch movements differ from language to language. For Dutch, ten perceptually relevant pitch movements are distinguished, for British English as many as 27 (Willems, 't Hart and Collier, 1988), and for German 11 (Adriaens, 1991).

Although the number of standard perceptually relevant pitch movements may differ from language to language, this number is always limited by the maximum number of categories that can be kept apart on each dimension. For direction this number is obviously not more than two, up or down. With respect to size it has been estimated that no more than three or four distinguishable intervals can be kept apart ('t Hart, 1981). Rate of change allows, within the bounds of a single syllable, only for one rise (and presumably one fall) to be discriminated from nonchanging pitch. Only gradual rises that extend over several syllables may perceptibly differ in rate of change ('t Hart, 1976). With regard to timing within the syllable, it appears that within a syllable of 200 ms, no more than three distinctive positions can be kept apart. The maximum number of abrupt pitch movements, occurring within a single syllable, for a particular language thus appears to be in the order of $2 \times 4 \times 1 \times 3 = 24$. This must be a comforting thought for students of intonation. Of course, the maximum number of possible pitch movements increases somewhat if pitch movements extending over more syllables (gradual rises and gradual falls) are included.

Perceptually, not all pitch movements have the same effect. Some rises and falls, such as the early rise and late fall in Dutch, serve as phonetic realizations of (pitch) accents, by lending perceptual prominence to particular syllables.

Others, such as the late rise and early fall in Dutch, seem more suited to mark some kind of non-finality, either in mid-utterance or at the end of an utterance.

2.5 Combining pitch movements: towards a grammar of intonation

Once one has defined an inventory of pitch movements for a particular language, it should be possible to generate sequences of such pitch movements. Such sequences would then constitute acceptable melodic realizations for speech utterances. Trying to do that, one will soon find out that not all possible sequences are acceptable. So, for example, in Dutch an accent-representing rise cannot be followed by another accent-representing rise without an intermediate fall. Also, studying the distribution of pitch movements in a corpus of utterances, it may become obvious that some pitch movements belong closer together than others: there appears to be a multilevel hierarchical structure to intonation. If we consider pitch movements themselves to constitute the lowest or first level of description, the second level is that of configurations, and the third that of contours.

A configuration is a close-knit intonational unit consisting of one or more consecutive pitch movements, for example a rise followed by a fall or a rise followed by a fall followed by a rise. Generally, constraints on combining pitch movements are much stricter within a configuration than at its boundaries. In their description of Dutch intonation 't Hart et al. distinguish Prefix configurations, Root configurations, and Suffix configurations, notions that closely resemble the time-honoured notions of Head, Nucleus and Tail in the British impressionistic tradition of intonation studies. Prefix configurations are optional and recursive. They always precede another Prefix or a Root. Root configurations are obligatory and non-recursive: each contour must contain only one and not more than one Root. Suffix configurations are optional and non-recursive. A Suffix always follows a Root.

Pitch contours are defined as lawful sequences of configurations. Each pitch contour extends over a clause (in some loose sense of the word clause, referring to a group of words that the speaker has chosen as belonging together, as having some kind of coherence). This entails that multi-clause sentences have as many contours as there are clauses. Because there are recursive elements in contour formation, the number of contours is unlimited.

Many sequences of Prefix, Root and Suffix appear to be unlawful. Therefore explicit rules are needed to generate the lawful sequences and exclude the unlawful ones. The inventory of pitch movements, their combinations in configurations, plus the set of rules generating the lawful contours, together constitute a grammar of intonation. Ideally, such a grammar of intonation generates all and only the acceptable pitch contours of the language. The predictions by the grammar of Dutch intonation were verified against a corpus of 1500 spontaneous and semi-spontaneous utterances, and found to account for 94 per cent of the contours in the corpus ('t Hart and Collier, 1975).

2.6 Basic intonation patterns

For both British English (Gussenhoven, 1983; Gussenhoven, 1984; Willems et al., 1988) and for Dutch (Collier and 't Hart, 1972; Collier, 1975) it has been shown that pitch contours can be classified into different families. Pitch contours belonging to the same family are put in the same class by native listeners when these are asked to sort utterances into a limited arbitrary number of subjective melodic categories. For both Dutch and English it appears that class membership is determined by one or more pitch movements belonging to the Root configuration. The pitch contours belonging to the same family are supposed to be manifestations of the same underlying "basic intonation pattern". In the grammar of intonation each basic intonation pattern can be defined as the family of generation paths that go through the Root configuration that corresponds to that pattern. For both British English and Dutch six such basic intonation patterns can be distinguished, probably carrying different attitudinal and/or emotional connotations. For Russian some ten such basic intonation patterns have been distinguished (Odé, 1989). Most of these basic intonation patterns are used rather infrequently. In Dutch, over 60 per cent of pitch contour tokens one encounters in everyday speech are realizations of a single basic intonation pattern, the so-called "hat pattern".

2.7 Text and tune

So far intonation has been dealt with here virtually without reference to the sequences of words on which it is superimposed in actual utterances. In order to select a fitting pitch contour for a particular sentence, or sequence of pitch contours in the case of longer sentences, one has at least to know two things about the sentence. One has to know which words are to be provided with a pitch accent on their lexically stressed syllable, and whether, and if so where, boundaries between successive clauses in the sentences are to be made. Once these things are known, acceptable pitch contours can be selected for all clauses from the ones generated by the grammar of intonation. Of course, for each clause or sentence with known accent placements, there still is a variety of different possible pitch contours, and each pitch contour, due to its inherent flexibility with respect to time, can be made to fit a variety of different clauses or sentences.

In normal human speech the speaker determines which words are to be accented and where clause boundaries are to be made according to rules and strategies that will be briefly discussed in section 4. In synthetic speech, for example in text-to-speech systems, such rules and strategies have to be approximated by automatic text analysis (Kulas and Rühl, 1985; Carlson and Granström, 1986b; Allen, Hunnicutt and Klatt, 1987; Quené and Kager, 1993; Dirksen and Quené, 1993). Once this is done, appropriate and acceptably sounding pitch contours can be generated automatically and synchronized with the synthetic speech. Generally, in synthetic speech rules for generating pitch contours are limited to pitch contours that are manifestations of a single, neutral sounding, basic intonation pattern, as there is no basis to select between different intonation patterns. (See also Carlson and Granström, SPEECH SYNTHESIS.)

The approach to the description of intonation sketched here, has the great advantage that it may lead to a set of rules that generate melodical equivalents to the vast majority of naturally occurring pitch curves in a particular language. This is achieved by severe reduction of reality by stylization and standardization. The result is that rule-generated equivalents of natural pitch curves, although on their own perfectly acceptable, are often much less lively than their natural counterparts. A long text read out with only synthetic pitch contours as generated by the grammar, may sound somewhat dull and monotonous. Future research in this area might be directed at capturing generalizations that would reintroduce some of the natural liveliness in synthetic pitch contours, for example by varying excursion size and tone register.

3 The rhythm of speech

3.1 Introduction

This section is concerned with the rhythm of speech. The very notion "rhythm of speech" suggests that two different utterances may share a common, underlying, property, called the same "rhythm". Intuitively, this can be brought to awareness by imitating the rhythmical pattern of an utterance with nonsense syllables, as "The MAN in the STREET" (where capitalized words are accented), imitated with "daDAdadaDA". Notice that one can do this at least in two different ways, either preserving the speech melody of the original utterance, or in a monotone. In case of the monotonous version we still can judge whether or not the imitation of the original rhythmical structure is successful. This suggests that it is possible, at least in first approximation, to study the rhythm of speech as a function of the temporal patterning of speech, without taking into account the melodic aspects.

As in the case of intonation, we will approach the rhythm of speech from the phonetic angle, concentrating on the ensemble of speech sound durations, that together constitute the temporal patterning of speech, attempting to focus on those aspects of temporal patterns that are relevant to the perceived rhythmical structure of speech, and de-emphasizing those aspects that are not. However, as will be shown below, the state of affairs with respect to rhythm is very different from the one in intonation. It will be made clear that different factors contributing to durational variation cannot so easily be separated. The primacy of perceptual structure, so helpful in the description of intonation to achieve a severe and useful reduction of capricious reality, teaches us that not only in production but also in perception temporal patterning is inherently complex and much less easily modeled. The corollary of this is that below we will not give primacy to a single unified approach to the study of temporal patterning, but rather will be more eclectic, asking attention for different approaches that may be seen as complementary. More particularly, we will discuss well-controlled experiments on so-called "reiterant" speech in 3.3, focusing on rhythmical speech patterns as it were in vitro, similar controlled experiments on real speech in 3.4, the many functions and quantitative interactions in temporal patterning in 3.5, statistical database studies, that seem to be indispensable as heuristic tools in this area, in 3.6, and rule systems for temporal patterning providing us with a perceptual testing ground in 3.7. But first we will discuss some basic aspects of the production and perception of speech sound durations in 3.2.

3.2 Speech sound durations: production and perception

Most sounds in nature are not indefinitely prolonged. They have an onset and an offset, and physical duration is determined by the time interval elapsing between onset and offset. Of course, perceived duration is determined by perceived onset and perceived offset, and an appropriate perceptual measure of time elapsed. This is not only so for the duration of sounds, but also for the duration of silent intervals between sounds.

In speech we rarely encounter isolated sounds. As speech develops in time, more or less abrupt changes in amplitude and spectral properties alternate with more or less homogeneous segments. Abrupt changes in the physical signal are caused by changes in the configuration of the vocal organs, such as opening and closing of the aperture of the vocal tract and onsets and offsets of vocal cord vibrations. Such changes demarcate both filled intervals, such as manifestations of vowels and fricatives, and silent intervals, as in manifestations of stop consonants. In oscillographic and spectrographic registrations of speech, where time is represented by spatial distance, one can measure the physical durations of such intervals. Figure 21.4 gives an oscillographic representation of an English utterance "the queen said, the knight is a monster".

In such registrations we can measure physical durations of vowel-like segments, nasal segments, fricative segments, silent intervals, noise bursts, etc., by making some assumptions about relevant criteria for segmenting the signal. In the case of clear and rapid changes in the signal such criteria are mostly straightforward, and segmentation accuracy is often more precise than human perception. In the case of less clear, slower changes such as in glides or in slurred speech, there may be more uncertainty both for the investigator and to human speech perception. Notice that the perceptual relevance of measured

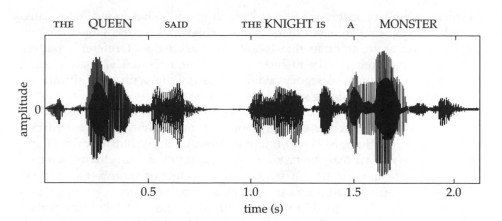

THE QUEEN SAID THE KNIGHT IS A MONSTER

Figure 21.4 Oscillographic representation of the utterance "The queen said, the knight is a monster".

durations depends on the level of perception one is interested in. For example, the duration of formant transitions at the beginning of the vowel in a CV combination, being part of connected speech, may be relevant to the perceived consonant, but irrelevant to the contribution of the vowel-like segment as a whole to the per-ceived rhythm of speech.

Differential thresholds for isolated non-speech or speech sounds with durations in between approximately 40 and 250 ms are in the order of 5 to 15 per cent (Ruhm, Mencke, Milburn, Cooper and Rose, 1966; Abel, 1972a), depending on the type of experiment. For silent intervals differential thresholds are somewhat higher (Abel, 1972b; Fujisaki, Nakamura and Imoto, 1973). Also, durations of silent intervals tend to be somewhat underestimated in comparison to those of filled intervals (Burghardt, 1973a, 1973b). Sound and silent interval durations shorter than about 40 ms and longer than about 250 ms are less accurately perceived than those in between these values. Very short intervals, shorter than roughly 40 ms for silent intervals and shorter than roughly 20 ms for filled intervals, do not seem to have subjective durations at all.

There is, mostly for practical reasons, relatively little research on just noticeable differences of speech sound durations being part of connected speech. However, it has been argued (Nooteboom and Doodeman, 1980) that we may infer the differential threshold, for example for vowel duration, from a binary forced choice phoneme classification task. In the experiment concerned the vowel of a Dutch word "taak", embedded in a longer utterance, was given a number of different durations. Long durations led to perceiving "taak" with long /a:/, short durations to perceiving the word "tak" with short /ɑ/. The transition of /ɑ/ to /a:/ as a function of vowel duration could be modeled by a cumulative normal distribution with a mean (the phoneme boundary) of approximately 90 ms, and a standard deviation in the order of 5 ms. This suggests that the duration of embedded segments can, if the need arises, be perceived with an accuracy that is at least as good as that found for isolated sounds. Of course in an experiment like this listeners hear the same utterance over and over again, and may thus establish a fixed temporal reference pattern that may hone their ability to hear small differences (cf. O'Shaughnessy, 1987:160–161). Using a category judgment technique with nine durational categories for an embedded vowel and an embedded fricative, being part of a longer sentence, Klatt and Cooper (1975) estimated differential thresholds of 25 ms and more. The task is difficult, however, and may overestimate differential thresholds. Huggins (1972) found differential thresholds of even 40 ms, but it may be argued that the task he used, asking in an "up-down" strategy whether a particular duration in an utterance is longer or shorter than normal, measured perceptual tolerance rather than perceptual acuity. Of course, perceptual tolerances may be more relevant to the purpose of this chapter than differential thresholds. One should notice, however, that perceptual tolerances measured for specific segments in specific utterances cannot easily be generalized to other segments and other contexts. Perceptual tolerances seem to vary considerably from one segment to another and one context to another in connected speech, and as yet we have no way of making adequate predictions of perceptual tolerances.

3.3 Prosodic temporal patterns: evidence from reiterant speech

Speech is not rhythmical in the strict sense that dance music is, with such a regular alternation of strong and weak elements in the stream of sound that the upcoming elements can be fairly precisely anticipated in psychological time from the preceding ones. Speech is rhythmical, however, in the looser sense that its development in time is controlled by some hierarchical mental pattern giving each syllable a certain strength that controls aspects of its production, among which is its duration. The resulting patterns are recognizable and can be imitated by users of the language, and lend speech an organization that helps its mental processing by the listener. Rhythmical imitations of speech utterances in sequences of identical nonsense syllables have been named "reiterant speech" by Nakatani and Schaffer (1978), but their use in speech research is much older than the name (Cf. Lindblom, 1968; Lindblom and Rapp, 1973; Nooteboom, 1972).

Figure 21.5 shows temporal patterns obtained with reiterant speech for Dutch words spoken in isolation, varying from one to four syllables, with stress on the first syllable that contains either the long vowel /a:/ or the short vowel /ɑ/. These data, among other things, exemplify the well known phenomenon of *compensatory shortening*: the more syllables follow the lexically stressed syllable within the same unit, the shorter its duration (and the durations of its segments). The data also clearly exemplify the phenomenon of *final lengthening*: the segment durations of the unstressed last syllable are considerably

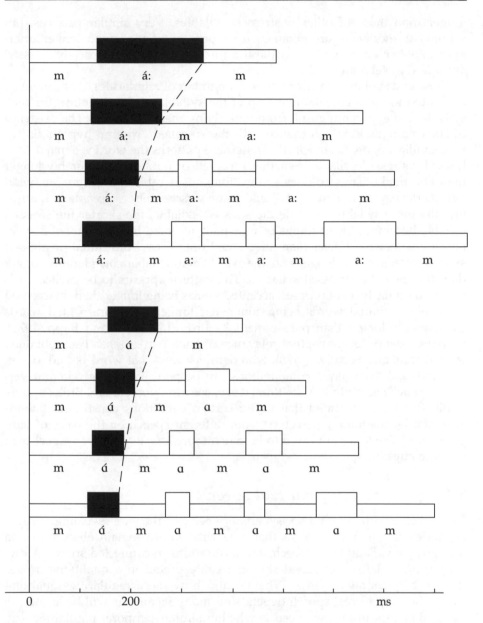

Figure 21.5 Schematized temporal patterns of reiterant versions of Dutch spoken words with stress on the first syllable, and varying from one to four syllables. Top: with repetitions of the syllable [ma:m], bottom: with repetitions of the syllable [mɑm].

longer than those of other unstressed syllables. Very similar patterns, but somewhat shortened, are obtained for words embedded with longer utterances, spoken either with or without a pitch accent on the lexically stressed syllable (Nooteboom, 1972).

These and similar data clearly reveal a number of regularities, that cannot be attributed to the segmental make up of the syllables, being identical for each syllable, but apparently result from underlying mental patterns. The existence of such patterns is in accordance with the so-called "rhythm hypothesis" of Kozhevnikov and Chistovich (1965). In these patterns the word is a major unit. Lexically stressed syllables, whether accented or not, are considerably longer than non-final unstressed ones and exhibit considerable *anticipatory compensatory shortening* (as in Figure 21.5) and some *perseveratory compensatory shortening* (the more syllables precede the stressed syllable, the shorter the stressed syllable becomes). Other things being equal, accented lexically stressed syllables are somewhat longer than unaccented ones. The word-initial unstressed syllable is somewhat longer and the word final syllable considerably longer than the medial unstressed syllables. The pattern appears to be cyclical: it is repeated on the level of phrases, accented words being longer than unaccented ones, phrase initial words being somewhat longer and phrase final words considerably longer than phrase medial words (Lindblom and Rapp, 1973). Partial evidence for perceptual relevance of such patterns has been obtained by Nakatani and Schaffer (1978), who demonstrated that word boundaries in trisyllabic adjective noun combinations can be perceived from reiterant versions of such short phrases. de Rooij (1979; see also Nooteboom, Brokx and de Rooij, 1979) demonstrated that under certain conditions constituent boundaries can be adequately perceived from reiterant speech on the basis of temporal cues. The latter appeared to be much more effective in this respect than melodic cues.

3.4 Confirmation from real speech

Experiments with reiterant speech are nice because they are revealing of regular underlying mental patterns that otherwise would remain obscure due to the extreme variability of speech sound durations in connected speech. However, the regularities obtained should be interpreted in a qualitative rather than in a quantitative sense. Whether and how these regularities quantitatively show up in real speech depends on many factors, as will be argued in 3.6. A first reassurance we need is whether similar temporal regularities can be demonstrated for real words and phrases, and whether such regularities can be shown to be part of what language users (implicitly) know about the way words and phrases in their language should sound. Both issues are, by way of example, addressed in Figure 21.6 with respect to the phenomenon of compensatory shortening.

The figure plots durations of the vowels, long /a:/ or short /ɑ/, of lexically stressed initial syllables of real Dutch words varying from one to four syllables, as a function of the number of syllables in the word. Three types of

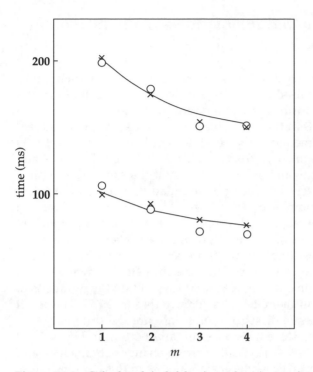

Figure 21.6 Calculated (solid line), spoken (crosses) and adjusted (circles) durations of stressed [a:] (top curve) and [ɑ] (bottom curve) as a function of the number of syllables in the word which remain to be produced at the beginning of the syllable concerned.

durations are plotted: durations measured in these words spoken in isolation, durations obtained in a method of adjustment with synthetically spoken versions of these words (see below), and durations calculated from a simple empirical rule $V = D/m^\alpha$, in which V is the vowel duration to be calculated, D is a standard duration for the vowel concerned, m is the number of syllables following in the word plus 1, and $^\alpha$ is a constant with the value 0.2 for both long /a:/ and short /ɑ/. Clearly compensatory shortening is strongly present in the spoken versions and well described by the empirical rule. In the method of adjustment used to obtain the third kind of data, subjects were asked to adjust, by turning a knob, the durations of the stressed vowels in synthetic versions of these words such that the word as a whole sounded as natural as possible. Again the pattern of compensatory shortening is accurately reproduced, showing that such regularities are part of the mental representation of speech. Similar results were obtained for a number of the regularities discussed in 3.3, such as stressed versus unstressed and initial and final lengthening (Nooteboom, 1972, 1973), demonstrating that, at least under certain conditions, patterns found in reiterant speech also show up in real words and that they are psychologically real.

3.5 *Multifunctionality and interactions in the temporal patterning in speech*

In the study of intonation we have seen that the natural course of pitch can be supplanted with a highly stylized approximation without noticeable changes to perception. This finding formed the foundation of highly simplified and standardized melodic models of the perceptually relevant structure of intonation. These models can immediately be used in synthetic speech virtually without adaptation to the segmental structure of speech, except for some simple synchronization rules. It would be nice and easy if the same trick applied to speech rhythm. We can try this out by manipulating a naturally spoken speech utterance of some complexity as follows. We have someone speak a reiterant version of that utterance. Both original utterance and the reiterant version are analyzed by means of Linear Prediction (see Liljencrants, SPEECH SIGNAL PROCESSING). In both original and reiterant version we mark each syllable boundary. After that we shrink and stretch, before resynthesis, all syllable durations in the original utterance so that they obtain the durations of the corresponding syllables in the reiterant utterance (Figure 21.7). The result of this exercise in many cases is disastrous. Not only are the differences between the two versions of the same utterance (top and bottom in Figure 21.7) easily perceived, but the perceived rhythmic pattern changes completely, and may become highly unnatural. The reader may note that in this demonstration experiment it is implicitly assumed that syllables are the basic units of timing in speech. It has also been suggested that rather intervals from vowel onset to vowel onset determine the perceived rhythmical patterns in speech (Huggins, 1968). Redoing the experiment lining up intervals between successive vowel onsets will produce results that are, although not identical, very similar. Either way, this simple classroom experiment immediately confronts us with the relative inviolability of temporal patterning of speech.

The reason for our failure is to be found in the multifunctional nature of speech sound durations, that are affected by a great many very divergent factors in production, and affect a great many very divergent perceived aspects of speech. Speech sound durations are affected by and carry information on both within syllable factors and between syllable factors. Examples of within syllable factors are segment identity, and the identities of preceding and following phonemic segments. Segment identity is, in many languages, involved in the opposition between phonologically long and short phonemes. On a more phonetic level, we observe for example that open vowels like /a/ have, other things being equal, longer durations than closed vowels like /e/ or /o/, simply because it takes more time to open the mouth further than to open it less (House, 1961; Nooteboom, 1972). It has also been found that the closed interval of a voiceless stop is much longer than the one in a voiced stop, and that this difference contributes to identification (Lisker, 1957; Slis and Cohen, 1969a and 1969b). A clear example of an effect of the following phonemic

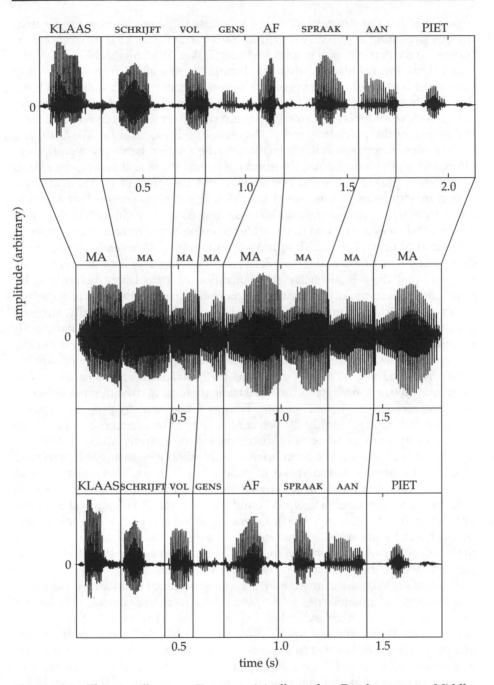

Figure 21.7 Three oscillograms. Top: an originally spoken Dutch utterance. Middle: a reiterant version of the same utterance, each syllable being spoken as [ma:]. Bottom: same as top, but with syllable durations made identical to those in the reiterant version.

segment is that the vowel preceding a voiceless stop consonant is longer than the one preceding a voiced stop within the same syllable. This difference contributes to the perception of stop voicedness (Lisker, 1957; Slis and Cohen, 1969a and 1969b). But we also see that the duration of the silent interval of a stop consonant is affected by the preceding vowel segment: after a long vowel this duration is markedly shorter than after a short vowel. In perception the duration of a closed interval of a stop consonant can affect the perceived phonological length of the preceding vowel (Nooteboom, Brokx and de Rooij, 1978).

Examples of between syllable factors are the relation between overall vocal effort and segment durations, the effects of lexical stress and accent, the effects of sentence, phrase and word boundaries, and the effect of rhythmical alternation in sequences of unstressed syllables. It has been shown that as vocal effort increases, vowel durations increase and consonant durations decrease. These differences are related to the wider opening of the mouth in loud speech compared to normal speech. It appeared impossible, however, to model these differences in a linear scaling model of the behaviour of lips and jaw. This suggests that there is extensive reorganization of articulatory behaviour, by which other perceptually relevant aspects of temporal patterning remain better preserved (Lindblom, 1989). Other things being equal, lexically stressed syllables are often considerably longer than lexically unstressed syllables, although this difference itself depends much on position within word and phrase. Perception of lexical stress depends to a large extent on the pattern of syllable durations (Lindblom, 1968; Nooteboom, 1972; Nakatani and Schaffer, 1978). Over and above the effect of lexical stress there is a considerable effect of sentence accents or phrasal accents. Eefting found that in prepared speech accented words are roughly 20 per cent longer than unaccented ones. This difference appears to be equally distributed over lexically stressed and unstressed syllables. It cannot be tampered with without reducing the perceived acceptability of speech and speed of processing (Eefting, 1991). Segments at word boundaries tend to be somewhat longer than segments within words. This difference contributes to word boundary detection (Nakatani and Schaffer, 1978; Quené, 1992; Eefting, 1991). Quené (1989) showed that in spoken versions of word pairs such as "known ocean" versus "no notion", excised from the utterances they were spoken in, word boundaries can be detected with 80 per cent accuracy on the basis of temporal patterning.

Segments in syllables immediately preceding sentence boundaries and major and minor phrase boundaries in the stream of speech are considerably longer than segments in other syllables, other things being equal (Klatt, 1976; Nooteboom, Brokx and de Rooij, 1978; van Santen, 1992; Campbell, 1992). Slootweg demonstrated that in sequences of three unstressed non-word initial and non-word final syllables in one spoken word, the middle one is rhythmically stronger and has a longer duration than the other two (Slootweg, 1988). Lehiste (1970) points out that, at least in some languages, speech tempo affects syllable durations differentially. In English, unstressed syllables are affected more than stressed syllables. It has been assumed that this is typical for so-called stress-timed languages in contrast to so-called syllable-timed languages

(Bertinetto, 1981). Stress-timed languages are supposed to have a tendency to make intervals consisting of a stressed syllable plus all following unstressed ones equally long; syllable-timed languages are supposed to have a tendency to make all syllables equally long. Den Os (1988) found little reason for this distinction in a systematic comparison between spoken Dutch, an alleged stress-timed language, and spoken Italian, supposedly a syllable-timed language. Presumably, the intuitive difference between stress- and syllable-timed languages has its origin in the presence versus absence of a phonological length opposition, and/or the presence versus absence of vowel reduction, and other aspects of the segmental make-up of syllables, such as the number of consonants permitted in consonant clusters.

The fact that there are so many different factors acting simultaneously on the perceptually relevant temporal patterns of speech makes life hard for speech researchers who want to give a systematic account of such temporal patterning. Life becomes even harder because there appear to be strong quantitative interactions between various factors. The well-known effect of compensatory shortening (see 3.3 and 3.4) on vowel durations is very different, both in milliseconds and in percentage, for different vowel phonemes, depending on their "compressibility". Not only vowel identity, but also the identities of preceding and following consonants affect vowel compressibility (Klatt, 1976), thereby changing the quantitative effect of compensatory shortening. This quantitative effect changes again, both in absolute and in relative terms, when speech tempo is changed. The higher the speech tempo, the less shortening we find (Nooteboom, 1992). Very brief vowels, like /ɪ/ before voiced stops, may not show any appreciable compensatory shortening at all, although in that case the syllable as a whole may still be shortened somewhat by shortening consonant durations surrounding the vowel.

The durational difference between lexically stressed and unstressed syllables and their segments is also far from fixed, and depends both on the type of segments in the syllable and on syllable position in word and utterance. In word medial and utterance medial position this difference between stressed and unstressed syllables may be considerable, in the order of hundreds of milliseconds, but in prepausal position the difference often is negligible, apparently because prepausal lengthening has exhausted the "stretchability" of the syllable. It is as if each particular segment type within a particular syllabic environment can only vary its duration between a maximum and a minimum that are typical for that segment in that environment (Klatt, 1976).

Such extreme interactions between many different factors affecting syllable and segment durations (of which many more examples are known, cf. van Santen, 1992) have the result that the systematic effects on speech sound durations of any one particular factor can only reliably be assessed when we take the effects of many other factors into account (Nooteboom, 1992). This has some consequences. One is that we cannot study or model the quantitative effects of rhythmical factors, presumably coinciding with the "between syllable factors" listed above, in isolation from "within syllable factors". Another is that one needs rather large databases and statistical tools to get an appropriate impression of the factors involved and their quantitative interactions. One also needs sophisticated quantitative models to account for the effects of these factors and their interactions.

So far we have concentrated on speech sound durations in stretches of speech between speech pauses. Speech pauses themselves are an integral part of temporal patterning, and play an important role in speech perception. Notice that one should make a distinction between acoustic silent intervals and perceived speech pauses. Not all silent intervals are perceived as speech pauses. For example silent intervals as part of the production of voiceless stop consonants are generally not perceived as speech pauses, unless their duration is abnormally long. Also subjectively speech pauses may be perceived where there is no silent interval, provided there is considerable final lengthening and/or a clear melodic boundary marker (Nooteboom, Brokx and de Rooij, 1978). So a subjectively perceived speech pause is triggered by final lengthening, whether or not it is accompanied by a melodic boundary marker (particular pitch movement and/or declination reset; see 2.4), and whether or not it is accompanied by a silent interval. Speech pauses, as cues to prosodic boundaries, are regularly used to demarcate major or minor phrases, and the particular acoustic realization seems to depend on the relation between the prosodic boundary and its position in the hierarchical constituent structure of the sentence being spoken (Harris and Umeda, 1974; Grosjean, Grosjean and Lane, 1979; Cooper and Paccia-Cooper, 1980; 't Hart et al., 1990). Production of speech pauses is to a large extent optional, and depends much on style of speech and speech tempo (Goldman-Eisler, 1968).

There are also quantitative interactions between the duration of silent intervals as cues to speech pauses on the one hand and the production and perception of segment durations in the preceding syllable on the other. The longer the silent interval, the more final lengthening is produced by the speaker and expected by the listener. This expectation can affect the perception of phonological length of the syllable nucleus (Nooteboom and Doodeman, 1981). There is also another kind of interaction: the actual durations of silent intervals at boundary positions in longer spoken sentences appear to be predictable from the average stress group duration (time interval between vowel onsets) in the preceding stretch of speech plus the number of phonemes in the stress group containing the speech pause (Fant and Kruckenberg, 1989). Fant and Kruckenberg also found that silent interval durations at prosodic boundaries are not stochastically distributed but seem to cluster around certain values, the longer ones being multiples of the shortest one.

3.6 Quantitative approaches to the study of temporal patterning

Researchers have many reasons to study the temporal organisation of speech. These reasons may be of a fundamental scientific nature, or may be technologically oriented. The first, more fundamental, reasons include for example a desire to elucidate the social, mental, physiological, or acoustic processes in speech communication (production and/or perception), or to find evidence for the psychological reality of linguistic units, patterns or rules. The second, more technological, reasons may stem from a wish to improve speech synthesis-by-rule or automatic speech recognition. This division between fundamentally motivated and technologically oriented research goals seems to be parallelled by a distinction between two types of data gathering. Fundamental research questions are generally approached with well controlled, but limited, stimulus materials, carefully designed for testing specific hypotheses. Examples abound in the literature. At the other end of the data-gathering dimension are statistical studies of speech segment durations based on more or less extensive corpuses of real, often connected, speech. Typically, such studies stem from technologically oriented research. Examples are provided by Barnwell (1971), Harris and Umeda (1974), Crystal and House (1982, 1988a, 1988b, 1988c, 1988d, 1990), Fant and Kruckenberg (1988a, 1988b, 1989), Fant, Nord and Kruckenberg (1986, 1987), Campbell (1990) and van Santen (1992).

Van Santen basically used as a corpus a set of isolated sentences, together containing 13,048 word tokens, spoken by a single male speaker. He investigated quantitative effects on vowel durations of the following seven factors:

— Vowel identity
— Identities of the surrounding segments
— Position of the vowel in the syllable: left- and right-open versus closed syllables
— Position of the syllable within the word (number of syllables that precede and follow in the word); or within the stress interval (the number of unstressed syllables that precede and follow the target vowel in the sentence)
— Stress status of the syllable
— Position of the word in the sentence: effects of phrase boundaries
— Accent status of the word.

(The effects of speaking rate and syntactic structure were explicitly not analysed.)

Except for stress intervals, all factors were found to have a considerable effect on vowel durations. Durations predicted from an eight parameter model incorporating these factors showed a correlation of 0.9 with the observed durations, accounting for 81 per cent of the variance.

Such statistical studies of speech sound durations have shown a number of systematic regularities in the temporal organisation of speech, sometimes confirming, at other times seemingly contradicting earlier findings. For example, Crystal and House (1989) found no evidence for compensatory shortening in American English. This is in agreement with the findings of Umeda (1975) for rapid connected speech, but is in contrast to what Harris and Umeda (1974) found for slower speech and is also in contrast to the findings of van Santen (1992).

Statistical studies of speech sound durations also consistently confirm that there are strong quantitative interactions between different factors affecting speech sound durations. These interactions can be modelled by equations combining additive terms with multiplicative terms. A well known example is the empirical rule proposed by Klatt (1976), which in its simple form can be written as:

$$DUR = k(D_{inh} - D_{min}) + D_{min}$$

in which:

DUR is the segment duration to be calculated,
k is a parameter describing a context effect, or any combination of such parameters,
D_{inh} is a table value standing for the segment-specific inherent duration,
D_{min} is a table value standing for the segment-specific minimal duration.

In this model, context parameters provide a multiplicative term, and segment-specific parameters provide additive terms. Furthermore, context parameters are functionally combined, under the implicit assumption that the order of the joint effects of these parameters is unaffected by other factors. The model was until recently never rigorously tested. van Santen and Olive (1989) show how to generalize models of this type mathematically and how such models can be tested by analyzing the covariances between sub-arrays of a multifactorial data matrix. van Santen and Olive applied their method of model analysis to a data base containing 304 different phrases of two nonsense words, read by one male speaker at two speaking rates. They showed for vowel durations that, contrary to Klatt's model, in their database the segment-specific factors need only a multiplicative term, and the context factor both a multiplicative and an additive term. They also showed that no factors could be functionally combined.

This approach is interesting because it allows the researcher to tune both the mathematical form of the model and the values of its parameters to real data. If this method of analysis could be applied to large databases of real connected speech, it holds the promise that we may finally come to grips with the complex and until now obscuring interactions between many factors that affect speech sound durations. Evidently, this will not only be of advantage to speech synthesis-by-rule, or automatic speech recognition, but may also provide an interesting testing ground for predictions made by models of speech production, and a rich source of testable hypotheses concerning speech perception.

Of course, there is no practical way in which we can be sure that the list of factors taken into account in this kind of modelling is exhaustive. Furthermore, the approach itself is not based on theories or models of speech production and speech perception, but rather represents the regularities in a database in the form of empirical rules. Predicting the effects of 'new' factors, that is factors that have hitherto been overlooked, should come from theoretical accounts of the mental, physiological, and acoustic processes in speech production and perception. Such accounts are often partial, not being part of any complete theory or model of all the processes involved in the production and perception of speech, and quantitative predictions are often very specific. Because of this, there remains a need for testing such predictions in vitro, in specifically designed laboratory experiments with well controlled stimulus materials. An approach as proposed by van Santen and Olive can never replace, but rather is complementary to, theoretical and experimental studies of different processes in the production and perception of speech.

3.7 Speech rhythm and rule systems for the temporal patterning of speech

In terms of rule systems for the temporal patterning of speech that could be used for example in speech synthesis by rule, we can operationalize the rhythmic rules as those rules that take care of aspects of temporal patterning that, at least qualitatively, show up in reiterant versions of real utterances. The remaining rules could be named syllable production rules. We can then imagine a rule system that first takes care of syllable production, producing an idealized temporal pattern for each syllable to be spoken, and then applies the rules responsible for speech rhythm. In fact, there are quite a few rule systems that are organized in this way (Campbell and Isard, 1991). One should realize, however, that due to the strong quantitative interactions discussed earlier, the rhythmic rules cannot be formulated in terms of constant additive or multiplicative values. Instead, they should contain parameters the values of which can only be filled in by going back to the level of syllable structure. Conversely, some aspects of syllable structure, such as assimilation, degemination, coarticulation and reduction, can only be adequately decided on after the rhythmic rules have applied, and the actual course of pitch generated in the intonation module can only be synchronized with the utterance after the complete temporal pattern has been generated. Generally the relations between parameter values and conditioning factors are given in lookup tables of considerable elaborateness, but in current rule systems the two-way interactions are often neglected. Due to this, synthetic speech, although intelligible, sounds often unnaturally over-articulated, and pitch fluctuations are sometimes inadequately sychronized with the segmental structure of the utterance. There is considerable room here for further study of the interactions between different aspects of speech production and for modelling such interactions.

The difficulty in setting up adequate rule systems for the temporal patterns of speech derives from the fact that the sequence of speech sound durations code so many different things simultaneously and interactively. This obscures the relation between the rather simple abstract rhythmical patterns of speech on the one hand and their realizations in speech as it is produced on the other. As illustrated in the beginning of this section on speech rhythm, it is deceivingly simple for humans to recognize and imitate rhythmical patterns of speech utterances. To have a machine perform the same feat is as yet far beyond our capabilities.

4 Some communicative functions of speech prosody

4.1 Introduction

What is the use of speech prosody in normal speech communication? In normal written or printed text there is, apart from punctuation and the use of capitals, very little that corresponds to prosodic patterns in speech. Yet many people easily read more words per minute than speakers can speak at their fastest rate. There is, however, a major difference between text and speech. Text is spatially presented, such that much of it is simultaneously present to the reader. Speech is not. At each moment in time the sound of speech is nothing more than a momentary disturbance of air pressure. One moment it is there, the next moment it is gone. Because speech is often listened to in the presence of other sounds, continuously decisions have to be made which successive sounds are to be integrated in the utterance being perceived and which are to be rejected as extraneous. Here prosody helps (4.2).

The fleeting nature of the sound of speech also has the consequence that human perceptual processing of speech draws heavily on human short term memory functions. It is all in the mind. A listener cannot go back to the physical stimulus during processing, because that stimulus has forever vanished in the past. Yet we notice that in normal speech a great many phonemes are very rapidly produced, becoming grossly degraded to the extent that they become unidentifiable without context, or even are completely deleted. We may imagine that if this were not so, speech would become much too slow for the listeners to keep attention focused on the contents of the message. As we learn from the comparison with reading, comprehension can go much faster than speech allows. But the less specified segmental structure is, the more support a listener needs from suprasegmental, prosodic cues. These cues can differentiate between more important and less important information as coded in accent patterns (4.3), and also organize the message in chunks that are easily processed by the listener, at the same time revealing aspects of the linguistic structure of the message (4.4).

These examples of communicative functions of speech prosody will be briefly described below. The list is not exhaustive. Prosody may to a certain extent also be used to characterize utterances as statements, questions, or exclamations

(Hadding-Koch and Studdert-Kennedy, 1964; Geluykens, 1987; 't Hart et al., 1990, pp. 111ff), to convey information on attitude and emotion (Crystal, 1969; Murray and Arnott, 1993), or to characterize certain styles of speech.

4.2 Auditory continuity and the separation of simultaneous voices

Cherry (1953) addressed himself to the question of how one recognizes what one person is saying when others are speaking at the same time, a phenomenon he referred to as the 'cocktail party effect'. Cherry mentioned as possible facilitating factors directional hearing, visual information, individual differences in voice characteristics and dialect and transitional probabilities. Although his main experiments were directed at directional hearing and transitional probability, he also observed that, when all the above-mentioned factors except transitional probability were eliminated by recording two messages spoken by the same speaker on the same magnetic tape, the result may sound "like a babel", but the messages can still be separated.

Darwin (1975) neatly demonstrated that pitch continuity is an important factor in "voice tracking". He presented listeners simultaneously with two different passages of speech, spoken by the same speaker, either or not switching from one ear to the other and vice versa during presentation. The stimulus material was so constructed that four conditions were obtained, a normal condition with no switch, a semantic change condition, in which pitch was continuous on each ear but the verbal message switched ears in the middle, an intonation change condition where the verbal message was continuous on each ear, but intonation switched ears in the middle, and a semantic and intonation change condition, in which both verbal message and intonation switched ears simultaneously. Listeners were instructed to attend to one ear only. Switching the intonation from one ear to the other caused a high percentage of intrusions of the unattended ear, showing that listeners track a voice in the presence of another voice (and in the absence of directional cues) mainly on the basis of pitch continuity.

From Darwin's experiment it is reasonable to assume that perceptual separation of simultaneous speech messages is easier for messages in different pitch ranges than for messages in the same pitch range, where the listener may inadvertently switch to the other message whenever the two pitches cross. This was shown to be correct by Brokx and Nooteboom (1982), in an experiment with resynthesized speech utterances from a single speaker, with artificially manipulated pitches. There were approximately 20 per cent less word perception errors with different than with the same pitch ranges.

Obviously, intelligibility of speech in the presence of other speech is better when the pitches or pitch ranges of the two competing messages are different than when they are the same. This effect can be related to the phenomenon of "perceptual fusion", occurring whenever two simultaneous sounds have identical pitches, and to "perceptual tracking": whenever the pitches of target and interfering speech cross each other, the listener runs the risk of inadvertently switching his attention from the target to the interfering speech.

4.3 Accent patterns and their role in speech communication

In the act of speaking, some words are accented by means of an accent-representing pitch movement on their lexically stressed syllable, with some concomitant cues such as some extra loudness and some lengthening of the word. Of course we can establish that a particular word is accented without worrying too much how the accent is realized in the act of speaking: the notion 'accent' is abstract with respect to its realisation, and as such basically refers to the same thing as the notions 'sentence stress' or 'word group stress' (Chomsky and Halle, 1968; Liberman, 1979; Selkirk, 1984).

To show how accents are used in speech communication we need to introduce the notion 'focus', used here as in Ladd (1980), Gussenhoven (1983), Selkirk (1984) and Baart (1987). A constituent, which can be a single word but also a word group or phrase, can be presented by the speaker as in focus (or +focus) by means of an accent on a single word that we call the prosodic head of the constituent. The position of the prosodic head within each potential constituent can be derived from syntactic structure. The reasons why a particular constituent can be put into focus, and thus receive an accent on its prosodic head, do not seem to be particularly well understood. But one of these reasons appears to be the 'newness' to the listener of the information contained in that constituent. Compare the following examples (accented words are capitalized):

(Who wrote that novel?)
(a) The dean of our FACULTY wrote that silly book

(Who wrote that novel?)
(b) The DEAN of our faculty wrote that silly book

In (a) the whole constituent "The dean of our FACULTY" is put into focus by the single accent on "FACULTY". The phrase "wrote that silly book" contains given or presupposed information and therefore stays out of focus. In (b) only "The DEAN" is brought into focus, because accentuation rules operating on the syntactic structure of constituents, determine that "DEAN" can never be the prosodic head of the whole constituent "the DEAN of our faculty". Obviously, the speaker presupposes that the listener knows that the author is someone of our faculty.

Speakers differ in the ways they use accent patterns, and often violate expectations of professional linguists in doing so. Still, it has been shown in acceptability experiments that in the ears of the listeners new information can hardly ever be acceptably associated with '–focus', whereas given information can rather often, although not always, acceptably be associated with both '–focus' and '+focus'. '+Focus' cannot only be perceived as signaling new information, but also as highlighting thematic relations with the context (Nooteboom and Kruyt, 1987). It has also been shown, in a speeded verification task in which listeners had to judge whether a particular utterance was or was not an accurate description of some situation on a visual display, that violation of the relation between newness versus givenness and accent patterns slows down comprehension (Terken and Nooteboom, 1987). Apparently, accent patterns play their modest part in speeding up human processing of speech.

4.4 Prosodic boundaries

A sequence of words like "the queen said the knight is a monster" can be read and spoken in at least two different ways: "the queen, said the knight, is a monster", or "the queen said, the knight is a monster". The ambiguity inherent in this sequence of words is disambiguated in speech by prosodic phrasing, producing either a strong prosodic boundary after "queen" and "knight" or after "said" (cf. Figure 21.8). Even when no such strong ambiguities are present, speakers nevertheless tend to divide their speech into prosodic phrases. Potential positions for prosodic phrase boundaries can be derived indirectly from syntactic trees, by assigning metrical trees to the syntactic trees, and then applying some simple phrasing rules to the metrical trees (Selkirk, 1984; Nespor and Vogel, 1986; Dirksen and Quené, 1993). Selkirk, and also Nespor and Vogel, distinguish between two types of phrases, I-phrases or intonational phrases, separated by major boundaries, and Phi-phrases or phonological phrases, separated by minor boundaries. Phi-phrases are combined into the hierarchically higher I-phrases. Dirksen and Quené, in the context of a text-to-speech system, attempt to implement some of the ideas of Selkirk and Nespor and Vogel in a set of computational rules. Instead of two hierarchically ordered types of phrases, they assume only one type of phrase boundary which may or may not be realized by a speech pause or final lengthening. Their phrasing rule, applied to metrical trees, states simply that a phrase boundary occurs between A and B if:

(a)   A and B are sisters
(b)   B is an XP, and
(c)   both A and B are accented,

where A and B are adjacent phrases, and XP is a maximal projection of an NP, VP or AP. The net result of this rule is that phrase boundaries are placed between 'major' phrases.

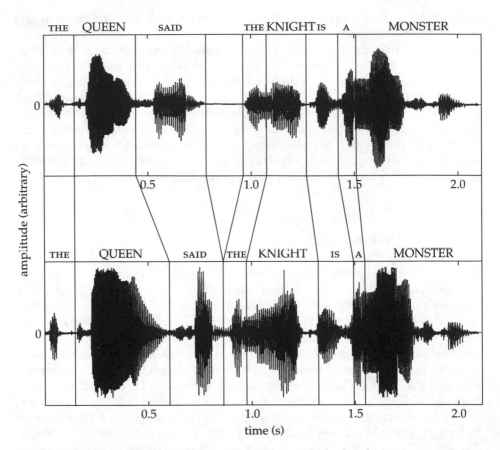

Figure 21.8 Two oscillograms. Top: "The queen said, the knight is a monster". Bottom: "The queen, said the knight, is a monster".

Actual speakers assume considerable freedom in choosing whether phrase boundaries are or are not realized by speech pauses. They are more liable to make speech pauses in slow and careful speech than in rapid and less careful speech. Whenever they make a melodically marked speech pause, however, it is likely to be made at a predictable phrase boundary. Speech pauses that are only realized in the temporal pattern and not in the speech melody, appear to be less closely related to syntactic and metrical structure, and may either be hesitation pauses, or pauses used to other stylistic ends (Blaauw, unpublished).

High quality speech without grammatical speech pauses within sentences can be highly intelligible and acceptable. But as soon as speech quality is less than normal, or speech is listened to in noisy conditions, the introduction of grammatical speech pauses can help to maintain intelligibility (Nooteboom, 1985). In general, it can be observed that the contributions of prosody to speech perception become more important when the segmental quality of speech or the listening conditions become less favorable.

NOTE

I am most grateful for critical comments on earlier drafts of this chapter by René Collier from IPO, Eindhoven, and Robert D. Ladd from the Department of Linguistics, University of Edinburgh. The following people helped me in several practical ways to put this chapter into shape: Leo Vogten from IPO, Eindhoven; Eleonora Blaauw, Guus de Krom, and Hugo Quené from OTS, Utrecht.

22 The Relation Between Phonetics and Phonology[1]

JOHN J. OHALA

1 Introduction

The question 'what is the relation between phonetics and phonology', like any question with historical and philosophical implications, cannot be answered objectively. Whenever an answer to this question is given it is inevitably subjective, grounded in the experience, beliefs, and prejudices of the answerer. This is no less true of my discussion here as of the views I survey from the past and the present. Nevertheless, I will try to make explicit the basis of my opinions so that those who have other views will be in a better position to evaluate my position and, perhaps, be persuaded by it.

To begin we must establish the defining characteristics of phonetics and phonology. Among the defects that I perceive in many prior attempts to define phonetics or phonology is specifying a field in a way which owes too much to modern theories and methods and which therefore implies that the field didn't even exist N years ago. To correct this defect it is necessary to take a broad historical view and to attempt to establish the recurring themes of the fields and aims of their practitioners. I believe that the defining characteristics of a discipline are not its methods and not its theories – the answers to questions – but rather the questions themselves. The methods used to get answers to questions and the candidate answers to the questions show periodic change; the questions themselves are remarkably long-lived and stem from the ordinary experience and puzzlings people have about spoken language. Ancient myths, oral and written, from many diverse cultures show, by the candidate answers given, that the following are some of the persistent questions people have had about spoken language:

(1) How did speech originate? Why do humans use speech but not other species? What is the relation between human speech and animals' cries? Is vocal communication possible across species?

(2) Why is there such diversity in the form of speech, i.e., between different linguistic communities and between generations of the same linguistic community?

(3) What is the physical structure of speech? How is it made? How is it perceived?

(4) How is speech represented in the brain?

(5) How does one learn to pronounce one's first language, a second language?

(6) How can we communicate effectively with speech under adverse conditions, over great distances, with high background noise? How can we effectively "freeze" ephemeral speech so that we can store spoken messages for later recall?

(7) How can we ameliorate speech communication deficits (e.g., cleft palate, stuttering, lisping, deafness)?

(8) How does meaning come to be associated with the sounds of language?

Although I would maintain that these are among the perennial questions about spoken language, it may happen that at any given time in history or in specific communities one or more may be the focus of inquiry with others neglected. For example, in the 18th century there was more focus on Qs. 1 and 2; in the 20th century, greater effort has been spent on Q. 4. Only some of these questions have received widely-accepted answers: Q. 2 was partially answered by the development of the comparative method in the 19th century; the accumulation of efforts devoted to Q. 3 over three centuries and more have given us an understanding of the physical structure of speech sufficient to make machines which speak and understand speech. Similarly, the invention of writing, the telephone, the hearing aid, surgical repair of cleft palate, etc. have provided some answers to Qs. 6 and 7. Q. 1 has yet to be satisfactorily answered and, indeed, the curiosity we have about all these aspects of speech will never be completely satisfied. It is the never-ending search for answers to these questions that unites everyone in the field, from von Kempelen to von Humboldt, from Grimm to Greenberg, from Helmholtz to Halle. Methods and theories come and go; the questions remain.

2 The relation between phonetics and phonology: some history

With this base it is now appropriate to survey opinions on the relation of phonetics and phonology. Sommerstein (1977:1) states:

> Phonology is a branch of linguistics; phonetics is often considered not to be. Phonetics deals with the capabilities of the human articulatory and auditory

systems with respect to the sounds and prosodic features available for use in language, and with the acoustic characteristics of these sounds and features themselves . . .

Phonology, in a sense, begins where phonetics leaves off. It is concerned with the ways in which the sounds and prosodic features defined by phonetics are actually used in natural languages. . . .

. . . there have been two main views on [the object of phonological inquiry] . . . 'What phonic features (a) serve in the language under investigation, or (b) are capable of serving in natural language, to distinguish one utterance from another?' [= *classical phonology*] . . . [the other] 'What are the principles determining the pronunciation of the words, phrases and sentences of a language; and to what extent are these principles derivable from more general principles determining the organization . . . of *all* human languages?' [= *generative phonology*].

From these and similar quotes from other texts one could characterize phonetics as concerned with discovering and describing the vocal sounds utilizable by humans, and studying articulation, acoustics, and perception; in other words approximately the domain of inquiry of Q. 3. Phonology is said to be concerned with how the sounds used in language pattern or function, how they are represented and used in the mental grammar of speakers; approximately Qs. 1 and 4 and perhaps 5. Phonetics deals with concrete, physical, manifestations of speech sounds; phonology with abstract, psychological manifestations, indeed, more generally, with the nature of human language and the genetic endowment which makes it possible. Phonetics is characterized as using the methods of the natural sciences; phonology of using the methods of the social sciences or perhaps of the humanities. (See also Kenstowicz and Kisseberth 1979:1; Hawkins 1984:7; Lass 1984:1; Clark and Yallop 1990:1–2.)

Curiously, in few of the texts I surveyed (admittedly not a thorough search) is there any mention of sound change, i.e., Q. 2, when the definition of phonology and its differentiation with phonetics is specified. Perhaps phonological change is assumed to be covered by the psychological focus if one assumes that "sound change is grammar change" (Kiparsky 1968). In any event, it is widely recognized that there is an intimate relation – some would say an identity – between the sound patterns which figure in synchronic, supposedly mental, grammars and the sound changes that occur in successive generations (Halle 1962; Kiparsky 1968; King 1969). It is safe to assume that an understanding of diachronic variation is essential to an understanding of the many sound patterns which occupy mainstream phonologists today: vowel harmony, spirantization, epenthesis, deletion, diphthongization, etc.

I would now like to contrast the contemporary view of the relation between phonetics and phonology with earlier attitudes on the matter, i.e., up to three centuries ago. Given that both 'phonetics' and 'phonology' did not necessarily exist as separately recognized disciplines in earlier centuries, I will instead look at the relation between the domains of study that are classified today as phonetic or phonological.

2.1 *Amman to Rousselot*

Johann Conrad Amman (1669–1724), like his contemporaries John Wallis and William Holder, delved into the study of the physical nature of speech because of his interest in teaching the deaf to speak (Amman 1694). But in pursuing this he made many original observations and analyses that would today be considered 'phonological': He proposed an elementary, binary, hierarchical system of phonetic features that still merits attention. In his system manner features dominated place features (see Miller and Nicely 1955, who found that manner distinctions are more resistant to confusion than place distinctions). He considered his system as a 'natural' hierarchy, i.e., in accord with nature, among other reasons, because substitutions of sounds in, for example, pathological speech, involve similar sounds at the lowest level of the hierarchy, not the highest; thus an alveolar 'semi-vowel' like <u>l</u> is substituted for another, <u>r</u>, or one nasal for another whereas vowels and consonants which are differentiated at the highest level, are rarely if ever substituted one for the other. Amman (like Wallis before him) also made some elementary phonological observations, e.g., "If any word terminates in **n** and the following word begins with **b** or **p**, . . . then in pronouncing the **n** we unconsciously change it, for the sake of euphony, into **m**, . . ."

Charles De Brosses (1709–1777) wanted to do for language what Descartes and Newton had done for the physical universe: derive it from first principles. The principal thesis of his work *Traité de la formation méchanique des langues, et de principes physiques de l'étymologie* (1765) was that the phonetic properties of words originally shared certain features of the things they designated (thus, he pointed out, words for *lip* often contain labial sounds, words for *nose* often contain nasal sounds, etc.). (See also Court de Gebelin 1776.) Thus he was concerned with Qs. 1 and 8, above. In pursuing this argument he found it useful to do a completely original anatomical–physiological analysis of speech sounds. I say 'original' because it was so far below what was known at his time that it is evident he must have done it without consulting contemporary sources. But it is not the sophistication of his analysis or the lack of it but rather the integration of what we now consider phonetics with phonology that is noteworthy. He invented two phonetic notations which enabled him to show the phonetic similarity of cognate words in diverse languages in spite of their having quite different spelling.

Erasmus Darwin (1731–1802), grandfather of Charles Darwin, in his work *The temple of nature* (1803) attempted to explain the origin of human society as well as language and speech. This work includes brief reports of his efforts at speech synthesis and what may be the first recorded instance of an instrumental phonetic study on a live, intact, speaker: To determine the place of articulation of vowels, he writes, "I rolled up some tin foil into cylinders about the size of my finger; and speaking the vowels separately through them [that is, inserting the cylinders into his mouth], found by the impressions made on them [i.e., where they were dented], in what part of the mouth each of the vowels was formed . . ." (p. 119). He also proposes 13 unary features for differentiating all human sounds (including the Welsh [a]): three basic places of articulation, oral resonance[2], nasal resonance, voiceless frication, voiced frication, etc.

Robert Willis (1800–1875), a Cambridge professor of mechanics ('engineering', to use the modern equivalent), in his 1830 work "On the vowel sounds", specified quantitatively a single characteristic vocal tract resonance for each vowel and claimed that their principal articulatory determinant was vocal tract length. He remarked that with some refinement of his study he should be able to provide "philologists with a correct measure for the shades of differences in the pronunciation of the vowels by different nations." In other words, he envisioned a universal, quantitative, acoustically-based specification of vowel quality (a goal that unfortunately still eludes us). His 'single resonance' theory of vowels, though superseded by Grassmann's (1854) and Helmholtz' (1863) subsequent work (the basis for the modern acoustic theory of vowels), bears a resemblance to modern auditorily-based theories of vowel quality, e.g., Fant and Risberg's F2-prime (Fant and Risberg (1963) and Hermansky's PLP (perceptual linear predictive) transform (1990)).

T. Hewitt Key (1799–1875), at first professor of Latin and later professor of comparative philology at London University (now University College) and at one time professor at the newly formed University of Virginia, attempted to apply Willis' theories to problems of sound change. In his paper "On vowel-assimilation, especially in relation to Professor Willis' experiment on vowel-sounds" (1855), he proposed explanations for vowel harmony and umlaut by invoking Willis' notion that vocal tract length is the main articulatory determinant of their quality. Although his explanations would not be judged worthy by modern standards, his account is an admirable attempt to integrate what he knew about acoustic phonetics and the traditional problems of historical phonology. His article also contains some memorable and still pertinent admonitions:

> [some scholars of language] have allowed themselves . . . to be led astray by paying more attention to the symbols of sound than to sounds themselves. . . . Scholars seldom unite the love of classical and scientific pursuits; and a paper [i.e., Willis'] of the highest value for philology might well fail to meet with all the attention it deserves from the students of language . . .

Rudolf von Raumer (1815–1876) in his paper "Die sprachgeschichtliche Umwandlung und die naturgeschichtliche Bestimmung der Laute" (1856) (translated by W.P. Lehmann (1967)) strongly advocated the integration of the latest phonetic research with historical phonological studies. He wrote:

> Through the discoveries of historical linguistic investigation, the significance of phonetics has been placed in a new light. The more the importance of phonetics

becomes recognized, the more apparent becomes the need to understand as clearly and precisely as possible its subject matter, namely the sounds themselves.

He attempted to give a more physiologically realistic interpretation to the first and second Germanic sound shifts in the light of philological and phonetic principles (based largely on Brücke 1856).

Karl Verner (1846–1896), one of the giants of 19th century linguistics whose paper "Eine Ausnahme der ersten Lautverschiebung" (1875) was a prime inspiration for the Neo-grammarian revolution, in his later years plunged into phonetic studies of accent in order to understand better how it could influence sound change. He was one of the first in Denmark to obtain an Edison phonograph. He then constructed an elaborate and quite sophisticated optical instrument which permitted him to enlarge the tiny grooves it traced on the metal foil when recording speech such that he could measure their waveforms and analyze them mathematically. Unfortunately all this effort did not produce significant results and was never published, except posthumously in his Collected Letters (Verner 1913; see also Jespersen 1933 and Fischer-Jørgensen 1979).

Abbé Pierre-Jean Rousselot (1846–1924), often called the father of experimental phonetics, introduced into phonetics the physiological methods of E.J. Marey, physician, pioneer in the study of locomotion, and the one who perfected the kymograph (with his invention, 'Marey's capsule'). Rousselot attempted to do for phonetics what Helmholtz had done for hearing and vision: reduce their function to known physiological principles. Indicative of his view of the broad integrative character of the phonetic sciences are two of his major works, first, his dissertation (1891) which was an attempt to give an instrumental phonetic account of the sound changes which shaped the dialect spoken in his home town,[3] and, second, the application of phonetics to the communication problems of the deaf (1903).

Many other examples of a similar sort could be given (see also Jacobi (1843), Bindseil (1838), Rapp (1836), Techmer (1880), Weymouth (1856), Grandgent (1896), Grammont (1930), Passy (1890), Panconcelli-Calzia (1904), Ellis (1877), Sweet (1899), Sievers (1881)). These all testify to the fact that there was no bar to the integration of what we would now label phonetics and phonology – a quite different attitude to what exists in the latter part of the 20th century.

2.2 Strains between phonetics and phonology

To be sure, there were some signs of tension between phonetics and phonology and Key's remarks quoted above reflect that. In addition there are the following remarks of Roudet (1910) (a student of Rousselot's) and Spargo (1931), the translator of Holger Pedersen's history of 19th century linguistics (1926), which by their intensity suggest that there were already some bitter feelings between the two fields.

... la phonétique fournit a l'étude théorique des langues anciennes et modernes une base indispensable, faute de laquelle une foule de faits linguistiques demeurent inintelligibles, faute de laquelle toute une part de la grammaire historique se réduit à un pur psittacisme, à une collection de formules verbales à peu près dénuées de signification réele. [Roudet (1910:v)]

... one important feature of [Pedersen's work] ... is the striking rôle assigned to the study of phonetics in increasing our knowledge of linguistics. It is shown clearly that every important advance during the last century and a quarter was made by a scholar who attacked his problem from the phonetic side. Surely this fact has its importance for the future of linguistic study, and suggests that the indifference to phonetics in many of the graduate schools in the United States is an evil presage for future progress. [Spargo 1931; in the preface, dated 1930, to his translation of Holger Pedersen's *Sprogvidenskaben i det nittende aarhundrede* (1924).]

But it would seem that the strained relations arose out of a difference in temperament or background: the bulk of those doing historical phonology had little or no training in or taste for phonetic work.[4] Rousselot, in the introduction to his *Principes* (1897–1908) offers a somewhat kinder view (p. 1):

... les procédes des sciences expérimentales sont assez étrangers aux linguistes. Une sorte de terreur superstitieuse s'emparé eux dès qu'il s'agit de toucher au mécanisme le plus simple. Il fallait donc leur montrer que la difficulté est moindre qu'ils ne se la figurent et leur faire entrevoir le champ immense que l'experimentation ouvre devant eux. [p. 1]

The picture that emerges from these brief vignettes from the history of phonetics and phonology up to the early decades of the 20th century is that there was no hardening of the division between phonology and phonetics (or speech technology and speech pathology). Those who studied speech pursued their research in whatever way was comfortable for them, depending on their training: medical, mathematical, physical, or philological, but with many unhesitating excursions into new methodological territory.

2.3   The split between phonetics and phonology

What precipitated the apparent split between phonetics and phonology later on in the 20th century? It is generally recognized that the division occurred due to the rise of structuralism, taught initially by Ferdinand de Saussure (1857–1913) and Jan Baudouin de Courtenay (1845–1929) but fully developed in phonology by the Prague School. In his 1939 work *Grundzüge der Phonologie* (trans. 1969 by C. Baltaxe), N.S. Trubetzkoy (1890–1938), a leader of the Prague School, distinguished

... the study of sound pertaining to the act of speech [phonetics] which is concerned with concrete physical phenomena, [and] would have to use the methods of the natural sciences, while the study of sound pertaining to the system of

language [phonology] would use only the methods of linguistics, or the humanities, or the social sciences. [p. 4]

In this way phonetics was placed outside of linguistics proper and phonology
was conceived of as an autonomous discipline. The emphasis on system or the
relationship between speech sounds and their function, rather than on the
substance of those sounds, represented a new concern and one which seemed
at the same time to open up new frontiers for phonological study and to
liberate the study of speech sounds from physical phonetics and all the bur-
dens of the methodology of the natural sciences.

Without a doubt phonology has a rich inheritance from Trubetzkoy and the
school which he helped to develop. In fact, some of Trubetzkoy's phonological
generalizations were based on intuitive phonetic grounds (though he felt he had
to apologize and explain at some length how this didn't imply that he thought
precise phonetic correlates of sound contrasts mattered). But Trubetzkoy's conception of phonetics was something of a stereotype:

> La phonétique actuelle se propose d'étudier les facteurs materiels des sons de la
> parole humaine: soit les vibrations de l'air qui leur correspondent, soit les posi-
> tions et les mouvements des organes qui les produisent.... Le phonéticien est
> necessairement atomiste ou individualiste ... Chaque son de la parole humaine
> ne peut être étudie qu'isolement, hors de tout rapport avec les autres sons de la
> même langue. (pp. 232–233)

A similar stereotype applied to astronomy would characterize its proper activity as merely looking at and cataloguing stars. No mention would be made of
cosmology, astrophysical theory, etc., i.e., attempts to generalize about the
birth, development and death of stars, the formation of galaxies, the origin of
the universe. This is the fallacy of equating the immediate, visible object of
study with the ultimate object of study. Though the immediate object of study
in phonetics (and in the psychological study of speech) may be the sounds of
speech observed at various stages in the speech chain, the ultimate objects of
study are the underlying *causes* of speech sound behavior, where "behavior"
includes the same broad domain that Johann Amman studied three centuries
ago, how laterals are produced, the assimilation of nasals to the place of articulation of following stops, the patterns of substitution of one speech sound
for another, the organization of speech sounds.

A few qualifications must be added to the above historical interpretation of
the origin of the split between phonetics and phonology. First, Trubetzkoy
was not alone in his attitude. As the earlier quote from Spargo reveals, North
American linguists had formed much the same opinion independently. Sapir's
emphasis on the psychological aspect of speech sounds (Sapir 1925) also led
to a depreciation of phonetics within linguistics:

> Mechanical and other detached methods of studying the phonetic elements of
> speech are, of course, of considerable value, but they have sometimes the unde-
> sirable effect of obscuring the essential facts of speech-sound psychology.

Second, there was also some opposition to Trubetzkoy's divorce of phonetics from phonology. Gyula Laziczius (1948 [1966]), a member of the Prague School, insisted on the essentially linguistic concerns of phonetics. Eberhard Zwirner (Zwirner and Zwirner 1966) emphasized that a proper experimental phonetic study of speech sounds must take into account the sounds' linguistic function. In fact, although Zwirner's views were not very influential in the development of the field, modern linguistic phonetics independently developed the same operating principles (see also Fischer-Jørgensen 1985). Furthermore, the British school of linguistics did not separate phonology and phonetics and, indeed, were much later than many other schools in adopting two separate names for the joint activity.

Third, it must be acknowledged that some of the new interests of phonology were more in the psychological domain (this was especially true of Baudouin de Courtenay's and Sapir's conception of phonology) and were not the typical focus of phonetic studies at that time. However, this situation has changed considerably today where there is substantial overlap between phonological, phonetic, and psychological studies of speech (e.g., Fowler 1981; Cutler and Norris 1988; Lahiri and Marslen-Wilson 1991; Ohala and Ohala 1995). Even so, although expressing an interest in the psychological aspect of speech, phonologists since Trubetzkoy's and Sapir's time have shown little initiative in adopting or developing rigorous psychological methods of studying sound patterns in language. The consequences of this neglect could be profound: many of the sound patterns in language claimed to be part of the native speaker's psychological endowment may simply be the residue of past sound changes which themselves came about primarily due to phonetic factors (Ohala 1992a). Other aspects of speakers' awareness of sound patterns in their language may stem from their knowledge of their language's orthography (Read et al. 1986; Morais and Kolinsky 1994; Jaeger 1984; Wang and Derwing 1986; Derwing 1992) which, being a cultural artefact, can hardly count as knowledge required of a competent native speaker.

It could also be claimed that there is a sense in which all phonological work does in fact incorporate some phonetics insofar as it uses terms such as 'obstruent', 'voice', etc. However, I would like to differentiate between two forms of phonetics (see also Ohala 1990a): one I call 'taxonomic' phonetics and the other 'scientific' phonetics. Taxonomic phonetics has provided us with traditional phonetic terms and symbols used to describe and classify speech sounds and has remained largely unchanged since the formation of the International Phonetic Association a century ago. Scientific phonetics, on the other hand, continues to change. It constantly expands its horizons; it develops new data, concepts, and methods; it rejects or revises earlier beliefs shown to be deficient, and, to the extent that the surviving beliefs or theories have congruence with the universe, it has practical payoff, e.g., in language teaching, speech pathology, and speech technology. Of course, it also has payoff in phonology: e.g., how would we be able to make sense of the inherent tendency of obstruents to become or remain voiceless if Husson's (1950) neurochronaxic theory of vocal cord vibration had not been effectively refuted? While autonomous phonology embraces taxonomic phonetics, for the most part it excludes scientific phonetics. A good bit of what is called and taught as "phonetics" in many universities – if it is taught at all – is exclusively taxonomic phonetics. Scientific phonetics is the intellectually most exciting form of the field – and one of the most successful and rigorous within linguistics (if one allows, of course, that it is part of linguistics). It addresses issues of fundamental importance for phonology. (See below.)

And it was not just the domain of inquiry that phonology left behind after its divorce from phonetics; it also abandoned phonetics' manner of bringing evidence to bear on theoretical claims. Over the decades the phonetic sciences had established a respectable degree of accountability in the way that generalizations and theories are proposed and defended. The degree of accountability in the field has been improved and tightened. As a result there is a relatively continuous and cumulative tradition on which to develop and refine both methods and theories. To give just one example, and one which has far-reaching implications for phonology and for the behavioral sciences in general: careful phonetic studies spanning a century have demonstrated, the tremendous amount of variation – essentially infinite in character – that exists in the speech signal (Ohala 1989). This synchronic variation parallels to a great extent documented diachronic variation which, in turn, gives rise to sound patterns studied by modern phonology: morphophonemic variations, phonotactic patterns, universal and language-particular patterns in languages' segment inventories, and allophonic variation. In addition, some patterns of variation parallel the phonological variation in language acquisition (first and second), as well as listeners' misperceptions over the telephone. Understanding variation in one of these domains has the potential to explain it in the other domains.

3 The relation between phonetics and phonology: philosophy

Anderson (1981) presents a useful scheme for discussing the relation of phonology with other disciplinary domains, e.g., phonetics, psychology, ethology, social and cultural factors, etc. Given Figure 22.1, where the thick-line circle represents the domain of "Language" (where, presumably, Phonology belongs) and the thinner-line circles intersecting it represent other disciplinary domains to which one may refer to explain specific aspects of language, the question may be stated: is there any area within Language which remains outside the intersection of these circles? Are there any phenomena that are uniquely linguistic and which 'cannot be explained as special cases of other systems.' Anderson endorses the Chomskyan position that language is a uniquely human

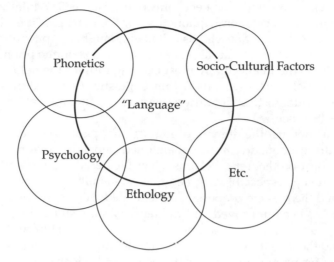

Figure 22.1   Venn diagram illustrating the overlapping domains of Linguistics and other disciplines; after Anderson (1981).

> mental organ . . . which is not reducible to features of other kinds (at least, within the limits of present knowledge in such areas as neurology, brain chemistry, the genetic control of development, etc.). It is exactly this area . . . that ought to occupy the central concern of linguists if they wish to arrive at an adequate conception of the essential and special nature of human Language.

There is, of course, no question that there will always be some things about language (or any other domain) that we will at the time be unable to explain by reference to physics, psychology, etc. These things should not be ignored but should be described. But to enshrine the things we are ignorant about as the central concern of linguistics is to misplace one's priorities. If one believes that there are irreducible phenomena in language then there will be no motivation to seek explanations for them. Indeed, left on its own, autonomous phonology endlessly recycles much the same data, trying out different labels and descriptive devices on it (markedness, abstract underlying forms, ordered rules, alpha-variables, atomic rules, upside-down rules, charm, optimality, a staggering variety of conditions and principles), all of which are attributed quite facilely to the new theoretical *deus ex machina*, "universal grammar". But it does this without achieving any greater insight into the mechanisms of speech. If one is committed to seek explanations for phenomena, not simply to relabel them, then there is a chance that the area of ignorance becomes smaller with time and as a spinoff will have practical benefits in speech technology, language teaching, and in communication disorders. Such a reductionist research strategy should not be misinterpreted, as it often is, as a requirement that every phenomenon in language *must* be immediately reducible to principles from other disciplinary domains. This is unreasonable; one might as well proclaim "let ignorance be abolished!" Rather, this is a strategy of what may be called "opportunistic reductionism": when an opportunity presents itself to explain something linguistic, that opportunity should be pursued and evaluated. (See also the exchanges between Lass 1980 and Ohala 1987; Pierrehumbert 1990 and Ohala 1990b; Pierrehumbert 1991 and J.J. Ohala and M. Ohala 1991.)

There is another sense in which Anderson's Venn diagram confuses the central issue of the relation between phonology and phonetics (and psychology, ethology, socio–cultural factors, etc.). When a given phenomenon is explained (reduced), it does not imply that one discipline "owns" those facts and therefore shrinks the "turf" of another discipline – in the case of linguistics, what Anderson refers to as the domain of 'Language per se'. When anthropologists cite linguistic evidence of name taboos from linguistics as support for posited societal structure, who owns the notion that there are hierarchical relations between individuals in a community? When neurologists discover localization of specific linguistic functions in the brain such as pronominalization, who owns the notion of modularity of these linguistic functions? If universals of sentence prosody (as well as size sound symbolism, facial expressions involving the mouth, and sexual dimorphism of the human vocal anatomy) are argued to be governed by the same ethological principles that determine the shape of other species's agonistic vocalizations (Ohala 1984, 1994a), which discipline owns the explanans? When Bantu specialists trace the introduction of the word for 'iron' in the various Bantu languages and paleontologists date the spread of iron smelting throughout sub-Saharan Africa, who owns the resulting picture of pre-historic Bantu migrations and the resulting spread of technology? Neither Linguistics nor other disciplines "lose ground" by such a cross-disciplinary union of data, methods, and theories. If anything, such a marriage increases the scope of all disciplines in the partnership. It is this idea, I think, that underlies the old, hopefully not out-dated, notion of the *unity of science*. (See below.)

Anderson qualified his view on the autonomy of linguistics by acknowledging that it applied 'within the limits of present knowledge'. But he does not make clear *how* the present limitations of knowledge are to be overcome. Shall linguists wait for those in other disciplines to provide answers to their questions or shall linguists themselves take the initiative?

4 The integration of phonetics and phonology

As argued by Laziczius and Zwirner, virtually all phonetic studies embrace and are guided by the phonological notion that speech sounds are part of a system and that the primary function of their physical make-up is to contrast with each other – both paradigmatically and syntagmatically. Thus many phonetic studies attempt to tease out the cues differentiating phonologically-specified contrasts using a corpus of minimal pairs or n-tuples. (See, e.g., Lisker and Abramson 1964, 1970; Lehiste 1967; Ladefoged 1963.) The common practice within phonetics of making a given measurement (e.g., vowel duration, formant frequency) on multiple tokens and reporting the means of these measurements is evidence that phonetics seeks some sort of pronunciation norm which is more abstract than any given speech token.

But the integration of phonetics and phonology is evident in other ways as well. I will briefly mention some of the traditional questions of phonology that can benefit from phonetic studies.

4.1 How is the pronunciation of words and other posited units of language represented and processed in the head of the speaker?

The first, most candid, answer to this question is: we don't know. Even such a fundamental issue as whether phoneme-sized segments are employed – or employed at **all** stages of encoding and decoding – has not been settled satisfactorily. There is an abundance of candidate answers given to the question of how speech is represented mentally but until they have been properly evaluated they are just speculations. Within phonology the basic criterion applied in evaluating claims about mental representation of language is **simplicity** and such related notions as **naturalness** and **elegance**. But these are quite subjective and we learn from the history of science that the workings of the universe do not always coincide with pre-conceived human preferences.[5]

Insofar as phonetic studies – or psychological studies (there is not always a clear distinction) – can shed light on the structure and processing of speech sounds in the mind of the speaker at some stages before the activation of muscle contractions and in the mind of the listener at some stages after the acoustic signal is transduced into an auditory signal, they may help us to discover other aspects of speech representation in the brain. Representative studies in this area (from among hundreds) include Stetson 1928; Kozhevnikov and Chistovich 1965; Lisker et al. 1962; Lieberman 1967; Ohala 1981, 1992b; Tuller and Kelso 1994; Cutler et al. 1986; Krakow 1994; Maddieson 1988.

4.2 How can we explain the occurrence of common cross-language sound patterns?

At least since the work of Passy (1890) and Rousselot (1891) parallels have been noted between synchronic, non-distinctive, variation in pronunciation, which can be discovered in fine-grained instrumental study of speech, and diachronic variation discovered via reconstruction or by the direct evidence in ancient texts. Moreover, the synchronic variation in many cases is understandable by reference to known physical phonetic principles. From this one may conclude that (a) many sound changes arise first as non-distinctive synchronic variation and (b) that it is physical principles that determine the direction of this variability, including articulation (the topological geometry of the vocal organs as well as their inertia and elasticity), aerodynamics, how given vocal tract configurations give rise to sound, and auditory principles. A cognitive element, e.g., how listeners may err in "parsing" the events in the speech signal, is also important (Ohala 1992a, 1993). Although speaker-specific and culture-specific psychological or cultural factors play some role in sound change (certainly in the actual triggering of sound changes), phonetic factors are the most important factors and those most amenable to experimental study in determining cross-language universals or tendencies for sound patterning, i.e., patterns in phoneme inventories, in phonotactics, as well as in morphophonemic or allophonic variation.

Though the physical constraints shaping speech sound behavior are universal, their influence on languages is probabilistic, not absolute, because there are often ways that they can be overcome. Similarly, gravity is universal but individuals are capable of walking upright; occasionally, however, they lose their balance and stumble and then gravity asserts itself and they fall.

I will briefly present two examples of phonetically-explained sound patterns (see also Kawasaki 1986, 1992; Ohala 1983, 1985, 1989, 1990d, 1992a, 1993, 1994a, in press a, b, c, d; Ohala and Lorentz 1977; M. Ohala and J.J. Ohala 1991; Wright 1986).

4.2.1 The "bias" against voiced obstruents

As is well known, there is a distinct "bias" against voiced obstruents in languages. Some languages, like Mandarin and Korean, have only voiceless stops and others, like English, which have both voiced and voiceless, show a lesser frequency of occurrence of voiced stops in running speech. Voicing in fricatives is even more infrequent than in stops. This pattern arises for the following reasons. Simplifying somewhat, vocal cord vibration has two requirements: first, the vocal cords must be lightly adducted, i.e., neither pressed against one another nor too far from the midline, and, second, there must be sufficient air flowing between the vocal cords. Assuming the first requirement is met, one of the principal factors influencing the second is the state of the supraglottal cavity. Obstruents, by definition, block the flow of air out of the vocal tract. During an obstruent the air accumulates in the air space between the point of constriction and the glottis; air pressure thus increases. Eventually the air pressure above the glottis will rise to approach that below the glottis. When the pressure differential across the glottis falls below a certain value (estimated at 1 to 2 cm. H_2O) the air flow will drop below the level necessary to maintain voicing. Vocal cord vibration will then stop. (See Ohala 1983, 1990c, 1994a.)

This is the principal reason for the bias against voiced obstruents. But there are many extensions and further elaborations of this principle.

The longer a stop closure is held, the more likely this constraint is to manifest itself. Thus voiced geminate stops often become devoiced, see Table 22.1.

Table 22.1   Geminate devoicing (Klingenheben 1927).

Original ("ursprüng")	Libanon-Neusyrischen	
naggīb	nakkīb	*trocken*
m^edaggel	mdukkel	*Lügner*
šaddar	šattar	*schickte*
zabben	zappen	*verkaufte*

Table 22.2   Development of implosives in Sindhi (Varyani 1974).

Prakrit	Sindhi	
*pabba	paɓuɳi	*lotus plant fruit*
gaddaha	gaɗahu	*donkey*
-(g)gam̊tʰi	ɠaɳdʰi	*knot*
bʰagga	bʰaːɠu	*fate*

    This aerodynamic constraint can be overcome (within limits) by enlarging the oral cavity during the obstruent closure in order to make more room for the accumulating air. Some enlargement happens passively due to the natural "give" or compliance of the vocal tract walls to impinging air pressure but even more enlargement can be done actively by lowering the tongue and jaw, letting the cheeks bulge out, raising the velum, lowering the larynx, etc. This factor must be responsible for the fact that the voiced implosives in Sindhi developed from geminate voiced stops, see Table 22.2. To maintain voicing during the long (geminate) stop closure the oral cavity volume was increased, including by lowering the larynx, and a sound change occurred when listeners took the cues for this active cavity enlargement as purposeful.

    However, the option of maintaining voicing by enlarging the oral cavity is less effective the further back the supraglottal closure is made because there is lesser surface area to yield to the impinging pressure and because there are few options for cavity enlargement. Thus Voiced uvular and velar stops, [ɢ], [g], therefore, are vulnerable; they may lose their voicing, their stop character, or both. This no doubt underlies the frequent absence of these sounds in languages which otherwise have one or more voiceless uvular or velar stops. See Table 22.3.

    Southern (Nobiin) Nubian exhibits a morphophonemic pattern where both the influence of geminates and the influence of place of articulation are manifested. See Table 22.4. Here an inflectional process meaning 'and' adds the suffix [ɔn] to a noun stem and geminates the final consonant. But if this final

Table 22.3 Stop inventories showing absence of voiced velars.

Thai	p	t	k
	pʰ	tʰ	kʰ
	b	d	
Chontal	p	t	k
	b	d	
	p′	t′	k′

Table 22.4 Morphophonemic variation in Nobiin Nubian (Bell 1971; Ohala and Riordan 1979).

Noun stem	Stem + 'and'	
fɑb	fɑbːɔn	*father*
sɛgɛd	sɛgɛtːɔn	*scorpion*
kad͡ʒ	kat͡ʃːɔn	*donkey*
mʊg	mʊkːɔn	*dog*

consonant is voiced, the geminate that results is voiceless, unless it is articulated at the furthest forward place: labial.

Statistics show that the bias against voicing in obstruents is even stronger in fricatives than in stops (Ohala 1983). Although this may at first glance seem puzzling because the fricatives, unlike stops, do involve some venting of the air accumulating behind the point of constriction, other factors are involved. Optimal voicing, as mentioned above, requires maximizing the $\Delta P_{transglottal} = P_{subglottal} - P_{oral}$. Optimal frication, on the other hand, requires maximizing $\Delta P_{transoral} = P_{oral} - P_{atmosphere}$. $P_{subglottal}$ and $P_{atmosphere}$ offers little or no opportunities for systematic, rapid, control. Therefore P_{oral} is the only parameter that can be controlled in order to optimize voicing and frication during voiced fricatives. But the one constraint would require keeping P_{oral} as low as possible and the other keeping it as high as possible. Obviously, it is not possible to do both simultaneously. Thus to the extent that voiced fricatives have good frication, they are liable to be devoiced (and this is true of the sibilant fricatives [z, ʒ]) and to the extent that they maintain their voicing, they are liable to have little or no frication (and this is true of the "weak" fricatives such as [β, v, ð, ɣ]; see Pickett 1980:155).

4.2.2 When nasal, labial velars behave like velars   The labial velar consonants [w, ʍ, k͡p, g͡b, ŋ͡m] have two simultaneous constrictions, one labial and

Table 22.5 Labial velars pattern as velars in assimilating nasals (Ohala and Lorentz 1977) Tswana passive verb formation (Cole 1955)

verb root + passive sfx		*passive verb stem*	
-bala	+ wa	-balwa	*to read*
BUT:			
-roma	+ wa	-roŋwa	*to send*
-akaɲa	+ wa	-akaɲːwa	*to think*

Kpelle definite formation (Welmers 1962)

Indefinite	*Definite*	
ɓɔ́ɔ	ʼmɔ́ɔi	*wax*
lúu	ʼnúui	*fog, mist*
ɣîlɑ	ʼɲilɑ̃	*dog*
wée	ʼŋwéei	*white clay*

Table 22.6 Labial velars patterning with labials and velars. Tenango Otomi (Blight and Pike 1976)

/h/ > [ɸ] / __ w
/n/ > [ŋ] / __ w

one velar. Nevertheless, when these sounds become nasal or have a nasal assimilating in place to them, insofar as the resulting nasal is other than labial velar, they pattern like velars, rarely or never as labials. See Table 22.5. In fact, this pattern appears even in languages where in other cases the labial velars pattern like labials, e.g., when interacting with or becoming obstruents. See Table 22.6. This pattern occurs due to the factors determining the acoustic differences between nasals. All nasal consonants have resonances from the pharyngeal-nasal air spaces; what differentiates one nasal from another is the length of the side cavity, the oral cavity, branching off of the pharyngeal-nasal passage. For this purpose it is the length of the oral cavity *measured from the pharynx forward* that matters. See Figure 22.2. In the case of a labial velar nasal, the effective length of this side cavity is that measured from the pharynx to the first, the velar, constriction. Thus labial velar nasals will tend to sound like simple velar nasals and listeners may interpret them thus.

As for why, when the labial velar approximant [w] becomes voiceless, it often becomes a labial or labio-dental, two principles can be cited. First, an

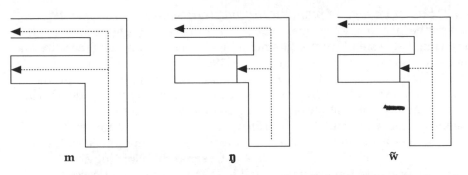

Figure 22.2   Schematic representation of the vocal tract during the production of [m], [ŋ], and [w̃]. The portion of the vocal tract contributing these sounds resonances are shown with the dashed lines and arrows. See text for details.

approximant can become an obstruent, i.e., give rise to turbulent noise, not due to any change in the supraglottal configuration but because air moves through the constriction with greater volume and thus with greater velocity. But in principle for [w] (or [ʍ]) there should be two more or less equal noise sources at the labial and the velar constrictions. But frication noise is inherently a high frequency sound and the downstream air space in the labial velar [w] constitutes a low-pass filter to the noise produced at the innermost, the velar, constriction. The frication noise at the velar place will be attenuated. Thus the noise generated at the outermost, the labial, constriction will dominate.

4.3 Phonetics and phonological theory

To the extent that phonetic explanations such as the above are judged successful they present challenges to phonological theory.

4.3.1 The relevance of language structure to sound change   First, it has been common since Prague school work on diachronic phonology in the 1930s (Jakobson 1931 [1972]) and subsequent work influenced by it, to propose that language structure, i.e., the system of contrasts, both paradigmatic and syntagmatic, play an important role in motivating sound change. For example, asymmetries in the segment inventory are claimed to motivate the "filling of the gaps" – so-called "pull chains" – or relieving the pressure due to crowding in one part of the segment inventory – so-called "push chains" (Martinet 1968). But the similar behavior of given speech sound types in different languages, briefly reviewed above, occurs in languages that have very different structure. One is left with the impression that the physical structure of the given speech sound is more of a determinant of its diachronic fate than are the character and patterning of its sister phones. The role of a language's sound structure in diachronic phonology deserves more careful study (see Ohala, in press a).

4.3.2 *Sound change is phonetically natural; should grammars be, too?*

Generative phonology assumes that speakers construct a grammar of their language that is simple and that simplicity correlates with the generality and naturalness of the grammatical rules (Halle 1962; Chomsky and Halle 1968:chapter 9). Natural and general rules thus have a preferred status in the grammar. In the past few decades there has been a continuing procession of devices and representations aimed at showing the generality and naturalness of the phonological processes embodied by rules, i.e., where the natural and general behavior of speech sounds falls out from the representation itself. Among these are features, marking conventions, autosegmental phonology, and feature geometry. But these representations fail in the vast majority of cases to represent the naturalness of phonological processes. For example, feature geometry, widely considered the most elaborate and phonetically-oriented phonological representation cannot reflect the naturalness of the processes discussed above:

(1)   why obstruents inhibit voicing
(2)   why place of articulation and the duration of a stop closure further modulate this inhibition
(3)   why implosives might develop out of geminate voiced stops
(4)   why there is a stronger bias against voiced fricatives than voiced stops
(5)   why labial velars tend to pattern as velars when nasal or interacting with nasals
(6)   why approximants become obstruents when devoiced
(7)   why labial velars tend to pattern as labials when becoming or interacting with obstruents

In defense of feature geometry it might be acknowledged that it is incapable of representing the naturalness of these processes since it does not incorporate phonetic principles based on aerodynamics and acoustics and such principles underlie 1–7. But if another, more elaborated, version of feature geometry were developed where the dependency relations of voicing on place and closure duration, etc., were incorporated then this defect could be corrected. I submit that such an elaboration if done would be identical to the phonetic models we have already (Ohala 1976, 1990c; Westbury and Keating 1985; Fant 1960; Stevens 1971, Scully 1990, etc.). But phonology has shown considerable reluctance to adopt the continuous, physical, models of speech and perhaps for good reason: it seems unlikely that the native speakers' grammars include physical principles such as Boyle's Law and the like. Among other things, grammars are thought to operate on discrete entities, not continuous parameters.

So there is an inherent problem: grammars are supposed to give priority to natural phonological rules but the ultimate embodiment of naturalness would require rules and representations that are psychologically implausible. The resolution of this problem may require re-thinking one of the fundamental assumptions of modern phonology: that phonetic naturalness plays any role in speakers' grammars. Do speakers, in fact, recognize the difference between phonetically natural and phonetically unnatural patterning of speech sounds? There is no substantial body of evidence suggesting that they do. The fact that phonetically-natural sound patterns can be found in languages does not necessarily mean that language users are aware of them. Many "natural" patterns exist in language (Ohala 1992c) – indeed, in the universe as a whole – that may escape the attention of the individual even though he knows in detail the individual objects or events which manifest the pattern. Were it otherwise, there would be much less history of science; every pattern and regularity of nature would be instantly evident to everyone who observed it. The phonological grammars in speakers' heads – i.e., the rules and representations that underlie native speakers' mastery of their language – may be coded using unanalyzed phoneme-like units and large look-up tables. The phonological concord evident in vowel harmony, for example, could be handled this way, though it may seem inelegant to the linguist who is aware of the general pattern that underlies it. However, a historical and phonetic account of how natural sound patterns arise in languages – also a proper concern of the phonologist – should involve as much physical phonetics as necessary to make a convincing explanatory scenario.

In conclusion, I personally advocate a characterization of phonology as the discipline that occupies itself with the questions listed at the start of this chapter and that seeks answers to the questions by employing the methods, data, and theories from phonetics (as well as psychology, social science (including history), ethology, etc.). Inherent in this view is that phonology should not be conducted as an autonomous discipline but rather should embrace any means that will help it to get the answers it seeks.

NOTES

1 Portions of this paper have appeared earlier in Ohala 1991.

2 Darwin used different terminology; I am 'translating' his terms into their approximate modern sense.

3 In the introduction to his *Principes de phonétique expérimentale* (1897–1908), Rousselot declared that the synchronic study of speech was intertwined with the study of the development of speech sounds in the past (p. 2).

4 There are exceptions, of course: von Raumer, Grandgent, Passy. On the other side, those who received their formative training in phonetics, there were many who were well-versed in traditional historical phonology, e.g., Rousselot (a student of the Romance philologist Gaston Paris).

5 The Ptolemaic school and even the great Copernicus labored under the assumption that planetary orbits consisted of circles or one or more circular epicycles – in part because the circle was regarded as the perfect geometrical shape: "... since the movement of the heavenly bodies ought to be the least impeded and most facile, the circle among plane

figures offers the easiest path of motion . . . ; likewise that, since of different figures having equal perimeters those having the more angles are the greater, the circle is the greatest plane figure . . . and the heavens are greater than any other body." [Ptolemy, *The Almagest*; from Hutchins (ed) 1952]. It wasn't until the work of Kepler at the end of the 16th century that astronomers accepted that orbits were ellipses. With great reluctance it was realized that nature didn't necessarily share Man's notions of what was simple and natural.

Part V Speech Technology

23   Speech Signal Processing

JOHAN LILJENCRANTS

1 Introduction

The speech signal is normally picked up as an analog electrical representation of the acoustic sound pressure as sensed by a microphone which can be analyzed, amplified, transmitted, or recorded using whatever kind of device is appropriate. Historically all processing like filtering, coding, analysis, and synthesis was done with analog devices, theoretically conceived and operating with continuous quantities like time, voltage, frequency, etc. In consequence of the technical evolution most processing today is more conveniently done with digital computing, in appliances for various purposes by special signal processors, in the laboratory often with personal or larger computers. This has allowed for an ever growing system complexity that could never realistically be implemented with analog systems. Also modern work often adopts signal processing tools and methods in higher level modelling such that the concept of a signal is wider than perhaps suggested by its naive original meaning. It is for instance commonplace to regard system parameters like formant frequencies as just another set of signals.

Digital signal processing (DSP) has expanded tremendously as a field of its own during the last few decades with important contributions from several diverse research disciplines, particularly those of speech and communications, statistics, and seismology not to mention mathematics. There is an abundant handbook literature on DSP, more often than not going into great mathematical detail, but the use of it is sometimes complicated by variant, but largely synonymous terminology and conventions that reflect the field background of the authors. This chapter gives a cursory presentation of some frequently used DSP concepts and applications that should be familiar to all speech workers. Formulas and examples of flow diagrams are shown for a few standard basic procedures, the main purpose being to assist the reader to identify them as such in the literature on theoretical developments and applications. The approach is directed into the domain of discrete signals rather than into the historic roots within classical continuous theory.

2 The discrete Fourier transform

A signal can be completely quantified in either of the two domains of time and of frequency. The classical invention of Fourier was to consider a signal to be constructed from a number of sinusoidally shaped components. For a periodic signal, one that repeats a pattern with a period T_0, he showed that it can be represented by a fundamental of frequency $1/T_0$ and a number of *harmonics*, all multiples of this frequency. The amplitudes and phases of these components constitute the amplitude and phase *spectrum* of the signal. This spectrum is discrete, it has spectral lines at the frequency intervals $\Delta f = 1/T_0$, but nothing between them. The spectrum is a prescription of how much to take of each frequency component in order to synthesize the time signal.

Let us assume our signal has no extreme temporal fine structure, such that the spectrum has a limited number of harmonics. One of these frequency components has the index number k, it represents the frequency $k \cdot \Delta f = k/T_0$ and may be denoted with a *complex* number X_k. The use of such a number is no more than a practical convention and an expedient to keep formulas simple. It can be expanded in alternate equivalent ways, for instance in terms of real and imaginary parts A_k and B_k, or magnitude $|X_k|$ and phase ϕ_k which for purposes like graphic plotting may be more appealing.

$$X_k = A_k + j\,B_k = |X_k|\;e^{j\phi k}$$

The formula to construct a sequence of N time samples x_n for one period is called the Inverse Discrete Fourier Transform, IDFT:

$$x_n = \frac{1}{N}\sum_{k=0}^{N-1} X_k e^{j(2\pi/N)kn}; \qquad n = 0\ldots N\text{-}1 \tag{1}$$

This compact mathematical notation should not hide the fact that there is a considerable quantity of computation involved; the formula is to be computed N times, once for every time sample x_n. And every such sample is built up as the sum of contributions from N different X_k. The second factor in each summed term is the sinusoidally shaped elementary function which can likewise be expanded as

$$e^{j(2\pi/N)\,kn} = \sin((2\pi/N)kn) + j\,\cos((2\pi/N)kn) \tag{2}$$

For a transform to be interesting it is of course required that it is invertible, we must be able to analyze a signal x to compute this prescription X_k. This amounts to solve X_k from a given set of x_n in the system (1) of N equations, and this mere procedure explains why we use N time samples x_n. The result is

$$X_k = \sum_{n=0}^{N-1} x_n e^{-j(2\pi/N)kn}; \qquad k = 0\ldots N\text{-}1 \tag{3}$$

in this notation known as the Discrete Fourier Transform, DFT. That the direct and inverse transforms are so similar is because the elementary shapes are *orthogonal*, that is, if you sum the product of two harmonics over the range N, then the result is zero unless the harmonics are of the same frequency.

The DFT exhibits a number of symmetries that come inherently from the sine and cosine shapes. A most important one is that if the time signal x_n is real (no imaginary part, as with all physical signals), then the spectrum is symmetrical such that $X_k = X^*_{-k}$, that is, the real part of the spectrum as well as its magnitude have even symmetry, $\text{Re}\{X_k\} = \text{Re}\{X_{-k}\}$, and the imaginary part and the phase have odd symmetry, $\text{Im}\{X_k\} = -\text{Im}\{X_{-k}\}$. In the same manner as the sequence X_k of frequency samples represent the spectrum of a periodic signal now the sequence x_n of time samples have a periodic spectrum, and we need to use only one of these spectrum periods; all the others are called *aliases*. In computing it is general practise to use positive subscripts only, so the convention is to use X_0 to X_{N-1} and with the symmetry point at $X_{N/2}$. The symmetry point should properly have been at zero frequency, but this is no problem in the discrete world since $X_{-k} = X_{N-k}$ in the next alias, identically.

Figure 23.1 shows a number of prototype examples of DFT time-frequency representation pairs. In a and b the time sequence is a unit impulse, x_n is zero for all n except at one place in each, at $n = 0$ and 3 respectively, and $N = 64$. The sequences are plotted in a 3D coordinate system of real and imaginary components vs. time or frequency indices respectively. This way you can also see the result in the form of magnitude and phase, displayed as lengths and inclinations of the thin lines extending from the frequency axis. When the pulse advances in time we observe that the magnitude of the DFT is constantly the same unit value, but the phase increases more rapidly with frequency, an example of the *delay theorem*. When the impulse advances one step, then the total frequency sequence will contain exactly one more revolution in phase. The ends of the sequence always meet. A programmer must be aware there is no X_{64} in Figure 23.1. That sample would be number 0 in the next alias, identical to X_0.

Further illustration of some symmetries is given in Figure 23.1c. Adding an equal pulse in number $64 - 3 = 61$ makes the time series even (and still real), and the transform is even and real. The transform is the sum of two spirals like in b, equal in magnitude and pitch, but opposite in direction of phase rotation. Similarly making an odd time series in d gives an odd and imaginary transform.

In the Figures 1c and d we can also for a moment switch in order to let the right hand graph represent time and the left hand represent frequency. We then see how the transform of a cosinusoid comes out as a pair of equal spectral lines at plus and minus the appropriate frequency. Changing the phase of the signal to make it a sinusoid, causes it to show up as a half revolution phase shift and an odd and real transform.

If we increase the frequency of a sinusoidal signal such that it contains one more cycle within the N samples, then the spectral line appears at the next

Time domain   Frequency domain

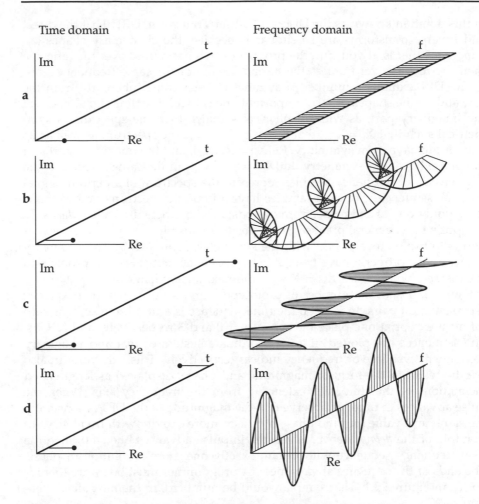

Figure 23.1 Prototype examples of three-dimensional time and frequency representations linked by the discrete Fourier transform. The signal real and imaginary components are shown horizontally and vertically, while the time and frequency axes extend away. a: a unit impulse with a white spectrum, b: delayed impulse gives phase increasing with frequency, c: even pulse pair gives real spectrum, d: odd pulse pair gives imaginary spectrum. The two domains can be interchanged when allowing for a scale factor.

sample in the frequency interval. Now, what happens if we transform a sinusoidal signal that does *not* have an integer number of periods within the time interval? The spectrum should perhaps then ideally be a line at some frequency that is not represented by any sample.

Remembering that the discrete spectrum we got represents the finite time signal repeated periodically, then when we join successive N sample time segments having a non-integer number of sine periods we will get a discontinuity

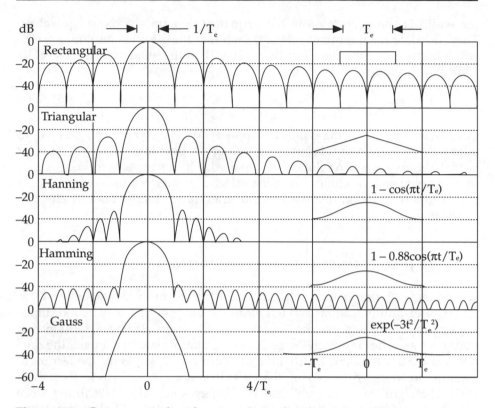

Figure 23.2 Common window functions (inserts) and their transforms.

at every joint. This will be seen in our spectrum as strong components extending over the entire frequency range.

The remedy is to modify the input prior to the transformation with a suitable *window* that has a gradual fall off toward the ends to reduce the discontinuity. Some well known windows and their transforms are shown in Figure 23.2. The *Hanning* window is an inverted cosine period, raised to give zero values at its ends. The *Hamming* window has the same basic shape, but is raised on a small pedestal. This is optimized such that the transform sidelobes are approximately the same level everywhere, about 43 dB below the main lobe. For even more stringent sidelobe requirements the Blackman or Kaiser windows can be used. Within the dynamic range shown they are similar to the truncated Gaussian shape at bottom of the figure, and which has a special interest since a Gaussian remains a Gaussian when transformed.

The window will impose an effective duration T_e for which the spectrum analysis is valid. This time is shorter than the total duration of the window, by a factor of 1, 2, and 3 in the cases of Figure 23.2. In the frequency domain what would ideally have been a single spectral line will be spread out as the shape of the window transform. The shown examples were scaled such that the width of the main lobes in the frequency domain are about equivalent. They illustrate the important rule of thumb that the effective resolution bandwidth in the spectrum, the effective bandwidth of the window main lobe at its −3dB points (approximately), is

$$B_e = 1/T_e \qquad (4)$$

The reason for windowing is thus to suppress artificial components that would otherwise arise from the abrupt truncation of the time interval to NT. The cost is that the frequency resolution is impaired. Or conversely, to keep a prescribed frequency resolution we must select a greater NT to accommodate a total window duration that is some moderate factor longer than its effective duration.

2.1 The fast Fourier transform algorithm

The amount of computation to perform the transform by the definition (3) is N^2 complex multiplications and additions, an amount that may be inordinate for larger N. The Fast Fourier Transform, FFT, is an elegant algorithm that optimizes an order in which the partial computations are performed, the final result is exactly the same as from the definition. FFT stands for the feature of computational speed in making the DFT, it is not a transform in itself as is DFT. The algorithm was published by Cooley and Tukey (1965) and since remains a prime standard tool in DSP making countless old and new developments practically usable. The total computational effort for FFT is proportional to $(N/2)*^2\log(N)$, where N is a power of 2, instead of N^2 as would be for the definition formula. For instance, with $N = 1024$ the reduction of computation is about 200-fold. Another merit of the FFT is that the accuracy of the result is improved because there are fewer rounding errors accumulated.

2.2 Other transforms

Having entered the domains of complex numbers and with Fourier derivations still valid it is no wide step to generalize the frequency variable from an imaginary $j\omega$ to a general complex quantity $s = \sigma + j\omega$, also including a real part which means the elementary function is a sinusoid which is exponentially increasing or decreasing as $e^{\sigma t}$. The continuous transform using this generalized frequency goes under the name of Laplace, and its discrete correspondent is in practice easily embraceable by the DFT.

The sinusoidal elementary building block is not the only one from which we can build up a world of signals. In fact any shape can be used, orthogonal shapes are preferred, but the Fourier method is standard for reasons of conceptual and mathematical simplicity as well as arithmetic efficiency. Over the times mathematicians have devised many other transforms, all with the same basic concept of building the time and/or the frequency representation from variants of an elementary shape, but differing in what exactly is this shape.

The last decade has seen a vivid activity in applying the concept of time-frequency distributions to speech analysis as well as other disciplines. This alternate development for the study of time-varying spectra originated as probability distributions in quantum physics, but its mathematical formalism can be used for power estimation. The best known of several such distributions, see for instance the review by Cohen (1989), is perhaps the Wigner-Ville distribution, WVD. This makes use of the *analytic signal* known from signal theory and which can be concisely described as the complex signal that arises when you filter away negative frequencies from a real physical signal, but retain the positive, an operation easily implemented by use of the DFT. Doing this involves a 'Hilbert transformer' which is a phase shifter in the time domain. This device is a kind of filter rather than a transform between domains, so its name can cause confusion.

3 Analog to digital conversion

We must be able to represent continuous analog signals as sequences of discrete numbers in order to treat them with digital devices. This process, the *analog to digital conversion*, A/D or ADC, can be broken down into two stages, the *sampling* and the *quantization*.

The sampling means that we measure a continuous signal at some specified intervals in time, and neglect what values the signal may have between those samples. Normally (but not necessarily) the time interval T between samples is constant such that we can define a *sampling rate* $f_s = 1/T$. In discrete theory the term rate is preferred to frequency which rather belongs in continuous theory, but in general usage they are mostly treated as synonyms. As just outlined, when we take N time samples, in all covering the time span $T_0 = NT$, then we also get N frequency samples, covering the frequency span $N/T_0 = 1/T$.

One point of essence is then that on our frequency axis with indices k the sampling rate is located at $k = N$. Another is that the symmetry requirement permits us to have only $N/2$ unique frequency samples, the other $N/2$ must be mirror values if the spectrum is to represent a real physical signal. This leads to one cornerstone of sampling theory: we can correctly handle only such signals that have no frequency components above half the sampling rate. Should there be any such higher frequency components their aliases will superimpose on those in our permitted range below $f_s/2$ and cause irreparable damage known as *aliasing distortion*. Therefore it is mandatory that an analog signal is band limited to $f_s/2$ by a pre-filter before it is sampled. The minimum sampling rate f_s is called the *Nyquist rate*, in some literature the term is unfortunately used for maximum allowable signal frequency $f_s/2$.

The other cornerstone of the sampling theorem is that we can reconstruct the original continuous signal exactly without loss of information, namely if we send the sampled signal through a lowpass (ideal) filter having its cut-off frequency at $f_s/2$. Then we will retrieve the base spectrum alone and remove all the higher frequency aliases. The reconstruction lowpass filter generates the missing signal shape between the samples and implements a special way of interpolation. Suppose the original signal indeed had some wiggles between the sampling points that are not present in the reconstruction. In that case it must also have had some too high frequency components for the sampling rate actually used. The second stage of A/D conversion is to represent the continuous range of sample values on a numerically quantized scale with a certain number of steps, we round off the continuous value to the nearest step. Each sample is assigned a numerical code for its value, and the accuracy depends on how many digits we care to use for this code which is normally binary. If we for instance use an 8 bit code, about the minimum to be practically usable, then the code can represent $2^8 = 256$ different steps on the scale. Through this incomplete description we introduce an error with a peak value of half a step which manifests as a pseudo random *quantization noise* superimposed on our signal. If we compare the maximum representable signal amplitude (256/2) to this noise amplitude we find a coarse approximation to the signal to noise ratio as 48 dB. A rule of thumb says we can expect about 6 dB of signal to noise ratio for each bit in the quantization; 10 bit quantizing would give 60 dB, and 16 bits 96 dB.

A quantizing scale with equal steps as with conventional A/D converters makes a noise background of constant level, irrespective of signal level. In speech coding for use in telephony 8 bit quantizers are normal, but where instead the steps on the scale are of unequal size, small steps for small signal amplitudes, and gradually larger steps with increasing amplitudes. There exist two slightly different international standards recognized as A-law and µ-law. These schemes render a signal to noise ratio that is only about 38 dB, but instead of being constant the noise background essentially follows at this distance below the actual signal level.

The development of consumer equipment for digital sound like CD and DAT includes a dramatic improvement of performance versus cost in ADC technology. A prime contributor is high speed circuitry which makes it possible to sample the signal at a much higher rate (several MHz) than needed from bandwidth considerations with the signals actually present. This means that lowpass filters for bandlimiting and reconstruction can be omitted at the analog side. Another is the use of so called delta-sigma quantizers that include a filtered feedback from the discrete to the continuous side with an effect to shape the spectrum of the quantizing noise. The total noise power is unaffected, but is concentrated at high frequencies such that its low frequency components are suppressed. Not until now has the bandlimiting lowpass filter, implemented as a digital filter with a performance close to ideal been introduced.

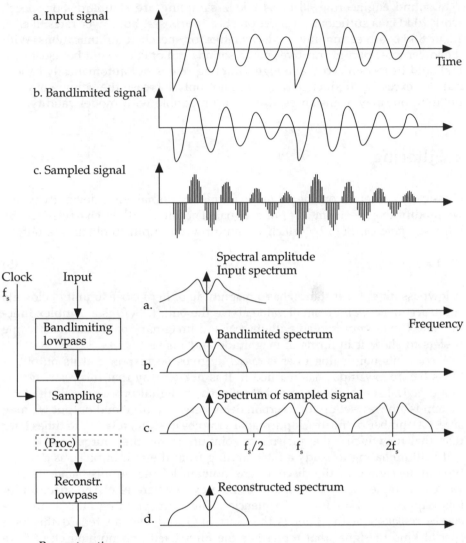

Figure 23.3 The stages in the sampling and reconstruction of an analog signal, top: time waveforms, bottom left: block diagram, bottom right: spectra.

The filter not only band limits the desired signal, but also removes a major part of the quantizer noise. This scheme is today perfected with such extreme noise suppression that precision conversion is attained with only a 1-bit sign detector toward the analog side. Finally most of the output samples are discarded (if ever computed), we only keep those (for instance ever 128th) necessary to make the resultant sampling rate at least twice the band limit.

In sound engineering 48 or 44.1 kHz sampling are standard. For speech work 20 kHz is sufficient for most practical purposes, but lower rates like 16, 12, or 8 kHz are commonly used, the latter for speech communications. With the lower rates part of fricative speech sounds can of course not be registered. It should be recognized that a high sampling rate is not automatically beneficial. An excessive frequency range will not only increase the volume of computation but may at instances also be incompatible with model validity.

4 Filtering

Classically a filter is considered in the frequency domain as a device by which we modify the spectrum $X(f)$ of a signal. The filter is then characterized by a *transfer function* $B(f)$ by which we multiply the input to obtain the output

$$Y(f) = X(f) \bullet B(f). \tag{5}$$

A lowpass filter, for instance, has a magnitude of $B(f)$ close to unity below its cutoff frequency, and a small value above the cutoff. $B(f)$ is a complex function and can be represented with its real and imaginary parts, but mostly one prefers to show it in terms of magnitude and phase.

A conventional analog filter is *causal*, it gives no response at its output at times before any input has reached it. It is noteworthy that this restriction is in a practical sense often somewhat relieved in digital processing. If the total system is anyway set up for a certain delay between input and output we may access a number of 'future' input signal samples in store, relating to times later than that for which we are currently computing the filter output.

It is illuminating to study a filter starting from the unit impulse as a prototype input signal. In the discrete time domain let the impulse have its unit value at sample number zero, and be zero everywhere else. The spectrum of this impulse $X(f) = 1$ for all frequencies. The corresponding output (the *frequency response*) of the filter is then just $B(f)$ and we can regard this as a special kind of signal that represents the filter itself and nothing else. If we now transform this signal into the time domain we get the filter time response, or *impulse response* $b(t)$. This gives an opening to examine one particular class of digital filters. We start with a known or prescribed impulse response manifest in a table of regularly spaced samples b_k. We then use these values to set up a number of multipliers in a device like in Figure 23.4a. Here an input pulse will travel along a chain of delay units, each with a delay equal to the sampling interval T. The signal is tapped between the delay units, multiplied with the appropriate b_k and forwarded via a summing unit to the output. If the input is a single impulse, then when it travels down the delay chain it is present at only one tap at a time and the output will take the corresponding value and thus reproduce the impulse response in sequence. And when the

a: All-zero – FIR – MA filter   b: All-pole – IIR – AR filter

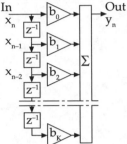 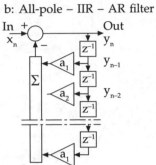

c: Pole-zero – (IIR) – ARMA filter   d: All-zero parcor filter

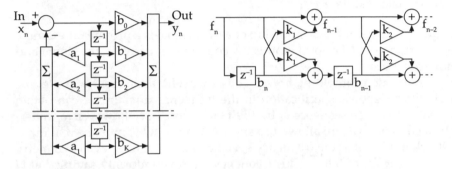

Figure 23.4 Block diagram representations of the computation formulas for elementary filter types.

input is a sequence x_n of a signal the output will be the sum of all the weighted and delayed samples. The general time domain notation for the filter is

$$y_n = \sum_{k=0}^{K} b_k x_{n-k} \tag{6}$$

This type of filter is called a *transversal* filter, or commonly a *FIR* filter, for *finite impulse response*, which emphasizes that in a practical implementation the delay chain must have a finite length. The output being a weighted average of $K + 1$ samples moving along with time n lies behind the term *moving average* (MA) filter in statistics terminology.

It also illustrates the kind of processing called *convolution* between b and x to find y. An important aspect is that to do the same operation in the frequency domain is just the simple multiplication of (5). And by the DFT/IDFT symmetry, multiplication in the time domain is equivalent to convolution in

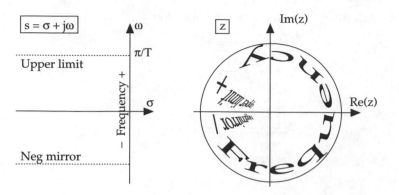

Figure 23.5   The conformal mapping of the complex frequency plane s, below half the sampling rate, and the z plane.

the frequency domain. The windowing of a time signal is a prominent example – the spectrum after transformation is the convolution between the signal and window transforms.

As a simplistic example of how to design a FIR filter from a prototype numeric filter response specification in the frequency domain we can obtain the impulse response sequence b_k by IDFT. It is necessary however to understand exactly what we are allowed to specify. Obviously b_k must be real numbers which implies that the frequency specification must have even symmetry from $-f_s/2$ to $+f_s/2$, or 0 to f_s. This frequency band is uniformly sampled at N intervals, so we cannot specify any details in the response with any better resolution than f_s/N. This implies that sharp frequency filtering requires such a large N that FIR filters sometimes are impractical for implementation in computers or signal processors. It is also important that the b_k sequence ends gracefully, for instance by the application of some window function. Design methods for FIR often become iterative for this reason, after windowing the frequency response is modified and must then be rechecked, conveniently with a DFT of the b_k.

4.1 The z transform

A central concept in DSP is the z transform. In discrete time systems this has a meaning correspondent to the Laplace transform in continuous systems. z is defined in complex frequency s and sample interval T by

$$z = e^{sT} = e^{\sigma T} \cdot e^{j\omega T} \quad or \quad z^{-1} = e^{-sT} \tag{7}$$

This constitutes a conformal mapping of every point in the s plane onto the z plane. A main feature is that the imaginary s axis, representing frequencies $j\omega$, is mapped on the unit circle in the z plane, Figure 23.5. The left half s plane, the allowed area for the poles of a filter if it is to be stable, is mapped to the interior of the circle. Conversely the z plane is mapped on an infinite sequence of horizontal stripes in the s plane, representing the baseband and its aliases due to the sampling. By virtue of the delay theorem z^{-1} can be seen as a *delay operator* that signifies a delay with the sampling interval time T. Each term in (6) can then be transformed as

$$b_k x_{n-k} \Rightarrow b_k X z^{-k} \tag{8}$$

such that the z transform of the time series expression (6) can simply be seen as

$$Y(z) = X(z) \sum_{k=0}^{K} b_k z^{-k} \tag{9}$$

where thus the sum is the z domain transfer function $B(z) = Y(z)/X(z)$.

This is an Kth order polynomial in z with the corresponding number of coefficients b_k. One of the things you can do with a polynomial is to set it to zero and solve the resulting equation. Then you get K (generally pairwise complex conjugate) values for z, and for each of them the transfer function is zero, they are referred to as the *zeroes* of the transfer function. Each value of z is represented by equivalent s domain values in the base band below half the sampling rate, and an infinite number of higher aliases.

In working with discrete systems it is often helpful to forget about the time domain and instead use the *lag* (z^{-1}) domain. Correspondingly the z domain is used as an, albeit distorted, replacement for the frequency domain. When you ultimately want some result expressed in frequency it is easy enough to compute that from z using the definition (7).

A very important trick that can be done with any kind of filter or other signal transmitting device is to connect it in a feedback loop as in Figure 23.4b. Doing this with our FIR device the configuration renders a new transfer function which is simply found by inspection as

$$A(z) = Y(z)/X(z) = 1/(1 + B(z)) \tag{10}$$

We now instead use coefficients a_i to distinguish the feedback case, and the convention is to put $a_0 = 1$ to settle a scale factor such that we can write

$$1/A(z) = 1 + \sum_{i=1}^{I} a_i z^{-i} \tag{11}$$

We then again have an expression with a polynomial with the important distinction that it is in the denominator of $A(z)$. Again solving for the roots, the values of z where the denominator polynomial is zero, we now get the *poles* of the new transfer function $A(z)$.

A specific consequence of the feedback mechanism is that once a signal sample has entered the system it will circulate through the network back to the input and generate new output samples for all future. This lies behind the term *infinite impulse response, IIR,* for this class of filters. This feedback device alone, with no zeroes in the numerator, is also called an *all-pole* filter, or in statistics terminology, an *AR* filter, then with reference to that its coefficients may be established by use of autoregressive methods.

Any filter can be modelled in terms of the two prototypes FIR and IIR in combination. The general recursion formula on how to compute the output samples y_n from the input samples x_n is then

$$y_n = \sum_{k=0}^{K} b_k x_{n-k} - \sum_{i=1}^{I} a_i y_{n-i} \tag{12}$$

visualized in Figure 23.4c. In the z domain, the filter transfer function $H(z) = Y(z)/X(z)$ is seen from

$$Y(z) \bullet \left(1 + \sum_{i=1}^{I} a_i z^{-i}\right) = X(z) \bullet \left(\sum_{k=0}^{K} b_k z^{-k}\right) \tag{13}$$

The AR part of the filter gives I complex conjugate poles and the MA part gives K complex conjugate zeroes. The higher of I and K define the *order* of this pole-zero, or ARMA filter.

Even if we can implement any filter directly with two such polynomials there is often a practical reason to refine the technique. Especially with higher order systems the coefficients may need to be specified with an accuracy that cannot be reached in processors with moderate word length. This can be overcome by various manipulations on the formulas to write them in alternative, but equivalent forms.

One way is to solve the polynomials for their roots. This may be a costly operation with high order systems since it must then be done iteratively. Once the roots are found the polynomial can be factored as the product of a number of first and second order polynomials. In the implementation this corresponds to that number of such low order filters, connected in sequence such that the output of one is input to the next. An example is the *cascade* formant speech synthesizer where each formant is implemented with a second order filter. Knowing the roots the polynomial can alternatively be expanded into a sum of partial fractions and this corresponds to a set of *parallel* filters, another speech synthesizer classic. Here all the filters are given the same input and the total output is the sum of the filter outputs. A more recent and technically advantageous development is the *lattice filter* structure to which we return below.

A sampled-data filter can be developed from well known templates in continuous theory, like the *Butterworth* (maximally flat frequency response) all-pole filters, and *elliptic filters* having poles and zeroes combined to render sharp filter cutoff between the pass and rejection frequency bands. Such descriptions in terms of poles and zeroes do not always perform well when transposed to the z domain because of interaction with the frequency aliases. One popular remedy is to pre-warp the frequency description with a *bilinear* transformation such that infinite frequency is mapped to $f_s/2$, that is, $z = -1$. In the handbook literature there are also numerous other methods on how to design the filter coefficients from given specifications in time or in frequency, some available as commercial programs.

5 Spectrum analysis

Spectrum analysis has always been a fundamental tool for description and parameter extraction in speech research. Two basic representations are predominant, the *spectrum section*, Figure 23.6, that pertains to a specified time interval and shows level versus frequency, and the *spectrogram*, Figure 23.7, with frequency versus time and the level portrayed as a shade of gray or color. The standard method of spectrography is to multiply the signal with a time window of suitable length and shape, Fourier transform this, and finally find the spectral level by the logarithm of the squared magnitude. To make a spectrogram this procedure is repeated with partly overlapping windows until the desired total time is covered. The most central issue in spectrography is to select the parameters of time resolution and frequency resolution. From the spectrogram we can localize an event timewise with a resolution that corresponds to the duration of the analysis window. The frequency resolution is inversely related to this duration as defined in (4). These resolutions define a 'logon' within which no further detail can be found. Classical selections for speech work from the time of the Sonagraph are 'narrow band' to resolve the voice harmonics, and 'wide band' to suppress these and instead reveal the formant structure and the timing details. Examples in Figure 23.7a and c show 4ms*250Hz and 20ms*50Hz. The essence of the now fashionable time-frequency distributions is that they, contrasting with the classical spectrogram, reveal time detail within the time span transformed. This has a price in that signals, more composite than for instance sine sweeps, exhibit what could be called intermodulation products or aliases, spurious peaks that make the distribution difficult to interpret. This effect can be moderated by various schemes of smoothing which however counteracts the purported improvement in resolution. Figure 23.7d shows results from an implementation with individually controllable time and frequency smoothing windows as suggested by Velez and Absher (1989). Here the smoothing is selected to make the spurious components barely visible. An example with less smoothing in Figure 23.7e shows typical spurious patterns

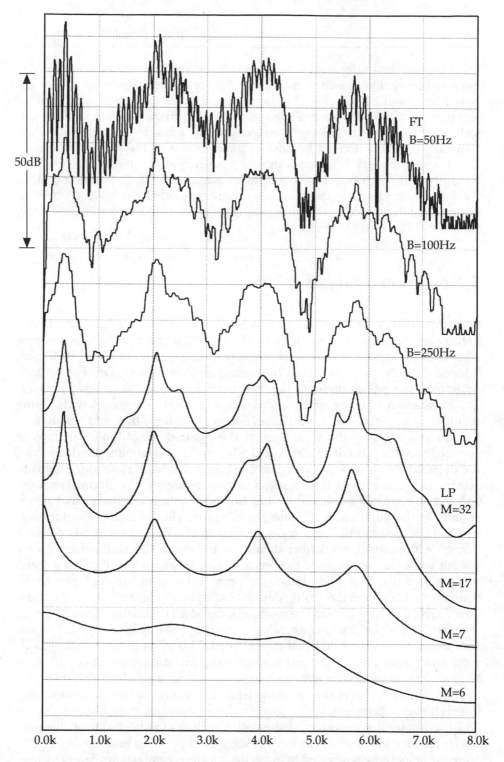

Figure 23.6 Spectrum sections of a vowel [e:] sampled at 16 kHz. The top three are Fourier spectra with different bandwidths to show or suppress the pitch harmonics. The bottom four are LP spectra of varying order. M = 17 would be the more adequate with the sampling rate used if the peaks were supposed to indicate formants.

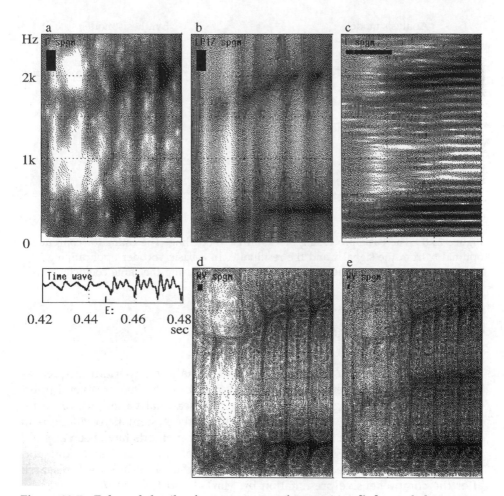

Figure 23.7 Enlarged details of spectrograms of a transition [le:] sampled at 16 kHz, annotated with 'logons' to indicate time and frequency resolutions.
a: conventional Fourier 'wideband' with 4ms*250Hz,
b: 17 coefficient autocorrelation LP with the same time window as a,
c: conventional Fourier 'narrowband' with 20ms*50Hz,
d: smoothed Wigner-Ville distribution with nominally 2ms*70Hz,
e: same, but 1ms*35Hz giving interlacing artificial pitch pulses and formant track.

and alias 'ghost' formants and pitch periods. The use of time-frequency distributions is promising but not yet established in speech. As Cohen (1989) remarks: 'Although it is now fashionable to say that the motivation for this approach is to improve on the spectrogram, it is historically clear that the main motivation was for a fundamental analysis and a clarification of the physical and mathematical ideas needed to understand what a time-varying spectrum is.'

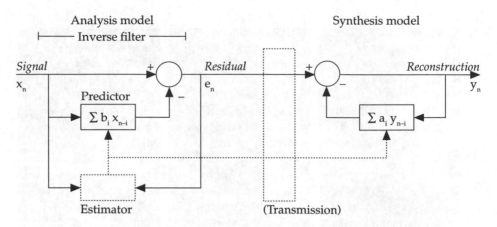

Figure 23.8   The basic processing blocks in LP modelling. The estimator computes optimal b_i from the signal x and the residual e. In a basic vocoder application a reconstructed version of the signal can be fabricated using the same coefficients in an IIR filter.

6 Linear prediction analysis

Prediction theory has an origin in statistics for analysis of periodic sequences of data, like daily temperature or population birth rate. One of several interesting aspects is that it gives a way to identify seasonal variations, or correspondingly with speech, for instance to identify the systematic oscillations in the waveform due to the formants. This or similar methods have been applied in many fields, in speech first by Saito and Itakura (1966), and Atal and Schroeder (1967), and became a widespread standard tool in speech research after the comprehensive presentation by Markel and Gray (1976).

An N:th order predictor would use N historic samples, each contributing to the prediction by some weight factor b_i, and then we use precisely the formula (6) for a FIR filter (excluding b_0, otherwise there would not be much of a prediction). This predictor is called *linear* because it uses a linear combination of the samples, but nothing like powers or products of them. The concept of linearity is an important one that implies that superposition is legal: assuming two different inputs to a system which would generate two different outputs – then the sum of the inputs also generates the sum of those outputs uniquely.

There exist several methods to arrive at the predictor coefficients, covered extensively in the standard textbook literature. One way to formulate the problem is to arrange the predictor in the circuit of Figure 23.8. The signal is compared to the prediction of it, and the resulting output difference is the *prediction error*, or *residual*. The solution amounts to finding values of the coefficients such that this error becomes as small as possible, normally using a minimum squares criterion. Two standard methods, known for historical rather than mathematical reasons as the *covariance* and the *autocorrelation* methods, differ in details and in the range of samples used. We do not enter the mathematics of them, this is well published, down to the level of source codes for their central subroutines, for instance in Markel and Gray (1976) or in the publication by the IEEE DSP committee (1979).

The covariance method is efficient in extracting a maximum of relevant information from a minimal amount of data, but may give problems in accuracy and stability. The more reliable results come with good quality input data, not corrupted by noise, and that reflect a stationary system. Even with a static articulatory position the vocal system is not stationary in this sense because the glottis presents a loading impedance that varies considerably over the glottal period, not to speak of the disturbing discontinuity at glottal closure which normally constitutes a major part of the excitation. The covariance method is considered to perform best when the data come from the part of a voiced speech period where the glottis is closed. An inherent property of the method is that the solution does not necessarily represent a stable filter, the roots of the predictor polynomial may be located outside the unit circle.

With the autocorrelation method one normally uses a larger number of samples for the computations, for speech typically at least 256, covering more than one pitch period. To reduce truncation effects the signal segment is normally weighted with a window like a Hamming window. Part of the processing, as its name suggests, is to compute autocorrelations of the samples which also includes an averaging process which will reduce the influence of noise. Moreover this method inherently gives a stable result.

Having found the coefficients that minimize the prediction error the configuration of Figure 23.8 will represent an *inverse filter*. This removes the spectrally prominent features (formants) in the signal and delivers a spectrally white residual at its output. The customary practice is to regard this as the inverse to the production filter in a source-filter production model. Whatever residual that remains of the speech wave after inverse filtering is categorized as the source. Ideally this white spectrum residue should be a pulse train in the case of voiced speech, or random noise with unvoiced. Usually it does exhibit prominent peaks at the instances of excitation of the vocal tract, and this in itself makes it a much used input for pitch determination algorithms. It also serves as a fundamental raw material for studies of the vocal source. To account for the effect from radiation in speech production the speech signal is normally high frequency preemphasized with a first order filter prior to LP analysis.

The impulse response of the inverse filter is an initial unit value followed by the predictor coefficients b_i. By Fourier transformation of this we obtain its frequency response, and turning this upside down we get the estimated 'LP spectrum' of the signal. Being a filter characteristic this lacks information on the signal level which however can easily be found from the signal directly.

Figure 23.6 compares Fourier and LP spectra of different orders. It is important to recognize that although the LP spectrum appears clean and regular as compared to the Fourier spectrum, and more like an ideal textbook shape of a spectrum with formants, it does not necessarily represent the speech signal in a more truthful way than the Fourier spectrum. Rather the LP spectrum *is* the ideal textbook shape, it is precisely a formant model of the signal. The number of formants that can appear is a priori decided by the number of LP coefficients. If you make an LP analysis with M coefficients you will get no more than $M/2$ formants, independent of what number of formants the signal may really have. The merit of LP is that you can prescribe M from your knowledge or desire of how many formants to find, and then the LP analysis will deliver the best matching model within this restriction.

The frame Figure 23.7b shows 17th order LP spectra in the format of a spectrogram. This representation is rarely used for visual display but is the more common as raw material for the estimation of formant patterns.

To get knowledge of the dimensionality from the signal alone has not been a primary concern for classical speech research but is intensely treated in the field of *system estimation*. Here speech serves as an example of a most challenging application because of its rapid variation in number and values of its system parameters. Numerous alternative methods have been developed to find LP parameters in a sequentially *adaptive* manner, and simple forms have reached enough maturity to be incorporated in mobile telecommunications systems, like ADPCM (adaptive predictive PCM), see e.g. Jayant and Noll (1984).

Batch or frame processing vs. such sequential processing is an often encountered dichotomy. The Fourier and LP analyses are typical examples of the first where the spectrum or the LP coefficients are determined for a frame of signal samples. The data of the whole frame is treated in one comprehensive and relatively complicated process, and also the result is a vector, a composite set of data. The data for the next execution of the algorithm is taken some frame step time later in the input sequence, with speech perhaps in the range 2–50 ms depending on application. The IIR and FIR filters with their simple recursion formulas exemplify sequential processes. Although the input is several samples the process delivers an output for only one sample time slot, and the process is then subsequently repeated in its entirety, each time displaced by one sample interval. Sometimes the desired processing can be obtained either way. You can for instance do a spectrum analysis framewise using the FFT or you can do it sequentially with a bank of parallel bandpass filters. Which is the computationally more efficient way can be inferred from the requirements of output temporal and spectral resolution. The inherent efficiency of FFT can in such cases justify apparently wasteful solutions like pooling several adjacent spectrum samples into one wider band analysis channel. Numerous methods have been developed to bridge such gaps, for instance special variations of the FFT with 'pruned' inputs or outputs, or the constant Q transform (Brown, 1991). The chirp-z transform (Rabiner et al, 1969) is for evaluation away from the frequency axis. Frequency warping can at instances be integrated within a process like in the warped LP outlined by Strube (1980).

7 Pitch extraction techniques

The extraction of pitch is one of the perennial problems of speech research, reviewed for instance by Hess (1983). The literature describes methods by the hundreds, constantly reporting improvements, but still an ideal method remains to be found. The reasons why a pitch determination algorithm (PDA) may fail are manifold, but prominent ones are that speech has a highly variable spectrum – the base for its information carrying capacity – as well as it shows considerable variation between speakers. These problems are likely to create difficulty when one attempts to measure or display accurate individual pitch periods within the laboratory. In practical applications like speech coding for communications we have the additional difficulties of band limiting, non-linear and phase distortions due to filtering and reverberation, and external noise. The more fundamental problem is however one of definition: what exactly is pitch? Most PDAs work on some specific feature connected with periodicity, and perform well if this feature is actually present. Suppose for instance a pitch meter that isolates the fundamental with a lowpass filter in order to measure its period. This will inevitably fail in cases where the fundamental has been removed by bandlimiting as in telephone speech, or in the presence of low frequency noise, even such that may not be perceived by a human listener.

Most practical measurement algorithms, not only for pitch, can be logically partitioned into a preprocessor, an estimator proper, and a postprocessor. The task of the preprocessor is to condition the signal, for instance by dynamic control of spectral preemphasis and gain, to create an optimal signal for the estimator. The postprocessor typically identifies and corrects errors, it could for instance replace a deviant sample with a value somehow derived from its neighboring samples. In all three subsystems the degree of sophistication can be arbitrarily selected which in part explains the vast number of PDAs in the literature.

The historically earlier PDAs were based on direct processing of the time signal, typically detecting peaks (Dolansky, 1955) or zero crossings. Another popular time domain idea is that successive pitch periods should be of approximately equal shape. This lies behind the autocorrelation and average magnitude difference methods (AMDF, Ross et al, 1974). If you compare two signal segments, located some time apart, then they should be maximally correlated (alternatively show a smallest difference) when this time equals the pitch period. The weakness of the time methods is that successive periods are not always very similar when articulation varies, or in the presence of reverberation or other disturbances. Some have as special merit that they reasonably locate some anchor point in each individual pitch period.

The other classical mainstream PDAs operate in the frequency domain and exploit the fact that a periodical signal has a number of evenly spaced harmonics. An initial process is then to Fourier transform the signal, and the PDA looks for the repetitive spectral peaks. The spectrum must then have sufficient resolution to show the individual harmonics which implies that the time interval transformed must have sufficient duration – you cannot detect a periodicity unless you look at more than one period. One way to detect the spectral periodicity is to compute the sum or product spectrum (Schroeder, 1968) or computationally efficient variations like subharmonic summation (Hermes, 1988). The principle is then that you make several versions of the spectrum with frequency axes rescaled by factors 1, 2, 3, etc., and then combine them by summing or multiplication. This way the harmonic peaks of a spectrum will give rise to a sharp coincidence peak while inharmonic components average out into a low floor.

Another way to identify the periodicity in the spectrum is to take the spectrum of the power spectrum. According to the Wiener-Kinchin theorem this amounts exactly to finding the autocorrelation function of the signal. A successful related variant is to first take the logarithm of the power spectrum – this makes all spectral lines have the same shape even if their levels vary with the formant envelope. The spectrum of the log power spectrum is called the *cepstrum*, with an abscissa of *quefrency*, the same dimension as time. This method and its vocabulary of permuted variants of the classical terms was conceived of in seismology by Bogert et al (1963), and was applied as a highly successful speech PDA by Noll (1967). A principal merit of this method is that it is largely insensitive to level variation and band limiting in the input – these only reflect as shift and truncation in the log spectrum. Thus the cepstral peak is largely of constant cepstral amplitude. A weakness appears when the signal has only a few harmonics (e.g. in the occlusion phase of a voiced plosive) or when the pitch is rapidly changing. In the latter case the higher harmonics in the log spectrum are smeared out and may overlap such that the periodic structure disappears. Figure 23.9 shows the cepstrum of a voiced sound. Its contents at quefrencies shorter than the pitch peak (the short-pass liftered cepstrum) is a Fourier description of the grosser features of the log spectrum like level, slope and formant density. These first few cepstral values are often used as input data to speech recognizers. In that application it is also customary to reshape the log spectrum on a warped frequency scale before Fourier transformation of it into the cepstrum. This is mostly done on the basis of the Bark scale which is applied to account for the frequency selective properties of the hearing mechanism. The intention is to represent the perceptually relevant information with a minimal amount of data, a prime interest both in communications applications and research.

Modern PDAs often use the machinery of an LP inverse filter as preprocessor to remove the formant structure from the speech wave, for instance Markel (1972), Un and Yang (1977), Ananthapadmanabha and Yegnanarayana (1979), Cheng and O'Shaughnessy (1989). The accuracy and robustness of modern PDAs are often sufficient for use in communications systems, but pitch extraction remains a dynamic field now trying to incorporate more complete modelling of the human auditory system, see Hermes (1993).

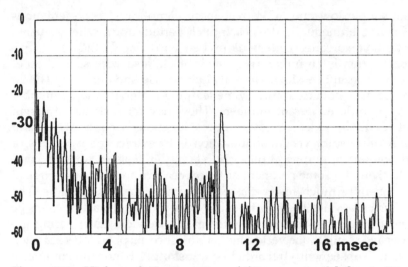

Figure 23.9 High resolution cepstrum of the same vowel [e:] as in Figs 23.6 and 7.

8 Speech synthesis and coding

Knowing the inverse filter it is elementary as outlined above to set up the inverse of it, that is the synthesis filter. Another important variation is that as part of the LP coefficients solution we find what in different terminologies is called, *reflexion, parcor* (Itakura and Saito, 1972), or k coefficients. They have correspondent filter implementations in the form of *lattice filters* (Makhoul, 1978; Friedlander, 1982) which can be set up in a variety of equivalent forms by use of mathematical transformations and such tricks as introducing backward prediction. These are similar to reflexion line filters, or wave filters (Fettweis and Meerkötter, 1975; Strube, 1982) and relate back to classical vocal tract modelling as a set of abutting transmission line sections of varying areas. From k one can thus construct such an area function that would give rise to the observed filtering. Yet another form is the logarithm of the area ratios, LAR, which have been found to be effective and robust descriptors in speech coding for communications. The possibility to estimate vocal tract area functions reliably is however limited. It depends critically on proper handling of such side factors as preemphasis and that assumptions of the model (for instance that of one-dimensional wave propagation) are valid in the frequency band defined via the sampling rate.

An early application of LP was in vocoders where the transmitted data were the coefficients, the pitch and the level. These exhibited a 'reedy' and somewhat unnatural character in the resynthesized voice, much due to the use of a simple pulse generator for synthesis excitation. For high quality vocoding different schemes have been developed to transmit the residual in more detail, ranging from simple low-rate PCM over more complicated representations with sets of multiple unequal pulses each pitch period, up to schemes using vector quantization, so called code-book excited vocoders, CELP.

Vector quantization is an important topic in itself, also with several other applications for speech. See Makhoul et al (1985) or Gersho and Gray (1992). Assume that we have collected, from some learning material, a large number of *vectors*, that is ordered *sets* of numbers. They may for instance represent pitch period residuals, spectrum shapes, area functions, or sets of formant frequencies. A purpose of vector quantization is to extract the essentials of such a large amount of empirical data and classify it. The vectors are compared to each other with some pertinent distance measure and they are grouped into classes, generally much fewer classes in number than the vectors. The members of each class are then sufficiently close in value that they can be averaged into a single representative entry in a codebook. Later, using the codebook, we have as input one vector and its closest correspondent is searched for. The quantity subsequently recorded or transmitted is not the composite vector itself, but only its ordinal number in the codebook. To hint the order of magnitude involved, a codebook to represent with reasonable fidelity the various spectral patterns used by a population of speakers might contain some 1000 vectors.

24 Some Approaches to Automatic Speech Recognition

W.A. AINSWORTH

1 Introduction

Speech recognition, a skill which every healthy child acquires with no apparent effort in the first few years of life, has proved remarkably difficult to achieve by machine. As in many fields, early attempts at solving subproblems such as digit recognition were encouraging (Dudley and Balashek, 1958), but the failure of attempts to generalize led to despondency and suggestions by some that the problem could not be solved (Pierce, 1969). Despite this there has been steady progress during the last few decades leading to a better understanding of the problems and the development of some successful systems, particularly for restricted domains.

Speech recognition is essentially a pattern recognition problem. Speech is a continuous acoustic signal which must be transformed into a sequence of discrete linguistic units. The problem is that neither the appropriate linguistic unit (word, syllable, phoneme) nor the boundaries between the segments corresponding to them are known. For this reason isolated word recognizers have been developed. The speaker is required to utter a sequence of words with pauses between them. However, although this unnatural mode of speaking simplifies the problem, it does not solve it.

Many problems arise in pattern recognition from different types of variabilities (Ainsworth, 1988). There is variability due to the speaker. Different speakers have different sized vocal tracts giving rise to formants with different ranges of frequencies. Males and females speak with different fundamental frequencies. Speakers from different regions and with different social backgrounds speak with different accents. Even the same speaker speaking the same phrase on different occasions will speak with different tempos. Speech will vary with the health and the emotional state of the speaker. In real situations the acoustic environment will change. Background noise will contaminate the speech waveform and reverberation will distort it. For recognition by

Speech ⟶ PRE-PROCESSOR ⟶ FEATURE EXTRACTOR ⟶ PATTERN MATCHER ⟶

Figure 24.1   Typical structure of a speech recognizer.

machine the acoustic waveform must be transformed into an electrical one by a microphone. The type of transducer and its position relative to the speaker will affect the signal. All these sources of variability must be addressed.

There are two main approaches to speech recognition: knowledge-based and statistical. In the knowledge-based approach, linguistic and acoustic knowledge concerning the units of speech, their structure and rules about how these units combine is used to determine what was said. In the statistical approach models of words or smaller units, which have been built by training them with large quantities of speech, are used to compute the probability of the correspondence between the models and the received sounds. Currently recognizers based on the statistical approach appear more successful as they are able to deal more readily with the variability which occurs with speech.

Most recognizers consist of a transducer, a preprocessing stage, a feature extraction stage, and a pattern matching or decision making stage as shown in Figure 24.1. In the next section various signal processing techniques which have been employed for feature extraction are discussed. Section 3 describes pattern recognition techniques and Section 4 knowledge-based techniques. Section 5 is concerned with noise problems: the sources of noise and how their effects may be alleviated. Speech recognizers are only useful when they are used by humans. In Section 6 some of the human factors are discussed.

2 Feature extraction

2.1 Frequency analysis

The oldest and most familiar technique for analyzing speech is frequency analysis. Consequently many feature extractors are based on this. The result of frequency analysis is usually displayed as a sound spectrogram, a two dimensional representation of the frequency-intensity-time structure of a speech sound (Figure 24.2). The features extracted are a sequence of vectors representing the spectra at each point in time.

These vectors are normally computed by digitizing the speech waveform at a rate of 10–20 kHz to produce a sampled waveform. An analysis interval of 10–30ms is chosen and this is multiplied by a Hamming or Hanning window to reduce spectral distortion caused by the window edges (for further description of these windows, see Liljencrants, SPEECH SIGNAL PROCESSING). An FFT

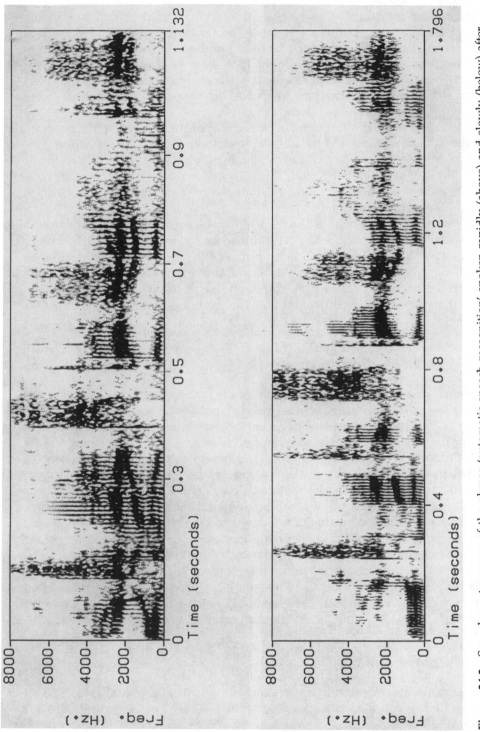

Figure 24.2 Sound spectrograms of the phrase 'automatic speech recognition' spoken rapidly (above) and slowly (below) after linear time normalization.

(fast Fourier transform (Cooley and Tukey, 1965)) is then computed from which the power spectrum is obtained. The window is then shifted by 5–10 ms and the process is repeated. The resulting sequence of vectors constitutes the features used in the pattern recognition stage of the process.

There are many variants of frequency analysis. In the past when computers were slower a bank of bandpass filters was often employed. This gives essentially the same information as the FFT.

The actual shape of the spectrum obtained depends on the relative positions of the analysis window and the start of the glottal period of the waveform. This source of variation can be reduced by aligning the analysis window to coincide with the start of the glottal period. This is known as pitch-synchronous analysis. In order for this to be successful preliminary analysis must be performed to detect the start of each glottal period.

One source of variability is the pitch of the voice itself. The effects of this on the spectrum may be reduced by cepstrum analysis (Noll, 1967, and Liljencrants, SPEECH SIGNAL PROCESSING). The logarithm of the spectrum is obtained, then the inverse Fourier transform of this is computed. The resulting signal, known as the cepstrum, contains a peak corresponding to the pitch. This is removed and the spectrum is again computed. The resulting feature vectors are less variable, but at the expense of extra computation.

2.2 *Linear prediction analysis*

Another way of separating the effects of the source (excitation pulses) from those of the filter (vocal tract) is by linear prediction analysis (Markel and Gray, 1976). The current value of a sampled waveform can be predicted from a linear combination of past values plus an error signal. The parameters by which the past values are multiplied are known as the linear prediction co-efficients (LPC). If these are chosen so as to minimize the error it can be shown that the error signal is in fact the excitation signal.

There are several techniques for estimating the linear prediction coefficients. In the autocorrelation method a window function is applied to the digitized waveform, as in frequency analysis, leading to a set of simultaneous equations which can be solved to give an estimate of the LPC. An alternative is the covariance method in which a finite part of the sampled waveform is used (see also Liljencrants, SPEECH SIGNAL PROCESSING). The covariance method is often applied pitch-synchronously. The set of LPC for each time interval can form a feature vector for input to the decision stage of the recognizer.

2.3 *Vector quantization*

A technique developed for speech coding, which is also useful for speech recognition, is vector quantization (Buzo et al, 1980; see also Liljencrants, SPEECH SIGNAL PROCESSING). If each vector has n elements, such as LPC, it can be represented by a point in an n-dimensional space. If this space is populated by points derived by analyzing a large amount of speech, some parts of the space will be densely populated and some sparsely populated. In vector quantization the space is divided into 2^m cells each containing approximately the same number of points. Each cell has an address consisting of m bits. A codebook is constructed with the address of the cell and the corresponding position of the centre of gravity of the cell in the n-dimensional space.

Codebooks may be constructed by computing the centre of gravity of the points in the space then choosing two points equidistant in opposite directions from that point along the major axis of the distribution. All points nearest to one point are placed in one cell and all points nearest to the other are placed in the other cell. The centres of gravity of these cells are then computed and the process repeated m times.

This codebook can be used to transform any vector (set of LPC) into an address and any address back into a vector which is near to the original. By choosing m appropriately, vector quantized speech may be restored with an acceptably small amount of distortion. For speech recognition the sequence of vectors can be replaced by a sequence of addresses, reducing the amount of computation at the next stage and, possibly, the amount of variation.

3 Pattern matching

3.1 Pattern classification techniques

A pattern classifier is a system for estimating the class to which a pattern belongs. Patterns may be thought of as points in an n-dimensional space. Figure 24.3 illustrates this for two-dimensional patterns. Levinson (1985) has suggested that there are three types of methods by which patterns may be classified: geometric, topological and probabilistic.

In the geometric methods the space is divided into regions by means of boundaries. The positions of these boundaries are chosen such that patterns of one class fall one side of the boundary and those of the other classes fall on the other side. In an n-dimensional space the boundaries of the regions will be surfaces. For ease of computation, hyperplanes are often employed as the decision surfaces, though the effectiveness of these depends upon the distribution of the points representing the pattern vectors in the space.

In the topological methods each pattern class is represented by one or more points in the hyperspace. An unknown pattern is classified by measuring the distance between the point representing the unknown pattern and the points representing the various classes. The point having the least distance is taken to represent the class of the unknown pattern. Topological methods require a distance measure to be defined. Often Euclidean distance, or square Euclidean distance, is used, but other more sophisticated measures such as that due to Itakura (1975) have been employed.

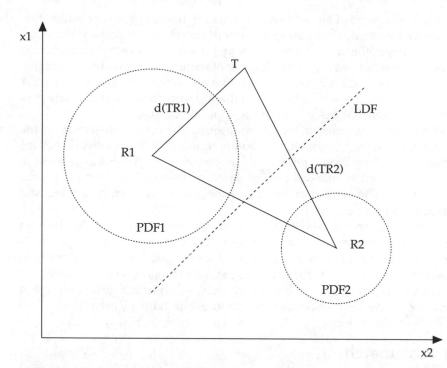

Figure 24.3   Geometric, topological and probabilistic classification of patterns in a two-dimensional feature space. The features are x_1 and x_2. R1 and R2 are the reference patterns and T is the test pattern. In a geometric classification T belongs to the same class as R1 because it lies on the same side of the linear discriminant function LDF. In a topological classification T belongs to the same class as R1 as the distance d(TR1) is less than the distance d(TR2). In a probabilistic classification T belongs to the same class as R1 if the probability density function PDF1 at T is greater than PDF2 at T.

In the probabilistic methods, a probability density function (PDF) is defined for each pattern in the space. The probability that an unknown pattern belongs to a certain class is estimated from the PDFs by choosing the class for which the value of its PDF is greatest at the point occupied by that pattern.

Speech sounds, of course, are represented by a sequence of pattern vectors and, hence, by a series of points in the space. In speech recognition the pattern classification techniques have to be extended to deal with this problem.

3.2 Time normalization

One of the main sources of variation in the speech of an individual is variations in the durations of the phonetic elements. We can speak slowly or quickly but, within limits, we are equally well understood. The designers of some early speech recognizers attempted to solve this problem by linear time normalization, that is by expanding or contracting an utterance uniformly in order to make it the same duration as the word in the vocabulary with which it was being matched. This also had the advantage of simplifying the pattern recognition as the distance between the patterns could be computed as the sum of the distances between corresponding feature vectors. This increased the recognition rate but ignored the fact when we speak quickly we shorten the durations of the more steady parts of the speech, such as the vowels, more than those parts of the speech where the spectra are changing rapidly (Figure 24.2).

One way of dealing with this problem is to employ nonlinear normalization based on dynamic programming (Bellman, 1957). In order to implement this the distance between every feature vector in the test word (length m vectors) and every feature vector in the template (length n vectors) with which it is being compared is computed forming a distance matrix with m×n elements. The ends of the two words (points (1,1) and (m,n)) must match so the problem is how to align the intervening vectors in such a way as to minimise the total distance between these points. This is achieved by computing the local minimum distance at each point which is calculated by taking for each vector in the template the minimum distance between it and the current vector in the test word (no timescale distortion), the next vector in the test word (contraction) and the last vector in the test word (expansion). As the points are continuous it is necessary to start at point (1,1) and compute the minimum cumulative distance at the neighbouring points and work progressively until the point (m,n) is reached. The result is the cumulative distance matrix. The distance at the point (m,n) is the total minimum distance between the words. This is computed for the test word and each of the templates. The word corresponding to the template which gives the least distance is chosen as the identity of the test word (Velichko and Zagoruyko, 1970; Sakoe and Chiba, 1978).

This technique, known as dynamic time warping (DTW), also gives the function by which the timescale of one word should be distorted to produce the optimum match with the other word. This function can be obtained by backtracking through the cumulative distance matrix from the point (m,n) to (1,1) by choosing the adjacent element which has the smallest value.

Provided that the templates are good exemplars of the words in the vocabulary a DTW recognizer works well for the speaker who trained it. In order for it to do so with many speakers more templates from other voices are required. One of the disadvantages of DTW recognizers is the amount of computation required to produce the distance matrices. With more templates this increases and the recognition time becomes unacceptably long. In order to speed up this process speech recognizers based on special architectures such as systolic arrays have been developed (Burr et al, 1984).

An alternative to having many templates is to combine all the templates of a word into an average template. However this ignores the spread of the

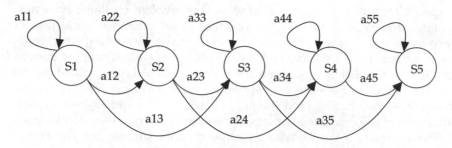

Figure 24.4   A left-to-right Markov model. At each instant in time the model stays in state S_i with a probability a_{ii} or moves to state S_j with a probability a_{ij}.

feature values so perhaps the variances of the features as well as their means should be used. This leads to the idea of employing statistical techniques.

3.3 Statistical techniques

The technique which has become most used for speech recognition is based on hidden Markov models (HMMs) (Jelinek, 1976; Levinson et al, 1983). A word can be represented by a sequence of feature vectors. The idea behind HMM recognizers is that a number of models can be built, one for each word in the vocabulary, and each model is able to generate a sequence of feature vectors. When a new word is spoken a sequence of feature vectors is produced and the probability of each model generating that sequence is calculated. The word corresponding to the model with highest probability is then chosen.

A Markov model has a number of states where the probability of being in one state depends only on the last state. Each state has a symbol associated with it. The model has an initial state vector which specifies the probability of being in each state at the start of the process and a transition matrix which specifies the probability, at each point in time, of changing to a new state or staying in the same state. The model is thus able to generate sequences of symbols and the probability of producing a particular sequence can be calculated.

In order to model spoken words a left-to-right Markov model is required, as shown in Figure 24.4. From each state the model can remain in the same state, move to the next state or skip to the next but one state with the probabilities shown. Each symbol can represent a feature vector so the model is capable of a sequence of feature vectors. Alternatively vector quantization may be used. Feature vectors may be transformed into symbols (addresses) with the codebook.

The probabilities in the initial state vectors and the transition matrices could be estimated by counting the frequency of occurrence of symbols and pairs of symbols in sequences produced by speaking the words in the vocabulary several times. In practice real speech requires a large number of feature

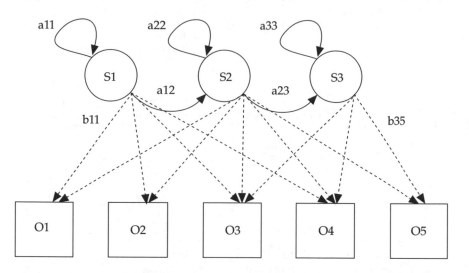

Figure 24.5 A hidden Markov model. At each instant in time the model stays in state S_i with a probability a_{ii} or moves to state S_j with a probability a_{ij}. However the state the model is in is hidden. An observer sees only the output O_k which is generated when the model is in state S_j with a probability b_{jk}.

vectors so in order to obtain good estimates a huge amount of training data would be needed. This can be reduced by employing hidden Markov models (HMMs).

A hidden Markov model is capable of emitting not just one symbol but any symbol with a certain probability (Figure 24.5). An observer sees the sequence of symbols but not the underlying state sequence. Hence the term hidden Markov model.

An HMM is characterized by its initial state vector, its transition matrix and an emission matrix, the probability of emitting a particular symbol when it is in a given state. HMMs are trained by estimating the probabilities in these matrices from the symbol sequences produced by a number of utterances of the word which the model is to represent. An efficient way of doing this is by means of the Baum–Welch algorithm (Baum, 1972). This is an iterative procedure involving intensive computation. However this needs to be done only during the training. During recognition much less computation is required.

The structure of an HMM recognizer is shown in Figure 24.6. During the training phase a number of repetitions of each word in the vocabulary is spoken and the probabilities in the transition and emission matrices and the initial state vector are estimated. In the recognition phase a word is spoken and analyzed to produce a sequence of symbols. The probability of each model generating that sequence is calculated and the word corresponding to the most likely model is chosen. The Viterbi algorithm which is based on dynamic programming is often used to calculate these probabilities (Viterbi, 1967).

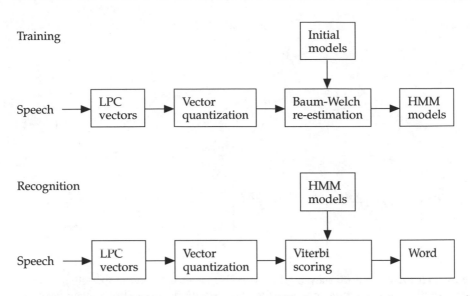

Figure 24.6 An HMM based speech recognizer. In the training mode examples of words in the vocabulary are analysed and used to estimate the parameters of the models. In recognition mode the models are used to compute the probability the input word was generated by each of the models.

There are many variations of this basic HMM. Software such as the HKT package (Young, 1992) is available for building HMM recognizers.

3.4 Neural networks

In recent years there have been a number of attempts to apply neural network techniques to speech recognition. Neural networks are based on neurons, the information processing units in the nervous systems of animals.

A neuron consists of a soma, or cell body, an axon and dendrites. Axons from other cells form connections with the dendrites and the soma. These connections may be excitatory or inhibitory. Electrical activity in the neighbouring cells causes ionic transport through the membranes of the connections changing the potential within the cell. If this exceeds a threshold, the cell discharges causing an electrical spike to be transmitted down the axon which in turn affects the discharge pattern of the cells with which it comes in contact. Excitatory inputs make the spike discharge more likely whereas inhibitory inputs prevent a discharge.

A multilayer perceptron (MLP) is a network of layers of artificial neurons. A typical MLP consists of an input layer, a hidden layer and an output layer (Figure 24.7). Each neuron receives connections from the previous layer and sends connections to the next layer. Associated with each input is a weight.

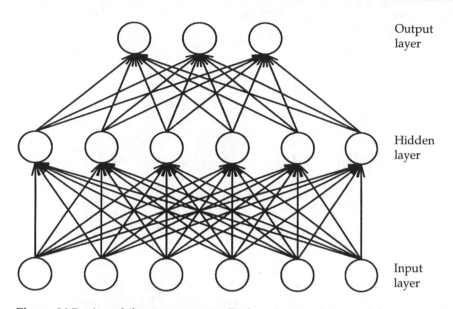

Output
layer

Hidden
layer

Input
layer

Figure 24.7 A multilayer perceptron. Each connection has a weight associated with it. Units in the hidden layer compute the activation function (Figure 24.8) of the sum of the weighted signals from the input layer and send the result to the output layer. The units in the output layer perform the same computation with the signals they receive from the hidden layer.

The neuron computes the activation function (Figure 24.8) of the weighted sum of the inputs and sends this value to the next layer. The MLP thus receives an input pattern and maps this into an output pattern. By adjusting the weights, any mapping function can be formed provided that there are at least two layers of adjustable weights and enough units in the hidden layer. If the input represents a pattern and each of the outputs represents the category of pattern an MLP can function as a pattern recognizer.

An MLP can be trained by presenting a pattern to the input and allowing it to compute the output. The target output is then presented and the difference between the actual output and this target output is used to adjust the weights in such a way that next time the pattern is presented the MLP will be more likely to produce the desired output. The rule for adjusting the weights is known as the back propagation algorithm and this training procedure is known as supervised learning (Rumelhart et al, 1986).

An MLP can be used as a vowel recognizer. Feature vectors derived from spoken vowels can be presented as input patterns and the outputs can represent the vowel categories. Vowels spoken by many speakers can be used to train the network so that a speaker independent vowel recognizer can be developed (McCulloch and Ainsworth, 1988). However in its simple form an MLP is not suitable for word recognition as it has no mechanism for dealing with the time varying nature of speech. A more elaborate network, a time-delay

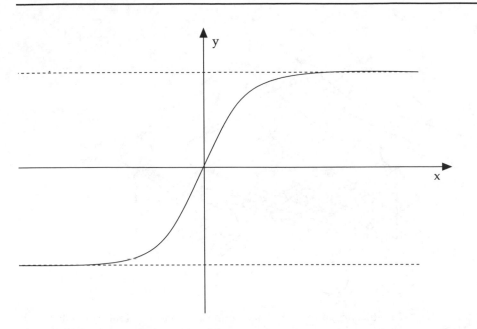

Figure 24.8   Activation function of a unit in an MLP.

neural network (TDNN), has been developed by Waibel et al (1989) for this purpose.

A TDNN designed to recognise the voiced plosives /b/, /d/ and /g/ is shown in Figure 24.9. It consists of four layers with 16 units in the input layer, 8 in the first hidden layer, 3 in the second and 3 output units. A spectral representation of a syllable is presented to the input. There are 16 frequency channels and 15 time frames of 10 ms. Each unit has as input a weighted sum of the current input plus the weighted sum of the n previous inputs, where n is 2 for the first hidden layer, 4 for the second and 8 for the output units. Time is mapped out spatially in Figure 24.9 so the weights to the delayed outputs are indicated by the total connectivity between each unit in one layer and a rectangular array of units in the previous layer. The forward pass can be considered as sliding a window of 3 time frames across the timescale of the input one step at a time.

Learning is achieved by modifying the weights according to the error back propagation algorithm. This causes a problem as it gives different weight changes for corresponding time-shifted weights. This is resolved by averaging the time-delayed weight changes.

The TDNN appears to work because it learns to recognise acoustic features such as F2 rise or vowel onset independently of where they occur in the time window. The main limitation is the fixed size of the window. For syllables this can be chosen appropriately but for speech in general temporal features can be much longer than 150 ms.

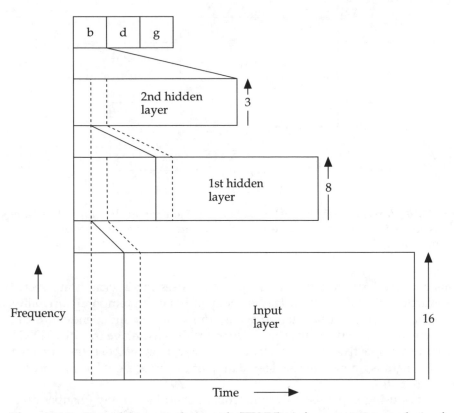

Figure 24.9 Time delay neural network (TDNN). A frequency-time analysis of a syllable is presented to the input layer. Units in a window activate the units in the first hidden layer which in turn activate those in the layers above. The window is swept along the time axis.

Another way to incorporate time into networks is to feed a state vector from the output back to the input after a delay (Figure 24.10). Such systems are known as recurrent neural networks (Jordan, 1986; Robinson, 1993). First a sequence of input vectors is presented to the network. These produce a corresponding sequence of output and state vectors. At the end of the sequence the final output and state vectors are compared with the target output and some arbitrary state vectors. This generates error signals which are fed back in the usual way. These are fed back through the time delay to provide the error signals for the penultimate state outputs. These are combined with the error signals produced by the comparison of the penultimate output and the penultimate target, and the whole process is repeated until the first input in the sequence is reached. The weights are then changed by an amount equal to the average weight changes produced by all the backward passes through the network.

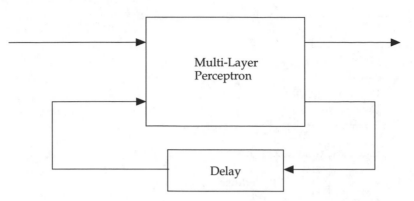

Figure 24.10   A recursive neural network. Some of the units in the output layer are fed back to the input layer after a delay so the system retains a memory of the previous inputs.

This network has a number of advantages. It uses the internal state vector to represent temporal position. This is a way of handling temporal variability as the path traversed in the state space is comparatively independent of the time taken to traverse the path. The network has the advantage over the TDNN of not imposing a fixed window length. However, in practice the effective window length is limited by the degradation of the error signal as one propagates back in time.

Instead of using supervised learning some networks employ unsupervised learning where categories are formed as a result of the statistical properties of the patterns rather than being imposed by a trainer. One such network has been developed by Kohonen (1984). This may be used to recognize time varying signals such as speech.

An input vector is presented to a two-dimensional array of units. Associated with each unit is a weight vector. At each unit the input vector is compared with the weight vector. The unit which most closely matches the input is chosen and its weight vector is moved nearer to the input vector. The weight vectors of neighbouring units are also adjusted. This algorithm is in effect a clustering algorithm producing an ordered mapping.

If spectral input vectors are used, such networks construct topological phoneme maps (or phonotopic maps). Continuous speech will excite a sequence of phoneme units. Each time an utterance is spoken it should excite the same shaped path in the two-dimensional space independently of the time taken to speak it (Tattersall, 1990).

Despite the development of neural networks for speech recognition none currently appear to work better than HMMs. Neural networks do, however, have a theoretical advantage. They are pattern discriminators whereas HMMs are models. If two models are similar they will give similar probabilities of being the model to have generated the observed sequence of vectors. A neural network, however, can be trained to exploit the differences and ignore the similarities.

One way to take advantage of this is to build a network which performs the same computations as an HMM and which has the parameters of the models as the weights of the network. The network can then be trained with speech data to adjust the weights by back propagation to improve its pattern discrimination performance (Bridle and Dodd, 1991).

3.5 Sub-word units

As mentioned earlier one of the problems in automatic speech recognition is choosing an appropriate unit. For some applications, such as digit recognition, where only a small vocabulary is required, the word is the natural unit. However as there are more than 100,000 words in common use in the English language the word is impractical for a general purpose recognizer. Not only would the storage required be large but also the training time would be impossible. Consequently sub-word units have been considered.

One possibility is the syllable. However there are some 10,000 of these in English so they have the same disadvantages as words but to a lesser degree. Another possibility is the demisyllable (Fujimura et al, 1977). Syllables have the structure $C_1 VC_2$ where C_1 and C_2 are optional consonant clusters and V is a vowel or diphthong. As the numbers of C_1 and C_2 are quite limited the number of demisyllables is much less than the number of syllables (it has been estimated to be about 2,000).

A further possibility is the phone. The problem here is that of context dependency. Phones have different acoustic forms depending upon the phones which precede and follow them. The solution is to use triphone units which are sounds of phone length which have both right and left transitional context properties included. A successful large vocabulary (997 words) speech recognition system called SPHINX has been built by Lee (1989) using 1,100 of these units. An HMM was built for each triphone using a large amount of training data. Word models are constructed by putting together appropriate triphone models and sentences are constructed from the word models in accordance with a finite state grammar which was constructed by analysing a number of sentences appropriate to a particular application. Speech recognition is performed using a Viterbi algorithm which obtains the optimum path through the word network generated by the grammar. The computational load is reduced using a beam search. A number of paths are traversed in parallel but when the cumulative probability for a path falls below a threshold that path is eliminated. Thus only the best paths remain and the one with the highest probability is selected as the recognised sentence.

4 Knowledge-based techniques

In the previous section a number of speech recognition techniques based on statistics were discussed. The systems were trained by giving them one or more examples of a word, or other unit, and the system was required to recognise other examples of the word by pattern matching using statistical measures. In a sense no knowledge of speech or language was built into the system. An alternative approach is to base recognition on the knowledge that phoneticians and linguists have acquired over the years by studying the structure of speech.

4.1 Linguistic knowledge

There are various sources of linguistic knowledge which may be of use in speech recognition: acoustic-phonetic knowledge, lexical knowledge, phonological knowledge, prosodic knowledge, syntactic knowledge and semantic knowledge.

Acoustic-phonetic knowledge expresses the relationship between the acoustic data and a phonetic transcription of the spoken utterance. The traditional approach to deriving a phonetic representation is by segmentation and labelling. This is usually achieved by first classifying each vector of the sound into a small number of acoustic categories such as steady-periodic, changing-periodic, noise, silence, etc. Adjacent vectors of the same type are then coalesced into phonemic-sized units. Rules are then applied to the features present in each segment to categorize the segments with phoneme-like labels. A steady-periodic segment with a low first formant frequency and a high second formant frequency, for example, might be labelled as an /i/. Sometimes a number of consecutive segments represent a phoneme unit. A period of silence followed by a brief noise burst followed by a changing-periodic segment may represent a voiceless plosive such as /t/.

This process, segmentation and labelling, is very error-prone as the manifestations of phonemes are subject to co-articulatory effects which are very context dependent. Consequently a number of structures have been developed for representing possible errors in the output. One of the most useful is the phonetic lattice. This is a two-dimensional array showing the n most likely phonemes in decreasing order of probability of occurrence at each point in time.

The task of the other knowledge sources is to transform the phonetic lattice into an acceptable sequence of words. A lexicon is necessary in this process. Words from the lexicon can be matched against parts of the lattice and the word sequences which best explain the acoustic data can be chosen. However, as the pronunciation of words depends upon their environments phonological rules are required to transform the 'ideal' forms of words found in the lexicon into the forms actually used in spoken sentences. A suitable structure for representing possible sequences of words is a word tree.

The order in which the words in a sentence are permitted to occur is determined by the rules of syntax. This syntactic knowledge enables sequences of words which form ungrammatical sentences but which otherwise match the phoneme lattice to be pruned from the word tree. In order to be effective, speech recognizers are sometimes designed to deal with sentences which obey the rules of finite-state grammars, i.e. where the next word depends only on the last n words. In practice n is often restricted to one so that the grammar too can be represented by network. The next level of complexity is known as a context-free grammar (Fu, 1982) but even this cannot generate all the structures found in natural language. More complex grammars, context-sensitive grammars, have been implemented in experimental speech recognition systems (Woods, 1974).

Prosodic knowledge can also be useful. The intonation contour can help identify the pattern of stressed syllables which in turn assists the word matching. This can also help distinguish statements from questions and thus limit possible word orders. Semantic knowledge could also be used if it can be expressed in a suitable form in order to ensure that the final sentence makes sense.

The structure in which the rules are applied is important (Ainsworth, 1988). In a bottom-up hierarchical system acoustic-phonetic rules are used to produce a phonetic lattice, from which a word tree is produced. The syntactic rules are then used to prune the tree, leaving possible sentences. However, errors produced at the bottom can propagate through the system making it impossible for the correct sentence to be found.

An alternative structure is a top-down system where hypotheses of possible sentences are made at a high level and these are passed to the lower levels for modification or rejection. This structure is also hierarchical which ensures that the rules are applied in a strict order. A more general structure is the blackboard system (Reddy et al, 1973) which allows each knowledge source to be used when it has a contribution to make.

4.2 Alternative systems

Green et al (1990) have argued that the form in which speech data is presented must be compatible with the knowledge structures used to explain it. Systems which apply threshold tests to the feature vectors fail to compare like with like. A phonetician 'reading' a spectrogram uses a combination of features such as 'dips' and 'peaks' in formant tracks, 'noise bursts' and 'formant transitions'. Combinations of such features lead to the hypothesis that a particular phoneme was probably articulated. Green et al have developed an intermediate representation between the acoustic parameters (the pattern vector) and the phonetic (symbolic) representation. They call this intermediate representation the 'speech sketch' by analogy with Marr's 'primal sketch' in vision (Marr, 1982).

Allerhand (1987) has suggested combining knowledge-based and pattern-matching transition model with discrete transition probabilities and continuous observation probabilities but with embedded structure to define the transition sequences. The embedded structure is a representation of phonological and linguistic knowledge. The model is based on a context-free grammar. The grammatical description of pattern structure is related to a numerical pattern representation through pattern-matching techniques. Unknown pattern vectors are assigned membership of a particular class with a probability. The probability is used in the parsing process and to identify unknown pattern sequences by maximum likelihood evidential reasoning (Devijver and Kittler, 1982).

4.3 Recognizer performance

The performance of a recognizer is often given as the percent of words correctly recognized or as an error rate. Such figures, however, are almost meaningless unless more details of the tests performed are given. The performance is dependent on many factors such as the size of the vocabulary and the similarity of the words therein, the noise environment and the speaker. In fact the experiments of Wyard (1993) suggest that the speaker may be the most important source of variation.

Nevertheless a number of tests have now been carried out with common databases so that some useful indication of current performance can be given. Lamel and Gauvin (1993) using a continuous density HMM with cepstral coefficients as features performed tests with the TIMIT, WSJ and BREF databases. The TIMIT database (Garofolo et al, 1993) consists of sets of constructed sentences read by a wide variety of American English speakers and has been widely used to evaluate speech recognition systems. A phone recognition rate of 73.4 per cent was obtained for a 39 phone set. With WSJ (Paul and Baker, 1992), which consists of extracts read from the Wall Street Journal, they obtained 74.4 per cent accuracy for a 46 phone set. This corresponds to 93.1 per cent word recognition accuracy. With BREF (Gauvain et al, 1990), which contains extracts from the French newspaper Le Monde, a 78.7 per cent accuracy was obtained with a 35 phone set.

Similar scores have been obtained with neural network based recognizers. Robinson (1991) reported a 75 per cent accuracy for a recurrent neural network recognizer with the TIMIT database.

In restricted domains a less than perfect recognizer can still be useful. Antoniol et al (1993) employed a speech recognizer for remote control of a mobile robot. With sentences such as 'Go ahead and turn into the next corridor on your left side' where the command can be correctly interpreted if only the underlined words are correctly recognized, they obtained 86.0 per cent word accuracy, 63.7 per cent complete sentence accuracy but 90.9 per cent sentence interpretation accuracy.

5 Noise problems

5.1 Applications

Speech recognizers offer their greatest potential usefulness in applications where the hands and eyes are occupied with other tasks. Examples of such applications are the driver of a vehicle who wishes to make a telephone call, the pilot of an aircraft who wishes to change radio communication channels and a quality control inspector on a production line in a factory. In all of these applications, however, speech is produced in a high level of ambient noise. This background noise interferes with the speech introducing extra variability and making it more difficult for the recognizer to avoid errors. Also in high levels of ambient noise speakers tend to speak louder which causes distortion as well as raising the level. This is known as the Lombard effect (Lombard, 1911).

5.2 Spectral subtraction

One of the most successful techniques for noise reduction is spectral subtraction. The background noise is continuously monitored and its spectrum computed. When a word is spoken this is detected and the spectrum of the speech plus the noise is computed. The spectrum of the noise immediately before the speech is then subtracted from the speech plus noise and the resulting spectral vectors passed to the pattern matching stage of the recognizer.

It has been found in practice that non-linear spectral subtraction is more effective in some applications (Lockwood et al, 1991). The noise power is multiplied by a function of the signal power, the noise power and maximum noise power at each frequency before it is subtracted from the speech plus noise power. Such algorithms have been shown to be particularly effective in a moving vehicle.

Such schemes only work well if the beginning and end points of the speech can be detected accurately and of course are only applicable to isolated word recognition.

5.3 Multi-microphone techniques

If the speech and noise arise from different locations the speech signal can be separated from the noise by means of two microphones. These may be placed so that one picks up the speech plus noise and the other only the noise, then the noise is subtracted from the other signal. In practice it is often impossible to pick up just the noise so, alternatively, the microphones may be placed symmetrically with respect to the speech source. Correlations between the signals in the two channels should then represent the speech signal.

Instead of two microphones an array of microphones may be employed. Provided the speech and the interfering noises come from different spatial locations it is possible to 'focus' the array on the speech by a technique known as adaptive beamforming (Grenier et al, 1990).

5.4 HMM enhancements

As well as making the feature extraction stage of a speech recognizer depend less on background noise the pattern matching stage can be made more robust with respect to variations caused by noise. In a typical HMM-based word recognizer the model spends much more time in a state than in moving to the next state. Whilst in a state it is expected that the input vectors remain the same, but they do not because of noise variations. However if a running average of the past vectors in that state is used in the computation of when to jump to the next state instead of the last vector, a more robust model is achieved (Beattie and Young, 1990).

Another approach is to build models of the noise as well as the speech. The computation of the probability of a particular model generating the input sequence of vectors is then changed to take account of both speech and noise by assuming that the two sources are additive or that one or the other is dominant at each point in time (Varga and Moore, 1990).

6 Human factors

The acceptability of a speech recognition system is crucially dependent on the user interface. Unless this interface provides the facilities which the user expects and in a way which he or she finds easy to use it is likely that the system will be rejected. One of the main problems is that recognition errors will occur occasionally no matter what provisions are made to minimise them. After all, even humans sometimes mishear what is said in a noisy environment. One task of the user interface is to provide a means of detecting and correcting these errors in an efficient manner.

The user interface must provide facilities for training the system. From the point of view of the user as little effort as possible should be devoted to this task but the system may give better performance if more training is performed. Consequently the interface should be designed to satisfy these constraints. The optimum training strategy and conditions should be employed and a means should be provided for the retraining of any vocabulary items which give rise to an unacceptable number of errors.

6.1 *Training*

User-dependent recognizers require at least some training before speech recognition can take place. During a training session the user pronounces the list of words which will then be the recognizer's total vocabulary. In principle the user can make any utterance when presented with a prompt. This could be a translation of the word into a known language or any code the user might wish to adopt. Provided the utterances are used consistently for training and use, recognizer performance should be satisfactory.

User-independent recognizers do not require training by each user. They depend instead on a large database containing many examples of the vocabulary words spoken by a variety of speakers, often over a range of acoustic conditions. It is an obvious advantage for a new user if he or she does not have to train the recognizer. Babini et al (1990) refer to an additional advantage conferred by speaker-independent systems: their performance is more robust in the presence of background noise. However, it is to be expected that a given user will not achieve such a high level of recognition performance with a speaker-independent recognizer as will be obtained with a speaker-dependent unit which he or she has trained.

Training is essential for speaker-dependent recognizers. In adaptation, the recognizer adapts some of the utterances employed in use to improve its models of the words to be recognised. Adaptation has been reported to improve the performance of speaker-independent recognizers (e.g. McInnes et al, 1987). The rationale is that the recognizer, at first dependent on information from speakers in general, improves its performance if it can also use data from the speech of the user. Similarly, performance may be expected to improve if acoustic conditions prevalent when the recognizer is in use differ from those which obtained when the recognizer was trained or the database compiled. Adaptation is, therefore, likely to benefit both user-dependent and user-independent recognizers. Adaptation should not be regarded as an alternative to training but rather as a supplement to it.

6.2 *Feedback*

Errors cannot be corrected unless feedback is provided for the user. The relative merits of visual and auditory feedback have been much discussed. Visual feedback is long-lasting but distracting for eyes-busy tasks: auditory feedback is convenient for these tasks but transient and if specific it is also slow. A common finding in the literature (e.g. Schurick et al, 1985) is that the modality preferred depends on the nature of the task. Giannotta (1990) cites an experiment in which drivers were given road information either visually on an anti-reflection screen or auditorily by loudspeakers. It was concluded that the auditory modality was preferable. The driver's visual system is already occupied with driving; it is not sensible to give additional information visually and also to require the driver to look away from the road.

6.3 Error correction

A variety of strategies can be employed for the error correction process. The simplest is one in which after an error is detected the user says 'no', 'cancel' or 'correction' and repeats the word. The recognizer is free to try the same word again, repeatedly. If the error persists this strategy is liable to result in considerable waste of time and much user frustration.

Another strategy is, following an error, for the machine to suggest the next most likely word on the basis of the output of the recognition algorithm. The correction process can be time consuming if the original utterance was atypical or if it occurred in the presence of loud background noise. The user does not have the opportunity of assisting the recognizer by repetition of the word, which can result in some frustration.

An alternative strategy is similar to simple repetition but the recognizer does not respond with words which have already been rejected by the user. This procedure often produces rapid correction of errors. However, if the user is mistaken and tries to correct a word which was in fact correct he or she will be obliged either to cancel the attempt and start again or to repeat the word until all the words in the active vocabulary have been tried and the recognizer can repeat its original suggestion. The advantage of escaping from the persistence of recognition errors which might occur with the simple repetition strategy make this strategy attractive.

Ainsworth and Pratt (1992) found, on average, fewer corrections were needed if the word that has been misrecognized was repeated. There are two possible explanations of this. An error may be caused by abnormal pronunciation, but when the user repeats the word he or she is likely to be more careful. Alternatively an error may be caused by the speech signal being masked by noise. Repeating the word gives the possibility of the word being spoken during a period when the background is less noisy, leading to correct recognition.

6.4 Wizard of Oz simulations

For some applications, such as speech driven word processing, it would be useful to know what recognition accuracy is necessary for such a system to be acceptable to users. One way of achieving this is by using a human operator, hidden from the user, to act as the recognizer and to type into the system what he or she hears. Recognition errors at a specified rate can be introduced automatically. This approach has been called 'Wizard of Oz' (Kelley, 1985 after Baum, 1900) simulation.

Gould et al (1983) simulated a listening typewriter and concluded that people would probably be able to compose letters by this method at least as efficiently as with traditional methods. However, Newell (1984) has pointed out that a speech-driven word processor must not only be able to accept dictation but also respond to spoken commands. Gould's editing facilities were rather primitive compared to those of a modern word processor, so Newell et al (1992) carried out further simulations.

They concluded that for a listening typewriter the recognition accuracy for speech to orthography must be better than 95 per cent, that such a system was barely acceptable for creative writing and that the input speeds were unlikely to exceed those of even a 'hunt and peck' typist. On the other hand some of the subjects were very positive and enthusiastic about the system.

7 Conclusions

A number of approaches to automatic speech recognition have been discussed. The most successful at present are those based on statistical modelling. This is remarkable as the models assume that speech consists of a sequence of steady sounds, which it patently does not. Current developments in neural networks demonstrate that it is possible to achieve similar results by this approach, the main problem being to adapt them to deal with time in a natural manner. Knowledge-based approaches have so far proved less fruitful, the difficulty being how to encode linguistic knowledge in an appropriate way.

Now that speech recognizers have a sufficiently good performance for them to be used in simple tasks, it is necessary to make them robust with respect to noise and to identify and solve the associated human factor problems.

25 Speaker Recognition and Forensic Phonetics

FRANCIS NOLAN

1 What is speaker recognition?

It is clear from everyday experience that the speech signal carries information about its producer. We are frequently able to tell who is speaking without seeing the speaker, for instance over the telephone or when the other person is out of sight round a corner. Given this fact alone, scientific curiosity might prompt us to investigate the cues which enable us to make such a judgment. But there are also specific circumstances in which it is crucial to be able to determine the identity of a speaker from speech alone, and this provides an even stronger motivation for research into how the speech signal encodes information about its producer, and how reliably that information can be re-covered. For instance, a witness to a crime or its victim may have heard the masked perpetrators speaking, and be asked if any of the voices was familiar. Or tape recordings of telephone conversations may have to be compared with the voice of a criminal suspect, as when a fraudulent foreign exchange deal has come to light, or when someone has been arrested in connection with a bomb threat or a malicious call to the emergency services.

There are many facets to speaker recognition, and this chapter will give an overview of methods and problems in this field. Throughout it will be taken as axiomatic that there are serious limitations on our knowledge of how iden-tity is encoded in the acoustic signal, and of how far an individual's speech is distinct from that of all other members of a speech community, and conse-quently applications of speaker recognition (particularly in the legal process) must always be approached cautiously.

Speaker recognition might be defined as any activity whereby a speech sample is attributed to a person on the basis of its phonetic–acoustic or per-ceptual properties. A distinction can be drawn between naive speaker recog-nition and technical speaker recognition (cf. Nolan, 1983:7). In naive speaker recognition, the recognition is performed by untrained observers – whether in the course of normal everyday life, for instance when answering the telephone or hearing a voice in the next room, or in the more dramatic circumstances of a crime. The decision is based on what is heard, and no special techniques are involved. The term technical speaker recognition probably first brings to mind the use of machines, and indeed much work on the comparison of recordings to establish identity does involve acoustic analysis by machine. The term, however, is intended also to include the application of a more traditional 'technique', namely the skilled analysis by listening which a traditionally trained phonetician can perform.

A second, more widely used, distinction is that between two classes of task under the heading of speaker recognition. These are generally known as speaker verification and speaker identification. In verification, the truth of an identity claim has to be assessed. For instance access by telephone to a bank account, or to other privileged information, might be controlled by checking the claimed identity of the caller. This might in principle be done 'naively', by a human recipient of the phone-call who is familiar with the voice of the account-holder. Normally, however, speaker verification implies techniques by which a computer automatically compares the voice of the caller to a stored reference sample of the speech of the person whose identity is being claimed. In speaker verification the speaker is likely to be cooperative, to be willing to produce and if necessary repeat a chosen utterance for comparison, and unlikely to be adopting any voice disguise – although day-to-day variation in the voice will have to be accommodated. Impostors, however, need to be excluded.

In speaker identification, on the other hand, which includes the usual forensic situation in the standard use of the term, the circumstances are in many ways rather more difficult. It will be hard to obtain from the suspect, even if he or she is cooperative, a sample of speech which is in all respects equivalent to the one which occurred during the crime, since freely spoken speech is not well imitated by reading, and many factors including the level of stress experienced by the speaker may be different. The criminal sample may involve disguise. Artefacts may have been introduced in the criminal sample by distortions in transmission (e.g. poor quality telephone lines) or recording (e.g. a tape recorder running at the wrong speed). So in terms of confounding circumstantial factors, speaker identification is the more challenging task. As for the kind of decision involved, speaker identification is often thought of as involving a difference from speaker verification because the task may be to match an unknown sample to one of a 'closed set' of 'suspects', and so all that is needed is to determine which suspect's speech is nearest the unknown speaker's sample; but although favoured as an experimental design for testing speaker identification techniques (because it allows correct identification rates for closed sets of different sizes to be compared across experiments), the 'closed set' is rare in real legal cases. More often, the forensic task is to compare two samples, one from a known speaker and one from an unknown source, and ultimately a criterion has to be applied to reach a decision as to whether the samples are similar enough to be from the same speaker. In this sense the *decision process* in forensic speaker identification is really like that in speaker verification (see Nolan, 1983:9–10; Doddington 1985:1652–3). Nonetheless, following by now established usage, forensic speaker recognition tasks will be classed as speaker 'identification'.

Whatever kind of speaker recognition is at issue, we need to understand what might be conceived of as 'speaker space'. This is a multi-dimensional space comprised of the dimensions along which speakers are differentiated – mean fundamental frequency and mean second formant frequency are just two examples of the very many dimensions involved. Each speaker is located at a point in this space, or, more accurately, because everyone's speech varies, each speaker occupies a region within the space. The tasks for research in speaker recognition include identifying the dimensions on which speakers are separated, discovering the variation which occurs for a given speaker on those dimensions, and, importantly, sampling the population at large to find out how common or rare particular values are.

2 What is forensic phonetics?

Since the recording of speech has become commonplace, law enforcers and courts have increasingly called on specialists to give expert opinions on speech samples, either in court or at the investigation stage. Often this has been a matter of trying to determine the identity of the speakers on recordings, or of inferring factors about a speaker's background (from regional accent, for instance); but it can also be a matter of determining what has been said (if the quality of the recording is poor), or whether a tape has been edited. In all these areas the phonetician or speech scientist has a contribution to make.

The resultant field of activity has become widely known as forensic phonetics – reflected for instance in the title of the 'International Association for Forensic Phonetics', founded in 1991. Forensic phonetics is an application of phonetics, and it is one which (particularly in the case of speaker identification) has been controversial. The controversy essentially stems from a doubt as to whether phonetics in fact provides sufficient knowledge which is relevant to this application.

The doubt arises in the case of speaker identification because the vast majority of phonetic research, both traditional and instrumental, starts from the assumption of a shared linguistic system, and looks at the phonetic properties realising that system. Differences between speakers, for instance in the formant frequencies of vowels, have been regarded theoretically as 'noise'. So whilst there are answers to questions like 'are there acoustic properties common to velar stops which set them apart from other stops', there is a shortage of answers to questions such as 'are there acoustic properties common to speaker X's stops which set them apart from those of other speakers'. This is not to say that there is no work on between-speaker differences – apart from anything else the need for automatic speech recognition systems to deal with a variety of speakers has motivated considerable work on between-speaker normalization (e.g. Klatt, 1986b; Deterding, 1990). But the work has almost all had the goal of finding principled ways of getting rid of between-speaker variation, rather than developing a theory of 'speaker space' comparable to the theory of 'phonetic space' which implicitly lies behind linguistic phonetics.

The alternative to phoneticians and speech scientists taking part in the forensic process is not, however, that evidence on speaker identity and other 'forensic phonetic' aspects would play no part in court cases; rather, if phonetically competent scientists do not offer the help sought by courts it will be provided by others who have much less understanding of the complexity of spoken communication (see e.g. Nolan, 1991). For this reason it is important for those qualified in phonetics and speech science, whether or not they have the inclination and time to become actively involved, to be closely aware of practices in their countries' legal systems.

3 How does one individual's speech differ from that of another?

We tend to think of a people having a 'voice' which we associate with them, but this handy way of thinking is potentially dangerous, firstly because a person's voice is far from constant, and secondly because it is not yet clear that what we could define as the person's voice is not shared by some other members of the speech community. The rest of this section deals with the factors which contribute to the individuality of a person's speech, and section 4 will discuss the limits on identifying an individual from speech.

3.1 Organic versus learned differences and beyond

A widely accepted view divides between-speaker differences into two categories, 'organic' and 'learned' (e.g. Wolf, 1972:2045). This is a reasonable first approximation. Human beings' vocal apparatus varies in size and detailed shape much as their external appearance does, and, since phonetic properties such as resonant frequencies and rate of vocal cord vibration depend on the dimensions of the vocal tract and larynx, one's physique clearly influences how one sounds (see Beck, ORGANIC VARIATION OF THE VOCAL APPARATUS and Ní Chasaide and Gobl, VOICE SOURCE VARIATION). On the other hand speech is more than a physical event. As children we learn one or more native languages, but in doing so we acquire more than the linguistic system which defines what we think of as a language. Children acquire a socially and regionally marked variety of pronunciation (even if it is the one popularly thought of as 'standard') according to their linguistic environment. This process continues to a smaller extent into adulthood. We thus construct for ourselves a linguistic phonetic system which marks us as belonging to a sub-group of the population; a group which, according to some, may consist of a single individual (see section 3.2).

The 'organic/learned' dichotomy, however, fails to show the true complexity of speaker individuality. In particular it fails to state explicitly that the two 'sources' of difference do not result in discretely different dimensions of variation in the speech signal. Thus, it is in formant frequencies that both vocal tract size and dialectal vowel differences will be manifest; and a person's fundamental frequency range will reflect both the structure of the larynx, and aspects of his or her intonation system. This is obvious to those familiar with speech, but the 'organic/learned' dichotomy runs the risk of being misinterpreted by others, particularly in the context of attempts to draw parallels between fingerprinting and speaker identification. A fingerprint is a direct trace of an organic difference, uncontaminated by 'learning'. If there were an equivalent in the phonetic domain, it might be a plaster cast of an individual's vocal tract in the configuration for an agreed vowel. In a recording of speech, on the other hand, the effects of organic differences are convolved with the effects of what the speaker has learnt, in the terms of the linguistic system and the choices from it made at a given moment.

The crux of the problem is that the mechanism (in the broadest sense of the word) producing speech is highly 'plastic' (see Nolan, 1983:27–8). A speaker's physique may define the limits of, say, a formant's frequency range and his or her laryngeal fundamental frequency, and possibly also a range of values which is optimal in the sense of requiring only moderate muscular activity to achieve; but, within the absolute limits, speakers have at their disposal very wide scope for controlled variation. As an example, a sample of male speech at the unusually high mean fundamental frequency of 170 Hz might be from a man with unusually short vocal cords speaking normally, or from a man with an habitual mean fundamental frequency of 120 Hz but wishing to convey great excitement, or from the second man imitating the first. This plasticity of the physical mechanism of speech is exploited for linguistic purposes (to realize elements of the phonology), for paralinguistic purposes (we vary our voices to convey anger, affection, and so on), and for non-linguistic purposes (for instance to disguise identity). And even if we leave aside volitional exploitation of the plasticity of the vocal tract, the organic basis of a person's speech is far from constant. States of ill health which affect the vocal organs, from minor colds through to cancer of the larynx, change the sound of the voice. In the shorter term, stress, fatigue, and intoxication also affect it. It is clear, then, that the physical mechanism producing speech is far from being like the constant pattern of whorls which leaves its trace in a fingerprint. The contribution of the physical mechanism will be dealt with in more detail in section 3.2.

The notion of plasticity can be extended to the linguistic system underlying the speech signal, which will be discussed in section 3.3. A linguistically fully functional member of a speech community commands a range of ways of speaking. He or she may articulate more clearly in a setting (e.g. public speaking) where it is important to convey complex information reliably, and take more phonetic short cuts (assimilation, vowel deletion, etc.) when talking casually with friends on topics of mutual familiarity; and may employ a variety of pronunciations ranging along a continuum of perceived social prestige depending on the setting and who is present. These kinds of sociolinguistic variation in the speech of an individual are a subject of study in themselves, but they are too often ignored in work on speaker identification.

Furthermore there is an area of potential individuality which falls between what is organic, and what is learned social behaviour. In implementing the resources of their linguistic mechanism, speakers have to map them onto their individual anatomy. Whilst the requirements of communication may determine many of the details of speech articulation, we may hypothesize that there may be aspects of speech production where each individual is free to find his or her own articulatory solution. The speaker's behaviour here is not 'learned' as part of the shared knowledge of the linguistic community; rather it is acquired, probably by trial and error. Little research has directly addressed this hypothesis, but potentially many differences of phonetic detail between speakers may arise in this way. Section 3.4 expands on this hypothesis.

So while the 'organic/learned' dichotomy provides a starting point for considering the source of a person's distinctive 'voice', a satisfactory account needs to take a more comprehensive view of speech communication. Nolan (1983: 2.3) develops a model of between-speaker differences which attempts to incorporate the factors discussed above, and others. It treats a speaker's voice as the interaction of constraints imposed by the physical properties of the vocal tract, and choices which a speaker makes in achieving communicative goals through the resources provided by the various components of his or her linguistic system. Some of the main points are summarized in the following sections.

3.2 Individuality in the physical mechanism: speech as anatomy made audible

If we accept that a person's speech anatomy defines absolute limits of acoustic variation and optimal ranges, how is this reflected in the acoustic signal? Here, as in speech analysis generally, it is useful to adopt a 'source-filter' model of speech production. In the case of many sounds, this means considering the larynx as a source of acoustic energy, and the supralaryngeal vocal tract as a filter or resonator which shapes that energy. The range of frequencies at which the vocal cords will vibrate, for instance, is determined by their length and mass, as is to some extent the detailed shape of the glottal source wave (in general, the thicker the vocal cords are the more complex will be their mode of vibration, and the richer in harmonics will be the glottal source waveform). Any anatomical irregularities, such as a nodule on a vocal cord, may introduce irregularities in the acoustic signal – the vocal cord vibration may be uneven from cycle to cycle, and there may be certain frequencies at which vibration is impossible. All this will contribute to the distinctiveness of a person's voice, assuming that the person is producing voiced speech and not whispering.

The vocal tract 'filter' also varies in size and shape. This is clearest in the differences between the vocal tracts of men and women. Not only are the dimensions of most men's vocal tracts larger than those of most women, but also there is a lack of 'isomorphism' – that is, a typical adult male vocal tract is not simply a scaled-up version of a typical female one, but is disproportionately longer in the pharynx. This means, among other things, that the relationship of male formant frequencies to female ones is non-linear, and vowel and formant specific (e.g. Fant, 1973). Such differences undoubtedly exist on a smaller scale within same-sex adult populations. An individual man's voice might be distinctive not only because, on average, his formant frequencies are rather high, but also because his formant configurations for various sounds are determined by a particular size relationship between different parts of his vocal tract.

The interplay of the laryngeal source and the vocal tract filter in determining the characteristics of a speaker's voice is highlighted if we ask what it means to say 'a high voice'. This percept might reflect an unusually high fundamental frequency (compared with the relevant population) resulting from small vocal cords, or from unusually high formant frequencies resulting from small cavity dimensions in the vocal tract, or both. Work on the perception of maleness and femaleness in the voice (e.g. Coleman, 1976) has shown that both fundamental frequency and formant frequencies contribute to hearers' decisions on whether a sample of speech is from a man or a woman, and other work (e.g. LaRiviere, 1975) has shown a similar combined contribution of the two factors to identification of individuals.

Laryngeal vibration is not the only source of acoustic energy in speech. The energy of fricatives is generated by air turbulence. In the case of [s], for instance, it is likely that the turbulence arises because air is forced through a narrow channel formed by the grooved blade of the tongue against the alveolar ridge, and also because the channel directs a jet of air onto the teeth causing further turbulence. The precise acoustic properties of this source will depend on the shape and size of a person's teeth. Individuality arising from this source should be present even in whispered speech, when the voicing source is not present. Claims for the usefulness of fricatives have been made in work on speaker recognition (e.g. LaRiviere, 1974; Künzel, 1987:93–4). Nonetheless it must be borne in mind that, for instance, a person's [s] is not directly determined by his or her dentition. If a tooth is broken or lost, for instance, it may well be possible for the articulation to be adjusted to make optimal use of the changed aerodynamic environment; and any speaker is capable of deliberately producing a more 'whistle-like' or a more 'hushy' [s]. Again, we see that anatomy imposes limits to variation, rather than absolute acoustic values.

The vocal tract 'filter' consisting of pharyngeal and oral cavities can be augmented by opening the velic port and coupling in the resonances of the nasal cavity. Nasal sounds have often attracted those looking for reliable cues to speakers' identity (e.g. Glenn and Kleiner, 1968) because the shape and size of the nasal cavity is both highly variable between speakers and not volitionally alterable. Nasals might thus be the best candidates to provide acoustic manifestations of anatomical individuality. There are, however, two factors which complicate the situation: firstly, the resonance effects of the nasal cavity are not available in isolation, but are combined in a complex way with those of the rest of the vocal tract (the shape of which is under volitional control); and, secondly, nasal resonances are highly susceptible to changes in health (contributing to the impression of someone having a cold in the head, for instance).

These examples are intended to give an indication of the ways that anatomy is reflected in the acoustic properties of a person's speech. The point has been stressed, however, that anatomy imposes limits on the acoustic effects available to an individual rather than absolute values. Speaking involves the use of an organic mechanism with considerable degrees of freedom.

3.3 Individuality in the linguistic mechanism: speech as behaviour

An act of speaking usually conveys more than a bare 'message'. What we tend to think of as the message may be accompanied by signals that indicate the attitude of the speaker (hostile, friendly, interested), help to regulate the flow of a conversation (inviting the listeners to contribute a 'turn', or fending them off), reinforce a social relationship between participants in an interaction (authority, intimacy), present the speaker's self image (competent, laid-back, timid), and so on (for more details, see Nolan, 1984). To the extent that speakers intend to convey these, they exploit what might be broadly termed their linguistic mechanism. This includes the lexical, syntactic, and prosodic resources of their language, together with some aspects of what is known as voice quality. Thus, for example, in responding to a welcome offer of dinner from a close friend we might say 'I'd love to', with an extensive rising falling intonation starting on *love*, a slightly breathy voice quality throughout, and no reduction of speaking rate at the end. The words convey the message; the intonation and voice quality convey our genuine enthusiasm and our interpretation of the relationship to the other person, and the lack of rallentando warns the listener not to interrupt because we intend to continue, perhaps to regret the impossibility of accepting.

This is by no means a complete or indeed uncontroversial analysis of what is conveyed in speaking. The point is to draw attention to the multi-faceted nature of spoken communication, because this is the background against which we must view potential sources of individuality in the speech signal. For instance, one person's speech might normally be characterized by a rather harsh phonation type, but this may still be overridden at times for communicational effect. With this in mind, let us proceed to consider how the linguistic mechanism varies from individual to individual. Because this chapter is concerned with an application of phonetics the focus will be exclusively on the sound-related aspects of the linguistic mechanism, but this is not meant to imply that there is no scope for individuality at the level of lexis, idiom, and syntax in speech, such as are dealt with in text-based studies (e.g. Eagleson, 1994; Smith, 1994).

Most obviously an individual has an accent. In general, this means that his or her speech allows them to be identified with a group. The group may be regionally defined ('having a Liverpool accent') or defined in terms of some kind of social strata ('a middle class accent'). Usually, in the urbanized English-speaking world at least, a speaker will be described in terms of both kinds of group ('a working class London accent'). Phonetically, accents are differentiated along all the phonetic parameters which speakers can control, specifically segmental phonology, prosody, and aspects of voice quality. For instance, a working class Edinburgh accent is distinct from an upper middle class London accent by virtue of its inventory of vowels and consonants together with their phonological behaviour and phonetic realizations, its prosodic patterns and their use, and its default voice quality (a tendency to whispery voice (Esling, 1978) as opposed to creaky voice in the latter accent).

Because accents subdivide the population speaking a language, they bring us some way towards identifying an individual. If the task is to compare an unknown recording with a closed set of possible known speakers, and the unknown sample manifests a clear and consistent New York accent, and the closed set contains only one New York accent with the rest British, then accent alone would allow a pretty confident identification. If there isn't a closed set to compare with, however, but merely a single suspect, and the question is whether or not the suspect is the speaker on the unknown recording, then the New York accent tells us very little – there are millions of New Yorkers.

But it is of course possible to carry the partitioning of the population further. We could define the 'New York' sample's accent more closely by seeing where its phonetic details place it in terms of sociolinguistic stratification (cf. Labov, 1966). Similarly, on the geographical dimension, dialectologists have traditionally delighted in separating smaller and smaller groups of speakers (generally in rural areas with stable populations) on the basis of pronunciation. There are claims, even, that this partitioning can be carried beyond social and regional groups, and that, ultimately, each person has his or her own dialect or 'idiolect' (see Baldwin, 1979). The idea seems to be that even the most narrowly defined linguistic variety leaves numerous phonetic choices open to the individual (e.g. *decision* with [ɪ] or [ə] in the first syllable, and [ʃ] or [ʒ] as the third consonant), and that a sufficient number of these will uniquely identify an individual. This is an interesting hypothesis, but it has not been subject to rigorous testing, and its application in speaker identification is questionable if it implicitly forms the basis of very positively stated identifications.

3.4 Individuality in phonetic implementation

Each speaker has to realize the complex resources of the learned and socially shared linguistic mechanism within the constraints of his or her anatomy. In implementing linguistic functions there may be scope for idiosyncrasy. For instance, there may be tight constraints imposed by a language on the auditory effects associated with a consonant and with a following vowel, but the transition between the two articulations – and hence the 'coarticulation' of the two segments – may allow for variation. The tongue position for the vowel might be adopted relatively early, making the consonant's secondary articulation highly dependent on the quality of the vowel; or relatively late, producing more of a transition in the early part of the vowel. Such between-speaker variation has been demonstrated by Su, Li, and Fu (1974) for nasal-plus-vowel sequences, and Nolan (1983:Ch.3) for lateral-plus-vowel sequences.

As indicated in section 3.1, the idea that some aspects of phonetic behaviour are not determined by the linguistic mechanism but are strategies worked out by individual speakers is, as yet, merely a hypothesis; but it is supported by observable differences between speakers in the dynamics and timing of articulations which go beyond what can be explained by anatomical differences and yet have no linguistic or social role.

3.5 *Speakers outside the normal range*

Virtually by definition the speakers who are most distinctive are those who lie outside the 'normal' range. Such speakers are usually those who have speech pathologies or impediments of varying degrees of severity, or whose command of a language is non-native. There is, of course, no clear boundary to the normal range – a speaker's [s] may be perceived by some as rather lispy, and go unnoticed by others. As in other aspects of speaker recognition, care must be taken not to jump to conclusions. Just because two recordings manifest a stutter does not mean they are necessarily of the same individual; and an apparently idiosyncratic foreign pronunciation may consist of features common to many speakers from the same language background.

Speech phenomena outside the normal range are, however, highly valuable in speaker identification. If, for instance, acoustic measurements and phonetic analysis of accent lead to a conclusion that two recordings are of the same male speaker, and (if it were possible realistically to quantify such probabilities, which it is not) that there is no more than a 10 per cent chance that they were from different speakers, the presence of a similar stutter in both recordings could reduce that to less than 0.2 per cent. This is because roughly one man in 50 stutters. In fact the probability that the same speaker is involved would be even higher because stutters vary, and so a close match in the characteristics of the stutter is of further value. The simultaneous presence of a lateralized [s] (a rare substitution of a sound like [ɬ], the Welsh 'll', for [s]) would be further strong evidence in favour of identity.

The usefulness of such phenomena for identification resides precisely in their rarity, and so they should perhaps not enter into an assessment of the potential for speaker recognition in the major part of the population. Nonetheless they do occur in some cases, and if analysed properly can be of considerable value for speaker identification.

4 The limiting factors in speaker recognition

Thinking particularly of the forensic application, there are many practical factors which limit the reliability of speaker recognition. Samples may be too short to give a complete enough representation of the speaker; the quality of recordings may be poor (background noise, distortion imposed in telephone transmission or tape recording); and there is always the possibility that a speaker is deliberately using voice disguise. Such factors may or may not apply in particular cases, but there are problems intrinsic to all speaker recognition: an individual's speech is not constant, and as yet we have little information on the distribution of features and values in the population as a whole.

A person's speech varies partly because the physical mechanism of speech undergoes changes. This is obvious when the person has a cold, often affecting the resonances of the nasal cavity and the mode of vibration of the vocal cords, or some serious laryngeal pathology. Less obvious are changes, for instance in fundamental frequency and phonation type, which are brought about by factors such as fatigue, stress, and the diurnal cycle in the short term, and ageing in the long term. References to research on such effects can be found in Laver (1979).

A person's speech also varies because of choices made in the use of the resources of the linguistic mechanism, exploiting its 'plasticity' as noted in section 3.1. These choices range from changes of loudness and pitch, at the least 'linguistic' end of a continuum, to changes in the segmental phonological system. Changes of loudness, mean pitch, pitch range, and phonation type, may depend on the physical circumstances of an interaction, for instance shouting over a bad telephone connection; or may be done to communicate affect, as when conveying anger. Use of the prosodic system, for instance, may vary according to speaking style. Intonation patterns are likely to be used more fully and explicitly to mark syntactic and informational structure in more formal, rehearsed speech than in informal, spontaneous speech; and the pattern chosen will also be affected by interpersonal factors, such as whether the speaker wishes to appear friendly and sympathetic to the interlocutor, distantly polite, rude, and so on.

The segmental phonetic system is also subject to variation, as has been charted extensively in sociolinguistic studies. Broadly, most individuals control a range of pronunciations along continua of phonetic explicitness and social prestige. In one recording, for instance, a speaker of London English might realize most occurrences of '-ing' as [ɪŋ], and in another as [ɪn]. The first variant is popularly regarded as 'standard', and a speaker who might use it almost exclusively in a formal context might, in a less formal context, replace it almost everywhere by [ɪn]. This is in no sense 'disguise'; it is part of the complex of social skills in which language plays a part. It does mean, however, that differences of pronunciation between speech samples cannot be taken blindly to indicate a difference of speakers. Their value can only be interpreted in the light of the facts of sociolinguistic and stylistic variation within a speech community.

The speech of an individual, then, is not a constant, either in terms of those properties which result primarily from the physical mechanism of speech, or those which are a function of the linguistic system. If we imagine the many parameters which characterize a speaker as defining a location in a multi-dimensional space (cf. section 1), we see that it is not a static point which characterizes the speaker but an area of variation. One of the fundamental issues in speaker recognition is whether each individual in the population occupies a unique area, or whether there is overlap, regardless of how many parameters are used to characterize the speakers. The fact that the answer to this is as yet simply not known places a limitation, in principle, on the reliability of any act of speaker recognition – a limitation which must always be acknowledged.

5 Naive speaker recognition

By the definition in section 1, naive speaker recognition is any attribution of identity performed by an untrained observer on the basis of speech samples. In some circumstances we may perform speaker verification – as when, for example, having asked 'who is it?' before unlocking a door, we rely partly on the familiarity of the voice answering to reassure us that it is a welcome caller. In the forensic sphere, the task is most likely to be one of identification. There is an extensive literature on naive speaker recognition, often under the heading of 'speaker recognition by listening' or 'SRL' (see for instance Bricker and Pruzansky (1976), who provide a broad survey of experiments on SRL). The term SRL is avoided here because it fails to acknowledge a category of 'listening' distinct from that done in everyday circumstances by naive listeners – specifically, auditory phoneticians using the traditional analysis techniques of phonetics, which will be discussed in section 7.1.

Naive speaker recognition in the forensic arena often goes under the heading 'Earwitness evidence'. The unseen perpetrator of a crime (an obscene telephone caller, masked raider, etc.) may be identified by the earwitness at the time of the crime as someone previously known to him or her, or the earwitness may subsequently be asked to make a judgment (often as in the context of a 'voice line-up' or 'voice parade') as to whether a suspect is the person who was heard during the crime. Bull and Clifford (1984) and Künzel (1994b) summarize some of the issues.

Most experiments on the reliability of earwitnesses take broadly the following form: subjects hear a recorded reference sample of speech, and then at some later time have to pick out the speaker of that sample from a voice 'parade' containing speech from that speaker and from a number of other speakers ('distractors'). Performance has been found to depend on a large number of factors, being improved for instance by listeners' prior familiarity with one or more voices (e.g. Hollien, Majewski, and Doherty, 1982; Schmidt-Nielsen and Stern, 1985; Künzel, 1990), listeners' active participation in a conversation with the target speaker as opposed to passive overhearing (Hammersley and Read, 1985), longer samples (e.g. Künzel, 1990), and 'recognizability' of the target voice (e.g. Papçun, Kreiman, and Davis, 1989). Bandwidth limitation, as found in telephone speech, can impair performance: Künzel (1990:35) reports, rather worryingly from the point of view of the legal context, that 'under less than ideal acoustic conditions . . . subjects show a considerable tendency to judge stimuli as coming from the same speaker, even if in reality these originate from different speakers'.

Delay between hearing the 'target' voice and performing the recognition task is a factor which has yielded a surprising variety of results. McGehee (1937), in what is generally acknowledged to be the first experiment directly relevant to earwitness performance, reports 83 per cent correct identification at two days, 68 per cent at two weeks, 35 per cent at three months, and 13 per cent (worse than chance) at five months. Clifford, Rathborn, and Bull (1981), in one of a series of experiments, obtained 50 per cent at 10 minutes, 43 per cent at 1 day, 39 per cent at 7 days, and 32 per cent at 14 days. Künzel (1990) found that the speaker of a 60 second familiarization sample was picked out from a closed set of five short samples better after 8 and 30 days than immediately after familiarization, and argues that it may be easier to compare the test samples if the reference sample is encoded in long term memory rather than short term memory (see Nolan, 1992a, for a discussion). Papçun, Kreiman, and Davis (1989), who find that the accuracy of 'heard previously' responses to voice samples declines over three intervals of one, two, and four weeks, propose that memory and recognition of voices work in terms of 'prototypes', and predict that listeners could actually perform at worse than chance levels at very long delays, 'because they will select prototypical voices instead of voices they originally heard'. They tentatively suggest that McGehee's (1937) worse than chance result (above) for the five month interval might be tapping this effect, although there are problems interpreting the early experiment.

A full survey and discussion of the wide variety of relevant experiments is beyond the scope of this summary, and indeed their interpretation in relation to the real world is often far from straightforward. But the far from perfect ability to recognize speakers which they reveal, and the number and complexity of factors affecting that ability which they demonstrate, do provide a necessary counterbalance to what may be a natural tendency to overestimate our skills in this area. Our apparent everyday ability to identify people we know well from their speech may lead to an over-optimistic view of the reliability of the ear in this task. It is easy to forget that when a friend phones, there is usually circumstantial evidence to help our identification, such as the time of day that person normally phones, and the greeting used. Courts of law need to be aware that the results of earwitness experiments do not suggest that naive speaker recognition is, of itself, particularly accurate. Clifford (1980:390) concludes:

> In the light of the extant literature and the present findings from our own research it must be deduced that the criminal justice system must exercise the greatest caution when utilizing voice identification in either case building or case prosecution.

It should also be noted that many experiments have involved a 'closed' test, that is, in terms of 'voice line-ups' or 'voice parades', one in which the subject knows in advance that the parade will contain the target speaker, and in effect merely has the task of selecting the sample which corresponds best to the remembered target voice – not of deciding whether, in absolute terms, that best match is good enough to be the same speaker. In the majority of real-life cases this latter decision does have to be made by the earwitness. In this connection, Clifford, Rathborn, and Bull (1981:207) caution that it seems probable that 'to present parades where target voices are *not* present and to warn witnesses that the target voice "may or may not be present" creates great difficulty'. This is not to say, of course, that witnesses' recall of voices is any worse than their recall of other factors.

6 Technical speaker verification

Work on technical speaker verification has aimed at building an automatic device which uses the voice to accept or reject identity claims, hence the term automatic speaker verification (ASV). There are many potential applications, mostly involving telephone interactions where other identity checks are not feasible, but also in locks and (potentially) cash machines. O'Shaughnessy (1987:Ch.11) and Furui (1994) provide useful introductions to some of the methodological and computational aspects of ASV, and Doddington (1985) includes a summary of issues relevant to ASV and an account of an operational system. This section will merely provide a general outline.

ASV research has tended to use speech signal processing techniques, usually adapted from automatic speech recognition, and has not drawn heavily on phonetic knowledge. In the simplest set-up, an utterance of a phrase from a speaker claiming to be a particular person is compared by computer with a stored reference template for that person, constructed on the basis of a number of repetitions by the speaker so as to accommodate at least some of the variation likely to be encountered. If the acoustic distance between the claimant's utterance and the stored reference is below a pre-set threshold, the claim is accepted. Where the threshold is set will determine the balance of probability between two wrong outcomes, namely occasionally rejecting a true claim and occasionally accepting an impostor, and the nature of the application will determine which kind of error is more acceptable. (If, instead, the claimant's utterance is compared to all stored speakers and the nearest chosen, the same system is performing closed set identification.)

The set-up described involves text dependent ASV, that is, the utterance is pre-agreed, and linguistically equivalent material is being compared. This, as noted in section 1, makes verification a potentially more constrained task than identification, where linguistically equivalent material may not be available for comparison. An identity claimant may produce a password or passphrase, or be prompted by the computer to produce a number of phrases in a particular order. If, alternatively, verification is to be independent of the text, then it needs to rely either on the automatic location and segmentation of particular phonetic events, which is far from trivial (cf. Doddington, 1985:1659), or on statistical properties of the speech which can be calculated over stretches of speech long enough to neutralize the effects of linguistic content (many seconds, in most cases), such as the long term average spectrum, and fundamental frequency statistics. Even then, much potentially speaker-specific information is lost, and so text dependent ASV seems more promising for most applications.

In text dependent ASV, the utterances to be compared are represented by time-varying parameters such as the fundamental frequency contour (e.g. Atal, 1972) or spectral shape represented as a sequence of linear prediction coefficients (e.g. Atal, 1974) or cepstral coefficients (e.g. Furui, 1981). (For further details see Ainsworth, SOME APPROACHES TO AUTOMATIC SPEECH RECOGNITION and Liljencrants, SPEECH SIGNAL PROCESSING.) The difference in value of the parameter at each successive point along the utterances is calculated, and the total difference compared to an empirically derived acceptance threshold. A problem which had to be solved was the fact that even the same speaker will not say an utterance at the same rate every time. If all segments were affected equally by rate changes, the test utterance could simply be stretched or compressed globally to match the duration of the reference utterance. In fact the rate changes are non-linear, and so a technique familiar in automatic speech recognition called dynamic time warping (DTW) is used differentially to stretch and compress different parts of the utterance, sometimes using the intensity contour as the basis of the alignment (Lummis, 1973; Rosenberg, 1976). In this way the distances measured should be between phonetically equivalent parts of the utterances, and should reflect speaker characteristics.

More recently, further techniques which have been used in automatic speech recognition have been extended to ASV, including hidden Markov modelling (e.g. Matsui and Furui, 1994), vector quantization (e.g. Soong, Rosenberg, Rabiner, and Juang, 1985), and neural nets (e.g. Farrell, Mammone, and Assahleh, 1994 and Ainsworth, SOME APPROACHES TO AUTOMATIC SPEECH RECOGNITION).

Finally, given the almost exclusive orientation of ASV research towards solutions in signal processing, it might be appropriate to note a related task where phonetic knowledge has been incorporated, namely automatic categorization of a speaker's accent. Barry, Hoequist and Nolan (1989) present a technique which automatically assigns a speaker to one of four major English regional accent groups on the basis of several pre-determined utterances. These are chosen to contain diagnostics for the different accents. In a sentence containing the words *father*, *path*, and *car*, a similar vowel quality for all three ([ɑː]) suggests Southern British, different for all three ([ɑ], [æ], [ɑˑ]) General American, and so on. The crucial events were identified in the input utterance by time-warping it to a segmented reference utterance, but all spectral comparisons were internal to the input signal, so that no normalization was needed prior to the accent decision. This method was devised as a preliminary to accent-switchable automatic speech recognition, but it would be interesting to explore whether it has applications in ASV. It could complement signal processing techniques by adding extra weight to those differences between samples resulting from differences in the linguistic mechanism, and free ASV from its exclusive reliance on 'low level' acoustic features (Doddington, 1985:1653).

7 Technical speaker identification

In the forensic arena the commonest speaker recognition task is to decide how likely it is that two recordings are from the same person. Often this involves a recording of an unknown speaker made during the commission of a crime, such as a bomb threat, or a kidnap demand, and a recording of a suspect. The latter may have been recorded surreptitiously, or be part of the interview record. Only if a recording is made specifically for comparison (with the suspect's consent) can the linguistic content be controlled to be the same as that on the unknown recording, and even then the impossibility of replicating the context of the unknown recording makes exact linguistic equivalence impossible. Often, then, the comparison has to be made on different material. Partly for this reason, fully automatic speaker identification has been overshadowed by methods relying on human input. There are two broad categories of method: those relying on human auditory perception, and those using acoustic analysis.

7.1 Auditory techniques

Many phoneticians and dialectologists are expert in the auditory analysis of speech. In particular, they can apply an agreed framework (usually the IPA) to the analysis of vowel and consonant quality. They are thus in a good position to analyse fine differences of pronunciation. How far this helps them to perform speaker identification depends, crucially, on the issue of idiolect mentioned in section 3.3. Is each speaker phonetically unique, sharing his or her exact pronunciation with no-one? And even if so, is the degree of detail required to define that individual as unique likely to be available from the amount of speech (often just a few seconds) available in many forensic cases?

The view in Baldwin (1979), and the predominant view in Baldwin and French (1990), is that a phonetician can indeed carry out speaker identification by auditory analysis alone ('I have found the auditory approach to be fully adequate for the task' – Baldwin and French (1990:9)). There is one sense in which this is uncontroversial. A phonetician familiar with the details of the relevant accents might analyse two recordings, and could come to the conclusion that they represented two distinct accents, and were both internally consistent (and therefore unlikely to be different as the result of disguise). A corollary of this would be to conclude that the recordings are not likely to be of the same speaker. This situation is unlikely to arise often, because marked differences in accents would rule out identity even to the lay ear. It might, however, arise if the accent difference was slight, and between two varieties not familiar to the investigating authorities.

In general, however, the technique is far from uncontroversial, especially when used to make very positive statements (cf. Baldwin and French, 1990:10) that two recordings are of the same individual. Nolan (1991) argues that the notion of 'idiolect' is an interesting hypothesis but one which has not been demonstrated, and that:

> In practice, given the degree of free variation found in the speech of one person, and the short samples normally available in forensic circumstances, I would expect idiolect to be of little value in separating speakers of a homogeneous accent. Unless and until extensive research vindicates the usefulness of idiolect in speaker identification, I believe we must work on the assumption that two samples with matching linguistic-phonetic properties can perfectly well be from different speakers. (Nolan 1991:489)

Having decided that two samples are identical in terms of accent, the auditory phonetician must either be content with a conclusion saying exactly that (and no more), or must attempt an analysis of other aspects of the samples. A comprehensive framework for the auditory analysis of voice quality exists (Laver, 1980), comparable to that of the IPA for phonetic quality. It is, however, a framework that categorizes those aspects of voice quality which are controllable by any speaker, and therefore does not directly address aspects of voice quality dependent on the individual. It has not, to my knowledge, been applied by those auditory phoneticians giving evidence in court. It can thus be questioned whether, once they get beyond fine dialectology, auditory phoneticians are applying any expertise over and above that of the lay listener. Indeed, one of the few experiments specifically to test phoneticians' abilities on various types of speaker identification task, that of Shirt (1984), showed that over a range of speaker identification tasks, on sets of speakers with similar accents, phoneticians performed overall 'only marginally better' than non-phoneticians. This experiment used short speech samples and therefore probably forced listeners to rely on voice quality rather than accent features. Köster (1987) found identification rates of 100 per cent by a group of five phoneticians on two tasks, the first involving speakers familiar to the listeners and the second unfamiliar voices, compared with 94 per cent and 89 per cent for a group of untrained listeners. But again, the evidence for superior processing of voice quality by phoneticians is not conclusive, since the phoneticians heard enhanced recordings over headphones whereas the naive listeners heard the original recordings via loudspeakers, and since the majority of the naive listeners' errors were contributed by a few subjects (pointing to the conclusion that there may be some individuals who are inherently bad at speaker recognition).

Skilled auditory phonetic analysis can undoubtedly tell us much of relevance to speaker identity, since, as we saw in section 3.3, an important part of the distinctiveness of a speaker results from the linguistic mechanism. Furthermore it is the phonetician who is most likely to understand the possible kinds of phonetic variation (section 4) which occur due to stylistic and contextual factors, and who is therefore in a position to evaluate the status of linguistic phonetic differences between samples. There is therefore an important role for skilled auditory phonetic analysis in speaker recognition (see section 7.3). But the position that it can, on its own, lead to firm positive identifications in forensic circumstances is not sustainable. As a real life demonstration of this, Nolan (1990) presents acoustic evidence showing how a positive identification made of a fraud suspect by two auditory phoneticians was wrong.

Hollien (1990:203–5) discusses a technique which exploits auditory skills in a different way. Paired comparisons of speech samples are presented, as in a perceptual discrimination experiment (using the ABX format), to phonetically trained and untrained listeners. Sometimes 'known' and 'unknown' speakers are paired, while other pairs are controls – either samples from the same speaker, or from different speakers (one or more speakers broadly similar to the samples under investigation are used, presumably). Assuming listeners make correct judgments on the control samples, if they are consistently able to discriminate the 'known' and 'unknown' samples, this suggests these samples are from different individuals, and if they are consistently unable to discriminate them, this points to them being from the same speakers. Not enough details are given to evaluate the potential of the technique fully, and its validity must depend in part on the care with which control speakers are selected, but it represents an interesting avenue for harnessing our natural abilities for speaker recognition in a structured way.

7.2 Acoustic techniques

If nothing else, acoustic analysis should allow for quantification of speaker-related aspects of speech which can be heard. But it can be argued (e.g. Nolan, 1994) that acoustic analysis, far from being 'simply another way of analyzing speech [in addition to auditory analysis]' (Baldwin and French, 1990:8), in fact also reveals information which our auditory system obscures, geared as it is to the extraction of *linguistic* information from the speech signal. As specific examples, we can potentially (and advantageously) hear as phonetically identical a vowel spoken by two different speakers even if the formant patterns are appreciably different, because our hearing system will integrate two close formants and treat them as equivalent to a single formant peak (e.g. Carlson, Fant, and Granström, 1975); and 'cue-trading', demonstrated in perceptual experiments, means that we may hear as phonetically the same sounds involving different mixes of acoustic cues – for instance a lower F2 transition compensating for a higher friction cut-off in [ʃ] (e.g. Repp, 1982).

However the use of acoustic analysis in speaker identification has, like that of auditory phonetic analysis, been controversial. In reality much of the opposition to both has been based on common factors – in brief, our relatively poor understanding of 'speaker space', and the issue of whether forensic opinions could properly be given in the absence of solid scientific evidence on the reliability of a technique. But in the case of acoustic techniques, a particularly acrimonious debate arose at the start.

Kersta (1962) claimed that visual comparison of spectrograms could provide 99 per cent accurate speaker identification. He applied the term 'voiceprint', emphasizing a supposed analogy with fingerprinting. Subsequently, even though other experiments yielded much lower levels of accuracy, evidence from 'voiceprints' (often couched in very incautious terms) was accepted in a number of courts in the USA. Furthermore a career began to emerge of 'voiceprint examiner', some examiners being policemen trained in the technique, which raised fears of a self-appointed clique gaining a monopoly on speaker identification. Such fears were reinforced by comments such as:

> A general speech scientist, with no general training in voice identification by use of spectrograms, can hardly give an opinion on this subject no matter how excellent are his credentials in the speech sciences. (Tosi, 1979:117)

Opposition came from phoneticians and speech scientists, objecting to the lack of scientific evidence that the technique worked, overstated conclusions, and basic errors of analysis. The early voiceprint work seems to have been based on largely subjective comparison of patterns; later, more explicit criteria were developed (see e.g. Tosi, 1979:Ch.4). Summaries of the controversy can be found in Nolan (1983:18–25, 197–206), and Hollien (1990:Ch.10), both of which give a negative view of 'voiceprinting'. Tosi (1979) presents the case of more moderate proponents of the technique, and Koenig (1986) gives an apparently favourable assessment of its use by the FBI in America as an investigative tool (but see criticisms by Shipp, Doherty, and Hollien (1987), responded to in Koenig, Ritenour, Kohus, and Kelly (1987)). By 1980 the tide had turned against acceptance of the technique in courts in the USA, and it has not been widely accepted elsewhere.

It is unfortunate that the early days of voiceprinting were marked by exaggerated claims and premature application, because the controversy almost certainly discouraged many reputable speech scientists from addressing the issue of speaker characteristics in their research. In fact many of the features noted in voiceprints undoubtedly reflect genuine between-speaker differences, and it is possible that progress could be made by formalising the intuitions of experienced voiceprint examiners, rather as the skills of spectrogram readers have formed the basis of one avenue of research into speech recognition (e.g. Zue, 1985).

The opposition to voiceprints often appears to focus on the fact that a human being is central to the process, and it is therefore subjective. This is an oversimplification. More objective methods of exploiting acoustic information in speaker identification are, for the foreseeable future, likely to entail a large amount of human involvement because (unlike in speaker verification) many contingent factors in the data have to be taken into account. The crucial advance from 'voiceprinting' lies in making the two main stages of analysis, parameter extraction and parameter comparison, as systematic and quantitative as possible. As a simple example, it might be seen in spectrograms that two samples differ in the general balance of energy between low and high frequencies. This can be quantified by computing the long-term average spectrum (LTAS) of the samples, and these can be compared mathematically using one of a number of distance measures. Human knowledge, however, will still be needed to select appropriate stretches of speech from forensic recordings over which to compute the LTAS, and interpret the resultant spectral distance in the light of factors such as whether the two samples were recorded over equivalent transmission channels.

Ideally, the acoustic parameters extracted should exhibit large between-speaker variation and low within-speaker variation, and be readily available in short samples, accurately measurable, and resistant to disguise or distortion. Early studies examined spectral properties of segments, and some (e.g. Glenn and Kleiner, 1968; Wolf, 1972) found promising discrimination of speakers in the spectra of nasal segments. But, as noted in section 3.2, nasal segments are particularly prone to change as a result of a speaker's state of health, and so at times may exhibit considerable within-speaker variation. Other segments may be somewhat less susceptible to dramatic within-speaker variation because of health, but undoubtedly vary according to factors such as prosodic context and overall speaking loudness. A practical demonstration of the value of spectral analysis of a segment is given in Nolan (1990), which is based on a fraud case. The English vowel /æ/ was analysed as it occurred in a substantial number of tokens of the words 'that' and 'back' in the incriminating recordings, in a sample of the defendant's speech, and also in a recording of a telephone call connected with a second similar fraud which the defendant could prove he had not made. The analysis showed a strong third formant at around 2.5 kHz for both fraud samples; this was consistently absent from the defendant's vowels, which instead showed weak third and fourth formants at around 3 and 4 kHz. On this basis, and the basis of other consistent differences in the defendant's speech, it was possible to conclude that he was most unlikely to be the speaker in the incriminating recordings.

Other parameters researched and utilized relate to the suprasegmental component of speech. Künzel (1987:82–85) discusses mean f_0 (fundamental frequency) and its standard deviation. He makes the important point that the usefulness of such measures depends on the distribution of values in the population as a whole, and presents a statistical frequency distribution of mean f_0 values for 100 male speakers and for 50 female speakers. For instance, only two percent of men have a mean f_0 lower than 90 Hz, and so if two samples are found to have their mean f_0 at 85 Hz and 87 Hz this is an important indicator of potential identity. On the other hand, values of 115 and 117 Hz fall right in the middle of the distribution (where large numbers of male speakers lie), and would have little to contribute to deciding whether the two samples are from the same speaker. Künzel also acknowledges the within-speaker variability of f_0 measures, which are affected by speaking louder, by mood changes, and speaking style.

Ultimately, given the plasticity inherent in speech production, it is unlikely that any isolated feature will adequately satisfy the criterion of low within-speaker variation relative to the between-speaker discrimination it affords. The only solution to this is the extraction of a substantial number of independent parameters. Hollien (1990:Ch.11) summarizes an approach to multiple parameter extraction and comparison in a semi automatic speaker identification system (known acronymically as SAUSI). The method is based on phonetically interpretable features of speech such as fundamental frequency statistics (as opposed to more abstract signal-processing features such as LPC coefficients). Further details can be found in Doherty (1976), Doherty and Hollien (1978), Hollien, Gelfer, and Huntley (1990), and Hollien, Hicks, and Oliver (1990). The method uses the notion of a 'vector', a characterization of a speaker by a number of quantitative parameters derived from a particular phonetic source. One such vector is derived from fundamental frequency, and comprises the sample's f_0 mean and standard deviation, together with values representing the statistical distribution of f_0-values over the sample. Other vectors incorporate information from the LTAS, from vowel formants, and from measurements to do with duration and speech rate. Combinations of vectors can then be used to calculate overall distances between speakers. Some vectors are likely to be sensitive to the confounding factors encountered in forensic samples; for instance the LTAS is particularly sensitive to characteristics of the communication channel, and to speaking effort (see Doddington, 1985:1658).

Another semi-automatic system, SASIS (Broderick, Paul, and Rennick, 1975; Wrench, 1980), relied on a human operator to identify equivalent phonetic events, and provided automatic evaluation of the distance between feature vectors relating to test and reference samples. Distances could be interpreted statistically in relation to data from a representative sample of speakers stored in the system. The failure of SASIS to achieve its promise (Künzel, 1987:129) may have been partly because of the susceptibility of spectral features to transmission factors, as mentioned above. Nonetheless the general philosophy of both SASIS and SAUSI, which involve extracting a variety of primary and derived features and comparing speakers (in effect) in a multi-dimensional acoustic–phonetic space, is likely to form part of all future practical approaches to technical speaker identification.

7.3 Combined auditory–acoustic techniques

Good auditory–phonetic analysis is the most effective way to capture those differences and similarities between samples which result from the linguistic system, while acoustic analysis provides for quantitative expression of audible differences and the discovery of differences which are not available in listening. Given the complementary strengths of the two approaches, it would be hard to argue coherently against using both in any task of speaker identification, assuming the quality of the samples available permit it. As a result, a combined auditory–acoustic approach is becoming widely accepted. In fact voiceprinting was rarely if ever exclusively a matter of examining spectrograms; Tosi (1979:111–15) details procedures for auditory examination of materials. But there is little to indicate that any thoroughgoing auditory–phonetic analysis played a part in the voiceprint approach.

Künzel (1987; 1994a:139–40), on the other hand, describes a combined approach which has become a benchmark for forensic speaker identification. It was developed at the German Bundeskriminalamt, and has been adopted, at least in broad outline, by several regional law enforcement agencies in Germany, and in other countries such as the Netherlands. It involves careful listening and analysis by a phonetician, who is able to identify and characterize features of accent and pathological or other audible idiosyncratic features. Acoustic analysis is carried out in part to give quantitative support to the specific features identified by ear, and in part to add independent parameters. In practice it is likely that auditory and acoustic analyses proceed interactively, with acoustic displays alerting the analyst to features worthy of further auditory attention. Ultimately the findings are interpreted in the light of population statistics, where these are available.

The direction for the future is, according to Künzel (1994a:140), 'to increase the number of parameters which can be expressed on . . . quantitative scales and thus broaden the objective basis for S[peaker] R[ecognition]'. This will by no means reduce the role of the human analyst, either in carrying out auditory phonetic analysis, guiding acoustic analysis, or interpreting results. Technical speaker identification, particularly in its usual forensic context, is a highly difficult task, and we will always need to exploit all reliable sources of information.

8 Content determination and tape authentication

Content determination is included in this chapter because, along with speaker identification, it constitutes a significant application of phonetic skills in forensics. The task is that of deciding what has been said in a recording of speech. Some of the techniques of relevance lie not in phonetics but in signal processing, since often the difficulty of deciphering the speech on a tape results from the poor quality of the recording. Selective filtering and other processing, increasingly carried out digitally, can enhance the audibility of the speech signal relative to other sound on the recording (see e.g. Koenig, 1988). But centrally phonetic techniques also have a part to play, especially where it is not possible to enhance intelligibility sufficiently because the unwanted noise overlaps the frequencies crucial for speech perception, or because the difficulty arises from a linguistic source, such as an unusual accent.

French (1990) summarizes the contribution which phonetics can make to content determination, and presents a case study in which the dispute centred on whether a doctor, speaking English with a Greek accent, had said *can* or *can't* in the context 'You ___ inject those things.' An auditory phonetic analysis, and an acoustic analysis in terms of vowel formant frequencies, were carried out on a large number of occurrences of *can* and *can't* as they occurred in another lengthy recorded interview with the doctor, and where they were unambiguous from the context and not in dispute. The two disputed instances were then also analysed. It emerged that the doctor made a consistent difference, albeit smaller than that of a native English speaker, between the two words, and that the two tokens in dispute were of the *can't* type.

Tape authentication is the task of deciding whether a recording is a true and complete record of acoustic events, or whether it has been edited, made selective by switching the tape recorder off and on, or otherwise manipulated. Here the task requires not primarily phonetic techniques, but those of acoustics or sound engineering, since the answer often lies in non-speech evidence on the tape such as switching transients or discontinuities in the physical substance of the tape (see Hollien, 1990:Ch.8; Koenig, 1990). An auditory examination of the recording by a phonetically trained listener may be a useful first step, however, particularly if there is no clear expectation as to where the recording may have been manipulated (Baldwin and French, 1990:61–2). Discontinuities in intonation contours, inappropriate sequences of intonation patterns, segmental shortening or lengthening where the phonological environment does not predict it, and similar unexpected phonetic phenomena can all point to the recorded speech signal being other than as the speaker produced it. It is likely that as digital editing and signal manipulation becomes more widespread, and the physical cues to such tampering more elusive, the focus will more often be on discontinuities of a phonetic kind, such as inappropriate sequences of intonation patterns.

9 Conclusion

It is clear that speaker recognition, and to a smaller extent content identification and tape authentication, will be growing areas for the exploitation of phonetic knowledge. Advances in technology will continue to bring gradual progress, particularly in the area of technical speaker verification. But a breakthrough in speaker recognition, particularly in speaker identification in the forensic context, will depend on a more complete model of 'speaker space' becoming available. That is, if we assume a multidimensional space defined by the acoustic and auditory phonetic parameters which can be analysed, we need to know what the relevant parameters are for separating speakers, how for a given speaker variation in acoustic and phonetic values is determined, and, for the population as a whole, to what extent the region in that space occupied by one speaker overlaps the regions occupied by other speakers. Research must be guided by a good understanding of the sources of between-speaker differences, and will have to take advantage of databases containing samples from large numbers of speakers.

Work on speaker recognition tends to have been driven by practical needs, and to have been carried out within the confines of pre-defined sub-disciplines (such as signal processing, auditory phonetics) for which the tasks of speaker recognition have been secondary applications. It is now time for the issues involved in speaker recognition to take a central place in phonetics, so that they can be tackled with the benefit of a fully integrated understanding of all aspects of human speech communication. The challenges, at both the conceptual and empirical levels, are considerable, but it is important that phoneticians accept them. Justice will depend on it.

26 Speech Synthesis

ROLF CARLSON AND BJÖRN GRANSTRÖM

1 Introduction

This chapter will review some of the more popular approaches to speech synthesis. Speech synthesis is not only one of the important applications of speech and language research but, in our opinion, a very valuable tool in the study of phonetics. We will point to some present and future applications of text-to-speech technology and describe some current trends in speech synthesis research.

Speech synthesis, during the last decade, has moved out of the research department and into everyday applications. Some of these applications actually employ prerecorded compiled digitized messages. Although a professional phonetician could contribute to creating procedures for optimizing the quality of such services, we will not focus on such methods in this chapter, but concentrate on the general aspects of speech synthesis as used in text-to-speech systems.

Electronic speech synthesis has developed over the last fifty years. In the publications by Fant (1960), Holmes, Mattingly, and Shearme (1964), Flanagan (1972), Klatt (1976), and Allen, Hunnicutt, and Klatt (1987), the foundations for speech synthesis based on acoustical or articulatory modelling can be found. The paper by Klatt (1987), gives an extensive review of the developments of speech synthesis techniques.

2 Speech synthesis in text-to-speech systems

The most widespread applications of speech synthesis techniques are in text-to-speech systems. Such systems can be thought of as comprehensive models of the process of reading aloud. Advanced versions of text-to-speech systems will hence contain components that are based on more than phonetic knowledge, even with a relatively wide definition of the phonetic sciences. In Figure

26.1, we have outlined a generic text-to-speech system. In its details it does not correspond to any specific system, but contains components found in many systems. In actually implemented systems, still on the research level or already commercialized, the developers have put varying emphasis on the different modules and have also found radically different solutions to the posed functional demands.

3 Components of a generic text-to-speech system

Looking at Figure 26.1 from top to bottom, we first see the input text module. This component typically identifies text of different kinds, such as digits, acronyms, and names. The input text can normally be mixed with other information, such as phonetic text or special symbols controlling either system functions or linguistic/phonetic processing. Some systems today have a multi-lingual capability. At least ideally, one would like language switching taking place automatically. Such components have been developed in projects such as the ESPRIT/POLYGLOT (Boves, 1991) and can be part of a foreign name pronunciation system (Church, 1986; Carlson, Granström, and Lindström, 1989; Vitale, 1991). The linguistic processing module varies a great deal in complexity and ambition in different systems. The balance between rules and lexicon is due to language structure and implementation constraints. The amount of syntactic analysis varies from simple local phrasing based primarily on function word identification to attempts at complete sentence parsing. The derived information is useful both for disambiguation of homographs and as an input to the prosodic description module. In this module the prosodic phrasing/stress and accent is determined. The components so far described (shaded in Figure 26.1) will not be discussed further in this chapter, but serve as a basis for phonetic processing in the text-to-speech system. The unshaded components will be described in greater detail below, but first we will discuss the issue of synthesis tools, something that has had a great impact on synthesis procedures and systems actually developed.

4 Notations and tools for speech synthesis

Development tools for text-to-speech systems have received considerable effort. Often the basis of such tools have followed the development of phonological theory. The work on generative phonology and especially the publication of The Sound Pattern of English by Chomsky and Halle (1968) led to a new kind of synthesis system based on rewrite rules (Carlson and Granström, 1976). Their ideas inspired researchers to create special rule compilers for text-to-speech developments in the early seventies. New software is still being

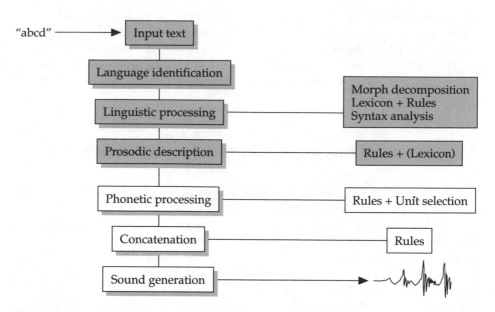

Figure 26.1   A generic text-to-speech system. Shaded modules are not discussed in detail in this chapter.

developed according to this basic principle, but the implementations vary depending on the developer's inclination. It is important to note that crucial decisions are often hidden in the systems. The rules may operate rule-by-rule or segment-by-segment. Other important decisions are based on the following questions: How is the backtrack organized? Are the default values in the phoneme library primarily referred to by labels or by features? These questions might seem trivial, but we see many examples of how the explicit design of a system influences the thinking of the researcher. With the greater emphasis on prosodic modelling and the related development of non-linear phonology (Pierrehumbert, 1987), synthesis procedures inspired by such theories have been created, as in the systems described by Hertz (1991), Hertz, Kadin, and Karplus (1985), Lazzaretto and Nebbia (1987), Ceder and Lyberg (1992) and van Leeuwen and te Lindert (1991, 1993). The common feature of these notations is that they keep information on different linguistic levels (tiers) separate in a more explicit way than the essentially linear representation based on generative phonology. This gives potentially higher flexibility, but also more complex notations. The rules now look more like two-dimensional schemes rather than one-line representations. This poses higher demands on the developers and their tools. Rather than conventional text editors, editors should preferably be graphic editors, where relations between tiers can easily be specified, as in the Speech Maker system developed at IPO (van Leeuwen and te Lindert, 1993). In Figure 26.2 this representation is compared to the one used in the KTH system. The rules describe how a letter "a" is pronounced as

(a)

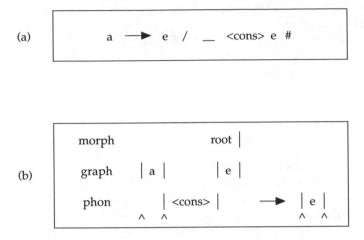

(b)

Figure 26.2 a) Notation according to the KTH "RULSYS" system. (Carlson and Granström, 1976) b) Notation according to the "Speech Maker" system developed at IPO (van Leeuwen and te Lindert, 1993).

[eɪ] if it occurs before a single consonant sound and a root final "e". In the KTH notation, the root boundary is introduced as the symbol "#" by earlier rules. After the rule application, the letter origin of the [eɪ] is lost, which puts higher demands on rule order.

5 Prosodic descriptions and implementations

Prosodic aspects of speech, primarily segmental duration and fundamental frequency (f_0) contours, have recently attracted an increasing interest in speech synthesis research. The general belief is that prosody is the key to the naturalness that is often lacking in current text-to-speech systems. Durational models, often based on the segmental duration model described by Klatt (1979) have been developed for several languages. This work is often based on labelled speech databases, where model predictions and database durations can be matched. The standard deviation of the prediction error is often found to be on the order of 25 msec (Carlson, 1991). Whether this is mostly due to inherent durational variability or to disregard for some important linguistic/pragmatic factors is not clear. Intonation is inherently more difficult to model. Automatic analysis of f_0 is still not reliable for all voices. Substantial variability exists among speakers. Local segmental context often affects the f_0 tracings, often referred to as inherent pitch or microprosody. Speech synthesis, as an alternative to speech analysis, has actually been used as a tool to better understand the important aspects of pitch contours. One important example of such work is the tradition at IPO on perceptually valid stylization (Collier, 1990). Several

other aspects of speech, such as voice source adjustments resulting in amplitude variations or variation in spectral shape, are also prosodically important.
General increase of articulatory distinctness in focal positions and relaxation
of articulators towards the end of phrases are often observed and are also
important to model in speech synthesis.

6   Units of speech synthesis

Modelling segmental coarticulation and other phonetic factors is an important
part of a text-to-speech system. The control part of a synthesis system calculates the parameter values at each time frame. Two main types of approaches
can be distinguished: rule-based methods that use an explicit formulation of
existing knowledge and the library-based methods that replace rules by a
collection of segment combinations of different unit lengths. Clearly both
approaches have their advantages. If the data is coded in terms of targets and
slopes, we need methods to calculate the parameter tracks. The efforts by
Holmes, Mattingly, and Shearme (1964) and the filtered square wave approach
by Liljencrants (1969) are some classical examples in this context. Some of the
problems of this approach will be discussed under the heading "articulatory
synthesis".

   One of the major problems in concatenative synthesis is to make the best
selection of units and to describe how to combine them. Two major factors
create problems: distortion because of spectral discontinuity at the connecting
points, and distortion because of the limited size of the unit set. Systems using
elements of different lengths depending on the target phoneme and its function have been explored by several research groups. In a paper by Olive (1990),
a new method was described to concatenate "acoustic inventory elements" of
different sizes. The system developed at ATR is also based on non-uniform
units (Sagisaka, Kaiki, Iwahashi, and Mimura, 1992).

   Special methods to generate a unit inventory have been proposed by the
research group at NTT in Japan (Hakoda, Nakajima, Hirokawa, and Mizuno,
1990; Nakajima and Hamada, 1988). The synthesis allophones are selected with
the help of the context-oriented clustering method, COC. The COC searches
for the phoneme sequences of different sizes that best describe the phoneme
realization.

   The context-oriented clustering approach is a good illustration of a current
trend in speech synthesis: automatic methods based on databases. The studies
are concerned with much wider phonetic contexts than before. (It might be
appropriate to remind the reader of similar trends in speech recognition.) It is
not possible to take into account all possible coarticulation effects by simply
increasing the number of units. At some point the total number might be too
high or some units might be based on a very few observations. In this case
a normalization of data might be a good solution before the actual unit is

chosen. Thus the system contains rules. However, the rules can be automatically trained from data the same way as in speech recognition (Philips, Glass, and Zue, 1991).

7 Sound generation techniques

Sound generation in speech synthesis can be divided into three main classes, waveform coding, analysis–synthesis and synthesis by rule. The analysis–synthesis method is defined as a method in which human speech is transformed into parameter sequences, which are stored. The output in such a system is created by a synthesis based on concatenation of the prestored parameters. In a synthesis-by-rule system, the output is generated with the help of rules which control a synthesis model such as a vocal tract model, a terminal analog or some kind of coding.

It is not an easy task to place different synthesis methods into unique classes. Some of the common "labels" are often used to characterize a complete system rather than the model it stands for. A rule-based system using waveform coding is a perfectly possible combination, as is speech coding using a terminal analog or a rule-based diphone system using an articulatory model.

The sound generating part of a synthesis system can be divided into two subclasses depending upon the dimensions in which the model is controlled. A vocal tract model can be controlled by spectral parameters such as frequency and bandwidth or shape parameters such as size and length. The source model that excites the vocal tract usually has parameters to control the shape of the source waveform. The combination of time-based and frequency-based controls is powerful in the sense that each part of the system is expressed in its most explanatory dimensions. A drawback of the combined approach can be that it makes interaction between the source and the filter difficult. However, the merits seem to be dominating.

7.1 "Canned speech"

The most radical solution to the synthesizer problem is simply to have a set of pre-recorded messages stored for reproduction. Simple coding of the speech wave might be performed in order to reduce the amount of memory needed. The quality is high, but the usage is limited to applications with few messages. If units smaller than sentences are used, the quality degenerates because of the problem of connecting the pieces without distortion and of overcoming prosodic inconsistencies. One important, and often forgotten, aspect in this context is that a vocabulary change can be an expensive and time-consuming process, since the same speaker and recording facility have to be used as with the original material. The whole system might have to be completely rebuilt in order to maintain equal quality of the speech segments. We will not discuss these methods further in this contribution.

7.2 Analysis–synthesis systems

Synthesis systems based on coding have as long a history as the vocoder. The underlying idea is that natural speech can be analyzed and stored in such a way that it can be assembled into new utterances. Synthesizers such as the systems from AT&T (Olive, 1977, 1990; Olive and Liberman, 1985), NTT (Hakoda et al., 1990; Nakajima and Hamada, 1988), and ATR (Sagisaka, 1988; Sagisaka, Kaiki, Iwahashi, and Mimura, 1992) are based on the source-filter technique where the filter is represented in terms of LPC or similar parameters. This filter is excited by a source model that can be of the same kind as the one used in terminal analog systems. The source must be able to handle all types of sounds: voiced, aspirative, and fricative.

7.3 Waveform manipulation techniques

Considerable success has been achieved by systems that base sound generation on concatenation of natural speech units (Moulines et al., 1990). Sophisticated techniques have been developed to manipulate these units. The PSOLA (Carpentier and Moulines, 1990) methods are based on a pitch-synchronous overlap-add approach for concatenating waveform pieces. The frequency domain approach, FD-PSOLA, is used to modify the spectral characteristics of the signal; the time domain approach, TD-PSOLA, provides efficient solutions for real-time implementation of synthesis systems. Earlier systems like SOLA (Roucos and Wilgus, 1985), and systems for diver's speech restoration also implemented direct processing of the waveform (Liljencrants, 1974).

The importance of PSOLA in phonetic research lies in its possibility of manipulating prosodically interesting parameters (duration, fundamental frequency and intensity) of natural speech without losing much of the original sound quality. In this respect it is quite superior to the speech coding techniques such as LPC that previously have been used for the same purpose. It must be stressed that it is a non-trivial task to perform optimal PSOLA synthesis. Many groups have been stimulated by the excellent work at CNET (Carpentier and Moulines, 1990) and have demonstrated much less convincing results. One of the key problems lies in precisely defining each glottal pulse in time, something that is theoretically difficult to do even for natural voices.

7.4 Voice source models

The traditional voice source model has been a simple or double impulse. This is one reason why different voices produced by text-to-speech systems from the last decade lack naturalness to a great extent. While the male voice sometimes has been regarded as being generally acceptable, an improved glottal source will open the way to more realistic synthesis of child and female voices and also to more naturalness and variation in male voices.

Most source models work in the time domain with different controls to manipulate the pulse shape (Ananthapadmanabha, 1984; Hedelin, 1984; Holmes, 1973; Klatt and Klatt, 1990; Rosenberg, 1971; Rothenberg, Carlson, Granström, and Lindqvist-Gauffin, 1975). One influential voice source model is the LF-model (Fant, Liljencrants, and Lin, 1985). It has a truncated exponential sinusoid followed by a variable cut-off -6dB/octave low-pass filter modelling the effect of the return phase, i.e., the time from maximum excitation of the vocal tract to complete closure of the vocal folds. Figure 26.3 explains the function of the control parameters. In addition to the amplitude and fundamental frequency control, two parameters influence the amplitudes of the two to three lowest harmonics, and one parameter the high-frequency content of the spectrum. Another vocal source parameter is the diplophonia parameter with which creak, laryngalization or diplophonia can be simulated (Klatt and Klatt, 1990). This parameter influences the function of the voiced source in such a way that every second pulse is lowered in amplitude and shifted in time.

The acoustic interactions between the glottal source and the vocal tract also have to be considered (Bickley and Stevens, 1986). One of the major factors in this respect is the varying bandwidth of the formants. This is especially true for the first formant which can be heavily damped during the open phase of the glottal source. However it is not clear that such a variation can be perceived by a listener. Listeners tend to be rather insensitive to bandwidth variation (Flanagan, 1972). When more complex models are to be included, the output from the model has to change from a glottal flow model to a model of the glottal opening. The subglottal cavities can then be included in an articulatory model.

Noise sources have attracted much less research effort compared to the voiced source. However, some aspects have been discussed by Stevens (1971), Shadle (1985), and Badin and Fant (1989). Typically, simple white noise is filtered by resonances which are stationary between each parameter frame. The new synthesizers do have some interaction between the voice source and the noise source, but the interaction is rather primitive. Realization of transient sounds and aspiration dependent on glottal opening are still under development.

7.5 *Terminal analog formant synthesizers*

The traditional text-to-speech systems use a terminal analog. The ambition with this kind of synthesizer is only that it should be able to produce the sounds (speech spectra) that are found in natural speech. The internal structure is not a model of acoustic speech production in the vocal tract. The basic

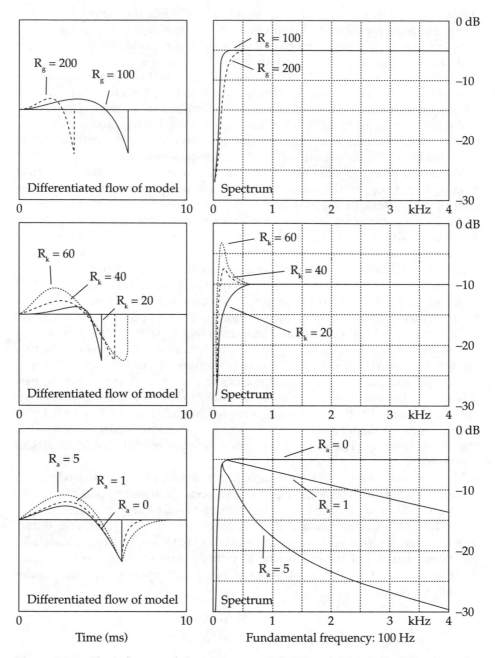

Figure 26.3   The influence of the parameters RG, RK and FA on the differentiated glottal flow pulse shape and spectrum. The spectra are preemphasized by 6 dB/octave. (After Göbl and Karlsson, 1991).

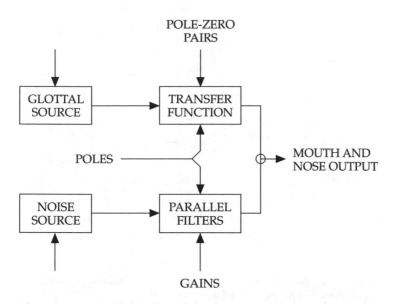

Figure 26.4 Block diagram of the main components of a terminal-analog speech synthesizer such as KLSYN88 (Klatt and Klatt, 1990). The vertical arrows on the sides of the boxes indicate arrays of control parameters. (After Stevens and Bickley, 1991).

concept is the combination of sound sources and filters, describing the transfer function. Building on the classical configuration by Klatt (1980), this principle is exemplified in Figure 26.4. The vocal tract transfer function is simulated by a sequence of second order filters in cascade while a parallel structure is used mostly for the synthesis of consonants. One important advantage of a cascade synthesizer is the automatic setting of formant amplitudes. The disadvantage is that it sometimes can be difficult to do detailed spectral matching between natural and synthesized spectra because of the simplified model. Parallel synthesizers such as the one developed by Holmes (1983) do not have this limitation.

The Klatt model is widely used in research both for general synthesis purposes and for perceptual experiments. A simplified version of this system is used in all commercial products that stem from MIT: MITalk (Allen, Hunnicutt, and Klatt, 1987), DECtalk, and the system at the Speech Technology Laboratory (Javkin et al., 1989). Similar configurations were used in the ESPRIT/ POLYGLOT project (Boves, 1991).

A formant terminal analog, GLOVE (Carlson, Granström, and Karlsson, 1991), based on the OVE synthesizer (Liljencrants, 1968), has been developed at KTH and is used in current text-to-speech modelling (Carlson, Granström, and Hunnicutt, 1982, 1991). In Figure 26.5, the structure of the Glove synthesizer is shown. The controllable parameters are indicated by two-letter symbols. To the left, the two sound sources can be seen. For mixed excitation the sources

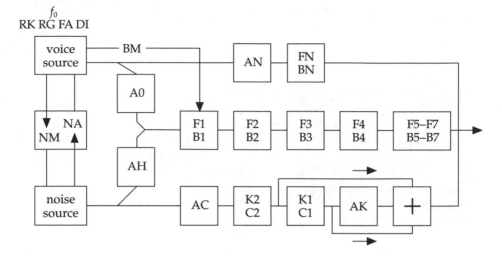

Figure 26.5   Block diagram of the main components of the terminal-analog speech synthesizer GLOVE. (Carlson, Granström, and Karlsson, 1991).

are connected in two ways. The parameter NM flow-modulates the noise source, typical for voiced fricatives. The parameter NA adds noise to the glottal source, as in breathy or whispered voices. The five parameters above the voice source are the glottal parameters referred to in the voice source section. The sound source signals are fed into the three parallel branches with poles and zeroes. All are controlled by amplitude parameters (AN, A0, AH and AC). The upper branch is primarily used for introducing an extra pole (and zero) in nasals and nasalized sounds. The middle branch is the main branch for sounds produced with glottal excitation and the lowest branch models sounds with supra-glottal excitation, such as stops and fricatives. This basic configuration can be augmented in several different ways. The interaction between the source and the vocal tract, which can be substantial, is in this case only modeled by the BM parameter that modulates the bandwidth of the first formant, dependent on glottal opening or more precisely, glottal flow. The main difference be-tween the Klatt and KTH traditions can be found in how the consonants are modelled. In the OVE case, a fricative is filtered by a zero-pole-pole configu-ration rather than the parallel branch in the Klatt synthesizer.

With the new capabilities of the terminal analog synthesizers, it is now possible to simulate most human voices, and to replicate an utterance without noticeable quality reduction. However, it is interesting to note that some voices are easier to model than others. Despite the progress, speech quality is not good enough in all applications of text-to-speech. The main reasons for the limited success in formant-based synthesis can be explained by incomplete phonetic knowledge. It should be noted that the transfer of knowledge from phonetics to speech technology has not been an easy process. Another reason is that the efforts using formant synthesis have not explored alternative control methods to the explicit rule-based description.

7.6 *Higher level parameters*

Since the control of a formant synthesizer can be a very complex task, some efforts have been made to help the developer. The "higher level parameters" described by Stevens and Bickley (1991), for example, explore an intermediate level that is more understandable from the developer's point of view compared to the detailed synthesizer specifications. The goal with this approach is to find a synthesis framework to simplify the process and to incorporate the constraints that are known to exist within the process. A formant frequency should not have to be adjusted specifically by the rule developer depending on nasality or glottal opening. This type of adjustment might be better handled automatically according to a well-specified model. The same process should occur with other parameters such as bandwidths and glottal settings. The approach requires detailed understanding of the relation between acoustic and articulatory phonetics.

7.7 *Articulatory models*

Ultimately an articulatory model will be the most interesting solution for the sound-generating part of text-to-speech systems. Development is going forward in this area, but the lack of reliable articulatory data and appropriate control strategies are still some of the bottlenecks. One possible solution that has attracted interest is to automatically train neural networks to control such a synthesizer. The work by Rahm, Kleijn, and Schroeter (1991) and Bailly, Laboissière, and Schwartz (1991) explores such methods. One promise of articulatory synthesis is that the controlling rules should be more simple and natural. Many of the phonetic details observed in natural speech will follow automatically if they depend on articulatory constraints included in the model. One case in point is the modelling of transitions between speech sounds and articulations. In the output of a formant synthesizer it is often observed that the formant transition between phones does not compare very well to natural transitions even if the segmental target values are well predicted. In the spectrogram in Figure 26.6, taken from a segment of natural speech, such a situation is obvious. In the transition between /j/ and /u:/, at approximately 1.23 sec, we can see that an interpolation between the /j/ and the /u:/ target will look very different in all formants except F1. The reason is that the formants change cavity affiliation. It is, for example, possible to imagine a continuity between F3 of /j/ and F2 of /u:/.

Articulatory models which are developed today stem from the basic work carried out at laboratories such as Bell, MIT and KTH some 30 years ago. In these models an approximation of the vocal tract is used either to calculate the

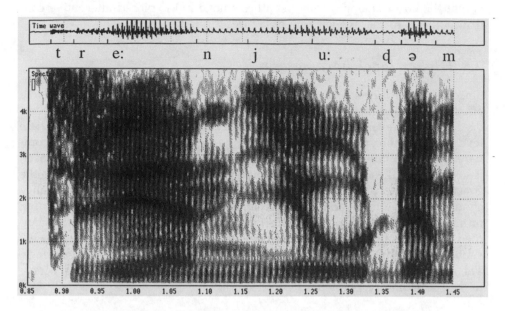

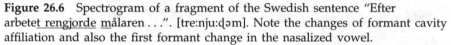

Figure 26.6 Spectrogram of a fragment of the Swedish sentence "Efter arbetet rengjorde målaren . . .". [treːnjuːɖəm]. Note the changes of formant cavity affiliation and also the first formant change in the nasalized vowel.

corresponding transfer filter or to filter a source waveform directly. Different vocal tract models have been used based on varying assumptions and simplifications. The models by Flanagan, Ishizaka, and Shipley (1975), Coker (1976), Mermelstein (1973), and Maeda (1990) have been studied by many researchers in the development of current articulatory synthesis.

The term "articulatory modelling" is often used in a rather loose way. The situation is explained in Figure 26.7. Often a so-called articulatory model only models a simplified area function, rather than describing the movements of articulators. Also, the distinction between static and dynamic models must be kept in mind when a synthesis approach is discussed. A complete model has to include several transformations from the control signal to the actual speech output. The relation between an articulatory gesture and a sequence of vocal tract shapes has to be modelled. Each shape should be transformed into some kind of tube model which has its acoustic characteristics. The vocal tract is then modelled in terms of an electronic network. At this point, the developer can choose to use the network as such to filter the source signal. Alternatively, the acoustics of the network can be expressed in terms of resonances which can control a formant-based synthesizer. The main difference is the domain, time or frequency, in which the acoustic events are simulated.

The developer has to choose at which level the controlling part of the synthesis system should connect to the synthesis model. All levels are possible and many have been used. One of the pioneering efforts using articulatory

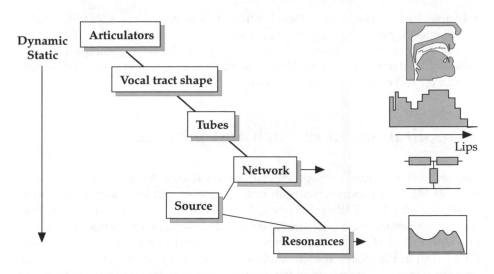

Figure 26.7 Different levels of the representation in an articulatory model for text-to-speech.

synthesis as part of a text-to-speech system was that of Bell Labs (Coker, 1976). Lip, jaw and tongue positions were controlled by rule. The final synthesis step was done by a formant based terminal analog. Recent efforts at KTH by Lin and Fant (1992) use a parallel synthesizer with parameters derived from an articulatory model.

In the development of articulatory modelling for text-to-speech we can take advantage of parallel work on speech coding based on articulatory modelling (Sondhi and Schroeter, 1987). This work not only focuses on synthesizing speech but also on how to extract appropriate vocal tract configurations. Thus, it will also help us to get articulatory data through an analysis–synthesis procedure. Another non-invasive technique to obtain articulatory data is the magnetic resonance imaging (MRI) technique, that is now replacing X-ray for many medical investigations. With this technique it is possible to get a three dimensional representation of the vocal tract without the health hazards of X-ray. The "exposure time" is still several seconds, implying that true dynamic registrations are not yet possible (see also Stone, LABORATORY TECHNIQUES FOR INVESTIGATING SPEECH ARTICULATION).

With a few exceptions, articulatory models have been only two dimensional. Progress in computing power and three dimensional CAD techniques are now starting to be exploited also in more comprehensive articulatory modelling. A related technique with immediate practical application is the synthesis of "talking faces" (Cohen and Massaro, 1993), where articulatory movements, as seen from the outside of the head, are synthesized. Such a face synthesis in combination with acoustic speech synthesis is expected to improve speech comprehension, especially for hard of hearing listeners.

In this section we have not dealt with the important work carried out to model speech production in terms of volumes, masses and airflow. The inclusion of such models still lies in the future beyond the next generation of text-to-speech systems, but the results of these experiments will improve the current articulatory and terminal analog models.

8 Applications in research and products

The original application of speech synthesis was as a research tool. The early work at Haskins Laboratories is an outstanding example of how speech synthesis, the so called Pattern Playback device, was used to investigate the perceptually relevant aspects of the "speech code." Work with similar ambitions, but with different synthesizers, were carried out at Bell Labs, MIT, KTH and Edinburgh in the 1950s. Speech synthesis is thus a well established part of the phonetics toolbox, where many tentative conclusions from speech analysis can be verified or discarded. It can also be used as an exploratory, interactive tool. With the development of more comprehensive speech synthesis schemes and advances in computer technology, the possibility of application in a text-to-speech system evolved. Reading machines for the visually impaired were proposed as an application as early as the late 1960s.

If one looks at the speech synthesis market today, it is obvious that a great share of the text-to-speech products is still used in devices for disabled persons (Carlson, Granström, and Hunnicutt, 1991). The widespread use of speech synthesis in personal computers and telecommunication services that was projected in the market studies some ten years ago has still not happened. The slower-than-expected improvement in speech quality is just one explanation. Voice response systems based on recorded speech and other competing methods of man-machine interaction might also have slowed down the market penetration of synthetic speech.

Many conceivable applications require a voice input and speech understanding and capability. This technology is inherently much more difficult, and current systems are thus less comprehensive than the speech synthesis technology. The research interest in voice dialogue systems is, however, currently very active. Many projects are concerned with automatic methods for two-way speech communication. The ATIS task within ARPA and the Voyager system at MIT, and European projects, such as the ESPRIT/SUNDIAL and SUNSTAR and national projects in Europe such as Verbmobil in Germany have this ambition. The integration in dialogue systems opens new possibilities for speech synthesis compared to ordinary text-to-speech, since much of the information that is hard to derive from text is "known" by the system. The problem of homograph disambiguation, syntactic analysis, prosodic phrasing and sentence stress assignment could at least in principle be solved by the dialogue component.

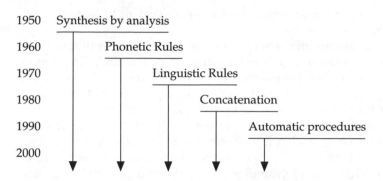

1950 Synthesis by analysis

1960   Phonetic Rules

1970   Linguistic Rules

1980   Concatenation

1990   Automatic procedures

2000

Figure 26.8 Important trends in speech-synthesis developments.

Many speech synthesis applications place special demands on the text-to-speech system. One important area is name pronunciation. Names are often pronounced according to other rules than the core vocabulary of a language. This is especially obvious in multi-language/multi-cultural societies such as in the USA. With the integration of Europe, name pronunciation has been made a topic of the Language Research and Engineering (LRE) project "Onomastica" with telecommunication and academic partners from some ten countries.

9 Trends in speech synthesis

During the last few decades speech synthesis has developed from manually controlled research tools to advanced text-to-speech products. The change is strongly related to our increased understanding of the speech production process, but perhaps to an even greater extent to the development in computer technology and signal processing techniques. In Figure 26.8 we have indicated some of the more important trends in this development. It is interesting to note that this development is rather incremental than revolutionary. Many of the old methods and problem areas indicated in the figure are still valid.

9.1 Multilingual synthesis

Many societies in the world are increasingly multilingual. The situation in Europe is an especially striking example of this. Most of the population is in touch with more than one language. This is natural in multilingual societies such as Switzerland and Belgium. Most schools in Europe have foreign languages on their mandatory curriculum from the early years. With the opening of the borders in Europe, more and more people will be in direct contact with several languages on an almost daily basis. For this reason text-to-speech devices, whether they are used professionally or not, ought to have a multi-lingual capability.

Based on this understanding, many synthesis efforts are multilingual in nature. The Polyglot project supported by the European ESPRIT program was a joint effort by several laboratories in several countries. The common software in this project was, to a great extent, language independent and the language-specific features were specified by rules, lexica and definitions rather than in the software itself. This is also the key to the multilingual effort at KTH. About one-third of the delivered systems by the INFOVOX company are multilingual. The synthesis developments pursued at companies such as ATR, CNET, DEC, and AT&T are all examples of multilingual projects. It is interesting to see that the research community in the world is rather small. Several of the efforts are joint ventures such as the co-operation between Japanese (ATR) and US partners. The Japanese company, Matsushita, even has a US branch (STL) for its English version, originally based on MITalk.

9.2 Style and personality

Currently available text-to-speech systems are not characterized by a great amount of flexibility, especially not when it comes to varying of voice or speaking style. On the contrary, the emphasis has been on a neutral way of reading, modelled after reading of non-related sentences. There is, however, a very practical need for different speaking styles in text-to-speech systems. Such systems are now used in a variety of applications and many more are projected as the quality is developed. The range of applications asks for a variation close to that found in human speakers. General use in reading stock quotations, weather reports, electronic mail or warning messages are examples in which humans would choose rather different ways of reading. Different voices are also important in speech prostheses so that non-speaking persons in the same environment have different voices. Apart from these practical needs in text-to-speech systems, there is the scientific interest in formulating our understanding of human speech variability in explicit models.

The current ambition in speech synthesis research is to model natural speech on a global level, allowing changes of speaker characteristics and speaking style. One obvious reason is the limited success in enhancing the general speech quality by only improving the segmental models. The speaker-specific aspects are regarded as playing a very important role in the acceptability of synthetic speech. This is especially true when the systems are used to signal semantic and pragmatic knowledge.

One interesting effort to include speaker characteristics in a complex system has been reported by the ATR group in Japan. The basic concept is to preserve speaker characteristics in interpreting systems (Abe, Shikano, and Kuwabara, 1990). The proposed voice conversion technique consists of two steps: mapping code-book generation of LPC parameters and a conversion synthesis using the mapping code book. The effort has stimulated much discussion, especially considering the application as such. The method has been extended from a frame-by-frame transformation to a segment-by-segment transformation (Abe, 1991).

One concern with this type of effort is that the speaker characteristics are specified through training without a specific higher level model of the speaker. It would be helpful if the speaker characteristics could be modelled by a limited number of parameters. Only a small number of sentences might in this case be needed to adjust the synthesis to one specific speaker. The needs in both speech synthesis and speech recognition are very similar in this respect.

A voice conversion system has been proposed that combines the PSOLA technique for modifying prosody with a source-filter decomposition which enables spectral transformations (Valbret, Moulines, and Tubach, 1992).

Duration-dependent vowel reduction has been one topic of research in this context (Lindblom, 1990). It seems that vowel reduction as a function of speech tempo is a speaker-dependent factor (van Son and Pols, 1989). Duration and intonation structures and pause insertion strategies reflecting variability in the dynamic speaking style are other important speaker-dependent factors. Parameters such as consonant–vowel ratio and source dynamics are typical parameters that have to be considered in addition to basic physiological variation.

The difference between male/female speech has been studied by a few researchers (e.g., Klatt and Klatt, 1990; Karlsson, 1992). Some systems use a female voice as reference speaker, e.g., Syrdal (1992). The male voice differs from the female in many respects not only based on physiological aspects. To a great extent speaking habits are formed by the social environment, dialect region, education and also by a communicative situation which may require formal or informal speech. The speaker characteristic aspects have to be viewed as a complete description of the speaker in which all aspects are linked to each other within a unique framework (Cohen, 1989; Eskénazi and Lacheret-Dujour, 1991).

For many applications of speech synthesis, paralinguistic information, such as attitudes and emotions are important. Experiments using DECtalk have been reported by Cahn (1990) in which a special "affect-editor" was developed to control the synthesizer. Its success in generating recognizable affects was confirmed in an experiment in which the affect intended was perceived as such for the majority of the presentations. Similar efforts have been reported by Murray, Arnott, Alm, and Newell (1991). The system HAMLET was developed for use in speech prostheses for the non-vocal, and was designed for incorporation into communication systems. The system uses DECtalk as an output device just as in the experiments by Cahn. Any of six emotions can be selected from a menu. The corresponding rules then operate on the phonemes and the voice quality settings, which are sent to the text-to-speech system.

The ultimate test of our descriptions is our ability to successfully synthesize not only different voices and accents but also different speaking styles (Bladon, Carlson, Granström, Hunnicutt, and Karlsson, 1987). Appropriate modelling of these factors will increase both naturalness and intelligibility of synthetic speech.

9.3 Data driven methods

When increasing our ambitions to multi-lingual, multi-speaker and multi-style synthesis it is obvious that we want to find at least semi-automatic methods to collect the necessary information, using speech and language databases. Traditionally, speech synthesis has been based on very labour-intensive optimization work. The notion "analysis by synthesis" has not been explored except by manual comparisons between hand-tuned spectral slices and a reference spectra. The work by Holmes and Pearce (1990) is a good example of how to speed up this process. With the help of a synthesis model, the spectra are automatically matched against analyzed speech. Automatic techniques such as this will probably also play an important role in making speaker-dependent adjustments. One advantage with these methods is that the optimization is done in the same framework as that to be used in the production. The synthesizer constraints are thus already imposed in the initial state.

Methods for pitch-synchronous analysis will be of major importance in this context. Experiments such as the one presented by Talkin and Rowley (1990) will lead to better estimates of pitch and vocal tract shape. These automatic procedures will, in the future, make it possible to gather a large amount of data. Lack of glottal source data is currently a major obstacle for the development of speech synthesis with improved naturalness.

Given a collection of parameter data from analyzed speech corpora, one is in a good position to look for coarticulation rules and context-dependent variations. The collection of speech corpora also facilitates possibilities to test duration and intonation models (Carlson and Granström, 1986a; Kaiki, Takeda, and Sagisaka, 1990; Riley, 1990; van Santen and Olive, 1990).

9.4 Evaluation techniques

The ultimate goal for all synthesis research with few exceptions is to produce as high speech quality as possible. The quality and the intelligibility of speech is usually a very difficult task to measure. No single measure is able to pinpoint where the problems are. The research in the University of Indiana group has pushed the evaluation methods further (Logan, Greene, and Pisoni, 1989). The speech community is still looking for a simple way to measure progress as a fast and reliable station on the synthesis development path. Thus, research tends to be heavily influenced by fast and subjective judgments by the developer in front of the computer screen. The recent work that has been done in the ESPRIT/SAM projects (Fourcin, Harland, Barry, and Hazan, 1989), the COCOSDA group and special workshops will set new standards for the

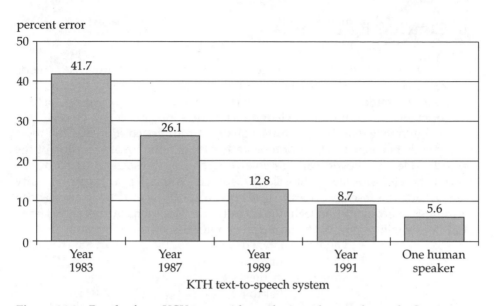

percent error

Figure 26.9 Results from VCV tests with synthetic and natural speech. Consonant errors are shown for several stages of development of the KTH system.

future. Evaluation serves several functions. One important objective is to be able to choose reliably between competing products, with boundary conditions given by a real application. Another function is to monitor progress in the development of a system. In the latter case it is essential to obtain information that pinpoints system weaknesses that could direct research. In this case it is important that the test procedures are well standardized, to ensure test/retest reliability. Several such tests have been defined and adopted by the SAM consortium. In Figure 26.9 the results from such a test are shown (Goldstein and Till, 1992). The procedure is a non-sense word test systematically evaluating the consonants intelligibility of a language in the context of the cardinal vowels /a/, /ɪ/, /ʊ/ (or the closest vowels in that language). The test is administered by a program running on a IBM/PC compatible computer. The detailed results can be displayed in several different ways, e.g., as confusion matrices. As seen from the figure, the segmental result from the most recently tested system is quite close to the performance of natural speech. This test, however, only evaluates one aspect of the synthesis system, but this aspect is of primary importance to the function of such a system. It is obvious that the output of all text-to-speech systems available today is noticeably inferior to the speech of most human speakers. However there are several reports on tests on a more global level that indicate that the comprehension of synthetic speech could be similar or even superior to natural speech (Delogu, Conte, Paoloni, and Sementina, 1992; Neovius and Raghavendra, 1993). This holds the promise that speech synthesis even now could be utilized in many applications outside the area of disability.

10 Concluding remarks

In this review we have touched upon a number of different synthesis methods and research goals to improve current text-to-speech systems. It might be germane to remind the reader that nearly all methods are based on historic development, where new knowledge has been added piece by piece to old knowledge rather than by a dramatic change of approach. Perhaps the most dramatic change is in the field of tools rather than in the understanding of the "speech code." However, considerable progress can be seen in terms of improved speech synthesis quality. Today, speech synthesis is a common facility even outside the research world, especially in speaking aids for persons with disabilities. New synthesis techniques under development in speech research laboratories will play a key role in future man-machine interaction.

References

Abbs, J. and Gilbert, B. (1973). A strain gauge transduction system for lip and jaw motion in two dimensions: design criteria and calibration data. *Journal of Speech and Hearing Research*, 16, 248–56.

Abbs, J. and Gracco, V.L. (1984). Control of complex motor gestures: orofacial muscle responses to load perturbations during speech. *Journal of Neurophysiology*, 51, 705–23.

Abbs, J., Gracco, V. and Blair, C. (1984). Functional muscle partitioning during voluntary movement: facial muscle activity for speech. *Experimental Neurology*, 85, 469–79.

Abbs, J., Gracco, V.L. and Cole, K. (1984). Control of multimovement coordination: sensorimotor mechanisms in speech motor programming. *Journal of Motor Behavior*, 16, 195–232.

Abbs, J.H., Nadler, R.D. and Fujimura, O. (1988). X-ray microbeam tracks the shape of speech. *SOMA*, 29–34.

Abe, M. (1991). A segment-based approach to voice conversion. *Proceedings of ICASSP–91*.

Abe, M., Shikano, K. and Kuwabara, H. (1990). Voice conversion for an interpreting telephone. *Proceedings of ESCA Workshop on Speaker Characterisation in Speech Technology*. Edinburgh.

Abel, S.M. (1972a). Duration discrimination of noise and tone bursts. *Journal of the Acoustical Society of America*, 51, 1219–23.

—— (1972b). Discrimination of temporal gaps. *Journal of the Acoustical Society of America*, 52, 519–24.

Abercrombie, D. (1957). Palatography. *Zeitschrift fur Phonetick*, 10, 21–5.

—— (1967). *Elements of general phonetics*. Edinburgh: Edinburgh University Press.

Abramson, A.S. (1977). Laryngeal timing in consonant distinction. *Phonetica*, 34, 295–303.

Abramson, A.S. and Lisker, L. (1970). Discriminability along the voicing continuum: cross-language tests. *Proceedings of the 6th International Congress of Phonetic Sciences*, 569–73. Prague: Academia.

Abry, C. and Lallouache, M.T. (1995). Le *MEM*: un modèle d´anticipation paramétrable par locuteur. Données sur l'arrondissement en français. *Bulletin du Laboratoire de la Communication Parlée*, Centre National de la Recherche Scientifique, Grenoble.

Ackermann, H., Hertrich, I. and Scharf, G. (1995). Kinematic analysis of lower lip movements in ataxic dysarthria. *Journal of Speech and Hearing Research*, 38, 1252–9.

Ackermann, H. and Ziegler, W. (1991). Articulatory deficits in Parkinsonian dysarthria: an acoustic analysis. *Journal of Neurology, Neurosurgery, and Psychiatry*, 54, 1093–8.

—— (1992). Die zerebellare dysarthrie – ein literaturübersicht [Cerebellar dysarthria – a review of literature]. *Fortschritte der Neurologie-Psychiatrie*, 60, 28–40.

Adams, M., Reich, A. and Flowers, C. (1989). Verbal fluency characteristics of normal and aphasic speakers. *Journal of Speech and Hearing Disorders*, 32, 871–9.

Adams, S.G. (1990). 'Rate and clarity of speech: an x-ray microbeam study'. Ph.D. dissertation, University of Wisconsin-Madison.

Adams, S.G., Weismer, G. and Kent, R.D. (1993). Speaking rate and speech movement velocity profiles. *Journal of Speech and Hearing Research*, 36, 41–54.

Adriaens, L.M.H. (1991). 'Ein Modell deutscher Intonation'. Ph.D. thesis. Eindhoven: Technical University of Eindhoven.

Ainsworth, W.A. (1988). *Speech recognition by machine*. London: Peter Peregrinus Ltd.

—— (ed.) (1992). *Advances in speech, hearing and language processing, Vol. 3*. London: JAI Press.

Ainsworth, W.A. and Pratt, S.R. (1992). Feedback strategies for error correction in speech recognition systems. *International Journal of Man-Machine Studies*, 36, 833–42.

Akansu, A.N. and Haddad, R.A. (1992). *Multiresolution signal decomposition: transforms, subbands and wavelets*. Boston: Academic Press.

Al-Bamerni, A. and Bladon, A. (1982). One-stage and two-stage patterns of velar coarticulation. *Journal of the Acoustical Society of America*, 72, S104.

Alexander, G.E., Delong, M.R. and Strick, P.L. (1986). Parallel organization of functionally segregated circuits linking basal ganglia and cortex. *Annual Review of Neuroscience*, 9, 357–81.

Alexander, M., Naeser, M. and Palumbo, C. (1990). Broca's area aphasias: aphasia after lesions including the frontal operculum. *Neurology*, 40, 353–62.

Alexander, R.McN. (1992). *The human machine*. New York: Columbia University Press.

Allen, J., Hunnicutt, M.S. and Klatt, D. (1987). *From text to speech. The MITalk system*. Cambridge: Cambridge University Press, Cambridge, MA: MIT Press.

Allerhand, M. (1987). *Knowledge-based speech pattern recognition*. London: Kogan Page Ltd.

Altman, P.L. and Dittner, D.S. (eds) (1962). *Committee on biological handbooks. Growth, including reproduction and morphological development*. Washington D.C.: Federation of American Societies for Experimental Biology.

Alwan, A. (1986). 'Acoustic and perceptual correlates of pharyngeal and uvular consonants'. S.M. thesis, Massachusetts Institute of Technology, Cambridge, MA.

Amerman, J.D., Daniloff, R. and Moll, K. (1970). Lip and jaw coarticulation for the phoneme /æ/. *Journal of Speech and Hearing Research*, 13, 147–61.

Amman, J.C. (1694). *The talking deaf man: or, a method proposed whereby he who is born deaf may learn to speak*. London: Hawkins.

Ananthapadmanabha, T.V. (1984). Acoustic analysis of voice source dynamics. *Speech Transmission Laboratory – Quarterly Progress and Status Report*, 2–3, 1–24. Royal Institute of Technology, Stockholm.

Ananthapadmanabha, T.S. and Yegnanarayana, B. (1979). Epoch extraction from linear prediction residual for identification of closed glottis interval. *IEEE Trans ASSP-27*, 309–19.

Anderson, M., Pierrehumbert, J.B. and Liberman, M.Y. (1984). Synthesis by rule of English intonation patterns. *Proceedings of ICASSP '84*, 1 (pp. 2.8.1–2.8.4). Piscataway, NJ: IEEE Service Center.

Anderson, S.R. (1981). Why phonology isn't "natural". *Linguistic Inquiry*, 12.493–539.

Antoniol, G., Cettolo, M. and Federico, M. (1993). Techniques for robust recognition in restricted domains. *Eurospeech '93*, 3, 2219–21.

Aronson, A.E. (1980). *Clinical voice disorders. An interdisciplinary approach*. New York: Thieme-Stratton Inc.

Aronson, A.E. and Lagerlund, T. (1991). Neural imaging studies do not prove the existance of brain abnormalities in spastic (spasmodic) dysphonia. *Journal of Speech and Hearing Research*, 34, 801–5.

Asanuma, H. (1989). *The motor cortex*. New York: Raven Press.

Asatryan, D. and Feldman, A. (1965). Functional tuning of the nervous system with control of movement or maintenance of a steady posture. I. Mechanographic analysis of the word of the joint or execution of a postural task. *Biofizika*, 10, 837–46 [English translation 925–35].

Atal, B.S. (1972). Automatic speaker recognition based on pitch contours. *Journal of the Acoustical Society of America*, 52, 1687–97.

—— (1974). Effectiveness of linear prediction characteristics of the speech wave for automatic speaker identification and verification. *Journal of the Acoustical Society of America*, 55, 1304–12.

Atal, B.S. and Hanauer, S. (1971). Speech analysis and synthesis by linear prediction of the speech wave. *Journal of the Acoustical Society of America*, 50, 637–55.

Atal, B.S., Chang, J.J., Mathews, M.V. and Tukey, J.W. (1978). Inversion of articulatory-to-acoustic transformation in the vocal tract by a computer-sorting technique. *Journal of the Acoustical Society of America*, 63, 1535–55.

Atal, B.S. and Remde, J.R. (1982). A new model of LPC excitation for producing natural-sounding speech at low bit rates, *Proceedings of ICASSP 82*, 1, 614–17.

Atal, B.S. and Schroeder, M.R. (1967). Predictive coding of speech signals. *Proceedings of 1967 Conference on Communication and Processing*, 360–1.

Aull, A.M. (1984). 'Lexical stress and its application in large vocabulary speech recognition'. M.S. thesis, Massachusetts Institute of Technology.

Baart, J.J.G. (1987). 'Focus, syntax, and accent placement'. Ph.D. thesis. Leyden: Leyden University.

Babini, G., Canavesio, F., Gatti, E., Gemme, P. and Schalk, T.B. (1990). A speaker independent voice dialling system for Italian in the cellular phone application. *CSELT Technical Reports*, 18, 201–5.

Bacon, S.P. and Viemeister, N.F. (1985). Temporal modulation transfer functions in normal-hearing and hearing-impaired subjects. *Audiology*, 24, 117–34.

Baddeley, A.D. (1986). *Working memory*. Oxford: Oxford University Press.

—— (1995). Working Memory. In M.S. Gazzaniga (ed.), *The cognitive neurosciences*. Cambridge: MIT Press.

Badin, P. (1989). Acoustics of voiceless fricatives: production theory and data. *Speech Transmission Laboratory – Quarterly Progress and Status Report*, 3, 33–55.

Badin, P. and Fant, G. (1984). Notes on vocal tract computation. *Speech Transmission Laboratory – Quarterly Progress and Status Report*, 2–3, 53–108.

—— (1989). Fricative modeling: some essentials. *Proceedings of European Conference on Speech Technology*, Paris.

Badin, P., Hertegard, S. and Karlsson, I. (1990). Notes on the Rothenberg mask. *Speech Transmission Laboratory – Quarterly Progress and Status Report*, 1, 1–7. Royal Institute of Technology, Stockholm.

Baer, T. (1975). 'Investigation of phonation using excised larynxes'. Ph.D. thesis, Massachusetts Institute of Technology, Cambridge, MA.

Baer, T., Alfonso, P. and Honda, K. (1988). Electromyography of the tongue muscles during vowels in /pVp/ environment. *Annual Bulletin of Research Institute of Logopedics and Phoniatrics*, University of Tokyo, 22, 7–19.

Baer, T., Gore, J., Boyce, S. and Nye, P. (1987). Application of MRI to the analysis of speech production. *Journal of Magnetic Resonance Imaging*, 5, 1–7.

Baer, T., Gore, J.C., Gracco, L.C. and Nye, P.W. (1991). Analysis of vocal tract shape and dimensions using magnetic resonance imaging: vowels. *Journal of the Acoustical Society of America*, 90, 799–828.

Baher, H. (1990). *Analog & digital signal processing*. Chichester: Wiley.

Bailly, G., Laboissière, R. and Schwartz, J.L. (1991). Formant trajectories as audible gestures: an alternative for speech synthesis. *Journal of Phonetics*, 19, 9–23.

Baldwin, J. (1979). Phonetics and speaker identification. *Medicine, Science and the Law*, 19, 231–2.

Baldwin, J. and French, P. (1990). *Forensic phonetics*. London: Pinter.

Bansal, R.K. (1966). 'The intelligibility of Indian English'. Ph.D. thesis, University of London.

Barkat, M. (1991). *Signal detection and estimation*. Boston: Artec House.

Barlow, S. and Abbs, J. (1983). Force transducers for the evaluation of labial, lingual, and mandibular motor impairments. *Journal of Speech and Hearing Research*, 26, 616–21.

Barlow, S. and Burton, M. (1990). Ramp-and-hold force control in the upper and lower lips: developing new neuromotor assessment applications in traumatically brain injured adults. *Journal of Speech and Hearing Research*, 33, 660–75.

Barlow, S. and Rath, E. (1985). Maximum voluntary closing forces in the upper and lower lips of humans. *Journal of Speech and Hearing Research*, 28, 373–6.

Barlow, S.M. and Farley, G.R. (1989). Neurophysiology of speech. In D.P. Kuehn, M.L. Lemme and J.M. Baumgartner (eds), *Neural bases of speech, hearing, and language* (pp. 146–200). Boston: College-Hill.

Barnwell, R.P. (1971). An algorithm for segment durations in a reading machine context. *Technological Report No. 279, Research Laboratory of Electronics*. Cambridge, MA: Massachusetts Institute of Technology.

Barry, M. (1991). Temporal modelling of gestures in articulatory assimilation. *Proceedings of the 12th International Congress of Phonetic Sciences*, 4, 14–17. Aix-en-Provence.

—— (1992). Palatalisation, assimilation and gestural weakening in connected speech. *Speech Communication*, 11, 393–400.

Barry, W.J., Hoequist, C.E. and Nolan, F. (1989). An approach to the problem of regional accent in automatic speech recognition. *Computer Speech and Language*, 3, 355–66.

Basbøll, H. (1974). The phonological syllable with special reference to Danish. *Annual Report of the Institute of Phonetics, Copenhagen*, 8, 39–128.

Batchelor, G.K. (1967). *An introduction to fluid dynamics*. Cambridge: Cambridge University Press.

Baudouin de Courtenay, J. (1895). *Versuch einer Theorie phonetischer Alternationen. Ein Capitel aus der Psychophonetik*. Strassburg: Karl J. Trübner.

Baum, F.L. (1900). *The wizard of Oz*. London: Wm. Collins and Sons.

Baum, L.E. (1972). An inequality and associated maximization technique in statistical estimation for probabilistic functions of a Markov process. *Inequalities*, 3, 1–8.

Baum, S.R., McFarland, D.H. and Diab, M. (1966). Compensation to articulatory perturbation: Perceptual data. *Journal of the Acoustical Society of America*, 99, 3791–3794.

Beattie, V.L. and Young, S.J. (1990). Speech recognition in noise: experiments using hidden Markov models. *Proceedings of the Institute of Acoustics*, 12 (10), 553–8.

Beauchamp, K.G. (1987). *Transforms for engineers: a guide to signal processing*. Oxford: Clarendon.

Beck, J.M. 'Organic variation and voice quality'. Ph.D. Dissertation, University of Edinburgh.

Beckman, M. and Shoji, A. (1984). Spectral and perceptual evidence for CV coarticulation in devoiced /si/ and /syu/ in Japanese. *Phonetica*, 41, 61–71.

Beckman, M.E. and Edwards, J. (1990). Lengthenings and shortenings and the nature of prosodic constituency. In J. Kingston and M.E. Beckman (eds), *Papers in laboratory phonology I* (pp. 152–78). Cambridge: Cambridge University Press.

—— (1994). Articulatory evidence for differentiating stress categories. In P.A. Keating (ed.), *Phonological structure and phonetic form: Papers in Laboratory Phonology II*. Cambridge: Cambridge University Press.

Beckman, M.E. and Pierrehumbert, J.B. (1986). Intonational structure in Japanese and English. *Phonology Yearbook*, 3, 255–309.

Bell, H. (1971). The phonology of Nobiin Nubian. *African Language Review*, 9, 115–59.

Bell-Berti, F. (1976). An electromyographic study of velopharyngeal function in speech. *Journal of Speech and Hearing Research*, 19, 225–40.

—— (1980). Velopharyngeal function: a spatial-temporal model. In N.J. Lass (ed.), *Speech and language, advances in basic research and practice* (pp. 291–316). New York: Academic Press.

Bell-Berti, F., Baer, T., Harris, K.S. and Niimi, S. (1979). Coarticulatory effects of vowel quality on velar function. *Phonetica*, 36, 187–93.

Bell-Berti, F. and Harris, K. (1974). More on the motor organization of speech gestures. *Haskins Laboratories Status Report on Speech Research*, 37/38, 73–7.

—— (1979). Anticipatory coarticulations: some implications from a study of lip rounding. *Journal of the Acoustical Society of America*, 65, 1268–70.

—— (1981). A temporal model of speech production. *Phonetica*, 38, 9–20.

—— (1982). Temporal patterns of coarticulation: lip rounding. *Journal of the Acoustical Society of America*, 71, 449–54.

Bell-Berti, F. and Krakow, R. (1991). Anticipatory velar lowering: a coproduction account. *Journal of the Acoustical Society of America*, 90, 112–23.

Bellanger, M. (1989). *Digital processing of signals: theory and practice* (2nd edn). Chichester: Wiley.

Bellman, R. (1957). *Dynamic programming*. Princeton: Princeton University Press.

Benade, A.H. (1976). *Fundamentals of musical acoustics*. New York: Oxford University Press.

Benguerel, A.P. and Cowan, H. (1975). Coarticulation of upper lip protrusion in French. *Phonetica*, 30, 41–55.

Benguerel, A.P., Hirose, H., Sawashima, M. and Ushijima, T. (1977a). Velar coarticulation in French. a fiberscopic study. *Journal of Phonetics*, 5, 149–58.

—— (1977b). Velar coarticulation in French: an electromyographic study. *Journal of Phonetics*, 5, 159–67.

—— (1978). Laryngeal control in French stop production: a fiberscopic, acoustic and electromyographic study. *Folia Phoniatrica*, 30, 175–98.

Benjamin, B.J. (1981). Frequency variability in the aged voice. *Journal of Gerontology*, 36, 722–6.

Benoit, C. (1986). Note on the use of correlation in speech timing. *Journal of the Acoustical Society of America*, 80, 1846–9.

Berg, J. van den (1958). Myoelastic-aerodynamic theory of voice production. *Journal of Speech and Hearing Research*, 1, 227–44.

Berg, J.W. van den, Zantema, J.T. and Doornenbal, Jr. P. (1957). On the air resistance and the Bernoulli effect of the human larynx. *Journal of the Acoustical Society of America*, 29, 626–31.

Bernhardt, B. (1992). Developmental implications of nonlinear phonological theory. *Clinical Linguistics*, 6, 259–281.

Bernstein, N. (1967). *The coordination and regulation of movements*. London: Pergamon Press.

Bertinetto, P. (1981). *Strutture prosodiche dell'Italiano*. Firenze: Academia della Crusca.

Bever, T.G. (1984). The road from behaviorism to rationalism. In H.L. Roitblat, T.G. Bever and H.S. Terrace (eds), *Animal Cognition*. Hillsdale, NJ: Lawrence Erlbaum Associates, pp. 61–75.

Bevis, R.R., Hayles, A.B., Isaacson, R.J. and Sather, A.H. (1977). Facial growth response to human growth hormone in hypopituitary dwarfs. *Angle Orthodontist*, 47, 193–205.

Bhaskararao, P. and Ladefoged, P. (1991). Two types of voiceless nasals. *Journal of the International Phonetic Association*, 21 (2), 80–8.

Bickerton, D. (1983). *Roots of language*. Ann Arbor: Karoma.

Bickley, C. (1991). Vocal-fold vibration in a computer model. In J. Gauffin and B. Hammerberg (eds), *Vocal fold physiology* (pp. 37–46). San Diego: Singular Publication Group Inc.

Bickley, C.A. (1982). Acoustic analysis and perception of breathy vowels. *Speech Communication Group Working Papers I*, Research Laboratory of Electronics, Massachusetts Institute of Technology, 71–82.

Bickley, C.B. and Stevens, K.N. (1986a). Effects of a vocal-tract constriction on the glottal source: data from voiced consonants. In K.S. Harris, T. Baer and C. Sasaki (eds), *Vocal fold physiology: laryngeal function in phonation and respiration* (pp. 239–53). San Diego: College Hill Press.

—— (1986b). Effects of a vocal-tract constriction on the glottal source: experimental and modelling studies. *Journal of Phonetics*, 14, 373–82.

Binder, J.R., Rao, S.M., Hammeke, T.A., Frost, J.A., Bandettini, P.A., Jesmanosicz and Hude, J.S. (1995). Lateralized human brain language systems demonstrated by task subtraction functional magnetic resonance imaging. *Archives of Neurology*, 52, 593–601.

Bindman, L. and Lippold, O. (1981). *The neurophysiology of the cerebral cortex*. Austin, TX: University of Texas Press.

Bindseil, H.E. (1838). *Abhandlungen zur allgemeinen vergleichenden Sprachlehre*. Hamburg: Publisher.

Binh, N. and Gauffin, J. (1983). Aerodynamic measurements in an enlarged static laryngeal model. *Speech Transmission Laboratory – Quarterly Progress and Status Report*, 2–3, 36–60.

Bizzi, E., Accornero, N., Chapple, W. and Hogan, N. (1984). Posture control and trajectory formation during arm movement. *Journal of Neuroscience*, 4, 2738–44.

Bizzi, E., Hogan, N., Mussa-Ivaldi, F. and Giszter, S. (1992). Does the nervous system use equilibrium-point control to guide single and multiple joint movements? *Behavioral and Brain Sciences*, 15, 603–13.

Bjork, A. (1966). Sutural growth of the upper face studied by the implant method. *Acta Odontologica Scandinavica*, 24, 10927.

Blaauw, E. (1994). The contribution of prosodic boundary markers to the perceptual difference between read and spontaneous speech. Submitted to *Speech Communication*.

Blackburn, C.C. and Sachs, M.B. (1990). The representation of the steady-state vowel /ɛ/ in the discharge patterns of cat anteroventral cochlear nucleus neurons. *Journal of Neurophysiology*, 63, 1191–212.

Bladon, A. and Al-Bamerni, A. (1976). Coarticulation resistance in English /l/. *Journal of Phonetics*, 4, 137–50.

Bladon, A., Carlson, R., Granström, B., Hunnicutt, S. and Karlsson, I. (1987). A text-to-speech system for British English, and issues of dialect and style. In J. Laver and M.A. Jack (eds), *Proceedings of European Conference on Speech Technology*, 1, 55–8. Edinburgh, September 1987.

Bladon, R.A. and Fant, C.G. (1978). A two-formant model and the cardinal vowels. *Speech Transmission Laboratory – Quarterly Progress and Status Report*, 1978/1, 1–8. Royal Institute of Technology, Stockholm.

Bladon, A. and Nolan, F. (1977). A video-fluorographic investigation of tip and blade alveolars in English. *Journal of Phonetics*, 5, 185–93.

Blahut, R.E. (1985). *Fast algorithms for digital signal processing*. Reading, MA.: Addison-Wesley.

Blahut, R.E. (1992). *Algebraic methods for signal processing and communications coding*. New York: Springer.

Blankenship, B., Ladefoged, P., Bhaskararao, P. and Chase, N. (1993). Phonetic structures of Khonoma Angami. *UCLA Working Papers in Phonetics*, 84, 127–41.

Bless, D. and Abbs, J.H. (eds) (1983). *Vocal fold physiology: contemporary research and clinical issues*. San Diego: College Hill Press.

Blight, R.C. and Pike, E.V. (1976). The phonology of Tenango Otomi. *International Journal of American Linguistics*, 42, 51–7.

Bloomer, H.H. (1971). Speech defects associated with dental abnormalities and malocclusions. In L.E. Travis (ed.), *Handbook of speech pathology and audiology*. New York: Appleton-Century-Crofts.

Bloomfield, L. (1933). *Language*. New York: H. Holt and Co.

Blumstein, S.E. and Stevens, K.N. (1980). Perceptual invariance and onset spectra for stop consonants in different vowel environments. *Journal of the Acoustical Society of America*, 67, 648–62.

Boashash, B. (ed.) (1992). *New methods in time-frequency analysis*. Sydney: Longman Cheshire.

Boettcher, F.A., Salvi, R.J. and Saunders, S.S. (1990). Recovery from short-term adaptation in single neurons in the cochlear nucleus. *Hearing Research*, 48, 125–44.

Bogert, B.P., Healy, M.J.R. and Tukey, J.W. (1963). The quefrency alanysis of time series for echoes: cepstrum, pseudo-autocovariance, cross-cepstrum, and saphe cracking. In M. Rosenblatt (ed.), *Proc. Symp. Time series analysis*, 209–43. N.Y.: John Wiley & Sons.

Bolinger, D. (1958). A theory of pitch accent in English. *Word*, 14, 109–49.

Bolla, K. (1980). A phonetic conspectus of Hungarian. The articulatory and acoustic features of Hungarian speech-sounds. *Magyar Fonetikai Füzetek* (Hungarian Papers in Phonetics). Vol. 6.

Bond, Z.S. and Garnes, S. (1980). Misperceptions of fluent speech. In R. Cole (ed.), *Perception and production of fluent speech* (pp. 115–32). Hillsdale, NJ: Erlbaum.

Bond, Z.S. and Small, L.H. (1983). Voicing, vowel and stress mispronunciations in continuous speech. *Perception & Psychophysics*, 34, 470–4.

Boomer, D.S. and Laver, J.D.M. (1968). Slips of the tongue. *British Journal of Disorders of Communication*, 3, 2–12.

Borden, G. and Harris, K.S. (1983). *Speech science primer: physiology, acoustics and perception of speech*. Baltimore, London: Wilkins and Wilkins.

Bosma, J.F. (1963). Maturation of function of the oral and pharyngeal region. *American Journal of Orthodontics*, 49, 94–104.

Botez, M.I. and Barbeau, A. (1971). Role of subcortical structures, and particularly of the thalamus, in the mechanisms of speech and language. *International Journal of Neurology*, 8, 300–20.

Bottini, G., Corcoran, R., Sterzi, R., Paulesu, E., Schenone, P. Scarpa, P. and Frackowiak, R.S. (1994). The role of the right hemisphere in the interpretation of figurative aspects of language: A positron emission tomography activation study. *Brain*, 117, 1241–53.

Bouhuys, A. (1977). *The physiology of breathing*. New York: Grune and Stratton.

Bourk, T.R. (1976). 'Electrical responses of neural units in the anteroventral cochlear nucleus of the cat'. Ph.D. Thesis, Massachusetts Institute of Technology, Cambridge, MA.

Boves, L. (1991). Considerations in the design of a multi-lingual text-to-speech system. *Journal of Phonetics*, 19 (1), pp. 25–36.

Bowen, B.A. and Brown, W.R. (1982). *VLSI systems design for digital signal processing, Vol. 1: signal processing and signal processors*. Englewood Cliffs: Prentice-Hall, Inc.

Boyce, S. (1990). Coarticulatory organization for lip rounding in Turkish and English. *Journal of the Acoustical Society of America*, 88, 2584–95.

Boyce, S., Krakow, R. and Bell-Berti, F. (1991). Phonological underspecification and speech motor organization. *Phonology*, 8, 219–36.

Boyce, S., Krakow, R., Bell-Berti, F. and Gelfer, C. (1990). Converging sources of evidence for dissecting articulatory movements into core gestures. *Journal of Phonetics*, 18, 173–88.

Boysson-Bardies, D. de (1993). Ontogeny of language-specific syllabic production. In D. de Boysson-Bardies, S. de Schonen, P. Jusczyk, P. MacNeilage and J. Morton (eds),

Developmental neurocognition: speech and face processing in the first year of life. Dordrecht: Kluwer Academic Publishers.

Boysson-Bardies, D. de and Vihman, M.M. (1991). Adaptation to language: evidence from babbling and first words in four languages. *Language*, 67, 297–319.

Boysson-Bardies, D. de, Vihman, M.M., Roug-Hellichius, L., Durand, C., Landberg, I. and Arao, F. (1992). Material evidence of infant selection from the target language. In C.A. Ferguson, L. Menn, and C. Stoel-Gammon (eds), *Phonological development: methods, results, implications*. Parkton, MD: York Press.

Boysson-Bardies, D. de, Halle, P., Sagart, L. and Durand, C. (1989). A cross-linguistic investigation of vowel formants in babbling. *Journal of Child Language*, 8, 511–24.

Boysson-Bardies, D. de, Sagart, L., Halle, P. and Durand, C. (1986). Acoustic investigations of cross-language variability in babbling. In B. Lindblom and R. Zetterstrom (eds), *Precursors to early speech*. New York: Stockton Press.

Boysson-Bardies, D. de, Sagart, L., and Durand, C. (1984). Discernible differences in the babbling of infants according to target language. *Journal of Child Language*, 11, 1–15.

Braine, M.D.S. (1976). Review of N.V. Smith; *The acquisition of phonology*. *Language*, 50, 270–99.

Braitenberg, V., Heck, D. and Sultan, F. (forthcoming). The detection and generation of sequences as a key to cerebellar function. Experiments and theory. *Behavioral and Brain Sciences*.

Branderud, P. (1985). Movetrak – a movement tracking system. *Proceedings of the French-Swedish Symposium on Speech*, 113–22, GALF, Grenoble, France, April 22–4, 1985.

Bregman, A.S. (1990). *Auditory scene analysis*. Cambridge, MA: MIT Press.

Bressler, S.L. (1995). Large-scale cortical networks and cognition. *Brain Research Reviews*, 20, 288–304.

Bricker, P.D. and Pruzansky, S. (1976). Speaker recognition. In N.J. Lass (ed.), *Contemporary issues in experimental phonetics*. New York: Academic Press.

Bridle, J.S. and Dodd, L. (1991). An alphanet approach to optimising input transformations for continuous speech recognition. *Proceedings of the IEEE International Conference on Acoustics, Speech and Signal Processing*.

Broderick, P.K., Paul, J.E. and Rennick, R.J. (1975). Semi-automatic speaker identification system. *Proceedings of the 1975 Carnahan Conference on Crime Countermeasures*. Lexington: University of Kentucky.

Brodmann, K. (1914). Physiologie des Gehirns, in die Allgemeine Chirurgie der Gehirnkrankheiten. *Neue Deutsch Chirurgia, Vol. 11* (p. 1). Stuttgart: Ferdinand Enke Verlag.

Brokx, J.P.L. and Nooteboom, S.G. (1982). Intonation and the perceptual separation of simultaneous voices. *Journal of Phonetics*, 10, 23–36.

Brook, D. and Wynne, R.J. (1988). *Signal processing: principles and applications*. London: Edward Arnold.

Brooks, V.B. (1986). *The neural basis of motor control*. New York: Oxford University Press.

Brosses, C. (1765). *Traité de la formation méchanique des langues, et de principes physiques de l'étymologie*. Paris: Chez Saillant, Vincent, Desaint.

Browman, C.P. (1978). Tip of the tongue and slip of the ear: implications for language processing. *UCLA Working Papers in Phonetics*, 42.

Browman, C.P. and Goldstein, L.M. (1985). Dynamic modeling of phonetic structure. In V.A. Fromkin (ed.), *Phonetic linguistics – Essays in honor of Peter Ladefoged* (pp. 35–53). New York: Academic Press.

—— (1986). Towards an articulatory phonology. In C. Ewan and J. Anderson (eds), *Phonology Yearbook 3* (pp. 219–52). Cambridge: Cambridge University Press.

—— (1989). Articulatory gestures as phonological units. *Phonology*, 6, 201–51.

—— (1990a). Gestural specification using dynamically-defined articulatory structures. *Journal of Phonetics*, 18, 299–320.

—— (1990b). Tiers in articulatory phonology, with some implications for casual speech. In J. Kingston and M.E. Beckman (eds), *Papers in laboratory phonology I: between the grammar and the physics of speech* (pp. 341–76). Cambridge: Cambridge University Press.

—— (1992). Articulatory phonology: an overview. *Phonetica*, 49, 155–80.

Brown, G., Currie, K.L. and Kenworthy, J. (1980). *Questions of intonation*. London: Croom Helm.

Brown, J.C. (1991). Calculation of a constant Q spectral transform. *Journal of the Acoustical Society of America*, 89 (1), 425–34.

Bruce, C., Desimone, R. and Gross, C.G. (1981). Visual properties of neurons in a polysensory area in superior temporal sulcus of the macaque. *Journal of Neurophysiology*, 46, 369–84.

Bruce, G. (1977). Swedish word accents in sentence perspective. *Travaux de l'Institut de Linguistique de Lund*. Lund: CWK Gleerup.

—— (1979). Word prosody and sentence prosody in Swedish. *Proceedings of the 9th International Congress of Phonetic Sciences*, 2, 388–94. Copenhagen.

Brücke, E. (1856). *Grundzüge der Physiologie und Systematik der Sprachlaute*. Wien.

Brugge, J.F. and Reale, R.A. (1985). Auditory cortex. In A. Peters and E.G. Jones (eds), *Cerebral cortex*, Vol. 4, (pp. 229–71). New-York: Plenum.

Buckingham, H.W. (1984). Localization of language in the brain. In R.C. Naremore (ed.), *Language Science* (pp. 243–80). San Diego: College-Hill.

Bull, R. and Clifford, B.R. (1984). Earwitness voice recognition accuracy. In G.L. Wells and E.F. Loftus (eds), *Eyewitness testimony: psychological perspectives*. Cambridge: Cambridge University Press.

Burghardt, H. (1973a). Die subjektive Dauer schmalbandiger Schalle bei verschiedenen Frequenzlagen. *Acustica*, 28, 278–84.

—— (1973b). Über die subjektive Dauer von Schallimpulsen und Schallpausen. *Acustica*, 28, 284–90.

Burr, D.J., Ackland, B.D. and Weste, N. (1984). Array configurations for dynamic time warping. *IEEE Transactions on Acoustics, Speech and Signal Processing*, 32, 119–28.

Burton, M.W., Baum, S.R. and Blumstein, S.E. (1989). Lexical effects on the phonetic categorization of speech: the role of acoustic structure. *Journal of Experimental Psychology: Human Perception and Performance*, 15, 567–75.

Busnel, R.G. and Classe, A. (1976). *Whistled languages*. New York: Springer-Verlag.

Butcher, A. and Weiher, E. (1976). An electropalatographic investigation of coarticulation in VCV sequences. *Journal of Phonetics*, 4, 59–74.

Buus, S. and Florentine, M. (1985). Gap detection in normal and impaired listeners: the effect of level and frequency. In A. Michelsen (ed.), *Time resolution in auditory systems* (pp. 159–79). New York: Springer-Verlag.

Buzo, A., Gray, A.H., Gray, R.M. and Markel, J.D. (1980). Speech coding based on vector quantization. *IEEE Transactions on Acoustics, Speech and Signal Processing*, 28, 562–74.

Byrd, D. (1993). 54,000 stops. *UCLA Working Papers in Phonetics*, 83, 97–115.

Cahn, J.E. (1990). The generation of affect in synthesized speech. *Journal of American Voice I/O Society*, 8.

Calford, M.B. and Semple, M.N. (1995). Monaural inhibition in cat auditory cortex. *Journal of Neurophysiology*, 71, 1876–91.

Caliguiri, M.P. (1989). The influence of speaking rate on articulatory hypokinesia in Parkinsonian dysarthria. *Brain and Language*, 36, 493–502.

Campbell, N. (1990). Evidence for a syllable-based model of speech timing. *Proceedings of the 1st International Congress of Spoken Language Processing* (pp. 9–12). Kobe: Acoustic Society of Japan.

—— (1992). Segmental elasticity and timing in Japanese speech. In Y. Tohkura, E. Vatikiotis-Bateson and Y. Sagisaka (eds), *Speech perception, production and linguistic structure* (pp. 403–18). Tokyo, Osaka, Kyoto: Ohmsha; Amsterdam, Washington, Oxford: IOS Press.

Campbell, W.N. and Isard, S.D. (1991). Segment durations in a syllable frame. *Journal of Phonetics*, 19, 37–47.

Cannito, M. (1991). Neurobiological interpretations of spasmodic dysphonia. In D. Vogel and M.P. Cannito (eds), *Treating disordered speech motor control* (pp. 275–317). Austin, TX: Pro-Ed.

Cannito, M.P., Kondraske, G.V. and Johns, D.F. (1991). Oral-facial sensorimotor function in spasmodic dysphonia. In C.A. Moore, K.A. Yorkston and D.R. Beukelman (eds), *Dysarthria and apraxia of speech: perspectives on management* (pp. 205–25). Baltimore, MD: Paul H. Brookes Co.

Cant, N.B. (1992). The cochlear nucleus: neuronal types and their synaptic organization. In D.B. Webster, A.N. Popper and R.R. Fay (eds), *The mammalian auditory pathway: neuroanatomy* (pp. 66–116). New York: Springer-Verlag.

Canter, G.J. (1963). Speech characteristics of patients with Parkinson's disease: I. Intensity, pitch, and duration. *Journal of Speech and Hearing Disorders*, 28, 221–9.

—— (1965a). Speech characteristics of patients with Parkinson's disease: II. Physiological support for speech. *Journal of Speech and Hearing Disorders*, 30, 44–9.

—— (1965b). Speech characteristics of patients with Parkinson's disease: III. Articulation diadochokinesis and overall speech adequacy. *Journal of Speech and Hearing Disorders*, 30, 217–24.

Caplan, D. (1987). *Neurolinguistics and linguistic aphasiology*. Cambridge: Cambridge University Press.

Cariani, P.A. (1995). Physiological correlates of periodicity pitch in the cochlear nucleus. *Abstracts of the Association for Research in Otolaryngology*, 18, 128.

Cariani, P.A. and Delgutte, B. (1993). Response of auditory-nerve fibers to concurrent vowels with same and different fundamental frequencies. *Abstracts of the Association for Research in Otolaryngology*, 16, 373.

—— (1996). Neural correlates of the pitch of complex tones. I. Pitch and pitch salience. *Journal of Neurophysiology* (in press).

Carlson, R. (1991). Duration models in use. *Proceedings of 12th International Congress of Phonetic Sciences*, 4, 278–81. 19–24 August 1991, Aix-en-Provence, France.

Carlson, R., Fant, C.G.M. and Granström, B. (1975). Two-formant models, pitch and vowel perception. In C.G.M. Fant and M.A.A. Tatham (eds), *Auditory analysis and perception of speech* (pp. 55–82). London: Academic.

Carlson, R. and Granström, B. (1976). A text-to-speech system based entirely on rules. *Conference Record of 1976 IEEE International Conference on ASSP*, Philadelphia, PA.

—— (eds) (1982). *The representation of speech in the peripheral auditory system*. Amsterdam: Elsevier.

—— (1986a). A search for durational rules in a real-speech data base. *Phonetica*, 43, 140–54.

—— (1986b). Linguistic processing in the KTH multi-lingual text-to-speech system. *Proceedings ICASSP 1986*, 2403–6. Tokyo.

Carlson, R., Granström, B. and Fant, G. (1970). Some studies concerning perception of isolated vowels. *Speech transmission Laboratory – Quarterly Progress and Status Report*, 2–3, 19–35. Royal Institute of Technology, Stockholm.

Carlson, R., Granström. B. and Hunnicutt, S. (1982). A multi-language text-to-speech module. *Proceedings of ICASSP 82*, 3, 1604–7. Paris.

—— (1991). Multilingual text-to-speech development and applications. In W.A. Ainsworth (ed.), *Advances in speech, hearing and language Processing*. London: JAI Press.

Carlson, R., Granström, B. and Karlsson, I. (1991). Experiments with voice modelling in speech synthesis. *Speech Communication*, 10, 481–9.

Carlson, R., Granström, B. and Lindström, A. (1989). Predicting name pronunciation for a reverse directory service. *Proceedings of European Conference on Speech Communication and Technology*, 1, 113–16. September 26–28, Paris.

Carney, L.H. (1990). Sensitivities of cells in the anteroventral cochlear nucleus of cat to spatiotemporal discharge patterns across primary afferents. *Journal of Neurophysiology*, 64, 437–56.

—— (1994). Spatiotemporal encoding of sound level: models for normal encoding and recruitment of loudness. *Hearing Research*, 76, 31–44.

Carney, L.H. and Geisler, C.D. (1986). A temporal analysis of auditory-nerve fiber responses to spoken stop consonant vowel syllables. *Journal of the Acoustical Society of America*, 79, 1896–914.

Carney, L.H. and Yin, T.C.T. (1989). Responses of low-frequency cells in the inferior colliculus to interaural time differences of clicks: excitatory and inhibitory components. *Journal of Neurophysiology*, 62, 144–61.

Carpentier, F. and Moulines, E. (1990). Pitch-synchronous waveform processing techniques for text-to-speech synthesis using diphones. *Speech communication*, 9 (5/6), 453–67.

Carrel, T. (1993). The effect of amplitude comodulation on extracting sentences from noise: evidence from a variety of contexts. *Journal of the Acoustical Society of America*, 93, 2327.

Carrell, T.D. and Opie, J.M. (1992). The effect of amplitude comodulation on auditory object formation in sentence perception. *Perception and Psychophysics*, 52, 437–45.

Carrow, E., Rivera, V., Mauldin, M. and Shamblin, L. (1974). Deviant speech characteristics in motor neuron disease. *Archives of Otolaryngology*, 100, 212–18.

Caruso, A.J. and Burton, E.K. (1987). Temporal acoustic measures of dysarthria associated with amyotrophic lateral sclerosis. *Journal of Speech and Hearing Research*, 30, 80–7.

Caspary, D.M., Rupert, A.L. and Moushegian, G. (1977). Neuronal coding of vowel sounds in the cochlear nuclei. *Experimental Neurology*, 54, 414–31.

Catford, J.C. (1964). Phonation types: the classification of some laryngeal components of speech production. In D. Abercrombie, D.B. Fry, P.A.D. MacCarthy, N.C. Scott and J.L.M. Trim (eds), *In honour of Daniel Jones* (pp. 26–37). London: Longmans.

—— (1977a). *Fundamental problems in phonetics*. Bloomington, IN: Indiana University Press.

—— (1977b). Mountain of tongues: the languages of the Caucasus. *Annual Review of Anthropology*, 6, 283–314.

Ceder, K. and Lyberg, B. (1992). Yet another rule compiler for text-to-speech conversion? *Proceedings of 1992 International Conference on Spoken and Language Processing* (pp. 1151–4). Banff, Canada.

Cha, C. and Patten, B. (1989). Amyotrophic lateral sclerosis: abnormalities of the tongue on magnetic resonance imaging. *Ann. Neurol.*, 25, 468–72.

Chan, D.S.F. and Brookes, D.M. (1989). Variability of excitation parameters derived from robust closed phase glottal inverse filtering. *Proceedings of European Conference on Speech Communication and Technology*, Paper 33.1, Paris.

Chanaud, R.C. and Powell, A. (1965). Some experiments concerning the hole and ring tone. *Journal of the Acoustical Society of America*, 37, 902–11.

Chandler, S.H. and Goldberg, L.J. (1984). Differentiation of the neural pathways mediating cortically induced and dopaminergic activation of the central pattern generator (CPG) for rhythmical jaw movements in the anesthetized guinea pig. *Brain Research*, 323, 297–301.

Charles-Luce, J. (forthcoming). Cognitive factors involved in incomplete neutralization. *Journal of Phonetics*.

Chater, N., Shillcock, R., Cairns, P. and Levy, J. (submitted). *Bottom-up explanation of phoneme restoration: comment on Elman and McClelland (1988)*.

Chen, H.-C. and Cutler, A. (submitted). *Lexical tone in Cantonese spoken-word recognition*.

Chen, M. (1970). Vowel length variation as a function of the voicing of the consonant environment. *Phonetica*, 22, 129–59.

—— (1995). Acoustic parameters of nasalized vowels in hearing-impaired and normal-hearing speakers. *Journal of the Acoustical Society of America*, 98, 2443–53.

—— (1996). Acoustic Correlates of Nasality, PhD Thesis, Massachusetts Institute of Technology.

Cheng, Y.M. and O'Shaughnessy, D. (1989). Automatic and reliable estimation of glottal closure instant and period. *IEEE Trans ASSP-37*, 1805–15.

Cherry, E.C. (1953). Some experiments on the recognition of speech, with one and with two ears. *Journal of the Acoustical Society of America*, 25, 975–9.

Chiba, T. and Kajiyama, M. (1941). *The vowel, its nature and structure*. Tokyo: Tokyo Kaiseikan.

Childers, D.G., Naik, J.M., Larar, J.N., Krishamurthy, A.K. and Moore, P. (1983). Electroglottography, speech, and ultra-high speed cinematography. In I.R. Titze and R.C. Scherer (eds), *Vocal fold physiology* (pp. 202–20). Denver: The Denver Center for Performing Arts.

Chistovich, L.A. and Lublinskaya, V.V. (1979). The centre of gravity effect in vowel spectra and critical distance between the formants: psychoacoustical study of the perception of vowel-like stimuli. *Hearing Research*, 1, 185–95.

Chistovich, L.A., Lublinskaya, V.V., Malinnikova, T.G., Ogorodnikova, E.A., Stoljarova, E.I. and Zhukov, S.J.S. (1982). Temporal processing of peripheral auditory patterns of speech. In R. Carlson and B. Granström (eds), *The representation of speech in the peripheral auditory system* (pp. 165–80). Amsterdam: Elsevier.

Chistovich, L.A., Sheikin, R. and Lublinskaya, V.V. (1979). 'Centers of gravity' and spectral peaks as determinants of vowel quality. In B. Lindblom and S. Öhman (eds), *Frontiers of speech communication research* (pp. 143–57). London: Academic Press.

Choi, J.D. and Keating, P. (1991). Vowel-to-vowel coarticulation in three Slavic languages. *UCLA Working Papers in Phonetics*, 78, 78–86.

Chomsky, N. (1972). *Language and mind*. New York: Harcourt Brace Jovanovich.

Chomsky, N. and Halle, M. (1968). *Sound pattern of English*. New York: Harper and Row.

Christianson, R., Lufkin, R. and Hanafee, W. (1987). Normal magnetic resonance imaging anatomy of the tongue, oropharynx, hypopharynx and larynx. *Dysphagia*, 1, 119–27.

Church, K. (1986). Stress assignment in letter to sound rules for speech synthesis. *Proceedings of ICASSP-86*, 4, 2423–6.

—— (1987). Phonological parsing and lexical retrieval. *Cognition*, 25, 54–69.

Clark, C., Bladon, A. and Mickey, K. (1986). Analysis and perception of sibilant fricatives: Shona data. *Journal of the Acoustical Society of America*, 80S1, S125.

Clark, J. and Yallop, C. (1990). *An introduction to phonetics and phonology*. Oxford/Cambridge, MA.: B. Blackwell.

Clements, G.N. (1985). The geometry of phonological features. *Phonology Yearbook*, 2, 225–52.

Clements, G.N. (1990). The role of the sonority cycle in core syllabification. In J. Kingston and M. Beckman (eds), *Papers in laboratory phonology*, 1, 283–333. Cambridge: Cambridge University Press.

Clifford, B.R. (1980). Voice identification by human listeners: on earwitness reliability. *Law and Human Behavior*, 4, 373–94.

Clifford, B.R., Rathborn, H. and Bull, R. (1981). The effects of delay on voice recognition accuracy. *Law and Human Behavior*, 5, 201–8.

Clumeck, H. (1976). Patterns of soft palate movements in six languages. *Journal of Phonetics*, 4, 337–51.

Cohen, A., Rossignol, S. and Grillner, S. (eds) (1988). *Neural control of rhythmic movements in vertebrates*. New York: Wiley.

Cohen, H. and Forget, H. (1995). Auditory cerebral lateralization following cross-gender hormone therapy. *Cortex*, 31, 565–573.

Cohen, H.M. (1989). 'Phonological structures for speech recognition'. Ph.D. Thesis, Computer Science Division, University of California, Berkeley, U.S.A.

Cohen, L. (1989). Time-frequency distributions – a review. *Proceedings of IEEE*, 77 (7), 941–81.

Cohen, M.M. and Massaro, D.W. (1993). Modelling coarticulation in synthetic visual speech. In N.M. Thalmannand and D. Thalmann (eds), *Computer animation 1993*. Tokyo: Springer Verlag.

Cohn, A.C. (1993). Nasalisation in English: phonology or phonetics. *Phonology*, 10, 43–81.

Coker, C.H. (1976). A model for articulatory dynamics and control. *Proceedings of IEEE*, 64, 452–60.

Cole, D.T. (1955). *An introduction to Tswana grammar*. London: Longmans, Green.

Cole, K., Gracco, V.L. and Abbs, J. (1984). Autogenic and nonautogenic sensorimotor actions in the control of multiarticulate hand movements. *Experimental Brain Research*, 56, 582–5.

Cole, R.A. and Jakimik, J. (1980). A model of speech perception. In R.A. Cole (ed.), *Perception and production of fluent speech* (pp. 133–63). Hillsdale, NJ: Erlbaum.

Cole, R.A. and Scott, B. (1974). Toward a theory of speech perception. *Psychological Review*, 81, 348–74.

Coleman, R.O. (1971). Male and female voice quality and its relationship to vowel formant frequencies. *Journal of Speech and Hearing Research*, 14, 565–77.

—— (1976). A comparison of the contributions of two voice quality characteristics to the perception of maleness and femaleness in the voice. *Journal of Speech and Hearing Research*, 19, 168–80.

Collier, R. (1975). Perceptual and linguistic tolerance in intonation. *International Review of Applied Linguistics*, 13, 293–308.

—— (1990). Multi-language intonation synthesis. *Journal of Phonetics*, 19 (1).

Collier, R. and Hart, J.'t (1972). Perceptual experiments on Dutch intonation. In A. Rigault and R. Charbonneau (eds), *Proceedings of the 7th international Congress of Phonetic Sciences* (pp. 880–4). The Hague, Paris: Mouton.

Collier, R., Lisker, L., Hirose, H. and Ushijima, T. (1979). Voicing in intervocalic stops and fricatives in Dutch. *Journal of Phonetics*, 7, 357–73.

Combes, J.M., Grossmann, A. and Tchamitchian, P. (eds) (1990). *Wavelets: time-frequency methods and phase space* (2nd edn). Berlin: Springer.

Connell, P. and Thompson, C. (1986). Flexibility of single-subject experimental designs. *Journal of Speech and Hearing Disorders*, 51, 204–14.

Connine, C.M. and Clifton, C. (1987). Interactive use of lexical information in speech perception. *Journal of Experimental Psychology: Human Perception and Performance*, 13, 291–9.

Connine, C.M., Clifton, C. and Cutler, A. (1987). Effects of lexical stress on phonetic categorization. *Phonetica*, 44, 133–46.

Conrad, B. and Schönle, P. (1979). Speech and respiration. *Archives of Psychiatry and Neurological Sciences*, 226, 251–68.

Conrad, W.A. (1985). Collapsible tube model of the larynx. In I.R. Titze and R.C. Scherer (eds), *Vocal fold physiology: biomechanics, acoustics and phonatory control* (pp. 328–48). Denver: Denver Center for the Performing Arts.

Cooke, J. (1980). The organization of simple, skilled movements. In G. Stelmach and J. Requin (eds), *Tutorials in motor behavior* (pp. 199–212). Amsterdam: North-Holland.

Cooke, M., Beet, S. and Crawford, S. (eds) (1993). *Visual representations of speech signals*. Chichester/New York: Wiley.

Cooley, J.W. and Tukey, J.W. (1965). An algorithm for the machine calculation of complex fourier series. *Mathematics of Computation*, 19, 297–301.

Cooper, D. and Folkins, J. (1981). *The spatial sampling problem in electromyographic studies of speech musculature.* Presented at 102nd meeting of Acoustical Society of America, Miami Beech, December, 1981.

—— (1982). *The temporal sampling problem in electromyographic studies of speech musculature.* Presented at 103rd meeting of Acoustical Society of America, Chicago, April, 1982.

Cooper, F.S., Delattre, P., Liberman, A.M., Borst, J. and Gerstman, L. (1952). Some experiments on the perception of synthetic speech sounds. *Journal of the Acoustical Society of America*, 24, 597–606.

Cooper, W. and Paccia-Cooper, J. (1980). *Syntax and speech.* Cambridge, MA: Harvard University Press.

Court de Gebelin (1776). *Histoire naturelle de la parole ou pris de l'origine du language & de la grammaire universelle.* Paris: Publisher.

Cowie, R.I. and Douglas-Cowie, E. (1983). Speech production in profound post-lingual deafness. In M.E. Lutman and M.P. Haggard (eds), *Hearing science and hearing disorders* (pp. 183–231). New York: Academic Press.

Craig, C. (1992). Effects of aging on time-gated word recognition performance. *Journal of Speech and Hearing Research*, 55, 234–8.

Cranen, B. (1991). Simultaneous modeling of EGG, PGG and glottal flow. In J. Gauffin and B. Hammerberg (eds), *Vocal fold physiology* (pp. 57–64). San Diego: Singular Publication Group Inc..

Cranen, B. and Boves, L. (1985). Pressure measurements during speech production using semiconductor miniature pressure transducers: impact on models for speech production, *Journal of the Acoustical Society of America*, 77, 1543–51.

—— (1987). On subglottal formant analysis. *Journal of the Acoustical Society of America*, 81, 734–46.

—— (1988). On the measurement of glottal flow. *Journal of the Acoustical Society of America*, 84, 888–900.

Crochiere, R.E. and Rabiner, L.R. (1983). *Multirate digital signal processing.* Englewood Cliffs: Prentice-Hall, Inc..

Crosson, B.A. (1992). *Subcortical functions in language and memory.* New York: Guildord Press.

Cruttenden, A. (1970). A phonetic study of babbling. *British Journal of Communication Disorders*, 5, 110–17.

Crystal, D. (1969). *Prosodic systems and intonation in English.* Cambridge: Cambridge University Press.

—— (1972). The intonation system of English. In D.L. Bolinger (ed.), *Intonation* (pp. 11–136). Middlesex: Penguin, Harmondsworth.

Crystal, T.H. and House, A.S. (1982). Segmental durations in connected-speech signals: preliminary results. *Journal of the Acoustical Society of America*, 72, 705–16.

—— (1988a). Segmental durations in connected-speech signals: current results. *Journal of the Acoustical Society of America*, 83, 1553–73.

—— (1988b). Segmental durations in connected-speech signals: syllabic stress. *Journal of the Acoustical Society of America*, 83, 1574–85.

—— (1988c). The duration of American English vowels: an overview. *Journal of Phonetics*, 16, 263–84.

—— (1988d). The duration of American English stop consonants: an overview. *Journal of Phonetics*, 16, 285–94.

—— (1990). Articulation rate and the duration of syllables and stress groups in connected speech. *Journal of the Acoustical Society of America*, 88, 101–12.

Cutler, A. (1976). Phoneme monitoring reaction time as a function of preceding intonation contour. *Perception & Psychophysics*, 20, 55–60.

—— (1986). Forbear is a homophone: lexical prosody does not constrain lexical access. *Language and Speech*, 29, 201–20.

—— (1987). Components of prosodic effects in speech recognition. *Proceedings of the 11th International Congress of Phonetic Sciences*, 1, 84–7, Tallinn, Estonia.

Cutler, A. and Butterfield, S. (1992). Rhythmic cues to speech segmentation: evidence from juncture misperception. *Journal of Memory and Language*, 31, 218–36.

Cutler, A. and Chen, H.-C. (1995). Phonological similarity effects in Cantonese word recognition. *Proceedings of the 13th International Congress of Phonetic Sciences*, 1, 106–9, Stockholm.

—— (in press) Lexical tone in Cantonese spoken-word processing. *Perception and Psychophysics*.

Cutler, A. and Clifton, C.E. (1984). The use of prosodic information in word recognition. In H. Bouma and D.G. Bouwhuis (eds), *Attention and performance X: control of language processes* (pp. 183–96). Hillsdale, NJ: Erlbaum.

Cutler, A. and Darwin, C.J. (1981). Phoneme-monitoring reaction time and preceding prosody: effects of stop closure duration and of fundamental frequency. *Perception & Psychophysics*, 29, 217–24.

Cutler, A., Mehler, J., Norris, D. and Segui, J. (1986). The syllable's differing role in the segmentation of French and English. *Journal of Memory and Language*, 25, 385–400.

—— (1987). Phoneme identification and the lexicon. *Cognitive Psychology*, 19, 141–77.

—— (1992). The monolingual nature of speech segmentation by bilinguals. *Cognitive Psychology*, 24, 381–410.

Cutler, A. and Norris, D. (1979). Monitoring sentence comprehension. In W.E. Cooper and E.C.T. Walker (eds), *Sentence processing: psycholinguistic studies presented to Merrill Garrett* (pp. 113–34). Hillsdale, NJ: Erlbaum.

—— (1988). The role of strong syllables in segmentation for lexical access. *Journal of Experimental Psychology: Human Perception and Performance*, 14, 113–21.

Cutler, A. and Otake, T. (1994). Mora or phoneme? Further evidence for language-specific listening. *Journal of Memory and Language*, 33, 824–44.

Dagenais, P. and Critz-Crosby, P. (1992). Comparing tongue positioning by normal-hearing and hearing-impaired children during vowel production. *Journal of Speech and Hearing Research*, 35, 35–44.

Damasio, A.R. (1989). Time-locked multiregional retroactivation: A system-level proposal for the neural substrates of recall and recognition. *Cognition*, 33, 25–62.

Damasio, A.R., Damasio, H., Rizzo, M., Varney, N. and Gersch, F. (1982). Aphasia with nonhemorrhagic lesions in the basal ganglia and internal capsule. *Archives of Neurology*, 35, 15–20.

Dang, J., Honda, K. and Suzuki, H. (1994). Morphological and acoustical analysis of the nasal and the paranasal cavities. *Journal of the Acoustical Society of America*, 96, 2088–100.

Daniloff, R. and Hammarberg, R. (1973). On defining coarticulation. *Journal of Phonetics*, 1, 239–48.

Daniloff, R. and Moll, K. (1968). Coarticulation of lip rounding. *Journal of Speech and Hearing Research*, 11, 707–21.

Darley, F.L., Aronson, A.E. and Brown, J.R. (1969a). Differential diagnostic patterns of dysarthria. *Journal of Speech and Hearing Research*, 12, 246–69.

—— (1969b). Clusters of deviant speech dimensions in the dysarthrias. *Journal of Speech and Hearing Research*, 12, 462–96.

—— (1975). *Motor speech disorders*. Philadelphia, PA: Saunders.

Dart, S. (1987). An aerodynamic study of Korean stop consonants: measurements and modeling. *Journal of the Acoustical Society of America*, 81 (1), 138–47.

—— (1991). Articulatory and acoustic properties of apical and laminal articulations. *UCLA Working Papers in Phonetics*, 79, 1–155.

Darwin, C.J. (1975). On the dynamic use of prosody in speech perception. In A. Cohen and S.G. Nooteboom (eds), *Structure and process in speech perception* (pp. 178–93). Berlin: Springer Verlag.

—— (1992). Listening to two things at once. In M.E.H. Schouten (ed.), *The auditory processing of speech* (pp. 133–47). Berlin: Mouton-De Gruyter.

Darwin, E. (1803). *The temple of nature*. London.

Daum, I. and Ackermann, H. (1995). Cerebellar contributions to cognition. *Behavioural Brain Research*, 67, 201–10.

Davidoff, R.A. (1990). The pyramidal tract. *Neurology*, 40, 332–9.

Davies, D.V. and Davies, F. (1962). *Grays anatomy* (33rd edn). London: Longmans, Green and Co. Ltd..

Davies, P.O.A.L. (1991). *Program suite VOAC*. Unpublished program documentation, Institute of Sound and Vibration Research, University of Southampton.

Davies, P.O.A.L., McGowan, R.S. and Shadle, C.H. (1993). Practical flow duct acoustics Applied to the vocal tract. In I.R. Titze (ed.), *Vocal fold physiology: frontiers in basic science* (pp. 93–142). San Diego: Singular Publishing Group Inc..

Davis, B.L. and MacNeilage, P.F. (1990). Acquisition of correct vowel production: a quantitative case study. *Journal of Speech and Hearing Research*, 33, 16–27.

—— (1994). Organization of babbling: a case study. *Language and Speech*, 37, 341–55.

—— (1995). The articulatory basis of babbling. *Journal of Speech and Hearing Research*.

Dawkins, R. (1986). *The blind watchmaker*. New York: Norton.

De Boer, E. (1976). On the "residue" and auditory pitch perception. In W.D. Keidel and W.D. Neff (eds), *Handbook of sensory physiology*, V/3 (pp. 479–583). Berlin: Springer-Verlag.

DeCasper, A.J. and Fifer, W.P. (1980). Of human bonding: newborns prefer their mother's voice. *Science*, 208, 1174–6.

Delattre, P. (1954). Les attributs acoustiques de la nasalité vocalique et consonantique. *Studia Linguistica*, 8, 103–9.

Delattre, P., Liberman, A.M. and Cooper, F.S. (1955). Acoustic loci and transitional cues for consonants. *Journal of the Acoustical Society of America*, 27, 769–73.

—— (1955). Acoustic loci and transitional cues for stop consonants. *Journal of the Acoustical Society of America*, 27, 769–73.

Delgutte, B. (1980). Representation of speech-like sounds in the discharge patterns of auditory-nerve fibers. *Journal of the Acoustical Society of America*, 68, 843–57.

—— (1982). Some correlates of phonetic distinctions at the level of the auditory nerve. In R. Carlson and B. Granström (eds), *The representation of speech in the peripheral auditory system* (pp. 131–50). Amsterdam: Elsevier.

—— (1984). Speech coding in the auditory nerve II: processing schemes for vowel-like sounds. *Journal of the Acoustical Society of America*, 75, 879–86.

—— (1986). Analysis of French stop consonants with a model of the peripheral auditory system. In J.S. Perkell and D.H. Klatt (eds), *Invariance and variability of speech processes* (pp. 163–77). Hillsdale, NJ: Erlbaum.

—— (1987). Peripheral auditory processing of speech information: implications from a physiological study of intensity discrimination. In M.E.H. Schouten (ed.), *The psychophysics of speech perception* (pp. 333–53). Dordrecht: Nijhof.

—— (1995). Physiological models for basic auditory percepts. In H. Hawkins and T. McMullen (eds), *Auditory computation*. New-York: Springer-Verlag.

Delgutte, B. and Cariani, P.A. (1992). Coding of the pitch of harmonic and inharmonic complex tones in the interspike intervals of auditory-nerve fibers. In M.E.H. Schouten (ed.), *The auditory processing of speech* (pp. 37–45). Berlin: Mouton-De Gruyter.

Delgutte, B. and Kiang, N.Y.S. (1984a). Speech coding in the auditory nerve I: vowel-like sounds. *Journal of the Acoustical Society of America*, 75, 866–78.

—— (1984b). Speech coding in the auditory nerve III: voiceless fricative consonants. *Journal of the Acoustical Society of America*, 75, 887–96.

—— (1984c). Speech coding in the auditory nerve IV: sounds with consonant-like dynamic characteristics. *Journal of the Acoustical Society of America*, 75, 897–907.

—— (1984d). Speech coding in the auditory nerve V: vowels in background noise. *Journal of the Acoustical Society of America*, 75, 908–18.

Dell, G.S. (1986). A spreading activation theory of retrieval in sentence production. *Psychological Review*, 93, 283–321.

Dell, G., Juliano, C. and Govindjee, A. (1993). Structure and content in language production: a theory of frame constraints in phonological speech errors. *Cognitive Science*, 17, 149–95.

Dell, G.S. and Newman, J.E. (1980). Detecting phonemes in fluent speech. *Journal of Verbal Learning and Verbal Behavior*, 19, 608–23.

Delogu, C., Conte, S., Paoloni, A. and Sementina, C. (1992). Two different methodologies for evaluating the comprehension of synthetic passages. *Proceedings of 1992 International Conference on Spoken Language Processing* (pp. 1231–4). Banff, Canada.

Delong, M.R., Georgopoulos, A.P., Crutcher, M.D., Mitchell, S.J., Richardson, R.T. and Alexander, G.E. (1984). Functional organization of the basal ganglia: contributions of single-cell recording studies. In E.V. Evarts (ed.), *Functions of the basal ganglia* (pp. 1017–61). London: Pitman.

Demb, J.B., Desmond, J.E., Wagner, A.D., Vaidya, C.J., Glover, G.H. and Gabriele, J.D. (1995). Semantic encoding and retrieval in the left inferior prefrontal cortex: A functional MRI study of task difficulty and process specificity. *Journal of Neuroscience*, 15, 5870–78.

Demonet, J.F., Price, C., Wise, R. and Frackowiak, R.S. (1994). Differential activation of right and left posterior sylvian regions by semantic and phonological tasks: A positron-emission tomography study in normal human subjects. *Neuroscience Letters*, 182, 25–8.

Demonet, J.F., Wise, R. and Frackowiak, R.S.J. (1993). Language functions explored in normal subjects by positron emission tomography. *Human Brain Mapping*, 1, 39–47.

Denes, P.B. and Pinson, E.N. (1973). *The speech chain: the physics and biology of spoken language*. New York: Anchor Press.

Deng, L. and Geisler, C.D. (1987). Response of auditory-nerve fibers to nasal consonant-vowel syllables. *Journal of the Acoustical Society of America*, 82, 1977–88.

Deng, L., Geisler, C.D. and Greenberg, S. (1988). A composite model of the auditory periphery for the processing of speech. *Journal of Phonetics*, 16, 109–23.

Dermaut, L.R. and O'Reilly, M.I.T. (1978). Changes in anterior facial height in girls during puberty. *Angle Orthodontist*, 48, 163–71.

Derwing, B.L. (1992). A "pause-break" task for eliciting syllable boundary judgments from literate and illiterate speakers: preliminary results for five diverse languages. *Language and Speech*, 35, 219–35.

D'Esposito, M., Detre, J.A., Alsop, D.C., Shin, R.K., Atlas, S. and Grossman, M. (1995). The neural basis of the central executive system of working memory. *Nature*, 368, 279–81.

Deterding, D.H. (1990). 'Speaker normalisation for speaker recognition'. PhD dissertation, University of Cambridge.

Devijer, P.A. and Kittler, J. (1982). *Pattern recognition: a statistical approach*. Englewood Cliffs: Prentice-Hall.

Dewson, J.H. III (1964). Speech sound discrimination by cats. *Science*, 144, 555–6.

Dickson, D.R. and Maue-Dickson, W. (1982). *Anatomical and physiological bases of speech*. Boston: Little, Brown and Company.

Dieber, M.P., Passingham, R.E., Colebatch, J.G., Friston, K.J., Nixon, P.D. and Frackowiak, R.S.J. (1991). Cortical areas and the selection of movement: a study with positron emission tomography. *Experimental Brain Research*, 84, 393–402.

Diener, H.-C. and Dichgans, J. (1992). Pathophysiology of cerebellar ataxia. *Movement Disorders*, 7, 95–108.

Diffloth, G. (1985). The registers of Mon vs. the spectrographist's tones. *UCLA Working Papers in Phonetics*, 60, 55–8.

Dirksen, A. and Quené, H. (1993). Prosodic analysis: the next generation. In V.J. van Heuven and L.C.W. Pols (eds), *Analysis and synthesis of speech* (pp. 131–46). Berlin, New York: Mouton de Gruyter.

Disner, S.F. (1983). Vowel quality: the relation between universal and language-specific factors. *UCLA Working Papers in Phonetics*, 58.

Divenyi, P.L. and Hirsh, I.J. (1974). Identification of temporal order in three-tone sequences. *Journal of the Acoustical Society of America*, 56, 144–51.

Dixit, R.P. (1978). Peak magnitude of supraglottal air pressure associated with affricated and nonaffricated stop consonant productions in Hindi. *Journal of Phonetics*, 6, 353–65.

—— (1987). Mechanisms for voicing and aspiration: Hindi and other languages compared. *UCLA Working Papers in Phonetics*, 67, 49–102.

—— (1989). Glottal gestures in Hindi plosives. *Journal of Phonetics*, 17, 213–37.

Dixit, R.P., Bell-Berti, F. and Harris, K. (1987). Palatoglossus activity during nasal/nonnasal vowels of Hindi. *Phonetica*, 44, 210–26.

Doble, E., Leiter, J., Knuth, S., Daubenspeck, J. and Bartlett, D. (1985). A noninvasive intraoral electromyographic electrode for genioglossus muscle. *Journal of Applied Physiology*, 58, 1378–82.

Doddington, G.R. (1985). Speaker recognition – identifying people by their voices. *Proceedings of the IEEE*, 73, 1651–64.

Doebelin, E.O. (1983). *Measurement systems: application and design* (3rd edn). London: McGraw-Hill International Book Co.

Dogil, G. (1988). *Linguistic phonetic features: a study in systematic phonetics*. L.A.U.D.: Duisburg.

Doherty, E.T. (1976). An evaluation of selected acoustic parameters for use in speaker identification. *Journal of Phonetics*, 4, 321–6.

Doherty, E.T. and Hollien, H. (1978). Multiple factor speaker identification of normal and distorted speech. *Journal of Phonetics*, 6, 1–8.

Doke, C.M. (1931). *A comparative study in Shona phonetics*. Johannesburg: University of the Witwatersrand Press.

Dolansky, L.O. (1955). An instantaneous pitch period indicator. *Journal of the Acoustical Society of America*, 27, 67–72.

Dolansky, L. and Tjernlund, P. (1968). On certain irregularities of voiced speech waveforms. *IEEE Trans.* AU-16.

Donald, M. (1991). *Origin of the modern mind: three stages in the evolution of culture and cognition*. Cambridge: Cambridge University Press.

Donegan, P.J. and Stampe, D. (1979). The study of natural phonology. In D.A. Dinnsen (ed.), *Current approaches to phonological theory*. Bloomington, IN: Indiana University Press.

Dooling, R.J., Okanoya, K. and Brown, S.D. (1989). Speech perception by budgerigars (melopsitaccus undulatus): the voiced-voiceless distinction. *Perception and Psychophysics*, 46, 65–71.

Dorman, M.F., Raphael, L.J. and Liberman, A.M. (1979). Some experiments on the sound of silence in phonetic perception. *Journal of the Acoustical Society of America*, 65, 1518–32.

Draper, M.H., Ladefoged, P. and Whitteridge, D. (1959). Respiratory muscles in speech. *Journal of Speech and Hearing Research*, 2, 16–27.

Dudgeon, D.E. and Mersereau, R.M. (1984). *Multidimensional digital signal processing*. Englewood Cliffs: Prentice-Hall, Inc.

Dudley, H. and Balashek, S. (1958). Automatic recognition of phonetic patterns in speech. *Journal of the Acoustical Society of America*, 30, 721–32.

Duez, D. (1991). Some evidence of second formant locus-nucleus patterns in spontaneous speech in French. *PERILUS*, XII, University of Stockholm, 109–26.

Duffy, J.R. (1995). *Motor speech disorders*. St. Louis, MO (USA): Mosby Year Book, Inc.

Dunn, M. (1993). 'The phonetics and phonology of geminate consonants: a production study'. Ph.D. dissertation, Yale University, New Haven.

Dupoux, E. and Mehler, J. (1990). Monitoring the lexicon with normal and compressed speech: frequency effects and the prelexical code. *Journal of Memory and Language*, 29, 316–35.

Durlach, N.I. and Colburn, H.S. (1978). Binaural phenomena. In E.C. Carterette and M.P. Friedman (eds), *Handbook of perception* (pp. 365–466). New York: Academic.

Duvoisin, R.C. (1986). Etiology of Parkinson's disease: current concepts. *Clinical Neuropharmacology*, 9 (Suppl. 1), S3–S11.

Dworkin, J.P. (1991). *Motor speech disorders: a treatment guide*. St. Louis, MO: Mosby Year Book.

Eagleson, R. (1994). Forensic analysis of personal written texts: a case study. In J. Gibbon (ed.), *Language and the law*. London: Longman.

Echols, C.H. (1993). A perceptually-based model of children's earliest productions. *Cognition*, 46, 245–96.

Echols, C.H. and Newport, E.L. (1992). The role of stress and position in determining first words. *Language Acquisition*, 2, 189–220.

Eddins, D.A., Hall, J.W. and Grose, J.H. (1992). Detection of temporal gaps as a function of frequency region and absolute noise bandwidth. *Journal of the Acoustical Society of America*, 91, 1069–77.

Edelman, G. (1992). *Bright air, brilliant fire*. New York: Basic Books.

—— (1993). Neural Darwinism: selection and reentrant signaling in higher brain function. *Neuron*, 10, 115–125.

Edwards, J., Beckman, M.E. and Fletcher, J. (1991). The articulatory phonetics of final lengthening. *Journal of the Acoustical Society of America*, 89, 369–82.

Eefting, W.Z.F. (1991). 'Timing in talking. Tempo variation in production and its role in perception'. Ph.D. thesis. Utrecht: Utrecht University.

Eek, A. (1973). Observations in Estonian palatalization: an articulatory study. *Estonian Papers in Phonetics*, 18–36.

Eggermont, J.J. (1995). Representation of a voice onset time continuum in primary auditory cortex of the cat. *Journal of the Acoustical Society of America*, 98, 911–920.

Ehret, G. (1992). Preadaptations in the auditory system of mammals for phonetic recognition. In M.E.H. Schouten (ed.), *The auditory processing of speech* (pp. 99–112). Berlin: Mouton-De Gruyter.

Eimas, P.D. and Corbit, J.D. (1973). Selective adaptation of linguistic feature detectors. *Cognitive Psychology*, 4, 99–109.

Eimas, P.D., Marcovitz Hornstein, S.B. and Payton, P. (1990). Attention and the role of dual codes in phoneme monitoring. *Journal of Memory and Language*, 29, 160–80.

Eimas, P.D. and Nygaard, L.C. (1992). Contextual coherence and attention in phoneme monitoring. *Journal of Memory and Language*, 31, 375–95.

Eimas. P.D., Siqueland, E.R., Jusczyk, P.W. and Vigorito, J. (1971). Speech perception in infants. *Science*, 171, 303–6.

Elbers, L. (1982). Operating principles in repetitive babbling: a cognitive continuity approach. *Cognition*, 12, 45–63.

Elert, C.-C. (1964). *Phonologic studies of quantity in Swedish*. Stockholm: Almqvist and Wiksell.

Ellis, A.J. (1877). *Speech in song, being the singer's pronouncing primer of the principal European languages for which vocal music is usually composed*. London: Novello, Ewer and Co.

Elman, J.L. and McClelland, J.L. (1986). Exploiting lawful variability in the speech wave. In J.S. Perkell and D.H. Klatt (eds), *Invariance and variability of speech processes* (pp. 360–80). Hillsdale, NJ: Erlbaum.

—— (1988). Cognitive penetration of the mechanisms of perception: compensation for coarticulation of lexically restored phonemes. *Journal of Memory and Language*, 27, 143–65.

Emery, J.L. (ed.) (1979). *The anatomy of the developing lung.* London: Heinemann; Spastics International Medical Publications.

Engstrand, O. (1981). Acoustic constraints or invariant input representation? An experimental study of selected articulatory movements and targets. *Reports from Uppsala University Department of Linguistics,* 7, 67–95.

—— (1983). Articulatory coordination in selected VCV utterances: a means-end view. *Reports from Uppsala University Department of Linguistics,* 10, 1–145.

—— (1989). Towards an electropalatographic specification of consonant articulation in Swedish. *PERILUS,* X, University of Stockholm, 115–56.

Engstrand, O. and Krull, D. (1994). Durational correlates of quantity in Swedish, Finnish and Estonian: cross-language evidence for a theory of adaptive dispersion. *Phonetica,* 51, 80–91.

Enlow, D.H. and Harris, D.B. (1964). A study of the postnatal growth of the mandible. *American Journal of Orthodontics,* 50, 25.

Erickson, D. and Fujimura, O. (1992). Acoustic and articulatory correlates of contrastive emphasis in repeated corrections. *Proceedings of 1992 International Conference on Spoken Language Processing,* 835–7.

Erickson, D., Liberman, M. and Niimi, S. (1977). The geniohyoid and the role of the strap muscle. *Haskins Laboratories Status Report on Speech Research,* SR-49, 97–102.

Eskénazi, M. and Lacheret-Dujour, A. (1991). Exploration of individual strategies in continuous speech. *Speech Communication,* 10, 249–64.

Esling, J.H. (1978). 'Voice quality in Edinburgh: a sociolinguistic and phonetic study'. Ph.D. dissertation, University of Edinburgh.

Estill, J., Fujimura, O., Sawada, M. and Beechler, K. (1995). Temporal perturbation and voice qualities. *Proceedings of IXth Vocal Fold Physiology Conference,* San Diego: Singular Publishing Co., Inc.

Evans, E.F. (1981). The dynamic range problem: place and time coding at the level of the cochlear nerve and nucleus. In J. Syka and L. Aitkin (eds), *Neuronal mechanisms of hearing* (pp. 69–95). New York: Plenum.

—— (1983). Pitch and cochlear nerve fibre temporal discharge patterns. In R. Klinke and R. Hartmann (eds), *Hearing – physiological bases and psychophysics* (pp. 140–6). Berlin: Springer-Verlag.

Evans, E.F. and Wilson, J.P. (1973). The frequency selectivity of the cochlea. In A.R. Møller (ed.), *Basic mechanisms in hearing* (pp. 519–54). London: Academic.

Everett, D.L. (1982). Phonetic rarities in Pirahã. *Journal of the International Phonetic Association,* 12, 94–6.

Ewan, W.G. and Krones, R. (1974). Measuring larynx movement using the thyroumbrometer. *Journal of Phonetics,* 2, 327–35.

Ewanowski, S.J. (1964). 'Selected motor speech behavior of patients with Parkinsonism'. Ph.D. dissertation, University of Wisconsin-Madison.

Faber, A. and Raphael, L. (1989). *Relationship of recorded emg signals to within and cross utterance acoustic variation.* Presented at Acoustical Society of America Conference, Syracuse, NY, May, 1989.

—— (submitted). *Posterior tongue grooving in front vowels: electromyographic evidence.*

Fairbanks, G., Herbert, E.S. and Hammond, J.M. (1949). An acoustical study of vocal pitch in seven and eight-year-old girls. *Child Development,* 20, 71–8.

Fairbanks, G., Wiley, J.H. and Lassman, F.M. (1949). An acoustical study of vocal pitch in seven and eight-year-old boys. *Child Development,* 20, 63–9.

Fant, G. (1956). On the predictability of formant levels and spectrum envelopes from formant frequencies. In M. Hall (ed.), *For Roman Jakobson: essays on the occasion of his sixtieth birthday.* The Hague: Mouton and Co.

—— (1960). *Acoustic theory of speech production.* The Hague: Mouton and Co.

—— (1962). Descriptive analysis of the acoustic aspects of speech. *Logos,* 5, 3–17. (Reprinted in Fant, F. (1973). *Speech sounds and features* (pp. 17–23). Cambridge, MA: MIT Press).

—— (1965). Formants and cavities. *Proceedings of the 5th International Congress of Phonetic Sciences* (pp. 120–41). Munster, 1964. Basel/New York: S. Karger.

—— (1968). Analysis and synthesis of speech processes. In B. Malmberg (ed.), *Manual of Phonetics* (pp. 173–277). Amsterdam: North-Holland.

—— (1970). Analysis and synthesis of speech processes. In B. Malmberg (ed.), *Manual of phonetics* (pp. 173–277). Amsterdam: North Holland.

—— (1972). Vocal tract wall effects, losses and resonance bandwidths. *Speech Transmission Laboratory – Quarterly Progress and Status Report* (Stockholm: Royal Institute of Technology), 2–3, 28–52.

—— (1973). A note on vocal tract size factors and nonuniform F-pattern scalings. In G. Fant, *Speech sounds and features*. Cambridge, MA: MIT Press.

—— (1979a). Glottal source and excitation analysis. *Speech Transmission Laboratory – Quarterly Progress and Status Report*, 1, 85–107. Royal Institute of Technology, Stockholm.

—— (1979b). Vocal source analysis – a progress report. *Speech Transmission Laboratory – Quarterly Progress and Status Report*, 3–4, 31–54. Royal Institute of Technology, Stockholm.

—— (1980). The relations between area functions and the acoustic signal. *Phonetica*, 57, 55–86.

—— (1982). The voice source – acoustic modeling. *Speech Transmission Laboratory – Quarterly Progress and Status Report*, 4, 28–48. Royal Institute of Technology, Stockholm.

Fant, G. and Kruckenberg, A. (1988a). Contributions to temporal analysis of read Swedish. *Department of Linguistics, Working papers No. 34* (pp. 37–41). Lund: Lund University.

—— (1988b). Some durational correlates of Swedish prosody. *Proceedings of the 7th FASE Symposium*, Vol. 2 (pp. 495–503). Edinburgh.

—— (1989). Preliminaries to the study of Swedish prose reading and reading style. *Speech Transmission Laboratory – Quarterly Progress and Status Report*, 2, 1–83. Royal Institute of Technology, Stockholm.

Fant, G., Kruckenberg, A., Liljencrants, J. and Båvegård, M. (1994). Voice source parameters in continuous speech. Transformation of LF-parameters. *Proceedings of the International Conference on Spoken Language Processing*, 3, 1451–4. Yokohama, Japan, 18–22 September, 1994.

Fant, G., Liljencrants, J. and Lin, Q. (1985). A four-parameter model of glottal flow. French-Swedish Seminar on Speech, Grenoble; also in *Speech Transmission Laboratory – Quarterly Progress and Status Report*, 4, 1–13. Royal Institute of Technology, Stockholm.

Fant, G., Martony, J., Rengman, U., Risberg, A. and Holmes, J.N. (1961). Recent progress in formant synthesis of connected speech. *Journal of the Acoustical Society of America*, 33, 834–5.

Fant, G., Nord, L. and Kruckenberg, A. (1986). Individual variations in text reading. A Data Bank pilot study. *Speech Transmission Laboratory, Quarterly Progress Report No. 4/1986* (pp. 1–7). Stockholm: Royal Institute of Technology.

—— (1987). Segmental and prosodic variabilities in connected speech. An applied Data Bank study. *Proceedings of 11th International Congress of Phonetic Sciences*, Vol. 6 (pp. 102–5). Tallinn: Estonian Academy of Sciences.

Fant, G. and Risberg, A. (1963). Auditory matching of vowels with two formant synthetic sounds. *Speech Transmission Laboratory – Quarterly Progress and Status Report*, Royal Institute of Technology [Stockholm]. STL-QPSR 4/1963, 7–11.

Farmer, A. (1980). Voice-onset time in cerebral palsied speakers. *Folia Phoniatrica*, 32, 267–73.

Farmer, J.D. (1990). A rosetta stone for connectionism. *Physica D*, 42, 153–87.

Farnetani, E. (1986). A pilot study of the articulation of /n/ in Italian using electro-palatography and airflow measurements. *15e Journées d'Etudes sur la Parole*, GALF, 23–6.

—— (1990b). V-C-V lingual coarticulation and its spatiotemporal domain. In W.J. Hardcastle and A. Marchal (eds), *Speech production and speech modelling* (pp. 93–130). Dordrecht: Kluwer.

—— (1991). Coarticulation and reduction in consonants: comparing isolated words and continuous speech. *PERILUS XIV*, University of Stockholm, Institute of Linguistics, 11–15.

—— (in press). Labial coarticulation. In W.J. Hardcastle (ed.), *Coarticulation in speech production*. Cambridge: Cambridge University Press.

Farnetani, E. and Busà, M.G. (1994). Italian clusters in continuous speech. *Proceedings of 1994 International Conference on Spoken Language Processing*, 1, 359–62, Yokohama, 18–22 September.

Farnetani, E. and Faber, A. (1992). Tongue-jaw coordination in vowel production: isolated words vs. connected speech. *Speech Communication*, 11, 411–19.

Farnetani, E. and Kori, S. (1986). Effects of syllable and word structure on segmental durations in spoken Italian. *Speech Communication*, 5, 17–34.

Farnetani, E. and Recasens, D. (1993). Anticipatory consonant-to-vowel coarticulation in the production of VCV sequences in Italian. *Language and Speech*, 36, 279–302.

Farnetani, E., Vagges, K. and Magno-Caldognetto, E. (1985). Coarticulation in Italian /VtV/ sequences: a palatographic study. *Phonetica*, 42, 78–99.

Farrell, K.R., Mammone, R.J. and Assahleh, K.T. (1994). Speaker recognition using neural networks and conventional classifiers. *IEEE Transactions on Speech and Audio Processing*, 2, 194–205.

Fear, B.D., Cutler, A. and Butterfield, S. (1995). The strong/weak syllable distinction in English. *Journal of the Acoustical Society of America*, 97, 1893–1904.

Feldman, A. (1966). Functional tuning of the nervous system during control of movement or maintenance of a steady posture. III. Mechanographic analysis of the execution by man of the simplest motor task. *Biophysics*, 11, 766–75.

Feldman, J.L. and Smith, J.C. (1989). Cellular mechanisms underlying modulation of breathing patterns in mammals. In M. Davis, B.L. Jacobs and R.L. Schoenfeld (eds), *Modulation of defined vertebrate neural circuits. Annals of the New York Academy of Sciences*, Vol. 563 (pp. 114–30).

Ferguson, C.A. (1986). Discovering sound units and constructing sound systems: it's child's play. In J.S. Perkell and D.H. Klatt (eds), *Invariance and variability in speech processes*. Hillsdale, NJ: Lawrence Erlbaum Associates.

Ferguson, C.A. and Farwell, C.B. (1975). Words and sounds in early language acquisition: English initial consonants in the first fifty words. *Language*, 51, 419–39.

Fernald, A. (1992). Human maternal vocalizations to infants as biologically relevant signals: an evolutionary perspective. In J.H. Barkow, L. Cosmides, and J. Tooby (eds), *The adapted mind: evolutionary psychology and the generation of culture*. Oxford: Oxford University Press.

Festen, J.M. (1993). Why do masker fluctuations as in interfering speech lower the speech-reception threshold? *Journal of the Acoustical Society of America*, 93, 2327.

Fettweis, A. and Meerkötter, K. (1975). On adaptors for wave digital filters. *IEEE Trans ASSP-23*, 516–25.

Filippo, C.L. de and Snell, K.B. (1986). Detection of a temporal gap in low-frequency narrow-band signals by normal hearing and hearing-impaired listeners. *Journal of the Acoustical Society of America*, 80, 1354–8.

Finitzo, T. and Freeman, F. (1989). Spasmodic dysphonia, whither and where: results of seven years of research. *Journal of Speech and Hearing Research*, 32, 541–55.

Firth, J.R. (1948). Sounds and prosodies. *Transactions of the Philological Society*, 127–52.

Fischer-Jørgensen, E. (1963). Beobachtungen über den Zusammenhang zwischen

Stimmhaftigkeit und intraoralem Luftdruck. *Zs. Phonetic, Sprachwissenschaft u. Kommunikationsforschung*, 16, 19–36.

—— (1964). Sound duration and place of articulation in Danish. *Zeitschrift fur Sprachwissenschaft und Kommunikationsforschung*, 17, 175–207.

—— (1967). Phonetic analysis of breathy (murmured) vowels in Gujerati. *Indian Linguistics*, 28, 71–139.

—— (1979). A sketch of the history of phonetics in Denmark until the beginning of the 20th century. *Annual Report of Institute of Phonetics, University of Copenhagen*, 13, 135–69.

—— (1985a). Review of Grundlagen der phonometrischen Linguistik (3rd ed.) by E. Zwirner and K. Zwirner. *Phonetica*, 42, 198–213.

—— (1985b). Some basic vowel features, their articulatory correlates, and their explanatory power in phonology. In V. Fromkin (ed.), *Phonetic Linguistics* (pp. 79–99). Orlando: Academic Press.

Fitzgibbons, P.L. (1983). Temporal gap detection in noise as a function of frequency, bandwidth and level. *Journal of the Acoustical Society of America*, 74, 67–72.

Flanagan, J.L. (1972). *Speech analysis synthesis and perception* (2nd edn). New York/Berlin: Springer-Verlag.

Flanagan, J.L. and Ishizaka, K. (1976). Automatic generation of voiceless excitation in a vocal cord-vocal tract speech synthesizer. *IEEE Transactions on Acoustics, Speech and Signal Processing*, 24, 163–70.

Flanagan, J.L., Ishizaka, K. and Shipley, K.L. (1975). Synthesis of speech from a dynamic model of the vocal cords and vocal tract. *Bell System Technical Journal*, 54, 485–506.

Flanagan, J.L. and Landgraf, L.L. (1968). Self-oscillating source for vocal-tract synthesizers. *IEEE Transactions on Audio and Electroacoustics*, AU-16, 57–64.

Flanagan, J.R., Ostry, D. and Feldman, A. (1990). Control of human jaw and multi-joint arm movements. In G. Hammond (ed.), *Cerebral control of speech and limb movements* (pp. 29–58). London: Springer-Verlag.

Flanagan, J.L. and Rabiner, L.R. (eds) (1973). *Speech synthesis*. Stroudsburg, PA: Dowden, Hutchinson and Ross.

Flanagan, J.L. and Saslow, M.G. (1958). Pitch discrimination for synthetic vowels. *Journal of the Acoustical Society of America*, 30, 435–42.

Flash, T. (1990). Organization of human arm trajectory control. In J. Winters and S. Woo (eds), *Multiple muscle systems: biomechanics and movement organization* (pp. 282–301). New York: Springer.

Flash, T. and Hogan, N. (1985). The coordination of arm movements: an experimentally confirmed mathematical model. *Journal of Neuroscience*, 5, 1688–703.

Flege, J., Fletcher, S. and Homiedan, A. (1988). Compensating for a bite block in /s/ and /t/ production: palatographic, acoustic, and perceptual data. *Journal of the Acoustical Society of America*, 83, 212–28.

Fletcher, H. (1940). Auditory patterns. *Reviews of Modern Physics*, 12, 47–65.

Fletcher, S. (1985). Speech production and oral motor skill in an adult with an unrepaired palatal cleft. *Journal of Speech and Hearing Disorders*, 50, 254–61.

—— (1989). Palatometric specification of stop, affricate and sibilant sounds. *Journal of Speech and Hearing Research*, 32, 736–48.

—— (1990). Recognition of words from palatometric displays, *Clinical Linguistics and Phonetics*, 4, 9–24.

Fletcher, S., Dagenais, P. and Critz-Crosby, P. (1991). Teaching consonants to profoundly hearing-impaired speakers using palatometry. *Journal of Speech and Hearing Research*, 34, 929–42.

Fletcher, S. and Hasegawa, A. (1983). Speech modification by a deaf child through dynamic orometric modeling and feedback. *Journal of Speech and Hearing Research*, 48, 178–85.

Fletcher, S., Hasegawa, A., McCutcheon, M. and Gilliom, J. (1979). Use of linguapalatal contact patterns to modify articulation in a deaf adult. In D. McPherson and M. Schwab (eds), *Advances in prosthetic devices for the deaf: a technical workshop* (pp. 127–33). Rochester: NTID Press.

Fletcher, S., McCutcheon, M. and Wolf, M. (1975). Dynamic palatometry. *Journal of Speech and Hearing Research*, 18, 812–19.

Fletcher, S. and Newman, D. (1991). [s] and [ʃ] as a function of linguapalatal contact place and sibilant groove width. *Journal of the Acoustical Society of America*, 89, 850–8.

Folkins, J. and Abbs, J. (1975). Lip and jaw motor control during speech: responses to resistive loading of the jaw. *Journal of Speech and Hearing Research*, 18, 207–20.

Folkins, J.W. and Brown, C.K. (1987). Upper lip, lower lip and jaw interactions during speech: comments on evidence from repetition-to-repetition variability. *Journal of the Acoustical Society of America*, 82, 1919–24.

Folkins, J.W. and Kuehn, D.P. (1982). Speech production. In N. Lass (ed.), *Speech, language and hearing* (pp. 246–85). Philadelphia: Saunders.

Folkins, J. and Zimmermann, G. (1982). Lip and jaw interaction during speech: responses to perturbation of lower-lip movement prior to bilabial closure. *Journal of the Acoustical Society of America*, 71, 1225–33.

Formby, C., Thomas, R.G. and Halsey, J.H. (1989). Regional cerebral blood flow for singers and nonsingers while speaking, singing, and humming a rote passage. *Brain and Language*, 36, 690–8.

Forrest, K., Weismer, G. and Turner, G.S. (1989). Kinematic, acoustic, and perceptual analysis of connected speech produced by Parkinsonian and normal geriatric adults. *Journal of the Acoustical Society of America*, 85, 2608–22.

Foss, D.J. and Blank, M.A. (1980). Identifying the speech codes. *Cognitive Psychology*, 12, 1–31.

Foss, D.J. and Gernsbacher, M.A. (1983). Cracking the dual code: toward a unitary model of phoneme identification. *Journal of Verbal Learning and Verbal Behavior*, 22, 609–32.

Foss, D.J., Harwood, D.A. and Blank, M.A. (1980). Deciphering decoding decisions: data and devices. In R.A. Cole (ed.), *Perception and production of fluent speech* (165–99). Hillsdale, NJ: Erlbaum.

Foss, D.J. and Swinney, D.A. (1973). On the psychological reality of the phoneme: perception, identification and consciousness. *Journal of Verbal Learning and Verbal Behavior*, 12, 246–57.

Foster (1990). *A textbook of orthodontics.*

Fourakis, M. (1991). Tempo, stress, and vowel reduction in American English. *Journal of the Acoustical Society of America*, 90, 1816–27.

Fourcin, A.J. (1981). Laryngographic assessment of phonatory function. In C.L. Ludlow and M.O. Hart (eds), *ASHA report 11: proceedings of the conference on the assessment of vocal pathology* (pp. 116–27). Rockville, Maryland: The American Speech-Language-Hearing Association.

Fourcin, A.J., Harland, G., Barry, W. and Hazan, V. (eds) (1989). *Speech input and output assessment – multilingual methods and standards.* Chichester: Ellis Horwood Limited.

Fowler, C.A. (1977). *Timing control in speech production.* Bloomington: Indiana University Linguistics Club.

—— (1980). Coarticulation and theories of extrinsic timing. *Journal of Phonetics*, 8, 113–33.

—— (1981). Production and perception of coarticulation among stressed and unstressed vowels. *Journal of Speech and Hearing Research*, 46, 127–49.

—— (1983). Realism and unrealism: a reply. *Journal of Phonetics*, 11, 303–22.

—— (1984). Segmentation of coarticulated speech in perception. *Perception & Psychophysics*, 36, 359–68.

—— (1985). Current perspectives on language and speech production: a critical overview. In R.G. Daniloff (ed.), *Speech Science* (pp. 193–278). London: Taylor and Francis.

—— (1986). An event approach to the study of speech perception from a direct-realist perspective. *Journal of Phonetics*, 14, 3–28.

—— (1992). Vowel duration and closure duration in voiced and unvoiced stops: there are no contrast effects here. *Journal of Phonetics*, 20, 143–65.

—— (1992). Phonological and articulatory characteristics of spoken language. *Haskins Laboratories Status Report on Speech Research*, 109/110, 1–12.

—— (1993). Phonological and articulatory characteristics of spoken language. In G. Blanken, J. Dittman, H. Grimm, J. Marshall and C-W. Wallesch (eds), *Linguistic disorders and pathologies: an international handbook* (pp. 34–46). Berlin: Walter de Gruyter.

Fowler, C., Rubin, P., Remez, R. and Turvey, M. (1980). Implications for speech production of a general theory of action. In B. Butterworth (ed.), *Language production I: speech and talk* (pp. 373–420). London: Academic Press.

Fowler, C.A. and Saltzman, E. (1993). Coordination and coarticulation in speech production. *Language and Speech*, 36, 171–95.

Fowler, C. and Smith, M. (1986). Speech perception as "vector analysis": an approach to the problems of segmentation and invariance. In J. Perkell and D. Klatt (eds), *Invariance and variability of speech processes* (pp. 123–36). Hillsdale, NJ: Lawrence Erlbaum.

Fowler, C. and Turvey, M. (1980). Immediate compensation in bite-block speech. *Phonetica*, 37, 306–26.

Fox, R.A. (1984). Effect of lexical status on phonetic categorization. *Journal of Experimental Psychology: Human Perception and Performance*, 10, 526–40.

Fox, R.A. and Unkefer, J. (1985). The effect of lexical status on the perception of tone. *Journal of Chinese Linguistics*, 13, 69–90.

Frauenfelder, U.H. and Segui, J. (1989). Phoneme monitoring and lexical processing: evidence for associative context effects. *Memory & Cognition*, 17, 134–40.

Frauenfelder, U.H., Segui, J. and Dijkstra, T. (1990). Lexical effects in phonemic processing: facilitatory or inhibitory? *Journal of Experimental Psychology: Human Perception and Performance*, 16, 77–91.

French, J.P. (1990). Analytic procedures for the determination of disputed utterances. In H. Kniffka (ed.), *Texte zu Theorie und Praxis forensischer Linguistik*. Tübingen: Max Niemeyer Verlag.

Freund, H.-J. (1987). Abnormalities of motor behavior after cortical lesions in humans. In S. Geiger, F. Plum and V. Mountcastle (eds), *Handbook of physiology, Vol. 5. The nervous system* (pp. 763–810). Bethesda, MD: American Physiological Society.

Friedlander, B. (1982). Lattice filters for adaptive processing. *Proceedings of IEEE*, 70 (8), 829–67.

Frisina, R.D., Smith, R.L. and Chamberlain, S.C. (1990). Encoding of amplitude modulation in the gerbil cochlear nucleus: I. A hierarchy of enhancement. *Hearing Research*, 44, 99–122.

Friston, J.J., Frith, C.D., Liddle, P.F. and Frackowiak, R.S. (1991). Investigating a network model of word generation with positron emission tomography. *Proceedings of the Royal Society of London: Biological Sciences*, 244 (1310), 101–6.

Friston, J.J., Tononi, G., Reeke, G.N., Jr., Sporns, O. and Edelman, G.M. (1994). Value-dependent selection in the brain: Simulation in a synthetic neural model. *Neuroscience*, 59, 229–43.

Fritzell, B., Hammarberg, B., Gauffin, J., Karlsson, I. and Sundberg, J. (1986). Breathiness and insufficient vocal fold closure. *Journal of Phonetics*, 14, 549–53.

Frøkjær-Jensen, B. (1967). A photo-electric glottograph. *Annual Report of the Institute of Phonetics of University of Copenhagen*, 2, 5–19.

—— (1968). Comparison between a Fabre glottograph and a photo-electric glottograph. *Annual Report of the Institute of Phonetics of University of Copenhagen*, 3, 9–16.

Fromkin, V.A. (1971). The non-anomalous nature of anomalous utterances. *Language*, 47, 27–52.

Fry, D.B. (1955). Duration and intensity as physical correlates of linguistic stress. *Journal of the Acoustical Society of America*, 27, 765–8.

—— (1958). Experiments in the perception of stress. *Language and Speech*, 1, 126–52.

Fu, K.S. (1982). *Syntactic pattern recognition and its applications*. Englewood Cliffs: Prentice-Hall.

Fujimura, O. (1958). Sound synthesizer with optical control. *Journal of the Acoustical Society of America*, 30, 56–7.

—— (1961a). Bilabial stop consonants: a motion picture study and its acoustical implications. *Journal of Speech and Hearing Research*, 4, 233–7.

—— (1961b). Some synthesis experiments on stop consonants in the initial position. *Quarterly Progress Report MIT, Research Laboratory of Electronics*, 61, 153–62.

—— (1962). Analysis of nasal consonants. *Journal of the Acoustical Society of America*, 34, 1865–75.

—— (1968). An approximation to voice aperiodicity. *IEEE Transactions of Audio Electroacoustics*, AU-16, 68–72.

—— (1971). Remarks on stop consonants: synthesis experiments and acoustic cues. In L. Hammerich, R. Jakobson, and E. Zwirner (eds), *Form and substance* (pp. 221–32). Copenhagen: Akademisk Forlag.

—— (1975). Syllable as a unit of speech recognition. *IEEE Transactions on Acoustics: Speech and Signal Processing*, 23, 82–6.

—— (1977). Recent findings on articulatory processes – velum and tongue movements as syllable features. In R. Carré, R. Descout, and M. Wajskop (eds), *Articulatory modeling and phonetics* (pp. 115–26). Grenoble: GALF Groupe de la Communication Parlée.

—— (1979). An analysis of English syllables as cores and affixes. *Zs. f. Phonetik, Sprachwissenschaft u. Kommunikationsforschung*, 32, 471–6.

—— (1986). Relative invariance of articulatory movements. In J.S. Perkell and D.H. Klatt (eds), *Invariance and variability in speech processes*. Hillsdale, NJ: Lawrence Erlbaum.

—— (1988). A note on voice fundamental frequency (pitch) in irregular voice. In O. Fujimura (ed.), *Vocal physiology: voice production, mechanisms and functions* (pp. 377–8). New York: Raven Press.

—— (1990a). Methods and goals of speech production research. *Language and Speech*, 33, 195–258.

—— (1990b). Articulatory perspectives of speech organization. In W.J. Hardcastle and A. Marchal (eds,) *Speech production and speech modeling* (pp. 323–42). Dordrecht: Kluwer Academic Publishers.

—— (1991). Remarks on phrasing and prosodic attachment. In C. Georgopoulos and R. Ishihara (eds), *Interdisciplinary approaches to language: essays in honor of S.-Y. Kuroda* (pp. 207–16). Dordrecht: Kluwer Academic Publishers.

—— (1992). Phonology and phonetics – A syllable-based model of articulatory organization. *Journal of the Acoustical Society of Japan (E)*, 13, 39–48.

—— (1994a). C/D model: a computational model of phonetic implementation. In E.S. Ristad (ed.), *Language computations (DIMACS series in discrete mathematics and theoretical computer science)*. (pp. 1–20). Providence, RI: American Mathematical Society.

—— (1994b). Syllable timing computation in the C/D model. In *Proceedings of 1994 International Conference on Spoken Language Processing*, 2, 519–22. Yokohama, Japan.

—— (1995a). Prosodic organization of speech based on syllables: the C/D model. *Proceedings of the 12th International Congress of Phonetic Sciences*, 3, 10–17.

—— (1995b). The syllable: its internal structure and role in prosodic organization. In

B. Palek (ed.), *LP 94: item order in natural languages.* (pp. 53–93). Prague: Charles University Press.

—— (ed.) (1994). *Vocal fold physiology.* San Diego: Singular Publication Group Inc.

Fujimura, O. and Kakita, Y. (1979). Remarks on quantitative description of the lingual articulation. In B. Lindblom and S. Öhman (eds), *Frontiers of speech communication research* (pp. 17–24). New York: Academic Press.

Fujimura, O. and Lindqvist, J. (1971). Sweep-tone measurements of vocal tract characteristics. *Journal of the Acoustical Society of America*, 49, 541–58.

Fujimura, O. and Lovins, J.B. (1978). Syllables as concatenative phonetic units. In A. Bell and J.B. Hooper (eds), *Syllables and segments* (pp. 107–20). Amsterdam: North Holland Publishers.

Fujimura, O., Macchi, M.J. and Lovins, J.B. (1977). Demisyllables and affixes for speech synthesis. *Proceedings of the Ninth International Congress on Acoustics* (pp. 5–13). Madrid, Spain.

Fujimura, O., Macchi, M.M. and Streeter, L.A. (1978). Perception of stop consonants with conflicting transitional cues: a cross-linguistic study. *Language and Speech*, 21, 337–46.

Fujimura, O. and Sawashima, M. (1971). Consonant sequences and laryngeal control. *Annual Bulletin of Research Institute of Logopedics and Phoniatrics*, University of Tokyo, 5, 1–13.

Fujimura, O., Tatsumi, I. and Kagaya, R. (1972). Computational processing of palatographic patterns. *Journal of Phonetics*, 1, 47–54.

Fujisaki, H. and Hirose, H. (1982). Modeling the dynamic characteristics of voice fundamental frequency with application to analysis and synthesis of intonation. *The 13th International Congress of Linguistics*, 57–70.

Fujisaki, H., Hirose, K. and Sugito, M. (1986). Comparison of acoustic features of word accent in English and Japanese. *Journal of the Acoustical Society of Japan (E)*, 7, 1–63.

Fujisaki, H., Nakamura, K. and Imoto, T. (1973). Auditory perception of duration of speech and nonspeech stimuli. *Annual Report of Engineering Research Institute* (p. 32). Tokyo: Faculty of Engineering, University of Tokyo.

Fujisaki, H. and Sudo, H. (1971). Synthesis by rule of prosodic features of connected Japanese. *Proceedings of the 7th International Congress on Acoustics*, Vol. 3 (pp. 133–6). Budapest: Akadémiai Kiadó.

Furui, S. (1981). Cepstral analysis technique for automatic speaker verification. *IEEE Transactions on Acoustics, Speech, and Signal Processing* ASSP-29, 254–72.

—— (1994). An overview of speaker recognition technology. *Proceedings of ESCA Workshop on Speaker Recognition, Identification, and Verification*, 1–9. Martigny, Switzerland, 5–7 April, 1994.

Furui, S. and Sondhi, M.M. (eds) (1992). *Advances in speech signal processing.* New York: Marcel Dekker, Inc.

Gandour, J. and Maddieson, I. (1976). Measuring larynx height in standard Thai using the cricothyrometer. *Phonetica*, 33, 241–67.

Ganong, W.F. (1980). Phonetic categorization in auditory word perception. *Journal of Experimental Psychology: Human Perception and Performance*, 6, 110–25.

Gårding, E. (1979). Sentence intonation in Swedish. *Phonetica*, 36, 207–15.

—— (1983). A generative model of intonation. In A. Cutler and D.R. Ladd (eds), *Prosody: models and measurements* (pp. 11–26). Berlin: Springer-Verlag.

Garn, S.M. and Clark, D.C. (1975). Nutrition, growth, development and maturation: findings from the ten-state nutrition survey of 1968–1970. *Pediatrics*, 56, 306–19.

Garofolo, J.S., Lamel, L.F., Fisher, W.M., Fiscus, J.G., Pallett, D.S. and Dahgren, D.L. (1993). *The DARPA TIMIT acoustic-phonetic continuous speech corpus CDROM*, NTIS order number PB91-100354.

Garrett, M. (1980). Levels of processing in sentence production. In B. Butterworth (ed.), *Language production I: speech and talk* (pp. 177–220). London: Academic Press.

Gauffin, J., Binh, N., Ananthapadmanabha, T. and Fant, G. (1983). Glottal geometry and volume velocity waveform. In D.M. Bless and J.H. Abbs (eds), *Vocal fold physiology* (pp. 194–201). San Diego, CA: College Hill Press.

Gauffin, J. and Sundberg, J. (1989). Spectral correlates of glottal voice source waveform characteristics. *Journal of Speech and Hearing Research*, 32, 556–65.

Gauvin, J.L., Lamel, L.F. and Eskénazi, M. (1990). Design considerations and text selection for BREF, a large French read-speech corpus, *Proceedings of 1990 International Conference on Spoken Language Processing*.

Gay, T. (1974). A cinefluorographic study of vowel production. *Journal of Phonetics*, 2, 255–66.

—— (1977). Cinefluorographic and EMG studies of articulatory organization. *Haskins Laboratories Status Reports*, SR-50, 77–93.

—— (1978). Effect of speaking rate on vowel formant movements. *Journal of the Acoustical Society of America*, 63, 223–30.

Gay, T., Boë, L. and Perrier, P. (1992). Acoustic and perceptual effects of changing vocal-tract constrictions for vowels. *Journal of the Acoustical Society of America*, 92, 1301–9.

Gay, T., Ushijima, T., Hirose, H. and Cooper, F. (1974). Effect of speaking rate on labial consonant-vowel articulation. *Journal of Phonetics*, 2, 47–63.

Geddes, L.A. and Baker, L.E. (1968). *Principles of applied biomedical instrumentation*. New York: John Wiley and Sons.

Geisler, C.D. and Gamble, T. (1989). Responses of "high-spontaneous" auditory-nerve fibers to consonant-vowel syllables in noise. *Journal of the Acoustical Society of America*, 85, 1639–52.

Gelfand, I., Gurfinkel, V., Fomin, S. and Tsetlin, M. (eds) (1971). *Models of the structural-functional organization of certain biological systems*. Cambridge, MA: MIT Press.

Gelfand, I., Gurfinkel, V., Tsetlin, M. and Shik, M. (1971). Some problems in the analysis of movements. In I. Gelfand, V. Gurfinkel, S. Fomin and M. Tsetlin (eds), *Models of the structural-functional organization of certain biological systems* (pp. 329–45). Cambridge, MA: MIT Press.

Gelfer, C.E., Harris, K.S. and Baer, T. (1987). Controlled variables in sentence intonation. In T. Baer, C. Sasaki and K.S. Harris (eds), *Vocal fold physiology: laryngeal function in phonation and respiration* (pp.). Boston: College Hill Press.

Gelfer, C.E., Harris, K.S. Collier, R. and Baer, T. (1985). Is declination actively controlled? In I. Titze (ed.), *Vocal fold physiology: physiology and biophysics of the voice*. Iowa City: Iowa University Press.

Geluykens, R. (1987). Intonation and speech act type. An experimental approach to rising intonation in queclaratives. *Journal of Pragmatics*, 11, 483–94.

Gentil, M. and Gay, T. (1986). Neuromuscular specialization of the mandibular motor system: speech versus non-speech movements. *Speech Communication*, 5, 69–82.

Gentner, D. (1987). Timing of skilled movements: test of the proportional duration model. *Psychological Review*, 94, 255–76.

Gerratt, B.R., Hanson, D.G. and Berke, G.S. (1986). Glottographic measures of laryngeal function in individuals with abnormal motor control. In T. Baer, C. Sasaki, and K.S. Harris (eds), *Laryngeal function in phonation and respiration* (pp. 521–32). Boston: College-Hill.

Gerratt, B.R., Till, J.A., Rosenbek, J.C., Wertz, R.T. and Boysen, A.E. (1992). Use and perceived value of perceptual and instrumental measures in dysarthria management. In C.A. Moore, K.M. Yorkston and D.R. Beukelman (eds), *Dysarthria and apraxia of speech: perspectives on management* (pp. 77–93). Baltimore, MD: Paul Brookes.

Gersho, A. and Gray R.M. (1992). *Vector quantization and signal compression*. Boston: Kluwer Academic.

Geschwind, N. and Galaburda, A.M. (1987). *Cerebral lateralization*. Cambridge, MA: MIT Press.

Ghez, C. (1991). Voluntary movement. In E. Kandel, J. Schwartz and T. Jessell (eds), *Principles of neural science* (pp. 534–47). New York: Elsevier.

Ghitza, O. (1988). Temporal non-place information in the auditory-nerve firing patterns as a front-end for speech recognition in a noisy environment. *Journal of Phonetics*, 16, 109–24.

Giannotta, C. (1990). *Etude de l'interface utilisateur dans un contexte d'utilisation de systèmes de reconnaissances embarqués*. Université de Valenciennes et du Hainaut-Cambresis, Laboratoire d'Automatique Industrielle et Humaine.

Gibbon, F. (1990). Lingual activity in two speech disordered children's attempts to produce velar/alveolar stop contrasts: evidence from electropalatographic (EPG) data. *British Journal of Disorders of Communication*, 25, 329–34.

Gibbon, F., Hardcastle, W. and Nicolaidis, K. (1993). Temporal and spatial aspects of lingual coarticulation in /kl/ sequences: a cross-linguistic investigation. *Language and Speech*, 36, 261–77.

Gibbs, R. (1991). Semantic analyzability in children's understanding of idioms. *Journal of Speech and Hearing Research*, 34, 613–20.

Gibson, J.J. (1966). *The senses considered as perceptual systems*. New York: Houghton-Mifflin.

Gierut, J. (1990). Differential learning of phonological opposition. *Journal of Speech and Hearing Research*, 33, 540–9.

Gimson, A.C. (1970). *An introduction to the pronunciation of English* (2nd edn). London: Edward Arnold.

Glasberg, B.R. and Moore, B.C.J. (1990). Derivation of auditory filter shapes from notched-noise data. *Hearing Research*, 47, 103–38.

Glass, L. and Mackey, M. (1988). *From clocks to chaos: the rhythms of life*. Princeton: Princeton University Press.

Glendinning, A.G., Nelson, P.A. and Elliott, S.J. (1990). Experiments on a compressed air loudspeaker. *Journal of Sound and Vibration*, 138, 479–91.

Glenn, J.W. and Kleiner, N. (1968). Speaker identification based on nasal phonation. *Journal of the Acoustical Society of America*, 43, 368–72.

Gobl, C. (1988). Voice source dynamics in connected speech. *Speech Transmission Laboratory – Quarterly Progress and Status Report*, 1, 123–59. Royal Institute of Technlogy Stockholm.

—— (1989). A preliminary study of acoustic voice quality correlates. *Speech Transmission Laboratory – Quarterly Progress and Status Report*, 4, 9–22. Royal Institute of Technology, Stockholm.

Gobl, C. and Karlsson, I. (1991). Male and female voice source dynamics. In Gauffin and Hammarberg (eds), *Proceedings of Vocal Fold Physiology Conference*. San Diego: Singular Publishing Group.

Gobl, C., Monahan, P., Fitzpatrick, L. and Ní Chasaide, A. (1994). A new approach to source-filter decomposition. *Proceedings of the 2nd Review Meeting of the Esprit/Basic Research Action no. 6975: SPEECH MAPS*. Royal Institute of Technology, Stockholm.

Gobl, C. and Ní Chasaide, A. (1988). The effects of adjacent voice/voiceless consonants on the vowel voice source: a cross language study. *Speech Transmission Laboratory – Quarterly Progress and Status Report*, 2–3, 23–59. Royal Institute of Technology, Stockholm.

—— (1992). Acoustic characteristics of voice quality. *Speech Communication*, 11, 481–90.

Gold, B. (1969). *Digital processing of signals*. New York: Lincoln Lab. Publ.

Goldinger, S.D., Luce, P.A. and Pisoni, D.B. (1989). Priming lexical neighbors of spoken words: effects of competition and inhibition. *Journal of Memory and Language*, 28, 501–18.

Goldinger, S.D., Luce, P.A., Pisoni, D.B. and Marcario, J.K. (1992). Form-based priming in spoken word recognition: the roles of competition and bias. *Journal of Experimental Psychology: Learning, Memory, and Cognition*, 18, 1211–38.

Goldinger, S.D., Pisoni, D.B. and Logan, J.S. (1991). On the nature of talker variability effects on recall of spoken word lists. *Journal of Experimental Psychology: Learning, Memory, and Cognition*, 19, 309–28.

Goldman-Eisler, F. (1968). *Psycholinguistics: experiments in spontaneous speech*. New York: Academic Press.

Goldsmith, J. (1979). *Autosegmental phonology*. New York: Garland.

—— (1990). *Autosegmental and metrical phonology*. Oxford: Basil Blackwell.

Goldstein, J.L. (1973). An optimum processor theory for the central formation of the pitch of complex tones. *Journal of the Acoustical Society of America*, 54, 1496–1516.

—— (1973). An optimum processor theory for the central formation of the pitch of complex tones. *Journal of the Acoustical Society of America*, 54, 1496–1516.

Goldstein, J.L. and Srulovicz, P. (1977). Auditory-nerve spike intervals as an adequate basis for aural spectrum analysis. In E.F. Evans and J.P. Wilson (eds), *Psychophysics and Physiology of Hearing* (pp. 337–45). London: Academic.

Goldstein, M. (1976). *Aeroacoustics*. New York: McGraw-Hill International Book Co.

Goldstein, M. and Till, O. (1992). Is % overall error rate a valid measure of speech synthesizer and natural speech performance at the segmental level? *Proceedings of 1992 International Conference on Spoken Language Processing* (pp. 1131–4). Banff, Canada.

Gordon, P.C. (1988). Induction of rate-dependent processing by coarse-grained aspects of speech. *Perception & Psychophysics*, 43, 137–46.

Gorecka, A. (1989). 'The phonology of articulation'. Ph.D. dissertation. Massachusetts Institute of Technology, Cambridge, MA.

Gould, J.D., Conti, J. and Hovanyecz, T. (1983). Composing letters with a simulated listening typewriter. *Communications ACM*, 26, 259–308.

Gracco, L.C., Gracco, V.L., Löfqvist, A. and Marek, K. (1992). An aerodynamic evaluation of Parkinsonian dysarthria: laryngeal and supralaryngeal manifestations. *Haskins Laboratories Status Report on Speech Research*, SR-111/112, 103–10.

Gracco, V.L. (1987). Multilevel control model for speech motor activity. In H.F.M. Peters and W. Hulsijn (eds), *Speech motor dynamics in stuttering* (pp. 57–76). New York: Springer.

—— (1988). Timing factors in the coordination of speech movements. *Journal of Neuroscience*, 8, 4628–39.

—— (1992). Sensorimotor mechanisms in speech motor control. *Haskins Laboratories Status Report on Speech Research*, SR-109/110, 27–44.

—— (1994). Some organizational characteristics of speech movement control. *Journal of Speech and Hearing Research*, 37, 4–27.

Gracco, V.L. and Abbs, J. (1985). Dynamic control of the perioral system during speech: kinematic analyses of autogenic and nonautogenic sensorimotor processes. *Journal of Neurophysiology*, 54, 418–32.

—— (1986). Variant and invariant characteristics of speech movements. *Experimental Brain Research*, 65, 156–66.

—— (1988). Central patterning of speech movements. *Experimental Brain Research*, 71, 515–26.

—— (1989). Sensorimotor characteristics of speech motor sequences. *Experimental Brain Research*, 75, 586–98.

Gracco, V.L. and Löfqvist, A. (1994). Speech motor coordination and control: evidence from lip, jaw, and laryngeal movements. *Journal of Neuroscience*, 14, 6585–97.

Grammont, M. (1933). *Traité de phonétique*. Paris: Librairie Delagrave.

Grandgent, C.H. (1896). Warmpth. *Publications of the Modern Language Association 11*. (New Series 4), 63–75.

Granit, R. (1970). *The basis of motor control*. London: Academic Press.

Grassmann, H. (1854). *Leitfaden der Akustik*. Programm des Stettiner Gymnasiums.

Green, D.M. (1973). Temporal acuity as a function of frequency. *Journal of the Acoustical Society of America*, 54, 373–9.

—— (1985). Temporal factors in psychoacoustics. In A. Michelsen (ed.), *Time resolution in auditory systems* (pp. 122–40). New York: Springer-Verlag.

—— (1988). *Profile analysis*. Oxford: Oxford University Press.

Green, P.D., Brown, G.D., Cooke, M.P., Crawford, M.D. and Simons, A.J.H. (1990). In W.A. Ainsworth (ed.), *Advances in speech, hearing and language processing*, Vol. 1, (pp. 149–92). London: JAI Press Ltd.

Greenberg, S. (1988). The ear as a speech analyzer. *Journal of Phonetics*, 16, 139–49.

Greenberg, S. and Rhode, W.S. (1987). Periodicity coding in cochlear nerve and ventral cochlear nucleus. In W.A. Yost and C.S. Watson (eds), *Auditory processing of complex sounds* (pp. 225–23). Hillsdale, NJ: Erlbaum.

Greene, M. and Mattheson, L. (1989). *The voice and its disorders* (5th edn). London: Whurr Publishers.

Greene, P. (1972). Problems of organization of motor systems. In R. Rosen and F. Snell (eds), *Progress in theoretical biology*, Vol. 2 (pp. 303–38). New York: Academic Press.

Greenwood, D.D. (1990). A cochlear frequency-position function for several species – 29 years later. *Journal of the Acoustical Society of America*, 87, 2592–605.

Grenier, G., Xu, M., Prado, J. and Liebenguth, D. (1990). An adaptive microphone array for speech input in cars. *Proceedings of ISATA '90*.

Grillner, S. and Wallen, P. (1985). Central pattern generators for locomotion, with special reference to vertebrates. *Annual Review of Neurosciences*, 8, 233–61.

Grose, J.H. and Hall, J.W. (1992). Comodulation masking release for speech stimuli. *Journal of the Acoustical Society of America*, 91, 1042–50.

Grosjean, F., Grosjean, L. and Lane, H. (1979). The patterns of silence: performance structures in sentence production. *Cognitive Psychology*, 11, 58–81.

Guay, A., Maxwell, D. and Beecher, R. (1978). A radiographic study of tongue position at rest and during the phonation of /s/ in Class III malocclusion. *Angle Orthodontics*, 48, 10–22.

Guenther, F.H. (1994a). Speech sound acquisition, coarticulation, and rate effects in a neural network model of speech production. *Technical Report CAS/CNS-94-012*, Boston University Center for Adaptive Systems.

—— (1994b). Skill acquisition, coarticulation, and rate effects in a neural network model of speech production. *Journal of the Acoustical Society of America*, 95, 3pSP18., 2924.

—— (1995a). Speech sound acquisition, coarticulation, and rate effects in a neural network model of speech production. *Psychological Review*, 102, 594–621.

Guenther, F.H. (1995b). A modeling framework for speech motor development and kinematic articulator control, *Proceedings of the XIIIth International Congress of Phonetic Sciences*, vol. 2, 92–9, Stockholm, Sweden, Aug. 13–19.

Guérin, B. (1983). Effects of the source-tract interaction using vocal fold models. In I.R. Titze and R.C. Scherer (eds), *Vocal fold physiology: biomechanics, acoustics and phonatory control* (pp. 482–99). Denver: Denver Center for the Performing Arts.

Guinan, J.J. Jr. (1996). The physiology of cochlear afferents. In P. Dallos, A.N. Popper and R.R. Fay (eds), *The cochlea*. New York: Springer (in press).

Guinan, J.J. and Gifford, M.L. (1988). Effects of electrical stimulation of efferent olivo-cochlear neurons on cat auditory nerve fibers. III. Tuning curves and thresholds at CF. *Hearing Research*, 37, 29–46.

Gussenhoven, C. (1983). Focus, mode and nucleus. *Journal of Linguistics*, 19, 377–417.

—— (1984). On the grammar and semantics of sentence accents. Dordrecht: Foris Publications.

Haddad, R.A. and Parsons, T.W. (1991). *Digital signal processing: theory, applications, and hardware*. New York: Computer Science.

Hadding-Koch, K. and Studdert-Kennedy, M. (1964). An experimental study of some intonation contours. *Phonetics*, 11, 175–85.

Haggard, M.P., Ambler, S. and Callow, M. (1970). Pitch as a voicing cue. *Journal of the Acoustical Society of America*, 47, 613–17.

Hakoda, K.S., Nakajima, T., Hirokawa and Mizuno, H. (1990). A new Japanese text-to-speech synthesizer based on COC synthesis method. *Proceedings of 1990 International Conference on Spoken Language Processing*. Kobe, Japan.

Hale, K., Krauss, M., Watahomigie, L.J., Yamamoto, A., Craig, C., Jeanne, L.M. and England, N.C. (1992). Endangered languages. *Language*, 68, 1–42.

Hall, J.W., Haggard, M.P. and Fernandes, M.A. (1984). Detection in noise by spectro-temporal pattern analysis. *Journal of the Acoustical Society of America*, 76, 50–6.

Hall, P.K., Jordan, L.S. and Robin, D.A. (1993). *Developmental apraxia of speech*. Austin, TX: Pro-Ed.

Halle, M. (1962). Phonology in generative grammar. *Word*, 18, 54–72.

—— (1983). On distinctive features and their articulatory implementation. *Natural Language and Linguistic Theory*, 1 (1), 91–105.

—— (1988). The immanent form of phonemes. In W. Hirsp (ed.), *Giving birth to cognitive science: a festschrift for George A. Miller*. Cambridge: Cambridge University Press.

Halle, M. and Stevens, K.N. (1971). A note on laryngeal features. *Quarterly Progress Report of the Research Laboratory of Electronics, MIT*, 101, 198–213.

—— (1990). Knowledge of language and the sounds of speech. In J. Sundberg, L. Nord and R. Carlson (eds). *Music, language, speech and brain*: Proceedings of an International Symposium at the Wenner-Gren Centre, Stockholm. (pp. 1–19). Basingstoke: MacMillan Press.

Halle, M. and Vergnaud, J.-R. (1980). Three dimensional phonology. *Journal of Linguistic Research*, 1 (1), 83–105.

Halliday, D. and Resnick, R. (1966). *Physics*. New York: John Wiley and Sons, Inc.

Hamlet, S. (1988). Speech compensation for prosthedontically created palatal asymmetries. *Journal of Speech and Hearing Research*, 31, 48–53.

Hamlet, S. and Stone, M. (1976). Compensatory vowel characteristics resulting from the presence of different types of experimental prostheses. *Journal of Phonetics*, 4, 199–218.

—— (1978). Compensatory alveolar consonant production induced by wearing a dental prosthesis. *Journal of Phonetics*, 6, 227–48.

Hamlet, S.L., Stone, M.L. and McCarthy, T. (1976). Persistence of learned motor patterns in speech. *Journal of the Acoustical Society of America*, 60, S66 (A).

Hammarberg, B., Fritzell, B. and Schiratzki, H. (1984). Teflon injection in 16 patients with paralytic dysphonia: perceptual and acoustic evaluation. *Journal of Speech and Hearing Disorders*, 49, 72–82.

Hamarberg, R. (1976). The methaphysics of coarticulation. *Journal of Phonetics*, 4, 353–63.

Hammersley, R.H., and Read, J.D. (1985). The effect of participation in a conversation on recognition and identification of the speakers' voices. *Law and Human Behavior*, 9, 71–81.

Hamon, C. (1988). *Procédé en dispositif de synthèse de la parole par addition-recouvrement de formes d'ondes*. Patent no. 8811517.

Hanson, D.G., Gerratt, B.R., Karin, R.R. and Berke, G.S. (1988). Glottographic measures of vocal fold vibration: an examination of laryngeal paralysis. *Laryngoscope*, 98, 541–60.

Haraguchi, S. (1977). *The tone pattern of Japanese: an autosegmental theory of tonology*. Tokyo: Kaitakusha.

Hardcastle, W. (1972). The use of electropalatography in phonetic research. *Phonetica*, 25, 197–215.

—— (1974). Instrumental investigations of lingual activity during speech: a survey. *Phonetica*, 29, 129–57.

—— (1976). *The physiology of speech production*. New York: Academic Press.

—— (1981). Experimental studies in lingual coarticulation. In R. Asher and E. Henderson (eds), *Towards a history of phonetics* (pp. 50–66). Edinburgh: Edinburgh University Press.

—— (1985). Some phonetic and syntactic constraints on lingual coarticulation during /kl/ sequences. *Speech Communication*, 4, 247–63.

—— (1994). EPG and acoustic study of some connected speech processes. *Proceedings of 1994 International Conference on Spoken Language Processing*, 2, 515–18, Yokohama, 18–22 September.

Hardcastle, W. and Barry, W. (1985). Articulatory and perceptual factors in /l/ vocalisation in English. *Work in progress* (Reading: Phonetics Laboratory, University of Reading), 5, 31–44.

—— (1989). Articulatory and perceptual factors in /l/ vocalisation in English. *Journal of the International Phonetic Association*, 15, 3–17.

Hardcastle, W. and Clark, J. (1981). Articulatory, aerodynamic and acoustic properties of lingual fricatives in English. *Phonetics Laboratory University of Reading Work in Progress*, 1, 27–44.

Hardcastle, W. and Edwards, S. (1992). EPG-based description of apraxic speech errors. In R. Kent (ed.), *Intelligibility in speech disorders* (pp. 287–328). Amsterdam: Benjamins.

Hardcastle, W., Gibbon, F. and Nicolaidis, K. (1991). EPG data reduction methods and their implications for studies of lingual coarticulation. *Journal of Phonetics*, 19, 251–66.

Hardcastle, W., Gibbon, R. and Jones, W. (1991). Visual display of tongue palate contact: electropalatography in the assessment and remediation of speech disorders. *British Journal of Disorders of Communication*, 26, 41–74.

Hardcastle, W., Morgan Barry, R. and Nunn, M. (1989). Instrumental articulatory phonetics in assessment and remediation: case studies with the electropalatograph. In J. Stengelhofen (ed.), *Cleft Palate: the nature and remediation of communication problems* (pp. 136–64). Edinburgh: Churchill Livingstone.

Hardcastle, W. and Roach, P. (1977). An instrumental investigation of coarticulation in stop consonant sequences. *Phonetics Laboratory University of Reading Works in Progress*, 1, 27–11.

Hardman, M.J. (1966). *Jaqaru: outline of phonological and morphological structure. (Janua Linguarum, Series Practice, 22)*. The Hague: Mouton.

Hardy, J.C. (1964). Lung function of athetoid and spastic quadriplegic children. *Developmental Medicine and Child Neurology*, 6, 378–88.

—— (1966). Suggestions for physiological research in dysarthria. *Cortex*, 3, 128–56.

Harrington, J. (1988). Stuttering, delayed auditory feedback, and linguistic rhythm. *Journal of Speech and Hearing Research*, 31, 36–47.

Harris, D.M. and Dallos, P. (1979). Forward masking of auditory-nerve fiber responses. *Journal of Neurophysiology*, 42, 1083–107.

Harris, K.S. (1971a). Action of the extrinsic tongue musculature in the control of tongue position. *Haskins Laboratories Status Reports*, SR 25/26, 87–96.

—— (1971b). Vowel stress and articulatory reorganization. *Haskins Laboratories Status Report on Speech Research*, SR-28, 167–78, New Haven.

—— (1981). Electromyography as a technique for laryngeal investigation. In C.L. Ludlow and M.O. Hart (eds), *ASHA report 11: proceedings of the conference on the assessment of vocal pathology* (pp. 70–87). Rockville, Maryland: The American Speech-Language-Hearing Association.

—— (1983). Coarticulation as a component in articulatory description. In R.G. Daniloff (ed.), *Articulation assessment and treatment issues* (pp. 147–67). San Diego: College-Hill Press.

Harris, K.S., Tuller, B. and Kelso, J.A.S. (1986). Temporal invariance in the production of speech. In J.S. Perkell and D.H. Klatt (eds), *Invariance and variability in speech processes* (pp. 243–67). Hillsdale, NJ: Lawrence Erlbaum.

Harris, M.S. and Umeda, N. (1974). Effect of speaking mode on temporal factors in speech: vowel duration. *Journal of the Acoustical Society of America*, 56, 1016–18.

Harshman, R., Ladefoged, P. and Goldstein, L. (1977). Factor analysis of tongue shapes. *Journal of the Acoustical Society of America*, 62, 693–707.

Hart, J.'t (1976). Psychoacoustic backgrounds of pitch contour stylization. *IPO Annual Progress Report*, 11 (pp. 11–19). Eindhoven: Institute for Perception Research.

——— (1981). Differential sensitivity to pitch distance, particularly in speech. *Journal of the Acoustical Society of America*, 69, 811–21.

Hart, J.'t and Collier, R. (1975). Integrating different levels of intonation analysis. *Journal of Phonetics*, 1, 309–27.

——— (1979). On the interaction of accentuation and intonation in Dutch. In *Proceedings of the 9th International Congress of Phonetic Sciences*, 2, 395–402. Copenhagen.

Hart, J.'t, Collier, R. and Cohen, A. (1990). *A perceptual study of intonation: an experimental phonetic approach to speech melody.* Cambridge: Cambridge University Press.

Hashimoto, Y., Katayama, Y., Murata, K. and Tanigushi, I. (1975). Pitch synchronous response of cat cochlear nerve fibers to speech sounds. *Japanese Journal of Physiology*, 25, 633–44.

Hashimoto, K. and Sasaki, K. (1982). On the relationship between the shape and position of the tongue for vowels. *Journal of Phonetics*, 10, 291–9.

Hattori, S. (1961). Prosodeme, syllable structure and laryngeal phonemes. In *Studies in descriptive and applied linguistics* (pp. 1–27). Tokyo: International Christian University.

Hattori, S., Yamamoto, K. and Fujimura, O. (1958). Nasalization of vowels in relation to nasals. *Journal of the Acoustical Society of America*, 30, 267–74.

Hawkins, P. (1984). *Introducing phonology.* London: Hutchinson.

Hawkins, S. and Stevens, K.N. (1983). A cross-language study of the perception of nasal vowels. *Journal of the Acoustical Society of America*, 73, Suppl. 1, S54.

——— (1985). Acoustic and perceptual correlates of the nasa-nonnasal distinction for vowels. *Journal of the Acoustical Society of America*, 77, 1560–75.

Haykin, S. (1984). *Introduction to adaptive filters.* New York: Macmillan.

Healy, A. and Cutting, J. (1976). Units of speech perception: phoneme and syllable. *Journal of Verbal Learning and Verbal Behavior*, 15, 73–83.

Hedelin, P. (1984). A glottal LPC-vocoder. *Proceedings of IEEE International Conference on Acoustics, Speech, and Signal Processing*, 1.6.1–1.6.4. San Diego.

——— (1986). High quality glottal LPC-vocoder. *Proceedings of IEEE International Conference on Acoustics, Speech, and Signal Processing*, 9.9.1–9.9.4. Tokyo.

Hegde, M. (1987). *Clinical research in communicative disorders.* Boston: College Hill.

Heinz, J.M. (1956). Fricative consonants. *MIT Research Laboratory of Electronics Quarterly Report*, Oct.–Dec., 5–7.

Helfrich, H. (1979). Age markers in speech. In K.R. Scherer and H. Giles (eds), *Social markers in speech* (pp. 63–107). Cambridge: Cambridge University Press.

Heller, H.H. and Widnall, S.E. (1970). Sound radiation from rigid flow spoilers correlated with fluctuating forces. *Journal of the Acoustical Society of America*, 47, 924–36.

Hellige, J.B. (1993). *Hemispheric asymmetry.* Cambridge, MA: Harvard University Press.

Helmholtz, H.L.F. von (1863). *Die Lehre von den Tonempfindungen als physiologische Grundlage für die Theorie der Musik.* Braunschweig: Vieweg und Sohn.

Henderson, E.J.A. (1965). The topography of certain phonetic and morphological characteristics of South East Asian languages. *Lingua*, 15, 400–34.

Hendry, S.H. (1987). Recent advances in understanding the intrinsic circuitry of the cerebral cortex. In S.P. Wise (ed.), *Higher brain functions* (pp. 241–83). New York: Wiley.

Henke, W.L. (1966). 'Dynamic articulatory model of speech production using computer simulation'. Doctoral Dissertation, MIT.

Hermansky, H. (1990). Perceptual linear predictive (PLP) analysis of speech. *Journal of the Acoustical Society of America*, 87, 1738–52.

Hermes, D.J. (1988). Measurement of pitch by subharmonic summation. *Journal of the Acoustical Society of America*, 83, 257–64.

—— (1993). Pitch analysis. In M. Cooke, S. Beet and S. Crawford (eds), *Visual representations of speech signals* (pp. 3–25). Chichester: Wiley.

Hermes, D.J. and Gestel, J.C. van (1991). The frequency scale of speech intonation. *Journal of the Acoustical Society of America*, 90, 97–102.

Hertegård, S. and Gauffin, J. (1992). Acoustic properties of the Rothenberg mask. *Speech Transmission Laboratory – Quarterly Progress and Status Report*, 2–3, 9–18. Royal Institute of Technology, Stockholm.

Hertz, S.R. (1991). Streams, phones, and transitions: towards a new phonological and phonetic model of formant timing. *Journal of Phonetics*, 19 (1).

Hertz, S.R., Kadin, J. and Karplus, K. (1985). The Delta rule development system for speech synthesis from text. *Proceedings of IEEE*, 73, 1589–1601.

Hess, W. (1983). *Pitch determination of speech signals: algorithms and devices*. Berlin: Springer.

—— (1992). Pitch and voicing determination. In S. Furui and M.M. Sondhi (eds), *Advances in speech signal processing* (pp. 3–48). New York: Marcel Dekker, Inc.

Heuer, H. (1991). Invariant timing in motor-program theory. In J. Fagard and P. Wolfe (eds), *The development of timing control and temporal organization in coordinated action* (pp. 37–68). Amsterdam: Elsevier.

Hiki, S. and Itoh, H. (1986). Influence of palate shape on lingual articulation. *Speech Communication*, 5, 141–58.

Hinton, V. and Luschei, E. (1992). Validation of a modern miniature transducer for measurement of interlabial contact pressure during speech. *Journal of Speech and Hearing Research*, 35, 245–51.

Hirahara, T., Cariani, P.A. and Delgutte, B. (1996). Representation of low-frequency vowel formants in the auditory nerve. *Abstracts of the Association for Research in Otolaryngology*, 19, 317.

Hirano, M. (1974). Morphological structure of the vocal cord as a vibrator and its variations. *Folia phoniatrica*, 26, 89–94, 1974.

—— (1981). *Clinical examination of voice*. New York: Springer Verlag.

—— (1991). Phonosurgical anatomy of the larynx. In C. Ford and D. Bless (eds), *Phonosurgery: assessment and surgical management of voice disorders*. New York: Raven Press.

Hirano, M., Kakita, Y., Ohmaru, K. and Kurita, S. (1982). Structure and mechanical properties of the vocal fold. In N. Lass (ed.), *Speech and language: advances in basic research and practice* (pp. 211–97). New York: Academic Press.

Hirano, M., Kurita, S. and Nakashima, T. (1981). The structure of the vocal folds. In K.N. Stevens and M. Hirano (eds), *Vocal fold physiology*. Tokyo: University of Tokyo Press.

—— (1983). Growth development and aging of the human vocal cords. In Bless, D.M. and Abbs, J.H. (eds), *Vocal Fold Physiology*. San Diego: College-Hill Press.

Hirano, M., Ohara, J. and Vennard, W. (1969). The function of laryngeal muscles in regulating fundamental frequency and intensity of phonation. *Journal of Speech Hearing Research*, 12, 616–28.

Hirano, M., Vennard, W. and Ohala, J. (1970). Regulation of register, pitch and intensity of voice. An electromyographic investigation of intrinsic laryngeal muscles. *Folia phoniatrica*, 22, 1–20.

Hirayama, M., Vatikiotis-Bateson, E., Kawato, M. and Honda, K. (1992). Neural network modeling of speech motor control. In J. Ohala, T. Neary, B. Derwing, M. Hodge and G. Wiebe (eds), *Proceedings of 1992 International Conference on Spoken Language Processing* (pp. 883–6). Edmonton: The University of Alberta.

Hirose, H. (1971). Electromyography of articulatory muscles: current instrumentation and technique. *Haskins Laboratories Status Reports*, SR 25/26, 73–86.

—— (1976). Posterior cricoarytenoid as a speech muscle. *Ann. Otol. Rhinol. Laryngol.*, 85, 334–343.

—— (1977). Laryngeal adjustment in consonant production. *Phonetica*, 34, 289–94.

—— (1985). Laryngeal electromyography. In G.M. English (ed.), *Otolaryngology*, Vol. 3 (pp. 1–14). St. Louis: Harper & Low.

—— (1986). Pathophysiology of motor speech disorders (dysarthria). *Folia Phoniatrica*, 38, 61–88.

—— (1988). High-speed digital imaging of vocal fold vibration. *Acta Otolaryngol (Stockholm)*, Supplement 458, 151–153.

Hirose, H. and Gay, T. (1972). The activity of the intrinsic laryngeal muscles in voicing control – An electro-myographic study. *Phonetica*, 25, 140–64.

Hirose, H. and Joshita, Y. (1991). Laryngeal behavior in patients with disorders of the central nervous system. In M. Hirano, J.A. Kirchner, and D.M. Bless (eds), *Neurolaryngology: recent advances* (pp. 258–66). San Diego: Singular Publishing Group.

Hirose, H., Kiritani, S. and Imagawa, S. (1988). High-speech digital image analysis of laryngeal behavior in running speech. In O. Fujimura (ed.), *Vocal physiology: voice production, mechanism and functions*. New York: Raven Press.

Hirose, H., Kiritani, S. and Sawashima, M. (1982). Patterns of dysarthric movement in patients with amyotrophic lateral sclerosis and pseudobulbar palsy. *Folia Phoniatrica*, 34, 106–12.

Hirose, H., Kiritani, S., Ushijima, T., Yoshioka, H. and Sawashima, M. (1981). Patterns of dysarthric movements in patients with Parkinsonism. *Folia Phoniatrica*, 33, 204–15.

Hirose, H. and Niimi, S. (1987). The relationship between glottal opening and the transglottal pressure differences during consonant production. In T. Baer, C. Sasaki and K. Harris (eds), *Laryngeal function in phonation and respiration* (pp. 381–90). Boston: A College-Hill Publication.

Hirose, H. and Ushijima, T. (1978). Laryngeal control for voicing distinction in Japanese consonant production. *Phonetica*, 35, 1–10.

Hirose, H., Yoshioka, H. and Niimi, S. (1979). A cross language study of laryngeal adjustment in consonant production. In H. Hollien and P. Hollien (eds), *Current issues in the phonetic sciences* (pp. 443–9). Amsterdam: John Benjamins B.V.

Hirsh, I.J. (1959). Auditory perception of temporal order. *Journal of the Acoustical Society of America*, 31, 759–67.

Hixon, T.J. and Collaborators (1987). *Respiratory function in speech and Song*. Boston: College Hill.

Hixon, T., Goldman, M. and Mead, J. (1973). Kinematics of the chest wall during speech production: volume displacements of the rib cage, abdomen, and lung. *Journal of Speech and Hearing Research*, 16, 78–115.

Hixon, T., Mead, J. and Goldman, M. (1976). Dynamics of the chest wall during speech production: function of the thorax, rib cage, diaphragm, and abdomen. *Journal of Speech and Hearing Research*, 19, 297–356.

Hockett, C. (1955). A manual of phonology. *International Journal of American Linguistics*, Memoir 11. Baltimore: Waverly Press.

Hodge, M.M. (1989). 'A comparison of spectral temporal measures across speaker age: implications for an acoustic characterization of speech production'. Ph.D. dissertation, University of Wisconsin, Madison.

Hoekstra, A. and Ritsma, R.J. (1977). Perceptive hearing loss and frequency selectivity. In E.F. Evans and J.P. Wilson (eds), *Psychophysics and physiology of hearing* (pp. 263–71). London: Academic Press.

Hoemeke, K.A. and Diehl, R.L. (1994). Perception of vowel height: the role of F_1-F_0 distance. *Journal of the Acoustical Society of America*, 96, 661–74.

Holder, W. (1669). *The elements of speech*. London: T.N. for J. Martyn.

Holger, D.K., Wilson, T.A. and Beavers, G.S. (1977). Fluid mechanics of the edgetone. *Journal of the Acoustical Society of America*, 62, 1116–28.

Hollerbach, J. (1990). Planning of arm movements. In D. Osherson, S. Kosslyn and

J. Hollerbach (eds), *Visual cognition and action. An invitation to cognitive science*, Vol. 2 (pp. 183–211). Cambridge, MA: MIT Press.

Hollien, H. (1990). *The acoustics of crime*. New York: Plenum.

Hollien, H., Dew, D. and Philips, P. (1971). Phonational frequency ranges of adults. *Journal of Speech and Hearing Research*, 14, 755–60.

Hollien, H., Gelfer, R. and Huntley, R. (1990). The natural speech vector concept in speaker identification. In J.P. Köster (ed.), *Neue Tendenzen in der angewandten Phonetik III*. Hamburg: Buske.

Hollien, H., Hicks, J.W. and Oliver, L.H. (1990). A semi-automatic system for speaker identification. In J.P. Köster (ed.), *Neue Tendenzen in der angewandten Phonetik III*. Hamburg: Buske.

Hollien, H. and Jackson, B. (1967). Normative SSF data on southern male university students. *Progress report to NIH, Grant NB-OX397*.

Hollien, H., Majewski, W. and Doherty, E.T. (1982). Perceptual identification of voices under normal, stress and disguise speaking conditions. *Journal of Phonetics*, 10, 139–48.

Holmberg, E.B., Hillman, R.E. and Perkell, J.S. (1988). Glottal airflow and transglottal air pressure measurements for male and female speakers in soft, normal, and loud voice. *Journal of the Acoustical Society of America*, 84, 511–29.

Holmes, G. (1917). The symptoms of acute cerebellar injuries due to gunshot injuries. *Brain*, 40, 461–535.

Holmes, J.N. (1973). Influence of glottal waveform on the naturalness of speech from a parallel formant synthesizer. *IEEE Transactions on Audio and Electroacoustics*, AU-21, 298–305.

—— (1975). Low-frequency phase distortion of speech recording. *Journal of the Acoustical Society of America* (Lett.), 58, 747–9.

—— (1983). Formant synthesizers, cascade or parallel. *Speech Communication*, 2, 251–73.

Holmes, J.N., Mattingly, I.G. and Shearme, J.N. (1964). Speech synthesis by rule. *Language and Speech*, 7, 127–43.

Holmes, W.J. and Pearce, D.J.B. (1990). Automatic derivation of segment models for synthesis-by-rule. *Proceedings of ESCA Workshop on Speech Synthesis*, Autrans, France.

Hombert, J.-M. (1978). Consonant types, vowel quality, and tone. In V. Fromkin (ed.), *Tone: a linguistic survey* (pp. 77–111). New York: Academic Press.

Homma, Y. (1981). Durational relationships between Japanese stops and vowels. *Journal of Phonetics*, 9, 273–81.

Honda, K. (1983). Relationship between pitch control and vowel articulation. In D.M. Bless and J.H. Abbs (eds), *Vocal fold physiology: contemporary research and clinical issues* (pp. 286–97). San Diego: College Hill Press.

—— (1996). Organization of tongue articulation for vowels. *Journal of Phonetics*, 24, 39–52.

Honda, K. and Fujimura, O. (1991). Intrinsic vowel F0 and phrase-final lowering: phonological versus biological explanations. In J. Gauffin and B. Hammarberg (eds), *Vocal fold physiology: acoustic, perceptual and physiological aspects of voice mechanisms* (pp. 149–57). San Diego: Singular Press.

Honjo, I. and Isshiki, N. (1980). Laryngoscopic and voice characteristics of aged persons. *Archives of Otolaryngology*, 106, 149–50.

Hoole, P. (1987). Bite-block speech in the absence of oral sensibility. *Proceedings of the 11th International Congress of Phonetic Sciences*, 4, 16–19, August 1–7, 1987, Tallinn, Estonia.

Hoole, J.P., Nguyen-Trong, N. and Hardcastle, W. (1993). A comparative investigation of coarticulation in fricatives: electropalatographic, electromagnetic and acoustic data. *Language and Speech*, 36, 235–60.

Hoole, P., Ziegler, W., Hartmann, E. and Hardcastle, W. (1989). Parallel electropalatographic and acoustic measures of fricatives. *Clinical Linguistics and Phonetics*, 3, 59–
69.

Hopkin, G.B. (1967). Neonatal and adult tongue dimensions. *Angle Orthodontist*, 37,
132–3.

—— (1978). *The dentition and speech*. Leaflet prepared for Speech Therapy students,
Edinburgh.

Houde, R. (1968). A study of tongue body motion during selected speech sounds. *SCRL
Monograph No. 2*. Santa Barbara: Speech Communications Research Laboratory.

House, A.S. (1961). On vowel duration in English. *Journal of the Acoustical Society of
America*, 33, 1174–8.

Houtgast, T. and Steeneken, H.J.M. (1973). The modulation transfer function in room
acoustics as a predictor of speech intelligibility. *Acustica*, 28, 66–73.

Houtsma, A.J.M. and Smurzynski, J. (1990). Pitch identification and discrimination for
complex tones with many harmonics. *Journal of the Acoustical Society of America*, 87,
304–10.

Howard, D., Patterson, K., Wise, R., Brown, W.D., Friston, K., Weiller, C. and Frackowiak,
R. (1992). The cortical localization of the lexicons. *Brain*, 115, 1769–82.

Hu, Y.-H., Qiou, Y.-G. and Zhong, G.-Q. (1990). Crossed aphasia in Chinese: a clinical
survey. *Brain and Language*, 39, 347–56.

Huang, C., Hsiao, C.F., Yang, B. and Mu, H. (1991). Auditory receptive area in the
cerebellar hemisphere is surrounded by somatosensory areas. *Brain Research*, 541,
251–6.

Huang, C., Liu, L. and Huang, R. (1988). The cerebellar auditory area in the cat and the
rat. *Association for Research in Otolaryngology*, 11, 85.

Hubel, D.H. and Wiesel, T.N. (1962). Receptive fields, binocular interaction and functional architecture in the cat's visual cortex. *Journal of Physiology*, 160, 106–54.

—— (1977). Functional architecture of macaque monkey visual cortex. *Proceedings of the
Royal Society of London*, 198, 1–59.

Huffman, M.K. (1987). Measures of phonation type in Hmong. *Journal of the Acoustical
Society of America*, 81, 495–504.

Huggins, A.W.F. (1968). The perception of timing in natural speech: compensation
within the syllable. *Language and Speech*, 11, 1–11.

—— (1972). Just noticeable differences for segment durations in natural speech. *Journal
of the Acoustical Society of America*, 51, 1270–8.

—— (1975). Temporally segmented speech. *Perception and Psychophysics*, 18, 149–57.

Hughes, O.M. and Abbs, J.H. (1976). Labial-mandibular coordination in the production
of speech: implications for the operation of motor equivalence. *Phonetica*, 33, 99–
121.

Humes, L. and Christopherson, L. (1991). Speech identification difficulties of hearing-
impaired elderly persons: the contributions of auditory processing deficits. *Journal
of Speech and Hearing Research*, 34, 686–93.

Humphrey, D.R. and Freund, H.-J. (eds) (1991). *Motor control: concepts and issues*. Chichester: Wiley.

Hunker, C. and Abbs, J.H. (1984). Physiological analyses of Parkinsonian tremors in the
orofacial system. In M.R. McNeil, J.C. Rosenbek and A.E. Aronson (eds), *The
dysarthrias* (pp. 69–100). San Diego, CA: College-Hill Press.

Hunker, C., Abbs, J.H. and Barlow, S.M. (1982). The relationship between parkinsonian
rigidity and hypokinesia in the orofacial system: a quantitative analysis. *Neurology*,
32, 755–61.

Hunt, M.J. (1978). Automatic correction of low-frequency phase distortion in analogue
magnetic recordings. *Acoustic Letters*, 2, 6–10.

—— (1987). Studies of glottal excitation using inverse filtering and an electroglottograph.

Proceedings of the 11th International Congress of Phonetic Sciences, Tallinn, Estonia, 3, 23–6.

Hunter, C.J. (1966). The correlation of facial growth with body height and skeletal maturity at adolescence. *Angle Orthodontist*, 36, 44–54.

Husson, R. (1950). Étude des phenomènes physiologiques et acoustiques fondamentaux de la voix chantée. Thèse de la Faculté de Science, Paris. *Revue Scientifique*, 88, 67–112, 131–46, 217–35.

Hutchins, R.M. (ed.) (1952). *Great books of the Western world. 16: Ptolemy, Copernicus, Kepler*. Chicago: Encyclopaedia Britannica.

Hyman, L. (1975). *Phonology theory and analysis*. New York: Holt, Rinehart and Winston.

IEEE Digital Signal Processing Committee (eds) (1979). *Programs for digital signal processing*. New York: IEEE Press.

Iijima, H., Miki, N. and Nagai, N. (1990). Finite-element analysis of a vocal cord model with muscle of nonhomogeneous elasticity. *Journal of the Acoustical Society of Japan*, (E)11, 53–6.

Imaizumi, S. (1985). Acoustic measures of pathological voice quality. *Journal of Phonetics*, 457–62.

Ingard, K.U. and Ising, H. (1967). Acoustic nonlinearity of an orifice. *Journal of the Acoustical Society of America*, 42, 6–17.

Ingerslev, C.H. and Solow, B. (1975). Sex differences in craniofacial morphology. *Acta Odontologica Scandinavica*, 33, 85–94.

Ingvar, D.H. and Schwartz, M.S. (1974). Blood flow patterns induced in the dominant hemisphere by speech and reading. *Brain*, 97, 273–88.

Irvine, D.R.F. (1986). *The auditory brainstem*. Berlin: Springer-Verlag.

Ishizaka, K. and Flanagan, J.L. (1972). Synthesis of voiced sounds from a two-mass model of the vocal cords. *Bell System Technical Journal*, 51, 1233–68.

Ishizaka, K. and Matsudaira, M. (1972). Fluid mechanical considerations of vocal cord vibration. *SCRL Monograph*, 8, April.

Ishizaka, K. Matsudaira, M. and Kaneko, T. (1976). Input acoustic-impedance measurement of the subglottal system. *Journal of the Acoustical Society of America*, 60, 190–7.

Isshiki, N. (1964). Regulating mechanisms of vocal intensity variation. *Journal of Speech and Hearing Research*, 7, 17–29.

Itakura, F. (1975). Minimum prediction residue principle applied to speech recognition. *IEEE Transactions on Acoustics, Speech and Signal Processing*, 23, 67–72.

Itakura, F. and Saito, S. (1972). On the optimum quantization of feature parameters in the PARCOR speech synthesizer. In J.L. Flanagan and L.R. Rabiner (eds) (1973), *Speech synthesis* (pp. 289–92). Stroudsburg, PA: Dowden, Hutchinson and Ross.

Ito, M. (1989). The roles of the cerebellum and basal ganglia in motor control. In K. Klivington (ed.), *The science of mind* (pp. 144–5). Cambridge, MA: MIT Press.

Jackson, L.B. (1986). *Digital filters and signal processing* (2nd edn) (1989). Boston-Dordrecht-Lancaster: Kluwer Academic Publ.

Jackson, M., Ladefoged, P., Huffman, M.K. and Antoñanzas-Barroso, N. (1985). Measures of spectral tilt. *UCLA Working Papers in Phonetics*, 61, 72–8.

—— (1986). Automated measures of spectral tilt. *UCLA Working Papers in Phonetics*, 62, 77–88.

Jacobi, W.A.T. (1843). *Beitrage zur deutschen Grammatik*. Berlin: T. Trautwein.

Jaeger, J.J. (1978). Speech aerodynamics and phonological universals. *Proceedings of the Fourteenth Annual Meeting of the Berkeley Linguistics Society*, 311–29.

—— (1984). Assessing the psychological status of the vowel shift rule. *Journal of Psycholinguistic Research*, 13, 13–36.

Jakobson, R. (1968). *Child language, aphasia, and phonological universals*. The Hague: Mouton.

—— (1972). Principles of historical phonology. [Translation by A.R. Keiler of Prinzipien der historischen Phonologie, *Travaux du Cercle Linguistique de Prague*, 1931, No. 4, pp. 247–67]. In A.R. Keiler (ed.), *A reader in historical and comparative linguistics* (pp. 121–38). New York: Holt, Rinehart and Winston.

Jakobson, R., Fant, G. and Halle, M. (1969). *Preliminaries to speech analysis*. Cambridge, MA: MIT Press.

Javkin, H.R. (1976). The perceptual basis of vowel duration differences associated with the voiced/voiceless distinction. *Report of the Phonology Laboratory*, University of California, Berkeley, 1, 78–92.

Javkin, H., Antoñanzas-Barroso, N. and Maddieson, I. (1987). Digital inverse filtering for linguistic research. *Journal of Speech and Hearing Research*, 30, 122–9.

Javkin, H., Hata, K., Mendes, L., Pearson, S., Ikuta, H., Kaun, A., DeHaan, G., Jackson, A., Zimmerman, B., Wise, T., Hewton, C., Gow, M., Matsui, K., Hara, N., Kitano, M., Lin, D.-H. and Lin, C.-H. (1989). A multi-lingual text-to-speech system. *Proceedings of ICASSP-89*.

Jayant, N.S. and Noll, P. (1984). *Digital coding of waveforms. Principles and applications to speech and video*. Englewood Cliffs: Prentice-Hall, Inc.

Jelinek, F. (1976). Continuous speech recognition by statistical methods. *Proceedings of the IEEE*, 64, 532–6.

Jespersen, O. (1933). Karl Verner. In *Linguistica. Selected papers in English, French, and German* (pp. 12–23). Copenhagen: Levin and Munksgård.

Jianfen, C. and Maddieson, I. (1989). An exploration of phonation types in Wu dialects of Chinese. *UCLA Working Papers in Phonetics*, 72, 139–60.

Joanette, Y. and Dudley, J.G. (1980). Dysarthric symptomatology of Friedrich's ataxia. *Brain and Language*, 10, 39–50.

Johnson, D.H. (1980). The relationship between spike rate and synchrony in responses of auditory-nerve fibers to single tones. *Journal of the Acoustical Society of America*, 68, 1115–22.

Johnson, K., Ladefoged, P. and Lindau, M. (1993). Individual differences in vowel production. *Journal of the Acoustical Society of America*, 94, 701–14.

Johnson-Davies, D. and Patterson, R.D. (1979). Psychophysical tuning curves: restricting the listening band to the signal region. *Journal of the Acoustical Society of America*, 65, 675–770.

Jonas, S. (1981). The supplementary motor region and speech emission. *Journal of Communication Disorders*, 14, 349–73.

Jones, D. (1969). *An outline of English phonetics* (9th edn). Cambridge: Heffer.

Jones, E.G. (1987). Ascending inputs to, and internal organization of, cortical motor areas. In G. Bock, M. O'Connor and J. Marsh (eds), *Motor areas of the cerebral cortex. CIBA Foundation Symposium*, 132 (pp. 21–39). Chichester: Wiley.

Joos, M. (1948). Acoustic phonetics. *Language Monographs*, 23 (Suppl. 24).

Jordan, M.I. (1986). Attractor dynamics and parallelism in a connectionist sequential machine. *Proceedings of the Eighth Annual Meeting of the Cognitive Science Society*. Hillsdale, NJ: Erlbaum.

—— (1990). Motor learning and the degrees of freedom problem. In M. Jeannerod (ed.), *Attention and Performance* XIII (pp. 796–836). Hillsdale, NJ: Erlbaum.

—— (1992). Constrained supervised learning. *Journal of Mathematical Psychology*, 36, 396–425.

Jordan, M.I. and Rumelhart, D.E. (1992). Forward models: supervised learning with a distal teacher. *Cognitive Science*, 16, 307–54.

Joris, P.X., Carney, L.H., Smith, P.H. and Yin, T.C.T. (1994). Enhancement of neural synchronization in the anteroventral cochlear nucleus. I. Response to tones at the characteristic frequency. *Journal of Neurophysiology*, 71, 1022–51.

Josephson, J.R. and Josephson, S.G. (eds) (1994). *Abductive inference: computation, philosophy, technology*. Cambridge: Cambridge University Press.

Jueptner, M., Rijntjes, M., Weiler, C., Faiss, J.H., Timmann, D., Mueller, S.P. and Diener, H.C. (1995). Localization of a cerebellar timing process using PET. *Neurology*, 45, 1540–5.

Jurgens, U. (1976). Projections from the cortical larynx area in the squirrel monkey. *Experimental Brain Research*, 25, 401–11.

—— (1992). On the neurobiology of vocal communication. In Papousek, M., Papousek, H. and Jurgens, U. (eds), *Nonverbal vocal communication: comparative and developmental approaches* (pp. 31–42). Cambridge: Cambridge University Press.

Jusczyk, P.W. (1992). Developing phonological categories from the speech signal. In C.A. Ferguson, L. Menn and C. Stoel-Gammon (eds), *Phonological development: methods, results, implications*. Parkton, MD: York Press.

Kaas, J.H. (1987). The organization and evolution of neocortex. In S.P. Wise (ed.), *Higher brain functions* (pp. 347–78). New York: Wiley.

Kagaya, R. (1975). Fiberoptic, electromyographic and acoustic analyses of Hindi stop consonants. *Annual Bulletin Research Institute of Logopedics and Phoniatrics*, University of Tokyo, 9, 27–46.

Kahane, J.C. (1983). A survey of age-related changes in the connective tissues of the human adult larynx. In D.M. Bless and J.H. Abbs (eds), *Vocal fold physiology: contemporary research and clinical issues*. San Diego: College Hill Press.

—— (1987). Connective tissue changes in the larynx and their effects on voice. *Journal of Voice*, 1, 27–30.

—— (1988). Anatomy and physiology of the organs of the peripheral speech mechanism. In J. Lass, L.V. McReynolds, J.L. Northern, and D.E. Yoder (eds), *Handbook of speech-language pathology and audiology*. Toronto/Philadelphia: B.C. Decker Inc.

Kahane, J.C. and Folkins, J.W. (1984). *Atlas of speech and hearing anatomy*. Columbus, Ohio: Bell and Howell Co.

Kahn, D. (1980). *Syllable-based generalizations in English phonology*. New York: Garland Publishing, Inc.

Kaiki, N., Takeda, K. and Sagisaka, Y. (1990). Statistical analysis for segmental duration rules in Japanese speech synthesis. *Proceedings of International Conference on Speech and Language Processing*, Kobe, Japan.

Kailath, T. (ed.) (1985). *Modern signal processing*. Washington: Hemisphere Publ.

Kane, P. and Ní Chasaide, A. (1992). A comparison of the dysphonic and normal voice source. *Journal of Clinical Speech and Language Studies*, 2, 17–29.

Kappas, A., Hess, U. and Scherer, K.R. (1991). Voice and emotion. In R.S. Feldman, and B. Rimé (eds), *Fundamentals of nonverbal behaviour* (pp. 200–38). Cambridge: Cambridge University Press.

Karbe, H., Wurker, M., Herholz, K., Ghaemi, M., Pietrzyk, U., Kessler, J. and Heiss, W.D. (1995). Planum temporale and Brodmann's area 22: Magnetic resonance imaging and high-resolution positron emission tomography demonstrate functional left-right asymmetry. *Archives of Neurology*, 52, 869–74.

Karlsson, I. (1985). Glottal waveforms for normal female speakers. *Speech Transmission Laboratory – Quarterly Progress and Status Report 1*, 31–6, Stockholm: Royal Institute of Technology.

—— (1990). Voice source dynamics for female speakers. *Proceedings of International Conference on Spoken Language Processing* (pp. 69–72). Kobe.

—— (1992a). 'Analysis and synthesis of different voices with emphasis on female speech'. D.Sc. thesis, Royal Institute of Technology, Stockholm.

—— (1992b). Modelling speaking styles in female speech synthesis. *Speech Communication*, 11, 491–7.

Karnell, M., Linville, R. and Edwards, B. (1988). Variations in velar position over time: a nasal videoendoscopic study. *Journal of Speech and Hearing Research*, 31, 405–16.

Katz, W., Krepke, C. and Tallal, P. (1991). Anticipatory coarticulation in the speech of adults and young children: acoustic, perceptual, and video data. *Journal of Speech and Hearing Research*, 34, 1222–32.

Katz, W., Machetanz, J., Orth, U. and Schonle, P. (1990). A kinematic analysis of anticipatory coarticulation in the speech of anterior aphasic subjects using electromagnetic articulography. *Brain and Language*, 38, 555–75.

Kawasaki, H. (1982). An acoustical basis for universal constraints on sound sequences. Univ. Calif., Berkeley, doctoral dissertation.

—— (1986). Phonetic explanation for phonological universals: the case of distinctive vowel nasalization. In J.J. Ohala and J.J. Jaeger (eds), *Experimental phonology* (pp. 81–103). Orlando, FL: Academic Press.

Kawase, T., Delgutte, B. and Liberman, M.C. (1993). Anti masking effects of the olivocochlear reflex. II. Enhancement of auditory-nerve response to masked tones. *Journal of Neurophysiology*, 70, 2533–49.

Kawato, M. (1991). Optimization and learning in neural networks for formation and control of coordinated movement. In D. Meyer (ed.), *Attention and Performance XIV*. New Jersey: Lawrence Erlbaum.

Kay, B., Saltzman, E. and Kelso, J.A.S. (1991). Steady-state and perturbed rhythmical movements: a dynamical analysis. *Journal of Experimental Psychology: Human Perception and Performance*, 17, 183–97.

Kay, R.H. and Mathews, D.R. (1972). On the existence in human auditory pathways of channels selectively tuned to the modulation present in frequency-modulated tones. *Journal of Physiology*, 225, 657–67.

Kean, M.-L. (1988). Brain structures and linguistic capacity. In F.J. Neumeyer (ed.), *Higher Brain Functions* (pp. 347–78). New York: Wiley.

Keating, P.A. (1984). Phonetic and phonological representation of stop consonant voicing. *Language*, 60, 286–319.

—— (1985). Universal phonetics and the organization of grammars. In V. Fromkin (ed.), *Phonetics linguistics: essays in honor of Peter Ladefoged* (pp. 115–32). Orlando: Academic Press.

—— (1988a). Underspecification in phonetics. *Phonology*, 5, 275–92.

—— (1988b). The window model of coarticulation: articulatory evidence. *UCLA Working Papers in Phonetics*, 69, 3–29.

—— (1990). Phonetic representations in a generative grammar. *Journal of Phonetics*, 18, 321–34.

—— (1995). Segmental phonology and non-segmental phonetics. *Proceedings of the 12th International Congress of Phonetic Sciences*, 3, 26–32.

Keating, P. and Lahiri, A. (1993). Fronted velars, palatalized velars and palatals. *Phonetica*.

Keele, S. (1968). Movement control in skilled motor performance. *Psychological Bulletin*, 70, 387–403.

Keele, S.W. and Ivry, R. (1990). Does the cerebellum provide a common computation for diverse tasks? In A. Diamond (ed.), *The development and neural bases of higher cognitive functions*. Annals of the New York Academy of Sciences, 608, 179–211.

Kelley, J.F. (1985). CAL – A natural language program developed with the Oz paradigm: implications for supercomputing systems. *Proceedings of the First International Conference on Supercomputing Systems*. New York: IEEE Computer Society Press.

Kelly, J. and Local, J. (1989). *Doing phonology: observing, recording, interpreting*. Manchester and New York: Manchester University Press.

Kelso, J.A.S., Holt, K., Kugler, P. and Turvey, M. (1980). On the concept of coordinative structures as dissipative structures: II. Empirical lines of convergence. In G. Stelmach and J. Requin (eds), *Tutorials in motor behavior* (pp. 49–70). Amsterdam: North-Holland.

Kelso, J.A.S., Saltzman, E. and Tuller, B. (1986). The dynamical perspective on speech production: data and theory. *Journal of Phonetics*, 14, 29–59.

Kelso, J.A.S. and Tuller, B. (1987). Intrinsic time in speech production: theory, methodology, and preliminary observations. In E. Keller and M. Gopnik (eds), *Motor and sensory processes of language*. Hillsdale, NJ: Lawrence Erlbaum.

Kelso, J.A.S., Tuller, B. and Harris, K.S. (1983). A "dynamic pattern" perspective on the control and coordination of movement. In P. MacNeilage (ed.), *The production of speech* (pp. 137–73). New York: Springer.

Kelso, J.A.S., Tuller, B., Vatikiotis-Bateson, E. and Fowler, C. (1984). Functionally specific articulatory cooperation following jaw perturbations during speech: evidence for coordinative structures. *Journal of Experimental Psychology: Human perception and performance*, 10, 812–32.

Kelso, J.A.S., Vatikiotis-Bateson, E., Saltzman, E.L. and Kay, B. (1985). A qualitative dynamic analysis of reiterant speech production: phase portraits, kinematics, and dynamic modeling. *Journal of the Acoustical Society of America*, 77, 266–80.

Kenstowicz, M. and Kisseberth, C. (1979). *Generative phonology: description and theory*. New York: Academic Press.

Kent, J.F., Kent, R.D., Rosenbek, J.C., Weismer, G., Martin, R., Sufit, R. and Brooks, B.R. (1992). Quantitative description of the dysarthria in women with amyotrophic lateral sclerosis. *Journal of Speech and Hearing Research*, 35, 723–33.

Kent, R. (1972). Some considerations in the cinefluorographic analysis of tongue movements during speech. *Phonetica*, 26, 16–32.

Kent, R.D. (1976a). Anatomical and neuromuscular maturation of the speech mechanism: evidence from acoustic studies. *Journal of Speech and Hearing Research*, 19, 421–47.

—— (1976b). Models of speech production. In N. Lass (ed.), *Contemporary issues in experimental phonetics* (pp. 79–104). New York: Academic Press.

—— (1983). The segmental organization of speech. In P.F. MacNeilage (ed.), *The Production of Speech* (pp. 57–89). New York: Springer Verlag.

—— (1990). The acoustic and physiologic characteristics of neurologically-impaired speech movements. In W.J. Hardcastle and A. Marchal (eds), *Speech production and speech modeling* (pp. 365–401). The Netherlands: Kluwer Academic Publishers.

—— (1992). The biology of phonological development. In C.A. Ferguson, L. Menn and C. Stoel-Gammon (eds), *Phonological development: models, research, implications*. Parkton, MD: York Press.

—— (forthcoming). Developments in the theoretical understanding of speech and its disorders. To appear in *Advances in Clinical Linguistics and Phonetics*, ed. by M.J. Ball.

Kent, R.D. and Adams, S.G. (1989). The concept and measurement of coordination in speech disorders. In S.A. Wallace (ed.), *Perspectives on the coordination of movement* (pp. 415–50). Amsterdam: Elsevier Science Publishers.

Kent, R.D., Adams, S.G. and Turner, G. (1996). Models of speech production. In N.J. Lass (ed.) *Principles of Experimental Phonetics* (pp. 3–45). St. Louis: Mosby.

Kent, R.D., and Bauer, H.R. (1985). Vocalizations of one year olds. *Journal of Child Language*, 12, 491–526.

Kent, R.D., Carney, P.J. and Severeid, L.R. (1974). Velar movement and timing: evaluation of a model for binary control. *Journal of Speech and Hearing Research*, 17, 470–88.

Kent, R.D. and Forner, L.L. (1980). Speech segment durations in sentence recitations by children and adults. *Journal of Phonetics*, 8, 157–68.

Kent, R.D., Kent, J.F., Weismer, G., Martin, R., Sufit, R.L., Brooks, B.R. and Rosenbek, J.C. (1989). Relationships between speech intelligibility and the slope of the second formant transitions in dysarthric subjects. *Clinical Linguistics and Phonetics*, 3, 347–58.

Kent, R.D., Kent, J.F., Weismer, G., Sufit, R.L., Rosenbek, J.C., Martin, R.E. and Brooks, B.R. (1990). Impairment of speech intelligibility in men with amyotrophic lateral sclerosis. *Journal of Speech and Hearing Disorders*, 55, 721–8.

Kent, R.D., Kim, H.-H., Weismer, G., Kent, J.F., Rosenbek, J.C., Sufit, R., Brooks, B.R.

and Workinger, M. (1994). Laryngeal disfunction in neurological disease: amyotrophic lateral sclerosis, Parkinson's disease, and stroke. *Journal of Medical Speech-Language Pathology*, 2, 157–76.

Kent, R.D., Martin, R.E. and Sufit, R.L. (1990). Oral sensation: a review and clinical prospective. In H. Winitz (ed.), *Human communication and its disorders: a review*, Vol. 3 (pp. 135–92). Norwood, NJ: Ablex Publishing Co.

Kent, R.D. and Moll, K.L. (1969). Vocal-tract characteristics of the stop cognates, *Journal of the Acoustical Society of America*, 46, 1549–55.

—— (1972). Cinefluorographic analyses of selected lingual consonants. *Journal of Speech and Hearing Research*, 15, 453–73.

—— (1972). Cinefluorographic analyses of lingual consonants. *Journal of Speech and Hearing Research*, 15, 453–73.

Kent, R.D. and Netsell, R. (1971). Effects of stress contrasts on certain articulatory parameters. *Phonetica*, 24, 23–44.

—— (1975). A case study of an ataxic dysarthric: cineradiographic and spectrographic observations. *Journal of Speech and Hearing Disorders*, 40, 115–34.

—— (1978). Articulatory abnormalities in athetoid cerebral palsy. *Journal of Speech and Hearing Disorders*, 43, 353–73.

Kent, R.D., Netsell, R. and Abbs, J. (1979). Acoustic characteristics of dysarthria associated with cerebellar disease. *Journal of Speech and Hearing Research*, 22, 627–48.

Kent, R.D., Netsell, R. and Bauer, L.L. (1975). Cineradiographic assessment of articulatory mobility in the dysarthrias. *Journal of Speech and Hearing Disorders*, 40, 467–80.

Kent, R.D., Osberger, M.J., Netsell, R. and Goldschmidt-Hustedde, C. (1987). Phonetic development in identical twins differing in auditory function. *Journal of Speech and Hearing Disorders*, 52, 64–75.

Kent, R.D. and Read, C. (1992). *The Acoustic Analysis of Speech*. San Diego: Singular Publishing Group, Inc.

Kent, R.D. and Rosenbek, J.C. (1982). Prosodic disturbance and neurologic lesion. *Brain and Language*, 15, 259–91.

Kent, R.D., Weismer, G., Kent, J.F. and Rosenbek, J.C. (1989). Toward explanatory intelligibility testing in dysarthria. *Journal of Speech and Hearing Disorders*, 54, 482–99.

Keppel, G. (1982). *Design and analysis* (2nd edn). Inglewood Cliffs: Prentice Hall.

Kersta (1962). Voiceprint identification. *Nature*, 196, 1253–7.

Kerswill, P. and Wright, S. (1989). On the limits of auditory transcription: a sociophonetic approach. *York Papers in Linguistics*, 14, 35–59.

Kertesz, A. (1989). Hemispheric dominance: its development and relation to speech disorders. *Folia Phoniatrica*, 41, 61–88.

Kesler, S.B. (1986). *Modern spectrum analysis, II*. New York: IEEE Press.

Kewly-Port, D. (1973). Computer processing of EMG signals at Haskins Laboratories. *Haskins Laboratories Status Report on Speech Research*, SR-33, 173–84.

—— (1982). Measurement of formant transitions in naturally produced stop consonant-vowel syllables. *Journal of the Acoustical Society of America*, 72, 379–89.

Kewley-Port, D., Pisoni, D.B. and Studdert-Kennedy, M. (1983). Perception of static and dynamic acoustic cues to place of articulation in initial stop consonants. *Journal of the Acoustical Society of America*, 73, 1779–93.

Key, T.H. (1855). On vowel-assimilation, especially in relation to Professor Willis's experiment on vowel-sounds. *Transactions of the Philological Society [London]*, 5, 191–204.

Kiang, N.Y.S. (1975). Stimulus representation in the discharge patterns of auditory neurons. In D.B. Tower (ed.), *The nervous system, Vol. 3: human communication and its disorders* (pp. 81–96). New York: Raven.

Kiang, N.Y.S. and Moxon, E.C. (1974). Tails of tuning curves of auditory-nerve fibers. *Journal of the Acoustical Society of America*, 55, 620–30.

Kiang, N.Y.S., Watanabe, T., Thomas, E.C. and Clark, L.F. (1965). *Discharge patterns of single fibers in the cat's auditory nerve*. Research Monograph 35. Cambridge, MA: MIT Press.

Kim, C.-W. (1970). A theory of aspiration. *Phonetica*, 21, 107–16.

Kim, D.O., Rhode, W.S. and Greenberg, S.R. (1986). Responses of cochlear nucleus neurons to speech signals: neural encoding of pitch, intensity and other parameters. In B.C.J. Moore and R.D. Patterson (eds), *Auditory frequency selectivity* (pp. 281–8). New York: Plenum.

King, R.D. (1969). *Historical linguistics and generative grammar*. Englewood Cliffs, NJ: Prentice-Hall.

Kingston, J. and Diehl, R.L. (1994). Phonetic knowledge. *Language*, 70, 419–54.

Kinsler, L.E., Frey, A.R., Coppens, A.B. and Sanders, J.V. (1982). *Fundamentals of acoustics* (3rd edn). New York: John Wiley and Sons.

Kiparsky, P. (1968). Linguistic universals and linguistic change. In E. Bach and R.T. Harms (eds), *Universals in linguistic theory* (pp. 170–202). New York: Holt, Rinehart and Winston.

Kiritani, S., Hirose, H. and Imagawa, H. (1993). High-speed digital image analysis of vocal cord vibration in diplophonia. *Speech Communication*, 13, 23–32.

Kiritani, S., Kakita, K. and Shibata, S. (1977). Dynamic palatography. In M. Sawashima and F. Cooper (eds), *Dynamic aspects of speech production* (pp. 159–70). Tokyo: Tokyo University Press.

Kirk, P., Ladefoged, J. and Ladefoged, P. (1994). Quantifying acoustic properties of modal, breathy and creaky vowels in Jalapa Mazatec. In T. Montler (ed.), *Festschrift for Larry Thompson*. Montana: University of Montana.

Kirk, P., Ladefoged, P. and Ladefoged, J. (1984). Using a spectrograph for measures of phonation types in a natural language. *UCLA Working Papers in Phonetics*, 59, 102–13.

—— (1976). Structure of a phonological rule component for a synthesis-by-rule program. *IEEE Transmission ASSP-24*.

—— (1979). Synthesis by rule of segmental durations in English sentences. In B. Lindblom and S. Öhman (eds), *Frontiers in Speech Communication Research* (pp. 287–99). New York: Academic Press.

—— (1973). Discrimination of fundamental frequency contours in speech: implications for models of pitch perception, *Journal of the Acoustical Society of America*, 53, 8–16.

—— (1976). Linguistic uses of segmental duration in English: acoustic and perceptual evidence. *Journal of the Acoustical Society of America*, 59, 1208–21.

—— (1980a). Software for a cascade/parallel formant synthesizer. *Journal of the Acoustical Society of America*, 67, 971–95.

—— (1980b). Speech perception: a model of acoustic-phonetic analysis and lexical access. In R.A. Cole (ed.), *Perception and production of fluent speech* (pp. 243–88). Hillsdale, NJ: Erlbaum.

—— (1986a). Detailed spectral analysis of a female voice. *Journal of the Acoustical Society of America*, 81, S80(A).

—— (1986b). The problem of variability in speech recognition and in models of speech perception. In J.S. Perkell and D.H. Klatt (eds), *Invariance and variability in speech processes*. Hillsdale, NJ: Lawrence Erlbaum Associates.

—— (1987a). Review of text-to-speech conversion for English. *Journal of the Acuostical Society of America*, 82 (3), 737–93.

—— (1989). Review of selected models of speech perception. In W.D. Marslen-Wilson (ed.), *Lexical representation and process* (pp. 169–226). Cambridge, MA: MIT Press.

Klatt, D.H. and Cooper, W.E. (1975). Perception of segment duration in sentence contexts. In A. Cohen and S.G. Nooteboom (eds), *Structure and process in speech perception* (pp. 69–89). Berlin: Springer Verlag.

Klatt, D.H. and Klatt, L.C. (1990). Analysis, synthesis, and perception of voice quality variation among female and male talkers. *Journal of the Acoustical Society of America*, 87, 820–57.

Klatt, D.H. and Stevens, K.N. (1969). Pharyngeal consonants. *Research Laboratory of Electronics Quarterly Report*, 93, 207–15. Massachusetts Institute of Technology, Cambridge, MA.

Klingenheben, A. (1927). Stimmtonverlust bei Geminaten. In *Festschrift Meinhof* (pp. 134–45). Hamburg: Kommissionsverlag von L. Friederichsen & Co.

Kluender, K.R. (1991). Effects of first formant onset on voicing judgments result from processes not specific to humans. *Journal of the Acoustical Society of America*, 90, 83–96.

—— (1994). Speech perception as a tractable problem in cognitive neuroscience. In *Handbook of psycholinguistics* (pp. 173–217). London: Academic.

Kluender, K.R., Diehl, R.L. and Killeen, P.R. (1987). Japanese quails can learn phonetic categories. *Science*, 237, 1195–7.

Kluender, K.R., Diehl, R.L. and Wright, B.A. (1988). Vowel-length differences before voiced and voiceless consonants: an auditory explanation. *Journal of Phonetics*, 16, 153–69.

Kluin, K.J., Gilman, S., Markel, D.S., Koeppe, R.A., Rosenthal, G. and Junck, L. (1988). Speech disorders in olivopontocerebellar atrophy correlate with positron emission tomography findings. *Annals of Neurology*, 23, 547–54.

Koenig, B.E. (1986). Spectrographic voice identification: a forensic survey. *Journal of the Acoustical Society of America*, 79, 2088–90.

—— (1988). Enhancement of forensic audio recordings. *Journal of the Audio Engineering Society*, 36, 884–94.

—— (1990). Authentication of forensic audio recordings. *Journal of the Audio Engineering Society*, 38, 3–33.

Koenig, B.E., Ritenour, D.V., Kohus, B.A. and Kelly, A.S. (1987). Reply to 'Some fundamental considerations regarding voice identification'. *Journal of the Acoustical Society of America*, 82, 688–9.

Kohler, K. (1976). The instability of word-final alveolar plosives in German: an electropalatographic investigation. *Phonetica*, 33, 1–30.

Kohler, K.J. (1990). Segmental reduction in connected speech in German: phonological facts and phonetic explanations. In W.J. Hardcastle and A. Marchal (eds), *Speech production and speech modelling* (pp. 69–92). Dordrecht: Kluwer Academic Publishers.

—— (1991). Cognitive-auditory constraints on articulatory reduction. *PERILUS XIV*, University of Stockholm, Institute of Linguistics, 11–15.

—— (1992). Gestural reorganization in connected speech: a functional viewpoint on "articulatory phonology". *Phonetica*, 49, 205–11.

Kohonen, T. (1984). *Self organisation and associative memory*. Berlin: Springer Verlag.

Koike, Y. and Hirano, M. (1973). Glottal-area time function and subglottal pressure variation. *Journal of the Acoustical Society of America*, 54, 1618–27.

Koizumi, T. and Taniguchi, S. (1990). A novel model of pathological vocal cords and its application to the diagnosis of vocal cord polyp. *Proceedings of International Conference on Spoken Language Processing* (pp. 73–6). Kobe.

Kollia, B. (1994). 'Functional organization of velar movements following jaw perturbation'. Ph.D. dissertation, The City University of New York.

Koopmans-van Beinum, F.J. and Stelt, van der (1986). Early stages in the development of speech movements. In Lindblom, B. and Zetterstrom, R. (eds), *Precursors of early speech*. Basingstoke, Hampshire: MacMillan.

Köster, J.P. (1987). Leistung von Experten und Naiven in der auditiven Sprechererkennung. In R. Weiss (ed.), *Festschrift für H. Wängler*. Hamburg: Buske.

Kozhevnikov, V.A. and Chistovich, L.A. (1965). *Speech: articulation and perception* (trans. US Department of Commerce, Clearing House for Federal Scientific and Technical Information), No. 30, 543. Washington D.C.: Joint Publications Research Service.

Krakow, R.A. (1989). Inter-articulator timing and syllable structure. *Meeting Handbook, Linguistic Society of America*, 38.

—— (1993). Nonsegmental influences on velum movement patterns: syllables, sentence, stress, and speaking rate. In M.K. Huffman, and R.A. Krakow (eds), *Nasals, nasalization, and the velum* (pp. 87–116). San Diego: Academic Press.

Kraniauskas, P. (1992). *Transforms in signals and systems*. Wokingham: Addison-Wesley.

Kröger, B.J. (1993). A gestural production model and its application to reduction in German. *Phonetica*, 50, 213–33.

Krull, D. (1987). Second formant locus patterns as a measure of consonant-vowel coarticulation. *PERILUS* V, University of Stockholm, 43–61.

—— (1989). Second formant locus patterns and consonant-vowel coarticulation in spontaneous speech. *PERILUS* X, University of Stockholm, 87–108.

Kubozono, H. (1993). *The organization of Japanese prosody*. Tokyo: Kurosio Publishers.

Kuehn, D.P. and Moll, K.L. (1976). A cineradiographic study of VC and CV articulatory velocities. *Journal of Phonetics*, 4, 303–20. Reprinted in R.D. Kent, B.S. Atal and J.L. Miller (1991), *Papers in speech communication: speech production* (pp. 527–65). Woodbury, NY: Acoustical Society of America.

Kuehn, D.P. and Moon, J.B. (1994). Levator veli palatini muscle activity in relation to intraoral air pressure variation, *Journal of Speech and Hearing Research*, 37, 1260–70.

Kuehn, D., Reich, A. and Jordan, J. (1980). A cineradiographic study of chin marker positioning: implications for the strain gauge transduction of jaw movement. *Journal of the Acoustical Society of America*, 67, 1825–7.

Kuehn, D., Templeton, P. and Maynard, J. (1990). Muscle spindles in the velopharyngeal musculature of humans. *Journal of Speech and Hearing Research*, 33, 488–93.

Kugler, P., Kelso, J.A.S. and Turvey, M. (1980). On the concept of coordinative structures as dissipative structures: I. Theoretical lines of convergence. In G. Stelmach and J. Requin (eds), *Tutorials in motor behavior* (pp. 3–47). Amsterdam: North-Holland.

Kugler, P.N. and Turvey, M.T. (1987). *Information, natural law, and the self-assembly of rhythmic movement*. Hillsdale, NJ: Lawrence Erlbaum Associates.

Kuhl, P.K. (1981). Discrimination of speech by nonhuman animals: basic auditory sensitivities conducive to the perception of speech-sound categories. *Journal of the Acoustical Society of America*, 70, 340–9.

—— (1987). Perception of speech and sound in early infancy. In P. Salapatek and L. Cohen (eds), *Handbook of infant perception Vol. 2*. New York: Academic Press.

—— (1993). Innate predispositions and the effects of experience in visual perception: the native language magnet theory. In D. de Boysson-Bardies, S. de Schonen, P. Jusczyk, P. MacNeilage and J. Morton (eds), *Developmental neurocognition: speech and face processing in the first year of life*. Dordrecht: Kluwer Academic Publishers.

Kuhl, P.K. and Meltzoff, A.N. (1982). The bimodal perception of speech in infancy. *Science*, 218, 1138–41.

Kuhl, P.K. and Miller, J.D. (1975). Speech perception by the chinchilla: voiced-voiceless distinction in alveolar plosive consonants. *Science*, 190, 69–72.

—— (1978). Speech perception by the chinchilla: identification functions for synthetic VOT stimuli. *Journal of the Acoustical Society of America*, 63, 905–17.

Kuhl, P.K. and Padden, D.M. (1982). Enhanced discriminability at the phonetic boundaries for the voicing feature in macaques. *Perception and Psychophysics*, 32, 542–50.

Kulas, W. and Rühl, H.W. (1985). Syntax – unrestricted conversion of text to speech for German. In R. de Mori and C.Y. Suen (eds), *New systems and architectures for automatic speech recognition and synthesis* (pp. 517–35).

Kumada, M., Niitsu, B., Niimi, S. and Hirose, H. (1992). A study on the inner structure of the tongue in the production of the 5 Japanese vowels by Tagging Snapshot MRI. *Annual Bulletin of Research Institute of Logopedics and Phoniatrics*, University of Tokyo, 26, 1–12.

Künzel, H.J. (1987). *Sprechererkennung: Grundzüge forensischer Sprachverarbeitung.* Heidelberg: Kriminalistik Verlag.

—— (1990). *Phonetische Untersuchungen zur Sprecher-Erkennung durch linguistisch naive Personen.* Stuttgart: Steiner.

—— (1994a). Current approaches to forensic speaker recognition. *Proceedings of ESCA Workshop on Speaker Recognition, Identification, and Verification,* 135–41. Martigny, Switzerland, 5–7 April, 1994.

—— (1994b). On the problem of speaker identification by victims and witnesses. *Forensic Linguistics,* 1, 45–57.

Kusakawa, N., Honda, K. and Kakita, Y. (1993). Construction of articulatory trajectories in the space of tongue muscle contraction force. *ATR Technical Report,* TR-A-0717 (in Japanese).

Kuypers, H.G.H.M. (1958a). Corticobulbar connections to the pons and lower brainstem in man. *Brain,* 81, 364–88.

—— (1958b). Some projections from the peri-central cortex to the pons and lower brain stem in monkey and chimpanzee. *Journal of Comparative Neurology,* 110, 221–55.

—— (1960). Central and cortical projections to motor and somato-sensory cell groups. *Journal of Anatomy,* 92, 198–218.

Kuzmzin, Y. (1962). Mobile palatography as a tool for acoustic study of speech sounds. *Proceedings of the 4th International Congress of Acoustics,* Copenhagen, 1962.

Kydd, W. and Belt, D. (1964). Continuous palatography. *Journal of Speech and Hearing Disorders,* 29, 489–94.

Laboissière, R., Ostry, D.J. and Feldman, A.G. (1996). Control of multi-muscle systems: Human jaw and hyoid movements, *Biological Cybernetics,* 74, 373–84.

Labov, W. (1966). *Social stratification of English in New York City.* Washington DC: Centre for Applied Linguistics.

Ladd, D.R. (1980). The structure of intonational meaning: evidence from English. Bloomington, IN: Indiana University Press.

—— (1986). *Intonational phrasing: the case for recursive prosodic structure.* Cambridge: Cambridge University Press.

—— (1988). Declination "reset" and the hierarchical organization of utterances. *Journal of the Acoustical Society of America,* 84, 530–44.

Ladd, D.R. and Silverman, K.E.A. (1984). Vowel intrinsic pitch in connected speech. *Phonetica,* 41, 31–40.

Ladd, D.R., Silverman, K.E.A., Tolkmitt, F., Bergmann, G. and Scherer, K.R. (1985). Evidence for the independent function of intonation contour type, voice quality and F0 range in signalling speaker affect. *Journal of the Acoustical Society of America,* 78, 435–44.

Ladefoged, P. (1957). Use of palatography. *Journal of Speech and Hearing Disorders,* 22, 764–74.

—— (1963). Some physiological parameters in speech. *Language and Speech,* 6, 109–19.

—— (1964). Igbirra notes and word-list. *Journal of West African Languages,* 1 (1), 27–37.

—— (1967a). Linguistic phonetics. *UCLA Working Papers in Phonetics,* 6.

—— (1967b). *Three areas of experimental phonetics.* London: Oxford University Press.

—— (1968). *A phonetic study of West African languages* (2nd edn). Cambridge: Cambridge University Press.

—— (1971). *Preliminaries to linguistic phonetics.* Chicago: The University of Chicago Press.

—— (1982). The linguistic use of different phonation types. *UCLA Working Papers in Phonetics,* 54, 28–39.

—— (1991). Instrumental phonetic fieldwork: techniques and results. In *Proceedings of 12th International Congress of Phonetic Sciences,* 4, 126–9. August, 1991. Aix-en-Provence, France.

—— (1993). *A course in phonetics* (3rd edn). New York: Harcourt Brace Jovanich.

Ladefoged, P. and Antoñanzas-Barroso, N. (1985). Computer measures of breathy phonation. *UCLA Working Papers in Phonetics*, 61, 79–86.

Ladefoged, P. and Bhaskararao, P. (1983). Non-quantal aspects of consonant production: A study of retroflex consonants. *Journal of Phonetics*, 11, 291–302.

Ladefoged, P., Cochran, A. and Disner, S. (1977). Laterals and trills. *Journal of the International Phonetic Association*, 7, 46–54.

Ladefoged, P. and Maddieson, I. (1996). *Sounds of the world's languages*. Oxford: Blackwells.

Ladefoged, P., Maddieson, I. and Jackson, M. (1988). Investigating phonation types in different languages. In O. Fujimura (ed.), *Vocal physiology: voice production, mechanisms and functions* (pp. 297–317). New York: Raven.

Ladefoged, P., Maddieson, I., Jackson, M. and Huffman, M.K. (1987). Characteristics of the voice source. *UCLA Working Papers in Phonetics*, 67, 119–25.

Ladefoged, P. and Traill, A. (1980). Phonological features and phonetic details of Khoisan languages. Bushman and Hottentot linguistic studies. In J.W. Snyman (ed.), *Papers of seminar held on 27 July, 1979* (pp. 132–66). Pretoria: University of South Africa.

—— (1984). Instrumental phonetic fieldwork. In R. Thelwall and J. Higgs (eds), *Studies in experimental phonetics in honor of E.T. Uldall*. Coleraine, Northern Ireland: University of Coleraine.

—— (1994). Clicks and their accompaniments. *Journal of Phonetics*, 22 (1), 33–64.

Ladefoged, P., Williamson, K., Elugbe, B. and Uwalaka, A. (1976). The stops of Owerri Igbo. *Studies in African Linguistics*, Supp. 6, 147–63.

Lagerquist, L.M. (1980). Linguistic evidence from paranomasia. *Papers from the Seventh Regional Meeting, Chicago Linguistic Society*, 185–91.

Lahiri, A. and Marslen-Wilson, W. (1991). The mental representation of lexical form: a phonological approach to the recognition lexicon. *Cognition*, 38, 245–94.

Laitman, J.T. and Crelin, E.S. (1975). Postnatal development of the basicranium and vocal tract region in man. In J.F. Bosma (ed.), *Symposium on development of the basicranium* (pp. 206–19). Bethesda: National Institute of Health.

Lakshminarayanan, A., Lee, S. and McCutcheon, M. (1990). *Vocal tract shape during vowel production as determined by magnetic resonance imaging*. Presented at 13th annual meeting of Society of Computed Body Tomography, Palm Springs, CA.

—— (1991). MR imaging of the vocal tract during vowel production. *Journal of Magnetic Resonance Imaging*, 1, 71–6.

Lamel, L.F. and Gauvin, J.L. (1993). High performance speaker-independent phone recognition using CDHMM, *Eurospeech '93*, 1, 121–4.

Lane, H. and Webster, J. (1991). Speech deterioration in postlingually deafened adults. *Journal of the Acoustical Society of America*, 89, 859–66.

Langner, G. (1992). A review: periodicity coding in the auditory system. *Hearing Research*, 60, 115–42.

LaRiviere, C. (1974). Speaker identification from turbulent portions of fricatives. *Phonetica*, 29, 246–52.

—— (1975). Contributions of fundamental frequency and formant frequencies to speaker identification. *Phonetica*, 31, 185–97.

Larsen, B., Skinhoj, E. and Lassen, N.A. (1978). Variations in regional cortical blood flow in the right and left hemispheres during automatic speech. *Brain*, 101, 193–209.

Larson, C.R. (1988). Brain mechanisms involved in the control of vocalization. *Journal of Voice*, 2, 301–11.

Lashley, K.S. (1951). The problem of serial order in behavior. In L.A. Jeffress (ed.), *Cerebral mechanisms in behavior* (pp. 112–36). New York: Wiley.

Lass, R. (1980). *On explaining language change*. Cambridge: Cambridge University Press.

—— (1984). *Phonology: an introduction to basic concepts*. Cambridge/New York: Cambridge University Press.

Lassen, N.A., Ingvar, D.H. and Skinhoj, E. (1978). Brain function and blood flow. *Scientific American*, 239, 62–71.

Lauter, J.L. (1995). Visions of speech and language: noninvasive imaging techniques and their applications to the study of human communication. In H. Winitz (ed.), *Current approaches to the study of language development and disorders*. Timonium, MD: York Press.

Laver, J. (1979). *Voice quality: a classified research bibliography*. Amsterdam: John Benjamins.

—— (1980). *The phonetic description of voice quality*. Cambridge: Cambridge University Press.

—— (1991). *The gift of speech*. Edinburgh: Edinburgh University Press.

—— (1994). *Principles of phonetics*. Cambridge: Cambridge University Press.

Laziczius, G. (1948). Phonétique et phonologie. *Lingua*, 1, 293–302. [Reprinted in *Selected writings of Gyula Laziczius* (pp. 95–104), 1966. The Hague: Mouton].

Lazzaretto, S., and Nebbia, L. (1987). SCYLA: speech compiler for your language. *Proceedings of European Conference on Speech Communication and Technology*, 1, 381–4. Edinburgh.

Leanderson, R., Meyerson, B.A. and Persson, A. (1972). Lip muscle function in Parkinsonian dysarthria. *Acta Otolaryngologica*, 74, 354–7.

Leblanc, R., Meyer, E., Bub, D., Zatorre, R.J. and Evans, A.C. (1992). Language localization with activation positron emission tomography scanning. *Neurosurgery*, 31, 369–73.

Lecanuet, J.-P. and Granier-Deferre, C. (1993). Speech stimuli in the fetal environment. In B. de Boysson-Bardies, S. de Schonen, P. Jusczyk, P. MacNeilage and J. Morton (eds), *Developmental neurocognition: speech and face processing in the first year of life*. Dordrecht: Kluwer Academic Publishers.

Lechevalier, B., Petit, M.C., Eustache, F., Lambert, J., Chapon, F. and Viader, F. (1989). Regional cerebral blood flow during comprehension and speech (in cerebrally healthy subject). *Brain and Language*, 37, 1–11.

Leden, H. von (1961). The mechanism of phonation. *Archives of Otolaryngology*, 74, 660.

Leden, H. von and Moore, P. (1961). The mechanism of the cricoarytenoid joint. *Arch. Otolaryng.*, 73, 541–50.

Lee, K.F. (1989). *Automatic speech recognition: the development of the SPHINX system*. Boston: Kluwer Academic Publishers.

Lee, T. (1983). An acoustical study of the register distinction in Mon. *UCLA Working Papers in Phonetics*, 57, 79–96.

Lee, W. (1984). Neuromotor synergies as a basis for coordinated intentional action. *Journal of Motor Behavior*, 16, 135–70.

Lefkowitz, D. and Netsell, R. (1993). Neuroanatomy of speech: an MRI atlas. *Journal of Medical Speech-Language Pathology*, 1, 3–26.

Lehiste, I. (1964). Acoustical characteristics of selected English consonants. *Folklore and Linguistics (Indiana University Research Center in Anthroplogy)*, 34, 10–50.

—— (1965). Some acoustic characteristics of dysarthric speech. *Bibliotheca Phonetica*, Fasc. 2, Basel: S. Karger.

—— (ed.) (1967). *Readings in acoustic phonetics*. Cambridge: MIT Press.

—— (1970). *Suprasegmentals*. Cambridge, MA: MIT Press.

Lehiste, I. and Peterson, G.E. (1961). Some basic considerations in the analysis of intonation. *Journal of the Acoustical Society of America*, 33, 419–25.

Lehman, M. and Sharf, D. (1989). Perception/production relationships in the development of the vowel duration cue to final consonant voicing. *Journal of Speech and Hearing Research*, 32, 803–15.

Lehmann, W.P. (1967). *A reader in nineteenth-century historical Indo-European linguistics*. Bloomington, IN: Indiana University Press.

Leiner, H.C., Leiner, A.L. and Dow, R.S. (1991). The human cerebro-cerebellar system: its computing, cognitive and language skills. *Behavioral and Brain Research*, 44, 113–28.

Lenneberg, E.H. (1967). *Biological foundations of language*. New York: Wiley.
Leshowitz, B. (1971). Measurement of the two-click threshold. *Journal of the Acoustical Society of America*, 49, 426–66.
Letterman, R. (1994). A phonetic study of Sinhala syllable rhymes. *Working Papers of the Cornell Phonetics Laboratory*, 9, 155–81.
Levelt, W.J.M. (1989). *Speaking: from intention to articulation*. Cambridge, MA: MIT Press.
—— (1992). Accessing words in speech production: stages, processes, representations. *Cognition*, 42, 1–22.
Levinson, S.E. (1985). A unified theory of composite pattern analysis for automatic speech recognition. In F. Fallside and W.A. Woods (eds), *Computer speech processing* (pp. 243–76). Englewood Cliffs: Prentice-Hall.
Levinson, S.E., Rabiner, L.R. and Sondhi, M.M. (1983). An introduction to the application of the theory of probabilistic functions of a Markov process to automatic speech recognition. *Bell Systems Technical Journal*, 62, 1035–74.
Levitt, H., Stromberg, H., Smith, C. and Gold, T. (1980). The structure of segmental errors in the speech of deaf children. *Journal of Communication Disorders*, 13, 419–41.
Liberman, A., Cooper, F.S., Shankweiler, D. and Studdert-Kennedy, M. (1967). Perception of the speech code. *Psychological Review*, 74, 431–61.
Liberman, A.M., Delattre, P.C., Cooper, F.S. and Gerstman, L.J. (1954). The role of consonant-vowel transitions in the perception of stop and nasal consonants. *Psychology Monographs*, 68, 1–13.
Liberman, A.M. and Ignatius, G.M. (1985). The motor theory of speech perception revised. *Cognition*.
Liberman, A.M., Ingemann, F., Lisker, L., Delattre, P. and Cooper, F.S. (1959). Minimal rules for synthesizing speech. *Journal of the Acoustical Society of America*, 31, 1490–9.
Liberman, A.M. and Mattingly, I.G. (1985). The motor theory of speech perception revised. *Cognition*, 21, 1–36.
—— (1989). A specialization for speech perception. *Science*, 243, 489–94.
Liberman, M. (1975). 'The intonational system of English'. Ph.D. dissertation, MIT.
—— (1979). *The intonational system of English*. New York: Garland.
Liberman, M. and Pierrehumbert, J. (1984). Intonational invariance under changes of pitch range and length. In M. Aronoff and R. Oehrle (eds), *Language and sound structure* (pp. 157–233). Cambridge, MA: The MIT Press.
Liberman, M. and Prince, A. (1977). On stress and linguistic rhythm. *Linguistic Inquiry*, 8, 249–336.
Liberman, M.C. (1978). Auditory-nerve response from cats raised in a low-noise environment. *Journal of the Acoustical Society of America*, 63, 442–55.
—— (1982a). Single-neuron labeling in the cat auditory nerve. *Science*, 216, 1239–41.
—— (1982b). The cochlear frequency map for the cat: labeling auditory-nerve fibers of known characteristic frequency. *Journal of the Acoustical Society of America*, 72, 1441–49.
—— (1991). Central projections of auditory-nerve fibers of differing spontaneous rates. I. Antero-ventral cochlear nucleus. *Journal of Comparative Neurology*, 313, 240–58.
Licklider, J.C.R. (1951). The duplex theory of pitch perception. *Experientia*, 7, 128–37.
Lidsky, T.I., Manetto, C. and Schneider, J.S. (1985). A consideration of sensory factors involved in motor functions of the basal ganglia. *Brain Research Review*, 9, 133–46.
Lieberman, P. (1963). Some effects of semantic and grammatical context on the production and perception of speech. *Language and Speech*, 6, 172–87.
—— (1967). *Intonation, perception, and language*. Cambridge, MA: MIT Press.
—— (1970). Towards a unified phonetic theory. *Linguistic Inquiry*, 1 (3), 307–22.
—— (1984). *The biology and evolution of language*. Cambridge, MA: Harvard University Press/MIT Press.
Lieberman, P., Crelin, E.S. and Klatt, D.H. (1972). Phonetic ability and related anatomy

of the newborn and adult human, Neanderthal man and the chimpanzee. *American Anthropologist*, 74, 287–307.

Liljencrants, J. (1968). The OVE III speech synthesizer. *IEEE Transmission on Audio and Electroacoustics*, Au-16, 1, 137–40.

—— (1969). Speech synthesizer control by smoothed step functions. *Speech Transmission Laboratory – Quarterly Progress and Status Report*, 4, 43–50. Royal Institute of Technology, Stockholm.

—— (1974). *Metoder för proportionell frekvenstransponering av en signal*. Swedish patent number 362975.

—— (1991a). A translating and rotating mass model of the vocal folds. *Speech Transmission Laboratory – Quarterly Progress and Status Report*, 1, 1–18.

—— (1991b). Numerical simulations of glottal flow. In J. Gauffin and B. Hammarberg (eds), *Proceedings of Vocal Fold Physiology III* (pp. 99–104). San Diego: Singular Pub. Co.

Liljencrants, J. and Lindblom, B. (1972). Numerical simulation of vowel quality systems: the role of perceptual contrast. *Language*, 48, 839–62.

Lin, Q. and Fant, G. (1992). An articulatory speech synthesizer based on a frequency domain simulation of the vocal tract. *Proceedings of ICASSP-92*.

Lindau, M. (1984). Phonetic differences in glottalic consonants. *Journal of Phonetics*, 12, 147–55.

—— (1985). The story of /r/. In V. Fromkin (ed.), *Phonetic Linguistics* (pp. 157–68). Orlando: Academic Press.

—— (1986). Testing a model of intonation in a tone language. *Journal of the Acoustical Society of America*, 80, 757–64.

Lindblom, B. (1963). Spectrographic study of vowel reduction. *Journal of Acoustic Society of America*, 35, 1773–81.

—— (1967). Vowel duration and a model of lip-mandible coordination. *Speech Transmission Laboratory – Quarterly Progress and Status Report*, Royal Institute of Technology, Stockholm, 1–29.

—— (1968). Temporal organization of syllable production. *Speech Transmission Laboratory, Quarterly Progress Report No. 2–3/1968* (pp. 1–5). Stockholm: Royal Institute of Technology.

—— (1982). The interdisciplinary challenge of speech motor control. In S. Griller, B. Lindblom, J. Lubker and A. Persson (eds), *Speech motor control*. Oxford: Pergamon.

—— (1983). Economy of speech gestures. In P.F. MacNeilage (ed.), *The Production of Speech* (pp. 217–45). New York: Springer Verlag.

—— (1984). Can the models of evolutionary biology be applied to phonetic problems? *Abstracts of the 10th International Congress of Phonetic Sciences*. Dordrecht: Foris Publications.

—— (1986). Phonetic universals in vowel systems. In J.J. Ohala and J. Jaeger (eds), *Experimental phonology* (pp. 13–44). Orlando: Academic Press.

—— (1989). Phonetic invariance and the adaptive nature of speech. In B.A.G. Elsendoorn and H. Bouma (eds), *Working models of human perception* (pp. 139–73). London: Academic Press.

—— (1990a). Explaining phonetic variation: a sketch of the H & H theory. In W.J. Hardcastle and A. Marchal (eds), *Speech production and speech modeling* (pp. 403–40), Dordrecht: Kluwer Academic Publishers.

—— (1990b). Models of phonetic variation and selection. *Phonetic Experimental Research, Institute of Linguistics, University of Stockholm (PERILUS)*, 11, 65–100.

—— (1992). Phonological units as adaptive emergents of lexical development. In C.A. Ferguson, L. Menn and C. Stoel-Gammon (eds), *Phonological development: models, research, implications* (pp.). Parkton, MD: York Press.

—— (1994). Role of articulation in speech perception: clues from production studies. *Journal of the Acoustical Society of America*, 95, 2848 (A).

Lindblom, B. and Engstrand, O. (1989). In what sense is speech quantal? *Journal of Phonetics*, 17, 107–21.

Lindblom, B., Lubker, J. and Gay, T. (1979). Formant frequencies of some fixed-mandible vowels and a model of speech-motor programming by predictive simulation. *Journal of Phonetics*, 7, 147–62.

Lindblom, B. and Maddieson, I. (1988). Phonetic universals in consonant systems. In L.M. Hyman and C.N.L. Routledge (eds), *Language, speech and mind: studies in honor of Victoria A. Fromkin* (pp. 62–80). London and New York: Routledge.

Lindblom, B., Pauli, S. and Sundberg, J. (1975). Modeling coarticulation in apical stops. In G. Fant (ed.), *Speech communication*, Vol. 2 (pp. 87–94). Uppsala: Almqvist and Wiksell.

Lindblom, B. and Rapp, K. (1973). Some temporal regularities of spoken Swedish. *PILUS* 21, 1–58. (Papers from the Institute of Linguistics). Stockholm: University of Stockholm.

Linder-Aronson, S., Woodside, D.G., Hellsing, E. and Enderson, W. (1993). Normalisation of incisor position after adenoidectomy. *American Journal of Dentofacial Orthopaedics*, 103, 412–17.

Linker, W. (1982). Articulatory and acoustic correlates of labial activity in vowels: A cross-linguistic study. *UCLA Working Papers in Phonetics*, 56.

Linville, R.N. (1982). 'Temporal aspects of articulation: some implications for speech motor control of stereotyped productions'. Ph.D. thesis, University of Iowa, Department of Speech Pathology and Audiology.

Linville, S.E. and Fisher, H.B. (1985). Acoustic characteristics of womens' voices with advancing age. *Journal of Gerontology*, 40, 324–30.

Lisker, L. (1957). Closure duration and the intervocalic voiced voiceless distinction in English. *Language*, 33, 42–9.

Lisker, L. and Abramson, A.S. (1964). A cross-language study of voicing in initial stops: acoustical measurements. *Word*, 20, 384–422. Reprinted in R.D. Kent, B.S. Atal, and J.L. Miller (1991). *Papers in speech communication: speech production* (pp. 671–88). Woodbury, NY: Acoustical Society of America.

Lisker, L. and Abramson, A. (1970). The voicing dimension: some experiments in comparative phonetics. In B. Hala, M. Romportl, and P. Janota (eds), *Proceedings of the 6th International Congress of Phonetic Sciences* (pp. 563–7). Prague: Czechoslovak Acad. of Sci.

Lisker, L., Cooper, F.S. and Liberman, A.M. (1962). The uses of experiment in language description. *Word*, 18, 82–106.

Liss, J.M. and Weismer, G. (1992). Qualitative acoustic analysis in the study of motor speech disorders. *Journal of the Acoustical Society of America*, 92, 2984–7.

Ljungqvist, M. and Fujisaki, H. (1985). A comparative study of glottal waveform models. *Technical Report of the Institute of Electronics and Communications Engineers*, Japan, EA85-58, 23–9.

Local, J. (1992). Modelling assimilation in non-segmental, rule-free synthesis. In Docherty, G.J. and Ladd, D.R. (eds), *Papers in Laboratory Phonology 2: Gesture, Segment, Prosody* (pp. 109–23). Cambridge: Cambridge University Press.

Locke, J.L. (1983). *Phonological acquisition and change*. New York: Academic Press.

—— (1990). Structure and stimulation in the ontogeny of spoken language. *Developmental Psychobiology*, 23, 621–43.

—— (1993). *The child's path to spoken language*. Cambridge, MA: Harvard University Press.

Locke, J.L. and Pearson, D.M. (1990). Linguistic significance of babbling: evidence from a tracheostomized infant. *Journal of Child Language*, 17, 1–16.

Lockwood, P., Gillot, J.M., Boudy, J. and Faucon, G. (1991). Experiments with a nonlinear spectral subtractor (NSS) for speech recognition in the car. *Proceedings of Eurospeech '91*.

Loeb, G.E., White, M.W. and Merzenich, M.M. (1983). Spatial crosscorrelation: a proposed mechanism for acoustic pitch perception. *Biological Cybernetics*, 47, 149–63.

Löfqvist, A. (1980). Interarticulator programming in stop production. *Journal of Phonetics*, 8, 475–90.

—— (1990). Speech as audible gestures. In W. Hardcastle and A. Marchal (eds), *Speech production and speech modeling* (pp. 289–322). Dordrecht: Kluwer.

—— (1991). Proportional timing in speech motor control. *Journal of Phonetics*, 19, 343–50.

—— (1992). Acoustic and aerodynamic effects of interarticulator timing in voiceless consonants. *Language and Speech*, 35, 13–28.

Löfqvist, A., Baer, T., McGarr, N.S. and Story, R.S. (1989). The cricothyroid muscle in voicing control. *Journal of the Acoustical Society of America*, 85, 1314–21.

Löfqvist, A. and Gracco, V.L. (1991). Discrete and continuous modes in speech motor control. Papers from the symposium current phonetics research paradigms: implications for speech motor control. *PERILUS*, XIV, 27–34. Stockholm: Institute of Linguistics.

—— (1994). Tongue body kinematics in velar stop production: influences of consonant voicing and vowel context. *Phonetica*, 51, 52–67.

Löfqvist, A., Gracco, V.L. and Nye, P. (1993). Recording speech movements using magnetometry: one laboratory's experience. In *Proceedings of the ACCOR workshop on electromagnetic articulography in phonetic research*. Forschungsberichte des Instituts für Phonetik und Sprachliche Kommunikation der Universität München, 31, 143–62.

Löfqvist, A. and Yoshioka, H. (1980). Laryngeal activity in Swedish obstruent clusters. *Journal of the Acoustical Society of America*, 63, 792–801.

—— (1981). Interarticulator programming in obstruent production. *Phonetica*, 38, 21–34.

—— (1984). Intrasegmental timing: laryngeal-oral coordination in voiceless consonant production. *Speech Communication*, 3, 279–89.

Logan, J.S., Greene, B.G. and Pisoni, D.B. (1989). Segmental intelligibility of synthetic speech produced by rule. *Journal of the Acoustical Society of America*, 86 (2), 566–81.

Logemann, J.A., Fisher, H.B., Boshes, B. and Blonsky, E. (1978). Frequency and co-occurrence of vocal tract dysfunction in the speech of a large sample of Parkinson patients. *Journal of Speech and Hearing Disorders*, 43, 47–57.

Lombard, E. (1911). Le signe de l'elevation de la voix. *Annales Maladies de l'Oreille, Larynx, Nez et Pharynx*, 37, 101–19.

Love, R.J. (1992). *Childhood motor speech disability*. New York: Macmillan Publishing Co.

Lowe, A.A. (1981). The neural regulation of tongue movements. *Progress in Neurobiology*, 15, 295–344.

Lubker, J. (1979). The reorganization time of bite-block vowels. *Phonetica*, 36, 273–93.

—— (1981). Temporal aspects of speech production: anticipatory labial coarticulation. *Phonetica*, 38, 51–65.

—— (1986). Articulatory timing and the concept of phase. *Journal of Phonetics*, 14, 133–7.

Lubker, J., Fritzell, B. and Lindqvist, J. (1970). Velopharyngeal function in speech: an electromyographic study. *Speech Transmission Laboratory Quarterly Progress Status Report*, 4, 9–20.

Lubker, J.F. and Gay, T. (1982). Anticipatory labial coarticulation: experimental, biological and linguistic variables. *Journal of the Acoustical Society of America*, 71, 437–48.

Luce, P.A. (1986). 'Neighborhoods of words in the mental lexicon'. Ph.D. dissertation, Indiana University (Technical Report No. 6). Indiana: Speech Research Laboratory, Indiana University.

Luchsinger, R. (1962). Voice disorders on an endocrine basis. In N.M. Levin (ed.), *Voice and speech disorders: medical aspects* (Chapter 2). Springfield: Thomas.

Ludlow, C. and Connor, N. (1987). Dynamic aspects of phonatory control in spasmodic dysphonia. *Journal of Speech and Hearing Research*, 30, 197–206.

Lufkin, R., Larsson, S. and Hanafee, W. (1983). Work in progress: NMR anatomy of the larynx and tongue base. *Radiology*, 148, 173–5.

Lummis, R. (1973). Speaker verification by computer using speech intensity for temporal registration. *IEEE Transactions on Audio and Electroacoustics* AU-21, 32–43.

Macchi, M.J. (1980). A phonetic dictionary for demisyllabic speech synthesis. In *ICASSP 80 Proceedings*, 2 (pp. 565–7). Piscataway, NJ: IEEE Service Center.

—— (1985). 'Segmental and suprasegmental features and lip and jaw articulators'. Ph.D. thesis, New York University.

Macchi, M.J. and Spiegel, M.F. (1990). Using a demisyllable inventory to synthesize names. *Proceedings Speech Technology '90*, 208–12.

Macken, M.A. (1978). Permitted complexity in phonological development: one child's acquisition of Spanish consonants. *Lingua*, 44, 219–53.

—— (1979). Developmental reorganization of phonology: a hierarchy of basic units of acquisition. *Lingua*, 49, 11–49.

—— (1992). Where's phonology. In C.A. Ferguson, L. Menn and C. Stoel-Gammon (eds), *Phonological development: models, research, implications*. Parkton, MD: York Press.

—— (1995). Phonological Acquisition. In J. Goldsmith (ed.) *Handbook of Phonological Theory*. Oxford: Basil Blackwell.

Macken, M.A. and Ferguson, C.A. (1983). Cognitive aspects of phonological development: model, evidence and issues. In K.E. Nelson (ed.), *Children's Language (Vol. 4)*. Hillsdale, NJ: Lawrence Erlbaum Associates.

Mackenzie, J., Laver, J. and Hiller, S.M. (1991). Structural pathologies of the vocal folds and phonation. In J. Laver, *The gift of speech*. Edinburgh: Edinburgh University Press.

MacNeilage, P. (1970). The motor control of serial ordering in speech. *Psychological Review*, 77, 182–96.

—— (1972). Speech physiology. In J.H. Gilbert (ed.), *Speech and cortical functioning* (pp. 1–72), New York: Academic Press.

—— (1987). The evolution of hemispheric specialization for manual function and language. In S.P. Wise (ed.), *Higher brain functions* (pp. 285–309). New York: Wiley and Sons.

—— (1994). Prolegomena to a theory of the sound pattern of the first language. *Phonetica*, 51, 184–94.

—— (Submitted). The frame-content theory of evolution of speech production.

MacNeilage, P.F. and Davis, B.L. (1990a). Acquisition of speech production: frames, then content. In M. Jeannerod (ed.), *Attention and performance XIII: motor representation and control*. Hillsdale, NJ: Lawrence Erlbaum Associates.

—— (1990b). Acquisition of speech production: the achievement of segmental independence. In Hardcastle, W.J. and Marchal, A. (eds), *Speech production and speech modelling*. Dordrecht: Kluwer Academic Publishers.

—— (1993). Motor explanations of babbling and early speech patterns. In B. de Boysson-Bardies, S. de Schonen, P. Jusczyk, P. MacNeilage and J. Morton (eds), *Developmental neurocognition: speech and face processing in the first year of life*. Dordrecht: Kluwer Academic Publishers.

MacNeilage, P., Hanson, R. and Krones, R. (1970). Control of the jaw in relation to stress in English. *Journal of the Acoustical Society of America*, 48, S119 (A).

MacNeilage, P. and Sholes, G. (1964). An electromyographic study of the tongue during vowel production. *Journal of Speech and Hearing Research*, 7, 211–32.

MacNeilage, P.F., Studdert-Kennedy, M.G. and Lindblom, B. (1987). Primate handedness reconsidered. *Behavioral and Brain Sciences*, 10, 247–303.

—— (1993). Hand signals. *The Sciences*, January/February issue.

Maddieson, I. (1984a). *Patterns of sounds*. Cambridge: Cambridge University Press.

—— (1984b). The effects on F0 of a voicing distinction in sonorants and their implications for a theory of tonogenesis. *Journal of Phonetics*, 12, 9–15.

—— (1985). Phonetic cues to syllabification. In V.A. Fromkin (ed.), *Phonetic linguistics: essays in honor of Peter Ladefoged* (pp. 203–21). New York: Academic Press.

—— (1989). Linguo-labials. In R. Harlow and R. Hooper (eds), *Proceedings of the Fifth International Congress of Austronesian Linguistics: Oceanic Languages* (pp. 349–75). Auckland: Linguistic Society of New Zealand.

—— (1991). Tone spacing. In J. Kelly and J. Local (eds), *Festschrift for Professor Jack Carnochan. York Papers in Linguistics*, 15, 149–75, University of York, Heslington.

—— (1992). The structure of segment sequences. In J.J. Ohala et al (eds), *Proceedings of the 1992 International Conference on Spoken Language Processing* (pp. 1–4). University of Alberta, Banff, Alberta: Addendum.

Maddieson, I. and Emmorey, K. (1984). Is there a valid distinction between voiceless lateral approximants and fricatives? *Journal of Phonetics*, 41, 181–90.

Maddieson, I. and Hess, S.A. (1987). The effect on F0 of the linguistic use of phonation type. *UCLA Working Papers in Phonetics*, 67, 112–18.

Maddieson, I. and Ladefoged, P. (1985). "Tense" and "lax" in four minority languages of China. *UCLA Working Papers in Phonetics*, 60, 59–83.

Maeda, S. (1976). 'A Characterization of American English Intonation'. Ph.D. Thesis, Department of Electrical Engineering, Massachusetts Institute of Technology, Cambridge, MA.

—— (1982a). The role of the sinus cavities in the production of nasal vowels. *Proceedings of ICASSP 82*, 911–14, Paris, France.

—— (1982b). Acoustic cues of vowel nasalization: a simulation study. *Journal of the Acoustical Society of America*, 72, Suppl. 1, S102.

—— (1987). On generation of sound in stop consonants. *Speech Communication Group Working Papers*, Research Laboratory of Electronics, Massachusetts Institute of Technology, 5, 1–14.

—— (1990). Compensatory articulation during speech: evidence from the analysis and synthesis of vocal tract shapes using an articulatory model. In W.L. Hardcastle and A. Marchal (eds), *Speech production and speech modelling* (pp. 131–49). Dordrecht: Kluwer Academic Publishers.

—— (1991). On articulatory and acoustic variabilities. *Journal of Phonetics*, 19, 321–31.

—— (1992). Articulatory modeling of the vocal tract. In *J. Physique IV*, 2 (pp. 307–14).

Maeda, S. and Honda, K. (1994). *From EMG to formant patterns of vowels: the implication of vowel systems spaces.* Presented at the ACCOR Workshop on Lingual Data and Modeling in Speech Production, Barcelona, 20–22 December.

Magen, H.S. (1989). 'An acoustic study of vowel-to-vowel coarticulation in English'. Ph.D. dissertation, Yale University, New Haven, CT.

Makhoul, J. (1978). A class of all-zero lattice digital filters: properties and applications. *IEEE Trans ASSP-26*, 304–14.

Makhoul, J., Roucos, S. and Gish, H. (1985). Vector quantization in speech coding. *Proceedings of IEEE 73-11*, 1551–88.

Makhoul, J., Vishwanathan, R., Schwartz, R. and Huggins, A.W.F. (1978). A mixed-source model for speech compression and synthesis. *Journal of the Acoustical Society of America*, 64, 1577–81.

Malécot, A. (1956). Acoustic cues for nasal consonants: an experimental study involving a tape-splicing technique. *Language*, 32, 274–84.

Malwar, H.S. (1992). *Signal processing with lapped transforms*. London: Artech House.

Mann, V.A. and Repp, B.H. (1981). Influence of preceding fricative on stop consonant perception. *Journal of the Acoustical Society of America*, 69, 548–58.

Manuel, S. (1987). 'Acoustic and perceptual consequences of vowel-to-vowel coarticulation in three Bantu languages'. Ph.D. Dissertation, Yale University, New Haven, CT.

—— (1990). The role of contrast in limiting vowel-to-vowel coarticulation in different languages. *Journal of the Acoustical Society of America*, 88, 1286–98.

Manuel, S. and Krakow, R. (1984). Universal and language particular aspects of vowel-to-vowel coarticulation, *Haskins Laboratories Status Report on Speech Research*, 77/78, 69–78.

Manuel, S. and Vatikiotis-Bateson, E. (1988). Oral and glottal gestures and acoustics of underlying [t] in English. *Journal of the Acoustical Society of America*, 84(51), 584(A).

Marchal, A. (1983). Coarticulatory patterns in stop sequences: EPG evidence. *Proceedings of the 10th International Congress of Phonetic Sciences* (p. 473). Utrecht: Foris Dordrecht.

—— (1988). Coproduction: EPG evidence. *Speech Communication*, 7, 287–95.

Markel, J.D. (1972). The SIFT algorithm for fundamental frequency estimation. *IEEE Trans* AU-20, 367–77.

Markel, J.D. and Gray, A.H. (1976). *Linear prediction of speech. Communication and cybernetics 12*. Berlin: Springer.

Marquardt, T.P. and Sussman, H.M. (1991). Developmental apraxia of speech: theory and practice. In D. Vogel and M.P. Cannito (eds), *Treating disordered speech motor control* (pp. 341–90). Austin, TX: Pro-Ed.

Marr, D. (1982). *Vision*. San Francisco: W.H. Freeman.

Marslen-Wilson, W.D. (1987). *Functional parallelism in spoken word-recognition. Cognition*, 25, 71–102.

—— (1990). Activation, competition, and frequency in lexical access. In G.T.M. Altmann (ed.), *Cognitive models of speech processing: psycholinguistic and computational perspectives* (pp. 148–72). Cambridge, MA: MIT Press.

Marslen-Wilson, W. and Warren, P. (1994). Levels of perceptual representation and process in lexical access: words, phonemes, and features. *Psychological Review*, 101, 653–75.

Martin, C.S., Mullennix, J.W., Pisoni, D.B. and Summers, W.V. (1989). Effects of talker variability on recall of spoken word lists. *Journal of Experimental Psychology: Learning, Memory, and Cognition*, 15, 676–84.

Martin, D. (1961). Some facies in the diseases of childhood. *Medical and Biological Illustration*, 11, 76–84.

Martin, P. (1982). Comparison of pitch detection by cepstrum and spectral comb analysis. *Proceedings of ICASSP*, 180–3.

Martin, R. and Haroldson, S. (1992). Stuttering and speech naturalness: audio and visual judgements. *Journal of Speech and Hearing Research*, 35, 521–8.

Martinet, A. (1955). *Economie des changements phonétiques*. Berne: Francke.

—— (1968). Phonetics and linguistic evolution. In B. Malmberg (ed.), *Manual of phonetics* (pp. 464–87). Amsterdam: North Holland.

Massaro, D.W. (1989). Testing between the TRACE model and the fuzzy logical model of speech perception. *Cognitive Psychology*, 21, 398–421.

Massey, B.S. (1984). *Mechanics of fluids* (5th edn). Wokingham: Van Nostrand Reinhold (UK) Co. Ltd.

Massey, N.S. (1994). 'Transients at stop consonant releases'. S.M. Thesis, Massachusetts Institute of Technology, Cambridge, MA.

Matsui, T. and Furui, S. (1994). Similarity normalization method for speaker verification based on a posteriori probability. *Proceedings of ESCA Workshop on Automatic Speaker Recognition, Identification and Verification*, 59–62, Martigny, Switzerland, 5–7 April 1994.

Matthews, P. (1972). *Mammalian muscle receptors and their central actions*. London: Edward Arnold.

Mattyear, C., MacNeilage, P.F. and Davis, B.L. (1994). *Vocants in oral and nasal contexts during canonical babbling*. Paper presented at the Annual Convention of the American Speech, Hearing and Language Association, New Orleans, Louisiana.

Mazo, M. (1992). Lament made visible: a study of paramusical elements in Russian lament. In B. Yung and J. Lam (eds), *Theme and variations: writings on music in honor of Rulan Chao Pian* (pp. 166–212). Cambridge, MA: Harvard University Department of Music.

Mazo, M., Erickson, D. and Harvey, T. (1994). Emotion and expression: temporal data on voice quality in Russian lament. In O. Fujimura and M. Hirano (eds), *Vocal fold physiology: voice quality control* (pp. 173–87). San Diego, CA: Singular Publ.

McCarthy, G., Blamire, A.M., Rothman, D.L., Gruetter, R. and Shulman, R.G. (1993). Echoplanar magnetic resonance imaging studies of frontal cortex activation during word generation in humans. *Proceedings of the National Academy of Sciences, U.S.A.*, 90, 4952–6.

McCarthy, J. and Prince, A. (in press). *Constraint interaction and prosodic morphology*.ms, University of Mass and Rutgers University.

McCarthy, R. and Warrington, E.K. (1984). A two-route model of speech production: evidence from aphasia. *Brain*, 107, 463–85.

McCawley, J. D. (1968). The role of semantics in a grammar. In E. Bach and R.T. Harms (eds), *Universals in linguistic theory*. New York: Holt Rinehart and Winston.

McClelland, J.L. (1991). Stochastic interactive processes and the effect of context on perception. *Cognitive Psychology*, 23, 1–44.

McClelland, J.L. and Elman, J.L. (1986). The TRACE model of speech perception. *Cognitive Psychology*, 18, 1–86.

McClelland, J. and Rumelhart, D. (eds) (1986). *Parallel distributed processing, Vol. 2: Psychological and biological models*. Cambridge, MA: MIT Press.

McCrea, D. (1992). Can sense be made of spinal interneuron circuits? *Behavioral and Brain Sciences*, 15, 633–43.

McCulloch, N.A. and Ainsworth, W.A. (1988). Speaker independent vowel recognition using a multi-layer perceptron. *Proceedings of the Seventh FASE Symposium*, 3, 851–8.

McCutcheon, M., Lee, S., Lakshminarayanan, A. and Fletcher, S. (1990). A comparison of glossometric measurements of tongue position with magnetic resonance images of the vocal tract. *Journal of the Acoustical Society of America*, S A.

McFarland, D.H. and Baum, S.R. (1995). Incomplete compensation to articulatory perturbation. *Journal of the Acoustical Society of America*, 97, 1865–73.

McGehee, F. (1937). The reliability of the identification of the human voice. *Journal of General Psychology*, 17, 249–71.

McGlone, R., Proffit, W. and Christiansen, R. (1967). Lingual pressures associated with alveolar consonants. *Journal of Speech and Hearing Research*, 10, 606–15.

McGowan, R.S. (1988). An aeroacoustic approach to phonation. *Journal of the Acoustical Society of America*, 83, 696–704.

—— (1992). Tongue-tip trills and vocal-tract wall compliance. *Journal of the Acoustical Society of America*, 91, 2903–10.

McInnes, F.R., Jack, M.A. and Laver, J. (1987). Experiments with template adaptation in an isolated word recognition system. In J. Laver and M.A. Jack (eds), *Proceedings of the European Conference on Speech Technology*, 2, 484–7. Edinburgh: CEP Consultants Ltd.

McKay, G.R. (1980). Medial stop gemination in Rembarrnga: a spectrographic study. *Journal of Phonetics*, 8, 343–352.

McKenna, K., Jabour, B., Lufkin, R. and Hanafee, W. (1990). Magnetic resonance imaging of the tongue and oropharynx. *Top Magn Reson Imaging*, 2, 49–59.

McNeil, M.R., Weismer, G., Adams, S. and Mulligan, M. (1990). Oral structure non-speech motor control in normal, dysarthric, aphasic, and apraxic speakers: isometric force and static position control. *Journal of Speech and Hearing Research*, 33, 255–68.

McNeill, D. and Lindig, K. (1973). The perceptual reality of phonemes, syllables, words, and sentences. *Journal of Verbal Learning and Verbal Behavior*, 12, 431–61.

McQueen, J.M. (1991a). The influence of the lexicon on phonetic categorization: stimulus quality in word-final ambiguity. *Journal of Experimental Psychology: Human Perception and Performance*, 17, 433–43.

—— (1991b). 'Phonetic decisions and their relationship to the lexicon'. Ph.D. dissertation, University of Cambridge.

—— (1993). Rhyme decisions to spoken words and nonwords. *Memory & Cognition*, 21, 210–22.

—— (submitted). *Lexical or non-lexical effects in compensation for coarticulation?*

McQueen, J.M., Norris, D. and Cutler, A. (1994). Competition in spoken word recognition: spotting words in other words. *Journal of Experimental Psychology: Learning, Memory, and Cognition*, 20, 621–38.

McReynolds, L. and Thompson, C. (1986). Review of the flexibility of single-subject designs. *Journal of Speech and Hearing Disorders*, 51, 194–203.

Meddis, R. and Hewitt, M.J. (1991). Virtual pitch and phase sensitivity of a computer model of the auditory periphery. I. Pitch identification. *Journal of the Acoustical Society of America*, 89, 2866–82.

—— (1992). Modeling the identification of concurrent vowels with different fundamental frequencies. *Journal of the Acoustical Society of America*, 91, 233–45.

Meditch, A. (1975). The development of sex-specific speech patterns in young children. *Anthropological Linguistics*, 17, 421–33.

Mehler, J. (1981). The role of syllables in speech processing: infant and adult data. *Philosophical Transactions of the Royal Society, Series B*, 295, 333–52.

Mehler, J., Dommergues, J.-Y., Frauenfelder, U.H. and Segui, J. (1981). The syllable's role in speech segmentation. *Journal of Verbal Learning and Verbal Behavior*, 20, 298–305.

Mehler, J., Jusczyk, P., Lambertz, G., Halsted, N., Bertoncini, J. and Amiel-Tison, C. (1988). A precursor of language acquisition in young infants. *Cognition*, 29, 143–78.

Mehta, G. and Cutler, A. (1988). Detection of target phonemes in spontaneous and read speech. *Language and Speech*, 31, 135–56.

Meltzoff, A.N. and Moore, M.K. (1993). Why faces are special to infants – On connecting the attraction of faces and infants' ability for imitation and cross-modal processing. In B. de Boysson-Bardies, S. de Schonen, P. Jusczyk, P. MacNeilage and J. Morton (eds), *Developmental neurocognition: speech and face processing in the first year of life*. Dordrecht: Kluwer Academic Publishers.

Menn, L. (1978). Phonological units in beginning speech. In A. Bell and J.B. Hooper (eds), *Syllables and segments*. Amsterdam: North Holland.

—— (1983). Development of articulatory, phonetic, and phonological capabilities. In B. Butterworth (ed.), *Language production, Vol. 2, Development, writing, and other processes*. New York: Academic Press.

Menn, L. and Matthei, E. (1992). The "Two-Lexicon" account of child phonology. In C.A. Ferguson, L. Menn and C. Stoel-Gammon (eds), *Phonological development: models, research, implications*. Parkton, MD: York Press.

Menzerath, P. and Lacerda, A. de (1933). *Koartikulation Steuerung und Lautabgrenzung*. Bonn: Ferdinand Dümmlers Verlag.

Meredith, M.A. and Stein, B.E. (1986). Visual, auditory, and somatosensory convergence on cells in superior colliculus results in multisensory integration. *Journal of Neurophysiology*, 56, 640–62.

Mermelstein, P. (1973). Articulatory model for the study of speech production. *Journal of the Acoustical Society of America*, 53, 1070–82.

Merrifield, W.R. (1963). Palantla Chinantec syllable types. *Anthropological Linguistics*, 5 (5), 1–16.

Meyer-Eppler, W. (1953). Zum Erzeugungsmechanismus der Gerauschlaute [On the generating mechanism of noise sounds]. *Zeitschrift für Phonetik*, 7, 196–212.

Michi, K., Suzuki, N., Yamashita, Y. and Imai, S. (1986). Visual training and correction of articulation disorders by use of dynamic palatography: serial observation in a case of cleft palate. *Journal of Speech and Hearing Disorders*, 51, 226–38.

Miller, G.A. and Nicely, P.E. (1955). Analysis of perceptual confusions among some English consonants. *Journal of the Acoustical Society of America*, 27, 338–53.

Miller, J.L. (1981). Effects of speaking rate on segmental distinctions. In P.D. Eimas and J.L. Miller (eds), *Perspectives on the study of speech* (pp. 39–74). Hillsdale, NJ: Erlbaum.

—— (1987). Mandatory processing in speech perception. In J.L. Garfield (ed.), *Modularity in knowledge representation and natural-language understanding* (pp. 309–24). Cambridge, MA: MIT Press.

Miller, J.L. and Dexter, E.R. (1988). Effects of speaking rate and lexical status on phonetic perception. *Journal of Experimental Psychology: Human Perception and Performance*, 14, 369–78.

Miller, J.L., Green, K. and Schermer, T. (1984). On the distinction between prosodic and semantic factors in word identification. *Perception & Psychophysics*, 36, 329–37.

Miller, J.L. and Jusczyk, P.W. (1989). Seeking the neurobiological bases of speech perception. *Cognition*, 33, 111–37.

Miller, M.I. and Sachs, M.B. (1983). Representation of stop consonants in the discharge patterns of auditory-nerve fibers. *Journal of the Acoustical Society of America*, 74, 502–17.

—— (1984). Representation of voiced pitch in the discharge patterns of auditory-nerve fibers. *Hearing Research*, 14, 257–79.

Miller, W.C. and Delong, M.R. (1988). Parkinsonian symptomatology: an anatomical and physiological analysis. In J.J. Joseph (ed.), Central determinants of age-related declines in motor function. *Annals of the New York Academy of Sciences*, 515, 287–302.

Mills, A.E. (1984). The acquisition of speech sounds in the visually handicapped child. In A.E. Mills (ed.), *Language acquisition in the blind child: normal and deficient*. San Diego, CA: College-Hill Press.

Milner, T. and Ijaz, M. (1990). The effect of accuracy constraints on three dimensional movement kinematics. *Neuroscience*, 35, 365–74.

Mitchell, P. and Kent, R. (1992). Phonetic variation in multisyllabic babbling. *Journal of Child Language*, 17, 247–65.

Mitra, S.K. and Kaiser, J.F. (1993). *Handbook for digital signal processing*. Chichester: Wiley.

Miyawaki, K. (1972). *A study of lingual articulation by use of dynamic palatography*. M.A. dissertation, Department of Linguistics, University of Tokyo.

—— (1974). A study of the musculature of the human tongue. *Annual Bulletin of Research Institute of Logopedics and Phoniatrics*, University of Tokyo, 8, 23–50.

Miyawaki, K., Hirose, H., Ushijima, T. and Sawashima, M. (1975). A preliminary report on the electromyographic study of the activity of lingual muscles. *Annual Bulletin of Research Institute of Logopedics and Phoniatrics*, University of Tokyo, 9, 91–106.

Miyawaki, K., Kiritani, S., Tatsumi, I. and Fujimura, O. (1974). Palatographic observations of VCV articulations in Japanese. *Annual Bulletin of Research Institute of Logopedics and Phoniatrics*, University of Tokyo, 8, 51–7.

Mizutani, T., Hashimoto, K., Wakumoto, M., Hamada, H. and Miura, T. (1988). *Analysis of tongue motion for the dental consonants based on high-speed palatographic data*. Second Joint Meeting of the Acoustical Society of America and Acoustical Society of Japan, Honolulu, HI.

Mohanan, K.P. and Mohanan, T. (1984). Lexical phonology of the consonant system in Malayalam. *Linguistic Inquiry*, 15, 575–602.

Mohr, B. (1971). Intrinsic variations in the speech signal. *Phonetica*, 23, 65–93.

Mohr, J.P., Pessin, M.S., Finkelstein, S., Funkenstein, H.H., Duncan, G.W. and Davis, K.R. (1978). Broca's aphasia: pathologic and clinical. *Neurology*, 28, 311–24.

Moll, K. and Daniloff, R. (1971). Investigation of the timing of velar movements during speech. *Journal of the Acoustical Society of America*, 50, 678–84.

Montague, J.C., Brown, W.S. and Hollein, H. (1974). Vocal fundamental characteristics of institutionalised Down's Syndrome children. *American Journal of Mental Deficiency*, 78, 414–18.

Moon, J.B. and Kuehn, D.P. (1994). *Effects of cleft palate on relative levels of levator veli palatini activity during speech*. Presented at the Conference on Motor Speech, Sedona, AZ, 24–28 March.

Moon, J.B., Kuehn, D.P. and Huisman, J.J. (1994). Measurement of velopharyngeal closure force during vowel production. *National Center for Voice and Speech Status and Progress Report*, 6, 53–60.

Moon, S.-J. (1991). An acoustic and perceptual study of undershoot in clear and citation-form speech. *PERILUS XIV*, University of Stockholm, Institute of Linguistics, 153–6.

Moon, S.-J. and Lindblom, B. (1989). Formant undershoot in clear and citation-form speech: a second progress report. *Quarterly Progress and Status Report*, Department of Speech Communication STL-KTH Stockholm, 121–3.

—— (1994). Interaction between duration, context, and speaking style in English stressed vowels. *Journal of the Acoustical Society of America*, 96, 40–55.

Moore, B.C.J. (1986). Parallels between frequency selectivity measured psychophysically and in cochlear mechanics. *Scandinavian Audiology Supplement*, 25, 139–52.

—— (1990). *Introduction to the psychology of hearing*. London: Academic.

—— (1993). Frequency analysis and masking. In B.C.J. Moore (ed.), *Handbook of perception and cognition, Vol. 6. Hearing* (in press). Orlando, FL: Academic Press.

Moore, B.C.J. and Glasberg, B.R. (1983). Suggested formulae for calculating auditory-filter bandwidths and excitation patterns. *Journal of the Acoustical Society of America*, 74, 750–3.

—— (1987). Formulae describing frequency selectivity as a function of frequency and level and their use in calculating excitation patterns. *Hearing Research*, 28, 209–25.

—— (1988). Effects of the relative phase of the components on the pitch discrimination of complex tones by subjects with unilateral and bilateral cochlear impairments. In H. Duifhuis, H. Wit and J. Horst (eds), *Basic issues in hearing* (pp. 421–30). London: Academic Press.

—— (1990). Frequency discrimination of complex tones with overlapping and non-overlapping harmonics. *Journal of the Acoustical Society of America*, 87, 2163–77.

Moore, B.C.J., Glasberg, B.R. and Peters, R.W. (1985). Relative dominance of individual partials in determining the pitch of complex tones. *Journal of the Acoustical Society of America*, 77, 1853–60.

Moore, B.C.J., Glasberg, B.R., Plack, C.J. and Biswas, A.K. (1988). The shape of the ear's temporal window. *Journal of the Acoustical Society of America*, 83, 1102–16.

Moore, B.C.J., Glasberg, B.R. and Shailer, M.J. (1984). Frequency and intensity difference limens for harmonics within complex tones. *Journal of the Acoustical Society of America*, 75, 550–61.

Moore, B.C.J. and Jorasz, U. (1992). Detection of changes in modulation depth of a target sound in the presence of other modulated sounds. *Journal of the Acoustical Society of America*, 91, 1051–61.

Moore, B.C.J. and O'Loughlin, B.J. (1986). The use of nonsimultaneous masking to measure frequency selectivity and suppression. In B.C.J. Moore (ed.), *Frequency Selectivity in hearing* (pp. 179–250). London: Academic Press.

Moore, B.C.J. and Ohgushi, K. (1993). Audibility of partials in inharmonic complex tones. *Journal of the Acoustical Society of America*, 93, 452–61.

Moore, B.C.J. and Peters, R.W. (1992). Pitch discrimination and phase sensitivity in young and elderly subjects and its relationship to frequency selectivity. *Journal of the Acoustical Society of America*, 91, 2881–93.

Moore, B.C.J., Peters, R.W. and Glasberg, B.R. (1993a). Detection of temporal gaps in sinusoids: effects of frequency and level. *Journal of the Acoustical Society of America*, 93, 1563–70.

Moore, B.C.J., Shailer, M.J., Hall, J.W. and Schooneveldt, G.P. (1993b). Comodulation masking release in subjects with unilateral and bilateral cochlear hearing impairment. *Journal of the Acoustical Society of America*, 93, 435–51.

Moore, C. (1992). The correspondence of vocal tract resonance with volumes obtained from magnetic resonance images. *Journal of Speech and Hearing Research*, 35, 1009–23.

Moore, C.A. and Scudder, R.R. (1989). Coordination of jaw muscle activity in parkinsonian movement: description and response to traditional treatment. In K. Yorkston and D.R. Beukelman (eds), *Clinical dysarthria* (pp. 147–63). San Diego: College-Hill Press.

Moore, C.A., Smith, A. and Ringel, R.L. (1988). Task specific organization of activity in human jaw muscles. *Journal of Speech and Hearing Research*, 31, 670–80.

Moore, J.K. (1987). The human auditory brainstem: a comparative view. *Hearing Research*, 29, 1–32.

Moore, T.J. and Cashin, J.L. (1976). Response of cochlear-nucleus neurons to synthetic speech. *Journal of the Acoustical Society of America*, 59, 1443–49.

Morais, J. and Kolinsky, R. (1994). Perception and awareness in phonological processing: the case of the phoneme. *Cognition*, 50, 287–97.

Morin-Surun, M.P., Boudinot, E., Sarraseca, H., Fortin, G. and Denavit-Saubie, M. (1992). Respiratory network remains functional in a mature guinea pig brainstem isolated in vitro. *Experimental Brain Research*, 90 (2), 375–83.

Moscowitz, B.A. (1991). The acquisition of language. In W.S.-Y. Wang (ed.), *The emergence of language: development and evolution*. New York: W.H. Freeman and Co.

Moulines, E., Emerard, F., Larreur, D., Le Saint Millon, J.L., Le Faucheur, L., Marty, F., Charpentier, F. and Sorin, C. (1990). A real-time French text-to-speech system generating high quality synthetic speech. *Proceedings of ICASSP-90*.

Mrayati, M., Carré, R. and Guérin, B. (1988). Distinctive regions and modes: a new theory of speech production. *Speech Communication*, 7, 257–86.

Muakkassa, K.F. and Strick, P.L. (1979). Frontal lobe inputs to primate motor cortex: evidence for four somatotopically organized "premotor" areas. *Brain Research*, 177, 176–82.

Mueller, P.B. (1971). Parkinson's disease: motor speech behavior in a selected group of patients. *Folia Phoniatrica*, 23, 333–46.

Mueller, P.B., Sweeney, R.J. and Baribeau, L.J. (1985). Senescence of the voice: morphology of excised male larynges. *Folia Phoniatrica*, 37, 134–8.

Mullennix, J.W. and Pisoni, D.B. (1990). Stimulus variability and processing dependencies in speech perception. *Perception & Psychophysics*, 47, 379–90.

Mullennix, J.W., Pisoni, D.B. and Martin, C.S. (1989). Some effects of talker variability on spoken word recognition. *Journal of the Acoustical Society of America*, 85, 365–78.

Muller, W., Abbs, J., Kennedy, J. and Larson, C. (1977). *Significance of biomechanical variables in lip movements for speech*. Presented at the American Speech and Hearing Association Convention, Chicago, IL.

Müller, E.M. and Abbs, J.H. (1979). Strain gauge transduction of lip and jaw motion in the midsagittal plane: refinement of a prototype system. *Journal of the Acoustical Society of America*, 65, 481–6.

Munhall, K. (1985). An examination of inter-articulator relative timing. *Journal of the Acoustical Society of America*, 78, 1548–53.

Munhall, K. and Löfqvist, A. (1992). Gestural aggregation in speech: laryngeal gestures. *Journal of Phonetics*, 20, 111–26.

Munhall, K., Löfqvist, A. and Kelso, J.A.S. (1994). Lip-larynx coordination in speech: effects of mechanical perturbations to the lower lip. *Journal of the Acoustical Society of America*, 95, 3605–16.

Munhall, K., Ostry, D. and Flanagan, J. (1991). Coordinate spaces in speech planning. *Journal of Phonetics*, 19, 293–307.

Munhall, K.G., Ostry, D.J. and Parush, A. (1985). Characteristics of velocity profiles of speech movements. *Journal of Experimental Psychology, Human Perception and Performance*, 11, 457–74.

Muraki, A., Mancuso, A., Harnsberger, H., Johnson, L. and Meads, G. (1983). CT of the oropharynx, tongue base and floor of the mouth: normal anatomy and range of variations, and applications in staging carcinoma. *Radiology*, 148, 725–31.

Murdoch, B.E., Chenery, H.J., Bowler, S. and Ingram, J.C.L. (1989). Respiratory function in Parkinson's subjects exhibiting a perceptible speech deficit: a kinematic and spirometric analysis. *Journal of Speech and Hearing Disorders*, 54, 610–26.

Murray, I.R. and Arnott, J.L. (1993). Toward the simulation of emotion in synthetic speech: a review of the literature on human vocal emotion. *Journal of the Acoustical Society of America*, 93, 1097–108.

Murray, I.R., Arnott, J.L., Alm, N. and Newell, A.F. (1991). A communication system for the disabled with emotional synthetic speech produced by rule. *Proceedings of European Conference on Speech Communication and Technology*, Genova, Italy.

Musiek, F.E. and Lamb, L. (1992). Neuroanatomy and neurophysiology of central auditory processing. In J. Katz, N. Stecker and D. Henderson (eds), *Central auditory processing: a transdisciplinary view* (pp. 11–38). St. Louis, MO: Mosby Year Book.

Mysak, E.D. (1959). Pitch and duration characteristics of older males. *Journal of Speech and Hearing Research*, 2, 4654.

Nakajima, S. and H. Hamada (1988). Automatic generation of synthesis units based on context oriented clustering. *Proceedings of ICASSP-88*.

Nakatani, L.H. and Schaffer, J.A. (1978). Hearing "words" without words. *Journal of the Acoustical Society of America*, 63, 234–45.

Nashner, L. and McCollum, G. (1985). The organization of human postural movements: a formal basis and experimental synthesis. *Behavioral and Brain Sciences*, 8, 135–72.

Negus, V.E. (1949). *The comparative anatomy and physiology of the larynx*. London: W. Heinemann Medical Books.

Neilson, P.D., Andrews, G., Guitar, B.E. and Quinn, P.T. (1979). Tonic stretch reflexes in lip, tongue, and jaw muscles. *Brain Research*, 178, 311–27.

Neilson, P.D. and O'Dwyer, N.J. (1983). Reproducibility and variability of speech muscle activity in athetoid dysarthria of cerebral palsy. *Journal of Speech and Hearing Research*, 27, 502–17.

Nelson, P.A. and Morfey, C.L. (1981). Aerodynamic sound production in low speed flow ducts. *Journal of Sound and Vibration*, 79, 263–89.

Nelson, W.L. (1977). Articulatory feature analysis – I. Initial processing considerations in spectral analyses. *Memorandum for file, Bell Laboratories*, Murray Hill, NJ.

—— (1983). Physical principles for economies of skilled movement. *Biological Cybernetics*, 46, 135–47.

Nelson, W.L., Perkell, J.S. and Westbury, J.R. (1984). Mandible movements during increasingly rapid articulations of single syllables: preliminary observations. *Journal of the Acoustical Society of America*, 75, 945–51.

Neovius, L. and Raghavendra, P. (1993). Comprehension of KTH text-to-speech with "listening speed" paradigm. *Proceedings of 3rd European Conference on Speech Communication and Technology*. Berlin, Germany.

Nespor, M. and Vogel, M. (1986). *Prosodic phonology*. Dordrecht: Foris Publications.

Netsell, R. (1984). A neurobiologic view of the dysarthrias. In M.R. McNeil, J.C. Rosenbek, and A.E. Aronson (eds), *The dysarthrias* (pp. 1–36). San Diego, CA: College-Hill Press.

Newell, A.F. (1984). Speech – the natural method of man-machine communication? *Proceedings of the First IFIP conference of human computer interaction*, 231–8. Amsterdam: North Holland.

Newell, A.F., Murray, I.R., Arnott, J.L., Dye, R., Cruickshank, G. and Carter, K.E.P. (1992). Human factors studies of speech-driven word processors: a simulated natural rate large vocabulary continuous speech recognition system. (1992). In W.A. Ainsworth (ed.), *Advances in speech, hearing and language processing*, 2, (pp. 253–79). London: JAI Press Ltd.

Newman, J.E. and Dell, G.S. (1978). The phonological nature of phoneme monitoring: a critique of some ambiguity studies. *Journal of Verbal Learning and Verbal Behavior*, 17, 359–74.

Newsom Davis, J. and Sears, T. (1970). The proprioceptive reflex control of the intercostal muscles during their voluntary activation. *Journal of Physiology*, 209, 711–38.

Ní Chasaide, A. and Gobl, C. (1993). Contextual variation of the vowel voice source as a function of adjacent consonants. *Language and Speech*, 36, 303–30.

Ní Chasaide, A., Gobl, C. and Monahan, P. (1992). A technique for analysing voice quality in pathological and normal speech. *Journal of Clinical Speech & Language Studies*, 2, 1–16.

—— (1993). Dynamic variation of the voice source in VCV sequences: intrinsic characteristics of selected consonants. *Proceedings of the 1st Review Meeting of the Esprit/ Basic Research Action No. 6975: SPEECH MAPS*, 2, 44 Grenoble, Institut de la Communication Parlée.

Nicolaidis, K., Hardcastle, W. and Gibbon, F. (1992). Bibliography of electropalatographic studies in English (1951–1992)-Parts I, II and III. *Speech Research Laboratory, University of Reading Work in Progress*, 7, 26–147.

Niitsu, M., Kumada, M., Niimi, S. and Itai, Y. (1992). Tongue movement during phonation: a rapid quantitative visualization using tagging Snapshot MR imaging. *Annual Bulletin of Research Institute of Logopedics and Phoniatrics*, University of Tokyo, 26.

Nippold, M., Martin, S. and Erskine, B. (1988). Proverb compensation in context: a developmental study with children and adolescents. *Journal of Speech and Hearing Research*, 31, 19–28.

Nishinuma, Y. and Rossi, M. (1981). Automatisation of prosodic analysis in French. *Study of sounds* (The Phonetic Society of Japan), 19, 155–69.

Nittrouer, S. (1991). Phase relations of jaw and tongue tip movements in the production of VCV utterances. *Journal of the Acoustical Society of America*, 90, 1806–15.

Nittrouer, S., Munhall, K., Kelso, J.A.S., Tuller, B. and Harris, K.S. (1988). Patterns of interarticulator phasing and their relation to linguistic structure. *Journal of the Acoustical Society of America*, 84, 1653–61.

Nolan, F. (1983). *The phonetic bases of speaker recognition*. Cambridge: Cambridge University Press.

—— (1984). Applying linguistics to synthesis. In G. Bristow (ed.), *Electronic speech synthesis*. London: Granada.

—— (1990). The limitations of auditory-phonetic speaker identification. In H. Kniffka (ed.), *Texte zu Theorie und Praxis forensischer Linguistik*. Tübingen: Max Niemeyer Verlag.

—— (1991). Forensic phonetics. *Journal of Linguistics*, 27, 483–93.

—— (1992a). Review of 'Phonetische Untersuchungen zür Sprecher-Erkennung durch linguistisch naive Personen' by H. Künzel. *Journal of Phonetics*, 20, 176–8.

—— (1992b). The descriptive role of segments: evidence from assimilation. In G.J. Docherty and D.R. Ladd (eds), *Papers in laboratory phonology II: gesture, segment, prosody* (pp. 261–80). Cambridge: Cambridge University Press.

—— (1994). Auditory and acoustic analysis in speaker recognition. In J. Gibbon (ed.), *Language and the law*. London: Longman.

Nolan, F. and Holst, T. (1993). *Modelling [s] to [ʃ] assimilation*. Presented at the 2nd ACCOR Workshop (ESPRIT) on Lingual Data and Modelling in Speech Production, Barcelona.

Noll, A.M. (1967). Cepstrum pitch determination. *Journal of the Acoustical Society of America*, 41, 293–309.

Nolte, J. (1981). *The human brain*. St. Louis: Mosby.

Noorden, L. van (1982). Two channel pitch perception. In M. Clynes (ed.), *Music, mind, and brain*, New York: Plenum.

Nooteboom, S.G. (1972). 'Production and perception of vowel duration. A study of durational properties of vowels in Dutch'. Ph.D. thesis. Utrecht: University of Utrecht.

—— (1973). The perceptual reality of some prosodic durations. *Journal of Phonetics*, 1, 25–45.

—— (1979). "Time" in the production and perception of speech. *Arbeitsberichte nr 12: Report of an interdisciplinary Colloquium held in the Phonetics Department of Kiel University*, February 22–24, 1979 (pp. 113–51). Kiel: Institut für Phonetik, Universität Kiel.

—— (1985). A functional view of prosodic timing. In J.A. Michon and J.L. Jackson (eds), *Time, mind, and behavior* (pp. 242–51). Berlin, Heidelberg, New York, Tokyo: Springer-Verlag.

Nooteboom, S.G., Brokx, J.P.L. and de Rooij, J.J. (1978). Contributions of prosody to speech perception. In W.J.M. Levelt and G.B. Flores d'Arcais (eds), *Studies in the perception of language* (pp. 75–107). New York: Wiley.

Nooteboom, S.G. and Doodeman, G.J.N. (1980). Production and perception of vowel length in spoken sentences. *Journal of the Acoustical Society of America*, 67, 276–87.

Nooteboom, S.G. and Eefting, W. (1992). To what extent is speech production controlled by speech perception? Some questions and some experimental evidence. In Y. Tohkura, E. Vatikiotis-Bateson and Y. Sagisaka (eds), *Speech perception, production and linguistic structure* (pp. 439–50). Amsterdam: IOS Press.

Nooteboom, S.G. and Kruyt, J.G. (1987). Accents, focus distribution, and the perceived distribution of given and new information: an experiment. *Journal of the Acoustical Society of America*, 82, 1512–24.

Nord, L. (1986). Acoustic studies of vowel reduction in Swedish. *Quarterly Progress and Status Report*, Department of Speech Communication STL-KTH Stockholm, 19–36.

Norris, D. (1993). Bottom-up connectionist models of "interaction". In G. Altmann and R. Shillcock (eds), *Cognitive models of speech processing: the second Sperlonga meeting* (pp. 211–34). Hillsdale, NJ: Erlbaum.

—— (1994). Shortlist: a connectionist model of continuous speech recognition. *Cognition*, 52, 189–234.

Norris, D. and Cutler, A. (1988). The relative accessibility of phonemes and syllables. *Perception & Psychophysics*, 43, 541–50.

Norris, D., McQueen, J.M. and Cutler, A. (1995). Competition and segmentation in spoken word recognition. *Journal of Experimental Psychology: Learning, Memory, and Cognition*, 21, 1209–28.

Nottebohm, F. (1991). Reassessing the mechanisms and origins of vocal learning in birds. *Trends in Neurosciences*, 14, 206–211.

Nusbaum, H.C., Walley, A.C., Carrell, T.D. and Ressler, W.H. (1982). Controlled perceptual strategies in phonemic restoration. *Progress Report*, 8, 83–103. Indiana: Speech Research Laboratory, Indiana University.

O'Dwyer, N.J. and Neilson, P.D. (1988). Voluntary muscle control in normal and athetoid dysarthric speakers. *Brain*, 111, 877–99.

O'Loughlin, B.J. and Moore, B.C.J. (1981). Improving psychoacoustical tuning curves. *Hearing Research*, 5, 343–6.

O'Reilly, M.T. (1979). A longitudinal growth study: maxillary length at puberty in females. *Angle Orthodontist*, 49, 2348.

O'Shaughnessy, D. (1976). 'Modelling fundamental frequency, and its relationship to syntax, semantics, and phonetics'. Ph.D. thesis. Cambridge, MA: MIT.

—— (1979). Linguistic features in fundamental frequency patterns. *Journal of Phonetics*, 7, 119–45.

—— (1987). *Speech communication: human and machine*. Reading, MA: Addison-Wesley Publishing Company.

Odden, D. (1991). Vowel geometry. *Phonology*, 8 (2), 261–90.

Odé, C. (1989). *Russian intonation: a perceptual description*. Amsterdam, Atlanta: Rodopi.

Ohala, J.J. (1976). A model of speech aerodynamics. *Report of the Phonology Laboratory (Berkeley)*, 1, 93–107.

—— (1978). The production of tone. In V. A. Fromkin (ed.), *Tone: a linguistic survey* (pp. 5–39). New York: Academic Press.

—— (1981). Speech timing as a tool in phonology. *Phonetica*, 38, 204–12.

—— (1983). The origin of sound patterns in vocal tract constraints. In P.F. MacNeilage (ed.), *The production of speech* (pp. 189–216). New York: Springer-Verlag.

—— (1984). An ethological perspective on common cross-language utilization of f_0 of voice. *Phonetica*, 41, 1–16.

—— (1985). Around *flat*. In V.A. Fromkin (ed.), *Phonetic linguistics. Essays in honor of Peter Ladefoged* (pp. 223–41). Orlando, FL: Academic Press.

—— (1987). Explanation in phonology: opinions and examples. In W.U. Dressler, H.C. Luschützky, O.E. Pfeiffer and J.R. Rennison (eds), *Phonologica 1984* (pp. 215–25). Cambridge: Cambridge University Press.

—— (1989). Sound change is drawn from a pool of synchronic variation. In L.E. Breivik and E.H. Jahr (eds), *Language change: contributions to the study of its causes*. [Series: *Trends in Linguistics*, Studies and Monographs No. 43] (pp. 173–98). Berlin: Mouton de Gruyter.

—— (1990a). There is no interface between phonetics and phonology. *Journal of Phonetics*, 18, 153–71.

—— (1990b). A response to Pierrehumbert's commentary. In J. Kingston and M. Beckman (eds), *Papers in laboratory phonology I: between the grammar and the physics of speech* (pp. 280–82). Cambridge: Cambridge University Press.

—— (1990c). Respiratory activity in speech. In W.J. Hardcastle and A. Marchal (eds), *Speech production and speech modelling* (pp. 23–53). Dordrecht: Kluwer Academic Press.

—— (1990d). The phonetics and phonology of aspects of assimilation. In J. Kingston and M. Beckman (eds), *Papers in laboratory phonology I: between the grammar and the physics of speech* (pp. 258–75). Cambridge: Cambridge University Press.

—— (1991). The integration of phonetics and phonology. *Proceedings of the 12th International Congress of Phonetic Sciences*, 1, 1–16. Aix-en-Provence, 19–24 August, 1991.

—— (1992a). What's cognitive, what's not, in sound change. In Günter Kellermann and M.D. Morrissey (eds), *Diachrony within synchrony: Language history and cognition* (pp. 309–355). Frankfurt/M: Peter Lang Verlag.

—— (1992b). The segment: primitive or derived? In G.J. Docherty and D.R. Ladd (eds), *Papers in laboratory phonology II: gesture, segment, prosody* (pp. 166–83). Cambridge: Cambridge University Press.

—— (1992c). The costs and benefits of phonological analysis. In P. Downing, S.D. Lima, and M. Noonan (eds), *The linguistics of literacy* (pp. 211–37). Amsterdam/ Philadelphia: J. Benjamins.

—— (1993a). Sound change as nature's speech perception experiment. *Speech Communication*, 13, 155–61.

—— (1993b). The perceptual basis of some sound patterns. In B.A. Connel and A. Arvaniti (eds), *Papers in laboratory phonology IV: phonology and phonetic evidence*. Cambridge: Cambridge University Press.

—— (1994a). The frequency code underlies the sound symbolic use of voice pitch. In L. Hinton, J. Nichols, and J.J. Ohala (eds), *Sound symbolism* (pp. 325–47). Cambridge: Cambridge University Press.

—— (1994b). Speech aerodynamics. In R.E. Asher and J.M.Y. Simpson (eds), *The encyclopedia of language and linguistics* (pp. 4144–8). Oxford: Pergamon.

—— (1995). A probable case of clicks influencing the sound patterns of some European languages. *Phonetica*.

—— (In press a). Nasal loss before voiceless fricatives: a perceptually-based sound change. In C.A. Fowler (ed.), *Revista di Linguistica. Special issue on phonetics and sound change*.

—— (In press b). Emergent obstruents. In D. Demolin and M. Dominicy (eds), *Studies in sound change*. Amsterdam: Benjamins.

Ohala, J.J. and Kawasaki, H. (1984). Prosodic phonology and phonetics. *Phonology Yearbook 1*, 113–28.

Ohala, J.J. and Lorentz, J. (1977). The story of [w]: an exercise in the phonetic explanation for sound patterns. *Berkeley Linguistic Society, Proceeding of Annual Meeting*, 3, 577–99.

Ohala, J.J. and Ohala, M. (1991). Reply to commentators. *Phonetica*, 48, 271–4.

—— (1993). Speech perception and lexical representation: the role of vowel nasalization in Hindi and English. In B.A. Connel and A. Arvaniti (eds), *Papers in laboratory phonology IV: phonology and phonetic evidence*. Cambridge: Cambridge University Press.

Ohala, J.J. and Riordan, C. (1979). Passive vocal tract enlargement during voiced stops. In J.J. Wolf and D.H. Klatt (eds), *Speech communication papers* (pp. 89–92). New York: Acoustical Society of America.

Ohala, M. (1980). *Aspects of Hindi phonology*. New Delhi: Motilal Banarsidass.

Ohala, M. and Ohala, J. (1991). Nasal epenthesis in Hindi. *Phonetica*, 48, 207–20.

Ohde, R.N. (1984). Fundamental frequency as an acoustic correlate of stop consonant voicing. *Journal of the Acoustical Society of America*, 75, 224–30.

Ohde, R.N. and Sharf, D.J. (1977). Order effect of acoustic segments of VC and CV syllables on stop and vowel identification. *Journal of Speech and Hearing Research*, 20, 543–54.

Ohde, R.N. and Stevens, K.N. (1983). Effect of burst amplitude on the perception of stop consonant place of articulation. *Journal of the Acoustical Society of America*, 74, 706–14.

Öhman, S.E.G. (1966). Coarticulation in VCV utterances: spectrographic measurements. *Journal of the Acoustical Society of America*, 39, 151–68.

—— (1967a). Word and sentence intonation: a quantitative model. *KTH-STL-QPSR*, 20–54.

—— (1967b). Numerical model of coarticulation. *Journal of the Acoustical Society of America*, 41, 310–20.

Ojemann, G.A. (1983). Brain organization for language from the perspective of electrical stimulation mapping. *Behavioral and Brain Sciences*, 6, 189–230.

Olive, J.P. (1977). Rule synthesis of speech from dyadic units. *Proceedings of ICASSP-77* (pp. 568–70).

—— (1990). A new algorithm for a concatenative speech synthesis system using an augmented acoustic inventory of speech sounds. *Proceedings of ESCA Workshop on Speech Synthesis*, Autrans, France.

Olive, J.P. and Liberman, M.Y. (1985). Text-to-speech – an overview. *Journal of the Acoustical Society of America*, Suppl 1, 78 (Fall), S6.

Oller, D.K. (1980). The emergence of the sounds of speech in infancy. In G. Yeni-Komshian, J.F. Kavanagh and C.A. Ferguson (eds), *Child phonology, Vol. 1, Production*. New York: Academic Press.

Oller, D.K. and Eilers, R.E. (1988). The role of audition in infant babbling. *Child Development*, 59, 441–9.

Oller, D.K., Eilers, R.E., Bull, D.H. and Carney, A.E. (1985). Prespeech vocalizations of a deaf infant: a comparison with normal metaphonological development. *Journal of Speech and Hearing Research*, 28, 47–63.

Oller, D.K. and Steffans, M.L. (1993). Syllables and segments in infant vocalizations. In M.S. Yavas (ed.), *First and second language phonology*. San Diego, CA: Singular Publishing.

Oller, D.K., Wieman, L.A., Doyle, W.J. and Ross, C. (1976). Infant babbling and speech. *Journal of Child Language*, 3, 1–11.

Ono, M., Kubik, S. and Abernathy, C.D. (1990). *Atlas of the cerebral sulci*. New York: Thieme.

Oppenheim, A.V. and Schafer, R.W. (1975). *Digital signal processing*. Englewood Cliffs: Prentice-Hall, Inc.

—— (1989). *Discrete-time signal processing*. Englewood Cliffs: Prentice-Hall, Inc.

Oppenheim, A.V., Willsky, A.S. and Young, I.T. (1983). *Signals and systems*. Englewood Cliffs: Prentice-Hall, Inc.

Orgogozo, J.M., Larsen, B., Roland, P.E., Melamed, E. and Lassen, N.A. (1979). Further studies on the supplementary motor area in man with rCBF method. *Acta Neurology Scandinavia*, Supplement 72, 60, 8–9.

Orrison, W.W. Jr., Lewine, J.D., Sanders, J.A. and Hartshorne, M.F. (1995). *Functional Brain Imaging*. St. Louis: Mosby.

Os, E.A.den (1988). 'Rhythm and tempo of Dutch and Italian'. Ph.D. thesis. Utrecht: Utrecht University.

Osberger, M.J. and McGarr, N.S. (1982). Speech production characteristics of the hearing-impaired. In N.J. Lass (ed.), *Speech and language: advances in basic research and practice* (pp. 221–84). New York: Academic Press.

Ostry, D.J., Cooke, J.D. and Munhall, K.G. (1987). Velocity curves of human arm and speech movements. *Experimental Brain Research*, 68, 37–46.

Ostry, D.J., Gribble, P.L. and Gracco, V.L. (forthcoming). Coarticulation in jaw movements in speech production: Is context sensitivity in speech kinematics centrally planned? *Journal of Neuroscience*.

Ostry, D.J. and Munhall, K.G. (1985). Control of rate and duration of speech movements. *Journal of the Acoustical Society of America*, 77, 640–8.

Otake, T., Hatano, G., Cutler, A. and Mehler, J. (1993). Mora or syllable? Speech segmentation in Japanese. *Journal of Memory and Language*, 32, 258–78.

Oviatt, S. (1980). The emerging ability to comprehend language: an experimental approach. *Child Development*, 50, 97–106.

Oyama, S. (1985). *The ontogeny of information: developmental systems and evolution*. New York: Cambridge University Press.

—— (1990). Commentary. The idea of innateness: Effects on language and communication research. *Developmental Psychobiology*, 23, 741–7.

—— (1993). Constraints and development. *Netherlands Journal of Biology*, 3, 6–16.

Palmer, A.R. (1990). The representation of spectra and fundamental frequencies of steady-state single- and double-vowel sounds in the temporal discharge patterns of guinea pig cochlear-nerve fibers. *Journal of the Acoustical Society of America*, 88, 1412–26.

Palmer, A.R., Rees, A. and Caird, D. (1990). Interaural delay sensitivity to tones and broadband signals in the guinea-pig inferior colliculus. *Hearing Research*, 50, 71–86.

Palmer, A.R. and Winter, I.M. (1992). Cochlear nerve and cochlear nucleus responses to the fundamental frequency of voiced speech sounds and harmonic complex tones. In Y. Cazals, L. Demany, and K. Horner (eds), *Auditory physiology and perception* (pp. 231–40). Oxford: Pergamon.

Palmer, A.R., Winter, I.M. and Darwin, C.J. (1986). The representation of steady-state vowel sounds in the temporal discharge patterns of the guinea-pig cochlear nerve and primarylike cochlear nucleus neurons. *Journal of the Acoustical Society of America*, 79, 100–13.

Palmer, A.R., Winter, I.M., Jiang, G. and James, N. (1994). Across-frequency integration by neurones in the ventral cochlear nucleus. In G.A. Manley, G.M. Klump, C.

Köppl, H. Fastl, H. Oeckinghous (eds), *Advances in hearing research.* Singapore: World Scientific (in press).

Palmer, J. (1973). Dynamic palatography. *Phonetica*, 28, 76–85.

Palmer, J.B. (1989). Electromyography of the muscles of oropharyngeal swallowing: basic concepts. *Dysphagia*, 6, 1–6.

Palmeri, T.J., Goldinger, S.D. and Pisoni, D.B. (1993). Episodic encoding of voice attributes and recognition memory for spoken words. *Journal of Experimental Psychology: Learning, Memory, and Cognition*, 19, 309–28.

Palombi, P.S., Backoff, P.M. and Caspary, D.M. (1994). Paired tone facilitation in dorsal cochlear nucleus neurons: a short-term potentiation model testable in vivo. *Hearing Research*, 75, 175–83.

Panconcelli-Calzia, G. (1904). *De la nasalité en Italien.* [Thèse présentée pour le doctorat de l'université de Paris]. Paris: Institut de Laryngologie et Orthopédie.

Pandit, P.B. (1957). Nasalization, aspiration and murmur in Gujarati. *Indian Linguistics*, 17, 165–72.

Pantoja, E. (1968). The laryngeal cartilages. Physiologic nonmineralization masquerading malignant destruction. *Archives of Otolaryngology*, 87, 416–21.

Papçun, G., Kreiman, J. and Davis, A. (1989). Long-term memory for unfamiliar voices. *Journal of the Acoustical Society of America*, 85, 913–25.

Papousek, M. and Papousek, H. (1989). Forms and functions of vocal matching in interactions between mothers and their precanonical infants. *First Language*, 9, 137–58.

Parent, A. and Hazrati, L.-N. (1995). Functional anatomy of the basal ganglia. I. The cortico-basal ganglia-thalamo-cortical loop. *Brain Research Reviews*, 20, 91–127.

Parsons, T. (1987). *Voice and speech processing.* New York: McGraw-Hill, Inc.

Passingham, R.D. (1987). From where does the motor cortex get its instructions? In S.P. Wise (ed.), *Higher brain functions* (pp. 67–97). Cambridge: Cambridge University Press.

Passy, P. (1890). *Etude sur les changements phonétiques et leur caractères généraux.* Paris: Librairie Firmin-Didot.

Pastel, L. (1987). 'Turbulent noise sources in vocal tract models'. S.M. Thesis, Massachusetts Institute of Technology, Cambridge, MA.

Pattee, H. (1977). Dynamic and linguistic modes of complex systems. *International Journal of General Systems*, 3, 259–66.

Patterson, J.H. and Green, D.M. (1970). Discrimination of transient signals having identical energy spectra. *Journal of the Acoustical Society of America*, 48, 894–905.

Patterson, R.D. (1976). Auditory filter shapes derived with noise stimuli. *Journal of the Acoustical Society of America*, 59, 640–54.

Patterson, R.D. and Moore, B.C.J. (1986). Auditory filters and excitation patterns as representations of frequency resolution. In B.C.J. Moore (ed.), *Frequency selectivity in hearing* (pp. 123–77). London: Academic Press.

Patterson, R.D. and Nimmo-Smith, I. (1980). Off-frequency listening and auditory filter asymmetry. *Journal of the Acoustical Society of America*, 67, 229–45.

Patterson, R.D. and Wightman, F.L. (1976). Residue pitch as a function of component spacing. *Journal of the Acoustical Society of America*, 59, 1450–9.

Paul, D. and Baker, J. (1992). The design for the Wall Street Journal-based CSR corpus. *DARPA Speech and Natural Language Workshop.* New York: Arden House.

Paulesu, E., Frith, C.D. and Frackowiak, R.S.J. (1993). The neural correlates of the verbal component of working memory. *Nature*, 362, 342–5.

Pedersen, H. (1924). *Sprogvidenskaben i det nittende aarhundrede.* Copenhagen. Gyldendalske Boghandel Nordisk Forlag.

Pelorson, X., Hirschberg, A., Hassel, R.R. van and Wijnands, A.P.J. (1994). Theoretical and experimental study of quasi-steady flow separation within the glottis during phonation. Application to a modified two-mass model. *Journal of the Acoustical Society of America*, 96, 3416–31.

Pelorson, X., Lallouache, T., Tourret, S., Bouffartigue, C. and Badin, P. (1994). Aerody-namical, geometrical and mechanical aspects of bilabial plosives production. *Proc. Int. Conf. on Spoken Lang. Proc.*, Yokohama, 599–602.

Penfield, W. and Roberts, L. (1959). *Speech and brain mechanisms*. Princeton, NJ: Princeton University Press.

Penfield, W. and Welch, K. (1951). The supplementary motor area of the cerebral cortex. *Archives of Neurology and Psychiatry*, 66, 289–317.

Penner, M.J. (1977). Detection of temporal gaps in noise as a measure of the decay of auditory sensation. *Journal of the Acoustical Society of America*, 61, 552–7.

Perkell, J.S. (1969). *Physiology of speech production: results and implications of a quantitative cineradiographic study*. Cambridge, MA: MIT Press.

—— (1974). 'A physiologically-oriented model of tongue activity during speech production'. Ph.D. thesis, Massachusetts Institute of Technology.

—— (1979). On the nature of distinctive features: implications of a preliminary vowel production study. In B. Lindblom and S. Öhman (eds), *Frontiers of speech communication research* (pp. 365–80). New York: Academic Press.

—— (1980). Phonetic features and the physiology of speech production. In B. Butterworth (ed.), *Language production* (pp. 337–72), London: Academic Press.

—— (1990). Testing theories of speech production: implications of some detailed analyses of variable articulatory data. In W.J. Hardcastle and A. Marchal (eds), *Speech production and speech modelling* (pp. 263–88). Dordrecht: Kluwer Academic Publishers.

—— (1996). Properties of the tongue help to define vowel categories: hypotheses based on physiologically-oriented modeling. *Journal of Phonetics*.

Perkell, J.S. and Chiang, C. (1986). Preliminary support for a 'hybrid model' of anticipatory coarticulation. *Proceedings of the 12th International Congress of Acoustics*, A3–6.

Perkell, J.S. and Cohen, M.H. (1989). An indirect test of the quantal nature of speech in the production of the vowels /i/, /a/ and /u/. *Journal of Phonetics*, 17, 123–33.

Perkell, J., Cohen, M. and Garabieta, I. (1988). Techniques for transducing movements of points on articulatory structures. *Journal of the Acoustical Society of America*, 84, Suppl. 1, S145A.

Perkell, J., Cohen, M., Svirksy, M., Matthies, M., Garabieta, I. and Jackson, M. (1992a). Electro-magnetic midsagittal articulometer (EMMA) systems for transducing speech articulatory movements. *Journal of the Acoustical Society of America*, 92, 3078–96.

Perkell, J., Lane, H., Svirsky, M. and Webster, J. (1992b). Speech of cochlear implant patients: a longitudinal study of vowel production. *Journal of the Acoustical Society of America*, 91, 2961–79.

Perkell, J.S. and Matthies, M.L. (1992). Temporal measures of anticipatory coarticulation for the vowel /u/: within- and cross-subject variability. *Journal of the Acoustical Society of America*, 91, 2911–25.

Perkell, J.S., Matthies, M.L., Svirsky, M.A. and Jordan, M.I. (1993). Trading relations between tongue-body raising and lip rounding in production of the vowel /u/: a pilot motor equivalence study. *Journal of the Acoustical Society of America*, 93, 2948–61.

—— (1995). Goal-based speech motor control: a theoretical framework and some preliminary data. *Journal of Phonetics*, 23, 23–35.

Perkell, J.S. and Nelson, W.L. (1985). Variability in production of the vowels /i/ and /a/. *Journal of the Acoustical Society of America*, 77, 1889–95.

Perlman, A., Luschei, E. and DuMond, C. (1989). Electrical activity from the superior pharyngeal constrictor during reflexive and non-reflexive tasks. *Journal of Speech and Hearing Research*, 32, 749–54.

Perrier, P., Ostry, D.J. and Laboissière, R. (1996). The equilibrium point hypothesis and its application to speech motor control, *Journal of Speech and Hearing Research*, 39.

Peters, M. (1992). Cerebral asymmetry for speech and the asymmetry in the path lengths for the right and left recurrent nerves. *Brain and Language*, 43, 349–52.

Petersen, S.E., Fox, P.T., Posner, M.I., Mintun, M. and Raichle, M.E. (1988). Positron emission tomographic studies of the cortical anatomy of single-word processing. *Nature*, London, 331, 585–9.

Peterson, G.E. and Barney, H.L. (1952). Control methods used in a study of the vowels. *Journal of the Acoustical Society of America*, 24, 175–84.

Peterson-Falzone, S.J. (1988). Speech disorders related to craniofacial structural defects: part 1. In J. Lass, L.V. McReynolds, J.L. Northern and D.E. Yoder (eds), *Handbook of speech-language pathology and audiology*. Toronto/Philadeplhia: B.C. Decker Inc.

Philips, M., Glass, J. and Zue, V. (1991). Automatic learning of lexical representations for subword unit based speech recognition systems. *Proceedings of European Conference on Speech Communication and Technology*.

Piatelli-Palmarini, M. (1989). Evolution, selection and cognition: from "learning" to parameter setting in biology and in the study of language. *Cognition*, 31, 1–44.

Picheny, M.A., Durlach, N.I. and Braida, L.D. (1986). Speaking clearly for the hard of hearing II: acoustic characteristics of clear and conversational speech. *Journal of Speech and Hearing Research*, 29, 434–46.

Pickett, J.M. (1980). *The sounds of speech communication*. Baltimore, MD: University Park Press.

Pickles, J.O. (1979). Psychophysical frequency resolution in the cat as determined by simultaneous masking, and its relation to auditory-nerve resolution. *Journal of the Acoustical Society of America*, 66, 1725–32.

—— (1980). Psychophysical frequency resolution in the cat studied with forward masking. In G. van den Brink and F.A. Bilsen (eds), *Psychophysical, physiological, and behavioral studies in hearing* (pp. 118–25). Delft: Delft U.P.

Pierce, J.R. (1969). Whither speech recognition. *Journal of the Acoustical Society of America*, 46, 1049.

Pierrehumbert, J. (1979). The perception of fundamental frequency declination. *Journal of the Acoustical Society of America*, 66, 363–8.

—— (1980). 'The phonology and phonetics of English intonation'. Ph.D. dissertation. Massachusetts Institute of Technology, Cambridge, MA.

—— (1981). Synthesizing intonation. *Journal of the Acoustical Society of America*, 70, 985–95.

—— (1987). *The phonetics of English intonation*. Bloomington: IULC.

—— (1989). A preliminary study of the consequences of intonation for the voice source. *Speech Transmission Laboratory – Quarterly Progress and Status Report*, 4, 23–36. Royal Institute of Technology, Stockholm.

—— (1990). On the value of reductionism and formal explicitness in phonological models: comments on Ohala's paper. In J. Kingston and M. Beckman (eds), *Papers in laboratory phonology I: between the grammar and the physics of speech* (pp. 276–9). Cambridge: Cambridge University Press.

—— (1991). The whole theory of sound structure. *Phonetica*, 48, 223–32.

Pierrehumbert, J.B. and Beckman, M.E. (1988). *Japanese tone structure*. Linguistic Inquiry Monograph, 17.

Pijper, J.R. de (1983). *Modelling British-English intonation*. Dordrecht, Cinnaminson: Foris Publications.

Pike, K.L. (1943). *Phonetics*. Ann Arbor: University of Michigan Press.

Pike, K.L. (1947). *Phonemics: a technique for reducing languages to writing*. Ann Arbor, Michigan: University of Michigan Press.

Pisoni, D.B. (1977). Identification and discrimination of the relative onset time of two component tones: implications for voicing perception in stops. *Journal of the Acoustical Society of America*, 61, 1352–61.

Pisoni, D.B. and Luce, P.A. (1987). Acoustic-phonetic representations in word recognition. *Cognition*, 25, 21–52.

Pitt, M.A. and Samuel, A.G. (1990a). Attentional allocation during speech perception: how fine is the focus? *Journal of Memory and Language*, 29, 611–32.

—— (1990b). The use of rhythm in attending to speech. *Journal of Experimental Psychology: Human Perception and Performance*, 16, 564–73.

—— (1993). An empirical and meta-analytic evaluation of the phoneme identification task. *Journal of Experimental Psychology: Human Perception and Performance*, 19, 699–725.

Platt, L.J., Andrews, G. and Howie, P.M. (1980). Dysarthria of adult cerebral palsy. II. Phonemic analysis of articulation errors. *Journal of Speech and Hearing Research*, 23, 41–55.

Platt, L.J., Andrews, G., Young, M. and Quinn, P.T. (1980). Dysarthria of adult cerebral palsy. I. Articulatory impairment. *Journal of Speech and Hearing Research*, 23, 28–40.

Plomp, R. (1964a). The ear as a frequency analyzer. *Journal of the Acoustical Society of America*, 36, 1628–36.

—— (1964b). The rate of decay of auditory sensation. *Journal of the Acoustical Society of America*, 36, 277–82.

—— (1967). Pitch of complex tones. *Journal of the Acoustical Society of America*, 41, 1526–33.

Ploog, D. (1992). The evolution of vocal communication. In H. Papousek, U. Jurgens and M. Papousek (eds), *Nonverbal vocal communication* (pp. 6–30). Cambridge: Cambridge University Press.

Poeck, K. and Kerschensteiner, M. (1975). Analysis of the sequential motor events in oral apraxia. In K. Zulch, O. Kreutzfeld and G. Galbraith (eds), *Otfried Foerster symposium* (pp. 98–109). Berlin: Springer.

Polit, A. and Bizzi, E. (1979). Characteristics of motor programs underlying arm movements in monkeys. *Journal of Neurophysiology*, 42, 183–94.

Port, D.K. (1971). The EMG data system. *Haskins Laboratories Status Report*, SR 25/26, 67–72.

Port, R.F. and O'Dell, M.L. (1985). Neutralization of syllable-final voicing in German. *Journal of Phonetics*, 13, 455–71.

Port, R.F., Reilly, W.T. and Maki, D.P. (1988). Use of syllable-scale timing to discriminate words. *Journal of the Acoustical Society of America*, 83, 265–73.

Porter, R.J. and Castellanos, F.X. (1980). Speech production measures of speech perception. *Journal of the Acoustical Society of America*, 67, 1349–56.

Poser, W.J. (1984). 'The phonetics and phonology of tone and intonation in Japanese'. Ph.D Thesis, MIT.

Posner, M.I., Petersen, S.E., Fox, P.T. and Raichle, M.E. (1988). Localization of cognitive operations in the human brain. *Science*, 240, 1627–31.

Potter, R., Kopp, G. and Green, H. (1947). *Visible speech*. New York: Van Nostrand Reinhold (reprinted in 1966 by Dover Press, New York).

Powell, A. (1961). On the edgetone. *Journal of the Acoustical Society of America*, 33, 395–409.

—— (1962). Vortex action in edgetones. *Journal of the Acoustical Society of America*, 34, 163–6.

Priemer, R. (1991). *Introductory signal processing*. Singapore: World Scientific.

Prince, A. (1980). A metrical theory for Estonian quantity. *Linguistic Inquiry*, 3, 511–62.

Prince, A. and Smolensky, P. (in press). *Optimality theory*. ms. Rutgers University and University of Colorado.

Proakis, J.G. and Manolakis, D.G. (1992). *Digital signal processing*. New York: Macmillan Publ. Co.

Ptacek, P.H. and Sander, E.K. (1966). Age recognition from the voice. *Journal of Speech and Hearing Research*, 9, 2737.

Ptacek, P.H., Sander, E.K., Maloney, W.H. and Jackson, C.C.R. (1966). Phonatory and related changes with advanced age. *Journal of Speech and Hearing Research*, 9, 353–60.

Putnam, A.H.B. (1988). Review of research in dysarthria. In H. Winitz (ed.), *Human communication and its disorders, A review 1988* (pp. 107–223). Norwood, NJ: Ablex Publishing Co.

Putnam, A.H.B. and Hixon, T.J. (1984). Respiratory kinematics in speakers in motor neuron disease. In M.R. McNeil, J.C. Rosenbek and A. Aronson (eds), *The dysarthrias: physiology-acoustics-perception-management* (pp. 37–67). San Diego, CA: College-Hill Press.

Quené, H. (1989). The influence of acoustic-phonetic word boundary markers on perceived word segmentation in Dutch. Unpublished doctoral thesis. Utrecht: University of Utrecht.

—— (1992). Durational cues for word segmentation in Dutch. *Journal of Phonetics*, 20, 331–50.

Quené, H. and Kager, R. (1993). Prosodic sentence analysis without parsing. In V.J. van Heuven and L.C.W. Pols (eds), *Analysis and synthesis of speech* (pp. 115–30). Berlin, New York: Mouton de Gruyter.

Rabiner, L.R. and Gold, B. (1975). *Theory and application of digital signal processing.* Englewood Cliffs: Prentice-Hall, Inc.

Rabiner, L.R. and Juang, B.H. (1986). An introduction to hidden Markov models. *IEEE ASSP Magazine*, 4–16.

Rabiner, L.R. and Rader, C.M. (eds) (1972). *Digital signal processing.* New York: IEEE Press.

Rabiner, L.R. and Schafer, R.W. (1978). *Digital processing of speech signals.* Englewood Cliffs: Prentice-Hall, Inc.

Rabiner, L.R., Schafer, R.W. and Rader, C.M. (1969). The chirp z-transform algorithm. *IEEE Trans* AU-17 (2), 86–92.

Rahm, M., Kleijn, B. and Schroeter, J. (1991). Acoustic to articulatory parameter mapping using an assembly of neural networks. *Proceedings of ICASSP-91.*

Ramig, L.A. (1986). Acoustic analyses of phonation in patients with Huntington's disease. *Annals of Otology, Rhinology, and Laryngology*, 95, 288–93.

Ramig, L.A. and Ringel, R.L. (1983). Effects of physiological aging on selected acoustic characteristics of voice. *Journal of Speech and Hearing Research*, 26, 22–30.

Ramig, L.O. (1995). Speech therapy for patients with Parkinson disease. In W.C. Koller and G. Paulson (eds), *Therapy of Parkinson disease*, 2nd ed. New York: Marcel Dekker, Inc.

Ramig, L.O., Bonitati, C.M., Lemke, J.H. and Horii, Y. (1994). Voice treatment for patients with Parkinson disease: development of an approach and preliminary efficacy data. *Journal of Medical Speech-Language Pathology*, 3, 191–209.

Ramig, L.O., Countryman, S., Thompson, L.L. and Horii, Y. (1995). Comparison of two forms of intensive speech treatment for Parkinson disease. *Journal of Speech and Hearing Research*, 38, 1232–51.

Raphael, L. and Bell-Berti, F. (1975). Tongue musculature and the feature of tension in English vowels. *Phonetica*, 32, 661–73.

Raphael, L.J., Dorman, M.F., Freeman, F. and Tobin, C. (1975). Vowel and nasal duration as cues to voicing in word-final stop consonants: spectrographic and perceptual studies. *Journal of Speech and Hearing Research*, 18, 389–400.

Rapp, K.M. (1836). Versuch einer Physiologie der Sprache nebst historischer Entwicklung der abendländischen Idiome nach physiologischen Grundsätzen. Stuttgart und Tübingen:. Cotta.

Raumer, R. von (1863). *Gesammelte sprachwissenschaftliche Schriften.* Frankfurt: Heyder & Zimmer.

Read, C., Zhang, Y., Nie, H. and Ding, B. (1986). The ability to manipulate speech sounds depends on knowing alphabetic writing. *Cognition*, 24, 31–44.

Reale, R.A. and Geisler, C.D. (1980). Auditory-nerve fiber encoding of two-tone approximations to steady-state vowels. *Journal of the Acoustical Society of America*, 67, 891–902.

Recasens, D. (1983). Timing and coarticulation for alveolo-palatals and sequences of alveolar + [j] in Catalan. *Haskins Laboratories Status Report on Speech Research*, 74/ 75, 97–112.

—— (1984a). V-to-C coarticulation in Catalan VCV sequences: an articulatory and acoustical study. *Journal of Phonetics*, 12, 61–73.

—— (1984b). Vowel-to-vowel coarticulation in Catalan VCV sequences. *Journal of the Acoustical Society of America*, 76, 1624–35.

—— (1987). An acoustic analysis of V-to-C and V-to-V coarticulatory effects in Catalan and Spanish V-C-V sequences. *Journal of Phonetics*, 15, 299–312.

—— (1989). Long range coarticulation effects for tongue dorsum contact in VCVCV sequences. *Speech Communication*, 8, 293–307.

—— (1991). On the production characteristics of apicoalveolar taps and trills. *Journal of Phonetics*, 19, 267–80.

Recasens, K. and Farnetani, E. (1990). Articulatory and acoustic properties of different allophones of /l/ in American English, Catalan and Italian. *Proceedings of 1990 International Conference on Spoken Language Processing*, 2, 961–4.

Reddy, D.R., Erman, L.D. and Neely, R.B. (1973). A model and a system for machine recognition of speech. *IEEE Transactions on Audio and Acoustics*, AU-21, 229–38.

Redman, R.S., Shapiro, B.L. and Gorlin, R.J. (1966). Measurement of normal and reportedly malformed palatal vaults. II. Normal juvenile measurements. *Journal of Dental Research*, 45, 266–9.

Remez, R.E., Rubin, P.E., Pisoni, D.B. and Carrell, T.C. (1981). Speech perception without traditional speech cues. *Science*, 212, 947–50.

Ren, H. (1985). Linguistically conditioned duration rules in a timing model for Chinese. *UCLA Working Papers in Phonetics*, 62, 34–50.

Repp, B. (1981). Phonetic trading relations and context effects: new experimental evidence for a speech mode of perception. *Psychological Bulletin*, 92, 81–110.

Repp, B.H. and Liberman, A.M. (1987). Phonetic category boundaries are flexible. In S.R. Harnad (ed.), *Categorical perception* (pp. 89–112). Cambridge: Cambridge University Press.

Rhode, W.S. (1995). Interspike intervals as a correlate of periodicity pitch in cat cochlear nucleus. *Journal of the Acoustical Society of America*, 97, 2413–29.

Rhode, W.S. and Greenberg, S. (1992). Physiology of the cochlear nuclei. In A.N. Popper and R.R. Fay (eds), *The mammalian auditory pathway: neurophysiology* (pp. 94–152). New York: Springer-Verlag.

—— (1994). Lateral suppression and inhibition in the cochlear nucleus of the cat. *Journal of Neurophysiology*, 71, 493–514.

Rhode, W.S., Oertel, D. and Smith, P.H. (1983). Physiological response properties of cells labeled intracellularly with horseradish peroxidase in cat ventral cochlear nucleus. *Journal of Comparative Neurology*, 213, 448–63.

Rhode, W.S. and Smith, P.H. (1986). Encoding time and intensity in the ventral cochlear nucleus of the cat. *Journal of Neurophysiology*, 56, 262–86.

Rietveld, A.C.M. and Gussenhoven, C. (1985). On the relation between pitch excursion size and prominence. *Journal of Phonetics*, 13, 299–308.

Riley, M. (1990). Tree-based modeling for speech synthesis. *Proceedings of ESCA Workshop on Speech Synthesis*, Autrans, France.

Ringel, R.L. and Chodzko-Zajko, W. (1987). Vocal indices of biological age. *Journal of Voice*, 1, 31–7.

Riordan, C.J. (1980). Larynx height during English stop consonants. *Journal of Phonetics*, 8, 353–60.

Risset, J.C. and Wessel, D.L. (1982). Exploration of timbre by analysis and synthesis. In D. Deutsch (ed.), *The psychology of music* (pp. 25–58). New York: Academic Press.

Ritsma, R.J. (1967). Frequencies dominant in the perception of the pitch of complex sounds. *Journal of the Acoustical Society of America*, 42, 191–9.

Roberts, R.A. and Mullis, C.T. (1987). *Digital signal processing*. Reading, MA.: Addison-Wesley.

Robinson, A. (1991). Several improvements to a recurrent error propagation phone recognition system, *Technical Report Cambridge University Engineering Department/TINFENG/TR.82*.

—— (1993). Artificial neural networks: the mole-grips of the speech scientist. In M. Cooke, S. Beet and M. Crawford (eds), *Visual representations of speech signals* (pp. 83–94). Chichester: John Wiley and Sons Ltd.

Robinson, E.A. (1982). A historical perspective of spectrum estimation. *Proceedings of IEEE*, 70 (9), 885–907.

Roland, P.E., Larsen, B., Lassen, N.A. and Skinhoj, E. (1980). Supplementary motor area and other cortical areas in organization of voluntary movements in man. *Journal of Neurophysiology*, 43, 118–36.

Romanes, G.J. (ed.) (1978). *Cunningham's manual of practical anatomy*, Vol. 3, Head, Neck and Brain (14th edn). Oxford: Oxford University Press.

Rona, R.J. (1981). Genetic and environmental factors in the control of growth in childhood. *British Medical Bulletin*, 37, 265–72.

Ronken, D. (1970). Monaural detection of a phase difference between clicks. *Journal of the Acoustical Society of America*, 47, 1091–9.

Rooij, J.J. de (1978). 'Speech punctuation. An acoustic and perceptual study of some aspects of speech prosody in Dutch'. Ph.D. thesis. Utrecht: University of Utrecht.

Rose, J.E., Brugge, J.F., Anderson, D.J. and Hind, J.E. (1967). Phase-locked responses to low-frequency tones in single auditory-nerve fibers of the squirrel monkey. *Journal of Neurophysiology*, 30, 769–93.

Rose, P. (1989). Phonetics and phonology of Yang tone phonation types in Zhenhai. *Cahiers Linguistiques Asia Orientale*, 18, 229–45.

Rosen, S. and Fourcin, A. (1986). Frequency selectivity and the perception of speech. In B.C.J. Moore (ed.), *Frequency selectivity in hearing* (pp. 373–487). London: Academic Press.

Rosenbek, J.C., Kent, R.D. and LaPointe, L.L. (1984). Apraxia of speech: an overview and some perspectives. In J.C. Rosenbek, M.R. McNeil, and A. Aronson (eds), *Apraxia of speech: physiology, acoustics, linguistics, and management*. San Diego, CA: College-Hill Press.

Rosenbek, J.C. and LaPointe, L.L. (1985). The dysarthrias: Descriptions, diagnosis, and treatment. In D.F. Johns (ed.), *Clinical management of neurogenic communicative disorders*. Boston, MA (USA): Little, Brown.

Rosenberg, A. (1976). Automatic speaker verification: a review. *Proceedings of the IEEE*, 64 (4), 475–86.

Rosenberg, A.E. (1971). Effect of glottal pulse shape on the quality of natural vowels. *Journal of the Acoustical Society of America*, 49, 583–98.

Rosenberg, E.A., Rabiner, L.R., Wilpon, G.J. and Kahn, D. (1983). Demisyllable-based isolated word recognition system. *IEEE Transactions on Acoustics, Speech and Signal Processing*, 31, 713.

Ross, M.J., Shaffer, H.L., Cohen, A., Freudberg, R. and Manley, H.J. (1974). Average magnitude difference function pitch extraction. *IEEE Trans ASSP-22*, 353–62.

Rothenberg, M. (1968). The breath stream dynamics of simple-released-plosive production. *Bibliotheca Phonetica*, 6, Basel: Karger.

—— (1973). A new inverse-filtering technique for deriving the glottal air flow waveform during voicing. *Journal of the Acoustical Society of America*, 53, 1632–45.

—— (1974). Glottal noise during speech. *Speech Transmission Laboratory – Quarterly Progress and Status Report*, 2–3, 1–10. Royal Institute of Technology, Stockholm.

—— (1977). Measurement of airflow in speech. *Journal of Speech and Hearing Research*, 20, 155–76.

—— (1981). Acoustic interaction between the glottal source and the vocal tract. In K.N. Stevens and M. Hirano (eds), *Vocal fold physiology* (pp. 305–23). Tokyo: University of Tokyo Press.

Rothenberg, M., Carlson, R., Granström, B. and Lindqvist-Gauffin, J. (1975). A three-parameter voice source for speech synthesis. *Proceedings of Speech Communication Seminar*, Stockholm 1974; In *Speech Communication*, 2, 235–43. Stockholm: Almqvist and Wiksell.

Rothman, J.S., Young, E.D. and Manis, P.B. (1993). Convergence of auditory-nerve fibers onto bushy cells in the ventral cochlear nucleus: implications of a computational model. *Journal of Neurophysiology*, 70, 2562–83.

Rothwell, J., Traub, M. and Marsden, C. (1982). Automatic and 'voluntary' responses compensating for disturbances of human thumb movements. *Brain Research*, 248, 33–41.

Roucos, S. and Wilgus, A. (1985). High quality time-scale modification for speech. *ICASSP-85* (pp. 493–6).

Roudet, L. (1910). *Elements de phonétique générale*. Paris: Librairie Universitaire.

Roug, L., Landberg, I. and Lundberg, L.J. (1989). Phonetic development in early infancy: a study of four Swedish children during the first 18 months of life. *Journal of Child Language*, 16, 19–40.

Rouiller, D.K. and Ryugo, D. (1984). Intracellular marking of physiologically characterized cells in the ventral cochlear nucleus. *Journal of Comparative Neurology*, 225, 167–86.

Rousselot, P.J. (1891). Les modifications phonétiques du langages. Paris: H. Welter.

—— (1897–1908). *Principes de phonétique expérimentale*. Paris: H. Welter.

—— (1903). *Phonétique expérimentale et surdité*. Paris.

—— (1924–5). *Principes de phonétique expérimentale*. Paris: Didier.

Rubin, P., Turvey, M.T. and Gelder, P. van (1976). Initial phonemes are detected faster in spoken words than in non-words. *Perception & Psychophysics*, 19, 394–8.

Ruhm, H.B., Mencke, E.O., Milburn, B., Cooper, W.A. and Rose, D.E. (1966). Differential sensitivity of duration of acoustic signals. *Journal of Speech and Hearing Research*, 9, 371–84.

Rumelhart, D.E., Hinton, G.E. and Williams, R.J. (1986). Learning internal representations by error propagation. In D.E. Rumelhart and J.L. McClelland (eds), *Parallel distributed processing: explorations in the microstructure of cognition*. Cambridge, MA: MIT Press.

Rumelhart, D. and McClelland, J. (eds) (1986). *Parallel distributed processing, Vol. 1: Foundations*. Cambridge, MA: MIT Press.

Rupert, A.L., Caspary, D.M. and Moushegian, G. (1977). Response characteristics of cochlear nucleus neurons to vowel sounds. *Annals of Otology*, 86, 37–48.

Ryalls, J. and Larouche, A. (1992). Acoustic integrity of speech production in children with moderate and severe hearing impairment. *Journal of Speech and Hearing Research*, 35, 88–95.

Ryan, W.J. and Burk, K.W. (1974). Perceptual and acoustic correlates of aging in the speech of males. *Journal of Communication Disorders*, 7, 181–92.

Ryding, E., Bradvik, V. and Ingvar, D.H. (1987). Changes of regional cerebral blood flow measured simultaneously in the right and left hemisphere during automatic speech and humming. *Brain*, 110, 1345–58.

Sachs, M.B. (1984). Speech encoding in the auditory nerve. In C. Berlin (ed.), *Hearing science* (pp. 263–308). San Diego: College Hill.

Sachs, M.B. and Abbas, P.J. (1974). Rate versus level functions for auditory-nerve fiber in cats: tone burst stimuli. *Journal of the Acoustical Society of America*, 56, 1835–47.

Sachs, M.B., Voigt, H.F. and Young, E.D. (1983). Auditory nerve representation of vowels in background noise. *Journal of Neurophysiology*, 50, 27–45.

Sachs, M.B., Winslow, R.L. and Blackburn, C.C. (1988). Representation of speech in the auditory periphery. In G.M. Edelman, W.E. Gall and W.M. Cowan (eds), *Auditory function* (pp. 747–74). New York: Wiley.

Sachs, M.B. and Young, E.D. (1979). Encoding of steady-state vowels in the auditory nerve: representation in terms of discharge rate. *Journal of the Acoustical Society of America*, 66, 470–9.

—— (1980). Effects of nonlinearities on speech encoding in the auditory nerve. *Journal of the Acoustical Society of America*, 68, 858–75.

Sagey, E.C. (1986). 'The representation of features and relations in non-linear phonology'. Ph.D. dissertation, MIT, Cambridge, MA.

Sagisaka, Y. (1988). Speech synthesis by rule using an optimal selection of non-uniform synthesis units. *Proceedings of ICASSP-88*.

Sagisaka, Y., Kaiki, N., Iwahashi, N. and Mimura, K. (1992). ATR v-TALK speech synthesis system. *Proceedings of 1992 International Conference on Speech and Language Processing* (pp. 483–6). Banff, Canada.

Saito, S. and Itakura, F. (1966). *The theoretical consideration of statistically optimum methods for speech spectral density* (in Japanese). Rep. no. 3107, Electr. Comm. Lab, NTT, Tokyo.

Sakoe, H. and Chiba, S. (1978). Dynamic programming algorithms optimization for spoken word recognition. *IEEE Transactions on Acoustics, Speech and Signal Processing*, 26, 43–9.

Salmelin, R., Hari, R., Lounasmaa, O.V. and Sams, M. (1994). Dynamics of brain activation during picture naming. *Nature*, 368, 463–5.

Salthouse, T. (1986). Perceptual, cognitive, and motoric aspects of transcription typing. *Psychological Bulletin*, 99, 303–19.

Saltzman, E. (1991). The task dynamic model in speech production. In H.F.M. Peters, W. Hulstijn and C.W. Starkweather (eds), *Speech motor control and stuttering* (pp. 37–52). Amsterdam: *Excerpta Medica*.

—— (1992). Biomechanic and haptic factors in the temporal patterning of limb and speech activity. *Human Movement Science*, 11, 239–51.

—— (1995). Intergestural timing in speech production: data and modeling. In *Proceedings of the XIIth International Congress of Phonetic Sciences*, Stockholm, Sweden. Vol. 2, 84–91.

Saltzman, E. and Munhall, K. (1989). A dynamical approach to gestural patterning in speech production. *Ecological Psychology*, 1, 333–82.

Saltzman, E., Löfqvist, A., Kinsella-Shaw, J., Rubin, P. and Kay, B. (1992). A perturbation study of lip-larynx coordination. In J. Ohala, T. Neary, B. Derwing, M. Hodge and G. Wiebe (eds), *Proceedings of 1992 International Conference on Spoken Language Processing, addendum* (pp. 19–22). Edmonton: The University of Alberta.

—— (1995). On the dynamics of temporal patterning in speech. In F. Bell-Berti and L. Raphael (eds), *Producing Speech: Contemporary Issues for Katherine Safford Harris*. Woodbury: American Institute of Phonetics.

Samuel, A.G. (1981a). Phonemic restoration: insights from a new methodology. *Journal of Experimental Psychology: General*, 110, 474–94.

—— (1981b). The role of bottom-up confirmation in the phonemic-restoration illusion. *Journal of Experimental Psychology: Human Perception and Performance*, 5, 1124–31.

—— (1987). Lexical uniqueness effects on phonemic restoration. *Journal of Memory and Language*, 26, 36–56.

Samuel, A.G. and Ressler, W.H. (1986). Attention within auditory word perception: insights from the phonemic restoration illusion. *Journal of Experimental Psychology: Human Perception and Performance*, 12, 70–9.

Sanes, J.N., Donoghue, J.P., Thangaraj, V., Edelman, R.R. and Warach, S. (1995). Shared neural substrates controlling hand movements in human motor cortex. *Science*, 268, 1775–77.

Sapir, E. (1925). *Sound patterns in language*. Language, 1, 37–51.

Sarter, M., Berntson, G.G. and Cacioppo, J.T. (1996). Brain imaging and cognitive neuroscience. *American Psychologist*, 51, 13–21.

Sauerland, E. and Mitchell, S. (1975). Electromyographic activity of intrinsic and extrinsic muscles of the human tongue. *Texas Reports on Biology and Medicine*, 33, 445–55.

Saussure, F. de (1916). *Cours de linguistique générale*. Lausanne and Paris: Payot.

Sawashima, M. (1968). Movements of the larynx in articulation of Japanese consonants. *Annual Bulletin of Research Institute of Logopedics and Phoniatrics, University of Tokyo*, 2, 11–20.

—— (1977). Fiberoptic observation of the larynx and other speech organs. In M. Sawashima and F.S. Cooper (eds), *Dynamic aspects of speech production* (pp. 31–46). Tokyo: University of Tokyo Press.

Sawashima, M. and Hirose, H. (1968). New laryngoscopic technique by use of fiber optics. *Journal of the Acoustical Society of America*, 43, 168.

—— (1983). Laryngeal gestures in speech production. In P.F. MacNeilage (ed.), *The production of speech* (pp. 11–38). New York: Springer-Verlag.

Sawusch, J.R. and Jusczyk, P.W. (1981). Adaptation and contrast in the perception of voicing. *Journal of Experimental Psychology: Human Perception and Performance*, 7, 1124–31.

Schafer, R.W. and Markel, J.D. (eds) (1979). *Speech analysis*. New York: IEEE Press.

Schalk, T. and Sachs, M.B. (1980). Nonlinearities in auditory-nerve fiber response to band limited noise. *Journal of the Acoustical Society of America*, 67, 903–13.

Scherer, K.R. (1987). Vocal assessment of affective disorders. In J.D. Maser (ed.), *Depression and expressive behavior*. Hillsdale, NJ: Lawrence Erlbaum Associates.

Scherer, K.R. and Giles, H. (eds) (1979). *Social markers in speech*. Cambridge: Cambridge University Press.

Scherer, K.R., Ladd, R.D. and Silverman, K.E.A. (1984). Vocal cues to speaker affect: testing two models. *Journal of the Acoustical Society of America*, 76, 1346–56.

Scherer, R.C. (1981). 'Laryngeal fluid mechanics: steady flow considerations using static models'. Ph.D. thesis, The University of Iowa, Iowa City.

Scherer, R.C. and Guo, C.-G. (1991). Generalized translaryngeal pressure coefficients for a wide range of laryngeal configurations. In J. Gauffin and B. Hammarberg (eds), *Proceedings of Vocal Fold Physiology III* (pp. 83–90). San Diego: Singular Pub. Co.

Schertel, L., Puppe, D., Schnepper, E., Witt, H. and zum Winkel, K. (1976). *Atlas of Xeroradiography*. W.B. Saunders Company: Philadelphia.

Schiff, H.B., Alexander, M.P., Naesser, M.A. and Galaburda, A.M. (1983). Aphemia: clinical-anatomic correlations. *Archives of Neurology*, 40, 720–7.

Schmidt, R. (1975). A schema theory for discrete motor skill learning. *Psychological Review*, 82, 225–60.

Schmidt-Neilsen, A. and Stern, K. (1985). Identification of known voices as a function of familiarity and narrow-band coding. *Journal of the Acoustical Society of America*, 77, 658–63.

Schönle, P.W. (1988). *Elektromagnetische Artikulographie*. Berlin: Springer.

Schönle, P., Grabe, K., Wenig, P., Hohne, J., Schrader, J. and Conrad, B. (1987). Electromagnetic articulography: use of alternating magnetic fields for tracking movements of multiple points inside and outside the vocal tract. *Brain and Language*, 31, 26–35.

Schönle, P. Muller, C. and Wenig, P. (1989). Echtzeitanalyse von orofacialen Bewegungen mit Hilfe der elektromagnetischen Artikulographie. *Biomed. Technik*, 34, 126–30.

Schouten, J.F. (1940). The residue and the mechanism of hearing. *Proceedings koninklijke Nederlandse Akademie van Wetenschappen* 43, 991–9.

—— (1970). The residue revisited. In R. Plomp and G.F. Smoorenburg (eds), *Frequency analysis and periodicity detection in hearing* (pp. 41–54). Lieden: Sijthoff.

Schouten, M.E.H. (ed.) (1987). *The psychophysics of speech perception*. Dordrecht: Nijhof.

—— (ed.) (1992). *The auditory processing of speech*. Berlin: Mouton-De Gruyter.

Schreiner, C.E. and Urbas, J.V. (1986). Representation of amplitude modulation in the auditory cortex of the cat. I. The anterior auditory field (AAF). *Hearing Research*, 21, 227–41.

Schroeder, M.R. (1967). Determination of the geometry of the human vocal tract by acoustic measurements. *Journal of the Acoustical Society of America*, 41, 1002–10.

—— (1968). Period histogram and product spectrum: new methods for fundamental-frequency measurement. *Journal of the Acoustical Society of America*, 43, 829–34.

—— (ed.) (1985). *Speech and speaker recognition*. Bibliotheca Phonetica 12. Basel: Karger.

Schurick, J.M., Williges, B.H. and Maynard, J.F. (1985). User feedback requirements with automatic speech recognition. *Ergonomics*, 28, 1543–55.

Schwartz, J.L., Beautemps, D., Arrouas, Y. and Escudier, P. (1992). Auditory analysis of speech gestures. In M.E.H. Schouten (ed.), *The auditory processing of speech* (pp. 239–52). Berlin: Mouton-De Gruyter.

Schwartz, M.F. and Rine, H.E. (1968). Identification of speakers from whispered vowels. *Journal of the Acoustical Society of America*, 44, 1736–7.

Scripture, E.W. (1916). Records of speech in disseminated sclerosis. *Brain*, 39, 455–77.

—— (1923). *The study of English speech by new methods of phonetic investigation*. London: Oxford University Press.

Scully, C. (1986). Speech production simulated with a functional model of the larynx and the vocal tract. *Journal of Phonetics*, 14, 407–13.

—— (1990). Articulatory synthesis. In W.J. Hardcastle and A. Marchal (eds), *Speech production and speech modelling* (pp. 151–86). Dordrecht: Kluwer Academic Press.

Segui, J. and Frauenfelder, U. (1986). The effect of lexical constraints upon speech perception. In F. Klix and H. Hagendorf (eds), *Human memory and cognitive capabilities: mechanisms and performances* (pp. 795–808). Amsterdam: North-Holland.

Segui, J., Frauenfelder, U. and Mehler, J. (1981). Phoneme monitoring, syllable monitoring and lexical access. *British Journal of Psychology*, 72, 471–7.

Selkirk, E.O. (1972). 'The phrase phonology of English and French'. Ph.D. dissertation, MIT.

—— (1984). *Phonology and syntax: the relation between sound and structure*. Cambridge, MA: MIT Press.

Seneff, S. (1988). A joint synchrony/mean-rate model of auditory speech processing. *Journal of Phonetics*, 16, 55–76.

Shadle, C.H. (1983). Experiments on the acoustics of whistling. *The Physics Teacher*, March, 148–54.

—— (1985). 'The acoustics of fricative consonants'. Ph.D. thesis. MIT, Cambridge, MA.

—— (1985). The acoustics of fricative consonants. *Research Laboratory of Electronics Quarterly Report*, 506. Massachusetts Institute of Technology, Cambridge, MA.

—— (1990). Articulatory-acoustic relationships in fricative consonants. In W.J. Hardcastle and A. Marchal (eds), *Speech production and speech modelling* (pp. 187–209). Dordrecht: Kluwer Academic Publishers.

—— (1991). The effect of geometry on source mechanisms of fricative consonants. *Journal of Phonetics*, 19, 409–24.

—— (1995). Modelling the noise source in voiced fricatives. *Proceedings of the 15th International Congress on Acoustics*. Trondheim.

Shadle, C.H., Barney, A.M. and Thomas, D.W. (1991). An investigation into the acoustics and aerodynamics of the larynx. In J. Gauffin and B. Hammarberg (eds), *Proceedings of Vocal Fold Physiology III* (pp. 73–82). San Diego: Singular Pub. Co.

Shadle, C.H. and Scully, C. (1995). An articulatory-acoustic-aerodynamic analysis of [s] in VCV sequences. *3rd Seminar on Speech Production: Models and Data*. Saybrook, CT.

Shah, P.J., Joshi, M.R. and Darnwala, N.R. (1980). The interrelationships between facial areas and other body dimensions. *Angle Orthodontist*, 50, 45–53.

Shailer, M.J. and Moore, B.C.J. (1983). Gap detection as a function of frequency, bandwidth and level. *Journal of the Acoustical Society of America*, 74, 467–73.

—— (1985). Detection of temporal gaps in band-limited noise: effects of variations in bandwidth and signal-to-masker ratio. *Journal of the Acoustical Society of America*, 77, 635–9.

—— (1987). Gap detection and the auditory filter: phase effects using sinusoidal stimuli. *Journal of the Acoustical Society of America*, 81, 1110–17.

Shaiman, S. (1989). Kinematic and electromyographic responses to perturbation of the jaw. *Journal of the Acoustical Society of America*, 86, 78–88.

Shaiman, S. and Abbs, J. (1987). Sensorimotor contributions to the temporal coordination of oral and laryngeal movements. *SMLC Preprints (Speech Motor Control Laboratories, University of Madison) Spring-Summer 1987*, 185–202.

Shamma, S. (1985). Speech processing in the auditory system. II: lateral inhibition and the central processing of speech evoked activity in the auditory nerve. *Journal of the Acoustical Society of America*, 78, 1622–32.

—— (1988). The acoustic features of speech sounds in a model of auditory processing: vowels and voiceless fricatives. *Journal of Phonetics*, 16, 77–91.

Shapiro, B.L., Redman, R.S. and Gorlin, R.J. (1963). Measurement of normal and reportedly abnormal palatal vaults. I. Normal adult measurements. *Journal of Dental Research*, 42, 1039.

Shapiro, D., Zernicke, R., Gregor, R. and Diestel, J. (1981). Evidence for generalized motor programs using gait pattern analysis. *Journal of Motor Behavior*, 13, 33–47.

Shattuck-Hufnagel, S. (1979). Speech errors as evidence of a serial-ordering mechanism in sentence production. In W. Cooper and E. Walker (eds), *Sentence processing* (pp. 295–342). Hillsdale, NJ: Lawrence Erlbaum.

—— (1983). Sublexical units and suprasegmental structure in speech production planning. In P. MacNeilage (ed.), *The production of speech* (pp. 109–36). New York: Springer-Verlag.

—— (1992). The role of word structure in segmental serial ordering. *Cognition*, 42, 213–59.

Shattuck-Hufnagel, S. and Klatt, D.H. (1979). The limited use of distinctive features and markedness in speech production: evidence from speech error data. *Journal of Verbal Learning and Verbal Behavior*, 18, 41–55.

Shaw, G.B. (1916). *Preface to Pygmalion*, Reprinted 1957. London: Penguin Books.

Shaywitz, B.A., Shawitz, S.E., Pugh, K.R., Constable, R.T., Skudlarski, P., Fulbright, R.K., Bronen, R.A., Fletcher, J.M., Shankweiler, D.P. and Katz, L. (1995). Sex differences in the functional organization of the brain for language. *Nature*, 373, 607–9.

Shepard, R.N. (1972). Psychological representation of speech sounds. In P.B. Denes and E.E. David Jr. (eds), *Human communication: a unified view*. New York: McGraw-Hill.

Shi, C. (1988). Tone and intonation in Mandarin. In G.N. Clements (ed.), *Working Papers of the Cornell Phonetics Laboratory* (pp. 83–109).

Shibata, S. (1968). A study of dynamic palatography. *Annual Bulletin of Research Institute of Logopedics and Phoniatrics*, University of Tokyo, 2, 28–36.

Shields, J.L., McHugh, A. and Martin, J.G. (1974). Reaction time to phoneme targets as a function of rhythmic cues in continuous speech. *Journal of Experimental Psychology*, 102, 250–5.

Shillcock, R. (1990). Lexical hypotheses in continuous speech. In G.T.M. Altmann (ed.), *Cognitive models of speech processing: psycholinguistic and computational perspectives* (pp. 24–49). Cambridge, MA: MIT Press.

Shipp, T., Doherty, E.T. and Hollien, H. (1987). Some fundamental considerations concerning voice identification. *Journal of the Acoustical Society of America*, 82, 687–8.

Shirt, M. (1984). An auditory speaker recognition experiment. *Proceedings of the Institute of Acoustics*, 6, 101–4.

Shore, S.E. (1995). Recovery of forward-masked responses in ventral cochlear nucleus neurons. *Hearing Research*, 82, 31–43.

Siebert, W.M. (1970). Frequency discrimination in the auditory system: place or periodicity mechanism? *Proceedings of the IEEE*, 58, 723–30.

Sievers, E. (1881). *Grundzüge der Phonetik*. Leipzig: Breitkopf & Hartel.

Silveri, M.C., Leggio, M.G. and Molinari, M. (1994). The cerebellum contributes to linguistic production: A case of agrammatic speech following a right cerebellar lesion. *Neurology*, 44, 2047–50.

Silverman, K.E.A. (1986). f_0 segmental cues depend on intonation: the case of the rise after voiced stops. *Phonetica*, 43, 76–91.

—— (1987). 'The structure and processing of fundamental frequency contours.' Ph.D. thesis, University of Cambridge.

Silverman, K.E.A., Beckman, M.E., Pitrelli, J.F., Pierrehumbert, J., Ostendorf, M., Wightman, C., Hirschberg, J. and Price, P. (1992). TOBI: a standard scheme for labeling prosody. *Proceedings of the 1992 International Conference on Spoken Language Processing*, 867–70.

Sinclair, D. (1978). *Human growth after birth* (3rd edn). Oxford: Oxford University Press.

Sinex, D.G. (1993). Auditory nerve fiber representation of cues to voicing in syllable-final stop consonants. *Journal of the Acoustical Society of America*, 94, 1351–62.

Sinex, D.G. and Geisler, C.D. (1983). Responses of auditory-nerve fibers to consonant-vowel syllables. *Journal of the Acoustical Society of America*, 73, 602–15.

Sinex, D.G. and McDonald, L. (1988). Average discharge rate representation of voice onset time in the chinchilla auditory nerve. *Journal of the Acoustical Society of America*, 83, 1817–927.

—— (1989). Synchronized discharge rate representation of voice onset time in the chinchilla auditory nerve. *Journal of the Acoustical Society of America*, 85, 1995–2004.

Sinex, D.G., McDonald, L. and Mott, J.B. (1991). Neural correlates of nonmonotonic temporal acuity for voice onset time. *Journal of the Acoustical Society of America*, 90, 2441–9.

Sinnott, J.M., Beecher, M.D., Moody, D.B. and Stebbins, W.C. (1976). Speech sound discrimination by monkeys and humans. *Journal of the Acoustical Society of America*, 60, 687–95.

Slaney, M. and Lyon, R.F. (1993). On the importance of time – a temporal representation of sound. In M. Cooke, S. Beet, M. Crawford (eds), *Visual representations of speech signals* (pp. 95–116). New York: Wiley.

Slis, I.H. and Cohen, A. (1969a and b). On the complex regulating the voiced-voiceless distinction, I and II. *Language and Speech*, 12, 80–102 and 137–56.

Slootweg, A. (1988). Metrical prominence and syllable duration. In P. Coopmans and A. Hulk (eds), *Linguistics and the Netherlands 1988* (pp. 139–48). Dordrecht: Foris Publications.

Slowiaczek, L.M. (1990). Effects of lexical stress in auditory word recognition. *Language and Speech*, 33, 47–68.

Slowiaczek, L.M. and Hamburger, M.B. (1992). Prelexical facilitation and lexical interference in auditory word recognition. *Journal of Experimental Psychology: Learning, Memory, and Cognition*, 18, 1239–50.

Smith, A. (1992). The control of orofacial movements in speech. *Critical Review in Oral Biology and Medicine*, 3, 233–67.

Smith, A. and Denny, M. (1990). High frequency oscillations as indicators of neural control mechanisms in human respiration, mastication, and speech. *Journal of Neurophysiology*, 63, 745–58.

Smith, B.L., Brown-Sweeney, S. and Stoel-Gammon, C. (1989). A quantitative analysis of reduplicated and variegated babbling. *A First Language*, 17, 147–53.

Smith, C. (1975). Residual hearing and speech production in deaf children. *Journal of Speech and Hearing Research*, 18, 795–811.

Smith, C.L. (1993). Prosodic patterns in the coordination of vowel and consonant gestures. In B.A. Connel and A. Arvaniti (eds), *Papers in laboratory phonology IV: phonology and phonetic evidence* (pp. 205–22). Cambridge: Cambridge University Press.

Smith, K. and Kier, W. (1989). Trunks, tongues, and tentacles: moving with skeletons of muscle. *American Scientist*, 77, 29–35.

Smith, N. (1973). *The acquisition of phonology: a case study*. Cambridge: Cambridge University Press.

Smith, R.L. (1979). Adaptation, saturation and physiological masking in single auditory-nerve fibers. *Journal of the Acoustical Society of America*, 65, 166–78.

Smith, T. (1971). A phonetic study of the function of the extrinsic tongue muscles. *UCLA Working Papers in Phonetics*, 18, 1–131.

Smith, W. (1994). Computers, statistics, and disputed authorship. In J. Gibbon (ed.), *Language and the law*. London: Longman.

Smith, W.S. and Fetz, E.E. (1987). Noninvasive brain imaging and the study of higher brain function in humans. In S.P. Wise (ed.), *Higher brain functions* (pp. 311–46). New York: Wiley and Sons.

Smoorenburg, G.F. (1987). Discussion of the physiological correlates of speech perception. In M.E.H. Schouten (ed.), *The psychophysics of speech perception* (pp. 393–9). Dordrecht: Nijhof.

Smoorenburg, G.F. and Linschoten, D.H. (1977). A neurophysiological study on auditory frequency analysis of complex tones. In E.F. Evans and J.P. Wilson (eds), *Psychophysics and physiology of hearing* (pp. 175–84). London: Academic.

Snyman, J.W. (1975). Zullhõasi fonologie en woordeboek. Cape Town: Balkena.

Sock, R., Ollila, L., Delattre, C., Zilliox, C. and Zohair, L. (1988). Patrons de phases dans le cycle acoustique de détente en français. *Journal Acoustique*, 1, 339–45.

Södersten, M. (1994). 'Vocal fold closure during phonation'. Ph.D. thesis, Studies in Logopedics and Phoniatrics No. 3, Huddinge University Hospital, Stockholm.

Södersten, M. and Lindestad, P.-Å. (1990). Glottal closure and perceived breathiness during phonation in normally speaking subjects. *Journal of Speech and Hearing Research*, 33, 601–11.

Södersten, M., Lindestad, P.-Å. and Hammarberg, B. (1991). Vocal fold closure, perceived breathiness, and acoustic characteristics in normal adult speakers. In J. Gauffin and B. Hammarberg (eds), *Proceedings of Vocal Fold Physiology III* (pp. 217–24). San Diego: Singular Pub. Co.

Solé, M.J. and Ohala, J. (1991). Differentiating between phonetic and phonological processes: the case of nasalization. *Proceedings of the 12th International Congress of Phonetic Sciences*, 2, 110–13, Aix-en-Provence.

Soloman, N., McCall, G., Trosset, M. and Gray, W. (1989). Laryngeal configuration and constriction during two types of whispering. *Journal of Speech and Hearing Research*, 32, 161–74.

Solomon, N.P. and Hixon, T.J. (1993). Speech breathing in Parkinson's disease. *Journal of Speech and Hearing Research*, 36, 294–310.

Sommerstein, A.H. (1977). *Modern phonology*. Baltimore: University Park Press.

Sondhi, M.M. and Schroeter, J. (1987). A hybrid time-frequency domain articulatory speech synthesizer. *IEEE Trans. ASSP*, 35 (7).

Sonesson, B. (1960). On the anatomy and vibratory pattern of the human vocal folds. *Acta Otolaryng*, Supplement 156, 1–58.

—— (1982). Vocal fold kinesiology. In S. Grillner, B. Lindblom, J. Lubker and A. Persson (eds), *Speech motor control* (pp. 113–17). Oxford: Pergamon Press.

Sonies, B. (1991). Ultrasound imaging and swallowing. In M. Donner and B. Jones (eds), *Normal and abnormal swallowing: imaging in diagnosis and therapy* (pp. 237–60). New York: Springer.

Soong, F., Rosenberg, A., Rabiner, L. and Juang, B. (1985). A vector quantization approach to speaker recognition. *Proceedings of the IEEE International Conference of ASSP*, 33, 387–90.

Sorokin, V.N., Gay, T. and Ewan, W.G. (1980). Some biomechanical correlates of jaw movement. *Journal of the Acoustical Society of America*, 68 (S1), S32 (A).

Spajić, S. (forthcoming). *Serbian affricates*.

Spajić, S., Ladefoged, P., Maddieson, I. and Sands, B. (1993). Phonetic structure of Dahalo. *UCLA Working Papers in Phonetics*, 84, 25–65.

Spargo, J.W. (1931). [Translator's preface]. *Pedersen, H. linguistic science in the nineteenth century: methods and results*. Cambridge, MA: Harvard University Press.

Spring, C., Erickson, D. and Call, T. (1992). Emotional modalities and intonation in spoken language. *Proceedings of 1992 International Conference on Spoken Language Processing*, 679–82.

Sproat, R.W. and Fujimura, O. (1993). Allophonic variation in English /l/ and its implications for phonetic implementation. *Journal of Phonetics*, 21, 291–311.

Square, P.A. and Martin, R.E. (in press). The nature and treatment of neuromotor speech disorders in aphasia. In R. Chapey (ed.), *Language intervention strategies in adult aphasia*, Vol. 3. Baltimore: Williams and Wilkins.

Srulovicz, P. and Goldstein, J.L. (1983). A central spectrum model: a synthesis of auditory nerve timing and place cues in monaural communication of frequency spectrum. *Journal of the Acoustical Society of America*, 73, 1266–76.

Stampe, D. (1969). *The acquisition of phonetic representation*. Papers from the Fifth Regional Meeting of the Chicago Linguistic Society, Chicago, Il.

Stanley, W.D., Dougherty, G.R. and Dougherty, R. (1984). *Digital signal processing*. Reston Publ. Co., Inc. (Prentice-Hall).

Stark, R.E. (1980). Stages of speech development in the first year of life. In G. Yeni-Komshian, J.F. Kavanagh and C.A. Ferguson (eds), *Child phonology, Vol. 1, Production*. New York: Academic Press.

—— (1983). Phonatory development in young normally hearing and hearing impaired children. In I. Hochberg, H. Levitt and M.J. Osberger (eds), *Speech of the hearing impaired: research, training, and personnel preparation*. Baltimore: University Park Press.

Stark, R.E., Rose, S.N. and McLagen, M. (1975). Features of infant sounds: the first eight weeks of life. *Journal of Child Language*, 2, 205–21.

Stathopoulos, E.T. and Weismer, G. (1983). Closure duration of stop consonants. *Journal of Phonetics*, 11, 395–400.

Steele, S.A. (1986). Interaction of vowel F0 and prosody. *Phonetica*, 43, 92–105.

Steeneken, H.J.M. and Houtgast, T. (1980). A physical method for measuring speech-transmission quality. *Journal of the Acoustical Society of America*, 69, 318–26.

Stein, B.R. and Meredith, M.A. (1990). Multisensory integration: neural and behavioral solutions for dealing with stimuli from different sensory modalities. In A. Diamond (ed.), *The development and neural bases of higher cognitive functions, annals of the New York Academy of Sciences*, 608, 51–70.

Steinschneider, Schroeder, C.E., M., Arezzo, J.C. and Vaughan, H.G. (1994). Speech-evoked activity in primary auditory cortex: effects of voice onset time. *Electroencephalography and Clinical Neurophysiology*, 92, 30–43.

—— (1995). Physiologic correlates of voice onset time boundary in primary auditory cortex (A1) of the awake monkey: temporal response patterns. *Brain and Language*, 48, 326–40.

Stemberger, J.P., Elman, J.L. and Haden, P. (1985). Interference between phonemes during phoneme monitoring: evidence for an interactive activation model of speech perception. *Journal of Experimental Psychology: Human Perception and Performance*, 11, 475–89.

Stent, G.S. (1981). Strength and weakness of the genetic approach to the development of the nervous system. *Annual Review of Neuroscience*, 4, 163–94.

Stephan, K.M., Fink, G.R., Passingham, R.E., Silbersweig, D., Ceballos-Baumann, A.O., Frith, C.D. and Frackowiak, R.S. (1995). Functional anatomy of the mental representation of upper extremity movements in healthy subjects. *Journal of Neurophysiology*, 73, 373–86.

Steriade, D. (1993). Closure, release, and nasal contours. In M. Huffman and R. Krakow (eds), *Phonetics and phonology 5* (pp. 401–70). New York: Academic Press.

Sternberg, S., Knoll, R.L., Monsell, S. and Wright, C.E. (1988). Motor programs and hierarchical organization in the control of rapid speech. *Phonetica*, 45, 175–97.

Stetson, R.H. (1928). *Motor phonetics. A study of speech movements in action.* [Archives neerlandaises de phonétique experimentale, Tome 3].

Stevens, K.L. and Keyser, S.J. (1989). Primary features and their enhancement in consonants. *Language*, 65, 81–106.

Stevens, K.N. (1971). Airflow and turbulence noise for fricative and stop consonants: static considerations. *Journal of the Acoustical Society of America*, 50 (4), 1180–92.

—— (1972). The quantal nature of speech: evidence from articulatory-acoustic data. In P.B. Denes and E.E. David Jr. (eds), *Human communication: a unified view* (pp. 51–66). New York: McGraw Hill.

—— (1977). Physics of laryngeal behavior and larynx modes. *Phonetica*, 34, 264–79.

—— (1980). Acoustic correlates of some phonetic categories. *Journal of the Acoustical Society of America*, 68, 836–42.

—— (1985a). Spectral prominences and phonetic distinctions in languages. *Speech Communication*, 4, 137–44.

—— (1985b). Evidence for the role of acoustic boundaries in the perception of speech sounds. In V. Fromkin (ed.), *Phonetic Linguistics* (pp. 243–55). New York: Academic Press.

—— (1988). Phonetic features and lexical access. *The Second Symposium on Advanced Man-Machine Interface through Spoken Language*, Hawaii.

—— (1989). On the quantal nature of speech. *Journal of Phonetics*, 17, 3–46.

—— (1993a). Modelling affricate consonants. *Speech Communication*, 13, 33–43.

—— (1993b). Models for the production and acoustics of stop consonants. *Speech Communication*, 13, 367–75.

—— (in preparation). *Acoustic phonetics.*

Stevens, K.N. and Bickley, C. (1991). Constraints among parameters simplify control of Klatt formant synthesizer. *Journal of Phonetics*, 19 (1).

Stevens, K.N. and Blumstein, S. (1978). Invariant cues for place of articulation in stop consonants. *Journal of the Acoustical Society of America*, 64, 1358–68.

—— (1981). The search for invariant acoustic correlates of phonetic features. In P. Eimas and J. Miller (eds), *Perspectives on the study of speech* (pp. 1–38). Hillsdale, NJ: Erlbaum.

Stevens, K.N., Fant, G. and Hawkins, S. (1987). Some acoustical and perceptual correlates of nasal vowels. In R. Channon and L. Shockey (eds), *In honor of Ilse Lehiste: Ilse Lehiste Puhendusteos* (pp. 241–54). The Netherlands: Foris Publications.

Stevens, K.N. and House, A.S. (1961). An acoustical theory of vowel production and some of its implications. *Journal of Speech and Hearing Research*, 4, 303–20.

Stevens, K.N., House, A.S. and Paul, A.P. (1966). Acoustic description of syllabic nuclei: an integration in terms of a dynamic model of articulation. *Journal of the Acoustical Society of America*, 40, 123–132.

Stewart, I. and Golubitsky, M. (1992). *Fearful symmetry.* Oxford: Blackwell.

Stoel-Gammon, C. (1983). Constraints on consonant-vowel sequences in early words. *Journal of Child Language*, 10, 455–7.

—— (1988). Prelinguistic vocalizations of hearing impaired and normally hearing subjects: a comparison of consonantal inventories. *Journal of Speech and Hearing Disorders*, 53, 303–15.

Stoel-Gammon, C. and Otomo, K. (1986). Babbling development in hearing-impaired and normally hearing subjects. *Journal of Speech and Hearing Disorders*, 51, 33–41.

Stone, M. (1990). A three-dimensional model of tongue movement based on ultrasound and x-ray microbeam data. *Journal of the Acoustical Society of America*, 87, 2207–17.

—— (1991). Imaging the tongue and vocal tract. *British Journal of Disorders of Communication*, 26, 11–23.

Stone, M., Faber, A. and Cordaro, M. (1991). Cross-sectional tongue movement and tongue-palate movement patterns in [s] and [ʃ] syllables. *Proceedings of the 12th International Congress of Phonetic Sciences*, 2, 354–7, Aix-en-Provence.

Stone, M., Faber, A., Raphael, L. and Shawker, T. (1992). Cross-sectional tongue shape and linguopalatal contact patterns in [s], [ʃ], and [l]. *Journal of Phonetics*, 20, 253–70.

Stone, M., Morrish, K., Sonies, B. and Shawker, T. (1987). Tongue curvature: a model of shape during vowels. *Folia Phoniatrica*, 39, 302–15.

Stone, M. and Shawker, T. (1986). An ultrasound examination of tongue movement during swallowing. *Dysphagia*, 1, 78–83.

Stone, M., Shawker, T., Talbot, T. and Rich, A. (1988). Cross-sectional tongue shape during vowels. *Journal of the Acoustical Society of America*, 83, 1586–96.

Strand, E.A., Buder, E.H., Yorkston, K.M. and Ramig, L.O. (1993). Differential phonatory characteristics of women with amyotrophic lateral sclerosis. *NCVS Status and Progress Report*, 4, 151–67.

Strube, H.W. (1980). Linear prediction on a warped frequency scale. *Journal of the Acoustical Society of America*, 68 (4), 1071–6.

—— (1982). Time-varying wave digital filters for modeling analog systems. *IEEE Trans ASSP*-30, 864–8.

Studdert-Kennedy, M.G. (1987). The phoneme as a perceptuomotor structure. In A. Allport, D. MacKay, W. Prinz and E. Scheerer (eds), *Language perception and production*. New York: Academic Press.

—— (1991). Language development from an evolutionary perspective. In N. Krasnegor, D. Rumbaugh, M. Studdert-Kennedy and R. Schiefelbusch (eds), *Biological foundations of language development*. Hillsdale, NJ: Lawrence Erlbaum Associates.

Su, L.-S., Li, K.-P. and Fu, K.S. (1974). Identification of speakers by use of nasal coarticulation. *Journal of the Acoustical Society of America*, 56, 1876–82.

Subtelny, J., Li, W., Whitehead, R. and Subtelny, J.D. (1989). Cephalometric and cineradiographic study of deviant resonance in hearing impaired speakers. *Journal of Speech and Hearing Disorders*, 54, 249–65.

Subtelny, J., Mestre, J. and Subtelny, J. (1964). Comparative study of normal and defective articulation of /s/ as related to malocclusion and deglutition. *Journal of Speech and Hearing Disorders*, 29, 264–85.

Suga, N. (1964). Recovery cycles and responses to frequency-modulated tone pulses in auditory neurones of echolocating bats. *Journal of Physiology (London)*, 175, 50–80.

—— (1992). Philosophy and stimulus design for neuroethology of complex-sound processing. *Philosophical Transactions of the Royal Society of London*, B 336, 423–8.

Summerfield, A.Q., Sidwell, A.S. and Nelson, T. (1987). Auditory enhancement of changes in spectral amplitude. *Journal of the Acoustical Society of America*, 81, 700–8.

Sundberg, J., Johansson, C., Wilbrand, H. and Ytterbergh, C. (1987). From sagittal distance to area: a study of transverse vocal tract cross-sectional area. *Phonetica*, 44, 76–90.

Sussman, H.M., MacNeilage, P.F. and Hanson, R.J. (1973). Labial and mandibular dynamics during the production of bilabial consonants: preliminary observations. *Journal of Speech and Hearing Research*, 16, 397–420.

Sussman, H.M., McCaffrey, H.A. and Matthew, S.A. (1991). An investigation of locus equations as a source of relative invariance for stop place categorization. *Journal of the Acoustical Society of America*, 90, 1309–25.

Sussman, H.M. and Westbury, J.R. (1981). The effects of antagonistic gestures on temporal and amplitude parameters of anticipatory labial coarticulation. *Journal of Speech and Hearing Research*, 24, 16–24.

Suzuki, N. and Michi, K. (1986). Dynamic Velography. *Proceedings of the XXth Congress of the International Association of Logopedics and Phoniatrics*, Tokyo, 172–3.

Suzuki, N., Sakuma, T., Michi, K. and Ueno, T. (1981). The articulatory characteristics of the tongue in anterior openbite: observation by use of dynamic palatography. *International Journal of Oral Surgery*, 10, 299–303.

Sweet, H. (1877). *Handbook of Phonetics*. Oxford: Clarendon. (Cited by Wood, S.A.J. (1993). Crosslinguistic cineradiographic studies of the temporal coordination of speech gestures. Working Papers, 40, Lund University, 251–63.)

—— (1899). *The practical study of languages. A guide for teachers and learners*. London: J.M. Dent.

Swinney, D. (1979). Lexical access during sentence comprehension: (re)consideration of context effects. *Journal of Verbal Learning and Verbal Behavior*, 18, 645–59.

—— (1981). Lexical processing during sentence comprehension: effects of higher order constraints and implications for representation. In T. Myers, J. Laver and J. Anderson (eds), *The cognitive representation of speech* (pp. 201–9). Amsterdam: North-Holland.

Syrdal, A.K. (1992). Development of a female voice for a concatenative synthesis text-to-speech system. *Journal of the Acoustical Society of America*, 92 (Fall), 5pSP12.

Syrdal, A.K. and Gopal, H.S. (1986). A perceptual model of vowel recognition based on the auditory representation of American English vowels. *Journal of the Acoustical Society of America*, 79, 1086–100.

Taft, L. (1984). 'Prosodic Constraints and Lexical Parsing Strategies'. Ph.D. thesis, University of Massachusetts.

Takashima, S., Ikezoe, J., Harada, K., Akai, Y., Hamada, S., Arisawa, J., Morimoto, S., Masaki, N., Kozuka, T. and Maeda, H. (1989). Tongue cancer: correlation of MR imaging and sonography with pathology. *American Journal of Neuroradiology*, 10, 419–24.

Talkin, D. and Rowley, M. (1990). Pitch-synchronous analysis and synthesis for TTS systems. *Proceedings of ESCA Workshop on Speech Synthesis*, Autrans, France.

Tanner, J.M. (1978). *Foetus into man: physical growth from conception to maturity*. London: Open Books.

Tattersall, G.D. (1990). Neural networks and speech processing. In W.A. Ainsworth (ed.), *Advances in speech, hearing and language processing*, Vol. 1 (pp. 107–48). London: JAI Press Ltd.

Teager, H.M. (1980). Some observations on oral air flow during phonation. *IEEE Transactions on Acoustics, Speech and Signal Processing*, 28: 5, 599–601.

Teager, H.M. and Teager, S.M. (1983). Active fluid dynamic voice production models, or there is a unicorn in the garden. In I.R. Titze and R.C. Scherer (eds), *Vocal fold physiology* (pp. 387–401). Denver: The Denver Center for Performing Arts.

Techmer, F. (1880). *Phonetik. Zur vergleichenden Physiologie der Stimme und Sprache*. Leipzig: Wilhelm Engelmann.

Terhardt, E. (1974). Pitch, consonance, and harmony. *Journal of the Acoustical Society of America*, 55, 1061–9.

Terken, J.M.B. and Nooteboom, S.G. (1987). Opposite effects of accentuation and deaccentuation on verification latencies for given and new information. *Language and Cognitive Processes*, 2, 145–63.

Terracol, J., Guerrier, Y. and Camps, F. (1956). Le sphincter glottique; étude anatamoclinique. *Annales d'Otolaryngologie* (Paris), 73: 451.

Terzuolo, C. and Viviani, P. (1979). The central representation of learned motor patterns. In R. Talbot and D. Humphrey (eds), *Posture and movement* (pp. 113–21). New York: Raven Press.

Thach, W.T., Goodkin, H.P. and Keating, J.G. (1992). The cerebellum and the adaptive co-ordination of movement. *Annual Review of Neuroscience*, 15, 403–42.

Thelen, E. (1991). Motor aspects of emergent speech: a dynamic approach. In N. Krasnegor, D. Rumbaugh, M. Studdert-Kennedy and R. Schiefelbusch (eds), *Biological foundations of language development*. Hillsdale, NJ: Lawrence Erlbaum Associates.

—— (1995). Motor development: a new synthesis. *American Psychologist*, 50, 79–95.

Thomas, C. (ed.) (1973). Taber's cyclopedic medical dictionary (12th edn). Philadelphia: F.A. Davis Co.

Thomas, D.G., Campos, J.J., Shucard, D.W., Ramsay, D.S. and Shucard, J. (1981). Semantic comprehension in infancy: a signal detection analysis. *Child Development*, 51, 798–803.

Thomas, T.J. (1986). A finite element model of fluid flow in the vocal tract. *Computer Speech and Language*, 1, 131–52.

Thomson, L. (1995). 'Listeners' judgements of intra-oral cancer patients (with anterior and posterior sites of tumour/surgical lesion), pre-operatively and post-operatively'. Dissertation in partial fulfilment of the requirements for the Honours degree in Speech Pathology and Therapy, Queen Margaret College, Edinburgh.

Thongkum, T.L. (1987). Another look at the register distinction in Mon. *UCLA Working Papers in Phonetics*, 67, 132–65.

—— (1988). Phonation types in Mon-Khmer languages. In O. Fujimura (eds), *Vocal physiology: voice production, mechanisms and functions* (pp. 319–34). New York: Raven Press.

Thorsen, N. (1980). A study of the perception of sentence intonation – evidence from Danish. *Journal of the Acoustical Society of America*, 67, 1014–30.

Thorsen, N.G. (1985). Intonation and text in standard Danish. *Journal of the Acoustical Society of America*, 80, 1205–16.

Tiede, M. (in preparation). *An MRI-based study of pharyngeal volume contrasts in Akan.*

Tikhonov, A. and Arsenin, V. (1977). *Solutions of ill-posed problems*. Washington, D.C.: W.H. Winstron.

Tikofsky, R.S. (1984). Contemporary aphasia diagnostics. In N.J. Lass (ed.), *Speech and language: advances in Basic research and practice*, Vol. 11 (pp. 1–111). New York: Academic Press.

Till, J.A. and Alp, L.A. (1991). Aerodynamic and temporal measures of continuous speech in dysarthric speakers. In C.A. Moore, K.M. Yorkston and D.R. Beukelman (eds), *Dysarthria and apraxia of speech: perspectives on management* (pp. 185–203). Baltimore: Paul H. Brookes.

Titze, I.R. (1973). The human vocal cords: a mathematical model. Part I. *Phonetica*, 28, 129–70.

—— (1974). The human vocal cords: a mathematical model. Part II, *Phonetica*, 29, 1–21.

—— (1988). The physics of small-amplitude oscillation of the vocal folds. *Journal of the Acoustical Society of America*, 83, 1536–52.

—— (1992). Phonation threshold pressure: a missing link in glottal aerodynamics. *Journal of the Acoustical Society of America*, 91, 2926–35.

—— (1994). *Principles of voice production*. Englewood Cliffs, NJ: Prentice Hall.

Titze, I.R. and Talkin, D.T. (1979). A theoretical study of the effects of various laryngeal configurations on the acoustics of phonation. *Journal of the Acoustical Society of America*, 66, 60–74.

Tognola, G. and Vignolo, L.A. (1980). Brain lesions associated with oral apraxia in stroke patients: a clinico-neuroradiological investigation with the CT scan. *Neuropsychologia*, 18, 257–72.

Tooby, J. and Cosmides, L. (1988). Can non-universal mental organs evolve? Constraints from genetics, adaptation and the evolution of sex. *Institute for Evolutionary Studies Technical Report*, 88–2.

—— (1995). Mapping the evolved functional organization of mind and brain. In M. Gazzaniga (ed.), *The cognitive neurosciences*. Cambridge, MA: MIT Press.

Tosi, (1979). *Voice identification: theory and legal applications*. Baltimore: University Park Press.

Tourne, L.P. (1991). Growth of the pharynx and its physiologic implications. *American Journal of Orthodontics and Dentofacial Orthopaedics*, 99, 129–39.

Traill, A. (1985). *Phonetic and Phonological studies of !Xóõ Bushman. (Quellen zur Khoisan-Forschung, 5)*. Hamburg: Helmut Buske.

—— (1991). Pulmonic control, nasal venting and aspiration in Khoisan languages. *Journal of the International Phonetic Association*, 21, 13–18.

Traill, A. and Jackson, M. (1987). Speaker variation and phonation types in Tsonga nasals. *UCLA Working Papers in Phonetics*, 67, 1–28.

Traub, M., Rothwell, J. and Marsden, C. (1980). A grab reflex in the human hand. *Brain*, 103, 869–84.

Traunmüller, H. (1981). Perceptual dimension of openness in vowels. *Journal of the Acoustical Society of America*, 69, 1465–75.

Trubetzkoy, N. (1933). La phonologie actuelle. Psychologie du Langage. *Journal de Psychologie*, 1–4, 227–46.

—— (1962). *Principes de phonologie* (first published 1939 edn). Paris: Klincksieck.

—— (1969). *Principles of phonology*. Berkeley, CA: University of California Press. [Original: 1939. *Grundzüge der Phonologie*. Prag].

Trudgill, P. (1974). *The social differentiation of English in Norwich*. Cambridge: Cambridge University Press.

Tsunoda, K., Niimi, S. and Hirose, H. (1994). The roles of the posterior cricoarytenoid and thyropharyngeus muscles in whispering speech and human evolution. *Folia Phoniatrica Logop.*, 46, 139–51.

Tsunoda, T. (1975). Functional differences between right- and left-cerebral hemispheres detected by the key-tapping method. *Brain and Language*, 2, 152–70.

—— (1989). Hemispheric dominance in Japan and the West. In K. Klivington (ed.), *The science and mind* (pp. 54–9). Cambridge, MA: MIT Press.

Tuller, B., Harris, K. and Gross, B. (1981). Electromyographic study of the jaw muscles during speech. *Haskins Laboratories Status Reports*, SR-59/60, 83–102.

Tuller, B. and Kelso, J.A.S. (1984). The timing of articulatory gestures: evidence for relational invariants. *Journal of the Acoustical Society of America*, 76, 1030–6.

—— (1994). Action theory and the production of speech. In R.E. Asher and J.M.Y. Simpson (eds), *The Encyclopedia of Language and Linguistics* (vol. 1, pp. 21–4). Oxford: Pergamon.

Turvey, M. (1977). Preliminaries to a theory of action with reference to vision. In R. Shaw and J. Bransford (eds), *Perceiving, acting and knowing: toward an ecological psychology* (pp. 211–65). Hillsdale, NJ: Lawrence Erlbaum.

—— (1990). *Coordination*. American Psychologist, 45, 938–53.

Tye-Murray, N. (1991). The establishment of open articulatory postures by deaf and hearing talkers. *Journal of Speech and Hearing Research*, 34, 453–9.

Umeda, N. (1975). Vowel duration in American English. *Journal of the Acoustical Society of America*, 58, 434–45.

—— (1977). Consonant duration in American English. *Journal of the Acoustical Society of America*, 61, 846–58.

Un, C.K. and Yang, S.C. (1977). A pitch extraction algorithm based on LPC inverse filtering and AMDF. *IEEE Trans ASSP-25*, 565–72.

Ushijima, T. and Hirose, H. (1974). Electromyographic study of the velum during speech. *Journal of Phonetics*, 2, 315–26.

Ushijima, T. and Sawashima, M. (1972). Fiberscopic observation of velar movements during Speech. *Annual Bulletin of Research Institute of Logopedics and Phoniatrics, University of Tokyo*, 6, 25–38.

Vagges, K., Ferrero, F.E., Magno-Caldognetto, E. and Lavagnoli, C. (1978). Some acoustic characteristics of Italian consonants. *Journal of Italian Linguistics*, 3, 68–85.

Vaissière, J. (1971). Contribution à la synthèse par règles du français, Thèse de troisième cycle, Grenoble.

—— (1983). Language-independent prosodic features. In A. Cutler and D.R. Ladd (eds), *Prosody: Models and Measurements* (pp. 53–66). Berlin: Springer Verlag.

—— (1988). Prediction of velum movement from phonological specifications, *Phonetica*, 45, 122–39.

Valbret, H., Moulines, E. and Tubach, J.P. (1992). Voice transformation using PSOLA technique. *Proceedings of ICASSP-92* (pp. I-145–I-148). San Fransisco, U.S.A.

van der Merwe, A. (forthcoming). A theoretical framework for the characterization of pathological speech sensorimotor control. In M. McNeil (ed.), *Sensorimotor Speech Disorders*.

van Leeuwen, H.C. and Lindert, E. te (1991). Speechmaker, text-to-speech synthesis based on a multilevel, synchronized data structure. *Proceedings of ICASSP-91*.

—— (1993). Speech maker: a flexible and general framework for text-to-speech synthesis, and its application to Dutch. *Computer Speech and Language*, 7 (2), 149–68.

van Santen, J.P.H. (1992). Contextual effects on vowel duration. *Speech Communication*, 11, 513–46.

van Santen, J.P.H. and Olive, J.P. (1989). The analysis of contextual effects on segmental duration. *Computer, Speech and Language*, 4, 359–90.

van Son, R.J.J.H. and Pols, L. (1989). Comparing formant movements in fast and normal rate speech. *Proceedings of European Conference on Speech Communication and Technology 89*.

Varga, A.P. and Moore, R.K. (1990). Hidden Markov model decomposition of speech and noise. *Proceedings of the IEEE International Conference on Acoustics, Speech and Signal Processing*, 845–8.

Varyani, P.L. (1974). Sources of implosives in Sindhi. *Indian Linguistics*, 35, 51–4.

Vatikiotis-Bateson, E. and Fletcher, J. (1992). Articulatory correlates of linguistically contrastive events: where are they? In Y. Tohkura, E. Vatikiotis-Bateson and Y. Sagisaka (eds), *Speech perception, production and linguistic structure* (pp. 341–58). Amsterdam: IOS Press.

Vatikiotis-Bateson, E., Hirayama, M., Honda, K. and Kawato, M. (1992). The articulatory dynamics of running speech: gestures from phonemes. In J. Ohala, T. Neary, B. Derwing, M. Hodge and G. Wiebe (eds), *Proceedings of 1992 International Conference on Spoken Language Processing* (pp. 887–90). Edmonton: The University of Alberta.

Vatikiotis-Bateson, E. and Kelso, J.A.S. (1990). Linguistic structure and articulatory dynamics: a cross language study. *Haskins Laboratories Status Report on Speech Research*, SR-103/104 67–94.

Vayra, M., and Fowler, C.A. (1992). Declination of supralaryngeal gestures in spoken Italian. *Phonetica*, 49, 48–60.

Veatch, T. (1992). /l/ and /ng/ effects on vowel nuclei in four dialects. *Journal of the Acoustical Society of America*, 91, 2388 (A).

Velez, E. and Absher, R. (1989). Transient analysis of speech signals using the Wigner time-frequency representation. *Proceedings of ICASSP '89*, 2242–5.

Velichko, V. and Zagoruyko, N.G. (1970). Automatic recognition of 200 words. *International Journal of Man-Machine Studies*, 2, 223–34.

Verner, K. (1875). Eine Ausnahme der ersten Lautverschiebung. *Z. f. vergleichende Sprachforschung*, 23, 97–130.

—— (1913). [Letters to Hugo Pipping]. *Oversigt over det kongelige danske videnskabernes selskabs forhandlinger*. No. 3, 161–211. København.

Verschuure, J. (1981). Pulsation patterns and nonlinearity of auditory tuning. II. Analysis of psychophysical results. *Acustica*, 49, 296–306.

Viemeister, N.F. (1979). Temporal modulation transfer functions based on modulation thresholds. *Journal of the Acoustical Society of America*, 66, 1364–80.

Vihman, M.M. (1992). Early syllables and the construction of phonology. In C.A. Ferguson, L. Menn and C. Stoel-Gammon (eds), *Phonological development: models, research, implications*. Timonium, MD: York Press.

—— (1996). *Phonological development and the origins of language in the child*. Oxford: Blackwell.

Vihman, M.M., Ferguson, C.A. and Elbert, M. (1986). Phonological development from babbling to speech. Common tendencies and individual differences. *Applied Psycholinguistics*, 7, 3–40.

Vihman, M., Macken, M., Miller, R., Simmons, H. and Miller, J. (1985). From babbling to speech: a reassessment of the continuity issue. *Language*, 60, 397–445.

Vitale, T. (1991). An algorithm for high accuracy name pronunciation by parametric speech synthesizer. *Computational linguistics*, 17 (3), 257–76.

Viterbi, A.J. (1967). Error bounds for convolution codes and an asymptotically optimal decoding algorithm. *IEEE Transactions*, IT-13, 260–9.

Viviani, P. and Terzuolo, C. (1980). Space-time invariance in learned motor skills. In G. Stelmach and J. Requin (eds), *Tutorials in motor behavior* (pp. 525–33). Amsterdam: North-Holland.

Voigt, H.F., Sachs, M.B. and Young, E.D. (1982). Representation of whispered vowels in discharge patterns of auditory-nerve fibers. *Hearing Research*, 8, 49–58.

Vroomen, J. and de Gelder, B. (1995). Metrical segmentation and lexical inhibition in spoken word recognition. *Journal of Experimental Psychology: Human Perception and Performance*, 21, 98–108.

Vroomen, J., van Zon, M. and de Gelder, B. (in press). Cues to speech segmentation: Evidence from juncture misperceptions and word spotting. *Memory and Cognition*.

Waddington, C.H. (1957). *The strategy of the genes*. London: Allen and Unwin.

Waibel, A. (1988). *Prosody and speech recognition*. London: Pitman.

Waibel, A., Hanazawa, T., Hinton, G., Shikano, J. and Lang, K.J. (1989). Phoneme recognition using time-delay neural networks. *IEEE Transactions on Acoustics, Speech and Signal Processing*, 37, 328–39.

Walker, G.W. and Kowalski, C.J. (1972). On the growth of the mandible. *American Journal of Physical Anthropology*, 36, 111–18.

Wang, H.S. and Derwing, B.L. (1986). More on English vowel shift: the back vowel question. *Phonology Yearbook*, 3, 99–116.

Wang, W.S.Y. and Peterson, G. (1958). Segment inventory for speech synthesis. *Journal of the Acoustical Society of America*, 30, 743–6.

Wann, J. and Nimmo-Smith, I. (1990). Evidence against the relative invariance of timing in handwriting. *Quarterly Journal of Experimental Psychology*, 42A, 105–19.

Warr, W.B. (1992). Organization of olivocochlear efferent systems in mammals. In D.B. Webster, A.N. Popper and R.R. Fay (eds), *The mammalian auditory pathway: neuroanatomy* (pp. 410–48). New York: Springer-Verlag.

Warren, E.H. and Liberman, M.C. (1989). Effects of contralateral sound on auditory-nerve responses. I. Contributions of cochlear efferents. *Hearing Research*, 37, 89–104.

Warren, R.M. (1970). Perceptual restoration of missing speech sounds. *Science*, 167, 392–3.

—— (1974). Auditory temporal discrimination by trained listeners. *Cognitive Psychology*, 6, 237–56.

Warren, R.M. and Obusek, C.J. (1971). Speech perception and phonemic restorations. *Perception & Psychophysics*, 9, 358–62.

Wäsz-Hockert, O., Lind, J., Vuorenkoski, I.V., Partanen, T. and Valanne, E. (1968). *Infant cry. A spectrographic and auditory analysis*. London: Heinemann.

Watanabe, T. and Katsuki, Y. (1974). Response patterns of single auditory neurons of the cat to species-specific vocalization. *Japanese Journal of Physiology*, 24, 135–55.

Watanabe, T. and Sakai, H. (1973). Responses of the collicular auditory neurons to human speech. I. Response to monosyllable /ta/. *Proceedings of the Japanese Academy*, 49, 291–6.

—— (1978). Responses of the cat's collicular auditory neuron to human speech. *Journal of the Acoustical Society of America*, 64, 333–7.

Waterson, N. (1971). Child phonology: a prosodic view. *Journal of Linguistics*, 7, 179–211.

—— (1987). *Prosodic phonology: the theory and its application to language acquisition and speech processing*. Newcastle upon Tyne: Grevatt & Grevatt.

Watkin, K. and Rubin, J. (1989). Pseudo-three-dimensional reconstruction of ultrasonic images of the tongue. *Journal of the Acoustical Society of America*, 85, 496–9.

Watson, E.H. and Lowrey, G.H. (1967). *Growth and development of children* (5th edn). Chicago: Year Book Medical Publishers.

Wei, S.H.Y. (1970). Craniofacial width dimensions. *Angle Orthodontist*, 40, 141–7.

Wein, B., Bockler, R., Huber, W., Klajman, S. and Willmes, K. (1990). Computer sonographic presentation of tongue shapes during formation of long German vowels (in German). *Ultraschall in Med.*, 11, 100–3.

Wein, B., Drobnitzky, M., Klajman, S. and Angerstein, W. (1991). Evaluation of functional positions of tongue and soft palate with MR imaging: initial clinical results. *Journal of Magnetic Resonance Imaging*, 1, 381–3.

Weismer, G. (1980). Control of the voicing distinction for intervocalic stops and fricatives: some data and theoretical considerations. *Journal of Phonetics*, 8, 427–38.

—— (1984). Articulatory characteristics of Parkinsonian dysarthria. In M.R. McNeil, J.C. Rosenbek and A. Aronson (eds), *The dysarthrias: physiology-acoustics-perception-management* (pp. 101–30). San Diego: College-Hill Press.

—— (1985). Speech breathing: contemporary views and findings. In R.G. Daniloff (ed.), *Recent advances in speech sciences* (pp. 47–72). San Diego: College-Hill Press.

—— (1988). Speech production. In N.J. Lass, L. McReynolds, J. Northern and D. Yoder (eds), *Handbook of speech, language, and hearing pathology* (pp. 215–52). Toronto: Brian Decker.

—— (1991). Assessment of articulatory timing. In J.A. Cooper (ed.), *Assessment of speech and voice production: research and clinical applications. NIDCD Monograph*, Vol. I (pp. 84–95). Bethesda, MD: NIDCD.

Weismer, G. and Forrest, K. (1992). Issues in motor speech disorders. Keynote addresses presented to the 1992 Clinical Dysarthria Conference, Boulder, CO.

Weismer, G. and Kent, R.D. (1993). The contribution of studies of disordered speech production to models and theories of normal speech production. Paper presented at the 3rd Seminar on Speech Production: Models and Data, Old Saybrook, CT.

Weismer, G., Kent, R.D., Hodge, M. and Martin, R. (1988). The acoustic signature for intelligibility test words. *Journal of the Acoustical Society of America*, 84, 1281–91.

Weismer, G. and Martin, R. (1992). Acoustic and perceptual approaches to the study of intelligibility. In R.D. Kent (ed.), *Intelligibility in speech disorders* (pp. 67–118). Amsterdam: John Benjamin.

Weismer, G., Martin, R., Kent, R.D. and Kent, J.F. (1992). Formant trajectory characteristics of males with ALS. *Journal of the Acoustical Society of America*, 91, 1085–98.

Weismer, G., Mulligan, M. and DePaul, R. (1986). Selected acoustic characteristics of the dysarthria associated with amyotrophic lateral sclerosis in young adults. Paper presented at the 3rd Clinical Dysarthria Conference, Tucson, AZ.

Weismer, G., Tjaden, K. and Kent, R.D. (1995a). Articulatory characteristics in motor speech disorders: relationship to models and theories of normal speech production. *Journal of Phonetics*, 23, 149–64.

—— (1995b). Speech production theory and articulatory behavior in motor speech disorders. In F. Bell-Berti and L.J. Raphael (eds), *Producing speech: contemporary issues: for Katherine Safford Harris* (pp. 35–50). New York: AIP Press.

Wells, J. (1982). *Accents of English*. (3 vols.) Cambridge: Cambridge University Press.

Welmers, W.E. (1973). *African language structures*. Berkeley: University of California Press.

Werker, J.F. and Tees, R.C. (1984). Cross-language speech perception: evidence for perceptual reorganization during the first year of life. *Infant Behavior and Development*, 7, 49–63.

Westbury, J.R. (1979). Aspects of the temporal control of voicing in consonant clusters in English. *Texas Linguistic Forum*, 14. Department of Linguistics, University of Texas, Austin, TX.

—— (1983). Enlargement of the supraglottal cavity and its relation to stop consonant voicing. *Journal of the Acoustical Society of America*, 73, 1322–36.

Westbury, J.R. and Keating, P.A. (1985). On the naturalness of stop consonant voicing. *Working Papers in Phonetics (UCLA)*, 60, 1–19.

Wever, E.G. and Bray, C.W. (1930). Auditory nerve impulses. *Science*, 71, 215–17.

Weymouth, R.F. (1856). On the liquids, especially in relation to certain mutes. *Transactions of the Philological Society* [London], 18–32.

Whalen, D. and Levitt, A. (1995). The intrinsic pitch of vowels. *Journal of Phonetics*, 24, 349–66.

Whitfield, I.C. and Evans, E.F. (1965). Responses of auditory cortical neurones to stimuli of changing frequency. *Journal of Neurophysiology*, 28, 655–72.

Wickelgren, W.A. (1969). Context-sensitive coding, associative memory, and serial order in (speech) behavior. *Psychological Review*, 76, 1–15.

Wiederhold, M.L. and Kiang, N.Y.S. (1970). Effects of electrical stimulation of the crossed olivocochlear bundle on single auditory nerve fibers in cat. *Journal of the Acoustical Society of America*, 48, 950–65.

Wiesendanger, M. (1986). Redistributive function of the motor cortex. *Trends in Neuroscience*, 93, 120–5.

Wiesendanger, M. and Wise, S.P. (1992). Current issues concerning the functional organization of motor cortical areas in non-human primates. In P. Chauvel, A.V. Delgado-Escueta et al. (eds), *Advances in Neurology*, 57, 117–34.

Wightman, C.W., Shattuck-Hufnagel, S., Ostendorf, M. and Price, P.J. (1992). Segmental durations in the vicinity of prosodic phrase boundaries. *Journal of the Acoustical Society of America*, 91, 1707–17.

Wilcox, K.A. and Horii, Y. (1980). Age and changes in vocal jitter. *Journal of Gerontology*, 35, 194–8.

Wilhelms-Tricarico, R. (1995). Physiological modeling of speech production: methods for modeling soft-tissue articulators. *Journal of the Acoustical Society of America*, 97, 3085–98.

—— (1996). A biomechanical and physiologically-based vocal tract model and its control. *Journal of Phonetics*, 24, 23–38.

Willems, M.J., Hart, J.'t and Collier, R. (1988). English intonation from a Dutch point of view. *Journal of the Acoustical Society of America*, 84, 1250–61.

Williams, C.E. and Stevens, K.N. (1972). Emotions and speech. *Journal of the Acoustical Society of America*, 52, 1238–50.

Williams, D., Bickley, C. and Stevens, K. (1992). Inventory of phonetic contrasts generated by high-level control of a formant synthesizer. *Proceedings of 1992 International Conference on Spoken Language Processing* (pp. 571–4). Banff, Canada.

Williams, H. (1989). Multiple representations and auditory-motor interactions in the avian song system. In M. Davis, B.L. Jacobs and R.I. Schoenfeld (eds), *Modulation of defined vertebrate neural circuits*. *Annals of the New York Academy of Sciences*, 563 (pp. 148–64).

Willis, R. (1830). On the vowel sounds, and on reed organ-pipes. *Transactions of the Cambridge Philosophical Society*, 3, 229–68.

Winer, B., Brown, D. and Michels, K. (1991). *Statistical principles in experimental design*. New York: McGraw-Hill.

Winfree, A. (1980). *The geometry of biological time*. New York: Springer.

Winkworth, A.L., Davis, P.J., Ellis, E. and Adams, R.D. (1994). Variability and consistency in speech breathing during reading: lung volumes, speech intensity and linguistic factors. *Journal of Speech and Hearing Research*, 37, 535–56.

Winslow, R.L., Barta, P.E. and Sachs, M.B. (1987). Rate coding in the auditory nerve. In W.A. Yost and C.S. Watson (eds), *Auditory processing of complex sounds* (pp. 212–24). Hillsdale, NJ: Erlbaum.

Winslow, R.L. and Sachs, M.B. (1987). Effect of electrical stimulation of the crossed olivocochlear bundle on auditory nerve response to tones in noise. *Journal of Neurophysiology*, 57, 1002–21.

Winter, I.M. and Palmer, A.R. (1990). Temporal responses of primarylike anteroventral cochlear nucleus units to the steady-state vowel /i/. *Journal of the Acoustical Society of America*, 88, 1437–41.

Winter, I.M., Robertson, D. and Yates, G.K. (1990). Diversity of characteristic frequency rate-intensity functions in guinea pig auditory nerve fibers. *Hearing Research*, 45, 191–202.

Wise, R., Chollet, F., Hadar, U., Friston, K., Hoffner, E. and Frackowiak, R. (1991). Distribution of cortical neural networks involved in word comprehension and word retrieval. *Brain*, 114, 1803–17.

Wolf, J.J. (1972). Efficient acoustic parameters for speaker recognition. *Journal of the Acoustical Society of America*, 51, 2044–56.

Wood, S. (1979). A radiographic analysis of constriction locations for vowels. *Journal of Phonetics*, 7, 25–43.

Woods, W.A. (1974). Motivation and overview of SPEECHLIS: an experimental prototype for speech understanding research. *IEEE Transactions on Acoustics, Speech and Signal Processing*, 23, 2–10.

Woodworth, R. (1899). The accuracy of voluntary movement. *Psychological Review*, 3, 1–114.

Workinger, M.S. and Kent, R.D. (1991). Perceptual analysis of the dysarthrias in children with athetoid and spastic cerebral palsy. In C.A. Moore, K.M. Yorkston, and D.R. Beukelman (eds), *Dysarthria and apraxia of speech: perspectives on management* (pp. 109–26). Baltimore, MD: Paul H. Brookes Co.

Wray, A. (1992). *The focusing hypothesis*. Amsterdam: John Benjamins.

Wrench, E.H. (1980). Speaker authentication. Operational test and evaluation. *ITT-Defense Communication Division Technical Report RADC-TR-80-64*. Rome Air Development Center, Griffiss Air Force Base, New York.

Wright, J.T. (1986). The behavior of nasalized vowels in the perceptual vowel space. In J.J. Ohala and J.J. Jaeger (eds), *Experimental phonology* (pp. 45–67). Orlando, FL: Academic Press.

Wright, S. and Kerswill, P. (1989). Electropalatography in the analysis of connected speech processes. *Clinical Linguistics and Phonetics*, 3, 49–57.

Wu, Z.L., Schwartz, J.L. and Escudier, P. (1992). Physiologically-based modules and detection of articulatory-based acoustic events. In W. Ainsworth (ed.), *Advances in speech, hearing and language processing*, Vol. 3, London: JAI Press.

Wyard, P. (1993). The relative importance of the factors affecting recogniser performance with telephone speech, *Eurospeech '93*, 3, 1085–8.

Yorkston, K.M., Beukelman, D.R. and Bell, K.R. (1988). *Clinical management of dysarthric speakers*. San Diego, CA: College-Hill Press.

Yorkston, K.M., Hammen, V.L., Beukelman, D.R. and Traynor, C.D. (1990). The effect of rate control on the intelligibility and naturalness of dysarthric speech. *Journal of Speech and Hearing Disorders*, 55, 350–60.

Yost, W.A. and Sheft, S. (1989). Across-critical-band processing of amplitude-modulated tones. *Journal of the Acoustical Society of America*, 85, 848–57.

Yost, W.A., Sheft, S. and Opie, J. (1989). Modulation interference in detection and discrimination of amplitude modulation. *Journal of the Acoustical Society of America*, 86, 2138–47.

Young, E.D. (1984). Response characteristics of neurons of the cochlear nuclei. In C. Berlin (ed.), *Hearing Science* (pp. 423–60). San Diego: College Hill.

Young, E.D. and Sachs, M.B. (1979). Representation of steady-state vowels in the temporal aspects of the discharge patterns of populations of auditory-nerve fibers. *Journal of the Acoustical Society of America*, 66, 1391–1403.

Young, R.K. (1993). *Wavelet theory and its applications*. Boston: Kluwer.

Young, S.J. (1992). HKT: hidden Markov model toolkit V1.4. *Speech Group*, Cambridge University Engineering Department.

Young, T. (1985). *Linear systems and digital signal processing*. Englewood Cliffs: Prentice-Hall, Inc.

Zeman, G. (1976). Analysis of the interrelationship between image quality and radiation exposure in Xeroradiography. *Sc.D. Dissertation, The Johns Hopkins University School of Hygiene and Public Health*.

Zentay, P.J. (1937). Motor disorders of the nervous system and their significance for speech. Part I. Cerebral and cerebellar dysarthrias. *Laryngoscope*, 47, 147–56.

Zera, J. and Green, D.M. (1993). Detecting temporal onset and offset asynchrony in multi-component complexes. *Journal of the Acoustical Society of America*, 93, 1038–52.

Ziegler, W. and Cramon, D.R. von (1983a). Vowel distortion in traumatic dysarthria. *Phonetica*, 40, 63–78.

—— (1983b). Vowel distortion in traumatic dysarthria: lip rounding versus tongue advancement. *Phonetica*, 40, 312–22.

—— (1986). Spastic dysarthria after acquired brain damage: an acoustic study. *British Journal of Disorders of Communication*, 21, 173–87.

Zsiga, E.C. (1993). 'Features, gestures, and the temporal aspects of phonological organization'. Ph.D. dissertation, Yale University.

Zue, V. (1985). The use of speech knowledge in automatic speech recognition. *Proceedings of the IEEE*, 73, 1602–15.

Zwicker, E. (1970). Masking and psychological excitation as consequences of the ear's frequency analysis. In R. Plomp and G.F. Smoorenburg (eds), *Frequency analysis and periodicity detection in hearing* (pp. 376–94). Leiden: Sijthoff.

Zwicker, E. and Feldtkeller, R. (1967). *Das Ohr als Nachtrichtenempfänger*. Stuttgart: Hirzel-Verlag.

Zwirner, E. and Zwirner, K. (1936). *Grundfragen der Phonometrie*. Basel.

Zwitserlood, P. (1989). The locus of the effects of sentential-semantic context in spoken-word processing. *Cognition*, 32, 25–64.

Zyski, B.J. and Weisinger, B.E. (1987). Identification of dysarthria types based on perceptual analyses. *Journal of Communication Disorders*, 20, 367–8.

Index

Note: page numbers in italics denote figures or tables where these are separated from their textual reference.